W9-BNR-168

# Introduction to Homeland Security, Second Edition

# Introduction to Homeland Security

## Second Edition

Jane A. Bullock

George D. Haddow

Damon Coppola

Erdem Ergin

Lissa Westerman

Sarp Yeletaysi

**Vincennes University
Shake Learning Resources Center
Vincennes, In 47591-9986**

ELSEVIER

AMSTERDAM • BOSTON • HEIDELBERG • LONDON
NEW YORK • OXFORD • PARIS • SAN DIEGO
SAN FRANCISCO • SINGAPORE • SYDNEY • TOKYO

Butterworth-Heinemann is an imprint of Elsevier

Acquisitions Editor: Mark Listewnik
Acquisitions Editor: Jennifer Soucy
Editorial Assistant: Kelly Weaver
Marketing Manager: Christian Nolin
Project Manager: Sarah Hajduk
Cover Designer: Eric DeCicco
Printer: Hing Yip Printing Company, Ltd.

Elsevier Butterworth–Heinemann
30 Corporate Drive, Suite 400, Burlington, MA 01803, USA
Linacre House, Jordan Hill, Oxford OX2 8DP, UK

**Library of Congress Cataloging-in-Publication Data**
Introduction to homeland security / Jane A. Bullock . . . [et al.].—2nd ed.
    p.    cm.
  Includes bibliographical references and index.
  ISBN 0-7506-7992-1 (hardcover : alk. paper)
  1. Terrorism—Prevention—Government policy—United States.  2. National security—United States.  3. Civil defense—United States.  4. Emergency management—United States.  I. Bullock, Jane A.
  HV6432.I58 2006
  363.32′0973—dc22                                                                 2005028924

**British Library Cataloguing-in-Publication Data**
A catalogue record for this book is available from the British Library.

ISBN 13: 978-0-7506-7992-3
ISBN 10: 0-7506-7992-1

For information on all Elsevier Butterworth–Heinemann publications
visit our Web site at www.books.elsevier.com

Printed in China
06 07 08 09 10 11   10 9 8 7 6 5 4 3 2 1

# Table of Contents

Contents

# Acknowledgments

The authors of this book would like to express their appreciation for the continued support and encouragement we have received from Dr. Jack Harrald and Dr. Joseph Barbera, codirectors of the Institute for Crisis, Disaster and Risk Management at George Washington University. These two individuals provide outstanding leadership to institutions and governments in designing and implementing homeland security projects. Greg Shaw, also part of the institute, contributed a large dose of practical advice and humor. We would like to acknowledge the many individuals whose research, analysis, and opinions helped to shape the content of this volume.

We would also like to thank Mark Listewnik and Jennifer Soucy at Elsevier for their assistance in conceiving this book and their patience and faith in us.

Finally, we recognize the thousands of professionals and volunteers who, through their daily pursuits, are giving form and substance to creating a more secure and safe homeland.

# Introduction

Since the events of September 11 and the subsequent anthrax attacks carried out through the U.S. mail system, governments, organizations, and individuals have significantly expanded their efforts, programs, and activities aimed at improving the security and safety of the nation and its people. The most comprehensive reorganization ever taken by the federal government resulted in the creation of the new Department of Homeland Security. Congress has proposed hundreds of new laws, many of which have passed, that have served to alter both the funding and the environment within which the countless federal, state, and local government agencies now approach and combat this new and increasing terrorist threat. And above these efforts, there have emerged many thousands of private citizens who have volunteered their time to make the nation's communities more secure.

FM-1    New York City, New York, September 16, 2001—Military and rescue workers stand amid the wreckage of the World Trade Center. (Photo by Andrea Booher/FEMA News Photo)

Public safety officials, particularly emergency managers, have found themselves in the forefront of the war on terror, preparing for and responding to the potential threat of attack. The intent of this book is to provide a primer on homeland security for emergency managers, students of emergency management, and for the countless public and private sector officials who find themselves suddenly thrust into the ever-expanding domain of homeland security.

The federal government defines homeland security as follows:

> "Homeland security is a concerted national effort to prevent terrorist attacks within the United States, reduce America's vulnerability to terrorism, and minimize the damage and recover from attacks that do occur."

Starting with this definition, the early chapters provide a historic perspective on the threat of terrorism, before and after September 11, with detailed descriptions of the extraordinary legislative and organizational actions that were taken in reaction to September 11 and in support of preventing future attacks. The text continues by providing a detailed examination of the various hazards and risks from which the nation's vulnerabilities to future terrorist events have arisen. Included in this chapter are many fact sheets describing individual terrorist agents. Several chapters describe the programs and actions being taken by government agencies, organizations, and the private sector to reduce or minimize the terrorist threat. We have focused on the areas of security (intelligence, border

FM-2   Arlington, Virginia, September 17, 2001—Work continues throughout the night at the site of the Pentagon terrorist attack. (Photo by Jocelyn Augustino/FEMA News Photo)

and transportation, infrastructure and information/ cyberspace); preparedness and mitigation (planning, initiatives, community and volunteers, private sector, best practices); communications (threat advisory system, public health strategies, public education); and new technologies (communications, information management, protective equipment).

A significant amount of the text has been devoted to response and recovery, as these two responsibilities are a primary focus of emergency managers. In the chapter that focuses upon these tasks, we describe the current state of first responder operations and applications, and discuss the major changes that are under way within the national response system network. Case studies are included to demonstrate practical application to the materials being presented. In addition, we have included full texts of critical guidance documents for use and reference. Wherever possible, budget and resource charts show past allocations and future projections. The concluding chapter has been provided to examine future issues that public safety, emergency management, and other types of professionals may confront as the nation continues to meet the challenges of establishing a secure homeland.

Please note that throughout this book, we make constant reference to the Federal Emergency Management Agency (FEMA). Prior to becoming the Emergency Preparedness and Response Directorate (EP&R) in the Department of Homeland Security (DHS), FEMA was an executive branch agency that reported directly to the president of the United States. Since being relocated within the new Department, FEMA has retained its name and many of its original functions (with exceptions noted throughout the text). And thus for clarity, the authors refer to FEMA by its original (and still used) title rather than EP&R throughout.

Homeland security is a new, ever-evolving discipline. The first edition was written very early in the new age of homeland security, and this second edition has accounted for the significant changes that have occurred in the intervening two years. However, due to the nature and speed with which these changes are

occurring, there are likely to be many more alterations to programs, activities, and even organizations that occur following the publication of this text. For that reason, we have included online references wherever possible so the reader will have access to information sites that can provide up-to-date information on program or organization changes, new initiatives, or simply more detail on specific issues.

Out of the tragic events of September 11 has come a monumental opportunity for the nation's government to improve its social and economic sustainability, at the national and community levels, from all threats and disasters—not just terrorism. Public safety officials and emergency managers champion the concept of an all-hazards approach, and despite some unique characteristics, terrorism can be incorporated into that approach as well. With the increased funding being provided, it is important that we have better-trained and better-equipped first responders; a stronger, less vulnerable national infrastructure; and an enhanced delivery system for public health and new technologies to improve and safeguard our information and communications networks.

These improvements will enhance our protection from hurricanes, energy and power outages, fires, and any other threat that comes our way. A new focus on research and development can lead to significant advances in the diverse fields of application that are grouped together under the umbrella of homeland security. Limiting ourselves to terrorism can set a dangerous course, but not, as this text will show, a precedent.

Considering there have been no major terrorist attacks since 9/11, as of the writing of this text, it is difficult to ascertain by how much the many actions described herein have reduced the nation's vulnerability to terrorism. Many believe that the lack of attacks itself is an indicator that the system is working.

Terrorism, like crime, will always exist, and as such, so will the drive that has pushed the many changes that have occurred since 2001. The authors' goal in writing this book was to provide as complete a source of practical information, programs, references, and best practices so that any emergency manager, public safety official, community leader or individual could engage in actions to help make their communities safer and more secure. In the end, achieving homeland security will not be accomplished by the federal government but by each individual, each organization, each business, and each community working together to make a difference.

# 1

# Historic Overview of the Terrorist Threat

INTRODUCTION

Harry Truman once said, "The only thing new is the history we don't know." For many Americans, the rush of activities by the government to pass new laws, reorganize government institutions, and allocate vast sums of money in the aftermath of the September 11, 2001, terrorist attacks may have seemed unprecedented. The reality is that actions of this nature in terms of both type and scope have happened in the past, and these historical experiences can offer some insight into the prospect of the future success or failure of the actions taken since the September 11 attacks.

The purpose of this chapter is to provide a historic perspective of the evolution of emergency management policies, statutes, and practices in the United States and to examine the chronology of events and actions leading up to and beyond September 11. This perspective will help frame the issues to be discussed in subsequent chapters of this book, which will detail the legislative, organizational, and operational underpinnings of America's homeland security structure.

This chapter provides summaries of the tragic events of September 11 including updated statistics, first responder anecdotes and perspectives, timelines,

and review of after-action reporters. Additional information is provided for three other major terrorist incidents: the 1993 World Trade Center bombing, the 1995 Oklahoma City bombing of the Murrah Federal Office Building, and the 2001 anthrax incidents in Washington, D.C.

## EMERGENCY MANAGEMENT IN THE UNITED STATES

In this section, we explore the historical, organizational, and legislative history of modern emergency management in the United States. We review some of the significant events and people who have shaped the emergency management discipline over the years. Understanding this history and evolution is important because it can provide insight into why emergency management concepts have been applied differently at different times.

There is no single definition of emergency management, and those that have been applied tend to be extremely broad and all encompassing. Additionally, in the United States the discipline of emergency management has expanded and contracted in response to events, the desires of Congress, and leadership styles.

Simply defined, emergency management is the discipline dealing with risk and risk avoidance. Risk represents a broad range of issues and includes an equally diverse set of players.

The range of situations that could possibly involve emergency management or various components of the emergency management system is extensive. Through time, as it has developed, emergency management has become integral to the security of our daily lives and has been integrated into our daily decisions. Emergency management is no longer called on only in times of disaster.

Emergency management has clearly become an essential role of government. The Constitution entrusted the states with responsibility for public health and safety—hence, responsibility for public risks—and assigns the federal government to a secondary, supportive role. The federal role was originally conceived such that it intervenes when the state, local, or individual entities are overwhelmed. This fundamental philosophy continues to guide the government function of emergency management.

The strong foundation of emergency management has been built over a period of many decades, and the validity of the discipline as a government function has never been in question. Entities and organizations fulfilling the mission of this function, likewise, have existed at the state and local level for a considerable time, even before the federal government became involved. But as history-defining events occurred, political philosophies changed, and the nation developed, the federal role in emergency management steadily increased to the point it is at today.

## EARLY HISTORY: 1800–1950

In 1803 a congressional act was passed to provide financial assistance to a New Hampshire town devastated by fire. This is the first example of the federal government becoming involved in a local disaster. Following this disaster it was not until the administration of Franklin Roosevelt began to use government as a tool to stimulate the economy that we saw a significant investment in emergency management functions in the federal government.

During the 1930s, the Reconstruction Finance Corporation and the Bureau of Public Roads were both granted the authority to make disaster loans available for repair and reconstruction of certain public facilities after disasters. The Tennessee Valley Authority (TVA) was created during this era to produce hydroelectric power and, as a secondary purpose, to reduce flooding in the region.

A significant piece of emergency management legislation, the Flood Control Act of 1934, was passed during this time. This act, which gave the U.S. Army Corps of Engineers increased authority to design and build flood control projects, ultimately made a significant and long-lasting impact on emergency management in this country. The Flood Control Act reflected the philosophy that man could control nature, thereby eliminating the risk of floods. The immediate-term success of this program promoted economic and population growth patterns along the nation's rivers, but history proved with a vengeance that such bold attempts at emergency management can be shortsighted and costly.

## THE COLD WAR AND THE RISE OF CIVIL DEFENSE: 1950s

The next notable period of emergency management evolution occurred during the 1950s. The Cold War era presented the potential for nuclear war and nuclear fallout as the principal disaster risk. Civil defense programs proliferated across communities during this time. Individuals and communities alike were encouraged to and did build bomb shelters to protect themselves and their families from a nuclear attack by the Soviet Union.

Almost every community appointed a civil defense director, and most states designed into their state government hierarchy a position whose incumbent managed civil defense activities in that state. These individuals tended to have military backgrounds, and their operations received little political or financial support from the state or local governments they served. Furthermore, the civil defense responsibilities they managed were often in addition to other duties.

Federal support for these activities was vested in the Federal Civil Defense Administration (FCDA), an organization with few staff and limited financial resources whose main role was to provide technical assistance. Despite these shortfalls, the local and state civil defense directors are the first recognized face of emergency management in the United States.

A companion office to the FCDA, the Office of Defense Mobilization, was established in the Department of Defense (DOD). The primary functions of this office were to allow for the quick mobilization of materials and the production and stockpiling of critical materials in the event of a war. It included a function called *emergency preparedness*. In 1958 these two offices were merged into the Office of Civil and Defense Mobilization.

The 1950s were a quiet time for large-scale natural disasters, but not devoid of them. Hurricane Hazel, a Category 4 hurricane, inflicted significant damage in Virginia and North Carolina in 1954; Hurricane Diane hit several mid-Atlantic and northeastern states in 1955; and Hurricane Audrey, the most damaging of the three storms, struck Louisiana and north Texas in 1957. Congressional response to these disasters followed a familiar pattern of ad hoc legislation to provide increased disaster assistance funds to the affected areas.

## NATURAL DISASTERS BRING CHANGES TO EMERGENCY MANAGEMENT: 1960s

As the 1960s began, three major natural disasters occurred. In a sparsely populated area of Montana in 1960, the Hebgen Lake earthquake struck, measuring 7.3 on the Richter scale, raising attention to the fact that the nation's earthquake risk extended far beyond California's borders. Later that year Hurricane Donna hit the west coast of Florida, and in 1961 Hurricane Carla blew across Texas. The incoming Kennedy administration decided to change the federal approach

to disasters. In 1961 it created the Office of Emergency Preparedness inside the White House to deal with these large-scale events. It distinguished these activities from the civil defense responsibilities, which remained in the Office of Civil Defense within DOD.

During the remainder of the 1960s, the United States was struck by a series of major natural disasters. The 1962 Ash Wednesday storm devastated more than 620 miles of shoreline on the East Coast, inflicting more than $300 million in damages. In 1964, in Prince William Sound, Alaska, an earthquake measuring 9.2 on the Richter scale garnered front-page news throughout the nation and the world. This Easter quake killed 123 people and generated a tsunami that affected beaches as far south as the Pacific Coast of California. Hurricane Betsy struck in 1965, and Hurricane Camille in 1969, together killing and injuring hundreds and causing hundreds of millions of dollars in damage along the Gulf Coast.

The response to these events, as with previous disasters, was the passage of ad hoc legislation for funds. However, the financial losses resulting from Hurricane Betsy's path across Florida and Louisiana engendered a discussion of insurance as a protection against future floods and a potential method to reduce continued government assistance after disasters. The unavailability of flood protection insurance on the standard homeowner policy, and the prohibitive cost of such insurance where it was available, prompted congressional interest. These discussions eventually led to the passage of the National Flood Insurance Act of 1968, which in turn created the National Flood Insurance Program (NFIP).

It is interesting to note how local and state governments have chosen to administer this flood risk program. At those levels, civil defense departments had usually been responsible for dealing with matters pertaining to risk and disasters. Although the NFIP pertained to these areas, responsibilities for the NFIP were given to local planning departments and state departments of natural resources. This is but one illustration of the fragmented and piecemeal approach to emergency management that began to evolve during the 1960s and continued during the following decade.

## THE CALL FOR A NATIONAL FOCUS TO EMERGENCY MANAGEMENT: 1970s

During the 1970s, responsibility for various emergency management tasks and functions was allotted to more than five separate federal departments and agencies, including the Department of Commerce (weather, warning, and fire protection), the General Services Administration (continuity of government, stockpiling, federal preparedness), the Treasury Department (import investigation), the Nuclear Regulatory Commission (power plants), and the Department of Housing and Urban Development (flood insurance and disaster relief).

With the passage of the Disaster Relief Act of 1974, prompted by the previously mentioned hurricanes and the San Fernando earthquake of 1971, the Department of Housing and Urban Development (HUD) possessed the most significant authority for natural disaster response and recovery through the NFIP, which it administered under the Federal Insurance Administration (FIA) and the Federal Disaster Assistance Administration (FDAA), which handled disaster response, temporary housing, and assistance. On the military side, there existed the Defense Civil Preparedness Agency (nuclear attack) and the U.S. Army Corps of Engineers (flood control). However, when one looked at the broad range of risks and potential disasters, more than 100 federal agencies were involved in some aspect of risk and disasters.

This pattern continued down to the state and, to a decreasing extent, local levels. Parallel organizations and programs added to confusion and turf wars, especially during disaster response efforts. The states and the governors grew increasingly frustrated over this fragmentation. In the absence of one clear federal lead agency in emergency management, a group of state civil defense directors led by Lacy Suiter of Tennessee and Erie Jones of Illinois launched a drive, by means of the National Governors Association (NGA), to consolidate federal emergency management activities in one agency.

With the election of Jimmy Carter, a former governor from Georgia, the effort gained steam. President Carter arrived in Washington already committed to streamlining all government agencies and seeking more control over key administrative processes. The state directors lobbied the NGA and Congress for a consolidation of federal emergency management functions. When the Carter administration finally proposed such an action, it was met with a receptive audience in the Senate. Congress had already expressed concerns about the lack of a coherent federal policy and the inability of states to know where to turn in the event of an emergency, so the state directors' concerns rang true for them.

In the midst of these discussions, an accident occurred at the Three Mile Island nuclear power plant in Pennsylvania, validating and further galvanizing the consolidation effort. This accident also brought national media attention to the lack of adequate off-site preparedness around commercial nuclear power plants and the role of the federal government in responding to such an event.

On June 19, 1978, President Carter transmitted to the Congress the Reorganization Plan Number 3 (3 CFR 1978, 5 U.S. Code 903). The intent of this plan was to consolidate emergency preparedness, mitigation, and response activities into one federal emergency management organization. The president stated that the plan would provide for the establishment of the Federal Emergency Management Agency (FEMA) and that the FEMA director would report directly to the president.

Reorganization Plan Number 3 transferred the following agencies or functions to FEMA: National Fire Prevention Control Administration (Department of Commerce), Federal Insurance Administration (HUD), Federal Broadcast System (Executive Office of the President), Defense Civil Preparedness Agency (DOD), Federal Disaster Assistance Administration (HUD), and the Federal Preparedness Agency (GSA).

Additional transfers of emergency preparedness and mitigation functions to FEMA were as follows: oversight of the Earthquake Hazards Reduction Program (Office of Science and Technology Policy), coordination of dam safety (Office of Science and Technology Policy), assistance to communities in the development of readiness plans for severe weather-related emergencies, coordination of natural and nuclear disaster warning systems, and coordination of preparedness and planning to reduce the consequences of major terrorist incidents.

The plan articulated several fundamental organizational principles.

> First, Federal authorities to anticipate, prepare for, and respond to major civil emergencies should be supervised by one official responsible to the president and given attention by other officials at the highest levels. Second, an effective civil defense system requires the most efficient use of all available resources. Third, whenever possible, emergency responsibilities should be extensions of Federal agencies. Fourth, Federal hazard mitigation activities should be closely linked with emergency preparedness and response functions. (Reorganization Plan Number 3 3 CFR 1978; 5 U.S. code 903)

After congressional review and concurrence, the Federal Emergency Management Agency was officially established by Executive Order 12127 of March 31, 1979 (44 FR 19367, 3 CFR, Comp., p. 376). A second executive order, Executive Order 12148, mandated reassignment of agencies, programs, and personnel into this new entity.

Creation of the new organization made sense. However, integrating the diverse programs, operations, policies, and people into a cohesive operation was a much bigger task than most people realized once the consolidation began, and its success required extraordinary leadership and a common vision. It also created immediate political problems. By consolidating these programs and the legislation that created them, the new agency would have to answer to 23 committees and subcommittees in Congress with oversight of its programs. Unlike most other federal agencies, it would have no organic legislation to support its operations and no clear champions to look to during the congressional appropriations process.

John Macy became the first director of FEMA, and his task was to unify an organization that was not only physically separated—parts of the agency were located in five different buildings around Washington—but also philosophically separate. Programs focused on nuclear war preparations were combined with programs focused on a new consciousness of the environment and floodplain management.

Macy focused his efforts by emphasizing the similarities between natural hazards preparedness and civil defense by developing a new concept called the Integrated Emergency Management System (IEMS). This system was an all-hazards approach that included direction, control, and warning as functions common to all emergencies—from small isolated events to the ultimate emergency of nuclear attack.

For all of Macy's good efforts, FEMA's departments continued to operate as individual entities pursuing their own interests and answering to their different congressional bosses. It was a period of few major disasters, so virtually no one noticed this problem of disjointedness.

## CIVIL DEFENSE REAPPEARS AS NUCLEAR ATTACK PLANNING: 1980s

The early and middle 1980s saw FEMA facing many challenges, but no significant natural disasters. The absence of the need for a coherent federal response to disasters, as was called for by Congress when it approved the establishment of FEMA, allowed FEMA to continue to exist as an organization of many parts.

In 1982 President Ronald Reagan appointed Louis O. Guiffrida as director of FEMA. Mr. Guiffrida, a California friend of Ed Meese, one of the president's closest advisers, had a background in training and terrorism preparedness at the state government level. General Guiffrida proceeded to reorganize FEMA consistent with administration policies and his own background. Top priority was placed on government preparedness for a nuclear attack. Resources within the agency were realigned, and additional budget authority was sought to enhance and elevate the national security responsibilities of the agency. With no real role for the states in these national security activities, the state directors who had lobbied for the creation of FEMA saw their authority and federal funding declining.

Because of congressional questions about the agency's operations, the Department of Justice and a grand jury began investigations of senior political officials at FEMA. These inquiries led to the resignation of Guiffrida and top aides in response to a variety of charges, including misuse of government funds.

President Reagan then selected General Julius Becton to be director of FEMA. General Becton was a retired military general and had been director of the Office of Foreign Disaster Assistance in the State Department. From a policy standpoint, he continued to emphasize the programs of his predecessor, but in a less visible manner. Becton himself expanded the duties of FEMA when he was asked by DOD to take over the program dealing with the off-site cleanup of chemical stockpiles on DOD bases. This program was fraught with problems, and bad feelings existed between the communities and the bases over the funds available to the communities for the cleanup. FEMA had minimal technical expertise to administer this program and depended on the DOD and the army for the funding. This situation led to political problems for the agency and did not lead to significant advancements in local emergency management operations as promised by DOD.

## AN AGENCY IN TROUBLE: 1989–1992

As Congress debated and finally passed major reform of federal disaster policy as part of the Stewart McKinney–Robert Stafford Act, the promise of FEMA and its ability to support a national emergency management system remained in doubt.

As the 1980s came to a close, FEMA was an agency in trouble. It suffered from severe morale problems, disparate leadership, and conflicts with its partners at the state and local levels over agency spending and priorities. In 1989 two devastating natural disasters called into question the continued existence of FEMA. In September, Hurricane Hugo slammed into North and South Carolina after first hitting Puerto Rico and the Virgin Islands. It was the worst hurricane in a decade, with more than $15 billion in damages and 85 deaths. FEMA was slow to respond, waiting for the process to work and for the governors to decide what to do. Senator Ernest Hollings (D–SC) personally called the FEMA director and asked for help, but the agency moved slowly. Hollings went on national television to berate FEMA in some of the most colorful language ever, calling the agency the "sorriest bunch of bureaucratic jackasses."

Less than a month later, the Bay Area of California was rocked by the Loma Prieta earthquake as the 1989 World Series got under way in Oakland Stadium. FEMA was not prepared to respond, but it was lucky. While FEMA had spent the last decade focused on nuclear attack planning, FEMA's state partners in emergency management, especially in California, had been preparing for a more realistic risk, an earthquake. Although damages were high, few lives were lost. This was a testament to good mitigation practices in building codes and construction that were adopted in California and some good luck relative to the time the earthquake hit.

In 1992, FEMA was not so lucky. In August of that year, Hurricane Andrew struck Florida and Louisiana and Hurricane Iniki struck Hawaii within months of each other (Figure 1-1). FEMA wasn't ready, and neither were FEMA's partners at the state level. The agency's failure to respond was witnessed by Americans all across the country as major news organizations followed the crisis. The efficacy of FEMA as the national emergency response agency was in doubt. After dispatching then-Secretary of Transportation Andrew Card to take over the response operation, President George H. W. Bush sent in the military.

FIGURE 1-1   Hurricane Andrew, Florida, August 24, 1992—Many houses, businesses, and personal effects suffered extensive damage from one of the most destructive hurricanes ever recorded in America. One million people were evacuated, and 54 died in this hurricane. (FEMA News Photo)

It was not just FEMA that failed during Hurricane Andrew; it was the whole federal emergency management process and system. In Hurricane Andrew, FEMA recognized the need to apply all of its resources to the response and began to use its national security assets for the first time in a natural disaster response. But these efforts came too late. Starting with Hurricane Hugo, public concern over natural disasters was high. People wanted and expected the government to be there to help in their time of need. FEMA seemed incapable of carrying out this essential government emergency management function.

In the aftermath of Hurricanes Andrew and Iniki, there came calls to abolish FEMA. Investigations by the General Accounting Office (GAO) and other governmental and nongovernmental watchdog groups called for major reforms. None of this was lost on the incoming Clinton administration.

## THE WITT REVOLUTION: 1993–2001

When President William Jefferson Clinton appointed James Lee Witt as FEMA director, he breathed life back into the troubled agency and introduced a whole new style of leadership. Witt was the first director with emergency management experience.

He was from a constituency that had played a major role in creating FEMA but had been forgotten—the state directors. With Witt, President Clinton had a politician with skill and credibility and, more important, an understanding of the importance of building partnerships and serving the customer.

Witt came in with a mandate to restore the trust of the American people that their government would be there for them during times of crisis. He initiated sweeping reforms both within and outside the agency. Inside FEMA, he reached out to all employees, implemented customer service training, and reorganized the agency to break down stovepipes. He supported the application of new technologies to the delivery of disaster services and emphasized mitigation and risk avoidance. Outside of the agency, he strengthened the relationships with state and local emergency managers and built new relationships with Congress, within the administration, and with the media. A hallmark of the Witt years at FEMA was open communication, both internally and externally.

Throughout the next several years, FEMA and its state and local partners would face almost every possible natural hazard, including killer tornadoes, ice storms, hurricanes, floods, wildfires, and drought.

When President Clinton elevated Witt to the position of director of FEMA and he became a member of Clinton's cabinet, the value and importance of emergency management were recognized. Witt used this newfound respect as an opportunity to lobby the nation's governors to include their state emergency management directors in their cabinets.

The Oklahoma City bombing in April 1995 represented a new phase in the evolution of emergency management. This event, which followed the first bombing of the World Trade Center in New York City in 1993, raised the issue of our nation's preparedness for terrorism events (Figure 1-2). Because emergency management responsibilities are defined by risks and the consequences of those risks, responding to terrorist threats was included. The Oklahoma City bombing tested this thesis and set the stage for interagency disagreements over which agency would be in charge of terrorism.

The Nunn–Lugar legislation of 1995 left open the question as to who would be the lead agency in terrorism. Many fault FEMA leadership for not quickly claiming that role, and the late 1990s were marked by several different agencies and departments assuming various roles in terrorism planning. The question of who should respond first to a terrorism incident—fire or police department, emergency management, or emergency medical personnel—was closely examined, but no clear answers emerged. The state directors looked to FEMA to claim the leadership role. In an uncharacteristic way, the leadership of FEMA vacillated on this issue. Terrorism was certainly part of the all-hazards approach to emergency management championed by FEMA, but the resources and technologies needed to address specific issues, such as weapons of mass destruction and the consequences of a chemical/biological attack, seemed well beyond the reach of the current emergency management structure.

While this debate continued, FEMA took an important step in its commitment to disaster mitigation by launching a national initiative to promote a new community-based approach called Project Impact: Building Disaster Resistant Communities. This program was designed to mainstream emergency management and mitigation practices into every community in America. Project Impact's goal was to incorporate decisions about risk and risk avoidance into the community's everyday decision-making processes. By building a disaster-resistant community, it was believed, Project Impact's members would promote sustainable economic development, protect and enhance their natural resources, and ensure a better quality of life for all citizens.

As the decade and century ended, with a noticeable lack of major technological glitches from Y2K (when the nation was unsure about what would happen to computer programs when the year changed from 1999 to 2000), FEMA was recognized as the preeminent emergency management system in the world. Other countries began to emulate the agency within their own governments, and Witt became an ambassador for emergency management overseas. State and local emergency management programs had grown, and

FIGURE 1-2    Oklahoma City, Oklahoma, April 26, 1995—A scene of the devastated Murrah Federal Office Building after the Oklahoma City bombing. (FEMA News Photo)

their value was recognized and supported by society. Private-sector and business continuity programs were flourishing. And with Hurricane Mitch, a vast international disaster, the world had even seen a change in American foreign policy toward promoting and supporting community-based mitigation projects.

The role and responsibility of emergency management had significantly increased, as had the partnerships supporting it. Its budget and stature had grown. Good emergency management became a way to get economic and environmental issues onto the table; it became a staple of discussion relative to a community's quality of life.

The profession of emergency management was attracting a different type of public servant. Political and management skills were critical, and candidates for state, local, and private emergency management positions were now being judged on the basis of their training and experience rather than their political connections. Undergraduate and advance degree programs in emergency management were flourishing at more than 65 national colleges and universities. It was now a respected, challenging, and sought-after profession.

## TERRORISM BECOMES MAJOR FOCUS: 2001

Prior to the attacks of September 11, 2001, the Nunn–Lugar–Domenici legislation (Defense against Weapons of Mass Destruction Act of 1996) provided the primary authority and focus for domestic federal preparedness activities for terrorism. Several agencies, including FEMA, the Department of Justice (DOJ), the Department of Health and Human Services (HHS), DOD, and the National Guard, were involved, and all jockeyed for leadership on the issue. Some attempts at establishing coordination systems were launched, but in general, these individual agencies pursued their own agendas. The obvious lack of direction caused significant confusion for state and local governments, who as a result were largely unprepared for terrorist acts. These state and municipal governments complained to the federal government of the need to address what they recognized as an excessive vulnerability to the will of terrorists. The TOPOFF exercise, held in 1999, involving Federal, State and local emergency officials in a first ever weapons of mass destruction exercise, reinforced these concerns and vividly demonstrated the problems that could arise in a real event.

With the election of George W. Bush, Joe Allbaugh was nominated and approved by Congress to lead FEMA. As a former chief of staff to Governor Bush in Texas and President Bush's campaign manager in the 2000 Presidential race, Allbaugh and Bush had a close personal relationship. As demonstrated by the relationship between Director Witt and President Clinton, such close rapport was clearly a positive aspect for the agency. Despite the fact that Allbaugh had an obvious weak emergency management background on his resume, the matter did not arise during his confirmation hearings.

As part of a major reorganization of the agency, Allbaugh recreated the Office of National Preparedness (ONP). This office was first established in the 1980s during the Guiffrida reign for planning for World War III and eliminated by Witt in 1992. The new director's actions raised some concerns among FEMA's constituents and FEMA staff, but their concerns fell on deaf ears in light of the fact that the office's mission was already moving toward an overall focus on terrorism adopted by the administration as a whole.

In a September 10, 2001, speech, Director Allbaugh spoke about his priorities as being firefighters, disaster mitigation, and catastrophic preparedness. These words seem prophetic in light of the events of September 11. As the events of that tragic day unfolded, FEMA activated the Federal Response Plan and response operations proceeded as expected in New York and in Virginia. Most of the agency's senior leaders, including the director, were in Montana, attending the annual meeting of the National Emergency Management Association (NEMA), an organization that represents state emergency management directors. The strength of the U.S. emergency management system was proven, however, as hundreds of response personnel initiated their operations within just minutes of the onset of events.

## THE CREATION OF THE DEPARTMENT OF HOMELAND SECURITY: 2001–2004

Almost immediately following the terrorist attacks, President Bush created by executive order the Office of Homeland Security within the White House. The same day that announcement was made, Pennsylvania Governor Tom Ridge was sworn in to lead the office with the rank of "assistant to the president." The office, having only 120 employees and what was derided as a prohibitively small budget in light of the gravity of the events the nation had just witnessed, began to be seen as just another government bureaucracy.

In March 2002, President Bush signed Homeland Security Presidential Directive 3 (HSPD-3), which stated that:

> The Nation requires a Homeland Security Advisory System to provide a comprehensive and effective means to disseminate information regarding the risk of terrorist acts to Federal, State, and local authorities and to the American people. Such a system would provide warnings in the form of a set of graduated "Threat Conditions" that would increase as the risk of the threat increases. At each Threat Condition, Federal departments and agencies would implement a corresponding set of "Protective Measures" to further reduce vulnerability or increase response capability during a period of heightened alert.
>
> This system is intended to create a common vocabulary, context, and structure for an ongoing national discussion about the nature of the threats that confront the homeland

and the appropriate measures that should be taken in response. It seeks to inform and facilitate decisions appropriate to different levels of government and to private citizens at home and at work.

The product outcome of this directive was the widely recognizable color-coded Homeland Security Advisory System (HSAS). The HSAS has been called on repeatedly since its inception to raise and lower the nation's alert levels between Elevated (yellow) and High (orange), though the frequency of these movements has decreased over time as standards for such movements have been developed.

On November 25, 2002, President Bush signed into law the Homeland Security Act of 2002 (HS Act) (Public Law 107-296), and announced that former Pennsylvania Governor Tom Ridge would become secretary of a new Department of Homeland Security (DHS) to be created through this legislation. This act, which authorized the greatest federal government reorganization since President Harry Truman joined the various branches of the armed forces under the Department of Defense, was charged with a threefold mission of protecting the United States from further terrorist attacks, reducing the nation's vulnerability to terrorism, and minimizing the damage from potential terrorist attacks and natural disasters.

The sweeping reorganization into the new department, which officially opened its doors on January 24, 2003, joined more than 179,000 federal employees from 22 existing federal agencies under a single, cabinet-level organization. Since that time, there have been many additions, movements, and changes to both the organizational makeup of the department and its leadership. The Department of Homeland Security, its importance within the framework of the U.S. government and society, and the changes that have taken place since its inception are discussed in much greater detail in Chapter 3.

## THE FUTURE: 2005 AND BEYOND

In the aftermath of the terrorist attacks on September 11, FEMA and the newly formed Department of Homeland Security, together with partners in emergency management, fire, police, and public health at the state and local government levels, have been charged with expanding and enhancing our nation's emergency management system. In the years following the creation of the Department of Homeland Security, billions of dollars have been allocated from the federal government to state and local governments in order to expand existing programs and establish new ones designed to meet the new terrorism threat.

Most notably within the United States, but also in many other countries around the world, a budgetary focus on the preparedness for and prevention of terrorist attacks has emerged and steadily increased. In the years that followed the September 11 attacks, there have been advancements in transportation security and commerce security, large increases in budgetary allowances for first responder terrorism training and related equipment acquisitions, the emergence of homeland security management structures at the state and local levels, a widespread public cognition of and preparedness for the terrorism threat, and many other positive changes. Whether as a result of these changes or in the absence of any significant attempts, there have been no major terrorist attacks within the borders of the United States since the attacks in 2001.

The focus on terrorism has, expectedly, altered much of the focus that once existed on the mitigation of and preparedness for natural and technological hazards, which by their very nature, are much more likely to occur. In fact, during this same time period that followed the events of September 11, the nation experienced severe flooding, extensive wildfires, record-breaking hurricanes, tornadoes, earthquakes, volcanic activity, drought, avalanches, ice storms, severe winter storms, and many more major and minor disaster events. The failure of the Federal response to Hurricane Katrina is a clear example of how the exclusive focus on terrorism prevention has marginalized the Federal government's and FEMA's capacity and capability to respond to a catastrophic natural disaster.

The professional and operational environment of emergency management has continued to grow, and the quality, skill base, technical demands, and caliber

FIGURE 1-3   New York City, New York, October 13, 2001—
New York firefighters at the site of the World Trade Center. (Photo
by Andrea Booher/FEMA News Photo)

of its practitioners have only increased (see Figure 1-3). The hyper-attention that is given to the terrorist threat has provided an unexpected opportunity to expand that base. The goal of this textbook is to provide the background and working knowledge of the disciplines, players and organizations that are part of this nation's homeland security efforts.

As has often occurred following previous defining events, the environment for emergency management will absorb the event and evolve to reflect its impacts. History has begun to repeat itself, and a focal shift to a more national approach to the problem has occurred, with an emphasis on preparedness through training and equipment. The resilience of the system allows for these midstream corrections. The long-term viability and measure of the influence of emergency management will continue to depend on its value to all citizens in all communities, everyday, not just during times of crisis.

A summary of the 1993 World Trade Center bombing, the 1995 Murrah Federal Building bombing and the September 11 attacks on the World Trade Center and the Pentagon follow.

## WORLD TRADE CENTER BOMBING

On February 23, 1993, a massive explosion occurred in the basement parking lot of the World Trade Center in New York City. The explosive device, which weighed more than 1,000 pounds, caused extensive damage to seven of the building's floors, six of which were below grade. A blast crater that resulted from the explosion measured 130 feet in width by 150 feet in length. More than 50,000 people were evacuated, 25,000 of which were in the twin towers of the Trade Center. The entire evacuation process required approximately 11 hours to complete (Fusco, 1993).

At the time, the response to the bombing was described as being the largest incident that the City of New York Fire Department (FDNY) had ever managed in its 128-year history. In terms of the number of fire units that responded, the event was described as being "the equivalent of a 16-alarm fire" (Fusco, 1993). The following list provides a summary of relevant data from the bombing event

- Deaths: 6
- Injuries: 1,042
- Firefighter injuries: 85 (one requiring hospitalization)
- Police officers injured: 35
- EMS workers injured: 1
- Firefighter, police, and EMS deaths: 0
- Number of people evacuated from WTC complex: approximately 50,000

FIGURE 1-4    Oklahoma City, Oklahoma, April 26, 1995—Search-and-rescue crews work to save those trapped beneath the debris after the Oklahoma City bombing. (FEMA News Photo)

- FDNY engine companies responding: 84
- FDNY truck companies responding: 60
- FDNY special units responding: 26
- FDNY personnel responding: 28 battalion chiefs, 9 deputy chiefs
- Percentage of FDNY on duty staff responding: 45%

*Source*: Fusco, 1993.

## MURRAH FEDERAL BUILDING BOMBING

On April 19, 1995, a massive truck bomb exploded outside of the Alfred P. Murrah Federal Building in downtown Oklahoma City. All told, 168 people died, including 19 children attending a day care program in the building. A total of 674 people were injured. The Murrah building was destroyed, 25 additional buildings in the downtown area were severely damaged or destroyed, and another 300 buildings were damaged by the blast. The ensuing rescue and recovery effort during the next 16 days involved, among many other resources, the dispatch of 11 FEMA urban search-and-rescue teams (Sidebar 1-1) from across the country to assist local and state officials search first for survivors and, ultimately, to recover victims' bodies (Figure 1-4) (The City of Oklahoma City, 1996).

**SIDEBAR 1-1**   **FEMA Urban Search and Rescue at Murrah Building Bombing in Oklahoma City, 1995**

At 9:02 A.M. on the morning of April 19, 1995, a bomb exploded from inside a Ryder truck under the Alfred P. Murrah Federal Building in Oklahoma City. The blast caused a partial collapse of all nine floors of the 20-year-old building, and 168 people died.

Rescuers from the Oklahoma City Fire Department entered the building unsure of whether or not the building would continue to support its own weight. Most of the steel support system had been blown out.

Within five hours of the blast the first FEMA urban search-and-rescue task force was deployed. By 6 P.M. the task force was in the building, searching for victims. One of the first assignments was to search the second floor nursery for victims.

Teams with search-and-rescue dogs began the search in the nursery. The dogs are trained to bark when they find live victims. No dogs barked that night.

Eleven of FEMA's 27 USAR task forces worked in the building, with representation from virtually every task force in the country. The FEMA teams coordinated with local fire departments, police departments, and military and Federal agencies during the search-and-rescue effort.

The rescue effort involved extensive stabilization of the fragmented building, rescuing of people trapped within tight spaces, rescues from high angles, breaking through concrete, and hazardous materials analysis and removal.

An innovative plan was developed to help rescuers deal with the psychological and emotional trauma of such a grisly scene. The plan allowed workers to be briefed in advance and prepared for what they were to experience; extensive debriefing sessions were also included.

*Source*: FEMA, www.fema.gov.

## SEPTEMBER 11 ATTACKS ON THE WORLD TRADE CENTER AND THE PENTAGON

On September 11, 2001, terrorists hijacked four planes and crashed them into the twin towers of the World Trade Center in New York City, the Pentagon in Washington, D.C., and a field in Pennsylvania (see Sidebar 1-2). These actions resulted in the collapse of both twin towers as well as a section of the Pentagon, and unprecedented deaths and injuries:

- Total deaths for all 9/11 attacks: 2,986
- Total injured for all 9/11 attacks: 2,337
- Total deaths in the World Trade Center towers: 2,595
- Total injured at World Trade Center: 2,261

- Total firefighter deaths at World Trade Center: 343
- Total police deaths at World Trade Center: 75
- Total deaths at Pentagon: 125
- Total injured at Pentagon: 76
- Total deaths American Flight 77, Pentagon: 64
- Total deaths United Airlines Flight 93, Pennsylvania: 45
- Total deaths American Airlines Flight 11, WTC North Tower: 92
- Total deaths United Airlines Flight 175, WTC South Tower: 65

*Sources*: www.september11news.com/911Art.htm and http://en.wikipedia.org/wiki/September_11,_2001_Terrorist_Attack.

September 11, 2001, Terrorist Attacks Timeline for the Day of the Attacks

*Note*: All times in New York Time (EDT). This is four hours before GMT.

Tuesday, September 11, 2001

7:58 A.M.: American Airlines Flight 11, a fully fueled Boeing 767 carrying 81 passengers and 11 crew members, departs from Boston Logan airport, bound for Los Angeles, California.

8:00 A.M.: United Airlines Flight 175, another fully fueled Boeing 767 carrying 56 passengers and 9 crew members, departs from Boston's Logan airport, bound for Los Angeles, California.

8:10 A.M.: American Airlines Flight 77, a Boeing 757 with 58 passengers and 6 crew members, departs from Washington's Dulles airport for Los Angeles, California.

8:40 A.M.: The FAA notifies NORAD about the suspected hijacking of American Airlines Flight 11.

8:42 A.M.: United Airlines Flight 93, a Boeing 757, takes off with 37 passengers and 7 crew members from Newark airport bound for San Francisco, following a 40-minute delay caused by congested runways. Its flight path initially takes it close to the World Trade Center.

8:43 A.M.: The FAA notifies NORAD about the suspected hijacking of United Airlines Flight 175.

8:46:26 A.M.: American Airlines Flight 11 crashes with a speed of roughly 490 miles per hour into the north side of the north tower of the World Trade Center, between floors 94 and 98. (Many accounts have given times that range between 8:45 A.M. and 8:50 A.M.) The building's structural type, pioneered in the late 1960s to maximize rentable floor space and featuring lightweight tubular design with no masonry elements in the facade, allows the jetliner to literally enter the tower, mostly intact. It plows to the building core, severing all three gypsum-encased stairwells and dragging combustibles with it. A massive shock wave travels down to the ground and up again. The combustibles, as well as the remnants of the aircraft, are ignited by the burning fuel. Because the building lacks a traditional full-cage frame and depends almost entirely on the strength of a narrow structural core running up the center, the fire at the center of the impact zone is in a position to compromise the integrity of all internal columns. People below the severed stairwells in the north tower start to evacuate. Officials in the south tower tell people shortly afterward by megaphone and office announcements that they are safe and can return to their offices. Some don't hear it; some ignore it and evacuate anyway; others congregate in common areas such as the 78th-floor sky lobby to discuss their options.

9:02:54 A.M.: United Airlines Flight 175 crashes with a speed of about 590 miles per hour into the south side of the south tower, banked between floors 78 and 84 in full view of media cameras. Parts of the plane leave the building at its east and north sides, falling to the ground six blocks away. A passenger on the plane, Peter Hanson, had called his father earlier from the plane reporting that hijackers were stabbing flight attendants in order to force the crew to open the cockpit doors.

8:46 A.M. to 10:29 A.M.: At least twenty people, primarily in the north tower, trapped by fire and smoke in the upper floors, jump to their deaths. There is some evidence that large central portions of the floor near the impact zone in the north tower collapsed soon after the plane hit, perhaps convincing some people that total collapse was imminent. One person at street level, firefighter Daniel Thomas Suhr, is hit by a jumper and dies. No form of airborne evacuation is attempted because the smoke is too dense for a successful landing on the roof of either tower, and New York City lacks helicopters specialized for horizontal rescue.

9:04 A.M. (approximately): The FAA's air route traffic control center in Boston stops all departures from airports in its jurisdiction (New England and eastern New York State).

*Continued*

FIGURE 1-5    New York City, New York, October 5, 2001—Rescue workers continue their efforts at the World Trade Center. (Photo by Andrea Booher/FEMA News Photo)

*Continued*

9:06 A.M.: The FAA bans takeoffs of all flights bound to or through the airspace of New York center from airports in that center and the three adjacent centers—Boston, Cleveland, and Washington. This is referred to as a first-tier groundstop and covers the Northeast from North Carolina north and as far west as eastern Michigan.

9:08 A.M.: The FAA bans all takeoffs nationwide for flights going to or through New York center airspace.

9:24 A.M.: President George W. Bush is interrupted with the news of the second crash as he participates in a class filled with Florida schoolchildren. He waits out the lesson then rushes into another classroom commandeered by the Secret Service. Within minutes he makes a short statement, calling the developments "a national tragedy," and is hurried aboard Air Force One.

9:24 A.M.: The FAA notifies NORAD's Northeast Air Defense Sector about the suspected hijacking of American Airlines Flight 77. The FAA and NORAD establish an open line to discuss American Airlines Flight 77 and United Airlines Flight 93.

9:26 A.M.: The FAA bans takeoffs of all civilian aircraft regardless of destination—a national groundstop.

9:37 A.M.: American Airlines Flight 77 crashes into the western side of the Pentagon and starts a violent fire. The section of the Pentagon hit consists mainly of newly renovated, unoccupied offices. Passenger Barbara K. Olson had called her husband, Solicitor General Theodore Olson, at the Justice Department twice from the plane to tell him about the hijacking and to report that the passengers and pilots were held in the back of the plane. As bright flames and dark smoke envelop the west side of America's military nerve center, all doubts about the terrorist nature of the attacks are gone.

9:45 A.M.: United States airspace is shut down. No civilian aircraft are allowed to lift off, and all aircraft in flight are ordered to land at the nearest airport as soon as practical. All air traffic headed for the United States is redirected to Canada. Later, the FAA announces that civilian flights are suspended until at least noon, September 12. The groundings last until September 14, but there are exemptions for Saudi families who fear retribution if they stay in the United States. Military and medical flights continue. This is the fourth time all commercial flights in the United States have been stopped, and the first time a suspension was unplanned. All previous suspensions were military related (Sky Shield I–III) and took place from 1960 to 1962.

9:45 A.M.: The White House and the Capitol are closed.

9:50 A.M. (approximately): The Associated Press reports that American Airlines Flight 11 was apparently hijacked after departure from Boston's Logan Airport. Within an hour, this report is confirmed for both Flight 11 and United Airlines Flight 175.

9:57 A.M.: President Bush is moved from Florida.

9:59:04 A.M.: The south tower of the World Trade Center collapses. A vast TV and radio audience reacts primarily with horrified astonishment. It is later widely reported that the collapse was not directly caused by the jetliner's impact but that the intense sustained heat of the fuel fire was mostly or wholly responsible for the loss of structural integrity. Later, a growing number of structural engineers assert that the fire alone would not have caused the collapse. Both towers made use of external load-bearing mini columns, and on one face of each building approximately 40 of these were severed by the jetliners. Had they been intact to efficiently distribute the increasing gravity load as the bunched core columns and joist trusses weakened in the fires, the towers might have stood far longer or perhaps indefinitely. Concrete in the towers' facades might have prevented most of the debris and fuel from reaching the building core. Investigations that may radically change skyscraper design (or result in a radical retreat to full-cage construction with high concrete-to-steel ratios as in pre-1960s skyscrapers) are ongoing.

10:03 A.M.: United Airlines Flight 93 crashes southeast of Pittsburgh in Somerset county, Pennsylvania. Other reports say 10:06 or 10:10. According to seismographic data readings, the time of impact was 10:06:05. The first reports from the police indicate that

*Continued*

no one on board survived. Later reports indicate that passengers speaking on cell phones had learned about the World Trade Center and Pentagon crashes and at least three were planning on resisting the hijackers. It is likely that the resistance led to the plane crashing before it reached its intended target. Reports stated that an eyewitness saw a white plane resembling a fighter jet circling the site minutes after the crash. These reports have limited credibility, although fighter jets had been scrambled to defend the Washington, D.C., region earlier. These jets, however, stayed within the immediate D.C. area.

10:10 A.M.: Part of the Pentagon collapses.

10:13 A.M.: Thousands are involved in an evacuation of the United Nations complex in New York.

10:15 A.M. (approximately): The Democratic Front for the Liberation of Palestine is reported to have taken responsibility for the crashes, but this is denied by a senior officer of the group soon after.

10:28:31 A.M.: The north tower of the World Trade Center collapses from the top down, as if being peeled apart. Probably as a result of the destruction of the gypsum-encased stairwells on the impact floors (most skyscraper stairwells are encased in reinforced concrete), no one above the impact zone in the north tower survives. The fact that the north tower stood much longer than the south one is later attributed to three facts: The region of impact was higher (which meant that the gravity load on the most damaged area was lighter), the speed of the airplane was lower, and the affected floors had their fireproofing partially upgraded. Also, the hottest part of the fire in the south tower burned in a corner of the structure, perhaps leading to a more concentrated failure of columns or joist trusses or both. The Marriott Hotel, located at the base of the two towers, is also destroyed.

10:35 A.M. (approximately): Police are reportedly alerted about a bomb in a car outside the State Department in Washington, D.C. Later reports claim that nothing happened at the State Department.

10:39 A.M.: Another hijacked jumbo jet is claimed to be headed for Washington, D.C. F-15s are scrambled and patrol the airspace above Washington, D.C., while other fighter jets sweep the airspace above New York City. They have orders, first issued by Vice President Cheney and later confirmed by President Bush, to shoot down any potentially dangerous planes that do not comply with orders given to them via radio.

10:45 A.M.: CNN reports that a mass evacuation of Washington, D.C., and New York has been initiated. The UN headquarters are already empty. A few minutes later, New York's mayor orders an evacuation of lower Manhattan.

10:50 A.M.: Five stories of part of the Pentagon collapse as a result of the fire.

10:53 A.M.: New York's primary elections are canceled.

11:15 A.M. (approximately): Reports surfaced that the F-15s over Washington had shot something down. There was no later confirmation of these reports.

11:16 A.M.: American Airlines confirms the loss of its two airplanes.

11:17 A.M.: United Airlines confirms the loss of Flight 93 and states that it is "deeply concerned" about Flight 175.

11:53 A.M.: United Airlines confirms the loss of its two airplanes.

11:55 A.M.: The border between the United States and Mexico is on highest alert, but has not been closed.

12:00 P.M. (approximately): President Bush arrives at Barksdale Air Force Base in Louisiana. He was on a trip in Sarasota, Florida, to speak about education but is now presumed to be returning to the capitol. He makes a brief and informal initial statement to the effect that terrorism on U.S. soil will not be tolerated, stating that "freedom itself has been attacked and freedom will be protected."

12:02 P.M.: The Taliban government of Afghanistan denounces the attacks.

12:04 P.M.: Los Angeles International Airport, the intended destination of Flight 11, Flight 77, and Flight 175 is shut down.

12:15 P.M.: San Francisco International Airport, the intended destination of United Airlines Flight 93, is shut down.

*Continued*

12:15 P.M. (approximately): The airspace over the 48 contiguous United States is clear of all commercial and private flights.

1:00 P.M. (approximately): At the Pentagon, fire crews are still fighting fires. The early response to the attack had been coordinated from the National Military Command Center, but that location had to be evacuated when it began to fill with smoke.

1:04 P.M.: President Bush puts the U.S. military on high alert worldwide. He speaks from Barksdale Air Force Base and leaves for the Strategic Air Command bunker in Nebraska.

1:27 P.M.: Mayor Anthony A. Williams of Washington, D.C., declares a state of emergency; the D.C. National Guard arrives on site.

2:30 P.M.: Senator John McCain characterizes the attack as an "act of war."

2:49 P.M.: At a press conference in New York, Mayor Rudy Giuliani is asked to estimate the number of casualties at the World Trade Center. He replies, "More than any of us can bear."

4:00 P.M.: National news outlets report that high officials in the federal intelligence community are stating that Usama Bin Ladin is the primary suspect in the attacks.

4:25 P.M.: The New York Stock Exchange, NASDAQ, and the American Stock Exchange report that they will remain closed on Wednesday, September 12.

5:20 P.M.: Salomon Brothers 7, commonly referred to as "7 World Trade Center," a 47-story building that had sustained what was originally thought to be light damage in the fall of the twin towers and was earlier reported on fire, collapses. Structural engineers are puzzled, and the investigation continues. The building was not designed by the same team responsible for the twin towers. The building contained New York's special emergency center, which may well have been intended for such a disaster as September 11.

6:00 P.M.: Explosions and tracer fire are reported in Kabul, the capital of Afghanistan, by CNN and the BBC. The Northern Alliance, involved in a civil war with the Taliban government, is later reported to have attacked Kabul's airport with helicopter gunships.

6:00 P.M.: Iraq announces the attacks are the fruit of "U.S. crimes against humanity" in an official announcement on state television.

6:54 P.M.: President Bush finally arrives at the White House. Executive authority through much of the day had rested with Vice President Cheney.

7:00 P.M.: Frantic efforts to locate survivors in the rubble that had been the twin towers continue. Fleets of ambulances have been lined up to transport the injured to nearby hospitals. They stand empty. "Ground Zero" is the exclusive domain of the FDNY and NYPD, despite volunteer steel and construction workers who stand ready to move large quantities of debris quickly. Relatives and friends displaying enlarged photographs of the missing printed on home computer printers are flooding downtown. The New York Armory, at Lexington Avenue and 26th Street, and Union Square Park, at 14th Street, become centers of vigil.

7:30 P.M.: The U.S. government denies any responsibility for reported explosions in Kabul.

8:30 P.M.: President Bush addresses the nation from the White House. Among his remarks: "Terrorist attacks can shake the foundations of our biggest buildings, but they cannot touch the foundation of America. These acts shatter steel, but they cannot dent the steel of American resolve."

9:00 P.M.: President Bush meets with his full National Security Council, followed roughly half an hour later by a meeting with a smaller group of key advisers. Bush and his advisers have evidence that Osama bin Laden is behind the attacks.

11:00 P.M.: There are reports of survivors buried in the rubble in New York making cell phone calls. These rumors were later proved to be wrong.

*Source*: www.wikipedia.com.

The response to these attacks by fire, police, and emergency medical teams was immediate, and their combined efforts saved hundreds if not thousands of lives, especially at the World Trade Center (Figure 1-5). The following facts provide additional insight into the situation faced by the responders that day:

- Year the World Trade Center was built: 1970
- Number of companies housed in the World Trade Center: 430
- Number working in World Trade Center on average working day before September 11: 50,000
- Average number of daily visitors: 140,000
- Maximum heat of fires, in degrees Fahrenheit, at World Trade Center site: 2,300
- Number of days underground fires at World Trade Center continued to burn: 69
- Number of days that workers dug up debris at Ground Zero, searching for body parts: 230
- Number of body parts collected: 19,500
- Number of bodies discovered intact: 291
- Number of victims identified by New York medical examiner: 1,102
- Number of death certificates issued without a body at request of victims' families: 1,616
- Number of people still classified as missing from the World Trade Center that day: 105
- Number of people who survived the collapse of the towers: 16

*Source*: http://observer.guardian.co.uk/waronterrorism/story/0,1373,776451,00.html and www.snopes.com/rumors/survivor.htm.

The addition of another stairway in each tower, the widening of existing stairways, and regular evacuation drills—actions implemented in the aftermath of the 1993 World Trade Center bombing—are all credited with facilitating the evacuation of thousands of office workers in the towers before they collapsed. Federal, state, and nongovernmental groups (e.g., Red Cross, Salvation Army) also responded quickly, establishing relief centers and dispensing critical services to victims and first responders. The following list illustrates the relief efforts that ensued:

- Cases opened: 55,494
- Mental health contacts made: 240,417
- Health services contacts made: 133,035
- Service delivery sites opened: 101
- Shelters opened: 60
- Shelter population: 3,554
- Meals/snacks served: 14,113,185
- Response vehicles assigned: 292
- Disaster workers assigned: 57,434

*Source*: www.redcrossalbq.org/04a_911statistics.html.

In addition to the stunning loss of life and the physical destruction caused by the attacks, two other losses are significant for their size and impact. First, 343 New York City firefighters and 75 New York City police officers were lost in the World Trade Center when the towers collapsed. So many first responders had never before been lost in a single disaster event in the United States, and their untimely deaths brought extraordinary attention to America's courageous and professional firefighters, police officers, and emergency medical technicians. They became the heroes of September 11, and this increased attention has resulted in increased funding for government programs that provide equipment and training for first responders. It has also resulted in a reexamination of protocols and procedures in light of the new terrorist threat. The examination of the after-action reports from the World Trade Center and the Pentagon in the next section of this chapter provides insight into the issues currently being addressed by the first responder community.

The second significant aspect of the September 11 attacks is the magnitude and the scope of the losses resulting from the attacks. The total economic impact on New York City alone is estimated to be between $82.8 and $94.8 billion. This estimate includes $21.8 billion in lost buildings, infrastructure, and tenant assets; $8.7 billion in the future earnings of those who died; and $52.3 to $664.3 billion gross city product (Thompson, 2002). The economic impact of the attacks were felt throughout the United States and the world, causing jobs to be lost and businesses to fail in communities hundreds and thousands of miles from Ground Zero:

- Value of U.S. economy: $11 trillion
- Estimated cost of attacks to United States based solely on property losses and insurance costs: $21 billion
- Amount of office space lost, in square feet: 13.5 million
- Estimated number of jobs lost in lower Manhattan area following September 11: 100,000
- Estimated number of jobs lost in the United States as a result of the attacks, by the end of 2002: 1.8 million
- Number of jobs lost in U.S. travel industry in the final 5 months of 2001: 237,000

- Amount allocated by Congress for emergency assistance to airline industry in September 2001: $15 billion

*Source*: http://observer.guardian.co.uk/waronterrorism/ story/0,1373,776451,00.html.

The federal government costs were extraordinary, and spending by FEMA on these events easily exceeded its spending on past natural disasters (see also Table 1-1): **Projected costs for the response and recovery efforts for Hurricane Katrina are expected to exceed $200 billion making Katrina the costliest disaster in U.S. History.**

- Direct emergency assistance from FEMA: $297 million
- Aid to individuals and families: $255 million

TABLE 1-1   **Top Ten Natural Disasters (Ranked by FEMA Relief Costs)**

| Event | Year | FEMA funding* |
| --- | --- | --- |
| World Trade Center attack (NY) | 2001 | $9.0 billion (projected) |
| Northridge earthquake (CA) | 1994 | $6.999 billion |
| Hurricane Georges (AL, FL, LA, MS, PR, VI) | 1998 | $2.254 billion |
| Hurricane Andrew (FL, LA) | 1992 | $1.848 billion |
| Hurricane Hugo (NC, SC, PR, VI) | 1989 | $1.307 billion |
| Midwest floods (IL, IA, KS, MN, MO, NE, ND, SD, WI) | 1993 | $1.141 billion |
| Hurricane Floyd (CT, DE, FL, ME, MD, NH, NJ, NY, NC, PA, SC, VT, VA) | 1999 | $1.186 billion |
| Tropical Storm Allison (FL, LA, MS, PA, TX) | 2001 | $970 million |
| Loma Prieta earthquake (CA) | 1989 | $865.7 million |
| Red River Valley floods (MN, ND, SD) | 1997 | $740.1 million |
| Hurricane Fran (MD, NC, PA, VA, WV) | 1996 | $621.8 million |

*Amount obligated from the President's Disaster Relief Fund for FEMA's assistance programs, hazard mitigation grants, federal mission assignments, contractual services, and administrative costs as of July 31, 2003. Figures do not include funding provided by other participating federal agencies, such as the disaster loan programs of the Small Business Administration and the Agriculture Department's Farm Service Agency. Note that funding amounts are stated in nominal dollars, unadjusted for inflation.

*Source*: Federal Emergency Management Agency (FEMA). 2003. "A Nation Remembers, A Nation Mourns." Washington, DC: FEMA (September).

TABLE 1-2   **Ten Most Costly World Insurance Losses, 1970–2001[a]**

| Date | Country | Event | Insured loss ($ millions)[b] |
|------|---------|-------|------------------------------|
| Sep. 11, 2001 | United States | Terrorist attack on WTC, Pentagon, and other buildings | $20,346[c] |
| Aug. 23, 1992 | United States, Bahamas | Hurricane Andrew | 20,185 |
| Jan. 17, 1994 | United States | Northridge, California, earthquake | 16,720 |
| Sep. 27, 1991 | Japan | Typhoon Mireille | 7,338 |
| Jan. 25, 1990 | France, United Kingdom, *et al.* | Winterstorm Daria | 6,221 |
| Dec. 25, 1999 | France, Switzerland, *et al.* | Winterstorm Lothar | 6,164 |
| Sep. 15, 1989 | Puerto Rico, United States, *et al.* | Hurricane Hugo | 5,990 |
| Oct. 15, 1987 | France, United Kingdom, *et al.* | Storm and floods | 4,674 |
| Feb. 25, 1990 | Western/Central Europe | Winterstorm Vivian | 4,323 |
| Sep. 22, 1999 | Japan | Typhoon Bart | 4,293 |

[a]Excluding liability.
[b]Adjusted to 2001 U.S. dollars by Swiss Re.
[c]Preliminary estimate for insured property damage and related coverage only.

*Source*:  Swiss Re, sigma, No. 1/2002, Insured Losses for Natural Catastrophes in the United States from Insurance Services Office, Inc.; and www.disasterinformation.org/stats.htm.

- Direct housing: 8,957 applications processed; 5,287 applications approved (59%)
- Mortgage and rental assistance: 11,818 applications processed; 6,187 applications approved (14%)
- Individual and family grant program: 43,660 applications processed; 6,139 applications approved (14%)
- Disaster unemployment: 6,657 claims processed; 3,210 claims approved (48%)
- Crisis counseling: $166 million
- Aid to government and nonprofits: $4.49 billion
- Debris removal: 437 million
- Overtime for New York Police Department (NYPD): $295.4 million
- Overtime for Fire Department New York: $105.6 million

*Source*: Federal Emergency Management Agency (FEMA). 2003. "A Nation Remembers, A Nation Mourns." Washington, DC: FEMA (September).

The insurance losses resulting from the September 11 events exceed all worldwide records for the 30-year period prior to September 11 and for any disaster event in U.S. history (Table 1-2 and Table 1-3): **Note, however, that the losses from the August 2005 Hurricane Katrina disaster are expected to exceed this number.**

- Amount of federal aid New York received within 2 months of the September 11 events: $9.5 billion
- Amount collected by the 11 September Fund: $501 million
- Percentage of fund used for cash assistance and services such as grief counseling for families of victims and survivors: 89

TABLE 1-3   **Ten Most Costly Catastrophes, United States**

| Date | Peril | Insured loss when event occurred ($ millions) | In 2001 dollars[a] |
|------|-------|-----------------------------------------------|--------------------|
| Sep. 2001 | World Trade Center[b] | $40,000.0 | $40,000.0 |
| Aug. 1992 | Hurricane Andrew | 15,500.0 | 19,565.6 |
| Jan. 1994 | Northridge, California, earthquake | 12,500.0 | 14,937.6 |
| Sep. 1989 | Hurricane Hugo | 4,195.0 | 5,991.4 |
| Sep. 1998 | Hurricane Georges | 2,900.0 | 3,150.9 |
| Jun. 2001 | Tropical Storm Allison | 2,500.0 | 2,500.0 |
| Oct. 1995 | Hurricane Opal | 2,100.0 | 2,440.4 |
| Sep. 1999 | Hurricane Floyd | 1,960.0 | 2,083.5 |
| Mar. 1993 | 20-State winter storm | 1,750.0 | 2,144.8 |
| Oct. 1991 | Oakland, California, fire | 1,700.0 | 2,210.5 |

[a]Adjusted to 2001 dollars by the Insurance Information Institute.
[b]Insurance Information Institute estimate of total losses.

*Source*: Insurance Services Office, Inc.; Insurance Information Institute; and www. disasterinformation.org/stats.htm.

- Quantity, in pounds, of food and supplies supplied by 11 September Fund at Ground Zero: 4.3 million
- Number of hot meals served to rescue workers by 11 September Fund: 343,000
- Number of displaced workers receiving job referrals: 5,000
- Amount of compensation sought by the families of civilian casualties of U.S. bombing in Afghanistan from the U.S. government: $10,000
- Amount of compensation sought for reckless misconduct and negligence from American Airlines by husband of September 11 victim: $50 million

*Source*: http://observer.guardian.co.uk/waronterrorism/story/0,1373,776451,00.html.

Additional information concerning these attacks and their impact is provided in subsequent chapters of the book.

## FIRST RESPONDER ISSUES

In July and August 2002, two September 11–related after-action reports were released: "Improving NYPD Emergency Preparedness and Response," prepared by McKinsey & Company for the New York City Police Department, and "Arlington County After-Action Report on the Response to the September 11 Terrorist Attack on the Pentagon," prepared for Arlington County, Virginia, by Titan Systems Corporation. Both reports are based on hundreds of interviews with event participants and reviews of organizational plans. These reports provide lessons learned and present hundreds of recommendations.

The NYPD report did not pass judgment on the success or failure of the NYPD on September 11 but rather assessed the NYPD's response objectives and instruments in order to identify 20 "improvement opportunities" for the NYPD, of which 6 merited immediate action:

- Clearer delineation of the roles and responsibilities of NYPD leaders
- Better clarity in the chain of command
- Radio communications protocols and procedures that optimize information flow
- More effective mobilization of members of the service
- More efficient provisioning and distribution of emergency and donated equipment
- A comprehensive disaster response plan, with a significant counterterrorism component.

*Source*: McKinsey & Company, 2002.

The Arlington County after-action report declared the response by the county and others to the Pentagon terrorist attack a success that "can be attributed to the efforts of ordinary men and women performing in extraordinary fashion" (Titan Systems Corporation, 2002). The terrorist attack on the Pentagon sorely tested the plans and skills of responders from Arlington County, Virginia; other jurisdictions; and the federal government. Appendix 1-1 presents some facts about September 11 at the Pentagon that were compiled in the report.

The Arlington County report contains 235 recommendations and lessons learned. Of these many recommendations, the report highlights examples of lessons learned in two categories: things that worked well and contributed to the overall success of the response and challenges encountered and overcome by responders that could serve as examples for other jurisdictions in the future. These lessons learned are presented in Appendix 1-2.

The events at the World Trade Center and the Pentagon vary significantly in size and impact, but from a responder's perspective, they are similar in terms of surprises and challenges. There are striking similarities between the "improvement opportunities" listed in the NYPD report and the "lessons learned" in the Arlington County report (Figure 1-6). While the specifics vary, both responses identified issues in five key areas:

- Command
- Communications
- Coordination
- Planning
- Dispatching personnel

Many of the actions taken after September 11 by government officials and emergency managers at the federal, state, and local levels reflect the need for changes in order to prepare for the next terrorist event.

## CONCLUSION

The terrorist attacks of September 11 have forever changed America and, in many ways, the world. This event has been termed the most significant disaster since the attack on Pearl Harbor, and the first national disaster. It seemed that every American knew someone or knew of someone who perished in the attacks, and surely every citizen felt the economic impact in the form of lost jobs, lost business, and an immediate reduction in the value of college savings and retirement accounts. Moreover, the perception that nobody was immune from the risk of becoming the next victim of terrorism spread quickly across the nation in the days and weeks that followed the attacks. The feelings of vulnerability were only strengthened in the wake of the October 2001 anthrax incidents and the sniper attacks in the Washington, D.C., metropolitan area on October 2002.

The expanded terrorism threat has created a new set of hazards (e.g., biological, chemical, radiological, and nuclear) that must be studied and understood to best prepare both our first responders and our citizens (see Chapter 4). New laws and executive orders that have been established to address the terrorism threat must strike a balance between our sense of security and our civil rights (see Chapter 2). A new and very large federal government agency, the Department of Homeland Security, has been formed from the parts of 22 other agencies and programs to coordinate and guide our nation's efforts in fighting terrorism on the domestic front (see Chapter 3). New funding programs have been established and there is a new focus for the nation's first responders.

FIGURE 1-6    Arlington, Virginia, March 7, 2002—A view of the Pentagon building shows the progress made in the reconstruction of the area damaged by the terrorist attack on the Pentagon on September 11, 2001. (Photo by Jocelyn Augustino/FEMA News Photo)

These significant changes are reflected not only in the daily lives of the American people but also in the way in which the country's emergency management system operates. The emergency management community must wonder if this new focus on terrorism will eventually reduce the system's capabilities at all levels of government and in the nongovernmental community to mitigate, prepare for, respond to, and recover from more common natural and technological disasters, as demonstrated in Hurricane Katrina.

It is important to recall that FEMA, as noted earlier in this chapter, has traversed this path before, when its focus was shifted from all-hazards to nuclear attack planning in the 1980s—with disastrous results for the agency and the victims of Hurricane Hugo, the Loma Prieta earthquake, and Hurricane Andrew. Though it can be argued that FEMA, in its new location within the Department of Homeland Security, is avoiding this fate, only time and experience will be effective judges. FEMA required a full 14 years to become an effective agency. DHS has a long way to go before reaching that distinction. Nobody, however, can predict what challenges the future will bring. As America's emergency management system adapts to the new terrorism risk, these will be the critical issues that must be addressed to ensure that it can effectively reduce the impact of all future disasters and mount a timely response when these events occur.

## REVIEW QUESTIONS

1. Identify the role the U.S. Constitution defines for federal, state, and local governments in the area of emergency management and public safety.
2. Which president established the Federal Emergency Management Agency (FEMA) and on what date? Which president established the Department of Homeland Security (DHS) and on what date?
3. Why did the National Governors Association and its members push the federal government to create FEMA? Why was DHS established?
4. After reviewing the difficulties that FEMA encountered in becoming a functioning emergency management agency, what issues do you anticipate DHS will en-counter in its evolution into a functioning government agency? Identify some lessons learned in the FEMA experience that could guide DHS actions in the future. Will history repeat itself as DHS matures as a government agency?
5. Throughout the history of emergency management in the United States, the priorities set for government emergency management agencies have been driven by the most widely perceived threat or hazard. How do you think the new threat of terrorism and the hazards associated with terrorism will impact the practice of emergency management in the United States at all levels of government (federal, state, and local) and in the business sector?

## REFERENCES

City of Oklahoma. 1996. "Alfred P. Murrah Federal Building Bombing, April 19, 1995."

Federal Emergency Management Agency (FEMA). 2003. "A Nation Remembers, A Nation Mourns." Washington, DC: FEMA (September).

Fire Protection Publications. Stillwater, OK: Oklahoma State University.

Fusco, A. L. 1993. "The World Trade Center Bombing: Report and Analysis." Emmitsburgs, MD: U.S. Fire Administration.

McKinsey & Company. 2002. "Improving NYPD Emergency Preparedness and Response." August 19, 2002.

Thompson, W. C. 2002. "One Year Later: The Fiscal Impact of 9/11 on New York City,", New York: Report Comptroller of the City of New York (September).

Titan Systems Inc. 2002. "Arlington County After-Action Report on the Response to the September 11 Terrorist Attack on the Pentagon." Washington, DC: Titan Systems Inc. (July).

# APPENDIX 1-1

## Notable Facts about September 11, 2001, at the Pentagon

- The first Arlington County emergency response unit arrived at the crash site less than 3 minutes after impact.
- Lieutenant Robert Medarios was the first Arlington County Police Department command-level official on site. He made a verbal agreement with a representative of the Defense Protective Service that Arlington County would lead the rescue efforts of all local and federal agencies.
- More than 30 urban search-and-rescue teams, police departments, fire departments, and federal agencies assisted Arlington's police and fire departments in the rescue. Some of these important partners included the Federal Bureau of Investigation, the Federal Emergency Management Agency, U.S. Park Police, Defense Protective Service, the Military District of Washington, the Metropolitan Washington Airport Authority, the Virginia Department of Emergency Management, and USAR teams from Albuquerque, New Mexico; Fairfax County, Virginia; Montgomery County, Maryland; and Memphis, Tennessee.
- Captain Dennis Gilroy and the team on Foam Unit 161 from the Fort Meyer Fire Station were on site at the Pentagon when Flight 77 crashed into the building. Firefighters Mark Skipper and Alan Wallace, who were next to the unit, received burns and lacerations but immediately began helping Pentagon employees, who were trying to escape from harm's way, out of the first-floor windows.
- Captain Steve McCoy and the crew of Engine 101 were on their way to fire staff training in Crystal City when they saw the plane flying low overhead and an explosion from the vicinity of the Pentagon. McCoy was the first person to call Arlington County's emergency communications center to report the plane crash.
- The Arlington County American Red Cross Chapter coordinated support from the Red Cross. The chapter had 80 trained volunteers at the time of the attack, but the organization's mutual-aid arrangements with other chapters garnered nearly 1,500 volunteers who helped support the emergency services personnel, victims, and their families.
- Business supporters set up temporary food service on the Pentagon parking lot for rescue workers. More than 187,940 meals were served to emergency workers. Many other businesses brought phones (so rescuers could call home), building materials, and other vital necessities.
- More than 112 surgeries on nine burn victims were performed in 3 weeks. One of the nine burn victims died after having more than 60% of her body burned. There were 106 patients that reported to area hospitals with various injuries.
- One hundred eighty-nine people died at the Pentagon—184 victims and 5 terrorists. On the morning of September 11, 1941, the original construction on the Pentagon began.

*Source*: Titan Systems Inc. 2002. "Arlington County After-Action Report on the Response to the September 11 Terrorist Attack on the Pentagon." Washington, DC: Titan Systems Inc. (July).

## APPENDIX 1-2
### Lessons Learned at the Pentagon

The Arlington County after-action report contains 235 recommendations and lessons learned, each of which must be understood within the context and setting of the Pentagon response. Some specifically apply to a particular response element or activity. Others address overarching issues that apply to Arlington County and other jurisdictions, particularly those in large metropolitan areas. They have not been weighted or prioritized. This is a task best left to those with operational responsibilities and budgetary authority.

**Capabilities Others Should Emulate**

1. *Incident Command System and Unified Command*: The primary response participants understood the ICS, implemented it effectively, and complied with its provisions. The Arlington County Fire Department, an experienced ICS practitioner, established its command presence literally within minutes of the attack. Other supporting jurisdictions and agencies, with few exceptions, operated seamlessly within the ICS framework. For those organizations and individuals unfamiliar with the ICS and Unified Command, particularly the military, which has its own clearly defined command and control mechanisms, the incident commander provided explicit information and guidance early during the response and elicited their full cooperation.

2. *Mutual aid and outside support*: The management and integration of mutual-aid assets and the coordination and cooperation of agencies at all government echelons, volunteer organizations, and private businesses were outstanding. Public safety organizations and chief administrative officers (CAOs) of nearby jurisdictions lent their support to Arlington County. The response to the Pentagon attack revealed the total scope and magnitude of support available

throughout the Washington metropolitan area and across the nation.

3. *Arlington County CEMP (Community Emergency Management Plan)*: The CEMP proved to be what its title implies. It was well thought out, properly maintained, frequently practiced, and effectively implemented. Government leaders were able to quickly marshal the substantial resources of Arlington County in support of the first responders, without interfering with tactical operations. County board members worked with counterparts in neighboring jurisdictions and elected federal and state officials to ensure a rapid economic recovery, and they engaged in frequent dialogue with the citizens of Arlington County.

4. *Employee Assistance Program (EAP)*: At the time of the Pentagon attack, Arlington County already had in place an aggressive, well-established EAP offering critical incident stress management (CISM) services to public safety and other county employees. In particular, the ACFD embraced the concept and encouraged all of its members to use EAP services. Thus it is not surprising that the members of the EAP staff were well received when they arrived at the incident site within 3 hours of the attack. During the incident response and in follow-up sessions weeks afterward, the EAP proved invaluable to first responders, their families, and the entire county support network. This is a valuable resource that must be incorporated in response plans.

5. *Training, exercises, and shared experiences*: The ACED has long recognized the possibility of a terrorist attack using weapons of mass destruction (WMD) in the Washington metropolitan area and has pursued an aggressive preparedness program for such an event, including

its pioneering work associated with the MMRS. In preparation for anticipated problems associated with the arrival of Y2K, Arlington County government thoroughly exercised the CEMP. In 1998 the FBI's Washington Field Office (WFO) established a fire liaison position to work specifically with area fire departments. Public safety organizations in the Washington metropolitan area routinely work together on events of national prominence and shared jurisdictional interests, such as presidential inaugural celebrations, visits by heads of state, international conferences such as the periodic International Monetary Fund (IMF) conference, and others. These organizations also regularly participate in training exercises, including those hosted by the Pentagon and MDW. All this and more contributed to the successful Pentagon response.

**Challenges That Must Be Met**

1. *Self-dispatching*: Organizations, response units, and individuals proceeding on their own initiative directly to an incident site, without the knowledge and permission of the host jurisdiction and the incident commander, complicate the exercise of command, increase the risks faced by bona fide responders, and exacerbate the challenge of accountability. WMD terrorist event response plans should designate preselected and well-marked staging areas. Dispatch instructions should be clear. Law enforcement agencies should be familiar with deployment plans and quickly establish incident site-access controls. When identified, self-dispatched resources should be immediately released from the scene, unless incorporated into the incident commander's response plan.

2. *Fixed and mobile command and control facilities*: Arlington County does not have a facility specifically designed and equipped to support the emergency management functions specified in the CEMP. The conference room currently used as the EOC does not have adequate space

and is not configured or properly equipped for that role. The notification and recall capabilities of the emergency communications center are constrained by equipment limitations, and there are no protected telephone lines for outside calls when the 9-1-1 lines are saturated. The ACED does not have a mobile command vehicle and relied on the use of vehicles belonging to other organizations and jurisdictions. The ACPD mobile command unit needs to be replaced or extensively modernized.

3. *Communications*: Almost all aspects of communications continue to be problematic, from initial notification to tactical operations. Cellular telephones were of little value in the first few hours, and cellular priority access service (CPAS) is not provided to emergency responders. Radio channels were initially oversaturated, and interoperability problems among jurisdictions and agencies persist. Even portable radios that are otherwise compatible were sometimes preprogrammed in a fashion that precluded interoperability. Pagers seemed to be the most reliable means of notification when available and used, but most firefighters are not issued pagers. The Arlington County EOC does not have an installed radio capacity and relied on portable radios coincidentally assigned to staff members assigned duties at the EOC.

4. *Logistics*: Arlington County, like most other jurisdictions, was not logistically prepared for an operation of the duration and magnitude of the Pentagon attack. The ACED did not have an established logistics function, a centralized supply system, or experience in long-term logistics support. Stock levels of personal protective equipment (PPE), critical high-demand items (such as batteries and breathing apparatus), equipment for reserve vehicles, and medical supplies for EMS units were insufficient for sustained operations. These challenges were overcome at the Pentagon with the aid of the more experienced Fairfax County Fire and Rescue Department logistics staff. A stronger standing

capacity, however, is needed for a jurisdiction the size of Arlington County.

5. *Hospital coordination*: Communications and coordination between EMS control at the incident site and area hospitals receiving injured victims were deficient. The coordination difficulties were not simple equipment failures. They represent flaws in the system present on September 11. Regional hospital disaster plans no longer require a clearinghouse hospital or other designated communications focal point for the dissemination of patient disposition and treatment information. Thus hospitals first learned of en route victims when contacted by transporting EMS units, and EMS control reconstructed much of the disposition information by contacting hospitals after the fact. Although the number of victims of the Pentagon attack were fewer than many anticipated, they were not insignificant. An incident with more casualties would have seriously strained the system.

*Source*: Titan Systems Inc. 2002. "Arlington County After-Action Report on the Response to the September 11 Terrorist Attack on the Pentagon." Washington, DC: Titan Systems Inc. (July).

# 2

# Statutory Authority

## INTRODUCTION

The Department of Homeland Security, and homeland security as we know it today, is primarily the result of legislation arising since the September 11, 2001, terrorist attacks. However, a movement to establish such broad-sweeping legislation was initiated long before those attacks took place. Terrorists, both domestic and international, have been striking the United States within and outside its borders for decades, though many had failed to take notice. Support for much of this precursory legislation was weak, and that which did pass rarely garnered front-page headlines. Institutional cultures in many of the agencies that may have been affected by this early legislation also served as a strong barrier to the fulfillment of goals.

The purpose of this chapter is to trace the series of statutes, presidential directives, and executive orders that have been issued and implemented to establish the authorities and the infrastructure within which the federal government must now address the terrorism hazard. Terrorism authorities were vague and not well established prior to September 11, and, as the 9/11 Commission discovered, not effective in coordinating terrorism prevention. The new legislation that has

emerged since September 11 has attempted to solve many of the recognized problems at the federal level. In doing so, massive changes have occurred in the organizational makeup of the federal government that have altered how terrorist attacks are managed.

Years after the September 11 attacks, these changes continue. Many of the original legislative actions taken were accused of being knee-jerk in nature, but are also heralded as being symbolic of a nation coming together in a time of need to address a common problem. As time passes, and the luxury of consideration is applied, it becomes obvious that changes must be made to the original laws that were enacted, and this process may go on for many more years to come.

A legislative timeline is provided with this chapter to provide reference for the progression of terrorism-related legislation, presidential directives, and executive orders that have occurred. For some of the more significant examples, including the USA PATRIOT Act of 2001 and the Homeland Security Act of 2002, detailed description and analysis are provided. The PATRIOT Act, which is notorious for its quick passage, placed new authority in the hands of the U.S. Justice Department to assist their efforts to identify and detain suspected terrorists operating in the United States. The Homeland Security Act resulted in the largest government reorganization since 1947, and established the Department of Homeland Security.

Also included in this chapter are reviews of Homeland Security Presidential Directive No. 5, the fiscal year (FY) 2006 budget for the Department of Homeland Security, and an analysis of the ongoing struggle by public officials to balance the need for increased security in the domestic war on terrorism and the need to protect the civil liberties of all Americans.

## NUNN–LUGAR–DOMENICI ACT

The contemporary roots of the Homeland Security Act of 2002 date back to the first term of the Clinton administration. Several major terror-related events occurred during Clinton's first three years in office, prompting the drafting and passage of the Nunn–Lugar–Domenici Weapons of Mass Destruction (WMD) Act (Public Law 104-201, September 23, 1996). These events included:

- 1993 bombing of the World Trade Center
- 1995 Oklahoma City bombing
- 1995 Tokyo subway sarin gas attacks

The primary result of the WMD Act was the provision of greater funding for training and equipment for the nation's first responders. This act addressed what could be done in the aftermath of a terrorist attack, but very little was done to change the way in which the federal government prevented terrorist acts from occurring in the first place. Always in the background, however, was a growing bipartisan movement calling for a less fragmented and more coordinated approach to combating terrorism.

## TERRORISM ANNEX TO THE FEDERAL RESPONSE PLAN

In 1996, during the Olympic competitions in Atlanta, Georgia, a bomb was detonated in a crowd, injuring dozens of people and killing one. The source of the attack was determined to have been domestic, apparently the act of a delusional individual, thereby negating any greater recognition by Americans of the need for better systems of terrorism prevention. This was, however, the third large terrorist attack on American soil in a period of 3 years, and as such it helped to build the steam behind the development of a terrorism annex to the Federal Response Plan (FRP). The criminal element of a terrorist attack, which had confounded previous responses to terrorism where the FRP had been invoked, was recognized as a component that needed special consideration (because it had not been addressed in the original FRP). This annex appended the original response document by dictating the coordination of the various federal agencies likely to respond to future terrorist events, including the events of September 11.

## THE THREE COMMISSIONS

In 1998, President Clinton and House Speaker Newt Gingrich petitioned Congress to form a 14-member panel called the United States Commission on National Security/21st Century (USCNS/21), also known as the Hart–Rudman Commission, to make strategic recommendations on how the U.S. government could ensure the nation's security in the coming years. The independent panel, created by Congress, was tasked with conducting a comprehensive review of American security with the goal of designing a national security strategy.

The commission's report, titled "Road Map for National Security: Imperative for Change," dated January 31, 2001, recommended the creation of a new independent National Homeland Security Agency (NHSA) with responsibility for planning, coordinating, and integrating various U.S. government activities involved in homeland security. This agency would be built on the Federal Emergency Management Agency (FEMA), with the Coast Guard, the Customs Service, and the U.S. Border Patrol [now part of U.S. Customs and Border Protection (CBP) within the Department of Homeland Security] transferred into it.

NHSA would assume responsibility for the safety of the American people as well as oversee the protection of critical infrastructure, including information technology. Obviously, the commission's recommendations were not heeded before 2001, but many of its findings would later be integrated into the justification and legislation behind the creation of the Department of Homeland Security (DHS).

Two other commissions were established to study the terrorist threat during these years: the Gilmore Commission and the Bremer Commission, as discussed next.

The Gilmore Commission, also known as the Advisory Panel to Assess Domestic Response Capabilities for Terrorism Involving Weapons of Mass Destruction, produced a series of annual reports beginning in 1999 (with the final report released in 2003). Each of these reports presented a growing base of knowledge concerning the WMD risk faced by the United States, and a recommended course of action required to counter that risk.

The Bremer Commission, also known as the National Commission on Terrorism, addressed the issue of the international terrorist threat. The commission was mandated by Congress to evaluate the nation's laws, policies, and practices for preventing terrorism, and for punishing those responsible for terrorist events. Its members drafted a report titled "Countering the Changing Threat of International Terrorism." This report, issued in the year 2000, arrived at the following conclusions:

- International terrorism poses an increasingly dangerous and difficult threat to America.
- Countering the growing danger of the terrorist threat requires significantly stepping up U.S. efforts.
- Priority one is to prevent terrorist attacks. U.S. intelligence and law enforcement communities must use the full scope of their authority to collect intelligence regarding terrorist plans and methods.
- U.S. policies must firmly target all states that support terrorists. Private sources of financial and logistical support for terrorists must be subjected to the full force and sweep of U.S. and international laws.
- A terrorist attack involving a biological agent, deadly chemicals, or nuclear or radiological material, even if it succeeds only partially, could profoundly affect the entire nation. The government must do more to prepare for such an event.
- The president and Congress should reform the system for reviewing and funding departmental counterterrorism programs to ensure that the activities and programs of various agencies are part of a comprehensive plan.

Each of these conclusions and recommendations would take on new meaning in the aftermath of the September 11 attacks, and would guide many of the changes incorporated into the Homeland Security Act of 2002. However, in the absence of a greater recognition of a terrorist threat within the borders of the United States, no major programs were initiated to combat the growing risk.

## PRESIDENTIAL DECISION DIRECTIVES 62 AND 63

As these commissions were conducting their research, President Clinton was addressing other recognized and immediate needs through the passage of several presidential decision directives (PDDs). Terrorist attacks continued to occur throughout the world, aimed at U.S. government, military, and private interests. In 1996, terrorists carried out a suicide bombing at U.S. military barracks (Khobar Towers) in Saudi Arabia, and in 1998, simultaneous bombings were carried out at the U.S. diplomatic missions in Kenya and Tanzania.

In May 1998, President Clinton issued Presidential Decision Directive 62 (PDD-62): "Combating Terrorism," which called for the establishment of the Office of the National Coordinator for Security, Infrastructure Protection and Counterterrorism. The directive's primary goal was to create a new and more systematic approach to fighting the terrorist threat.

PDD-62 reinforced the mission of many U.S. agencies involved in wide array of counterterrorism activities. The new national coordinator was tasked with overseeing a broad variety of relevant policies and programs including counterterrorism, critical infrastructure protection, WMD preparedness, and consequence management.

Soon after this directive, President Clinton issued Presidential Decision Directive 63 (PDD-63), "Protecting America's Critical Infrastructure." This directive tasked all of the departments of the federal government with assessing the vulnerabilities of their cyber and physical infrastructures and with working to reduce their exposure to new and existing threats.

## ATTORNEY GENERAL'S FIVE-YEAR INTERAGENCY COUNTERTERRORISM AND TECHNOLOGY CRIME PLAN

In December 1998, as mandated by Congress, the Department of Justice (DOJ), through the Federal Bureau of Investigation (FBI), began a coordinated project with other agencies to develop the Attorney General's Five-Year Interagency Counterterrorism and Technology Crime Plan. The FBI emerged as the federal government's principal agency for responding to and investigating terrorism. Congress had intended the plan to serve as a baseline for the coordination of a national strategy and operational capabilities to combat terrorism. This plan represented a substantial interagency effort, including goals, objectives, performance indicators, and recommended specific agency actions to help resolve interagency problems. It clearly did not, however, tear down the walls that prevented interagency sharing of information, as evidenced by the failures that resulted in the success of the 9/11 terrorists.

## GENERAL ACCOUNTING OFFICE FINDINGS

The Department of Justice asserted that the Attorney General's Five-Year Interagency Counter-

terrorism and Technology Crime Plan, considered together with related PDDs as described earlier, represented a comprehensive national strategy to address the terrorist threat. However, after a thorough review, the General Accounting Office (GAO), Congress's investigative arm, concluded that additional work remained that would build on the progress that the plan represented. The GAO contended that a comprehensive national security strategy was lacking.

The GAO report "Combating Terrorism: Comments on Counterterrorism Leadership and National Strategy" (GAO-01-55T), released March 27, 2001, stated that the DOJ plan did not have measurable outcomes and suggested, for example, that it should include goals that improve state and local response capabilities. The report argued that without a clearly defined national strategy, the nation would continue to miss opportunities to focus and shape counterterrorism programs to meet the impending threat. It also made the criticism that the DOJ plan lacked a coherent framework to develop and evaluate budget requirements for combating terrorism since there was no signal focal point. The report claimed that no single entity was acting as the federal government's top official accountable to both the president and Congress for the terrorism hazard, and that fragmentation existed in both coordination of domestic preparedness programs and in efforts to develop a national strategy.

The GAO released another report in early September 2001 entitled "Combating Terrorism: Selected Challenges and Related Recommendations" (GAO-01-822), which it finalized in the last days before the terrorist attacks occurred in Washington and New York. The report stated that the federal government was ill equipped and unprepared to counter a major terrorist attack, claiming also that—from sharing intelligence to coordinating a response—the government had failed to put in place an effective critical infrastructure system. It further stated that

> Federal efforts to develop a national strategy to combat terrorism . . . have progressed, but key challenges remain. The initial step toward developing a national strategy is to conduct a national threat and risk assessment . . . at the

national level (agencies) have not completed assessments of the most likely weapon-of-mass destruction agents and other terrorist threats. . . .

To prevent terrorist attacks, the GAO recommended:

- A national strategy to combat terrorism and computer-based attacks
- Better protection for the nation's infrastructure
- A single focal point to oversee coordination of federal programs
- Completion of a threat assessment on likely WMD and other weapons that might be used by terrorists
- Revision of the Attorney General's Five-Year Interagency Counterterrorism and Technology Crime Plan to better serve as a national strategy
- Coordination of research and development to combat terrorism.

In a later report regarding Homeland Security, "Key Elements to Unify Efforts Are Underway but Uncertainty Remains" (GAO-02-610), the GAO called for more of the same in terms of needing central leadership and an overarching strategy that identifies goals and objectives, priorities, measurable outcomes, and state and local government roles in combating terrorism since the efforts of more than 40 federal entities and numerous state and local governments were still fragmented. It also called for the term *homeland security* to be defined properly since to date it had not.

## SEPTEMBER 11, 2001

The attacks on the World Trade Center in New York City and the Pentagon in Arlington, Virginia, on September 11, 2001, could arguably be considered the first national disaster event, outside of wartime, in the history of the United States. It is the first disaster in this country that impacted all Americans, leaving all citizens and communities with an unrelenting sense of vulnerability. The economic consequences of these attacks, felt in all parts of our country and, in fact,

around the world, make this disaster event truly global in scope.

The attacks involved the hijacking of four commercial airliners by 19 trained terrorists. Three of the four planes were flown into major American landmarks: the two World Trade Center Twin Towers, and the headquarters of the U.S. military. The fourth, whose target may never be conclusively known, was prevented from reaching its target by passengers on the plane who overpowered its four terrorist hijackers. Almost 3,000 people were killed, and billions of dollars in property damage resulted. The full economic impacts, which include everything from lost revenues to increased spending on terrorism preparedness, may never be known.

This was not a simple act, but one that required years of surveillance, funding, training, intelligence gathering, practice, and breaching of U.S. immigration law. There were many instances during this time, as evidenced in the report of the National Commission on Terrorist Attacks Upon the United States (9/11 Commission), which was created to investigate the causes of the 9/11 attacks and means to prevent similar attacks from occurring in the future, where individual agencies involved in counterterrorist activities recognized one or more of these activities. However, insufficient coordination between the agencies prevented the federal government system from piecing together the larger picture of what exactly was occurring and, as such, the terrorists were ultimately successful in their mission.

## IMMEDIATE RESPONSE TO THE 9/11 TERRORIST ATTACKS

In the immediate aftermath of the September 11 attacks, as the search-and-rescue teams were still sifting through the debris and wreckage for survivors in New York, Pennsylvania, and Virginia, the federal government was analyzing what had just happened and what it could quickly do to begin the process of ensuring such attacks could not be repeated. It was recognized that nothing too substantial could take place void of longer term study and congressional review, but the circumstances mandated that real changes begin without delay.

On September 20, 2001, just 9 days after the attacks, President George W. Bush announced that an Office of Homeland Security would be established within the White House by executive order. Directing this office would be Pennsylvania Governor Tom Ridge. Ridge was given no real staff to manage, and the funding he would have at his disposal was minimal. The actual order, catalogued as Executive Order 13228, was given on October 8, 2001. In addition to creating the Office of Homeland Security, this order created the Homeland Security Council, "to develop and coordinate the implementation of a comprehensive national strategy to secure the United States from terrorist threats or attacks."

Four days later, on September 24, 2001, President Bush announced that he would be seeking passage of an act entitled "Uniting and Strengthening America by Providing Appropriate Tools Required to Intercept and Obstruct Terrorism," which would become better known as the PATRIOT Act of 2001. This act, which introduced a large number of controversial legislative changes in order to significantly increase the surveillance and investigative powers of law enforcement agencies in the United States (as it states) to ". . . deter and punish terrorist acts in the United States and around the world," was signed into law by the president on October 26 after very little deliberation in Congress.

On October 29, 2001, President Bush issued the first of many homeland security presidential directives (HSPDs), which were specifically designed to "record and communicate presidential decisions about the homeland security policies of the United States" (HSPD-1, 2001). Sidebar 2-1 lists several of the HSPDs, their stated purposes, and their dates of issuance.

---

SIDEBAR 2-1   **Select Homeland Security Presidential Directives**

HSPD-1: Organization and Operation of the Homeland Security Council—October 29, 2001

HSPD-2: Combating Terrorism through Immigration Policies—October 29, 2001

HSPD-3: Creation of the Homeland Security Advisory System—March 11, 2002

HSPD-4: National Strategy to Combat WMDs—September 17, 2002

HSPD-5: Management of Domestic Incidents [Creation of a National Incident Management System (NIMS)]—February 28, 2003

HSPD-6: Integration and Use of Screening Information [Creation of the Terrorist Threat Integration Center (TTIC)]—September 16, 2003

HSPD-7: Critical Infrastructure Identification, Prioritization, and Protection—December 17, 2003

HSPD-8: Strengthen National Preparedness ("Establish policies to strengthen the preparedness of the United States to prevent and respond to threatened or actual domestic terrorist attacks, major disasters, and other emergencies by requiring a national domestic all-hazards preparedness goal, establishing mechanisms for improved delivery of Federal preparedness assistance to State and local governments, and outlining actions to strengthen preparedness capabilities of Federal, State, and local entities.")—December 17, 2003

HSPD-9: Defense of U.S. Agriculture and Food—February 3, 2004

HSPD-10: Defense from Biological Weapons—April 28, 2004

HSPD-11: Comprehensive Terrorist Screening Procedures—August 27, 2004

HSPD-13: Maritime Security—December 21, 2004

On March 21, 2002, President Bush signed Executive Order 13260 establishing the President's Homeland Security Advisory Council (PHSAC) and Senior Advisory Committees for Homeland Security.

## Legislative, Presidential Directive, and Executive Order Timeline

*November 18, 1988*—Executive Order (EO) 12656—Assignment of Emergency Preparedness Responsibilities. This executive order defines a national security emergency as any occurrence that seriously degrades or threatens the national security of the United States. Terrorist incidents were not specifically mentioned except for DOJ responsibilities. The National Security Council is assigned responsibility for developing and administering this policy. The director of the Federal Emergency Management Agency (FEMA) shall assist in the implementation of and management of national security emergency management preparedness policy by coordinating with other federal departments. FEMA is responsible for coordinating, supporting, developing, and implementing the following: civil national security emergency preparedness and response programs, continuity of government functions, and civil-military support. This EO was in draft and coordination for five years.

*November 18, 1988*—EO 12657—FEMA Assistance in Emergency Preparedness Planning at Commercial Nuclear Power Plants Responsibilities. This EO allows FEMA to initially respond in coordinating federal response activities when advance state and local commitments (e.g., response planning) are absent or inadequate off site at commercial nuclear power plants. FEMA is authorized to assume any necessary command and control function, or delegate such function to another federal agency, in the event that no competent state and local authority is available to perform such function.

*November 23, 1988*—President Reagan signs into law the Robert T. Stafford Disaster Relief and Emergency Assistance Act [Public Law (P.L.) 100-707] amending the Federal Disaster Relief Act of 1974.

*March 23, 1989*—EO 12673 delegates Stafford Act authority with some exceptions (principally declarations) to the director of FEMA.

*April 1992*—Federal Response Plan (FRP) is issued. This plan "established a process and structure for the systematic, coordinated, and effective delivery of Federal assistance to address the consequences of any major disaster or emergency declared under the Robert T. Stafford Disaster Relief and Emergency Assistance Act, as amended." Under the "Scope" section, the FRP states "[I]n some instances, a disaster or emergency may result in a situation [that] affects the national security of the United States. For those instances, appropriate national security authorities and procedures will be utilized to address the national security requirements of the situation." Law enforcement emergencies are defined under "Policies," and procedures are referenced under which DOJ and Department of Defense (DOD) personnel respond to law enforcement emergencies under 28 CFR Part 65 and 10 USC 331–333.

*November 30, 1993*—P.L. 103-160 §1704. Joint Resolution of Congress on FEMA terrorism-preparedness planning provides that "[I]t is the sense of Congress that the president should strengthen Federal interagency emergency planning by the Federal emergency management agency and other appropriate Federal, state, and local agencies for development of a capability for early detection and warning of and response to (1) potential terrorist use of chemical or biological agents or weapons; and (2) emergencies or natural disasters involving industrial chemicals or the widespread outbreak of disease."

*June 3, 1994*—EO 12919—National Defense Industrial Resources Preparedness. This EO delegates authorities and addresses national defense industrial resource policies and programs under the Defense Production Act of 1950, as amended, except for the amendments to Title III of the act in the Energy Security Act of 1980 and excludes telecommunication authorities under EO 12472. Under this order the FEMA director (1) serves as an adviser to the National Security Council on issues of national security resource preparedness and on the use of the authorities and functions delegated by this order; (2) provides for the central coordination of the plans and programs incident to authorities and functions delegated under this order, and provides guidance and procedures approved by the assistant to the president for National Security Affairs to the federal departments and agencies under this order; (3) establishes procedures, in consultation with federal departments and agencies assigned functions under this order, to resolve in a timely and effective manner conflicts and issues that may arise in implementing the authorities and functions delegated under this order; and (4) reports to the president periodically concerning all program activities conducted pursuant to this order.

*November 1994*—P.L. 103-337. This law repeals the Federal Civil Defense Act. In new Title VI of the Stafford Act, the policy of the federal government is for FEMA to provide necessary direction, coordination and guidance, and necessary assistance, as authorized in the title so that a comprehensive emergency preparedness system exists for all hazards in the United States. FEMA is directed to (1) prepare federal response plans and programs for the emergency preparedness of the United States and (2) sponsor and direct such plans and programs to coordinate such plans and programs with state efforts. The FEMA director may request such reports on state plans and operations for emergency preparedness as may be necessary to keep the president, Congress, and the states advised of the status of emergency preparedness in the United States. Interstate emergency preparedness compacts are authorized to (1) assist and encourage the states to negotiate and enter into interstate emergency preparedness compacts; (2) facilitate uniformity between state compacts and consistency with federal emergency response plans and programs; (3) assist and coordinate the activities under state compacts; and (4) aid and assist reciprocal state emergency preparedness legislation that will permit mutual aid in the event of a hazard that cannot be adequately met or controlled by a state or political subdivision thereof. Public Law 103-337 amended P.L. 93-288 as previously amended by P.L. 100-707.

*January 22, 1995*—Director of FEMA establishes the Office of National Security Coordination, which reports directly to him.

*March 19, 1995*—Sarin gas attack on a subway in Tokyo, Japan.

*April 19, 1995*—The Murrah Federal Office Building in Oklahoma City is bombed. Within 7 hours of the explosion, President Clinton signs an emergency declaration. This is the first use of the president's authority under the Stafford Act to "self-initiate" an emergency declaration for emergencies with federal involvement.

*June 21, 1995*—Presidential Decision Directive 39. This directive states that it is the policy of the United States to use all appropriate means to deter, defeat, and respond to all terrorist attacks on our territory and resources, both people and facilities, wherever they occur. Established that DOJ personnel have lead responsibility for crisis management, and FEMA personnel have lead responsibility for consequence management. FEMA chairs the Senior Interagency Group for Training and Preparedness.

*April 24, 1996*—Antiterrorism and Effective Death Penalty Act of 1996, P.L. 104-132 [110 Stat. 1255]. Congress funds first responder and firefighter training by grants. United States Fire Administration receives funds from DOJ to conduct first responder training.

*May 1, 1996*—Federal Radiological Emergency Response Plan (FRERP) signed by FEMA Director James L. Witt. The FRERP addresses radiological sabotage and terrorism and states that a coordinated response to contain or mitigate a threatened or actual release of radioactive material would be essentially the same whether it resulted from an accidental or deliberate act. Therefore, sabotage and terrorism are not treated as separate types of emergencies, rather they are considered a complicating dimension of (radiological emergencies).

*July 15, 1996*—EO 13010—Critical Infrastructure Protection. This EO established the President's Commission on Critical Infrastructure Protection (PCCIP) and the Critical Infrastructure Protection Working Group (CIPWG). Certain national infrastructures are so vital that their incapacity or destruction would have a debilitating impact on the defense or economic security of the United States. It is essential that the government and private sector work together to develop a strategy for protecting them and ensuring their continued operation. These infrastructures include telecommunications, transportation, water supply systems, emergency services (including medical, police, fire, and rescue), and continuity of government.

*1996*—Anti-Terrorism and Effective Death Penalty Act (P.L. 104-132). The president signs a law authorizing FEMA and the DOJ's Office of Justice Programs to fund and develop an emergency response to terrorism training program for fire, emergency medical service, and public safety personnel. Annual appropriation to DOJ is shared with FEMA through FY 2002. DOJ administers grants through its State and Local Domestic Preparedness Office (SLDPO) in its Office of Justice Assistance (not in the FBI).

*September 23, 1996*—Defense Against Weapons of Mass Destruction Act (P.L. 104-201), also called Nunn–Lugar legislation. The president signs a law directing the DOD to lead, for 3 years, domestic preparedness for responding to and managing the consequences of a terrorist attack using WMD. The law authorizes transfer of this responsibility to another agency after 3 years with presidential concurrence.

*February 7, 1997*—FEMA director adopts the Terrorism Incident Annex (TIA) to the Federal Response Plan. This annex provides federal emergency planners with information and a framework within which to address the consequences of terrorist attacks.

*May 22, 1998*—Presidential Decision Directives (PDDs) 62, "Combating Terrorism," and 63, "**Protecting America's Critical Infrastructure**" are signed by President Clinton. The president designates a national coordinator for security, infrastructure protection, and counterterrorism (Richard Clarke of National Security Council staff) who is not to direct agencies' activities but is to integrate the government's policies and programs on unconventional threats to the homeland and Americans abroad, including terrorism. The national coordinator oversees the broad variety of relevant policies and programs including counterterrorism, protection of critical infrastructure, preparedness, and consequence management for WMD. The national coordinator works within the National Security Council process and reports to the president through the assistant to the president for National Security Affairs and produces an annual security preparedness report. The national coordinator will also provide advice regarding budgets for counterterrorism programs and lead in the development of guidelines that might be needed for crisis management.

*August 7, 1998*—Bombings of the U.S. embassies in Nairobi, Kenya, and Dares Salaam, Tanzania.

*April 1999*—The Federal Response Plan is revised after full interagency coordination to incorporate the 11 changes published to the plan since 1992. The FRP was also revised to ensure consistency with current policy guidance; integrate recovery and mitigation functions into the response structure; and describe relationships to other emergency operations plans. The revised FRP as adopted includes four new support annexes (community relations, donations management, logistics management, and occupational safety and health), the terrorism incident annex, and two new appendices (FRP changes and revision, and an overview of a disaster operation).

*May 2000*—Congressionally mandated No-Notice Operation TOPOFF Exercise, simulating terrorist attacks in both Denver, Colorado, and Portsmouth, New Hampshire. Communication difficulties and the lack of a lead agency severely hinder operations in both locations. The DOJ is assigned executive responsibility for after-action reports.

*July 25, 2000*—House of Representatives passes HR 4210, which would have established a President's Council on Domestic Terrorism Preparedness composed of the president, directors of FEMA and Office of Management and Budget (OMB), the attorney general, the secretary of defense, the assistant to the president for national security affairs, and additional members appointed by the president. Purposes were to (1) improve federal assistance to state and local emergency preparedness and response for domestic terrorist attacks, (2) designate the President's Council to coordinate federal efforts, and (3) update federal authorities to reflect increased risk of terrorist attacks. Because the Senate did not act, this legislation died in the 106th Congress.

*February 8, 2001*—Introduction of HR 525, the Preparedness Against Domestic Terrorism Act of 2001. This resolution amends the Stafford Act to include acts of terrorism or other catastrophic events within its definition of "major disaster" for purposes of authorized disaster relief. It requires the president (then-current law authorized the director of FEMA) to be responsible for carrying out federal emergency preparedness plans and programs. It includes into the definition of hazards as covered under the Stafford Act a domestic terrorist attack involving a weapon of mass destruction. It also establishes the President's Council on Domestic Preparedness to eliminate duplication within federal terrorism-preparedness programs. It requires the council to (1) publish a domestic terrorism-preparedness plan and an annual implementation strategy; (2) designate an entity to assess the risk of terrorist attacks against transportation, energy, and other infrastructure facilities; and (3) establish voluntary minimum guidelines for preparedness programs. Finally, it authorizes the council to attend meetings of the National Security Council pertaining to domestic terrorist-attack preparedness matters, subject to the direction of the president.

*March 21 and 29, 2001*—The introduction of HR 1158, which establishes a National Homeland Security Agency, and HR 1292, requiring the president to develop and implement a strategy for homeland security. It is anticipated that these bills will be combined with HR 525 addressing preparedness against acts of domestic terrorism.

*September 11, 2001*—Terrorist attacks on the World Trade Center and the Pentagon. President George W. Bush issues a disaster declaration for New York City within 6 hours after Governor Pataki's state disaster declaration (approximately 6 hours after the initial attack at 8:43 A.M. EDT).

*September 14, 2001*—President Bush signs a declaration of national emergency as a result of the terrorist attacks at the World Trade Center, the Pentagon, and the continuing and immediate threat of further attacks on the United States.

*September 15, 2001*—Congress approves a $40 billion expenditure on disaster relief and anti- and counterterrorism (HR 2888).

*October 8, 2001*—President Bush signs an EO establishing the Office of Homeland Security and the Homeland Security Council, to be headed by the assistant to the president for homeland security. Former Pennsylvania Governor Tom Ridge was sworn in as the first director of Homeland Security. (EO 13228 published at 66 *Federal Register* 51812–51817.)

*November 2002*—President Bush signs P.L. 107–296, establishing Department of Homeland Security effective January 24, 2003.

*November 25, 2002*—S. 1214: Maritime Transportation Security Act of 2002.

*November 26, 2002*—H.R. 3210: Terrorism Risk Insurance Act of 2002.

*January 24, 2003*—The Department of Homeland Security is activated.

*April 29, 2003*—H.R. 1770: Smallpox Emergency Personnel Protection Act of 2003.

*December 6, 2003*—S. 1152: Firefighting Research and Coordination Act.

*July 20, 2004*—S. 15: Project BioShield Act of 2004.

*August 8, 2004*—H.R. 2443: Coast Guard and Maritime Transportation Act of 2004.

*October 24, 2004*—H.R. 2828: Water Supply, Reliability, and Environmental Improvement Act.

*December 17, 2004*—S. 2845: National Intelligence Reform Act of 2004.

### The Patriot Act of 2001

The PATRIOT Act of 2001 (P.L. 107-56), officially titled "Uniting and Strengthening America by Providing Appropriate Tools Required to Intercept and Obstruct Terrorism (USA PATRIOT Act) Act of 2001," was signed into law by President Bush on October 26, 2001. This legislation was introduced in the U.S. House of Representatives by Representative F. James Sensenbrenner, Jr. (R–WI) on October 23, 2001, "to deter and punish terrorist acts in the United States and around the world, to enhance law enforcement investigatory tools, and for other purposes" (www.congress.gov, 2003).

Under normal circumstances, legislation, especially that which has broad-sweeping reach and which brings into question constitutional rights, requires years and even decades of deliberation before it is finally passed—if that day ever comes. Considering the PATRIOT Act was passed less than a month after the event that inspired it, with almost no significant deliberation, it can be considered an anomalous case, and one that, considering its comprehensive nature and its impact on civil liberties, deserves more detailed description (summaries of the PATRIOT Act's ten titles are presented in Appendix 2-1 at the end of this chapter, and a full summary of the PATRIOT Act is presented in Appendix 2.)

The principal focus of the PATRIOT Act is to provide law enforcement agencies with the proper legal authority to support their efforts to collect information on suspected terrorists, to detain people suspected of being or aiding terrorists and terrorist organizations, to deter terrorists from entering and operating within the borders of the United States, and to further limit the ability of terrorists to engage in money-laundering activities that support terrorist actions. The major provisions of the PATRIOT Act are as follows:

- Relaxes restrictions on information sharing between U.S. law enforcement and intelligence officers on the subject of suspected terrorists.
- Makes it illegal to knowingly harbor a terrorist.
- Authorizes "roving wiretaps," which allows law enforcement officials to get court orders to wiretap any phone a suspected terrorist would use. The provision was needed, advocates said, with the advent of cellular and disposable phones.

- Allows the federal government to detain non-U.S. citizens suspected of terrorism for up to 7 days without specific charges (original versions of the legislation allowed for the holding of suspects indefinitely).
- Allows law enforcement officials greater subpoena power for e-mail records of terrorist suspects.
- Triples the number of border patrol personnel, customs service inspectors, and Immigration and Naturalization Service inspectors at the

northern border of the United States and provides $100 million to improve technology and equipment on the U.S. border with Canada.
- Expands measures against money laundering by requiring additional record keeping and reports for certain transactions and requiring identification of account holders.
- Eliminates the statute of limitations for prosecuting the most egregious terrorist acts but maintains the statute of limitation on most crimes at 5 to 8 years.

The PATRIOT Act immediately sparked concern among citizens and organizations involved in protecting the civil rights and liberties of all Americans, though this concern only became more vocal as the time between the attacks increased due to the emotional sensitivities associated with what had transpired. The critics that have emerged, and which continue to emerge in growing numbers as the act is repeatedly renewed, have questioned the constitutionality of several of the act's provisions, and have expressed grave concerns regarding the methods by which some of those new authorities will be used by law enforcement agencies in their pursuit of terrorists.

The U.S. attorney general at the time, John Ashcroft, and the Department of Justice that operated under his direction, countered that these authorities are necessary if the U.S. government is to more effectively track and detain terrorists. Regardless, the act very quickly began generating lawsuits, resistance from community officials, and concern about the way its provisions were being used and abused outside of their intended scope in a way that affected everyday Americans with no association with terrorist activi-

ties. Sidebars 2-2, 2-3, and 2-4 present three media accounts providing different perspectives on the PATRIOT Act.

In the months and years since the act's passage, numerous communities across the country have passed resolutions opposing parts or all of the act's contents. According to a memo drafted in September 2003 by the director of intergovernmental affairs in the city of San Jose, California, "over 150 local governments and three states have adopted resolutions opposing parts or all of the measure." The memo notes that "in California, the Counties of Santa Clara, Contra Coast, San Mateo, Marin, Santa Cruz, San Francisco, Lake, Mendocino and Yolo have all passed resolutions against all or parts of the Act. The cities of Palo Alto, Los Gatos, Santa Cruz, Oakland, Richmond, Hayward, Berkeley and Union City have also passed their own resolutions." Similar resolutions have been passed in the cities of Denver, Detroit, Honolulu, Minneapolis, and Seattle (Shotwell, 2003). A copy of the San Jose resolution passed on September 23, 2003, is presented in Sidebar 2-5.

## SIDEBAR 2-2   Patriot Act Perspective—How the New Antiterrorism Bill Could Affect You

By Lance Gay, Scripps Howard News Service (published October 26, 2001)

WASHINGTON—Do you use your local library's computers or a cyber-cafe to surf the Internet? If a suspected terrorist used the computer before you, the FBI can use "sneak and peek" warrants to collect your surfing habits and look at your e-mails.

Do you rent rooms? If that quiet upstairs boarder turns out to be a suspected terrorist, you could be charged with the new crime of "harboring" a terrorist.

Do you make a lot of large cash deposits in the bank? The CIA and other intelligence agencies will be alerted to find out if you are involved in money laundering.

Those are just a few of the sweeping changes that will affect Americans under the antiterrorism bill that Congress sent to President Bush on Thursday. It vastly expands the powers of the FBI and CIA to monitor Internet surfing, intercept e-mails, and look at bank transactions and other personal records of Americans just on mere suspicion that someone is involved in terrorist activities.

Congressional leaders say the new law—dubbed the Uniting and Strengthening America by Providing the Appropriate Tools Required to Intercept and Obstruct Terrorism, or U.S.A. Patriot Act—closes loopholes that have allowed terrorists to operate cells in the United States like those involved in the Sept. 11 attacks.

Critics, ranging from the Electronic Privacy Information Center, the Gun Owners of America, and the American Civil Liberties Union, says the U.S.A. Patriot Act is so broadly drafted it could disrupt the lives of ordinary Americans.

Lawmakers admitted the powers they are giving the government are extraordinary and sought to dampen civil liberties concerns by including "sunset" provisions in the legislation, allowing many to exist only until Dec. 31, 2005.

Some even admitted they expect the new law will cause problems. "There will be some abuses, and if there are abuses we can reverse it. It sunsets in four years," said Sen. Paul Wellstone, D–MN.

In most cases, Federal agents will have to get advance wiretap approval from the foreign Intelligence Surveillance Court. About the only thing known publicly about the seven-member panel created in 1978 that sits secretly in the basement of the Justice Department is that it has never rejected an FBI request for a secret warrant. Open warrants, much more common, get approval in regular Federal courts.

Here's how the U.S.A. Patriot Act could affect your life:

- The FBI is given new authority for Internet searches and can ask the secret court for a warrant to monitor Internet activities of anyone suspected of terrorism. If that involves use of Internet connections at libraries or cyber-cafes, the FBI can collect all the e-mails and information on Internet sites visited but would have to get another warrant to read e-mail texts of those who aren't targets of the investigation. "The net is cast so broadly, a lot of innocent communications are caught up," said David Sobel, general counsel of the Electronic Privacy Information Center.

- The FBI is authorized to investigate anyone believed linked either to international terrorism or someone involved in "domestic terrorism." Although not thought to be directly involved in terrorism themselves, these people could be charged with "harboring" a suspected terrorist or "providing material support" to a suspect. Anyone involved in providing assistance to a suspected terrorist, no matter how minor, is affected.

- Make a deposit that a bank clerk thinks is suspicious or in violation of some state or Federal law, or that involves more than $10,000, and the reports will be turned over to Federal intelligence agencies, including the CIA, without any notification to you. Under a 1992 law, banks file such reports only with the Treasury Department. The U.S.A. Patriot Act allows intelligence agencies to obtain this information to track money-laundering activities.

- Credit, medical, and student records can be retrieved secretly by Federal agencies on anyone suspected of involvement in terrorism, after approval by the secret court, regardless of state privacy laws.

- The U.S.A. Patriot Act defines domestic terrorism as "an attempt to intimidate or coerce a civilian population" or change "the policy of the government by intimidation or coercion." The American Civil Liberties Union says that definition is so broad it could cover political dissent by activists involved in protests against world trade, animal rights, or environmental concerns if police conclude their activities endanger human lives.

- Using a secret warrant, the FBI can break into offices or homes to conduct secret searches. Agents don't need probable cause, just a suspicion of involvement in a crime. Laura Murphy, director of the Washington office of the American Civil Liberties Union, said that poses major Fourth Amendment search-and-seizure concerns. There would be no notification of what was found in the secret searches.

- Immigrants and non-citizens could be detained for up to 7 days before charges are filed. Those charged with immigration violations, including overstaying visas, can be deported. If their home countries refuse to take them back, they can be held indefinitely.

- Information collected during grand jury proceedings could be shared by the FBI with the CIA, giving the CIA domestic information it has been restricted in the past from receiving.

William Webster, a former director of both the FBI and the CIA, said that while Congress is granting very broad powers to Federal agencies, there's a check requiring Federal judges to review what Federal agents are doing. "I'm comfortable as long as the courts have a role to play," said Webster, a former judge. John Velleco, director of Federal affairs for Gun Owners of America, said the government already has sufficient powers to investigate and deal with terrorists.

Jeff Kerr, general counsel for People for the Ethical Treatment of Animals, said his organization is concerned that police could use the new domestic terrorism provisions against social activists. "There's a fine line that has to be guarded very carefully here," he said. "Something that is educational to one person may be coercive to someone else—a boycott, for example, against any industry. Is that intimidating and coercive?"

*Source*: *Star Tribune*, October 26, 2001, www.startribune.com.

### SIDEBAR 2-3   Patriot Act Perspective—ACLU Files against Patriot Act

From Kevin Bohn, CNN Washington Bureau, July 30, 2003

WASHINGTON (CNN)—The American Civil Liberties Union [on July 30, 2003] filed the first lawsuit against the Patriot Act, the antiterrorism law passed after the attacks of September 11, 2001. The lawsuit claims one section of the law authorizing searches of records, including those of businesses, libraries, and bookstores, is unconstitutional.

"This lawsuit challenges the constitutionality of Section 215 of the U.S.A. Patriot Act, which vastly expands the power of the Federal Bureau of Investigation to obtain records and other 'tangible things' of people not suspected of criminal activity," the lawsuit states.

The ACLU filed the lawsuit in U.S. District Court in Michigan on behalf of six mostly Arab and Muslim-American groups. The groups claim the provisions of the law allowing the searches violates the Constitution's First, Fourth, and Fifth amendments. They include the Muslim Community Association of Ann Arbor, Arab Community Center for Economic and Social Services, and the Islamic Center of Portland, Masjed As-Saber.

Without directly commenting on the suit, Justice Department spokeswoman Barbara Comstock defended the act in a written statement, saying it was "a long overdue measure to close gaping holes" in the government's antiterrorism efforts. She described Section 215 as having "a narrow scope that scrupulously respects First Amendment rights, requires a court order to obtain any business records, and is subject to congressional reporting and oversight on a regular basis."

Justice Department officials say the section can be used only in a narrow set of circumstances, including to obtain foreign intelligence information about people who are neither American citizens nor lawful permanent residents, and to defend the United States against foreign spies or international terrorists. "Section 215 cannot be used to investigate garden-variety crimes, or even domestic terrorism," Comstock said in her statement.

Those bringing the lawsuit contend it is too easy to get approval for a search under Section 215. "To obtain a Section 215 order, the FBI need only assert that the records or personal belongings are 'sought for' an ongoing foreign intelligence, counterintelligence, or international terrorism investigation," the lawsuit says.

"The FBI is not required to show probable cause—or any reason—to believe that the target of the order is a criminal suspect or foreign agent." Previously, such broad powers were permitted only in investigations of suspected agents of foreign powers. Section 215 expanded the type of information that can be subpoenaed and broadened the scope to add probes into al Qaeda and other terrorism suspects.

Another controversial element of the Patriot Act involves what are called "sneak and peek" searches of homes and other locations in which the owners are informed only after the search has been conducted. Last week, the House of Representatives voted to bar the Justice Department from executing such searches under the act.

In a letter last week to House Speaker Rep. Dennis Hastert, R–Illinois, the department said the idea of delaying notification of such searches is "to prevent tipping off terrorists in the war on terror" and is a "long-existing, crime-fighting tool."

In February, the ACLU and a coalition of other civil liberties groups asked the U.S. Supreme Court to overturn new, more lenient standards for wiretaps in foreign intelligence investigations.

Before the Patriot Act, foreign intelligence had to be a "primary" purpose of the investigation. Now, foreign intelligence has to be a "significant" purpose. The court overseeing the issuance of wiretaps had ruled against that interpretation last year, saying it was too broad.

*Source*: CNN, July 30, 2003, www.cnn.com.

SIDEBAR 2-4   **Patriot Act Perspective: Communities Shun Patriot Act**

By Gus Taylor, *The Washington Times*, July 21, 2003

About 165 communities nationwide have passed resolutions condemning the USA Patriot Act. But one little city in northern California has taken its opposition a step further, making it a misdemeanor for city employees to cooperate in enforcing the Federal antiterrorism measure.

In March, Arcata officials set down a $57 fine for those who don't "promptly notify the city manager" if Federal law-enforcement authorities contact them seeking help in an investigation, interrogation, or arrest under the provisions of the act.

But a city fine would be nothing compared with the penalties an Arcata official faces for obstructing a Federal probe, a Justice Department spokesman said. "Obviously, the folks [in Arcata] who voted for this ordinance haven't read the law," said Justice Department spokesman Mark C. Corallo. "This is not the FBI or the Justice Department acting unilaterally," Mr. Corallo said. "Just like any other criminal investigation, these are tools that are not just legal, but they are constitutional and they are tools that have been available for law-enforcement authorities for decades."

The Patriot Act's most-criticized provision, for so-called roving wiretaps, merely allows investigators to "track a terrorist, instead of having to get multiple warrants for every phone the guy uses," Mr. Corallo explained.

Still, critics say, the reason so many communities are denouncing the Patriot Act is because they believe the measure passed in the wake of the September 11 attacks vastly expands the power of Federal investigators, not only for investigating terrorism suspects but also for probing into the lives of ordinary Americans.

Most of the resolutions being signed against the 340-page act condemn its provisions that compel libraries and bookstores to assist Federal investigators in monitoring the reading habits of suspects.

Timothy H. Edgar, the legislative counsel for the American Civil Liberties Union, said that a far more frightening provision of the Patriot Act is one that "allows investigators to sneak into your house with a warrant and conduct a search and not notify you until much later, if at all."

Further, according to a report issued earlier this month by the ACLU, the act gives the FBI "access to highly personal 'business records' including financial, medical, mental health, library, and student records with no meaningful judicial oversight."

The report continues: "Federal officials actually can obtain a court order for records of the books you borrow from libraries or buy from bookstores, without showing probable cause of criminal activity or intent, and the librarian or bookseller cannot even tell you that the government is investigating what you read."

Justice Department officials say such criticisms are arbitrary, noting that investigators still are required to get permission from a Federal judge to obtain records about the reading habits of suspects. Mr. Corallo said the wave of objections to the Patriot Act has done little more than illustrate some Americans' "incredible ignorance of Federal law."

But Arcata officials aren't second-guessing themselves; they take pride in their city's stance. "A lot of people are becoming more aware of the problems with the Patriot Act," says Arcata Mayor Bob Ornelas.

"We were the first to put it in our municipal code," he said. "It's one thing to have a proclamation; we have an ordinance saying you can't engage in the Patriot Act where it violates people's constitutional rights."

Arcata, a town of about 16,000 nearly 300 miles north of San Francisco, made headlines as a haven of liberalism in the early 1990s when its city council became first in the country with a Green Party majority.

But Mr. Ornelas and others point out that liberals aren't the only ones objecting to the Patriot Act. "From the NAACP to the NRA, people are working together on these resolutions," says ACLU spokesman Damon Moglin, in reference to the National Association for the Advancement of Colored People and the National Rifle Association.

"We see this as being a true grass-roots response." The ACLU's July 3 report says "more than 16 million people in 26 states have passed resolutions" condemning the Patriot Act and that among them are some "traditionally conservative locales, such as Oklahoma City, . . . Alaska, Hawaii, and Vermont."

*Source*: *The Washington Times*, July 21, 2003, http://www.washtimes.com/national/20030720-115938-3269r.htm.

---

**SIDEBAR 2-5    A Resolution of the Council of the City of San Jose, California, to Defend the Bill of Rights and Civil Liberties**

Passed September 23, 2003

WHEREAS, the City of San Jose ("City") has a long and distinguished tradition of protecting the civil rights and civil liberties of its residents; and

WHEREAS, the City has a diverse population, including immigrants, students, and working people, whose contributions to the community are vital to its character and function; and

WHEREAS, fundamental constitutional rights and liberties are essential to the preservation of a just and democratic society; and

WHEREAS, several new Federal laws, regulations, and executive orders issued since the terrorist attacks of September 11, 2001, including the adoption of certain provisions of the USA PATRIOT Act (collectively, the "Act"), now threaten these fundamental constitutional rights and liberties, including:

- Freedom of speech and religion;
- Right to privacy;
- Right to counsel and due process in judicial proceedings;
- Right to equal protection before the law; and
- Protection from unreasonable searches and seizures; and

WHEREAS, the powers granted under the Act threaten the civil rights and civil liberties of San Jose residents, and particularly affect those of Arab-American, Muslim, and South Asian backgrounds; and

WHEREAS, thirty years ago California voters overwhelmingly adopted a Constitutional right to privacy to protection against a "proliferation of government snooping and data collecting [that] is threatening to destroy our traditional freedoms"; and

WHEREAS, the failure to defend civil liberties during World War II led to the incarceration of 120,000 Americans of Japanese descent in California and other western states as well as the incarceration of German and Italian Americans, and Hungarian, Romanian and Bulgarian Americans; and

WHEREAS, during the 1930s and the 1950s, the U.S. government systematically rounded up and deported thousands of Mexican immigrants and Americans of Mexican descent;

NOW, THEREFORE, BE IT RESOLVED BY THE COUNCIL OF THE CITY OF SAN JOSE THAT THE CITY COUNCIL HEREBY:

1. Affirms its strong support for fundamental constitutional rights and its opposition to (1) the provisions of the Act that infringe on important civil liberties and (2) any future legislation, rules, regulations or executive orders that strengthen, reinforce, broaden, or otherwise expand the provisions of the Act that infringe on civil liberties.

2. Affirms its strong opposition to terrorism but also affirm that any efforts to fight terrorism not be waged at the expense of the fundamental civil rights and liberties of the people of the City of San Jose, and the United States.

3. Affirms its strong support for the constitutional rights of immigrant communities in San Jose and oppose racial profiling and the scapegoating of immigrants.

4. Directs the City Manager to send a letter and a copy of this Resolution to the City of San Jose's U.S. Senate and Congressional Delegation urging them to (1) work to repeal all provisions of the Act that infringe on civil liberties and (2) to oppose any future legislation, rules, regulations or executive orders that strengthen, reinforce, broaden, or otherwise expand the provisions of the Act that infringe on civil liberties. A copy of the letter and the resolution shall also be sent to President Bush and Attorney General John Ashcroft.

5. Encourages City departments to (1) determine how the new Federal powers under the Act are affecting residents of the City of San Jose; (2) monitor requests for cooperation in investigations utilizing those new powers on an ongoing basis; and (3) regularly report their findings to the City Manager for submission to the City Council.

6. Directs the City Manager to ensure that the San Jose Police Department and other departments, to the extent legally possible, not officially assist or voluntarily cooperate with investigations, interrogations or arrest procedures, public or clandestine that are in violation of individuals' constitutionally protected civil rights or civil liberties.

7. Urges Congress to identify decisions and policy directives from the Justice Department and the immigration authorities that are discriminatory and require them to be changed.

8. Urges Congress to exercise more oversight to ensure that powers granted under the Patriot Act and other Federal laws are not abused.

9. Urges Congress to require the Department of Justice (DOJ) and Department of Homeland Security (DHS) to document and report to Congress their uses of power under the Patriot Act in a way that the American people can be assured that abuses are not occurring.

10. Urges Congress to require the Inspector General for the DHS to investigate civil rights violations and report to the Congress like the Office of the Inspector General for the DOJ.

11. Urges Congress to increase the funding of the Office of the Inspector General in both the DOJ and DHS so that they can fully investigate complaints in both the DOJ and the DHS.

12. Urges Congress to make sure that the DOJ and DHS promptly and fully respond to and implement the recommendations from their Inspector Generals.

*Source*: American Civil Liberties Union, www.aclu.org/SafeandFree/SafeandFree.cfm?ID=13900&c=207.

## SIDEBAR 2-6   USA PATRIOT Act Expirations

The temporary provisions of the PATRIOT Act, with a December 31, 2005 expiration date, are as follows:

201—wiretapping in terrorism cases

202—wiretapping in computer fraud and abuse felony cases

203(b)—sharing wiretap information

203(d)—sharing foreign intelligence information

204—Foreign Intelligence Surveillance Act (FISA) pen register/trap and trace exceptions

206—roving FISA wiretaps

207—duration of FISA surveillance of non-U.S. persons who are agents of a foreign power

209—seizure of voice mail messages pursuant to warrants

212—emergency disclosure of electronic surveillance

214—FISA pen register/trap and trace authority

215—FISA access to tangible items

217—interception of computer trespasser communications

218—purpose for FISA orders

220—nationwide service of search warrants for electronic evidence

223—civil liability and discipline for privacy violations, and

225—provider immunity for FISA wiretap assistance

*Source*: Congressional Research Service, www.au.af.mil/au/awc/awcgate/crs/rs21704.pdf.

The lawmakers who enacted the Patriot Act were aware that controversy would accompany most of its provisions for a long time to come. Many of these lawmakers, if not all of them, are in fact concerned about the welfare and civil liberties of citizens, so they set within the legislation various "sunset" clauses that stipulate dates of expiration for many of the legal authorities granted to law enforcement agencies. The first major round of expirations was set for December 31, 2005. Debate about the various components of the act was heated, unlike in the weeks following the September 11 attacks. With the luxury of time, politics and constituent concerns become a factor in many lawmakers' decisions, and extended analysis and provisional arrangements are possible without the belief that such delays will cause harm or prevent any major breakthroughs in the war on terror. It is likely that the back-and-forth volley with civil liberties will continue for years to come, and it is certain that the direction these debates take will ultimately be a factor of whether or not future terrorist attacks occur—thereby either negating or reinforcing the perceived need for citizens to weaken their own civil liberties in the name of security. Sidebar 2-6 illustrates the PATRIOT Act provisions that were up for renewal on December 31, 2005.

Understandably, the Department of Justice, as the greatest operational benefactor of the provisions stipulated by the Patriot Act, has issued supportive documentation to proclaim its position on the benefits of the act. Many of the investigations currently being carried out by DOJ officials, and those from other agencies such as the Central Intelligence Agency (CIA) and the National Security Agency (NSA), are either augmented or fully dependent on the survivability of the PATRIOT Act, and, with the support of President George W. Bush, these organizations have fought strongly to garner citizen support.

It is expected that most PATRIOT Act authorities will persist. In June 2005, the House of

Representatives voted 238–187 to block the DOJ and the FBI from using the PATRIOT Act to "peek at library records and bookstore sales slips" (Taylor, 2005). This was the first time any one of the selected provisions in the PATRIOT Act containing an expiration date was addressed. Whether or not these actions can result in actual removal of sections of the legislation remains to be seen.

Sidebar 2-7 is an excerpt from a fact sheet published by the Department of Justice in support of the PATRIOT Act in the months during which renewal was being considered by Congress. This fact sheet is interesting in terms of its contrast with the descriptive verbiage used by those in opposition as displayed in Sidebars 2-2 through 2-4.

---

**SIDEBAR 2-7    U.S. Department of Justice Fact Sheet—USA PATRIOT Act Overview**

**What Is the PATRIOT Act?**

The Department of Justice's first priority is to prevent future terrorist attacks. Since its passage following the September 11 attacks, the PATRIOT Act has played a key role in a number of successful operations to protect innocent Americans from terrorists. In passing the PATRIOT Act, Congress provided for modest, incremental changes in the law. Congress took existing legal principles and adapted them to preserve the lives and liberty of the American people given the challenges posed by global terrorist threats.

Congress enacted the PATRIOT Act by overwhelming, bipartisan margins, arming law enforcement, intelligence, and homeland security officers with new tools to detect and prevent terrorism: The USA PATRIOT Act was passed nearly unanimously by the Senate 98–1, and 357–66 in the House of Representatives, with bipartisan support. The Act improves our counter-terrorism efforts in several ways:

1. The PATRIOT Act facilitates information sharing and cooperation among government agencies so that they can better "connect the dots." The Act removed the major legal barriers that prevented the law enforcement, intelligence, and national defense communities from talking and coordinating their work to protect the American people and our national security. Now FBI agents, Federal prosecutors, and intelligence officials can protect our communities by "connecting the dots" to uncover terrorist plots before they are completed while respecting constitutional rights.

2. The PATRIOT Act allows terrorism investigators to use the tools that were already available to investigate organized crime and drug trafficking. Many of the tools the Act provides to law enforcement to fight terrorism have been used for decades to fight organized crime and drug dealers, and have been reviewed and approved by the courts. Specifically, the PATRIOT Act:

   • Allows law enforcement to use surveillance against more crimes of terror, such as use of chemical weapons and other weapons of mass destruction.

   • Allows Federal agents to follow sophisticated terrorists trained to evade detection. For years, Federal judges across America have authorized law enforcement to use "roving wiretaps" to investigate non-terrorism crimes, including drug offenses and racketeering. A roving wiretap can be authorized by a Federal judge to apply to a particular suspect, rather than a particular phone or communications device. Because international terrorists are sophisticated and trained to thwart surveillance by rapidly changing locations and communication devices, the Act authorized agents to seek court permission to use the same techniques in national security investigations to track terrorists.

- Allows law enforcement to conduct investigations without tipping off terrorists. If criminals are tipped off too early to an investigation, they are likely to flee, destroy evidence, intimidate or kill witnesses, cut off contact with associates, or take other action to evade arrest. Therefore, Federal courts in narrow circumstances long have allowed law enforcement to delay for a limited time when the subject is told that a judicially-approved search warrant has been executed. Notice is always provided, but the reasonable delay gives law enforcement time to identify the criminal's associates, eliminate immediate threats to our communities, and coordinate the arrests of multiple individuals without tipping them off beforehand. These delayed-notification search warrants have been used for decades, have proven crucial in drug and organized crime cases, and have been upheld by courts as fully constitutional. The Act simply codified the procedure for obtaining them.

- Allows Federal agents to ask a court for an order to obtain business records in national security terrorism cases. Examining business records often provides the key that investigators are looking for to catch terrorists, and, traditionally, to solve a wide range of crimes. Investigators might seek specific records from a hardware store or chemical wholesaler, for example, to determine the identity of a suspected terrorist who purchased materials to construct a bomb, or specific bank records to identify the source of money used to finance terrorist attacks.

Law enforcement authorities have always been able to obtain business records in criminal cases through grand jury subpoenas, and for example, via administrative subpoenas in drug investigations. Previously—in national security cases where use of the grand jury process was too risky or otherwise not appropriate (e.g., because disclosure of the fact that the subpoena had been issued could potentially tip off suspected terrorists to the existence of the investigation)—investigators had limited tools to obtain certain business records. Under Section 215 of the Act, the government can now ask a Federal court to order production of the same type of records that are available through grand jury subpoenas (which typically do not require specific court approval). This Federal court, however, can issue these orders only after: (1) the government demonstrates that the records concerned are sought for an authorized investigation to obtain foreign intelligence information not concerning a U.S. person; or (2) to protect against international terrorism or clandestine intelligence activities, provided that any such investigation of a U.S. person is not conducted solely on the basis of activities protected by the First Amendment.

3. The PATRIOT Act updates the law to reflect new technologies and new threats. The Act brought the law up-to-date with the new technologies actually used by terrorists, so America no longer has to fight a digital-age battle with legal authorities left over from the era of rotary telephones. It allows law enforcement officials to move more quickly to prevent attacks by asking a Court to authorize a nationwide search warrant. Before the PATRIOT Act, law enforcement personnel were required to obtain a series of search

warrants, one-by-one, from a series of different judges everywhere suspected terrorists may be hiding documents about planned attacks or other evidence. Today, however, terrorism investigations often span a number of districts, and obtaining multiple warrants in multiple jurisdictions can create risky and unnecessary delays. Now warrants can be obtained in any district in which terrorism-related activities occurred, regardless of where they will be executed.

4. The PATRIOT Act increases the penalties for those who commit terrorist crimes. Americans are threatened as much by the terrorist who pays for a bomb as by the one who detonates it. That's why the PATRIOT Act imposed tough new penalties on those who commit and support terrorist operations, both at home and abroad. In particular, the Act:

- Prohibits individuals from knowingly harboring terrorists who have committed or are about to commit a variety of terrorist offenses, such as: destruction of aircraft; use of nuclear, chemical, biological, or other weapons of mass destruction; bombing of government property; sabotage of nuclear facilities; and aircraft piracy.

- Enhances the maximum penalties for various crimes likely to be committed by terrorists: including arson, destruction of energy facilities, material support to terrorists and terrorist organizations, and destruction of national-defense materials.

- Enhances a number of conspiracy penalties, including for arson, killings in Federal facilities, attacking communications systems, material support to terrorists, sabotage of nuclear facilities, and interference with flight crews.

- Punishes terrorist attacks on mass transit systems; punishes bioterrorists; and eliminates or lengthens the statutes of limitations for certain terrorism crimes.

*Source*: U.S. Department of Justice, www.nunes.house.gov/documents/PatriotActOverview.pdf.

## HOMELAND SECURITY ACT OF 2002

The legislation to establish a Department of Homeland Security was first introduced in the U.S. House of Representatives by Texas Representative Richard K. Armey on June 24, 2003. Similar legislation was introduced into the Senate soon after. After differences between the two bills were quickly ironed out, the Homeland Security Act of 2002 (P.L. 107-296) was passed by both houses and signed into law by President Bush on November 25, 2002.

The Homeland Security Act provided authorization for a full range of federal government changes that came in response to not only the events of September 11, but the perceived inefficiencies in the government organization and operation that directly resulted in the vulnerabilities that allowed for such an event, and by

logic, possible future attacks by similar terrorist organizations, to occur. The act established the Department of Homeland Security within the executive branch, with the DHS secretary reporting directly to the president. The act, which is outlined in Appendix 2-2 of this chapter and in Chapter 3 with regards to its organizational changes and makeup, outlined the DHS management structure, identified those agencies and programs to be migrated to the DHS, and detailed the roles and responsibilities of the five directorates that make up the DHS: Information Analysis and Infrastructure Protection, Science and Technology, Border and Transportation Security, Emergency Preparedness, and Response and Management. The act called for the migration of the Secret Service and the Coast Guard to the DHS and transfers the Bureau of Alcohol, Tobacco, Firearms, and

Explosives from the Treasury Department to the DOJ. The act also established within the executive office of the president the Homeland Security Council to advise the president on homeland security matters and the Office for State and Local Coordination and Preparedness reporting to the DHS secretary. A summary of selected sections under each of the act's titles is presented in Appendix 2-2.

## HOMELAND SECURITY PRESIDENTIAL DIRECTIVE NO. 5

On February 28, 2003, the White House released Homeland Security Presidential Directive No. 5 (HSPD-5) to enhance the ability of the United States to manage domestic incidents. The directive proclaimed that this would be done through the establishment of a single, comprehensive National Incident Management System (NIMS).

HSPD-5 tasked the DHS secretary to develop and administer NIMS, and subsequently a National Response Plan (NRP), which would replace the oft-applied and highly acclaimed Federal Response Plan. HSPD-5 set a time frame for the development of initial versions of these documents, consultation with other federal agencies, and adoption by state and local departments and agencies. As of January 2005, all of these actions had taken place. Excerpts from the text of HSPD-5 are presented in Sidebar 2-8.

NIMS was designed to integrate emergency management practices, including mitigation, preparedness, response, and recovery, at all government levels, including federal, state, and local, into a comprehensive national framework. NIMS's central mission is to enable responders at all levels to work together more effectively to manage domestic incidents regardless of the cause, size, or complexity. The benefits of the NIMS, as stated by FEMA, include the following:

- Standardized organizational structures, processes and procedures
- Standards for planning, training and exercising, and personnel qualification standards

- Equipment acquisition and certification standards
- Interoperable communications processes, procedures, and systems
- Information management systems
- Supporting technologies—voice and data communications systems, information systems, data display systems and specialized technologies

The NRP is a single, comprehensive framework for the management of domestic incidents, which almost always involve many participants from all levels of government. The plan directly addresses the prevention of terrorist attacks, as well as the reduction in vulnerability to all natural and man-made hazards. Finally, it attempts to offer guidance on minimizing the damage and assisting in the recovery from any type of incident that occurs.

NIMS and the NRP are explained in much greater detail in Chapter 7.

## FUTURE LEGISLATION

Numerous considerations exist for future legislation and executive action concerning homeland security. One area currently under discussion in Congress is how communities, families, and individuals can become better prepared to respond to terrorism attacks. In September 2003, congressional members of the House Select Committee on Homeland Security proposed the Preparing America to Respond Effectively (PREPARE) Act of 2003 (full title, "To amend the Homeland Security Act of 2002 to establish a task force to determine essential capabilities for State and local jurisdictions to prevent, prepare for, and respond to acts of terrorism, to authorize the Secretary of Homeland Security to make grants to State and local governments to achieve such capability, and for other purposes"), which was billed as a comprehensive approach to prepare the nation to respond to acts of terrorism. The major elements of the PREPARE Act were as follows:

- Meeting the needs of first responders
- Making sense of threat alerts
- Improving information sharing
- Providing interoperable communications and equipment
- Encouraging participation of "second responders"
- Educating schoolchildren to be prepared

On October 5, 2003, this bill was referred to the Subcommittee on Telecommunications and the Internet and has yet to move. A bill summary of the PREPARE Act is presented as Appendix 2-3. Sidebar 2-9 illustrates the range of homeland security and terrorism legislation currently under consideration in the U.S. Congress.

---

SIDEBAR 2-8  **Excerpts from Homeland Security Presidential Directive No. 5: Management of Domestic Incidents**

**Purpose**

To enhance the ability of the United States to manage domestic incidents by establishing a single, comprehensive national incident management system.

**Policy**

- To prevent, prepare for, respond to, and recover from terrorist attacks, major disasters, and other emergencies, the US government (USG) shall establish a single, comprehensive approach to domestic incident management. The objective of the USG is to ensure that all levels of government across the nation have the capability to work efficiently and effectively together, using a national approach to domestic incident management. In these efforts, with regard to domestic incidents, the USG treats crisis management and consequence management as a single, integrated function, rather than as two separate functions.
- The secretary of Homeland Security is the principal Federal official for domestic incident management. Pursuant to the Homeland Security Act of 2002, the secretary is responsible for coordinating Federal operations within the United States to prepare for, respond to, and recover from terrorist attacks, major disasters, and other emergencies. The secretary

shall coordinate the Federal government's resources utilized in response to or recovery from terrorist attacks, major disasters, or other emergencies if and when any one of the following four conditions applies: (1) a Federal department or agency acting under its own authority has requested the assistance of the secretary; (2) the resources of state and local authorities are overwhelmed and Federal assistance has been requested by the appropriate state and local authorities; (3) more than one Federal department or agency has become substantially involved in responding to the incident; or (4) the secretary has been directed to assume responsibility for managing the domestic incident by the president.

- Nothing in this directive alters, or impedes the ability to carry out, the authorities of Federal departments and agencies to perform their responsibilities under law. All Federal departments and agencies shall cooperate with the secretary in the secretary's domestic incident management role.
- The Federal government recognizes the roles and responsibilities of State and local authorities in domestic incident management. Initial responsibility for managing domestic incidents generally falls on state and local authorities. The Federal government will assist state

and local authorities when their resources are overwhelmed, or when Federal interests are involved. The secretary will coordinate with state and local governments to ensure adequate planning, equipment, training, and exercise activities. The secretary will also provide assistance to state and local governments to develop all-hazards plans and capabilities, including those of greatest importance to the security of the United States, and will ensure that state, local, and Federal plans are compatible.

- The Federal government recognizes the role that the private and nongovernmental sectors play in preventing, preparing for, responding to, and recovering from terrorist attacks, major disasters, and other emergencies. The secretary will coordinate with the private and nongovernmental sectors to ensure adequate planning, equipment, training, and exercise activities and to promote partnerships to address incident management capabilities.

- The attorney general has led responsibility for criminal investigations of terrorist acts or terrorist threats by individuals or groups inside the United States, or directed at United States citizens or institutions abroad, where such acts are within the Federal criminal jurisdiction of the United States, as well as for related intelligence collection activities within the United States, subject to the National Security Act of 1947 and other applicable law, EO 12333, and attorney general–approved procedures pursuant to that executive order. Generally acting through the Federal Bureau of Investigation, the attorney general, in cooperation with other Federal departments and agencies engaged in activities to protect our national security, shall also coordinate the activities of the other members of the law enforcement community to detect, prevent, preempt, and disrupt terrorist attacks against the United States. Following

a terrorist threat or an actual incident that falls within the criminal jurisdiction of the United States, the full capabilities of the United States shall be dedicated, consistent with United States law and with activities of other Federal departments and agencies to protect our national security, to assisting the attorney general to identify the perpetrators and bring them to justice. The attorney general and the secretary shall establish appropriate relationships and mechanisms for cooperation and coordination between their two departments.

- Nothing in this directive impairs or otherwise affects the authority of the secretary of defense over the Department of Defense, including the chain of command for military forces from the president as commander in chief, to the secretary of defense, to the commander of military forces, or military command and control procedures. The secretary of defense shall provide military support to civil authorities for domestic incidents as directed by the president or when consistent with military readiness and appropriate under the circumstances and the law. The secretary of defense shall retain command of military forces providing civil support. The secretary of defense and the secretary shall establish appropriate relationships and mechanisms for cooperation and coordination between their two departments.

- The secretary of state has the responsibility, consistent with other United States government activities to protect our national security, to coordinate international activities related to the prevention, preparation, response, and recovery from a domestic incident, and for the protection of United States citizens and United States interests overseas. The secretary of state and the secretary shall establish appropriate relationships and mechanisms for cooperation and coordination between their two departments.

- The assistant to the president for Homeland Security and the assistant to the president for National Security Affairs shall be responsible for interagency policy coordination on domestic and international incident management, respectively, as directed by the president. The assistant to the president for Homeland Security and the assistant to the president for National Security Affairs shall work together to ensure that the United States' domestic and international incident management efforts are seamlessly united.

- The secretary shall ensure that, as appropriate, information related to domestic incidents is gathered and provided to the public, the private sector, state and local authorities, Federal departments and agencies, and, generally through the assistant to the president for Homeland Security, to the president. The secretary shall provide standardized, quantitative reports to the assistant to the president for Homeland Security on the readiness and preparedness of the nation—at all levels of government—to prevent, prepare for, respond to, and recover from domestic incidents.

- Nothing in this directive shall be construed to grant to any assistant to the president any authority to issue orders to Federal departments and agencies, their officers, or their employees.

**Tasking**

- The heads of all Federal departments and agencies are directed to provide their full and prompt cooperation, resources, and support, as appropriate and consistent with their own responsibilities for protecting our national security, to the secretary, the attorney general, the secretary of defense, and the secretary of state in the exercise of the individual leadership responsibilities and missions assigned above.

- The secretary shall develop, submit for review to the Homeland Security Council, and administer a National Incident Management System (NIMS). This system will provide a consistent nationwide approach for Federal, State, and local governments to work effectively and efficiently together to prepare for, respond to, and recover from domestic incidents, regardless of cause, size, or complexity. To provide for interoperability and compatibility among Federal, State, and local capabilities, the NIMS will include a core set of concepts, principles, terminology, and technologies covering the incident command system; multi-agency coordination systems; unified command; training; identification and management of resources (including systems for classifying types of resources); qualifications and certification; and the collection, tracking, and reporting of incident information and incident resources.

- The secretary shall develop, submit for review to the Homeland Security Council, and administer a National Response Plan (NRP). The secretary shall consult with appropriate assistants to the president (including the assistant to the president for Economic Policy) and the director of the office of Science and Technology Policy, and other such Federal officials as may be appropriate, in developing and implementing the NRP. This plan shall integrate Federal government domestic prevention, preparedness, response, and recovery plans into one all-discipline, all-hazards plan. The NRP shall be unclassified. If certain operational aspects require classification, they shall be included in classified annexes to the NRP.

- The NRP, using the NIMS, shall, with regard to response to domestic incidents, provide the structure and mechanisms for national level policy and operational direction for Federal support to state and local incident managers and for exercising direct Federal authorities and responsibilities, as appropriate.

- The NRP will include protocols for operating under different threats or threat levels; incorporation of existing Federal emergency and incident management plans (with appropriate modifications and revisions) as either integrated components of the NRP or as supporting operational plans; and additional operational plans or annexes, as appropriate, including public affairs and intergovernmental communications.

- The NRP will include a consistent approach to reporting incidents, providing assessments, and making recommendations to the president, the secretary, and the Homeland Security Council.
- The NRP will include rigorous requirements for continuous improvements from testing, exercising, experience with incidents, and new information and technologies.

*Source*: Office of the Press Secretary, the White House.

---

**SIDEBAR 2-9   Select Legislation Relating to Homeland Security and Terrorism under Consideration**

## 2005

S. 1266—An original bill to permanently authorize certain provisions of the USA PATRIOT Act of 2001, to reauthorize a provision of the Intelligence Reform and Terrorism Prevention Act of 2004, to clarify certain definitions in the Foreign Intelligence Surveillance Act of 1978, to provide additional investigative tools necessary to protect the national security, and for other purposes. (Scheduled for Debate; June 15, 2005)

H.R. 2237—To help protect the public against the threat of chemical attacks. (Introduced; June 14, 2005)

H.R. 2101—To amend the Homeland Security Act of 2002 to direct the Secretary of Homeland Security to develop and implement the READICall emergency alert system. (Introduced; May 18, 2005)

S. 1052—A bill to improve transportation security, and for other purposes. (Introduced; May 16, 2005)

H.R. 2351—To provide for the safety and security of United States railroads, passengers, workers, and

communities, and to establish an assistance program for families of passengers involved in rail accidents. (Introduced; May 12, 2005)

H.R. 1794—To direct the Secretary of Homeland Security to procure the development and provision of improved and up-to-date communications equipment for the New York City Fire Department, including radios. (Introduced; May 12, 2005)

H.R. 1544—Faster and Smarter Funding for First Responders Act of 2005 (Passed House; May 11, 2005)

S. 1013—A bill to improve the allocation of grants through the Department of Homeland Security, and for other purposes. (Introduced; May 11, 2005)

S. 1032—A bill to improve seaport security. (Introduced; May 11, 2005)

H.R. 1763—To increase criminal penalties relating to terrorist murders, deny Federal benefits to terrorists, and for other purposes. (Introduced; May 9, 2005)

S. 975—A bill to provide incentives to increase research by private sector entities to develop medical countermeasures to prevent, detect, identify, contain, and treat illnesses, including those associated with biological, chemical, nuclear, or radiological weapons attack or an infectious disease outbreak, and for other purposes. (Scheduled for Debate; May 8, 2005)

H.R. 1731—To improve the security of the Nation's ports by providing Federal grants to support Area Maritime Transportation Security Plans and to address vulnerabilities in port areas identified in approved vulnerability assessments or by the Secretary of Homeland Security. (Introduced; May 8, 2005)

S. 969—A bill to amend the Public Health Service Act with respect to preparation for an influenza pandemic, including an avian influenza pandemic, and for other purposes. (Introduced; April 27, 2005)

H.R. 1805—To establish the position of Northern Border Coordinator in the Department of Homeland Security. (Introduced; April 26, 2005)

S. 629—Railroad Carriers and Mass Transportation Protection Act of 2005 (Scheduled for Debate; April 24, 2005)

H.R. 1562—To protect human health and the environment from the release of hazardous substances by acts of terrorism. (Introduced; April 21, 2005)

H.R. 1795—To amend the Robert T. Stafford Disaster Relief and Emergency Assistance Act to modify the terms of the community disaster loan program, to authorize assistance under that program for losses related to the terrorist attacks of September 11, 2001, and for other purposes. (Introduced; April 20, 2005)

S. 378—Reducing Crime and Terrorism at America's Seaports Act of 2005 (Scheduled for Debate; April 20, 2005)

H.R. 285—To amend the Homeland Security Act of 2002 to enhance cybersecurity, and for other purposes. (Introduced; April 19, 2005)

S. 855—A bill to improve the security of the Nation's ports by providing Federal grants to support Area Maritime Transportation Security Plans and to address vulnerabilities in port areas identified in approved vulnerability assessments or by the Secretary of Homeland Security. (Introduced; April 19, 2005)

S. 773—A bill to ensure the safe and secure transportation by rail of extremely hazardous materials. (Introduced; April 12, 2005)

S. 3—A bill to strengthen and protect America in the war on terror. (Introduced; April 5, 2005)

S. 729—A bill to establish the Food Safety Administration to protect the public health by preventing food-borne illness, ensuring the safety of food, improving research on contaminants leading to food-borne illness, and improving security of food from intentional contamination, and for other purposes. (Introduced; April 5, 2005)

S. 737—A bill to amend the USA PATRIOT Act to place reasonable limitations on the use of surveillance and the issuance of search warrants, and for other purposes. (Introduced; April 5, 2005)

H.R. 1320—To secure the borders of the United States, and for other purposes. (Introduced; March 29, 2005)

H.R. 1419—To require that Homeland Security grants related to terrorism preparedness and prevention be awarded based strictly on an assessment of risk, threat, and vulnerabilities. (Introduced; March 29, 2005)

H.R. 796—To authorize the Secretary of Homeland Security to make grants to address homeland security preparedness shortcomings of units of municipal and county government. (Introduced; March 9, 2005)

H.R. 895—To provide for interagency planning for preparing for, defending against, and responding to the consequences of terrorist attacks against the

Yucca Mountain Project, and for other purposes. (Introduced; March 9, 2005)

S. 573—A bill to improve the response of the federal government to agroterrorism and agricultural diseases. (Introduced; March 9, 2005)

S. 572—A bill to amend the Homeland Security Act of 2002 to give additional biosecurity responsibilities to the Department of Homeland Security. (Introduced; March 9, 2005)

H.R. 1116—To direct the Secretary of Homeland Security to carry out activities to assess and reduce the vulnerabilities of public transportation systems. (Introduced; March 4, 2005)

S. 12—A bill to combat international terrorism, and for other purposes. (Introduced; March 1, 2005)

H.R. 228—To establish a realistic, threat-based allocation of grant funds for first responders. (Introduced; February 18, 2005)

H.R. 173—To prevent and respond to terrorism and crime at or through ports. (Introduced; February 18, 2005)

H.R. 418—REAL ID Act of 2005 (Passed House; February 17, 2005)

S. 376—A bill to improve intermodal shipping container transportation security. (Introduced; February 15, 2005)

H.R. 665—To prevent access by terrorists to nuclear material, technology, and expertise, to establish an Office of Nonproliferation Programs in the Executive Office of the President, and for other purposes. (Introduced; February 10, 2005)

S. 317—A bill to protect privacy by limiting the access of the Government to library, bookseller, and other personal records for foreign intelligence and counterintelligence purposes. (Introduced; February 8, 2005)

**2004**

S. 2635—A bill to establish an intergovernmental grant program to identify and develop homeland security information, equipment, capabilities, technologies, and services to further the homeland security needs of the United States and to address the homeland security needs of Federal, State, and local governments. (Passed Senate; November 24, 2004)

S. 2393—Aviation Security Advancement Act (Scheduled for Debate; November 19, 2004)

S. 3010—Firefighters Special Operation Task Force Act (Introduced; November 19, 2004)

H.R. 5392—Volunteer First Responder Fairness Act of 2004 (Introduced; November 18, 2004)

S. 2980—Nunn–Lugar Cooperative Threat Reduction Act of 2004 (Introduced; November 16, 2004)

H.R. 5329—Disaster Area Health and Environmental Monitoring Act of 2004 (Introduced; October 10, 2004)

H.R. 5326—To provide additional security for nuclear facilities under certain circumstances. (Introduced; October 7, 2004)

H.R. 5259—Safe Food Act of 2004, and S. 2910—Safe Food Act of 2004 (Introduced; October 6, 2004)

H.R. 5082—Public Transportation Terrorism Prevention and Response Act of 2004 (Scheduled for Debate; October 6, 2004)

S. 666—Biological, Chemical, and Radiological Weapons Countermeasures Research Act (Introduced; October 5, 2004)

H.R. 5217—Railroad Security and Public Awareness Act of 2004 (Introduced; October 4, 2004)

H.R. 5223—National Intelligence Reform Act of 2004 (Introduced; October 4, 2004)

S. 2884—Public Transportation Terrorism Prevention Act of 2004 (Passed Senate; October 4, 2004)

S. 2273—Rail Security Act of 2004 (Passed Senate; October 3, 2004)

H.R. 5130—Secure Borders Act (Introduced; September 30, 2004)

H.R. 5159—Community Security Act (Introduced; September 27, 2004)

S. 2840—National Intelligence Reform Act of 2004 (Scheduled for Debate; September 26, 2004)

H.R. 5150—National Intelligence Reform Act of 2004 (Introduced; September 23, 2004)

H.R. 5132—Rail and Public Transportation Security Act of 2004 (Introduced; September 23, 2004)

H.R. 5121—To further protect the United States aviation system from terrorist attacks. (Introduced; September 21, 2004)

S. 2279—Maritime Transportation Security Act of 2004 (Passed Senate; September 21, 2004)

H.R. 5118—Prevention of Terrorist Access to Destructive Weapons Act of 2004 (Introduced; September 20, 2004)

S. 2811—9-11 Act (Introduced; September 14, 2004)

H.R. 5068—Department of Homeland Security Cybersecurity Enhancement Act of 2004 (Introduced; September 13, 2004)

H.R. 5054—Hardened Containers for Air Cargo Security Act of 2004 (Introduced; September 9, 2004)

H.R. 5050—Director of National Intelligence Act of 2004 (Introduced; September 8, 2004)

S. 430—Agriculture Security Preparedness Act (Introduced; September 8, 2004)

H.R. 4056—Commercial Aviation MANPADS Defense Act of 2004 (Passed House; September 6, 2004)

H.R. 4810—Direct Funding for First Responders Act of 2004 (Introduced; August 3, 2004)

H.R. 4883—Terrorism Against Animal-Use Entities Prohibition Improvement Act of 2004 (Introduced; August 3, 2004)

S. 779—Wastewater Treatment Works Security and Safety Act (Introduced; July 21, 2004)

S. 2726—Flight Attendant Security Training Act (Introduced; July 21, 2004)

S. 2679—Tools to Fight Terrorism Act of 2004 (Scheduled for Debate; July 18, 2004)

S. 2665—Weapons of Mass Destruction Prohibition Improvement Act of 2004 (Introduced; July 14, 2004)

H.R. 4830—Private Sector Preparedness Act of 2004 (Introduced; July 14, 2004)

H.R. 4824—Extremely Hazardous Materials Transportation Security Act of 2004 (Introduced; July 13, 2004)

S. 2653—Reducing Crime and Terrorism at America's Seaport Act of 2004 (Introduced; July 13, 2004)

S. 2632—First Responders Homeland Defense Act of 2004 (Scheduled for Debate; July 8, 2004)

H.R. 3712—United States Seaport Multiyear Security Enhancement Act (Introduced; June 8, 2004)

H.R. 4454—Ecoterrorism Prevention Act of 2004 (Introduced; May 31, 2004)

H.R. 4355—Secure COAST Act (Introduced; May 19, 2004)

H.R. 4108—High Risk Nonprofit Security Enhancement Act of 2004 (Introduced; May 19, 2004)

H.R. 4361—Safe TRAINS Act (Introduced; May 13, 2004)

S. 994—Chemical Facilities Security Act of 2004 (Scheduled for Debate; May 10, 2004)

H.R. 4126—Cockpit Security Technical Corrections and Improvements Act of 2004 (Introduced; April 2, 2004)

H.R. 4008—Anti-Terrorism Protection of Mass Transportation and Railroad Carriers Act of 2004 (Introduced; April 2, 2004)

H.R. 4104—Intelligence Transformation Act of 2004 (Introduced; April 2, 2004)

S. 2239—First Responders Homeland Defense Act of 2004 (Introduced; March 25, 2004)

S. 930—Emergency Preparedness and Response Act of 2003 (Scheduled for Debate; February 25, 2004)

H.R. 3798—Secure Existing Aviation Loopholes Act (Introduced; February 12, 2004)

**2003**

S. 1152—Firefighting Research and Coordination Act (Enacted; December 6, 2003)

H.R. 3644—Homeland Security Technology Improvement Act of 2003 (Introduced; December 4, 2003)

H.R. 3562—Prevent Act of 2003 (Introduced; November 20, 2003)

H.R. 2512—First Responders Funding Reform Act of 2003 (Introduced; November 20, 2003)

S. 1882—Terrorist Apprehension Act (Introduced; November 18, 2003)

S. 1866—Security Enhancement Act of 2003 (Scheduled for Debate; November 17, 2003)

H.R. 3456—Port Anti-Terrorism and Security Act of 2003 (Introduced; November 13, 2003)

S. 1657—A bill to amend Section 44921 of Title 49, United States Code, to provide for the arming of cargo pilots against terrorism. (Passed Senate; November 13, 2003)

S. 1043—Nuclear Infrastructure Security Act of 2003 (Scheduled for Debate; November 6, 2003)

H.R. 3040—Pretrial Detention and Lifetime Supervision of Terrorists Act of 2003 (Introduced; October 21, 2003)

H.R. 3307—Stop Terrorism of Property Act of 2003 (Introduced; October 21, 2003)

H.R. 3274—Regional Comprehensive Emergency Preparedness, Response, and Coordination Act of 2003 (Introduced; October 21, 2003)

H.R. 3227—National Preparedness Standards Act (Introduced; October 13, 2003)

H.R. 3158—PREPARE Act (Introduced; October 5, 2003)

H.R. 3016—Combating Terrorism Financing Act of 2003 (Introduced; October 2, 2003)

H.R. 3179—Anti-Terrorism Intelligence Tools Improvement Act of 2003 (Introduced; September 24, 2003)

H.R. 3173—Nuclear Terrorist Threat Reduction Act (Introduced; September 23, 2003)

S. 1039—Wastewater Treatment Works Security Act of 2003 (Scheduled for Debate; September 16, 2003)

S. 1606—Pretrial Detention and Lifetime Supervision of Terrorists Act of 2003 (Introduced; September 9, 2003)

S. 1604—Terrorist Penalties Enhancement Act of 2003 (Introduced; September 9, 2003)

S. 1587—Reducing Crime and Terrorism at America's Seaport Act of 2003 (Introduced; September 4, 2003)

H.R. 2570—State Threat Alert Reimbursement (STAR) Act of 2003 (Introduced; September 3, 2003)

H.R. 2708—Nuclear Infrastructure Security Act of 2003 (Introduced; September 3, 2003)

H.R. 2926—Nuclear Waste Terrorist Threat Assessment and Protection Act (Introduced; September 3, 2003)

S. 929—Max Cleland Over-the-Road Bus Security and Safety Act of 2003 (Passed Senate; September 3, 2003)

H.R. 2901—Chemical Facility Security Act of 2003 (Introduced; August 7, 2003)

S. 1507—Library, Bookseller, and Personal Records Privacy Act (Introduced; July 30, 2003)

S. 1552—Protecting the Rights of Individuals Act (Introduced; July 30, 2003)

S. 1441—Protection against Terrorist Hoaxes Act of 2003 (Introduced; July 21, 2003)

H.R. 2726—National Defense Rail Act (Introduced; July 15, 2003)

S. 746—Anti-Terrorism and Port Security Act of 2003 (Introduced; July 13, 2003)

H.R. 2537—Emergency Warning Act of 2003 (Introduced; June 19, 2003)

H.R. 1118—Staffing for Adequate Fire and Emergency Response Firefighters Act of 2003 (Introduced; June 3, 2003)

H.R. 2329—Global Pathogen Surveillance Act of 2003 (Introduced; June 3, 2003)

S. 165—Air Cargo Security Improvement Act (Passed Senate; May 8, 2003)

H.R. 1449—First Responder and Emergency Preparedness Block Grant Program for Local Governments (Introduced; April 2, 2003)

H.R. 1389—Homeland Emergency Response Act of 2003 (Introduced; March 24, 2003)

H.R. 1392—To require inspection of all cargo on commercial trucks and vessels entering the United States. (Introduced; March 21, 2003)

S. 609—Restoration of Freedom of Information Act of 2003 (Introduced; March 12, 2003)

H.R. 891—Dirty Bomb Prevention Act (Introduced; March 10, 2003)

H.R. 703—Law Enforcement Partnership to Combat Terrorism Act (Introduced; March 6, 2003)

H.R. 1049—Arming Cargo Pilots Against Terrorism Act (Introduced; March 5, 2003)

H.R. 1007—Homeland Security Block Grant Act of 2003 (Introduced; March 4, 2003)

S. 466—First Responders Partnership Grant Act of 2003 (Introduced; February 27, 2003)

H.R. 764—First Responders Expedited Assistance Act of 2003 (Introduced; February 13, 2003)

S. 329—Neighborhood Security Act of 2003 (Introduced; February 6, 2003)

S. 311—Commercial Airline Missile Defense Act (Introduced; February 5, 2003)

S. 315—First Responders Partnership Grant Act of 2003 (Introduced; February 5, 2003)

S. 266—Antiterrorism Intelligence Distribution Act of 2003 (Introduced; January 30, 2003)

H.R. 356—Terrorist Elimination Act of 2003 (Introduced; January 27, 2003)

H.R. 105—Homeland Emergency Responders Organization Act of 2002 (Introduced; January 8, 2003)

S. 104—National Defense Rail Act (Introduced; January 7, 2003)

## 2002

H.R. 3609—Pipeline Safety Improvement Act of 2002 (Enacted; December 17, 2002)

H.R. 3394—Cyber Security Research and Development Act (Enacted; November 27, 2002)

S. 1456—Critical Infrastructure Information Security Act of 2001 (Introduced; November 20, 2002)

H.R. 5710—Homeland Security Information Sharing Act (Passed House; November 14, 2002)

S. 3148—Biological, Chemical, and Radiological Weapons Countermeasures Research Act of 2002 (Introduced; October 16, 2002)

S. 3121—Nuclear and Radiological Terrorism Threat Reduction Act of 2002 (Introduced; October 15, 2002)

H.R. 5490—Tribal Government Homeland Security Coordination and Integration Act (Introduced; September 29, 2002)

H.R. 5483—Regional Comprehensive Emergency Preparedness, Coordination, and Recovery Act of 2002 (Introduced; September 25, 2002)

H.R. 5441—Homeland Emergency Responders Organization Act of 2002 (Introduced; September 24, 2002)

H.R. 5420—Port Protection Act of 2002 (Introduced; September 18, 2002)

H.R. 4864—Anti-Terrorism Explosives Act of 2002 (Introduced; September 17, 2002)

S. 2846—Security and Liberty Preservation Act (Introduced; July 31, 2002)

S. 2887—Homeland Security Information Sharing Act (Introduced; July 31, 2002)

H.R. 3448—Public Health Security and Bioterrorism Preparedness and Response Act of 2002 (Enacted; June 11, 2002)

S. 2579—Community Protection from Chemical Terrorism Act (Introduced; June 4, 2002)

**2001**

H.R. 3285—Federal–Local Information Sharing Partnership Act of 2001 (Introduced; March 6, 2002)

H.R. 3209—Anti-Hoax Terrorism Act of 2001 (Passed House; December 12, 2001)

H.R. 3435—Empowering Local First Responders To Fight Terrorism Act of 2001 (Introduced; December 7, 2001)

S. 1661—Deadly Biological Agent Control Act of 2001 (Introduced; November 8, 2001)

H.R. 3153—State Bioterrorism Preparedness Act (Introduced; October 29, 2001)

S. 1546—Biological Chemical Attack bill (Introduced; October 14, 2001)

S. 1551—Protecting the Food Supply from Bioterrorism Act (Introduced; October 14, 2001)

H.R. 3110—Transportation Security Enhancement Act of 2001 (Introduced; October 14, 2001)

H.R. 3069—Securing American Families Effectively (SAFE) Act (Introduced; October 8, 2001)

S. 1508—Biological and Chemical Attack Preparedness Act (Introduced; October 3, 2001)

H.R. 2928—Keeping America Safe Act of 2001 (Introduced; September 27, 2001)

H.R. 2958—Passenger Airline Safety and Security Act (Introduced; September 25, 2001)

S. 1453—Preparedness against Terrorism Act of 2001 (Introduced; September 20, 2001)

H.R. 2795—Agroterrorism Prevention Act of 2001 (Introduced; September 9, 2001)

H.R. 2583—Environmental Terrorism Reduction Act (Introduced; August 5, 2001)

H.R. 1158—National Homeland Security Agency Act (Introduced; April 23, 2001)

H.R. 1292—Homeland Security Strategy Act of 2001 (Introduced; March 29, 2001)

H.R. 19—Terrorist Elimination Act of 2001 (Introduced; January 3, 2001)

*Source*: www.govtrack.us.

## 9/11 COMMISSION

To allow for a full investigation into the terrorist attacks of September 11, 2001, and to make recommendations as to how such attacks could be prevented in the future, Congress created the National Commission on Terrorist Attacks Upon the United States, more commonly known as the "9/11 Commission." The 9/11 Commission was created by Public Law 107-306, and signed by President George W. Bush on November 27, 2002. In addition to other tasks, this law required the commission to investigate "facts and circumstances relating to the terrorist attacks of September 11, 2001," including those relating to intelligence agencies; law enforcement agencies; diplomacy; immigration, nonimmigrant visas, and border control; the flow of assets to terrorist organizations; commercial aviation; the role of congressional oversight and resource allocation; and other areas determined relevant by the commission for its inquiry.

The commission was provided with an initial $3 million to carry out its tasks. When the investigation became much more involved than originally expected, Congress appropriated an additional $12 million in two separate allocations, bringing the total cost of the investigation to $15 million. In fulfilling its mission, the members and staff of the commission interviewed more than 1,200 individuals in 10 countries, reviewed more than 2.5 million documents, and held 19 days of public hearings, during which it received testimony from more than 160 federal, state, and local officials, and experts from the private sector.

On July 22, 2004, after 20 months of research and investigation, the 9/11 Commission released its final report. In this report, the commission issued 37 recommendations to help prevent future terrorist attacks, divided into sections detailing a global strategy and a government reorganization necessary to implement such a strategy. The commission summarized its recommended global strategy into three subject areas:

1. Attacking terrorists and their organizations
2. Preventing the continued growth of Islamist terrorism
3. Protecting and preparing for terrorist attacks

To implement this strategy, the commission proposed a five-part plan to build a coherent, unified effort across the various U.S. government agencies that would be involved:

1. Closing the foreign–domestic divide by linking intelligence and operational planning in a new National Counterterrorism Center
2. Bringing the intelligence community together under a national intelligence director and national intelligence centers

3. Encouraging information sharing throughout government through decentralized networks
4. Centralizing and strengthening congressional oversight of intelligence and homeland security issues
5. Strengthening the national security workforce within the FBI and clarifying the missions of the departments of Defense and Homeland Security.

A summary of the 9/11 Commission's report is provided at the end of this chapter in Appendix 2-4.

## BUDGET APPROPRIATIONS

Each year, the budget appropriation for the Department of Homeland Security is established and proposed by the Executive Office, and then debated and enacted by Congress. The DHS budget has steadily increased since the 2003 inception of the department. In FY 2004, the DHS budget was $29,868,930,000. This amount was raised to $31,991,413,000 in FY 2005, a 6.63% increase over FY 2003. For FY 2006, the president requested a DHS budget of $34,152,143,000, or 6.33% over the 2005 figures.

It is easy to argue that the creation of the DHS demonstrated the fact that securing the United States is considered a high-priority item on the Bush administration agenda. With budget figure values that are so high, however, the question of sustainability must be addressed. Supporting such a large federal effort requires the commitment of both the Congress, and the citizens who elect those officials. With the memory of September 11 still fresh, many people do not have a problem with dedicating so much taxpayer money to ensuring national security. However, this support is likely to wane as time passes without successive attacks. The problem with this thinking is that, unfortunately, it is not in line with the full functions of the DHS.

DHS serves many needs besides the prevention of terrorism. Simply examining the former duties of many of the agencies absorbed, as will be discussed in Chapter 3, helps to define these responsibilities. For example, the Coast Guard, one of the largest agencies absorbed and the recipient of 20% of the DHS budget, has many tasks that do not relate to terrorism including search and rescue and environmental protection, to name a few. The funding for these tasks, however, is often lumped together with general "counterterrorism appropriations" just by the nature of it being included in the DHS budget. It will be contingent on the abilities of the DHS leadership to educate the American public about this disconnect in understanding for people to better justify in their minds what this large sum of money is supporting, outside of terrorism, for the DHS budget to remain sustainable.

The DHS budget is explored in more detail, in relation to each departmental component, in Chapter 3. Sidebar 2-10, a DHS fact sheet explaining the FY 2006 DHS budget request, explores the budget and the five major themes to be addressed in that fiscal year.

---

### SIDEBAR 2-10    Fact Sheet: U.S. Department of Homeland Security FY 2006 Budget Request

President George W. Bush's FY 2006 budget request includes a total of $34.1 billion for the Department of Homeland Security. This is an increase of seven percent over the enacted FY 2005 funding, excluding Project BioShield. This year's request demonstrates the Administration's continued commitment to making further improvements to the nation's homeland security.

Among the entities with significant budgetary increases are Immigration and Customs Enforcement with a 13.5 percent increase and the U.S. Coast Guard with an increase of more than nine percent.

The budget includes the establishment of the Domestic Nuclear Detection Office (DNDO). The DNDO will develop, acquire and support the deployment and improvement of a domestic system to detect and report attempts to import, assemble, or transport a nuclear explosive device, fissile material or radiological material intended for illicit use.

The budget proposes to consolidate the various DHS screening activities with the formation of the Office of Screening Coordination and Operations (SCO) within the Border and Transportation Security (BTS) directorate. This new organization would enhance terrorist-related screening through comprehensive, coordinated procedures that detect, identify, track and interdict people, cargo and other entities and objects that pose a threat to homeland security.

The effectiveness of state and local homeland security assistance can be increased through an approach that closes the most critical gaps in terrorism prevention and preparedness capabilities. Over $2 billion in grants for states and urban areas would be based on assessments of risk and vulnerability, as well as the needs and priorities identified in state and regional homeland security plans. The proposed Targeted Infrastructure Protection program would provide $600 million in integrated grants, enabling DHS to supplement state, local and regional government efforts in their protection of critical national infrastructures such as seaports, mass transit, railways, and energy facilities.

In FY 2006, DHS seeks to consolidate the research, development, test and evaluation (RDT&E) activities within the DHS Science and Technology (S&T) directorate. This consolidation, in the amount of $127 million, will bring the scientific and engineering personnel and other RDT&E resources of the Department under a single accountable authority.

The Department requests $49.9 million to begin to establish a regional structure for DHS and integrate and identify efficiencies within information technology, facilities, and operations centers across DHS. Of the 22 agencies that were brought together to form the Department, twelve have regional and field structures ranging in size from three to thirty offices distributed throughout the nation.

The budget revolves around five major themes: Revolutionizing the Borders; Strengthening Law Enforcement; Improving National Preparedness and Response; Leveraging Technology; and Creating a 21st Century Department.

**Revolutionizing the Borders**

- **Weapons of Mass Destruction (WMD) Detection Technology**—The budget includes $125 million to purchase additional Radiation Portal Monitors (RPMs) and pilot advanced next generation RPMs to detect both gamma and neutron radiation at our borders.
- The **Container Security Initiative (CSI)**, which focuses on pre-screening cargo before it reaches our shores, will have a preventive and deterrence effect on the use of global containerized shipping of WMD and other terrorist equipment. An increase of $5.4 million over FY 2005 is included in CBP's budget for CSI, for a total request of $138.8 million.
- **CBP Targeting Systems** aid in identifying high-risk cargo and passengers. The budget includes a total of $28.3 million for these system initiatives, which includes a $5.4 million increase.
- **America's Shield Initiative (ASI)** enhances electronic surveillance capabilities along the northern and southern land borders of the U.S. by improving the sensor and video surveillance equipment deployed to guard against the entry of illegal aliens, terrorists, WMDs and contraband into the U.S. The budget includes $51.1 million, an increase of $19.8 million.

- **US-VISIT**, which is proposed for consolidation within the SCO, increases from $340 million to $390 million. The increase will provide for the accelerated deployment of US-VISIT at the land borders and enhance access for border personnel to immigration, criminal and terrorist information.
- The **Customs Trade Partnership Against Terrorism (C-TPAT)** focuses on partnerships all along the entire supply chain, from the factory floor, to foreign vendors, to land borders and seaports. The budget includes an increase of $8.2 million, for a total amount of $54.3 million.
- **Border Patrol Staffing** would increase along the southwest border and coastal areas, in part to replace some Border Patrol agents shifted to the northern border as required by the Patriot Act. An increase of 210 agents and $36.9 million is included in the budget for the Border Patrol. This increases the Border Patrol Agents to 10,949.
- **Long Range Radar** technology is used by the Office of Air and Marine Operations to detect and intercept aircraft attempting to avoid detection while entering the U.S. CBP and the Department of Defense will assume responsibility for operating and maintaining these systems from the FAA beginning in FY 2006. CBP's share is $44.2 million in the budget.

**Strengthening Law Enforcement**

- The **Armed Helicopter for Homeland Security Project** increases by $17.4 million in the budget. These funds will provide equipment and aircraft modifications to establish armed helicopter capability at five USCG Air Stations. A total of $19.9 million is included in the budget for this project.
- The **Integrated Deepwater System** increases by $242 million to a total of $966 million in FY 2006 to continue the acquisition of the

USCG's Maritime Security Cutter–Large, complete design of the Maritime Security Cutter–Medium, promote completion of the Multi-Mission Cutter Helicopter (re-engineered and electronically upgraded HH-65 helicopter) and significantly improve fixed and rotary wing aircraft capabilities.

- The **Response Boat-Medium Project** increases the effort to replace the USCG's 41-foot utility boats and other large non-standard boats with assets more capable of meeting all of the USCG's multi-mission operational requirements by $10 million. A total of $22 million is proposed in the budget for this effort.
- The **Federal Air Marshal Service (FAMS)** seeks a total of $688.9 million. This funding will allow ICE to protect air security and promote public confidence in our civil aviation system.
- **Detention and Removal** within ICE increases by $176 million for detention and removal activities. Total increases for this program are approximately 19 percent above the FY 2005.
- **Federal Flight Deck Officers (FFDO)/Crew Member Self-Defense (CMSD) Training** is increased by $11 million in FY 2006 for a total of $36.3 million. This allows for the expansion of the semi-annual firearm re-qualification program for FFDO personnel and to fund the first full year of the CMSD training program.

**Improving National Preparedness and Response**

- **Federal assistance for our nation's first responder community**. The budget includes $3.6 billion for grants, training, and technical assistance administered by the Office of State and Local Government Coordination and Preparedness (SLGCP). This funding will support state and local agencies as they equip, train, exercise, and assess preparedness for emergencies regardless of scale or cause.
- **Enhanced Catastrophic Disaster Planning** is budgeted at $20 million for FEMA to work with states and localities, as well as other Federal agencies, to develop and implement plans that will improve the ability to respond to and to recover from catastrophic disasters.
- The **Office of Interoperability and Compatibility (OIC)** within the S&T Directorate will allow the Department to expand its leadership role in interoperable communications that could be used by every first responder agency in the country. The OIC has currently identified three program areas: communications, equipment, and training. With $20.5 million in FY 2006, the OIC will plan and begin to establish the training and equipment programs, as well as continue existing communication interoperability efforts through the SAFECOM Program.
- Replacement of the USCG's **High Frequency (HF) Communications System**, funded at $10 million in the budget, will replace unserviceable, shore-side, high power high frequency transmitters, significantly improving long-range maritime safety and security communications.
- The **Rescue 21** project is funded at $101 million in the budget to continue recapitalizing the Coast Guard's coastal zone communications network. This funding will complete system infrastructure and network installations in 14 regions and begin development of regional designs for the remaining 11 regions.

**Leveraging Technology**

- **Low Volatility Agent Warning System** is a new FY 2006 initiative totaling $20 million. Funding is included to develop a system that will serve as the basis for a warning and identification capability against a set of chemical agents whose vapor pressure is too low to be detected by conventional measures.

- **Counter-MAN Portable Air Defense Systems (C-MANPADS)** funding is increased by $49 million to a total of $110 million in the budget. This program will continue to research the viability of technical countermeasures for commercial aircraft against the threat of shoulder-fired missiles.
- **Cyber Security** is enhanced in the budget to augment a 24/7 cyber threat watch, warning, and response capability that would identify emerging threats and vulnerabilities and coordinate responses to major cyber security incidents. An increase of $5 million is proposed in the budget for this effort, bringing the program total to $73.3 million.
- **Secure Flight/Crew Vetting** requests an increase of $49 million to field the system developed and tested in FY 2005. The funds will support testing, information systems, connectivity to airlines and screen systems and daily operations. This also includes an increase of $3.3 million for crew vetting.
- The budget includes $174 million to complete installation of **High Speed Operational Connectivity (Hi-SOC)** to passenger and baggage screening checkpoints to improve management of screening system performance.
- **Emerging Checkpoint Technology** is enhanced by $43.7 million in FY 2006 to direct additional resources to improve checkpoint explosives screening. This assures that TSA is on the cutting edge, ahead of the development of increasingly well-disguised prohibited items. This proposed increase will result in investing more than $100 million invested in FY 2005 and FY 2006 for new technology to ensure improved screening of all higher risk passengers.
- **Homeland Secure Data Network (HSDN)** includes $37 million in the budget. These

funds will streamline and modernize the classified data capabilities in order to facilitate high quality and high value classified data communication and collaboration.

- The **Homeland Security Operations Center (HSOC)** funding is increased by $26.3 million bringing its FY 2006 funded level to $61.1 million. This includes an increase of $13.4 million for the Homeland Security Information Network (HSIN) and an increase of $12.9 million to enhance HSOC systems and operations.

### Creating a 21st Century Department

- **Electronically Managing enterprise resources for government effectiveness and efficiency (eMerge2)** funding of $30 million in the budget to continue implementation of a DHS-wide solution that delivers accurate, relevant and timely resource management information to decision makers. By delivering access to critical information across all components, the Department will be able to better support its many front-line activities.
- **MAX HR** funding of $53 million is to continue the design and deployment of a new human resources system. As outlined in final regulations, issued jointly on February 1, 2005, by Secretary Ridge and the Director of the Office of Personnel Management (OPM) Kay Coles James, the MAX HR system provides greater flexibility and accountability in the way employees are paid, developed, evaluated, afforded due process and represented by labor organizations. The goal is a 21st century personnel system that enhances mission-essential flexibility and preserves core civil service principles and the merit system.
- The **Information Sharing and Collaboration (ISC)** program will affect the policy, procedures, technical, process, cultural, and organi-

zational aspects of information sharing and collaboration, including coordinating ISC policy with other Federal agencies, drafting technical and operational needs statements, performing policy assessments and analyzing

new requirements. The total funding for FY 2006 will be $16.5 million.

*Source*: Department of Homeland Security, www.dhs.gov/ dhspublic/interapp/press_release/press_release_0613.xml.

## CONCLUSION

The issue of terrorism and the methods by which the federal government should prepare for and respond to terrorist threats did not suddenly appear after the devastating events of September 11. As this chapter has shown, concerns about potential threats to the United States have been recognized and actions taken to address them since the early 1980s. Precipitating events, such as the earlier bombing of the World Trade Center in 1993 and attacks on U.S. embassies and installations abroad, caught the attention not only of the investigative and intelligence agencies, but also of Congress and the White House.

The domestic terrorist bombing of the Murrah Federal Office Building in Oklahoma City vividly demonstrated that conflicts existed regarding incident command and control at the federal level. Although members of Congress passed legislation they believed would adequately address these conflicts, the competition, and a lack of resources, they failed to address the concerns and needs of first responders at the state and local levels. Despite these shortfalls, the federal response worked surprisingly well on September 11. However, the enormous loss of lives among civilians and the first responder community demanded and pro-

duced a flurry of activity to ensure that this tragedy would not be repeated. Two of the most far-reaching pieces of legislation, the PATRIOT Act and the Homeland Security Act, dramatically changed the power, organization, and functions of the federal government. The PATRIOT Act gave the attorney general and the DOJ unsurpassed authority over the civil rights and liberties of individuals. Combining 22 federal entities with a mandate to establish a safe and secure homeland, the Homeland Security Act represents the largest single reorganization of the federal government since World War II.

Whether these actions have created a safer, more secure homeland will require many more years to determine. As the federal government further reorganizes, authorized funding is making its way to the states. Legislation addressing loopholes continues to emerge, and problems associated with the original, fast-action legislation is being exposed and addressed. The United States is in a state of legislative recalibration. Nonetheless, all the authorities are in place; and the major legislation has been passed. Historians will surely assess the effectiveness of the U.S. response to the threat of terror based on the success of these acts, and whether their implementation has accomplished the goals of a safe and secure homeland.

## REVIEW QUESTIONS

1. What are the two principal purposes for establishing legislation to support government homeland security activities and programs?

2. What are the principal functions of the PATRIOT Act, the Homeland Security Act, and Homeland Security Presidential Directive No. 5?

3. What issues have been raised concerning some of the authorities granted government agencies in the PATRIOT Act?

4. If you were a member of Congress, what types of standards would you propose to measure the effectiveness of the spending that is occurring for homeland security? How would you propose to determine if the spending has raised individual, community, and private sector preparedness for the new terrorist threat? How would these measurements be enforced and by what government agency(s) at what level of government (federal, state, and/or local)?

5. What additional statutory authorities and resources do you think emergency managers require in order to function effectively in homeland security? Should certain preparedness and mitigation actions and activities be made mandatory like building codes and seat belt use? Should greater emphasis be placed on enforcement of current and future restrictions and requirements? Should additional resources become part of a regular annual appropriation at all levels of government? How would the impact of the new authorities and resources be measured to ensure that they are successfully applied?

## REFERENCES

American Civil Liberties Union, San Jose, CA Resolution. 2003. <www.aclu.org/SafeandFree/SafeandFree.cfm?ID=13900&c=207>

Baldwin, T. E. 2002. "Historical Chronology of FEMA Consequence Management, Preparedness and Response to Terrorism." Argonne, IL: Argonne National Laboratory.

Bohn, K. 2003. "ACLU Files against Patriot Act." CNN (July 30). <www.cnn.com>

Doyle, Charles. 2004. "CRS Report for Congress: USA PATRIOT Act Sunset: A Sketch" (January 7). <www.au.af.mil/au/awc/awcgate/crs/rs21704.pdf>

Gay, L. 2001. "How the New Antiterrorism Bill Could Affect You." Scripps Howard News Service (October 26). <www.startribune.com>

Library of Congress. July 21, 2003. <www.congress.gov>

Paul, Ron. 2005. "Reconsidering the Patriot Act, Texas Straight Talk: A Weekly Column" (May 2). <www.house.gov/paul/tst/tst2005/tst050205.htm>

Rubin, C. B., William R. Cummings, and Irmak Renda-Tanali. 2003. "Terrorism Time Line: Major Focusing Events and U.S. Outcomes (1993–2002)" (May). Washington, DC: Self-published.

Shotwell, Betsy. 2003. "Memorandum to Honorable Mayor and city Council, USA PATRIOT Act and Patriot Act II" (September 19). <www.sanjoseca.gov/cty_clk/9_23_03docs/09_23_03_3.4.pdf>

Taylor, Andrew. 2005. "House Votes to Limit Patriot Act Rules." The Associated Press (June 16). <www.washingtonpost.com/wp-dyn/content/article/2005/06/15/AR2005061502674.html>

U.S. Department of Justice. 2005. "USA PATRIOT Act Overview: What Is the Patriot Act?" <www.nunes.house.gov/documents/PatriotActOverview.pdf>

*The Washington Post.* 2005. "Patriot Second Act" (June 13). <www.washingtonpost.com/wp-dyn/content/article/2005/06/12/AR2005061201436.html>

The White House. 2004. "Fact Sheet: President Bush Calls for Renewing the USA PATRIOT Act" (April 18). <www.whitehouse.gov/news/releases/2004/04/20040419-4.html>

## APPENDIX 2-1
### Patriot Act of 2001—Summary of Titles

*Title I: Enhancing Domestic Security against Terrorism*—Establishes in the treasury the counterterrorism fund.

*Title II: Enhanced Surveillance Procedures*—Amends the Federal criminal code to authorize the interception of wire, oral, and electronic communications for the production of evidence of: (1) specified chemical weapons or terrorism offenses; and (2) computer fraud and abuse.

*Title III: International Money-Laundering Abatement and Anti-Terrorist Financing Act of 2001; International Money-Laundering Abatement and Financial Anti-Terrorism Act of 2001*—Sunsets this act after the first day of FY 2005 if Congress enacts a specified joint resolution to that effect.
- *Subtitle A: International Counter Money Laundering and Related Measures*—Amends Federal law governing monetary transactions to prescribe procedural guidelines under which the secretary of the Treasury (the secretary) may require domestic financial institutions and agencies to take specified measures if the secretary finds that reasonable grounds exist for concluding that jurisdictions, financial institutions, types of accounts, or transactions operating outside or within the United States, are of primary money laundering concern. Includes mandatory disclosure of specified information relating to certain correspondent accounts.
- *Subtitle B: Bank Secrecy Act Amendments and Related Improvements*—Amends Federal law known as the Bank Secrecy Act to revise requirements for civil liability immunity for voluntary financial institution disclosure of suspicious activities. Authorizes the inclusion of suspicions of illegal activity in written employment references.
- *Subtitle C: Currency Crimes*—Establishes as a bulk cash smuggling felony the knowing concealment and attempted transport (or transfer) across U.S. borders of currency and monetary instruments in excess of $10,000, with intent to evade specified currency reporting requirements.

*Title IV: Protecting the Border*
- *Subtitle A: Protecting the Northern Border*—Authorizes the attorney general to waive certain Immigration and Naturalization Service (INS) personnel caps with respect to ensuring security needs on the northern border.
- *Subtitle B: Enhanced Immigration Provisions*—Amends the Immigration and Nationality Act to broaden the scope of aliens ineligible for admission or deportable due to terrorist activities to include an alien who: (1) is a representative of a political, social, or similar group whose political endorsement of terrorist acts undermines U.S. antiterrorist efforts; (2) has used a position of prominence to endorse terrorist activity or to persuade others to support such activity in a way that undermines U.S. antiterrorist efforts (or the child or spouse of such an alien under specified circumstances); or (3) has been associated with a terrorist organization and intends to engage in threatening activities while in the United States.
- *Subtitle C: Preservation of Immigration Benefits for Victims of Terrorism*—Authorizes the attorney general to provide permanent resident status through the special immigrant program to an alien (and spouse, child, or grandparent under specified circumstances) who was the beneficiary of a petition filed on or before September 11, 2001, to grant the alien permanent residence as an employer-sponsored immigrant or of an application for labor certification if the petition or application was rendered null because of the

disability of the beneficiary or loss of employment due to physical damage to, or destruction of, the business of the petitioner or applicant as a direct result of the terrorist attacks on September 11, 2001 (September attacks) or because of the death of the petitioner or applicant as a direct result of such attacks.

*Title V: Removing Obstacles to Investigating Terrorism*—Authorizes the attorney general to pay rewards from available funds pursuant to public advertisements for assistance to the DOJ to combat terrorism and defend the nation against terrorist acts, in accordance with procedures and regulations established or issued by the attorney general, subject to specified conditions, including a prohibition against any such reward of $250,000 or more from being made or offered without the personal approval of either the attorney general or the president.

*Title VI: Providing for Victims of Terrorism, Public Safety Officers, and Their Families*
- *Subtitle A: Aid to Families of Public Safety Officers*—Provides for expedited payments for: (1) public safety officers involved in the prevention, investigation, rescue, or recovery efforts related to a terrorist attack; and (2) heroic public safety officers. Increases Public Safety Officers Benefit Program payments.
- *Subtitle B: Amendments to the Victims of Crime Act of 1984*—Amends the Victims of Crime Act of 1984 to: (1) revise provisions regarding the allocation of funds for compensation and assistance, location of compensable crime, and the relationship of crime victim compensation to means-tested Federal benefit programs and to the September 11 victim compensation fund; and (2) establish an antiterrorism emergency reserve in the Victims of Crime Fund.

*Title VII: Increased Information Sharing for Critical Infrastructure Protection*—Amends the Omnibus Crime Control and Safe Streets Act of 1968 to extend Bureau of Justice Assistance regional information-sharing-system grants to systems that enhance the investigation and prosecution abilities of participating Federal, state, and local law enforcement agencies in addressing multi-jurisdictional terrorist conspiracies and activities. Authorizes appropriations.

*Title VIII: Strengthening the Criminal Laws Against Terrorism*—Amends the Federal criminal code to prohibit specific terrorist acts or otherwise destructive, disruptive, or violent acts against mass transportation vehicles, ferries, providers, employees, passengers, or operating systems.

*Title IX: Improved Intelligence*—Amends the National Security Act of 1947 to require the director of Central Intelligence (DCI) to establish requirements and priorities for foreign intelligence collected under the Foreign Intelligence Surveillance Act of 1978 and to provide assistance to the attorney general (AG) to ensure that information derived from electronic surveillance or physical searches is disseminated for efficient and effective foreign intelligence purposes. Requires the inclusion of international terrorist activities within the scope of foreign intelligence under such act.

*Title X: Miscellaneous*—Directs the inspector general of the Department of Justice to designate one official to review allegations of abuse of civil rights, civil liberties, and racial and ethnic profiling by government employees and officials.

*Source*: www.congress.gov.

# APPENDIX 2-2
## Summary of the Homeland Security Act of 2002

### TITLE I: DEPARTMENT OF HOMELAND SECURITY

(Sec. 101)—Establishes a Department of Homeland Security (DHS) as an executive department of the United States, headed by a secretary of Homeland Security (secretary) appointed by the president, by and with the advice and consent of the Senate, to:

1. prevent terrorist attacks within the United States;
2. reduce the vulnerability of the United States to terrorism;
3. minimize the damage, and assist in the recovery, from terrorist attacks that occur within the United States;
4. carry out all functions of entities transferred to DHS;
5. ensure that the functions of the agencies and subdivisions within DHS that are not related directly to securing the homeland are not diminished or neglected except by a specific act of Congress;
6. ensure that the overall economic security of the United States is not diminished by efforts, activities, and programs aimed at securing the homeland; and
7. monitor connections between illegal drug trafficking and terrorism, coordinate efforts to sever such connections, and otherwise contribute to efforts to interdict illegal drug trafficking.

Vests primary responsibility for investigating and prosecuting acts of terrorism in Federal, state, and local law enforcement agencies with proper jurisdiction except as specifically provided by law with respect to entities transferred to DHS under this act.

(Sec. 102)—Directs the secretary to appoint a special assistant to carry out specified homeland security liaison activities between DHS and the private sector.

(Sec. 103)—Creates the following:

1. a deputy secretary of Homeland Security;
2. an undersecretary for Information Analysis and Infrastructure Protection;
3. an undersecretary for Science and Technology;
4. an undersecretary for Border and Transportation Security;
5. an undersecretary for Emergency Preparedness and Response;
6. a director of the Bureau of Citizenship and Immigration Services;
7. an undersecretary for Management;
8. not more than 12 assistant secretaries; and
9. a general counsel.

Establishes an inspector general (to be appointed under the Inspector General Act of 1978). Requires the following individuals to assist the secretary in the performance of the secretary's functions:

1. the commandant of the Coast Guard;
2. the director of the Secret Service;
3. a chief information officer;
4. a chief human capital officer;
5. a chief financial officer; and
6. an officer for Civil Rights and Civil Liberties.

### TITLE II: INFORMATION ANALYSIS AND INFRASTRUCTURE PROTECTION

Subtitle A: Directorate for Information Analysis and Infrastructure Protection; Access to Information (Sec. 201)—Establishes in the department:

1. a directorate for Information Analysis and Infrastructure Protection, headed by an under-

secretary for Information Analysis and Infrastructure Protection;

2. an assistant secretary for Information Analysis; and

3. an assistant secretary for Infrastructure Protection.

Requires the undersecretary to:

1. access, receive, and analyze law enforcement and intelligence information from Federal, state, and local agencies and the private sector to identify the nature, scope, and identity of terrorist threats to the United States, as well as potential U.S. vulnerabilities;

2. carry out comprehensive assessments of vulnerabilities of key U.S. resources and critical infrastructures;

3. integrate relevant information, analyses, and vulnerability assessments to identify protection priorities;

4. ensure timely and efficient department access to necessary information for discharging responsibilities;

5. develop a comprehensive national plan for securing key U.S. resources and critical infrastructures;

6. recommend necessary measures to protect such resources and infrastructure in coordination with other entities;

7. administer the Homeland Security Advisory System;

8. review, analyze, and make recommendations for improvements in policies and procedures governing the sharing of law enforcement, intelligence, and intelligence-related information and other information related to homeland security within the Federal government and between the Federal government and state and local government agencies and authorities;

9. disseminate department homeland security information to other appropriate Federal, state, and local agencies;

10. consult with the director of Central Intelligence (DCI) and other appropriate Federal intelligence, law enforcement, or other elements to establish collection priorities and strategies for information relating to the terrorism threats;

11. consult with state and local governments and private entities to ensure appropriate exchanges of information relating to such threats;

12. ensure the protection from unauthorized disclosure of homeland security and intelligence information;

13. request additional information from appropriate entities relating to threats of terrorism in the United States;

14. establish and utilize a secure communications and information technology infrastructure for receiving and analyzing data;

15. ensure the compatibility and privacy protection of shared information databases and analytical tools;

16. coordinate training and other support to facilitate the identification and sharing of information;

17. coordinate activities with elements of the intelligence community, Federal, state, and local law enforcement agencies, and the private sector; and

18. provide intelligence and information analysis and support to other elements of the department. Provides for:
    a. staffing, including the use of private sector analysts; and
    b. cooperative agreements for the detail of appropriate personnel.

Transfers to the secretary the functions, personnel, assets, and liabilities of the following entities:

1. the National Infrastructure Protection Center of the Federal Bureau of Investigation (other than the Computer Investigations and Operations Section);

2. the National Communications System of the Department of Defense;
3. the Critical Infrastructure Assurance Offices of the Department of Commerce;
4. the National Infrastructure Simulation and Analysis Center of the Department of Energy and its energy security and assurance program; and
5. the Federal Computer Incident Response Center of the General Services Administration.

Amends the National Security Act of 1947 to include as elements of the intelligence community the department elements concerned with analyses of foreign intelligence information.

Subtitle B: Critical Infrastructure Information— Critical Infrastructure Information Act of 2002 (Sec. 213)—Allows a critical infrastructure protection program to be so designated by either the president or the secretary.

Subtitle C: Information Security—(Sec. 221)— Requires the secretary to establish procedures on the use of shared information that:

1. limit its re-dissemination to ensure it is not used for an unauthorized purpose;
2. ensure its security and confidentiality;
3. protect the constitutional and statutory rights of individuals who are subjects of such information; and
4. provide data integrity through the timely removal and destruction of obsolete or erroneous names and information.

Subtitle D: Office of Science and Technology— (Sec. 231)—Establishes within the Department of Justice (DOJ) an Office of Science and Technology whose mission is to:

1. serve as the national focal point for work on law enforcement technology (investigative and forensic technologies, corrections technologies, and technologies that support the judicial process); and
2. carry out programs that improve the safety and effectiveness of such technology and improve

technology access by Federal, state, and local law enforcement agencies.

Sets forth office duties, including:

1. establishing and maintaining technology advisory groups and performance standards;
2. carrying out research, development, testing, evaluation, and cost-benefit analyses for improving the safety, effectiveness, and efficiency of technologies used by Federal, state, and local law enforcement agencies; and
3. operating the regional National Law Enforcement and Corrections Technology Centers (established under this subtitle) and establishing additional centers.

Requires the office director to report annually on office activities.

## TITLE III: SCIENCE AND TECHNOLOGY IN SUPPORT OF HOMELAND SECURITY

(Sec. 301)—Establishes in DHS a directorate of Science and Technology, headed by an undersecretary for Science and Technology to be responsible for:

1. advising the secretary regarding research and development (R&D) efforts and priorities in support of DHS missions;
2. developing a national policy and strategic plan for identifying priorities, goals, objectives, and policies for, and coordinating the Federal government's civilian efforts to identify and develop countermeasures to chemical, biological, radiological, nuclear, and other emerging terrorist threats;
3. supporting the undersecretary for Information Analysis and Infrastructure Protection by assessing and testing homeland security vulnerabilities and possible threats;

4. conducting basic and applied R&D activities relevant to DHS elements, provided that such responsibility does not extend to human health-related R&D activities;

5. establishing priorities for directing, funding, and conducting national R&D and procurement of technology systems for preventing the importation of chemical, biological, radiological, nuclear, and related weapons and material and for detecting, preventing, protecting against, and responding to terrorist attacks;

6. establishing a system for transferring homeland security developments or technologies to Federal, state, and local government and private sector entities;

7. entering into agreements with the Department of Energy (DOE) regarding the use of the national laboratories or sites and support of the science and technology base at those facilities;

8. collaborating with the secretary of agriculture and the attorney general in the regulation of certain biological agents and toxins as provided in the Agricultural Bioterrorism Protection Act of 2002;

9. collaborating with the secretary of health and human services and the attorney general in determining new biological agents and toxins that shall be listed as select agents in the Code of Federal Regulations;

10. supporting U.S. leadership in science and technology;

11. establishing and administering the primary R&D activities of DHS;

12. coordinating and integrating all DHS R&D activities;

13. coordinating with other appropriate executive agencies in developing and carrying out the science and technology agenda of DHS to reduce duplication and identify unmet needs; and

14. developing and overseeing the administration of guidelines for merit review of R&D projects throughout DHS and for the dissemination of DHS research.

## TITLE IV: DIRECTORATE OF BORDER AND TRANSPORTATION SECURITY

Subtitle A: Undersecretary for Border and Transportation Security—(Sec. 401)—Establishes in DHS a directorate of Border and Transportation Security to be headed by an undersecretary for Border and Transportation Security. Makes the secretary, acting through the undersecretary for Border and Transportation Security, responsible for:

1. preventing the entry of terrorists and the instruments of terrorism into the United States;

2. securing the borders, territorial waters, ports, terminals, waterways, and air, land, and sea transportation systems of the United States;

3. carrying out the immigration enforcement functions vested by statute in, or performed by, the commissioner of Immigration and Naturalization immediately before their transfer to the undersecretary;

4. establishing and administering rules governing the granting of visas or other forms of permission to enter the United States to individuals who are not citizens or aliens lawfully admitted for permanent residence in the United States;

5. establishing national immigration enforcement policies and priorities;

6. administering the customs laws of the United States (with certain exceptions);

7. conducting the inspection and related administrative functions of the Department of Agriculture transferred to the secretary; and

8. ensuring the speedy, orderly, and efficient flow of lawful traffic and commerce in carrying out the foregoing responsibilities.

(Sec. 403)—Transfers to the secretary the functions, personnel, assets, and liabilities of:

1. the U.S. Customs Service;
2. the Transportation Security Administration;
3. the Federal Protective Service of the General Services Administration (GSA);

4. the Federal Law Enforcement Training Center of the Department of the Treasury; and
5. the Office for Domestic Preparedness of the Office of Justice Programs of the Department of Justice (DOJ).

Subtitle B: United States Customs Service—(Sec. 411)—Establishes in DHS the U.S. Customs Service (transferred from the Department of the Treasury but with certain customs-revenue functions remaining with the secretary of the Treasury). Authorizes the secretary of the Treasury to appoint up to 20 new personnel to work with DHS personnel in performing customs revenue functions.

Subtitle C: Miscellaneous Provisions—(Sec. 421)—Transfers to the secretary the functions of the secretary of Agriculture relating to agricultural import and entry inspection activities under specified animal and plant protection laws. Requires the secretary of agriculture and the secretary to enter into an agreement to effectuate such transfer and to transfer periodically funds collected pursuant to fee authorities under the Food, Agriculture, Conservation, and Trade Act of 1990 to the secretary for activities carried out by the secretary for which such fees were collected. Directs the secretary of agriculture to transfer to the secretary not more than 3,200 full-time equivalent positions of the Department of Agriculture.

Subtitle D: Immigration Enforcement Functions—(Sec. 441)—Transfers from the commissioner of Immigration and Naturalization to the undersecretary for Border and Transportation Security all functions performed under the following programs and all personnel, assets, and liabilities pertaining to such programs, immediately before such transfer occurs:

1. the border patrol program;
2. the detention and removal program;
3. the intelligence program;
4. the investigations program; and
5. the inspections program.

Subtitle E: Citizenship and Immigration Services—(Sec. 451)—Establishes in DHS a Bureau of Citizenship and Immigration Services, headed by the director of the Bureau of Citizenship and Immigration Services, who shall:

1. establish the policies for performing and administering transferred functions;
2. establish national immigration services policies and priorities; and
3. implement a managerial rotation program. Authorizes the director to implement pilot initiatives to eliminate the backlog of immigration benefit applications. Transfers all Immigration and Naturalization Service (INS) adjudications and related personnel and funding to the director.

Establishes for the bureau positions of:

1. chief of Policy and Strategy;
2. legal adviser;
3. budget officer; and
4. chief of the Office of Citizenship to promote citizenship instruction and training for aliens interested in becoming naturalized U.S. citizens.

Subtitle F: General Immigration Provisions—(Sec. 471)—Abolishes INS upon completion of all transfers from it as provided for by this act.

## TITLE V: EMERGENCY PREPAREDNESS AND RESPONSE

(Sec. 501)—Establishes in DHS a directorate of Emergency Preparedness and Response, headed by an undersecretary.

(Sec. 502)—Requires the responsibilities of the secretary, acting through the undersecretary, to include:

1. helping to ensure the effectiveness of emergency response providers to terrorist attacks, major disasters, and other emergencies;
2. with respect to the Nuclear Incident Response Team, establishing and certifying compliance with standards, conducting joint and other

exercises and training, and providing funds to the Department of Energy and the Environmental Protection Agency for homeland security planning, training, and equipment;

3. providing the Federal government's response to terrorist attacks and major disasters;

4. aiding recovery from terrorist attacks and major disasters;

5. building a comprehensive national incident management system with Federal, state, and local governments to respond to such attacks and disasters;

6. consolidating existing Federal government emergency response plans into a single, coordinated national response plan; and

7. developing comprehensive programs for developing inter-operative communications technology and helping to ensure that emergency response providers acquire such technology.

(Sec. 503)—Transfers to the secretary the functions, personnel, assets, and liabilities of:

1. the Federal Emergency Management Agency (FEMA);

2. the Integrated Hazard Information System of the National Oceanic and Atmospheric Administration, which shall be renamed FIRESAT;

3. the National Domestic Preparedness Office of the FBI;

4. the Domestic Emergency Support Teams of DOJ;

5. the Office of Emergency Preparedness, the National Disaster Medical System, and the Metropolitan Medical Response System of HHS; and

6. the Strategic National Stockpile of HHS.

## TITLE VI: MANAGEMENT

(Sec. 701)—Makes the secretary, acting through the undersecretary for Management, responsible for the management and administration of DHS. Details

certain responsibilities of the undersecretary with respect to immigration statistics. Transfers to the undersecretary functions previously performed by the Statistics Branch of the Office of Policy and Planning of the Immigration and Naturalization Service (INS) with respect to:

1. the border patrol program;

2. the detention and removal program;

3. the intelligence program;

4. the investigations program;

5. the inspections program; and

6. INS adjudications.

## TITLE VII: COORDINATION WITH NON-FEDERAL ENTITIES; INSPECTOR GENERAL; UNITED STATES SECRET SERVICE; COAST GUARD; GENERAL PROVISIONS

Subtitle A: Coordination with Non-Federal Entities—(Sec. 801)—Establishes within the office of the secretary the office for State and Local Government Coordination to oversee and coordinate department homeland security programs for and relationships with state and local governments.

Subtitle C: United States Secret Service—(Sec. 821)—Transfers to the secretary the functions of the United States Secret Service, which shall be maintained as a distinct entity within DHS.

Subtitle F: Federal Emergency Procurement Flexibility—(Sec. 852)—Provides that the simplified acquisition threshold to be applied for any executive agency in the procurement of property or services that are to be used to facilitate the defense against or recovery from terrorism or nuclear, biological, chemical, or radiological attack and that are carried out in support of a humanitarian or peacekeeping operation or a contingency operation shall be:

1. $200,000 for a contract to be awarded and performed, or a purchase to be made, inside the United States; or

2. $300,000 for a contract to be awarded and performed, or a purchase to be made, outside the United States.

Subtitle I: Information Sharing—Homeland Security Information Sharing Act—(Sec. 891)—Expresses the sense of Congress that Federal, state, and local entities should share homeland security information to the maximum extent practicable, with special emphasis on hard-to-reach urban and rural communities.

## TITLE IX: NATIONAL HOMELAND SECURITY COUNCIL

(Sec. 901)—Establishes within the executive office of the president the Homeland Security Council to advise the president on homeland security matters.

(Sec. 903)—Includes as members of the council:

1. the president;
2. the vice president;
3. the secretary;
4. the attorney general; and
5. the secretary of defense.

(Sec. 904)—Requires the council to:

1. assess the objectives, commitments, and risks of the United States in the interest of homeland security and make recommendations to the president; and
2. oversee and review Federal homeland security policies and make policy recommendations to the president.

## TITLE X: INFORMATION SECURITY— FEDERAL INFORMATION SECURITY MANAGEMENT ACT OF 2002

(Sec. 1001)—Revises government information security requirements. Requires the head of each agency operating or exercising control of a national security system to ensure that the agency:

1. provides information security protections commensurate with the risk and magnitude of the harm resulting from the unauthorized access, use, disclosure, disruption, modification, or destruction of the information; and
2. implements information security policies and practices as required by standards and guidelines for national security systems. Authorizes appropriations for FY 2003 through 2007.

## TITLE XI: SUBTITLE B: TRANSFER OF THE BUREAU OF ALCOHOL, TOBACCO, AND FIREARMS TO THE DEPARTMENT OF JUSTICE

(Sec. 1111)—Establishes within DOJ, under the attorney general's authority, the Bureau of Alcohol, Tobacco, Firearms, and Explosives (the bureau). Transfers to DOJ the authorities, functions, personnel, and assets of the Bureau of Alcohol, Tobacco and Firearms (BATF), which shall be maintained as a distinct entity within DOJ, including the related functions of the secretary of the Treasury.

## TITLE XIV: ARMING PILOTS AGAINST TERRORISM—ARMING PILOTS AGAINST TERRORISM ACT

(Sec. 1402)—Amends Federal law to direct the undersecretary of transportation for security (in the Transportation Security Administration) to establish a two-year pilot program to:

1. deputize volunteer pilots of air carriers as Federal law enforcement officers to defend the flight decks of aircraft against acts of criminal violence or air piracy (Federal flight deck officers); and

2. provide training, supervision, and equipment for such officers. Requires the undersecretary to begin the process of training and deputizing qualified pilots to be Federal flight deck officers under the program. Allows the undersecretary to request another Federal agency to deputize such officers.

## TITLE XV: TRANSITION—SUBTITLE A: REORGANIZATION PLAN

(Sec. 1502)—Requires the president, within 60 days after enactment of this act, to transmit to the appropriate congressional committees a reorganization plan regarding:

1. the transfer of agencies, personnel, assets, and obligations to DHS pursuant to this act; and
2. any consolidation, reorganization, or streamlining of agencies transferred to DHS pursuant to this Act.

(Sec. 1503)—Expresses the sense of Congress that each House of Congress should review its committee structure in light of the reorganization of responsibilities within the executive branch by the establishment of DHS.

*Source*: www.congress.gov.

## APPENDIX 2-3

### Bill Summary: Preparing America to Respond Effectively (PREPARE) Act of 2003, H.R. 3158

The Preparing America to Respond Effectively Act (PREPARE Act) is a comprehensive approach to prepare the nation to respond to acts of terrorism. The legislation improves the first responder funding system; bolsters information sharing, threat warnings, communications, and equipment interoperability; integrates private companies and the public into response plans; and provides grants to educate schoolchildren to be prepared. Major elements of the legislation include the following:

#### MEETING THE NEEDS OF FIRST RESPONDERS

The PREPARE Act moves beyond the current debate over the first responder grant system by creating a method to identify and provide what cities, counties, and states need in order to be prepared to handle a terrorist attack. As the Council on Foreign Relations Task Force recently stated, "The absence of a functioning methodology to determine national requirements for emergency preparedness constitutes a public policy crisis. Establishing national standards that define levels of preparedness is a critical first step toward determining the nature and extent of additional requirements and the human and financial resources needed to fulfill them." The Gilmore commission's most recent report to Congress states, ". . . without a comprehensive approach to measuring how well we are doing with the resources being applied at any point in time, there will be very little prospect for answering the question 'How well prepared are we?' "

The PREPARE Act addresses these findings by creating a task force on standards for terrorism preparedness, which will develop a methodology for local and state governments to use to determine what resources (e.g., personnel, equipment, training, etc.) are needed to be prepared for a terrorist attack. For the first time, we will know how prepared we are and where more preparation is needed.

The act then creates PREPARE grants to provide every jurisdiction with what it needs to be prepared to defend against terrorist attack, meeting the highest priority needs first. Currently, there is no way to establish priorities. The act consolidates all terrorism preparedness grants in one DHS office in order to streamline interaction with state and local officials.

## MAKING SENSE OF THREAT ALERTS

The PREPARE Act requires the Department of Homeland Security (DHS) to reform the threat advisory system so it can issue alerts to the affected geographic area or industry sector. The act mandates that DHS will notify Congress before issuing threat advisories, provide threat information, and recommend actions at the state and local level, for the general public and the private sector, as appropriate. In addition, the act requires the department to reimburse personnel costs incurred by local and state governments when the threat level is increased.

## IMPROVING INFORMATION SHARING

The PREPARE Act requires the Administration to clarify DHS's responsibilities for sharing and receiving information with local and state governments. The act provides support for obtaining security clearances and equipment that local and state law enforcement officials need to receive and use classified intelligence.

## PROVIDING INTEROPERABLE COMMUNICATIONS AND EQUIPMENT

The PREPARE Act requires DHS, with other agencies, to ensure that first responder equipment and training standards are developed and that such equipment is interoperable within the first responder communities. The act authorizes $20 million to give every state and major metropolitan area the immediate capability to connect radios of different responder agencies.

## ENCOURAGING PARTICIPATION OF "SECOND RESPONDERS"

The PREPARE Act recognizes that local and state emergency officials are the first to respond to a terrorist attack. The act, however, also takes into account the public volunteers, the private companies, and other groups that play important roles in the longer term response. The PREPARE Act stresses the importance of public training and education, and expands current programs to link company resources with emergency response.

## EDUCATING SCHOOLCHILDREN TO BE PREPARED

The PREPARE Act authorizes a three-year grant program for public elementary and secondary schools to develop and implement instruction regarding age-appropriate skills to prepare for and respond to a man-made emergency or a natural disaster.

*Source*: www.congress.gov.

## APPENDIX 2-4
### Excerpts from the Executive Summary of the 9/11 Commission Report

### GENERAL FINDINGS

Since the plotters were flexible and resourceful, we cannot know whether any single step or series of steps would have defeated them. What we can say with confidence is that none of the measures adopted by the U.S. government from 1998 to 2001 disturbed or even delayed the progress of the al Qaeda plot. Across the government, there were failures of imagination, policy, capabilities, and management.

### IMAGINATION

The most important failure was one of imagination. We do not believe leaders understood the gravity of the threat. The terrorist danger from Bin Ladin and al Qaeda was not a major topic for policy debate among the public, the media, or in the Congress. Indeed, it barely came up during the 2000 presidential campaign.

Al Qaeda's new brand of terrorism presented challenges to U.S. governmental institutions that they were not well-designed to meet. Though top officials all told us that they understood the danger, we believe there was uncertainty among them as to whether this was just a new and especially venomous version of the ordinary terrorist threat the United States had lived with for decades, or [if] it was indeed radically new, posing a threat beyond any yet experienced.

As late as September 4, 2001, Richard Clarke, the White House staffer long responsible for counterterrorism policy coordination, asserted that the government had not yet made up its mind how to answer the question: "Is al Qida a big deal?" A week later came the answer.

### POLICY

Terrorism was not the overriding national security concern for the U.S. government under either the Clinton or the pre-9/11 Bush administration.

The policy challenges were linked to this failure of imagination. Officials in both the Clinton and Bush administrations regarded a full U.S. invasion of Afghanistan as practically inconceivable before 9/11.

### CAPABILITIES

Before 9/11, the United States tried to solve the al Qaeda problem with the capabilities it had used in the last stages of the Cold War and its immediate aftermath. These capabilities were insufficient. Little was done to expand or reform them.

The CIA had minimal capacity to conduct paramilitary operations with its own personnel, and it did not seek a large-scale expansion of these capabilities before 9/11. The CIA also needed to improve its capability to collect intelligence from human agents.

At no point before 9/11 was the Department of Defense fully engaged in the mission of countering al Qaeda, even though this was perhaps the most dangerous foreign enemy threatening the United States.

America's homeland defenders faced outward. NORAD itself was barely able to retain any alert bases at all. Its planning scenarios occasionally considered the danger of hijacked aircraft being guided to American targets, but only aircraft that were coming from overseas.

The most serious weaknesses in agency capabilities were in the domestic arena. The FBI did not have the capability to link the collective knowledge of agents in the field to national priorities. Other domestic agencies deferred to the FBI.

FAA capabilities were weak. Any serious examination of the possibility of a suicide hijacking could have suggested changes to fix glaring vulnerabilities—expanding no-fly lists, searching passengers identified by the CAPPS screening system, deploying federal air marshals domestically, hardening cockpit doors, alerting air crews to a different kind of hijacking possibility than they had been trained to expect. Yet the FAA did not adjust either its own training or training with NORAD to take account of threats other than those experienced in the past.

## MANAGEMENT

The missed opportunities to thwart the 9/11 plot were also symptoms of a broader inability to adapt the way government manages problems to the new challenges of the twenty-first century. Action officers should have been able to draw on all available knowledge about al Qaeda in the government. Management should have ensured that information was shared and duties were clearly assigned across agencies, and across the foreign–domestic divide.

There were also broader management issues with respect to how top leaders set priorities and allocated resources. For instance, on December 4, 1998, DCI Tenet issued a directive to several CIA officials and the DDCI for Community Management, stating: "We are at war. I want no resources or people spared in this effort, either inside CIA or the Community." The memorandum had little overall effect on mobilizing the CIA or the intelligence community. This episode indicates the limitations of the DCI's authority over the direction of the intelligence community, including agencies within the Department of Defense.

The U.S. government did not find a way of pooling intelligence and using it to guide the planning and assignment of responsibilities for joint operations involving entities as disparate as the CIA, the FBI, the State Department, the military, and the agencies involved in homeland security.

## SPECIFIC FINDINGS

### UNSUCCESSFUL DIPLOMACY

Beginning in February 1997, and through September 11, 2001, the U.S. government tried to use diplomatic pressure to persuade the Taliban regime in Afghanistan to stop being a sanctuary for al Qaeda, and to expel Bin Ladin to a country where he could face justice. These efforts included warnings and sanctions, but they all failed.

The U.S. government also pressed two successive Pakistani governments to demand that the Taliban cease providing a sanctuary for Bin Ladin and his organization and, failing that, to cut off their support for the Taliban. Before 9/11, the United States could not find a mix of incentives and pressure that would persuade Pakistan to reconsider its fundamental relationship with the Taliban.

From 1999 through early 2001, the United States pressed the United Arab Emirates, one of the Taliban's only travel and financial outlets to the outside world, to break off ties and enforce sanctions, especially those related to air travel to Afghanistan. These efforts achieved little before 9/11.

Saudi Arabia has been a problematic ally in combating Islamic extremism. Before 9/11, the Saudi and U.S. governments did not fully share intelligence information or develop an adequate joint effort to track and disrupt the finances of the al Qaeda organization. On the other hand, government officials of Saudi Arabia at the highest levels worked closely with top U.S. officials in major initiatives to solve the Bin Ladin problem with diplomacy.

### LACK OF MILITARY OPTIONS

In response to the request of policymakers, the military prepared an array of limited strike options for attacking Bin Ladin and his organization from May 1998 onward. When they briefed policymakers, the military presented both the pros and cons of those strike options and the associated risks. Policymakers expressed frustration with the range of options presented.

Following the August 20, 1998, missile strikes on al Qaeda targets in Afghanistan and Sudan, both senior military officials and policymakers placed great emphasis on actionable intelligence as the key factor in recommending or deciding to launch military action against Bin Ladin and his organization. They did not want to risk significant collateral damage, and they did not want to miss Bin Ladin and thus make the United States look weak while making Bin Ladin look strong. On three specific occasions in 1998–1999, intelligence was deemed credible enough to warrant planning for possible strikes to kill Bin Ladin. But in each case the strikes did not go forward, because senior policymakers did not regard the intelligence as sufficiently actionable to offset their assessment of the risks.

The Director of Central Intelligence, policymakers, and military officials expressed frustration with the lack of actionable intelligence. Some officials inside the Pentagon, including those in the special forces and the counterterrorism policy office, also expressed frustration with the lack of military action. The Bush administration began to develop new policies toward al Qaeda in 2001, but military plans did not change until after 9/11.

## PROBLEMS WITHIN THE INTELLIGENCE COMMUNITY

The intelligence community struggled throughout the 1990s and up to 9/11 to collect intelligence on and analyze the phenomenon of transnational terrorism. The combination of an overwhelming number of priorities, flat budgets, an outmoded structure, and bureaucratic rivalries resulted in an insufficient response to this new challenge.

Many dedicated officers worked day and night for years to piece together the growing body of evidence on al Qaeda and to understand the threats. Yet, while there were many reports on Bin Ladin and his growing al Qaeda organization, there was no comprehensive review of what the intelligence community knew and what it did not know, and what that meant. There was no National Intelligence Estimate on terrorism between 1995 and 9/11.

Before 9/11, no agency did more to attack al Qaeda than the CIA. But there were limits to what the CIA was able to achieve by disrupting terrorist activities abroad and by using proxies to try to capture Bin Ladin and his lieutenants in Afghanistan. CIA officers were aware of those limitations.

To put it simply, covert action was not a silver bullet. It was important to engage proxies in Afghanistan and to build various capabilities so that if an opportunity presented itself, the CIA could act on it. But for more than three years, through both the late Clinton and early Bush administrations, the CIA relied on proxy forces, and there was growing frustration within the CIA's Counterterrorist Center and in the National Security Council staff with the lack of results. The development of the Predator and the push to aid the Northern Alliance were products of this frustration.

## PROBLEMS IN THE FBI

From the time of the first World Trade Center attack in 1993, FBI and Department of Justice leadership in Washington and New York became increasingly concerned about the terrorist threat from Islamist extremists to U.S. interests, both at home and abroad. Throughout the 1990s, the FBI's counterterrorism efforts against international terrorist organizations included both intelligence and criminal investigations. The FBI's approach to investigations was case-specific, decentralized, and geared toward prosecution. Significant FBI resources were devoted to after-the-fact investigations of major terrorist attacks, resulting in several prosecutions.

The FBI attempted several reform efforts aimed at strengthening its ability to prevent such attacks, but these reform efforts failed to implement organization-wide institutional change. On September 11, 2001, the FBI was limited in several areas critical to an effective preventive counterterrorism strategy. Those working counterterrorism matters did so despite limited intelligence collection and strategic analysis capabilities, a limited capacity to share information both internally and externally, insufficient training, perceived legal barriers to sharing information, and inadequate resources.

## PERMEABLE BORDERS AND IMMIGRATION CONTROLS

There were opportunities for intelligence and law enforcement to exploit al Qaeda's travel vulnerabilities. Considered collectively, the 9/11 hijackers

- included known al Qaeda operatives who could have been watch-listed;
- presented passports manipulated in a fraudulent manner;
- presented passports with suspicious indicators of extremism;
- made detectable false statements on visa applications;
- made false statements to border officials to gain entry into the United States; and
- violated immigration laws while in the United States.

Neither the State Department's consular officers nor the Immigration and Naturalization Service's inspectors and agents were ever considered full partners in a national counterterrorism effort. Protecting borders was not a national security issue before 9/11.

## PERMEABLE AVIATION SECURITY

Hijackers studied publicly available materials on the aviation security system and used items that had less metal content than a handgun and were most likely permissible. Though two of the hijackers were

on the U.S. TIPOFF terrorist watch-list, the FAA did not use TIPOFF data. The hijackers had to beat only one layer of security—the security checkpoint process. Even though several hijackers were selected for extra screening by the CAPPS system, this led only to greater scrutiny of their checked baggage. Once on board, the hijackers were faced with aircraft personnel who were trained to be non-confrontational in the event of a hijacking.

## FINANCING

The 9/11 attacks cost somewhere between $400,000 and $500,000 to execute. The operatives spent more than $270,000 in the United States. Additional expenses included travel to obtain passports and visas, travel to the United States, expenses incurred by the plot leader and facilitators outside the United States, and expenses incurred by the people selected to be hijackers who ultimately did not participate.

The conspiracy made extensive use of banks in the United States. The hijackers opened accounts in their own names, using passports and other identification documents. Their transactions were unremarkable and essentially invisible amid the billions of dollars flowing around the world every day.

To date, we have not been able to determine the origin of the money used for the 9/11 attacks. Al Qaeda had many sources of funding and a pre-9/11 annual budget estimated at $30 million. If a particular source of funds had dried up, al Qaeda could easily have found enough money elsewhere to fund the attack.

## AN IMPROVISED HOMELAND DEFENSE

The civilian and military defenders of the nation's airspace—FAA and NORAD—were unprepared for the attacks launched against them. Given that lack of preparedness, they attempted and failed to improvise an effective homeland defense against an unprecedented challenge.

The events of that morning do not reflect discredit on operational personnel. NORAD's Northeast Air Defense Sector personnel reached out for information and made the best judgments they could based on the information they received. Individual FAA controllers, facility managers, and command center managers were creative and agile in recommending a nationwide alert, ground-stopping local traffic, ordering all aircraft nationwide to land, and executing that unprecedented order flawlessly.

At more senior levels, communication was poor. Senior military and FAA leaders had no effective communication with each other. The chain of command did not function well. The President could not reach some senior officials. The Secretary of Defense did not enter the chain of command until the morning's key events were over. Air National Guard units with different rules of engagement were scrambled without the knowledge of the President, NORAD, or the National Military Command Center.

## EMERGENCY RESPONSE

The civilians, firefighters, police officers, emergency medical technicians, and emergency management professionals exhibited steady determination and resolve under horrifying, overwhelming conditions on 9/11. Their actions saved lives and inspired a nation.

Effective decision-making in New York was hampered by problems in command and control and in internal communications. Within the Fire Department of New York, this was true for several reasons: the magnitude of the incident was unforeseen; commanders had difficulty communicating with their units; more units were actually dispatched than were ordered by the chiefs; some units self-dispatched; and once units arrived at the World Trade Center, they were neither comprehensively accounted for nor coordinated. The Port Authority's response was hampered by the

lack both of standard operating procedures and of radios capable of enabling multiple commands to respond to an incident in unified fashion. The New York Police Department, because of its history of mobilizing thousands of officers for major events requiring crowd control, had a technical radio capability and protocols more easily adapted to an incident of the magnitude of 9/11.

## CONGRESS

The Congress, like the executive branch, responded slowly to the rise of transnational terrorism as a threat to national security. The legislative branch adjusted little and did not restructure itself to address changing threats. Its attention to terrorism was episodic and splintered across several committees. The Congress gave little guidance to executive branch agencies on terrorism, did not reform them in any significant way to meet the threat, and did not systematically perform robust oversight to identify, address, and attempt to resolve the many problems in national security and domestic agencies that became apparent in the aftermath of 9/11.

So long as oversight is undermined by current congressional rules and resolutions, we believe the American people will not get the security they want and need. The United States needs a strong, stable, and capable congressional committee structure to give America's national intelligence agencies oversight, support, and leadership.

## ARE WE SAFER?

Since 9/11, the United States and its allies have killed or captured a majority of al Qaeda's leadership; toppled the Taliban, which gave al Qaeda sanctuary in Afghanistan; and severely damaged the organization. Yet terrorist attacks continue. Even as we have thwarted attacks, nearly everyone expects they will come. How can this be?

The problem is that al Qaeda represents an ideological movement, not a finite group of people. It initiates and inspires, even if it no longer directs. In this way it has transformed itself into a decentralized force. Bin Ladin may be limited in his ability to organize major attacks from his hideouts. Yet killing or capturing him, while extremely important, would not end terror. His message of inspiration to a new generation of terrorists would continue.

Because of offensive actions against al Qaeda since 9/11, and defensive actions to improve homeland security, we believe we are safer today. But we are not safe. We therefore make the following recommendations that we believe can make America safer and more secure.

## RECOMMENDATIONS

Three years after 9/11, the national debate continues about how to protect our nation in this new era. We divide our recommendations into two basic parts: What to do, and how to do it.

### WHAT TO DO? A GLOBAL STRATEGY

The enemy is not just "terrorism." It is the threat posed specifically by Islamist terrorism, by Bin Ladin and others who draw on a long tradition of extreme intolerance within a minority strain of Islam that does not distinguish politics from religion, and distorts both.

The enemy is not Islam, the great world faith, but a perversion of Islam. The enemy goes beyond al Qaeda to include the radical ideological movement, inspired in part by al Qaeda, that has spawned other terrorist groups and violence. Thus our strategy must match our means to two ends: dismantling the al Qaeda network and, in the long term, prevailing over the ideology that contributes to Islamist terrorism.

The first phase of our post-9/11 efforts rightly included military action to topple the Taliban and pursue al Qaeda. This work continues. But long-term success demands the use of all elements of national power: diplomacy, intelligence, covert action, law enforcement, economic policy, foreign aid, public diplomacy, and homeland defense. If we favor one tool while neglecting others, we leave ourselves vulnerable and weaken our national effort.

What should Americans expect from their government? The goal seems unlimited: Defeat terrorism anywhere in the world. But Americans have also been told to expect the worst: An attack is probably coming; it may be more devastating still.

Vague goals match an amorphous picture of the enemy. Al Qaeda and other groups are popularly described as being all over the world, adaptable, resilient, needing little higher-level organization, and capable of anything. It is an image of an omnipotent hydra of destruction. That image lowers expectations of government effectiveness.

It lowers them too far. Our report shows a determined and capable group of plotters. Yet the group was fragile and occasionally left vulnerable by the marginal, unstable people often attracted to such causes. The enemy made mistakes. The U.S. government was not able to capitalize on them.

No president can promise that a catastrophic attack like that of 9/11 will not happen again. But the American people are entitled to expect that officials will have realistic objectives, clear guidance, and effective organization. They are entitled to see standards for performance so they can judge, with the help of their elected representatives, whether the objectives are being met.

We propose a strategy with three dimensions: (1) attack terrorists and their organizations, (2) prevent the continued growth of Islamist terrorism, and (3) protect against and prepare for terrorist attacks.

#### Attack Terrorists and Their Organizations

- Root out sanctuaries. The U.S. government should identify and prioritize actual or potential terrorist sanctuaries and have realistic country or regional strategies for each, utilizing every element of national power and reaching out to countries that can help us.

- Strengthen long-term U.S. and international commitments to the future of Pakistan and Afghanistan.
- Confront problems with Saudi Arabia in the open and build a relationship beyond oil, a relationship that both sides can defend to their citizens and includes a shared commitment to reform.

### Prevent the Continued Growth of Islamist Terrorism

In October 2003, Secretary of Defense Donald Rumsfeld asked if enough was being done "to fashion a broad integrated plan to stop the next generation of terrorists." As part of such a plan, the U.S. government should

- Define the message and stand as an example of moral leadership in the world. To Muslim parents, terrorists like Bin Ladin have nothing to offer their children but visions of violence and death. America and its friends have the advantage—our vision can offer a better future.
- Where Muslim governments, even those who are friends, do not offer opportunity, respect the rule of law, or tolerate differences, then the United States needs to stand for a better future.
- Communicate and defend American ideals in the Islamic world, through much stronger public diplomacy to reach more people, including students and leaders outside of government. Our efforts here should be as strong as they were in combating closed societies during the Cold War.
- Offer an agenda of opportunity that includes support for public education and economic openness.
- Develop a comprehensive coalition strategy against Islamist terrorism, using a flexible contact group of leading coalition governments and fashioning a common coalition approach on issues like the treatment of captured terrorists.
- Devote a maximum effort to the parallel task of countering the proliferation of weapons of mass destruction.

- Expect less from trying to dry up terrorist money and more from following the money for intelligence, as a tool to hunt terrorists, understand their networks, and disrupt their operations.

### Protect against and Prepare for Terrorist Attacks

- Target terrorist travel, an intelligence and security strategy that the 9/11 story showed could be at least as powerful as the effort devoted to terrorist finance.
- Address problems of screening people with biometric identifiers across agencies and governments, including our border and transportation systems, by designing a comprehensive screening system that addresses common problems and sets common standards. As standards spread, this necessary and ambitious effort could dramatically strengthen the world's ability to intercept individuals who could pose catastrophic threats.
- Quickly complete a biometric entry—exit screening system, one that also speeds qualified travelers.
- Set standards for the issuance of birth certificates and sources of identification, such as driver's licenses.
- Develop strategies for neglected parts of our transportation security system. Since 9/11, about 90 percent of the nation's $5 billion annual investment in transportation security has gone to aviation, to fight the last war.
- In aviation, prevent arguments about a new computerized profiling system from delaying vital improvements in the "no-fly" and "automatic selectee" lists. Also, give priority to the improvement of check-point screening.
- Determine, with leadership from the President, guidelines for gathering and sharing information in the new security systems that are needed, guidelines that integrate safeguards for privacy and other essential liberties.

- Underscore that as government power necessarily expands in certain ways, the burden of retaining such powers remains on the executive to demonstrate the value of such powers and ensure adequate supervision of how they are used, including a new board to oversee the implementation of the guidelines needed for gathering and sharing information in these new security systems.
- Base federal funding for emergency preparedness solely on risks and vulnerabilities, putting New York City and Washington, D.C., at the top of the current list. Such assistance should not remain a program for general revenue sharing or pork-barrel spending.
- Make homeland security funding contingent on the adoption of an incident command system to strengthen teamwork in a crisis, including a regional approach. Allocate more radio spectrum and improve connectivity for public safety communications, and encourage widespread adoption of newly developed standards for private-sector emergency preparedness—since the private sector controls 85 percent of the nation's critical infrastructure.

## HOW TO DO IT? A DIFFERENT WAY OF ORGANIZING GOVERNMENT

The strategy we have recommended is elaborate, even as presented here very briefly. To implement it will require a government better organized than the one that exists today, with its national security institutions designed half a century ago to win the Cold War. Americans should not settle for incremental, ad hoc adjustments to a system created a generation ago for a world that no longer exists.

Our detailed recommendations are designed to fit together. Their purpose is clear: to build unity of effort across the U.S. government. As one official now serving on the front lines overseas put it to us: "One fight, one team."

We call for unity of effort in five areas, beginning with unity of effort on the challenge of counterterrorism itself:

- unifying strategic intelligence and operational planning against Islamist terrorists across the foreign-domestic divide with a National Counterterrorism Center;
- unifying the intelligence community with a new National Intelligence Director;
- unifying the many participants in the counterterrorism effort and their knowledge in a network-based information sharing system that transcends traditional governmental boundaries;
- unifying and strengthening congressional oversight to improve quality and accountability; and
- strengthening the FBI and homeland defenders.

### Unity of Effort: A National Counterterrorism Center

The 9/11 story teaches the value of integrating strategic intelligence from all sources into joint operational planning—with *both* dimensions spanning the foreign-domestic divide.

- In some ways, since 9/11, joint work has gotten better. The effort of fighting terrorism has flooded over many of the usual agency boundaries because of its sheer quantity and energy. Attitudes have changed. But the problems of coordination have multiplied. The Defense Department alone has three unified commands (SOCOM, CENTCOM, and NORTHCOM) that deal with terrorism as one of their principal concerns.
- Much of the public commentary about the 9/11 attacks has focused on "lost opportunities." Though characterized as problems of "watch-listing," "information sharing," or "connecting the dots," each of these labels is too narrow. They describe the symptoms, not the disease.
- Breaking the older mold of organization stovepiped purely in executive agencies, we propose a National Counterterrorism Center (NCTC) that

would borrow the joint, unified command concept adopted in the 1980s by the American military in a civilian agency, combining the joint intelligence function alongside the operations work.

- The NCTC would build on the existing Terrorist Threat Integration Center and would replace it and other terrorism "fusion centers" within the government. The NCTC would become the authoritative knowledge bank, bringing information to bear on common plans. It should task collection requirements both inside and outside the United States.
- The NCTC should perform joint operational planning, assigning lead responsibilities to existing agencies and letting them direct the actual execution of the plans.
- Placed in the Executive Office of the President, headed by a Senate-confirmed official (with rank equal to the deputy head of a cabinet department) who reports to the National Intelligence Director, the NCTC would track implementation of plans. It would be able to influence the leadership and the budgets of the counterterrorism operating arms of the CIA, the FBI, and the departments of Defense and Homeland Security.
- The NCTC should *not* be a policymaking body. Its operations and planning should follow the policy direction of the president and the National Security Council.

### Unity of Effort: A National Intelligence Director

Since long before 9/11—and continuing to this day—the intelligence community is not organized well for joint intelligence work. It does not employ common standards and practices in reporting intelligence or in training experts overseas and at home. The expensive national capabilities for collecting intelligence have divided management. The structures are too complex and too secret.

- The community's head—the Director of Central Intelligence—has at least three jobs: running the

CIA, coordinating a 15-agency confederation, and being the intelligence analyst-in-chief to the president. No one person can do all these things.

- A new National Intelligence Director should be established with two main jobs: (1) to oversee national intelligence centers that combine experts from all the collection disciplines against common targets—like counterterrorism or nuclear proliferation; and (2) to oversee the agencies that contribute to the national intelligence program, a task that includes setting common standards for personnel and information technology.
- The national intelligence centers would be the unified commands of the intelligence world—a long-overdue reform for intelligence comparable to the 1986 Goldwater-Nichols law that reformed the organization of national defense. The home services—such as the CIA, DIA, NSA, and FBI—would organize, train, and equip the best intelligence professionals in the world, and would handle the execution of intelligence operations in the field.
- This National Intelligence Director (NID) should be located in the Executive Office of the President and report directly to the president, yet be confirmed by the Senate. In addition to overseeing the National Counterterrorism Center described above (which will include both the national intelligence center for terrorism and the joint operations planning effort), the NID should have three deputies:
  - For foreign intelligence (a deputy who also would be the head of the CIA)
  - For defense intelligence (also the undersecretary of defense for intelligence)
  - For homeland intelligence (also the executive assistant director for intelligence at the FBI or the undersecretary of homeland security for information analysis and infrastructure protection)
- The NID should receive a public appropriation for national intelligence, should have authority to hire and fire his or her intelligence deputies, and

should be able to set common personnel and information technology policies across the intelligence community.

- The CIA should concentrate on strengthening the collection capabilities of its clandestine service and the talents of its analysts, building pride in its core expertise.
- Secrecy stifles oversight, accountability, and information sharing. Unfortunately, all the current organizational incentives encourage overclassification. This balance should change; and as a start, open information should be provided about the overall size of agency intelligence budgets.

### Unity of Effort: Sharing Information

The U.S. government has access to a vast amount of information. But it has a weak system for processing and using what it has. The system of "need to know" should be replaced by a system of "need to share."

- The President should lead a government-wide effort to bring the major national security institutions into the information revolution, turning a mainframe system into a decentralized network. The obstacles are not technological. Official after official has urged us to call attention to problems with the unglamorous "back office" side of government operations.
- But no agency can solve the problems on its own—to build the network requires an effort that transcends old divides, solving common legal and policy issues in ways that can help officials know what they can and cannot do. Again, in tackling information issues, America needs unity of effort.

### Unity of Effort: Congress

Congress took too little action to adjust itself or to restructure the executive branch to address the emerging terrorist threat. Congressional oversight for intelligence—and counterterrorism—is dysfunctional. Both Congress and the executive need to do more to minimize national security risks during transitions between administrations.

- For intelligence oversight, we propose two options: either a joint committee on the old model of the Joint Committee on Atomic Energy or a single committee in each house combining authorizing and appropriating committees. Our central message is the same: the intelligence committees cannot carry out their oversight function unless they are made stronger, and thereby have both clear responsibility and accountability for that oversight.
- Congress should create a single, principal point of oversight and review for homeland security. There should be one permanent standing committee for homeland security in each chamber.
- We propose reforms to speed up the nomination, financial reporting, security clearance, and confirmation process for national security officials at the start of an administration, and suggest steps to make sure that incoming administrations have the information they need.

### Unity of Effort: Organizing America's Defenses in the United States

We have considered several proposals relating to the future of the domestic intelligence and counterterrorism mission. Adding a new domestic intelligence agency will not solve America's problems in collecting and analyzing intelligence within the United States. We do not recommend creating one.

- We propose the establishment of a specialized and integrated national security workforce at the FBI, consisting of agents, analysts, linguists, and surveillance specialists who are recruited, trained, rewarded, and retained to ensure the development of an institutional culture imbued with a deep expertise in intelligence and national security.

At several points we asked: Who has the responsibility for defending us at home? Responsibility for America's national defense is shared by the Department of Defense, with its new Northern Command, and by the Department of Homeland Security. They must have a clear delineation of roles, missions, and authority.

- The Department of Defense and its oversight committees should regularly assess the adequacy of Northern Command's strategies and planning to defend against military threats to the homeland.

- The Department of Homeland Security and its oversight committees should regularly assess the types of threats the country faces, in order to determine the adequacy of the government's plans and the readiness of the government to respond to those threats.

*Source*: The National Commission on Terrorist Attacks Upon the United States, 2004. www.9-11commission.gov.

# 3

# Organizational Actions

## INTRODUCTION

Prior to the September 11, 2001, terrorist attacks, the Nunn–Lugar–Domenici legislation provided the primary authority and focus for domestic federal preparedness activities for terrorism. Several agencies—including the Federal Emergency Management Agency (FEMA), Department of Justice (DOJ), Department of Health and Human Resources (DHHS), Department of Defense (DOD), and the National Guard—were involved in the terrorism issue, and all were jockeying for the leadership position. Several attempts at coordination among these various agencies were launched, but in general, each agency pursued their own agenda. The single factor that provided the greatest distinction between these agencies related to the levels of funding they received, with DOD and DOJ controlling the majority of what was allocated. State and local governments generally found themselves confused by the federal government's approach, and likewise felt unprepared as a result. While many of these state and local agencies appealed to the federal government to recognize local vulnerabilities and to establish stronger systems to accommodate anticipated needs, the majority rarely considered the possibility of an attack at all. The 1999 TOPOFF (short for "Top Officials") terrorism exercise was successful only in that it highlighted many of the concerns of state and local agencies, and vividly demonstrated to all participants the problems that would ultimately arise during a real event.

The events of September 11 were a real-world validation of the fact that the American emergency management system was unprepared to manage an emergency situation resulting from catastrophic terrorism, including prevention, preparedness, and response needs. Understandably, these events precipitated a major shift in the way the terrorism hazard was handled by all levels of government, beginning with the federal government.

There are five groups that must be fully engaged to be successful in the nation's war on terrorism: the diplomatic community, the intelligence community, the military, law enforcement (including investigations), and emergency management. The principal goal of the first four members of this group—the diplomatic community, intelligence community, the military, and law enforcement agencies—is to reduce, if not eliminate, the risk of future terrorist attacks on American citizens both within the nation's borders and abroad. Each of these performs a separate but critical function in the overall effort.

The goal of emergency management, however, is unique in that it addresses not the terrorists themselves but the consequences of their actions. The emergency management community attempts to both eliminate the ability of these actions to find success, through mitigation and preparedness activities like hardening targets and educating the public, and to respond to them effectively when they do occur and result in negative consequences. The emergency management community's main goal is not to stop the terrorists, but to reduce future loss of life, injuries, property damage, and economic disruption.

As President George W. Bush and many of his advisers have repeatedly recognized in both speeches and briefings, the question of the next terrorist attack is not one of *if,* but rather of *when* it will occur. It has therefore become incumbent for emergency managers to apply the same diligence to preparing for the next bombing or bioterror event as they have for the next hurricane or flood or tornado. The focus of emergency management in the war on terrorism has been and will remain on reducing the effects of future terrorist attacks on first responders, the general public, the business community, the economy, and the American way of life. Clearly, this is no small undertaking.

The establishment of a Department of Homeland Security (DHS) in 2002 represented a landmark change within the federal community, most notably for emergency management. This consolidation of federal agencies required to fight the war on terrorism followed similar logic to that which resulted in the creation of FEMA in 1979. At that time, President Jimmy Carter, at the request of the nation's governors, consolidated all of the federal agencies and programs involved in disaster relief, preparedness, and mitigation into one single federal agency, FEMA. It took 15 years and several reorganizations for FEMA to become a functioning agency. The question now is how long it will take the DHS to become fully functional.

The FEMA director reported directly to the president and, in 1996, President Bill Clinton elevated the director of FEMA to cabinet status. However, when FEMA was absorbed into the DHS, the secretary of homeland security joined the president's cabinet and the FEMA director no longer reported directly to the president. These adjustments in FEMA's organizational status have resulted in the terrorism-oriented mission of the DHS being imposed heavily on FEMA's all-hazards mission and regular programming priorities.

Prior to September 11, at the request of President Bush, FEMA established the Office of National Preparedness (in May 2001) to focus attention on the (then) largely undefined terrorist threat and other national security issues. This was the first step in refocusing the attention of FEMA's public safety mission from the all-hazards emergency management approach embraced by the Clinton administration to one of public security. The shift in focus was greatly accelerated by the events of September 11 and has since been embraced by state and local emergency management operations across the country. What impact the failure of the Hurricane Katrina response will have on this current focus on terrorism prevention at all levels of government has yet to be determined.

A similar shift of focus in FEMA occurred in 1981 at the beginning of the Reagan administration when all-hazards disaster management planning was replaced by a program that focused primarily on nuclear response planning. Until the end of President George H. W. Bush's administration, FEMA resources and personnel therefore focused their attention of ensuring continuity of government operations in the event of a nuclear attack, with little attention paid to natural hazard management. Ultimately, FEMA found itself unprepared to deal with a series of catastrophic natural disasters that started with Hurricane Hugo in 1989 and culminated with Hurricane Andrew in 1992.

Nobody can predict if the U.S. government is in the process of repeating history, but one must question whether the current change in focus away from the all-hazard approach of the 1990s could result in a weakening of FEMA's future natural disaster management capabilities. Certainly, the ineffective response to Hurricane Katrina in 2005 raises many of the same issues and concerns that were raised in the aftermath of Hurricane Andrew in 1992.

What is unique about the changes that are occurring today is that they are not isolated to one, or a few government agencies, but to virtually all of them. By nature of the terrorist threat itself, every government agency, as an extension of the U.S. government itself, is certainly a plausible terrorist target. Every government agency, by nature of its actions, has some specialty to offer in the fight against terrorism, be it financial, environmental, transportation related, health related, and so on. This chapter will examine how the legislative changes discussed in Chapter 2, and the organizational actions both within and in spite of these laws, have redefined the emergency management mechanisms at all levels of government. The Department of Homeland Security, in particular, will be explained in detail.

## THE DEPARTMENT OF HOMELAND SECURITY (DHS)

On November 25, 2002, President Bush signed into law the Homeland Security Act of 2002 (HS Act) (Public Law 107-296), and announced that former Pennsylvania Governor Tom Ridge would become secretary of a new Department of Homeland Security (DHS) to be created through this legislation. This act, which authorized the greatest federal government reorganization since President Harry Truman joined the various branches of the armed forces under the Department of Defense, was charged with a threefold mission of protecting the United States from further terrorist attacks, reducing the nation's vulnerability to terrorism, and minimizing the damage from potential terrorist attacks and natural disasters.

The sweeping reorganization into the new department, which officially opened its doors on January 24, 2003, joined more than 179,000 federal employees from 22 existing federal agencies, under a single, cabinet-level organization. The legislation, which was not restricted to the newly created department, also transformed several other federal agencies that at first glance may have appeared only remotely affiliated with the homeland security mission. To the affected government employees, millions of concerned American citizens, the entire world media, and even the terrorists themselves, it was clear that the U.S. government was entering a new era.

The creation of the DHS was the culmination of an evolutionary legislative process that began largely in response to criticism that increased interagency cooperation between federal intelligence organizations could have prevented the September 11 terrorist attacks. Based on the findings of several pre–September 11 commissions, it appeared that the country needed a centralized federal government agency whose primary reason for existence would be to coordinate the security of the "homeland" (a term that predated the attacks). The White House and Congress were both well aware that any homeland security czar position they conceived would require both an adequate staff and a large budget to succeed. Thus, in early 2002 deliberations began to create a new cabinet-level department that would fuse many of the security-related agencies dispersed throughout the federal government.

For several months during the second half of 2002, Congress jockeyed between differing versions of the homeland security bill in an effort to establish legislation that was passable yet effective. Lawmakers were particularly mired on the issue of the rights of the 179,000 affected employees—an issue that prolonged the legislative process considerably. Furthermore, efforts to incorporate many of the intelligence-gathering and investigative law enforcement agencies, namely, the National Security Agency (NSA), the Federal Bureau of Investigation (FBI), and the Central Intelligence Agency (CIA), into the legislation failed.

Despite these delays and setbacks, after the 2002 midterm elections, the Republican seats that were gained in both the House and Senate gave the president the leverage he needed to pass the bill without further deliberation (House of Representatives, 299–121 on November 13, 2002; Senate, 90–99 on November 19, 2002). While the passage of this act represented a significant milestone, the implementation phase to come presented a tremendous challenge; a concern that was echoed by several leaders from the agencies that were to be absorbed. On November 25, 2002, President Bush submitted his reorganization plan (as required by the legislation), which mapped out the schedule, methodology, and budget for the monumental task at hand.

Secretary Ridge was given exactly 1 year to develop a comprehensive structural framework for the DHS, and to name new leadership for all five directorates and other offices created under the legislation. Beginning on March 1, 2003, almost all of the federal agencies named in the act began their move, whether literally or symbolically, into the new department. Those remaining followed on June 1, 2003, with all incidental transfers completed by September 1, 2003. Although a handful of these agencies remained intact after the move, most were fully incorporated into one of four new directorates: Border and Transportation Security (BTS), Information Analysis and Infrastructure Protection (IAIP), Emergency Preparedness and Response (EP&R), and Science and Technology (S&T). A fifth directorate, Management, incorporated parts of the existing administrative and support offices within the merged agencies.

In addition to the creation of the Department of Homeland Security (see Figure 3-1 and Sidebar 3-1), which is described in detail later in this chapter, the HS Act made several changes to other federal agencies and their constituent partners, and created several new programs. A list of the most significant is presented below:

- Established a National Homeland Security Council within the Executive Office of the President, which assesses U.S. objectives, commitments, and risks in the interest of homeland security, oversees and reviews federal homeland security policies, and makes recommendations to the president.
- Transferred the Bureau of Alcohol, Tobacco and Firearms (ATF) from the Department of the Treasury to the Department of Justice (DOJ).
- Explicitly prohibited both the creation of a national ID card and the proposed Citizen Corps "Terrorism Information and Prevention System"

(Operation TIPS, which encouraged transportation workers, postal workers, and public utility employees to identify and report suspicious activities linked to terrorism and crime.) The act also reaffirmed the Posse Comitatus Act, which prohibits the **U.S. military** from being used a domestic police force except under constitutional or congressional authority (the Coast Guard is exempt from this act).

- The Arming Pilots against Terrorism Act, incorporated into the HS Act, allowed pilots to defend aircraft cockpits with firearms or other "less-than-lethal weapons" against acts of criminal violence or air piracy, and provides antiterrorism training to flight crews.
- The Critical Infrastructure Information Act (2002), incorporated in the HS Act, exempts certain components of critical infrastructure from Freedom of Information Act (FOIA) regulations.
- The Johnny Michael Spann Patriot Trusts were created to provide support for surviving spouses, children, or dependent parents, grandparents, or siblings of various federal employees who die in the line of duty as result of terrorist attacks, military operations, intelligence operations, or law enforcement operations.

On November 30, 2004, following the presidential election, DHS Secretary Ridge announced his resignation. After an initial nomination of NYPD commissioner Bernard Kerik for the position, which was withdrawn due to the immigration status of an employee in his home, Federal Judge Michael Chertoff was named to lead the agency.

## HOMELAND SECURITY DEPARTMENT SUBCOMPONENTS AND AGENCIES

The Department of Homeland Security is a massive agency, juggling numerous responsibilities between a staggeringly wide range of program areas, employing approximately 180,000 people, and managing a massive multi-billion-dollar budget and an

- September 11, 2001—Terrorists attacks occur in Washington, D.C., New York, and Pennsylvania.
- September 20, 2001—In an address to congress, President Bush announces the creation of the Office of Homeland Security (OHS) and the appointment of Tom Ridge as director.
- October 8, 2001—President swears in Tom Ridge as assistant to the president for homeland security and issues an executive order creating the OHS.
- October 9, 2001—President swears in General Wayne Downing as director of the Office of Combating Terrorism (OCT) and issues an executive order creating the OCT.
- October 16, 2001—President Bush issues an executive order establishing the president's Critical Infrastructure Protection Board to coordinate and have cognizance of federal efforts and programs that relate to protection of information systems.
- October 26, 2001—President Bush signs the USA PATRIOT Act.
- October 29, 2001—President Bush chairs the first meeting of the Homeland Security Council (HSC) and issues Homeland Security Presidential Directive No. 1 (HSPD-1), establishing the organization and operation of the HSC, and HSPD-2, establishing the Foreign Terrorist Tracking Task Force and increasing immigration vigilance.
- November 8, 2001—President Bush announces that the Corporation for National and Community Service (CNCS) will support homeland security, "mobilizing more than 20,000 Senior Corps and AmeriCorps participants."
- November 8, 2001—President Bush creates the Presidential Task Force on Citizen Preparedness in the War against Terrorism to "help prepare Americans in their homes, neighborhoods, schools, workplaces, places of worship and public places from the potential consequences of terrorist attacks."
- November 15, 2001—FEMA announces Individual and Family Grant program for disaster assistance.
- January 30, 2002—President Bush issues an executive order establishing the U.S.A. Freedom Corps, encouraging all Americans to serve their country for the equivalent of at least 2 years (4,000 hours) over their lifetimes.
- February 4, 2002—President Bush submits the president's budget for FY 2003 to Congress, directing $37.7 billion to homeland security (up from $19.5 billion in FY 2002).
- March 12, 2002—President Bush establishes the Homeland Security Advisory System (HSPD-3).
- March 19, 2002—President Bush issues an executive order establishing the President's Homeland Security Advisory Council.
- September 17, 2002—President declares the National Strategy to Combat Weapons of Mass Destruction (HSPD-4).
- November 25, 2002—President Bush signs the Homeland Security Act of 2002 (HR 5005) as Public Law 107-296. Tom Ridge is announced as secretary, Navy Secretary Gordon England is nominated as deputy secretary of the DHS, and Drug Enforcement Agency (DEA) Administrator Asa Hutchinson is nominated as the undersecretary of border and transportation security.
- January 24, 2003—Sixty days after it was signed, the Homeland Security Act becomes effective.
- February 28, 2003—President Bush calls for the creation of the National Incident Management System (NIMS) through HSPD-5.
- March 1, 2003—Most affected federal agencies are incorporated into the DHS.
- June 1, 2003—All remaining affected federal agencies are incorporated into the DHS.

*Source*: Compiled from multiple sources by Damon Coppola, January 2003.

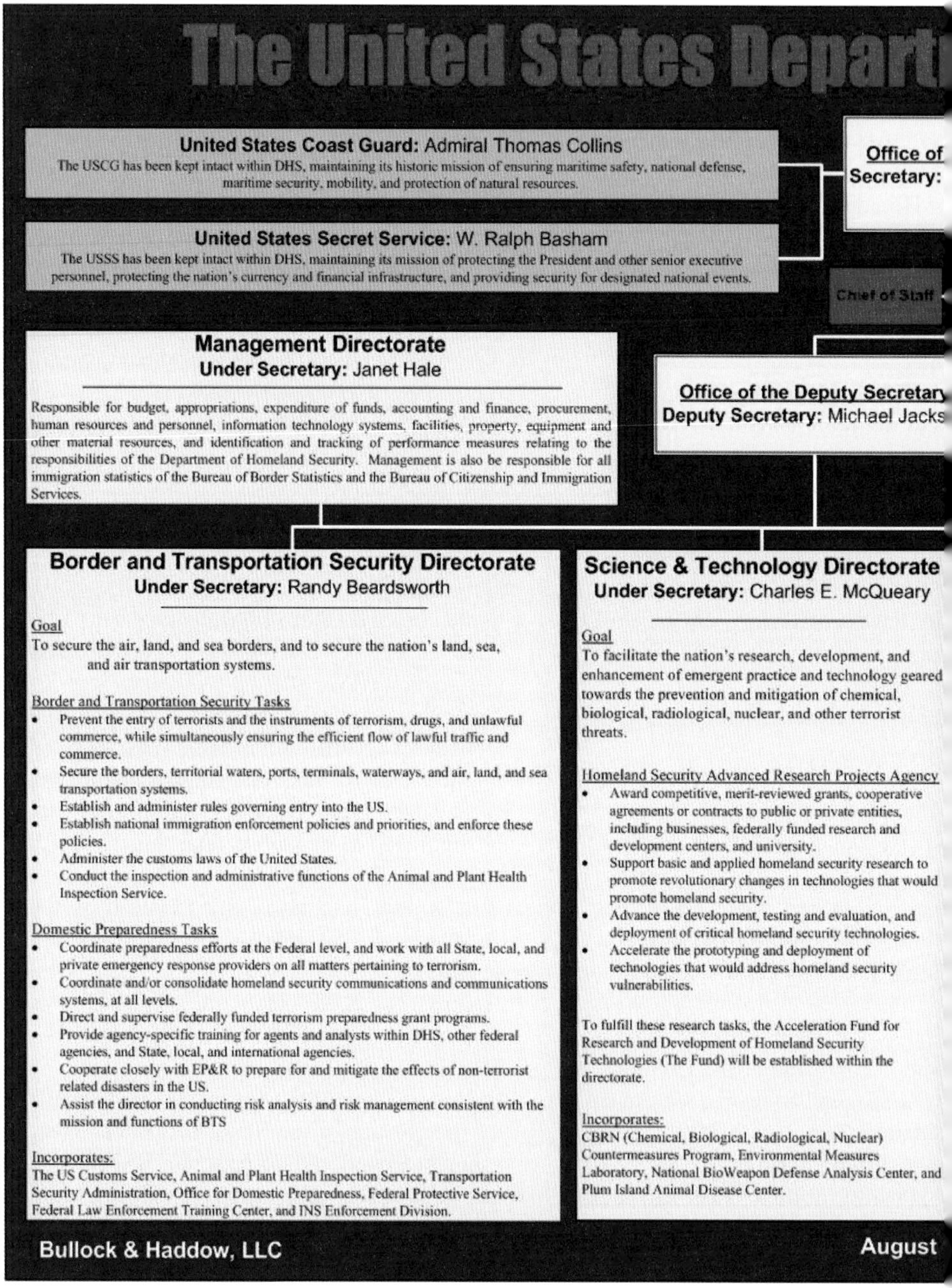

## The United States Depart

**United States Coast Guard:** Admiral Thomas Collins

The USCG has been kept intact within DHS, maintaining its historic mission of ensuring maritime safety, national defense, maritime security, mobility, and protection of natural resources.

**Office of Secretary:**

**United States Secret Service:** W. Ralph Basham

The USSS has been kept intact within DHS, maintaining its mission of protecting the President and other senior executive personnel, protecting the nation's currency and financial infrastructure, and providing security for designated national events.

**Chief of Staff**

### Management Directorate
**Under Secretary:** Janet Hale

Responsible for budget, appropriations, expenditure of funds, accounting and finance, procurement, human resources and personnel, information technology systems, facilities, property, equipment and other material resources, and identification and tracking of performance measures relating to the responsibilities of the Department of Homeland Security. Management is also responsible for all immigration statistics of the Bureau of Border Statistics and the Bureau of Citizenship and Immigration Services.

**Office of the Deputy Secretary**
**Deputy Secretary:** Michael Jacks

### Border and Transportation Security Directorate
**Under Secretary:** Randy Beardsworth

Goal
To secure the air, land, and sea borders, and to secure the nation's land, sea, and air transportation systems.

Border and Transportation Security Tasks
- Prevent the entry of terrorists and the instruments of terrorism, drugs, and unlawful commerce, while simultaneously ensuring the efficient flow of lawful traffic and commerce.
- Secure the borders, territorial waters, ports, terminals, waterways, and air, land, and sea transportation systems.
- Establish and administer rules governing entry into the US.
- Establish national immigration enforcement policies and priorities, and enforce these policies.
- Administer the customs laws of the United States.
- Conduct the inspection and administrative functions of the Animal and Plant Health Inspection Service.

Domestic Preparedness Tasks
- Coordinate preparedness efforts at the Federal level, and work with all State, local, and private emergency response providers on all matters pertaining to terrorism.
- Coordinate and/or consolidate homeland security communications and communications systems, at all levels.
- Direct and supervise federally funded terrorism preparedness grant programs.
- Provide agency-specific training for agents and analysts within DHS, other federal agencies, and State, local, and international agencies.
- Cooperate closely with EP&R to prepare for and mitigate the effects of non-terrorist related disasters in the US.
- Assist the director in conducting risk analysis and risk management consistent with the mission and functions of BTS

Incorporates:
The US Customs Service, Animal and Plant Health Inspection Service, Transportation Security Administration, Office for Domestic Preparedness, Federal Protective Service, Federal Law Enforcement Training Center, and INS Enforcement Division.

### Science & Technology Directorate
**Under Secretary:** Charles E. McQueary

Goal
To facilitate the nation's research, development, and enhancement of emergent practice and technology geared towards the prevention and mitigation of chemical, biological, radiological, nuclear, and other terrorist threats.

Homeland Security Advanced Research Projects Agency
- Award competitive, merit-reviewed grants, cooperative agreements or contracts to public or private entities, including businesses, federally funded research and development centers, and university.
- Support basic and applied homeland security research to promote revolutionary changes in technologies that would promote homeland security.
- Advance the development, testing and evaluation, and deployment of critical homeland security technologies.
- Accelerate the prototyping and deployment of technologies that would address homeland security vulnerabilities.

To fulfill these research tasks, the Acceleration Fund for Research and Development of Homeland Security Technologies (The Fund) will be established within the directorate.

Incorporates:
CBRN (Chemical, Biological, Radiological, Nuclear) Countermeasures Program, Environmental Measures Laboratory, National BioWeapon Defense Analysis Center, and Plum Island Animal Disease Center.

**Bullock & Haddow, LLC**                                           **August**

FIGURE 3-1    DHS organizational chart. (Designed by Damon Coppola for Bullock & Haddow, funding provic Foundation. Revised July 2005)

# of Homeland Security

**Office of State and Local Government Coordination and Preparedness (SLGCP)**
**Office of National Capital Region Coordination**
**Office of Civil Rights and Civil Liberties**
**Office of the Executive Secretary**
**Special Asst. to the Secretary, Private Sector Coordination**

**Office of International Affairs**
**Office of Public Affairs**
**Office of the Inspector General**
**Counter Narcotics Office**
**Office of Legislative Affairs**
**Office of the General Counsel**

## Bureau of Citizenship and Immigration Services (BCIS)

Will establish new immigration policies, practices, and priorities of DHS, and will administer immigration laws and perform services such as immigrant sponsorship, adjustment of status, work authorization and other permits, naturalization for citizenship, and asylum or refugee processing.

## Office of the Citizenship and Immigration Ombudsman

Will assist individuals and employers in resolving problems with the Bureau of Citizenship and Immigration Services, and provide oversight and improvement recommendations for the administrative practices of that Bureau. This office will essentially be a 'customer service' agent for BCIS, appointing at least one local ombudsman for each state.

## Bureau of Shared Services

Will coordinate the resources required and utilized by the two immigration-related bureaus of DHS (BCIS, and the Bureau of Border Security within the Border and Transportation Security Directorate), which cannot ever be combined or share budgets according to the legislation of the Homeland Security Act of 2002.

## Information Analysis & Infrastructure Protection Directorate
### Under Secretary: Robert Stephan

**Goal**
To identify and assess current and future terrorist threats, assess and mitigate risks to the nation's critical infrastructure systems, and disseminate threat information.

**Information Analysis Tasks**
- Identify and assess the nature and scope of terrorist threats, and detect such threats. Administer the five-color coded Homeland Security Advisory System.
- Ensure efficient access by DHS to all related information gathered or analyzed, and disseminate relevant homeland security information externally to DHS.
- Establish and utilize a secure but compatible National Security and Emergency Preparedness communications system for the Federal government.
- Conduct Training for Federal, State, and local governments in information identification, analysis, and sharing.

**Infrastructure Protection Tasks**
- Conduct a comprehensive risk assessment of US Critical Infrastructure, and develop a comprehensive plan for securing its components.
- Work with other agencies at the Federal, State, local, and private levels to recommend protection measures, and provide technical assistance and crisis management support upon request.
- Coordinate with other Federal government agencies to provide specific warning information to State, local, private, public, and other agencies.

**Incorporates:**
Critical Infrastructure Assurance Office, Federal Computer Incident Response Center, National Communications System, National Infrastructure Protection Center, National Infrastructure Simulation and Analysis Center, and Energy Security and Assurance Program.

## Emergency Preparedness and Response Directorate
### Under Secretary: R. David Paulison

**Goal**
To prepare for and respond to natural and technological disasters and terrorism.

**Emergency Preparedness and Response Tasks**
- Coordinate with local and State first responders to manage disasters requiring federal government assistance, and to recover from their damaging effects.
- Practice a comprehensive, risk-based approach, employing a program of preparedness, prevention, prevention, and recovery.
- Proactively help communities and citizens avoid becoming victims, utilizing public education and volunteerism to achieve this goal.
- Develop a curriculum for and manage the training and evaluation of local, State, and Federal emergency responders.
- Maintain administration of the National Flood Insurance Program.
- Continue training and research responsibilities of the USFA
- Continue to offer mitigation grant programs, including the Hazards Mitigation Grant Program, the Pre-Disaster Mitigation Program, and the Flood Mitigation Assistance Program.
- Administer the Citizen Corps Program, which includes:
  - Citizen Corps Councils
  - Community Emergency Response Teams (CERT)
  - Citizen Preparedness Publications
  - Volunteers in Police Service (VIPS)
  - Medical Reserve Corps
  - Neighborhood Watch

**Incorporates:**
Federal Emergency Management Agency, Strategic National Stockpile, National Disaster Medical System, Nuclear Incident Response Team, Domestic Emergency Support Teams, and National Domestic Preparedness Office.

**Designed by Damon Coppola for the Annie E. Casey Foundation**

ambitious list of tasks and goals. The department leverages resources within federal, state, and local governments, coordinating the ongoing transition of multiple agencies and programs into a single, integrated agency focused on protecting the American people and their homeland. In total, more than 87,000 different governmental jurisdictions at the federal, state, and local level have homeland security responsibilities.

At the federal level, the DHS organizational composition still remains in a state of flux. Scattered readjustments have occurred throughout its first years of existence, with multiple offices being passed between the department's components. Though it seemed by the end of DHS Secretary Tom Ridge's years of service that the basic organizational makeup had been established, incoming DHS Secretary Chertoff has proposed several fundamental changes to the department's organization. The following sections describe the major components that constitute the Department of Homeland Security, explain their current organizational positioning, and detail the proposed changes to this organizational structure proposed by Secretary Chertoff.

## OFFICE OF THE SECRETARY

The secretary of homeland security, a cabinet-level official within the executive branch, leads the department. The first DHS secretary, who served from the department's opening day in March 2003 until February 2005, was former Pennsylvania Governor Tom Ridge. The current DHS secretary is Michael Chertoff, who formerly served as United States Circuit Judge for the Third Circuit Court of Appeals.

The secretary and his or her staff are responsible for managing the overall direction of the department. This office oversees the activities of the department. In conjunction with other federal, state, local, and private entities, as part of a collaborative effort to strengthen the nation's borders, the Office of the Secretary sets the direction for intelligence analysis and

infrastructure protection, improved use of science and technology to counter weapons of mass destruction, and the creation of comprehensive response and recovery initiatives. Within the Office of the Secretary are multiple program and issue-related offices that contribute to the overall homeland security mission. These offices include:

- Office of the Chief Privacy Officer
- Office of Civil Rights and Civil Liberties
- Office of Counter Narcotics
- Office of General Counsel
- Office of the Inspector General
- Office of Legislative Affairs
- Office of National Capital Region Coordination
- Office of the Private Sector
- Office of Public Affairs
- Office of State and Local Government Coordination and Preparedness
- United States Citizenship and Immigration Services

Several agencies that existed elsewhere in the federal government prior to September 11 were transferred into the Department of Homeland Security intact and also report directly to the Office of the Secretary. Most notable of these agencies are the U.S. Coast Guard and the U.S. Secret Service. These agencies, and three of those from the preceding list that were created within the Office of the Secretary—the Office of the Inspector General, the Office of State and Local Government Coordination and Preparedness, and the United States Citizenship and Immigration Services (USCIS)—are described individually in the following subsections.

### The U.S. Coast Guard

The U.S. Coast Guard (USCG), under the direction of Commandant Thomas H. Collins, was transferred to the DHS as an intact agency on March 1, 2003. The primary function of the Coast Guard within the DHS remains consistent with its historic mission, as identified in the following five functional areas:

- Maritime safety
- National defense
- Maritime security
- Mobility
- Protection of natural resources

As lead federal agency for maritime safety and security, the USCG protects several of the nation's vital interests; the personal safety and security of the American population; the natural and economic resources of the United States; and the territorial integrity of the country from both internal and external threats, natural and man-made. As a military, maritime service, the USCG is responsible for a blend of humanitarian, law enforcement, regulatory, diplomatic, and military duties—all for which it is entirely qualified—to provide maritime security, maritime safety, protection of natural resources, maritime mobility, and national defense services.

The USCG was recognized after September 11 as being a well-equipped military force with established jurisdiction within U.S. territory. Immediately following September 11, the importance of this fact was not lost on federal government officials who witnessed how, as naval ships were quickly leaving the nation's ports to protect themselves, the Coast Guard's ships were moving into position inside those same ports.

Since entering the DHS, the U.S. Coast Guard has received a significant boost in its budget allocation, which has been used primarily to update a fleet of ships and aircraft that was considered outdated in relation to the other armed services (as part of the ongoing Integrated Deepwater System project). Additionally, many more employees have been added to the agency's payroll. As of 2005, the Coast Guard employed 40,739 military and 6,373 civilian employees, for a total of 47,112 people. In addition to these, the USCG maintains 8,100 selected reserve and 31,400 auxiliary employees. Between FY 2004 and FY 2006, the USCG saw its budget rise first from $6.994 billion to $7.559 billion in FY 2005, and then again to $8.147 billion in FY 2006. This accounts for 20% of the total DHS budget in FY 2006 (see Figure 3-2).

### U.S. Secret Service

The U.S. Secret Service (USSS), under the leadership of W. Ralph Basham, was transferred to the DHS

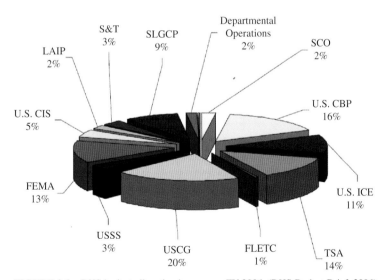

**FIGURE 3-2**   DHS budget allocation by agency, FY 2006. (DHS Budget Brief, 2006)

as an intact agency on March 1, 2003. The Secret Service was able to continue its historic mission of protecting the president and senior executive personnel, in addition to protecting the country's currency and financial infrastructure and providing security for designated national events (e.g., the Super Bowl and the Olympics). The USSS is also responsible for the protection of the vice president, immediate family members of these senior officials, the president-elect and vice president-elect, or other officers next in the order of succession to the Office of the President and members of their immediate families, presidential candidates, visiting heads of state and their accompanying spouses, and, at the direction of the president, other distinguished foreign visitors to the United States and official representatives of the United States performing special missions abroad. Former presidents, their spouses, and minor children are also offered USSS protection for life.

The USSS also protects the executive residence and grounds in the District of Columbia, buildings in which White House offices are located, the official residence and grounds of the vice president in the District of Columbia, foreign diplomatic missions located in the Washington metropolitan area, the headquarters buildings and grounds of the DHS and Treasury Department, and such other areas as directed by the president. The USSS is also responsible for telecommunications fraud, computer and telemarketing fraud, fraud relative to federally insured financial institutions, and other criminal and noncriminal cases. USSS is organized into two major components, one focused on protection and the other focused on investigation.

All of these people, places, and events that are protected represent key components of the nation's government and heritage. They are all, in addition to their intended roles, symbols of the country, and therefore prime terrorist targets. The loss of any of these, whether due to terrorist or other means, would threaten the security of the nation, and therefore their protection is integral to the homeland security of the nation. In 2005, the USSS employed 6,526 people. Their budget allocation has gained slightly each year,

rising from $1.334 billion in FY 2004 to $1.404 billion in FY 2006. This accounts for about 3% of the total DHS budget for FY 2006.

### The Office of the Inspector General

The DHS Office of Inspector General (OIG) was established by the HS Act, by amendment to the Inspector General Act of 1978. Inspector General Clark Kent Ervin was the first to hold the post. The inspector general has a dual reporting responsibility, both to the DHS secretary and to Congress. The OIG serves as an independent and objective inspection, audit, and investigative body that safeguards public tax dollars by promoting effectiveness, efficiency, and economy in DHS programs and operations, and by preventing and detecting fraud, abuse, mismanagement, and waste in such programs and operations.

Considering the massive changes that have resulted from the creation of DHS, and the billions of dollars that have been dedicated to the department's mission, an office such as this is critical. In 2005, OIG maintained a staff of 540 people. The OIG budget has remained relatively constant during the period of FY 2004 to FY 2006, with an allocation of approximately $83 million. Clark Kent Ervin left the post of inspector general on December 8, 2004, and was replaced by Assistant Inspector General Richard L. Skinner.

### Office of State and Local Government Coordination and Preparedness

The Office of State and Local Government Coordination and Preparedness (SLGCP) is the federal government's lead agency responsible for preparing the nation against terrorism by assisting state, local, and tribal jurisdictions and regional authorities as they prevent, deter, and respond to terrorist acts. To ensure that first responders and public safety officials are properly equipped, trained, and prepared to confront a terror-related or weapons of mass destruction (WMD) event, SLGCP facilitates and coordinates DHS programs with state and local partners and provides significant financial assistance, exercise support, technical assistance, and training resources to government agencies and public safety professionals across the nation.

SLGCP awards grants to every state and territory in the United States, as well as to metropolitan regions and other critical areas identified as either high risk, of economic and symbolic national importance, or both. Also, SLGCP provides support and resources for the planning and execution of national or regional exercises (e.g., the TOPOFF exercise series), technical assistance, and other counterterrorism expertise. Finally, SLGCP administers the Assistance to Fire Fighters Grant Program in cooperation with the U.S. Fire Administration, which provides financial assistance directly to fire departments at the local government level for procurement of equipment, training, and vehicles that better protect the public, firefighters, and emergency medical service personnel.

SLGCP became a "one-stop shop" for grants in 2005. The office redesigned its grant application process, resulting in a more efficient and effective grant funding process. The new design was intended to simplify what was considered a difficult and confusing grant system, so that critically needed funding would make it to state and local governments in the quickest manner possible. The Homeland Security Grant Program (HSGP) consolidated six programs into one application to better coordinate funding and administration. These programs included the State Homeland Security Program (SHSP), Urban Areas Security Initiative (UASI), Law Enforcement Terrorism Prevention Program (LETPP), Citizen Corps Program (CCP), Emergency Management Performance Grant (EMPG), and Metropolitan Medical Response System (MMRS).

SLGCP maintained a staff of 256 people in FY 2005. The office's FY 2006 allocation of $3.565 billion accounts for 9% of the total DHS budget. Much more information on this office is provided in Chapter 7.

## United States Citizenship and Immigration Services

The U.S. Citizenship and Immigration Services (USCIS) is the component of the DHS that facilitates legal immigration for people seeking to enter, reside, or work in the United States. The office is responsible for "ensuring the delivery of the right immigration benefit to the right person at the right time, and no benefit to the wrong person." USCIS has established three priorities to accomplish this task:

1. Eliminating the immigration benefit application backlog
2. Improving customer service
3. Enhancing national security

Before September 11, all immigration issues were handled by the U.S. State Department through their consular services section, and through the Immigration and Naturalization Service (INS) of the Department of Justice. The State Department, which handled the granting of permission to apply for entry into the United States from overseas posts, has maintained its role since the government reorganization has taken place. The INS, however, which handled the creation of and enforcement of immigration policy within the United States, was absorbed into the DHS and broken into three distinct offices. USCIS was given responsibility for the immigration services (applications for residence, for instance), Immigration and Customs Enforcement (ICE) is responsible for enforcing immigration law within the United States, and Customs and Border Protection (CBP) enforces those same laws at the U.S. ports of entry and the borders.

USCIS processes more than 7 million applications each year. The office maintained a staff of 10,207 in FY 2005, and saw their budget rise from $1.550 billion in FY 2004 to $1.854 billion in FY 2006.

## THE FIVE DIRECTORATES

The Department of Homeland Security contains five major divisions, which have been named *directorates*: Border and Transportation Security,

Emergency Preparedness and Response, Information Analysis and Infrastructure Protection, Science & Technology, and Management. Each of these divisions is led by an undersecretary. If Secretary Chertoff's reorganization plan is approved by Congress, these directorates will be altered considerably, as is illustrated in the later section describing his proposal. The five directorates, as they have existed since the creation of DHS, are described next.

## DIRECTORATE OF BORDER AND TRANSPORTATION SECURITY

The largest of the five directorates, Border and Transportation Security (BTS) incorporates all of the functions of the following six former federal agencies: the U.S. Customs Service, the INS Enforcement Division, the Animal and Plant Health Inspection Service, the Transportation Security Administration (TSA), the Office for Domestic Preparedness (ODP), and the Federal Protective Service (FPS). The goal of BTS is to secure the air, land, and sea borders (including security at ports and immigration enforcement) and to secure the nation's land, sea, and air transportation systems. Its stated primary goal is "to prevent the entry of terrorists and the instruments of terrorism while simultaneously ensuring the efficient flow of lawful traffic and commerce."

BTS is administered by the undersecretary for BTS, who is assisted by an assistant secretary for border security. This office maintains an enormous budget, divided among four primary programs, as described next. The administrative costs of the central office are covered by a $10.617 million allocation, while the four individual offices within the directorate have an impressive combined operating budget of $16.875 billion. The BTS directorate includes the following components:

- Transportation and Security Administration
- Customs and Border Protection
- Immigration and Customs Enforcement
- Federal Law Enforcement Training Center

## Transportation and Security Administration (TSA)

The Transportation Security Administration (TSA) protects the nation's transportation systems in order to ensure the freedom of movement for both people and commercial goods and services. Through the passage of the Aviation and Transportation Security Act (ATSA), inspired as a result of recognized failures in the private security systems that contributed to the September 11 attacks, overall aviation transportation security became a direct federal responsibility. TSA's focus is on identifying risks to the transportation sector, prioritizing them, and managing them to acceptable levels through a variety of means, while working to mitigate the impact of incidents that may occur.

TSA began as an agency focused on airline security, which was understandable considering that the September 11 terrorists capitalized on lax security measures to attack the nation. However, their focus has steadily expanded to address other transportation modes such as intercity buses, rail travel, and ferry travel. In terms of both dollars and people, their primary focus clearly remains on aviation security. TSA's specific responsibilities include ensuring thorough and efficient screening of all aviation passengers and baggage through an appropriate mix of federalized and privatized screeners and technology. This screener workforce consists primarily of 45,000 passenger and baggage screeners located at 453 commercial and privatized airports throughout the country.

U.S. air carriers transport approximately 12.5 million tons of cargo, of which 2.8 million tons fly on board commercial passenger planes and 9.7 million tons are shipped in cargo planes (which, still today, are not inspected to the same degree as cargo that is shipped on the passenger carriers). TSA has been given the responsibility to devise and implement a system to screen, inspect, or otherwise ensure the security of all cargo that is to be transported aboard aircraft—a task that will likely require many years and significant financial investment.

TSA is also tasked with managing the security risk to the U.S. surface transportation systems. They are confronted with the paradox of trying to ensure the freedom of movement of people and commerce while preventing the same for terrorists. The March 11, 2004 attacks in Madrid, Spain, involved satchel explosives on commuter trains. In the United States, and throughout most of the world, passengers on these systems are not given security inspections to the same degree as air travellers or at all, which highlights the difficulty of such issues. In the United States, these systems include nine billion passenger trips per year throughout the nation's various mass transit systems, more than 161,000 miles of interstate and national highways and their integrated bridges and tunnels, and nearly 800,000 shipments of hazardous materials (95% by truck). To address this difficult endeavor, TSA is working in partnership with other DHS and DOT components.

On June 4, 2005, retired Army Col. Kenneth S. Kasprisin was named acting assistant secretary for homeland security and acting administrator of TSA. The TSA maintained an employee base of 52,504 in FY 2005 (primarily federal airport security screeners), and saw its budget rise steadily from $4.578 billion in FY 2004 to $5.562 billion in FY 2006. This amounts to 14% of the total DHS budget for FY 2006.

### Customs and Border Protection

U.S. Customs and Border Protection (CBP) is responsible for protecting the nation's borders, at and between official ports of entry. CBP is responsible for ensuring that all persons and cargo entering the United States do so both legally and safely. CBP inspectors are responsible for preventing cross-border smuggling of such contraband as controlled substances, WMDs, and illegal plants and animals. They also ensure that travelers and immigrants have appropriate documentation necessary to enter the country legally. Other tasks include preventing the illegal export of U.S. currency or other negotiable instruments, the export of stolen goods such as vehicles, and the export of strategically sensitive technologies that could be used overseas to compromise both the security and the strategic and economic position of the United States. The

Border Patrol, which operates under the direction of CBP, is responsible for controlling all of America's 7,500 miles of land borders between ports of entry, and 95,000 miles of maritime border in partnership with the USCG.

CBP officials are also deployed overseas at major international seaports, through application of the Container Security Initiative (CSI). This project was established to allow agents to prescreen shipping containers in order to detect and interdict WMDs and other illicit material before they arrive in the United States. CBP's entry specialists and trade compliance personnel enforce U.S. trade and tariff laws and regulations in order to ensure that a fair and competitive trade environment exists for the United States. CBP's Air and Marine Operations Division patrols the nation's borders to interdict illegal drugs and terrorists before entry into the United States, and provides surveillance and operational support to special national security events.

CBP makes direct contact with more than 500 million people crossing the borders through ports each year, and with tens of thousands of shippers, drivers, pilots, and importers associated with more than 25 million officially declared trade entries. In FY 2005, CBP maintained a staff of 40,828, and saw budgets rise steadily from $5.997 billion in FY 2004 to $6.725 billion in FY 2006.

### Immigration and Customs Enforcement

As the largest investigative arm of the DHS, U.S. Immigration and Customs Enforcement (ICE) enforces federal immigration and customs laws. Through the Federal Protective Service and the Federal Air Marshal Service, ICE also facilities security in the air and on federal property. The primary mission of ICE is to detect vulnerabilities and prevent violations that threaten national security. The various components of this directorate are as follows:

- *Investigations* is responsible for investigating a range of domestic and international activities arising from the movement of people and goods that violate immigration and customs laws and threaten national security.

- The *Federal Air Marshal Service (FAMS)* is responsible for promoting confidence in our nation's civil aviation system through the effective deployment of federal air marshals to detect, deter, and defeat hostile acts targeting U.S. air carriers, airports, passengers, and crews.
- *Detention and Removal* is responsible for promoting the public safety and national security by ensuring the departure from the United States of all removable aliens through the fair enforcement of the nation's immigration laws.
- The *Federal Protective Service (FPS)* is responsible for policing, securing, and ensuring a safe environment in which federal agencies can conduct their business by reducing threats posed against more than 8,800 federal government facilities nationwide.
- *Intelligence* is responsible for the collection, analysis, and dissemination of strategic and tactical intelligence data in support of ICE and DHS.

ICE works to protect and serve the United States and its people by deterring, interdicting, and investigating threats arising from the movement of people and goods into and out of the United States, and by policing and securing federal government facilities across the nation. In FY 2005, ICE employed 15,440 employees, and saw allocations rise steadily from $3.616 billion in FY 2004 to $4.364 billion in FY 2006.

### Federal Law Enforcement Training Center

The Federal Law Enforcement Training Center (FLETC) serves as the federal government's principal provider of federal law enforcement personnel training. FLETC relies on research, training, and education to conduct its shared mission of protecting U.S. democratic institutions, ensuring public safety, and preserving law and order.

FLETC provides for the training needs of more than 81 federal agencies that carry out enforcement

responsibilities. The center also provides training and technical assistance to state and local law enforcement entities, and plans, develops, and presents formal training courses and practical exercise applications related to international law enforcement training. The center offers numerous basic law enforcement training programs of varying lengths, designed specifically for the duties and responsibilities of the personnel to be trained, and conducts numerous advanced and specialized training programs found nowhere else in the country.

FLETC currently operates four training sites throughout the United States. Its headquarters and primary training site is located in Glynco, Georgia. Two other field locations, both of which provide both basic and advanced training, are located in Artesia, New Mexico, and Charleston, South Carolina. The fourth training site, in Cheltenham, Maryland, provides in-service and requalification training for officers and agents in the Washington, D.C., area. In cooperation with the State Department, FLETC also operates an International Law Enforcement Academy in Gabarone, Botswana. FLETC maintained a staff of 959 in FY 2005, and saw budget allocations rise from $192 million in FY 2004 to $224 million in FY 2006.

### Directorate of Emergency Preparedness and Response

The Directorate of Emergency Preparedness and Response (EP&R) is responsible for ensuring that the United States is prepared for all types of disasters, whether they are natural, technological, or terrorism related (Figure 3-3). EP&R has been built on the foundation of the Federal Emergency Management Agency (FEMA), which was transferred relatively intact into this directorate.

EP&R has expanded on FEMA's existing efforts to reduce the loss of life and property and to protect the nation's institutions from all types of hazards through a comprehensive, risk-based emergency management program of preparedness, prevention (mitigation), response, and recovery. One of its primary missions, as stated by DHS, is to "further the evolution of the

FIGURE 3-3   New York City, New York, October 4, 2001—Relief efforts continued day and night at the site of the World Trade Center. (Photo by Andrea Booher/FEMA News Photo)

emergency management culture from one that reacts to disasters to one that proactively helps communities and citizens avoid becoming victims." In addition, the directorate develops and manages a national training and evaluation system, designs curriculums, sets standards, and rewards performance in local, state, and federal training efforts.

EP&R focuses on risk mitigation, in advance of disasters, by promoting a concept of "disaster-resistant communities." To do this, they provide federal support for local governments that promote structures and communities that reduce their vulnerabilities. EP&R coordinates with private industry, the insurance sector, mortgage lenders, the real estate industry, homebuilding associations, citizens, and others, in order to create what they consider "model communities" in high-risk areas.

EP&R has been granted the leadership role, through the National Response Plan (NRP) and the Robert T. Stafford Disaster Relief and Emergency Assistance Act, to manage the DHS response to any sort of natural, technological, or terrorist attack disaster. This directorate is also in charge of coordinating the involvement of other federal response teams, such as the National Guard, in the event of a major incident. In accordance with the new National Response Plan, FEMA also leads federal government relief and recovery efforts that follow major declared disasters. These response and recovery processes are illustrated in much greater detail in Chapter 7.

EP&R continues to offer four mitigation grant programs that were formerly and still managed by FEMA: the Hazards Mitigation Grant Program, the Pre-Disaster Mitigation Program, the Flood Mitigation Assistance Program, and the U.S. Fire Administration's "Fire Grants."

FEMA's Citizen Corps Program continues within the EP&R Directorate as well. Citizen Corps provides funding for the formation and training of local Citizen Corps Councils, which increase local involvement (in Citizen Corps), develop community action plans, perform threat assessments, identify local resources for homeland security, and locally coordinate the Citizen Corps programs. The existing programs, administered by several federal agencies both internal and external to homeland security, involve leaders from law enforcement, fire, and emergency medical services, businesses, community-based institutions, schools, places of worship, health care facilities, public works, and other key community sectors. Current Citizen Corps programs include the following (Citizen Corps activities are documented in greater detail in Chapter 6 of this book):

- Community Emergency Response Teams (CERT), administered by DHS
- Volunteers in Police Service (VIPS) program, administered by DOJ
- Medical Reserve Corps, administered by HHS
- Neighborhood Watch programs, administered by DOJ
- Fire Corps Program, administered by the USA Freedom Corps and several nongovernmental partners
- Citizen-preparedness publications, which are public education guides that seek to increase individual knowledge and preparedness for crime, terrorism, and disasters at home, in neighborhoods, at places of work, and in public spaces

EP&R maintained a staff of 4,858 in FY 2005, of which 2,593 were full-time personnel and 2,265 were on call to be activated in times of disaster. EP&R saw allocations rise from $5.554 billion in FY 2004 to $7.541 billion in FY 2005, mostly because of biode-

fense funding. However, biodefense funding was cut from the EP&R budget in FY 2006, dropping the amount the directorate received to $5.365 billion. This amount accounts for 13% of the total DHS budget. The FEMA budget can be increased by congress through emergency appropriations to cover the costs of catastrophic disasters—as was the case following the September 11 attacks.

### Directorate of Information Analysis and Infrastructure Protection

The Directorate of Information Analysis and Infrastructure Protection (IAIP) is responsible for intelligence analysis and infrastructure protection operations within DHS. IAIP has developed the capability to receive, analyze, and assess a broad range of information concerning terrorist threats, to issue warnings to the public and law enforcement agencies, and to take or enable appropriate preventive and protective action.

IAIP has worked to help integrate terrorist threat information and analysis produced by the intelligence and law enforcement community to develop a comprehensive picture of threats to the United States, map that information against vulnerabilities of America's critical infrastructure, and issue timely, actionable warnings, advisories and preventive measures.

Within IAIP is the Homeland Security Operations Center (HSOC), which constantly monitors terrorism, and issues terrorist threat advisories under the color-coded Homeland Security Advisory System (HSAS). IAIP has been assigned the primary responsibility for sharing threat information with and fostering collaboration among all appropriate federal, state, local, tribal, and foreign governments, and private-sector entities through the creation of a secure information sharing environment. Prior to their existence, there was no organized sharing mechanism, which, in part, made local terrorism preparedness other than generalized actions almost impossible. IAIP also develops protective plans to reduce the risk to and mitigate vulnerabilities in the nation's critical infrastructure and key assets.

This directorate fully incorporated the functions of six former federal agencies:

- The Critical Infrastructure Assurance Office
- The Federal Computer Incident Response Center
- The National Communications System
- The National Infrastructure Protection Center
- The National Infrastructure Simulation and Analysis Center
- The Energy Security and Assurance Program

The IAIP undersecretary conducts his or her tasks through two assistant secretaries: the assistant secretary for information analysis and the assistant secretary for infrastructure protection. The divisions these two assistant secretaries are charged with divide the IAIP tasks as follows:

### Information Analysis

- Identify and assess the nature and scope of terrorist threats to the nation (relevant to actual and potential vulnerabilities), and detect such threats.
- Administer the color-coded HSAS.
- Identify priorities (in coordination with the assistant secretary for infrastructure protection) for infrastructure protection measures by all government, private, and other agencies.
- Ensure efficient access by DHS to all related information gathered or analyzed, and disseminate relevant homeland security information to other agencies within the federal government and to appropriate state, local, and private-sector entities.
- Recommend improvement to the collection and sharing of information processes related to homeland security within the federal government and between federal, state, and local agencies.
- Establish and utilize a secure but fully compatible National Security and Emergency Preparedness (NS/EP) communications system for the federal government, including a secure information technology infrastructure.
- Conduct training for federal, state, and local governments in information identification, analysis, and sharing.

### Infrastructure Protection

- Conduct a comprehensive risk assessment of the U.S. critical infrastructure.
- Develop a comprehensive national plan for securing the U.S. critical infrastructure, including systems for power production; generation and distribution; information technology and telecommunications; electronic, financial, and property record storage and transmissions; and emergency preparedness communications, as well as the physical assets that support such systems; and other infrastructure, such as food, water, and health care.
- Work with other agencies at the federal, state, local, and private-sector level to recommend protection measures and provide technical assistance and crisis management support on request.
- Coordinate with other federal government agencies to provide specific warning information and advice to state, local, private, public, and other agencies.

IAIP maintained a full-time staff of 873 people in FY 2005. Their budget allocation has remained relatively constant, rising from $834 million in FY 2004 to $894 million in FY 2005, and down again to $873 million in FY 2006. This accounts for only 2% of the total DHS budget.

### Directorate of Science and Technology

The Science and Technology (S&T) Directorate provides leadership for directing, funding, and conducting research, development, test, and evaluation (RDT&E), and procurement of technologies and systems that can prevent the importation of chemical, biological, radiological, nuclear, and related weapons and material, and will help the national protect against and respond to terrorist threats. The S&T Directorate partners and coordinates with federal, state, and local government and private-sector entities in conducting its activities, and is working to establish a system to transfer the fruits of these homeland security developments and technologies into DHS's operational elements.

Through S&T research and development activities, DHS hopes to enhance its ability to execute all of its stated missions, now and in the future, and to help the nation meet its homeland security RDT&E needs.

The HS Act of 2002 effectively abolished the Office of Science and Technology that existed within the National Institute of Justice (which still exists within the DOJ) and transferred all applicable functions to S&T. Within the directorate, the Homeland Security Advanced Research Projects Agency (HSARPA) and the Acceleration Fund for Research and Development of Homeland Security Technologies (the "Fund") were created to carry out the S&T mission. HSARPA was established to "award competitive, merit-reviewed grants, cooperative agreements or contracts to public or private entities, including businesses, Federally funded research and development centers, and universities." The Fund was created to manage the finances used to support those goals.

S&T maintained a staff of 387 full-time employees in FY 2005. The S&T budget allocation rose steadily from $913 million in FY 2004 to $1.368 million in FY 2006. This accounts for 3% of the total DHS FY 2006 budget. The S&T directorate is expanded on in much greater detail in Chapter 9.

### Office of Management

The Undersecretary for Management is responsible for budget, appropriations, expenditure of funds, accounting and finance; procurement; human resources and personnel; information technology systems; facilities, property, equipment, and other material resources; and identification and tracking of performance measurements relating to the responsibilities of the DHS. The FY 2006 DHS budget includes $665 million to carry out this mission. There were 821 employees involved in management activities in DHS, both within and outside of the Management Directorate, in FY 2005.

The DHS goals from its strategic plan are summarized in Sidebar 3-2.

---

### SIDEBAR 3-2  Select Strategic Goals for Protection and Response from the U.S. Department of Homeland Security Strategic Plan

In February 2004, in order to better organize the new department and to provide guidance to the 180,000 DHS employees transferred to the new agency, DHS released its own strategic plan. The plan contains vision and mission statements, strategic goals, and objectives that are intended to provide the framework guiding the actions that make up the department's daily operations. The strategic goals are as follows:

**Strategic Goal 1: Awareness**

Identify and understand threats, assess vulnerabilities, determine potential impacts and disseminate timely information to our homeland security partners and the American public.

- Objective 1.1—Gather and fuse all terrorism-related intelligence; analyze and coordinate access to information related to potential terrorist or other threats.
- Objective 1.2—Identify and assess the vulnerability of critical infrastructure and key assets.
- Objective 1.3—Develop timely, actionable and valuable information based on intelligence analysis and vulnerability assessments.
- Objective 1.4—Ensure quick and accurate dissemination of relevant intelligence information to homeland security partners, including the public.

**Strategic Goal 2: Prevention**

Detect, deter and mitigate threats to our homeland.

- Objective 2.1—Secure our borders against terrorists, means of terrorism, illegal drugs and other illegal activity.

- Objective 2.2—Enforce trade and immigration laws.
- Objective 2.3—Provide operational end users with the technology and capabilities to detect and prevent terrorist attacks, means of terrorism and other illegal activities.
- Objective 2.4—Ensure national and international policy, law enforcement and other actions to prepare for and prevent terrorism are coordinated.
- Objective 2.5 Strengthen the security of the Nation's transportation systems.
- Objective 2.6—Ensure the security and integrity of the immigration system.

**Strategic Goal 3: Protection**

Safeguard our people and their freedoms, critical infrastructure, property and the economy of our nation from acts of terrorism, natural disasters, or other emergencies.

- Objective 3.1 Protect the public from acts of terrorism and other illegal activities.
- Objective 3.2—Reduce infrastructure vulnerability from acts of terrorism.
- Objective 3.3—Protect against financial and electronic crimes, counterfeit currency, illegal bulk currency movement and identity theft.
- Objective 3.4—Secure the physical safety of the President, Vice President, visiting world leaders and other protectees.
- Objective 3.5—Ensure the continuity of government operations and essential functions in the event of crisis or disaster.

- Objective 3.6—Protect the marine environment and living marine resources.
- Objective 3.7—Strengthen nationwide preparedness and mitigation against acts of terrorism, natural disasters, or other emergencies.

**Strategic Goal 4: Response**

Lead, manage and coordinate the national response to acts of terrorism (Figure 3-4), natural disasters, or other emergencies.

- Objective 4.1—Reduce the loss of life and property by strengthening nationwide response readiness.
- Objective 4.2—Provide scalable and robust all-hazard response capability.
- Objective 4.3—Provide search and rescue services to people and property in distress.

**Strategic Goal 5: Recovery**

Lead national, state, local and private sector efforts to restore services and rebuild communities after acts of terrorism, natural disasters, or other emergencies.

- Objective 5.1—Strengthen nationwide recovery plans and capabilities.
- Objective 5.2—Provide scalable and robust all-hazard recovery assistance.

*Source*: U.S. Department of Homeland Security Strategic Plan. www.dhs.gov.

## SECRETARY CHERTOFF'S DHS REORGANIZATION PLAN

On July 13, 2005, DHS Secretary Michael Chertoff released a six-point agenda that would be used to guide a reorganization of the department aimed at streamlining its efforts. The agenda followed an initial review that Chertoff initiated immediately on assuming the leadership position. The review was designed to closely examine the department in order to discover ways in which leadership could better manage risk in terms of threat, vulnerability, and consequence; prioritize policies and operational missions according to this risk-based approach; and establish a series of preventive and protective steps that would increase

FIGURE 3-4   New York City, New York, September 20, 2001—A dust-covered office in a building near the World Trade Center. (Photo by Andrea Booher/FEMA News Photo)

security at multiple levels. According to the six-point agenda, changes that will occur at DHS will focus on the following:

- Increasing overall preparedness, particularly for catastrophic events
- Creating better transportation security systems to move people and cargo more securely and efficiently
- Strengthening border security and interior enforcement and reforming immigration processes
- Enhancing information sharing (with partners)
- Improving financial management, human resource development, procurement and information technology within the department

- Realigning the department's organization to maximize mission performance

Secretary Chertoff announced several new policy initiatives that will be included in the overhaul of the department, including these:

- A new approach to securing borders through additional personnel, new technologies, infrastructure investments, and interior enforcement—coupled with efforts to reduce the demand for illegal border migration by channeling migrants seeking work into regulated legal channels
- Restructuring the current immigration process to enhance security and improve customer service

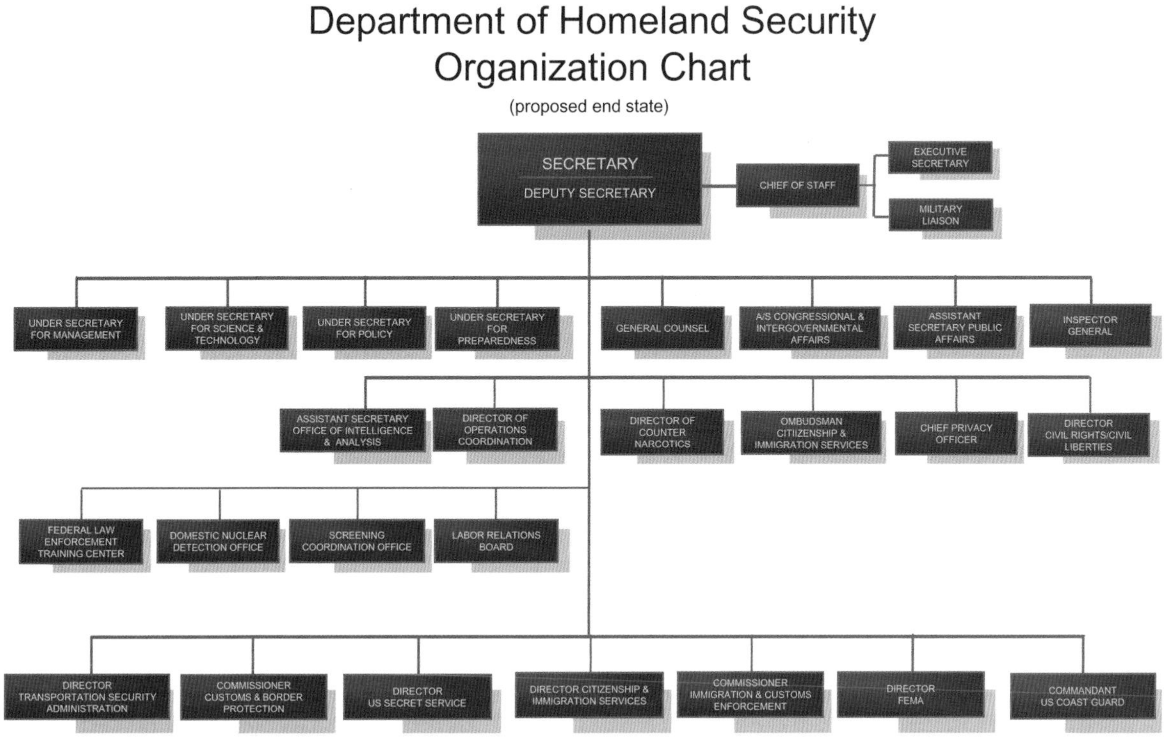

# Department of Homeland Security
# Organization Chart

(proposed end state)

FIGURE 3-5   Proposed new DHS organizational chart, as defined by Secretary Chertoff's six-point agenda. (Department of Homeland Security, 2005)

- Reaching out to state homeland security officials to improve information exchange protocols, refine the Homeland Security Advisory System, support state and regional data fusion centers, and address other topics of mutual concern
- Investing in DHS personnel by providing professional career training and other development efforts

One of the most significant changes that is to occur as result of the six-point agenda is an organizational restructuring of the department (Figure 3-5). Chertoff asserts that these changes are being made "to increase [the Department's] ability to prepare, prevent, and respond to terrorist attacks and other emergencies." Changes to be performed include the following:

- A new Directorate of Policy will be created "to centralize and improve policy development and coordination" (Figure 3-6). This directorate will be led by an undersecretary on enactment of legislation, and will serve as the primary department-wide coordinator for policies, regulations, and other initiatives. This directorate is being created to ensure the consistency of policy and regulatory development across various parts of the department as well as to perform long-range strategic policy planning. It will assume the policy coordination functions previously performed by the Border and Transportation Security Directorate. It will also create a single point of contact for internal and external stakeholders by consolidating or colocating similar activities from across the department. This new directorate will include these offices:
  - Office of International Affairs
  - Office of Private Sector Liaison

# Department of Homeland Security
## Organization Chart—Policy

(proposed end state)

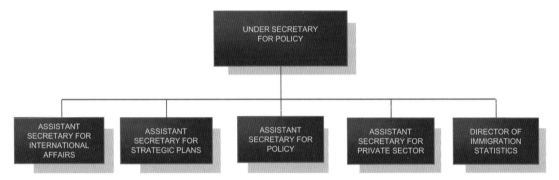

FIGURE 3-6    Proposed new DHS Policy Directorate organizational chart. (Department of Homeland Security, 2005)

– Office of Immigration Statistics
– Office of Strategic Plans
• A new Office of Intelligence and Analysis will be created to "strengthen intelligence functions and information sharing." This office will ensure that information is gathered from all relevant field operations and other parts of the intelligence community; analyzed with a mission-oriented focus; is informative to senior decision makers; and disseminated to the appropriate federal, state, local, and private-sector partners. Led by a chief intelligence officer who reports directly to the secretary, this office will be comprised of analysts within the former information analysis directorate and draw on the expertise of other DHS components with intelligence collection and analysis operations.
• A new "director of operations coordination" position will be created to "improve coordination and efficiency of operations." This official will work to enable DHS to more effectively conduct joint operations across all organizational elements; coordinate incident management activities; and utilize all resources within the department to translate intelligence and policy

into immediate action. The Homeland Security Operations Center, which serves as the nation's nerve center for information sharing and domestic incident management on a full-time basis, will be a critical part of this new office.
• The Information Analysis and Infrastructure Protection Directorate will be renamed the Directorate for Preparedness and consolidate preparedness assets from across the department (Figure 3-7). The Directorate for Preparedness will facilitate grants and oversee nationwide preparedness efforts supporting first responder training, citizen awareness, public health, infrastructure security, and cyber security and ensure proper steps are taken to protect high-risk targets. The directorate will be managed by an undersecretary and include the following:
– A new assistant secretary for cyber security and telecommunications, responsible for identifying and assessing the vulnerability of critical telecommunications infrastructure and assets; providing timely, actionable, and valuable threat information; and leading the national response to cyber and telecommunications attacks

# Department of Homeland Security
## Organization Chart—Preparedness

(proposed end state)

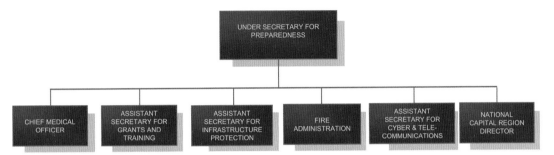

FIGURE 3-7    New DHS Preparedness Directorate organizational chart. (Department of Homeland Security, 2005)

- A new chief medical officer, responsible for carrying out the department's responsibilities in coordinating the response to biological attacks—and to serve as a principal liaison between DHS and the Department of Health and Human Services, the Centers for Disease Control and Prevention, the National Institutes of Health, and other key parts of the biomedical and public health communities
- Assistant secretary for infrastructure protection
- Assets of the Office of State and Local Government Coordination and Preparedness responsible for grants, training, and exercises
- U.S. Fire Administration
- Office of National Capitol
• FEMA will report directly to the secretary of homeland security in order to "improve national response and recovery efforts by focusing FEMA on its core functions." Under the new DHS proposed by the agenda, FEMA will focus on response and recovery.
• The Federal Air Marshal Service will be moved from the Immigration and Customs Enforcement bureau to the Transportation Security Administration to "increase operational coordination and strengthen efforts to meet this common goal of aviation security."

• A new Office of Legislative and Intergovernmental Affairs will be created, which will merge certain functions among the Office of Legislative Affairs and the Office of State and Local Government Coordination in order to "streamline intergovernmental relations efforts and better share homeland security information with members of Congress as well as state and local officials."
• The Office of Security will be moved such that it will be under the direction of the undersecretary for management "in order to better manage information systems, contractual activities, security accreditation, training and resources."

Of these changes that are taking place, there is one that stands out above the rest as being particularly troubling—the disassembly of the Directorate of Emergency Preparedness and Response (EP&R). Though it makes perfect sense that FEMA should be a stand-alone agency within the department—especially considering the fact that the functions of FEMA fully dominated the directorate as it stood—it is somewhat inexplicable as to why FEMA would be stripped of its preparedness and mitigation functions. This action, it would seem, is a complete reversal in the 30-year trend toward the comprehensive approach toward emergency management: mitigation, preparedness, response, and recovery.

United Press International reported that critics both within FEMA and outside of DHS, especially from within the first responder community, feel that the change is a sure sign that DHS is making a significant departure from the traditional "all-hazards" approach to emergency management, which would see terrorism as but one of many hazards encompassing each community's hazard profile.

## OTHER AGENCIES PARTICIPATING IN COMMUNITY-LEVEL FUNDING

As mentioned in the introduction to this chapter, the Department of Homeland Security may be the most recognized embodiment of federal homeland security action and have the most central role in its implementation, but it is not alone in the federal government by any means in this mission. Several other federal agencies outside of the new department have both maintained and created programs that address homeland security. Many of these also fund or support homeland security efforts at the state and local levels as well. Several of these programs, as discussed next, are either in the transitional or developmental phase but have already begun active participation within the greater homeland security context.

## U.S.A. FREEDOM CORPS

The U.S.A. Freedom Corps is an umbrella organization within the Executive Office of the President that includes the Peace Corps, the Corporation for National and Community Service (CNCS), and Citizen Corps. CNCS and Citizen Corps, which operate domestically, are discussed here.

### Corporation for National and Community Service

The CNCS administers several individual volunteer-based but grant-funded programs, including

AmeriCorps, Senior Corps, and Learn and Serve America:

- *AmeriCorps* is a network of national service programs that "engage more than 50,000 Americans each year in intensive service to meet critical needs in education, public safety, health, and the environment." AmeriCorps members serve through more than 2,100 nonprofit and nongovernmental agencies, public agencies, and faith-based organizations, tutoring and mentoring youth, building affordable housing, teaching computer skills, cleaning parks and streams, running after-school programs, and helping communities respond to disasters. These programs engage more than 2 million Americans of all ages and backgrounds in service each year.
- *Senior Corps* is a network of programs that "tap the experience, skills, and talents of older citizens to meet community challenges." It includes three programs: Foster Grandparents, Senior Companions, and the Retired and Senior Volunteer Program. More than a half-million Americans ages 55 and older assist local nonprofits, public agencies, and faith-based organizations in carrying out their missions.
- *Learn and Serve America* is a program that "supports service-learning programs in schools and community organizations that help nearly one million students from kindergarten through college meet community needs, while improving their academic skills and learning the habits of good citizenship." Service learning is defined as an educational method by which participants learn and develop through active participation in service that is conducted in and meets the needs of a community.

In July 2002, the Corporation for National and Community Service announced an initiative aimed at increasing citizen participation in homeland security. That year, CNCS awarded 43 grants totaling $10.3 million to communities, government agencies, and voluntary organizations to fund volunteer programs whose activities focused on the homeland security needs of communities. Since that time CNCS has continued to support community-level homeland security projects, including several of the following, which illustrate their accomplishments:

- AmeriCorps members serving in a program sponsored by the Florida Department of Elder Affairs recruited more than 600 disaster services volunteers who contributed more than 12,000 hours of service, distributed more than 200,000 disaster services publications, and reached nearly 2,500 residents with presentations on safety.
- AmeriCorps members serving with the Green River Area Development District in rural Kentucky utilized data from a Global Positioning System to map out information about fire stations, emergency shelters, hazardous materials (HAZMAT) storage facilities, medical facilities, and nursing homes.
- Just blocks from the World Trade Center site, Pace University AmeriCorps members trained 250 people in English, Chinese, and Spanish in emergency preparedness techniques, created a resource list that consolidates all important emergency numbers, and built a "Downtown Needs" website that serves as a volunteer clearinghouse for 2,000 organizations in the downtown area.
- AmeriCorps members in the California Safe Corps taught disaster preparedness classes to more than 1,000 community members, recruited more than 100 new volunteers who have provided more than 250 hours of service, and assisted more than 200 victims of disasters.
- In Iowa, AmeriCorps members made presentations on disaster preparedness at 400 schools across the state.

A list of the original grantees and their proposed activities is presented in Appendix 6.

## Citizen Corps Program

Citizen Corps is the arm of U.S.A. Freedom Corps that provides opportunities for citizens who want to help make their communities more secure. Since its establishment, at which time President George W. Bush called for 2 years of volunteer service from every American citizen, almost 24,000 people from all 50 states and U.S. territories have volunteered to work with one or more of the Citizen Corps programs. These include the following:

- *Citizen Corps Councils (CCC)* are established at the state and local level to promote, organize, and run the various programs that fall under the Citizen Corps umbrella. Funding for these councils is provided by the federal government through grant awards. As of July 2005, there were Citizen Corps Councils in 55 States and U.S. territories, 1,673 local communities, all of which serve 68% of the total population of the United States.
- *Community Emergency Response Teams (CERTs)* began in Los Angeles, California, in 1983. City administrators there recognized that in most emergency situations, average citizens—neighbors, coworkers, and bystanders, for example—were often on the scene during the critical moments before professional help arrived. These officials acted on the belief that, by training average citizens to perform basic search and rescue, first aid, and other critical emergency response skills, they would increase the overall resilience of the community. Additionally, should a large scale disaster like an earthquake occur, where first response units would be stretched very thin, these trained citizens would be able to augment official services and provide an important service to the community.

Beginning in 1993, FEMA began to offer CERT training on a national level, providing funding to cover start-up and tuition costs for programs. Since that time, CERT programs have been established in more than 1,831 communities in all 50 states, the District of Columbia, and several U.S. territories. CERT teams remain active in the community before a disaster strikes, sponsoring events such as drills, neighborhood cleanup, and disaster-education fairs. Trainers offer periodic refresher sessions to CERT members to reinforce the basic training and to keep participants involved and practiced in their skills. CERT members also offer other nonemergency assistance to the community with the goal of improving the overall safety of the community.

- *Volunteers in Police Service (VIPS)* was created in the aftermath of September 11, 2001, to address the increased demands on state and local law enforcement. The basis of the program is that civilian volunteers are able to support police officers by doing much of the behind-the-scenes work that does not require formal law enforcement training, thereby allowing officers to spend more of their already strained schedules on the street. Though the concept is not new, the federal support for such programs is.

  VIPS draws on the time and recognized talents of civilian volunteers. Volunteer roles may include performing clerical tasks, serving as an extra set of "eyes and ears," assisting with search-and-rescue activities, and writing citations for accessible parking violations, just to name a few. As of July 2005, there were 1,178 official VIPS programs registered throughout the United States.

- The *Medical Reserve Corps (MRC)* was founded after the 2002 State of the Union Address to establish teams of local volunteer medical and public health professionals who can contribute their skills and experience when called on in times of need. The program relies on volunteers who are practicing and retired physicians, nurses, dentists, veterinarians, epidemiologists, and other health professionals, as well as other citizens untrained in public health but who can contribute to the community's normal and disaster public health needs in other ways (which may include interpreters, chaplains, legal advisers, etc.)

  Local community leaders develop their own MRC units and recruit local volunteers that address the specific community needs. For exam-

ple, MRC volunteers may deliver necessary public health services during a crisis, assist emergency response teams with patients, and provide care directly to those with less serious injuries and other health-related issues. MRC volunteers may also serve a vital role by assisting their communities with ongoing public health needs (e.g., immunizations, screenings, health and nutrition education, and volunteering in community health centers and local hospitals). The MRC unit decides, in concert with local officials (including the local Citizen Corps Council), on when the community Medical Reserve Corps is activated during a local emergency. As of July 2005, there were 282 MRC programs established throughout the United States.

- The *Neighborhood Watch Program* has been in existence for more than 30 years in cities and counties throughout the United States. The program is based on the concept that neighbors who join together to fight crime will be able to increase security in their surrounding areas and, as result, provide an overall better quality of life for residents. Understandably, after September 11, when terrorism became a major focus of the U.S. government, the recognized importance of programs like Neighborhood Watch took on much greater significance.

  The Neighborhood Watch program is not maintained by the National Sheriff's Association, which founded the program initially. At the local level, the Citizen Corps Councils help neighborhood groups that have banded together to start a program to carry out their mission. Many printed materials and other guidance are available for free to help them carry out their goals.

  Neighborhood watch programs have successfully decreased crime in many of the neighborhoods where they have been implemented. In total, as of June 2005, there were 10,153 programs spread out throughout the United States and the U.S. territories. In addition to serving a crime prevention role, Neighborhood Watch has also been used as the basis for bringing neighborhood residents together to focus on disaster preparedness and terrorism awareness; to focus on evacuation drills and exercises; and even to organize group training, such as the CERT training.

- *Fire Corps* was created in 2004 under the umbrella of U.S.A. Freedom Corps and Citizen Corps. The purpose of the program, like the VIPS program with the police, was to enhance the ability of fire departments to utilize citizen advocates and provide individuals with opportunities to support their local fire departments with both time and talent.

  Fire Corps was created as a partnership between the International Association of Fire Chiefs' Volunteer Combination Officers Section (VCOS), the International Association of Fire Fighters (IAFF), and the National Volunteer Fire Council (NVFC). By participating in the program, concerned and interested citizens can assist in their local fire department's activities through tasks such as administrative assistance, public education, fund-raising, data entry, accounting, public relations, and equipment and facility maintenance, just to name a few examples.

  Any fire department that allows citizens to volunteer support service is considered a Fire Corps program, but programs can become official through registering with a local, county, or state CCC, if one exists. Official Fire Corps programs will be provided with assistance on how to implement a nonoperational citizen advocates program, or improve existing programs. A Fire Corps National Advisory Committee has been established under the program in order to provide strategic direction and collect feedback from the field. As of July 2005, there were 294 established Fire Corps programs throughout the United States and the U.S. territories.

While some of these programs are new, some, such as Neighborhood Watch, have been in place for more than a decade. More information on these programs is provided in Chapter 7.

## U.S. DEPARTMENT OF AGRICULTURE

Considering the wide assortment of impacts that both terrorism and other natural disasters (such as plant and animal diseases) could have on the both the U.S. food supply and on the U.S. economy, agriculture has assumed a very important role in the overall homeland security approach of the United States. Shortly after September 11, the U.S. Department of Agriculture (USDA) formed a Homeland Security Council (within USDA) to develop a department-wide plan and coordinate efforts among all USDA agencies and offices. Their efforts have since focused on three identified key areas of concern:

- Food supply and agricultural production
- Protection of USDA facilities
- USDA staff and emergency preparedness

The following section describes how USDA has fulfilled its homeland security mission to date.

### Protecting U.S. Borders from Invasive Pests and Diseases

USDA is contributing to the DHS effort to keep foreign agricultural pests and diseases from entering the country. More veterinarians and food import surveillance officers have been posted at borders and ports of entry for this mission. Though approximately 2,600 members of the USDA border inspection force were transferred to DHS, USDA has continued to train inspectors and set policy for plants, animals and commodities entering the United States.

In March 2004, the DHS Bureau of Customs and Border Protection's Border Patrol (BP) announced the 2004 Arizona Border Control Initiative. This initiative was aimed at protecting the border with Mexico. The initiative required increased cooperation between DHS and the USDA Forest Service in allowing more access to public lands on the border. Forest Service resource managers have worked within environmental laws to enhance the BP's effectiveness without disturbing the environment, and Forest Service law enforcement personnel have assisted the

BP in deterring illegal activities on National Forest System lands.

### Protecting the Health of Farm Animals, Crops, and Natural Resources

USDA created a National Surveillance Unit within its Animal and Plant Health Inspection Service's (APHIS) Veterinary Services program. The unit provides a focal point for the collection, processing, and delivery of surveillance information used to make risk analyses and to take further action. The unit designs surveillance strategies and coordinates and integrates surveillance activities, to protect the health and enhance the marketability of livestock and poultry.

In an effort to develop a more comprehensive approach to animal health surveillance, USDA appointed a national surveillance system coordinator. USDA also works with universities and state veterinary diagnostic laboratories around the country to create plant and animal health laboratory networks in order to increase the nation's capability to respond in an emergency. USDA developed guidance documents to help remind farmers and ranchers of steps they can take to secure their operations.

USDA has provided $43 million to states, universities, and tribal lands to increase homeland security prevention, detection, and response efforts. USDA also developed the National Animal Health Reserve Corps, which has resulted in the registration of almost 300 private veterinarians who will assist local communities during times of emergency.

USDA is currently working under a $25 million project to develop rapid tests for biological agents considered to pose the most serious threats to our agricultural system, including foot and mouth disease, rinderpest, and soybean and wheat rust.

### Ensuring a Safe Food Supply

USDA has enhanced security at all food safety laboratories around the country, and expanded its abilities to test for "nontraditional" biological, chemical, and radiological agents. USDA established an Office of Food Security and Emergency Preparedness, which now serves as the lead coordinating body in the development of the infrastructure and capacity to prevent, prepare for, and respond to terrorism aimed at U.S. food supply. USDA also drafted and distributed guidance for field and laboratory personnel about what to do when the HSAS is raised to either Orange or Red levels.

New import surveillance liaison inspectors have been hired by the department, who are stationed around the United States to enhance surveillance of imported products. Using a food security plan they developed, USDA has conducted training for employees, veterinarians, and inspectors on threat prevention and preparedness activities. USDA food safety labs have maintained a lead role in creating a network to integrate the U.S. laboratory infrastructure and surge capacity at the local, state, and federal levels.

### Protecting Research and Laboratory Facilities

USDA has spent $88.2 million for security assessments, background investigations, physical security upgrades, and additional security personnel at research and laboratory facilities. Security countermeasures have been implemented based on the findings of these assessments. Furthermore, all USDA laboratories where dangerous agents and toxins are used are held to the requirements of the Agricultural Bioterrorism Protection Act of 2002.

### Emergency Preparedness and Response

A department-wide National Interagency Incident Management System (NIIMS), based on the successful system utilized by USDA's Forest Service, has being implemented. This system includes incident command and control systems, coordination systems, training and qualification systems, and publication management systems. USDA's NIIMS uses the same systems within USDA for incident management as those standardized for the nation under the National Incident Management System (NIMS), which is described in Chapter 7.

The construction of an APHIS Emergency Operations Center (AEOC), which is used to coordinate and support emergency response within APHIS, has been completed. The AEOC, which enhances APHIS's ability to provide leadership during national emergencies, has already been utilized on several occasions, including the exotic Newcastle disease outbreak, the monkey pox outbreak, and the confirmations of bovine spongiform encephalopathy (BSE) in both Canada and the United States.

### Protecting Other Infrastructure

USDA Forest Service law enforcement officers continue to conduct security assessments of research facilities and air tanker bases nationwide. USDA's Forest Service continues to enhance efforts to protect National Forest System lands and facilities, including dams, reservoirs, pipelines, water treatment plants, power lines, and energy production facilities on government property.

### Securing Information Technology

USDA has conducted tests of their network systems to assess threat levels. USDA upgraded the security status of key information technology personnel and conducted training and planning sessions to strengthen the department's continuity of operations plans.

## DEPARTMENT OF COMMERCE

The Department of Commerce promotes homeland security through actions conducted in three of its many offices and agencies. These include:

- The Bureau of Industry and Security
- The National Institute for Standards and Technology
- The National Oceanographic and Atmospheric Administration

### Bureau of Industry and Security

The mission of the Bureau of Industry and Security (BIS) is to advance U.S. national security, foreign policy, and economic interests. BIS's activities include regulating the export of sensitive goods and technologies and enforcing export control and public safety laws; cooperating with and assisting foreign countries on export control; helping U.S. industry to comply with international arms control agreements; and monitoring the U.S. defense industrial base to ensure that it is capable of handling national and homeland security needs. This agency gained more notoriety after September 11, when concerns about certain technologies and arms that could be used by terrorists abroad were raised. The bureau has enjoyed an increase in funding as result of these changes.

### National Institute for Standards and Technology

The National Institute for Standards and Technology (NIST) has provided significant contributions to the homeland security of the nation by assisting in the measurement infrastructure used to establish safety and security standards. NIST labs, which are detailed in Chapter 9, have enjoyed an increase in funding levels since September 11, and have developed technologies that are used for such actions as establishing standards for and measuring the safety and security of buildings, for the development of biometric identification systems, and for various radiation detection systems utilized at U.S. and foreign ports, among many others. NIST laboratories involved, at least partially, in homeland security include these:

- The Building and Fire Research Laboratory
- Chemical Science and Technology Laboratory
- Materials Science and Engineering Laboratory
- Physics Laboratory
- Technology Services

### National Oceanographic and Atmospheric Administration

The National Oceanographic and Atmospheric Administration (NOAA) has been involved in disaster management since long before the creation of the DHS. NOAA monitors meteorological conditions, makes forecasts about storm risks, and recommends preparedness measures to FEMA and other federal, state, and local government agencies. The NOAA National Weather Service (NWS), under which the All-Hazards Radio Warning Network is managed, is another vital component to the overall homeland security needs of the nation. Though not focused on terrorism, the weather radio system is capable of being activated in the event of any type of disaster, regardless of its origin, to provide timely warning to people who may be in danger.

## DEPARTMENT OF EDUCATION

The Department of Education is responsible, among other things, for taking a leadership position in establishing standards and technical assistance for school safety. Schools are not only vulnerable to the effects of natural and technological disasters, but have been identified by many terrorism experts to be a primary target for terrorist activities due to the emotional factor involved with the injury or death of children. Both before and since September 11, there have been many terrorist or other attacks in schools throughout the world, including in Beslan, Russia, and in Cambodia—both of which resulted in fatalities—and elsewhere. Attacks on schools, exemplified by the 1999 Columbine attacks, provide further justification of the required homeland security role that is filled by the Department of Education.

The office of Safe and Drug Free Schools was created in September 2002 to manage all Department of Education activities related to safe schools, crisis response, alcohol and drug prevention, and health and well-being of students. Today, this office is responsible for leading the homeland security efforts of the department. Millions of dollars in funding have been made available to schools by the Department of Education through this office, including $30 million in both FY 2003 and FY 2004, to help them to better address emergency planning issues.

Emergency planning guidance and technical assistance are major concerns of the Department of Education, and this area of expertise is also handled through the Office of Safe and Drug Free Schools. Through the

development and maintenance of a website (www.ed. gov/emergencyplan), the Department of Education has created what they call a "one-stop-shop" for schools to locate information to plan for all types of disasters, whether they are natural, terrorist, or other.

### Environmental Protection Agency

The Environmental Protection Agency (EPA) has played a very important role in emergency management and homeland security for decades. The EPA was one of the signatory agencies of the Federal Response Plan (FRP), and today plays a major role in the National Response Plan (NRP; this response-related role is detailed in Chapter 7). The EPA is concerned primarily with emergencies involving the release, or threatened release, of oil, radioactive materials, or hazardous chemicals that have the potential to affect communities and the surrounding environment. These releases may be accidental, deliberate, or the result of a natural disaster. EPA works with a variety of private and public entities to prevent, prepare for, and respond to spills and other environmental emergencies. EPA's website provides information for these entities to be able to better prevent spills and releases and to better respond to them when they occur.

The EPA has a responsibility for preparing for and responding to terrorist threats involving WMDs. Because of its inherent role in protecting human health and the environment from possible harmful effects of certain chemical, biological, and nuclear materials, the EPA is actively involved in counterterrorism planning and response efforts. The EPA supports federal counterterrorism programs through the following four mechanisms:

1. Helping state and local responders to plan for emergencies
2. Coordinating with key federal partners
3. Training first responders
4. Providing resources in the event of a terrorist incident

Several offices within the agency are involved in these efforts, including these three:

- The Chemical Emergency Preparedness and Prevention Office
- Office of Superfund Remediation and Technology Innovation
- Office of Air and Radiation

## Chemical Emergency Preparedness and Prevention Office

In 1985, one year after the Bhopal, India, chemical accident that killed thousands of people, the EPA established the Chemical Emergency Preparedness and Prevention Office (CEPPO). Through this office, EPA has taken a leading role within the federal government in building programs to respond to and prevent chemical accidents. CEPPO works with numerous federal, state, local, and tribal governments; industry groups; environmental groups; labor organizations; and community groups to help them better understand the risks posed by chemicals in their communities, to manage and reduce those risks, and to deal with emergencies.

CEPPO works with its state and local partners to develop new approaches to deal with emergency preparedness and accident prevention. They assist local emergency planning committees (LEPCs) and state emergency response commissions (SERCs) by providing leadership, issuing regulations, developing technical guidance, and enabling these committees to develop their own unique emergency planning systems appropriate to their individual needs.

CEPPO also works closely with the National Response Team (NRT) to help states and localities better prepare for, respond to, and prevent accidents. The NRT consists of 16 federal agencies with interests and expertise in various aspects of emergency response specifically to pollution incidents.

CEPPO's website links to general information and subject-specific data about the Emergency Planning and Community Right-to-Know Act (EPCRA), the risk management planning requirements of the Clean Air Act, up-to-date information on chemical accidents, as well as publications, regulations, conference listings, and links to other databases to help regula-

tors, SERCs, LEPCs, industry, and the public find out more about chemical emergency preparedness and accident prevention.

Programs developed by CEPPO include these:

- *Risk Management Plans* (RMPs)—RMPs, submitted from industry in June 1999, require certain facilities to tell the public and CEPPO what they are doing to prevent accidents and how they plan to operate safely and manage their chemicals in a responsible way.
- *RMP\*Info*™—Summaries of facility risk management programs are available to the public via the Internet. The data are useful to environmental groups, state and local agencies, community organizations, and the public in understanding the chemical risks in their communities.
- *Counterterrorism*—CEPPO is working with communities on how local emergency plans can address deliberate chemical releases and provide suggestions for rapid response.

## Office of Superfund Remediation Technology Innovation

The Office of Superfund Remediation Technology Innovation (OSRTI), called the Office of Emergency and Remedial Response (OERR) until 2003, manages the Superfund program. The Superfund program was created to protect citizens from the dangers posed by abandoned or uncontrolled hazardous waste sites. Congress established Superfund in 1980 by passing the Comprehensive Environmental Response, Compensation, and Liability Act (CERCLA). CERCLA gives the federal government the authority to respond to hazardous substance emergencies, and to develop long-term solutions for the nation's most serious hazardous waste problems.

## Office of Air and Radiation

The Office of Air and Radiation (OAR) develops national programs, technical policies, and regulations for controlling air pollution and radiation exposure. OAR is concerned with energy conservation and pollution prevention, indoor and outdoor air quality, industrial air pollution, pollution from vehicles and engines, radon, acid rain, stratospheric ozone depletion, and radiation protection. With regard to homeland security, this office is responsible for emergency response to radiation disasters, helping to design and implement air protection measures, monitoring ambient air (including project BioWatch and monitoring the air around the World Trade Center disaster), and maintaining a national air monitoring system.

In March 2004, the EPA Homeland Security Collaborative Network (HSCN) was established to facilitate the agency's collective approach to analyzing homeland security issues while formulating policy recommendations and actions cooperatively. The following is a list of EPA program offices that are members of the HSCN and a brief description of their homeland security tasks (where appropriate):

- Office of Air and Radiation (OAR)
  - See earlier description
- Office of Administration and Resource Management (OARM)
  - EPA facilities and employee security
  - Physical critical infrastructure protection
  - Design buildout of sensitive, classified information facilities/secured access facilities (SCIFs/SAFs)
  - Monitoring of Homeland Security Advisory System (HSAD) threat conditions
- Office of the Chief Financial Officer (OCFO)
- Office of Enforcement and Compliance Assurance (OECA)
  - Civil and criminal enforcement
  - Incident response
  - Counterterrorism support
  - Forensics
- Office of Environmental Information (OEI)
  - Information protection and access policy
  - Information infrastructure and cyber protection
  - Information technology
  - Data management
- Office of Prevention, Pesticides, and Toxic Substances (OPPTS)
  - Food and agriculture security support

- Emergency exemption requests
- Acute Exposure Guideline Limits (AEGLs)
- Chemical data/expertise on pesticides and industrial chemicals
- Licensing authority for antimicrobials to inactivate pathogens and pesticides
- Establishment of rules for storage/disposal of pesticides and pesticide applicator certification program
- Office of Research and Development (ORD)
  - Water security research
  - Building decontamination
  - Rapid risk assessment
- Office of Solid Waste and Emergency Response (OSWER)
  - Chemical industry infrastructure support
  - Building and critical infrastructure decontamination
  - Emergency response
  - Lab capacity
  - Continuity of operations plan/continuity of government (COOP/COG)
  - Superfund
- Office of Water (OW)
  - Drinking water and wastewater infrastructure protection
  - Training, simulations, exercises
  - Best water security practices
  - Vulnerability assessments and emergency response plans
  - Tools for preparedness and emergency response
  - Framework for monitoring/surveillance network
  - Financial assistance to states and tribes
  - Information sharing with sector and partners
- Region 6
  - Lead EPA region for homeland security responsibilities

## NRP SIGNATORIES

Many other federal agencies other than those just listed are involved in homeland security efforts, though most of these actions occur as result of their contractual obligations set out in the new National Response Plan (NRP). Though these actions will be described in greater detail in Chapter 7, the following is a list of the federal agencies that participate in the response to disasters within the United States:

- Department of Agriculture
- Department of Commerce
- Department of Defense
- Department of Education
- Department of Energy
- Department of Health and Human Resources
- Department of Homeland Security
- Department of Housing and Urban Development
- Department of the Interior
- Department of Justice
- Department of Labor
- Department of State
- Department of Transportation
- Department of the Treasury
- Department of Veterans Affairs
- Central Intelligence Agency
- Environmental Protection Agency
- Federal Bureau of Investigation
- Federal Communications Commission
- General Services Administration
- National Aeronautics and Space Administration
- National Transportation Safety Board
- Nuclear Regulatory Commission
- Office of Personnel Management
- Small Business Administration
- Social Security Administration
- Tennessee Valley Authority
- United States Agency for International Development
- U.S. Postal Service

## ACTIVITIES BY STATE AND LOCAL ORGANIZATIONS

State and local governments have expended considerable human and financial resources to secure their jurisdictions from the perceived threat of terrorism. Though considerable amounts of federal funding have gone to helping state and local agencies to better prepare for the terrorist threat, much of these efforts have been performed without any federal compensation. Also, each time the DHS Homeland Security Advisory System (HSAS) threat level has been raised, or when a major event that is identified as being a possible terrorist target is held within a jurisdiction, local leaders must divert sparse financial and human resources from other areas of need to adequately address those threats. As a result of these strains, the organizations' representative of state and local governments became actively engaged in the debates over the creation of the HS Act of 2002 and have remained active in homeland security process ever since.

As early as September 2002, the municipal organizations, which include the U.S. Conference of Mayors (USCM), the National League of Cities (NLC), the National Association of Counties (NACo), and the National Governors Association (NGA), and the emergency management organizations, which include the National Emergency Management Association (NEMA) and the International Association of Emergency Managers (IAEM), began fighting for first responder funding for state and local governments and about the way the money was allocated—whether it would be to the states or directly to the local municipalities. Clearly, these organizations were and continue to be involved in informing the federal government's approach to funding state and local homeland security efforts. Each of these organizations is discussed next.

## UNITED STATES CONFERENCE OF MAYORS

The U.S. Conference of Mayors (USCM) is the official nonpartisan organization of the nation's 1,183 U.S. cities with populations of 30,000 or more. Each city is represented in the conference by its chief elected official, the mayor. The primary roles of the USCM are to:

- Promote the development of effective national urban/suburban policy
- Strengthen federal–city relationships
- Ensure that federal policy meets urban needs

- Provide mayors with leadership and management tools
- Create a forum in which mayors can share ideas and information

The conference has historically assumed a national leadership role, calling early attention to serious urban problems and pressing successfully for solutions.

In December 2001, the USCM released "A National Action Plan for Safety and Security in America's Cities." The document was prepared as part of the Mayors Emergency Safety and Security Summit held in Washington, D.C., on October 23–25, 2001. It contained recommendations in four priority areas: transportation security, emergency preparedness, federal–local law enforcement, and economic security. In this document, the mayors made the following critical point:

> It is important to understand that while the fourth area, economic security, is viewed as the ultimate goal of a nation, it cannot be achieved in the absence of the first three. That is, securing our transportation system, maximizing our emergency response capability, and coordinating our law enforcement response to threats and incidents at all levels are viewed as prerequisites to eliminating the anxiety that has accelerated the nation's economic downturn, and to achieving economic security for the nation.

The principal areas of concern in federal–local law enforcement for the mayors are communications, coordination, and border-city security. In the transportation security section, the mayors' paper presents recommendations concerning security issues in each of the major transportation modes: airport, transit, highway, rail, and port.

USCM leadership has repeatedly expressed concern that a significant amount of funding from the federal government has not reached the cities for combating terrorism. The mayors expressed that they have been working on initiatives related to homeland security, largely without any federal assistance. Select initiatives, related to communities, that they mentioned include the following: (1) conducting exercises to help prepare for emergencies and improve response capabilities, (2) expanding public information and education efforts, and (3) conducting vulnerability assessments of potential key targets.

Funding for cities remains the principal focus of the USCM in the area of homeland security. In September 2003, the USCM released a report entitled, "First Mayors' Report to the Nation: Tracking Homeland Security Funds Sent to the 50 State Governments" (U.S. Conference of Mayors, 2003). Through release of the report, the USCM website announced that 90% of cities had not received funds from the largest federal homeland security program designed to assist first responders by the federally set deadline of August 1, 2003. The report also found that more than half of the cities have either not been consulted or have had no opportunity to influence state decision making about how to use and distribute funding. USCM priorities are listed in Sidebar 3-3.

---

### SIDEBAR 3-3   Selected U.S. Conference of Mayors' Homeland Security Priorities

**Emergency Preparedness**

1. Of the approximately $10 billion Federal terrorism budget identified by the OMB, only 4.9 percent is allocated to state and local first response activities. And, of this limited amount, most goes to the states rather than directly to America's cities and major population centers.

2. In the event of a catastrophic disaster, most communities will run short of critical emergency response resources (e.g., life-saving equipment, PPE, respirators, etc.) in six hours, and Federal help won't arrive for 12 hours. Pre-positioned equipment pods should be strategically located throughout the United States to re-supply local responders. The lim-

ited funding now available to the Department of Justice for equipment pods should be increased.

3. Effective preparedness efforts require an empowered community and the involvement of community representatives in the development of emergency response plans. The public should be educated in basic life-saving techniques so that bystanders can provide assistance to those injured until help arrives.

4. There must be communication system interoperability to insure clear communication among city departments and Federal, regional, state, and other local entities responding to disasters.

5. The compatibility, security and reliability of Federal, state, regional, and local emergency telecommunications systems must be assured.

**Economic Security**

1. Unemployment insurance should be expanded to provide benefits to those directly and indirectly affected by disaster-related job loss, and unemployment benefits should be extended from 26 to 78 weeks for all workers. Eligibility requirements should be modified to provide equal benefits to those who lost their jobs as a result of the economic downturn but who are ineligible for regular benefits, such as temporary and part-time workers and former Temporary Assistance to Needy Family (TANF) recipients. This would allow workers to be hired for community service jobs.

2. Funding of job training programs for dislocated workers, adults, and youth under the Workforce Investment Act (WIA) should be sufficient to enable those who are laid off, especially if they are low-skilled workers, to get upgrade training, basic skills training, and ESL education.

3. Free or low-cost health insurance should be provided to low-income families affected by the September 11 attack. Federal subsidies for COBRA for individuals who are unemployed due to the economic downturn should be provided.

4. The rescission in the FY 2001 dislocated workers appropriation should be restored.

5. It should be recognized that young workers served by WIA, especially those in Youth Opportunity Grant programs, will most likely be the first laid off in a recession and that many of these youth are high-school dropouts who need job training and financial subsidies.

*Source*: U.S. Conference of Mayors, www.usmayors.org.

The USCM has established a Homeland Security Monitoring Center to monitor the flow of homeland security funds from the federal government to states and localities. This focus on funding was at the heart of a March 12, 2004, message from Tom Cochran, executive director of the USCM, in a website column that stated, "Our goal is to do one thing: get the money down to our first responders on the front line in cities throughout America" (U.S. Conference of Mayors, 2004a). At its 72nd Annual Meeting in Boston in 2004, the USCM adopted a resolution entitled, "Federal Homeland Security Funding for First Responders" that is presented in Sidebar 3-4.

In June 2004, the USCM released a report of a survey that was conducted to assess the flow of federal homeland security funds through the states to the cities. Their study found that 52% of the 231 cities surveyed had not received any money at all, nor had they been notified that they will receive money from the state-block grant program, which is the largest homeland security program designed to assist first responders.

**SIDEBAR 3-4    2004 Adopted Resolutions at the 72nd USCM Annual Meeting: Federal Homeland Security Funding for First Responders**

- **WHEREAS,** America's mayors are 100 percent committed to the homeland war against terrorism; and
- **WHEREAS,** cities throughout the nation have already dedicated unprecedented, and mostly unbudgeted, resources to the new war on terrorism as detailed in surveys released by the Conference of Mayors; and
- **WHEREAS,** over $7 billion in new funding has been appropriated by Congress for Fiscal Years 2003 and 2004 for first responder assistance; and
- **WHEREAS,** despite a major lobbying effort by the nation's mayors—in partnership with local first responders including police chiefs, fire chiefs, police officers and fire officers— the majority of this funding has been sent through the states; and
- **WHEREAS,** two 50 state surveys conducted by the Conference of Mayors Homeland Security Monitoring Center in September of 2003 and January of 2004 found that a majority of cities had not yet received funding from the largest Federal first responder program; many states had chosen to send funding to regional or county governments; and problems exist regarding the involvement of cities in state planning processes; and
- **WHEREAS,** because each state can establish its own funding distribution plan, local governments do not have a predictable source of funding that can be integrated into local homeland security plans; and
- **WHEREAS,** there has not been established a detailed, transparent monitoring system to track the Federal funding through the states to local governments and first responders; and
- **WHEREAS,** President Bush acknowledged that a logjam existed in the states on this funding during the Conference of Mayors' 72nd Winter Meeting in January of 2004, and pledged to help "un-stick" the funds; and
- **WHEREAS,** Department of Homeland Security (DHS) Secretary Tom Ridge immediately responded to the President's statements by forming a special Task Force on State and Local Homeland Security Funding, with the Conference of Mayors top three officers and Criminal and Social Justice Committee Chair serving as members; and
- **WHEREAS,** that DHS Task Force has been working to refine the existing funding system through the states to ensure that funding reaches local first responders quickly and efficiently; and
- **WHEREAS,** the DHS Task Force has identified a number of structural problems that have accounted for funding difficulties including, but not limited to, the reimbursement nature of the program and the multiple layers of governmental involvement in funding distribution; and
- **WHEREAS,** the Task Force did not address the issue of direct funding; and
- **WHEREAS,** the Administrations FY 2005 budget includes a request for $3.2 billion in additional first responders assistance, and with the exception of the $500 million requested for fire grants, the remaining funding would continue to flow through the states; and
- **WHEREAS,** reauthorization bills currently moving forward in the United States Senate and House of Representatives would significantly alter the nature of the first responder program, including a provision in the Senate bill to provide high threat funding directly to local governments without a state pass-through,

- **NOW, THEREFORE, BE IT RESOLVED** that the United States Conference of Mayors calls on the Congress to pass, and the President to sign, legislation creating a new formula-based first responder funding program with direct local assistance and maximum flexibility to cover costs such as equipment, communications interoperability, training, exercises, planning, critical infrastructure protection, and overtime related to homeland security; and
- **BE IT FURTHER RESOLVED** that Congress should approve retroactive changes to

ensure that the more than $7 billion in the pipeline, as well as future appropriations, can be quickly and efficiently accessed by local governments and first responders including eliminating the reimbursement nature of the first responder program and providing pass-through deadlines for when funding is sent by the states to counties or regional governments.

*Source*: U.S. Conference of Mayors, www.usmayors.org/uscm/resolutions/72nd_conference/csj_01.asp.

## National League of Cities

The National League of Cities (NLC) is the oldest and largest national organization representing municipal governments throughout the United States. The NLC serves as a resource to and is an advocate for the more than 18,000 cities, villages, and towns it represents. More than 1,600 municipalities of all sizes pay dues to NLC and actively participate as leaders and voting members in the organization. The National League of Cities provides numerous benefits to its network of members, including:

- Advocates for cities and towns in Washington, D.C., through full-time lobbying and grassroots campaigns.
- Promotes cities and towns through an aggressive media and communications program that draws attention to city issues and enhances the national image of local government.
- Provides programs and services that give local leaders the tools and knowledge to better serve their communities.
- Keeps leaders informed of critical issues that affect municipalities and warrant action by local officials.

- Strengthens leadership skills by offering numerous training and education programs.
- Recognizes municipal achievements by gathering and promoting examples of best practices and honoring cities and towns with awards for model programs and initiatives.
- Partners with state leagues to supplement resources and strengthen the voice of local government in the nation's capital and all state capitols.
- Provides opportunities for involvement and networking to help city officials seek ideas, share solutions, and find common ground for the future.

Like the USCM, the NLC has also focused on the first responder funding issue. It conducted a letter-writing campaign to the White House and Congress to build support for the original allocation of first responder funds. In 2002, NLC proposed a $75.5 billion stimulus package that would include $10 billion for unmet homeland security needs.

In January 2003, NLC President Karen Anderson appointed a special Working Group on Homeland Security to serve a NLC's front line resource on the subject. That group worked to prepare resources to

---

**SIDEBAR 3-5    2005 Advocacy Priority—The Issue: Funding for First Responders**

The nation's cities and towns need a well-funded, improved grant program to respond to terrorism threats in highly-populated and high-threat areas. Local governments seek funding that allows jurisdictions to prepare for possible terrorist threats, with flexibility to use the funds for a range of risks based on their state homeland security plans.

**Message to Congress**

- *Preserve direct funding.* Preserve direct funding to local governments and regions based on the congressionally mandated 80 percent pass-through requirement from states to local governments.
- *Improve homeland and hometown security.* Improve security by increasing funding for Urban Area Security Grants and the State Homeland Security Grant program.
- *Preserve funding.* Preserve funding for both homeland security programs such as Law Enforcement Terrorism Prevention grants, the Urban Search and Rescue program and the Metropolitan Medical Response System, and traditional first responder and emergency management programs that existed before September 11, 2001.

- *Provide flexibility.* Provide flexibility for local governments to use homeland security funds to offset overtime expenditures during national high alerts, counterterrorism activities, and training exercises.
- *Create a Federal clearinghouse.* Create a web-based Federal clearinghouse of best practices and updated voluntary national consensus standards.
- *Waive cost-sharing requirements.* Waive matching or cost-sharing requirements for local governments.

**Request to Congress**

- Enact an authorization bill that provides funding for first responders to target terrorism threats in highly-populated and high-threat areas, with maximum flexibility to use the funds for a range of risks based on their state homeland security plans.
- Fully fund the State Homeland Security Grant program, Urban Area Security Grants, and other critical homeland security programs.

*Source*: National League of Cities, www.nlc.org/content/Files/PFRHomeland%20Security1.pdf.

---

help city officials in carrying out their new roles as the "front line of hometown defense."

The NLC has continued to lobby Congress and the Executive Office to increase or maintain funding support to strengthen "hometown" and homeland security, and develop extensive policy on these issues. The NLC reports the results of surveys on municipal responses to terrorism regarding vulnerable targets and the need for federal guidance and support. A variety of publications that NLC generates offer practical guidance to local officials to assist in their ongoing

efforts to develop and refine local and regional homeland security plans.

In 2005, homeland security remains a top priority for the NLC. The two primary NLC issues are first responder funding and public safety communications. Presented in Sidebar 3-5 is text from an NLC document on funding for first responders.

In 2005, the NLC developed a policy statement on homeland security that was included in its "National Municipal Policy." The policy statement addresses the following topics:

- Prevention, planning, and mitigation
- Disaster response and recovery
- Training and technical assistance
- Disaster insurance
- Domestic terrorism
- Border security
- Immigration enforcement
- Profiling

An abridged copy of the NLC policy statement is presented in Sidebar 3-6.

The NLC has developed two publications to assist local governments in participating in homeland security:

- "Homeland Security: Federal Resources for Local Governments" (www.nlc.org/nlc_org/site/files/reports/fedlresrc.pdf)

- "Homeland Security: Practical Tools for Local Governments" (www.nlc.org/nlc_org/site/files/reports/terrorism.pdf)

## NATIONAL ASSOCIATION OF COUNTIES

The National Association of Counties (NACo) was created in 1935, and remains the only national organization that represents county governments in the United States. NACo maintains a membership of more than 2,000 counties (over 80% of the U.S. population), but represents all of the nation's 3,066 counties to the White House and to Congress.

NACo is a full-service organization that provides many services to its members, including legislative, research, technical, and public affairs assistance. The

---

**SIDEBAR 3-6    NLC 2005 National Municipal Policy on Homeland Security, Disaster Preparedness, and Response**

### Problem Statement

The lives lost, property damaged, and economic hardships suffered due to criminal and terrorist acts and natural, manufactured and technological disasters pose severe problems for individual residents, communities, businesses and all levels of government. Local governments are the first level of government to respond to most disasters and emergencies and must be regarded as the focal point of all disaster mitigation and recovery activities. The Federal government should provide funding directly to local governments for homeland security, emergency preparedness and response.

An effective system must be developed to ensure that Federal and state emergency management officials conduct substantive consultations with local officials for key decision-making affecting homeland security, disaster preparedness and response at the local level. Federal and state technical and financial assistance should be structured to allow local officials maximum flexibility in meeting identified needs. The potential for hazardous or radioactive material spills, pipeline accidents, large scale social disorders, and domestic terrorism compels all levels of government to coordinate efforts to protect communities. Such coordination must result in a comprehensive national homeland security and disaster preparedness strategy. The Department of Homeland Security must continue to have a central office for coordinating local and state domestic preparedness activities. Regional plans and cooperation must be fostered through this central office.

### Prevention, Planning, and Mitigation

The highest priority of all levels of government in addressing disaster and terrorism issues should be prevention and mitigation. Mitigation saves lives and reduces injuries; reduces economic losses;

maintains and protects critical infrastructure; and reduces the liability borne by local governments and elected officials.

Knowing that improved safety from disasters in the future relies on what we can learn from the disasters of today, the Federal government should collect data on the effects of disasters and lessons learned from the analysis of such data should be disseminated to aid state and local disaster-related efforts. Similarly, the Federal government should provide assistance to state and local governments to help them conduct annual hazard and risk assessments to determine the vulnerability of particular areas or structures to disasters or terrorist acts based on historical and/or intelligence information.

The Federal government can also help mitigate potential disasters by working closely with local governments to develop a useful uniform emergency warning. The Federal government must also educate and train local emergency services on the effects of disasters and lessons on the warning system and what precautions need to be taken.

The Federal government should provide an adequate level of funding for local emergency preparedness and disaster planning and management. Such funding should allow a city to tailor its disaster preparedness planning to the special circumstances and needs of the area, particularly to any facilities and densely populated areas that have the potential to be terrorist targets, as well as provide local governments with appropriate emergency response equipment and communication as necessary. In addition to directly assisting cities and towns in their mitigation efforts, NLC urges the Federal government to:

- Require Federal agencies to develop and coordinate pre- and post-disaster mitigation programs for the types of emergencies they manage;
- Develop a comprehensive evaluation of risk factors for potential terrorist targets;

- Make their mitigation training programs more accessible and affordable and ensure that proven mitigation technology is more widely publicized and utilized;
- Support local governments in their efforts to encourage the public and private sectors to retrofit existing structures to reduce future losses from natural disasters and to locate new construction outside of high-risk areas such as flood plains, coastal areas or on or near earthquake faults;
- Encourage lending institutions to incorporate mitigation provisions as conditions for loans;
- Sufficiently fund agricultural counterterrorism and food safety efforts; and
- Adopt strict standards for the enforcement and transport of hazardous materials.

**Disaster Response and Recovery**

Federal programs should be structured to support municipal governments with adequate funding and authority to immediately and effectively respond to all types of disasters, including training and equipping first responders and the public and private medical community. The Federal government must increase funding to local governments for preparedness and response, including processes to resolve equity issues in disaster relief efforts. The Federal government must ensure that local governments and their first responders have the resources and capacity to address and respond to NBC incidents, and should coordinate with state and local governments for public education regarding NBC incidents. Additionally, the Federal government should assist in the establishment and training of interdisciplinary, multi-jurisdictional search and rescue teams in each state to respond to and recover from natural and manufactured disasters.

**Training and Technical Assistance**

The Federal government must provide technical assistance and regional training devoted to disaster preparedness and response. This technical assistance should include the gathering and regular dissemination of information to local governments on general disaster issues and terrorist threats as well as specific disasters where they occur. This sensitive information must be shared with local government without jeopardizing national security. As part of its technical assistance efforts, the Federal government should encourage regions to share resources and equipment needed for preparedness and response through mutual aid agreements and regional coordination.

## Disaster Insurance

In the wake of recent high-cost natural disasters and terrorist attacks, a number of insurance companies have been unable to properly cover the losses of their policy holders because the industry was overexposed to loss. Since the 9/11 terrorist attacks, the industry has virtually eliminated its coverage of terrorism, and if available, it is prohibitively expensive. This limited ability to obtain natural disaster insurance also has restricted or stopped property transfers in some real estate markets. The Federal government has stepped in to provide assistance to the states whose residents have lost coverage from their insurance companies, but often this assistance comes at the expense of other Federal programs. The costs to the Federal government continue to increase as people cannot or do not seek private insurance to help cover losses from natural disasters. Similarly, the Federal government must address reinsurance for acts of terrorism.

## Domestic Terrorism

The Federal government should help local authorities by providing appropriate training to local governments in terrorism prevention. Public safety personnel must be taught and provided the necessary equipment to manage a situation involving WMDs. Information or intelligence on likely or imminent acts of terrorism must be shared across agency lines and with local enforcement agencies in potential impact areas. A policy for sharing certain classified information on threats or potential threats of terrorism with first responders must be implemented. Both Federal financial assistance and Federal personnel should be provided to the local government immediately when terrorist acts take place. The Federal government must include local governments in Federal plans and operations relative to issues in their jurisdictions and provide legal assistance to local governments that have high profile public or private targets within their boundaries.

## Border Security

NLC supports increased coordination and cooperation between Federal, state and local law enforcement agencies to achieve operational control of our nation's borders. Local law enforcement should not be conscripted into Federal border patrol service. If the Federal government does require local law enforcement to act on its behalf, absolute immunity and/or indemnification should be given so that localities are not liable for the actions taken on the Federal government's behalf. All costs associated with enforcement, training and equipment for these duties should be paid directly to the local jurisdiction by the Federal government.

## Profiling

NLC supports Federal legislation and action which eliminates discrimination in the enforcement of our criminal justice system. NLC opposes profiling of suspects based solely on race, ethnic origin, religion or other similar factors. In addition, the Federal government should assist local law enforcement agencies in their efforts to provide education and training for law enforcement officers regarding appropriate investigative and enforcement techniques.

*Source*: National League of Cities, www.nlc.org/content/Files/ 2005%20NMP%20PSCP%20Chapter%20w%20toc.pdf.

association acts as a liaison with other levels of government, works to improve public understanding of counties, serves as a national advocate for counties, and provides them with resources to help them find innovative methods to meet the challenges they face. NACo is involved in a number of special projects that deal with such issues as the environment, sustainable communities, volunteerism, and intergenerational studies.

In 2001, NACo created a "Policy Agenda to Secure the People of America's Counties." This policy paper stated that "Counties are the first responders to terrorist attacks, natural disasters and major emergencies" (National Association of Counties, 2002). NACo established a 43-member NACo Homeland Security

Task Force that, on October 23, 2001, prepared a set of 20 recommendations in four general categories concerning homeland security issues: public health, local law enforcement and intelligence, infrastructure security, and emergency planning and public safety.

Like the other municipal organizations listed earlier, NACo is vitally interested in homeland security funding issues. This interest is exemplified in its opposition to proposed cuts in state and local bioterrorism funding included in the Bush Administration's FY 2006 budget request (see Sidebar 3-7).

In February 2004, NACo surveyed several of the nation's "core counties," which are those counties that are most representative of each of the nation's high-threat urban areas included in the DHS Urban Areas

---

**SIDEBAR 3-7  Excerpts from the NACo Resolution in Support of HHS' State and Local Bioterrorism Grant Program**

The Department of Health and Human Services' State and local bioterrorism preparedness grant program comprises the foundation of an effective national strategy for preparedness and emergency response to bioterrorism. Preparedness incorporates more than the immediate response to threats such as biological and chemical terrorism; it also encompasses the broader components of public health infrastructure that provide the essential foundation for immediate and effective emergency responses.

The President's FY 2006 budget request disproportionately cuts funding for local and state governmental public health. The request would reduce the budget for the Centers for Disease Control [and Prevention] (CDC) bioterrorism preparedness funding for state and local health departments by $130 million. Additionally, the budget request proposes the complete elimination of the $131 million Preventive Health and Health Services block grant, of which about 40% goes to local entities. Overall, the

President's budget would cut CDC by over 6% and the Health Resources and Services Administration (HRSA) by over 11%. In fact, overall cuts to Federal discretionary health funding would total $1 billion and will cause widespread harm to the nation's ability to respond to future public health and terrorist threats.

County public health agencies are being asked to address a growing number of health threats and problems, including influenza, vaccine shortages and preparedness for bioterrorism. The cut of 14% in bioterrorism preparedness funding for public health departments is wholly inconsistent with national goals to improve preparedness for terrorism. Such a cut will cause counties to move backward, rather than forward, in preparing their communities for terrorist threats.

(Adopted by the NACo Board of Directors, March 7, 2005).

*Source*: National Association of Counties, www.naco.org.

Security Initiative (UASI; see Chapter 7). The survey solicited information about each county's involvement in the UASI and how well the process worked from their perspective. The results of the survey are presented in Sidebar 3-8.

## NATIONAL GOVERNORS ASSOCIATION

The National Governors Association (NGA)—the bipartisan organization of the nation's governors—promotes visionary state leadership, shares best practices, and speaks with a unified voice on national policy. Its members are the governors of the 50 states and five territories. The NGA bills itself as the collective voice of the nation's governors and one of Washington, D.C.'s most respected public policy organizations. NGA provides governors and their senior staff members with services that range from representing states on Capitol Hill and before the administration on key federal issues to developing policy reports on innovative state programs and hosting networking seminars for state government executive branch officials. The NGA Center for Best Practices focuses on state innovations and best practices on issues that range from education and health to

technology, welfare reform, and the environment. NGA also provides management and technical assistance to both new and incumbent governors.

In August 2002, the Center for Best Practices of the NGA released "States' Homeland Security Priorities." A list of 10 major priorities and issues was identified by the NGA center through a survey of states and territories state homeland security offices (NGA Center for Best Practices, 2002). These priorities clearly illustrated the main concerns of the state leadership in regards in light of the massive changes that were occurring at the federal level, and included the following:

- Coordination must involve all levels of government;
- The Federal government must disseminate timely intelligence information to the states;
- The states must work with local governments to develop interoperable communications between first responders, and adequate wireless spectrum must be set aside to do the job;
- State and local governments need help and technical assistance to identify and protect critical infrastructure;
- Both the states and Federal government must focus on enhancing bioterrorism preparedness

---

### SIDEBAR 3-8   Excerpts from NACo UASI Survey Report

During FY 2003, the DHS Office of Domestic Preparedness (ODP) created the Urban Areas Security Initiative (UASI). This initiative is designed to combat terrorism in the United States by targeting Federal funding to high threat urban areas. These areas have been determined to be high threats because they house significant national, state or business infrastructure, governmental systems and population centers and are considered most vulnerable to terrorist attacks. Each urban area is made up of a core city and county and includes jurisdictions

that are contiguous and have established formal mutual aid agreements.

A core county is where the core city of the urban area is located. The funds were to address the unique equipment, training, planning, exercise and operation needs of these large urban areas. After the designation of the 30 urban high threat areas, each state worked with ODP to complete the process to determine the allocation for each urban area. The funds were then awarded to the states, each of which was responsible, through its State

Administrative Agency, for managing the submission of assessments and strategies from each urban area that was eligible to receive funds.

In mid-February 2004, the National Association of Counties sent a survey to the core county in each of these high threat urban areas. This survey was designed to find out whether these targeted areas were receiving these much needed funds. In addition, the survey asked each responding county to comment on how the funding distribution process has worked in their states. Fifteen core counties completed the survey, representing 12 of the 20 states that had been awarded at that time.

### Findings

Core counties were asked if their states had kept them well informed about the process it followed to submit a plan to the ODP to make their urban area eligible for UASI funds.

- **One hundred percent** of responding core counties, except Washington, DC, responded yes to that question.
- When asked if the core county participated in discussions with their states about the distribution of these funds, **80 percent** of responding core counties report discussions with their states.
- Of the 3 core counties that indicated that they did not participate, all were in states where another core county responded that they had participated in such discussions. The states are California, Ohio and Texas.

Core counties were next asked it they had participated in discussions with the other participating local governments in their high threat area. All 15 responding counties (**100%**) report having these discussions.

Core counties were asked what percentage of the funds was asked for each of the four major expenditure areas.

- Of the four, training, exercises, equipment and planning, in **80 percent** of the core counties the largest percentage of the funds was requested for equipment. These requests ranged from a low of **30 percent** to a high of **100 percent**.
- Only Miami-Dade County and Multnomah County requested that the largest percentage of their funds be in the area of training.

Core counties were asked if they had received any of their UASI funds as of the date of their response to this survey.

- **Forty-seven percent** of responding counties responded yes.
- **Fifty-three percent** responded that they have not.
- These amounts ranged from a high of $18.5 million down to $40,000.
- When asked what percentage of the anticipated funds they had received, **81 percent** report receiving from **0 to 25 percent**.
- Only San Francisco County reports receiving **100 percent** of its funds, which amount to more than $18.5 million.
- Only **47 percent** of the core counties, representing 6 states, say that the state has appropriated its own funds to assist with homeland security efforts.
- **Thirty-three percent** of core counties did not know whether their states had appropriated these funds.

Among the core counties, **73 percent** report that they have used their own general operating funds to enhance homeland security efforts. **One hundred percent** of the core counties report that the planning and funding process for the UASI grant program has better prepared their counties for responding to a terrorist threat.

*Source*: National Association of Counties, www.naco.org/ContentManagement/ContentDisplay.cfm?ContentID=16077.

and rebuilding the nation's public health system to address 21st century threats;

- The Federal government should provide adequate Federal funding and support to ensure that homeland security needs are met;
- The Federal government should work with states to protect sensitive security information, including restricting access to information available through "freedom of information" requests;
- An effective system must be developed that secures points of entry at borders, airports, and seaports without placing an undue burden on commerce;
- The National Guard has proven itself to be an effective force during emergencies and crises. The mission of the National Guard should remain flexible, and Guard units should primarily remain under the control of the governor during times of crises;
- Federal agencies should integrate their command systems into existing state and local incident command systems (ICS) rather than requiring state and local agencies to adapt to Federal command systems.

*Source*: NGA Center for Best Practices, Issue Brief, August 19, 2002.

The NGA Center for Best Practices (NGAC) provides support to the governors in their management of new homeland security challenges as they arise and the overall homeland security domain that exists as a result of September 11. NGAC provides these officials with technical assistance and policy research and facilitates their participation in national discussions and initiatives. Center activities focus on states' efforts to protect critical infrastructure, develop interoperable communications capabilities, and prepare for and respond to bioterrorism, agroterrorism, nuclear and radiological terrorism, and cyber terrorism (as it impacts the government's ability to obtain, disseminate, and store essential information). The NGA does recognize that, while terrorism must be a priority, natural and man-made disasters will continue to demand timely and coordinated responses from local, state, and federal government agencies.

The National Governor's Association position on homeland security is presented in Sidebar 3-9.

In August 2004, the NGA conducted a survey of state and territorial homeland security directors. A summary of the survey results is presented in the NGA Issues Brief covered in Sidebar 3-10.

## NATIONAL EMERGENCY MANAGEMENT ASSOCIATION

The National Emergency Management Association (NEMA) is a nonpartisan, nonprofit association that works to enhance public safety. NEMA is focused on the all-hazards approach to emergency management. NEMA began in 1974 when state directors of emergency services first united in order to exchange information on common emergency management issues in their constituencies. State emergency management directors form the core membership, but members also include key state staff, homeland security advisers, federal agencies, nonprofit organizations, private-sector companies, and concerned individuals.

NEMA's mission is to:

- Provide national leadership and expertise in comprehensive emergency management.
- Serve as a vital emergency management information and assistance resource.
- Advance continuous improvement in emergency management through strategic partnerships, innovative programs, and collaborative policy positions.

Following September 11, NEMA created the National Homeland Security Consortium, which includes key state and local organizations, elected officials, the private sector, and others with roles and responsibilities for homeland security prevention, preparedness, response, and recovery activities. Participating organizations began meeting in 2002. The consortium is an outgrowth of those initial discussions regarding the need for enhanced communication and

## SIDEBAR 3-9   NGA Position on Homeland Security

Although the Constitution delegates to Congress the power and responsibility to provide for the common defense, most of the responsibility for providing homeland defense rests with state and local governments. Governors, with the support of the Federal government and local jurisdictions, are responsible for ensuring the ability of state, territorial, and local authorities to deal with natural disasters and other types of major emergencies, including a terrorist incident. State homeland security efforts (infrastructure assets, people resources, and coordination) are critical components of the National Strategy for Homeland Security.

NGA policy and positions with regard to Homeland Security issues are guided by the following principles:

- There should be a base capacity in every state, which means that every state should receive some funds.
- The Department of Homeland Security should provide guidance to states for developing equipment and training standards for adequate levels of protection and preparedness.

- There should be flexibility in the allowable uses of grant funds.
- Governors and other high-ranking state and territorial officials need to receive timely and critical intelligence information related to terrorist threats.
- The traditional first responder programs that existed prior to September 11, 2001 should continue to be funded.
- There should be predictable and sustainable long-term funding of homeland security programs.
- All Federal funding, resources, programs and activities involving state and local governments must be coordinated through the nation's Governors for maximum effectiveness and efficiency.
- The role of the business community and the impact on the economic viability of a community when faced with recovery from a terrorist attack must be considered.

*Source*: National Governor's Association, www.nga.org/nga/lobbyIssues/1,1169,D_4898,00.html.

---

coordination between disciplines and levels of government. The consortium is now recognized by DHS and works in partnership with other federal agencies such as the Centers for Disease Control and Prevention. The mission of the consortium is to provide a forum wherein key ideas on homeland security can be shared among and between different levels of government.

### Terrorism-Related Activity among State Emergency Managers

A good indicator of the manner in which each of the state governments approaches the terrorism issue

is the priorities set by their emergency managers. A survey of state homeland security structures by NEMA conducted in June 2002 found that all 50 states maintain primary point of contact for antiterrorism/homeland security efforts. At that time, these contacts were located in the following state government offices:

- Governor's office—12 states
- Military/adjutant general—12 states
- Emergency management—10 states
- Public safety—9 states
- Law enforcement—3 states
- Attorney general—2 states

## SIDEBAR 3-10   NGA Survey Results

An NGA homeland security survey was completed in August 2004 by 38 of the 55 state and territorial homeland security directors. The survey found homeland security has quickly become a bipartisan priority for governors across the nation. In the weeks, months and years since Sept. 11, states have rallied to plan, coordinate and implement a number of initiatives to prevent and respond to terrorist acts. States have also expanded their internal security capacity and worked with Federal and local partners toward building a comprehensive network of resources to implement homeland security initiatives.

Despite a general lack of precedent to assist their work, states have made great strides in protecting their borders and preventing future attacks. While each state homeland security strategy is tailored to specific needs, the survey found several like-minded strategies have been employed, including:

- Establishing statewide emergency operations centers (100 percent of respondents);
- Designing exercises to train first responders while identifying weaknesses in agency response plans (98 percent);
- Focusing attention on bioterrorism preparedness and acting to amend policies and laws

related to isolation and quarantine practices (95 percent); and
- Developing mutual assistance agreements with neighboring states for sharing National Guard resources, equipment and personnel (94 percent).

The survey also polled states to determine their top 10 priorities—those which still need to be addressed to meet the homeland security challenges facing states in the future. States identified the following top three priorities:

- Achieving interoperability—the ability for emergency responders to communicate with one another during an incident;
- Enhancing states' ability to collect, analyze and disseminate intelligence by creating "fusion centers" for intelligence sharing among Federal, state, and local government was the second priority; and
- Protecting critical infrastructure, including identifying and protecting essential daily functions such as telecommunications, transportation and banking.

*Source*: National Governors Association, www.nga.org/center/divisions/1,1188,C_ISSUE_BRIEF^D_7987,00.html.

- Lieutenant governor—2 states
- Land commissioner—1 state

*Source*: National Conference of State Legislatures, 2005.

As of July 2005, these numbers had changed, reflecting a more thought-out approach to placement of these officials in the overall context of state government affairs. Many states had even created dedicated homeland security offices. These figures are as follows:

- Office of Homeland Security—14 states
- Public safety/law enforcement—14 states
- Emergency management—9 states
- Military/adjutant general—7 states
- Governor's office—2 states
- Attorney general—2 states
- Lt. governor—1 state
- Counterterrorism Office—1 state

On October 1, 2001, NEMA released a "White Paper on Domestic Preparedness" that was supported by the Adjutants Generals Association of the United States, the International Association of Emergency Managers (which represents local emergency management officials), and the National Guard Association of America. The document states that "NEMA thinks it critical that the following enhancements be incorporated into a nationwide strategy for catastrophic disaster preparedness" (National Emergency Management Association, 2001). A total of 22 enhancements were presented in the white paper in three general categories: emergency preparedness and response, health and medical, and additional WMD recommendations. A partial list of these enhancements is presented in Sidebar 3-11.

The NEMA white paper presents "enhancements" that address coordination, communications, command, information sharing, funding, technology, and public health system and preparedness issues. Also included were the use of National Guard assets and increasing the capabilities of state–local urban search and rescue. Expanding the FEMA Fire Grant program and establishment of a standardized national donations protocol were also included in the paper.

Many states are moving ahead in terrorism and homeland security planning and other activities. A report compiled by the White House Office of Homeland Security (2002) found activities in many states,

---

**SIDEBAR 3-11   Partial List of Enhancements Presented in the NEMA Paper on Domestic Preparedness**

**Emergency Preparedness and Response**

- Congress should provide to the states immediate Federal funding for full-time catastrophic disaster coordinators in moderate and high-risk local jurisdictions of the United States. *(did happen)*
- States need financial assistance to improve catastrophic response and Continuity of Operations Plans (COOP) and Continuity of Government (COG) for states. *(did happen)*
- Interstate and intrastate mutual assistance must be recognized and supported by the Federal government as an expedient, cost-effective approach to disaster response and recovery. *(recognized in the NRP)*
- FEMA, state, and local emergency managers must implement renewed emphasis on family and community preparedness to ensure Americans have the skills necessary to survive a catastrophic disaster. *(did happen)*
- A standardized national donations management protocol is needed to address the outpouring of food, clothing, supplies, and

other items that are commonly sent to impacted states localities following a disaster. *(addressed in the NRP)*

**Health and Medical**

- The medical surge capacity must be strengthened. The emergency management, medical, and public health professions must work with lawmakers to ensure each region of our nation has a certain minimum surge capacity to deal with mass casualty events. *(in process)*
- State–local disaster medical assistance teams should be developed across the country, with standardized equipment, personnel, and training. *(in process)*

**Additional WMD Recommendations**

- The Department of Justice should immediately release the FY00 and FY01 equipment funds in order to begin implementation of these recommendations and then require a basic statewide strategy in order to receive FY02 funds; and further, provide funding to states to administer the equipment program. *(equipment funds now handled by DHS)*

- Congress and the Department of Defense should authorize homeland defense as a key Federal defense mission tasking for the National Guard. State and local Urban Search and Rescue capabilities should be developed across the country, with the standardized equipment, personnel, and training. *(did happen)*
- National interagency and intergovernmental information management protocols are needed to support information sharing (i.e., damage/situation reports, warning/intelligence reports, resource coordination). *(in process)*
- Better Federal interagency coordination is needed to assist states in identifying and accessing the full range of Federal resources and assistance available to them. *(has happened through the DHS Office of State and Local Coordination and Preparedness)*
- FEMA's fire grant program should be expanded and modified to strengthen regional and national, not just local, fire protection capabilities to respond to catastrophic disasters. *(has not happened)*
- There is a need for technology transfer from the Federal government and technology contractors to state and local governments to support an automated decision support system. *(has not happened)*

*Source*: National Emergency Management Association, "White Paper of Domestic Preparedness, October 1, 2001.

cities, and counties in the following four general areas:

- Developing plans
- Information sharing
- Responding to biological threats
- Protecting critical infrastructure

## INTERNATIONAL ASSOCIATION OF EMERGENCY MANAGERS

The International Association of Emergency Managers (IAEM) is a nonprofit organization dedicated to promoting the goals of saving lives and protecting property during emergencies and disasters. Founded in 1952 as the U.S. Civil Defense Council, it became the National Coordinating Council on Emergency Management in 1985, and changed its name to the International Association of Emergency Managers in 1998.

The association brings together emergency managers and disaster response professionals from all levels of government, as well as the military, the private sector, and volunteer organizations in the United States and around the world. The purpose of IAEM is to serve the emergency management community by:

- Encouraging the development of disaster-resistant communities to reduce the effect of disasters on life and property
- Acting as a clearinghouse for information on comprehensive management issues
- Providing a forum for creative and innovative problem solving on emergency management issues
- Maintaining and expanding standards for emergency management programs and professionals
- Fostering informed decision making on public policy in the emergency management arena

The IAEM often issues policy briefs that relay the position of the nation's and the world's emergency managers, about salient issues being debated or considered in Congress. An example of one of these position papers, issued in early 2005, is provided in Sidebar 3-12.

**SIDEBAR 3-12  IAEM Position Paper on Emergency Management
Performance Grants, 2005**

**Issue**: President's 06 Budget Request for the Department of Homeland Security for EMPG

- Cuts the funding from 05 appropriated $180,000,000 to $170,000,000.
- Does not retain the program as a separate account.

**Action Requested**: Increase the funding to $280 million and maintain as a separate account.

- The program has been underfunded for decades.
- The current estimate of the shortfall is $264 million. A $100 million increase would begin to address the shortfall.

- Emergency performance management grants, called "the backbone of nation's emergency management system" in an Appropriations Conference Report, constitute the only source of direct federal funding for state and local governments to provide basic emergency coordination and planning capabilities including those related to homeland security. This is a shared cost.
- We need to be building capacity not reducing it.

*Source*: IAEM,
www.iaem.com/resources/ADVOCACY/postionpapers.htm.

## LOCAL GOVERNMENT TERRORISM ACTIVITIES

Emergency preparedness, mitigation, response, and recovery all occur at the local community level. It is at the local level that the critical planning, communications, technology, coordination, command, and spending decisions matter the most. The priorities of groups such as the National Conference of Mayors and the National Association of Counties are to represent these very concerns shared by local communities about what is necessary for them to become resilient from the threat of terrorism. The drive toward a reduction in vulnerability from terrorism has spawned a series of new requirements in preparedness and mitigation planning for most local-level officials that, prior to September 11, rarely considered such issues.

Both NACo and the USCM policy papers identified issues in the areas of command, coordination, communications, funding and equipment, training, and mutual aid. These two organizations recognized

and proclaimed the local concerns about protecting critical community infrastructure, including the public health system, most of which is maintained and secured at the local level by local government law enforcement, fire, and health officials.

The events of September 11 brought to the surface the notion that the security of community infrastructure, which was suddenly recognized as a potential target for terrorist attacks, was vital to the security of the nation as a whole. Community infrastructure has always been vulnerable to natural and other technological disaster events—so much so that FEMA's largest disaster assistance program, Public Assistance, is designed to fund the rebuilding of community infrastructure damaged by a disaster event. However, local government officials and local emergency managers were suddenly finding themselves dedicating a greatly increased amount of funding and personnel to protecting and securing community infrastructure from the increased threat of terrorist attack. They have also had to boost the abilities of the local public health system, which has been recognized by the federal government as the most likely area where an outbreak caused by a bioterrorism agent will be identified.

To illustrate several of the new issues that local governments, most notably the smaller, rural governments, have had to consider in light of the new terrorist threat, the following checklist designed for the City of Boone, North Carolina, is provided. This checklist is excerpted from that municipality's technological annex developed for the town's All-Hazards Planning and Operations Manual in March 2002:

- Identify the types of terrorist events that might occur in the community.
- Plan emergency activities in advance to ensure a coordinated response to terrorist attacks.
- Build capabilities necessary to respond effectively to the consequences of terrorism.
- Identify the type or nature of a terrorist attack when it does happen.
- Implement the planned response quickly and efficiently.
- Recover from the incident.

The response to terrorism is similar in many ways to that of other natural or man-made disasters for which Boone has already prepared. Through additions and modifications, the development of a completely separate system could be avoided. Training and public education have been vital to enhancing preparedness, and understanding the process by which available federal financial assistance is acquired has drastically increased local capacity. The following are the general types of activities that Boone has needed to take to meet the above-mentioned objectives:

- Strengthen information and communications technology.
- Establish a well-defined incident command structure that includes the FBI.
- Strengthen local working relationships and communications.
- Educate health care and emergency response communities about identification of bioterrorist attacks and agents.

- Educate health care and emergency response community about medical treatment and prophylaxis for possible biological agents.
- Educate local health department about state and federal requirements and assistance.
- Maintain locally accessible supply of medications, vaccines, and supplies.
- Address health-care-worker safety issues.
- Designate a spokesperson to maintain contact with the public.
- Develop comprehensive evacuation plans.
- Become familiar with state and local laws relating to isolation/quarantine.
- Develop or enhance local capability to prosecute crimes involving WMD or the planning of terrorism events.
- Develop, maintain, and practice an infectious diseases emergency response plan.
- Practice with surrounding jurisdictions to strengthen mutual agreement plans.
- Outline the roles of federal agency assistance in planning and response.
- Educate the public in recognizing events and ways to respond as individuals.
- Stay current.

*Source:* Town of Boone. 2002. *All-Hazards Planning and Operations Manual, Technological Hazards Annex.* Boone, NC: Town of Boone (March).

## CONCLUSION

Emergency management in the United States was forever changed by the events of September 11, 2001, and many would say for the better. This opinion is in wide dispute, however, for a variety of reasons that are unique to each successive level of government, primarily in terms of a loss of dedication to more traditional, nonterrorism hazards. Regardless, it is undeniable that emergency management, and now homeland security, have been thrust to the forefront of the public and the policy agendas, and are one of many primary concerns of federal, state, and local administrators.

For local governments, terrorism is a new threat that greatly expands their already strained safety and security requirements, and adds to a long list of needs and priorities. But the threat of terrorism is one that cannot be ignored, and state and local governments have not done so. At these local levels, the drastic increase in funding that has provided training and equipment to local first responders has been greeted with mixed emotion. Many recipients feel it has remained singular in focus, addressing mainly the terrorism threat. Historically, and including the 2001 terrorist attacks, natural disasters have taken many more lives and have caused much more financial harm. These natural and technological hazards will continue to pose a threat and will continue to result in disaster. It is undeniable that a more comprehensive approach to building the capacity of the local government to respond would provide more long-term benefits. Whether or not these local government agencies will be better prepared overall remains to be seen.

At the state level, governors and state emergency management directors have resisted the push toward local control, and have been accused on many occasions of holding out federal homeland security funding from the local governments for which it was intended. In many circumstances it was determined that these accusations were correct. But state officials feel the same concerns about the terrorist threat as do the locals, and have called for better coordination, new communications technologies, and, as always, more and more funding.

At the federal government level, the changes that have resulted with regard to emergency management have been the most visible—and the most dramatic. The creation in 2002 of the Department of Homeland Security, which absorbed FEMA and most of the former federal government disaster management programs, has resulted in DHS taking the lead in addressing these new issues. This new agency has been tested on several occasions, as will be displayed throughout this text, and has enjoyed relatively mixed but primarily positive success. Under the leadership of DHS, many federal disaster response, recovery, and mitigation programs have so far fared well, though their priorities have seen a drastic shift to accommodate the new terrorist concern. In general, the United States has taken the typical response to a new problem in that it reorganized and committed huge amounts of funding to reducing the newly recognized problem.

Sidebar 3-13 lists websites where additional information about the organizations discussed in this chapter can be found.

---

**SIDEBAR 3-13   Select Websites for Additional Information**

AmeriCorps: www.americorps.org

Animal and Plant Health Inspection Service: www.aphis.usda.gov

Citizen Corps: www.citizencorps.gov

Corporation for National and Community Service: www.nationalservice.org

Department of Homeland Security: www.dhs.gov

Federal Emergency Management Agency: www.fema.gov

Immigration and Nationalization Service: www.ins.gov

Medical Reserve Corps: www.medicalreservecorps.gov

Office for Domestic Preparedness: www.ojp.usdoj.gov/odp

Office for National Preparedness: www.fema.gov/onp

National Association of Counties: www.naco.org

National Governors Association: www.nga.org

National League of Cities: www.nlc.org

Neighborhood Watch: www.usaonwatch.org

Senior Corps: www.seniorcorps.org

Transportation Security Administration: www.tsa.dot.gov

United States Coast Guard: www.uscg.mil

United States Conference of Mayors: www.usmayors.org

United States Customs Service: www.customs.ustreas.gov

United States Secret Service: www.ustreas.gov/usss/

U.S.A. Freedom Corps: www.usafreedomcorps.gov

Volunteers in Police Service: www.policevolunteers.org

## REVIEW QUESTIONS

1. What is the principal role of emergency management in homeland security? Identify the other major players and their roles in homeland security.

2. Identify the five principal directorates of the Department of Homeland Security and discuss their respective missions.

3. Discuss the role of federal agencies other than DHS in homeland security.

4. Make the case for retaining an all-hazards approach to emergency management that includes terrorism and its associated hazards as one of many hazards. Discuss the pros and cons of such an approach as it relates to all four phases of emergency management: mitigation, preparedness, response, and recovery.

5. If you had been in charge of establishing the Department of Homeland Security (DHS), would you have included the Federal Emergency Management Agency in DHS or would you have retained it as an independent executive branch agency reporting directly to the president? Discuss the possible ramifications of moving FEMA into DHS in terms of FEMA's mission, programs, and reporting structure. The director of FEMA no longer reports directly to the president; will this be a problem in future natural and terrorist related disasters? What will the impact of FEMA's inclusion in DHS be on the nation's emergency management system?

## REFERENCES

National Association of Counties (NACo). 2002. "Counties and Homeland Security: Policy Agenda to Secure the People of America's Counties." Washington, DC: NACo (August). <http://www.naco.org/programs/homesecurity?policyplan.cfm>

National Association of Counties. 2004. "Homeland Security Funding—The Urban Areas Security Initiative: A Survey Report." <www.naco.org/ContentManagement/ContentDisplay.cfm?ContentID=16077>

National Association of Counties. 2005. "Resolution in Support of HHS' State and Local Bioterrorism Grant Program" (March 7). <www.naco.org/Template.cfm?Section=homeland_security&

template=/ContentManagement/ContentDisplay.cfm&ContentID=15321>

National Conference of State Legislatures. 2005. "State Offices of Homeland Security." <www.ncsl.org/programs/legman/nlssa/sthomelandoffcs.htm>

National Emergency Management Association. 2001. "White Paper on Domestic Preparedness" (October 1). www.nemaweb.org

National Emergency Management Association. 2002. "NEMA Reports on State Homeland Security Structures" (June). <www.nemaweb.org/ShowExtendedNewscfm? ID=171>

National Governors Association. 2003. "EC-5. Homeland Security Comprehensive Policy." <www.nga.org/nga/legislativeUp-date/1,1169,C_POLICY_POSITION^D_5102,00.html>

National Governors Association. 2005. "Homeland Security: NGA Position." <www.nga.org/nga/lobbyIssues/1,1169,D_4898,00.html>

National Governors Association. 2005. "Issue Brief: Homeland Security in the States: Much Progress, More Work" (January 24). <www.nga.org/cda/files/0502homesec.pdf>

National Governors Association. 2005. "Survey: States Make Strides in Homeland Security, Challenges Remain." <www.nga.org/center/divisions/1,1188,C_ISSUE_BRIEF^D_7987,00.html>

National Governors Association Center for Best Practices (NGAC). 2002. "Issue Brief: States' Homeland Security Priorities." Washington, DC: NGAC (August 19).

National League of Cities. 2005. "2005 Advocacy Priority—The Issue: Funding for First Responders." <www.nlc.org/content/Files/PFRHomeland%20Security1.pdf>

National League of Cities. 2005. "2005 National Municipal Policy." <www.nlc.org/content/Files/2005%20NMP%20PSCP%20Chapter%20w%20toc.pdf>

U.S. Conference of Mayors. 2001. "A National Action Plan for Safety and Security in America's Cities" (December). <www.usmayors.org/uscm/home.asp>

U.S. Conference of Mayors. 2003. "Homeland Security Report: 90 Percent of Cities Left Without Funds from Largest Federal Homeland Security Program" (September 29). <www.usmayors.org/uscm/us_mayor_newspaper/documents/09_29_03/homeland_report.asp>

U.S. Conference of Mayors. 2004a. "Executive Director's Column" (March 12). <www.usmayors.org/uscm/us_mayor_newspaper/documents/03_15_04/cochran.asp>

U.S. Conference of Mayors. 2004b. "2004 Adopted Resolutions 72nd Annual Meeting Boston." <www.usmayors.org/uscm/resolutions/72nd_conference/csj_01.asp>

# 4

# Terrorist-Related Hazards

## INTRODUCTION

For most of the nation's municipalities, urban and rural alike, the threat or risk posed by terrorism has introduced an expanded set of hazards. These new hazards fall into four principal categories often referred to by the acronym CBRNE: chemical, biological, radiological/nuclear, and explosive. These CBRNE hazards must now be considered in concert with the myriad traditional natural and technological hazards such as hurricanes, tornadoes, floods, earthquakes, fires, hazardous materials transportation and storage accidents, power outages, and releases at nuclear power plants.

There are two significant differences between these new hazards and the more traditional ones. First, much is known about the traditional hazards as a result of years of research, actual occurrence, and response and recovery from these hazards. We can now predict with a fair amount of accuracy the track of a hurricane. We know enough about the destructive force of a tornado to design and build safe rooms. We have spent the better part of a century trying, with increasing success, to control flooding. We have developed building codes and standards that protect structures from earthquakes, fires, and wind damage.

We have enough experience in responding to disaster events caused by these hazards to ensure that our first responders have effective protective gear and are trained and exercised in the best response protocols and practices.

While research is ongoing and new practices continue to be discovered, the emergency management community in this country is well trained and experienced in dealing with the long list of traditional hazard events. This is not the case with the new hazards presented by the terrorist threat. Knowledge of the properties and the destructive qualities of the various chemical and biological threats is limited at best, even in the agencies charged with knowing the most about these hazards. The first responder community, the state and local emergency managers, and the general public remain almost completely uninformed about these hazards, and have little or no experience in facing their consequences. The same is largely true with community and national leaders, and the news media.

It took decades of research and practice for all parties to become fluent in the traditional mix of natural and technological disasters. Not surprisingly, it will take time before we all can reach a comfort level with our knowledge of the new hazards.

The second notable difference between the traditional and new terrorism hazards is the manner in which we come to encounter each. Traditional hazards occur because of natural processes, whether geological, meteorological, or hydrological, or because of some human accident, oversight, or negligence. Hurricanes, tornadoes, and earthquakes are inherently natural hazard events that have occurred for eons, regardless of the presence of humans. Hazardous materials spills, releases at nuclear power plants, and transportation accidents, for example, have traditionally been just that—accidents. The new terrorism hazards differ from these natural and technological hazards in that their genesis is intentional, and their primary purpose is death and destruction. These hazards are weapons in every sense of the word, unique in that they primarily target civilian populations instead of military assets, and they are used specifically to advance political, ideological, or religious agendas. No hurricane or earthquake has ever advanced a human agenda.

## DIFFICULTY OF PREDICTING TERROR ATTACKS IN THE UNITED STATES

A risk index published on August 18, 2003, by the World Markets Research Center (WMRC), a business intelligence firm based in London, ranked the United States fourth among the top five countries most likely to be targeted for a terrorist attack within the 12-month period that followed (www.wmrc.com). The index also predicted that "another September 11-style terrorist attack in the United States is highly likely." Colombia, Israel, and Pakistan ranked in the top three positions, respectively. After the United States, the Philippines, Afghanistan, Indonesia, Iraq, India, and Britain, which tied with Sri Lanka, rounded out the top ten. North Korea ranked as the least likely country to experience a terrorist attack within the next year. The index assessed the risk of terrorism to some 186 countries and their interests based on five criteria: "motivation of terrorists; the presence of terror groups; the scale and frequency of past attacks; effi-

cacy of the groups in carrying out attacks; and how many attacks were thwarted by the country." Explaining the U.S. ranking, the index stated that while the presence of militant Islamic networks within the United States is less extensive than in Western Europe, "U.S.-led military action in Afghanistan and Iraq has exacerbated anti-U.S. sentiment." (*Source*: *Homeland Security Monitor*, August 19, 2003)

This rank designation made issues such as detection, containment, control, quarantine, and vaccination—to name just a few—significant factors in developing new response and recovery practices for first responders. Political affairs and events across the globe have factored heavily in efforts to prepare populations and to mitigate the impacts of these new hazards on those populations and on critical infrastructure, communities, economies, and the normality of daily life.

During the months that followed the WMRC risk prediction, the actual incidence of terrorism followed drastically different patterns than expected. These differences highlight the difficulty of predicting intentional hazards such as terrorism that are dynamic and respond to social, political, economic, and other anthropologically generated factors. Table 4-1 presents a list of terrorist events that occurred between February 2004 and February 2005, adapted from an AON Corporation study. This table illustrates how great uncertainty factors into any terrorism risk prediction.

The lack of knowledge about these new hazards and the fact that they will be used deliberately to attack us has resulted in the perception by nearly all Americans that they are potential terrorist victims. (See Sidebar 4-1.) Unlike hurricanes or tornadoes, which tend to have geographical boundaries, the terrorist threat and the new hazards must be considered national risks. People in Montana do not worry about hurricanes, and it rarely floods in the desert of Nevada. There have been few if any tornadoes reported in Maine. But all people consider themselves, however remotely, potential victims of terrorism, and the reality of the new hazards only reinforces this risk perception. A list of selected chemical, biological,

TABLE 4-1   **Top 40 Countries Ranked by Number of Terrorist Attacks from February 2004 through February 2005**

| Rank | Country | Number of attacks | Rank | Country | Number of attacks |
|---|---|---|---|---|---|
| 1 | Iraq | 2,922 | 21 | China | 16 |
| 2 | Israel/Palestine | 1,242 | 22 | Yemen | 14 |
| 3 | India | 512 | 23 | France | 13 |
| 4 | Nepal | 388 | 24 | Lebanon | 11 |
| 5 | Russia | 346 | 24 | Greece | 11 |
| 6 | Pakistan | 282 | 26 | Serbia & Montenegro | 10 |
| 7 | Afghanistan | 145 | 27 | Georgia | 9 |
| 8 | Thailand | 97 | 28 | Sudan | 7 |
| 9 | Bangladesh | 90 | 28 | Somalia | 7 |
| 10 | Turkey | 73 | 28 | Germany | 7 |
| 11 | Algeria | 50 | 28 | Bulgaria | 7 |
| 12 | Philippines | 43 | 32 | Uzbekistan | 6 |
| 13 | Colombia | 38 | 32 | Ukraine | 6 |
| 14 | United Kingdom | 37 | 32 | Kuwait | 6 |
| 15 | Saudi Arabia | 34 | 32 | Myanmar | 6 |
| 16 | Indonesia | 33 | 32 | Bosnia | 6 |
| 17 | Sri Lanka | 31 | 37 | Madagascar | 5 |
| 18 | United States | 27 | 37 | Laos | 5 |
| 19 | Spain | 23 | 37 | Kazakhstan | 5 |
| 20 | Italy | 17 | 37 | Czech Republic | 5 |

*Source*: AON Corporation, *2005 Terrorism Risk Map.*

radiological, and nuclear incidents compiled by the Central Intelligence Agency (CIA) is presented in Sidebar 4-2.

The first step in reducing this fear is to better understand these new hazards and how individuals, communities, and countries can deal with them. The purpose of this chapter is to present basic information concerning the four new CBRNE hazards. Most of this information has been taken from the websites and reports maintained and prepared by the Centers for Disease Control and Prevention (CDC) and the Federal Emergency Management Agency (FEMA). In many cases, the authors have reprinted the information provided by the CDC, FEMA, and others in its original form in order to present the most accurate and succinct information for each hazard.

## SIDEBAR 4-1   Where Will Terrorists Strike? Different Theories . . .

One of the greatest problems facing the new Department of Homeland Security is trying to determine where terrorists will strike next. Major U.S. cities are considered the most likely targets for terrorist attacks, as evidenced by risk-based funding for terrorism that has clearly targeted urban centers with the greatest amount of counterterrorism related funding. There are, however, opinions that conflict with this majority assessment.

In 2003, Deputy Secretary of Health and Human Services Claude Allen stated that rural America should be considered among the most likely sites for the next terror attack in the United States, especially a bioterrorism attack. Deputy Secretary Allen stated that "Some rural communities are among the most vulnerable to attack, simply because of their proximity to a missile silo or to a chemical stockpile. Other rural communities are vulnerable simply because they mistakenly believe that terrorism is an urban problem and they are safe from attack." While Allen said the federal government has increased funding for bioterrorism preparedness, he also noted that rural areas are vulnerable given their "limited infrastructure for public health as well as fewer health care providers and volunteer systems."

In March 2004, CSO Online, an industry journal for security executives, conducted a survey that asked where in the United States terrorists would likely strike next. The results of the poll indicated that these industry experts felt the next target would be the airline industry (3%), a seaport (7%), a large public event (23%), an urban mass transit system (27%), or a "different and unexpected target" (41%). Considering the efforts that are under way to block an attack on known or expected targets, it would follow in this line of thinking that terrorists would seek to exploit an unknown target that would likely be "soft," or more vulnerable to attack. Citing another major area of vulnerability, a Princeton University research group found that most Internet experts feel that a devastating cyber-attack will occur within the next 10 years, possibly affecting business, utilities, banking, communications, and other Internet-dependent components of society.

On June 23, 2005, the U.S. Senate Foreign Relations Committee released a report stating that there was a 50% chance of a major, WMD-based attack, between 2005 and 2010, somewhere in the world. The report was based on a poll of 85 national security and nonproliferation experts. The reports found that the risks of biological or chemical attacks were comparable to or slightly higher than the risk of a nuclear attack, but that there is a "significantly higher" risk of a radiological attack.

*Sources: Homeland Security Monitor, August 28, 2003; ClickZ Network, January 9, 2005; CSO Online, March 25, 2004, Associated Press, June 23, 2005.*

---

SIDEBAR 4-2   **Selected Examples of Chemical, Biological, Radiological, and Nuclear Incidents**

- *February 2004:* U.S. Senate Majority Leader Bill Frist received a letter containing ricin powder. Several staff members needed decontamination, but no injuries or fatalities occurred as result of the attack.
- *October 2003:* A metallic container was discovered at a Greenville, South Carolina, postal facility with ricin in it. The small container was in an envelope along with a threatening note. Authorities did not believe this was a terrorism-related incident. The note expressed anger against regulations overseeing the trucking industry.
- *August 2002:* Ansar al-Islam, a Sunni militant group, was reported to have tested ricin powder as an aerosol on animals such as donkeys and chickens and perhaps even an unwitting

human subject. No more specific details have been released.

- *February 2002:* Italian authorities arrested as many as nine Moroccan nationals who may have been plotting to poison the water supply of the U.S. embassy in Rome. Authorities confiscated a detailed map of Rome's underground water system, highlighting the location of the U.S. embassy's pipes. The suspects also had 4 kilograms of potassium ferrocyanide in their possession.

- *December 2001:* According to press reporting, the military wing of HAMAS (Palestinian Islamic Resistance Movement) claimed that the bolts and nails packed into explosives detonated by a suicide bomber had been dipped into rat poison.

- *October 2001:* U.S. and international law enforcement authorities stepped up investigations in the United States and abroad to determine the sources of confirmed cases of anthrax exposures in Florida, New York, and Washington, D.C. In the past several years, there have been hundreds of hoaxes involving anthrax in the United States. In the aftermath of the September 11 terrorist attacks against the United States, these anthrax scares have spread across the globe and have exacerbated international concerns. The confirmed anthrax cases involved letters sent through the mail to the U.S. Congress and several media organizations. More than 50 individuals were exposed to *B. anthracis* spores, including 18 who became infected, and 5 people died from inhalation anthrax—the first reported cases in the United States in 25 years. U.S. and international health organizations have treated thousands of individuals associated with these incidents.

- *September 2001:* Colombian police accused the Revolutionary Armed Forces of Colombia (FARC) of using improvised grenades filled with poisonous gas during an attack on the city of San Adolfo in the Huila Department. According to media accounts, four policemen died and another six suffered respiratory problems from the attack.

- *January 2000:* According to press reports, a Russian general accused Chechen rebels of delivering poisoned wine and canned fruit to Russian soldiers in Chechnya.

- *November 1999:* Raw materials for making ricin were seized by law-enforcement authorities during the arrest of a U.S. citizen who threatened to poison two Colorado judges.

- *June 1998:* U.S. law enforcement authorities arrested two members of the violent secessionist group called the Republic of Texas for planning to construct a device with toxins to kill selected government officials. A U.S. federal court convicted them in October 1998 for threatening to use a weapon of mass destruction.

- *December 1996:* Sri Lankan press noted that government authorities warned the military in the northern region not to purchase food or stamps from local vendors, because some stamps had been found laced with cyanide.

- *July 1995:* Four improvised chemical devices (ICDs) were found in restrooms at the Kayabacho, Tokyo, and Ginza subway stations and the Japanese railway's Shinjuku station. Each device was slightly different but contained the same chemicals.

- *May 1995:* An ICD was left in Shinjuku station in Tokyo. The device consisted of two plastic bags, one containing sodium cyanide and the other sulfuric acid. If the device had not been neutralized, the chemicals would have combined to produce a cyanide gas.

- *May 1995:* A U.S. citizen, and member of the neo-Nazi Aryan Nations, acquired three vials of *Yersinia pestis*, the bacteria that causes plague, from a Maryland lab. Law enforcement officials recovered the unopened material and arrested the individual. No delivery system was recovered, and no information indicated the subject's purpose in obtaining the bacteria.

- *March 20, 1995:* Members of the Japanese cult Aum Shinrikyo used ICDs to release sarin nerve gas in the Tokyo subway station. Twelve people died, and thousands of others were hospitalized or required medical treatment.
- *March 15, 1995:* Three briefcases were left at locations in the Kasumigaseki train station in Tokyo. No injuries resulted, but an Aum Shinrikyo member later confessed that this was a failed biological attack with *Botulinum* toxin.
- *January 1995:* Tajik opposition members laced champagne with cyanide at a New Year's celebration, killing six Russian soldiers and the wife of another soldier, and sickening other revelers.
- *June 27, 1994:* A substance identified as sarin was dispersed using a modified van in a residential area near Matsumoto; 7 persons died, and more than 200 people were injured. Reportedly, an Aum Shinrikyo member confessed that the cult targeted three judges who lived there to prevent them from returning an adverse decision against the cult.
- *1993:* A U.S. citizen was detained by the Canadian Customs Service as he attempted to enter Canada from Alaska. A white powdery substance was confiscated and later identified through laboratory analysis as ricin. The individual, traveling with a large sum of cash, told officials that he was carrying the poison to protect his money.
- *1992:* Four individuals were convicted by a U.S. federal court for producing ricin and advocating the violent overthrow of the government. The subjects, who had espoused extremist, antigovernment, antitax ideals, specifically had targeted a deputy U.S. marshal who previously had served papers on one of them for tax violations.
- *1984:* An outbreak of salmonella poisoning that occurred in Oregon during a 2-week period was linked to the salad bars of eight restaurants. More than 700 people were affected, but no fatalities occurred. Investigators of the outbreak determined that two members of the Rajneesh religious sect produced and dispensed salmonella bacteria in the restaurants, in order to influence a local election by incapacitating opposition voters.

*Sources*: CIA. (2002) *Terrorism: Guide to Chemical, Biological, Radiological, and Nuclear Weapons Indicators* CNN, February 4, 2004; CNS Reports, February 3, 2004.

## CONVENTIONAL EXPLOSIVES AND SECONDARY DEVICES

Conventional explosives have existed for centuries, since explosive gunpowder, invented by the Chinese for use in firecrackers, was modified for use in weaponry. Traditional and improvised explosive devices (IEDs) are the easiest weapons to both obtain and use. Instructions for their assembly and use are widely available in print and on the Internet, as well as through the institutional knowledge of informal criminal networks. These widely available weapons, when skillfully used, can inflict massive amounts of destruction to property and can cause significant injuries and fatalities to humans. Conventional explosives are most troubling as a WMD in light of their ability to effectively disperse chemical, biological, or radiological agents.

Conventional explosives and IEDs can be either explosive or incendiary in nature. Explosives use the physical destruction caused by the expansion of gases that result from the ignition of "high- or low-filler" explosive materials to inflict damage or harm. Examples of explosive devices include simple pipe bombs, made from common plumbing materials; satchel charges, which are encased in a common looking bag such as a backpack, and left behind for later detonation; letter or package bombs, delivered through the mail; or a car bomb, which can be used to deliver a large amount of explosives. Incendiary devices, also referred to as firebombs, rely on the ignition of fires to cause damage or harm. Examples include Molotov cocktails (gas-filled bottles capped with a burning rag) and napalm bombs.

Explosions and fires can be delivered as a missile, or projectile device, such as a rocket, rocket-propelled grenade (RPG), mortar, or air-dropped bomb. Nontraditional explosive delivery methods are regularly discovered, and include the use of fuel-filled commercial airliners flown into buildings as occurred on September 11, 2001. Because these weapons rely on such low technology and are relatively easy to transport and deliver, they are the most commonly utilized terrorist device. Though suicide bombings, in which bombers manually deliver and detonate the device on or near their person, are becoming more common, most devices are detonated through the use of timed, remote (radio, cell phone), or other methods of transmission (light sensitivity, air pressure, movement, electrical impulse, etc.).

Although more than 70% of terrorist attacks involve the use of conventional explosives, less than 5% of actual and attempted bombings are preceded by any kind of threat or warning. These devices can be difficult to detect because most easily attainable explosive materials are untraceable. Commercial explosives in the United States are now required to contain a chemical signature that can be used to trace their source should they be used for criminal means, but this accounts for only a fraction of materials available to terrorists. What is particularly troubling about

these devices is that it is easy to detonate multiple explosives in single or multiple municipalities, and secondary explosives can be used to target bystanders and officials who are responding to the initial, often smaller, explosion. Because of the often graphic nature of the carnage resulting from explosives, and the widespread fear associated with their historic use, these weapons are very effective as a terror-spreading devices. (*Source*: FEMA, 2002)

## CHEMICAL AGENTS

Like explosives, chemical weapons have existed for centuries and have been used repeatedly throughout history. The most significant and first organized modern use of chemical weapons was during World War I. In Belgium, during a German attack against allied forces in World War I (WWI), German troops released 160 tons of chlorine gas into the air, killing more than 10,000 soldiers and injured another 15,000. In total, 113,000 tons of chemical weapons were used in WWI, killing more than 90,000 and injuring 1.3 million.

Chemical weapons are created for the sole purpose of killing, injuring, or incapacitating people. They can enter the body through inhalation, ingestion, or through the skin or eyes. Many different kinds of chemicals have been developed as weapons, falling under six general categories that are distinguished according to their physiological effect on victims:

1. Nerve agents (Sarin, VX)
2. Blister agents (mustard gas, lewisite)
3. Blood agents (hydrogen cyanide)
4. Choking/pulmonary agents (phosgene)
5. Irritants [tear gas, capsicum (pepper) spray]
6. Incapacitating agents (BZ, Agent 15)

Terrorists can deliver chemical weapons by several mechanisms. Aerosol devices spread chemicals in liquid, solid (generally powdered), or gas form by causing tiny particulates of the chemical to be suspended into the air. Explosives can be used to spread the chemicals through the air as well. Containers that hold chemicals, either for warfare or everyday use (such as a truck or train tanker), can be breached, exposing the chemical to the air. Chemicals can also be mixed with water or placed into food supplies. Chemicals that are easily absorbed through the skin can be placed directly onto a victim to cause harm or death.

Chemical attacks, in general, are recognized immediately (some indicators of the possible use of chemical agents are listed in Sidebar 4-3), though it may be unclear until further testing has taken place whether the attack was chemical or biological in nature. Chemical weapons can be persistent, remaining in the affected area for long after the attack, or nonpersistent. Nonpersistent chemicals tend to evaporate quickly, are lighter than air, and lose their ability to

harm or kill after about 10 or 15 minutes in open areas. In unventilated rooms, any chemical can linger for a considerable time.

The effect on victims is usually fast and severe. Identifying what chemical has been used presents special difficulties, and responding officials (police, fire, EMS, HAZMAT) and hospital staff treating the injured are at risk from their effects. Without proper training and equipment, there is little these first response officials can do in the immediate aftermath of a chemical terrorist attack. (*Source*: FEMA, 2002)

A list of chemical agents compiled by the CDC is presented in Sidebar 4-4. Facts sheets about cyanide, sulfur mustard (mustard gas), sarin, ricin, and chlorine, which have been compiled from the CDC website, are presented in Sidebars 4-5 through 4-9, respectively, and Sidebar 4-10 lists resources for finding more information about these chemical agents.

---

SIDEBAR 4-3 **General Indicators of Possible Chemical Agent Use**

- Stated threat to release a chemical agent
- Unusual occurrence of dead or dying animals
  - For example, lack of insects, dead birds
- Unexplained casualties
  - Multiple victims
  - Surge of similar 911 calls
  - Serious illnesses
  - Nausea, disorientation, difficulty breathing, or convulsions
  - Definite casualty patterns
  - Unusual liquid, spray, vapor, or powder

  - Droplets, oily film
  - Unexplained odor
  - Low-lying clouds/fog unrelated to weather
- Suspicious devices, packages, or letters
  - Unusual metal debris
  - Abandoned spray devices
  - Unexplained munitions

*Source*: Federal Emergency Management Agency. (2002). *Interim Planning Guide for State and Local Government: Managing the Emergency Consequences of Terrorist Incidents.* Washington, DC: FEMA (July).

## SIDEBAR 4-4    List of Chemical Agents

Compiled by the Centers for Disease Control and Prevention

Abrin
Adamsite (DM)
Agent 15
Ammonia
Arsenic
Arsine (SA)
Benzene
Bromobenzylcyanide (CA)
BZ
Cannabinoids
Chlorine (CL)
Chloroacetophenone (CN)
Chlorobenzylidenemalononitrile (CS)
Chloropicrin (PS)
Cyanide
Cyanogen chloride (CK)
Cyclohexyl sarin (GF)
Dibenzoxazepine (CR)
Diphenylchlorarsine (DA)
Diphenylcyanoarsine (DC)
Diphosgene (DP)
Distilled mustard (HD)
Ethyldichloroarsine (ED)
Ethylene glycol
Fentanyls and other opioids
Hydrofluoric acid
Hydrogen chloride
Hydrogen cyanide (AC)
Lewisite (L, L-1, L-2, L-3)
LSD
Mercury
Methyldichloroarsine (MD)
Mustard gas (H) (sulfur mustard)

Mustard/lewisite (HL)
Mustard/T
Nitrogen mustard (HN-1, HN-2, HN-3)
Nitrogen oxide (NO)
Paraquat
Perflurorisobutylene (PHIB)
Phenodichlorarsine (PD)
Phenothiazines
Phosgene (CG)
Phosgene oxime (CX)
Phosphine
Potassium cyanide (KCN)
Red phosphorus (RP)
Ricin
Sarin (GB)
Sesqui mustard
Sodium azide
Sodium cyanide (NaCN)
Soman (GD)
Stibine
Strychnine
Sulfur mustard (H) (mustard gas)
Sulfur trioxide-chlorosulfonic acid (FS)
Super warfarin
Tabun (GA)
Teflon and perflurorisobutylene (PHIB)
Thallium
Titanium tetrachloride (FM)
VX
White phosphorus
Zinc oxide (HC)

*Source*: Centers for Disease Control and Prevention, www.bt.
cdc.gov/agent/agentlistchem.asp.

SIDEBAR 4-5   **Facts about Cyanide**

### What Is Cyanide?

- Cyanide is a rapidly acting, potentially deadly chemical that can exist in various forms.
- Cyanide can be a colorless gas, such as hydrogen cyanide (HCN) or cyanogen chloride (CNCl), or a crystal form such as sodium cyanide (NaCN) or potassium cyanide (KCN).
- Cyanide sometimes is described as having a "bitter almond" smell, but it does not always give off an odor, and not everyone can detect the odor when it does exist.
- Cyanide is also known by the military designations AN (for hydrogen cyanide) and CK (for cyanogen chloride).

### Where Cyanide Is Found and How It Is Used

- Hydrogen cyanide, under the name Zyklon B, was used as a genocidal agent by the Germans in World War II.
- Reports have indicated that during the Iran–Iraq War in the 1980s, hydrogen cyanide gas may have been used along with other chemical agents against the inhabitants of the Kurdish city of Halabja in northern Iraq.
- Cyanide is naturally present in some foods and in certain plants such as cassava. Cyanide is contained in cigarette smoke and the combustion products of synthetic materials such as plastics. Combustion products are substances given off when things burn.
- In manufacturing, cyanide is used to make paper, textiles, and plastics. It is present in the chemicals used to develop photographs. Cyanide salts are used in metallurgy for electroplating, metal cleaning, and removing gold from its ore. Cyanide gas is used to exterminate pests and vermin in ships and buildings.
- If accidentally ingested (swallowed), chemicals found in acetonitrile-based products that are used to remove artificial nails can produce cyanide.

### How People Can Be Exposed to Cyanide

- People may be exposed to cyanide by breathing air, drinking water, eating food, or touching soil that contains cyanide.
- Cyanide enters water, soil, or air as a result of both natural processes and industrial activities. In air, cyanide is present mainly as gaseous hydrogen cyanide.
- Smoking cigarettes is probably one of the major sources of cyanide exposure for people who do not work in cyanide-related industries.

### How Cyanide Works

- Poisoning caused by cyanide depends on the amount of cyanide a person is exposed to, the route of exposure, and the length of time that a person is exposed.
- Breathing cyanide gas causes the most harm, but ingesting cyanide can be toxic as well.
- Cyanide gas is most dangerous in enclosed places where the gas will be trapped.
- Cyanide gas evaporates and disperses quickly in open spaces, making it less harmful outdoors.
- Cyanide gas is less dense than air, so it will rise.
- Cyanide prevents the cells of the body from getting oxygen. When this happens, the cells die.
- Cyanide is more harmful to the heart and brain than to other organs because the heart and brain use a lot of oxygen.

### Immediate Signs and Symptoms of Cyanide Exposure

- People exposed to a small amount of cyanide by breathing it, absorbing it through their skin,

or eating foods that contain it may have some or all of the following symptoms within minutes:
- Rapid breathing
- Restlessness
- Dizziness
- Weakness
- Headache
- Nausea and vomiting
- Rapid heart rate
- Exposure to a large amount of cyanide by any route may cause these other health effects as well:
  - Convulsions
  - Low blood pressure
  - Slow heart rate
  - Loss of consciousness
  - Lung injury
  - Respiratory failure leading to death
- Showing these signs and symptoms does not necessarily mean that a person has been exposed to cyanide.

### What the Long-Term Health Effects May Be

Survivors of serious cyanide poisoning may develop heart and brain damage.

### How People Can Protect Themselves and What They Should Do If They Are Exposed to Cyanide

- First, get fresh air by leaving the area where the cyanide was released. Moving to an area with fresh air is a good way to reduce the possibility of death from exposure to cyanide gas.
  - If the cyanide release was outside, move away from the area where the cyanide was released.
  - If the cyanide release was indoors, get out of the building.
- If leaving the area that was exposed to cyanide is not an option, stay as low to the ground as possible.
- Remove any clothing that has liquid cyanide on it. If possible, seal the clothing in a plastic bag, and then seal that bag inside a second plastic bag. Removing and sealing the clothing in this way will help protect people from any chemicals that might be on their clothes.
- If clothes were placed in plastic bags, inform either the local or state health department or emergency coordinators upon their arrival. Do not handle the plastic bags.
- Rinse the eyes with plain water for 10 to 15 minutes if they are burning or if vision is blurred.
- Wash any liquid cyanide from the skin thoroughly with soap and water.
- If cyanide is known to be ingested (swallowed), do not induce vomiting or give fluids to drink.
- Seek medical attention right away. Dial 911 and explain what has happened.

### How Cyanide Poisoning Is Treated

Cyanide poisoning is treated with specific antidotes and supportive medical care in a hospital setting. The most important thing is for victims to seek medical treatment as soon as possible.

*Source*: Centers for Disease Control and Prevention, www.cdc.gov.

SIDEBAR 4-6   **Facts about Sulfur Mustard**

### What Is Sulfur Mustard?

- Sulfur mustard is a type of chemical warfare agent. These kinds of agents are called vesicants, or blistering agents, because they cause blistering of the skin and mucous membranes on contact.
- Sulfur mustard is also known as "mustard gas or mustard agent" or by the military designations H, HD, and HT.
- Sulfur mustard sometimes smells like garlic, onions, or mustard and sometimes has no odor. It can be a vapor (the gaseous form of a liquid), an oily-textured liquid, or a solid.
- Sulfur mustard can be clear to yellow or brown when it is in liquid or solid form.

### Where Sulfur Mustard Is Found and How It Is Used

- Sulfur mustard is not found naturally in the environment.
- Sulfur mustard was introduced in World War I as a chemical warfare agent. Until recently, it was available for use in the treatment of a skin condition called psoriasis. Currently, it has no medical use.

### How People Can Be Exposed to Sulfur Mustard

- If sulfur mustard is released into the air as a vapor, people can be exposed through skin contact, eye contact, or breathing. Sulfur mustard vapor can be carried long distances by wind.
- If sulfur mustard is released into water, people can be exposed by drinking the contaminated water or getting it on their skin.
- People can be exposed by coming in contact with liquid sulfur mustard.
- Sulfur mustard can last from 1 to 2 days in the environment under average weather conditions and from weeks to months under very cold conditions.

- Sulfur mustard breaks down slowly in the body, so repeated exposure may have a cumulative effect (that is, it can build up in the body).

### How Sulfur Mustard Works

- Adverse health effects caused by sulfur mustard depend on the amount to which people are exposed, the route of exposure, and the length of exposure time.
- Sulfur mustard is a powerful irritant and blistering agent that damages the skin, eyes, and respiratory (breathing) tract.
- It damages DNA, a vital component of cells in the body.
- Sulfur mustard vapor is heavier than air, so it will settle in low-lying areas.

### Immediate Signs and Symptoms of Sulfur Mustard Exposure

- Exposure to sulfur mustard is usually not fatal. When sulfur mustard was used during World War I, it killed fewer than 5% of the people who were exposed and got medical care.
- People may not know right away that they have been exposed because sulfur mustard often has no smell or has a smell that might not cause alarm.
- Typically, signs and symptoms do not occur immediately. Depending on the severity of the exposure, symptoms may not occur for 2 to 24 hours. Some people are more sensitive to sulfur mustard than are other people and may have symptoms sooner.
- Sulfur mustard can have the following effects on specific parts of the body:
  - *Skin:* Redness and itching of the skin may occur 2 to 48 hours after exposure and change eventually to yellow blistering of the skin.

- *Eyes:* Irritation, pain, swelling, and tearing may occur within 3 to 12 hours of a mild to moderate exposure. A severe exposure may cause symptoms within 1 to 2 hours and may include the symptoms of a mild or moderate exposure plus light sensitivity, severe pain, or blindness (lasting up to 10 days).
- *Respiratory tract:* Runny nose, sneezing, hoarseness, bloody nose, sinus pain, shortness of breath, and cough may occur within 12 to 24 hours of a mild exposure and within 2 to 4 hours of a severe exposure.
- *Digestive tract:* Abdominal pain, diarrhea, fever, nausea, and vomiting may occur.
- Showing these signs and symptoms does not necessarily mean that a person has been exposed to sulfur mustard.

### What the Long-Term Health Effects May Be

- Exposure to sulfur mustard liquid is more likely to produce second- and third-degree burns and later scarring than is exposure to sulfur mustard vapor. Extensive skin burning can be fatal.
- Extensive breathing in of the vapors can cause chronic respiratory disease, repeated respiratory infections, or death.
- Extensive eye exposure can cause permanent blindness.
- Exposure to sulfur mustard may increase a person's risk for lung and respiratory cancer.

### How People Can Protect Themselves and What They Should Do If They Are Exposed to Sulfur Mustard

- Because no antidote exists for sulfur mustard exposure, the best thing to do is avoid it.

Immediately leave the area where the sulfur mustard was released. Try to find higher ground, because sulfur mustard is heavier than air and will settle in low-lying areas.
- If avoiding sulfur mustard exposure is not possible, rapidly remove the sulfur mustard from the body. Getting the sulfur mustard off as soon as possible after exposure is the only effective way to prevent or decrease tissue damage to the body.
- Quickly remove any clothing that has liquid sulfur mustard on it. If possible, seal the clothing in a plastic bag, and then seal that bag inside a second plastic bag.
- Immediately wash any exposed part of the body (eyes, skin, etc.) thoroughly with plain, clean water. Eyes need to be flushed with water for 5 to 10 minutes. Do *not* cover eyes with bandages, but do protect them with dark glasses or goggles.
- If someone has ingested sulfur mustard, do *not* induce vomiting. Give the person milk to drink.
- Seek medical attention right away. Dial 911 and explain what has happened.

### How Sulfur Mustard Exposure Is Treated

The most important factor is removing sulfur mustard from the body. Exposure to sulfur mustard is treated by giving the victim supportive medical care to minimize the effects of the exposure. Though no antidote exists for sulfur mustard, exposure is usually not fatal.

*Source*: Centers for Disease Control and Prevention, www.cdc. gov.

SIDEBAR 4-7   **Facts about Sarin**

### What Is Sarin?

- Sarin is a human-made chemical warfare agent classified as a nerve agent. Nerve agents are the most toxic and rapidly acting of the known chemical warfare agents. They are similar to certain kinds of pesticides (insect killers) called organophosphates in terms of how they work and what kind of harmful effects they cause. However, nerve agents are much more potent than organophosphate pesticides.
- Sarin originally was developed in 1938 in Germany as a pesticide.
- Sarin is a clear, colorless, and tasteless liquid that has no odor in its pure form. However, sarin can evaporate into a vapor (gas) and spread into the environment.
- Sarin is also known as GB.

### Where Sarin Is Found and How It Is Used

- Sarin and other nerve agents may have been used in chemical warfare during the Iran–Iraq War in the 1980s.
- Sarin was used in two terrorist attacks in Japan in 1994 and 1995.
- Sarin is not found naturally in the environment.

### How People Can Be Exposed to Sarin

- Following release of sarin into the air, people can be exposed through skin contact or eye contact. They can also be exposed by breathing air that contains sarin.
- Sarin mixes easily with water, so it could be used to poison water. Following release of sarin into water, people can be exposed by touching or drinking water that contains sarin.
- After contamination of food with sarin, people can be exposed by eating the contaminated food.
- A person's clothing can release sarin for about 30 minutes after it has come in contact with

sarin vapor, which can lead to exposure of other people.
- Because sarin breaks down slowly in the body, people who are repeatedly exposed to sarin may suffer more harmful health effects.
- Because sarin vapor is heavier than air, it will sink to low-lying areas and create a greater exposure hazard there.

### How Sarin Works

- The extent of poisoning caused by sarin depends on the amount of sarin to which a person was exposed, the way the person was exposed, and the length of time of the exposure.
- Symptoms will appear within a few seconds after exposure to the vapor form of sarin and within a few minutes up to 18 hours after exposure to the liquid form.
- All the nerve agents cause their toxic effects by preventing the proper operation of the chemical that acts as the body's "off switch" for glands and muscles. Without an "off switch," the glands and muscles are constantly being stimulated. They may tire and no longer be able to sustain breathing function.
- Sarin is the most volatile of the nerve agents, which means that it can easily and quickly evaporate from a liquid into a vapor and spread into the environment. People can be exposed to the vapor even if they do not come in contact with the liquid form of sarin.
- Because it evaporates so quickly, sarin presents an immediate but short-lived threat.

### Immediate Signs and Symptoms of Sarin Exposure

- People may not know that they were exposed because sarin has no odor.

- People exposed to a low or moderate dose of sarin by breathing contaminated air, eating contaminated food, drinking contaminated water, or touching contaminated surfaces may experience some or all of the following symptoms within seconds to hours of exposure:
  - Runny nose
  - Watery eyes
  - Small, pinpoint pupils
  - Eye pain
  - Blurred vision
  - Drooling and excessive sweating
  - Cough
  - Chest tightness
  - Rapid breathing
  - Diarrhea
  - Increased urination
  - Confusion
  - Drowsiness
  - Weakness
  - Headache
  - Nausea, vomiting, and/or abdominal pain
  - Slow or fast heart rate
  - Low or high blood pressure
- Even a small drop of sarin on the skin can cause sweating and muscle twitching where sarin touched the skin.
- Exposure to large doses of sarin by any route may result in the following harmful health effects:
  - Loss of consciousness
  - Convulsions
  - Paralysis
  - Respiratory failure possibly leading to death
- Showing these signs and symptoms does not necessarily mean that a person has been exposed to sarin.

## What the Long-Term Health Effects Are

Mild or moderately exposed people usually recover completely. Severely exposed people are not likely to survive. Unlike some organophosphate pesticides, nerve agents have not been associated with neurological problems lasting more than 1 to 2 weeks after the exposure.

## How People Can Protect Themselves and What They Should Do If They Are Exposed to Sarin

- Recovery from sarin exposure is possible with treatment, but the antidotes available must be used quickly to be effective. Therefore, the best thing to do is avoid exposure:
  - Leave the area where the sarin was released and get to fresh air. Quickly moving to an area where fresh air is available is highly effective in reducing the possibility of death from exposure to sarin vapor.
    - If the sarin release was outdoors, move away from the area where the sarin was released. Go to the highest ground possible because sarin is heavier than air and will sink to low-lying areas.
    - If the sarin release was indoors, get out of the building.
- If people think they may have been exposed, they should remove their clothing, rapidly wash their entire body with soap and water, and get medical care as quickly as possible.
- Removing and disposing of clothing:
  - Quickly take off clothing that has liquid sarin on it. Any clothing that has to be pulled over the head should be cut off the body instead of pulled over the head. If possible, seal the clothing in a plastic bag. Then seal the first plastic bag in a second plastic bag. Removing and sealing the clothing in this way will help protect people from any chemicals that might be on their clothes.
  - If clothes were placed in plastic bags, inform either the local or state health department or emergency personnel upon their arrival. Do not handle the plastic bags.
  - If helping other people remove their clothing, try to avoid touching any contaminated

areas, and remove the clothing as quickly as possible.
- Washing the body:
  - As quickly as possible, wash any liquid sarin from the skin with large amounts of soap and water. Washing with soap and water will help protect people from any chemicals on their bodies.
  - Rinse the eyes with plain water for 10 to 15 minutes if they are burning or if vision is blurred.
- If sarin has been swallowed, do not induce vomiting or give fluids to drink.

- Seek medical attention immediately. Dial 911 and explain what has happened.

### How Sarin Exposure Is Treated

Treatment consists of removing sarin from the body as soon as possible and providing supportive medical care in a hospital setting. Antidotes are available for sarin. They are most useful if given as soon as possible after exposure.

*Source*: Centers for Disease Control and Prevention, www.cdc.gov.

---

SIDEBAR 4-8   **Facts about Ricin**

### What Is Ricin?

- Ricin is a poison that can be made from the waste left over from processing castor beans.
- It can be in the form of a powder, a mist, or a pellet, or it can be dissolved in water or weak acid.
- It is a stable substance. For example, it is not affected much by extreme conditions such as very hot or very cold temperatures.

### Where Is Ricin Found and How Is It Used?

- Castor beans are processed throughout the world to make castor oil. Ricin is part of the waste "mash" produced when castor oil is made. Amateurs can make ricin from castor beans.
- Ricin has some potential medical uses, such as in bone marrow transplants and cancer treatment (to kill cancer cells).

### How Can People Be Exposed to Ricin?

- It would take a deliberate act to make ricin and use it to poison people. Accidental exposure to ricin is highly unlikely.

- People can breathe in ricin mist or powder and be poisoned.
- Ricin can also get into water or food and then be swallowed.
- Pellets of ricin, or ricin dissolved in a liquid, can be injected into people's bodies.
- Depending on the route of exposure (such as injection), as little as 500 micrograms of ricin could be enough to kill an adult. A 500-microgram dose of ricin would be about the size of the head of a pin. A much greater amount would be needed to kill people if the ricin were inhaled (breathed in) or swallowed.
- Ricin poisoning is not contagious. It cannot be spread from person to person through casual contact.
- In 1978 Georgi Markov, a Bulgarian writer and journalist who was living in London, died after he was attacked by a man with an umbrella. The umbrella had been rigged to inject a poison ricin pellet under Markov's skin.
- Some reports have indicated that ricin may have been used in the Iran–Iraq war during the

1980s and that quantities of ricin were found in al Qaeda caves in Afghanistan.

### How Does Ricin Work?

- Ricin works by getting inside the cells of a person's body and preventing the cells from making the proteins they need. Without the proteins, cells die, and eventually the whole body can shut down and die.
- Specific effects of ricin poisoning depend on whether ricin was inhaled, swallowed, or injected.

### What Are the Signs and Symptoms of Ricin Exposure?

- *Inhalation:* Within a few hours of inhaling significant amounts of ricin, the likely symptoms would be coughing, tightness in the chest, difficulty breathing, nausea, and aching muscles. Within the next few hours, the body's airways (such as the lungs) would become severely inflamed (swollen and hot), excess fluid would build up in the lungs, breathing would become even more difficult, and the skin might turn blue. Excess fluid in the lungs would be diagnosed by X-rays or by listening to the chest with a stethoscope.
- *Ingestion:* If someone swallows a significant amount of ricin, he or she would have internal bleeding of the stomach and intestines that would lead to vomiting and bloody diarrhea. Eventually, the person's liver, spleen, and kidneys might stop working, and the person could die.
- *Injection:* Injection of a lethal amount of ricin at first would cause the muscles and lymph nodes near the injection site to die. Eventually, the liver, kidneys, and spleen would stop working, and the person would have massive bleeding from the stomach and intestines. The person would die from multiple organ failure.
- Death from ricin poisoning could take place within 36 to 48 hours of exposure, whether by injection, ingestion, or inhalation. If the person lives longer than 5 days without complications, he or she will probably not die.
- Showing these signs and symptoms does not necessarily mean that a person has been exposed to ricin.

### How Is Ricin Poisoning Treated?

- No antidote exists for ricin. Ricin poisoning is treated by giving the victim supportive medical care to minimize the effects of the poisoning. The types of supportive medical care would depend on several factors, such as the route by which the victim was poisoned (that is, by inhalation, ingestion, or injection). Care could include such measures as helping the victim breathe and giving him or her intravenous fluids and medications to treat swelling.

### How Do We Know for Sure People Have Been Exposed to Ricin?

- If we suspect that people have inhaled ricin, a possible clue would be that a large number of people who had been close to each other suddenly developed fever, cough, and excess fluid in their lungs. These symptoms could be followed by severe breathing problems and possibly death.
- No widely available, reliable test exists to confirm that a person has been exposed to ricin.

### What Can People Do If They Think They May Have Been Exposed to Ricin?

Unintentional ricin poisoning is highly unlikely. CDC has no reports of intentional ricin poisoning. If people think they might have been exposed to ricin, however, they should contact the regional poison control center at 1-800-222-1222.

*Source:* Centers for Disease Control and Prevention, www.cdc.gov.

SIDEBAR 4-9   **Facts about Chlorine**

### What Is Chlorine?

- Chlorine is an element used in industry and found in some household products.
- Chlorine is sometimes in the form of a poisonous gas. Chlorine gas can be pressurized and cooled to change it into a liquid so that it can be shipped and stored. When liquid chlorine is released, it quickly turns into a gas that stays close to the ground and spreads rapidly.
- Chlorine gas can be recognized by its pungent, irritating odor, which is like the odor of bleach. The strong smell may provide an adequate warning to people that they have been exposed.
- Chlorine gas appears to be yellow-green in color.
- Chlorine itself is not flammable, but it can react explosively or form explosive compounds with other chemicals such as turpentine and ammonia.

### Where Chlorine Is Found and How It Is Used

- Chlorine was used during World War I as a choking (pulmonary) agent.
- Chlorine is one of the most commonly manufactured chemicals in the United States. Its most important use is as a bleach in the manufacture of paper and cloth, but it is also used to make pesticides (insect killers), rubber, and solvents.
- Chlorine is used in drinking water and swimming pool water to kill harmful bacteria. It is also used as part of the sanitation process for industrial waste and sewage.
- Household chlorine bleach can release chlorine gas if it is mixed with other cleaning agents.

### How People Can Be Exposed to Chlorine

- People's risk for exposure depends on how close they are to the place where the chlorine was released.

- If chlorine gas is released into the air, people may be exposed through skin contact or eye contact. They may also be exposed by breathing air that contains chlorine.
- If chlorine liquid is released into water, people may be exposed by touching or drinking water that contains chlorine.
- If chlorine liquid comes into contact with food, people may be exposed by eating the contaminated food.
- Chlorine gas is heavier than air, so it would settle in low-lying areas.

### How Chlorine Works

- The extent of poisoning caused by chlorine depends on the amount of chlorine a person is exposed to, how the person was exposed, and the length of time of the exposure.
- When chlorine gas comes into contact with moist tissues such as the eyes, throat, and lungs, an acid is produced that can damage these tissues.

### Immediate Signs and Symptoms of Chlorine Exposure

- During or immediately after exposure to dangerous concentrations of chlorine, the following signs and symptoms may develop:
  - Coughing
  - Chest tightness
  - Burning sensation in the nose, throat, and eyes
  - Watery eyes
  - Blurred vision
  - Nausea and vomiting
  - Burning pain, redness, and blisters on the skin if exposed to gas; skin injury similar to frostbite if exposed to liquid chlorine
  - Difficulty breathing or shortness of breath (may appear immediately if high concentra-

tions of chlorine gas are inhaled, or may be delayed if low concentrations of chlorine gas are inhaled)
  – Fluid in the lungs (pulmonary edema) within 2 to 4 hours
- Showing these signs or symptoms does not necessarily mean that a person has been exposed to chlorine.

### What the Long-Term Health Effects Are

- Long-term complications from chlorine exposure are not found in people who survive a sudden exposure unless they suffer complications such as pneumonia during therapy. Chronic bronchitis may develop in people who develop pneumonia during therapy.

### How People Can Protect Themselves and What They Should Do If They Are Exposed to Chlorine

- Leave the area where the chlorine was released and get to fresh air. Quickly moving to an area where fresh air is available is highly effective in reducing exposure to chlorine.
  – If the chlorine release was outdoors, move away from the area where the chlorine was released. Go to the highest ground possible, because chlorine is heavier than air and will sink to low-lying areas.
  – If the chlorine release was indoors, get out of the building.
  – If you think you may have been exposed, remove your clothing, rapidly wash your entire body with soap and water, and get medical care as quickly as possible.
- Removing and disposing of clothing:
  – Quickly take off clothing that has liquid chlorine on it. Any clothing that has to be pulled over the head should be cut off the body instead of pulled over the head. If possible, seal the clothing in a plastic bag. Then seal the first plastic bag in a second plastic

bag. Removing and sealing the clothing in this way will help protect you and other people from any chemicals that might be on your clothes.
  – If you placed your clothes in plastic bags, inform either the local or state health department or emergency personnel upon their arrival. Do not handle the plastic bags.
  – If you are helping other people remove their clothing, try to avoid touching any contaminated areas, and remove the clothing as quickly as possible.
- Washing the body:
  – As quickly as possible, wash your entire body with large amounts of soap and water. Washing with soap and water will help protect people from any chemicals on their bodies.
  – If your eyes are burning or your vision is blurred, rinse your eyes with plain water for 10 to 15 minutes. If you wear contacts, remove them before rinsing your eyes, and place them in the bags with the contaminated clothing. Do not put the contacts back in your eyes. You should dispose of them even if you do not wear disposable contacts. If you wear eyeglasses, wash them with soap and water. You can put the eyeglasses back on after you wash them.
- If you have ingested (swallowed) chlorine, do not induce vomiting or drink fluids.
- Seek medical attention right away. Dial 911 and explain what has happened.

### How Chlorine Exposure Is Treated

No antidote exists for chlorine exposure. Treatment consists of removing the chlorine from the body as soon as possible and providing supportive medical care in a hospital setting.

*Source*: Centers for Disease Control and Prevention, www. cdc.org.

SIDEBAR 4-10   **Additional Information on Cyanide, Sulfur Mustard, Sarin, Ricin, and Chlorine**

For more information on cyanide, sulfur mustard, sarin, ricin, and chlorine, contact one of the following:

- Regional poison control center: 1-800-222-1222
- Centers for Disease Control and Prevention
  - Public response hotline (CDC)
    - English: 1-888-246-2675
    - Español: 1-888-246-2857
    - TTY: 1-866-874-2646
  - Emergency Preparedness and Response website at www.fema.gov
  - E-mail inquiries: cdcresponse@ashastd.org
  - Mail inquiries: Public Inquiry, Bioterrorism Preparedness and Response Planning, Centers for Disease Control and Prevention, Mailstop C-18, 1600 Clifton Road NE, Atlanta, GA 30333
- Agency for Toxic Substances and Disease Registry (ATSDR): 1-888-422-8737
  - E-mail inquiries: atsdric@cdc.gov
  - Mail inquiries: Agency for Toxic Substances and Disease Registry Division of Toxicology, Mailstop E-29, 1600 Clifton Road NE, Atlanta, GA 30333
  - Centers for Disease Control and Prevention (CDC), National Institute for Occupational Safety and Health (NIOSH), Pocket Guide to Chemical Hazards.

*Source*: Centers for Disease Control and Prevention, www.cdc.org.

## BIOLOGICAL AGENTS

Biological or "germ" weapons are live organisms (either bacteria, viruses, or the toxic by-products generated by living organisms) used to cause illness, injury, or death in humans, livestock, or plants. Awareness of the potential use of bacteria, viruses, and toxins as a weapon has existed since long before the 2001 anthrax mail attacks. As early as the 14th century, in fact, we have evidence of biological warfare, when the Mongols used plague-infected corpses to spread disease among enemies. Because of advances in weapons technology that has allowed much more successful use of bioweapons over much greater geographic limits, biological weapons elicit great concern from counterterrorism officials and emergency planners alike.

Bioweapons can be dispersed either overtly or covertly. Their use can be extremely difficult to recognize because their negative consequences may take hours, days, or even weeks, to emerge. This is especially true with bacteria and viruses, though toxins generally elicit an immediate response. Recognition is made through a range of methods, including identification of a credible threat, the discovery of weapons materials (dispersion devices, raw biological material, or weapons laboratories), and correct diagnosis of affected humans, animals, or plants. Detection depends on a collaborative public health monitoring system, trained and aware physicians, patients who choose to seek medical care, and equipment suitable for confirming diagnoses. Bioweapons are unique in this capacity, in that detection is likely to be made not by a first responder, but by members of the public health community.

The devastating potential of bioweapons is confounded by the fact that people normally have no idea that they have been exposed. During their incubation period, when they do not exhibit symptoms but are contagious to others, they can spread the disease. Incubation periods can be as short as several hours but as long as several weeks, allowing for wide geographic spreading due to the efficiency of modern travel. The spread of the SARS virus (which was not a terrorist attack) throughout all continents of the world is evidence of this phenomenon.

Biological weapons are also effective at disrupting economic and industrial components of society, when they target animals or plants. Terrorists could potentially spread a biological agent over a large geographic area, undetected, causing significant destruction of crops. If the agent spread easily as is often the case with natural diseases such as Dutch elm disease, the consequences could be devastating to an entire industry. Cattle diseases such as foot and mouth disease and mad cow disease, which occur naturally, could be used for sinister purposes with little planning, resources, or technical knowledge. In 1918, the German army did just this, spreading anthrax and other diseases through exported livestock and animal feed. With globalization, such actions would require much less effort to conduct.

The primary defense against the use of biological weapons is recognition, which is achieved through proper training of first responders and public health officials. Early detection, before the disease or illness has spread to critical limits, is key to preventing a major public health emergency.

Biological agents are grouped into three categories, designated A, B, and C. Category A agents are those that have great potential for causing a public health catastrophe, and which are capable of being disseminated over a large geographic area. Examples of Category A agents are anthrax, smallpox, plague, botulism, tularemia, and viral hemorrhagic fevers. Category B agents are those that have low mortality rates, but which may be disseminated over a large geographic area with relative ease. Category B agents

include salmonella, ricin, Q fever, typhus, and glanders. Category C agents are common pathogens that have the potential for being engineered for terrorism or weapon purposes. Examples of Category C agents are hantavirus and tuberculosis. (*Sources:* FEMA, 2002; Wikipedia, 2005, www.wikipedia.org)

Some indicators of biological attack are as follows:

- Stated threat to release a biological agent
- Unusual occurrence of dead or dying animals
- Unusual casualties
  - Unusual illness for region/area
  - Definite pattern inconsistent with natural disease
- Unusual liquid, spray, vapor, or powder
  - Spraying, suspicious devices, packages, or letters

*Source*: Federal Emergency Management Agency. (2002). *Interim Planning Guide for State and Local Anthrax Government: Managing the Emergency Consequences of Terrorist Incidents.* Washington, DC: FEMA (July).

A list of biological agents compiled by the Centers for Disease Control and Prevention is presented in Sidebar 4-11. Facts sheets compiled from the CDC website for the following selected biological agents are presented in Sidebars 4-12 through 4-18:

- Anthrax
- Smallpox
- Plague
- Salmonellosis
- Typhoid fever
- Botulism
- Tularemia

---

**SIDEBAR 4-11  List of Biological Agents**

Compiled by the Centers for Disease Control and Prevention

Anthrax (*Bacillus anthracis*)

Botulism (*Clostridium botulinum* toxin)

Brucellosis (*Brucella* species)

Cholera (*Vibrio cholerae*)

E. coli O157:H7 (*Escherichia coli*)

Epsilon toxin (*Clostridium perfringens*)

Emerging infectious diseases such as Nipah virus and hantavirus

Glanders (*Burkholderia mallei*)

Melioidosis (*Burkholderia pseudomallei*)

Typhoid fever (*Salmonella typhi*)

Typhus fever (*Rickettsia prowazekii*)

Plague (*Yersinia pestis*)

Psittacosis (*Chlamydia psittaci*)

Q fever (*Coxiella burnetii*)

Ricin toxin from *Ricinus communis* (castor beans)

Salmonellosis (*Salmonella* species)

Smallpox (variola major)

Staphylococcal enterotoxin B

Tularemia (*Francisella tularensis*)

Viral encephalitis [alphaviruses (e.g., Venezuelan equine encephalitis, eastern equine encephalitis, western equine encephalitis)]

Viral hemorrhagic fevers [filoviruses (e.g., Ebola, Marburg) and arenaviruses (e.g., Lassa, Machupo)]

Water safety threats [e.g., *Vibrio cholerae*, Shigellosis (*Shigella*), *Cryptosporidium parvum*]

*Source*: Centers for Disease Control and Prevention, www.bt.cdc.gov/agent/agentlist.asp.

---

### SIDEBAR 4-12   Facts about Anthrax

**What Is Anthrax**

Anthrax is a serious disease caused by *Bacillus anthracis*, a bacterium that forms spores. A bacterium is a very small organism made up of one cell. Many bacteria can cause disease. A spore is a cell that is dormant (asleep) but may come to life with the right conditions.

There are three types of anthrax:

- Skin (cutaneous)
- Lungs (inhalation)
- Digestive (gastrointestinal)

**How Do You Get It?**

Anthrax is not known to spread from one person to another. Humans can become infected with anthrax by handling products from infected animals or by breathing in anthrax spores from infected animal products, such as wool. People also can become infected with gastrointestinal anthrax by eating undercooked meat from infected animals. Anthrax also can be used as a weapon. This happened in the United States in 2001. Anthrax was deliberately spread through the postal system by sending letters with powder containing anthrax. This caused 22 cases of anthrax infection.

**How Dangerous Is Anthrax?**

The CDC classifies agents with recognized bioterrorism potential into three priority areas (A, B, and C). Anthrax is classified a Category A agent. Category A agents are those that do the following:

- Pose the greatest possible threat for a bad effect on public health
- May spread across a large area or need public awareness
- Need a great deal of planning to protect the public's health

In most cases, early treatment with antibiotics can cure cutaneous anthrax. Even if untreated, 80% of people who become infected with cutaneous anthrax do not die. Gastrointestinal anthrax is more serious because between one-fourth and more than half of cases lead to death. Inhalation anthrax is much more severe. In 2001, about half of the cases of inhalation anthrax ended in death.

## What Are the Symptoms?

The symptoms of anthrax are different depending on the type of the disease:

- *Cutaneous:* The first symptom is a small sore that develops into a blister. The blister then develops into a skin ulcer with a black area in the center. The sore, blister, and ulcer do not hurt.
- *Gastrointestinal:* The first symptoms are nausea, loss of appetite, bloody diarrhea, and fever, followed by severe stomach pain.
- *Inhalation:* The first symptoms of inhalation anthrax are like those associated with cold or flu and can include a sore throat, mild fever, and muscle aches. Later symptoms include cough, chest discomfort, shortness of breath, tiredness, and muscle aches. (*Caution:* Do not assume that just because a person has cold or flu symptoms that they have inhalation anthrax.)

## How Soon Do Infected People Get Sick?

Symptoms can appear within 7 days of coming in contact with the bacterium for all three types of anthrax. For inhalation anthrax, symptoms can appear within a week or can take up to 42 days to appear.

## How Is Anthrax Treated?

Antibiotics are used to treat all three types of anthrax. Early identification and treatment are important. Treatment is different for a person who is exposed to anthrax but is not yet sick. Health care providers will use antibiotics (such as ciprofloxacin, doxycycline, or penicillin) combined with the anthrax vaccine to prevent anthrax infection.

Treatment after infection usually calls for a 60-day course of antibiotics. Success depends on the type of anthrax and how soon treatment begins.

## Can Anthrax Be Prevented?

There is a vaccine to prevent anthrax, but it is not yet available to the general public. Anyone who may be exposed to anthrax, including certain members of the U.S. armed forces, laboratory workers, and workers who may enter or reenter contaminated areas, may get the vaccine. Also, in the event of an attack using anthrax as a weapon, people exposed would get the vaccine.

## What Should I Do If I Think I Have Been Exposed to Anthrax?

If you are showing symptoms of anthrax infection, call your health care provider right away.

Contact local law enforcement immediately if you think that you may have been exposed to anthrax. This includes being exposed to a suspicious package or envelope that contains powder.

## What Is CDC Doing to Prepare for a Possible Anthrax Attack?

CDC is working with state and local health authorities to prepare for an anthrax attack. Activities include the following:

- Developing plans and procedures to respond to an anthrax attack
- Training and equipping emergency response teams to help state and local governments control infection, gather samples, and perform tests; educating health care providers, media, and the general public about what to do in the event of an attack
- Working closely with health departments, veterinarians, and laboratories to watch for suspected cases of anthrax; developing a national electronic database to track potential cases of anthrax
- Ensuring that there are enough safe laboratories for quick testing of suspected anthrax cases
- Working with hospitals, laboratories, emergency response teams, and health care providers to make sure they have the supplies they need in case of an attack

*Source:* Centers for Disease Control and Prevention, www.cdc.gov.

SIDEBAR 4-13   **Facts about Smallpox**

## What Smallpox Is

Smallpox is a serious, contagious, and sometimes fatal infectious disease. There is no specific treatment for smallpox disease, and the only prevention is vaccination. The name *smallpox* is derived from the Latin word for "spotted" and refers to the raised bumps that appear on the face and body of an infected person.

There are two clinical forms of smallpox. *Variola major* is the severe and most common form of smallpox, with a more extensive rash and higher fever. There are four types of *variola major* smallpox: ordinary (the most frequent type, accounting for 90% or more of cases); modified (mild and occurring in previously vaccinated persons); flat; and hemorrhagic (both rare and very severe). Historically, *variola major* has an overall fatality rate of about 30%; however, flat and hemorrhagic smallpox usually are fatal. *Variola minor* is a less common presentation of smallpox and a much less severe disease, with death rates historically of 1% or less.

Smallpox outbreaks have occurred from time to time for thousands of years, but the disease is now eradicated after a successful worldwide vaccination program. The last case of smallpox in the United States was in 1949. The last naturally occurring case in the world was in Somalia in 1977. After the disease was eliminated from the world, routine vaccination against smallpox among the general public was stopped because it was no longer necessary for prevention.

## Smallpox Disease

- *Incubation period:* Duration: 7 to 17 days. Not contagious. Exposure to the virus is followed by an incubation period during which people do not have any symptoms and may feel fine. This incubation period averages about 12 to 14 days but can range from 7 to 17 days. During this time, people are not contagious.

- *Initial symptoms (prodrome):* Duration: 2 to 4 days. Sometimes contagious (smallpox may be contagious during the prodome phase, but is most infectious during the first 7 to 10 days after onset of rash). The first symptoms of smallpox include fever, malaise, head and body aches, and sometimes vomiting. The fever is usually high, in the range of 101° to 104°F. At this time, people are usually too sick to carry on their normal activities.

- *Early rash:* Duration: about 4 days. Most contagious. A rash emerges first as small red spots on the tongue and in the mouth. These spots develop into sores that break open and spread large amounts of the virus into the mouth and throat. At this time, the person becomes most contagious.

- *Rash distribution:* Around the time the sores in the mouth break down, a rash appears on the skin, starting on the face and spreading to the arms and legs and then to the hands and feet. Usually the rash spreads to all parts of the body within 24 hours. As the rash appears, the fever usually falls and the person may start to feel better. The distribution of the rash in smallpox is distinguished from that of chickenpox in that it tends to concentrate more on the face and extremities rather than on the face and trunk (see Figure 4-1).

  By the third day of the rash, the rash becomes raised bumps. By the fourth day, the bumps fill with a thick, opaque fluid and often have a depression in the center that looks like a belly button. (This is a major distinguishing characteristic of smallpox.) Fever often will rise again at this time and remain high until scabs form over the bumps.

- *Pustular rash:* Duration: about 5 days. Contagious. The bumps become pustules—sharply raised, usually round and firm to the touch as

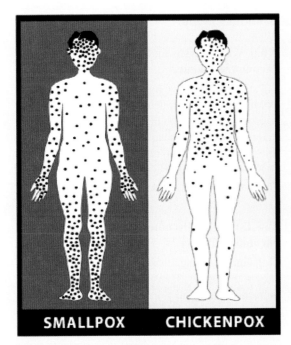

FIGURE 4-1   Rash distribution in (*left*) smallpox and (*right*) chickenpox.

if there's a small round object under the skin. People often say the bumps feel like BB pellets embedded in the skin.

- *Pustules and scabs:* Duration: about 5 days. Contagious. The pustules begin to form a crust and then scab. By the end of the second week after the rash appears, most of the sores have scabbed over.
- *Resolving scabs:* Duration: about 6 days. Contagious. The scabs begin to fall off, leaving marks on the skin that eventually become pitted scars. Most scabs will have fallen off 3

weeks after the rash appears. The person is contagious to others until all of the scabs have fallen off.

- *Scabs resolved:* Not contagious. Scabs have fallen off. Person is no longer contagious.

**Where Smallpox Comes from**

Smallpox is caused by the variola virus that emerged in human populations thousands of years ago. Except for laboratory stockpiles, the variola virus has been eliminated. However, in the aftermath of the events of September and October 2001, there is heightened concern that the variola virus might be used as an agent of bioterrorism. For this reason, the U.S. government is taking precautions for dealing with a smallpox outbreak.

**Transmission**

Generally, direct and fairly prolonged face-to-face contact is required to spread smallpox from one person to another. Smallpox also can be spread through direct contact with infected body fluids or contaminated objects such as bedding or clothing. Rarely, smallpox has been spread by virus carried in the air in enclosed settings such as buildings, buses, and trains. Humans are the only natural hosts of variola. Smallpox is not known to be transmitted by insects or animals.

A person with smallpox is sometimes contagious with onset of fever (prodrome phase), but the person becomes most contagious with the onset of rash. At this stage the infected person is usually very sick and not able to move around in the community. The infected person is contagious until the last smallpox scab falls off.

*Source:* Centers for Disease Control and Prevention, www.cdc.gov.

SIDEBAR 4-14  **Facts about Plague**

### What Is Plague?

Plague is a disease caused by *Yersinia pestis* (*Y. pestis*), a bacterium found in rodents and their fleas in many areas around the world.

### Why Are We Concerned about Pneumonic Plague as a Bioweapon?

*Yersinia pestis* used in an aerosol attack could cause cases of the pneumonic form of plague. One to 6 days after becoming infected with the bacteria, people would develop pneumonic plague. Once people have the disease, the bacteria can spread to others who have close contact with them. Because of the delay between being exposed to the bacteria and becoming sick, people could travel over a large area before becoming contagious and possibly infecting others. Controlling the disease would then be more difficult. A bioweapon carrying *Y. pestis* is possible because the bacterium occurs in nature and could be isolated and grown in quantity in a laboratory. Even so, manufacturing an effective weapon using *Y. pestis* would require advanced knowledge and technology.

### Is Pneumonic Plague Different from Bubonic Plague?

Yes. Both are caused by *Yersinia pestis*, but they are transmitted differently and their symptoms differ. Pneumonic plague can be transmitted from person to person; bubonic plague cannot. Pneumonic plague affects the lungs and is transmitted when a person breathes in *Y. pestis* particles in the air. Bubonic plague is transmitted through the bite of an infected flea or exposure to infected material through a break in the skin. Symptoms include swollen, tender lymph glands called *buboes*. Buboes are not present in pneumonic plague. If bubonic plague is not treated, however, the bacteria can spread through the bloodstream and infect the lungs, causing a secondary case of pneumonic plague.

### What Are the Signs and Symptoms of Pneumonic Plague?

Patients usually have fever, weakness, and rapidly developing pneumonia with shortness of breath, chest pain, cough, and sometimes bloody or watery sputum. Nausea, vomiting, and abdominal pain may also occur. Without early treatment, pneumonic plague usually leads to respiratory failure, shock, and rapid death.

### How Do People Become Infected with Pneumonic Plague?

Pneumonic plague occurs when *Yersinia pestis* infects the lungs. Transmission can take place if someone breathes in *Y. pestis* particles, which could happen in an aerosol release during a bioterrorism attack. Pneumonic plague is also transmitted by breathing in *Y. pestis* suspended in respiratory droplets from a person (or animal) with pneumonic plague. Respiratory droplets are spread most readily by coughing or sneezing. Becoming infected in this way usually requires direct and close (within 6 feet) contact with the ill person or animal. Pneumonic plague may also occur if a person with bubonic or septicemic plague is untreated and the bacteria spread to the lungs.

### Does Plague Occur Naturally?

Yes. The World Health Organization reports 1,000 to 3,000 cases of plague worldwide every year. An average of 5 to 15 cases occur each year in the western United States. These cases are usually scattered and occur in rural to semirural areas. Most cases are of the bubonic form of the disease. Naturally occurring pneumonic plague is uncommon, although small outbreaks do occur. Both types of plague are readily controlled by standard public health response measures.

### Can a Person Exposed to Pneumonic Plague Avoid Becoming Sick?

Yes. People who have had close contact with an infected person can greatly reduce the chance of becoming sick if they begin treatment within 7 days of their exposure. Treatment consists of taking antibiotics for at least 7 days.

### How Quickly Would Someone Get Sick If Exposed to Plague Bacteria through the Air?

Someone exposed to *Yersinia pestis* through the air—either from an intentional aerosol release or from close and direct exposure to someone with plague pneumonia—would become ill within 1 to 6 days.

### Can Pneumonic Plague Be Treated?

Yes. To prevent a high risk of death, antibiotics should be given within 24 hours of the first symptoms. Several types of antibiotics are effective for curing the disease and for preventing it. Available oral medications are a tetracycline (such as doxycycline) or a fluoroquinolone (such as ciprofloxacin). For injection or intravenous use, streptomycin or gentamicin antibiotics are used. Early in the response to a bioterrorism attack, these drugs would be tested to determine which is most effective against the particular weapon that was used.

### Would Enough Medication Be Available in the Event of a Bioterrorism Attack Involving Pneumonic Plague?

National and state public health officials have large supplies of drugs needed in the event of a bioterrorism attack. These supplies can be sent anywhere in the United States within 12 hours.

### What Should People Do If They Suspect They or Others Have Been Exposed to Plague?

Get immediate medical attention. To prevent illness, a person who has been exposed to pneumonic plague must receive antibiotic treatment without delay. If an exposed person becomes ill, antibiotics must be administered within 24 hours of the first symptoms to reduce the risk of death. Immediately notify local or state health departments so they can begin to investigate and control the problem right away. If bioterrorism is suspected, the health departments will notify the CDC, FBI, and other appropriate authorities.

### How Can Someone Reduce the Risk of Getting Pneumonic Plague from Another Person or Giving It to Someone Else?

People having direct and close contact with someone with pneumonic plague should wear tightly fitting disposable surgical masks. Patients with the disease should be isolated and medically supervised for at least the first 48 hours of antibiotic treatment. People who have been exposed to a contagious person can be protected from developing plague by receiving prompt antibiotic treatment.

### How Is Plague Diagnosed?

The first step is evaluation by a health worker. If the health worker suspects pneumonic plague, samples of the patient's blood, sputum, or lymph node aspirate are sent to a laboratory for testing. Once the laboratory receives the sample, preliminary results can be ready in less than two hours. Confirmation will take longer, usually 24 to 48 hours.

### How Long Can Plague Bacteria Exist in the Environment?

*Yersinia pestis* is easily destroyed by sunlight and drying. Even so, when released into air, the bacterium will survive for up to 1 hour, depending on conditions.

### Is a Vaccine Available to Prevent Pneumonic Plague?

Currently, no plague vaccine is available in the United States. Research is in progress, but we are not likely to have vaccines for several years or more.

*Source*: Centers for Disease Control and Prevention, www.cdc.gov.

**What Is Salmonellosis?**

Salmonellosis is an infection with a bacteria called *Salmonella*. Most persons infected with *Salmonella* develop diarrhea, fever, and abdominal cramps 12 to 72 hours after infection. The illness usually lasts 4 to 7 days, and most persons recover without treatment. However, in some persons the diarrhea may be so severe that the patient needs to be hospitalized. In these patients, the *Salmonella* infection may spread from the intestines to the bloodstream and then to other body sites and can cause death unless the person is treated promptly with antibiotics. The elderly, infants, and those with impaired immune systems are more likely to have a severe illness.

**What Sort of Germ Is *Salmonella*?**

The *Salmonella* germ is actually a group of bacteria that can cause diarrheal illness in humans. They are microscopic living creatures that pass from the feces of people or animals to other people or other animals. There are many different kinds of *Salmonella* bacteria. *Salmonella* serotype *typhimurium* and *Salmonella* serotype *enteritidis* are the most common in the United States. *Salmonella* has been known for more than 100 years to cause illness. The bacteria were discovered by an American scientist named Salmon, for whom they are named.

**How Can *Salmonella* Infections Be Diagnosed?**

Many different kinds of illnesses can cause diarrhea, fever, or abdominal cramps. Determining that *Salmonella* is the cause of the illness depends on laboratory tests that identify *Salmonella* in the stools of an infected person. These tests are sometimes not performed unless the laboratory is instructed specifically to look for the organism. Once *Salmonella* has been identified, further testing can determine its specific type, and which antibiotics could be used to treat it.

**How Can *Salmonella* Infections Be Treated?**

*Salmonella* infections usually resolve in 5 to 7 days and often do not require treatment unless the patient becomes severely dehydrated or the infection spreads from the intestines. Persons with severe diarrhea may require rehydration, often with intravenous fluids. Antibiotics are not usually necessary unless the infection spreads from the intestines, then it can be treated with ampicillin, gentamicin, trimethoprim/sulfamethoxazole, or ciprofloxacin. Unfortunately, some *Salmonella* bacteria have become resistant to antibiotics, largely as a result of the use of antibiotics to promote the growth of feed animals.

**Are There Long-Term Consequences to a *Salmonella* Infection?**

Persons with diarrhea usually recover completely, although it may be several months before their bowel habits are entirely normal. A small number of persons who are infected with *Salmonella* will go on to develop pains in their joints, irritation of the eyes, and painful urination. This is called *Reiter's syndrome*. It can last for months or years, and can lead to chronic arthritis, which is difficult to treat. Antibiotic treatment does not affect whether the person later develops arthritis.

**How Do People Catch *Salmonella*?**

*Salmonella* live in the intestinal tracts of humans and other animals, including birds. *Salmonella* are usually transmitted to humans by eating foods contaminated with animal feces. Contaminated foods usually look and smell normal. Contaminated foods are often of animal origin, such as beef, poultry, milk, or eggs, but all foods, including vegetables, may become contaminated. Many raw foods of animal origin are frequently contaminated, but, fortunately, thorough cooking kills *Salmonella*. Food may also become contaminated by the unwashed hands of an infected food handler who forgot to wash his or her hands with soap after using the bathroom.

*Salmonella* may also be found in the feces of some pets, especially those with diarrhea, and people can become infected if they do not wash their hands after contact with these feces. Reptiles are particularly likely to harbor *Salmonella*, and people should always wash their hands immediately after handling a reptile, even if the reptile is healthy. Adults should also be careful that children wash their hands after handling a reptile.

### What Can a Person Do to Prevent This Illness?

There is no vaccine to prevent salmonellosis. Because foods of animal origin may be contaminated with *Salmonella*, people should not eat raw or undercooked eggs, poultry, or meat. Raw eggs may be unrecognized in some foods, such as homemade hollandaise sauce, Caesar and other salad dressings, tiramisu, homemade ice cream, homemade mayonnaise, cookie dough, and frostings. Poultry and meat, including hamburgers, should be well cooked, not pink in the middle. Persons also should not consume raw or unpasteurized milk or other dairy products. Produce should be thoroughly washed before consuming.

Cross-contamination of foods should be avoided. Uncooked meats should be kept separate from produce, cooked foods, and ready-to-eat foods. Hands, cutting boards, counters, knives, and other utensils should be washed thoroughly after handling uncooked foods. Hands should be washed before handling any food, and between handling different food items.

People who have salmonellosis should not prepare food or pour water for others until they have been shown to no longer be carrying the *Salmonella* bacterium.

People should wash their hands after contact with animal feces. Because reptiles are particularly likely to have *Salmonella*, everyone should immediately wash his or her hands after handling reptiles. Reptiles (including turtles) are not appropriate pets for small children and should not be in the same house as an infant.

### How Common Is Salmonellosis?

Every year, approximately 40,000 cases of salmonellosis are reported in the United States. Because many milder cases are not diagnosed or reported, the actual number of infections may be thirty or more times greater. Salmonellosis is more common in the summer than winter. Children are the most likely to get salmonellosis. Young children, the elderly, and the immunocompromised are the most likely to have severe infections. It is estimated that approximately 600 persons die each year with acute salmonellosis.

### What Else Can Be Done to Prevent Salmonellosis?

It is important for the public health department to know about cases of salmonellosis. It is important for clinical laboratories to send isolates of *Salmonella* to the city, country, or state public health laboratories so the specific type can be determined and compared with other *Salmonella* cases in the community. If many cases occur at the same time, it may mean that a restaurant, food, or water supply has a problem which needs correction by the public health department.

Some prevention steps occur every day without your even thinking about it. Pasteurization of milk and treating municipal water supplies are highly effective prevention measures that have been in place for many years. In the 1970s, small pet turtles were a common source of salmonellosis in the United States, and in 1975 the sale of small turtles was halted in this country. Improvements in farm animal hygiene, in slaughter plant practices, and in vegetable and fruit harvesting and packing operations may help prevent salmonellosis caused by contaminated foods. Better education of food industry workers in basic food safety and restaurant inspection procedures may prevent cross-contamination and other food-handling errors that can lead to outbreaks. Wider use of pasteurized eggs in restaurants, hospitals, and nursing homes is an important prevention measure. In the future, irradiation or other treatments may greatly reduce contamination of raw meat.

### What Is the Government Doing about Salmonellosis?

The CDC monitors the frequency of *Salmonella* infections in the country and assists the local and state health departments to investigate outbreaks and devise control measures. CDC also conducts research to better identify specific types of *Salmonella*. The Food and Drug Administration inspects imported foods and milk pasteurization plants, promotes better food preparation techniques in restaurants and food processing plants, and regulates the sale of turtles. The FDA also regulates the use of specific antibiotics as growth promoters in food animals. The U.S. Department of Agriculture monitors the health of food animals, inspects egg pasteurization plants, and is responsible for the quality of slaughtered and processed meat. The U.S. Environmental Protection Agency regulates and monitors the safety of our drinking water supplies.

### How Can I Learn More about This and Other Public Health Problems?

You can discuss any medical concerns you may have with your doctor or other heath care provider. Your local city or country health department can provide more information about this and other public health problems that are occurring in your area.

General information about the public health of the nation is published every week in the *Morbidity and Mortality Weekly Report*, by the CDC in Atlanta, Georgia. Epidemiologists in your local and state health departments are tracking a number of important public health problems, investigating special problems that arise, and helping to prevent them from occurring in the first place or from spreading if they do occur.

### What Can I Do to Prevent Salmonellosis?

- Cook poultry, ground beef, and eggs thoroughly before eating.
- Do not eat or drink foods containing raw eggs or raw unpasteurized milk.
- If you are served undercooked meat, poultry, or eggs in a restaurant, don't hesitate to send it back to the kitchen for further cooking.
- Wash hands, kitchen work surfaces, and utensils with soap and water immediately after they have been in contact with raw meat or poultry.
- Be particularly careful with foods prepared for infants, the elderly, and the immunocompromised.
- Wash hands with soap after handling reptiles or birds, or after contact with pet feces.
- Avoid direct or even indirect contact between reptiles (turtles, iguanas, other lizards, snakes) and infants or immunocompromised persons.
- Don't work with raw poultry or meat and an infant (e.g., feed, change diaper) at the same time.
- Mother's milk is the safest food for young infants. Breastfeeding prevents salmonellosis and many other health problems.

*Source*: Centers for Disease Control and Prevention, www.cdc.gov.

**SIDEBAR 4-16   Facts about Typhoid Fever**

Typhoid fever is a life-threatening illness caused by the bacterium *Salmonella typhi* (*S. typhi*). In the United States about 400 cases occur each year, and 70% of these are acquired while traveling internationally. Typhoid fever is still common in the developing world, where it affects about 12.5 million persons each year.

Typhoid fever can be prevented and can usually be treated with antibiotics. Anyone planning to travel outside the United States should know about typhoid fever and what steps they can take to protect themselves.

### How Is Typhoid Fever Spread?

*Salmonella typhi* lives only in humans. Persons with typhoid fever carry the bacteria in their bloodstream and intestinal tract. In addition, a small number of persons, called *carriers*, recover from typhoid fever but continue to carry the bacteria. Both ill persons and carriers shed *S. typhi* in their feces (stool).

You can get typhoid fever if you eat food or drink beverages that have been handled by a person who is shedding *S. typhi* or if sewage contaminated with *S. typhi* bacteria gets into the water you use for drinking or washing food. Therefore, typhoid fever is more common in areas of the world where hand washing is less frequent and water is likely to be contaminated with sewage.

Once *S. typhi* bacteria are eaten or drunk, they multiply and spread into the bloodstream. The body reacts with fever and other signs and symptoms.

### Where in the World Do You Get Typhoid Fever?

Typhoid fever is common in most parts of the world except in industrialized regions such as the United States, Canada, western Europe, Australia, and Japan. Therefore, if you are traveling to the developing world, you should consider taking pre-

cautions. During the past 10 years, travelers from the United States to Asia, Africa, and Latin America have been especially at risk.

### How Can You Avoid Typhoid Fever?

Two basic actions can protect you from typhoid fever:

1.  Avoid risky foods and drinks.
2.  Get vaccinated against typhoid fever.

It may surprise you, but watching what you eat and drink when you travel is as important as being vaccinated. This is because the vaccines are not completely effective. Avoiding risky foods will also help protect you from other illnesses, including travelers' diarrhea, cholera, dysentery, and hepatitis A.

### "Boil It, Cook It, Peel It, or Forget It"

- If you drink water, buy it bottled or bring it to a rolling boil for 1 minute before you drink it. Bottled carbonated water is safer than uncarbonated water.
- Ask for drinks without ice unless the ice is made from bottled or boiled water. Avoid popsicles and flavored ices that may have been made with contaminated water.
- Eat foods that have been thoroughly cooked and that are still hot and steaming.
- Avoid raw vegetables and fruits that cannot be peeled. Vegetables such as lettuce are easily contaminated and are very hard to wash well.
- When you eat raw fruit or vegetables that can be peeled, peel them yourself. (Wash your hands with soap first.) Do not eat the peelings.
- Avoid foods and beverages from street vendors. It is difficult for food to be kept clean on the street, and many travelers get sick from food bought from street vendors.

TABLE 4-2  **Typhoid Vaccines Available in the United States**

| Vaccine name | How given | Number of doses necessary | Time between doses | Total time needed for vaccination | Minimum age for vaccination | Booster needed every |
|---|---|---|---|---|---|---|
| Ty21a (Vivotif Berna, Swiss Serum and Vaccine Institute) | 1 capsule by mouth | 4 | 2 days | 2 weeks | 6 years | 5 years |
| ViCPS (Typhim Vi, Pasteur Merieux) | Injection | 1 | N/A | 1 week | 2 years | 2 years |

*Note*:  The parenteral heat-phenol-inactivated vaccine (manufactured by Wyeth-Ayerst) has been discontinued.

## Getting Vaccinated

If you are traveling to a country where typhoid is common, you should consider being vaccinated against typhoid. Visit a doctor or travel clinic to discuss your vaccination options. Remember that you will need to complete your vaccination at least 1 week before you travel so that the vaccine has time to take effect. Typhoid vaccines lose effectiveness after several years; if you were vaccinated in the past, check with your doctor to see if it is time for a booster vaccination. Taking antibiotics will not prevent typhoid fever; antibiotics only help treat it. Table 4-2 provides basic information on typhoid vaccines that are available in the United States.

## What Are the Signs and Symptoms of Typhoid Fever?

Persons with typhoid fever usually have a sustained fever as high as 103° to 104°F (39° to 40°C). They may also feel weak or have stomach pains, headache, or loss of appetite. In some cases, patients have a rash of flat, rose-colored spots. The only way to know for sure if an illness is typhoid fever is to have samples of stool or blood tested for the presence of *S. typhi*.

## What Do You Do If You Think You Have Typhoid Fever?

If you suspect you have typhoid fever, see a doctor immediately. If you are traveling in a foreign country, you can usually call the U.S. consulate for a list of recommended doctors. You will probably be given an antibiotic to treat the disease. Three commonly prescribed antibiotics are ampicillin, trimethoprim/sulfamethoxazole, and ciprofloxacin. Persons given antibiotics usually begin to feel better within 2 to 3 days, and deaths rarely occur. However, persons who do not get treatment may continue to have fever for weeks or months, and as many as 20% may die from complications of the infection.

## Typhoid Fever's Danger Doesn't End When Symptoms Disappear

Even if your symptoms seem to go away, you may still be carrying *S. typhi*. If so, the illness could return, or you could pass the disease to other people. In fact, if you work at a job where you handle food or care for small children, you may be barred legally from going back to work until a doctor has determined that you no longer carry any typhoid bacteria.

If you are being treated for typhoid fever, it is important to do the following:

- Keep taking the prescribed antibiotics for as long as the doctor has asked you to take them.
- Wash your hands carefully with soap and water after using the bathroom, and do not prepare or serve food for other people. This will lower the chance that you will pass the infection on to someone else.
- Have your doctor perform a series of stool cultures to ensure that no *S. typhi* bacteria remain in your body.

*Source*: Centers for Disease Control and Prevention, www.cdc.gov.

---

SIDEBAR 4-17   **Facts about Botulism**

### What Is Botulism?

Botulism is a rare but serious paralytic illness caused by a nerve toxin that is produced by the bacterium *Clostridium botulinum*. There are three main kinds of botulism. Food-borne botulism is caused by eating foods that contain the botulism toxin. Wound botulism is caused by toxin produced from a wound infected with *Clostridium botulinum*. Infant botulism is caused by consuming the spores of the botulinum bacteria, which then grow in the intestines and release toxin. All forms of botulism can be fatal and are considered medical emergencies. Food-borne botulism can be especially dangerous because many people can be poisoned by eating a contaminated food.

### What Kind of Germ Is *Clostridium botulinum*?

*Clostridium botulinum* is the name of a group of bacteria commonly found in soil. These rod-shaped organisms grow best in low oxygen conditions. The bacteria form spores that allow them to survive in a dormant state until exposed to conditions that can support their growth. There are seven types of botulism toxin designated by the letters A through G; only types A, B, E, and F cause illness in humans.

### How Common Is Botulism?

In the United States an average of 110 cases of botulism are reported each year. Of these, approximately 25% are food-borne, 72% are infant botulism, and the rest are wound botulism. Outbreaks of food-borne botulism involving two or more persons occur most years and usually are caused by eating contaminated home-canned foods. The number of cases of food-borne and infant botulism has changed little in recent years, but wound botulism has increased because of the use of black-tar heroin, especially in California.

### What Are the Symptoms of Botulism?

The classic symptoms of botulism include double vision, blurred vision, drooping eyelids, slurred speech, difficulty swallowing, dry mouth, and muscle weakness. Infants with botulism appear lethargic, feed poorly, are constipated, and have a weak cry and poor muscle tone. These are all symptoms of the muscle paralysis caused by the bacterial toxin. If untreated, these symptoms may progress to cause paralysis of the arms, legs, trunk, and respiratory muscles. In food-borne botulism, symptoms generally begin 18 to 36 hours after eating a contaminated food, but they can occur as early as 6 hours or as late as 10 days.

### How Is Botulism Diagnosed?

Physicians may consider the diagnosis if the patient's history and physical examination suggest botulism. However, these clues are usually not enough to allow a diagnosis of botulism. Other diseases, such as Guillain-Barré syndrome, stroke, and myasthenia gravis, can appear similar to botulism, and special tests may be needed to exclude these other conditions. These tests may include a brain scan, spinal fluid examination, nerve conduction test (electromyography, or EMG), and a Tensilon test for myasthenia gravis. The most direct way to confirm the diagnosis is to demonstrate the *Botulinum* toxin in the patient's serum or stool by injecting serum or stool into mice and looking for signs of botulism. The bacteria can also be isolated from the stool of persons with food-borne and infant botulism. These tests can be performed at some state health department laboratories and at CDC.

### How Can Botulism Be Treated?

The respiratory failure and paralysis that occur with severe botulism may require a patient to be on a breathing machine (ventilator) for weeks, plus intensive medical and nursing care. After several weeks, the paralysis slowly improves. If diagnosed early, food-borne and wound botulism can be treated with an antitoxin that blocks the action of toxin circulating in the blood. This can prevent patients from worsening, but recovery still takes many weeks. Physicians may try to remove contaminated food still in the gut by inducing vomiting or by using enemas. Wounds should be treated, usually surgically, to remove the source of the toxin-producing bacteria. Good supportive care in a hospital is the mainstay of therapy for all forms of botulism. Currently, antitoxin is not routinely given for treatment of infant botulism.

### Are There Complications from Botulism?

Botulism can result in death due to respiratory failure. However, in the past 50 years the proportion of patients with botulism who die has fallen from about 50% to 8%. A patient with severe botulism may require a breathing machine as well as intensive medical and nursing care for several months.

Patients who survive an episode of botulism poisoning may have fatigue and shortness of breath for years and long-term therapy may be needed to aid recovery.

### How Can Botulism Be Prevented?

Botulism can be prevented. Food-borne botulism has often been from home-canned foods with low acid content, such as asparagus, green beans, beets, and corn. However, outbreaks of botulism have also been linked to more unusual sources, such as chopped garlic in oil, chili peppers, tomatoes, improperly handled baked potatoes wrapped in aluminum foil, and home-canned or fermented fish. Persons who do home canning should follow strict hygienic procedures to reduce contamination of foods. Oils infused with garlic or herbs should be refrigerated. Potatoes that have been baked while wrapped in aluminum foil should be kept hot until served or refrigerated. Because the botulism toxin is destroyed by high temperatures, persons who eat home-canned foods should consider boiling the food for 10 minutes before eating it to ensure safety. Instructions on safe home canning can be obtained from country extension services or from the U.S. Department of Agriculture. Because honey can contain spores of *Clostridium botulinum* and this has been a source of infection for infants, children younger than 12 months of age should not be fed honey. Honey is safe for persons 1 year of age and older. Wound botulism can be prevented by promptly seeking medical care for infected wounds and by not using injectable street drugs.

### What Are Public Health Agencies Doing to Prevent or Control Botulism?

Public education about botulism prevention is an ongoing activity. Information about safe canning is widely available for consumers. State health departments and CDC offices have persons knowledgeable about botulism available to consult with physicians 24 hours a day. If antitoxin is needed to treat a patient, it can be quickly delivered to a physician anywhere in the country. Suspected outbreaks of botulism are quickly investigated, and if they involve a commercial product, the appropriate control measures are coordinated among public health and regulatory agencies. Physicians should report suspected cases of botulism to a state health department.

*Source*: Centers for Disease Control and Prevention, www.cdc.gov.

---

SIDEBAR 4-18   **Facts about Tularemia**

### What Is Tularemia?

Tularemia is an infectious disease caused by a hardy bacterium, *Francisella tularensis*, found in animals (especially rodents, rabbits, and hares).

### How Do People Become Infected with the Tularemia Bacteria?

Typically, persons become infected through the bites of arthropods (most commonly, ticks and deerflies) that have fed on an infected animal, by handling infected animal carcasses, by eating or drinking contaminated food or water, or by inhaling infected aerosols.

### Does Tularemia Occur Naturally in the United States?

Yes. It is a widespread disease of animals. Approximately 200 cases of tularemia in humans are reported annually in the United States, mostly in persons living in the south-central and western states. Nearly all cases occur in rural areas and are associated with the bites of infective ticks and biting flies or with the handling of infected rodents, rabbits, or hares. Occasional cases result from inhaling infectious aerosols and from laboratory accidents.

### Why Are We Concerned About Tularemia as a Bioweapon?

*Francisella tularensis* is highly infectious: A small number of bacteria (10 to 50 organisms) can cause disease. If *F. tularensis* were used as a bioweapon, the bacteria would likely be made airborne for exposure by inhalation. Persons who inhale an infectious aerosol would generally experience severe respiratory illness, including life-threatening pneumonia and systemic infection, if they were not treated. The bacteria that cause tularemia occur widely in nature and could be isolated and grown in quantity in a laboratory, although manufacturing an effective aerosol weapon would require considerable sophistication.

### Can Someone Become Infected with the Tularemia Bacteria from Another Person?

No. People have not been known to transmit the infection to others, so infected persons do not need to be isolated.

### How Quickly Would Someone Become Sick If Exposed to the Tularemia Bacteria?

The incubation period for tularemia is typically 3 to 5 days, with a range of 1 to 14 days.

### What Are the Signs and Symptoms of Tularemia?

Depending on the route of exposure, the tularemia bacteria may cause skin ulcers, swollen and painful lymph glands, inflamed eyes, sore throat, oral ulcers, or pneumonia. If the bacteria were inhaled, symptoms would include the abrupt onset of fever, chills, headache, muscle aches, joint pain, dry cough, and progressive weakness. Persons with pneumonia can develop chest pain, difficulty breathing, bloody sputum, and respiratory failure. Forty percent or more of persons with the lung and systemic forms of the disease may die if they are not treated with appropriate antibiotics.

### What Should Someone Do If They Suspect They or Others Have Been Exposed to the Tularemia Bacteria?

Seek prompt medical attention. If a person has been exposed to *Francisella tularensis*, treatment with tetracycline antibiotics for 14 days after exposure may be recommended. Local and state health departments should be immediately notified so an investigation and control activities can begin quickly. If the exposure is thought to be due to criminal activity (bioterrorism), local and state health departments will notify CDC, the FBI, and other appropriate authorities.

### How Is Tularemia Diagnosed?

When tularemia is clinically suspected, the health care worker will collect specimens, such as blood or sputum, from the patient for testing in a diagnostic or reference laboratory. Laboratory test results for tularemia may be presumptive or confirmatory. Presumptive (preliminary) identification may take less than 2 hours, but confirmatory testing will take longer, usually 24 to 48 hours.

### Can Tularemia Be Effectively Treated with Antibiotics?

Yes. After potential exposure or diagnosis, early treatment is recommended with an antibiotic from the tetracycline (such as doxycycline) or fluoroquinolone (such as ciprofloxacin) class, which are taken orally, or the antibiotics streptomycin or gentamicin, which are given intramuscularly or intravenously. Sensitivity testing of the tularemia bacterium can be done in the early stages of a response to determine which antibiotics would be most effective.

### How Long Can *Francisella tularensis* Exist in the Environment?

*Francisella tularensis* can remain alive for weeks in water and soil.

### Is There a Vaccine Available for Tularemia?

In the past, a vaccine for tularemia has been used to protect laboratory workers, but it is currently under review by the Food and Drug Administration.

*Source*: Centers for Disease Control and Prevention, www.cdc.gov.

## NUCLEAR/RADIOLOGICAL

Nuclear and radiological weapons are those that involve the movement of energy through space and through material. There are three primary mechanisms by which terrorists can use radiation to carry out an attack: detonation of a nuclear bomb, dispersal of radiological material, or an attack on a facility housing nuclear material (power plant, research laboratory, storage site, etc.)

Nuclear weapons are the most devastating of the various attack forms listed earlier. They are also the most difficult to develop or acquire, so are considered the lowest threat of the three in terms of terrorist

potential. A nuclear weapon causes damage to property and harm to life through two separate processes. First, a blast is created by the detonation of the bomb. An incredibly large amount of energy is released in the explosion, which is the result of an uncontrolled chain reaction of atomic splitting. The initial shock wave, which destroys all built structures within a range of up to several miles, is followed by a heat wave reaching tens of millions of degrees close to the point of detonation. High winds accompany the shock and heat waves.

The second process by which nuclear weapons inflict harm is through harmful radiation. This radiation and radiological material is most dangerous close to the area of detonation, where high concentrations can cause rapid death, but particles reaching high into the atmosphere can pose a threat several hundreds of miles away under the right meteorological conditions. Radiation can also persist for years after the explosion occurs.

Radiological dispersion devices (RDDs) are simple explosive devices that spread harmful radioactive material upon detonation, without the involvement of a nuclear explosion. These devices are often called "dirty bombs." Radiological dispersion devices also exist that do not require explosives for dispersal. Though illnesses and fatalities very close to the point of dispersal are likely, these devices are more likely to be used to spread terror. Like many biological and chemical weapons, it may be difficult to initially detect that a radiological attack has occurred. Special detection equipment and the training to use it are a prerequisite. Sidebar 4-19 lists some indicators of a radiological release.

A third scenario involving nuclear/radiological material entails an attack on a nuclear facility. There

are many facilities around the country where nuclear material is stored, including nuclear power plants, hazardous materials storage sites, medical facilities, military installations, and industrial facilities. An attack on any of these facilities could result in a release of radiological material into the atmosphere, which would pose a threat to life and certainly cause fear among those who live nearby.

If a radiological or nuclear attack were to occur, humans and animals would experience both internal and external consequences. External exposure results from any contact with radioactive material outside the body, while internal exposure requires ingestion, inhalation, or injection of radiological materials. Radiation sickness results from high doses of radiation, and can result in death if the dosage was high enough. Other effects of radiation exposure can include redness or burning of the skin and eyes, nausea, damage to the body's immune system, and a higher lifetime risk of developing cancer. (*Source*: FEMA, 2002)

A fact sheet developed by the CDC on a radiation event is presented in Sidebar 4-20.

---

SIDEBAR 4-19   **General Indicators of Possible Nuclear Weapon/Radiological Agent Use**

- Stated threat to deploy a nuclear or radiological device
- Presence of nuclear or radiological equipment
- Spent fuel canisters or nuclear transport vehicles

- Nuclear placards/warning materials along with otherwise unexplained casualties.

*Source*: Federal Emergency Management Agency. (2002). *Interim Planning Guide for State and Local Government: Managing the Emergency Consequences of Terrorist Incidents.* Washington, DC: FEMA (July).

---

SIDEBAR 4-20   **Facts about a Radiation Emergency**

**What Is Radiation?**

- Radiation is a form of energy that is present all around us.
- Different types of radiation exist, some of which have more energy than others.

- Amounts of radiation released into the environment are measured in units called curies. However, the dose of radiation that a person receives is measured in units called rem.

**How Can Exposure Occur?**

- People are exposed to small amounts of radiation every day, both from naturally occurring sources (such as elements in the soil or cosmic rays from the sun), and man-made sources. Man-made sources include some electronic equipment (such as microwave ovens and television sets), medical sources (such as X-rays, certain diagnostic tests and treatments), and from nuclear weapons testing.

- The amount of radiation from natural or man-made sources to which people are exposed is usually small; a radiation emergency (such as a nuclear power plant accident or a terrorist event) could expose people to small or large doses of radiation, depending on the situation.

- Scientists estimate that the average person in the United States receives a dose of about one-third of a rem per year. About 80% of human exposure comes from natural sources, and the remaining 20% comes from man-made radiation sources—mainly medical X-rays.

- Internal exposure refers to radioactive material that is taken into the body through breathing, eating, or drinking.

- External exposure refers to an exposure to a radioactive source outside of our bodies.

- Contamination refers to particles of radioactive material that are deposited anywhere that they are not supposed to be, such as on an object or on a person's skin.

**What Happens When People Are Exposed to Radiation?**

- Radiation can affect the body in a number of ways, and the adverse health effects of exposure may not be apparent for many years.

- These adverse health effects can range from mild effects, such as skin reddening, to serious effects such as cancer and death, depending on the amount of radiation absorbed by the body (the dose), the type of radiation, the route of exposure, and the length of time a person was exposed.

- Exposure to very large doses of radiation may cause death within a few days or months.

- Exposure to lower doses of radiation may lead to an increased risk of developing cancer or other adverse health effects later in life.

**What Types of Terrorist Events Might Involve Radiation?**

- Possible terrorist events could involve introducing radioactive material into the food or water supply, using explosives (such as dynamite) to scatter radioactive materials (called a "dirty bomb"), bombing or destroying a nuclear facility, or exploding a small nuclear device.

- Although introducing radioactive material into the food or water supply most likely would cause great concern or fear, it probably would not cause much contamination or increase the danger of adverse health effects.

- Although a dirty bomb could cause serious injuries from the explosion, it most likely would not have enough radioactive material in a form that would cause serious radiation sickness among large numbers of people. However, people who were exposed to radiation scattered by the bomb could have a greater risk of developing cancer later in life, depending on their dose.

- A meltdown or explosion at a nuclear facility could cause a large amount of radioactive material to be released. People at the facility would probably be contaminated with radioactive material and possibly be injured if there was an explosion. Those people who received a large dose might develop acute radiation syndrome. People in the surrounding area could be exposed or contaminated.

- Clearly, an exploded nuclear device could result in a lot of property damage. People would be killed or injured from the blast and might be contaminated by radioactive material. Many people could have symptoms of acute radiation syndrome. After a nuclear explosion, radioactive fallout would extend over a large region far from the point of impact, potentially increasing people's risk of developing cancer over time.

### What Preparations Can I Make for a Radiation Emergency?

- Your community should have a plan in place in case of a radiation emergency. Check with community leaders to learn more about the plan and possible evacuation routes.
- Check with your child's school, the nursing home of a family member, and your employer to see what their plans are for dealing with a radiation emergency.
- Develop your own family emergency plan so that every family member knows what to do.
- At home, put together an emergency kit that would be appropriate for any emergency. The kit should include the following items:
  - A flashlight with extra batteries
  - A portable radio with extra batteries
  - Bottled water
  - Canned and packaged food
  - A hand-operated can opener
  - A first-aid kit and essential prescription medications
  - Personal items such as paper towels, garbage bags, and toilet paper.

### How Can I Protect Myself During a Radiation Emergency?

- After a release of radioactive materials, local authorities will monitor the levels of radiation and determine what protective actions to take.
- The most appropriate action will depend on the situation. Tune to the local emergency

response network or news station for information and instructions during any emergency.
- If a radiation emergency involves the release of large amounts of radioactive materials, you may be advised to "shelter in place," which means to stay in your home or office; or you may be advised to move to another location.
- If you are advised to shelter in place, you should do the following:
  - Close and lock all doors and windows.
  - Turn off fans, air conditioners, and forced-air heating units that bring in fresh air from the outside. Only use units to recirculate air that is already in the building.
  - Close fireplace dampers.
  - If possible, bring pets inside.
  - Move to an inner room or basement.
  - Keep your radio tuned to the emergency response network or local news to find out what else you need to do.
- If you are advised to evacuate, follow the directions that your local officials provide. Leave the area as quickly and orderly as possible. In addition:
  - Take a flashlight, portable radio, batteries, first-aid kit, supply of sealed food and water, hand-operated can opener, essential medicines, and cash and credit cards.
  - Take pets only if you are using your own vehicle and going to a place you know will accept animals. Emergency vehicles and shelters usually will not accept animals.

### Should I Take Potassium Iodide During a Radiation Emergency?

- Potassium iodide (KI) should only be taken in a radiation emergency that involves the release of radioactive iodine, such as an accident at a nuclear power plant or the explosion of a nuclear bomb. A "dirty bomb" most likely will not contain radioactive iodine.

- A person who is internally exposed to radio-active iodine may experience thyroid disease later in life. The thyroid gland will absorb radioactive iodine and may develop cancer or abnormal growths later on. KI will saturate the thyroid gland with iodine, decreasing the amount of harmful radioactive iodine that can be absorbed.

- KI only protects the thyroid gland and does not provide protection from any other radiation exposure.
- Some people are allergic to iodine and should not take KI. Check with your doctor about any concerns you have about potassium iodide.

*Source*: Centers for Disease Control and Prevention, www.cdc. gov.

## PREPAREDNESS AND SHELTERING IN PLACE

Sidebar 4-21 discusses how the general population can prepare for a bioterror or chemical attack. Preparedness against dispersion of a chemical agent is further discussed in Sidebar 4-22, about sheltering in place in the event of a chemical attack.

## COMBINED HAZARDS

Terrorists can combine two or more attack methods to achieve a synergistic effect. By doing so, they can increase the efficacy of each agent in terms of their potential to destroy, harm, or kill, creating a sum total consequence that is more devastating than had each agent been used individually. A dirty bomb, in which

---

SIDEBAR 4-21    **Preparedness and Response for a Bioterror or Chemical Attack**

**What Should I Do to Be Prepared?**

We continue to hear stories of the public buying gas masks and hoarding medicine in anticipation of a possible bioterrorist or chemical attack. We do not recommend either. [P]eople should not be scared into thinking they need a gas mask. In the event of a public health emergency, local and state health departments will inform the public about the actions individuals need to take.

**Does Every City Have an Adequate Emergency Response System, Especially One Geared for a Bioterrorist Attack? How Quickly Can It Be Implemented?**

The emergency response system varies from community to community on the basis of each community's investment in its public health infra-structure. Some components of these emergency systems can be implemented very quickly, while others may take longer.

**Are Hospitals Prepared to Handle a Sudden Surge in Demand for Health Care?**

The preparedness level in hospitals depends on the biological agent used in an attack. Because a sudden surge in demand could overwhelm an individual hospital's resources, hospitals collaborate with other hospitals in their area in order to respond to a bioterrorist attack on a citywide or regional basis. Hospitals are required to maintain disaster response plans and to practice applying them as part of their accreditation process. Many components of such plans are useful in responding to bioterrorism. Specific plans for bioterrorism have been added to the latest accreditation requirements of the Joint Commission on Accreditation of Healthcare Organizations. In an emergency, local medical care capacity will be supplemented with federal resources.

### Are Health Department Labs Equipped for/Capable of Doing Testing?

CDC, the Association of Public Health Laboratories, and other officials are working together to ensure that all state health departments are capable of obtaining results of tests on suspected infectious agents. The nation's laboratories are generally classified as Level A, B, C, or D. Level A laboratories are those typically found in community hospitals and are designated to perform initial testing on all clinical specimens. Public health laboratories are usually Level B; these laboratories can confirm or refute preliminary test results and can usually perform antimicrobial susceptibility tests. Level C laboratories, which are reference facilities and can be public health laboratories, perform more rapid identification tests. Level D laboratories are designed to perform the most sophisticated tests and are located in federal facilities such as CDC. CDC is currently working with public and private laboratory partners to develop a formal national laboratory system linking all four levels.

Every state has a laboratory response network (LRN) contact. The LRN links state and local public health laboratories with advanced-capacity laboratories, including clinical, military, veterinary, agricultural, water, and food-testing laboratories. Laboratorians should contact their state public health laboratory to identify their local LRN representative.

### Water Safety: With All This Talk about Possible Biochemical Agents, Just How Safe Is Our Water? Should I Be Disinfecting My Water Just in Case?

The U.S. public water supply system is one of the safest in the world. The general public should continue to drink and use water just as they would under normal conditions. Your local water treatment supplier and local governments are on the alert for any unusual activity and will notify you immediately in the event of any public health threat. At this point, we have no reason to believe that additional measures need to be taken.

The U.S. Environmental Protection Agency (EPA) is the lead federal agency that makes recommendations about water utility issues. The EPA is working closely with the CDC and the U.S. Departments of Defense and Energy to help water agencies assess their systems, determine actions that need to be taken to guard against possible attack, and develop emergency response plans. For more information, visit http://www.epa.gov/safewater.

*Source*: Centers for Disease Control and Prevention, www.cdc. gov.

---

SIDEBAR 4-22 **Chemical Agents: Facts about Sheltering in Place**

### What "Sheltering in Place" Means

Some kinds of chemical accidents or attacks may make going outdoors dangerous. Leaving the area might take too long or put you in harm's way. In such a case it may be safer for you to stay indoors than to go outside. "Shelter in place" means to make a shelter out of the place you are in. It is a way for you to make the building as safe as possible to protect yourself until help arrives. You should not try to shelter in a vehicle unless you have no other choice. Vehicles are not airtight enough to give you adequate protection from chemicals.

### How to Prepare to Shelter in Place

Choose a room in your house or apartment for your shelter. The best room to use for the shelter is a room with as few windows and doors as possible. A large room, preferably with a water supply, is desirable—something like a master bedroom that is connected to a bathroom. For chemical events, this room should be as high in the structure as possible to avoid vapors (gases) that sink. This guideline is different from the sheltering-in-place technique used in tornadoes and other severe weather, when the shelter should be low in the home. You might not be at home if the need to shelter in place ever arises, but if you are at home, the following items would be good to have on hand. (Ideally, all of these items would be stored in the shelter room to save time.)

- First-aid kit
- Food and bottled water. Store 1 gallon of water per person in plastic bottles as well as ready-to-eat foods that will keep without refrigeration at the shelter-in-place location. If you do not have bottled water, or if you run out, you can drink water from a toilet tank (not from a toilet bowl).
- Flashlight, battery-powered radio, and extra batteries for both
- Duct tape and scissors
- Towels and plastic sheeting
- A working telephone

### How to Know If You Need to Shelter in Place

- You will hear from the local police, emergency coordinators, or government officials on the radio and on television if you need to shelter in place.
- If there is a "code red" or "severe" terror alert, you should pay attention to radio and television broadcasts to know right away whether a shelter-in-place alert is announced for your area.
- If you are away from your shelter-in-place location when a chemical event occurs, follow the instructions of emergency coordinators to find the nearest shelter. If your children are at

school, they will be sheltered there. Unless you are instructed to do so, do not try to get to the school to bring your children home.

### What to Do

Act quickly and follow the instructions of your local emergency coordinators. Every situation can be different, so local emergency coordinators might have special instructions for you to follow. In general, do the following:

- Go inside as quickly as possible.
- If there is time, shut and lock all outside doors and windows. Locking them may provide a tighter seal against the chemical. Turn off the air conditioner or heater. Turn off all fans, too. Close the fireplace damper and any other place that air can come in from the outside.
- Go in the shelter-in-place room, and shut the door.
- Tape plastic over any windows in the room. Use duct tape around the windows and doors and make an unbroken seal. Use the tape over any vents into the room and seal any electrical outlets or other openings. Sink and toilet drain traps should have water in them (you can use the sink and toilet as you normally would). If it is necessary to drink water, drink the stored water, not water from the tap.
- Turn on the radio. Keep a telephone close at hand, but don't use it unless there is a serious emergency.

Sheltering in this way should keep you safer than if you are outdoors. Most likely, you will be in the shelter for no more than a few hours. Listen to the radio for an announcement indicating that it is safe to leave the shelter. After you come out of the shelter, emergency coordinators may have additional instructions on how to make the rest of the building safe again.

*Source*: Centers for Disease Control and Prevention, www.cdc. gov.

radiological material is added to a conventional explosive, illustrates this effect. The explosive causes physical damage from the expansion of gases, while the radiological material causes severe health effects. The combination of the two causes both physical damage and harmful radiation, but the dispersal of the radiological material is over a much larger area, and the debris from the conventional explosive becomes dangerous beyond the original explosion due to radiological contamination. Sidebar 4-23 is a fact sheet of information compiled by the CDC on dirty bombs.

Explosives can also be used to deliver chemical or biological weapons. This presents a dangerous scenario in that trauma resulting from the explosion will demand immediate attention from responders, who may enter a contaminated attack scene without first recognizing or taking the time to check if a biological or chemical agent is present. Victims who are rushed to hospitals can cause secondary infections or injuries to EMS and hospital staff. Additionally, contaminated debris can help to spread certain viruses that may not otherwise have so easily entered the body.

When multiple chemicals, biological agents, or a combination of the two are used in an attack, the consequences can confound even those considered experts. The combination of symptoms resulting from multiple injuries or infections will make diagnosis extremely difficult, because these diagnoses often depend on a defined set of effects. The multiple agents will cause physiological effects in humans, animals, or plants that do not fit any established models. The extra time required for identification of the agents used will undoubtedly cause an overall increase in the efficacy of the terrorist attack.

## ROLE OF CDC IN PREPAREDNESS AND RESPONSE

The Centers for Disease and Control and Prevention is a full partner in the nation's emergency management system. With the advent of the new hazards, the CDC has assumed a significant role in defining the characteristics of these hazards and how they may be used as terrorist weapons. This information is critical in preparing first responders, community leaders, businesspeople, and individuals to deal with these hazards. These data are also useful in the design and development of protective gear and clothing, mitigation and prevention measures, and response and cleanup protocols and practices.

CDC has developed two fact sheets on preparedness and response and the CDC's role in the event of a radiological event that are presented in Sidebars 4-24 and 4-25.

## CONCLUSION

The new hazards of terrorism have required a significant investment in education of the general public, local officials, the media, and our first responders. This requirement is equaled by the need to invest in training, protective equipment and gear, specialized technical capabilities, and enhancements of our public health networks. The new hazards represent an opportunity to begin to integrate those responsible for mitigating, preparing, responding to, and recovering from any disaster. It is an opportunity to include public health concerns into our disaster planning and to incorporate the private sector, which involves prominent players because these new hazards affect financial and communications infrastructures. The R&D efforts associated with these new hazards will surely result in advances across a broad spectrum of human activities from medicine to communications technology, and to safer personal protective equipment (PPE). Most importantly, these new hazards, and the financial resources connected with addressing them, can provide an opportunity to actually embrace and apply an all-hazards approach to achieving a homeland that is more secure from the threat of weapons of mass destruction.

SIDEBAR 4-23  **Facts about Dirty Bombs**

Because of recent terrorist events, people have expressed concern about the possibility of a terrorist attack involving radioactive materials, possibly through the use of a "dirty bomb" and the harmful effects of radiation from such an event. The Centers for Disease Control and Prevention has prepared this fact sheet to help people understand what a dirty bomb is and how it may affect their health.

**What Is a "Dirty Bomb"?**

A dirty bomb, or radiological dispersion device, is a bomb that combines conventional explosives, such as dynamite, with radioactive materials in the form of powder or pellets. The idea behind a dirty bomb is to blast radioactive material into the area around the explosion. This could possibly cause buildings and people to be exposed to radioactive material. The main purpose of a dirty bomb is to frighten people and make buildings or land unusable for a long period of time.

**Dirty Bomb versus Atomic Bombs in Hiroshima and Nagasaki**

The atomic explosions that occurred in Hiroshima and Nagasaki were conventional nuclear weapons involving a fission reaction. A dirty bomb is designed to spread radioactive material and contaminate a small area. It does not include the fission products necessary to create a large blast like those seen in Hiroshima and Nagasaki.

**Sources of the Radioactive Material**

There has been a lot of speculation about where terrorists could get radioactive material to use in a dirty bomb. The most harmful radioactive materials are found in nuclear power plants and nuclear weapons sites. However, increased security at these facilities makes obtaining materials from them more difficult.

Because of the dangerous and difficult aspects of obtaining high-level radioactive materials from a nuclear facility, there is a greater chance that the radioactive materials used in a dirty bomb would come from low-level radioactive sources. Low-level radioactive sources are found in hospitals, on construction sites, and at food irradiation plants. The sources in these areas are used to diagnose and treat illnesses, sterilize equipment, inspect welding seams, and irradiate food to kill harmful microbes.

**Dangers of a Dirty Bomb**

If low-level radioactive sources were to be used, the primary danger from a dirty bomb would be the blast itself. Gauging how much radiation might be present is difficult when the source of the radiation is unknown. However, at the levels created by most probable sources, not enough radiation would be present in a dirty bomb to cause severe illness from exposure to radiation.

**Past Use of Dirty Bombs**

According to a United Nations report, Iraq tested a dirty bomb device in 1987 but found that the radiation levels were too low to cause significant damage. Thus, Iraq abandoned any further use of the device.

**What People Should Do after an Explosion**

Radiation cannot be seen, smelled, felt, or tasted by humans. Therefore, if people are present at the scene of an explosion, they will not know whether radioactive materials were involved at the time of the explosion. If people are not too severely injured by the initial blast, they should attempt the following:

- Leave the immediate area on foot. Do not panic. Do not take public or private transportation such as buses, subways, or cars because if radioactive materials were involved, they may contaminate cars or the public transportation system.

- Go inside the nearest building. Staying inside will reduce your exposure to any radioactive material that may be on dust at the scene.
- Remove your clothes as soon as possible, place them in a plastic bag, and seal it. Removing clothing will remove most of the contamination caused by external exposure to radioactive materials. Saving the contaminated clothing would allow testing for exposure without invasive sampling.
- Take a shower or wash yourself as best you can. Washing will reduce the amount of radioactive contamination on your body and will effectively reduce total exposure.
- Be on the lookout for information. Once emergency personnel can assess the scene and the damage, they will be able to tell people whether radiation was involved.

Even if people do not know whether radioactive materials were present, following these simple steps can help reduce their injury from other chemicals that might have been present in the blast.

**If Radioactive Materials Were Involved**

Keep televisions or radios tuned to local news networks. If a radioactive material is released, people will be told where to report for radiation monitoring and blood tests to determine whether they were exposed to the radiation as well as what steps to take to protect their health.

**Risk of Cancer from a Dirty Bomb**

Some cancers can be caused by exposure to radiation. Being at the site where a dirty bomb exploded does not guarantee that people were exposed to the radioactive material. Until doctors are able to check people's skin with sensitive radiation detection devices, it will not be clear whether they were exposed. Just because people are near a radioactive source for a short time or get a small amount of radioactive material on them does not mean that they will get cancer. Doctors will be able to assess risks after the exposure level has been determined.

*Source*: Centers for Disease Control and Prevention, www.cdc.gov.

---

SIDEBAR 4-24   **Preparedness and Response**

**What Should I Do to Be Prepared?**

We continue to hear stories of the public buying gas masks and hoarding medicine in anticipation of a possible bioterrorism or chemical attack. We do not recommend either. As Secretary Thompson said recently, people should not be scared into thinking they need a gas mask. In the event of a public health emergency, local and state health departments will inform the public about the actions individuals need to take.

**Does Every City Have an Adequate Emergency Response System, Especially One Geared for a Bioterrorist Attack? How Quickly Can It Be Implemented?**

The emergency response system varies from community to community on the basis of each community's investment in its public health infrastructure. Some components of these emergency systems can be implemented very quickly, while others may take longer.

## Are Hospitals Prepared to Handle a Sudden Surge in Demand for Health Care?

The preparedness level in hospitals depends on the biological agent used in an attack. Because a sudden surge in demand could overwhelm an individual hospital's resources, hospitals collaborate with other hospitals in their area in order to respond to a bioterrorist attack on a citywide or regional basis. Hospitals are required to maintain disaster response plans and to practice applying them as part of their accreditation process. Many components of such plans are useful in responding to bioterrorism. Specific plans for bioterrorism have been added to the latest accreditation requirements of the Joint Commission on Accreditation of Healthcare Organizations. In an emergency, local medical care capacity will be supplemented with federal resources.

## Are Health Department Labs Equipped/Capable of Doing Testing?

CDC, the Association of Public Health Laboratories, and other officials are working together to ensure that all state health departments are capable of obtaining results of tests on suspected infectious agents. The nation's laboratories are generally classified as Level A, B, C, or D.

- Level A laboratories are those typically found in community hospitals and are designated to perform initial testing on all clinical specimens.
- Level B; these laboratories can confirm or refute preliminary test results and can usually perform antimicrobial susceptibility tests.
- Level C laboratories, which are reference facilities and can be public health laboratories, perform more rapid identification tests.

- Level D laboratories are designed to perform the most sophisticated tests and are located in federal facilities such as CDC.

CDC is currently working with public and private laboratory partners to develop a formal National Laboratory System linking all four levels.

Every state has a Laboratory Response Network (LRN) contact. The LRN links state and local public health laboratories with advanced-capacity laboratories, including clinical, military, veterinary, agricultural, water, and food-testing laboratories. Laboratorians should contact their state public health laboratory to identify their local LRN representative.

## With All This Talk about Possible Biochemical Agents, Just How Safe Is Our Water? Should I Be Disinfecting My Water Just in Case?

The United States public water supply system is one of the safest in the world. The general public should continue to drink and use water just as they would under normal conditions. Your local water treatment supplier and local governments are on the alert for any unusual activity and will notify you immediately in the event of any public health threat. At this point, we have no reason to believe that additional measures need to be taken.

The U.S. Environmental Protection Agency (EPA) is the lead federal agency that makes recommendations about water utility issues. The EPA is working closely with the CDC and the U.S. Departments of Defense and Energy to help water agencies assess their systems, determine actions that need to be taken to guard against possible attack, and develop emergency response plans. For more information, visit http://www.epa.gov/safewater.

*Source*: Centers for Disease Control and Prevention, www.cdc.gov.

## SIDEBAR 4-25   CDC's Roles in the Event of a Radiological Terrorist Event

Because of recent terrorist events, people may be concerned about the possibility of a terrorist attack involving radioactive materials. People may wonder what the Centers for Disease Control and Prevention (CDC) would do to protect people's health if such an event were to occur. CDC has prepared this fact sheet to help people understand the roles and responsibilities of CDC during such an incident.

**Lead Federal Agencies**

In the event of a radiological accident or terrorist attack, the agency that is responsible for the site of the incident also has responsibility for responding to the emergency and protecting the people, property, and environment around the area. For example, if the incident occurs on property owned by the federal government, such as a military base, research facility, or nuclear facility, then the federal government takes responsibility. In areas that are not controlled by the federal government, the state and local governments have the responsibility to respond to the emergency and protect people, property, and the environment (see Figure 4-2).

Regardless of whether the state, local, or federal government is responsible for responding to the emergency, a federal agency would be sent to the terrorist incident site and would act as the lead federal agency (LFA). This agency would work with the state and local government and might be the Nuclear Regulatory Commission (NRC), the Federal Bureau of Investigation (FBI), or another agency, depending on what type of incident occurred (accidental or intentional release of radioactive materials) and where it occurred (nuclear power plant versus a spilled radioactive material in an urban or suburban area). The LFA would implement the Federal Radiological Emergency Response Plan (FRERP); within this plan, the Department of Health and Human Services

(HHS) has the major role in protecting people's health through the following measures:

- Monitoring, assessing, and following up on people's health
- Ensuring the safety of workers involved in and responding to the incident
- Ensuring that the food supply is safe
- Providing medical and public health advice

**CDC's Roles**

As part of HHS, CDC would be the chief public health entity to respond to a radiological incident, whether accidental or intentional. As the chief public health entity, CDC's specific roles and responsibilities would include the following:

- Assessing the health of people affected by the incident
- Assessing the medical effects of radiological exposures on people in the community, emergency responders and other workers, and high-risk populations (such as children, pregnant women, and those with immune deficiencies)
- Advising state and local health departments on how to protect people, animals, and food and water supplies from contamination by radioactive materials
- Providing technical assistance and consultation to state and local health departments on medical treatment, follow-up, and decontamination of victims exposed to radioactive materials
- Establishing and maintaining a registry of people exposed to or contaminated by radioactive materials

**CDC's Partners**

To carry out its roles, CDC would work with many other agencies to ensure that people's health

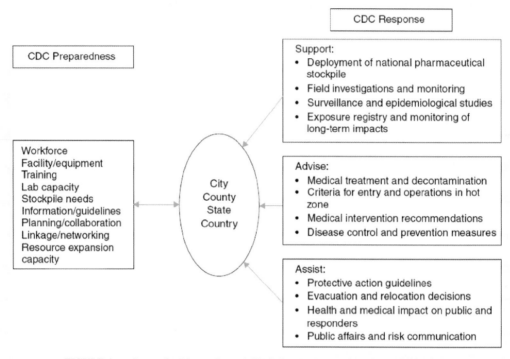

FIGURE 4-2    Centers for Disease Control (CDC) Preparedness and Response Capabilities.

is protected. These agencies may include the following:

- State and local health departments
- Department of Defense (DOD)
- Department of Energy (DOE)
- Department of Transportation (DOT)
- HHS
  - Food and Drug Administration (FDA)
  - Agency for Toxic Substances and Disease Registry (ATSDR)
  - Office of Emergency Response (OER)
  - Health Resources and Services Administration (HRSA)
  - Substance Abuse and Mental Health Services Administration (SAMHSA)
- Environmental Protection Agency (EPA)
- FBI

- Federal Emergency Management Agency (FEMA)
- NRC
- Department of Agriculture (USDA)

**CDC's Actions**

In the hours and days following a radiological incident, CDC would assist and advise the LFA and the state and local health departments on recommendations that the community would need to accomplish the following:

- Protect people from radioactive fallout
- Protect people from radioactive contamination in the area
- Safely use food and water supplies from the area
- Assess and explain the dangers in the area of the incident

If necessary, CDC would also deploy the National Pharmaceutical Stockpile, a federal store of drugs and medical supplies set aside for emergency situations. In addition, CDC would give workers in the area information on the following:

- The amount of time they can safely work in an area contaminated with radioactive materials
- Equipment needed to protect themselves from radiation and radioactive materials
- Types of respiratory devices needed to work in the contaminated area
- How to use radiation monitoring devices

**Radiation Exposure Registry**

After an incident involving radioactive materials, CDC would work with ATSDR to establish an exposure registry. The purpose of this registry would be to monitor people's exposure to radiation and perform dose reconstructions to determine the exact amount of radiation to which people were exposed. This registry would help CDC determine the necessary long-term medical follow-up for those who were affected by the incident.

*Source*: Centers for Disease Control and Prevention, www.cdc. gov.

## REVIEW QUESTIONS

1. Discuss the two major differences between traditional hazards (i.e., hurricanes, floods, tornadoes, earthquakes, hazardous materials incidents) and the new hazards associated with terrorism.
2. What are five major categories of hazards associated with terrorism?
3. Discuss the appropriate responses to the new hazards associated with terrorism. For each hazard, when is it appropriate to shelter in place, evacuate, and/or quarantine?
4. Understanding the new hazards associated with terrorism will be critical to reducing the fear among the public of these hazards. This was done very successfully in the past in understanding and dispelling the fear surrounding traditional hazards. How would you design and implement a public education campaign concerning the new hazards? What information would you present and how?
5. As a member of Congress, what role do you perceive for the federal government in researching these new hazards, identifying appropriate response and preparedness measures, and educating the public? What role would you have if you were a governor? What role would you have if you were a mayor or county executive?

## REFERENCE

Federal Emergency Management Agency (FEMA). (2002). *Managing the Emergency Consequences of Terrorist Incidents— Interim Planning Guide for State and Local Governments.* Washington, DC: FEMA.

# 5

# Safety and Security

## INTRODUCTION

The United States of America experienced the most extensive terrorist attack on its soil on September 11, 2001. This attack precipitated many changes in the American way of life, as well as in the political structure and organization of the American government. Securing the safety of the American people inside the borders of their homeland became a critical priority. On September 20, 2001, only 9 days after the attacks, President George W. Bush began what would become a major governmental transformation when he announced the establishment of the Office of Homeland Security within the White House, and appointed Tom Ridge, then governor of Pennsylvania, as his homeland security chief. Some months later, after originally rejecting the idea, President Bush proposed the creation of a cabinet-level Department of Homeland Security, whose primary purpose would be to unify those agencies responsible for homeland security missions and achieve greater accountability in the execution of those missions. On November 19, 2002, the U.S. Senate voted overwhelmingly to create a Department of Homeland Security (DHS), spurring the most extensive reorganization of the federal government since the 1940s. This chapter will focus on the key components of safety and security in the context of homeland security that already existed and that have arisen as a result of these changes. We will also identify many of the important stakeholders in charge of these components.

This chapter will discuss how safety and security are maintained in the United States through an examination of the many agencies that make up the U.S. intelligence community, and the agencies and programs that serve to control the nation's borders, transportation systems, commerce, information systems, and infrastructure.

## THE INTELLIGENCE COMMUNITY

Within the U.S. government, the intelligence community has developed such that its many components (agencies and offices) are spread out across the vast range of civilian and military departments. Like most national governments, the government of the United States has always performed some form of intelligence gathering and processing activities. However, the Cold War era was the period that most significantly pushed the expansion of intelligence activities that ultimately resulted in the extensive intelligence community that exists as we know it today. The cadre of federal employees that form the intelligence function of government grew by the mid-1980s to include more than 100,000 people, disbursed throughout 25 individual organizations specializing in the collection and analysis of information. More than $30 billion of the federal budget was dedicated to their collective activities. Considering the highly secretive and critical information needs of the government during this period of showdown between the world's great superpowers, such growth is not surprising.

After the Cold War ended, the number of agencies and employees was reduced by consolidation of activities and reduction of budgetary allocations. The military intelligence services saw the greatest of these cuts. Total reductions in the employee base were about 20%. Because the intelligence capacity grew so large during the Cold War era, however, a vast intelligence capacity remains despite these cuts. Today's U.S. government intelligence capacity involves a full range of activities and operations:

- *Technical collection*: The gathering of intelligence through the use of technical devices such as satellites, aircraft, and ship- and land-based antenna arrays
- *Human source collection*: The use of agents (recruited foreign nationals) and attaches, and interviews with individuals who have traveled to or reside in areas of interest
- *Open-source collection*: The collection of books, newspapers, and reports, recording radio and television broadcasts, and the exploitation of computer databases
- *Shared intelligence*: Intelligence gathered through meetings conducted with foreign intelligence services and information exchanges
- *Counterintelligence*: The study and penetration of foreign intelligence and security services
- *Covert action*: Influence placed on foreign political events without the United States role being admitted
- *Intelligence analysis, production, and dissemination*: The evaluation of information, the display

of that information in printed, electronic, or video form, and the transmission of that information to "customers"

These activities are performed by four individual organizations within the federal government:

- The Central Intelligence Agency (CIA)
- The National Security Agency (NSA)
- The National Reconnaissance Office (NRO)
- The National Imagery and Mapping Agency (NIMA)

Several other smaller agencies, which fall under the Department of Defense or other civilian intelligence organizations, also perform these duties to a lesser degree (Richelson *et al.*, 2003). The next sections will give a brief explanation of the background, duties, and organization of those agencies.

## THE CENTRAL INTELLIGENCE AGENCY

The recognized intelligence needs of modern warfare that surfaced during World War II resulted in the creation of America's first central intelligence organization, the Office of Strategic Services (OSS). The OSS was created to perform a variety of functions, including traditional espionage, covert action (ranging from propaganda to sabotage), counterintelligence, and intelligence analysis. The OSS represented a revolution in U.S. intelligence, not only because of the varied functions performed by a single, national agency, but also because of the breadth of its intelligence interests and its use of scholars to produce finished intelligence.

In the aftermath of World War II, the OSS was disbanded, officially ceasing all operations on October 1, 1945 by executive order from President Truman. However, several of its branches were retained and were distributed among other governmental departments. For instance, the X-2 (Counterintelligence) and Secret Intelligence branches were transferred to the War Department to form the Strategic Services Unit, and the Research and Analysis Branch was transferred into the Department of State. (Smith, 1983)

As Truman was ordering the termination of the OSS, he was also commissioning studies to determine the requirements of and changes to the U.S. intelligence structure in the post–World War II climate. Based on these studies, the National Intelligence Authority (NIA) and its operational element, the Central Intelligence Group (CIG), were created. The CIG was initially responsible for coordinating and synthesizing the reports produced by the military service intelligence agencies and the FBI, but it soon after assumed the task of secret intelligence collection.

National security needs and the intelligence reorganization were addressed by the National Security Act of 1947. The Central Intelligence Agency (CIA) was established as an independent agency within the executive office of the president to replace the CIG. According to the act, the CIA was to have five functions:

1. To advise the National Security Council in matters concerning such intelligence activities of the government departments and agencies as relate to national security
2. To make recommendations to the National Security Council for the coordination of such intelligence activities of the departments and agencies of the government as relate to national security
3. To correlate and evaluate the intelligence relating to national security, and to provide for the appropriate dissemination of such intelligence within the government using, where appropriate, existing agencies and facilities
4. To perform for the benefit of existing intelligence agencies such additional services of common concern as the National Security Council determines can be more effectively accomplished centrally
5. To perform other such functions and duties related to intelligence affecting the national security as the National Security Council may from time to time direct. (U.S. Congress, 1983)

The organizational structure of the CIA as it exists today began to take shape in the early 1950s under Director Walter Bedell Smith. In 1952, the Office of Policy Coordination was transferred under CIA control and merged with the secret intelligence-gathering Office of Special Operations to form the Directorate of Plans. That same year, the offices involved in intelligence research and analysis were placed under a Directorate of Intelligence. A third unit, the Directorate of Administration, was established to perform administrative functions.

The principal functions of the Directorate of Plans were clandestine collection and covert action. A separate directorate was later formed to perform technical collection operations, but before that time the Directorate of Plans was heavily involved in the development and operation of overhead collection systems like the U-2 spy plane and CORONA reconnaissance satellite. In 1973, the Directorate of Plans became the Directorate of Operations. Today, its functions include clandestine collection, covert action, counternarcotics and counterterrorism activities, and counterintelligence.

A fourth directorate, the Directorate of Research, was established in 1962. This directorate consolidated in one unit all agency components involved in technical collection activities. In 1963, it was renamed the Directorate of Science and Technology and assumed control of scientific intelligence analysis. Its present functions include the following:

- Developing technical collection systems
- Collecting intelligence from embassy sites (in cooperation with the National Security Agency)
- Recording foreign radio and television broadcasts (through its Foreign Broadcast Information Service)
- Developing and producing technical devices (such as bugging devices, hidden cameras, and weaponry) for agents and officers
- Providing research and development in support of intelligence collection and analysis

Until late 1996, the directorate also managed the National Photographic Interpretation Center (NPIC), which interpreted satellite and aerial reconnaissance imagery. NPIC was absorbed by the newly established National Imagery and Mapping Agency. (Richelson *et al.*, 2003)

In its current organization the different major branches of CIA have the following responsibilities (see Figure 5-1):

### The Office of Terrorism Analysis

The Office of Terrorism Analysis (OTA) is the analytic component of the DCI Counterterrorism Center. OTA analysts work to inform policymakers and support the intelligence, law enforcement, homeland security, and military communities by performing the following tasks:

- Tracking terrorists and the activities of states that sponsor them, and assessing terrorist vulnerabil-

ities by analyzing their ideology and goals, capabilities, associates, and locations
- Analyzing worldwide terrorist threat information and patterns to provide warnings aimed at preventing terrorist attacks
- Monitoring worldwide terrorism trends and patterns, including emerging and nontraditional terrorist groups, evolving terrorist threats or operational methods, and possible collusion between terrorist groups
- Identifying, disrupting, and preventing international financial transactions that support terrorist networks and operations

### The DCI Crime and Narcotics Center

The Crime and Narcotics Center (CNC) collects and analyzes information on international narcotics

FIGURE 5-1   CIA organizational chart.

trafficking and organized crime for policymakers and the law enforcement community. CNC's workforce is diverse, utilizing individuals with a variety of backgrounds, experience, and specialties. CNC strategic analysts focus on long-term trends and keep U.S. policymakers up to speed on fast-breaking events. They analyze the impact of the drug trade and of organized crime on U.S. national security, follow trafficking methods and routes, and monitor cooperation between organized crime groups, traffickers, and terrorists. Targeting analysts use sophisticated tools to identify key individuals, organizations, trends, and components in criminal organizations. They help guide intelligence operations and support law enforcement investigations by analyzing the information as it is collected, often from the field, and assist in efforts to put these organizations out of business. Operational support specialists and program managers provide fast-paced operational research, management, and support to colleagues overseas. They develop substantive expertise on organized crime and narcotics issues, and often travel to support operations or collect information.

### DCI Weapons Intelligence, Nonproliferation, and Arms Control Center

The DCI Weapons Intelligence, Nonproliferation, and Arms Control Center (WINPAC) provides intelligence support aimed at protecting the United States and its interests from all foreign weapons threats. WINPAC officers are a diverse group with a variety of backgrounds and work experiences, and include mathematicians, engineers (nuclear, chemical/biological, mechanical, and aerospace, among others), physicists, economists, political scientists, computer specialists, and physical scientists. On any given day, those analysts could be answering a question from the president, assessing information about a foreign missile test, or developing new computational models to determine blast effects. A key part of its mission includes studying the development of the entire spectrum of threats, from weapons of mass destruction (nuclear, radiological, chemical, and biological weapons) to advanced conventional weapons such as lasers, advanced explosives, and armor, as well as all types of missiles, including ballistic, cruise, and surface-to-air missiles. The center studies systems from their earliest development phase through production, deployment, and transfers to other countries, and monitors strategic arms control agreements. WINPAC also supports military and diplomatic operations.

### Counterintelligence Center/Analysis Group

The Counterintelligence Center/Analysis Group (CIC/AG) identifies, monitors, and analyzes the efforts of foreign intelligence entities against U.S. persons, activities, and interests. CIC/AG analysts focus on two specific types of counterintelligence threats to U.S. national security: transnational threats, such as the counterintelligence aspect of terrorism, or the threats posed by emerging or changing technologies to the U.S. government's intelligence operations and information systems. CIC/AG also tracks threats posed by foreign intelligence services and monitors their activities.

### Information Operations Center/Analysis Group

The Information Operations Center/Analysis Group (IOC/AG) evaluates foreign threats to U.S. computer systems, particularly those that support critical infrastructures. The group provides its analysis to the president, his senior advisers, high-level officials on cyber issues in the Departments of Defense, State, and Treasury, and to senior private-sector officials responsible for operating critical infrastructures. IOC/AG analysts consider potential threats from state and nonstate actors and evaluate a wide array of information, including foreign intentions, plans, and capabilities.

### Office of Asian Pacific, Latin American, and African Analysis

The Office of Asian Pacific, Latin American, and African Analysis (APLAA) studies the political, economic, leadership, societal, and military developments in Asia, Latin America, and Sub-Saharan Africa.

### Office of Near Eastern and South Asian Analysis

The Office of Near Eastern and South Asian Analysis (NESA) provides policymakers with comprehensive analytic support on Middle Eastern and North African countries, as well as on the South Asian nations of India, Pakistan, and Afghanistan.

### Office of Russian and European Analysis

The Office of Russian and European Analysis (OREA) provides intelligence support on a large set of countries that have long been of crucial importance to the United States as allies or as adversaries and are likely to continue to occupy a key place in U.S. national security policy. OREA officers are a mix of generalists and specialists who concentrate on issues ranging from ethnic conflict in the Balkans to the U.S.–Russian relationship.

### Office of Transnational Issues

The Office of Transnational Issues (OTI) produces analytic assessments on critical intelligence-related issues that transcend regional and national boundaries. Drawing on a broad range of experts in engineering, science, and social science disciplines, OTI's analysis addresses energy and economic security, illicit financial activities, societal conflicts, humanitarian crises, and the long-term military and economic strategic environment.

### Office of Policy Support

The Office of Policy Support (OPS) customizes defense intelligence (DI) analysis and presents it to a wide variety of policy, law enforcement, military, and foreign liaison recipients.

### Office of Collection Strategies and Analysis

The Office of Collection Strategies and Analysis (CSAA) provides comprehensive intelligence collection expertise to the DI, a wide range of senior agency and intelligence community officials, and key national policymakers. CSAA analysts work with colleagues in the CIA's Directorate of Operations and Directorate of Science and Technology, the Department of Defense, the National Security Agency, the National Geospatial-Intelligence Agency, the National Reconnaissance Office, and other Intelligence Community agencies to craft new approaches to solving complex collection issues. (CIA, 2005)

The CIA is probably the most widely recognized of the various U.S. intelligence agencies, primarily because of its celebrated and cinematized involvement in covert action, and also because of the central role it plays in providing intelligence to the president. However, as noted earlier, there are several U.S. intelligence agencies, some of which rival the CIA in influence and exceed it in budget. The most important of these other agencies are the three "national" agencies: the National Security Agency, the National Reconnaissance Office, and the National Geospatial-Intelligence Agency. Each of these is described in detail next.

## NATIONAL SECURITY AGENCY

On May 20, 1949, Secretary of Defense Louis Johnson established the Armed Forces Security Agency (AFSA) and placed it under the command of the Joint Chiefs of Staff. In theory, the AFSA was to direct the communications intelligence and electronic intelligence activities of the military service signals intelligence units (at the time, the Army Security Agency, Naval Security Group, and Air Force Security Service). In practice, however, the AFSA had little power, and its functions were characterized as activities not performed by the service units.

On October 24, 1952—the same day that he sent a (now-declassified) top secret eight-page memorandum entitled "Communications Intelligence Activities" to the secretaries of state and defense—President Truman abolished the AFSA and transferred its personnel to the newly created National Security Agency (NSA). As its name indicated, the new agency was to have national, not just military, responsibilities. In 1971, NSA became the National Security Agency/Central Security Service (NSA/CSS). The second half of NSA's title, which is rarely used, refers to its role in coordinating the signals intelligence activities of the military services (Richelson, 1999). Today the NSA has two primary responsibilities: information assurance and signals intelligence.

NSA's Information Assurance Directorate (IAD) is dedicated to providing information assurance solutions that serve to protect U.S. information systems from harm. This mission involves many activities, including these:

- Detecting, reporting, and responding to cyber threats
- Making encryption codes to securely pass information between systems
- Embedding information assurance measures directly into the emerging global information grid
- Building secure audio and video communications equipment
- Making tamper-proof products
- Providing trusted microelectronics solutions
- Testing the security of its partners' and its customers' systems
- Providing operational security assistance
- Evaluating commercial software and hardware against set standards.

The Signals Intelligence directorate of NSA collects, processes, and disseminates foreign signals intelligence (SIGINT). It provides information in the form of SIGINT products and services that enables the U.S. government to make critical decisions. NSA's SIGINT mission provides military leaders and policymakers with intelligence to ensure national defense and to advance U.S. global interests. This information is specifically limited to that which focuses on foreign powers, organizations, or persons and international terrorists. NSA responds to requirements of its intelligence partners and customers, which include all departments and levels of the United States Executive Branch. (NSA, 2005)

## NATIONAL RECONNAISSANCE OFFICE

The National Reconnaissance Office (NRO) was established on September 6, 1961, to coordinate CIA reconnaissance activities with those of the Department of Defense. NRO's primary function has been to oversee the research and development, procurement, deployment, and operation of imaging, signals intelligence, and ocean surveillance satellites. It awards contracts, oversees the research and development efforts of contractors, supervises the launch of the payloads, and, in conjunction with the CIA and NSA, operates these spacecraft. It has also been involved in the research, development, and procurement of selected aerial reconnaissance systems, such as the SR-71. From its inception until September 18, 1992, when its existence was formally acknowledged, the NRO operated as a classified organization. A major restructuring of NRO also began to be implemented in 1992, which turned the NRO into a functional organization instead of a stand alone organization. (Richelson *et al.*, 2003)

In its current setting, the NRO designs, builds, and operates the nation's reconnaissance satellites. NRO products, provided to an expanding list of customers such as the CIA and the Department of Defense (DOD), can warn of potential trouble spots around the world, help plan military operations, and monitor the environment. The NRO is a DOD agency and is staffed by DOD and CIA personnel. The NRO has historically been one of the most clandestine intelligence organizations in the United States, but many parts of its operations have now been declassified. For example, the location of its headquarters, in Chantilly, Virginia, was declassified in 1994. In February 1995, CORONA, a photoreconnaissance program in operation from 1960 to 1972, was declassified and 800,000

CORONA images were transferred to the National Archives and Records Administration. In December 1996, the NRO announced for the first time, in advance, the launch of a reconnaissance satellite. (NRO, 2005)

## NATIONAL GEOSPATIAL-INTELLIGENCE AGENCY

By the mid-1990s, imagery was the basis for both imagery intelligence and map-based imagery products, and the intelligence community wished to centralize the management of both of these functions. The National Imagery and Mapping Agency (NIMA), formally proposed by the secretary of defense and director of the CIA in November 1995, was established on October 1, 1996. Through this creation, NIMA joined four existing imagery interpretation and mapping organizations: the National Photographic Interpretation Center, the Defense Mapping Agency, the CIA's Office of Imagery Analysis, the DIA's Office of Imagery Analysis, the Central Imagery Office. Other offices absorbed into the new agency included the Defense Dissemination Program Office and elements of the Defense Airborne Reconnaissance Office and National Reconnaissance.

Initially NIMA was organized into three main directorates: operations, systems and technology, and corporate affairs. Three key units within the Operations Directorate were Imagery Analysis, Geospatial Information and Services, and the Central Imagery Tasking Office. The latter was responsible for allocating targets to imagery collection systems and determining when the imagery was obtained. Formed from several defense and intelligence agencies, NIMA merged imagery, maps, charts, and environmental data to produce what has been coined *geospatial intelligence*. The Imagery Analysis Unit combined the activities of NPIC and the CIA and DIA imagery analysis organizations, while the Geospatial Information and Services Unit provided the mapping, charting, and geodesy products formerly provided by the DMA. The unit was responsible for producing strategic and tactical maps, charts, and databases, and spe-

cialized products to support current and advanced weapons and navigation systems. (Richelson *et al.*, 2003)

Between 1995 and 1998, NIMA products helped resolve many national and international issues, including long-standing border differences between Peru and Ecuador and between Israel and Southern Lebanon. NIMA products also supported the Dayton Peace Accord efforts in the Balkans. In February 2000, the space shuttle *Endeavor*'s shuttle radar topography mission (SRTM) provided the most detailed measurements of the planet's elevation ever gathered—data that will prove invaluable in supporting the National Geospatial-Intelligence Agency's geospatial-intelligence efforts.

NIMA played a critical role in homeland security following the attacks of September 11. In the response and recovery phases of the disaster in New York City, NIMA partnered with the U.S. Geological Survey (USGS) to survey the World Trade Center site and determine the extent of the destruction. Then, in 2002, NIMA partnered with federal organizations to provide geospatial assistance to the 2002 Winter Olympics in Utah.

On November 24, 2003, the president signed the 2004 Defense Authorization Bill, which included a provision to change NIMA's name to the National Geospatial-Intelligence Agency (NGA).

## NATIONAL INTELLIGENCE DIRECTORATE

The National Commission on Terrorist Attacks Upon the United States (the 9/11 Commission) recommended in its final report:

> The current position of Director of Central Intelligence should be replaced by a National Intelligence Director with two main areas of responsibility: (1) to oversee national intelligence centers on specific subjects of interest across the U.S. government and (2) to manage the national intelligence program and oversee the agencies that contribute to it.

In efforts to move forward with the commission's recommendation, Senators Susan Collins and Joe Lieberman, and Speaker of the House of Representatives Dennis Hastert, separately introduced legislation to create the national intelligence director (NID) position. Both bills sought to establish a presidentially nominated, Senate-confirmed position of NID, who would serve as the head of the intelligence community's 15 distinct intelligence agencies, including the CIA. Both bills also sought to establish a separate Senate-confirmed director of central intelligence, who would manage the CIA, and would be prohibited from serving simultaneously as the NID.

The House of Representatives passed the Collins–Lieberman Intelligence Reform and Terrorism Prevention Act on December 7, 2004, by a vote of 336 to 75. On December 8, 2004, the bill was approved by an 89-to-2 vote in the U.S. Senate and was sent to the president for his signature. The president signed the bill and nominated John Negroponte, the former U.S. ambassador to the United Nations and recently U.S. ambassador to Iraq, for the position of national intelligence director on February 17, 2005. John Negroponte was confirmed by the Senate on April 21, 2005, and was officially sworn in on May 18, 2005.

In this new position, John Negroponte will be expected to ensure coordination and cooperation between all intelligence communities in the United States. As the director of national intelligence, he will have the authority to do the following:

- Create national intelligence centers to incorporate capabilities from across the intelligence community in order to accomplish intelligence missions.
- Control the national intelligence budget in terms of dollar amounts and distribution among different intelligence agencies.
- Transfer personnel and funds to ensure that the intelligence community is flexible and can respond to emerging threats.
- Create a Privacy and Civil Liberties Board to protect privacy and civil liberties concerns potentially created by proposals to fight terrorism.
- Establish an information-sharing network to break down the stovepipes that currently impede

the flow of information between federal, state and local agencies and the private sector. (Congressional Research Service, 2004a, 2004b)

## BORDER CONTROL

The borders of any country are strategically important because of the critical role they play in the economic vitality and commerce of the country. Increasing globalization of economic systems and transportation networks has made it possible for every community in the United States to be connected to the outside world through a vast system of airports, seaports, pipelines, roadways, and waterways. Borders are gateways for imported and exported goods to and from the country; therefore, their effectiveness and efficiency are important measures for the trade capacity and capability of the country. Borders also have an important role for the international tourism and travel capability of the country.

At the same time, borders provide access into the country, through both major and clandestine entry points, for illegal immigrants and goods. Therefore, the security and control of borders is of the utmost importance in the drive to mitigate the risk posed by the penetration of unwanted or dangerous people and goods into the country. The movement of smugglers, drug dealers, criminals, terrorists, illegal drugs, conventional weapons, smuggled goods, biological agents, and weapons of mass destruction (WMD) are all examples of potential dangerous goods that people may try to move across the country's borders.

The United States has 5,525 miles of border with Canada and 1,989 miles with Mexico. The maritime border includes 95,000 miles of shoreline and a 3.4 million square mile exclusive economic zone. Each year, more than 500 million people cross the borders into the United States, and approximately 330 million of them are not U.S. citizens (White House, 2005, www.whitehouse.gov).

Enhanced border and transportation security was a primary focus of the methodology behind creation of the DHS. The DHS consolidated the various agencies responsible for the safety, security, and control of the borders under the Directorate of Border and Transportation Security. Those agencies include the Immigration and Customs Enforcement Agency (previously named the Immigration and Naturalization Service), the Customs and Border Protection Agency (previously named the Customs Service), the U.S. Coast Guard (USCG), the Animal and Plant Health Inspection Service (APHIS), and the Transportation Security Agency (TSA).

The DHS Directorate of Border and Transportation Security (DHS-BTS), along with the Department of Justice, is charged with this protective mission as defined by several statutory authorities including the Homeland Security Act of 2002 and the National Response Plan (NRP). The Department of Agriculture (USDA), the USCG, the Department of Commerce (DOC), the DOD, the Department of Energy (DOE), the Department of the Interior (DOI), the Environmental Protection Agency (EPA), the National Aeronautics and Space Administration (NASA), the Social Security Administration, and the U.S. Postal Service are mentioned as support agencies for border and transportation security in the NRP.

The following section summarizes the duties of agencies that have a direct role in border control and security.

## DHS/U.S. COAST GUARD

The Coast Guard is the lead federal agency for maritime drug interdiction and shares lead responsibility for air interdiction with the U.S. Customs Service. As such, it is a key player in combating the flow of illegal drugs into the United States. The Coast Guard's mission is to reduce the supply of drugs from its source by denying smugglers the use of air and maritime routes in the Transit Zone, a 6 million square mile area that includes the Caribbean, Gulf of Mexico, and Eastern Pacific. In patrolling this vast area, the Coast Guard coordinates closely with other federal agencies and countries located within the region to

disrupt and deter the flow of illegal drugs. Coast Guard drug interdiction accounts for a high number of drug seizures performed by the U.S. government, including more than 50% of all seizures of cocaine each year. In FY 2002 alone, USCG cocaine seizures alone had an estimated import value of approximately $3.9 billion. (USCG, 2005, www.uscg.mil).

As the primary maritime law enforcement agency, the Coast Guard is tasked with enforcing immigration law at sea. The Coast Guard conducts patrols and coordinates with other federal agencies and foreign countries to interdict undocumented migrants at sea, denying them entry via maritime routes to the United States, its territories, and possessions. By interdicting migrants at sea, the Coast Guard is able, by law, to quickly return them to their countries of origin without the costly processes required if they successfully enter the United States. Specifically, the Coast Guard's mission includes:

- *Maritime safety*: Eliminate loss of life, injuries and physical damage associated with maritime transportation, fishing, and recreational boating.
- *National defense*: Defend the nation as one of the five U.S. armed services. Enhance regional stability in support of the National Security Strategy, utilizing the Coast Guard's unique and relevant maritime capabilities.
- *Maritime security*: Protect America's maritime borders from all intrusions by (a) halting the flow of illegal drugs, aliens, and contraband into the United States through maritime routes; (b) preventing illegal fishing; and (c) suppressing violations of federal law in the maritime arena.
- *Mobility*: Facilitate maritime commerce and eliminate interruptions and impediments to the efficient and economical movement of goods and people, while maximizing recreational access to and enjoyment of the water.
- *Protection of natural resources*: Eliminate environmental damage and the degradation of natural resources associated with maritime transportation, fishing, and recreational boating. (DHS, 2005)

TABLE 5-1   **USCG Budget Allocation, FY 2004–2006**

| USCG budget review ($ in 1,000s) | FY 2004 enacted | FY 2005 enacted | FY 2006 pres. budget | FY 2006 ± FY 2005 |
|---|---|---|---|---|
| Search & rescue | $990,999 | $999,934 | $1,045,208 | $45,274 |
| Marine safety | $491,074 | $526,357 | $544,633 | $18,276 |
| Aids to navigation | $953,485 | $988,639 | $1,083,296 | $94,657 |
| Ice operations | $186,825 | $215,619 | $174,327 | −$41,292 |
| Marine environmental protection | $350,649 | $377,101 | $426,643 | $49,542 |
| Living marine resources | $748,152 | $861,848 | $958,651 | $96,803 |
| Drug interdiction | $916,429 | $985,590 | $1,114,700 | $129,110 |
| Migrant interdiction | $254,380 | $267,528 | $301,460 | $33,932 |
| Other law enforcement | $105,628 | $72,438 | $76,070 | $3,632 |
| Port waterways and coastal security | $1,853,034 | $2,091,427 | $2,219,394 | $127,967 |
| National defense | $143,567 | $172,079 | $202,530 | $30,451 |
| TOTAL | $6,994,222 | $7,558,560 | $8,146,912 | $588,352 |
| Less rescissions of prior year carryover | −$85,385 | −$16,000 | | |
| Adjusted budget authority | **$6,908,837** | **$7,542,560** | **$8,146,912** | **$604,352** |

*Source*: *USCG Budget Overview, DHS Budget in Brief Document*, 2005.

Table 5-1 displays the USCG budget for FY 2004–2006, broken down by program, and Sidebar 5-1 lists the USCG's accomplishments in 2005.

Another important responsibility of the U.S. Coast Guard is its role as the lead federal agency during federal responses to oil and hazardous material incidents—a responsibility the Coast Guard shares with the Environmental Protection Agency (EPA). The EPA or the USCG, depending on whether the incident affects inland or coastal zones, serves as the primary agency for emergency support function 10 (ESF #10) actions under the NRP. For incidents where DHS/USCG is the primary agency, the USCG Chief of the Office of Response serves as the lead for ESF #10. During these incidents, the USCG assumes the following responsibilities:

• Maintains close coordination between DHS/ USCG headquarters and the affected area and district offices; the EPA, as appropriate; the Interagency Incident Management Group (IIMG); the National Response Coordination Center (NRCC); other ESFs; and the National Response Team (NRT).

• Provides damage reports, assessments, and situation reports to support ESF #5 (emergency management).

• Facilitates resolution of any conflicting demands for hazardous materials response resources and ensures coordination between NRT and IIMG activities, and Regional Response Team (RRT) and the Joint Field Office (JFO) activities, as appropriate. Coordinates (through headquarters) the provision of backup support from other districts to the affected area.

• Provides technical, coordination, and administrative support and personnel, facilities, and communications for ESF #10. Coordinates,

SIDEBAR 5-1   **Accomplishments of the U.S. Coast Guard in 2005**

- *Ongoing delivery of the Integrated Deepwater System (IDS)*: construction of the first two Maritime Security Cutters–Large to be delivered in FY 2007 and 2008, respectively; initial design of the Maritime Patrol Coastal (WPC) and the Maritime Security Cutter–Medium; production of the first two Maritime Patrol Aircraft and two Vertical Unmanned Aerial Vehicles (VUAVs) to be delivered in FY 2006; continued development of a Common Operating Picture at shore-based command centers, an Integrated Logistics Support System and legacy sustainment/enhancement projects for all major cutters and aircraft, including continued reengineering of the HH-65 short-range helicopter fleet.

- *Implementation of the Maritime Transportation Security Act (MTSA) of 2002*: In FY 2005 the USCG added 500 personnel to develop, review, and approve approximately 9,000 domestic vessel security plans and 3,200 domestic facility plans; develop 48 area maritime security plans and committees; perform 55 domestic Port Security Assessments; develop a national Maritime Transportation Security Plan, verify security plan implementation on 8,100 foreign vessels and continue conducting foreign port security assessments on 100+ countries conducting direct trade with United States.

- *Continuation of the Great Lakes Icebreaker (GLIB) project*, which will reach full operating capability in FY 2006.

- *Continuation of the Rescue 21 project*, recapitalizing the USCG's coastal zone communications network, to ensure completion by the end of FY 2007.

- *Adding nearly 100 new personnel* to support planning and coordination of all USCG mission at command centers.

- *Continuing implementation of the nationwide Automatic Identification System (AIS)*, significantly enhancing maritime domain awareness (MDA) and improving the USCG's ability to detect maritime security threats farther from the nation's ports.

- *Procurement of new Response Boats*: Continue recapitalization of the USCG's obsolete, nonstandard utility boats and increase the USCG's presence in critical ports and coastal zones.

- *Commence Airborne Use of Force (AUF) implementation* on the USCG's entire fleet of helicopters by arming existing helicopters at various air stations. AUF capability will improve performance of all homeland security missions, including enhanced protection of U.S. ports.

- *Continue C-130J Maritime Patrol Aircraft (MPA) missionization*: This project will provide additional MPA resources, enhancing MDA and resulting in increased ability to detect, identify, and monitor maritime security threats such as illegal drug traffickers. Armed with MPA surveillance information, USCG operational commanders can optimize use of surface assets and rotary-wing aircraft through targeted interdiction of known threats.

- *Added 55 billets for enhancing intelligence collection and oversight* as a member of the national intelligence community. The staff will support critical maritime intelligence support nodes, the USCG Central Adjudication Facility (CGCAF) at the Security Center in Chesapeake, Virginia, and program management at the strategic level.

*Source*: Department of Homeland Security (DHS). 2005. *Budget in Brief Document 2006*. Washington, DC: DHS.

integrates, and manages the overall federal effort to detect, identify, contain, clean up, or dispose of or minimize releases of oil or hazardous materials, or prevent, mitigate, or minimize the threat of potential releases.

- Provides OSCs for incidents within its jurisdiction (including for the coastal zone response for incidents for which EPA is the primary agency, but the incident affects both the inland and coastal zone). (National Response Plan, 2004)

## DHS/BUREAU OF CUSTOMS AND BORDER PROTECTION

U.S. Customs and Border Protection (CBP) is the single agency responsible for protecting the sovereign borders of the United States at and between the official ports of entry. CBP is considered the "front line" in protecting the nation against terrorist attacks. CBP also ensures national economic security by regulating and facilitating the lawful movement of goods and persons across U.S. borders.

The U.S. Border Patrol is the primary operational agency within the Bureau of Customs and Border Protection, which is responsible from protecting the borders. Therefore, it is the mobile uniformed law enforcement arm of the Department of Homeland Security. The primary mission of the Border Patrol is the detection and apprehension of illegal aliens and smugglers of aliens at or near the land border. This is accomplished by maintaining surveillance, following up leads, responding to electronic sensor alarms and aircraft sightings, and interpreting and following tracks. Some of the major activities include maintaining traffic checkpoints along highways leading from border areas, conducting city patrols and transportation checks, and antismuggling investigations. Since 1994 the Border Patrol has made more than 11.3 million apprehensions nationwide. In FY 2001, Border Patrol agents apprehended almost 1.2 million persons for illegally entering the country. An increase in smuggling activities has pushed the Border Patrol to the front line of the U.S. war on drugs. Its role as the primary drug-interdiction organization along the Southwest border continues to expand (see Sidebar 5-2). In FY 2001, Border Patrol agents seized more than 18,500 pounds of cocaine and more than 1.1 million pounds of marijuana, with a total street value of more than $1.4 billion.

CBP officials are also deployed overseas at major international seaports through the Container Security Initiative (CSI) to prescreen shipping containers to detect and interdict terrorists' weapons and other illicit material before arrival on U.S. shores. Through programs like CSI, CBP is partnering with foreign nations and private industry to expand the nation's zone of security and ensure that U.S. borders are not the last line of defense. CBP's entry specialists and trade compliance personnel also enforce U.S. trade and tariff laws and regulations in order to ensure a fair and competitive trade environment as stipulated by existing international agreements and treaties. CBP's Air and Marine Operations Division patrols the nation's borders to interdict illegal drugs and terrorists before entry into the United States and provides surveillance and operational support to special national security events. (DHS, 2005)

One component of border security (also included in the Arizona Border Control Initiative) that is gaining increased recognition for its abilities is the use of the Hermes 450 unmanned aerial vehicles (UAVs). These remote-guided airplanes have already begun monitoring the border regions in the hunt for illegal movements. By using the unmanned vehicles for border protection—their first nonmilitary use—DHS will enjoy much greater border coverage and will be able to respond much faster to incidents in rugged areas of the country. Additionally, the recordings made by the UAVs will provide evidence for convicting apprehended criminals in court. The high-tech airplanes are an indication of the technological advancements that will more and more dictate both the direction and the success of homeland security in the United States.

Table 5-2 illustrates the Customs and Border Protection budget allocations for FY 2004–2006.

## SIDEBAR 5-2  DHS Arizona Border Control Initiative

The Arizona Border Control Initiative is a joint effort by several DHS agencies to improve border protection and reduce the number of trespassing aliens from the Mexican border into the United States. The goal of the initiative is to establish federal, state, and local coordinated efforts to achieve operational control of the Arizona border and support of the DHS priority mission of antiterrorism, detection, arrest, and deterrence of all cross-border illicit trafficking, to significantly impair the ability of the smuggling organizations to operate, to decrease the rate of violent crime, and to reduce the need for social services in southern Arizona.

The Arizona Border Control (ABC) Initiative will build on the combined assets within Homeland Security of Customs and Border Protection (CBP), Immigration and Customs Enforcement (ICE), the Transportation Security Administration (TSA), the Department of the Interior (DOI), and other federal agencies. Close liaison will be maintained with the Tohono O'odham Nation and state and local law enforcement.

The initiative will activate 60 additional U.S. Border Patrol agents who are specially trained in search, rescue, and remote tactical operations. They will be deployed temporarily to support the ABC Initiative. These agents are able to deliver life-saving medical treatment in remote parts of the Arizona desert when necessary. Two hundred experienced Border Patrol agents were permanently assigned to Arizona in summer 2005 bringing the Tucson Sector to more than 2,000 agents.

The Department of Interior will support and coordinate patrol activity on DOI-entrusted lands, which includes assigning a full-time coordinator to the ABC Initiative. The ABC Initiative includes additional aviation resources to be assigned for border surveillance of illegal activities. In this capacity, Unmanned Aerial Vehicles (UAVs) have been used beginning in early June 2005 along the border. Funding for this project comes from the FY 2004 budget in Homeland Security's Science and Technology Directorate.

Immigration and Customs Enforcement Air and Marine Operations fly additional hours patrolling the area with both helicopters and fixed-wing aircraft. CBP/Border Patrol has assigned four additional A-Star 350 helicopters to assist with these efforts. Air and Marine Operations and the Border Patrol will use additional aircraft to rapidly transport search, rescue, and enforcement assets to remote areas of the Arizona desert.

The program may include the use of hundreds of civilian volunteers (The Minuteman Program) to monitor a 20-mile stretch of Arizona's border with Mexico. The use of volunteers for law enforcement purposes, which was tested during a one-month pilot program with success, has been found highly controversial by civil liberties and human rights groups. "We think there's a real danger of something bad occurring," said Mark Potok, director of the Intelligence Project, which monitors hate groups. "People around the country, on white supremacist and neo-Nazi Web sites, are talking about going down there."

*Sources*: DHS, 2005; *USA Today*, 2005.

TABLE 5-2   **CBP Budget Allocation, FY 2004–2006**

| DHS CBP budget review ($ in 1,000s) | FY 2004 enacted | FY 2005 enacted | FY 2006 pres. budget | FY 2006 ± FY 2005 |
|---|---|---|---|---|
| Headquarters management and administration | $1,364,974 | $1,172,838 | $1,250,033 | $77,195 |
| Border security inspections and trade facilitation at points of entry (POE) | $1,564,955 | $1,682,883 | $1,738,024 | $55,141 |
| Border security inspections and trade facilitation and control at POE | $1,440,500 | $1,546,962 | $1,606,427 | $59,465 |
| Air and marine operations—salaries | — | $131,436 | $136,060 | $4,624 |
| Air and marine interdiction, operations, maintenance, and procurement | — | $257,535 | $292,780 | $35,245 |
| Automation modernization | $438,519 | $449,909 | $458,009 | $8,100 |
| Construction | $89,830 | $91,718 | $93,418 | $1,700 |
| Less rescission of prior year carryover | — | −$63,010 | — | $63,010 |
| Gross discretionary | $4,898,778 | $5,270,271 | $5,574,751 | $304,480 |
| Reappropriation | $3,000 | — | — | — |
| Customs unclaimed goods | $8,113 | $8,113 | $8,113 | — |
| Fee accounts | $1,082,203 | $1,070,000 | $1,136,912 | $66,912 |
| TOTAL budget authority | $5,992,094 | $6,348,384 | $6,719,776 | $371,392 |

*Source*: *CBP Budget Overview, DHS Budget in Brief Document*, 2005.

## DHS/BUREAU OF IMMIGRATION AND CUSTOMS ENFORCEMENT

The immigration enforcement component of the Bureau of Immigration and Customs Enforcement (BICE) promotes public safety and national security by deterring illegal migration, preventing immigration-related crimes, and removing individuals, especially criminals, who are unlawfully present in the United States. This mandate is carried out by the Immigration Investigations, Detention and Removal, and Intelligence programs.

Traditionally the primary mission of the customs enforcement component of BICE has been to combat various forms of smuggling. Over time, however, this mission has been expanded to other violations of law involving terrorist financing, money laundering, arms

trafficking (including WMD), technology exports, commercial fraud, and child pornography, to name a few. In total, BICE enforces more than 400 different laws and regulations, including those of 40 other agencies.

Within the new organization of the Department of Homeland Security, the primary mission of BICE is to detect vulnerabilities and prevent violations that threaten national security. There are several distinct divisions that carry out separate tasks within this collective mission. The Investigations Division is responsible for investigating a range of domestic and international activities arising from the movement of people and goods that violate immigration and customs laws and threaten national security. The Federal Air Marshal Service (FAMS) is responsible for promoting confidence in the nation's civil aviation system through the deployment of federal air marshals to

TABLE 5-3  **BICE Budget Allocation, FY 2004–2006**

| DHS BICE budget review ($ in 1,000s) | FY 2004 enacted | FY 2005 enacted | FY 2006 pres. budget | FY 2006 ± FY 2005 |
|---|---|---|---|---|
| Salaries & expenses | $2,138,359 | $2,438,494 | $2,892,281 | $453,787 |
| Federal air marshals | $622,704 | $662,900 | $688,860 | $25,960 |
| Federal protective service | $424,211 | $478,000 | $487,000 | $9,000 |
| Automation modernization | $39,764 | $39,605 | $40,150 | $545 |
| Air & marine interdiction | $208,960 | — | — | — |
| Construction | $26,617 | $26,179 | $26,546 | $367 |
| Rescission of prior year carryover funds | −$54,000 | — | — | — |
| Gross discretionary | $3,406,615 | $3,645,178 | $4,134,837 | $489,659 |
| Fee accounts | $209,000 | $200,000 | $229,433 | $29,433 |
| TOTAL budget authority | $3,615,615 | $3,845,178 | $4,364,270 | $519,092 |

*Source*: *BICE Budget Overview, DHS Budget in Brief Document*, 2005.

detect, deter, and defeat hostile acts targeting U.S. air carriers, airports, passengers, and crews. The Detention and Removal Division is responsible for promoting the public safety and national security by ensuring the departure from the United States of all removable aliens through enforcement of immigration laws (see Sidebar 5-3). The Federal Protective Service (FPS) is responsible for policing, securing, and ensuring a safe environment in which federal agencies can conduct their business by reducing threats posed against more than 8,800 federal government facilities nationwide. Intelligence is responsible for the collection, analysis, and dissemination of strategic and tactical intelligence data in support of BICE and DHS. Table 5-3 illustrates the Bureau of Immigration and Customs Enforcement budget for FY 2004–2006.

## TRANSPORTATION SAFETY AND SECURITY

Transportation is a general term that refers to the movement of things or people from one location to another. However, in today's modern world, where transportation systems are intertwined into a global network that moves millions of people and products throughout the world on a daily basis, such simple definitions do not give justice to the complexity that exists in this sector. Furthermore, the safety and security needs to address such a complex system are equally complex and interconnected. Historically, the United States has relied on the private sector for both the transportation network and the promise of domestic transportation safety and security. The events of September 11, 2001, however, illustrated the vulnerabilities of our systems and spurred a massive change in the existing approaches. Transportation security and the identification and reduction of vulnerabilities within the vast transportation networks have since experienced significant challenges and changes. Because of the complexity of these systems as a whole and the complexity of the subsystems included, this has not been an easy task.

In the United States, the Department of Transportation (DOT) and the DHS Directorate of Border and Transportation Security (BT&S) are the main stakeholders ensuring transportation safety and security. The Transportation Security Agency (TSA) is the main agency under the BT&S directorate that addresses the system's security of the transportation infrastructure.

### SIDEBAR 5-3    **The US-VISIT Program**

US-VISIT is a DHS program that enhances the nation's entry and exit system. It enables the United States to effectively verify the identity of incoming visitors and confirm compliance with visa and immigration policies. The program's goals are to enhance the security of U.S. citizens and visitors who travel in and out of the country, to expedite legitimate travel and trade, to ensure the integrity of the immigration system while safeguarding the personal privacy of visitors.

The changes that are associated with the implementation of the new system start at U.S. posts and embassies abroad when the prospective foreign visitor to the United States applies for a U.S. visa. The applicant gets both of her index fingers digitally scanned and those images are saved in a database where other relevant information about the applicant is saved. The fingerprints are later used to verify the identity of the visitor when he or she enters or leaves the country.

On arrival in the United States, as part of the enhanced procedures, most visitors traveling on visas will have two fingerprints scanned by an inkless device and a digital photograph taken. All of the data and information are then used to assist the border inspector in determining whether or not to admit the traveler. These enhanced procedures add only seconds to the visitor's overall processing time.

All data obtained from the visitor is securely stored as part of the visitor's travel record. This information is made available only to authorized officials and selected law enforcement agencies on a need-to-know basis in their efforts to help protect against those who intend to harm American citizens or visitors.

The most notable change for international visitors is the new exit procedure. Most visitors who require a visa will eventually need to verify their departure. This checkout process will be completed by use of automated self-service workstations in the international departure areas of airports and seaports. By scanning travel documents and capturing fingerprints on the same inkless device, the system validates the visitor's identity, verifies his or her departure, and confirms his or her compliance with U.S. immigration policy.

*Source*: DHS, www,dhs.gov, 2004.

---

TSA's security focus is on identifying risks, prioritizing them, managing these risks to acceptable levels, and mitigating the impact of potential incidents that may arise as result of these risks. Sharing of information among agencies and stakeholders—including intelligence information—has become a cornerstone of its risk management model. Recognizing that differences exist between transportation modes, TSA has needed to adapt to the complex and unique needs of both passenger and cargo security, in an attempt to instill citizen confidence in the security of the transportation system. TSA's stated guiding principle is that it will focus on the leveraging of prevention services, new technologies, best practices, public education, stakeholder outreach, and regulation compliance across transportation modes.

TSA provides security to the nation's transportation systems with a primary focus on aviation security. TSA's specific responsibilities include screening of all aviation passengers and baggage through a mix of federalized and privatized screeners and technology. This screener workforce consists primarily of the 45,000 passenger and baggage screeners located at 448 commercial airports. TSA screeners augment screening through the most modern technologies, including metal detectors, X-ray machines, explosives trace detection machines, and explosives detection systems.

TABLE 5-4   **TSA Budget Allocation, FY 2004–2006**

| DHS TSA budget review ($ in 1,000s) | FY 2004 enacted | FY 2005 enacted | FY 2006 pres. budget | FY 2006 ± FY 2005 |
|---|---|---|---|---|
| Aviation security | $3,724,114 | $4,578,523 | $4,984,784 | $406,261 |
| Surface transportation security | $261,449 | $115,000 | $32,000 | −$83,000 |
| Transportation security support | $592,480 | $711,852 | $545,008 | −$166,844 |
| TOTAL budget authority | $4,578,043 | $5,405,375 | $5,561,792 | $156,417 |

*Source*: *TSA Budget Overview, DHS Budget in Brief Document*, 2005.

U.S. air carriers annually transport approximately 12.5 million tons of cargo, 2.8 million tons of which is now secured on passenger planes. The remaining 9.7 million tons of freight, shipped in cargo planes, remains a unique threat to the nation. TSA is working on the development of a screening operation to ensure the security of this cargo as well, though no system is yet in place, nor is the funding for one available.

TSA is also tasked with managing the security risk to the U.S. surface transportation systems. These systems include 9 billion passenger trips per year on the nation's mass transit systems, more than 161,000 miles of interstate and national highways and their integrated bridges and tunnels, and nearly 800,000 shipments of hazardous materials (95% of which are made by truck). These systems have come under heightened security considerations since the repeat bombings of the London subway and bus systems in July 2005. For these systems, TSA will address these security responsibilities in partnership with other components of the DHS as well as the Department of Transportation and other departments. Table 5-4 illustrates the budget allocation for the Transportation Security Agency for FY 2004–2006.

## AIR TRANSPORTATION SAFETY AND SECURITY

The primary agency for aviation safety is the Office of System Safety of the Federal Aviation Administra-

tion (FAA) within the Department of Transportation (DOT). The principal function of the office is to develop and implement improved tools and processes for hazard identification, risk assessment, and risk management. The office attempts to facilitate effective use of air safety data, both inside and outside the agency for the purpose of improving overall aviation safety. The office provides international leadership in monitoring airline safety, and identifies emerging aviation safety issues and concerns. It has become a focal point for aviation safety data and information worldwide as a result.

The agency has many goals:

- To create an environment that facilitates and encourages sharing aviation safety information
- To identify appropriate data and analysis techniques and make them readily available to the international aviation community
- To develop tools to help identify safety issues
- To promote system safety methodologies within and outside the FAA
- To maximize impact of safety resource investments
- To develop, market, and promote safety information (FAA, 2005, www.faa.gov)

The Aviation and Transportation Security Act (P.L. 107-71), signed by the president on November 19, 2001, created the Transportation Security Administration (TSA) in the Department of Transportation. (As described earlier, the agency was later on moved into

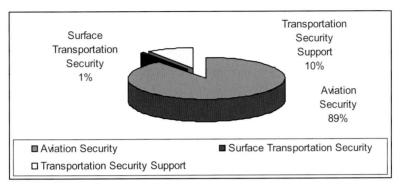

FIGURE 5-2   Components of the TSA budget. (*Source:* DHS, 2005)

the Department of Homeland Security under the Directorate for Border & Transportation Security.) This law made many fundamental changes in the way transportation security is performed and managed in the United States. For instance, this law for the first time made aviation security a direct federal responsibility. In addition, all transportation security activities are now managed by one agency. Because of the events of September 11, aviation security is one of the highest priority responsibilities of TSA, and the agency expends significant budget and human resources to develop strategies and implement necessary technologies to prevent any future terrorist events connected to the abuse of the aviation system and air transportation. Figure 5-2 displays the internal budget allocations of the TSA, illustrating its heavy bias toward aviation security. It is expected that, in light of the continuing threat posed by terrorists to public transportation systems, these trends will change.

Since its initial full year of funding in 2003, TSA has accomplished several important projects that seek to improve air transportation security. The 2003 budget for TSA totaled $4.8 billion, an increase of more than $3.5 billion from 2002 funding levels. The 2003 budget included the costs of well over 30,000 airport security personnel, including screeners, law enforcement personnel, and screener supervisors. The budget also included funding for the purchase of explosive detection systems that had to be in place to screen all checked baggage by December 31, 2002, and their maintenance. The 2003 budget was also the first year reflecting full funding of the greatly expanded federal air marshal program.

The president requested a budget of $4.82 billion for TSA for FY 2004, which is over $1 billion more than the agency spent in FY 2003. The FY 2004 budget was spent primarily on four programs, among which the aviation security program is the largest with a $4.22 billion (86%) of the overall budget. The aviation security program consisted of a passenger screening program for which $1.80 billion was allocated, a baggage screening program with a budget of $944 million, and a security direction and enforcement program for which $1.47 billion was allocated. (TSA, www.dhs.gov, 2005)

In FY 2005, the agency accomplished the following air transportation security-related projects:

- Developed a standardized approach to physical aviation security measures at the nation's airports and began development of the Freight Assessment Authenticating Model
- Supported the air cargo improvements being tested and developed to include Hardened Unit Load Devices

- Began inline installation of Explosive Detection Systems (EDS) machines at select airports
- Continued to strengthen and expand airport contract screening opportunities at those airports wishing to opt out of federal screening
- Developed a program to perform assessments of the state of security and vulnerability of general aviation facilities
- Deployed inspectors to enhance existing resources at high threat airports and engage in inspection and screening of aircraft, facilities, and cargo, pursuant to DHS adjustments in security conditions
- Continued screening operations based on security requirements and increased efficiencies in business processes
- Began a 2-year, $100 million investment in emerging explosives technologies at passenger screening checkpoints
- Continued to deploy Federal Flight Deck Officers (FFDO) aboard flights representing the last possible line of defense against on-board passengers intending to inflict harm to the aircraft and the aviation system

The FY 2006 budget request for the Transportation Security Administration, a sign of the continued importance of this federal responsibility, includes (in addition to most of the existing programs to date) funding for the following initiatives:

- Emerging checkpoint explosive detection technologies ($43.7 million)
- Screener workforce base realignment ($179.981 million)
- High-speed operational connectivity (Hi-SOC) ($174 million)
- Flight crew training ($11 million)
- Repair station inspections ($6 million)

## TRUCKING SECURITY

Trucking is an important component of transportation security because a significant portion of haz-ardous materials (HAZMAT) in the United States is being transported by trucks on highways and roads. TSA is tasked with managing the security risk to the U.S. surface transportation systems while ensuring the freedom of movement of people and commerce. For these systems, TSA addresses these security responsibilities in partnership with other components of the DHS as well as the DOT and other departments.

A serious HAZMAT incident is defined by the DOT's Research and Special Programs Administration (RISPA) as an incident that involves a fatality or major injury caused by the release of a hazardous material, the evacuation of 25 or more persons as a result of release of a hazardous material or exposure to fire, a release or exposure to fire that results in the closure of a major transportation artery, the alteration of an aircraft flight plan or operation, the release of radioactive materials from Type B packaging, the release of over 11.9 gallons or 88.2 pounds of a severe marine pollutant, or the release of a bulk quantity (over 119 gallons or 882 pounds) of a hazardous material. Table 5-5 illustrates the number of these serious incidents that have occurred on U.S. highways between 1995 and 2004.

Because a significant portion of HAZMAT transportation is done by trucks, trucking has become an important issue in securing homeland safety and improving the security of the U.S. transportation systems. The Office of Hazardous Materials Safety of DOT/RISPA is responsible for coordinating a national safety program for the transportation of hazardous materials by air, rail, highway, and water in the United States. The Code of Federal Regulations (CFR) 49 Part 107 documents the steps being taken to enhance hazardous material transportation security. Subchapter C, Part 107, specifically discusses regulations for HAZMAT transportation on U.S. highways. The subparts of the document include information about regulations for loading and unloading of HAZMAT transportation vehicles, segregation and separation of HAZMAT vehicles and shipments in transit, accidents, and regulations applying to hazardous material on motor vehicles carrying passengers for hire. To supplement safety efforts, the DHS, Office of Screen-

TABLE 5-5   **Classification of Serious HAZMAT Incidents in the United States by the Mode of Transportation and Yearly Frequencies**

| Mode | 1995 | 1996 | 1997 | 1998 | 1999 | 2000 | 2001 | 2002 | 2003 | 2004 | Total |
|---|---|---|---|---|---|---|---|---|---|---|---|
| Air | 817 | 925 | 1,031 | 1,386 | 1,582 | 1,419 | 1,083 | 732 | 751 | 995 | 10,721 |
| Highway | 12,869 | 12,034 | 11,932 | 13,111 | 14,953 | 15,063 | 15,806 | 13,505 | 13,599 | 12,977 | 135,849 |
| Railway | 1,155 | 1,112 | 1,102 | 989 | 1,073 | 1,058 | 899 | 870 | 802 | 753 | 9,813 |
| Water | 12 | 6 | 5 | 11 | 8 | 17 | 6 | 10 | 10 | 15 | 100 |
| Total | 14,853 | 14,077 | 14,070 | 15,497 | 17,616 | 17,557 | 17,794 | 15,117 | 15,162 | 14,740 | 156,483 |

*Source*: Hazardous Materials Information System, U.S. Department of Transportation.

ing Coordination and Operations (SCO) within the B&TS Directorate initiated hazardous materials trucker background checks in 2005 in an effort to secure the highways and trucks.

In 2005, the TSA provided grants totaling $4,828,569 to trucking companies in 2005 for the following priorities:

1. **Participant Identification and Recruitment**:
   a. *Motor carriers*: Identify and recruit motor carriers (truck, bus, school transportation) that will actively participate and support Highway Watch training and activity reporting goals and who agree to adopt recommended "best practices."
   b. *Individual drivers*: Develop methodologies to identify and recruit active current drivers to include independent, unaffiliated drivers, passenger carriers, and other vehicle fleets to expand the program.
   c. *Responder/law enforcement*: Develop methodology to identify and recruit first responder/enforcement entities that will actively support Highway Watch goals regarding driver training and activity reporting, and will adopt recommended "best practices" within their entities.
2. **Training**: Create highway security training programs designed specifically for each service segment of the motor carrier industry, driver,

first responder and law enforcement communities to ensure that trainees understand the difference between those incidents that require reporting as potential threats to homeland security and those incidents that are more rightly fielded as highway safety emergencies.

3. **Communications**: Highway Watch Call Center: Maintain a full-service (24/7) communications/call center staffed with well-trained responders who will provide nationwide first responder/enforcement contact numbers and electronic linkage to registered participants, and be capable of re-directing calls to law enforcement and first responders for immediate action or to the Highway Information Sharing and Analysis Center (ISAC) for investigation as terrorist threats.
4. **Information Analysis and Distribution**: The applicant will provide management consulting services and oversight in cooperation with ODP leadership to maintain the Highway Information Sharing and Analysis Center (ISAC), located at the Transportation Security Operations Center (TSOC) in Herndon, Virginia. This center is dedicated exclusively to highway and highway transport-related security needs and issues. The applicant will provide recommendations, implementation strategies, and a completed plan for continued Highway ISAC operations. Responsibilities may include identifying the

appropriate role of a highway-specific ISAC, identification of benefits of highway-specific ISAC separation from existing rail or other centers, optimal configuration and location of a new ISAC, and optimal staffing or implementation strategies.

*Source*: DHS, Office of Domestic Preparedness, *Fiscal Year 2005 Trucking Security Grant Program Application Kit.*

The Bureau of Customs and Border Protection in 2005 requested $125 million for a WMD Detection Technology Program. The need for this purchase of additional radiation portal monitors is considered critically important because the equipment will provide CBP with a passive, nonintrusive means of screening trucks and other vehicles for the presence of radiological materials, which will allow for much faster and effective processing of time-sensitive cargo.

## PORTS AND SHIPPING SECURITY

Ports are important facilities of the U.S. transportation infrastructure, and vital to the economic prosperity of the country. Seventy-seven U.S. ports are open to international trade, import, and export, 30 of which account for almost 99% of all international maritime trade activity. Securing maritime transportation is a critical task for the DHS, because a successful terrorist attack on any major U.S. port could result in significant loss of life, tremendous physical damage, and serious disruption to the economy and commerce of the United States and its trade partners. Two major departments, DOT and DHS, share responsibility for securing the maritime transportation system and the ports.

The USCG has its own maritime strategy for homeland security, where duties, responsibilities and strategic missions of the agency are clearly defined. The homeland security mission of the Coast Guard is to protect the U.S. maritime domain and the U.S. marine transportation system and deny their use and exploitation by terrorists as a means for attacks on

U.S. territory, population, and critical infrastructure and to prepare for and, in the event of attack, conduct emergency response operations. When directed by the supported or supporting commander, the USCG conducts military homeland defense operations. The Coast Guard is the lead federal agency for maritime homeland security. In accomplishing its homeland security mission, the strategic goals of the Coast Guard are as follows:

- Increase maritime domain awareness.
- Conduct enhanced maritime security operations.
- Close port security gaps.
- Build critical security capabilities.
- Leverage partnerships to mitigate security risks.
- Ensure readiness for homeland defense operations.

The DHS Transportation Security Agency's main role in maritime and port security has been in providing grants to support port security and related issues. Of TSA's FY 2004 budget, $86 million was spent on maritime and land safety, and $55 million for the Transportation Worker Identification Card (TWIC) program, which is a federal program to improve security by establishing a transportation system-wide common credential, used across all modes, for all transportation workers requiring unescorted physical and logical access to secure areas of the transportation system.

The DHS and USCG Port and Maritime Security Strategy consists of a layered approach that aims to minimize potential threats that may be posed while U.S.-bound ships and vessels are overseas, while they are in transit (i.e., while they are moving in between continents and countries), and while they are within the U.S. waterways. There are separate initiatives that are intended to minimize the vulnerabilities in each of those layers. These initiatives include the following:

**Initiatives for overseas vulnerability reduction:**

1. **24-Hour Advanced Manifest Rule—Awareness**: All sea carriers with the exception of bulk carriers and approved break bulk cargo are

required to provide proper cargo descriptions and valid consignee addresses 24 hours before cargo is loaded at the foreign port for shipment to the United States through the Sea Automated Manifest System. Failure to meet the 24-hour Advanced Manifest Rule results in a "do not load" message and other penalties. Through this program, administered by DHS's Customs and Border Protection (CBP), the department has greater awareness of what is being loaded onto ships bound for the United States and the advance information enables DHS to evaluate the terrorist risk from sea containers.

2. **Container Security Initiative (CSI)—Awareness & Prevention**: Under the CSI program, the screening of containers that pose a risk for terrorism is accomplished by teams of CBP officials deployed to work in concert with their host nation counterparts. Nineteen of the top 20 ports have agreed to join CSI and are at various stages of implementation. These 20 ports account for approximately 68% of sea containers shipped to the United States. CSI operational seaports include Rotterdam, LeHavre, Bremerhaven, Hamburg, Antwerp, Singapore, Yokohama, Tokyo, Hong Kong, Göteborg, Felixstowe, Genoa, La Spezia, Busan, Durban, Vancouver, Montreal, Halifax and Port Klang. Through CSI, potential suspect containers are targeted and identified before being loaded onto vessels. Phase 2 of CSI will enable the DHS to extend port security protection from 68% of container traffic to more than 80%.

3. **Customs-Trade Partnership against Terrorism (C-TPAT)—Awareness & Prevention**: Through C-TPAT, thousands of importers, carriers, brokers, forwarders, ports and terminals and foreign manufacturers have taken the necessary steps to secure their supply chains. Under the C-TPAT initiative, business participants providing verifiable security information are eligible for special benefits. The security enhancements put in place by C-TPAT participant allow DHS to devote more resources to high-risk shipments.

4. **International Ship and Port Facility Security (ISPS) Code—Awareness & Prevention**: By July 1, 2004, countries around the world will have implemented the first multilateral ship and port security standard ever created. The ISPS Code requires vessels and port facilities to conduct security assessments, develop security plans and hire security officers. By establishing a standard for security, the world has increased its ability to prevent maritime related attacks by making ports around the world more aware of unusual or suspicious activity.

5. **International Port Security Program—Awareness & Prevention**: Under this effort, the U.S. Coast Guard and the host nations will work jointly to evaluate the countries' overall compliance with the ISPS Code. The Coast Guard will use the information gained from these visits to improve the United State's own security practices and to determine if additional security precautions will be required for vessels arriving in the United States from other countries.

6. **Operation Safe Commerce (OSC)—Awareness & Prevention**: This pilot program analyzes security in the commercial supply chain and tests solutions to close security gaps. The technologies tested through the program will enhance maritime cargo security, protect the global supply chain, and facilitate the flow of commerce. DHS has awarded $58 million in grants to the private sector since its inception. The ports of Seattle and Tacoma, Los Angeles, and Long Beach and the Port Authority of New York/New Jersey are participating in the pilot program. The Department will award another $17 million within 2005 to participating private sector companies.

**Initiatives for "in-transit" vulnerability reduction:**

1. **Smart Box Initiative—Prevention**: One core element of Container Security Initiative is using

smarter, "tamper evident" containers that will better secure containerized shipping. Designed to be "tamper evident," the Smart Box couples an internationally approved mechanical seal affixed to an alternate location on the container door with an electronic container security device designed to deter and detect tampering of the container door. If someone attempts to open the cargo door after it has been sealed, the Smart Box device on the door would reflect that there had been an attempted intrusion into the container. Together with the results of technology testing, Operation Safe Commerce, DHS will have valuable information to assist in developing performance standards for container security.

2. **Ship Security Alert System—Response**: Like a silent alarm in a bank, a SSAS allows a vessel operator to send a covert alert to shore for incidents involving acts of violence (such as piracy or terrorism), indicating the security of the ship is under threat or has been compromised. The International Ship and Port Facility Security Code requires new passenger and cargo ships of at least 500 gross tons to install this equipment by July 1, 2004. Existing passenger vessels and cargo vessels must have the equipment installed prior to the first radio survey after July 1, 2004, or by July 1, 2006. Other types of vessels may carry and use SSAS voluntarily.

3. **Automated Targeting System (ATS)—Awareness**: CBP's ATS serves as the premier tool for performing transactional risk assessments and evaluating potential national security risks posed by cargo and passengers arriving by sea, air, truck, and rail. Using prearrival information and input from the intelligence community, this rules-based system identifies high-risk targets before they arrive in the United States.

4. **96-Hour Advance Notice of Arrival—Awareness & Prevention**: Ships must notify the Coast Guard 96 hours before arriving in a U.S. port and provide detailed information on the crew, passenger, cargo and voyage history. This infor-

mation is analyzed using databases and intelligence information, including reviewing previous security problems with the vessel or illegal activity on the part of the crew. Part of this analysis will also account for the security environment in previous ports of call. By obtaining this information well in advance of a vessels arrival, the U.S. Coast Guard is able to make determinations about which vessels require additional attention, including security precautions such as an at-sea boarding or armed escort during transit to and from port.

**Initiatives for vulnerability reduction "in U.S. Waters and on U.S. shores":**

1. **National Targeting Center (NTC)—Prevention & Response**: The priority mission of CBP's NTC is to provide tactical targeting and analytical research support for CBP antiterrorism efforts. Experts in passenger and cargo targeting at the NTC operate around the clock using tools like the Automated Targeting System (ATS) to identify tactical targets and support intradepartmental and interagency antiterrorist operations. The NTC also supports operations in the field including the Container Security Initiative (CSI) personnel stationed at critical foreign ports throughout the world.

2. **Maritime Intelligence Fusion Centers—Prevention**: Located in Norfolk, Virginia, and Alameda, California, these units compile and synthesize intelligence products from the federal, state and local level dealing with maritime security. These intelligence products are then disseminated to homeland security professionals across the country responsible for securing ports and waterways.

3. **High Interest Vessels Boardings—Prevention**: Before they are allowed to enter port, all vessels are screened for the security risk they pose to the United States based on information about the vessel's cargo, size, voyage, security

history, and any intelligence information. Those identified as higher risk are targeted for offshore boardings to ensure potential security issues are addressed prior to entry into port. In addition, the Coast Guard randomly selects vessels for security boardings to ensure an element of unpredictability and thus deterrence. Specially trained Coast Guard teams board the boats through traditional water-based methods or via fast roping from helicopters.

4. **Operation Port Shield—Prevention**: Operation Port Shield focuses on the implementation and enforcement of the new security measures implemented under the international requirements or MTSA between June 15 and December 31, 2004. Under this verification program, the Coast Guard will be boarding every vessel, at sea or at the dock, on its first visit to a U.S. port on or after July 1 to ensure that the vessel is compliant with U.S. security standards. These program officers will also visit foreign countries to evaluate antiterrorism measures in place at ports abroad.

5. **Automatic Identification System—Awareness**: AIS is a type of vessel-tracking equipment that automatically sends detailed ship information to other ships and shore-based agencies, allowing for comprehensive, virtually instantaneous vessel tracking and monitoring, increasing security and safety in shipping channels. Currently, most vessels required to use this technology are large vessels on international voyages. The Coast Guard is exploring possible ways to expand these requirements to other vessels and other U.S. waters.

6. **Area Maritime Security Committees— Awareness, Prevention & Response**: The Coast Guard has established committees in all the nation's ports to coordinate the activities of all port stakeholders, including other federal, local and state agencies, industry and the boating public. These groups are tasked with collaborating on plans to secure their ports so the

resources of an area can be best used to deter, prevent and respond to terror threats.

7. **Port Security Assessment Program— Awareness**: This program is aimed at increasing the information and best practices available to port officials across the country to help them make decisions about how to reduce the vulnerability of their ports. The Coast Guard is in the process of closely examining the key infrastructure in the nation's 55 most economically and strategically important ports for potential vulnerabilities. In addition to these assessments, the Coast Guard is creating a system to display key port information in an electronic geospatially referenced format to serve as a database that can be easily searched for national, regional and local information.

8. **Port Security Grants—Awareness, Prevention & Response**: The Port Security Grant Program provides federal resources for projects to enhance facility and operational security for critical national seaports. Funds assist ports in analyzing vulnerabilities and then closing gaps in security through physical enhancements like access control gates, fencing, lighting and advanced communication and surveillance systems. The program also funds the implementation of security strategies to prevent and respond to terror threats. During the past 3 years, $516 million in grants have been allocated and another $50 million are currently pending review.

9. **Non-Intrusive Inspection Technology (NII)—Prevention**: Nonintrusive inspection (NII) technologies allows U.S. Customs and Border Protection to screen a larger portion of the stream of commercial traffic in less time while facilitating legitimate trade. CBP officers use large-scale gamma ray and X-ray imaging systems to safely and efficiently screen conveyances for contraband, including weapons of mass destruction. These units can scan the interior of a full-size 40-foot container in under a minute. Inspectors also use personal

radiation detectors to scan for signs of radioactive materials, as well as special high-tech tools such as density meters and fiber-optic scopes to peer inside suspicious containers. Finally, if necessary, containers are opened and unloaded for a more intensive manual inspection.

10. **Maritime Safety and Security Teams (MSSTs)—Prevention & Response**: MSSTs are a Coast Guard rapid response force assigned to vital ports and capable of nationwide deployment via air, ground, or sea transportation to meet emerging threats. MSSTs were created in direct response to the terrorist attacks on September 11, 2001. They have unique capabilities, including explosive-detection dogs, personnel trained to conduct fast-roping deployments from a helicopter to a hostile vessel, and antiterrorism/force protection small boat handling training. Eight teams are currently in operation and five more are scheduled to be commissioned by early 2005.

11. **Guarding In-Between the Ports—Prevention**: Coast Guard, CBP Border Patrol, and Immigration and Customs Enforcement's Air and Marine Operations units are responsible for patrolling and securing the nation's borders between the ports of entry. During FY 2004 to date, DHS personnel have apprehended more than 770,000 illegal aliens on land and over 9,000 at sea. By adding additional personnel, equipment, and technology, the Department of Homeland Security has been able to broaden the areas of coverage. Through strong enforcement operations and the state of the art technology at the borders, the department has enhanced its operational effectiveness on the front line.

12. **Operation Drydock—Awareness & Prevention**: Operation Drydock, a Coast Guard and FBI investigation into national security threats and document fraud associated with U.S. merchant mariner credentials, revealed nine individuals linked to terrorist groups that were holding maritime credentials. Merchant mariner credentials are often used as an identification document that allows mariners to come and go from the ship while it is docked in a foreign port. This investigation, enhancements to the criminal background check process for applicants, and increased security features on the cards themselves have increased the U.S. government's ability to monitor crews of the U.S. merchant fleet.

13. **Transportation Workers Identity Card (TWIC)—Awareness & Prevention**: The goal of the TWIC program is to develop a secure uniform credential to prevent potential terrorist threats from entering sensitive areas of the transportation system. When implemented, the TWIC program will ensure that credentials contain a biometric identifier to positively authenticate identities of TWIC holders. By having one universally recognized credential, workers avoid paying for redundant cards and background investigations to enter secure areas at multiple facilities. The prototype phase will be conducted at 35 facilities in six states including the ports of Los Angeles and Long Beach, California, and the 14 major port facilities in the state of Florida. The prototype is funded with $50 million included in Homeland Security's Transportation Security Administration budget and up to 200,000 port workers are expected to participate.

14. **America's Waterways Watch—Awareness**: The goal of America's Waterway Watch is to help prevent acts of terrorism and other illegal activity that jeopardizes maritime homeland security by having members of the maritime and recreational boating industries, as well as the boating public, recognize and report to appropriate authorities suspicious activity that may be an indicator of potential terrorism. Any observations of suspicious or unusual activity could be extremely valuable to the national security and may provide clues to help uncover patterns of possible terrorist activity. Reports

can be made to the Coast Guard, local law enforcement, or by calling 1-877-24-WATCH.

*Source*: DHS, *Secure Seas, Open Ports, "Keeping Our Waters Safe, Secure and Open for Business."* **June 21, 2004, http://whitepapers.zdnet.co.uk/ 0,39025945,60121606p-39001102q,00.htm**.

## BUS TRANSPORTATION SECURITY

Bus transportation is an often-neglected link in the nation's transportation networks, and represents a potential vulnerability to homeland security efforts. The bus transportation system is likely to eventually become a target of terrorists because the system has comparatively less protection against terrorist attacks, which makes it "soft" for terrorists searching for less risky but high-consequence attacks.

The motor coach industry, which includes regularly scheduled point-to-point service and chartered tour operations, carried more than 774 million passengers in the United States in 2000, 28% more passengers than carried by domestic commercial airlines and 33 times more passengers than carried by Amtrak. The 12 Class 1 bus companies, defined by the Bureau of Statistics as having revenues of at least $10 million annually, carried approximately 33 million passengers in 2000. There are worrisome precedents for the potential for security breaches on buses. In the United States, Greyhound drivers and passengers were the targets of at least four serious assaults in 2002, one killing seven passengers and another injuring 33 passengers, and at least three other serious security breaches. These incidents occurred in several states throughout the country. While steps have been taken to improve security, serious work remains to be done before the system can be considered secure.

To support the intercity bus transportation sector, TSA provided $20 million in grants for intercity bus security projects. More than 60 private bus operators received these grants to complete their proposed projects to improve the security of their staff, customers, and operations. The priorities that TSA was looking

for in the 2003 proposals that it reviewed to select the grantees were as follows:

1. Protecting or isolating the driver
2. Monitoring, tracking, and communication technologies for over-the-road buses
3. Implementing and operating passenger and baggage screening programs at terminals and over-the-road buses
4. Developing an effective security assessment/ security plan that identifies critical security needs and vulnerabilities
5. Training drivers, dispatchers, ticket agents, and other personnel in recognizing and responding to criminal attacks and terrorist threats, evacuation procedures, passenger screening procedures, and baggage inspection

The Department of Homeland Security provided $9,657,138 of intercity bus security grants to bus companies in 2005. Those grants were provided to projects that were proposed in following topics:

1. **Passenger and Baggage Screening for Prevention and Detection of IEDs and Chemical, Biological, Radiological, and Nuclear Devices at Terminals Located in Defined UASI Jurisdictions**
   - Explosive agent detection sensors
   - Chemical/biological/radiological agent detection sensors
   - Canines (start-up costs and training)
   - Positive ID ticketing procedures
   - Baggage matching to passengers
   - Baggage screening technology (X-ray, explosive detection)
   - Passenger screening (metal detectors, explosive detection, behavioral screening)
   - Limited access for passenger waiting and loading areas
   - Passenger manifest
2. **Facility Security Enhancements for Prevention and Detection of IEDs and Chemical, Biological, Radiological, and Nuclear Devices at Terminals and Bus Lots Located in Defined UASI Jurisdictions**

- Explosive agent detection sensors
- Chemical/biological/radiological agent detection sensors
- Canines (start-up costs and training)
- Intrusion detection
- Video surveillance systems
- Secure entry ID systems
- Employee identification
- Improved lighting
- Fencing and secured gates

3. **Vehicle/Driver Security, Monitoring, Tracking, and Communications**
- Explosive agent detection sensors
- Chemical/biological/radiological agent detection sensors
- Canines (start-up costs and training)
- Interoperable communications systems
- GPS tracking systems
- On-board camera systems
- Fixed personnel protection (driver shields, etc.)
- Interlock security devices
- Kill switch technology

4. **Training and Exercises**
- Behavioral screening training for front-line employees
- Antiterrorism training
- Antihijacking training
- Public and employee awareness programs
- Multidisciplinary, multijurisdictional terrorism exercises

*Source*: DHS, *Fiscal Year 2005 Intercity Bus Security Grant Program Application Kit.*

The president's 2006 budget for the Department of Homeland Security included the continuation of the $10,000,000 funding for intercity bus security grants. Those grants will be provided to projects with respect to the revised funding priorities.

## RAILWAY TRANSPORTATION SECURITY

The railroad system is another highly utilized and valuable component of the U.S. transportation infra-

structure that must now be protected against potential terrorist and other vulnerabilities. DHS made its most noticeable references to the protection of the railway system in the *National Strategy for the Physical Protection of Critical Infrastructure and Key Assets* and in the announcement of the *Operation Liberty Shield.*

The *National Strategy for the Physical Protection of Critical Infrastructure and Key Assets* document mentions potential vulnerabilities and talks about possible terrorist attack scenarios to the railroad system, and it identifies four priorities for improvement in the railroad security:

1. *The need to develop improved decision-making criteria regarding the shipment of hazardous materials*: DHS and DOT, coordinating with other federal agencies, state and local governments, and industry, will facilitate the development of an improved process to ensure informed decision making with respect to hazardous materials shipment.

2. *The need to develop technologies and procedures to screen intermodal containers and passenger baggage*: DHS and DOT will work with sector counterparts to identify and explore technologies and processes to enable efficient and expeditious screening of rail passengers and baggage, especially at intermodal stations.

3. *The need to improve security of intermodal transportation*: DHS and DOT will work with sector counterparts to identify and facilitate the development of technologies and procedures to secure intermodal containers and detect threatening content. DHS and DOT will work with the rail industry to devise or enable a hazardous materials identification system that supports the needs of first responders yet avoids providing terrorists with easy identification of a potential weapon.

4. *The need to clearly delineate roles and responsibilities regarding surge requirements*: DHS and DOT will work with industry to delineate infrastructure protection roles and responsibilities to enable the rail industry to address surge requirements for resources in the case of cata-

strophic events. Costs and resource allocation remain a contentious issue for the rail sector. DHS and DOT will also convene a working group consisting of government and industry representatives to identify options for the implementation of surge capabilities, including access to federal facilities and capabilities in extreme emergencies.

The national physical protection strategy clearly identifies the transportation of HAZMAT within the railroad infrastructure as the greatest vulnerability of the system. This assessment was reiterated by Admiral James Loy, former TSA administrator, in a meeting with the North American Rail Shippers Association where he identified the following as the primary threats to the railway system: (1) hazardous material, (2) nuclear and radiological material, (3) food and livestock, and (4) intermodal containers.

In response to Admiral Loy's assessment, DOT and DHS released a document regarding the HAZMAT transportation vulnerability and measures to be taken to minimize the terrorist threat to the system. This document provides background information on the improvements accomplished in the railroad system since September 11. It discusses the security task force established by the Association of American Railroads (AAR) to assess vulnerabilities in several critical areas, such as physical assets, information technology, chemicals and hazardous materials, defense shipments, train operations, and passenger security. In March 2003, DHS announced *Operation Liberty Shield*, which details the following steps to enhance railway security:

1. *To improve rail bridge security*: State governors have been asked to provide additional police or National Guard forces at selected bridges.
2. *To increase railroad infrastructure security*: Railroad companies will be asked to increase security at major facilities and key rail hubs.
3. *AMTRAK security measures*: AMTRAK will implement security measures consistent with private rail companies.
4. *To increase railroad hazardous material safety*: At the request of the Department of Transporta-

tion, private railroad companies will monitor shipments of hazardous material and increase surveillance of trains carrying this material.

On April 8, 2004, the Senate's Commerce, Science, and Transportation Committee approved the Rail Security Act of 2004, which authorized an increase in rail security funding by $1.1 billion, over the initial funding of only $65 million. The Rail Security Act, as proposed, requires DHS to conduct a vulnerability assessment of the nation's rail systems and report back to Congress with its findings. The vulnerability assessment would require a review of freight and passenger rail transportation, including the identification and evaluation of critical assets and infrastructures; threats to those assets and infrastructures; vulnerabilities that are specific to rail transportation of hazardous materials; and security weaknesses. Based on the assessment, DHS would develop prioritized recommendations for improving the security of rail infrastructure and facilities, terminals, tunnels, bridges, and other at-risk areas; deploying weapons detection and surveillance equipment; training employees; and conducting public outreach campaigns.

The bill authorized $5 million for FY 2005 for the vulnerability assessment and development of recommendations. The bill also requires DHS to conduct a pilot program of random security screening of passengers and baggage at five passenger rail stations served by Amtrak. The program included testing a wide range of explosives-detection technologies, devices and methods, and a requirement that intercity rail passengers produce government-issued photo identification prior to boarding.

To comply with the act, TSA began the prototype phase of its Transportation Worker Identity Credential (TWIC) program on November 17, 2004, on five pilot sites that were initially port facilities. Each site uses biometric technology to provide authorized transportation workers access to controlled areas. Using fingerprint and iris scan technology, the TWIC tied the transportation worker to the credential and threat assessment and can be used in conjunction with access control to critical components of the nation's transportation infrastructure. The TWIC program is designed to enhance security at U.S. transportation facilities while boosting the efficiency of commercial activity. The program, still in its pilot phase, will later be enlarged to include railway facilities.

The Association of American Railroads coordinated and conducted a comprehensive risk analysis covering the entire railway industry. This scope of this risk assessment included the train operations, communication and cyber security aspects, identification and protection of critical assets, transportation of hazardous materials, and identification of a military liaison. The association worked closely with the federal intelligence community and security experts and identified and prioritized more than 1,300 critical assets. As a result of the vulnerability analysis, more than 50 permanent changes were made to procedures and operations, including restricted access to facilities, increased tracking of certain shipments, enhanced employee security training, and cyber security improvements. In addition to those measures it was decided that one rail police officer should sit on the FBI's National Joint Terrorism Task Force and two rail analysts should sit in the Department of Homeland Security intelligence offices to help evaluate data at the top secret level. The association created a DOD-certified, full-time operations center, working at the secret level to monitor and evaluate intelligence on potential threats and communicate with railroads through the Railway Alert Network (RAN). A Surface Transportation Information Sharing and Analysis Center (ST-ISAC)—operating at the top secret level—was also created to collect, analyze and disseminate information on physical and cyber security threats. (Association of American Railroads, 2004)

The TSA provided the top 10 mass transit and passenger rail agencies with TSA-certified explosives detection canine teams to aid in the identification of explosives materials within the mass transit/rail transportation system. The pilot inspection program was named the Transit and Rail Inspection Pilot (TRIP), which is a first-time rail security technology study conducted by the DHS in cooperation with several other entities. TRIP was conducted in three phases. TRIP Phase I occurred at the New Carrollton,

Maryland, rail station and evaluated the use of technologies for screening rail passengers and their baggage prior to boarding a train. TRIP Phase II occurred at Union Station in Washington, D.C., and tested the use of screening equipment for checked baggage and cargo prior to their loading onto an Amtrak passenger train, as well as screening of unclaimed baggage and temporarily stored items inside Union Station. TRIP Phase III occurred on board a Shoreline East commuter rail car. The goal of Phase III was to evaluate the use of existing technologies installed on a rail car to screen passengers and their baggage for explosives, while the rail car is in transit.

In addition to the TRIP program, the TSA hired and deployed 100 surface transportation (rail) inspectors to enhance the level of national transportation security by leveraging private and public partnerships through a consistent national program of compliance reviews, audits, and enforcement actions pertaining to required standards and directives.

The DHS FY 2005 Freight Rail Security Program was appropriated total funds of $5 million. The funding priorities for the program were as follows:

1. **Development of a Rail Corridor Risk Management Tool**: The focus of this priority is on the development of a web-based Rail Corridor Risk Management Tool (RCRMT) for use by the federal, state, and local governments and private industry. The RCRMT is expected to leverage existing technologies and accepted risk management practices already in use by DHS and DOT where feasible, and incorporate new technologies and elements where necessary. In addition, the RCRMT must complement and support the rail corridor assessments currently being conducted by TSA, IAIP, and FRA in eight locations nationwide. This project also has to include the development of a comprehensive training curriculum for use of the RCRMT by state and local governments and industry. The final stage of the program includes a field test of the RCRMT and associated training program in Chicago, Illinois. Chicago is the hub of the

nation's rail transportation system, and is the busiest freight railroad gateway in North America. One-third of rail and truck cargo moves to, from, or through the Chicago region. This project must leverage the work and existing structure of the Chicago Region Environmental and Transportation Efficiency Program (CREATE), a partnership of railroad industry, federal, state, and local government officials. Total funding available for this project priority is $3 million.

2. **Development of a Rail Corridor Hazmat Response and Recovery Tool**: DOT is in the process of updating and revising regulatory requirements previously implemented under PHMSA docket HM-232—*Hazardous Materials: Security Requirements for Offerors and Transporters of Hazardous Materials,* published on March 25, 2003 (68 FR 14509), as a result of responses to a request for comments published on August 16, 2004 (69 FR 50987) and experiences obtained through the joint DHS/DOT toxic inhalation hazard working group. One aspect the departments are considering is the requirement to conduct safety/security risk analyses of current, and alternative, TIH routes. These requirements, if adopted, would mandate carriers to evaluate the safety and security risks present on each TIH route and at each railroad facility (yard, storage location, dispatching center) along the route, noting the specific measures the railroad has taken to ameliorate the noted risks. Among the factors to be considered in the analysis are:

- Volume of material transported
- Presence or absence of signals and train control systems along route (dark vs. signaled territory)
- Track conditions
- Proximity to iconic targets or environmentally sensitive areas
- Population density along route
- Venues along route (stations, events, places of congregation)
- Emergency response capabilities along route

- Trip length for route
- Areas of high vulnerability along route
- Presence of passenger traffic along route (shared track)
- Number and types of grade crossings and public access points
- Grade and grade curvature
- Hazard detection equipment installed along the right-of-way
- Single vs. double track
- Density and speed of train operations

To address these challenges, the Rail Corridor Hazmat Response and Recovery Tool (RCHRRT) project exists to focus on the development of a web-based tool that would support assessment of routes based on risk, and assist federal, state, and local emergency response and recovery agencies in allocating appropriate resources in the most needed TIH rail corridors and rail segments. Specifically, the RCHRRT exists to provide:

- A protocol for performing route-specific risk reviews to identify and evaluate HAZMAT risk factors and to inform route selection decisions. The protocol will identify risk factors and alert levels of communities along specific routes, but it will not attempt to quantify associated risks.
- Route-specific risk indices for specific routes that measure relative route-level risks for HAZMAT shipments, and which can be implemented without an extensive, time-consuming effort to identify, manipulate, and compile data.
- A rail HAZMAT transportation risk model to quantify the likelihood and consequences of HAZMAT releases due to railroad accidents that accounts for emergency response capabilities where applicable. The model should be able to meet key user requirements without requiring an excessively complex and time-consuming development effort.

The RCHRRT is also expected to complement and benefit from the activities proposed in the first project. Whereas the RCRMT is intended to advise and inform decisions about security and countermeasure enhancements, RCHRRT would provide state and local emergency managers with a tool that would significantly enhance their response planning and incident response and recovery capabilities related to rail operations. The RCHRRT must leverage existing commercial and government off-the-shelf solutions, which would in turn facilitate connectivity with a broader user community. The final stage of the project will include a field test of the tool in Chicago. As with the RCRMT, this project must leverage the work and existing structure of the CREATE partnership. This would also allow for side-by-side usage of the two tools to determine their compatibility and potential for integration. Total funding available for this project priority is $500,000.

3. **Development and Demonstration of "Safe Haven" Concepts for In-Route TIH Shipments**: The "safe haven" concept will provide an enhanced level of security for "lock-down" facilities that handle bulk TIH shipments. The strategy will also focus on expediting the movement of trains carrying bulk TIH from lock-down facilities to customers' secured facilities or other rail lock-down facilities. The first phase of this project must involve the evaluation of potential procedures and technologies to reduce access to railcars carrying TIH materials. This evaluation would include consideration of the alert level security actions developed by the railroad and chemical industries (customer storage of hazardous materials on leased track, reducing inventory in yards and plants, protocols for handling and securing in-route shipments, and coordination with FBI WMD district offices). The second phase of the project must include field tests of the solution sets at several sights along the New Jersey Freight Rail Corridor. These field tests would be conducted in partnership with industry, as well as applicable

State and local authorities. Total funding available for this project priority is $1.5 million.

*Source*: DHS, *Fiscal Year 2005 Freight Rail Security Program Application Kit.*

## INFORMATION SECURITY AND NATIONAL NETWORK INFRASTRUCTURE SECURITY

Information security is defined as the techniques, technical measures, and administrative measures used to protect information assets from deliberate or inadvertent unauthorized acquisition, damage, disclosure, manipulation, modification, loss, or use (McDaniel, 1994). The term *network infrastructure security* refers to the protection of the physical infrastructure of data networks and peripherals, such as fiber-optic cables, routers, switches, and servers that allow data in digital format to be transferred from one location to another one or process it to meet user demands.

These two systems are linked because most of the complex systems are digitally controlled, wherein data transfer and processing is done by large telecommunication networks and servers, with clients connected to them in a network fashion. The fact that complex systems are digitally controlled brings a potential vulnerability to those systems. The possible scenario that proposes terrorists can gain access to these controlling systems is not an unrealistic one. Once the terrorists have gained control of the system, they can abuse it in such a way as to cause major damage to human life and the government, thereby creating major economic disruption. To cause this harm, it is not even necessary for the terrorists to be physically co-located within the system facilities, or even within the United States. This type of terrorist behavior is called *cyber terrorism.*

DHS acts as the coordinating body of the U.S. government to secure the cyberspace and the network infrastructure in the United States. The Directorate of Information Analysis & Infrastructure Protection (IAIP) and the Directorate of Science and Technology of DHS are the main units within the department that identify and assess current and future terrorist threats, assess and mitigate risks to the nation's critical infrastructure systems, and disseminate threat information. Some of the tasks of the IAIP related to this issue are as follows:

1. To identify and assess the nature and scope of terrorist threats, and detect such threats, and administer the color-coded Homeland Security Advisory System
2. To ensure efficient access by DHS to all related information gathered or analyzed, and disseminate relevant homeland security information externally to DHS
3. Establish and utilize a secure but compatible national security and emergency preparedness communications system for the federal government
4. Conduct training for federal, state, and local governments in information identification, analysis, and sharing

When the directorate was formed in 2003, by the Homeland Security Act of 2002, it incorporated the Critical Infrastructure Assurance Office, Federal Computer Incident Response Center, National Communications System, National Infrastructure Protection Center, National Infrastructure Simulation and Analysis Center, and Energy Security and Assurance Program, each of which previously managed some component of the overall infrastructure protection task. (Coppola, 2003)

IAIP protects the cyber-infrastructure from terrorist attack by unifying and focusing the key cyber-security activities performed by the Critical Infrastructure Assurance Office and the National Infrastructure Protection Center (FBI). The directorate augments those capabilities with the response functions of the National Cyber Security Division's (NCSD's) U.S. Computer Emergency Response Team (US-CERT). Because the information and telecommunications sectors are increasingly interconnected, DHS also assumes the functions and assets of the National Communications System (within DOD), which coordinates emergency preparedness for the telecommunications sector.

US-CERT is a partnership between DHS and the public and private sectors. The team was established in 2003 to protect the nation's Internet infrastructure. US-CERT coordinates defense against and responses to cyber attacks across the nation. The team is charged with protecting the nation's Internet infrastructure by coordinating defense against and response to cyber attacks. It is responsible for analyzing and reducing cyber threats and vulnerabilities, disseminating cyber threat warning information, and coordinating incident response activities. US-CERT interacts with federal agencies, industry, the research community, state and local governments, and others to disseminate reasoned and actionable cyber security information to the public.

The Directorate of Science and Technology (S&T) is also involved in the protection of critical infrastructure and information. Some strategic objectives of S&T, for example, are to develop methods and capabilities to test and assess threats and vulnerabilities, to prevent technological surprise, and to anticipate emerging threats. Such threats include cyber threats as well. S&T established the Cyber Security Research and Development Center in March 2004. The center is the umbrella under which the DHS's cyber security R&D activities are coordinated and performed. Charged with creating partnerships between government and private industry, the venture capital community, and the research community, the center develops and fortifies security technology to better protect the cyber infrastructure of the United States. The Homeland Security Advanced Research Projects Agency (HSARPA) is responsible for funding the center's research and development. As part of its cyber security mission, HSARPA uses the center to focus cyber security research, development, and test and evaluation activities and to involve expertise from academic, private industry, and federal and national laboratories. HSARPA invests in programs offering the potential for revolutionary changes in technologies that promote homeland security and accelerates the prototyping and deployment of technologies intended to reduce homeland vulnerabilities.

SRI International, an independent, nonprofit research institute, provides technical, managerial, and administrative support for the center. SRI provides the center with expertise in information security and the creation of innovative business models and partnerships.

The center supports the DHS's responsibility to secure a substantial portion of the nation's critical infrastructure (including information and telecommunications, transportation, postal and shipping, emergency services, and government continuity). Because DHS does not own or control this infrastructure, it faces unique challenges related to technologies that must be developed and deployed in support of the DHS mission.

The National Plan for Research and Development in Support of Critical Infrastructure Protection of 2004 suggests that the critical infrastructure of the United States including its cyberspace should operate under a national "Common Operating Picture" (COP). COP is defined as the communication and computing system architecture around which the nation's critical infrastructures operate in a safe and secure fashion. The plan identifies nine critical areas that have to be prioritized in terms of research and development for the sake of critical infrastructure protection and the achievement of COP:

- Detection and sensor systems
- Protection and prevention
- Entry and access portals
- Insider threats
- Analysis and decision support systems
- Response, recovery, and reconstitution
- New and emerging threats and vulnerabilities
- Advanced infrastructure architectures and systems design
- Human and social issues

Almost every one of these areas has a cyber security component. In particular, they are:

### Detection and Sensor Systems

This CIP R&D scope includes developing sensors to detect intruders to cyber infrastructures, including sensors that monitor and report the status and condition of the infrastructure. In addition, there are detection and sensing R&D tasks that are not related to a particular device, but rather to ways of processing sensor data to extract anomalies and identify patterns that are part of the CIP R&D scope. In cyber systems, the sensors may take the form of intelligent autonomous software agents that can travel throughout a computing or communications network. These networked systems of sensors must be smart, self-organizing, self-healing, and capable of analysis and reporting. Cyber intrusion detection considers surveillance in many forms, as well as the interpretation of that surveillance data in digital network space. For example, wireless technologies are increasingly crucial to automation, communication, and information technology systems pervasive throughout the critical infrastructure sectors. However, they are already vulnerable due to limited security, and face increased risks from mobile wireless nodes that can enter, traverse, and leave the network.

### Protection and Prevention

The cyber infrastructure is threatened by infiltration of a network from the outside; exfiltration, disclosure, exposure, or corruption of stored data, or rendering stored data inaccessible; interception, interruption, or redirection of data flows or communications; malicious (untrusted) software agents; compromised (trusted) software applications or hardware components; local or widespread disruption of services; and compromised or usurped (hijacked) machines. To achieve the envisioned secure communications network, CIP is challenged to develop effective protection against cyber intruders such as intelligent software agents that can quarantine and disable software intruders. Protection from cyber intrusion is a challenge due to the rapidly evolving nature of computer systems, the increased application of computer-based technologies, and the ever-increasing sophistication of intruders and insiders. Within the vast array of legacy, current, and planned systems there are weaknesses that can be accessed by cyber intruders ranging from novices to professionals.

Another protection and prevention task is to prevent or minimize disruption and denial-of-service and access attacks. Fairly common in today's sophisticated network systems and the Internet, such attacks can be devastating. Overwhelming a process by forcibly inserting tasks, dramatically increasing demands on a system, or denying availability of needed resources such as communication systems can result in serious consequences. These actions can divert attention, consume resources, and displace capability making other portions of both physical and cyber critical infrastructure systems more vulnerable. To minimize the impacts of such attacks, protective identification, confirmation, and authorization access measures must be rigorous and well managed. Systems should be designed in a manner such that they provide redundancy, rerouting options, and self-healing or self-sustaining attributes to rapidly restore or at least provide a minimum level of service until recovery actions can be implemented for both cyber and physical systems.

### Entry and Access Portals

Cyber portals for the exchange of critical data and information will require widely available and technologically advanced protections that are well beyond the basic password systems commonly used today. They also will require adaptation to attacks that are continuously changing and evolving. Emerging security issues will require that physical portals (entryways, checkpoints) and cyber portals (network access, secure transmissions) manage increasingly similar scopes of information, to include accurate identification, authentication, data protection, and information exchange regarding people, material, or information. Future needs of both physical portals and cyber portals can benefit from similar ongoing applied R&D approaches, communication standards development, and engineering requirements. Focus areas for entry and access portals are identification, authentication, authorization, access control, tracking, and dynamic

situational control (which refers to the ability of a system to infer actions or intent and potentially control or direct the outcome of a given security situation).

### Response, Recovery, and Reconstitution

Certain classes of attacks in cyberspace can be detected very quickly. In fact, in some cases it is even possible to detect indications of an attack prior to its actual onset. For such attacks, taking the correct action quickly enough makes it possible not only to reduce the effects of an attack, but also to possibly avert it altogether. On increasingly shortening time scales, closely coupled automated sensing of, and response to, malicious activity is viewed not simply as a damage mitigation approach, but as a key protective strategy. Important research areas in this context include analysis to automatically determine appropriate corrective actions, and effective coupling of both the analytical approaches and the technological interfaces associated with detection and response systems, which may be comprised of hardware, software, or both. Because some types of attacks (such as worms) are capable of propagating very quickly, the speed associated with detection, analysis, and response capability becomes critical. It is generally accepted that for some attacks, any response that requires human intervention, either to help identify an attack, to determine appropriate action, or to take corrective action, is doomed to failure because the attack would propagate too quickly and would effectively outrun the response. The implication here is that in addition to improving the capabilities of automated detection, analysis, and response approaches, technological advances are also needed along a different dimension to increase their speed. For those responding, having access to a secure Internet will provide critical access to "experts at a distance" as they are conduits for experts in science, engineering, technology, decision making, alternative actions, and much more from other responder communities. The COP will provide awareness of other events that might affect their actions and use or availability of resources that may be critical if there is a coordinated multipoint attack or multiple impacts from a natural disaster. Unattended devices such as robotic platforms must be developed to provide the information essential for effective decision support made available through the COP.

### New and Emerging Threats and Vulnerabilities

New software virus architectures that arrive in pieces and self-assemble later and new, more damaging network infestations that appear, perform, and self-destruct leaving no forensic trail are considered as potential emerging cyber threats and vulnerabilities and the CIP R&D plan identifies the need to start the preparedness efforts to deal with such threats and vulnerabilities when they become real.

### Advanced Infrastructure Architectures and Systems Design

Networking and systems research that produced the Internet has yielded radical change and a society globally focused on information. In addition to rapid communication, the Internet provides a cyber computational grid by enabling high-performance and clustered, smaller computers, and massive data centers that are connected and shared. Internet-based sharing of computational facilities and data resources has created opportunities for collaborative virtual working environments, and virtual control of sensing and control systems for monitoring, operation, prediction, and control within the country's CI sector networks. However, the current architecture of the Internet and the tools within it are largely insecure. Protecting these systems against a knowledgeable community of adversaries requires massive overhaul to make them fully secure.

To develop the next generation of cyber infrastructure, research needs must address its architecture and design, by building the fundamental basis on new concepts for robust and secure networking, systems software for real-time sensing and control, and integrated data acquisition, information management, and simulation technology. The Internet of the future must be designed with its incorporation in the nation's critical infrastructure sectors in mind. Cyber systems must be capable of detecting and responding to a large number of threats that change frequently over the course of even a few hours or days. Next-generation cyber systems and control systems will be designed in the early planning stages to incorporate security-related standards, secure hardware designs, common secure communication protocols, and other requirements and guidelines. New cyber platforms need to leverage advances in grid-based computing concepts, increasingly powerful computer systems on-a-chip, and wireless communications technology. Advanced systems will include self-organizing networks that can spontaneously communicate and collaborate with other networks in a larger system. These "smart" networks can adjust their roles and deliver new levels of communication and computing capacity. Codesign of physical and information systems needs improvement. Design and systems infrastructure approaches are needed that enable safe, reliable, automatic transition from failure to recovery modes. Current systems are generally static in their designs; new research is needed to enable safe dynamic composition and specialization of open, cooperating systems as they are deployed. Design capability is particularly lacking for reactive, reconfigurable, high-confidence systems.

DHS has released a document, titled *National Strategy to Secure Cyberspace*, that defines how it will ensure information security and protect cyberspace. In this document the three strategic objectives to secure cyberspace are listed as follows:

1. Prevent cyber attacks against America's critical infrastructures.
2. Reduce national vulnerability to cyber attacks.
3. Minimize damage and recovery time from cyber attacks that do occur.

The *National Strategy to Secure Cyberspace* articulates five national priorities as discussed next.

### Priority 1: A National Cyberspace Security Response System

Rapid identification, information exchange, and remediation can often mitigate the damage caused by malicious cyberspace activity. For those activities to be effective at a national level, the United States needs a partnership between government and industry to perform analyses, issue warnings, and coordinate response efforts. Privacy and civil liberties must be protected in the process. Because no cyber security plan can be impervious to concerted and intelligent attack, information systems must be able to operate while under attack and have the resilience to restore full operations quickly. The *National Strategy to Secure Cyberspace* identifies eight major actions and initiatives for cyberspace security response:

1. Establish a public-private architecture responding to national-level cyber incidents.
2. Provide for the development of tactical and strategic analysis of cyber attack vulnerability assessments.
3. Encourage the development of a private-sector capability to share a synoptic view of the health of cyberspace.
4. Expand the Cyber Warning and Information Network to support the DHS in coordinating crisis management for cyberspace security.
5. Improve national incident management.
6. Coordinate processes for voluntary participation in the development of national public–private continuity and contingency plans.
7. Exercise cyber security continuity plans for federal systems.
8. Improve and enhance public–private information sharing involving cyber attacks, threats, and vulnerabilities.

### Priority 2: A National Cyberspace Security Threat and Vulnerability Reduction Program

By exploiting vulnerabilities in cyber systems, an organized attack may endanger the security of the United States' critical infrastructures. The vulnerabilities that most threaten cyberspace occur in the information assets of critical infrastructure enterprises themselves and their external supporting structures, such as the mechanisms of the Internet. Lesser secured sites on the interconnected network of networks also present potentially significant exposures to cyber attacks. Vulnerabilities result from weaknesses

in technology and because of improper implementation and oversight of technological products. The *National Strategy to Secure Cyberspace* identifies eight major actions and initiatives to reduce threats and related vulnerabilities:

1. Enhance law enforcement's capabilities for preventing and prosecuting cyberspace attacks.
2. Create a process for national vulnerability assessments to better understand the potential consequences of threats and vulnerabilities.
3. Secure the mechanisms of the Internet, improving protocols and routing.
4. Foster the use of trusted digital control systems/supervisory control and data acquisition systems.
5. Reduce and remediate software vulnerabilities.
6. Understand infrastructure interdependencies and improve the physical security of cyber systems and telecommunications.
7. Prioritize federal cyber security research and development agendas.
8. Assess and secure emerging systems.

### Priority 3: A National Cyberspace Security Awareness and Training Program

Many cyber vulnerabilities exist because of a lack of cyber security awareness on the part of computer users, systems administrators, technology developers, procurement officials, auditors, chief information officers (CIOs), chief executive officers, and corporate boards. Such awareness-based vulnerabilities present serious risks to critical infrastructures regardless of whether they exist within the infrastructure itself. A lack of trained personnel and the absence of widely accepted, multilevel certification programs for cyber security professionals complicate the task of addressing cyber vulnerabilities. The *National Strategy to Secure Cyberspace* identifies four major actions and initiatives for awareness, education, and training:

1. Promote a comprehensive national awareness program to empower all Americans, businesses, the general workforce, and the general population to secure their own parts of cyberspace.

2. Foster adequate training and education programs to support the nation's cyber security needs.
3. Increase the efficiency of existing federal cyber security training programs.
4. Promote private-sector support for well-coordinated, widely recognized professional cyber security certifications.

### Priority 4: Securing Governments' Cyberspace

Although governments administer only a minority of the nation's critical infrastructure computer systems, governments at all levels perform essential services in the agriculture, food, water, public health, emergency services, defense, social welfare, information and telecommunications, energy, transportation, banking and finance, chemicals, and postal shipping sectors that depend on cyberspace for their delivery. Governments can lead by example in cyberspace security, including fostering a marketplace for more secure technologies through their procurement. The *National Strategy to Secure Cyberspace* identifies five major actions and initiatives for the securing of governments' cyberspace:

1. Continuously assess threats and vulnerabilities to federal cyber systems.
2. Authenticate and maintain authorized users of federal cyber systems.
3. Secure federal wireless local-area networks.
4. Improve security in government outsourcing and procurement.
5. Encourage state and local governments, consider establishing information technology security programs, and participate in information sharing and analysis centers with similar governments.

### Priority 5: National Security and International Cyberspace Security Cooperation

America's cyberspace links the United States to the rest of the world. A network of networks spans the planet, allowing malicious actors on one continent to act on systems thousands of miles away. Cyber attacks cross borders at light speed, and discerning the source of malicious activity is difficult. America must be capable of safeguarding and defending its critical systems and networks. Enabling the ability to do so requires a system of international cooperation to facilitate information sharing, reduce vulnerabilities, and deter malicious actors. The *National Strategy to Secure Cyberspace* identifies six major actions and initiatives to strengthen U.S. national security and international cooperation:

1. Strengthen cyber-related counterintelligence efforts.
2. Improve capabilities for attack attribution and response.
3. Improve coordination for responding to cyber attacks within the U.S. national security community.
4. Work with industry and through international organizations to facilitate dialogue and partnerships among international public and private sectors focused on protecting information infrastructures and promoting a global "culture of security."
5. Foster the establishment of national and international watch-and-warning networks to detect and prevent cyber attacks as they emerge.
6. Encourage other nations to accede to Council of Europe Convention on Cyber Crime or to ensure that their laws and procedures are at least as comprehensive.

*Source*: Department of Homeland Security (DHS). 2003. *National Strategy to Secure Cyberspace*, www.dhs.gov (February).

## UTILITIES AND INDUSTRIAL FACILITIES

Utilities are the lifelines of American society. They include essential daily needs such as electricity, energy, water, sewerage, and telecommunication that are characterized as critical infrastructure. Today's complex terrorist attacks target people and economies, as well as important critical infrastructure such as these utilities, in order to cause destruction of property and disruption of society and commerce. For this reason, utilities are recognized as an important terrorist target and their protection is seen as a critical national security priority.

Protection of the U.S. utilities' infrastructures is, understandably, another of DHS's many security responsibilities. The Directorate of Information Analysis and Infrastructure Protection (IAIP) is the operational branch of DHS responsible for protecting the nation's utility infrastructure. However, this task is complex and extremely difficult. For one thing, almost 85% of the utility infrastructure of the United States is owned or operated by the private sector. Therefore, strong relationships and coordination between DHS and the private sector are essential to successfully protect these facilities. A separate section is dedicated for the role of private sector in homeland security, discussed below. The following section will address federal initiatives dedicated to protecting the utility infrastructure of the United States.

The primary publication guiding the federal protection of utilities is, again, the *National Strategy for the Physical Protection of Critical Infrastructures and Key Assets* from DHS. The document covers utilities protection in its "Water," "Energy," and "Telecommunication" subtitles.

## WATER

The nation's water sector is critical from both a public health and an economic standpoint. The water sector consists of two basic, yet vital, components: freshwater supply and wastewater collection and treatment (wastewater treatment will be mentioned later). Sector infrastructures are diverse, complex, and distributed, ranging from systems that serve a few customers to those that serve millions. On the supply side, the primary focus of critical infrastructure protection efforts is the nation's 170,000 public water systems. These utilities depend on reservoirs, dams, wells, and

aquifers, as well as treatment facilities, pumping stations, aqueducts, and transmission pipelines.

The water sector has taken great strides to protect its critical facilities and systems. For instance, government and industry have developed vulnerability assessment methodologies for both drinking water and wastewater facilities and trained thousands of utility operators to conduct them. In response to the Public Health Security and Bio-Terrorism Preparedness and Response Act of 2002, the Environmental Protection Agency (EPA) has developed baseline threat information to use in conjunction with vulnerability assessments. EPA has provided assistance to state and local governments for drinking water systems to enable them to undertake vulnerability assessments and develop emergency response plans. To improve the flow of information among water-sector organizations, the industry has begun development of its sector-ISAC.

Water-ISAC is the first sector-wide information sharing and analysis center for the water sector. Since its creation in December 2002, the Water-ISAC has served as a secure forum for gathering, analyzing, and sharing security-related information. The center is funded by the EPA, but also receives income from subscription fees for its online notification system. The Water-ISAC's notification system is an Internet-based, rapid notification system and information resource focused on threats to America's drinking water and wastewater systems, and is the only centralized, up-to-the-minute resource of its kind serving the water sector. The Water-ISAC functions as a subscription service that gathers and quickly disseminates alerts, expert analyses, and other information specific to the water community. The system provides services such as timely e-mail alerts about potential and actual physical or cyber attacks against drinking or wastewater systems; information on water security from the federal law enforcement, intelligence, public health, and environment agencies; access to an extensive database of information on chemical, biological, and radiological agents; notifications about cyber vulnerabilities and technical fixes, research, reports, and other water security-related information; a highly secure means for quickly reporting incidents; vulnerability assessment tools and resources; guidance about emergency preparedness and response; the ability to participate in and review secure electronic forums on water security topics; and helpful summaries of open-source security information. (Water-ISAC, 2005, www.waterisac.org)

Several federal agencies are working together to improve the warehousing of information regarding contamination threats, such as the release of biological, chemical, and radiological substances into the water supply, and how to respond to their presence in drinking water. With respect to identifying new technologies, the EPA has an existing program that develops testing protocols and verifies the performance of innovative technologies. It has initiated a new program to verify monitoring technologies that may be useful in detecting or avoiding biological or chemical threats.

To support the water industry, the EPA has been providing grants for vulnerability assessments and related security improvements at large drinking water utilities since 2003. EPA's funding priority is to provide grant assistance to large (regularly serving 100,000 people or more) publicly owned community drinking water systems, for up to $115,000 to each eligible utility to develop/revise a vulnerability assessment (V/A), emergency response/operating plan (EOP), security enhancement plans and designs, or a combination of these efforts.

In 2003 and 2004 EPA awarded grants for counterterrorism coordination activities by the states and territories, a total of $5 million for each year. The grant program was continued in the FY 2005 president's budget and was appropriated in the Consolidated Appropriations Act of 2005. Under this FY 2005 appropriation in the State and Tribal Assistance Grants (STAG) account, $4.96 million is now available to the EPA for award to states and territories to continue the support of counterterrorism coordination activities in protecting the nation's drinking water systems. According to the distribution scheme of those funds, each state will receive a minimum of $50,000 and each territory at least $16,700.

In 2004 EPA allocated $1 million in funding for small wastewater system security training. The goal of the grant was to increase security among small and medium-sized wastewater systems. Short-term objectives of the program included incorporating immediate basic security enhancements, improving the capacity for emergency response, and accomplishing vulnerability assessments. Another objective was to implement long-range security measures and institutionalize security-related issues into existing wastewater programs. The funding was to be used for the sole purpose of providing on-site training assistance or classroom wastewater security training activities to wastewater utilities on the use of the wastewater security vulnerability assessment tools, emergency response plan development and upgrades, and physical system security enhancements.

The basic human need for water and the concern for maintaining a safe water supply are driving factors for water infrastructure protection. Public perception regarding the safety of the nation's water supply is also significant, as is the safety of people who reside or work near water facilities. To set priorities among the wide range of protective measures that should be taken, the water sector is focusing on the types of infrastructure attacks that could result in significant human casualties and property damage or widespread economic consequences. In general, there are four areas of primary concentration:

1. Physical damage or destruction of critical assets, including intentional release of toxic chemicals
2. Actual or threatened contamination of the water supply
3. Cyber attack on information management systems or other electronic systems
4. Interruption of services from another infrastructure

To address these potential threats, the sector requires additional focused threat information in order to direct investments toward enhancement of corresponding protective measures. The water sector also requires increased monitoring and analytic capabilities to enhance detection of biological, chemical, or radiological contaminants that could be intentionally introduced into the water supply. Some enterprises are already in the process of developing advanced monitoring and sampling technologies, but additional resources from the water sector will likely be needed.

Environmental monitoring techniques and technologies and appropriate laboratory capabilities require enhancement to provide adequate and timely analysis of water samples to ensure early warning capabilities and assess the effectiveness of cleanup activities should an incident occur. Specific innovations needed include new broad-spectrum analytical methods, monitoring strategies, sampling protocols, and training.

Currently, approaches to emergency response and the handling of security incidents at water facilities vary according to state and local policies and procedures. With regard to the public reaction associated with contamination or perceived contamination, it is essential that local, state, and federal departments and agencies coordinate their protection and response efforts. Maintaining the public's confidence regarding information provided and the timeliness of the message is critical. Suspected events concerning water systems to date have elicited strong responses that involved taking systems out of service until their integrity could be verified, announcing the incident to the public, and issuing "boil water" orders.

The operations of the water sector depend extensively on other sectors. The heaviest dependence is on the energy sector. For example, running pumps to move water and wastewater and operating drinking water and wastewater treatment plants require large amounts of electricity. Water infrastructure protection initiatives are guided both by the challenges that the water sector faces and by recent legislation. Additional protection initiatives include efforts to do the following:

1. *Identify high-priority vulnerabilities and improve site security*: EPA, in concert with DHS, state and local governments, and other water-sector leaders, will work to identify processes and technologies to better secure key points of storage and distribution, such as dams, pumping stations, chemical storage facilities, and treatment plants. EPA and DHS will also continue to provide tools, training, technical assistance, and limited financial assistance for research on VA methodologies and risk management strategies.

2. *Improve sector monitoring and analytic capabilities*: EPA will continue to work with sector representatives and other federal agencies to improve information on contaminants of concern and to develop appropriate monitoring and analytical technologies and capabilities.

3. *Improve sector-wide information exchange and coordinate contingency planning*: DHS and EPA will continue to work with the sector coordinator and the Water-ISAC to coordinate timely information on threats, incidents, and other topics of special interest to the water sector. DHS and EPA will also work with the sector and the states to standardize and coordinate emergency response efforts and communications protocols.

4. *Work with other sectors to manage unique risks resulting from interdependencies*: DHS and EPA will convene cross-sector working groups to develop models for integrating priorities and emergency response plans in the context of interdependencies between the water sector and other critical infrastructures.

## ENERGY

Energy drives the foundation of many of the sophisticated processes at work in American society today. It is essential to the economy, national defense, and virtually all aspects of a modern quality of life. The energy sector is commonly divided into two segments in the context of critical infrastructure protection: electricity and oil and natural gas.

The electricity sector services almost 130 million households and institutions. The United States as a nation consumed nearly 3.6 trillion kilowatt-hours in 2001. Oil and natural gas facilities and assets are also widely distributed, consisting of more than 300,000 production sites, 4,000 off-shore platforms, more than 600 natural gas processing plants, 153 refineries and more than 1,400 product terminals, and 7,500 bulk stations.

### Electricity

Almost every form of productive activity— whether in businesses, manufacturing plants, schools, hospitals, or homes—requires electricity. Electricity is also necessary to produce other forms of energy, such as refined oil. Were a widespread or long-term disrup-

tion of the power grid to occur, many of the activities critical to the economy and national defense—including those associated with response and recovery—would be impossible.

The North American electric system is an interconnected, multinodal distribution system that accounts for virtually all the electricity supplied to the United States, Canada, and a portion of Baja California Norte, Mexico. The physical system consists of three major parts: generation, transmission and distribution, and control and communications.

Generation assets include fossil fuel plants, hydroelectric dams, and nuclear power plants. Transmission and distribution systems link areas of the national grid (see Figure 5-3). Distribution systems manage and control the distribution of electricity into homes and businesses. Control and communications systems

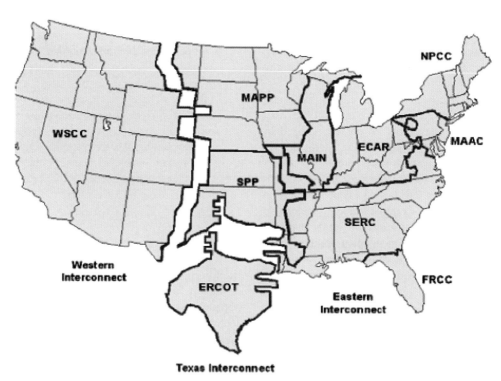

FIGURE 5-3    U.S. power grid and regional commissions. (*Source:* North American Electric Reliability Council)

operate and monitor critical infrastructure components.

The North American electric system is the world's most reliable, a fact that can be attributed to industry efforts to identify single points of failure and system interdependencies and to institute appropriate backup processes, systems, and facilities. The North American Electric Reliability Council (NERC), in charge of developing guidelines and procedures for ensuring electricity system reliability, is a nonprofit corporation made up of 10 regional reliability councils, whose voluntary membership represents all segments of the electricity industry, including public and private utilities from the United States and Canada. Through NERC, the electricity sector coordinates programs to enhance security for the electricity industry. Sidebar 5-4 discusses a blackout that affected about 50 million Americans and Canadians.

The electricity sector is highly regulated even as the industry is being restructured to increase competition. The Federal Energy Regulatory Commission (FERC) and state utility regulatory commissions regulate some of the activities and operations of certain electricity industry participants. The Nuclear Regulatory Commission (NRC) regulates nuclear power reactors and other civilian nuclear facilities, materials, and activities.

The electricity sector is highly complex, and its numerous component assets and systems span the North American continent. The stakeholders in the sector are diverse in size, capabilities, and focus. Currently, individual companies pay for levels of protection that are consistent with their resources and customer expectations. Typically, these companies seek to recover the costs of new security investments through proposed rate or price increases. Under current federal law, however, there is no assurance that electricity industry participants would be allowed to recover the costs of federally mandated security measures through such rate or price increases.

Another challenge for the electricity industry is effective, sector-wide communications. The owners and operators of the electric system are a large and heterogeneous group. Industry associations serve as clearing houses for industry-related information, but not all industry owners and operators belong to such organizations.

Data needed to perform thorough analyses on the infrastructure's interdependencies is not readily available. A focused analysis of the time-phased effects of one infrastructure on another, including loss of operations metrics, would help identify dependencies and establish protection priorities and strategies.

For certain transmission and distribution facilities, providing redundancy and increasing generating capacity provide greater reliability of electricity service. However, this approach faces several challenges. Long lead times, possible denials of rights-of-way, state and local site selection requirements, "not-in-my-back-yard" (NIMBY) community perspectives, and uncertain rates of return when compared with competing investment needs are hurdles that may prevent owners and operators of electricity facilities from investing sufficiently in security and service assurance measures.

Building a less vulnerable electricity grid is a priority for protecting the national electricity infrastructure. Work is ongoing to develop a national R&D strategy for the electricity sector. Additionally, FERC has developed R&D guidelines, and the Department of Energy's (DOE) National Grid Study contains recommendations focused on enhancing physical and cyber security for the transmission system.

The electricity industry has a history of taking proactive measures to ensure the reliability and availability of the electricity system. Individual enterprises also work actively in their communities to address public safety issues related to their systems and facilities. Since September 11, 2001, the sector has reviewed its security guidelines and initiated a series of intra-industry working groups to address specific aspects of security. It has created a utility-sector security committee at the chief executive officer level to enhance planning, awareness, and resource allocation within the industry.

The sector as a whole, with NERC as the sector coordinator, has been working in collaboration with DOE since 1998 to assess its risk posture in light of

## SIDEBAR 5-4  The August 14, 2003, Blackout in the United States and Canada

On August 14, 2003, large portions of the Midwest and Northeast United States and Ontario, Canada, experienced an electric power blackout. The outage affected an area with an estimated 50 million people and 61,800 megawatts (MW) of electric load in the states of Ohio, Michigan, Pennsylvania, New York, Vermont, Massachusetts, Connecticut, New Jersey, and the Canadian province of Ontario. The blackout began a few minutes after 4:00 p.m. Eastern Daylight Time (16:00 EDT), and power was not restored for 4 days in some parts of the United States. Parts of Ontario suffered rolling blackouts for more than a week before full power was restored. Estimates of total costs in the United States range between $4 billion and $10 billion (U.S. dollars). In Canada, gross domestic product was down 0.7% in August, there was a net loss of 18.9 million work-hours, and manufacturing shipments in Ontario were down $2.3 billion (Canadian dollars).

A joint commission from the United States and Canada was tasked to investigate why this blackout happened and what can be done to prevent it from happening again. The commission found out that a wide range of events, problems, or actions initiated or contributed to the initiation of the power outage.

Examples of such causes include but are not limited to human decisions by various organizations that affected conditions of the power grid that day, deficiencies in corporate policies, lack of adherence to industry policies, and inadequate technical decisions.

The commission provided its recommendations under four separate subtitles: (1) Institutional Issues Related to Reliability, (2) Support and Strengthen NERC's Actions of February 10, 2004, (3) Physical and Cyber Security of North American Bulk Power Systems, and (4) Canadian Nuclear Power Sector.

For the sake of this chapter only the recommendations regarding the physical and cyber security of North American bulk power systems will be provided. Those recommendations are:

- Implement NERC IT standards.
- Develop and deploy IT management procedures.
- Develop corporate-level IT security governance and strategies.
- Implement controls to manage system health, network monitoring, and incident management.
- Initiate U.S.–Canada risk management study.
- Improve IT forensic and diagnostic capabilities.
- Assess IT risk and vulnerability at scheduled intervals.
- Develop capability to detect wireless and remote wireline intrusion and surveillance.
- Control access to operationally sensitive equipment.
- NERC should provide guidance on employee background checks.
- Confirm NERC ES-ISAC as the central point for sharing security information and analysis.
- Establish clear authority for physical and cyber security.
- Develop procedures to prevent or mitigate inappropriate disclosure of information.

*Source*: Adapted from U.S.–Canada Power System Outage Task Force. 2004. *Final Report on the August 14, 2003 Blackout in the United States and Canada: Causes and Recommendations* (April 5).

the new threat environment, particularly with respect to the electric system's dependence on information technology and networks. In the process, the sector has created an awareness program that includes a "Business Case for Action" for industry senior executives, a strategic reference document titled *An Approach to Action for the Electric Power Sector*, and security guidelines related to physical and cyber security.

With respect to managing security information, the sector has established an indication, analysis, and warning program that trains utilities on incident reporting and alert notification procedures. The sector has also developed threat alert levels for both physical and cyber events, which include action-response guidelines for each alert level.

The industry has also established an Electricity Sector Information Sharing and Analysis Center (ES-ISAC) to gather incident information, relay alert notices, and coordinate daily briefs between the federal government and electric grid operators around the country. ES-ISAC is operated by the North American Electric Reliability Council on behalf of the electricity sector. The most active program of the ES-ISAC is the Indications, Analysis, and Warnings (IAW) Program. The program consists of a set of guidelines for reporting operational and cyber incidents that adversely affect the electric power infrastructure. The IAW Standard Operating Procedure (SOP) defines the criteria and thresholds for event reporting. The program's primary objective is the development of a national-level system that will provide timely, reliable, and actionable warnings of threats and impending attacks on critical power infrastructures. Incident information submitted by government agencies and the private sector is being utilized to develop key indicators of threats and attacks. The objectives include maintaining the health and capabilities of critical customers served by the infrastructures. (ES-ISAC, www.eeiac.comn/d)

Power management control rooms are probably the most protected aspect of the electrical network. NERC's guidelines require a backup system and/or manual work-arounds to bypass damaged systems.

FERC is also working with the sector to develop a common set of security requirements for all enterprises in the competitive electric supply market.

Additional electricity sector protection initiatives include efforts to do the following:

1. *Identify equipment stockpile requirements*: DHS and DOE will work with the electricity sector to inventory components and equipment critical to electric-system operations and to identify and assess other approaches to enhance restoration and recovery to include standardizing equipment and increasing component interchangeability.

2. *Reevaluate and adjust nationwide protection planning, system restoration, and recovery in response to attacks*: The electric power industry has an excellent process and record of reconstitution and recovery from disruptive events. Jointly, industry and government need to evaluate this system and its processes to support the evolution from a local and regional system to an integrated national response system. DHS and DOE will work with the electricity sector to ensure that existing coordination and mutual aid processes can effectively and efficiently support protection, response, and recovery activities as the structure of the electricity sector continues to evolve.

3. *Develop strategies to reduce vulnerabilities*: DHS and DOE will work with state and local governments and the electric power industry to identify the appropriate levels of redundancy of critical parts of the electric system, as well as requirements for designing and implementing redundancy in view of the industry's realignment and restructuring activities.

4. *Develop standardized guidelines for physical security programs*: DHS and DOE will work with the sector to define consistent criteria for criticality, standard approaches for vulnerability and risk assessments for critical facilities, and physical security training for electricity sector personnel. (DHS, 2003a)

## Oil and Natural Gas

The oil and natural gas industries are closely integrated. The oil infrastructure consists of five general components: oil production, crude oil transport, refining, product transport and distribution, and control and other external support systems. Oil and natural gas production include exploration, field development, on- and off-shore production, field collection systems, and their supporting infrastructures. Crude oil transport includes pipelines (160,000 miles), storage terminals, ports, and ships. The refinement infrastructure consists of about 150 refineries that range in size and production capabilities from 5,000 to over 500,000 barrels per day. Transport and distribution of oil includes pipelines, trains, ships, ports, terminals and storage, trucks, and retail stations.

The natural gas industry consists of three major components: exploration and production, transmission, and local distribution. The United States produces roughly 20% of the world's natural gas supply. There are 278,000 miles of natural gas pipelines and 1,119,000 miles of natural gas distribution lines in the United States. Distribution includes storage facilities, gas processing, liquid natural gas facilities, pipelines, city gates, and liquefied petroleum gas storage facilities.

The pipeline and distribution segments of the oil and natural gas industries are highly regulated. Oversight includes financial, safety, and site selection regulations. The exploration and production side of the industry is less regulated, but it is affected by safety regulations and restrictions concerning property access. Sidebar 5-5 illustrates a unique side to the oil and gas industry: the possible use of oil and gas as weapons.

Protection of critical assets requires both heightened security awareness and investment in protective equipment and systems. One serious issue is the lack of metrics to determine and justify corporate security expenditures. In the case of natural disasters or accidents, there are well-established methods for determining risks and cost-effective levels of investments in protective equipment, systems, and methods for

managing risk (e.g., insurance). It is not clear what levels of security and protection are appropriate and cost effective to meet the risks of terrorist attack.

The first government responders to a terrorist attack on most oil and natural gas sector facilities will be local police and fire departments. In general, these responders need to improve their capabilities and preparedness to confront well-planned, sophisticated attacks, particularly those involving CBR weapons. Fortunately, because of public safety requirements related to their operations and facilities, the oil and natural gas industries have substantial protection programs already in place.

Quick action to repair damaged infrastructure in an emergency can be impeded by a number of hurdles, including the long lead time needed to obtain local, state, and federal construction permits or waivers; requirements for environmental reviews and impact statements; and lengthy processes for obtaining construction rights-of-way for the placement of pipelines on adjoining properties if a new path becomes necessary. The availability of necessary materials and equipment and the uniqueness of such equipment are also impediments to rapid reconstitution of damaged infrastructure.

The current system for locating and distributing replacement parts needs to be enhanced significantly. The components themselves range from state-of-the-art systems to mechanisms that are decades old. While newer systems are standardized, many of the older components are unique and must be custom manufactured. Moreover, there is extensive variation in size, ownership, and security across natural gas facilities. There are also a large number of natural gas facilities scattered over broad geographical areas—a fact that complicates protection.

Oil and natural gas sector protection initiatives include efforts to do the following:

1. *Plan and invest in research and development for the oil and gas industry to enhance robustness and reliability*: Utilizing the federal government's national scientific and research capabilities, DHS and DOE will work with oil and

## SIDEBAR 5-5   Oil and Gas as Weapons

There is a unique risk associated with the oil and gas sector. Other kinds of critical infrastructure are deemed to be vulnerable to disasters primarily due to the adverse economical or human consequences should they be damaged or destroyed. This holds true for the oil and gas sectors as well, but there are additional, unique hazards associated with these two sectors. Both oil and gas are highly flammable materials, which are very hazardous if they are not adequately obtained, processed, stored, and transported. For these reasons, the two resources have become highly attractive to terrorists.

For terrorists targeting oil or gas, the target itself is a weapon that is designed for ignition. The involvement of oil or gas materials in a terrorist attack can drastically enlarge the scope of the incident and in some cases create secondary disasters that overshadow the primary ones. The September 11 attacks are an example of such a disaster. Initially the incident was perceived as an accident where an airliner crashed into a high-rise building. But since the airliners that crashed into the towers carried approximately 10,000 gallons of unused jet fuel each at the time of impact, the incident became not only a physical crash incident, but also a highly technical and very difficult high-rise fire incident. Were it not for the excess fuel, it is unlikely that the buildings would have collapsed, but the fire that started burning as a result of that fuel increased the temperature of the buildings' structures to temperatures as high as 1,500°F.

According to the FEMA report about the collapse of the towers, this heat was transferred over the huge steel blocks in the center of the building, which acted as the primary load carriers of the buildings. When steel gets as hot as 1,500°F it quickly loses the physical properties that it typically has in its solid state. The steel softens and eventually melts, thereby reducing its strength significantly, making it impossible to carry the load it was designed to carry. September 11 was, therefore, an incident where jet fuel was used as a primary weapon against civilians.

The ignition of the oil fields and wells by Saddam Hussein during the first Gulf War (Operation Desert Storm) is also another example of oil being used as a weapon. Liquid fuel fires are also extremely difficult to fight especially when the amount of involved fuel is significant (see Figure 5-4). The best responders can usually do is control the fire (making sure that it does not spread to other locations) and then use adequate foam to insulate the fire from the air and to use water to cool down the surroundings at the fire's base.

natural gas sector stakeholders to develop an appropriate strategy for research and development to support protection, response, and recovery requirements.

2. *Develop strategies to reduce vulnerabilities*: DHS and DOE will work with state and local governments and industry to identify the appropriate levels of redundancy of critical components and systems, as well as requirements for designing and enhancing reliability.

3. *Develop standardized guidelines for physical security programs*: DHS and DOE will work with the oil and natural gas industry representatives to define consistent criteria for criticality, standard approaches for vulnerability and risk assessments for various facilities, and physical security training for industry personnel.

4. *Develop guidelines for measures to reconstitute capabilities of individual facilities and systems*: DHS and DOE will convene an advisory task

FIGURE 5-4    Petroleum fire. (*Source*: U.S. Army)

force of industry representatives from the sector, construction firms, equipment suppliers, oil engineering firms, state and local governments, and federal agencies to identify appropriate planning requirements and approaches.

5. *Develop a national system for locating and distributing critical components in support of response and recovery activities*: DHS and DOE will work with industry to develop regional and national programs for identifying parts, requirements, notifying parties of their availability, and distributing them in an emergency. (DHS, 2003a)

The first Information Analysis and Sharing Center for the oil and natural gas sector has been established with participation from the sector's stakeholders. The

Oil and Gas Sector Homeland Security Coordinating Council serves as a broad industry-wide network for coordinating ongoing industry initiatives, government partnerships, and responsibilities, but most importantly in communications with DHS on issues relating to sector coordination. This council represents more than 90% of the sector's owners and operators. The mission of the council is to foster and facilitate the coordination of oil and natural gas sector-wide voluntary activities and initiatives designed to improve critical infrastructure protection and homeland security. Objectives of the council include, but are not limited to, the following:

• Provide broad industry representation for critical infrastructure protection and homeland security and related matters for the oil and natural gas sector and for voluntary sector-wide partnership efforts.

- Provide a forum for policy discussion and coordination, with implementation of policy through the council members.
- Foster and promote coordination and cooperation among participating sector constituencies on critical infrastructure protection and homeland security related activities and initiatives, including the Energy-ISAC.
- Establish and promote broad sector activities and initiatives that improve critical infrastructure protection and homeland security.
- Identify barriers to and recommend initiatives to improve sector-wide voluntary critical infrastructure protection and homeland security information and knowledge sharing and the timely dissemination processes for critical information sharing among all sector constituencies.
- Improve sector awareness of critical infrastructure protection and homeland security issues, available information, sector activities/initiatives and opportunities for improved coordination.

*Source*: Oil and Gas Sector Homeland Security Co-ordinating Council. 2004. *September 2004 Update.*

Critical infrastructure protection in the oil and gas sector is an exceptionally challenging task for several reasons. First, as mentioned earlier, the flammable nature of those materials make them natural targets for terrorists. Second, the overall operations of the oil and gas sectors are distributed over a very large geographical area with different types of infrastructures that need to be protected. Every single node within that infrastructure is vulnerable. Included in that vast infrastructure are drilling facilities, refineries, pipelines, highways, ports, and offshore facilities. Last but not least; an added challenge comes from the necessity to protect the different transportation modes used by the oil and gas sectors. Ground transportation and maritime transportation are the two most commonly used means by those sectors. Protecting each mode requires unique expertise, making such protection very costly and resource intensive.

## TELECOMMUNICATIONS

The telecommunications sector is constantly evolving because of the rapid rate by which technology in this sector advances, pressures from business and competition, and changes in the regulatory environment. Despite its dynamic nature, the sector has consistently provided robust and reliable communication services and processes designed to meet the needs of business and government. In the modern threat environment, the sector faces significant challenges to protect its vast and dispersed critical assets, both cyber based and physical. Because the government and critical infrastructure industries rely heavily on the public telecommunications infrastructure for vital communications services, the sector's vulnerabilities and protection initiatives are particularly important.

Every day the sector must contend with traditional natural and human-based threats to its physical infrastructure, such as weather events, unintentional cable cuts, and the technology threat (e.g., physical and cyber sabotage). The September 11 attacks revealed the threat terrorism poses to the telecommunications sector's physical infrastructure. While it was not a direct target of the attacks, the telecommunications sector suffered significant collateral damage. In the future, certain concentrations of key sector assets themselves could become attractive direct targets for terrorists, particularly with the increased use of collocation facilities. The telecommunications infrastructure withstood the September 11 attacks in overall terms and demonstrated remarkable resiliency because damage to telecommunications assets at the attack sites was offset by diverse, redundant, and multifaceted communications capabilities. Priorities for telecommunications carriers are service reliability, cost balancing, security, and effective risk management postures. The government places high priority on the consistent application of security across the infrastructure. Although private- and public-sector stakeholders share similar objectives, they have different perspectives on what constitutes acceptable risk and how to achieve security and reliability. Therefore, an agreement on a sustainable security threshold and corresponding security requirements remains elusive.

Because of growing interdependencies among the various critical infrastructure components, a direct or indirect attack on any of them could result in cascading effects across the others. Such interdependencies increase the need to identify critical assets and secure them against both physical and cyber threats. Critical infrastructures rely on a secure and robust telecommunications infrastructure.

Redundancy within the infrastructure is critical to ensure that single points of failure in one infrastructure will not create an adverse impact in others. It is vital that government and industry work together to characterize the state of diversity in the telecommunications architecture. They must also collaborate to understand the topography of the physical components of the architecture to establish a foundation for defining a strategy to ensure physical and logical diversity.

Despite significant challenges, the telecommunications marketplace remains competitive, and customer demand for services is steady, if not increasing. An economic upturn within the industry could rapidly accelerate service demands. The interplay of market forces and FCC oversight will ensure the continuance of service delivery to sustain critical telecommunications functions. Nevertheless, recent economic distress has forced companies to spend their existing resources on basic network operations rather than recapitalizing, securing, and enhancing the infrastructure, which could amplify the financial impact of necessary infrastructure protection investments.

Given the reality of the physical and cyber threats to the telecommunications sector, government and industry must continue to work together to understand vulnerabilities, develop countermeasures, establish policies and procedures, and raise awareness necessary to mitigate risks. The telecommunications sector has a long, successful history of collaboration with government to address concerns over the reliability and security of the telecommunications infrastructure. The sector has undertaken a variety of new initiatives to further ensure both reliability and quick recovery and reconstitution. Within this environment of increasing emphasis on protection issues, public–private partnership can be further leveraged to address a number of key telecommunications initiatives, including efforts to do the following:

1. *Define an appropriate threshold for security*: DHS will work with industry to define an appropriate security threshold for the sector and develop a set of requirements derived from that definition. DHS will work with industry to close the gap between respective security expectations and requirements. Reaching agreement on a methodology for ensuring physical diversity is a key element of this effort.

2. *Expand infrastructure diverse routing capability*: DHS will leverage and enhance the government's capabilities to define and map the overall telecommunications architecture. This effort will identify critical intersections among the various infrastructures and lead to strategies that better address security and reliability.

3. *Understand the risks associated with vulnerabilities of the telecommunications infrastructure*: The telecommunications infrastructure, including the PSTN, the Internet, and enterprise networks, provides essential communications for governments at all levels and other critical infrastructures. DHS will work with the private sector to conduct studies to understand physical vulnerabilities within the telecommunications infrastructure and their associated risks. Studies will focus on facilities where many different types of equipment and multiple carriers are concentrated.

4. *Coordinate with key allies and trading partners*: More than ever our nation has a common reliance on vital communications circuits and processes with our key allies and trading partners. DHS will work with other nations to consider innovative communications paths that provide priority communications processes to link our governments, global industries, and networks in such a manner that vital communications are ensured. (DHS, 2003a)

DHS is currently in the process of undertaking a major telecommunications security overhaul. The project is called Homeland Secure Data Network (HSDN). DHS is seeking $37 million in FY 2006 funding for the HSDN to address requirements for secure classified, computer-to-computer connectivity. The HSDN effort will streamline and modernize the classified data capabilities of DHS in order to facilitate high-quality and high-value classified data communication and collaboration within DHS and with other federal agencies and organizations, including DOD. Based on modern network and telecommunications designs, the HSDN will optimize both the classified data exchanges between DHS offices, and other networks of classified data such as the Anti-Drug Network, U.S. Customs & Border Protection (ADNET), Automatic Digital Network (AUTODIN), and Defense Message System (DMS). It will provide a scalable infrastructure, capable of supporting the growth and evolution of the DHS mission. (DHS, 2005)

The private and nonprofit stakeholders in the telecommunications sector are also actively working toward ensuring a higher level of protection and security of their critical infrastructures. One of such initiatives is the Telecommunications Infrastructure Information Sharing and Analysis Center (Telecom-ISAC). The Telecom-ISAC mission is to facilitate voluntary collaboration and information sharing among government, the telecommunications industry, and the national critical infrastructure protection goals; to gather information on vulnerabilities, threats, intrusions, and anomalies from multiple sources; and to perform analysis with the goal of averting or mitigating impact on the telecommunications infrastructure. The scope of the Telecom-ISAC's mission is all hazards, which include natural and man-made disasters and physical and cyber attacks.

Operational goals of Telecom-ISAC include, but are not limited to, facilitation of voluntary collaboration to support both government and industry information sharing requirements, fostering working liaisons with external sources and liaison partners, adding value and providing information not available elsewhere, filtering appropriately, performing high-quality analyses, and ensuring protection of information and the rights of data owners. The National Communication System operates the on-site and full-time Telecom-ISAC watch and analysis operation (WAO). The WAO consists of senior analysts closely integrated with the government NCC operations staff and industry representatives from Telecom-ISAC member companies. The Telecom-ISAC watch and analysis operation serves a dual function as the operational arm of the Telecom-ISAC and as one of DHS's Information Analysis and Infrastructure Protection watch and analysis centers. Information received by Telecom-ISAC is shared with participating entities only if the originator of information approves its release to anyone or any entity.

The Telecom Industry Association (TIA) is another important DHS partner in its efforts to protect the telecommunication critical infrastructure. TIA is active in both the standards and public policy arenas of homeland security and related critical infrastructure protection. The association supports interoperable communications for first responders and has worked with the public safety community for many years to create standards for such equipment. TIA currently has a large number of American National Standards supporting homeland security, emergency communications, and the needs of first responders. The association continues to work with the public safety community at the federal, state, and local levels through various activities to enhance and upgrade these standards and support emergency and security initiatives.

As a sector coordinator and neutral industry forum, TIA provided input to the National Response Plan Private Sector Support Annex working via Telecom-ISAC and the DHS Private Sector Office. TIA and its member companies have been actively engaged with communications network security/critical infrastructure protection (and asset) protection issues. Critical infrastructure protection responsibilities for the sector include raising awareness of vulnerabilities and risks to the sector and its infrastructure; assisting the sector to eliminate/mitigate its vulnerabilities; facilitating establishment and operation of sector information sharing and analysis centers (ISACs); developing cooperative efforts with other countries and international organizations to achieve compatible security policies and strategies; and providing industry with information on results from complementary U.S. government research and development on critical infrastructure and assets protection. TIA is partnering with DHS to support the requirements of those responsibilities for the telecommunications sector.

## PIPELINES

The United States has a vast pipeline infrastructure, consisting of many hundreds of thousands of miles of pipes, many of which are buried underground. These lines move a variety of substances, such as crude oil, refined petroleum products, and natural gas. Pipeline facilities already incorporate a variety of stringent safety standards that account for the potential effects a disaster could have on surrounding areas. Moreover, most elements of pipeline infrastructures are designed such that they can be quickly repaired or bypassed to mitigate localized disruptions. Destruction of one or even several of its key components could not disrupt the entire system. As a whole, the response and recovery capabilities of the pipeline industry are well proven, and most large control-center operators have established extensive contingency plans and backup protocols.

Pipelines are not independent entities but rather integral parts of industrial and public service networks. Loss of a pipeline could have an impact on a wide array of facilities and industrial factories that depend on reliable fuel delivery to operate.

Several hundred thousand miles of pipeline span the country, and it is unrealistic to expect total security for all facilities. As such, protection efforts focus on infrastructure components whose impairment would have significant effects on the energy markets and the economy as a whole. For the pipeline industry, determining what to protect and when to protect it is a factor in cost-effective infrastructure protection. During

periods of high demand, such as the winter months, pipeline systems typically operate at peak capacity and are more important to the facilities and functions they serve.

The pipeline industry as a whole has an excellent safety record, as well as in-place crisis management protocols to manage disruptions as they occur. Nevertheless, many of the products that pipelines deliver are inherently volatile. Hence, their protection is a significant issue.

Pipelines cross numerous international, state, and local jurisdictional boundaries. The range of stakeholders creates a confusing—and sometimes conflicting—-array of regulations and security programs for the industry to manage, especially with respect to the ability of pipeline facilities to recover, reconstitute, and reestablish service quickly after a disruption. The pipeline industry's increasing interdependencies with the energy and telecommunications sectors necessitate cooperation with other critical infrastructures during protection and response planning. Individually, companies have difficulty assessing the broader implications of an attack on their critical facilities. These interdependencies call for cross-sector coordination for them to be truly responsive to national concerns. Additionally, some issues concerning recovery or reconstitution will require at least regional planning within the industry, as well as the sharing of sensitive business information that may run into proprietary concerns.

Historically, individual enterprises within this sector have invested in the security of their facilities to protect their ability to deliver oil and gas products. Representatives from major entities within this sector have examined the new terrorist risk environment. As a result, they have developed a plan for action, including industry-wide information sharing. Within the federal sector, DHS and DOT's Office of Pipeline Safety have major responsibility for enhancing pipeline security. DOT has developed a methodology for determining pipeline facility criticality and a system of recommended protective measures that are synchronized with the threat levels of the Homeland Security Advisory System.

However, operationally, several challenges still need to be met. As mentioned earlier, the DOT's Office of Pipeline Safety historically had the responsibility of ensuring the security of the U.S. pipeline infrastructure by developing standards and guidelines, arranging site visits, and organizing drills. However in the aftermath of the establishment of DHS, the Transportation Safety Agency within the department and the Pipeline Security Program Office within the agency have also become important players in securing the pipeline infrastructure. According to the Pipeline Security Program Office, the office engages in following activities:

1. Develops security standards for pipeline infrastructure and for hazardous materials movement.
2. Implements protective and preventive measures to mitigate risk and avert terrorist activities and other threats.
3. Builds and maintains strong stakeholder relations, coordination, education, and outreach for transportation industry security issues.
4. Monitors adherence to and compliance with standards, requirements, and regulations.

These activities partially overlap with the activities of the Office of Pipeline Safety. While one office's primary responsibility is the safety of the pipelines, and the others' is the security of the pipelines, operationally the difference in activities is not great. While the agencies' offices are currently cooperating, there is no formal agreement between the TSA and the OPS that makes this cooperation official.

Additional pipeline mode protection initiatives include efforts to do the following:

1. *Develop standard reconstitution protocols*: DHS, in collaboration with DOE, DOT, and industry, will initiate a study to identify, clarify, and establish authorities and procedures as needed to reconstitute facilities as quickly as possible after a disruption.
2. *Develop standard security assessment and threat deterrent guidelines*: DHS, in collabora-

tion with DOE and DOT, will work with state and local governments and the pipeline industry to develop consensus security guidance on assessing vulnerabilities, improving security plans, implementing specific deterrent and protective actions, and upgrading response and recovery plans for pipelines.

3. *Work with other sectors to manage risks resulting from interdependencies*: DHS, in collaboration with DOE and DOT, will convene cross-sector working groups to develop models for integrating protection priorities and emergency response plans. (DHS, 2003a)

Since September 11, industry and federal, state, and local governments have taken significant steps to secure the nation's critical energy infrastructure. Efforts have ranged from increasing surveillance of pipelines and conducting more thorough employee background checks to further restricting access to pipeline facilities and Internet mapping systems. Private companies have also formed task forces with federal, state, and local law enforcement officials to share security information and develop emergency notification and response plans.

Along with issuing new security measures in 2002, DOT developed criteria to evaluate an operator's implementation of those measures. Each operator was asked to submit a statement certifying that he or she had a security plan and had instituted the appropriate security procedures.

Today, 95% of oil pipeline operators have already implemented the measures and returned confirmation statements to DOT. The remaining 5% are primarily small operators that are in other businesses but run pipelines between plant facilities.

Some additional steps oil pipeline operators have taken include the following:

• Developing direct relationships with FBI regional field personnel
• Obtaining secret level security clearances for selected operational personnel to ensure that threat information can be communicated directly from federal officials to the company

- Joining government–industry threat information dissemination services
- Installing additional surveillance cameras and physical barriers to entrances at certain facilities
- Conducting response drills using terrorist scenarios as a basis for training personnel and working with new federal law enforcement officials
- Using guard patrol at certain facilities during certain threat condition levels
- Limiting access to facilities and permitting entrance only after positive identification. (Cooper, 2003)

In addition to procedural improvements, the pipeline sector is also undergoing major improvements in its utilization of science and technology to make the infrastructure safer and more secure. Some of the more recent technologies being used by pipeline security organizations to secure their infrastructure are as follows:

- **SCADA encryption**: SCADA systems are commonly used software packages in the pipeline industry that remotely monitor and control system status and functions, such as valve openings and pipeline pressure, from a central control point, often called a master station. The commands that are sent over the existing network to control the infrastructure are normally not encrypted. However, in today's sophisticated networking environment with its increased number of cyber threats, those messages really need to be encrypted in order not to be accessed by hackers or terrorists. To ensure proper encryption of the messages, the American Gas Association (AGA) recently released recommendations for procedures that pipelines and other energy utilities can use to encrypt their SCADA transmissions between master stations and remote sites. The new design will provide robust 1,024-bit-key encryption, the same level used by banks.
- **GASNET**: The Gasline Network Sensor System (GASNET™) is a distributed network of multipurpose sensors for communicating information on the real time state of a natural gas distribution

network to utility operators. The goal of GASNET is to help optimize the functioning of the nation's natural gas distribution infrastructure. When in use, GASNET will be an inexpensive way to monitor the status of pipelines over large areas, and it could later incorporate the ability to take further security-related measurements.

- **Wide-range sensing**: Sandia National Laboratories is studying shoulder-mounted devices that use backscatter absorption gas imaging (BAGI) technology. The devices would be used to detect chemical leaks that are not visible to the naked eye. While the technology has existed for years, in its newest incarnation it would be able to instantaneously survey a large area for gas leaks. The device could potentially be mounted on vans or on survey aircraft.
- **Explorer robots**: Robots that explore pipelines already exist, and they are improving. In conjunction with the Department of Energy and Carnegie Mellon University's National Robotics Engineering Consortium, the New York Gas Group has developed the so-called EXPLORER robot, essentially an untethered moving camera that monitors pipeline conditions in real time. The EXPLORER robot is equipped with a miniaturized fish-eye imager that sends pictures of the pipeline to a monitor above ground through a wireless connection. Because it provides pictures of a pipe's interior in real time, the system provides an accurate, complete view of a pipeline's health.
- **Acoustic Detecting and Locating Gas Pipeline Infringement**: West Virginia University has been assessing acoustic technology that "listens" for the unique sound wave generated when a pipeline break releases a large discharge of gas after being damaged. The objective of this project is to develop a centralized and automated acoustic monitoring system to detect leaks in, and infringements on, high-pressure natural gas pipelines. This system will detect the unique sound waves and vibrations that are generated when a pipeline break releases gas due to land-

slides, excavations, demolitions, or other sudden disturbances. The system will be designed to monitor background noise inside the pipe and identify any new frequencies that might signal a pipeline rupture or pipeline infringement.

*Sources*: Security Management and the U.S. Department of Energy.

## PUBLIC WORKS

The phrase *public works*, in its general definition, refers to all facilities and services provided by the government (usually state and local governments) to meet the basic sanitary needs and comfort of its citizens. Common responsibilities of public works departments include waste management, recycling, street lighting, trash removal, water management, and wastewater management.

Although these facilities are localized, they represent a collective high vulnerability because of the potentially high and widespread health consequences in the case of a successful terrorist attack on one or more of the facilities. Water treatment plants, wastewater plants, and landfills are three widely cited examples of these vulnerable facilities.

## WATER TREATMENT PLANTS

When a water supply facility takes untreated water from a river or reservoir, the water often contains dirt and tiny pieces of leaves and other organic matter, as well as trace amounts of certain contaminants. At their treatment plants, the facilities often add chemicals called coagulants to the water, which act on the water as it flows very slowly through tanks to remove these contaminants by forming clumps that settle to the bottom. The water usually follows this procedure by flowing through filters to remove even the smallest contaminants, such as harmful viruses and bacteria.

The most common drinking water treatment, considered by many to be one of the most important sci-entific advances of the 20th century, is disinfection. To perform this task, most water facilities add chlorine or another disinfectant to kill bacteria and other germs. Water supply facilities use other treatments as needed, according to the quality of their source water. For example, systems whose water is contaminated with organic chemicals can treat their water with activated carbon, which adsorbs or attracts the chemicals dissolved in the water.

The disinfection and purification of water is a rather complex process. It consists of several subprocesses such as prechlorination, coagulation, flocculation, sedimentation, filtration, fluoridation, post-chlorination, and corrosion control treatment. These steps are needed in order to produce water that will meet federal and state drinking water standards that is free of pathogens and suitable for public consumption.

As Figure 5-5 demonstrates, the water goes through several subprocesses until it is purified, and each of these subprocesses, especially the ones that involve chemical additives, are vulnerable to potential terrorist attacks. The terrorists can secretly change the additives with hazardous materials that they acquired beforehand and therefore change the contents of the city water into a potential chemical weapon against the served population. Water with extremely high or low pH can be very dangerous and even poisonous for the body. Extreme chemical changes with the water can usually be detected quickly; however, even so, the panic, stress, and potential psychological effects of such a terrorist attack can be devastating.

Terrorists can introduce biological agents that do not naturally exist inside the groundwater for which the water treatment systems do not have any countermeasures. Live, infectious bacteria can be transported to the city and housing with the water, and can infect people when they drink the water, thereby initiating a serious public health consequence. This risk has been determined to be very low, because of the amount of pathogen that would have to be introduced to cause high enough concentrations that would sicken the population, but it is still a very real risk. For this reason, the ability to detect biological attacks is

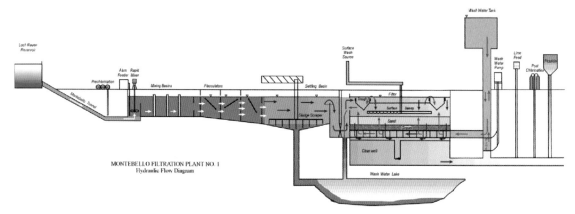

MONTEBELLO FILTRATION PLANT NO. 1
Hydraulic Flow Diagram

FIGURE 5-5   The water treatment process diagram of Montebello Water Treatment Plant in Baltimore, Maryland. (*Source:* http://
cityservices.baltimorecity.gov/dpw/waterwastewater03/waterquality5a.html)

considered an important issue that is still very much open for research and improvement.

Drinking water utilities today find themselves facing these new responsibilities. While their mission has always been to deliver a dependable and safe supply of water to their customers, the challenges inherent in achieving that mission have expanded to include security and counterterrorism. In the Public Health Security and Bioterrorism Preparedness and Response Act of 2002, Congress recognized the need for drinking water systems to undertake a more comprehensive view of water safety and security. The act amended the Safe Drinking Water Act and specified actions community water systems and the EPA must take to improve the security of the nation's drinking water infrastructure.

In its *Strategic Plan for Homeland Security*, EPA has six critical infrastructure protection goals. One of them states, "EPA will work with the states, tribes, drinking water and wastewater utilities (water utilities), and other partners to enhance the security of water and wastewater utilities."

In accomplishing this goal, EPA is planning to use the following approaches:

1. EPA will work with the states, tribes, associations and others to provide tools, training, and technical assistance to assist water utilities in

conducting vulnerability assessments, implementing security improvements, and effectively responding to terrorist events. In FY 2002, while developing tools and providing training for all utilities, EPA provided direct grants to large drinking water utilities for vulnerability assessments, security enhancement designs, and/or emergency response plans. EPA will work with states, tribes, associations, and water utilities to identify needs and provide assistance for vulnerability assessments for medium and small utilities, and for high-priority security enhancements identified in the water utility vulnerability assessments for all systems. As plans are completed, emphasis on implementation of security enhancements will continue to increase.

By the end of FY 2003, EPA expects all water utility managers to have access to basic information to understand potential water threats, and basic tools to identify security needs. By the end of FY 2003, all large community drinking water utilities shall have identified key vulnerabilities and shall be prepared to respond to any emergency. By the end of 2004, all medium community drinking water utilities shall be similarly positioned. By 2005, unacceptable security risks at water utilities across the country will be significantly reduced through completion of appropriate vulnerability assessments; design of security enhancement plans; development of emergency response plans; and implementation of security enhancements. The 2003 budget of EPA included $3.214 billion for safe water that is more than 41% of its total budget (EPA, 2003). The 2004 budget of EPA included $2.95 billion and the 2005 budget included $2.94 billion for safe water. For fiscal year 2006 the EPA budget included $2.81 billion for clean and safe water, which accounted for 37.2% of its annual budget.

2. EPA will work with the DHS, other federal agencies, universities, and the private sector to solicit and review methods to prevent, detect, and respond to chemical, biological, and radiological contaminants that could be intentionally introduced in drinking water systems and wastewater utilities; review methods and means by which terrorists could disrupt the supply of safe drinking water or take other actions against water collection, pretreatment, treatment, storage, and distribution facilities; and review methods and means by which alternative supplies of drinking water could be provided in the event of a disruption.

3. EPA will work with states, tribes, and water utilities to implement water security practices in ongoing water utility operations. EPA will also work with states and tribes to build security concerns into ongoing review systems (e.g., sanitary survey, capacity development, operator certification, and treatment optimization program for drinking water systems and pretreatment program, environmental management systems, and operator certification programs for wastewater).

EPA expects that beginning in FY 2003, water utilities will incorporate security measures as a standard aspect of day-to-day operations and EPA, states, and tribes will review security measures at water utilities on a continuous basis. Through ongoing practice and review, water utilities' managers and employees will optimize security measures.

4. EPA will work with other government agencies, utility organizations, and water utilities to establish formal communication mechanisms to facilitate the timely and effective exchange of information on water utility security threats and incidents.

5. EPA and DHS will work together to foster coordination among federal, state, tribal, and local emergency responders, health agencies, environmental and health labs, the medical community, and the law enforcement community at all levels (federal, state, and local) concerning response to potential terrorist actions against water utilities. This will be achieved through training and support of simulations and emergency response exercises.

6. EPA will work with other critical infrastructure sectors to further understand and reduce the impact on water utilities of terrorist attacks on related infrastructure as well as the impacts of attacks on water utilities on other critical infrastructure. (EPA, n/d)

In March 2004 the EPA released its *Water Security Research and Technical Support Action Plan.* The plan details potential risks and vulnerabilities associated with the water systems and other possible waterborne threats. The plan identifies the following priorities that are related to the protection of water treatment plants:

- Protecting drinking water systems from physical and cyber threats
- Identifying drinking water threats, contaminants, and threat scenarios
- Improving analytical methodologies and monitoring systems for drinking water
- Containing, treating, decontaminating, and disposing of contaminated water and materials
- Planning for contingencies and addressing infrastructure interdependencies
- Targeting impacts on human health and informing the public about risks. (EPA, n/d)

## WASTEWATER PLANTS

Wastewater is the spent, or used water, originating in homes, businesses, farms, and industry that contains enough harmful material to negatively affect water quality. Wastewater includes both domestic sewage and industrial waste from manufacturing sources. Metals, organic pollutants, sediment, bacteria, and viruses all may be found in wastewater. As a result, untreated wastewater has the potential to cause serious harm to the environment and threaten human life.

EPA regulates the discharge and treatment of wastewater under the Clean Water Act. The National Pollutant Discharge Elimination System (NPDES) issues permits to all wastewater dischargers and treatment facilities. These permits establish specific discharge limits, monitoring and reporting requirements, and may also require these facilities to undertake special measures to protect the environment from harmful pollutants.

The basic function of wastewater treatment is to enable the processes by which water is purified. There are two basic stages in the treatment of wastes; primary and secondary. In the primary stage, solids are allowed to settle and are removed from the wastewater. The secondary stage uses biological processes to further purify wastewater. In some instances, these two stages are combined into one operation.

The nation's wastewater infrastructure consists of approximately 16,000 publicly owned wastewater treatment plants, 100,000 major pumping stations, 600,000 miles of sanitary sewers, and another 200,000 miles of storm sewers, with a total value of more than $2 trillion. Taken together, the sanitary and storm sewers form an extensive network that runs near or beneath key buildings and roads, the heart of business and financial districts, and the downtown areas of major cities and is contiguous to many communication and transportation networks.

There are several vulnerabilities and risks associated with the wastewater treatment infrastructure. A potential scenario is the abuse of the wastewater collected in wastewater treatment plant by terrorists and its use as a biological or chemical weapon. The terrorists can accomplish this by diverting the waste into the clean water and making it toxic. Another scenario would be a direct attack on one of the wastewater facilities where hazardous materials are filtered from the wastewater and stored for further processing. The blast on such a facility (assuming that it contains nuclear waste, such as waste from nuclear power plants) can have the effects of a dirty bomb, making the removal of the contaminated debris very difficult and risky for the first responders. The primary consequences, however, would be environmental and psychological.

Vulnerability assessments and risk reduction programs are necessary to minimize the potential impacts of terrorist attacks to these facilities. As mentioned in the previous section, EPA has programs to improve water security and wastewater security. One of the important programs of EPA, in cooperation with the Association of Metropolitan Sewerage Agencies (AMSA), released two new Vulnerability Self Assessment Tools (VSAT$^{TM}$), one for joint water/wastewater utilities and another for small-medium sized water utilities. VSAT water/wastewater provides the valuable online vulnerability assessment capabilities to utilities providing both wastewater treatment and water supply services. Its new counterpart, VSAT$^{TM}$ water, will do the same for both public and private water utilities. These new software tools, developed by AMSA for EPA, provide an approach to evaluate, prioritize, and remediate vulnerabilities based upon five critical utility assets—-physical plant, information technology, knowledge base, employees, and customers.

Another program by EPA to improve safety and security on wastewater plants is the Wastewater Treatment Plant Operator On-Site Assistance Training Program. The goal of the program is to provide direct on-site assistance to operators at small underserved community wastewater treatment facilities, in order to help the facility achieve and maintain consistent permit compliance, maximizing the community's investment in improved water quality. In a cooperative effort with EPA, states, state coordinators, municipalities, and operators, the assistance endeavor focuses on issues such as wastewater treatment plant capacity, operation training, maintenance, administrative management, financial management, troubleshooting, and laboratory operations. The program identifies any need to repair or build new facilities to meet existing or future permit limits, assists the town during the process of selecting consultants and design review, recommends ways to improve preventive maintenance of equipment and structures, and often reduces energy and chemical costs through more efficient operation techniques.

A significant contribution to EPA's wastewater treatment security efforts came from the Water Environment Research Foundation (WERF). In 2003 WERF was awarded a cooperative research grant from the U.S. EPA's Office of Water to coordinate seven new projects to protect the nation's wastewater infrastructure and public health. The $2.1 million grant for a time frame of 2003–2007 will fund seven projects to assist in addressing a broad spectrum of issues related to security and public health protection of water and wastewater infrastructure, as well as risk communications in the event of potential threats or terrorist attacks. Projects that were funded were as follows:

- *Identify, screen, and treat contaminants in water/wastewater*: The goal of the project is to identify methods to screen for common biological, chemical, and radiological compounds and then determine the removal efficacy of wastewater treatment processes.
- *Security measures for computerized and automated systems at wastewater facilities*: The project is providing guidance to utilities on how to secure and protect automated systems and will document currently available technology to detect and correct such security breaches.
- *Contingency planning for wastewater treatment facilities*: The project is helping water and wastewater treatment facilities and their communities nationwide develop individual contingency plans in the event of an emergency.

- *Communicating with your local government and community*: The project is aimed at helping public agencies, such as water and wastewater utilities and elected officials, effectively communicate with the public.
- *Software and guidance for assessing and inventorying wastewater treatment infrastructure*: The project's goal is to provide a valuable tool for utilities to identify and categorize their underground and aboveground assets and then to better assess their system condition.
- *Feasibility testing/demonstration of support systems for use in wastewater treatment plants (WWTP)*: The project tests the feasibility of using computer models, decision trees, or other expert systems to ensure public and ecosystem health by learning from and preventing future WWTP system upsets.

*Sources*: Association of Metropolitan Sewage Agencies, 2004; Water Environment Research Foundation, n/d.

## LANDFILLS

Although conservation, reuse, recycling, and composting have reduced municipal waste, most of the waste that is generated still ends up in landfills. At present, there are more than 3,000 landfills in the United States. Many are modern, well-engineered facilities that are located, designed, operated, monitored, and financed to ensure compliance with federal regulations. These regulations include restrictions that require landfills to be located away from wetlands, floodplains, and other restricted areas; clay-reinforced liners; operating practices that reduce odor and control insects and rodents; groundwater monitoring; postclosure care; and corrective action to clean up landfill sites. In addition, the EPA encourages the use of landfill gas as a renewable fuel source through its Landfill Methane Outreach Program.

Location restrictions ensure that landfills are built in suitable geological areas away from faults, wetlands, floodplains, or other restricted areas. Liners are geo-membrane or plastic sheets reinforced with 2 feet of clay on the bottom and sides of landfills. Operating practices such as compacting and covering waste frequently with several inches of soil help reduce odor; control litter, insects, and rodents; and protect public health. Groundwater monitoring requires testing groundwater wells to determine whether waste materials have escaped from the landfill. Closure and post-closure care includes covering landfills and providing long-term care of closed landfills. Corrective action controls and cleans up landfill releases and achieves groundwater protection standards. Financial assurance provides funding for environmental protection during and after landfill closure (i.e., closure and post-closure care). However, there are still some risks and vulnerabilities associated with landfills.

More than 40 million tons of hazardous waste is produced in the United States each year. It is produced by large industrial facilities such as chemical manufacturers, electroplating companies, petroleum refineries, and by more common businesses such as dry cleaners, auto repair shops, hospitals, exterminators, and photo processing centers. The EPA has produced a list of more than 500 hazardous wastes and works closely with businesses and state and local authorities to make sure these wastes are properly treated and disposed of. The EPA conducts risk management studies to ascertain the potential health effects of exposure to these wastes and oversees Superfund and other programs that clean up contaminated waste sites.

Radioactive waste is produced by a number of activities, including nuclear power generation, mining, medicine, and industry. Some radioactive waste can remain hazardous for thousands of years. The EPA works with the Nuclear Regulatory Commission (NRC), DOT, DOE, and local authorities to regulate the storage and disposal of radioactive waste. The EPA is responsible for developing environmental standards that apply to radioactive waste disposal facilities. The EPA ensures that waste facilities comply with all federal environmental laws and regulations.

The physical security of landfill sites still poses a potential terrorist threat. Recognizing the amount of hazardous toxic waste every year in the United States and the existence of radiological waste, the physical security of landfill sites rises in importance. A scenario in which terrorists attack and blow up a landfill where radiological waste was stored could potentially cause a major disaster. Given that terrorists look for easy targets with the largest potential impact, this scenario is fairly realistic. If physical security of landfills cannot be ensured, they then become an easy, or soft, target of terrorist attacks.

Currently there are a few local and state initiatives to improve physical security of landfills, and federal support, while essential to providing greater physical security, has been limited. EPA, in cooperation with DHS, is the appropriate source for technical and financial assistance. However, because of other competing priorities, there has been limited attention paid to coordinate the initiatives and support state, local, and publicly held landfill sites for improved physical security.

## ROLE OF PRIVATE SECTOR IN HOMELAND SECURITY AND CHANGES IN BUSINESS CONTINUITY AND CONTINGENCY PLANNING

The terrorist attacks of September 11 affected thousands of private businesses; not just businesses in New York or near the Pentagon, but businesses that were as far away as Hawaii and Seattle. The attacks killed nearly 3,000 people, most of whom were employees of private corporations that had offices in or near the World Trade Center (WTC). Some companies lost hundreds of employees. In downtown Manhattan, almost 34.5 million square feet of office space was destroyed. Totaling $50 to $70 billion dollars in insured losses, the WTC attack became the most catastrophic economic disaster in U.S. history. Most of these direct economic losses were incurred by the private sector. In addition to the physical resources and systems lost by businesses in the WTC, changes in public behavior following the attacks had a severe impact on travel, tourism, and other businesses. Because the biggest portion of the impact was absorbed by the private sector, September 11 demanded that the private sector focus on understanding the philosophy and implementing programs for corporate crisis management.

The changes in private sector crisis management after September 11 can be analyzed in two perspectives: (1) the changing expectations of the private sector of the new federal role (DHS) in helping achieve greater homeland and (2) the self-reassessment of the private sector in terms of corporate crisis management and business continuity. Our reference point in addressing the changing expectations of the federal government from the private sector will be several major federal documents and strategies, such as the *National Strategy for Homeland Security* and official press releases from relevant departments and agencies. While addressing the change of internal processes and procedures among the private sector, we will refer to publications and press releases that address changes in particular companies and try to find general trends between different approaches.

## EXPECTATIONS FOR DHS FROM THE PRIVATE SECTOR

The *National Strategy for Homeland Security* defines the basic approach of DHS and briefly describes the characteristics of the partnership the department is planning to achieve with the private sector. Given the fact that almost 85% of the infrastructure of the United States is owned or managed by the private sector, there is no doubt that the private sector must be included as a major stakeholder in homeland security. Reducing the vulnerabilities and securing the private sector means the same as securing the vast portion of U.S. infrastructure and economic viability.

According to the *National Strategy for Homeland Security*, a close partnership between the government and private sector is essential to ensuring that existing vulnerabilities to terrorism in the critical infrastructure are identified and eliminated as quickly as possible. The private sector is expected to conduct risk assessments on their holdings and invest in systems to protect key assets. The internalization of these costs is interpreted by the DHS as not only a matter of sound corporate governance and good corporate citizenship but also an essential safeguard of economic assets for shareholders, employees, and the nation. (DHS, 2002)

The *National Strategy for the Protection of Physical Infrastructure and Key Assets* provides more direct clues about what the DHS expects from the private sector as a partner and stakeholder in homeland security. The strategy defines the private sector as the owner and operator of the bulk of U.S. critical infrastructures and key assets and mentions that private-sector firms prudently engage in risk management planning and invest in security as a necessary function of business operations and customer confidence. Moreover, since in the present threat environment the private sector generally remains the first line of defense for its own facilities, the DHS expects private sector owners and operators to reassess and adjust their planning, assurance, and investment programs to better accommodate the increased risk presented by deliberate acts of violence.

Since the events of September 11, many businesses have increased their threshold investments and undertaken enhancements in security in an effort to meet the demands of the new threat environment. For most enterprises the level of investment in security reflects implicit risk-versus-consequence trade-offs, which are based on (1) what is known about the risk environment and (2) what is economically justifiable and sustainable in a competitive marketplace or in an environment of limited government resources. Given the dynamic nature of the terrorist threat and the severity of the consequences associated with many potential attack scenarios, the private sector naturally looks to the government for better information to help make its crucial security investment decisions. The private sector is continuing to look for better data, analysis, and assessment from DHS to use in the corporate decision-making process.

Similarly, the private sector looks to the government for assistance when the threat at hand exceeds an enterprise's capability to protect itself beyond a reasonable level of additional investment. In this light the federal government promises to collaborate with the private sector (and state and local governments) to ensure the protection of nationally critical infrastructures and assets; provide timely warning and ensure the protection of infrastructures and assets that face a specific, imminent threat; and promote an environment in which the private sector can better carry out its specific protection responsibilities. (DHS, 2003b)

A good example of partnership between the private sector and the DHS are the sectoral Information Sharing and Analysis Centers (ISAC). ISACs are established by the owners and operators of a national critical infrastructure to better protect their networks, systems, and facilities within the coordination of DHS. ISACs serve as central points to gather, analyze, sanitize, and disseminate private-sector information to both industry and the DHS. These centers also analyze and distribute information received from the DHS to the private sector. The objectives of this program are to seek participation from all sector segments/entities, representation of all segments on ISAC Advisory Board in order to establish two-way trusted information sharing program between ISAC entities and the DHS, and to provide cleared industry expertise to assist DHS in evaluating threats and incidents. Currently ISACs exist and are being created in a variety of critical infrastructure sectors such as electric power (NERC), water supply/wastewater (AMWA), telecommunications (NCS/NCC), information technology (LLC, ISS), financial services (LLC., SAIC), chemicals (ACC/ChemTrec), food (FMI), emergency fire services (USFA), interstate (NASCIO), emergency law enforcement (NIPC/ELES), trucking (ATA), maritime (Coast Guard) (ISAC not yet announced), research and education networks (Indiana University), real estate (Real Estate Roundtable), airports (ACI-NA), surface transportation (LLC, AAR/EWA), and energy (oil and gas) (LLC, SAIC). (DHS, 2003b)

The most recent and the most clarifying DHS document that defines the relationships between the private sector and the DHS is the *Interim National Infrastructure Plan* (NIPP) of February 2005. This plan defines the mechanisms that serve to build those relationships and creates a system where the government and private entities can work in harmony to achieve a higher level of protection for critical infrastructures and key resources of the United States.

As mentioned earlier, the primary building block of this relationship is the formation of sectoral Information Sharing and Analysis Centers, which promote the coordination, cooperation, best practices, lessons learned, information flow, and information sharing among sector specific entities. The NIPP defines another coordination body for the achievement of the public–private integration. Those coordinating bodies are called Critical Infrastructure and Key Resources Sector Coordinating Councils. They are private-sector coordinating mechanisms that comprise private sector infrastructure owners and operators and supporting associations, as appropriate. Sector coordinating councils bring together the entire range of infrastructure protection activities and issues to a single entity.

One role of the sector coordinating councils is to identify or establish and support the information sharing mechanisms (ISMs) that are most effective for their sector, drawing on existing mechanisms (e.g., ISACs) or creating new ones as required. The NIPP also creates Critical Infrastructure and Key Resources Government Coordinating Councils, which are government coordinating councils for each sector comprised of representatives from DHS, the SSA, and the appropriate supporting federal departments and agencies. The government coordinating councils work with and support the efforts of the sector coordinating councils to plan, implement, and execute sufficient and necessary broad-based sector security, planning, and information sharing to support the nation's homeland security mission.

As indicated by the NIPP, the private sector will be engaged by DHS, in collaboration with the relevant SSAs, to promote awareness of and feedback on the NIPP framework and to solicit their involvement in the national CIP program. The private sector will also be working with the appropriate SSAs to begin implementation of the SSPs for their sectors. As the interim NIPP is implemented, the private sector will be provided with more coordinated data calls from government agencies, enhanced engagement through sector coordinating councils, and subsequent versions of the NIPP and SSPs will reflect discussions among DHS, the SSAs, and other stakeholders, including the private sector.

The NIPP serves as a guide for the private sector to identify and implement the procedures to protect the critical infrastructure against specific threats and the general threat environment. There are five major goals identified in the plan, and objectives to meet those goals are also listed. Those goals and the respective objectives are as follows:

- **Goal 1: Protect CI/KR against plausible and specific threats.** Objectives to meet goal include:
  - Increase awareness of the threat environment across CI/KR sectors
  - Integrate threat and vulnerability information into specific vulnerability reduction prioritization decisions
  - Use vulnerability assessment information when responding to specific threats
  - Identify and implement protective measures against specific threats
- **Goal 2: Long-term reduction of CI/KR vulnerabilities in a comprehensive and integrated manner.** Objectives to meet goal include:
  - Develop and maintain comprehensive national inventory of CI/KR assets and vulnerabilities that includes cyber, physical, and human aspects of each asset, including intangibles
  - Complete mapping of interdependencies among assets and across CI/KR sectors
  - Conduct vulnerability assessments for the Nation's critical infrastructure and key resources for both specific and general threats
  - Integrate infrastructure protection activities with those called for in other national-level plans to avoid overlaps and gaps

- Reduce general vulnerabilities within and across sectors where needed
- **Goal 3: Maximize efficient use of resources for infrastructure protection.** Objectives to meet goal include:
  - Prioritize possible protective measures considering return-on-investment in light of inherent vulnerabilities, existing protective measures, and (when applicable) threat information
  - Encourage and support SSA responsibility for sectors to leverage sector-specific expertise
  - Identify market-based incentives for voluntary action by owners and operators
  - Ensure lessons learned and best practices are captured and shared for evolution into sector-accepted operational practices over time
- **Goal 4: Build partnerships among federal, state, local, tribal, international, and private-sector stakeholders to implement CIP programs.** Objectives to meet goal include:
  - Delineate roles, responsibilities, and accountability for actions
  - Develop necessary organizations, staffing, and training to carry out responsibilities
  - Request appropriate authorities and funding to allow actions to be implemented
  - Establish mechanisms for coordination and information exchange among partners
  - Develop mechanisms for tracking involvement and progress
- **Goal 5: Continuously track and improve national protection.** Objectives to meet goal include:
  - Develop mechanisms for tracking national- and sector-level vulnerabilities and progress in reducing those vulnerabilities
  - Make infrastructure protection activities and metrics part of the organization's overall operational metrics to reinforce the importance of CIP initiatives and activities
  - Develop a national risk profile (a high-level summary of the risk and protection for all sectors) to align threats with strategic decision making

– Develop an information sharing system to support rapid dissemination of lessons learned

These goals are to be achieved using the national risk management framework as defined by the NIPP. The framework is similar for specific and general threat environments (see Figure 5-6); therefore, we will not address both frameworks separately.

DHS has acknowledged that it is well aware that effective protection of the critical infrastructure in the United States is only achievable through direct involvement of and strong partnership with the private sector. The private sector is not only an integral part of the national infrastructure protection effort, but it lies in the center of all protection strategies designed by DHS. That said, DHS is responsible for creating the environment where public- and private-sector entities talk to each other and work together to achieve a well-established national goal. Understanding the needs of each sector, building trust among officials and decision makers, making plausible assumptions, and setting realistic milestones are all key success factors. The real challenge is addressing cross-sectoral vulnerabilities due to interdependencies where involvement of multiple sectors is necessary for sustainable protection of a critical infrastructure and creation of realistic recovery objectives and procedures. Creation of cross-sector vulnerability assessment teams and utilization of multiple-sector expertise is critical to successfully plan for contingencies that may simultaneously hit interdependent critical infrastructures.

## CORPORATE CRISIS MANAGEMENT, BUSINESS CONTINUITY, AND CONTINGENCY PLANNING: THE NEW COST OF DOING BUSINESS

September 11 was the most devastating day in modern history for American corporations. The attack in New York City was a direct attack on not only the symbols of corporate American, but on the businesses themselves. The private sector lost human resources, expertise, buildings, office space, data, records, and

revenue. Some of these losses were irreplaceable, such as people and buildings. The affected companies also suffered time-dependent and continuous losses such as business interruption, loss of customer trust, and employee loyalty. The property and human losses could not have been prevented because the private sector itself could not have stopped the hijacked planes from crashing into the towers. However, effective corporate crisis management and business continuity planning absolutely could have, and in many places did, minimize the continuous losses.

To put this discussion in perspective, the following statistics and charts are provided to illustrate the vulnerability of the private sector in terms of terrorist actions. The Department of State report *Patterns of Global Terrorism 2001* reports on the total number of facilities struck by international terrorist attacks (see Figure 5-7). The statistics show attacks with respect to the year they occurred and the type of facility struck (e.g., private sector, government, diplomat, military). These figures are important because they show changing trends in the type of facilities terrorists have chosen to attack. There is a common belief that terrorists are more likely to attack military and government facilities, because of the stated political ideologies of the terrorist groups. However, the facts prove this theory wrong. In actuality, it is the soft-target private-sector facilities that have most commonly been victimized by the scourge of terrorism.

Clearly, a reduction in the number of attacks on businesses worldwide occurred after 2001. This reduction may be attributable to several factors that have changed since that time. One of these factors is the increased global effort to reduce terrorist acts. This effort is primarily led by the United States and its allies, which are the most likely targets but also which have spent billions on preventing such attacks. As terror cells become more and more international and decentralized, international cooperation and intelligence sharing become critical to prevent acts of terrorism. Since 2001, significant amounts of resources have been allocated to achieve this goal, and this may serve as a contributing factor to the reduced number of terrorist attacks.

| GENERAL THREAT ENVIRONMENT | SPECIFIC THREAT ENVIRONMENT |
|---|---|
| INPUT: General Threat Information | INPUT: Specific Threat Information |

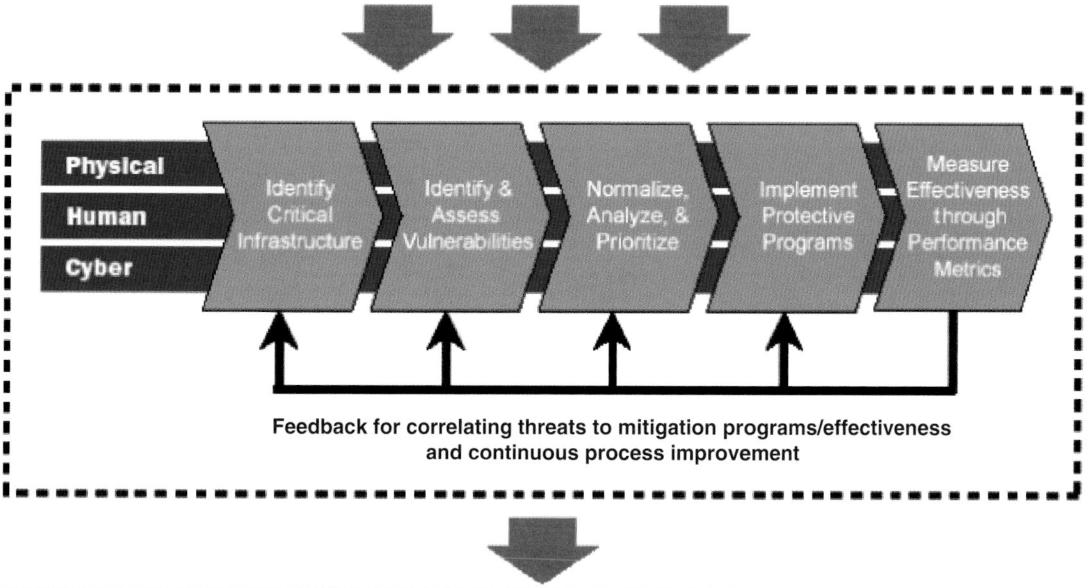

| A GENERAL THREAT ENVIRONMENT | SPECIFIC THREAT ENVIRONMENT |
|---|---|
| OUTCOMES:<br>• Vulnerability Reduction<br>• National Risk Profile<br>• Prioritized Assets<br>• Effective Resource Allocation<br>• Enhanced Preparedness<br>• Voluntary Actions<br>• Potential Legislation/Regulation | OUTCOMES:<br>• Identification and Implementation of Focused Protective Actions<br>• Preparedness for Specific Threats |

FIGURE 5-6   Framework for general and specific threat information. (*Source*: National Infrastructure Protection Plan, pp. 12, 25)

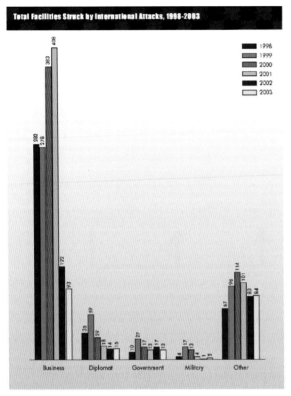

**Total Facilities Struck by International Attacks, 1998-2003**

Legend: 1998, 1999, 2000, 2001, 2002, 2003

FIGURE 5-7   Total facilities struck by terrorist attacks (worldwide), 1998–2003. (*Source:* Department of State, *Patterns of Global Terrorism*, 2003)

However, the preceding explanation does not account for why the reduction in the total number of attacks to businesses is steeper compared to other potential targets. As we can see in Figure 5-7, the number of terrorist attacks to hit businesses was reduced from 409 in 2001, to 122 in 2002 and to 93 in 2003, whereas such reductions were not as significant for either diplomatic facilities, government buildings, or military or other facilities.

Businesses have historically been targets of terrorist primarily because they have been perceived as soft targets that are easier to attack and minimally protected. After the 9/11 attacks the vulnerability of businesses to disasters such as terrorism became obvious. Businesses learned with a tragic experience that they constitute a potential target for terrorists. So they began to invest more into their security, risk management, crisis management, and business continuity programs. Research shows that all sophisticated terrorists carefully observe their prospective targets before deciding on their actual target.

This process often results with the selection of the softest target, that is, the one that is easiest to hit. Therefore, not only the operational benefit of those programs, but also their visibility is very important to serve as a deterring factor for the terrorists. For example, if a terrorist organization aims to damage the tourism industry in a country, it may plan to explode a bomb in a hotel. As terrorists choose which hotel they are going to attack, they will look at a few alternatives and select the one with the least amount of visible security. In short, the involvement and preparedness of the business sector is much higher today, compared to 2001. This may have acted as a deterring factor for the terrorists to look for business targets. The reduction in the number of incidents impacting business may be attributable to businesses "hardening" themselves as opposed to being perceived as "soft" targets.

Another factor that is changing private-sector perceptions is insurance and losses. The Insurance Information Institute has charted the distribution of different types of insured damage from the September 11 attacks and it presents some interesting facts (see Figure 5-8 graph). The most notable figure in this graph is the amount of damage from business interruption: $9.8 billion (31% of all estimated damage) of the total damage is caused by business interruption. This is a significant portion of the damage, one over which we have some degree of control if adequate preplanning and business impact analysis can be maintained before the crisis. Because of the 1993 WTC bombing and the potential Y2K threat, private-sector members located inside the WTC complex were among the most prepared stakeholders; however, there is always space for improvements and things to be learned from each new event.

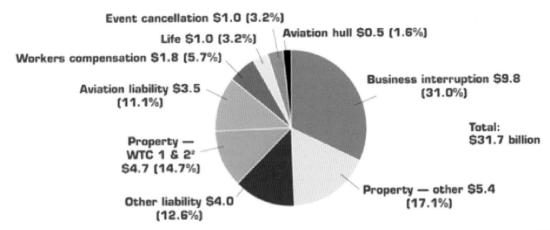

FIGURE 5-8    September 11, 2001, insurance industry loss estimates ($ in billions). (*Source:* Insurance Information Institute, 2004)

## CONCLUSION

Safety and security are two key concepts in the scope of homeland security. However, they are both difficult to ensure to the levels most citizens would prefer. The complexity of the systems and infrastructure we depend on today only increases our overall vulnerability and increases the difficulty of mitigating the risks we face. In addition to our personal vulnerabilities, we also face much systematic vulnerability, which will affect the society in case the risk becomes a reality.

The public and private sectors are under constant risk from natural, technological, and terrorist threats. To deal with those distinct vulnerabilities, the homeland security approach should be inclusive and interactive rather than top down and exclusive. Only with the participation of different stakeholders and the public can those systematic vulnerabilities be detected and improved. The interdependency of systems makes it almost impossible to improve safety and security on a subsystem level. In light of this observation, homeland security can only be ensured if it can bring together people from all levels of the public, governmental, and private sectors, as well as academia and NGOs.

## REVIEW QUESTIONS

1. What are the key intelligence agencies in the United States? Briefly comment on their roles in terms of homeland security.
2. Describe how intelligence has evolved in the United States.
3. What is the role of the private sector in homeland security? What are your suggestions to improve private-

sector participation and coordination with the Department of Homeland Security?
4. What are the different transportation modes in the United States? How does the U.S. government protect each?
5. Name three different forms of critical infrastructure. For each, describe their vulnerabilities to terrorism, and what is being done at the federal level to reduce these vulnerabilities.

# REFERENCES

*Agency Responsibilities by Functional Areas, Functions and Tasks.* NRP Initial Plan Draft, Appendix A, Table 6.2.

Association of American Railroads. 2004. <www.aar.org/ Rail_Safety/Security.pdf>

Association of Metropolitan Sewage Agencies (AMSA). 2004. *Wastewater Sector Security Link* vol 1, no. 1. <http://newsman­ager.commpartners.com/amsawssl/issues/2004-06-17.html>

Blumenthal, H. 2003. *Department of Human Services. Private Sector Information Sharing: ISAC Program.* Government Symposium on Information Sharing and Homeland Security (July 1).

Central Intelligence Agency. 2005. <www.cia.gov>

CFR 49, May 5, 2003, <www.myregs.com/dotrspa/>

*Classification of Serious HAZMAT Incidents in the United States by the Mode of Transportation and Yearly Frequencies.* <http://hazmat.dot.gov/files/hazmat/10year/10yearfrm.htm>

Congressional Research Service. 2004a. *The National Intelligence Director and Intelligence Analysis.* RS21984.

Congressional Research Service. 2004b. *The Proposed Authorities of a National Intelligence Director: Issues for Congress and Side-by-Side Comparison of S.2845, H.R. 10, and Current Law.* RL32506.

Cooper, B. 2003. *Protecting Pipelines from Terrorist Attack* (April). <www.enewsbuilder.net/aopl/e_article 000141902.cfm>

Coppola, D. P. 2003. *Annotated Organizational Chart for the Department of Homeland Security.* Washington, DC: Bullock & Haddow, LLC.

Department of Homeland Security (DHS). 2002. *National Strategy for Homeland Security.* Washington, DC: DHS (July). <www.dhs.gov>

Department of Homeland Security. 2003a. *National Strategy for the Protection of Physical Infrastructure and Key Assets.* Washington, DC: DHS (February).

Department of Homeland Security. 2003b. *Private Sector Information Sharing: ISAC Program.* Government Symposium on Information Sharing and Homeland Security.

Department of Homeland Security. 2005. <www.dhs.gov>

Department of Transportation Maritime Administration Statistics. n/d. <www.marad.dot.gov/Marad_Statistics/Con-Pts-02.htm>

Environmental Protection Agency. 2003. *Budget 2003.* pp. xv–2. <www.epa.gov/ocfo/budget/2003/2003bib.pdf>

Environmental Protection Agency (EPA). n/d. *How Wastewater Treatment Works . . . Basics.* Washington, DC: EPA, p. 1.

Greenberg, W. J. 2003. "September 11, 2001: A CEO's Story." *Harvard Business Review*, pp. 7–8.

Harrald, C., Coppola, D. P., and Yeletaysi, S. 2003. "Assessing the Financial Impacts of the World Trade Center Attacks on Pub

licly Held Corporations." TIEMS Conference Proceedings (June).

*The National Plan for Research and Development in Support of Critical Infrastructure Protection of 2004*, pp. 23–67).

http://cityservices.baltimorecity.gov/dpw/waterwastewater03/water quality5.html

http://hazmat.dot.gov/files/hazmat/serious_new_def.htm

http://nsarchive.chadwyck.com/esp_essay.htm

http://post911timeline.org/Timeline/

http://securitysolutions.com/ar/security_grants_target_wastewater/

http://www.amsa-cleanwater.org

http://www.asy.faa.gov/asy_internet/about.htm

http://www.bice.gov/graphics/customs.htm

http://www.bice.gov/graphics/immig.htm

http://www.buses.org/pressroom/PROutput.cfm?PRID=232

http://www.cbp.gov/xp/cgov/enforcement/border_patrol/overview. xml

http://www.dot.gov

http://www.epa.gov/ebtpages/wasthazardouswaste.html

http://www.epa.gov/ebtpages/wastradioactivewaste.html

http://www.epa.gov/ebtpages/wastwastelandfills.html

http://www.epa.gov/ebtpages/watewastewater.html

http://www.epa.gov/epaoswer/non-hw/muncpl/disposal.htm

http://www.epa.gov/owm/mab/smcomm/104g/index.htm#report

http://www.epa.gov/safewater/dwh/treat.html

http://www.epa.gov/safewater/security/

http://www.epa.gov/safewater/security/index.html

http://www.house.gov/transportation/press/press2003/release77. html

http://www.oig.dot.gov/item_details.php?item=997

http://www.tsa.gov/public/display?content=85

http://www.tsa.gov/public/display?theme=39&content=79

http://www.tsa.gov/public/display?theme=44&content=680

http://www.tsa.gov/public/interweb/assetlibrary/TSA_FY2004_ budget_briefing_(public).ppt

http://www.uscg.mil/hq/g-o/g-opl/mle/amio.htm

http://www.uscg.mil/hq/g-o/g-opl/mle/drugs.htm

http://www.whitehouse.gov/deptofhomeland/sect3.html

http://www.whitehouse.gov/news/releases/2002/06/20020618-5.html

https://www.nasdac.faa.gov

Kavanaugh, P. 2002. *Current State of Crisis Management as an Industry in Canada.* The Health Canada Emergency Preparedness Forum (October 28).

Lerbinger, O. 1997. *The Crisis Manager.* New York: Lawrence Erlbaum Associates.

McDaniel, G., ed., 1994. *IBM Dictionary of Computing.* New York: McGraw-Hill.

*National Strategy to Secure Cyberspace.* 2003 (February). <www.dhs.gov>

National Reconnaissance Office. 2005.

National Security Agency. 2005. <www.nsa.gov>

NRP Initial Plan Draft, p. 26, 2003. Department of Homeland Security.

*Operation Liberty Shield: Press Briefing by Secretary Ridge.* 2003 (March 15). <www.dhs.gov/dhspublic/display?content=520>

Richelson, J. T. 1999. *The U.S. Intelligence Community*, 4th ed. Boulder, CO: Westview Press.

Richelson, J. T., Gefter, J., Waters, M., *et al.* 2003. *U.S. Espionage and Intelligence, 1947–1996.* Digital National Security Archive.

Smith, Bradley F. 1983. *The Shadow Warriors: OSS, and the Origins of the CIA.* New York: Basic Books.

Transportation Security Administration. n/d. *Intercity Bus Security Grants, Attachment A.* TSA Program Announcement 02MLPA0002. <www.tsa.gov/public/interweb/assetlibrary/ATTACH_A_Background.pdf>

U.S. Congress. 1983. *Compilation of Intelligence Laws and Related Laws and Executive Orders of Interest to the National Intelligence Community.* Washington, DC: U.S. Government Printing Office.

*USA Today.* 2005. "Border Patrols Growing in Arizona" (March 29). <www.usatoday.com/news/nation/2005-03-29-borders_x.htm>

*USA Company—Managing Risk in a War Zone.* The Economist Intelligence Unit Ltd., 2001.

Water Environment Research Foundation (WERF). n/d. *Protecting Wastewater Infrastructure and Human Health.* <www.werf.org/Collection/security.cfm>

# 6

# Mitigation, Prevention, and Preparedness

Mitigation and preparedness constitute one-half of the classic emergency management cycle, with response and recovery completing the sequence (see Figure 6-1). Mitigation and preparedness generally occur before a disaster ever occurs, though postdisaster mitigation and preparedness, conducted in recognition that similar events are likely in the future, make these two activities somewhat general to the entire emergency management cycle. This is in contrast to response and recovery, which by definition are only possible in the aftermath of a disastrous event.

In its classical meaning, *mitigation* refers to a sustained action taken to reduce or eliminate risk to people and property from hazards and their effects. Mitigation activities address either or both of the two components of risk, which are probability (likelihood) and consequence. By mitigating either of these components, the risk becomes much less of a threat to the affected population. In the case of natural disasters, the ability of man to limit the probability of a hazard is highly dependent on the hazard type, with some hazards such as hurricanes or tornadoes impossible to prevent, while avalanches, floods, and wildfires are examples of hazards for which limiting the rate of

occurrence is possible. In general, however, mitigation efforts for natural hazards tend to focus upon improved consequence management. In terms of manmade disasters, however, there is a much greater range of opportunities to minimize both the probability and the consequences of potential incidents, and both are applied with equal intensity. Mitigation in terms of terrorism, which is a much more complicated process, is discussed later in this chapter.

Preparedness can be defined as a state of readiness to respond to a disaster, crisis, or any other type of emergency situation. In general, preparedness activities can be characterized as the human component of predisaster hazard management. Training and public education are the most common preparedness activities, and, when properly applied, they have great potential to help people survive disasters. While preparedness activities do little to prevent a disaster from occurring, they are very effective at ensuring people know what to do once the disaster has happened.

The concepts of mitigation and preparedness have been altered since September 11, 2001, when terrorism became viewed as the primary threat facing America. As such, terms like *terrorism prevention* and *terrorism preparedness* have become more popular. One must question, in light of these new terms,

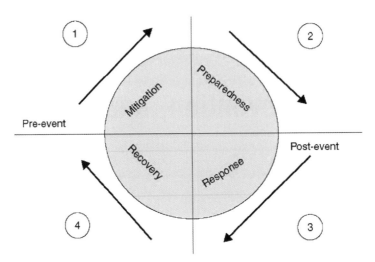

FIGURE 6-1   The four classical phases of disaster management.

whether or not there is any real difference between the traditional definitions of preparedness and mitigation and what is being conducted in light of the new terrorism hazard.

The National Response Plan (NRP), released in December 2004 to replace the Federal Response Plan as the national framework for disaster management, provides insight into this issue. Although this new plan does not directly define the phases of incident management, it introduces to users the sequential terminology of *prevention, preparedness, response, recovery,* and *mitigation.* The use of this terminology reflects two major changes with respect to the classical incident management approach in the United States. The first change is that mitigation is placed last in this cycle of incident management, which could indicate to readers that the activity (in the context of the plan) is perceived as a postincident one. This is significant mainly because it is altering a set terminology, which has already been widely understood and accepted within the emergency management discipline, feasibly resulting in unnecessary confusion. The second change, which is surely the more radical of the two, is the introduction of the term *prevention* not

only as a concept but also as a distinct phase in the incident management cycle. The plan defines prevention as "actions taken to avoid an incident or to intervene to stop an incident from occurring, which involve actions taken to protect lives and property." The NRP, like the FRP, is a comprehensive plan developed according to the all-hazards approach, but the inclusion of *prevention* as a separate incident phase (especially in light of the preceding definition) gives rise to the question of whether the NRP is focused primarily on terrorism incident management. Prevention, it would seem (in accordance with the definition provided), does not seem applicable to most natural disasters. (NRP, www.dhs.gov, 2004)

Whether deemed prevention or mitigation, proactive incident management is crucial for minimizing the loss of human life, injuries, financial losses, property damage, decreased quality of life, and interruption of business activities. Specific methods of prevention and mitigation change from hazard to hazard, and incident to incident, but the goals are the same.

Using the all-hazards approach, whether you are mitigating for earthquakes or floods or preparing for a potential terrorist threat, the classic mitigation planning process is an effective guide to the overall process. The traditional mitigation planning process, still conducted by the Federal Emergency Management Agency (FEMA) today under its Department of Homeland Security (DHS) umbrella, consists of four stages: (1) identifying and organizing resources; (2) conducting a risk or threat assessment and estimating losses; (3) identifying mitigation measures that will reduce the effects of the hazards and creating a strategy to deal with the mitigation measures in priority order; and (4) implementing the measures, evaluating the results, and keeping the plan up-to-date. This chapter will expand on these concepts.

## MITIGATION PLANS, ACTIONS, AND PROGRAMS

Mitigation activities include many different methods and strategies that have the common goal of reducing the risk associated with potential hazards. To provide a deeper understanding of mitigation, it is important to first understand the nature of natural, man-made, and terrorism risk.

There are many different definitions of risk, each of which may be appropriate within specific circumstances. Stan Kaplan (1997), an acclaimed risk management expert, argues that rather than providing a full definition of risk, one must ask three major questions in considering a specific hazard: (1) What can happen? (2) How likely is it? (3) What are the consequences? This indirect definition provides a much more flexible starting point with which to begin our discussion of risk and how to mitigate it. It also sheds additional light on the complexity of treating risks, which are clearly dynamic in nature. How we consider

those risks—and rank them according to our concern—is a factor of the combined answers of those three questions. For instance, though traffic accidents occur on a daily basis, their consequences tend to be relatively minor. Very large meteor strikes, on the other hand, are incredibly rare, but when they do occur, their consequences are globally catastrophic. Each hazard must be considered for its individual characteristics, and it is up to the individual, community, or society that is making the analysis to determine what level of effort will be made to address each according to these individual risk components.

The uncertainty component of risk, contained within the probability of disastrous event occurrence, places the greatest burden on those who are treating a full portfolio of risks that must be compared in relation to each other. Uncertainty forces us to ask ourselves questions that are often difficult and based more on expert judgment than on concrete evidence, such as "What is the probability that a 7.0-magnitude earthquake will happen in San Francisco Bay within the next 10 years?" or "What is the probability that terrorists will attack and damage a nuclear power plant in the United States?" The probability component of risk is important because it is an equally weighted parameter that helps us to quantify and prioritize mitigation actions when dealing with multiple risks. The determination of probabilities for events is often a difficult and complicated process. While several quantitative methods and tools are available that can be used to determine probabilities, these tend to be incomplete and very often too difficult for communities to use. Qualitative methods have been developed to ease this problem, which in turn allows for much easier comparison of risk by communities attempting to treat their risks. Sidebar 6-1 illustrates but one example of a system of estimation used to establish qualitative risk likelihood rankings.

The second component of risk, hazard consequence, is a detailed examination of the total unwanted impact of the disaster to the community, government, or the interested stakeholders. Consequence is often given an assigned monetary value in order to facilitate comparison with other hazards, but there are many intangible consequences that are very difficult to quantify in such absolute terms but which have to be considered as well if a comprehensive risk analysis is expected (see Table 6-1). Interestingly, the consequences of disasters also have a probabilistic nature. In practice, it is quite hard to assign a single monetary value to the expected damage; probability distributions are used to model the most likely damage estimates. For this reason, qualitative applications of consequence estimation have also been developed. Sidebar 6-2 is but one example.

---

SIDEBAR 6-1   **Qualitative Representation of Likelihood**

This particular qualitative representation system uses words to describe the chance of an event occurring. Each word or phrase has a designated range of possibilities attached to it. For instance, events could be described as follows:

- *Certain*: >99% chance of occurring in a given year (one or more occurrences per year)
- *Likely*: 50%–99% chance of occurring in a given year (one occurrence every 1 to 2 years)
- *Possible*: 5%–49% chance of occurring in a given year (one occurrence every 2 to 20 years)
- *Unlikely*: 2%–5% chance of occurring in a given year (one occurrence every 20 to 50 years)

- *Rare*: 1%–2% chance of occurring in a given year (one occurrence every 50 to 100 years)
- *Extremely rare*: <1% chance of occurring in a given year (one occurrence every 100 or more years)

Note that this is just one of a limitless range of qualitative terms and values assigned that can be used to describe the likelihood component of risk. As long as all hazards are compared using the same range of qualitative values, the actual determination of likelihood ranges attached to each term does not necessarily matter.

---

SIDEBAR 6-2   **Qualitative Representation of Consequence**

As was true with the qualitative representation of likelihood, words or phrases that have associated meanings can be used to describe the effects of a past disaster or the anticipated effects of a future one. These measurements can be assigned to deaths, injuries, or costs (oftentimes, the qualitative measurement of fatalities and injuries is combined). The following is one example of a qualitative measurement system for injuries and deaths:

- *Insignificant*: No injuries or fatalities
- *Minor*: Small number of injuries but no fatalities; first-aid treatment required
- *Moderate*: Medical treatment needed but no fatalities; some hospitalization
- *Major*: Extensive injuries, significant hospitalization; fatalities
- *Catastrophic*: Large number of fatalities and severe injuries; extended and large numbers requiring hospitalization

TABLE 6-1   **Tangible and Intangible Consequences of Disasters**

| Consequences | Measure | Losses | |
| --- | --- | --- | --- |
| | | Tangible | Intangible |
| Deaths | Number of people | Loss of economically active individuals | Social and psychological effects on remaining community |
| Injuries | Number and injury severity | Medical treatment needs, temporary loss of economic activity by productive individuals | Social and psychological pain and recovery |
| Physical damage | Inventory of damaged elements by number and damage level | Replacement and repair cost | Cultural losses |
| Emergency operations | Volume of manpower, man-days employed, equipment and resources expended to relief | Mobilization cost, investment in preparedness capability | Stress and overwork in relief participants |
| Disruption to economy | Number of working days lost, volume of production lost | Value of lost production | Opportunities, competitiveness, reputation |
| Social disruption | Number of displaced persons, homeless | Temporary housing, relief, economic production | Psychological, social contacts, cohesion, community morale |
| Environmental impact | Scale and severity | Cleanup costs, repair costs | Consequences of poorer environment, health risks, risk of future disaster |

*Source*: United Nations Development Programme. 1994. *Vulnerability and Risk Assessment*, 2nd ed. Cambridge: Cambridge Architectural Research Limited.

Once both of these factors (probability and consequence) have been determined, it is possible to compare risks against each other, primarily for the purposes of treating the risks through mitigation and preparedness. Normally, only limited funds exist for this purpose and, as such, not all risks can be treated. Risk comparison allows for a prioritization of risk, which can help those performing mitigation and preparedness ensure that they are spending their limited funds most wisely. Table 6-2 provides one example of a risk matrix that can be used to compare risks to each other.

Having provided a basic description of the components of risk, it is appropriate to move on to the mitigation of risk. In applying mitigation, risk managers try to minimize either or both of the two risk factors:

probability and consequence. In practice, however, it is not always easy, or even possible, to address both. And because each risk is unique, there are different strategies that must be identified, assessed, and then applied to each if any level of success is expected. For example, assume one seeks to minimize the risk of an earthquake. How can one minimize the probability of it happening? In terms of modern science, unfortunately, there are no known options to do so, and this is true for many natural hazards despite man's best efforts. However, one can still mitigate the risk of that earthquake by minimizing its consequences. For the earthquake risk, several known and proven strategies are available to minimize such consequences, such as adopting and enforcing earthquake-resistant building codes, educating the public about earth-

TABLE 6-2   **Example of a Risk Matrix Used in Risk Assessment**

Qualitative Risk Analysis Matrix—Level of Risk

| Likelihood | Consequences | | | | |
|---|---|---|---|---|---|
| | Insignificant | Minor | Moderate | Major | Catastrophic |
| Almost certain | High | High | Extreme | Extreme | Extreme |
| Likely | Moderate | High | High | Extreme | Extreme |
| Possible | Low | Moderate | High | Extreme | Extreme |
| Unlikely | Low | Low | Moderate | High | Extreme |
| Rare | Low | Low | Moderate | High | High |

*Source*: Emergency Management Australia. 2000. *Emergency Risk Management: Applications Guide.* Australian Emergency Manual Series.

quakes, and developing robust earthquake response plans.

In dealing with the newly expanded terrorism risk, the mitigation strategy would likely take on a much different approach. In this case, the opportunity to minimize the likelihood of the event's occurrence is very possible, and has been done countless times with great success. Through actionable intelligence about terrorist activities, their location, their networks, and communication strategies, it is possible to stop them before they proceed with their actions. Therefore, theoretically, the probability component of terrorism risk can be reduced through mitigation (or "prevention"). Of course, minimizing this likelihood component is a very complex task, requiring governments to expend very large amounts of money to build and manage necessary systems, establish international partnerships, and build networks to identify and detain terrorists.

The consequence component of terrorism risk can also be mitigated. However, unlike most natural disas-

ters that have a limited range of possible consequences, the options available to terrorists are limited only by their imagination. Terrorists have limitless targets, including facilities, infrastructure, and organizations, so many different strategies must be employed to minimize the impacts of terrorist attacks to each of these potential targets. DHS has developed a manual titled *Reference Manual to Mitigate Potential Terrorist Attacks against Buildings* (see Sidebar 6-3). This manual discusses the importance of minimizing the impacts of potential terrorist attacks against buildings. Buildings, however, are but one target. Presumably, it may be impossible to mitigate all possible consequences only because to do so would surely exhaust even the richest nation's financial resources. It would seem, then, that the best measures would seek multiple-use solutions, such as building a robust mass casualty public health system that would not only serve to mitigate the impact of terrorism on humans, but mitigate the consequences of other natural and technological hazards that also may affect the population.

## SIDEBAR 6-3    FEMA 426: Reference Manual to Mitigate Potential Terrorist Attacks against Buildings

The Federal Emergency Management Agency (FEMA) developed the *Reference Manual to Mitigate Potential Terrorist Attacks against Buildings* to provide needed information on how to mitigate the effects of potential terrorist attacks. The intended audience includes the building sciences community of architects and engineers working for private institutions. The manual supports FEMA's mission (to lead America to prepare for, prevent, respond to, and recover from disasters) and the Strategic Plan's Goal 3 (to prepare the nation to address the consequences of terrorism), all of which will be done within the all-hazards framework and the needs of homeland security.

The building science community, as a result of FEMA's efforts, has incorporated extensive building science into designing and constructing buildings against natural hazards (earthquake, fire, flood, and wind). To date, the same level of understanding has not been applied to man-made hazards (terrorism/intentional acts) and technological hazards (accidental events). Since September 11, 2001, terrorism has become a dominant domestic concern. Security can no longer be viewed as a stand-alone capability that can be purchased as an afterthought and put in place. Life, safety, and security issues must become a design goal from the beginning.

The objective of this manual is to reduce physical damage to structural and nonstructural components of buildings and related infrastructure and also to reduce resultant casualties during conventional bomb attacks, as well as attacks using chemical, biological, and radiological agents. Although the process is general in nature and applies to most building uses, this manual is most applicable for six specific types of facilities:

- Commercial office facilities
- Retail commercial facilities
- Light industrial and manufacturing facilities
- Health care facilities
- Local schools (K–12)
- Higher education (university) facilities

Chapter 1 presents selected methodologies to integrate threat/hazard, asset criticality, and vulnerability assessment information. This information becomes the input for determining relative levels of risk. Higher risk hazards require mitigation measures to reduce risk. The chapter also provides an assessment checklist that compiles many best practices to consider during the design of a new building or renovation of an existing building.

Chapter 2 discusses architectural and engineering design considerations (mitigation measures), starting at the perimeter of the property line, and includes the orientation of the building on the site. Therefore this chapter covers issues outside the building envelope.

Chapter 3 provides the same considerations for the building—its envelope, systems and interior layout.

Chapter 4 provides a discussion of blast theory to understand the dynamics of the blast pressure wave, the response of building components and a consistent approach to define levels of protection.

Chapter 5 presents chemical, biological, and radiological measures that can be taken to mitigate vulnerabilities and reduce associated risks for these terrorist tactics or technological hazards.

Appendices A, B, and C contain acronyms, general definitions, and CBR definitions, respectively.

Appendix D describes electronic security systems and design considerations.

Appendices E and F present a comprehensive bibliography of publications and the associations and organizations capturing the building security guidance needed by the building sciences community, respectively.

*Source*: FEMA 426, June 2003.

Terrorism is not a new hazard. Throughout history there have been terrorist organizations and terrorist attacks in many parts of the world, including North America, Europe, and Australia; however, the September 11 attacks resulted in such severe consequences that, not unexpectedly, terrorism became the primary issue on the U.S. government's agenda.

Mitigating the terrorism risk is important in order to minimize potential damage that may result from what is known to be a very real threat, but it is vital to remember that combating terrorism is a complex and long-term task, one that requires both patience and sacrifice. Therefore, all stakeholders—including the government, the public, the private sector, the media and academia—need to appreciate the benefit of applying mitigation on an all-hazards approach such that all known risks are treated, not only terrorism. Clearly, as has been shown in the years following the September 11 attacks, there are much more likely hazards—hurricanes and floods being the greatest—that have much greater potential to cause harm in terms of both likelihood and consequence. Hurricane Katrina is just one of many recent examples.

DHS continues to provide funding for predisaster and postdisaster mitigation projects through FEMA, though according to DHS Secretary Michael Chertoff's reorganization plan, the mitigation and preparedness capacity may be moved outside of this traditional location. Although typically applied to natural disasters, the Hazards Mitigation Grant Program and the predisaster mitigation programs could support terrorism mitigation through an all-hazards approach.

## FEMA MITIGATION DIVISION

The Mitigation Division within FEMA is responsible for a majority of the U.S. government's hazard mitigation activities, including the National Flood Insurance Program. This division performs several organizational activities that serve to promote protection, prevention, and partnerships at the federal, state, local, and individual levels. The overall mission of this division is to protect lives and prevent the loss of

property from natural and other hazards. The Mitigation Division does employ the all-hazards approach, through a comprehensive, risk-based emergency management program focused on both preparedness and, since the introduction of the increased terrorism risk, prevention. The Mitigation Division administers the nationwide, risk-reduction programs and congressionally authorized efforts discussed in the following subsections.

### National Flood Insurance Program

The U.S. Congress established the National Flood Insurance Program (NFIP) with the passage of the National Flood Insurance Act of 1968. The NFIP is a federal program enabling property owners in participating communities to purchase insurance as a protection against flood losses in exchange for state and community floodplain management regulations that reduce future flood damages. Flood insurance is designed to provide an alternative to disaster assistance to reduce the escalating costs of repairing damage to buildings and their contents caused by floods. Flood damage is reduced by nearly $1 billion a year through communities implementing sound floodplain management requirements and property owners purchasing of flood insurance. Additionally, buildings constructed in compliance with NFIP building standards suffer approximately 80% less damage annually than those not built in compliance. And, every $3 paid in flood insurance claims saves $1 in disaster assistance payments. (*Source*: FEMA, *National Flood Insurance Program*, www.fema.gov, 2005)

The president's 2006 budget includes $295 million for the Flood Insurance and Flood Map Modernization Programs. In addition to that, the budget includes approximately $2.1 billion for the National Flood Insurance Fund Account.

### National Dam Safety Program

The Dam Safety and Security Act of 2002, which was signed into law on December 2, 2002, addressed safety and security for dams through coordination by

FEMA. The 2002 act includes resources for the development and maintenance of a national dam safety information network and the development by the National Dam Safety Review Board of a strategic plan that establishes goals, priorities, and target dates to improve the safety and security of dams in the United States.

Under the leadership of FEMA, state assistance funds have enabled all participating states to better their dam safety programs through increased inspections, emergency action planning, and the purchase of needed equipment. A national research program in dam safety has been created, that is focusing on priorities and developing technological tools that drive data collection and analysis toward a better understanding of risk and remediation needs. In the training arena, FEMA has been able to expand existing training programs and begin new training programs to enhance the sharing of expertise between the federal and state sectors. (*Source*: FEMA, *National Dam Safety Program,* 2005)

### National Earthquake Hazards Reduction Program

The National Earthquake Hazards Reduction Program (NEHRP) was established by the Earthquake Hazards Reduction Act of 1977 to "reduce the risks of life and property from future earthquakes in the U.S." In 1980, the act was amended to include the National Institutes of Standards and Technology (NIST, then the National Bureau of Standards) and to designate the newly created FEMA as the lead agency. FEMA coordinated NEHRP until 2003, when legislation transferred FEMA's management role in the program to NIST. In this capacity FEMA planned and managed federal response to earthquakes, funded state and local preparedness exercises, and supported seismic design and construction techniques for new buildings and retrofit guidelines for existing buildings.

As part of this program, the United States Geological Survey (USGS) conducts and supports earth science investigations into the origins of earthquakes, predicts earthquake effects, characterizes earthquake

hazards, and disseminates earth science information. Additionally, the National Science Foundation (NSF) funds earthquake engineering research, basic earth science research, and earthquake-related social science.

In addition to its lead management role for the program, NIST conducts and supports engineering studies to improve seismic provisions of building codes, standards, and practices for buildings and lifelines. (*Source*: FEMA, NEHRP, www.fema.gov/hazards/earthquakes/nehrp/about.shtm)

The roles of the four agencies were further clarified in the 1990 NEHRP Reauthorization Act, which cast their primary responsibilities as follows:

### Federal Emergency Management Agency

- Translates research results into technical publications.
- Supports state and local governments by providing multiple-hazard loss estimation capability for use in planning and response.
- Prepares technical documents aimed at improving the seismic safety of new and existing buildings.
- Works with national standards organizations to develop seismic standards for new and existing lifelines.
- Prepares and disseminates information about building codes and practices.

### National Institutes of Standards and Technologies

- Promotes better building practices among architects and engineers.
- Works with national standards organizations to develop improved seismic standards for new and existing lifelines.
- Chairs and provides the secretariat for the Interagency Committee on Seismic Safety in Construction (ICSSC), which recommends practices and policies to reduce earthquake hazards in

federally owned, leased, assisted, and regulated facilities.

## National Science Foundation

- Supports research on plate tectonics.
- Funds engineering research on geotechnical, structural, architectural, and lifeline systems.
- Supports research on the social and economic aspects of earthquake hazard mitigation.
- Supports the education of new scientists and engineers in the field.

## United States Geological Survey

- Provides national and regional seismic hazard and risk maps.
- Conducts engineering seismology studies of the ground-shaking phenomenon.
- Develops methods and standardized procedures for forecasting earthquakes.
- Supports an external cooperative grants research program.
- Operates national seismograph networks.

### National Hurricane Program

The National Hurricane Program conducts and supports many projects and activities that help protect communities and their residents from hurricane hazards. The mitigation component of the program aims to reduce the damage caused by hurricane winds and flooding through improvements in the built environment, including residential and nonresidential buildings and their utility systems. The activities of the program include, but are not limited to, assessing building performance after significant hurricanes and coastal storms, developing designs for hazard-resistant construction in new buildings and retrofitting techniques for existing buildings, and recommending improvements in state and local regulatory programs.

## FEMA's Mitigation Grant Programs

FEMA currently has three mitigation grant programs: the Hazards Mitigation Grant Program, the Pre-Disaster Mitigation Program, and the Flood Mitigation Assistance program. Each is described next.

### Hazards Mitigation Grant Program

Authorized under Section 404 of the Stafford Act, the Hazard Mitigation Grant Program (HMGP) provides grants to states and local governments to implement long-term hazard mitigation measures after a major disaster declaration. The purpose of the program is to reduce the loss of life and property due to natural disasters and to enable mitigation measures to be implemented during the immediate recovery from a disaster declaration. The purpose of the program is to reduce the loss of life and property due to natural disasters and to enable mitigation measures to be implemented during the immediate recovery from a disaster.

Hazard Mitigation Grant Program funding is only available in states following a presidential disaster declaration. Eligible applicants are as follows:

- State and local governments
- Indian tribes or other tribal organizations
- Certain private nonprofit organizations

Individual homeowners and businesses may not apply directly to the program; however, a community may apply on their behalf. HMGP funds may be used to fund projects that will reduce or eliminate the losses from future disasters. Projects must provide a long-term solution to a problem—for example, elevation of a home to reduce the risk of flood damages as opposed to buying sandbags and pumps to fight the flood. In addition, a project's potential savings must be more than the cost of implementing the project. Funds may be used to protect either public or private property or to purchase property that has been subjected to, or is in danger of, repetitive damage.

### Pre-Disaster Mitigation Program

The Pre-Disaster Mitigation (PDM) Program was authorized by §203 of the Robert T. Stafford Disaster Assistance and Emergency Relief Act (Stafford Act), 42 USC, as amended by §102 of the Disaster Mitigation Act of 2000. Funding for the program is provided through the National Pre-Disaster Mitigation Fund to assist states and local governments (to include Indian tribal governments) in implementing cost-effective hazard mitigation activities that complement a comprehensive mitigation program. All applicants must be participating in the National Flood Insurance Program (NFIP) if they have been identified through the NFIP as having a special Flood Hazard Area (a Flood Hazard Boundary Map [FHBM] or Flood Insurance Rate Map [FIRM] has been issued). In addition, the community must not be suspended or on probation from the NFIP.

In 44 CFR Part 201, Hazard Mitigation Planning, criteria are established for state and local hazard mitigation planning authorized by §322 of the Stafford Act, as amended by §104 of the DMA. After November 1, 2003, local governments and Indian tribal governments applying for PDM funds through the states will have to have an approved local mitigation plan prior to the approval of local mitigation project grants. States will also be required to have an approved standard state mitigation plan in order to receive PDM funds for state or local mitigation projects after November 1, 2004. Therefore, the development of state and local multiple-hazard mitigation plans is key to maintaining eligibility for future PDM funding. The president's FY 2006 budget includes a total of $178 million for the Pre-Disaster Mitigation Fund and National Flood Mitigation Fund combined.

### Flood Mitigation Assistance Program

The Flood Mitigation Assistance (FMA) Program provides funding to assist states and communities in implementing measures to reduce or eliminate the long-term risk of flood damage to buildings, manufactured homes, and other structures insurable under the National Flood Insurance Program (NFIP). Three types of grants are available under FMA: planning, project, and technical assistance grants. FMA planning grants are available to states and communities to prepare flood mitigation plans. NFIP–participating communities with approved flood mitigation plans can apply for FMA project grants. FMA project grants are available to states and NFIP–participating communities to implement measures to reduce flood losses. Ten percent of the project grant is made available to states as a technical assistance grant. These funds may be used by the state to help administer the program. Communities receiving FMA planning and project grants must be participating in the NFIP. An example of eligible FMA projects includes the elevation, acquisition, and relocation of NFIP–insured structures.

Funding for the program is provided through the National Flood Insurance Fund, and FMA is funded at $20 million nationally (see Table 6-3). States are encouraged to prioritize FMA project grant applications that include repetitive loss properties. The FY 2001 FMA emphasis encourages states and communities to address target repetitive loss properties identified in the agency's repetitive loss strategy. These include structures with four or more losses and structures with two or more losses in which cumulative payments have exceeded the property value. State and communities are also encouraged to develop plans that address the mitigation of these target repetitive loss properties. (FEMA, www.fema.gov)

## PREVENTION ACTIONS AND PROGRAMS

Prevention refers to actions taken to avoid an incident or to intervene in an effort to stop an incident from occurring, in an effort to protect lives and property. According to DHS, the NRP may be implemented for threats or potential incidents of national significance to prevent or intervene in order to lessen the impact of an incident. Prevention activities may include heightened inspections; improved surveillance and security operations; public health and

TABLE 6-3 **FEMA Budget Update**

| DHS FEMA budget review ($ in 1,000s) | FY 2004 enacted | FY 2005 enacted | FY 2006 pres. budget | FY 2006 ± FY 2005 |
|---|---|---|---|---|
| Disaster relief fund and disaster loans | $1,768,067 | $2,042,947 | $2,140,567 | $97,620 |
| Office of the Under Secretary; PMRR; ARO; public health; radiological; emergency preparedness | $476,621 | $479,465 | $490,980 | $11,515 |
| Pre-Disaster Mitigation Fund and National Flood Mitigation Fund | $169,115 | $120,000 | $178,062 | $58,062 |
| Emergency food and shelter | $152,097 | $153,000 | $153,000 | — |
| Flood insurance and flood map modernization | $289,292 | $292,593 | $295,922 | $3,329 |
| Cerro Grande | $37,837 | — | — | — |
| Rescission of prior year carryover | −$3,000 | −$5,000 | — | $5,000 |
| Gross discretionary | $2,890,029 | $3,083,005 | $3,258,531 | $175,526 |
| Biodefense | $884,749 | $2,507,776 | — | −$2,507,776 |
| National Flood Insurance Fund Account | $1,778,753 | $1,950,251 | $2,106,757 | $156,506 |
| TOTAL | $5,553,531 | $7,541,032 | $5,365,288 | −$2,175,744 |

*Source: FEMA Budget in Brief 2006 Document.*

agricultural surveillance and testing; immunizations, isolation, or quarantine; and, as appropriate, specific law enforcement operations aimed at deterring, preempting, interdicting, or disrupting illegal activity and apprehending potential perpetrators and bringing them to justice. (NRP, www.dhs.gov., 2005)

As the prevention activities described by DHS imply, most of these activities are related to the prevention of terrorist incidents. Prevention actions related to terrorism threats and incidents include law enforcement activities and protective activities. All federal law enforcement activities are coordinated by the attorney general, generally acting through the FBI. During an incident, initial prevention efforts include, but are not limited to, the following actions:

- Collect, analyze, and apply intelligence and other information.
- Conduct investigations to determine the full nature and source of the threat.
- Implement countermeasures such as surveillance and counterintelligence.

- Conduct security operations, including vulnerability assessments, site security, and infrastructure protection.
- Conduct tactical operations to prevent, interdict, preempt, or disrupt illegal activity.
- Conduct attribution investigations, including an assessment of the potential for future related incidents.
- Conduct activities to prevent terrorists, terrorist weapons, and associated materials from entering or moving within the United States.

As defined within the NRP, any activity that intends to prevent terrorist attacks can be qualified as a prevention measure. Several specific DHS prevention programs are discussed in greater detail in Chapter 5.

Several of the recommendations made by the 9/11 Commission, discussed in Chapter 4, also include a prevention component. Several are provided for illustrative purposes here:

- **Prevention of proliferation of weapons of mass destruction and their acquisition by terrorist groups**: The 9/11 Commission underlines that about two dozen terrorist groups including al-Qaeda have attempted to acquire or develop chemical, biological, radiological, and nuclear weapons. Most of those weapons can be developed relatively inexpensively if the necessary knowledge is available to terrorists. The possible consequences of an attack involving those weapons are very likely to be devastating. Therefore, preventing the proliferation of such weapons or materials that are necessary in their development is a critical task that needs to be performed. The commission recommends that the United States has to work with the international community to get this done. The commission recommends that the United States should sustain its support for the Cooperative Threat Reduction Program, which aims to secure the weapons and highly dangerous materials still scattered in Russia and other countries of the Soviet Union.
- **Prevention of financial strength and flexibility of terrorist organizations**: The United States and its allies made an effort to paralyze the financial networks of terrorists in the recent aftermath of 9/11. This effort aimed to reduce or eliminate the ability of terrorist groups to support their operations and maintain their existence. The experience showed that tracking and blocking of money that is potentially connected to terrorist groups is a very difficult job that demands not only international cooperation, but also the convenience of national laws of international partners. Therefore, other innovative ways of reducing the financial strength and flexibility of terrorist organizations is necessary.
- **Prevention of terrorist travel**: With the advancements in and increased frequency of international travel, terrorist groups were able to gain the mobility to conduct attacks in different parts of the world. This gives an opportunity to governments to identify the terrorist as they enter the transportation system or the country through its border checkpoints. This is a critical task that may prevent some terrorist attacks or at least the penetration of terrorists from one country to another one. But the fact that terrorists also use local resources and people in their activities makes the challenge even tougher.
- **Prevention of terrorist access to critical infrastructures and key assets**: The 9/11 Commission recommends that the improvements being made to protect U.S. borders such as use of terrorist lists, biometric screening, biometric passports, and other threat-related information be shared with and implemented at access points to critical infrastructures and key assets. Such assets may include nuclear power plants, dams and other infrastructures of national significance and consequences.

*Source*: Adapted from the Recommendations of the 9/11 Commission, Chapter 12, *"What to Do? A Global Strategy."*

## PREPAREDNESS ACTIONS AND PROGRAMS

Preparedness within the field of emergency management can best be defined as a state of readiness to respond to a disaster, crisis, or any other type of emergency situation. It includes those activities, programs, and systems that exist before an emergency that are used to support and enhance response to an emergency or disaster.

Preparedness is important to the overall emergency management cycle because it provides for the readiness and testing of all actions and plans before actual application occurs in response to a real event or disaster. There is a close connection between mitigation and preparedness. Often, emergency managers argue over whether a specific action should be considered mitigation or preparedness. Oftentimes the lines of distinction become fuzzy, and exact determination impossible. In its most simple terms, preparedness is more about planning for the best response, whereas

FIGURE 6-2   Emmitsburg, Maryland, March 10, 2003—An incident command system course is held at FEMA's National Emergency Training Center, one of dozens of courses offered there each year for first responders, emergency managers, and educators. (Photo by Jocelyn Augustino/FEMA News Photo)

mitigation includes all the actions that are attempts to prevent the need for a disaster response or to minimize the scope of the needed response.

Examples of preparedness for natural hazards are organizing evacuation drills from buildings in case of fires or other threats, providing first response training to employees so that they can assist each other and their neighbors in small emergencies (see Figure 6-2), and preparing a family disaster plan that covers topics such as the designation of a location where family members will meet if they get separated during an event and what personal papers (e.g., prescriptions, insurance records) they might need in the aftermath of an event. More specific examples include the logistical planning for tugboats operating around oil refineries such that they become responsible for responding

to fire emergencies in the refinery, or providing training and relocating necessary hazardous materials (HAZMAT) teams to areas where the risk of radiological emergencies is higher, such as nuclear power plants.

In the aftermath of September 11, terrorism preparedness has become a more pressing issue. The risk of terrorists gaining access to and using weapons of mass destruction, such as biological, chemical, and radiological agents, forced the U.S. government to establish an adequate response capability, capacity, and expertise to protect American citizens against a potential attack and respond to it, in case these weapons are used. Citizens, who are the most likely targets of these attacks, must be adequately prepared if any response effort is to be successful. DHS has been given the responsibility for this task, though several other federal government agencies, including the Centers for Disease Control and Prevention (CDC) and the Department of Education for example, provide guidance on a full range of terrorism preparedness activities.

The Department of Homeland Security's Emergency Preparedness and Response Directorate (EP&R) has as its goal "to prepare for and respond to natural and technological disasters and terrorism." The directorate, which incorporated FEMA, the Strategic National Stockpile, the National Disaster Medical System (NDMS), the Nuclear Incident Response Team, the Domestic Emergency Support Teams, and the National Domestic Preparedness Office, produces and publishes several documents that help citizens and businesses to perform self-preparedness actions in light of the new terrorism threat. Unfortunately, the arsenal of weapons available to the growing cadre of international terrorists is expanding, and as these weapons are identified and understood, the public must be educated accordingly. Sidebars 6-4 through 6-6, and Sidebar 4-22 in Chapter 4, provide examples of these terrorist weapons, and the guidance provided by DHS, CDC, and FEMA for citizen preparedness.

---

**SIDEBAR 6-4    CDC Guidance for Evacuation Preparedness for Chemical Weapons**

Some kinds of chemical accidents or attacks may make staying put dangerous. In such cases, it may be safer for you to evacuate or leave the immediate area. You may need to go to an emergency shelter after you leave the immediate area.

**How to Know If You Need to Evacuate**

You will hear from the local police, emergency coordinators, or government on the radio or television if you need to evacuate. If there is a "code red" or "severe" terror alert, you should pay attention to radio and television broadcasts so that you will know right away if an evacuation order is made for your area.

**What to Do**

Act quickly and follow the instructions of local emergency coordinators. Every situation can be different, so local coordinators may give you special instructions to follow for a particular situation. Local emergency coordinators may direct people to evacuate homes or offices and go to an emergency shelter. If so, emergency coordinators will tell you how to get to the shelter. If you have children in school, they may be sheltered at the school. You should not try to get to the school if the children are being sheltered there.

The emergency shelter will have most supplies that people need. The emergency coordinators will tell you which supplies to bring with you. Be sure to bring any medications you are taking. If you have time, call a friend or relative in another state to tell him or her where you are going and that you are safe. Local telephone lines may be jammed in an emergency, so you should plan ahead to have an out-of-state contact with whom to leave messages. If you do not have private transportation, make plans in advance of an emergency to identify people who can give you a ride.

Evacuating and sheltering in this way should keep you safer than if you stayed at home or at your workplace. You will most likely not be in the shelter for more than a few hours. Emergency coordinators will let you know when it is safe to leave the shelter.

*Source*: Centers for Disease Control and Prevention, www.cdc. gov, 2005.

SIDEBAR 6-5    **FEMA "Are You Ready" Protective Measures for a Nuclear Blast**

### Before a Nuclear Blast

To prepare for a nuclear blast, you should do the following:

- Find out from officials if any public buildings in your community have been designated as fallout shelters. If none have been designated, make your own list of potential shelters near your home, workplace, and school. These places would include basements or the windowless center area of middle floors in high-rise buildings, as well as subways and tunnels.
- If you live in an apartment building or high-rise, talk to the manager about the safest place in the building for sheltering and about providing for building occupants until it is safe to go out.
- During periods of increased threat increase your disaster supplies to be adequate for up to two weeks.

Taking shelter during a nuclear blast is absolutely necessary. There are two kinds of shelters: blast and fallout. The following describes the two kinds of shelters:

- Blast shelters are specifically constructed to offer some protection against blast pressure, initial radiation, heat, and fire. But even a blast shelter cannot withstand a direct hit from a nuclear explosion.
- Fallout shelters do not need to be specially constructed for protecting against fallout. They can be any protected space, provided that the walls and roof are thick and dense enough to absorb the radiation given off by fallout particles.

### During a Nuclear Blast

The following are guidelines for what to do in the event of a nuclear explosion. If an attack warning is issued:

- Take cover as quickly as you can, below ground if possible, and stay there until instructed to do otherwise.
- Listen for official information and follow instructions.

If you are caught outside and unable to get inside immediately:

- Do not look at the flash or fireball—it can blind you.
- Take cover behind anything that might offer protection.
- Lie flat on the ground and cover your head. If the explosion is some distance away, it could take 30 seconds or more for the blast wave to hit.
- Take shelter as soon as you can, even if you are many miles from ground zero where the attack occurred—radioactive fallout can be carried by the winds for hundreds of miles. Remember the three protective factors: Distance, shielding, and time.

### After a Nuclear Blast

Decay rates of the radioactive fallout are the same for any size nuclear device. However, the amount of fallout will vary based on the size of the device and its proximity to the ground. Therefore, it might be necessary for those in the areas with highest radiation levels to shelter for up to a month. The heaviest fallout would be limited to the area at or downwind from the explosion, and 80% of the fallout would occur during the first 24 hours. People in most of the areas that would be affected could be allowed to come out of shelter within a few days and, if necessary, evacuate to unaffected areas.

### Returning to Your Home

Remember the following:

- Keep listening to the radio and television for news about what to do, where to go, and places to avoid.
- Stay away from damaged areas. Stay away from areas marked "radiation hazard" or "HAZMAT." Remember that radiation cannot be seen, smelled, or otherwise detected by human senses.

*Source*: Federal Emergency Management Agency, www.fema. gov, 2005.

---

### SIDEBAR 6-6    DHS Ready.Gov Guidance on Explosions

**If There Is an Explosion**

- Take shelter against your desk or a sturdy table.
- Exit the building ASAP.
- Do not use elevators.
- Check for fire and other hazards.
- Take your emergency supply kit if time allows.

**If There Is a Fire**

- Exit the building ASAP.
- Crawl low if there is smoke
- Use a wet cloth, if possible, to cover your nose and mouth.
- Use the back of your hand to feel the upper, lower, and middle parts of closed doors.
- If the door is not hot, brace yourself against it and open slowly.
- If the door is hot, do not open it. Look for another way out.
- Do not use elevators
- If you catch fire, do not run. Stop-drop-and-roll to put out the fire.

- If you are at home, go to a previously designated meeting place.
- Account for your family members and carefully supervise small children.
- Never go back into a burning building.

**If You Are Trapped in Debris**

- If possible, use a flashlight to signal your location to rescuers.
- Avoid unnecessary movement so that you don't kick up dust.
- Cover your nose and mouth with anything you have on hand. (Dense-weave cotton material can act as a good filter. Try to breathe through the material.)
- Tap on a pipe or wall so that rescuers can hear where you are.
- If possible, use a whistle to signal rescuers.
- Shout only as a last resort. Shouting can cause a person to inhale dangerous amounts of dust.

*Source*: Department of Homeland Security, www.dhs.gov, 2005.

---

## PREPAREDNESS AGAINST BIOLOGICAL AND CHEMICAL ATTACKS AND ACCIDENTS

Preparedness against biological and chemical attacks and accidents poses a distinct challenge due to the unique consequences they inflict and the relatively limited experience of emergency management professionals in dealing with them. This unique challenge is being addressed by many local, state, federal, private, and nonprofit agencies throughout the United States. In fact, the majority of preparedness funding under the Department of Homeland Security targets these WMD hazards.

## SPECIFIC CHALLENGES FOR BIOLOGICAL/CHEMICAL TERRORISM INCIDENT MANAGEMENT

Deliberate biological or chemical incidents will present critical challenges to both the parties under attack and those in charge of managing the incident that results. These agents, as with all weapons of mass destruction, present public health threats that are not typically seen in either day-to-day or even major incidents of natural or unintentional man-made nature. As such, the methods by which citizens and response officials can prepare for these attacks have only just begun to emerge in the past few months and years. Chemical incidents do occur with regularity, but it is very rare for them to deliberately target a human population.

Both chemical and biological agents, when used as a weapon, have a significant potential to overwhelm the capabilities of the public health infrastructure. There have been several attempts to design a comprehensive framework to prepare for and manage mass casualty medical incidents. The specific response challenges that those defining new preparedness methods must take into account are listed here:

- The existence of a chemical or biological attack may be hard to verify, due to delayed consequences or symptoms.
- The incident may involve multiple jurisdictions, which may make it much more difficult to organize a coordinated response.
- It may be time consuming to identify and isolate the type and source of the chemical or biological agent present on site.
- The incident may have a pinpoint target where a specific crowd is targeted, or may be designed to impact a larger geographic area and even larger crowds, both of which will likely create large crowds of morbidities if not mortalities.
- If large numbers of the public are impacted by the incident, the demand for health care may quickly exceed local, or even regional, medical resources.

- The identification of the involved chemical(s) or biological agent(s) may consume the capacity of local medical laboratories making it mandatory to integrate use of neighboring laboratories.
- Resources of the medical system may be consumed by not only the victims, but also by those who perceive themselves as possible victims who may not be real victims.
- The emergency management officials may have to make extremely difficult public policy decisions very quickly, where lives may have to be sacrificed to save other lives.
- It may be necessary to quarantine the impacted region to insulate the nonimpacted geographies from potential contamination.
- The medical units may have to triage arriving victims if the incoming demand dramatically exceeds the capacity of available resources.
- To decontaminate the impacted geographies and those who were contaminated by the release, necessary decontamination systems, equipment, and human resources may be necessary at multiple locations.
- The medical system may not only have to deal with the physical disease caused by the chemical or biological release, but also with the mental impacts of the "mass paranoia" the incident may have triggered.

The challenges just listed are only a small subset of potential challenges that have to be met. Individual events will present individual response factors that may or may not be known beforehand. To address these issues, physical (equipment, tools, technology), financial, knowledge, and human resources are all necessary. More importantly, a comprehensive system to address these challenges is necessary, and the adequate utilization of such a system demands the provision of training and exercises to those who will be dependent on such a system in a time of crisis. Sidebar 6-7 presents the CDC's strategic plan for preparedness and response in the event of a biological or chemical attack.

SIDEBAR 6-7   **CDC's Strategic Plan for Preparedness and Response to Biological and Chemical Terrorism**

The CDC has developed a plan, titled the *Strategic Plan for Preparedness and Response to Biological and Chemical Terrorism*, that identifies preparedness and prevention; detection and surveillance; diagnosis and characterization of biological and chemical agents; response; and communication as the five focus areas for comprehensive mass casualty health incident management. Each of these is described next.

**Preparedness and Prevention**

Detection, diagnosis, and mitigation of illness and injury caused by biological and chemical terrorism are complex processes that involve numerous partners and activities. Meeting this challenge requires special emergency preparedness in all cities and states. CDC provides public health guidelines, support, and technical assistance to local and state public health agencies as they develop coordinated preparedness plans and response protocols. CDC also provides self-assessment tools for terrorism preparedness, including performance standards, attack simulations, and other exercises.

**Detection and Surveillance**

Early detection is essential for ensuring a prompt response to a biological or chemical attack, including the provision of prophylactic medicines, chemical antidotes, or vaccines. CDC is integrating surveillance for illness and injury resulting from biological and chemical terrorism into the U.S. disease surveillance systems, while developing new mechanisms for detecting, evaluating, and reporting suspicious events that might represent covert terrorist acts. As part of this effort, CDC and state and local health agencies form partnerships with front-line medical personnel in hospital emergency departments, hospital care facilities, poison control centers, and other offices to enhance detection and

reporting of unexplained injuries and illnesses as part of routine surveillance mechanisms for biological and chemical terrorism.

**Diagnosis and Characterization of Biological and Chemical Agents**

CDC and its partners created a multilevel laboratory response network (LRN). The LRN and its partners will maintain an integrated national and international network of laboratories that are fully equipped to respond quickly to acts of chemical or biological terrorism, emerging infectious diseases, and other public health threats and emergencies.

**Response**

A comprehensive public health response to a biological or chemical terrorist event involves epidemiologic investigation, medical treatment and prophylaxis for affected persons, and the initiation of disease prevention or environmental decontamination measures. CDC assists state and local health agencies in developing resources and expertise for investigating unusual events and unexplained illnesses. If requested by a state health agency, CDC will deploy response teams to investigate unexplained or suspicious illnesses or unusual etiologic agents and provide on-site consultation regarding medical management and disease control. To ensure the availability, procurement, and delivery of medical supplies, devices, and equipment that might be needed to respond to terrorist-caused illness or injury, CDC maintains a national pharmaceutical stockpile.

**Communication Systems**

U.S. preparedness to mitigate the public health consequences of biological and chemical terrorism depends on the coordinated activities of well-trained health-care and public health personnel throughout the United States who have access to up-to-the minute emergency information. Effective communication with the public through the news media will also be essential to limit terrorists' ability to induce public panic and disrupt daily life.

*Source*: Centers for Disease Control and Prevention, 2005. *Biological and Chemical Terrorism: Strategic Plan for Preparedness and Response*.

## COMPREHENSIVE MEDICAL AND HEALTH INCIDENT MANAGEMENT SYSTEM: MaHIM

The Medical and Health Incident Management System (MaHIM) designed by Drs. Joseph A. Barbera and Anthony G. Macintyre is one of the most recent and most comprehensive analytical tools designed to help communities develop their own medical mass casualty incident management capacity. The system not only focuses on developing local capacities, but also proposes a framework that can be used to integrate interjurisdictional capacities, should the incident spread beyond local jurisdictional borders.

The goal of the framework is to define as a single system the medical and public health functions and processes required for adequate management of a mass casualty incident. The system has been designed with an all-hazards approach where special consideration is given to bioterrorism.

The MaHIM system defines the goal of medical consequence management in a mass casualty incident as follows: to maximally limit morbidity (injury or illness) and mortality (deaths) in the population exposed to a major hazard, and to return the community to normalcy as soon as possible. The three primary medical objectives to attain this goal are as follows:

1. **Reduce hazard exposure**: Avoid or minimize the hazard exposure to patients and the population after hazard "release."
2. **Increase hazard resistance**: Maximize patient and population resistance to the hazard impact after exposure.

3. **Promote/achieve healing from hazard effects**: Maximize the rate and degree of patient and population healing from the hazard impact.

To achieve these goals, the system utilizes principles of effective local and regional organization to provide a detailed description of necessary medical and health emergency operations, and the associated subfunctions and processes. The system underlines the importance of *responsibility* and *authority*. It defines the operational requirements for surge capacity, and provides detailed explanations about support functions critical to system's operation. Figure 6-3 details the MaHIM Management Process.

MaHIM provides a new vision for the health and emergency medical service communities, and gives them an actionable tool with which they can now structure their preparedness and management efforts in a more systematic fashion. The system describes in detail all functional areas that should be included in a comprehensive mass casualty health incident management system. The system is currently being implemented in Arlington County, Virginia, as part of a pilot project. The project includes restructuring the county's entire emergency medical system. A more detailed functional description of the system can be downloaded at the following location: www.gwu.edu/~icdrm/publications/MaHIM%20Model%20Web%20Version%20FEB%2003.pdf. (*Sources*: Barbera, J. A., and A. G. Macintyre. 2002. *Medical and Health Incident Management (MaHIM) System: A Comprehensive Functional System Description for Mass Casualty Medical and Health Incident Management*.

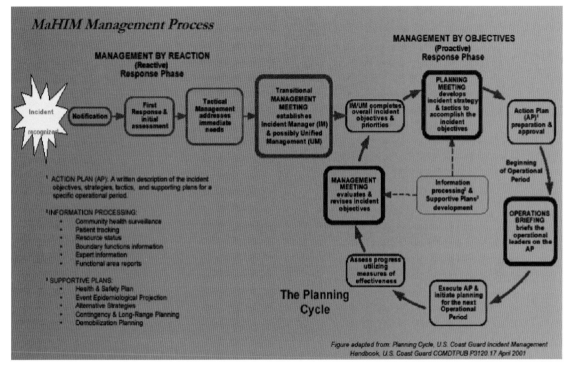

FIGURE 6-3   MaHIM management process. (Adapted from "Planning Cycle," *U.S. Coast Guard Incident Management Handbook,* U.S. Coast Guard COMDTPUB P3120, April 17, 2001)

Washington, DC: Institute for Crisis, Disaster, and Risk Management, The George Washington University (October); Barbera, J. A., and A. G. Macintyre. Presentation at the ICDRM/SAIC Monthly Emergency Management Forum)

## NUCLEAR AND RADIOLOGICAL PREPAREDNESS

The Nuclear Regulatory Commission (NRC) is the primary federal government agency in charge of regulating the commercial radiological operations within the United States. The NRC's mission is to regulate the nation's civilian use of by-product, source, and special nuclear materials to ensure adequate protection of public health and safety, to promote the common defense and security, and to protect the envi-

ronment. The NRC's regulatory mission covers three main areas:

- *Reactors*: Commercial reactors for generating electric power and research and test reactors used for research, testing, and training
- *Materials*: Uses of nuclear materials in medical, industrial, and academic settings and facilities that produce nuclear fuel
- *Waste*: Transportation, storage, and disposal of nuclear materials and waste, and decommissioning of nuclear facilities from service

A key component of the mission of the NRC is to ensure adequate preparedness measures are in place to protect the health and safety of the public. These actions are taken to avoid or reduce radiation dose exposure and are sometimes referred to as *protective measures.*

The overall objective of NRC's Emergency Preparedness (EP) program is to ensure that nuclear power plant operators are capable of implementing adequate measures to protect public health and safety in the event of a radiological emergency. As a condition of their license, operators of these nuclear power plants must develop and maintain EP plans that meet comprehensive NRC EP requirements. Increased confidence in public protection is obtained through the combined inspection of the requirements of emergency preparedness and the evaluation of their implementation.

The NRC maintains oversight of the capability of nuclear power plant operators to protect the public by conducting thorough inspections. The NRC maintains four regional offices (Region I in King of Prussia, Pennsylvania; Region II in Atlanta, Georgia; Region III in Lisle, Illinois; and Region IV in Arlington, Texas) that implement the NRC's inspection program. In addition to these regionally based inspectors, the NRC places "resident inspectors" at each of the nation's operating nuclear plants to carry out the inspection program on a day-to-day basis.

The NRC assesses the capabilities of nuclear power plant operators to protect the public by requiring the performance of a full-scale exercise at least once every 2 years that includes the participation of government agencies. These exercises are performed in order to maintain the skills of the emergency responders and to identify and correct weaknesses. They are evaluated by NRC regional inspectors and FEMA regional evaluators. Between the times when these 2-year exercises are conducted, additional drills are conducted by the nuclear power plant operators that are evaluated by the resident inspectors. (*Source*: Nuclear Regulatory Commission, www.nrc.gov/what-we-do/emerg-preparedness/protect-public.html)

## TERRORISM PREPAREDNESS AND MITIGATION: COMMUNITY ISSUES

The terrorism threat knows no geographic, social, or economic boundaries. Every citizen and every community is potentially at risk. While DHS focuses on federal and state efforts to prepare for and combat terrorism, local communities are struggling to address the terrorism risk. The following sections will explain several initiatives that have been launched to deal with community issues concerning the terrorist threat.

## CORPORATION FOR NATIONAL AND COMMUNITY SERVICE

The mission of the Corporation for National and Community Service (CNCS), an independent federal agency under the White House, is to provide opportunities for Americans of all ages and backgrounds to engage in service that addresses the nation's educational, public safety, environmental, and other human needs to achieve direct and demonstrable results and to encourage all Americans to engage in such service. In doing so, the corporation fosters civic responsibility, strengthens the ties that bind citizens together as a people, and provides educational opportunities for those who make a substantial commitment to service.

The Corporation for National and Community Service provides opportunities for Americans of all ages and backgrounds to serve their communities and country through three programs: Senior Corps, AmeriCorps, and Learn and Serve America. Members and volunteers serve with national and community nonprofit organizations, faith-based groups, schools, and local agencies to help meet community needs in education, the environment, public safety, homeland security, and other critical areas. The corporation is part of USA Freedom Corps, a White House initiative to foster a culture of citizenship, service, and responsibility and help all Americans answer the president's call to service.

Senior Corps taps the skills, talents, and experience of more than 500,000 Americans ages 55 years and older to meet a wide range of community challenges through three programs: RSVP, Foster Grandparents, and Senior Companions. RSVP volunteers conduct safety patrols for local police departments, participate in environmental projects, provide intensive educational services to children and adults, and respond to natural disasters, among other activities. Foster Grandparents serve one-on-one as tutors and mentors to young people with special needs. Senior Companions help homebound seniors and other adults maintain independence in their own homes.

Fifty thousand Americans are serving their communities 20 to 40 hours a week through AmeriCorps. Most of AmeriCorps' members are selected by and serve with local and national nonprofit organizations such as Habitat for Humanity, the American Red Cross, City Year, Teach for America, and Boys and Girls Clubs of America, as well as with a host of smaller community organizations, both secular and faith based. AmeriCorps operates in a decentralized manner that gives a significant amount of responsibility to states and local nonprofit groups. Roughly three-quarters of all AmeriCorps grant funding goes to governor-appointed state service commissions, which award grants to nonprofit groups to respond to local needs. Most of the remainder of the grant funding is distributed by the corporation directly to multistate and national organizations through a competitive grants process. AmeriCorps*NCCC (National Civilian Community Corps) is a residential program for more than 1,200 members ages 18 to 24. Based on a military model, it sends members in teams of 10 to 14 to help nonprofit groups provide disaster relief, preserve the environment, build homes for low-income families, tutor children, and meet other challenges. Because members are trained in CPR, first aid, and mass care and can be assigned to new duties on short notice, they are particularly well suited to meet the emerging homeland security needs of the nation.

Learn and Serve America provides grants to schools, colleges, and nonprofit groups to support efforts to engage students in community service linked to academic achievement and the development of civic skills. This type of learning, referred to as *service learning*, improves communities while preparing young people for a lifetime of responsible citizenship. In addition to providing grants, Learn and Serve America serves as a resource on service and service learning to teachers, faculty members, schools, and community groups.

The Corporation for National and Community Service is an important initiative for homeland security efforts at the local community level because it provides a significant portion of the total federal funding that goes to volunteer organizations and local communities that are trying to improve their homeland security capabilities.

On July 18, 2002, the corporation announced that it had acquired more than $10.3 million in grants. These grants supported 37,000 volunteers for homeland security in public safety, public health, and disaster mitigation and preparedness. The corporation announced on September 10, 2003, the renewal of 17 of the grants from the previous year totaling nearly $4.5 million for homeland security volunteer projects that were developed in the aftermath of the September 11 terrorist attacks. (See Appendix 6 for a full list of corporation grantees and descriptions of their proposed homeland security programs.)

In January 2004, the Corporation for National and Community Service announced the availability of $3.2 million in funding for organizations addressing homeland security concerns by engaging students in service learning activities in their schools and communities. The funding was made available through the Corporation's Learn and Serve America program, which provides grants to schools, colleges, and nonprofits to support programs that connect classroom learning with community service. The Homeland Security initiative aims to engage young people ages 5 to 17 in planning for and responding to health, safety, and security concerns in their schools or communities, including natural disasters, school violence, medical emergencies, or terrorist acts. Examples of the kinds of activities that could be supported include engaging students in service learning projects to develop school crisis plans, distribute preparedness kits, conduct school safety audits and drills, provide health education, inventory and maintain emergency supplies, or provide language assistance to non-English-speaking populations.

In February 2004, the Corporation for National and Community Service announced the renewal of 13 AmeriCorps homeland security grants to support 362

AmeriCorps members serving in public safety, public health, and disaster relief and preparedness projects across the country. The grants totaled $3.5 million and supported AmeriCorps projects in 20 states. The grantees included 12 state or local groups and one national organization, the American Red Cross. The grants support AmeriCorps members' efforts to recruit volunteers; develop disaster response plans; teach disaster preparedness to students; assist firefighting and police operations; train people in first aid and CPR; respond to national and local disasters; and develop partnerships with organizations involved in homeland security such as Citizen Corps councils and Neighborhood Watch Programs. (Sidebar 6-8 discusses neighborhood security.) Results from the 2003 activities sponsored by the grants included these:

- AmeriCorps members serving in a program sponsored by the Florida Department of Elder Affairs have recruited over 600 disaster services volunteers who contributed more than 12,000 hours of service, distributed over 200,000 disaster services publications, and reached nearly 2,500 residents with presentations on safety.
- Serving with the Green River Area Development District in rural Kentucky, AmeriCorps members have utilized data from a Global Positioning System to map out information about fire stations, emergency shelters, HAZMAT storage facilities, medical facilities and nursing homes.
- Just blocks from the World Trade Center site, Pace University AmeriCorps members have trained 250 people in English, Chinese, and Spanish in emergency preparedness techniques, created a resource list that consolidates all important emergency numbers, and built a "Downtown Needs" website that serves as a volunteer clearinghouse for 2,000 organizations in the downtown area.
- AmeriCorps members in the California Safe Corps have taught disaster preparedness classes to more than 1,000 community members, recruited more than 100 new volunteers who

have provided over 250 hours of service, and assisted more than 200 victims of disasters.
- In Iowa, AmeriCorps members have made presentations on disaster preparedness at 400 schools across the state.

In March 2004, the Corporation for National and Community Service announced the availability of a new $4 million grant for nonprofit organizations and public agencies for projects to engage volunteers in homeland security efforts in their communities. The grants are for projects that engage volunteers, especially those ages 55 years and over, in helping communities prepare for and respond to all types of emergencies and disasters. The CNCS expects to make approximately 12 awards, ranging from $100,000 to $500,000 each. The grants will cover 1 year of program activity, but funding for a second and third year may be provided contingent on performance and availability of funds. Examples of the kinds of activities that could be supported include engaging volunteers to assist fire or police departments; assisting in disaster response, search and rescue, first aid, coordination of emergency supplies; establishing communication links for relief workers; organizing immunization programs; and educating the public on preparing for potential disasters or terrorist attacks.

In the summer of 2004, the devastation wrought by Hurricanes Charley and Frances in Florida prompted the CNCS to muster as much assistance as possible to the state. More than 600 national service volunteers have been deployed to provide both direct services and leverage the support of thousands of additional volunteers. The CNCS worked with state and federal disaster officials to deploy even more volunteers as needed. Here are some examples of national service response:

- 128 AmeriCorps*NCCC members, who worked out of Red Cross shelters and delivered relief supplies to Red Cross centers throughout the affected areas.
- 42 State AmeriCorps members volunteered with Christian Contractors Association and the Army

Corps of Engineers in placing tarps on damaged roofs.

- 12 AmeriCorps*VISTA members from Red Cross of North Central Florida trained community volunteers in CPR and first aid and engaged in damage assessments related to sink holes and flooding.
- 57 senior volunteers with City of Orlando Special Volunteer Program assisted with staffing a Citizen Information hotline, shelter operations, and distributing ice after the storm. Many of these senior volunteers served 24-hour shifts during the storm.
- RSVP of Seminole County closed offices to set up a volunteer reception center to register and process volunteers and assist in recovery efforts in Sanford, Florida. Volunteers manned the Emergency Operation Center, and senior volunteers worked around the clock to handle citizen calls and assist special needs clients who did not evacuate during the storms.

- Youth in Learn and Serve America programs like ManaTEENS helped with food and donation drives, assisted with animal evacuations, and helped at Volunteer Reception Centers placing unaffiliated volunteers in De Soto County.

AmeriCorps members and Senior Corps volunteers specially trained in disaster relief have responded to disasters in more than 30 states. The corporation has a long track record of working with FEMA and other relief agencies in helping run emergency shelters, assisting law enforcement, providing food and shelter, managing donations, and helping families and communities rebuild. Hundreds of national service volunteers have directly assisted victims of the September 11 terrorist attacks by providing family services, organizing blood drives, raising funds, and counseling victim's families. (*Sources*: www.nationalservice.org/news/factsheets/homeland.html and www.nationalservice.org/news/homeland.html)

## SIDEBAR 6-8   DHS Secretary Ridge Cites Neighborhood Security as Instrumental to Homeland Security

In Falcon Heights, Minnesota, a program that trains residents to respond to potential terrorist attacks is becoming a model for other cities and states. Falcon Heights Mayor Sue Gehrz, St. Paul Mayor Randy Kelly, and other officials were joined by Homeland Security Secretary Tom Ridge at a symposium in St. Paul exploring how Americans can protect their food supply, workplaces, and homes. "The potential destruction to life and property from man-made disasters is so large that communities can no longer assume" that agencies in neighboring communities will be available to help, Gehrz said. "That means more individuals need to be trained to assist their families and neighbors until help arrives," she said.

"The only way you can secure the homeland is to make sure the hometowns are secure," Ridge told about 350 people at the symposium. The nation has strengthened security in many ways since the terror attacks of 2001, yet it still needs a greater degree of readiness, he said. "We need to consolidate most of our computer systems and databases in one seamless operation, make it easier for police to communicate with each other, with the rest of federal government, right down to the state and locals," he said.

Since the September 11 attacks, the residents of Falcon Heights have worked together to plan a response to terror attacks, Gehrz said. They have created a community manual on their "intergenerational organizing model" and provided it to more than 70 Minnesota cities and counties. It has been used in Florida, South Carolina, and Washington, DC.

In Falcon Heights, which has a population of 5,600, 65 "neighborhood liaisons" have collected the names, addresses, and phone numbers of people on their blocks, identifying who has medical training or other specialized skills or equipment that might be useful in a disaster, Gehrz said. A neighborhood commission worked with the Red Cross to provide free first-aid training for 62 residents. Police have trained 11 residents how to direct traffic during emergencies. Others will receive 21 hours of training in how to respond to emergencies. "Involving all ages helps reduce fear and protect civil rights," said Gehrz, who is trained as a psychologist. "One of the primary goals of terrorism is to make people feel isolated and vulnerable."

*Source*: "Falcon Heights Security Efforts Are Becoming a National Model," *Star Tribune*, June 20, 2003, p. 19A.

## CITIZEN CORPS

Following the tragic events that occurred on September 11, 2001, state and local government officials have increased opportunities for citizens to become an integral part of protecting the homeland and supporting local first responders. Officials agree that the formula for ensuring a more secure and safer homeland consists of preparedness, training, and citizen involvement in supporting first responders. In January 2002, President George W. Bush launched USA Freedom Corps to "capture the spirit of service that has emerged throughout our communities following the terrorist attacks."

Citizen Corps, a vital component of USA Freedom Corps, was created to help coordinate volunteer activities that can make communities safer, stronger, and better prepared to respond to emergencies. It provides opportunities for people to participate in a range of measures to make their families, their homes, and their communities safer from the threats of crime, terrorism, and disasters of all kinds.

Citizen Corps is coordinated nationally by FEMA. In this capacity, FEMA works closely with other federal entities, state and local governments, first responders and emergency managers, the volunteer community, and the White House Office of the USA Freedom Corps. One of the initiatives supported by Citizen Corps is the Community Emergency Response Teams (CERT). The program trains citizens to be better prepared to respond to emergency situations in their communities. When emergencies happen, CERT members can give critical support to first responders, provide immediate assistance to victims, and organize spontaneous volunteers at a disaster site. CERT members can also help with nonemergency projects that help improve the safety of the community.

The CERT course is taught in the community by a trained team of first responders who have completed a CERT Train-the-Trainer course conducted by their state training office for emergency management, or FEMA's Emergency Management Institute (EMI), located in Emmitsburg, Maryland. CERT training includes disaster preparedness, disaster fire suppression, basic disaster medical operations, and light search and rescue operations. More information on CERT can be found by accessing the CERT website at www.citizencorps.gov/programs/cert.shtm.

Undersecretary of DHS for Emergency Preparedness and Response Mike Brown announced in May 2003 the availability of $19 million in grant money to train citizens to be better prepared to respond to emergency situations in their communities through local CERT. The grant money represents the FY 2003 funds made available to expand the CERT program and is in addition to $17 million distributed through the FY 2002 supplemental appropriation. FEMA distributed the funds for state and local level CERT programs to each state and territory according to the formula developed through the Patriot Act. The CERT grants allowed states to fund new programs and to expand existing teams. FEMA has a goal of training 400,000 citizens through the CERT program during the next two years throughout the United States.

Another important initiative from the Citizen Corps is the Medical Reserve Corps (MRC) program, which coordinates the skills of practicing and retired physicians, nurses, and other health professionals, as well as other citizens interested in health issues who are eager to volunteer to address their community's ongoing public health needs and to help their community during large-scale emergency situations.

Local community leaders develop their own Medical Reserve Corps units and identify the duties of the MRC volunteers according to specific community needs. For example, MRC volunteers may deliver necessary public health services during a crisis, assist emergency response teams with patients, and provide care directly to those with less serious injuries and other health-related issues. More information on the MRC program can be found at www.citizencorps.gov/programs/medical.shtm.

The Neighborhood Watch Program (NWP) and Volunteers in Police Service (VIPS) programs are other homeland security–related projects of the Citizen Corps.

A relatively new partner program of the Citizen Corps initiative is the Fire Corps program. Launched in 2004, Fire Corps is a partnership between the International Association of Fire Chiefs' Volunteer and Combination Officers Section (IAFC/VCOS), the International Association of Fire Fighters (IAFF), the National Volunteer Fire Council (NVFC), and the U.S. Fire Administration (USFA). Its mission is to help career, volunteer, and combination fire departments supplement existing personnel resources by recruiting citizen advocates. In June 2005 the program signed up its first 250 fire departments in its "citizen advocates" program. The purpose of the program is to help fire departments expand existing programs—or assist in developing new ones—that recruit citizens who

donate their time and talents to support the fire service in nonoperational roles.

The FY 2004 Homeland Security Appropriations Bill provided a budget of $40 million to the Citizen Corps program. In 2005 Congress reduced the available funding to $15 million even though the president's budget asked for $50 million. The president's FY 2006 budget requested from Congress $50 million for the program.

## THE SAFE CONFERENCE

The first annual conference on "The Community and Homeland Security," in cooperation with the SAFE project, took place in San Francisco on March 27 and 28, 2003. The aim of the conference was to bring together local leaders from several states, leaders responsible for shaping homeland security programs and activities in their communities, with representatives from federal, state, local, nonprofit, private, and international organizations working on homeland security–related issues. The conference allowed all these practitioners, participants, and representatives to voice their concerns and to share their experiences and gave them their first opportunity not only to work together to identify existing problems with homeland security at the local level but to propose possible solutions to these problems (see Sidebar 6-9). A copy of the full conference report on the SAFE Conference is presented in Appendix 9.

Four principal areas of concern on the community level emerged from the discussions in the conference:

1. *Resources*: Greater access to resources to fund homeland security programs and projects at the community level
2. *Information*: Greater access to practical information about application, eligibility, recruitment, retention, and other concerns
3. *Programming*: The need for innovative and effective programming ideas
4. *Customizing*: The need to focus on diverse and "special needs" populations

To create more resources and to use available resources more effectively, the following ideas were developed in the conference:

- Block grants to communities are an efficient means for providing federal funding for community homeland security efforts.
- Communities should partner with the National Governor's Association, the United States Conference of Mayors, the League of Cities, and other professional associations seeking federal funding for community homeland security efforts.
- Creative funding ideas practiced in communities around the country need to be identified and widely disseminated among community homeland security officials.
- New partnerships need to be established with the country's business and philanthropic communities to leverage their resources for community homeland security efforts.

Suggestions for improving access to accurate and timely information regarding homeland security issues included the following:

- Establishing an information clearinghouse to catalog homeland security information sources
- Establishing a web-based "chat room" for community officials to exchange ideas and best practices and to discuss current issues
- Establishing a "funding exchange" to share ideas on funding sources and creative funding ideas
- Partnering with the Department of Homeland Security and state homeland security operations to facilitate the flow of information on federal and state programs and funding opportunities to community officials.

In addition to the homeland security programming currently in place (e.g., CERT training, Medical RSVP), conference participants identified a need to design and implement programs that fully leveraged the capabilities of volunteers in the community. Several ideas were considered, including the following:

- The SAFE Project, designed to develop volunteer programs in support of community emergency management and homeland security operations
- The development of Community Emergency Networks (CENs) designed to facilitate communications between community residents and local homeland security officials before, during, and after a disaster or terrorism incident

Some of the ideas developed in the conference regarding the "special needs" populations were as follows:

- Reprogramming Community Development Block Grant (CDBG) funding targeted for "special needs" populations to include homeland security efforts
- Establishing "language and culture banks" in communities to facilitate communications and information flow between public safety and emergency officials and "special needs" populations
- Partnering with national associations and groups that represent the interests of special needs populations such as the elderly, veterans, minority populations, children, and the disabled
- Partnering with foundations and other philanthropic organizations, such as the Annie E. Casey Foundation, which focuses its efforts and funding in disadvantaged communities
- Partnering with local emergency management/homeland security and public health operations to help these groups identify and serve special needs populations in the community

The existence of voluntary activities for homeland security, such as the SAFE conference, is important because such activities bring together different stakeholders, provide an opportunity to share expertise and best practices, and create an environment in which public–private partnerships can be initiated and brainstorming can occur.

## SIDEBAR 6-9   SAFE Conference: The Community and Homeland Security

The National Council on Crime and Delinquency (NCCD) and the SAFE Project (Securing America's Future for Everyone) hosted the first annual conference on "The Community and Homeland Security" on March 27 and March 28, 2003, in San Francisco, California. The conference brought over 60 local leaders from around the country, leaders who are responsible for shaping homeland security programs and activities in their communities together with representatives from federal, state, and local government and nonprofit, private, and international organizations working on homeland security–related issues.

The conference allowed participants to voice their concerns and share experiences and gave them their first opportunity not only to work together to identify existing problems with Homeland Security at the local level but also to propose possible solutions. The following excerpts from the conference highlight the myriad needs identified by community leaders relating to preparedness efforts at the community level:

The primary concern of those in attendance was well stated by Carol Lopes (Berkeley, California), who said, "Though there has been a lot of progress, we are willfully unprepared. Community and neighborhood preparedness is the centerpiece of today's work. Our responsibility is to prepare a community before a disaster and assist after a disaster strikes. We must train a cadre of emergency prepared individuals who will interface well with first responders."

Said Chuck Supple (GO SERV): "We must engage citizens to address problems in their own communities to have the greatest possible impact in Community Homeland Security."

Said Valli Wasp (Austin, Texas): "Preparedness must be addressed locally. We need to take this to

'homes'—get rid of the 'land,' get rid of the 'security'—this is about people protecting their homes. If you want people to listen to you, you have to go to where they live."

Said Eileen Garry (U.S. Department of Justice): "Every good idea I have ever heard came from the local level."

One participant expressed concern that "making us fundraisers, in addition to our programmatic [tasks], really stretches municipalities' resources thin. The raw numbers of people required for fundraising exhausts programs." However, such fundraising actions are recognized as vital to any program's success, echoed by Doris Milldyke (Kansas) who said, "Money is the first goal, volunteers are the second."

Ann Patton (Tulsa, Oklahoma) stated, "An information clearinghouse would be invaluable," while Doris Milldyke (Kansas) noted that information on VIPS, MRS, and other programs is "notoriously difficult to find," adding, "we need a golden key for information on getting grants."

Chuck Supple (California GO SERV) stated this position well in saying, "We've probably only thought of a 'minutia' of the areas where volunteers would be useful."

Ana-Marie Jones (Oakland, California) warned that "special needs communities are often isolated from services," adding that "[programs] must have a trusted leader who either speaks or has access to the languages of all representative groups—you need more than a 'Spanish press release.'" She suggested that participants "involve special needs communities before the disaster" to be effective.

*Source*: Coppola, D., G. D. Haddow, and J. A. Bullock. 2003. *A Report on the First Annual Conference on "The Community and Homeland Security"* (March). www.nccd-crc.org/new/chs_conference_1.pdf.

## THE AMERICAN RED CROSS

The American Red Cross has always been one of the most important partners of the federal, state, and local governments in disaster preparedness and relief operations. Some of the daily community operations of the Red Cross chapters include senior services, caregivers' support, provision of hospital and nursing home volunteers, lifeline (an electronic personal emergency response service), transportation to medical/doctor's appointments and other essential trips, food pantry and hot lunch programs, homeless shelters and transitional housing services, school clubs and community service learning programs and projects, youth programs (violence and substance abuse prevention, peer education and mentoring, leadership development camps), food and rental assistance, language banks, and community information and referral.

Besides its common missions, the Red Cross is also trying to find itself an appropriate place in the new homeland security environment. Some of the Red Cross chapters have already developed homeland security programs, in which they provide training for volunteers from local communities.

From the first $10.3 million in federal grants provided to involve citizen volunteers in homeland security efforts in 2002, the American Red Cross received $1,778,978, which was distributed by the national headquarters to many individual chapters. The recipient of the greatest portion of these funds was the Greater New York chapter, which received $500,000 of the funds for the recruitment, training, and mobilization of 5,000 new disaster volunteers equipped to respond to another terrorist attack on a local level. These volunteers will work with Red Cross service delivery units in New York to train additional volunteers, exponentially increasing the city's force of disaster relief workers.

In 2002, another $371,978 was given to the American Red Cross National Headquarters for a nationwide program aimed at increasing volunteers in communities most vulnerable to terrorist attacks. The grant supported a yearlong program with 30 Community Preparedness Corps (CPC) members working in 19 chapters. Corps members worked in chapters to ensure that all community members—totaling some 27,000,000—have a "family disaster response plan." They tailored plans for those with language barriers and disabilities and for children and the elderly. At the same time, CPC volunteers focused on minimizing intolerance across the country by teaching international humanitarian law and the principles of the International Red Cross Movement (humanity, independence, neutrality, impartiality, voluntary service, unity, and universality).

Corps members also recruited and trained an estimated 400 new volunteers and instructors who made the educational programs available to additional vulnerable communities. Ultimately, corps members working through Red Cross chapters will create a network of hundreds of skilled volunteers across the country.

Additional grants have since been awarded to Red Cross chapters nationwide. In California, funds have been dedicated to the implementation of homeland security measures in Los Angeles, San Francisco, and Sacramento. The Oregon Trail Chapter was awarded a grant funding 400 new volunteers who will perform 1,500 hours of service of disaster preparedness. On the East Coast, the Red Cross developed "Disaster Resistant Neighborhood" programs across eight wards of Washington, D.C. Through the program these communities created disaster response plans. The southeast Pennsylvania chapter received a grant to create an alliance of more than 100 nonprofits in the Philadelphia area to form the Southeast Pennsylvania Voluntary Organization Active in Disaster (VOAD) to help citizens prevent, prepare for, and respond to disasters.

In 2003, the American Red Cross participated in the Top Officials (TOPOFF) 2 national training exercise. Red Cross used this exercise to practice the screening of emergency shelter residents and supplies for radiation exposure, the logistical support when national stockpiles of medications were mobilized, and keeping the public informed as the national threat level reached the highest "red" alert. In the same year the Red Cross was actively involved with the development of the new National Response Plan. The American Red Cross was the only nongovernmental organization that was invited to the discussions.

Throughout 2004, the Red Cross taught 11 million Americans critical lifesaving skills such as first aid, water safety, caregiving, CPR, and the use of automated external defibrillators (AEDs). In addition, the number of people attending presentations or demonstrations for Together We Prepare, community disaster education awareness, and the Masters of Disasters program climbed 6% to 3.9 million. Those programs aim to create safer families and communities.

Another 2004 initiative from the Red Cross involved expanding to diverse audiences with important preparedness and other information. To achieve this goal, the Red Cross expanded and detailed its Spanish-language website and first-aid and preparedness print materials. In cooperation with the CDC the Red Cross initiated a multiyear project to develop and disseminate terrorism preparedness materials to the public.

The American Red Cross has always been a consistent and contributing partner of all disaster-related community issues. It has continuously provided products and services to restore the quality of life in communities hit by disasters. With its nationwide organization and widely distributed network of volunteer resources, the Red Cross is and will be an essential partner and supporter of the Homeland Security effort.

## THE ROLE OF THE PRIVATE SECTOR IN MITIGATION AND PREPAREDNESS ACTIVITIES

The events of September 11 brought to light the importance of private-sector involvement in crisis, emergency, and disaster management. Since that time, an ever-expanding list of private entities has begun focusing on their needs in this area. This section will discuss the essentials of private-sector business continuity planning and disaster management. Most of the components discussed next have been learned as a result of experience with natural disasters or manmade accidents; however, the September 11 attacks have proved that those important components of classical crisis management are also important for terrorism risk management.

- **Business impact analysis (BIA)**: The management level analysis by which an organization assesses the quantitative (financial) and qualitative (nonfinancial) impacts, effects, and loss that might result if the organization were to suffer a business-interrupting event. Performing BIA as a preparedness measure is important because findings from BIA are used to make decisions concerning business continuity management strategy.
- **Crisis communications planning**: Decision making about how crisis communications will be performed during an emergency is important because communication is a critical success factor for effective crisis management. Preventing rumors about your corporation as well as telling your story before someone else does it for you is only possible via a predefined communication policy.
- **IT and systems infrastructure redundancy planning**: There are different techniques and approaches regarding the enforcement of systems redundancy. Each company is unique, with its own IT and system needs and processes; therefore, customized approaches have to be employed to build more reliable systems infrastructure (e.g., backup databases, software, hardware, network redundancy).
- **Geographic location and backup sites**: The selection of the geographic location of headquarters and offices and the distribution of key executives in those buildings are strategically important decisions with regard to minimizing potential losses (both human and physical) during a disaster. The availability of backup sites that allow employees to continue operations in case of physical loss of or damage to a primary

facility is a key success factor, one that is, unfortunately, usually difficult to justify in terms of cost and benefit.

- **Transportation planning**: The transportation infrastructure is among the most sensitive infrastructures to emergency and disaster situations. Overloaded transportation infrastructure during crisis is usually a reason for micro-disasters in the midst of bigger ones. Therefore realistic transportation planning is important for a successful response.

- **Crisis leadership**: Research and experience has shown that during crisis situations people (e.g., employees, staff, customers) need someone to tell them what is going on and explain what is being done about it, even if the information this

person communicates is obsolete or redundant. Strong leadership also helps other people to regain self-esteem and motivates them to commit to the efforts to overcome the crisis.

- **Insurance**: It is important for companies to have a feasible but protective insurance policy. Realistic risk assessments and modeling are necessary to establish this economic feasibility.

There surely are other components of private-sector risk mitigation and preparedness that are not mentioned in this text, however these are the most important across the broad range of business types and sizes (Kayyem and Chang, 2002; Smith, 2002). Sidebar 6-10 provides an antiterror checklist designed by DHS to help the private sector respond to terrorism.

---

SIDEBAR 6-10   **Private-Sector Homeland Security Checklist**

The Department of Homeland Security released the following antiterror checklist for the private sector in its May 2003 Homeland Security Information Bulletin:

- Maintain situational awareness of world events and ongoing threats.
- Ensure all levels of personnel are notified via briefings, e-mail, voice mail, and signage of any changes in threat conditions and protective measures.
- Encourage personnel to be alert and immediately report any situation that may constitute a threat or suspicious activity.
- Encourage personnel to avoid routines, vary times and routes, preplan, and keep a low profile, especially during periods of high threat.
- Encourage personnel to take notice and report suspicious packages, devices, unattended briefcases, or other unusual materials immediately; inform them not to handle or attempt to move any such object.

- Encourage personnel to keep their family members and supervisors apprised of their whereabouts.
- Encourage personnel to know emergency exits and stairwells.
- Increase the number of visible security personnel wherever possible.
- Rearrange exterior vehicle barriers, traffic cones, and roadblocks to alter traffic patterns near facilities and cover by alert security forces.
- Institute/increase vehicle, foot, and roving security patrols varying in size, timing, and routes.
- Implement random security guard shift changes.
- Arrange for law enforcement vehicles to be parked randomly near entrances and exits.
- Review current contingency plans and, if not already in place, develop and implement procedures for receiving and acting on threat information; alert notification procedures;

terrorist incident response procedures; evacuation procedures; bomb threat procedures; hostage and barricade procedures; chemical, biological, radiological, and nuclear (CBRN) procedures; consequence and crisis management procedures; accountability procedures; and media procedures.

- When the aforementioned plans and procedures have been implemented, conduct internal training exercises and invite local emergency responders (fire, rescue, medical, and bomb squads) to participate in joint exercises.
- Coordinate and establish partnerships with local authorities to develop intelligence and information-sharing relationships.
- Place personnel on standby for contingency planning.
- Limit the number of access points, and strictly enforce access control procedures.
- Approach all illegally parked vehicles in and around facilities, question drivers, and direct them to move immediately; if owner cannot be identified, have vehicle towed by law enforcement.
- Consider installing telephone caller I.D.; record phone calls, if necessary.

- Increase perimeter lighting.
- Deploy visible security cameras and motion sensors.
- Remove vegetation in and around perimeters; maintain regularly.
- Institute a robust vehicle inspection program to include checking under the undercarriage of vehicles, under the hood, and in the trunk. Provide vehicle inspection training to security personnel.
- Deploy explosive detection devices and explosive detection canine teams.
- Conduct vulnerability studies focusing on physical security, structural engineering, infrastructure engineering, and power, water, and air infiltration, if feasible.
- Initiate a system to enhance mail and package screening procedures (both announced and unannounced).
- Install special locking devices on manhole covers in and around facilities.
- Implement a counter-surveillance detection program.

*Source*: Continuity Central, May 21, 2003.

## CORPORATE PREPAREDNESS AND RISK MANAGEMENT IN THE SARBANES–OXLEY ERA

The Sarbanes–Oxley Act of 2002, written by Senator Paul Sarbanes (D–Maryland) and Representative Paul Oxley (R–Ohio), was created to protect investors by improving the accuracy and reliability of corporate disclosures. The act is in direct response to financial fraud discovered in the cases of both Enron and WorldCom. However, it was created to cover issues beyond fraud (establishing a public company account-

ing oversight board, auditor independence, corporate responsibility and enhanced financial disclosure), and is now a driving force behind corporate business continuity planning. Though the phrase *business continuity planning* is not once mentioned in the language of the act, continuity professionals claim that Section 404 of the act implies such measures must be taken for compliance. Section 404 of the act reads as follows:

SEC. 404. MANAGEMENT ASSESSMENT OF INTERNAL CONTROLS.
(a) RULES REQUIRED—The Commission shall prescribe rules requiring each annual report

required by section 13(a) or 15(d) of the Securities Exchange Act of 1934 (15 U.S.C. 78m or 78o(d)) to contain an internal control report, which shall

(1) state the responsibility of management for establishing and maintaining an adequate internal control structure and procedures for financial reporting; and

(2) contain an assessment, as of the end of the most recent fiscal year of the issuer, of the effectiveness of the internal control structure and procedures of the issuer for financial reporting.

(b) INTERNAL CONTROL EVALUATION AND REPORTING—With respect to the internal control assessment required by subsection (a), each registered public accounting firm that prepares or issues the audit report for the issuer shall attest to, and report on, the assessment made by the management of the issuer. An attestation made under this subsection shall be made in accordance with standards for attestation engagements issued or adopted by the Board. Any such attestation shall not be the subject of a separate engagement.

*Source*: Sarbanes Oxley Act of 2002, http://thomas. loc.gov/cgi-bin/query/F?c107:6:./temp/~c107X5G Hak:e143423.

Section 404 of Sarbanes–Oxley Act requires companies to include an internal control report that states the responsibility of management for establishing and maintaining an adequate internal controls structure and procedures for financial reporting in their annual report. On top of that it requires the management to ensure that the effectiveness of the internal control structure is assessed on an annual basis. The section also requires the external auditing entity to report on management's assessment of the effectiveness of the company's internal controls and procedures with respect to standards defined by the Public Company Accounting Oversight Board. Compliance with the act became effective in April 2005 for most companies.

Even though the section still focuses on financial record management and process control, in order to really ensure those things, it is almost a prerequisite for the company to ensure adequate protection and continuity of its entire core processes. This is where the "business continuity" aspect of the act becomes part of the picture.

To protect the financial processes and records from misconduct or fraud, and to ensure data integrity and resilience, the first step is to identify the risks, threats, and vulnerabilities that may endanger those expectations defined by the act. This is possible through a comprehensive risk and vulnerability assessment followed by a business impact analysis (BIA) to identify the business consequences of possible adverse incidents. The BIA is usually considered as one of the main building blocks of business continuity planning, because its findings usually help the corporations identify and prioritize the risks it has to mitigate, and provide an understanding of recovery goals.

At its current stage it is early to comment on whether there is a full consensus between what the Sarbanes–Oxley Act demands from corporation and how the corporations interpret those expectations and what they are going to do about it. But it is at least true that business continuity concepts will adequately fit to address some of the expectations of the act. Business continuity service providers seem to capitalize on this connection and enlarge the market for their services and products. The fact that the Sarbanes–Oxley Act puts the top management as the holder of the pure responsibility for compliance makes it inevitable for those corporations to increase their investments for compliance. Business continuity is one of the answers.

An article that appeared in a sectoral journal (disaster-resource.com) dedicated to explain the impact of the Sarbanes–Oxley Act to the business continuity field discusses that compliance may require further than basic business continuity planning. The article explains that the act will make it inevitable to involve senior management in the planning process, to make them think and find solutions beyond their organizations, paying more attention to service level agreements, continuity of vendors, and suppliers. (*Sources*: Benvenuto, N., 2004. "The Relationship between Business Continuity and Sarbanes–Oxley," www.protiviti.com/downloads/PRO/pro-us/articles/

FeatureArticle_20040312.html, Sarbanes Oxley Act of 2002; Berman, Al, "Business Continuity in a Sarbanes–Oxley World." *Disaster Recovery Journal,* Spring 2004, www.drj.com/articles/spr04/1702-01.html; and Williams, B. "Sarbanes–Oxley: Another Driver for Business Continuity Management," www.disaster-resource.com/articles/03p_029.shtml.)

## BEST PRACTICES

The nature of crisis, emergency, and risk management is very complicated: No matter how much one may discuss the process in the theoretical sense, the complexity of the actual environment in which they must try to implement practical applications cannot be fully appreciated. The two case studies that follow will document private-sector experience with disaster and a multi-governmental approach to preparedness.

The first of the following cases details the experience of Cantor Fitzgerald, a private company devastated by September 11 attacks. Although the case is mainly concerned with response and recovery, it is included in the mitigation and preparedness chapter because it clearly illustrates the importance mitigation and preparedness play in the response to a disaster.

### CASE STUDY 1
### Cantor Fitzgerald

(Summarized from the original work of Edward Cone and Sean Gallagher)

For Joseph Noviello, September 11 began at 6:30 a.m. with a phone call confirming that an annual fishing trip with colleagues at the Cantor Fitzgerald bond trading firm was still on, despite some foul weather offshore. Minutes later, the most intense two days of his life would begin as the first plane hijacked by terrorists crashed into Cantor's building.

Watching on TV from his Manhattan apartment, Noviello had no way of knowing what lay in store.

Clearly, this was a disaster of a proportion neither he, nor likely anyone in his position, had dealt with before. Fortunately, he had a plan to follow.

That plan may have saved the company. No firm suffered a worse fate, in terms of lives lost on September 11, than Cantor Fitzgerald and its electronic marketplace unit, eSpeed. More than 700 employees of the two companies died in the destruction of the World Trade Center's north tower, where Cantor and eSpeed shared their headquarters and a vital computer center. Yet eSpeed was up and running when the bond market reopened at 8 a.m. on September 13, little more than 47 hours after the disaster.

"The difference for us was the planning we had in place," says Noviello, 36, who was promoted to eSpeed's chief information officer after the disaster. eSpeed's systems were built on a dual architecture that replicated all machines, connections, and functionality at the World Trade Center and at a Rochelle Park site, with a third facility in London.

eSpeed, which operates as a freestanding business and also serves as the trading engine for its parent company, lost 180 employees, including about half of its U.S.-based technology staff. But eSpeed had several important assets left. Most of the top technology executives had been out of the office, including Matt Claus, eSpeed's current CTO and Noviello's right-hand man, who had been scheduled to go on the fishing trip.

The response atmosphere was tense, with people unsure as to what had happened to their friends or colleagues. "For days, every time a new face came in the door it was an emotional release," says Noviello. "There was a disaster-recovery contact list, but people were seeking to find each other not for work but to find out who was OK."

Beyond the technical questions were operational details such as advising staff on public transportation options to the suburban site, reestablishing shifts, and making sure there were counselors on duty. Conference calls every two hours kept track of milestones and objectives. "We were talking at 2 a.m., at 4 a.m.," says Noviello. "Who is sleeping during something like this? Work is great therapy."

None of this effort would have succeeded without the duplicate architecture in Rochelle Park. Yet Cantor started moving into the facility only in February. From day one, Rochelle Park was seen as a concurrent system, not a disaster-recovery site.

All that redundancy would be stretched to the limit as eSpeed worked to overcome the technical hurdles between the company and the opening of the bond market Thursday morning. Two of those hurdles were huge: the loss of eSpeed's private network connections and the destruction of the company's ability to handle fulfillment of trades.

The first problem was solved by allowing customers who had overseas offices connected to Cantor's London data center to reroute across their own networks to London. eSpeed worked with customers to reconfigure their servers to point to London and moved or expanded the permissions on customer accounts to connect to that site. For customers without overseas private networks, eSpeed worked to get them access over the Internet until the customers could get their high-speed connections hooked into the Rochelle Park facility.

To solve the second issue, help arrived in the form of one of eSpeed's competitors. ICI/ADP, another electronic trading company, offered to take care of eSpeed's clearing and settling of transactions through its own connection to banks. By Wednesday night the eSpeed team had mapped its financial back-office system to ADP's system and had successfully sent test transactions to J.P. Morgan Chase & Co. and other banks. The cooperation of other companies, including vendors and fellow financial firms, turned out to be essential to Cantor/eSpeed's quick recovery.

The firm was weakened by the loss of so many people and the related shutdown of its voice-broker business. But it survived as a viable business. Thanks to planning, the company can keep operating, even if something should happen to Rochelle Park. Its data center in London will serve as the mirror site going forward.

And going forward, the company's systems should be even more resilient. "We are learning a lot of lessons as we are restoring the system," says Noviello,

FIGURE 6-4   Washington, D.C., May 13, 2003—FEMA's Emergency Support Team employees were TOPOFF2 exercise participants as well as assistants with the response and recovery efforts for the tornadoes that hit the South and Midwest. (Photo by Lauren Hobart/FEMA News Photo)

including how to automate more aspects of bringing systems back up. "And we are not restoring our bad habits."

*Source*: Case study summarized from *Baseline Magazine*, www.baselinemag.com/print_article/0,3668, a17022,00.asp.

The second case provided is adapted from a governmental preparedness activity, a drill that simulated a radiological and biological terrorist attack to the United States called TOPOFF 2 (see Figure 6-4).

## CASE STUDY 2
## TOPOFF 2

On Monday, May 12, 2003, a fake dirty bomb was detonated in downtown Seattle, releasing radioactive material throughout the metropolitan area. At the same time in Chicago, hospitals were inundated with patients complaining of flu-like symptoms associated with pneumonic plague.

Fortunately, the mastermind of both scenarios was not a terrorist group but, rather, the federal government. With a price tag of $16 million, TOPOFF 2 has been the most expensive, comprehensive emergency preparedness exercise ever undertaken.

Designed to test and improve the response capacity of "top officials" in the event of a weapons of mass destruction attack, TOPOFF 2 included more than 8,000 participants from 19 federal agencies, such as the Centers for Disease Control and Prevention (CDC) and the federal Emergency Management Agency (FEMA), as well as state and local emergency responders and the American Red Cross—the only nongovernmental agency included in the exercise.

The goals of TOPOFF 2 were to improve the nation's capacity to manage extreme events; create broader frameworks for the operation of expert crisis and consequence management systems; validate authorities, strategies, plans, policies, procedures, and protocols; and build a sustainable, systematic national exercise program to support the national strategy for homeland security.

The fake crisis began around lunchtime on Monday, with the detonation of a radioactive dirty bomb near a coffee roasting plant in Seattle. Two cars were set afire, releasing plumes of smoke. A small explosion was created. Actors playing victims began to moan and cry. A mock television-news crew broke through a police barrier to get at the action. Some of the first emergency workers on the scene ran through the wreckage. Others ambled.

Emergency response staff at all 17 King County hospitals immediately swung into action, directed by Harborview Medical Center's Emergency Services department. Staff members were able to follow the crisis on a virtual TV network set up exclusively for the drill.

A short time later, Harborview employees learned the explosive device contained radioactive material, although they didn't know what kind of radiation it involved. The decontamination team—designated emergency response medical staff, plus engineering and public safety personnel—was called in and began setting up a heated decontamination tent on the road by the hospital's emergency response wing.

Only six people arrived in the first 90 minutes of the crisis, and the rest trickled in later in the afternoon.

In the end, Harborview treated about 30 patients, all of whom "survived."

Just 24 hours later and halfway across the country, the scene was quite different as very sick people began turning up in emergency responses in Chicago and across Illinois. Their devastating symptoms were quickly diagnosed as pneumonic plague, unleashed in a biological attack by the same terrorist group.

Thirty-six people "died" among the more than 300 infected. At hospitals across the state, infected patients—volunteers wearing bright yellow T-shirts printed with "Role Player"—mixed in with real patients to test hospitals' ability to meet the crisis amid business as usual. Every once in a while, a volunteer would produce a card indicating that he or she had died.

Even more victims were represented by faxes pouring into the hospital containing a name, a diagnosis, a brief medical history, and a summary of physical findings. These "paper patients" were triaged and treated as live bodies, subject to the same hospital resource allocations.

Richard Fantus, M.D., chief of Trauma Services at Advocate Illinois Masonic Medical Center on Chicago's north side, acted as incident commander for his hospital. "We knew early on that something unusual was going on because of what was coming across the mock news network and the communications we received from the public health department," Fantus said.

But he noted that diagnosing all the emergency arrivals was not as straightforward as expected. "Victims came in with various symptoms, many having nothing to do with plague. Some had had heart attacks, some were pregnant, and some had the respiratory symptoms of SARS. Just as in real life, we had to identify who was likely to have been exposed and triage them according to respiratory symptoms," he says. "Staff was gowned and masked and everyone suspected of exposure immediately went into respiratory isolation."

Vivian Chamberlain was an actor who played a passerby when the false bomb exploded. She had to pretend that her eardrums had burst from the force of the bogus blast.

As the first patient to arrive by ambulance at Bellevue's Overlake Hospital Medical Center, Chamberlain screamed and shook, her ears bleeding, her face marked by soot. But before her injuries could be treated, Chamberlain had to be "decontaminated" of radiation.

Her gurney was wheeled into a $30,000 tent set up in the parking lot and manned by hospital staffers wearing "Level C ensembles," sealed jumpsuits with head masks and respirators costing $950 each.

Chamberlain was put on a back board and her T-shirt and shorts were cut off. Four moon-suited workers scrubbed her body with long-handled brushes and hosed her down with unheated water from a nearby fire hydrant.

"It was awful. It was freezing cold," Chamberlain later said of the "decon" shower as she stood shivering in a hospital gown, a white sheet draped over her shoulders.

All did not go smoothly. One male "victim," who was portraying someone with psychiatric problems, refused to put up a fight as instructed by the paper tag on his hand. Prodding by nurses at first could not persuade the shy young man. Finally getting with the program, he "escaped" from the roped-off area. Then hospital guards refused to capture him, saying their jurisdiction was only inside the perimeter.

"You guys need to get him *now*!" bellowed Vickie Nostrant, a veteran emergency-room nurse and one of 70 hospital staffers participating. The guards immediately complied. The incident is a small example of glitches the exercise is designed to reveal, nurses said.

At the same time agencies from around the Puget Sound area responded to the mock crisis in Seattle, and some institutions set up their own simultaneous drills.

At Pacific Lutheran University near Tacoma, students and others acted out a terrorist attack that featured a mock car bomb and a hostage situation.

As part of the overall exercise, events took place in Washington, D.C., and Chicago, where a mock bioterror attack was staged at Midway Airport, and a raid was made on a terrorists' lair. City, county, and federal officials proclaimed the drill a success.

For example, Seattle County Executive Ron Sims said he and others discovered how much work is involved in rerouting the county's transportation system. Because of the mock radiation, numerous bus lines had to be rerouted, a move that affected mass transit in King, Pierce, and Snohomish counties.

After each day's activities, local and federal officials in each city met to discuss how things went. Within a month, a 2-day conference for all participants was planned to review the exercise. By September, a full report was submitted outlining strengths and vulnerabilities.

*Sources*: www.dhs.gov/dhspublic/display?content735; www.redcross.org/news/ds/terrorism/030512TOPOFF. html; www.aamc.org/newsroom/reporter/august03/ bioterrorism.htm; www.emergencypreparednessweek. ca/mr_nr_050202_e.shtml; http://seattletimes.nwsource. com/html/localnews/134726076_topoff13m.html; www.envoyworldwide.com/News/ContinuityInsights. pdf.

## EXERCISES TO FOSTER PREPAREDNESS

The Homeland Security Council (HSC), in partnership with the DHS, and state and local homeland security agencies, has developed 15 all-hazards planning scenarios for use in national, federal, state, and local homeland security preparedness activities. These scenarios are designed to be the foundational structure for the development of national preparedness standards from which homeland security capabilities can be measured. The scenario presented in Sidebar 6-11 illustrates the HSC guidance on preparedness for a major earthquake.

## SIDEBAR 6-11   HSC Scenario 9: Major Earthquake

**Executive Summary**

- **Casualties**: 1,400 fatalities; 100,000 hospitalizations
- **Infrastructure Damage**: 150,000 buildings destroyed, 1 million buildings damaged
- **Evacuations/Displaced Persons**: 300,000 households
- **Contamination**: From hazardous materials, in some areas
- **Economic Impact**: Hundreds of billions
- **Potential for Multiple Events**: Yes, aftershocks
- **Recovery Timeline**: Months to years

**Scenario Overview**

**General Description**: Earthquakes occur when the plates that form under the Earth's surface suddenly shift, and most earthquakes occur at the boundaries where the plates meet. A fault is a fracture in the Earth's crust along which two blocks of the crust have slipped with respect to each other. The magnitude of an earthquake, usually expressed by the Richter Scale, is a measure of the amplitude of the seismic waves. The intensity, as expressed by the Modified Mercalli Scale, is a subjective measure that describes how strong a shock was felt at a particular location.

The Richter Scale is logarithmic so that a recording of 7, for example, indicates a disturbance with ground motion ten times as large as a recording of 6. A quake of magnitude 2 is the smallest quake normally felt by people. Earthquakes with a Richter value of 6 or more are commonly considered major; great earthquakes have magnitude of 8 or more. The Modified Mercalli (MM) Scale expresses the intensity of an earthquake's effects in a given locality in values ranging from I to XII. The most commonly used adaptation covers the range of intensity from the condition of "I—Not felt except by a very few

under especially favorable conditions," to "XII—Damage total. Lines of sight and level are distorted. Objects thrown upward into the air."

In this scenario, a 7.2-magnitude earthquake occurs along a fault zone in a major metropolitan area (MMA) of a city. MM Scale VIII or greater intensity ground shaking extends throughout large sections of the metropolitan area, greatly impacting a six-county region with a population of approximately 10 million people. Subsurface faulting occurs along 45 miles of the fault zone, extending along a large portion of highly populated local jurisdictions, creating a large swath of destruction. Soil liquefaction occurs in some areas, creating quicksand-like conditions.

**Timeline/Event Dynamics**: While scientists have been predicting a moderate to catastrophic earthquake in the region sometime in the future, there were no specific indications that an earthquake was imminent in the days and weeks prior to this event.

Damage includes a large multi-state area of several hundred square miles. Rapid horizontal movements associated with the earthquake shift homes off their foundations and cause some tall buildings to collapse or "pancake" as floors collapse down onto one another. Shaking is exaggerated in areas where the underlying sediment is weak or saturated with water. (Note: In the central and eastern United States, earthquake waves travel more efficiently than in the western United States. An earthquake of a given size in the central and eastern United States may cause damage over a much broader area than the same size earthquake in California.)

Several hours later, an aftershock of magnitude 8.0 occurs. Based on past events, additional aftershocks are possible. Sizable aftershocks (7.0 to 8.0 in magnitude) may occur for months after the original jolt.

**Secondary Hazards/Events**: As a result of the earthquake, hazardous contamination impacts of concern include natural gas compression stations and processing plants, oil refineries and major tank farms, and natural gas/crude oil pipelines. In addition, more than 2,000 spot fires occur and widespread debris results. Flooding may occur due to levee failures and breaks in water mains and sewage systems.

Transportation lines and nodes; power generation and distribution; communications lines; fuel storage and distribution; and various structures (ranging from dams to hospitals) may be damaged and will require damage assessment in order to continue operating. Reduced availability of services will be disruptive and costly.

Ground shaking from the earthquake has generated massive amounts of debris (more than 120 million tons) from collapsed structures. In addition, fuel pumps in several gas stations have sustained damages, leaking thousands of gallons of gasoline into the streets. There are numerous reports of toxic chemical fires, plumes with noxious fumes, and spills. Several other local waste treatment facilities have reported wastewater and sewage discharges. A large refining spill has contaminated the port facility and is spilling into the harbor. Significant concern for spilled hazardous materials from storage, overturned railcars, and chemical stockpiles make progress very slow as triage is conducted.

**Key Implications**: Approximately 1,400 fatalities occur as a direct result of the earthquake. More than 100,000 people are injured and continue to overwhelm area hospitals and medical facilities, most of which have sustained considerable damage. Approximately 18,000 of the injured require hospitalization. As many as 20,000 people are missing and may be trapped under collapsed buildings and underground commuter tunnels.

More than 1 million buildings were at least moderately damaged (40% of the buildings) and

more than 150,000 buildings have been completely destroyed.

Service disruptions are numerous to households, businesses, and military facilities. Medical services are overwhelmed and functioning hospitals are limited. Fire and Emergency Medical Services (EMS) stations and trucks were also damaged. Bridges and major highways are down or blocked and damaged runways have caused flight cancellations. There are widespread power outages and ruptures to underground fuel, oil, and natural gas lines. Water mains are broken. Wastewater primary receptors have broken, closing down systems and leaking raw sewage into the streets. As a result, public health is threatened.

More than 300,000 households have been displaced, and many businesses have lost employees and customers. The port has been adversely affected in its capacity to provide export/import and loading/unloading capabilities, and damage to vital parts of the communications infrastructure has resulted in limited communications capabilities.

The disruption to the nation's economy could be severe because the earthquake impacts major supply and transportation centers. Reconstruction, repairs, disposal, and replacement of lost infrastructure will cost billions of dollars. Replacement of lost private property and goods could also cost billions. An overall national economic downturn is probable in the wake of this event.

**Mission Areas Activated**

**Prevention/Deterrence/Protection**: After the earthquake occurs, actions should be taken to protect critical facilities from terrorist attacks and to maintain civil order.

**Emergency Assessment/Diagnosis**: Disaster assessments and aerial reconnaissance are necessary. Using real-time seismic data, the federal Emergency Management Agency (FEMA) runs an earthquake model to provide a preliminary "best guess" at the level of expected damage, subject to confirmation or modification through remote sensing and field assessments. Assessment teams must be deployed and remote sensing initiated.

**Emergency Management/Response**: Hazardous material spills must be managed. Emergency medical treatment, shelters, and food must be provided. A Joint Information Center (JIC) is established, and search and rescue teams must be placed on alert, some of which should be activated and deployed. Public utilities and other basic-needs services must be repaired as quickly as possible, and damage assessments should be conducted.

**Incident/Hazard Mitigation**: Federal support will be required to coordinate the development of plans to execute mitigation efforts to lessen the effects of future disasters. Mitigation to minimize or avoid future impacts would largely be an issue for recovery and restoration.

**Public Protection**: Structural engineers are inspecting critical building, bridge, freeway, waste facilities, etc., and inspection teams are deployed to inspect hundreds of homes for safe habitability.

**Victim Care**: The massive number of injured and displaced persons requires a warning order for the activation of Task Forces for the delivery of mass care and health and medical services. Temporary housing strategies must be considered.

**Investigation/Apprehension**: N/A (natural disaster).

**Recovery/Remediation**: Hazardous materials will contaminate many areas, and decontamination and site restoration will be a major challenge. (*Source*: DHS and the Homeland Security Council)

## CONCLUSION

Mitigation, prevention, and preparedness programs are vital to the safety and security of the nation. Since the onset of civilized societies, people have worked to limit their vulnerability to hazards once they recognized that those hazards existed. Since the attacks of September 11, the focus of mitigation has shifted primarily to mitigation, prevention, and preparedness for terrorist attacks, but the real threat has proven to be the traditional natural and man-made hazards that existed both before and after the attacks began. It is the responsibility of government, one that rests most clearly on the Department of Homeland Security, to protect the nation from the consequences of disastrous events. For that reason, it is vital that the all-hazards approach to mitigation, prevention, and preparedness be maintained.

## REVIEW QUESTIONS

1. What are the initiatives that help local communities to mitigate/prepare against potential terrorist attacks? Why is community preparedness an important component of Homeland Security?
2. What mitigation/preparedness role does the private sector have in terms of Homeland Security? Do you believe that the private sector learned lessons from the 9/11 terrorist attacks?
3. Try to define *terrorism mitigation* using the common definition of mitigation in terms of the all-hazards approach. (*Hint*: Define risk as a combination of probability and consequence, and list all potential activities that can reduce both components of the potential terrorist event.)
4. What is the importance of international consensus and cooperation for terrorism mitigation/preparedness?

5. Take a quick look at the FEMA document, FEMA 426: *Reference Manual to Mitigate Potential Terrorist Attacks against Buildings* (available at www.fema.gov). What are the two most important factors to minimize damage given by car bombs to buildings?

6. Does your family have a disaster plan? If not, start developing one. The preparedness website of the Department of Homeland Security (www.ready.gov) will help you with necessary steps to prepare your plan.

## REFERENCES

www.aamc.org/newsroom/reporter/august03/bioterrorism.htm

www.citizencorps.gov/councils/ http://www.citizencorps.gov/programs/cert.shtm

www.citizencorps.gov/programs/medical.shtm

Cone, E., and G. Sean. "Cantor Fitzgerald—Forty Seven Hours." <www.baselinemag.com/print_article/0,3668,a=17022,00.asp>

Coppola, D. P. 2003. *Annotated Organizational Chart for the Department of Homeland Security.* Washington, DC: Bullock & Haddow, LLC.

Coppola, D. P. 2003. *A Report on the First Annual Conference on "The Community and Homeland Security.* Washington, DC: Haddow and Bullock, LLC (March).

Department of Homeland Security (DHS). 2003. *Family Preparedness Guide.* Washington, DC: DHS. <www.ready.gov>

www.dhs.gov/dhspublic/display?content=735

www.dhs.gov/dhspublic/display?content=1395

www.disasterrelief.org/Disasters/020918security/

www.emergencypreparednessweek.ca/mr_nr_050202_e.shtml http://www.envoyworldwide.com/News/ContinuityInsights.pdf

Federal Emergency Management Agency. *FEMA 426: Reference Manual to Mitigate Potential Terrorist Attacks against Buildings.* <www.fema.gov/fima/antiterrorism>

www.fema.gov/nwz03/nwz03_123.shtm http://www.medicalreservecorps.gov/faq.htm

Kaplan, S. 1997. "The Words of Risk Analysis." *Risk Analysis*, vol. 17, no. 4, p. 408.

Kayyem, N. J., and E. P. Chang. 2002. "Beyond Business Continuity: The Role of the Private Sector in Preparedness Planning." Belfer Center for Science and International Affairs, John F. Kennedy School of Government, Harvard University, Cambridge, MA, http://bcsia.ksg.harvard.edu/publication.cfm?ctype=paper&item_id=345, August 2002, pp. 3–4.

www.nationalservice.org/news/factsheets/homeland.html

www.nationalservice.org/news/homeland.html

www.redcross.org/faq/0,1096,0_383_,00.html

www.redcross.org/news/ds/terrorism/030512TOPOFF.html

www.salvationarmysouth.org/isabel-9-23-03.htm

seattletimes.nwsource.com/html/localnews/134726076_topoff13m.html

Smith, J. D. 2002. "Business Continuity Management: Good Practice Guidelines." United Kingdom: Business Continuity Institute, p. 231, http://www.thebci.org/

"The Terrorist Attack with Sarin in Tokyo." 1995. <www.sos.se/SOS/PUBL/REFERENG/9803020E.htm>

# 7

# Response and Recovery

When a natural disaster such as a flood, earthquake, or hurricane occurs, or when a technological incident or terrorist attack happens, local police, fire, and emergency medical personnel are generally the first to respond. Their mission is to rescue and attend to the victims, suppress any secondary fires that may have resulted, secure and police the disaster area, and begin the process of restoring order. They are supported in this effort by local emergency management personnel and community government officials.

As the saying "practice makes perfect" goes, the past decade has provided an unprecedented number of natural and man-made disasters to test the capacity of these first responders and the nation's response system as a whole. In the vast majority of these cases, the system and its participants were considered to be efficient and effective. However, the unexpected terrorist attacks of September 11, 2001, and the anthrax events shortly thereafter, revealed certain weaknesses in this system that clearly needed to be addressed. Although the immediate response to the World Trade Center attacks actually showed the national system to be working well, there followed an unprecedented loss of lives among both civilians and first responders (Figure

7-1). Certain primary and support systems that were in place at the time did not perform as well as expected, and many established procedures were not followed.

In the aftermath of this watershed event, national, local, state, and local government agencies all initiated an evaluation process to improve on existing response procedures and protocols in light of the new knowledge and experience attained through the response to the 9/11 events. The spectacular nature of the events, and the apparent threat of subsequent events of equal or greater magnitude, mandated the generation of numerous after-action evaluations, which in turn have led to changes and improvements in the procedures and protocols that first responders will use in future events. Considering the devious dangerous potential of future terrorism events, many of these evaluations have focused attention on a relatively new concept: how best to protect first responders from harm in future attacks.

The federal government responded to this shift in response procedures by updating the Federal Response Plan. A new prescriptive and functional document, the National Response Plan (NRP), is the product of these efforts. This change was justified under the belief that, because the nature of threats facing the United States had become more complex, and

FIGURE 7-1    New York City, New York, September 27, 2001—An aerial view of the rescue and recovery operations under way in lower Manhattan at the site of the collapsed World Trade Center. (Photo by Bri Rodriguez/FEMA News Photo)

because the effect of future natural, technological, and terrorist events could cause detriment to the American way of life, a "unified national effort" is required to prepare for the response to these events before they occur again. The team members assembled to create this document were charged with making this new national response system as efficient and effective as possible, and to focus on utilizing a unified approach to managing incidents that would result in a significant reduction in the vulnerability of the United States to all hazards.

The National Response Plan, which resulted from these collective efforts, and which was released in January 2005, is billed as an all-discipline, all-hazards plan. The NRP was designed to establish a single,

comprehensive framework for the management of domestic incidents, which will likely involve many participants from all levels of government. The plan directly addresses the prevention of terrorist attacks, as well as the reduction in vulnerability to all natural and man-made hazards. Finally, it attempts to offer guidance on minimizing the damage and assisting in the recovery from any type of incident that occurs.

Although the plan places a clear emphasis on retaining the primary responsibility for initial incident response at the local level, and with the locally available assets and special capabilities for prevention, it includes a more aggressive integration between agencies in charge and seeks to establish a workable unified approach to the management of incidents, especially those involving the criminal element of terrorism.

To carry out the coordinated response approach prescribed in the National Response Plan, the federal government created the National Incident Management System (NIMS). On March 1, 2004, former DHS Director Tom Ridge announced the release of NIMS and stated that it was created in order to "provide a consistent nationwide approach for federal, state, and local governments to work effectively and efficiently together to prepare for, respond to, and recover from domestic incidents, regardless of cause, size, or complexity."

Overall, the changing nature of threats (e.g., greater population exposure, possible use of weapons of mass destruction) has been the motivator for developing a new approach to response operations. This new approach has sought to initiate a profound transformation on the response community at the state and local levels through implementation of the following four goals:

- To unify crisis and consequence management as a single, integrated function, rather than two separate functions, and integrate all existing federal emergency response plans into a single document (the NRP)
- To provide interoperability and compatibility among federal, state, and local capabilities (through NIMS)
- To enhance response and preparedness capabilities of first responders and state and local governments against all kinds of hazards and threats by providing extensive funding for equipment, training, planning, and exercises
- To integrate the private sector and the business communities at a greater extent into response activities and responsibilities in order to increase resources in hand

It is the purpose of this chapter to describe the functional and operational performance of the U.S. response system, to identify and describe the changes brought by the Department of Homeland Security (DHS), and to discuss their consequences. Chapter highlights in this regard include legislative and budgetary issues, local and state response capacities, volunteer group response mechanisms, an overview of the Incident Command System and the National Incident Management System (NIMS), the National Response Plan (FRP), and the recovery function as well as the various programs available to assist in recovery.

## RESPONSE PROCESSES

Whenever the emergency number, 911, is called for assistance for an emergency of any size, whether it be a traffic accident, a tornado sighting, or someone showing signs of a viral disease, the first responders to take the call are always local. But when the size of the disaster or incident is so large that response requirements exceed the capabilities of local responders, and the costs of inflicted damage exceed what the local government could possibly cover, the mayor or county executive will turn to the governor and state government for assistance in responding to the event and in helping the community to recover. Each state has an established system in place whereby the governor decides whether or not to intervene with personnel (including the state emergency management agency and the state National Guard), equipment, or funding. Should the disaster exceed the abilities of the state to recover, however, then there is the possibility that a national disaster has occurred.

The new National Response Plan dictates the rules by which states initiate an appeal for assistance, and by which that assistance is granted should the president so choose to declare the disaster. The process for reporting disasters is similar to the former process stipulated under the Federal Response Plan, though some fundamental changes have occurred. The following section gives a brief overview of the new process, which is described in greater detail later in this chapter.

1. Should the governor decide, based on information and damage surveys generated by

FIGURE 7-2  Denver, Colorado, March, 7, 2003—Michael Brown, undersecretary of homeland security for emergency preparedness and response and director of the Federal Emergency Management Agency, has a roundtable meeting with Colorado first responders and community leaders about FEMA's entry into the Department of Homeland Security. (Photo by Michael D. Rieger/FEMA News Photo)

community and state officials, or predictions of impending disaster or terrorist threat, that the size of the actual or anticipated disaster event has or will exceed the state's capacity to respond, the governor will make a formal request to the president for a presidential major disaster declaration. The request is prepared by state officials in cooperation with regional staff from the Federal Emergency Management Agency (FEMA) (Figure 7-2). At the federal level, the governor's request is analyzed first by the Homeland Security Operations Center (HSOC), which is the primary national hub for domestic incident management operational coordination. The DHS secretary, using information provided by the HSOC regarding the possible or actual incident, makes a recommendation to the president about whether or not a declaration is warranted. The president considers the DHS secretary's recommendation, and decides whether or not to declare the disaster an *incident of national significance*. What consti-

tutes an incident of national significance is described in Sidebar 7-1.

2. Once an incident of national significance has been declared, the secretary of homeland security and/or senior staff designated by the secretary determine the need to activate components of the NRP to conduct further assessment of the situation, initiate interagency coordination, share information with affected jurisdictions, and/or initiate the deployment of resources. At this time, federal departments and agencies are notified by the HSOC, and may be called on to staff the Interagency Incident Management Group (IIMG) and National Response Coordination Center (NRCC).

3. If an incident has already occurred, the NRP priority shifts to immediate and short-term response activities. The purpose of these activities is to preserve lives, protect property, and prevent further harm to the environment. The social, economic, and political structures of the affected community or communities are protected as well. Response actions could include the participation of law enforcement officers, fire officials, emergency medical services (mass care, public health, and medical services), officials involved in infrastructure restoration, environmental protection officials, and more.

4. Either during (if appropriate) or immediately following the response phase, the long-term recovery is initiated.

When a major disaster strikes in the United States, or when the threat of disaster is imminent, the aforementioned chronology describes how the most sophisticated and advanced emergency management system in the world responds and begins the recovery process. The fundamental pillars on which the system is built are, and continue to be, coordination and cooperation among a significant number of federal, state, and local government agencies; volunteer organizations; and, more recently, the business community.

---

**SIDEBAR 7-1   Incidents of National Significance**

The NRP bases the definition of incidents of national significance on situations related to the following four criteria set forth in Homeland Security Presidential Directive No. 5 (HSPD-5):

1. A federal department or agency acting under its own authority has requested the assistance of the secretary of homeland security.
2. The resources of state and local authorities are overwhelmed and federal assistance has been requested by the appropriate state and local authorities. Examples include:
   a. Major disasters or emergencies as defined under the Stafford Act; and
   b. Catastrophic incidents.
3. More than one federal department or agency has become substantially involved in responding to an incident. Examples include:

a. Credible threats, indications or warnings of imminent terrorist attack, or acts of terrorism directed domestically against the people, property, environment, or political or legal institutions of the United States or its territories or possessions; and
b. Threats or incidents related to high-profile, large-scale events that present high-probability targets such as National Special Security Events (NSSEs) and other special events as determined by the secretary of homeland security, in coordination with other federal departments and agencies.
4. The secretary of homeland security has been directed to assume responsibility for managing a domestic incident by the president.

*Source*: Department of Homeland Security (DHS). 2005. *The National Response Plan*. Washington, DC: DHS.

---

## LEGISLATIVE ACTIONS

The establishment of the state of homeland security as it exists today involved several bills and laws, essentially determined by homeland and national security presidential directives delivered during the years following the 9/11 attacks. The most significant include:

- The USA PATRIOT Act of 2001
- The Aviation and Transportation Security Act of 2001
- The SA 4470 Amendment
- The Public Health Security and Bioterrorism Preparedness and Response Act of 2002
- The Enhanced Border Security and Visa Entry Reform Act of 2002
- The Maritime Transportation Security Act of 2002
- The Homeland Security Act of 2002

These laws, among many other goals, attempted to clearly define the mission and organization of emergency management and terrorism preparedness in the United States. The single greatest change that resulted from these laws in the spectrum of emergency management—and also in terms of the changes that have occurred within the federal government itself—was the creation of the Department of Homeland Security. The new department created through this legislation, which integrated 22 existing federal agencies under a single cabinet-level official for the purpose of streamlining emergency management and counterterrorism activities, was vigorously debated, but finally came into existence in March 2003.

The Federal Emergency Management Agency (FEMA), which was included in this transfer, and which retained its pre-FEMA trademark name, was transferred largely intact to form one of the five DHS directorates, the Directorate of Emergency Preparedness and Response (EP&R). The EP&R mission as defined by the Homeland Security Act of 2002 is similar to that of FEMA: to ensure that the nation is prepared for catastrophes—whether natural or technological disasters or terrorist assaults—but there is now clearly a new focus that considers more carefully the terrorism hazard. This new directorate not only supports the original federal government national response and recovery strategy, but it has dedicated much of its resources to enhancing the abilities of first responders at the local level to carry out that same mission.

DHS has emphasized through its public relations efforts that it will make every effort to build on FEMA's original mission of response and recovery. They assure that DHS will continue FEMA's efforts to reduce the loss of life and property and to protect the nation's institutions from all types of hazards through risk-based emergency management. In a continuation of FEMA's mitigation role, but using new nomenclature, DHS asserts that it will further the evolution of the emergency management culture from one that reacts to disasters to one that proactively helps communities and citizens avoid becoming victims— with *prevention* being the term of choice to replace *mitigation*.

The Homeland Security Act of 2002 describes the responsibilities of the directorate as follows:

1. Helping to ensure the preparedness of emergency response providers for terrorist attacks, major disasters, and other emergencies
2. Establishing standards, conducting exercises and training, evaluating performance, and providing funds in relation to the Nuclear Incident Response Team (defined in Section 504 of the bill)
3. Providing the federal government's response to terrorist attacks and major disasters
4. Aiding the recovery from terrorist attacks and major disasters
5. Working with other federal and nonfederal agencies to build a comprehensive national incident management system

6. Consolidating existing federal government emergency response plans into a single, coordinated national response plan
7. Developing comprehensive programs for developing interoperative communications technology and ensuring that emergency response providers acquire such technology

The responsibility of providing the federal government's response to terrorist attacks and major disasters—item 3 above—is explained in detail in the act, and includes the following:

- Coordinating the overall response to terrorist attacks
- Directing the Domestic Emergency Support Team (DEST), the Strategic National Stockpile (SNS), the National Disaster Medical System (NDMS), and the Nuclear Incident Response Team (each described later in this chapter)
- Overseeing the Metropolitan Medical Response System (MMRS) and coordinating other federal response resources

It is important to note that the new responsibilities of FEMA are not intended to detract from other important functions transferred to DHS, which are also included in the EP&R Directorate, such as those of the United States Fire Administration (USFA). In almost all areas, DHS has fully preserved the authority to carry out the original functions of FEMA, including support for community initiatives that promote homeland security.

The following agencies were transferred to the EP&R Directorate:

- The Federal Emergency Management Agency (FEMA)
- The Integrated Hazard Information System of the National Oceanic and Atmospheric Administration (NOAA), which was renamed "FIRESAT"
- The National Domestic Preparedness Office (NDPO) of the Federal Bureau of Investigation (FBI)

TABLE 7-1   **Local Response Related Legislation**

| Bill | Title | Homeland purpose |
|------|-------|------------------|
| HR 3153 | State Bioterrorism Preparedness Act of 2001 | To assist states in preparing for, and responding to, biological or chemical terrorist attacks. |
| HR 3435 | Empowering Local First Responders To Fight Terrorism Act of 2001 | To provide for grants to local first responder agencies to combat terrorism and be a part of homeland defense. |
| HR 3615 | Protecting Our Schools Homeland Defense Act of 2002 | To amend the Public Health Service Act to direct the secretary of Health and Human Services to make grants to train school nurses as "first responders" in the event of a biological or chemical attack. |
| HR 5169 | Wastewater Treatment Works Security Act of 2002 | To improve the defense and response of publicly owned water treatment plants against terrorist attacks by assessing risks and locating vulnerabilities. |
| S 1520 | State Bioterrorism Preparedness Act of 2002 | To assist states in preparing for, and responding to, biological or chemical attack. |
| S 1602 | Chemical Security Act of 2001 | To protect the public against the threat of a chemical terrorist attack. |
| S 1746 | Nuclear Security Act of 2001 | To strengthen security at sensitive nuclear facilities. |
| S 2664 | First Responder Terrorism Preparedness Act of 2002 | To establish an Office of National Preparedness to coordinate terrorism preparedness and response. |

*Source*: www.acca.com/infopaks/homeland/legislativechart.pdf.

- The Domestic Emergency Support Teams (DEST) of the Department of Justice (DOJ)
- The Office of Emergency Preparedness (OEP), the National Disaster Medical System (NDMS), and the Metropolitan Medical Response System (MMRS) of the Department of Health and Human Services (HHS)
- The Strategic National Stockpile (SNS) of HHS

Other legislation that addresses local response issues is presented briefly in Table 7-1.

## BUDGET

The Department of Homeland Security receives one of the largest shares of the federal budget. Each year since its creation, its associated budget requests and funds granted have increased. In 2004, this amount was $35.6 million, which rose to $38.5 million in 2005, and to more than $41 million (requested) in 2006. Of this total allocation, approximately 13% has been dedicated to the EP&R Directorate, for which FEMA is the primary agency. Table 7-2 depicts the various EP&R programs funded under the DHS budget, including changes from the period FY 2004 through FY 2006 (as proposed).

## LOCAL RESPONSE

On an operational level, minor disasters occur daily in communities around the United States. Local fire, police, and emergency medical personnel respond to these events in a routine, systematic, and well-planned course of action (Figure 7-3). Firefighters, police officers, and emergency medical technicians respond to the scene and take immediate actions. Their job is to secure the scene and maintain order, rescue and treat those who are injured, contain and suppress fire or hazardous conditions, and retrieve the dead. Here are some notable facts about first responders that assert

TABLE 7-2 **FEMA Budgets ($ in 1,000s)**

| EP&R Component | FY 2004 | FY 2005 | FY 2006 Proposed |
|---|---|---|---|
| Disaster Relief Fund and disaster loans | 1,768,067 | 2,042,947 | 2,140,567 |
| Office of the Under Secretary; PMRR; ARO; public health; radiological emergency preparedness | 476,621 | 479,465 | 490,980 |
| Pre-Disaster Mitigation Fund and National Flood Mitigation Fund | 169,115 | 120,000 | 178,062 |
| Emergency food and shelter | 152,097 | 153,000 | 153,000 |
| Flood insurance and flood map modernization | 289,292 | 292,593 | 295,922 |
| Cerro Grande | 37,837 | 0 | 0 |
| Rescission of prior year carryover | −3,000 | −5,000 | 0 |
| Gross discretionary | 2,890,029 | 3,083,005 | 3,258,531 |
| Biodefense | 884,749 | 2,507,776 | 0 |
| National Flood Insurance Fund Account | 1,778,753 | 1,950,251 | 2,106,757 |
| **TOTALS** | **5,553,531** | **7,541,032** | **5,365,288** |

*Source*: FEMA Budget-In-Brief, Fiscal Year 2006.

their role as the real front line in the nation's defense from disasters of all categories:

- There are more than 1 million firefighters in the United States, of which approximately 750,000 are volunteers.
- Local police departments have an estimated 556,000 full-time employees, including about 436,000 sworn enforcement personnel.
- Sheriffs' offices reported about 291,000 full-time employees, including about 186,000 sworn personnel.
- There are more than 155,000 nationally registered emergency medical technicians (EMT).

*Source*: Department of Homeland Security, www.dhs. gov.

The actions of local first responders are driven by procedures and protocols developed by the responding agency agencies themselves (e.g., fire, police, and emergency medical). Most communities in the United States have developed community-wide emergency plans, now as mandated by the Disaster Mitigation Act of 2000 (DMA2000), that incorporate these procedures and protocols. In the aftermath of the Sep-

tember 11 terrorist events, many communities are reviewing and reworking their community emergency plans to include procedures and protocols for responding to all forms of terrorist attacks including bioterrorism and weapons of mass destruction (WMD). These changes are most often driven by the funds allocated for specific requirements and the programs that are designed at the federal level.

The federal government, as described earlier in the section on budgets, has supported the local level first responders heavily through funding. This funding has provided support through four primary areas:

- *Planning*: Support of state and local governments in developing comprehensive plans to prepare for and respond to a terrorist attack
- *Equipment*: Assistance for state and local first responder agencies for the purchase of a wide range of equipment needed to respond effectively to a terrorist attack, including personal protective equipment, chemical and biological detection systems, and interoperable communications gear
- *Training*: Resources to train firefighters, police officers, and emergency medical technicians to respond and operate in response to terrorist

FIGURE 7-3   New York City, New York, October 5, 2001—Rescue workers continue their efforts at the World Trade Center. (Photo by Andrea Booher/FEMA News Photo)

attacks, most notably for those that result in a chemical or biological environment

- *Exercises*: Support for a coordinated, regular program of exercises that improve response capabilities, practice mutual aid, and assess operational improvements and deficiencies.

## FIRST RESPONDER ROLES AND RESPONSIBILITIES

The roles and responsibilities of first responders are usually detailed in the community emergency plan. Citing the responsibilities of first responders after a terrorist incident provides a useful example of the scope of the changes that first responders are experiencing.

The following points are the main objectives for the first responders to a terrorist incident:

- Protect the lives and safety of the citizens and other first responders.
- Isolate, contain, and/or limit the spread of any cyber, nuclear, biological, chemical, incendiary, or explosive devices.
- Identify the type of agent and/or devices used.
- Identify and establish control zones for the suspected agent used.
- Ensure emergency responders properly follow protocol and have appropriate protective gear.
- Identify the most appropriate decontamination and/or treatment for victims.
- Establish victim services.

- Notify emergency personnel, including medical facilities, of dangers and anticipated casualties and proper measures to be followed.
- Notify appropriate state and federal agencies.
- Provide accurate and timely public information.
- Preserve as much evidence as possible to aid in the investigation process.
- Protect critical infrastructure.
- Oversee fatality management.
- Develop and enhance medical EMS.
- Protect property and environment.

*Source*: Bullock & Haddow, LLC, 2003.

## LOCAL EMERGENCY MANAGERS

It is usually the responsibility of the designated local emergency manager to develop and maintain the community emergency plans. Often, this individual shares a dual responsibility in local government, such as fire or police chief, and serves only part time as the community's emergency manager. The profession of local emergency management has been maturing since the 1980s. There are more opportunities for individuals to receive formal training in emergency management in our country. There are currently more than 80 junior college, undergraduate, and graduate programs that offer courses and degrees in emergency management and related fields. Additionally, FEMA's Emergency Management Institute (EMI) located in Emmitsburg, Maryland, offers emergency management courses on campus and through distance learning programs. EMI has also worked closely with junior colleges, colleges, universities, and graduate schools to develop course work and curriculums in emergency management. Details of EMI's Certified Emergency Manager Program are as follows:

- The International Association of Emergency Managers (IAEM) created the Certified Emergency Manager program to raise and maintain professional standards. It is an internationally recognized program that certifies achieve-

ments within the emergency management profession.
- CEM certification is a peer-review process administered through the International Association of Emergency Managers. You do not have to be an IAEM member to be certified, although IAEM membership does offer you a number of benefits that can assist you through the certification process. Certification is maintained in 5-year cycles.
- The CEM program is served by a CEM commission that is composed of emergency management professionals, including representatives from allied fields, education, the military, and private industry.
- Development of the CEM program was supported by the Federal Emergency Management Agency (FEMA), the National Emergency Management Association (NEMA), and a host of allied organizations.

*Source*: International Association of Emergency Managers, www.iaem.org.

More and more communities have designated emergency managers responsible for guiding response and recovery operations. Training and education programs in emergency management are expanding dramatically, resulting in a growing number of professionally trained and certified local emergency managers. The maturing of this profession can only lead to more effective and efficient local responses to future disaster events.

The role and responsibilities of the individual designated as the county emergency manager is also defined by the County Emergency Plan, and they show the same variance as those of the first responders on account of the widening of the incident/threats spectrum. Although no specific guidelines are given for the new roles of local managers, the essential differences will be based on the following:

- Changes in procedures for handling terrorist incidents
- Changes in response equipment

- Changes in responding agencies and protocols of cooperation
- Changes in local/state/federal operation plans

## FUNDING FOR FIRST RESPONDERS

The federal government has spent more than $13 billion on funding for first responders since the September 11 terrorist attacks, in clear recognition of their importance not only in the fight against terrorism, but also to acknowledge their role in protecting citizens from all forms of disaster. Since 2001, this has been done through the provision of funding through several programs, which often change from year to year as needs and programs are evaluated, adjusted, and reevaluated. Several of these programs and funding levels from recent years are discussed next.

On October 18, 2004, the president signed the DHS Appropriations Act of 2005, which set the levels of funding for FY 2005 homeland security activities. In an effort to streamline and better coordinate funding to the states and territories, DHS established the Office of State and Local Government Coordination and Preparedness (SLGCP), whose primary task was to prepare the nation for acts of terrorism. SLGCP, in turn, develops and implements national programs to enhance the capacity of state and local agencies to respond to terrorism (particularly those involving WMDs) and natural disasters, through coordinated training, exercises, equipment acquisition, and technical assistance. Through the SLGCP Office for Domestic Preparedness (ODP), state and local emergency prevention, preparedness, and response personnel received approximately $3 billion in funding in FY 2005 to carry out this mission.

SLGCP, through ODP, consolidated application requests and the administration of six programs, including the State Homeland Security Program, the Urban Areas Security Initiative, the Law Enforcement Terrorism Prevention Program, the Citizen Corps Program, the Emergency Management Performance Grants, and the Metropolitan Medical Response System Program Grants. All six programs were integrated into the Homeland Security Grant Program (HSGP).

The federal government provided a total of $5.056 billion in grants during FY 2003, and $3.102 billion in grants during FY 2004, to help state and local responders, public health agencies, and emergency managers prepare for disasters. There was considerable dispute between the states during these years, addressed at the congressional level, about how these funding levels should be determined. There were two schools of opposing thought—one that felt funding should include a minimum amount per state, based on the assumption that nobody can say for sure where the terrorists will strike next, and another that felt that the funding should be risk based, going to those states with populated urban centers containing obvious terrorist targets. The calculation that determined the amount allocated to each state as a factor of how many people reside in that state—the "per capita funding"— was often used to illustrate how states like Alaska were receiving much more funding per person that states believed to be obvious targets, such as New York or California. In 2005, it was decided by Congress that risk factors would be considered in the determination of funding levels for each state. Table 7-3 illustrates the state funding levels, including these per capita figures. Sidebar 7-2 highlights several of these grants, in this case those awarded during the period of September 2004 to May 2005.

TABLE 7-3  **FY 2005 Homeland Security Appropriations to the States**

| State/territory | State homeland security program | Urban areas security initiative | Law enforcement terrorism prevention program | Citizen Corps program | Emergency management performance grants | MMRS | Totals |
|---|---|---|---|---|---|---|---|
| Alabama | 17,688,796 | N/a | 6,432,290 | 224,559 | 2,896,618 | 910,368 | 28,152,631 |
| Alaska | 9,368,591 | N/a | 3,406,760 | 118,934 | 1,529,911 | 455,184 | 14,879,381 |
| Arizona | 20,021,731 | 9,996,463 | 7,280,630 | 254,176 | 3,241,450 | 910,368 | 41,704,818 |
| Arkansas | 13,854,701 | N/a | 5,038,073 | 175,885 | 2,264,789 | 227,592 | 21,561,040 |
| California | 84,613,815 | 148,278,663 | 30,768,660 | 1,074,172 | 13,790,111 | 4,096,656 | 282,622,077 |
| Colorado | 17,796,658 | 8,718,395 | 6,471,512 | 225,929 | 2,903,630 | 682,776 | 36,798,900 |
| Connecticut | 15,491,248 | N/a | 5,633,181 | 196,661 | 2,531,746 | 227,592 | 24,080,428 |
| Delaware | 9,732,926 | N/a | 3,539,246 | 123,559 | 1,588,053 | N/a | 14,983,784 |
| Washington, DC | 9,184,053 | 82,000,000 | 3,339,656 | 116,592 | 1,503,841 | N/a | 96,144,140 |
| Florida | 44,728,450 | 30,885,716 | 16,264,891 | 567,828 | 7,244,714 | 1,593,144 | 101,284,742 |
| Georgia | 26,726,187 | 13,333,567 | 9,718,613 | 339,289 | 4,345,323 | 455,184 | 54,918,163 |
| Hawaii | 10,683,582 | 6,454,763 | 3,884,939 | 135,628 | 1,743,745 | 227,592 | 23,130,249 |
| Idaho | 10,918,426 | N/a | 3,970,337 | 138,609 | 1,777,897 | N/a | 16,805,270 |
| Illinois | 35,298,886 | 48,000,000 | 12,835,959 | 448,119 | 5,782,151 | 227,592 | 102,592,707 |
| Indiana | 21,349,773 | 5,664,822 | 7,763,554 | 271,035 | 3,491,346 | 455,184 | 38,995,714 |
| Iowa | 14,326,334 | N/a | 5,209,576 | 181,873 | 2,345,389 | 227,592 | 22,290,764 |
| Kansas | 13,849,934 | N/a | 5,036,340 | 175,825 | 2,266,809 | 455,184 | 21,784,091 |
| Kentucky | 16,861,675 | 5,000,000 | 6,131,518 | 214,059 | 2,756,510 | 455,184 | 31,418,947 |
| Louisiana | 17,679,253 | 14,531,675 | 6,428,819 | 224,438 | 2,895,235 | 910,368 | 42,669,788 |
| Maine | 10,787,521 | N/a | 3,922,735 | 136,948 | 1,761,346 | N/a | 16,608,549 |
| Maryland | 19,806,423 | 11,437,517 | 7,224,154 | 252,204 | 3,242,045 | 227,592 | 42,249,934 |
| Massachusetts | 21,863,377 | 28,075,000 | 7,950,319 | 277,556 | 3,587,028 | 682,776 | 62,436,056 |
| Michigan | 29,739,930 | 17,584,608 | 10,814,538 | 377,549 | 4,875,422 | 682,776 | 64,074,873 |
| Minnesota | 18,895,426 | 5,763,411 | 6,871,064 | 239,877 | 3,086,137 | 455,184 | 35,311,099 |
| Mississippi | 14,190,727 | N/a | 5,160,264 | 180,151 | 2,322,271 | 227,592 | 22,081,006 |
| Missouri | 20,288,866 | 15,253,865 | 7,377,769 | 257,567 | 3,318,388 | 455,184 | 46,951,640 |
| Montana | 9,949,207 | N/a | 3,617,894 | 126,305 | 1,624,359 | N/a | 15,317,765 |
| Nebraska | 11,724,020 | 5,148,300 | 4,263,280 | 148,836 | 1,915,921 | 455,184 | 23,655,542 |
| Nevada | 12,806,048 | 8,456,728 | 4,657,472 | 162,598 | 2,073,887 | 227,592 | 28,386,325 |
| New Hampshire | 10,748,552 | N/a | 3,908,565 | 136,453 | 1,754,428 | 227,592 | 16,775,590 |
| New Jersey | 26,626,137 | 19,353,418 | 9,682,232 | 338,019 | 4,356,164 | 455,184 | 60,811,154 |
| New Mexico | 12,016,319 | N/a | 4,369,571 | 152,547 | 1,960,687 | 227,592 | 18,726,716 |

TABLE 7-3   (*continued*)

| State/territory | State homeland security program | Urban areas security initiative | Law enforcement terrorism prevention program | Citizen Corps program | Emergency management performance grants | MMRS | Totals |
|---|---|---|---|---|---|---|---|
| New York | 49,417,927 | 221,082,907 | 17,970,155 | 627,360 | 8,114,323 | 1,137,960 | 298,350,633 |
| North Carolina | 26,126,856 | 5,479,243 | 9,500,675 | 331,680 | 4,260,009 | 682,776 | 46,381,239 |
| North Dakota | 9,336,232 | N/a | 3,394,993 | 118,523 | 1,526,451 | N/a | 14,376,200 |
| Ohio | 32,668,546 | 26,131,917 | 1,879,471 | 414,727 | 5,363,019 | 1,365,552 | 77,823,233 |
| Oklahoma | 15,552,074 | 5,570,181 | 5,655,300 | 197,434 | 2,543,443 | 455,184 | 29,973,615 |
| Oregon | 15,655,892 | 10,491,037 | 5,693,052 | 198,752 | 2,553,324 | 227,592 | 34,819,649 |
| Pennsylvania | 34,676,612 | 33,801,680 | 12,609,677 | 440,219 | 5,687,940 | 455,184 | 87,671,312 |
| Rhode Island | 10,291,661 | N/a | 3,742,422 | 130,653 | 1,681,441 | 227,592 | 16,073,769 |
| South Carolina | 16,925,018 | N/a | 6,154,552 | 214,863 | 2,761,710 | 227,592 | 26,283,735 |
| South Dakota | 9,618,052 | N/a | 3,497,474 | 122,101 | 1,571,539 | N/a | 14,809,166 |
| Tennessee | 20,585,357 | N/a | 7,485,584 | 261,331 | 3,362,684 | 910,368 | 32,605,325 |
| Texas | 55,743,279 | 49,842,990 | 20,270,283 | 707,661 | 9,046,712 | 2,958,696 | 138,569,621 |
| Utah | 13,046,325 | N/a | 4,744,118 | 165,623 | 2,124,715 | 227,592 | 20,308,373 |
| Vermont | 9,304,415 | N/a | 3,383,424 | 118,120 | 1,520,181 | N/a | 14,326,139 |
| Virginia | 23,921,666 | N/a | 8,698,787 | 303,685 | 3,894,890 | 1,365,552 | 38,184,581 |
| Washington | 21,211,105 | 11,994,012 | 7,713,129 | 269,275 | 3,459,280 | 682,776 | 45,329,577 |
| West Virginia | 11,877,517 | N/a | 4,319,097 | 150,785 | 1,941,687 | N/a | 18,289,086 |
| Wisconsin | 19,787,345 | 6,325,872 | 7,195,398 | 251,200 | 3,236,049 | 455,184 | 37,251,048 |
| Wyoming | 9,049,826 | N/a | 3,290,846 | 114,888 | 1,478,311 | N/a | 13,933,869 |
| Puerto Rico | 16,344,796 | N/a | 5,943,562 | 207,497 | 2,673,229 | N/a | 25,169,085 |
| Virgin Islands | 2,890,316 | N/a | 1,051,024 | 36,693 | 633,753 | N/a | 4,611,785 |
| American Samoa | 2,779,462 | N/a | 1,010,713 | 35,285 | 454,033 | N/a | 4,279,493 |
| Guam | 2,990,093 | N/a | 1,087,307 | 37,959 | 590,228 | N/a | 4,705,587 |
| Northern Mariana Islands | 2,805,231 | N/a | 1,020,084 | 35,612 | 472,042 | N/a | 4,332,970 |
| Republic of the Marshall Islands | N/a | N/a | N/a | N/a | 50,075 | N/a | 50,075 |
| Federated States of Micronesia | N/a | N/a | N/a | N/a | 50,075 | N/a | 50,075 |
| **TOTALS** | **1,062,285,226** | **854,656,750** | **386,285,537** | **13,485,708** | **173,828,492** | **28,221,408** | **2,518,763,121** |

*Source*:  DHS, 2004.

**SIDEBAR 7-2**  **Examples of Grants for States, Cities, Urban Areas, and First Responders**

- *May 13, 2005*: $140 million was awarded under the Port Security Grant Program, to protect the nation's ports from acts of terrorism. The grants were based on a formula that considers three elements: threat, vulnerability, and consequence.
- *April 14, 2005*: $17.1 million awarded for shipping container security under the Operation Safe Commerce Container Cargo Security Program.
- *April 12, 2005*: $141 million awarded under the Transit Security Grant Program, to protect the nation's rail, intracity bus, and ferry systems.
- *March 2, 2005*: $91.3 million was awarded under the Buffer Zone Protection Program, to secure areas surrounding critical infrastructure and other key resource sites (identified as chemical facilities, dams, and nuclear plants).
- *December 3, 2004*: $1.66 billion was made available to all 50 states, the territories, and Washington, D.C., under the Homeland Security Grant Program. The funding is used for equipment, training, planning and exercises.

- *December 3, 2004*: $866 million was made available under the Urban Area Security Initiative (UASI) to provide additional support for the same concerns funded in t he HSGP, but for urban areas that have greater identified security needs.
- *September 30, 2004*: $46 million in funding was granted under the Metropolitan Medical Response System (MMRS) grant program, to help 114 jurisdictions enhance and maintain integrated, systematic preparedness capacities for local response to WMD high-casualty events until significant external assistance arrives.
- *September 13, 2004*: $9.9 million in grants was awarded to private bus operators to improve security on intercity bus routes.
- *September 13, 2004*: $49 million awarded in Port Security grants, to enhance security at the nation's ports and maritime facilities.

*Source*: Department of Homeland Security press releases, www. dhs.gov.

In accordance with the DHS Appropriations Act of 2005, FY 2005 allocations were determined by a formula using a base amount of 0.75% of the total allocation for each state (including the District of Columbia and the Commonwealth of Puerto Rico), and 0.25% of the total allocation for each U.S. territory with the balance of funds being distributed on a population-share basis. FY 2005 UASI funding allocations, however, were determined by a formula based on credible threat, presence of critical infrastructure, vulnerability, population, population density, law enforcement investigative and enforcement activity, and the existence of formal mutual aid agreements.

Tables 7-3 and 7-4 illustrate these levels of funding.

The following programs were funded in FY 2005 under the DHS Appropriations Act of 2005:

- **State Homeland Security Program (SHSP)**: SHSP provided financial assistance directly to each of the states and territories to prevent, respond to, and recover from acts of terrorism. SHSP supported the implementation of the State Homeland Security Strategy to address the identified planning, equipment, training, and exercise needs. In addition, SHSP supported the imple-

TABLE 7-4   **Federal Homeland Security Allocations to States in 2003 and 2004, Including Per-Capita Funding Totals**

| State | FY 03 total | FY 03 per capita | FY 04 total | FY 04 per capita | State | FY 03 total | FY 03 per capita | FY 04 total | FY 04 per capita |
|---|---|---|---|---|---|---|---|---|---|
| Alabama | $83.0 | $18.44 | $39.8 | $8.84 | Nevada | $43.9 | $19.95 | $38.9 | $17.68 |
| Alaska | $33.9 | $56.50 | $21.0 | $35.00 | New Hampshire | $37.9 | $29.15 | $24.1 | $18.54 |
| Arizona | $85.6 | $15.56 | $56.6 | $10.29 | New Jersey | $128.1 | $14.90 | $92.4 | $10.74 |
| Arkansas | $55.9 | $20.70 | $31.2 | $11.56 | New Mexico | $43.1 | $22.68 | $26.9 | $14.16 |
| California | $446.7 | $12.73 | $330.9 | $9.43 | New York | $418.2 | $21.78 | $191.5 | $10.03 |
| Colorado | $82.2 | $18.27 | $48.4 | $10.76 | North Carolina | $113.3 | $13.65 | $65.9 | $7.94 |
| Connecticut | $62.0 | $17.71 | $45.1 | $12.89 | North Dakota | $33.4 | $55.67 | $20.9 | $34.83 |
| Delaware | $30.6 | $38.25 | $21.8 | $27.25 | Ohio | $157.1 | $13.78 | $106.3 | $9.32 |
| DC | $33.6 | $56.00 | $20.6 | $34.33 | Oklahoma | $61.9 | $17.69 | $34.9 | $9.97 |
| Florida | $205.8 | $12.32 | $138.0 | $8.26 | Oregon | $69.0 | $19.71 | $43.1 | $12.31 |
| Georgia | $107.3 | $12.48 | $71.9 | $8.36 | Pennsylvania | $200.6 | $16.31 | $116.7 | $9.49 |
| Hawaii | $41.0 | $34.17 | $23.9 | $19.92 | Rhode Island | $33.9 | $30.82 | $23.0 | $20.91 |
| Idaho | $39.9 | $30.69 | $24.5 | $18.85 | South Carolina | $73.2 | $17.85 | $38.0 | $9.27 |
| Illinois | $206.4 | $16.38 | $119.6 | $9.49 | South Dakota | $34.6 | $43.25 | $21.6 | $27.00 |
| Indiana | $93.6 | $14.18 | $58.0 | $8.79 | Tennessee | $95.7 | $16.50 | $56.2 | $9.69 |
| Iowa | $62.9 | $21.69 | $32.2 | $11.10 | Texas | $284.8 | $13.06 | $163.1 | $7.48 |
| Kansas | $56.1 | $20.78 | $31.2 | $11.56 | Utah | $46.3 | $20.13 | $29.1 | $12.65 |
| Kentucky | $76.2 | $18.59 | $46.8 | $11.41 | Vermont | $33.2 | $55.33 | $20.9 | $34.83 |
| Louisiana | $84.6 | $18.80 | $54.1 | $12.02 | Virginia | $104.7 | $14.34 | $60.8 | $8.33 |
| Maine | $43.8 | $33.69 | $24.2 | $18.62 | Washington | $128.4 | $21.05 | $64.7 | $10.61 |
| Maryland | $87.6 | $15.93 | $62.1 | $11.29 | West Virginia | $47.4 | $26.33 | $26.7 | $14.83 |
| Massachusetts | $111.6 | $17.44 | $71.9 | $11.23 | Wisconsin | $85.7 | $15.87 | $54.5 | $10.09 |
| Michigan | $134.3 | $13.43 | $80.7 | $8.07 | Wyoming | $30.5 | $61.00 | $20.3 | $40.60 |
| Minnesota | $81.3 | $16.26 | $62.3 | $12.46 | Puerto Rico | $57.5 | $14.74 | $36.7 | $9.41 |
| Mississippi | $62.1 | $21.41 | $31.9 | $11.00 | US Virgin Is. | $8.0 | $80.00 | $6.7 | $67.00 |
| Missouri | $108.3 | $19.00 | $69.4 | $12.18 | American Samoa | $7.1 | $118.33 | $6.3 | $105.00 |
| Montana | $38.8 | $43.11 | $22.3 | $24.78 | Guam | $7.9 | $39.50 | $6.8 | $34.00 |
| Nebraska | $44.9 | $26.41 | $26.3 | $15.47 | Northern Marianas | $7.2 | $102.86 | $6.3 | $90.00 |
| **TOTALS** | | | | | | **$5,056.8** | **N/a** | **$3,102.1** | **N/a** |

*Source*: CRS Report RL32463, August 16, 2004.

mentation of NIMS, Homeland Security Presidential Directive No. 8: *National Preparedness*, and the National Response Plan (NRP).

- **Urban Areas Security Initiative (UASI)**: UASI provided financial assistance to address the unique planning, equipment, training, and exercise needs of high risk urban areas, and to assist them in building an enhanced and sustainable capacity to prevent, respond to, and recover from threats or acts of terrorism. Funds under FY 2005 UASI were also available to protect nonprofit organizations located within designated urban areas.

- **Law Enforcement Terrorism Prevention Program (LETPP)**: LETPP provided law enforcement communities with funds to support the following prevention activities: information sharing to preempt terrorist attacks; target hardening to reduce vulnerability of selected high value targets; recognition and mapping of potential or developing threats; counterterrorism and security planning; interoperable communications; and interdiction of terrorists before they can execute a threat or intervention activities that prevent terrorists from executing a threat. These funds could be used for planning, organization, training, exercises, and equipment.

- **Citizen Corps Program (CCP)**: Citizen Corps is the department's grass-roots initiative to actively involve all citizens in hometown security through personal preparedness, training, and volunteer service. CCP funds were used to support Citizen Corps Councils with efforts to engage citizens in preventing, preparing for, and responding to all hazards, including planning and evaluation, public education and communication, training, participation in exercises, providing proper equipment to citizens with a role in response and management of Citizen Corps volunteer programs and activities.

- **Emergency Management Performance Grants (EMPG)**: EMPG funds were used to support comprehensive emergency management at the state and local levels and to encourage the improvement of mitigation, preparedness, response, and recovery capabilities for all hazards. Funds provided under EMPG were also used to support activities that contributed to the capability to manage consequences of acts of terrorism.

- **Metropolitan Medical Response System (MMRS) Program**: MMRS funds supported MMRS jurisdictions in further enhancement of their integrated, systematic mass casualty incident preparedness to respond to mass casualty events during the first hours of a response, the time crucial to lifesaving and population protection, until significant external assistance can arrive.

In FY 2006, these grant programs changed slightly, in terms of the amount of funding proposed and the specific programs that were to be offered. These grants, and their respective proposed levels of funding, include (and are described if not detailed above) the following:

- **Urban Area Security Initiative (UASI)/ Regional Grants—$1.02 billion**
- **Targeted Infrastructure Protection Grants— $600 million**: This program will address a broad range of homeland security needs focused on enhancing the protection of critical facilities and national infrastructure, include major transportation, energy, and commerce facilities. Targeted infrastructure protection grants will be allocated with the assistance of Information Analysis and Infrastructure Protection (IAIP) Directorate, the U.S. Coast Guard, the Transportation Safety Administration (TSA), and the Domestic Nuclear Detection Office (DNDO) based on the most up-to-date assessments of existing vulnerabilities and emerging threats.
- **State Homeland Security Grants—$1.02 billion**: This formula grant, formerly based on population, will be changed such that it will now be awarded on a discretionary basis incorporating

evaluations of risk, and an application-based review of need, and consistency with national priorities. The minimum grant size, to ensure that all states receive some funding, will be no less than 0.25 percent the funding total, or approximately $2.6 million. The SLGCP is currently working with state and local government partners to prioritize the basic preparedness capabilities that each state should have. At least 20 percent of funds awarded will be dedicated to support law enforcement terrorism prevention activities.

- **Citizen Corps—$50 million**

*Source*: Department of Homeland Security. *Budget-In-Brief, Fiscal Year 2006.*

## STATE RESPONSE

Each of the 50 states and six territories that make up the United States maintains a state government Office of Emergency Management. However, where the emergency management office resides in state government varies from state to state. In California the Office of Emergency Services (OES) is located in the Office of the Governor; in Tennessee the Tennessee Emergency Management Agency (TEMA) reports to the adjunct general. In Florida the emergency management function is located in the Office of Community Affairs. National Guard adjutant generals manage state emergency management offices in just under a quarter of the states and territories, down from more than 50% just 2 years ago. All other state emergency management offices are led by civilian employees. A current list of state emergency management directors is presented in Appendix 5. There is no explicit change in most of the state response systems; the procedures remain the same while at the federal level the contact with the states is made through DHS instead of FEMA.

Funding for state emergency management offices comes principally from DHS and state budgets. His-

torically, FEMA has provided up to $175 million annually to the states to fund state and local government emergency management activities. This money is used by state emergency management agencies to hire staff, conduct training and exercises, and purchase equipment. A segment of this funding is targeted for local emergency management operations as designated by the state. State budgets provide funding for emergency management operations, but this funding historically has been inconsistent, especially in those states with minimal annual disaster activity. The principal resource available to governors in responding to a disaster event in their state is the National Guard. The resources of the National Guard that are used for disaster response include personnel, communications systems and equipment, air and road transport, heavy construction and earth-moving equipment, mass care and feeding, equipment, and emergency supplies such as beds, blankets, and medical supplies.

Response capabilities and capacities are strongest in those states and territories that experience high levels of annual disaster activity. But now, all states and territories with critical assets must strive to reinforce their capabilities against the possibility of a terrorist incident. North Carolina is one of the states that regularly faces the risk of hurricanes and floods. How the North Carolina Department of Emergency Management describes its response process on its website provides a good example state response functions.

The division's emergency response functions are coordinated in a proactive manner from the State Emergency Operations Center located in Raleigh, North Carolina. Proactive response strategies used by the division include the following:

- Area commands that are strategically located in an affected region to assist with local response efforts using state resources
- Central warehousing operations managed by the state that allow for immediate delivery of bottled water, ready-to-eat meals, blankets, tarps, and the like; field deployment teams manned by division

and other state agency personnel that assist severely affected counties; coordinate and prioritize response activity

- Incident action planning that identifies response priorities and resource requirements 12 to 24 hours in advance

The State Emergency Response Team (SERT), which is comprised of top-level management representatives of each state agency involved in response activities, provides the technical expertise and coordinates the delivery of the emergency resources used to support local emergency operations.

When resource needs are beyond the capabilities of state agencies, mutual aid from other unaffected local governments and states may be secured using the Statewide Mutual Aid agreement or Emergency Management Assistance compact. Federal assistance may also be requested through the Federal Emergency Response Team, which collocates with the SERT during major disasters. (*Source*: North Carolina Department of Emergency Management, www.dem.dcc.state.nc.us)

The changes to occur in the role and responsibilities of the state emergency managers will be based on the same principles as the local managers (i.e., changes in procedures to handle terrorist incidents; response equipment; responding agencies and protocols of cooperation; and in local/state/federal operation plans). Described next are the responsibilities of the governor for the public safety and welfare of his or her people as stated in the National Response Plan (NRP). The governor:

- Is responsible for coordinating state and local resources to address effectively the full spectrum of actions to prepare for and respond to man-made incidents, including terrorism, natural disasters, and other contingencies
- Has extraordinary powers during a contingency to suspend authority, to seize property, to direct evacuations, and to authorize emergency funds
- Plays a key role in communicating to the public, in requesting federal assistance, when state capabilities have been exceeded or exhausted, and in

helping people, businesses, and organizations to cope with disasters

- May also encourage local mutual aid and implement authorities for the state to enter into mutual aid agreements with other states and territories to facilitate resource sharing

*Source*: Department of Homeland Security (DHS). 2005. *The National Response Plan.* Washington, DC: DHS.

## VOLUNTEER GROUP RESPONSE

Volunteer groups are often on the front line of any disaster response. National groups such as the American Red Cross and the Salvation Army maintain rosters of local chapters of volunteers who are trained in emergency response. These organizations work with local, state, and federal authorities to address the immediate needs of disaster victims. These organizations provide shelter, food, and clothing to disaster victims who have had to evacuate or lost their homes to disasters large and small.

In addition to the Red Cross and the Salvation Army, there are numerous volunteer groups across the country that provide aid and comfort to disaster victims. The National Volunteer Organizations Against Disasters (NVOAD) comprises 34 national member organizations, 52 state and territorial VOADs, and a growing number of local VOADs involved in disaster response and recovery operations around the country and abroad. Formed in 1970, NVOAD helps member groups at a disaster location to coordinate and communicate in order to provide the most efficient and effective response. A list of the NVOAD member organizations is as follows:

- Adventist Community Services
- American Baptist Men USA
- American Disaster Reserve
- American Radio Relay League
- American Red Cross
- America's Second Harvest

- Ananda Marga Universal Relief Team
- Catholic Charities USA
- Christian Disaster Response
- Christian Reformed World Relief Committee
- Church of the Brethren
- Church World Service
- Convoy of Hope
- Disaster Psychiatry Outreach
- Episcopal Relief and Development
- Friends Disaster Service
- Humane Society of the United States
- International Aid
- International Critical Incident Stress Foundation
- International Relief Friendship Foundation
- Lutheran Disaster Response
- Mennonite Disaster Services
- Mercy Medical Airlift
- National Emergency Response Team
- National Organization for Victim Assistance
- Nazarene Disaster Response
- Northwest Medical Teams International
- The Points of Light Foundation
- Presbyterian Church
- REACT International
- The Salvation Army
- Society of St. Vincent De Paul
- Southern Baptist Disaster Relief
- United Jewish Communities
- United Methodist Committee on Relief
- Volunteers in Technical Assistance
- Volunteers of America
- Wider Church Ministries, United Church of Christ
- World Vision

*Source*: National Volunteer Organizations Against Disasters, 2005.

## DHS VOLUNTEER PROGRAMS

Volunteerism has been an integral part of life in the United States for decades. After the September 11, 2001, terrorist attacks, this pattern remained true. What did occur, however, is that many people who were already volunteers, as well as many people who had not been volunteering but were suddenly drawn to do so, sought out ways in which they could contribute to making their communities more secure. The federal government responded to this concern through the creation of USA Freedom Corps, which was created "in an effort to capture those opportunities [to contribute to community security] and to foster a culture of service, citizenship, and responsibility."

Citizen Corps is the arm of U.S.A. Freedom Corps that provides opportunities for citizens who want to help make their communities more secure. Since its establishment, at which time President George W. Bush called for 2 years of volunteer service from every American citizen, almost 24,000 people from all 50 states and U.S. territories have volunteered to work with one or more of the Citizen Corps programs. These include the following:

- Citizen Corps Councils
- Community Emergency Response Teams (CERT)
- Volunteers in Police Service (VIPS)
- Medical Reserve Corps
- Neighborhood Watch
- Fire Corps

While some of these programs are new, some, such as Neighborhood Watch, have been in place for more than a decade. Brief information about the programs and their response component follow along with Sidebar 7-3, which is a fact sheet about the Citizen Corps prepared by DHS.

## CITIZEN CORPS COUNCILS

Citizen Corps Councils (CCCs) are established at the state and local level to promote, organize, and run the various programs that fall under the Citizen Corps umbrella. Funding for these councils is provided by the federal government through grant awards. As of July 2005, there were Citizen Corps Councils in 55 states and U.S. territories, 1,758 local communities, all of which serve 68% of the total population of the

**FIGURE 7-4**    Map of Citizen Corps Councils in the United States and its territories. (*Source*: Citizen Corps, 2005)

United States. Figure 7-4 displays the geographic coverage of the CCCs.

## COMMUNITY EMERGENCY RESPONSE TEAMS

The Community Emergency Response Team (CERT) program began as in Los Angeles, California, in 1983. City administrators there recognized that in most emergency situations, average citizens—neighbors, coworkers, and bystanders, for example—were often on scene during the critical moments before pro-

fessional help arrives. These officials acted on the belief that, by training average citizens to perform basic search and rescue, first aid, and other critical emergency response skills, they would increase the overall resilience of the community. Additionally, should a large-scale disaster like an earthquake occur, where first response units would be stretched very thin, these trained citizens would be able to augment official services and provide an important service to the community.

Beginning in 1993, FEMA began to offer CERT training on a national level, providing funding to

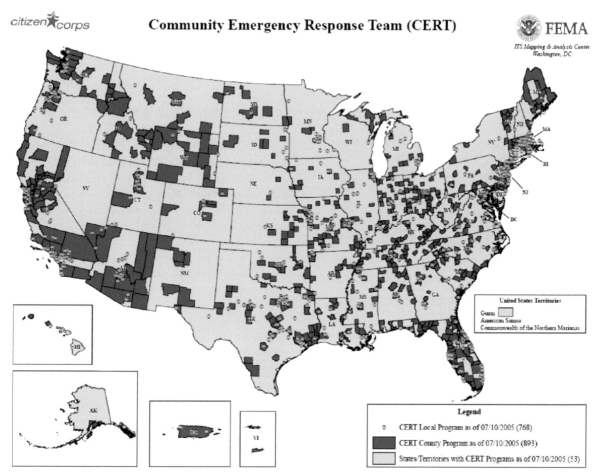

FIGURE 7-5    CERT programs in the United States and its territories. (*Source*: FEMA, 2005)

cover startup and tuition costs for programs. Since that time, CERT programs have been established in more than 1,947 communities in all 50 states, the District of Columbia, and several U.S. territories. CERT teams remain active in the community before a disaster strikes, sponsoring events such as drills, neighborhood cleanup, and disaster-education fairs. Trainers offer periodic refresher sessions to CERT members to reinforce the basic training and to keep participants involved and practiced in their skills. CERT members also offer other nonemergency assistance to the community with the goal of improving the overall safety of the community. Figure 7-5 illustrates the geographic coverage of CERT in the United States.

## VOLUNTEERS IN POLICE SERVICE PROGRAM

Since September 11, 2001, the demands on state and local law enforcement have increased dramatically. Limited resources at the community level have resulted from these increased demands, and regular police work has ultimately suffered. To address these shortfalls, the Volunteers in Police Service (VIPS) program was created. The basis of the program is that civilian volunteers are able to support police officers by doing much of the behind-the-scenes work that does not require formal law enforcement training, thereby allowing officers to spend more of their already strained schedules on the street. Though the concept is not new, the federal support for such programs is.

VIPS draws on the time and recognized talents of civilian volunteers. Volunteer roles may include performing clerical tasks, serving as an extra set of "eyes and ears," assisting with search and rescue activities, and writing citations for accessible parking violations, just to name a few. As of July 2005, there were 1,178 official VIPS programs registered throughout the United States.

## MEDICAL RESERVE CORPS PROGRAM

The Medical Reserve Corps (MRC) was founded after the 2002 State of the Union Address, to establish teams of local volunteer medical and public health professionals who can contribute their skills and experience when called on in times of need. The program relies on volunteers who are practicing and retired physicians, nurses, dentists, veterinarians, epidemiologists, and other health professionals, as well as other citizens untrained in public health but who can contribute to the community's normal and disaster public health needs in other ways (which may include interpreters, chaplains, legal advisers, etc.).

Local community leaders develop their own Medical Reserve Corps units and recruit local volunteers who address the specific community needs. For example, MRC volunteers may deliver necessary public health services during a crisis, assist emergency response teams with patients, and provide care directly to those with less serious injuries and other health-related issues. MRC volunteers may also serve a vital role by assisting their communities with ongoing public health needs (e.g., immunizations, screenings, health and nutrition education, and volunteering in community health centers and local hospitals). The MRC unit decides, in con-

cert with local officials (including the local Citizen Corps Council) on when the community Medical Reserve Corps is activated during a local emergency. As of July 2005, there were 282 MRC programs established throughout the United States.

## NEIGHBORHOOD WATCH PROGRAM

The Neighborhood Watch program has been in existence for more than 30 years in cities and counties throughout the United States. The program is based on the concept that neighbors who join together to fight crime will be able to increase security in their surrounding areas and, as result, provide an overall better quality of life for residents. Understandably, after September 11, when terrorism became a major focus of the U.S. government, the recognized importance of programs like Neighborhood Watch took on much greater significance.

The Neighborhood Watch program is not maintained by the National Sheriff's Association, which founded the program initially. At the local level, the Citizen Corps Councils help neighborhood groups that have banded together to start a program to carry out their mission. Many printed materials and other guidance are available for free to help them carry out their goals.

Neighborhood Watch programs have successfully decreased crime in many of the neighborhoods where they have been implemented. In total, as of June 2005, there were 10,153 programs spread out throughout the United States and the U.S. territories. In addition to serving a crime prevention role, Neighborhood Watch has also been used as the basis for bringing neighborhood residents together to focus on disaster preparedness and terrorism awareness; to focus on evacuation drills and exercises; and even to organize group training, such as the CERT training.

## FIRE CORPS

The Fire Corps was created in 2004 under the umbrella of USA Freedom Corps and Citizen Corps.

FIGURE 7-6 Arlington, VA, March 7, 2002—A nighttime view of the Pentagon building shows the progress made in the reconstruction of the area damaged by the terrorist attack on the Pentagon on September 11, 2001. (Photo by Jocelyn Augustino/FEMA News Photo)

The purpose of the program, like the VIPS program with the police, was to enhance the ability of fire departments to utilize citizen advocates and provide individuals with opportunities to support their local fire departments with both time and talent.

Fire Corps was created as a partnership between the International Association of Fire Chiefs' Volunteer Combination Officers Section (VCOS), the International Association of Fire Fighters (IAFF), and the National Volunteer Fire Council (NVFC). By participating in the program, concerned and interested citizens can assist in their local fire department's

activities through tasks such as administrative assistance, public education, fund-raising, data entry, accounting, public relations, and equipment and facility maintenance, just to name a few examples.

Any fire department that allows citizens to volunteer support service is considered a Fire Corps program, but programs can become official through registering with a local, county, or state CCC, if one exists. Official Fire Corps programs will be provided with assistance on how to implement a nonoperational citizen advocates program or how to improve existing programs. A Fire Corps National Advisory Committee

SIDEBAR 7-3 **Citizen Corps Fact Sheet**

- Four million more Americans participated in volunteer service in FY 2003 than in FY 2002. The total number of volunteers in FY 2003 was 63.8 million.
- Since January 2002, more than 52,000 people have each completed 20 hours of Community Emergency Response Team training, which equates to more than 1 million hours.
- There are currently more than 68,000 volunteers in the Volunteers in Police Service program and over 1,178 registered programs. Volunteers have provided more than 1 million hours of service.
- Since its inception in 2002, Medical Reserve Corps has grown to more than 27,000 members. There are 282 communities with federally funded Medical Reserve Corps units and

- another 45 that have been started with private funding.
- There are now 10,153 Neighborhood Watch groups and 1,708 law enforcement agencies registered on www.usaonwatch.org.
- Fire Corps was started in May 2004. In its first year of existence, almost 300 Fire Corps programs were created.
- The CERT program aimed to double the number of participants, with over 400,000 individuals completing the 20-plus hours of training, by the end of 2004. Train-the-Trainer sessions have been held in all 56 states and territories in order to expand the program throughout the United States.

*Source*: Department of Homeland Security, www.dhs.gov.

has been established under the program in order to provide strategic direction and collect feedback from the field. As of July 2005, there were 294 established Fire Corps programs throughout the United States and the U.S. territories.

- The Domestic Emergency Support Teams of the Department of Justice
- The Office of Emergency Preparedness
- The National Disaster Medical System
- The Metropolitan Medical Response System
- The Strategic National Stockpile

## DHS RESPONSE AGENCIES

The different agencies that were brought into DHS and merged to form the EP&R Directorate of DHS are as follows:

- The Federal Emergency Management Agency (FEMA)
- The Integrated Hazard Information System of the National Oceanic and Atmospheric Administration
- The National Domestic Preparedness Office of the Federal Bureau of Investigation

## FEDERAL EMERGENCY MANAGEMENT AGENCY

The Federal Emergency Management Agency—a former independent agency that became part of the new DHS in March 2003—is tasked with responding to, planning for, recovering from, and mitigating against disasters. Its responsibilities in the new DHS are as follows:

- Coordinate with local and state first responders to manage disasters requiring federal assistance and to recover from their effects.
- Administer the Disaster Relief Fund.

- Practice a comprehensive, risk-based approach, employing a program of preparedness, prevention, response, and recovery.
- Proactively help communities and citizens avoid becoming victims, utilizing public education and volunteerism to achieve this goal.
- Maintain administration of the National Flood Insurance Program.
- Continue training and responsibilities of the U.S. Fire Administration.
- Continue to offer mitigation grant programs, including the Hazards Mitigation Grant Program, the Pre-Disaster Mitigation Program, and the Flood Mitigation Assistance Program.
- Administer the Citizen Corps Program.

## INTEGRATED HAZARD INFORMATION SYSTEM

The Integrated Hazard Information System (IHIS) was transferred from the National Oceanic and Atmospheric Administration (NOAA). At the time of transfer, its name was changed to "FIRESAT." IHIS, originally named the Hazards Support System (HSS), was a classified information system developed by the Department of Defense (DOD) in 1997 to compile data obtained from various satellites and sensors, such as those used to detect ballistic missiles and others which continuously monitor weather conditions in the United States. In late 2000, after DOD tested the system, HSS was turned over to the U.S. Geological Survey (USGS) in the Department of the Interior and renamed IHIS, where it would be used to detect wildfires and volcanic eruptions around the world. However, Congress directed USGS to cease expenditures on IHIS, apparently because of concerns about unauthorized reprogramming of those funds. Since then, no funding has been authorized for IHIS. The agreement by Congress and the administration to move IHIS to DHS included "the transfer of workstations, software, documentation, and its communications component." However, the president did not request funding for FIRESAT for FY 2004. (Congressional Research Service, Report RS21367)

## NATIONAL DOMESTIC PREPAREDNESS OFFICE

The National Domestic Preparedness Office (NDPO), within the Department of Justice (DOJ), coordinated all federal efforts, including those of the DOD, FEMA, the Department of Health and Human Services (HHS), the Department of Energy (DOE), and the Environmental Protection Agency (EPA), to assist state and local first responders with planning, training, equipment, and exercise necessary to respond to a conventional or nonconventional WMD incident.

The NDPO was transferred into the new DHS and relocated to be part of the EP&R Directorate. Among the functions of the NDPO cited on the DHS website are the following:

- Serve as a single program and policy office for WMD to ensure that federal efforts are in harmony and represent the most effective and cost-efficient support to the state and local first responder community
- Coordinate the establishment of training curriculum and standards for first responder training to ensure consistency based on training objectives and to tailor training opportunities to meet the needs of the responder community
- Facilitate the efforts of the federal government to provide the responder community with detection, protection, analysis, and decontamination equipment necessary to prepare for, and respond to, an incident involving WMD
- Provide state and local governments with the resources and expertise necessary to design, conduct, and evaluate exercise scenarios involving WMD
- Communicate information to the state and local emergency response community

## THE DOMESTIC EMERGENCY SUPPORT TEAM (DEST)

The Domestic Emergency Support Team (DEST) is designed to be an interagency team of experts, operating on a stand-by basis, which can be quickly mobilized. This team, even within DHS, is led by the FBI to provide an on-scene commander (Special Agent in Charge) with advice and guidance in situations involving weapons of mass destruction (WMDs), or other significant domestic threats. The DEST guidance could range from information management and communications support to instructions on how to best respond to the detonation of a chemical, biological, or nuclear weapon, or a radiological dispersal device. As specialized pre-designated teams, DEST has no permanent staff at DHS, the FBI, or at any other federal agency.

## OFFICE OF EMERGENCY PREPAREDNESS

The Office of Emergency Preparedness (OEP) was responsible for oversight, coordination, and management of emergency preparedness and response and recovery activities in the Department of Health and Human Services prior to its transfer to DHS. There were two principal programs of OEP that now exist within DHS under separate functional units. They are the National Disaster Medical System (NDMS) and the Metropolitan Medical Response System (MMRS) and are described in further detail later.

Before its move into DHS, OEP served as the lead for Emergency Support Function (ESF) #8 within the Federal Response Plan—Health and Medical. Under the National Response Plan, HHS has maintained this responsibility under the new ESF #8, Public Health and Medical Services. The tasks performed by the NDMS and MMRS, which were fulfilled within ESF #8, are still performed as before but under different direction.

## THE NATIONAL DISASTER MEDICAL SYSTEM

The National Disaster Medical System (NDMS), which originally resided within the Office of Emergency Preparedness of HHS, is now located within the DHS EP&R Directorate, under the direction of FEMA's Response Division Operations Branch. NDMS is a federally coordinated system that is responsible for supporting federal agencies in the management and coordination of the federal medical response to major emergencies and federally declared disasters. In doing so, it establishes a single, integrated national medical response capability for assisting state and local authorities in dealing with the medical and health effects of major disasters. NDMS also cares for casualties of U.S. military operations overseas who have been airlifted back to the United States.

NDMS consists of more than 8,000 volunteer health professionals and support personnel organized into disaster assistance teams that can be activated and deployed anywhere in the country to assist state and local emergency medical services. Several operational units within NDMS assist in this function:

- *Disaster Medical Assistance Team (DMAT)*—A DMAT is a group of professional and para-professional medical personnel, supported by logistical and administrative staff, designed to provide medical care during a disaster or other event. Each team has a sponsoring organization, such as a major medical center, public health or safety agency, nonprofit, public, or private organization that signs a Memorandum of Agreement (MOA) with DHS. The DMAT sponsor organizes the team and recruits members, arranges training, and coordinates the dispatch of the team.
- *Disaster Mortuary Operational Response Team (DMORT)*—DMORTs, like DMATs, are composed of private citizens, each with a particular field of expertise, who are activated in the event of a disaster. During an emergency response, DMORTs work under the guidance of local authorities by providing technical assistance and personnel to recover, identify, and process deceased victims. Teams are composed of funeral directors, medical examiners, coroners, pathologists, forensic anthropologists, medical records technicians and transcribers, fingerprint specialists, forensic odontologists, dental assis-

tants, X-ray technicians, mental health specialists, computer professionals, administrative
support staff, and security and investigative
personnel. Their duties include setting up temporary morgue facilities, victim identification,
forensic dental pathology, forensic anthropology,
and processing, preparation, and disposition of
remains.

- *Veterinary Medical Assistance Team (VMAT)*—
VMATs are composed of private citizens who are
activated in the event of a disaster. During an
emergency response, VMATs work under the
guidance of local authorities by providing technical assistance and veterinary services. Teams
are composed of clinical veterinarians, veterinary
pathologists, animal health technicians (veterinary technicians), microbiologist/virologists,
epidemiologists, toxicologists and various scientific and support personnel. Their tasks include
assessing the medical needs of animals, medical
treatment and stabilization of animals, animal
disease surveillance, zoonotic disease surveillance and public health assessments, technical
assistance to ensure food and water quality, hazard mitigation, animal decontamination, and biological and chemical terrorism surveillance.

- *Federal Coordinating Centers (FCCs)*—FCCs
recruit hospitals and maintain local nonfederal
hospital participation in the NDMS, coordinate
exercise development and emergency plans with
participating hospitals and other local authorities
in order to develop patient reception, transportation, and communication plans, and during system activation, coordinate the reception and
distribution of patients being evacuated to the
area.

- *National Pharmacy Response Team (NPRT)*—
NPRTs are located in each of the 10 Department
of Homeland Security regions. NPRTs are activated in times of disaster to assist in chemo-
prophylaxis (preventive medicine) or the
vaccination of hundreds of thousands, or even
millions of Americans. They may be activated in
any scenario that is expected to require the assis-

tance of hundreds of pharmacists, pharmacy
technicians, and students of pharmacy.

- *National Nurse Response Team (NNRT)*—
NNRTs are specialty DMATs designed for use in
scenarios expected to require the activation of
hundreds of nurses to assist in chemoprophy-
laxis, a mass vaccination program, or a scenario
that overwhelms the nation's supply of nurses
in responding to a WMD event. The NNRTs are
directed by the NDMS in conjunction with a
regional team leader in each of the 10 standard
federal regions. Each NNRT is composed of
approximately 200 civilian nurses. National
Nurse Response Team members are required to
maintain appropriate certifications and licensure
within their discipline, stay current in treatment
recommendations for diseases compatible with
weapons of mass destruction, complete web-
based training courses in disaster response,
humanitarian relief, bioterrorism, and other
relevant training, participate in regular training
exercises, and be available to deploy when
needed.

## THE METROPOLITAN MEDICAL RESPONSE SYSTEM

The Metropolitan Medical Response System
(MMRS) provides funding to cities that upgrade and
improve their own planning and preparedness to
respond to mass casualty events. The concept for the
program began in 1995 in the Washington, D.C., metropolitan area with the creation of the Metropolitan
Medical Strike Team (MMST). This first team, which
pooled resources from several adjoining jurisdictions,
was created primarily for the response to chemical
incidents, but was able to provide on-site emergency
health and medical services following WMD terrorist
incidents.

The MMST concept was expanded to several
cities under the guidance and funding of the federal
government through the authority of the Defense
Against Weapons of Mass Destruction Act of 1996

(Nunn–Lugar–Domenici legislation). The program's name was changed to the Metropolitan Medical Response System to highlight its national system-oriented approach.

In 2003, the MMRS was transferred to FEMA under DHS as stipulated by the Homeland Security Act of 2002. Later, in October 2004, the program was moved again into the Office of Domestic Preparedness (ODP), but still within DHS under the Office of State and Local Government Coordination and Preparedness (SLGCP). Today, the program has grown from the 25 created in 1995 to almost 130 municipalities.

The current MMRS efforts focus on immediate site-specific response capabilities:

- Enhance existing capabilities.
- Develop overall systems plans.
- Raise awareness of WMD agents.

- Develop enhanced capability to operate in contaminated environments.
- Develop specialized treatment protocols for WMD victims.

The MMRS plans to carry out this mission through the following goals:

- Integrate biological preparedness into the overall planning process.
- Develop plans for mass prophylaxis of exposed and potentially exposed populations.
- Develop plans for mass patient care.
- Develop plans for mass fatality management.
- Develop plans for environment surety.

Sidebar 7-4 gives a more detail description of the MMRS capabilities and the difference it makes at the local level.

---

SIDEBAR 7-4   **MMRS Capabilities and Impacts**

**MMRS Capabilities**

- Initial identification of agents
- Ability to perform operations in OSHA levels A, B, and C personal protective equipment, avoiding secondary responder casualties
- Enhanced triage, treatment, and decontamination capabilities at the incident site and definitive care facilities
- Maintenance of local caches sufficient to treat 1,000 patients exposed to chemical agents
- Ability to transport uncontaminated/decontaminated patients to area hospitals for definitive care
- Ability to maintain a viable health system
- Ability to transport patients to participating NDMS hospitals throughout the nation
- Mechanisms to activate mutual aid support from local, state, and federal emergency response agencies
- Ability to integrate additional response assets into the ongoing incident command structure

**MMRS Local Level Impacts**

- Requires development of response plans unique for each city.
- Creates integrated immediate response structure.
- Creates additional local and regional support networks.
- Integrates with local mass casualty plans.
- Brings together and encourages city planning agencies to interact where they never interacted before.
- Encourages and initiates hospital WMD planning.
- Encourages local health care providers to develop appropriate medical treatment protocols.

*Source*: Department of Health and Human Services, www.hhs.gov.

## THE STRATEGIC NATIONAL STOCKPILE

The Strategic National Stockpile (SNS) began in 1999, when Congress charged HHS and CDC with the establishment of the capability to provide a resupply of large quantities of essential medical materiel to states and communities during an emergency within 12 hours of the federal decision to deploy to that region. The system that was developed was called the National Pharmaceutical Stockpile (NPS).

As stipulated in the Homeland Security Act of 2002, on March 1, 2003, the NPS was transferred from HHS to DHS, and was given the new titled Strategic National Stockpile. The program was established so that it could be managed jointly by DHS and HHS, and to be able to work with governmental and nongovernmental partners to continually seek ways to upgrade the nation's public health capacity to respond to national emergencies.

During a national emergency, state, local, and private stocks of medical materiel will be depleted quickly. The SNS is designed to help all state and local first responders bolster their response to a national emergency, through the provision of specially designed 12-hour Push Packages, private vendors, or a combination of both, depending on the situation. Like most federal response programs, the SNS is not a first response tool, but one that supplements the initial local response efforts.

The SNS is a national repository of antibiotics, chemical antidotes, antitoxins, life support medications, IV administration supplies, airway maintenance supplies, and medical/surgical items. The SNS is designed to supplement and resupply state and local public health agencies in the event of a national emergency anywhere and at anytime within the United States or its territories. The system is also set up to allow for the acquisition of additional pharmaceuticals and/or medical supplies not maintained directly by the SNS through the use of private vendors (which can ship supplies to arrive within 24 to 36 hours of the request). In some areas, the vendors, which are preregistered under the program, can actually provide the first wave of supplies that arrive.

Sidebar 7-5 gives an overview of how the SNS functions, and how its components interact with local and state organizations.

---

SIDEBAR 7-5   **The Strategic National Stockpile**

The Strategic National Stockpile (SNS) program is committed to have 12-hour Push Packages delivered anywhere in the United States or its territories within 12 hours of a federal decision to deploy. The 12-hour Push Packages have been configured to be immediately loaded onto either trucks or commercial cargo aircraft for the most rapid transportation. Concurrent to SNS transport, the SNS program will deploy its Technical Advisory Response Unit (TARU). The TARU staff will coordinate with state and local officials so that the SNS assets can be efficiently received and distributed on arrival at the site.

DHS will transfer authority for the SNS materiel to the state and local authorities once it arrives at the designated receiving and storage site. State and local authorities will then begin the breakdown of the 12-hour Push Package for distribution. SNS TARU members will remain on site in order to assist and advise state and local officials in putting the SNS assets to prompt and effective use.

The decision to deploy SNS assets may be based on evidence showing the overt release of an agent that might adversely affect public health. It is more likely, however, that subtle indicators, such as unusual morbidity and/or mortality identified

through the nation's disease outbreak surveillance and epidemiology network, will alert health
officials to the possibility (and confirmation) of a
biological or chemical incident or a national emergency. To receive SNS assets, the affected state's
governor's office will directly request the deployment of the SNS assets from CDC or DHS. DHS,
HHS, CDC, and other federal officials will evaluate
the situation and determine a prompt course of
action.

The SNS program is part of a nationwide preparedness training and education program for state
and local health care providers, first responders, and
governments (to include federal officials, governors' offices, state and local health departments,
and emergency management agencies). This train-

ing explains the SNS program's mission and operations and also alerts state and local emergency
response officials to the important issues they must
plan for in order to receive, secure, and distribute
SNS assets.

To conduct this outreach and training, CDC and
SNS program staff are currently working with
DHS, HHS agencies, regional emergency response
coordinators at all of the U.S. Public Health Service
regional offices, state and local health departments,
state emergency management offices, the Metropolitan Medical Response System cities, the Department of Veterans' Affairs, and the Department of
Defense.

*Source*: Centers for Disease Control and Prevention, www.cdc.
gov.

## URBAN SEARCH AND RESCUE

The concept of formally maintained Urban Search
and Rescue (US&R or USAR) teams began in the
early 1980s. The Fairfax County (Virginia) Fire and
Rescue and the Metro-Dade County (Florida) Fire
Department each created specialized search and rescue teams trained for rescue operations in collapsed
buildings. Urban search and rescue involves the location, rescue (extrication), and initial medical stabilization of victims trapped in confined spaces. Structural
collapse is most often the cause of victims being
trapped, but victims may also be trapped in transportation accidents, mines, and collapsed trenches.
The initial teams created to carry out these tasks were
so successful in this specialty that they were often sent
abroad on missions, representing the U.S. government
relief efforts, through support of the Department of
State and the Office of Foreign Disaster Assistance
(OFDA) of the United States Agency for International
Development (USAID). These teams have deployed

to Mexico City, the Philippines, and Armenia, providing vital search and rescue support in earthquake-
induced disasters in each of these areas.

Beginning in 1991, urban search and rescue
became a component of federal response operations
under the Federal Response Plan, when the US&R
concept was incorporated as an individual emergency
support function. From that starting point, the size of
the US&R system grew considerably, with FEMA
sponsoring the creation of 25 national urban search
and rescue task forces. There are now a total of 28
national task forces, staffed and equipped to conduct
round-the-clock search and rescue operations following any disaster that requires their specialized talents
and equipment. In 2003, when FEMA was transferred
into DHS, the US&R system transferred with FEMA,
intact. FEMA, under DHS, maintains its primary
agency designation under ESF #9, Urban Search and
Rescue.

Sidebar 7-6 provides information about how the
teams are structured and how they operate.

## SIDEBAR 7-6   The Urban Search and Rescue Teams

If a disaster event warrants national US&R support, DHS will deploy the three closest task forces within 6 hours of notification and additional teams as necessary. The role of these task forces is to support state and local emergency responders' efforts to locate victims and manage recovery operations.

- Each task force consists of two 31-person teams, four canines, and a comprehensive equipment cache. For every US&R task force, there are 62 positions. To ensure that a full team can respond to an emergency, the task forces have at the ready more than 130 highly trained members.
- A task force is really a partnership between local fire departments, law enforcement agencies, federal and local governmental agencies, and private companies.
- A task force is totally self-sufficient for the first 72 hours of a deployment.
- The equipment cache used to support a task force weighs nearly 60,000 pounds and is worth about $1.4 million. Add the task force members to the cache, and you can completely fill a military C-141 transport or two C-130s.
- US&R task force members work in four areas of specialization: search, to find victims trapped after a disaster; rescue, which includes safely digging victims out of tons of collapsed concrete and metal; technical, made up of structural specialists who make rescues safe for the rescuers; and medical, which cares for the victims before and after a rescue.

- In addition to search and rescue support, DHS provides hands-on training in search and rescue techniques and equipment, technical assistance to local communities, and in some cases federal grants to help communities better prepare for US&R operations.
- The bottom line in US&R: Someday lives may be saved because of the skills these rescuers gain. These first responders consistently go to the front lines when the nation needs them most.
- Not only are these first responders a national resource that can be deployed to a major disaster or structural collapse anywhere in the country, they are also the local firefighters and paramedics who answer local 911 calls.
- Events such as the 1995 bombing of the Alfred P. Murrah Federal Office Building in Oklahoma City, the Northridge earthquake, the Kansas grain elevator explosion in 1998, and earthquakes in Turkey and Greece in 1999 underscore the need for highly skilled teams to rescue trapped victims.
- What the task force can do: Conduct physical search and rescue in collapsed buildings; provide emergency medical care to trapped victims; deploy search and rescue dogs; assess and control gas, electric service, and hazardous materials; and evaluate and stabilize damaged structures.

*Source*: Federal Emergency Management Agency, www.fema.gov; and Department of Homeland Security, www.dhs.gov.

## MARITIME SEARCH AND RESCUE

The United States Coast Guard (USCG) is one of only two federal agencies (including the United States Secret Service) that transferred into the new Department of Homeland Security as an independent entity, thus reporting directly to the secretary of homeland security as opposed to one of the five directorates. The USCG maintains several distinct missions within

DHS, but one of those, search and rescue, has resulted in strong cooperation with FEMA and the EP&R Directorate. Specifically, USCG maintains the authority and responsibility for the various tasks related to maritime search and rescue.

Maritime search and rescue (SAR) is one of the Coast Guard's oldest missions. Minimizing the loss of life, injury, property damage, or loss by rendering aid to persons in distress and property in the maritime environment has always been a Coast Guard priority. Coast Guard SAR response involves multiple-mission stations, cutters, aircraft, and boats linked by communications networks. The Coast Guard is the SAR coordinator for U.S. aeronautical and maritime search and rescue regions that are near America's oceans, including Alaska and Hawaii. To meet this responsibility, the Coast Guard maintains SAR facilities on the East, West, and Gulf coasts; in Alaska, Hawaii, Guam, and Puerto Rico; and on the Great Lakes and inland U.S. waterways.

The USCG maintains that, in performing their SAR goal, they are guided by two program objectives:

1. Save at least 93% of those people at risk of death on waters over which the Coast Guard has SAR responsibility.
2. Prevent the loss of at least 80% of the property that is at risk of destruction on the waters over which the Coast Guard has SAR responsibility.

Additionally, USCG maintains standards of operation by which they plan to fulfill these goals and objectives:

- *Response Standards*:
  - *Readiness*: Search and rescue unit ready to proceed within 30 minutes of notification of a distress.
  - *Transit*: Search and rescue unit on scene, or within the search area, within 90 minutes of getting under way.
- *VHF-FM Distress Net Standard*: 100 percent VHF-FM continuous coverage to receive a 1-W signal out to 20 nautical miles around the U.S. Atlantic, Pacific, Gulf of Mexico, and Great Lakes coasts. This is the primary distress alerting and SAR communications method for U.S. coastal waters.
- *406-MHz Emergency Position Indicating Radio Beacon (EPIRB)*: Maximum use of the 406-MHz EPIRB in the offshore environment. The beacon's superior alerting, position indicating, and signaling capabilities significantly improve system effectiveness and efficiency. Beacon registration provides useful SAR response information and mitigates false alarm response costs. Currently about 70% of U.S. beacons are registered.
- *Command and Control Standard*: Initiate action within 5 minutes of initial notification of a distress incident. Process and evaluate information about the SAR incident and determine appropriate action.
- *Computer Assisted Search Planning (CASP) System Standard*: Use CASP for planning guidance for all cases involving incidents outside the 30 fathom mark when:
  - The duration of an incident has or could have exceed 24 hours, and
  - There is uncertainty concerning the incident time, incident location, or type of search object(s) involved.
- *Automated Mutual-Assistance Vessel Rescue (AMVER) System Standard*: Use AMVER for identification of rescue resources for all cases involving incidents on the high seas. The Coast Guard actively seeks to increase participation in this voluntary reporting system. Each year, more vessels participate in the system and more lives are saved.
- *SAR Planner Training Standard for SAR Mission Coordinators*: 100 percent attendance and completion of resident SAR planner training at the National SAR School for Area, District, Section, and Group SAR planners.

The Coast Guard currently maintains six separate programs under the Maritime Search and Rescue Program, as briefly described in Sidebar 7-7.

## SIDEBAR 7-7   U.S. Coast Guard Search and Rescue Programs

### Rescue 21

The Coast Guard currently uses the National Distress and Response System to monitor for maritime distress calls and coordinate response operations. The system consists of a network of VHF-FM antenna sites with analog transceivers that are remotely controlled by regional communications centers and rescue boat stations providing coverage out to approximately 20 nautical miles from the shore in most areas.

### Salvage Assistance and Technical Support

The Marine Safety Center Salvage Assistance and Response Teams provide on-scene technical support during maritime catastrophes in order to predict events and mitigate their impact.

### Operational Command, Control, and Communications

The National Strike Force Coordination Center (NSFCC) provides oversight and strategic direction to the strike teams, ensuring enhanced interoperability through a program of standardized operating procedures for response, equipment, training, and qualifications. The NSFCC conducts at least six major government-led spill response exercises each year under the National Preparedness for Response Exercise program; maintains a national logistics network, using the Response Resource Inventory; implements the Coast Guard Oil Spill Removal Organization program; and administers the National Maintenance Contract for the Coast Guard's $30 million inventory of propositioned spill response equipment.

### AMVER

AMVER (Automated Mutual-assistance Vessel Rescue) is a ship-reporting system for search and rescue. It is a global system that enables identification of other ships in the area of a ship in distress, which could then be sent to its assistance. AMVER information is used only for search and rescue and is made available to any rescue coordination center in the world responding to a search and rescue case. The Coast Guard actively seeks to increase participation in this voluntary reporting system. Each year, more vessels participate in the system and more lives are saved. Currently, ships from more than 143 nations participate.

AMVER represents "free" safety insurance during a voyage by improving the chances for aid in an emergency. By regular reporting, someone knows where a ship is at all times on its voyage in the event of an emergency. AMVER can reduce the time lost for vessels responding to calls for assistance by orchestrating a rescue response, utilizing ships in the best position or with the best capability to avoid unnecessary diversions in response to a Mayday or SOS call.

### Pollution Control

The Response Operations Division develops and maintains policies for marine pollution response. They also coordinate activities with the international community, intelligence agencies, and the federal government in matters concerning threats or acts of terrorism in U.S. ports and territorial waters.

### The National Strike Force

The National Strike Force (NSF) was established in 1973 as a direct result of the Federal Water Pollution Control Act of 1972. The NSF's mission is to provide highly trained, experienced personnel and specialized equipment to Coast Guard and other federal agencies to facilitate preparedness and response to oil and hazardous substance pollution incidents in order to protect public health and the environment. The NSF's area of responsibility covers all Coast Guard districts and federal response regions.

The strike teams provide rapid response support in incident management, site safety, contractor performance monitoring, resource documentation, response strategies, hazard assessment, oil spill dis-persant and operational effectiveness monitoring, and high-capacity lightering and offshore-skimming capabilities.

*Source*: Department of Homeland Security, www.dhs.gov.

## OTHER RESPONSE AGENCIES

The agencies listed in the preceding section all operate directly under the Department of Homeland Security, and in most cases, under the Federal Emergency Management Agency. However, several other agencies also provide emergency response capabilities to the federal response system, operating in their respective organizations without any clear day-to-day contact with DHS. These agencies can all be called on to provide their services in times of need, whether an incident of national significance occurs or not. These departments and agencies are discussed next.

## THE FEDERAL BUREAU OF INVESTIGATION

The Federal Bureau of Investigation (FBI), part of the Department of Justice, is the lead federal agency (LFA) for crisis management and investigation of all terrorism-related matters, including incidents involving a WMD. Within the FBI's role as LFA, the FBI federal on-scene commander (OSC) coordinates the overall federal response until the attorney general transfers the LFA role to DHS EP&R (Figure 7-7). The main concerned units within the FBI are as follows:

- *FBI Domestic Terrorism/Counterterrorism Planning Section (DTCTPS)*: The DTCTPS serves as the point of contact (POC) to the FBI field offices and command structure as well as other federal agencies in incidences of terrorism, the use or suspected use of WMD, and/or the evaluation of threat credibility. If the FBI's Strategic Information and Operations Center (SIOC) is operational for exercises or actual incidents, the DTCTPS ill provide staff personnel to facilitate the operation of SIOC.
- *FBI Laboratory Division*: Within the FBI's Laboratory Division reside numerous assets, which can deploy to provide assistance in a terrorism/WMD incident. The Hazardous Materials Response Unit (HMRU) personnel are highly trained and knowledgeable and are equipped to direct and assist in the collection of hazardous and/or toxic evidence in a contaminated environment.
- *FBI Critical Incident Response Group (CIRG)*: The Crisis Management Unit (CMU), which conducts training and exercises for the FBI and has developed the concept of the Joint Operations Center (JOC), is available to provide on-scene assistance to the incident and integrate the concept of the JOC and the Incident Command System (ICS) to create efficient management of the situation.

## DEPARTMENT OF DEFENSE

In the event of a terrorist attack or an act of nature on American soil resulting in the release of chemical, biological, radiological, or nuclear material or high-yield explosive (CBRNE) devices, the local law enforcement, fire, and emergency medical personnel who are first to respond may become quickly overwhelmed by the magnitude of the attack. The Department of Defense (DOD) has many unique war-fighting support capabilities, both technical and operational, that could be used in support of state and

FIGURE 7-7   New York City, New York, September 18, 2001—FBI members look on toward the wreckage at the World Trade Center. (Photo by Andrea Booher/FEMA News Photo)

local authorities, if requested by DHS, as the lead federal agency, to support and manage the consequences of such a domestic event.

When requested, the DOD will provide its unique and extensive resources in accordance with the following principles. First, DOD will ensure an unequivocal chain of responsibility, authority, and accountability for its actions to ensure the American people that the military will follow the basic constructs of lawful action when an emergency occurs. Second, in the event of a catastrophic CBRNE event, DOD will always play a supporting role to the LFA in accordance with all applicable law and plans. Third, DOD support will emphasize its natural role, skills, and structures to mass mobilize and provide logistical support. Fourth, DOD will purchase equipment and provide support in areas that are largely related to its war-fighting mission. Fifth, reserve component forces are DOD's forward-deployed forces for domestic consequence management.

All official requests for DOD support to CBRNE consequence management (CM) incidents are made by the LFA to the executive secretary of the DOD. While the LFA may submit the requests for DOD assistance through other DOD channels, immediately upon receipt, any request that comes to any DOD element shall be forwarded to the executive secretary. In each instance the executive secretary will take the necessary action so that the deputy secretary can determine whether the incident warrants special operational management. In such instances, upon issuance of secretary of defense guidance to the chairman of the Joint Chiefs of Staff (CJCS), the Joint Staff will translate the secretary's decisions into military orders for these CBRNE-CM events, under the policy oversight of the ATSD(CS). If the deputy secretary of defense determines that DOD support for a particular CBRNE-CM incident does not require special consequence management procedures, the secretary of the Army will exercise authority as the DOD executive agent through normal director of Military Support, Military Support to Civil Authorities (MSCA) procedures, with policy oversight by the ATSD(CS).

Additionally, DOD has established 10 Weapons of Mass Destruction Civil Support Teams (WMD-CST), each composed of 22 well-trained and equipped full-time National Guard personnel. Upon secretary of defense certification, one WMD-CST will be stationed in each of the 10 FEMA regions around the country, ready to provide support when directed by their respective governors. Their mission is to deploy rapidly, assist local responders in determining the precise nature of an attack, provide expert technical advice, and help pave the way for the identification and arrival of follow-on military assets. By congressional direction, DOD is in the process of establishing and training an additional 17 WMD-CSTs to support the U.S. population. Interstate agreements provide a process for the WMD-CST and other National Guard assets to be used by neighboring states. If national security requirements dictate, these units may be transferred to federal service.

In August 2005, the Department of Defense announced that it had, for the first time, created operational plans of war that included U.S. territory, primarily for use in the response to a major terrorist attack within the nation's borders. The plans are based on 15 possible attack scenarios that assume simultaneous attacks throughout the country.

Northern Command, the military sector created in 2002 whose territory includes the United States, developed the domestic war plans. In the event of military involvement, according to these plans, ground troop responsibilities would range from crowd control to high-end, full-scale disaster management following attacks that utilize WMDs.

What is important to note about these plans, the first of their kind, is that they maintain in explicit verbiage that military assets utilized in a domestic incident will be provided in support of civilian response units, including police, fire, and EMS officials. They do allow, however, for the military to assume command in mass casualty situations where local response units are clearly overwhelmed and no longer able to adequately perform their duties.

These military plans are based on two separate documents, entitled CONPLAN 2002 and CONPLAN 0500 (CONPLAN is short for "Concept Plan"). CONPLAN 2002 was drafted to centralize missions of domestic basis into a single document, covering land, sea, and air operations. The plan covers the pre- and post-attack timeframes, which enables the military to help prevent terrorist attacks from occurring (either within or outside the United States). CONPLAN 0500, on the other hand, covers the organizational response to the 15 hypothetical scenarios mentioned earlier. These two plans have yet to gain approval of the secretary of defense.

These plans represent a great advancement for military planning. Though it was always assumed that the military may have to lend support in the response to a large-scale terrorist attack within the United States, no formalized plans had been created to dictate how that would be carried out. Through these plans, the military will be able to formalize both its responsibilities and capabilities, and will likely be able to exercise in this role before its members are required to perform.

Organizations that are concerned with civil liberties have raised alarm about the idea of greater military involvement in homeland security operations. These groups feel that such defined military involvement could go against the 1878 Posse Comitatus Act, which prevents military forces from participating in domestic law enforcement in any form (this act was reiterated in the Homeland Security Act of 2002). However, military drafters of the two CONPLANs assert that the military role would fall under Article 2 of the Constitution, which allows the president to use the military to defend the nation as he sees fit, which is allowable under the Posse Comitatus Act (*Washington Post,* 2005).

## DEPARTMENT OF ENERGY

Through its Office of Emergency Response, the Department of Energy (DOE) manages radiological emergency response assets that support both crisis and consequence management response in the event of an incident involving a WMD. DOE is prepared to respond immediately to any type of radiological accident or incident with its radiological emergency response assets.

Through its Office of Nonproliferation and National Security, DOE coordinates activities in nonproliferation, international nuclear safety, and communicated threat assessment. DOE maintains the following capabilities that support domestic terrorism preparedness and response:

- *Aerial Measuring System (AMS)*: AMS is an aircraft-operated radiation detection system that uses fixed-wing aircraft and helicopters equipped with state-of-the-art technology instrumentation to track, monitor, and sample airborne radioactive plumes and/or detect and measure radioactive material deposited on the ground.
- *Atmospheric Release Advisory Capability (ARAC)*: ARAC is a computer-based atmospheric dispersion and deposition modeling capability operated by Lawrence Livermore National Laboratory (LLNL) and its role in an emergency begins when a nuclear, chemical, or other hazardous material is, or has the potential of being, released into the atmosphere. ARAC's capability consists of meteorologists and other technical staff using three-dimensional computer models and real-time weather data to project the dispersion and deposition of radioactive material in the environment.
- *Accident Response Group (ARG)*: ARG is DOE's primary emergency response capability for

responding to emergencies involving U.S. nuclear weapons. ARG members will deploy with highly specialized, state-of-the-art equipment for weapons recovery and monitoring operations. ARG advance elements focus on initial assessment and provide preliminary advice to decision makers.

- *Federal Radiological Monitoring and Assessment Center (FRMAC)*: For major radiological emergencies affecting the United States, the DOE establishes a FRMAC. The center is the control point for all federal assets involved in the monitoring and assessment of off-site radiological conditions. FRMAC provides support to the affected states, coordinates federal off-site radiological environmental monitoring and assessment activities, maintains a technical liaison with tribal nations and state and local governments, responds to the assessment needs of the LFA, and meets the statutory responsibilities of the participating federal agency.
- *Nuclear Emergency Search Team (NEST)*: NEST is DOE's program for dealing with the technical aspects of nuclear or radiological terrorism. Response teams vary in size from a five-person technical advisory team to a tailored deployment of dozens of searchers and scientists who can locate and then conduct or support technical operations on a suspected nuclear device.
- *Radiological Assistance Program (RAP)*: Under RAP, DOE provides, upon request, radiological assistance to DOE program elements, other federal agencies, state, tribal, and local governments, private groups, and individuals. RAP provides resources (trained personnel and equipment) to evaluate, assess, advise, and assist in the mitigation of actual or perceived radiation hazards and risks to workers, the public, and the environment.
- *Radiation Emergency Assistance Center/Training Site (REAC/TS)*: The REAC/TS is managed by DOE's Oak Ridge Institute for Science and Education in Oak Ridge, Tennessee, and it maintains a 24-hour response center staffed with

personnel and equipment to support medical aspects of radiological emergencies.

- *Communicated Threat Credibility Assessment*: DOE is the program manager for the Nuclear Assessment Program (NAP) at LLNL. The NAP is a DOE-funded asset specifically designed to provide technical, operational, and behavioral assessments of the credibility of communicated threats directed against the U.S. government and its interests.
- *Nuclear Incident Response*: This program provides expert personnel and specialized equipment to a number of federal emergency response entities that deal with nuclear emergencies, nuclear accidents, and nuclear terrorism. The emergency response personnel are experts in such fields as device assessment, device disablement, intelligence analysis, credibility assessment, and health physics.

## DEPARTMENT OF HEALTH AND HUMAN SERVICES

The Department of Health and Human Services (HHS), as the lead federal agency for Emergency Support Function (ESF) #8 (health and medical services), provides coordinated federal assistance to supplement state and local resources in response to public health and medical care needs following a major disaster or emergency. Additionally, HHS provides support during developing or potential medical situations and has the responsibility for federal support of food, drug, and sanitation issues. Resources are furnished when state and local resources are overwhelmed and public health and/or medical assistance is requested from the federal government.

HHS, in its primary agency role for ESF #8, coordinates the provision of federal health and medical assistance to fulfill the requirements identified by the affected state/local authorities having jurisdiction. Included in ESF #8 is overall public health response; triage, treatment, and transportation of victims of the disaster; and evacuation of patients out of the disaster area, as needed, into a network of military services,

veterans affairs, and preenrolled nonfederal hospitals located in the major metropolitan areas of the United States.

ESF #8 utilizes resources primarily available from

1. Within HHS
2. ESF #8 support agencies
3. The National Disaster Medical System
4. Specific nonfederal sources (major pharmaceutical suppliers, hospital supply vendors, international disaster response organizations, and international health organizations)

Other than the agencies integrated under FEMA, the CDC may also be used in response activities. CDC is the federal agency responsible for protecting the public health of the country through prevention and control of diseases and for response to public health emergencies. CDC works with national and international agencies to eradicate or control communicable diseases and other preventable conditions. The CDC's Bioterrorism Preparedness and Response Program oversees the agency's effort to prepare state and local governments to respond to acts of bioterrorism. In addition, CDC has designated emergency response personnel throughout the agency who are responsible for responding to biological, chemical, and radiological terrorism. CDC has epidemiologists trained to investigate and control outbreaks or illnesses, as well as laboratories capable of quantifying an individual's exposure to biological or chemical agents.

## ENVIRONMENTAL PROTECTION AGENCY

The Environmental Protection Agency (EPA) is chartered to respond to WMD releases under the National Oil and Hazardous Substances Pollution Contingency Plan (NCP) regardless of the cause of the release. EPA is authorized by the Comprehensive Environmental Response, Compensation, and Liability Act (CERCLA); the Oil Pollution Act; and the Emergency Planning and Community Right-to-Know Act to support federal, state, and local responders in counterterrorism.

EPA will provide support to the FBI during crisis management in response to a terrorist incident. In its crisis management role, the EPA on-scene commander (OSC) may provide the FBI special agent in charge (SAC) with technical advice and recommendations, scientific and technical assessments, and assistance (as needed) to state and local responders. The EPA's OSC will support DHS during consequence management for the incident. EPA carries out its response according to the FRP, ESF #10, and Hazardous Materials. The OSC may request an environmental response team that is funded by EPA if the terrorist incident exceeds available local and regional resources. EPA is the chair of the National Response Team (NRT).

## DEPARTMENT OF AGRICULTURE

It is the policy of the U.S. Department of Agriculture (USDA) to be prepared to respond swiftly in the event of national security, natural disaster, technological, and other emergencies at the national, regional, state, and county levels to provide support and comfort to the people of the United States. USDA has a major role in ensuring the safety of food for all Americans. One concern is bioterrorism and its effect on agriculture in rural America, namely, crops in the field, animals on the hoof, and food-safety issues related to food in the food chain between the slaughterhouse and/or processing facilities and the consumer.

- *The Office of Crisis Planning and Management (OCPM)*: This USDA office coordinates the emergency planning, preparedness, and crisis management functions and the suitability for employment investigations of the department.
- *USDA State Emergency Boards (SEBs)*: The SEBs have responsibility for coordinating USDA emergency activities at the state level.
- *The Farm Service Agency*: This USDA agency develops and administers emergency plans and controls covering food processing, storage, and

wholesale distribution; distribution and use of seed; and manufacture, distribution, and use of livestock and poultry feed.
- *The Food and Nutrition Service (FNS)*: This USDA agency provides food assistance in officially designated disaster areas on request by the designated state agency. Generally, the food assistance response from FNS includes authorization of Emergency Food Stamp Program benefits and use of USDA-donated foods for emergency mass feeding and household distribution, as necessary. FNS also maintains a current inventory of USDA-donated food held in federal, state, and commercial warehouses and provides leadership to the FRP under ESF #11, Food.
- *Food Safety and Inspection Service*: This USDA agency inspects meat and meat products, poultry and poultry products, and egg products in slaughtering and processing plants; assists the Food and Drug Administration in the inspection of other food products; develops plans and procedures for radiological emergency response in accordance with the Federal Radiological Emergency Response Plan (FRERP); and provides support, as required, to the FRP at the national and regional levels.
- *Natural Resources Conservation Service*: This USDA agency provides technical assistance to individuals, communities, and governments relating to proper use of land for agricultural production; provides assistance in determining the extent of damage to agricultural land and water; and provides support to the FRP under ESF #3, Public Works and Engineering.
- *Agricultural Research Service (ARS)*: This USDA agency develops and carries out all necessary research programs related to crop or livestock diseases; provides technical support for emergency programs and activities in the areas of planning, prevention, detection, treatment, and management of consequences; provides technical support for the development of guidance information on the effects of radiation, biological, and chemical agents on agriculture; develops

and maintains a current inventory of ARS-controlled laboratories that can be mobilized on short notice for emergency testing of food, feed, and water safety; and provides biological, chemical, and radiological safety support for USDA.

- *Economic Research Service*: This USDA agency, in cooperation with other departmental agencies, analyzes the impacts of the emergency on the U.S. agricultural system, as well as on rural communities, as part of the process of developing strategies to respond to the effects of an emergency.
- *Rural Business-Cooperative Service*: This USDA agency, in cooperation with other government agencies at all levels, promotes economic development in affected rural areas by developing strategies that respond to the conditions created by an emergency.
- *Cooperative State Research, Education, and Extension Service (CSREES)*: This USDA agency coordinates use of land-grant and other cooperating state college and university services and other relevant research institutions in carrying out all responsibilities for emergency programs.
- *Rural Housing Service*: This USDA agency will assist the Department of Housing and Urban Development by providing living quarters in unoccupied rural housing in an emergency situation.
- *Rural Utilities Service*: This USDA agency will provide support to the FRP under ESF #12, Energy, at the national level.
- *Office of Inspector General (OIG)*: This USDA office is the department's principal law enforcement component and liaison with the FBI. OIG, in concert with appropriate federal, state, and local agencies, is prepared to investigate any terrorist attacks relating to the nation's agriculture sector, to identify subjects, interview witnesses, and secure evidence in preparation for federal prosecution. As necessary, OIG will examine USDA programs regarding counterterrorism-related matters.

- *Forest Service (FS)*: This USDA agency will prevent and control fires in rural areas in cooperation with state, local, and tribal governments and appropriate federal departments and agencies. They will determine and report requirements for equipment, personnel, fuels, chemicals, and other materials needed for carrying out assigned duties.

## NUCLEAR REGULATORY COMMISSION

The Nuclear Regulatory Commission (NRC) is the lead federal agency (in accordance with the Federal Radiological Emergency Response Plan) for facilities or materials regulated by NRC or by an NRC Agreement State. NRC's counterterrorism-specific role, at these facilities or material sites, is to exercise the federal lead for radiological safety while supporting other federal, state, and local agencies in crisis and consequence management.

- *Radiological Safety Assessment*: NRC will provide the facility (or for materials, the user) technical advice to ensure on-site measures are taken to mitigate off-site consequences; serve as the primary federal source of information regarding on-site radiological conditions and off-site radiological effects; will support the technical needs of other agencies by providing descriptions of devices or facilities containing radiological materials and assessing the safety impact of terrorist actions and of proposed tactical operations of any responders. Safety assessments will be coordinated through NRC liaison at the Domestic Emergency Support Team (DEST), Strategic Information and Operations Center (SIOC), Command Post (CP), and Joint Operations Center (JOC).
- *Protective Action Recommendations*: NRC will contact state and local authorities and offer advice and assistance on the technical assessment of the radiological hazard and, if requested, provide advice on protective actions for the

FIGURE 7-8    New York City, New York, September 21, 2001—Rescue operations continue far into the night at the World Trade Center. (Photo by Andrea Booher/FEMA News Photo)

public. NRC will coordinate any recommendations for protective actions through NRC liaison at the CP or JOC.

- *Responder Radiation Protection*: NRC will assess the potential radiological hazards to any responders and coordinate with the facility radiation protection staff to ensure that personnel responding to the scene are observing the appropriate precautions.
- *Information Coordination*: NRC will supply other responders and government officials with timely information concerning the radiological aspects of the event. NRC will liaison with the Joint Information Center to coordinate information concerning the federal response.

## THE NATIONAL INCIDENT MANAGEMENT SYSTEM

A difficult issue in any response operation is determining who is in charge of the overall response effort at the incident. This concept of control, or leadership, is most commonly referred to in the emergency management community as *incident command*. With the significant shift in legislation brought about by the creation of the Department of Homeland Security, and the new emphasis on terrorism, this issue of incident command was in danger of becoming even more difficult and, likewise, confusing and even conflicting. To address the concerns that many officials at the local, state, and federal levels expressed in light of the changes that were occurring in the emergency management world, President George W. Bush called on the secretary of homeland security, by means of Homeland Security Presidential Directive No. 5, to develop a nationally based incident command system. The purpose of this system, it was assumed, was to provide a consistent nationwide approach for federal, state, tribal, and local governments to work together to prepare for, prevent, respond to and recover from domestic incidents—regardless of their cause, size or complexity.

On March 1, 2004, following the collective efforts of state and local government officials, representatives from a wide range of public safety organizations, and the Department of Homeland Security, the product result of HSPD-5 was released. The National Incident Management System (NIMS), as it is called, incorporated existing knowledge, lessons learned, and best practices into a new comprehensive national approach to domestic incident management and command that appeared to fully account for the many recent changes in federal response requirements that resulted for the reasons mentioned above. This document was created such that it addressed all jurisdictional levels and all functional disciplines involved in emergency management.

The NIMS represents a core set of doctrine, principles, terminology, and organizational processes to enable the management of disasters at all government levels. One very important aspect of this new framework is that it recognized the value of an existing system, the Incident Command System (ICS), and stressed the importance of effective incident command as a way of better managing disaster events. The well-known National Commission on Terrorist Attacks Upon the United States (the 9/11 Commission) identified ICS as an answer to many of the coordination problems that arose during the response to the September 11 attacks, and recommended a national adoption of ICS to enhance command, control, and communications capabilities during disaster response.

To better understand the processes by which NIMS helps in the management of events requiring multiple levels of government, it is necessary to have a brief understanding of the Incident Command System. The ICS was developed in California in 1970 after a devastating wildfire. During the after-action analysis of the response to the fire, which caused hundreds of millions of dollars in damage, killed 16 people, and left hundreds of families without homes, it was recognized that problems with communications and with coordination between different agencies made operations much less effective than they could have been. Following this analysis, Congress mandated that a system be created to address these coordination issues, and the result was a system called FIRESCOPE ICS, developed by the U.S. Forest Service, the California Department of Forestry and Fire Protection, the Governor's Office of Emergency Services, and several local and county fire departments.

FIRESCOPE ICS effectively standardized the response to wildfires in California. It resulted in a common terminology being used by all responding agencies, which significantly reduced the confusion. It established common procedures to be applied to firefighting, which significantly reduced the amount of time needed to coordinate between two or more agencies that would be working together on attacking a fire. Several "field tests" had shown that the system was effective, and by 1981 it was being applied throughout Southern California. So effective was FIRESCOPE ICS at standardizing coordination to wildfire events, that departments began to apply its methods to other events unrelated to wildfires. It was soon recognized as being effective for the response to floods, hazardous materials (HAZMAT) spills and leaks, earthquakes, and even major transportation accidents.

There are multiple functions in the ICS. They include common use of terminology, integrated communications, a unified command structure, resource management, and action planning. There is a planned set of directives that includes assigning one coordinator to manage the infrastructure of the response and assigning personnel, deploying equipment, obtaining resources, and working with the numerous agencies that respond to the disaster scene. In most instances, the local fire chief or fire commissioner is designated the incident commander.

The ICS was designed to remain effective at each of the following three levels of incident escalation:

1. Single jurisdiction and/or single agency
2. Single jurisdiction with multiagency support
3. Multijurisdictional and/or multiagency support

There are five major management systems within the ICS. They include command, operations, planning, logistics, and finance. Each is described here:

1. The command section includes developing, directing, and maintaining communication and collaboration with the multiple agencies on site, as well as working with local officials, the public, and the media to provide up-to-date information regarding the disaster.
2. The operations section handles the tactical operations, coordinates the command objectives, develops tactical operations, and organizes and directs all resources to the disaster site.
3. The planning section provides the necessary information to the command center to develop the action plan to accomplish the objectives. This section also collects and evaluates information as it is made available.
4. The logistics section provides personnel, equipment, and support for the command center. This section handles the coordination of all services that are involved in the response from locating rescue equipment to coordinating the response for volunteer organizations such as the Salvation Army and the Red Cross.
5. The finance section is responsible for the accounting for funds used during the response and recovery aspect of the disaster. The finance section monitors costs related to the incident and provides accounting procurement time recording cost analyses.

Under the ICS, there is almost always a single incident commander. However, even under this single command figure, the ICS allows for something called a *unified command* (UC). Unified command is often used when there is more than one agency with incident jurisdiction or when incidents cross political jurisdictions. Within this UC framework, agencies are able to work together through the designated members of the UC, often with a senior official from each agency or discipline participating in the UC, to establish a common set of objectives and strategies and a single plan of action. Due to the nature of disasters, multiple government agencies often need to work together to monitor the response and manage the large number of personnel responding to the scene. ICS allows for the integration of the agencies to operate under a single response management.

Though it is upon this ICS system that NIMS was built, it goes beyond the initial scope of the original system. This is to be expected, of course, considering the exponentially greater size of the largest incidents that will be managed under NIMS, although NIMS could be used effectively to manage small single-jurisdictional events such as house fires or automobile accidents. NIMS establishes standardized incident management processes, protocols, and procedures that all responders, whether they are federal, state, tribal, or local, can use to coordinate and conduct their cooperative response actions. Using these standardized procedures, it is presumed that all responders will be able to share a common understanding, and will be able to work together with very little mismatch. The following are the key components of the new incident management system:

- **Incident Command System (ICS)**. NIMS establishes ICS as a standard incident management organization with five functional areas—command, operations, planning, logistics, and finance/administration—for management of all major incidents. To ensure further coordination, and during incidents involving multiple jurisdictions or agencies, the principle of unified command has been universally incorporated into NIMS. This unified command not only coordinates the efforts of many jurisdictions, but provides for and ensures joint decisions on objectives, strategies, plans, priorities, and public communications.

- **Communications and Information Management**. Standardized communications during an incident are essential, and NIMS prescribes interoperable communications systems for both incident and information management. NIMS recognizes that responders and managers across all agencies and jurisdictions must have common access to the full operational picture, thereby allowing for efficient and effective incident response.
- **Preparedness**. Preparedness incorporates a range of measures, actions, and processes accomplished before an incident happens. NIMS preparedness measures include planning, training, exercises, qualification and certification, equipment acquisition and certification, and publication management. NIMS stresses that each of these measures helps to ensure that preincident actions are standardized and consistent with mutually agreed-on doctrine. NIMS further places emphasis on mitigation activities to enhance preparedness. Mitigation includes public education and outreach, structural modifications to reduce the loss of life or destruction of property, code enforcement in support of zoning rules, land management, and building codes, and flood insurance and property buy-out for frequently flooded areas.
- **Joint Information System (JIS)**. The Joint Information System provides the public with timely and accurate incident information and unified public messages. This system employs Joint Information Centers (JICs) and brings incident communicators together during an incident to develop, coordinate, and deliver a unified message. This is performed under the assumption that it will ensure federal, state, and local levels of government are releasing the same information during an incident.
- **NIMS Integration Center (NIC)**. To ensure that NIMS remains an accurate and effective man-

agement tool, a NIMS NIC will be established by the DHS secretary to assess proposed changes to NIMS, capture and evaluate lessons learned, and employ best practices. The NIC will provide strategic direction and oversight, supporting both routine maintenance and continuous refinement of the system and its components over the long term. It will also develop and facilitate national standards for NIMS education and training, first responder communications and equipment, typing of resources, qualification and credentialing of incident management and responder personnel, and standardization of equipment maintenance and resources. Finally, the NIC will continue to use the collaborative process of federal, state, tribal, local, multidiscipline, and private authorities to assess prospective changes to NIMS.

Figure 7-9 illustrates how NIMS was developed on the structure originally outlined in the Incident Command System. The National Response Plan, which guides the federal support of state, country, tribal, and local response to disasters, was built on the NIMS framework. Together, these three coordinated concepts have likely helped to further eliminate coordination problems that may have existed before in the absence of such complementary systems.

## THE FEDERAL RESPONSE

Almost every facet of the nation's emergency response system have undergone changes to some degree as a result of the reaction to the September 11 terrorist attacks on America. While some of the more significant adjustments have occurred at the federal level, most notably the creation of the Department of Homeland Security, all state and most local agencies have followed their lead. As for the response to major disasters—those requiring action by multiple levels of government—these changes have resulted in a shift toward increased federal control and direction. This shift is most notable with regard to events

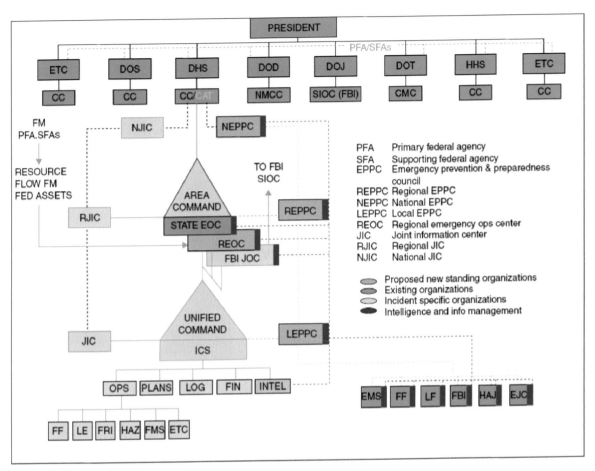

FIGURE 7-9   National structure for NIMS operations.

that include criminal elements such as intentional disasters (e.g., sabotage or civil unrest) and terrorist-driven threats or events. These changes have all been formalized through the transformation of the federal response framework from the old Federal Response Plan (FRP)—which was successfully applied during several terrorist event responses including the Murrah Federal Building bombing and the September 11 attacks—to the new National Response Plan (NRP).

The federal response can be initiated in two ways: A governor can request a presidential disaster declara-

tion or the president can declare a presidential emergency upon damage to federal entities (as was the case for the Discovery tragedy). Additionally, the president, through FEMA, can predeploy resources (personnel and equipment) to a location where a disaster declaration is imminent due to an impending disaster. Under the NRP, all of these authorities remain unchanged. It is important to note that, although a formal declaration does not have to be signed by the president for the federal government to begin response, the governor of the affected state must make a formal request for assistance to occur, and must

**FIGURE 7-10**   New York City, New York, September 27, 2001—Search dogs proved very helpful to the search and rescue teams throughout the cleanup effort at the World Trade Center. (Photo by Bri Rodriguez/FEMA News Photo)

specify in the request the specific needs of the disaster area. The presidential major disaster declaration process is presented in Sidebar 7-8.

Under the NRP, the president maintains the ultimate discretion in making a disaster declaration. There are no set criteria by which he or she is bound, no government regulations to guide which events are declared disasters and which are not. FEMA has developed a number of factors it considers in making its recommendation to the president, including individual property losses per capita, level of damage to existing community infrastructure, level of insurance coverage, repetitive events, and other subjective factors. But in the end, the decision to make the declaration is the president's alone. One major change in the

verbiage of the plan, as changed in the NRP, concerns the prevention of terrorist attacks. In situations where the Homeland Security Operations Center determines that a terrorist threat exists for which federal intervention is required to prevent an incident from occurring, DHS provides support as necessary under the direction of the attorney general, through the Federal Bureau of Investigation.

A presidential disaster declaration can be made in as short a time as a few hours, as was the case in the 1994 Northridge earthquake, the 1995 Oklahoma City bombing, and the September 11 World Trade Center attacks (Figure 7-10). Sometimes it takes weeks for damages to be assessed and the capability of state and local jurisdictions to fund response and recovery efforts to be evaluated. Should the governor's request be turned down by the president, the governor has the right to appeal, an appeal that will be considered, especially if new damage data become available and is included in the appeal.

Presidential declarations are routinely sought for such events as floods, hurricanes, earthquakes, and tornadoes. In recent years, governors have become more inventive and have requested presidential disaster declarations for snow removal, drought, West Nile virus, and economic losses caused by failing industries, such as the Northwest salmon spawning decline.

Once a disaster declaration has been made, the full range of federal government resources becomes available to assist the affected state or states. The federal assistance is guided through the invocation of the National Response Plan, which is detailed later in this chapter. Through this plan, and under the guidance of the Department of Homeland Security, 32 signatory federal agencies and the American Red Cross provide all forms of assistance as dictated under the 15 emergency support functions (also detailed later in this chapter). A declaration also paves the way for federal funding to pay for response activities at all government levels (including reimbursing the expenses of federal agencies that do respond), and certain recovery costs to individuals, businesses, nonprofit agencies, and public entities.

From 1976 to September 2004, there were 1,079 presidential disaster declarations, averaging 38.2 declarations per year (Table 7-5). As an illustration of disaster declaration activity in a single year, in 1999 there were 50 major disaster declarations in 38 states:

- 18 for hurricanes (13 alone for Hurricane Floyd)
- 11 for tornadoes
- 7 for floods
- 6 for winter storms
- 6 for severe storms
- 1 for a flash flood
- 1 for winter freeze

Before the creation of the National Response Plan, there were several individual response plans that

TABLE 7-5  **Total Major Disaster Declarations, 1976–2004**

| Year | Disaster declarations |
| --- | --- |
| 1976 | 30 |
| 1977 | 22 |
| 1978 | 25 |
| 1979 | 42 |
| 1980 | 23 |
| 1981 | 15 |
| 1982 | 24 |
| 1983 | 21 |
| 1984 | 34 |
| 1985 | 27 |
| 1986 | 28 |
| 1987 | 23 |
| 1988 | 11 |
| 1989 | 31 |
| 1990 | 38 |
| 1991 | 43 |
| 1992 | 45 |
| 1993 | 32 |
| 1994 | 36 |
| 1995 | 32 |
| 1996 | 75 |
| 1997 | 44 |
| 1998 | 65 |
| 1999 | 50 |
| 2000 | 45 |
| 2001 | 45 |
| 2002 | 49 |
| 2003 | 46 |
| 2004 | 68 |
| Total | 1,069 |
| Average | 38.2 |

*Source*: FEMA, www.fema.gov.

guided the government response to several different kinds of emergencies or disasters. However, HSPD-5 directed DHS to develop the National Response Plan such that all existing federal plans were integrated into that one document or directly linked through formal coordination mechanisms—giving it the distinction of serving as the single guide for federal response. The following list contains the various plans and operation guidelines integrated or linked under the NRP:

- The Federal Response Plan (FRP)
- The Federal Radiological Emergency Response Plan (FRERP)
- The Domestic Terrorism Concept of Operations Plan (CONPLAN)
- The Mass Mitigation Emergency Plan (Distant Shore)
- The National Oil Spill and Hazardous Substances Pollution Contingency Plan (NCP)

The National Response Plan accommodates the needs of events covered under the FRERP, CON-PLAN, Distant Shore, and NCP, as well as several newly identified or newly addressed issues through the incorporation of several *incident annexes*. These include the following:

- Biological Incident
- Catastrophic Incident
- Cyber Incident
- Food and Agriculture Incident (not yet developed)
- Nuclear/Radiological Incident
- Oil and Hazardous Materials Incident
- Terrorism Incident Law Enforcement and Investigation

Later in this chapter, the annexes just listed will be detailed.

---

SIDEBAR 7-8  **Presidential Major Disaster Declaration Process**

Listed here are the guidelines to states for the disaster declaration process:

- Contact is made between the governor of the affected state (including the District of Columbia), or territory, and the FEMA/EPR regional office. This contact may take place prior to or immediately following the disaster.
- State and federal officials conduct a preliminary damage assessment (PDA) to estimate the extent of the disaster and its impact on individuals and public facilities. This information is included in the governor's request to show that the disaster is of such severity and magnitude that effective response is beyond the capabilities of the state and the local governments and that federal assistance is necessary. Normally, the PDA is completed prior

to the submission of the governor's request. However, when an obviously severe or catastrophic event occurs, the governor's request may be submitted prior to the PDA. Nonetheless, the governor must still make the request.

- Based on the PDA findings, the governor submits a request to the president through the FEMA/EPR regional director for either a major disaster or an emergency declaration and identifying the affected counties. As part of the request, the governor must take appropriate action under state law and direct execution of the state's emergency plan. The governor has to provide in the request information on the nature and amount of state and local resources that have been or will be committed to alleviating the results of the disaster, provide an estimate of the amount and severity of damage and the impact on the private and public sector, and provide an estimate of the type and amount of assistance needed under the Stafford Act.

- The FEMA/EPR regional office submits a summary of the event and a recommendation based on the results of the PDA to FEMA/EPR headquarters, along with the governor's request, to FEMA headquarters in Washington.
- Upon receipt of these documents, FEMA headquarters' senior staff, through the Homeland Security Operations Center (HSOC), convene to discuss the request and determine the

recommendation to be made to the president through the secretary of homeland security.

- The recommendation of the secretary of homeland security is forwarded to the White House for review.
- Based on the governor's request, the president may declare that a major disaster or emergency exists, thereby activating the National Response Plan and setting in motion the full the array of available federal programs to assist in the response and recovery effort.

*Source*: Federal Emergency Management Agency. 2003. *Federal Response Plan* (January), www.fema.gov.

## NATIONAL RESPONSE PLAN

The National Response Plan is an all-discipline, all-hazards emergency operations plan that establishes a single, comprehensive framework for the management of disasters within the United States and its territories (Figure 7-11). It provides the structure and mechanisms for the coordination of federal support to state, local, and tribal incident managers and for exercising direct federal authorities and responsibilities. The NRP also defines the action that will be taken at all government levels to (1) help to prevent terrorist attacks within the United States, (2) reduce the vulnerability to all natural and man-made hazards, and (3) minimize the damage and assist in the recovery from any type of incident that occurs.

The National Response Plan is a signed, binding agreement among 32 federal departments and agencies, the American Red Cross, and the National Voluntary Organizations Active in Disasters (NVOADs). The NRP supports implementation of the Robert T. Stafford Disaster Relief and Emergency Assistance Act, as amended (42 USC 5121, et seq.), as well as individual agency statutory authorities; and incorporates the actions of several former federal emergency operations plans developed to address specific hazards. The fundamental goal of the NRP is to maximize available federal resources in support of response and

recovery actions taken by state and local emergency officials (see Sidebar 7-9).

The NRP, using the NIMS, establishes mechanisms to accomplish the following:

1. Maximize the integration of incident-related prevention, preparedness, response, and recovery activities.
2. Improve coordination and integration of federal, state, local, tribal, regional, private-sector, and nongovernmental organization partners.
3. Maximize efficient utilization of resources needed for effective incident management and the protection and restoration of identified critical infrastructure and other key resources.
4. Improve incident management communications and increase situational awareness across jurisdictions and between the public and private sectors.
5. Facilitate emergency mutual aid and federal emergency support to state, local, and tribal governments.
6. Facilitate federal-to-federal interaction and emergency support.
7. Provide a proactive and integrated federal response to catastrophic events.
8. Address links to other federal incident management and emergency response plans developed for specific types of incidents or hazards.

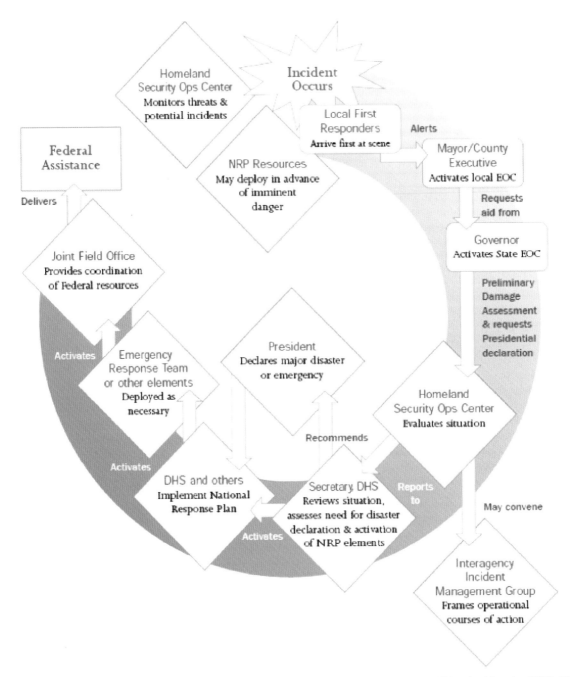

FIGURE 7-11    Initial federal involvement under the National Response Plan. (*Source:* Department of Homeland Security (DHS). 2005. *The National Response Plan.* Washington, DC: DHS)

There are four operating principles that are integral in the successful implementation of the NRP:

1. The NRP does not call for FEMA, DHS, or any other federal department or agency to take over direction and control of a disaster relief effort— it is likely that no governor would allow that to happen. On the contrary and often in contrast to public perception, the NRP defines how DHS and its fellow federal agencies, the American Red Cross, and the NVOADs will support state and local governments in the disaster relief effort. Direction and control of all presidentially declared major disasters remain in the hands of the governor and local officials.
2. The NRP is the only working agreement in existence that involves one federal agency directing the activities of a large number of other federal agencies. This agreement is truly unique in U.S. federal government. Basically, all signatories to the FRP agree to follow the direction of DHS, through FEMA, in providing disaster assistance from their respective agencies. Nowhere else in the federal government are the full resources of so many federal agencies brought to bear on a single civil problem.
3. The NRP includes a series of agreements between DHS, the participating federal agencies, the American Red Cross, and the NVOADs that clearly define the types of services and resources that FEMA expects each agency to be able to provide in the event of a presidential declaration. In other words, each participating agency agrees to retain the capability to deploy personnel, services, and other resources on a 24-hour on-call basis. Also, agencies are expected to have contract vehicles in place that allow for rapid procurement of contractor services and products. This ensures that when DHS requests services and resources from a participating agency, they are available and ready to go immediately.
4. What really makes the FRP work is money. DHS, through FEMA, is able to support all

FIGURE 7-12   New York City, New York, November 7, 2001— FEMA interpreter Richie Park explains tele-registration procedures and disaster assistance options to business owner Betsy Chun at the Disaster Assistance Service Center in New York City. (Photo by Larry Lerner/ FEMA News Photo)

NRP-guided activities out of its annual Disaster Relief Fund (DRF) or from supplemental funding made available for major catastrophes by Congress (Figure 7-12). In FY 2005, Congress funded $2.2 billion for the DRF, which FEMA uses to pay for services and products provided by NRP partner agencies. This means that NRP partner agencies do not have to tap existing budgets that are already programmed for disaster spending and ensures that these agencies will respond quickly to the direction of DHS/FEMA to support state and local efforts. FEMA "mission assigns" specific tasks to those agencies capable of completing these tasks, and it is already understood that FEMA will reimburse the NRP partner agencies per a preexisting agreement concerning costs of services.

The signatory partners of the National Response Plan are as follows:

- Department of Agriculture
- Department of Commerce
- Department of Defense
- Department of Education
- Department of Energy

- Department of Health and Human Resources
- Department of Homeland Security
- Department of Housing and Urban Development
- Department of the Interior
- Department of Justice
- Department of Labor
- Department of State
- Department of Transportation
- Department of the Treasury
- Department of Veterans Affairs
- Central Intelligence Agency
- Environmental Protection Agency
- Federal Bureau of Investigation
- Federal Communications Commission

- General Services Administration
- National Aeronautics and Space Administration
- National Transportation Safety Board
- Nuclear Regulatory Commission
- Office of Personnel Management
- Small Business Administration
- Social Security Administration
- Tennessee Valley Authority
- United States Agency for International Development
- U.S. Postal Service
- American Red Cross
- National Voluntary Organizations Active in Disaster

---

**SIDEBAR 7-9  Types of Federal Disaster Assistance Available**

The National Response Plan (NRP) makes available the following types of assistance:

**Pre-Incident Services**

- Interagency information and intelligence sharing is conducted to enable counterterrorism activities.

Resources and staff can be prepositioned to ensure effective response in anticipation of a disaster.

**Immediate Relief Delivery—Response Actions**

- Assets are mobilized and resources are deployed to support the incident.
- Teams with specialized capabilities such as the NDMS, the HHS Secretary's Emergency Response Team, the Epidemic Intelligence Service, HHS behavioral health response teams, the U.S. Public Health Service Commissioned Corps, and Urban Search and Rescue teams are deployed.
- A Joint Field Office (JFO) and other field facilities are established to provide incident management, public health, and other community support.

- Assistance is provided to support immediate law enforcement, fire, ambulance, and emergency medical service actions; emergency flood fighting; evacuations; transportation system detours; emergency public information; actions taken to minimize additional damage; urban search and rescue; the establishment of facilities for mass care; the provision of public health and medical services, food, ice, water, and other emergency essentials; debris clearance; the emergency restoration of critical infrastructure; control, containment, and removal of environmental contamination; and protection of responder health and safety.
- During the response to a terrorist event, law enforcement actions to collect and preserve evidence and to apprehend perpetrators are conducted.

**Assistance to Speed Recovery and Reduce Damage from Future Occurrences**

- Loans and grants to repair or replace damaged housing and personal property are provided.

- Grants to repair or replace roads and public buildings, incorporating to the extent practical hazard-reduction structural and nonstructural measures, are provided.
- Technical assistance to identify and implement mitigation opportunities to reduce future losses is provided.

- Other assistance, including crisis counseling, tax relief, legal services, and job placement may also be provided.

*Source*: Department of Homeland Security (DHS). 2005. *The National Response Plan*. Washington, DC: DHS.

## SITUATIONS WHERE THE NATIONAL RESPONSE PLAN IS APPLIED

The NRP applies to all incidents occurring within the United States. These incidents can be classified as follows:

1. An "emergency" or "major disaster"
2. A threat or act of "terrorism" that the secretary, in consultation with the attorney general, determines is of sufficient magnitude to warrant implementation of this plan
3. Any other occasion or instance in which one or more of the following conditions or thresholds applies: (a) A federal department or agency acting under its own authority has requested the assistance of the secretary; (b) the resources of state and local authorities are overwhelmed and federal assistance has been requested by the

appropriate state and local authorities; (c) more than one federal department or agency has become substantially involved in responding to the incident; or (d) the secretary has been directed to assume responsibility for managing the incident by the president

A considerable change has occurred between the FRP and the NRP with regard to whom the plan applies. The NRP is a plan that now applies to all federal departments and agencies; state and local authorities requesting federal assistance; state and local authorities accepting federal preparedness assistance through grants, contracts, or other activities; and private and nongovernmental entities partnering with the federal government in relation to domestic incident management activities. Sidebar 7-10 lists the key tenets of the NRP, and Sidebar 7-11 covers some of the new terminology used in the NRP.

### SIDEBAR 7-10   NRP Assumptions

The NRP reflects certain key tenets as set forth in HSPD-5, namely, that the NRP be:

1. *A single plan*: The NRP integrates existing federal domestic awareness, prevention, preparedness, response, and recovery plans into one base plan, addressing functional areas common to most contingencies, with annexes

to describe unique procedures required under special circumstances.

2. *An "all-hazards/all-disciplines" plan*: Current emergency plans are designed to deal with only certain types of contingencies. The NRP is a single plan that is flexible enough to accommodate all hazards and covering all of the disciplines required for con-

ducting activities throughout the life cycle of an incident. Under the NRP, "hazards" refers to the full range of possible contingencies, including:

a. Natural disasters, such as floods, earthquakes, hurricanes, tornadoes, droughts, and epidemics

b. Accidents, such as chemical spills, industrial accidents, radiological or nuclear incidents, explosions, and utility outages

c. Civil or political incidents, including mass migrations, the domestic effects of war, nation-state attacks, and unrest or disorder resulting from riots, public demonstrations, and strikes

d. Terrorist or criminal incidents, including chemical, biological, radiological, nuclear, explosive, or cyber threats or attacks

e. Significant events and designated special events requiring security, such as inaugurals, State of the Union addresses, the Olympics, and international summit conferences

3. *A plan that emphasizes unity of effort among all levels of government*: The NRP is a national plan that emphasizes unity of effort among all levels of government. Under this plan, federal, state, and local governments, along with private organizations and the American public, work as partners to manage domestic contingencies efficiently and effectively.

4. *A plan that integrates crisis and consequence management*: In keeping with the presidential directive, the NRP will "treat crisis management and consequence management as a single, integrated function, rather than as two separate functions."

5. *A plan that places the same emphasis on awareness, prevention, and preparedness as traditionally has been placed on response and recovery*: Traditionally, response plans have been exactly what their name implies—plans for responding to and recovering from an incident or contingency. In the aftermath of September 11, 2001, however, preventing terrorism and reducing our nation's vulnerabilities through preparedness have become top priorities. The NRP sets forth a new concept of a "response" plan by covering five domains: awareness, prevention, preparedness, response, and recovery.

*Source*: Department of Homeland Security (DHS). 2005. *The National Response Plan*. Washington, DC: DHS.

---

### SIDEBAR 7-11  "Life Cycle" of Incident Management Activities—New Definitions

The language defining the application of the NRP differs significantly from the classic mitigation–preparedness–response–recovery terminology used in the FRP. It is best described as having five domains within which domestic incident management activities occur: awareness, prevention, preparedness, response, and recovery. Each of these is defined in the following list:

- **Awareness**—Refers to the continual process of collecting, analyzing, and disseminating intelligence, information, and knowledge to allow organizations and individuals to anticipate requirements and to react effectively.

- **Prevention**—Refers to actions taken to avoid an incident, to intervene to stop an incident from occurring, or to mitigate an incident's effects.

- **Preparedness**—Refers to the activities necessary to build and sustain performance across all of the other domains.

- **Response**—Refers to the activities necessary to address the immediate and short-term effects of an incident, which focus primarily on the actions necessary to save lives, to protect property, and to meet basic human needs.

- **Recovery**—Refers to those actions necessary to restore the community back to normal and

to bring the perpetrators of an intentional incident to justice.

*Source*: Department of Homeland Security (DHS). 2005. *The National Response Plan*. Washington, DC: DHS.

## ORGANIZATION OF THE NATIONAL RESPONSE PLAN

The National Response Plan consists of five separate components:

- **Base Plan**—Describes the structure and processes comprising a national approach to domestic incident management designed to integrate the efforts and resources of federal, state, local, tribal, private-sector, and nongovernmental organizations. The base plan includes planning assumptions, roles and responsibilities, concept of operations, incident management actions, and plan maintenance instructions.
- **Appendixes**—Provide other relevant, more detailed supporting information, including terms, definitions, acronyms, authorities, and a compendium of national interagency plans.
- **Emergency Support Function (ESF) Annexes**—Detail the missions, policies, structures, and responsibilities of federal agencies for coordinating resource and programmatic support to states, tribes, and other federal agencies or other jurisdictions and entities during incidents of national significance. The introduction to the ESF annexes summarizes the functions of ESF coordinators and primary and support agencies.
- **Support Annexes**—Provide guidance and describe the functional processes and administrative requirements necessary to ensure efficient and effective implementation of NRP incident management objectives.
- **Incident Annexes**—Address contingency or hazard situations requiring specialized applica-

tion of the NRP. The incident annexes describe the missions, policies, responsibilities, and coordination processes that govern the interaction of public and private entities engaged in incident management and emergency response operations across a spectrum of potential hazards. These annexes are typically augmented by a variety of supporting plans and operational supplements.

## ROLES AND RESPONSIBILITIES

The National Response Plan defines the roles and responsibilities of all levels of government that are guided under the plan. It also defines the roles and responsibilities of the nongovernmental organizations, private sector, and citizens who are involved in support of the management of emergency incidents.

### State, Local, and Tribal Governments

The NRP recognizes that police, fire, public health and medical, emergency management, public works, environmental response, and other personnel are often the first to arrive and the last to leave an incident site. However, it is also recognized that in certain cases, a federal agency in the local area may act as a first responder, and the local assets of federal agencies may be used to advise or assist state or local officials in accordance with agency authorities and procedures. The NRP specifically defines the responsibilities of the governor, local chief executive officer (usually the mayor), or the tribal chief executive officer for incidents that occur on reservations. Each of these is described below.

As a state's chief executive, the governor is responsible for the public safety and welfare of the people of that state or territory. The governor:

1. Is responsible for coordinating state resources to address the full spectrum of actions to prevent, prepare for, respond to, and recover from incidents in an all-hazards context to include terrorism, natural disasters, accidents, and other contingencies.
2. Under certain emergency conditions, typically has police powers to make, amend, and rescind orders and regulations.
3. Provides leadership and plays a key role in communicating to the public and in helping people, businesses, and organizations cope with the consequences of any type of declared emergency within state jurisdiction.
4. Encourages participation in mutual aid and implements authorities for the state to enter into mutual aid agreements with other states, tribes, and territories to facilitate resource sharing.
5. Is the commander-in-chief of state military forces (National Guard when in state active duty or Title 32 status and the authorized state militias).
6. Requests federal assistance when it becomes clear that state or tribal capabilities will be insufficient or have been exceeded or exhausted.

A mayor or city or county manager, as a jurisdiction's chief executive, is responsible for the public safety and welfare of the people of that jurisdiction. The local chief executive officer:

1. Is responsible for coordinating local resources to address the full spectrum of actions to prevent, prepare for, respond to, and recover from incidents involving all hazards including terrorism, natural disasters, accidents, and other contingencies.
2. Dependent on state and local law, has extraordinary powers to suspend local laws and ordinances, such as to establish a curfew, direct evacuations, and, in coordination with the local health authority, to order a quarantine.
3. Provides leadership and plays a key role in communicating to the public, and in helping people, businesses, and organizations cope with the consequences of any type of domestic incident within the jurisdiction.
4. Negotiates and enters into mutual aid agreements with other jurisdictions to facilitate resource sharing.
5. Requests state and, if necessary, federal assistance through the governor of the state when the jurisdiction's capabilities have been exceeded or exhausted.

The tribal chief executive officer is responsible for the public safety and welfare of the people of that tribe. The tribal chief executive officer, as authorized by tribal government:

1. Is responsible for coordinating tribal resources to address the full spectrum of actions to prevent, prepare for, respond to, and recover from incidents involving all hazards including terrorism, natural disasters, accidents, and other contingencies.
2. Has extraordinary powers to suspend tribal laws and ordinances, such as to establish a curfew, direct evacuations, and order a quarantine.
3. Provides leadership and plays a key role in communicating to the tribal nation, and in helping people, businesses, and organizations cope with the consequences of any type of domestic incident within the jurisdiction.
4. Negotiates and enters into mutual aid agreements with other tribes/jurisdictions to facilitate resource sharing.
5. Can request state and federal assistance through the governor of the state when the tribe's capabilities have been exceeded or exhausted.
6. Can elect to deal directly with the federal government. (Although a state governor must request a presidential disaster declaration on behalf of a tribe under the Stafford Act, federal agencies can work directly with the tribe within existing authorities and resources.)

## The Federal Government

The Homeland Security Act of 2002 established DHS to prevent terrorist attacks within the United States; reduce the vulnerability of the United States to terrorism, natural disasters, and other emergencies; and minimize the damage and assist in the recovery from terrorist attacks, natural disasters, and other emergencies. The act also designates DHS as "a focal point regarding natural and man-made crises and emergency planning."

Pursuant to HSPD-5, the secretary of homeland security is responsible for coordinating federal operations within the United States to prepare for, respond to, and recover from terrorist attacks, major disasters, and other emergencies. HSPD-5 further designates the secretary of homeland security as the "principal federal official" for domestic incident management.

In this role, the secretary is also responsible for coordinating federal resources utilized in response to or recovery from terrorist attacks, major disasters, or other emergencies if and when any of the following four conditions applies:

1. A federal department or agency acting under its own authority has requested DHS assistance.
2. The resources of state and local authorities are overwhelmed and federal assistance has been requested.
3. More than one federal department or agency has become substantially involved in responding to the incident.
4. The secretary has been directed to assume incident management responsibilities by the president.

The NRP also defines the responsibilities of many other federal agencies, but their specific roles and responsibilities are primarily dictated by the emergency support functions, which are described later in this chapter.

## Nongovernmental and Volunteer Organizations

The NRP recognized the importance of nongovernmental organizations (NGOs), which collaborate with first responders, governments at all levels, and other agencies and organizations providing relief services to sustain life, reduce physical and emotional distress, and promote recovery of disaster victims when assistance is not available from other sources. The American Red Cross, the most critical NGO with regards to its contribution to emergency management in the United States, not only provides relief at the local level, but also coordinates one of the emergency support functions of the NRP—ESF #6.

The National Voluntary Organizations Active in Disaster (NVOAD) is a consortium of more than 30 recognized national organizations of volunteers active in disaster relief. The NRP recognizes the important role these organizations play, by stating in the NRP that they provide significant capabilities to incident management and response efforts at all levels. Wildlife rescue and rehabilitation activities conducted during a pollution emergency are just one example of the services provided by these agencies that are not covered by the federal government.

## The Private Sector

The National Response Plan seeks to increase cooperation between DHS, other primary and support agencies from throughout the federal government, and private-sector entities. The NRP asserts that this cooperation is for the purpose of sharing information, forming strategic plans to handle emergencies, and to prevent, prepare for, respond to, and recover from incidents of national significance. The roles, responsibilities, and participation of the private sector during incidents of national significance, according to the NRP, vary based on the nature of the organization and the type and impact of the incident.

Private-sector organizations support the NRP by sharing information, identifying risks, performing vulnerability assessments, developing emergency response and business continuity plans, enhancing their overall readiness, implementing appropriate prevention and protection programs, and donating or otherwise providing goods and services through contractual arrangement or government purchases to assist in response to and recovery from an incident.

Certain organizations are required by law to bear the cost associated with planning and response, regardless of cause. In the case of an incident of national significance, these private-sector organizations are expected to mobilize and employ the resources necessary and available in accordance with their plans to address the consequences of incidents at their own facilities or incidents for which they are otherwise responsible.

The various roles played by private-sector organizations could include the following:

- *Impacted organizations or infrastructure*—Organizations affected by direct or indirect consequences of the incident.
- *Response resource*—Organizations that provide response resources (donated or compensated) during an incident—including specialized teams, equipment, and advanced technologies—through local public–private emergency plans, mutual aid agreements, or requests from government and private-sector-volunteered initiatives.
- *Regulated and/or responsible party*—Owners/operators of certain regulated facilities or hazardous operations may bear responsibilities under the law for preparing for and preventing incidents from occurring, and responding to an incident once it occurs. For example, federal regulations require owners/operators of NRC-regulated nuclear facilities and activities to maintain emergency (incident) preparedness plans, procedures, and facilities and to perform assessments, prompt notifications, and training for a response to an incident.
- *State/local emergency organization member*—Organizations may serve as an active partner in local and state emergency preparedness and response organizations and activities.

### Citizen Participation in the NRP

Citizens participate in "prevention, preparedness, response, recovery, and mitigation" through their involvement with citizen groups. The Citizen Corps is

the federal organization that offers funding and direction to many homeland security–based citizen programs. Local Citizen Corps Councils implement Citizen Corps programs, which include Community Emergency Response Teams (CERTs), Medical Reserve Corps, Neighborhood Watch, Volunteers in Police Service, and affiliated programs; provide opportunities for special skills and interests; develop targeted outreach for special needs groups; and organize special projects and community events. Other programs unaffiliated with Citizen Corps also provide organized citizen involvement opportunities in support of federal response to major disasters and events of national significance.

## CONCEPT OF OPERATIONS

### The President of the United States

The president leads the nation in responding to all incidents of national significance. As necessary, the assistant to the president for homeland security convenes interagency meetings to coordinate policy issues. However, White House–level coordination mechanisms are not described in detail in the NRP. During actual or potential incidents of national significance, the overall coordination of federal incident management activities is executed through the secretary of homeland security.

### The Secretary of Homeland Security

The secretary of homeland security utilizes multiagency structures at the headquarters, regional, and field levels to coordinate efforts and provide appropriate support to the incident command structure. At the federal headquarters level, incident information sharing, operational planning, and deployment of federal resources are coordinated by the Homeland Security Operations Center (HSOC), and its component element, the National Response Coordination Center (NRCC). Strategic-level interagency incident management coordination is performed by the Interagency Incident Management Group (IIMG), which also serves as an advisory group to the DHS secretary.

At the regional level, interagency resource coordination and multiagency incident support are provided by the Regional Response Coordination Center (RRCC). In the field, the DHS secretary is represented by the principal federal officer (PFO) and/or the federal coordinating officer (FCO) and the federal resource coordinator (FRC) as needed. See Sidebar 7-12 for further explanation of these roles. Overall federal support to the incident command structure on scene is coordinated through the Joint Field Office (JFO).

For terrorist incidents, the primary responsibilities for coordinating and conducting all federal law enforcement and criminal investigation activities are executed by the attorney general acting through the FBI. During a terrorist incident, the local FBI special agent in charge (SAC) coordinates these activities with other members of the law enforcement community, and works in conjunction with the PFO, who coordinates overall federal incident management activities.

## ORGANIZATIONAL STRUCTURE

The national structure for incident management established in the NRP provides a progression of coordination and communication from the local level to the regional and to the national headquarters level. In accordance with NIMS, resource and policy issues are addressed at the lowest organizational level practica-

---

### SIDEBAR 7-12   NRP Leadership Roles Explained—The PFO and FCO

**Principal Federal Official**—The PFO is personally designated by the secretary of homeland security to facilitate federal support to the established ICS Unified Command structure and to coordinate overall federal incident management and assistance activities across the spectrum of prevention, preparedness, response, and recovery. The PFO ensures that incident management efforts are maximized through effective and efficient coordination. The PFO provides a primary point of contact and situational awareness locally for the secretary of homeland security. The Secretary is not restricted to DHS officials when selecting a PFO.

The PFO does not direct or replace the incident command structure established at the incident, nor does the PFO have directive authority over the SFLEO, FCO, or other federal and state officials. Other federal incident management officials retain their authorities as defined in existing statutes and directives. The PFO coordinates the activities of the SFLEO, FCO, and other federal officials involved in incident management activities acting under their own authorities. The PFO also provides a channel for media and public communications and an interface with appropriate jurisdictional officials pertaining to the incident. Once formally designated, PFOs relinquish the conduct of all normal duties and functions. PFOs may not be "dual-hatted" with any other roles or responsibilities that could detract from their overall incident management responsibilities.

**Federal Coordinating Officer (FCO)**—The FCO is the official selected by the secretary of homeland security to act as his or her representative in the field. This officer is appointed to manage federal resource support activities related to Stafford Act (presidentially declared) disasters and emergencies. The FCO is responsible for coordinating the timely delivery of federal disaster assistance resources and programs to the affected state and local governments, individual victims, and the private sector.

*Source*: Department of Homeland Security (DHS). 2005. *The National Response Plan*. Washington, DC: DHS.

ble, most appropriately the local level. If the issues cannot be resolved at that level, they are forwarded up to the next level for resolution. In accordance with NIMS, the NRP includes the following command and coordination structures:

- ICPs on-scene using the Incident Command System (ICS)/Unified Command
- Area Command (if needed)
- State, local, tribal, and private-sector EOCs
- JFO, which is responsible for coordinating federal assistance and supporting incident management activities locally
- RRCC and HSOC, which serve as regional and national-level multiagency situational awareness and operational coordination centers
- IIMG, which serves as the national headquarters-level multiagency coordination entity for domestic incident management
- HSC and other White House organizations, which serve as the national-level multiagency coordination entities to advise and assist the president on homeland security and other policy issues

The NRP organizational structure addresses both site-specific incident management activities and the broader regional or national issues related to the incident, such as impacts to the rest of the country, immediate regional or national actions required to avert or prepare for potential subsequent events, and the management of multiple threats or incidents. The role of regional coordinating structures varies depending on the situation. Many incidents may be coordinated by regional structures primarily using regional assets. Larger, more complex incidents may require direct coordination between the JFO and national level, with regional structures continuing to play a supporting role.

## NRP ORGANIZATIONAL ELEMENTS

The successful application of the NRP depends on many organizational elements existing at many gov-

ernment levels, including people from many different backgrounds. Each of these elements fits within a defined organizational structure within the NRP, fulfilling well-defined roles. The following section describes each of these organizational elements.

### The Homeland Security Council and the National Security Council

The assistant to the president for homeland security and the assistant to the president for national security affairs are responsible for interagency policy coordination regarding domestic and international incident management, respectively, as directed by the president. Following an initial assessment by the DHS Secretary, interagency policy issues, and courses of action framed by the IIMG, executive orders and directives are elevated for resolution through the Homeland Security Council (HSC)/National Security Council (NSC) system.

### Policy Coordination Committees

Policy coordination committees (PCCs) may be convened at the request of any NRP member agency on an emergency basis (based on a threat, an incident of national significance, or a policy issue of an urgent nature) to coordinate policy issues for the White House.

### Interagency Incident Management Group

The Interagency Incident Management Group (IIMG) is a multiagency coordination entity that facilitates management for incidents of national significance. The DHS secretary can activate the IIMG based on the nature, severity, magnitude, and complexity of the threat or incident. The IIMG is comprised of senior representatives from DHS components, other federal departments and agencies, and NGOs, as required. When activated, the IIMG:

- Serves as a focal point for federal strategic incident management planning and coordination.

- Maintains situational awareness of threat assessments and ongoing incident-related operations and activities.
- Provides decision-making support for threat or incident-related prevention, preparedness, response, and recovery efforts.
- Synthesizes information, frames issues, and makes recommendations to the DHS secretary on threat actions (including the HSAS alert level), operational courses of action, and the use of federal resources.
- Assesses national impacts of the incident(s) as well as those associated with the actual or proposed federal response.
- Anticipates evolving federal resource and operational requirements according to the specifics of the situation.
- Maintains ongoing coordination with the PFO and the JFO Coordination Group.
- Coordinates with the FBI on terrorism-related issues.
- Facilitates interagency operational coordination and coordination with other public and private entities required for implementation of decisions and directions from the president or other appropriate White House entities.
- Develops strategies for implementing existing policies and provides incident information to DHS and the White House to facilitate policy-making.

## Homeland Security Operations Center

The Homeland Security Operations Center (HSOC) is the primary national hub for incident management operational coordination. The HSOC is a standing, full-time organization that joins the functions of law enforcement, national intelligence, emergency response, and private-sector reporting. The HSOC attempts to facilitate information sharing and operational coordination between federal, state, local, tribal, and nongovernmental EOCs. HSOC roles and responsibilities include:

- Establishing and maintaining real-time communications links to other federal EOCs at the national level, as well as appropriate state, tribal, local, regional, and nongovernmental EOCs and relevant elements of the private sector
- Maintaining communications with private-sector critical infrastructure and key resources information sharing entities
- Maintaining communications with federal incident management officials
- Coordinating resources pertaining to domestic incident management, and the protection against and prevention of terrorists attacks
- Coordinating with the Terrorist Screening Center (TSC), FBI SIOC, National Counterterrorism Center (NCTC), and other federal government entities for terrorism-related threat analysis and incident response, consistent with applicable executive orders
- Providing general domestic situational awareness, common operational picture, and support to and acting upon requests for information from the IIMG and DHS leadership and
- Acting as the primary conduit for the White House Situation Room and IIMG for domestic situational awareness.

## FBI Strategic Information Operations Center (FBI SIOC)

The FBI Strategic Information Operations Center (FBI SIOC) is the central organizational body for all federal intelligence, law enforcement, and investigations activities related to domestic terrorism. The SIOC serves as an information clearinghouse to law enforcement agencies and criminal investigations. Housed within the SIOC is the National Joint Terrorism Task Force (NJTTF), whose mission is to enhance communications, coordination, and cooperation among federal, state, local, and tribal agencies representing the intelligence, law enforcement, defense, diplomatic, public safety, and homeland security communities by providing a point of fusion for terrorism intelligence and by supporting Joint Terrorism Task Forces (JTTFs) throughout the United States.

### National Counterterrorism Center (NCTC)

The National Counterterrorism Center (NCTC) serves as the primary federal organization for analyzing and integrating all intelligence possessed or acquired by the U.S. government pertaining to terrorism and counterterrorism (except in circumstances where the terrorism is determined to be fully domestic in origin). The NCTC also conducts strategic operational planning for counterterrorism activities, integrating all instruments of national power, including diplomatic, financial, military, intelligence, homeland security, and law enforcement activities within and among agencies. It assigns operational responsibilities to agencies for counterterrorism activities. In addition, the NCTC serves as the central and shared knowledge bank on known and suspected terrorists and international terror groups, as well as their goals, strategies, capabilities, and networks of contacts and support. The NCTC ensures that agencies, as appropriate, have access to and receive all-source intelligence support needed to execute their counterterrorism plans or perform independent, alternative analysis.

### Joint Field Office

The Joint Field Office (JFO) is a multiagency coordination center that is established locally, close to the incident, that replaces the Disaster Field Office (DFO) structure that existed under the FRP. It provides a central location or coordination of federal, state, local, tribal, nongovernmental, and private-sector organizations with incident-related responsibility, using the scalable organizational structure of NIMS ICS. The JFO does not, however, manage on-scene operations; instead, it focuses on providing support to on-scene efforts and conducting broader support operations that may extend beyond the incident site.

As described in NIMS, the JFO may also incorporate intelligence and information as a sixth element outside the regular ICS. This element may be included as a position in the Coordination Staff, a unit within the Planning Section, a branch within the Operations Section, or as a separate General Staff Section. Law enforcement activities are managed through the Joint Operations Center (JOC), which becomes an operational branch of the JFO during terrorist-related incidents of national significance. Threat situations or incidents that impact multiple states or localities may require separate JFOs. In these situations, one of the JFOs may be identified (typically in the most heavily impacted area) to provide strategic leadership and coordination for the overall incident management effort.

## THE EMERGENCY SUPPORT FUNCTIONS OF THE NATIONAL RESPONSE PLAN

The emergency support functions (ESFs) provide the structure for coordinating federal interagency support during incidents of national significance. The ESF structure includes mechanisms used to provide federal support to states and federal-to-federal support, both for declared disasters and emergencies under the Stafford Act and for non–Stafford Act incidents. Some departments and agencies provide resources for response, support, and program implementation during the early stage of an event, while others are more prominent in the recovery phase.

### ESF Notification and Activation

The National Response Coordination Center (NRCC), a component of the Homeland Security Operations Center (HSOC), develops and issues operation orders to activate individual ESFs based on the scope and magnitude of the threat or incident. ESF primary agencies are notified of the operations orders and time to report to the NRCC by the FEMA Operations Center. At the regional level, ESFs are notified by the Regional Response Coordination Center (RRCC). ESF primary agencies notify and activate support agencies as required for the threat or incident, to include support to specialized teams. Each ESF is required to develop standard operating procedures (SOPs) and notification protocols and to maintain current rosters and contact information.

### ESF Coordinator

The ESF coordinator has ongoing responsibilities throughout the prevention, preparedness, response, recovery, and mitigation phases of incident management. The role of the ESF coordinator is carried out through a "unified command" approach as agreed on collectively by the designated primary agencies. Responsibilities of the ESF coordinator include:

- Preincident planning and coordination
- Maintaining ongoing contact with ESF primary and support agencies
- Conducting periodic ESF meetings and conference calls
- Coordinating efforts with corresponding private-sector organizations
- Coordinating ESF activities relating to catastrophic incident planning and critical infrastructure preparedness as appropriate

### ESF Primary Agencies

A federal agency designated as an ESF primary agency serves under the federal coordinating officer (FCO) to accomplish the ESF mission. When an ESF is activated in response to an incident of national significance, the primary agency is responsible for:

- Orchestrating federal support within their functional area for an affected state
- Providing staff for the operations functions at fixed and field facilities
- Notifying and requesting assistance from support agencies

- Managing mission assignments and coordinating with support agencies, as well as appropriate state agencies
- Working with appropriate private-sector organizations to maximize use of all available resources
- Supporting and keeping other ESFs and organizational elements informed of ESF operational priorities and activities
- Executing contracts and procuring goods and services as needed
- Ensuring financial and property accountability for ESF activities
- Planning for short-term and long-term incident management and recovery operations
- Maintaining trained personnel to support interagency emergency response and support teams

### ESF Support Agencies

Under each ESF are listed several federal and other agencies that provide supplementary support to the coordinating and primary agencies and fulfill the missions of the ESF. When an ESF is activated in response to an incident of national significance, support agencies are responsible for:

- Conducting operations, when requested by DHS or the designated ESF primary agency, using their own authorities, subject-matter experts, capabilities, or resources
- Participating in planning for short-term and long-term incident management and recovery operations and the development of supporting operational plans, SOPs, checklists, or other job aids, in concert with existing first responder standards
- Assisting in the conduct of situational assessments
- Furnishing available personnel, equipment, or other resource support as requested by DHS or the ESF primary agency

- Providing input to periodic readiness assessments
- Participating in training and exercises aimed at continuous improvement of prevention, response, and recovery capabilities
- Identifying new equipment or capabilities required to prevent or respond to new or emerging threats and hazards, or to improve the ability to address existing threats
- Nominating new technologies to DHS for review and evaluation that have the potential to improve performance within or across functional areas
- Providing information or intelligence regarding their agency's area of expertise

When requested, and on approval of the secretary of defense, the Department of Defense (DOD) provides Defense Support of Civil Authorities (DSCA) during domestic incidents. Accordingly, DOD is considered a support agency to all ESFs. The 15 ESFs, a brief description of the activities conducted and managed in each ESF, and the identity of the coordinating agency or agencies in each ESF, are provided below.

### The 15 Emergency Support Functions of the NRP

The NRP employs a functional approach that groups under 15 ESFs the types of direct federal assistance that a state is most likely to need. Each ESF is headed by one or more coordinating agencies designated on the basis of its authorities, resources, and capability in that functional area. Federal response assistance is provided using some or all ESFs as necessary. Federal ESF representatives coordinate with their counterpart state agencies.

The ESFs provide the structure for coordinating federal interagency support for incidents of national significance. The ESF structure includes mechanisms used to provide federal support to states and federal-to-federal support, both for declared disasters and emergencies under the Stafford Act and for non–Stafford Act incidents. The ESF structure

provides mechanisms for interagency coordination during all phases of incident management. Some departments and agencies provide resources for response, support, and program implementation during the early stage of an event, while others are more prominent in the recovery phase. The following list describes the ESFs:

- *ESF #1, Transportation, Department of Transportation*: Supports DHS, assisting federal agencies; state, local, and tribal governmental entities; and voluntary organizations requiring transportation for an actual or potential incident of national significance. Through the Department of Transportation (DOT)'s coordination role, ESF #1 integrates the DOT responsibility for emergency management of the transportation system (EMTS) in the prevention/mitigation, preparedness, recovery, infrastructure restoration, safety, and security of the nation and its transportation system.
- *ESF #2, Communications, Department of Homeland Security*: Ensures the provision of federal communications support to federal, state, local, tribal, and private-sector response efforts during an incident of national significance. This ESF supplements the provisions of the National Plan for Telecommunications Support in Non-Wartime Emergencies, also referred to as the National Telecommunications Support Plan (NTSP).
- *ESF #3, Public Works and Engineering, U.S. Army Corps of Engineers*: Assists DHS by coordinating and organizing the capabilities and resources of the federal government to facilitate the delivery of services, technical assistance, engineering expertise, construction management, and other support to prevent, prepare for, respond to, and/or recover from an incident of national significance. Activities within the scope of this function include conducting preincident and postincident assessments of public works and infrastructure; executing emergency contract

support for lifesaving and life-sustaining services; providing technical assistance to include engineering expertise, construction management, and contracting and real estate services; providing emergency repair of damaged infrastructure and critical facilities; and implementing and managing the DHS/Emergency Preparedness and Response/Federal Emergency Management Agency (DHS/EPR/FEMA) Public Assistance Program and other recovery programs.

- *ESF #4, Firefighting, U.S. Forest Service*: Enables the detection and suppression of wildland, rural, and urban fires resulting from, or occurring coincidentally with, an incident of national significance.

- *ESF #5, Emergency Management, Federal Emergency Management Agency*: Serves as the support ESF for all federal departments and agencies across the spectrum of domestic incident management from prevention to response and recovery. ESF #5 facilitates information flow in the preincident prevention phase in order to place assets on alert or to preposition assets for quick response. During the postincident response phase, ESF #5 is responsible for support and planning functions, and activities include those functions that are critical to support and facilitate multiagency planning and coordination for operations involving potential and actual incidents of national significance. This includes alert and notification, deployment and staffing of DHS emergency response teams, incident action planning, coordination of operations, logistics and material, direction and control, information management, facilitation of requests for federal assistance, resource acquisition and management (to include allocation and tracking), worker safety and health, facilities management, financial management, and other support as required.

- *ESF #6, Mass Care, Housing, and Human Services, Federal Emergency Management Agency*: Supports state, regional, local, and tribal government and nongovernmental organization (NGO)

efforts to address the nonmedical mass care, housing, and human services needs of individuals and/or families impacted by incidents of national significance. Mass care involves the coordination of nonmedical mass care services to include sheltering of victims, organizing feeding operations, providing emergency first aid at designated sites, collecting and providing information on victims to family members, and coordinating bulk distribution of emergency relief items. Housing involves the provision of assistance for short- and long-term housing needs of victims. Human services include providing victim-related recovery efforts such as counseling, identifying support for persons with special needs, expediting processing of new federal benefits claims, assisting in collecting crime victim compensation for acts of terrorism, and expediting mail services in affected areas.

- *ESF #7, Resource Support, General Services Administration*: Assists DHS, supporting federal agencies and state, local, and tribal governments requiring resource support prior to, during, and/or after incidents of national significance. Resource support consists of emergency relief supplies, facility space, office equipment, office supplies, telecommunications, contracting services, transportation services (in coordination with ESF #1), security services, and personnel required to support immediate response activities.

- *ESF #8, Public Health and Medical Services, Department of Health and Human Services*: Provides the mechanism for coordinated federal assistance to supplement state, local, and tribal resources in response to public health and medical care needs (to include veterinary and/or animal health issues when appropriate) for potential or actual incidents of national significance and/or during a developing potential health and medical situation.

- *ESF #9, Urban Search and Rescue, Federal Emergency Management Agency*: Rapidly deploys components of the National US&R

Response System to provide specialized lifesaving assistance to state, local, and tribal authorities during an incident of national significance. US&R activities include locating, extricating, and providing on-site medical treatment to victims trapped in collapsed structures.

- *ESF #10, Oil and Hazardous Materials, Environmental Protection Agency*: Provides federal support in response to an actual or potential discharge and/or uncontrolled release of oil or hazardous materials during incidents of national significance when activated. The federal government also may respond to oil and hazardous materials incidents of national significance using mechanisms of the National Oil and Hazardous Substances Pollution Contingency Plan (NCP) without activating ESF #10. Those procedures are described in the Oil and Hazardous Materials Incident Annex.

- *ESF #11, Agriculture and Natural Resources, Department of Agriculture*: Supports state, local, and tribal authorities and other federal agency efforts to address (1) provision of nutrition assistance; (2) control and eradication of an outbreak of a highly contagious or economically devastating animal/zoonotic disease, highly infective exotic plant disease, or economically devastating plant pest infestation; (3) assurance of food safety and food security, and (4) protection of natural and cultural resources and historic properties (NCH) resources prior to, during, and/or after an incident of national significance.

- *ESF #12, Energy, Department of Energy*: Intended to restore damaged energy systems and components during a potential or actual incident of national significance. Under Department of Energy (DOE) leadership, ESF #12 is an integral part of the larger DOE responsibility of maintaining continuous and reliable energy supplies for the United States through preventive measures as well as restorative actions.

- *ESF #13, Public Safety and Security, Department of Homeland Security, Department of Justice*: Provides a mechanism for coordinating and providing federal-to-federal support or federal support to state and local authorities to include noninvestigative/noncriminal law enforcement, public safety, and security capabilities and resources during potential or actual incidents of national significance. ESF #13 capabilities support incident management requirements including force and critical infrastructure protection, security planning and technical assistance, technology support, and public safety in both preincident and postincident situations. ESF #13 generally is activated in situations requiring extensive assistance to provide public safety and security and where state and local government resources are overwhelmed or are inadequate, or in preincident or postincident situations that require protective solutions or capabilities unique to the federal government.

- *ESF #14, Long-Term Community Recovery and Mitigation, Federal Emergency Management Agency*: Provides a framework for federal government support to state, regional, local, and tribal governments, nongovernmental organizations (NGOs), and the private sector designed to enable community recovery from the long-term consequences of an incident of national significance. This support consists of available programs and resources of federal departments and agencies to enable community recovery, especially long-term community recovery, and to reduce or eliminate risk from future incidents, where feasible.

- *ESF #15, External Affairs, Department of Homeland Security*: Ensures that sufficient federal assets are deployed to the field during a potential or actual incident of national significance to provide accurate, coordinated, and timely information to affected audiences, including governments, media, the private sector, and the local populace. ESF #15 provides the resource support and mechanisms to implement the National Response Plan—Incident Communications Emergency Policy and Procedures (NRP-

ICEPP) described in the NRP Public Affairs Support Annex.

Table 7-6 lists the various roles assumed by the different federal agencies with regard to the 15 ESFs.

## The Incident Annexes of the National Response Plan

The incident annexes address contingency or hazard situations requiring specialized application of the NRP. The annexes describe the following components for each of the specialized incident types:

- **Policies**: Each annex explains unique authorities pertinent to that incident, the special actions or declarations that may result, and any special policies that may apply.
- **Situation**: Each annex describes the incident situation as well as the planning assumptions, and outlines the approach that will be used if key assumptions do not hold (for example, how authorities will operate if they lose communication with senior decision makers).
- **Concept of Operations**: Each annex describes the concept of operations appropriate to the incident, integration of operations with NRP elements, unique aspects of the organizational approach, notification and activation processes, and specialized incident-related actions. Each annex also details the coordination structures and positions of authority that are unique to the type of incident, the specialized response teams or unique resources needed, and other special considerations.
- **Responsibilities**: Each incident annex identifies the coordinating and cooperating agencies involved in an incident-specific response; in some cases this responsibility is held jointly by two or more departments.

Each of the incident annexes is described in the following subsections.

### Biological Incident Annex

**Coordinating Agency**: Department of Health and Human Services

The purpose of the Biological Incident Annex is to outline the actions, roles, and responsibilities associated with response to a disease outbreak of known or unknown origin requiring federal assistance. Actions associated with the Biological Incident Annex can take place with or without a presidential Stafford Act declaration or a public health emergency declaration by the secretary of health and human services (HHS). However, the policies included in the annex apply only to potential or actual incidents of national significance.

The annex outlines biological incident response actions including threat assessment notification procedures, laboratory testing, joint investigative/response procedures, and activities related to recovery. The broad objectives of the federal government's response to a biological terrorism event, pandemic influenza, emerging infectious disease, or novel pathogen outbreak are to:

- Detect the event through disease surveillance and environmental monitoring.
- Identify and protect the population(s) at risk.
- Determine the source of the outbreak.
- Quickly frame the public health and law enforcement implications.
- Control and contain any possible epidemic (including providing guidance to state and local public health authorities).
- Augment and surge public health and medical services.
- Track and defeat any potential resurgence or additional outbreaks.
- Assess the extent of residual biological contamination and decontaminate as necessary.

### Catastrophic Incident Annex

**Coordinating Agency**: The Department of Homeland Security

**TABLE 7-6** The Various Roles Assumed by Federal Agencies in Support of the 15 ESFs

| Agency | #1—Transportation | #2—Communications | #3—Public Works and Engineering | #4—Firefighting | #5—Emergency Management | #6—Mass Care, Housing, and Human Services | #7—Resource Support | #8—Public Health and Medical Services | #9—Urban Search and Rescue | #10—Oil and Hazardous Materials Response | #11—Agriculture and Natural Resources | #12—Energy | #13—Public Safety and Security | #14—Long-term Community Recovery and Mitigation | #15—External Affairs |
|---|---|---|---|---|---|---|---|---|---|---|---|---|---|---|---|
| USDA | | | S | | S | S | | S | | S | C/P | S | | P | S |
| USDA/FS | S | S | S | C/P | S | S | S | S | S | S | | | S | | |
| DOC | S | S | S | S | S | | S | | | S | S | S | S | P/S | S |
| DOD | S | S | S | S | S | S | S | S | S | S | S | S | S | S | S |
| DOD/USACE | | | C/P | S | S | S | | S | S | S | S | S | S | S | |
| ED | | | | | S | | | | | | | | | | S |
| DOE | S | | S | | S | | S | S | | S | S | C/P | S | S | S |
| HHS | | | S | | S | S | | C/P | S | S | S | | | P/S | S |
| DHS | S | S | S | | S | S | S | S | S | S | S | S | C/P/S | S | C |
| DHS/EPR/FEMA | | S | P | S | C/P | C/P | | | C/P | S | | | | C/P | P |
| DHS/IAIP/NCS | | C/P | | | | | | | | | | S | | | |
| DHS/USCG | S | | S | S | | | | S | S | P | | | S | | |
| HUD | | | | | S | S | | | | | | | | P | S |
| DOI | S | S | S | S | S | S | | | | S | P | | S | S | S |
| DOJ | S | | | | S | S | | S | S | S | S | | C/P/S | | S |
| DOL | | | S | | S | S | S | S | S | S | S | S | | S | S |
| DOS | S | | | | S | | | S | | S | S | S | | | S |
| DOT | C/P | | S | | S | S | S | S | S | S | S | S | | S | S |
| TREAS | | | | | S | S | | | | | | | | P | S |
| VA | | | S | | S | S | S | S | | | | | S | | S |
| EPA | | | S | S | S | | | S | | C/P | S | S | S | S | S |
| FCC | | S | | | S | | | | | | | | | | S |
| GSA | S | S | S | | S | S | C/P | S | | | S | S | | | S |
| NASA | | | | | S | | S | | S | | | | | S | S |
| NRC | | | S | | S | | | | | | S | | S | | S |
| OPM | | | | | S | | S | | | | | | | | S |
| SBA | | | | | S | S | | | | | | | | P | S |
| SSA | | | | | | S | | | | | | | S | | S |
| TVA | | | S | | S | | | | | | | S | | S | S |
| USAID | | | | | | | | S | S | | | | | | S |
| USPS | S | | | | S | S | | S | | | S | | S | | S |
| ARC | | | S | | S | P | | S | | | S | | | S | S |

C = ESF coordinator
P = Primary agency
S = Support agency

*Source*: Department of Homeland Security (DHS). 2005. *The National Response Plan*. Washington, DC: DHS.

The Catastrophic Incident Annex to the National Response Plan (NRP-CIA) establishes the context and overarching strategy for implementing and coordinating an accelerated, proactive national response to a catastrophic incident. A more detailed and operationally specific NRP Catastrophic Incident Supplement (NRP-CIS) that is designated "For Official Use Only" has not been released for public view, and is therefore published independently of the NRP base plan and annexes.

A catastrophic incident, as defined by the NRP, is any natural or man-made incident, including terrorism, that results in extraordinary levels of mass casualties, damage, or disruption severely affecting the population, infrastructure, environment, economy, national morale, and/or government functions. A catastrophic incident could result in sustained national impacts over a prolonged period of time; almost immediately exceeds resources normally available to state, local, tribal, and private-sector authorities in the impacted area; and significantly interrupts governmental operations and emergency services to such an extent that national security could be threatened. All catastrophic incidents are automatically considered incidents of national significance. These factors drive the urgency for coordinated national planning to ensure accelerated federal/national assistance.

Recognizing that federal and/or national resources are required to augment overwhelmed state, local, and tribal response efforts, the NRP-CIA establishes protocols to preidentify and rapidly deploy key essential resources (e.g., medical teams, urban search and rescue teams, transportable shelters, and medical and equipment caches) that are expected to be urgently needed/required to save lives and contain incidents.

Accordingly, upon designation by the secretary of homeland security of a catastrophic incident, federal resources—organized into incident-specific "packages"—deploy in accordance with the NRP-CIS and in coordination with the affected state and incident command structure.

Only the secretary of homeland security or a designee may initiate implementation of the NRP-CIA. All deploying federal resources remain under the control of their respective federal department or agency during mobilization and deployment. Unless it can be credibly established that a mobilizing federal resource identified in the NRP-CIS is not needed at the catastrophic incident venue, that resource deploys. An important factor associated with NRP-CIA designated disasters is that federal assets unilaterally deployed in accordance with the NRP-CIS do not require a state cost-share.

Responsibilities of the DHS as coordinating agency under the NRP-CIS, include the following:

- Establish that a catastrophic incident has occurred and implement the NRP-CIA.
- Notify all federal departments and agencies to implement the NRP-CIA and the NRP-CIS.
- Upon implementation of the NRP-CIA:
  - Activate and deploy (or prepare to deploy) DHS-managed teams, equipment caches, and other resources in accordance with the NRP-CIS.
  - Identify, prepare, and "operationalize" facilities critical to supporting the movement and reception of deploying federal resources.
  - Activate national-level facilities and capabilities in accordance with the NRP-CIS and standard NRP protocols.
  - Establish and maintain communications with incident command authorities to ensure a common and current operating picture regarding critical resource requirements.
  - Make every attempt to establish contact with the impacted state(s) to coordinate the employment of federal resources in support of the state.

Responsibilities of the cooperating agencies under the NRP-CIS are as follows. When notified by the HSOC that the secretary of homeland security has implemented the NRP-CIA, federal departments and agencies (and the American Red Cross):

- Activate and deploy (or prepare to deploy) agency- or ESF-managed teams, equipment caches, and other resources in accordance with the NRP-CIS.

- Commence ESF responsibilities as appropriate.
- Commence assessments of the probable consequences of the incident and projected resource requirements.
- Commence development of shorter and longer term response and recovery strategies.

The NRP-CIS provides a list of the specific actions that are initiated on activation of the NRP-CIA. The following federal departments and agencies and other organizations are assigned specific responsibilities as cooperating agencies:

- Department of Agriculture
- Department of Defense
- Department of Energy
- Department of Health and Human Services
- Department of Homeland Security
- Department of Transportation
- Department of Veterans Affairs
- Environmental Protection Agency
- American Red Cross

Departments and agencies assigned primary responsibility for one or more functional response areas under the NRP-CIS appendixes are identified here:

- **Mass Care**: American Red Cross
- **Search and Rescue**: Department of Homeland Security
- **Decontamination**: Department of Homeland Security, Environmental Protection Agency, and Department of Health and Human Services
- **Public Health and Medical Support**: Department of Health and Human Services
- **Medical Equipment and Supplies**: Department of Health and Human Services
- **Patient Movement**: Department of Health and Human Services and Department of Defense
- **Mass Fatality**: Department of Health and Human Services
- **Housing**: Department of Homeland Security
- **Public and Incident Communications**: Department of Homeland Security
- **Transportation**: Department of Transportation

- **Private-Sector Support**: Department of Homeland Security
- **Logistics**: Department of Homeland Security

### Cyber Incident Annex

**Coordinating Agencies**: Department of Defense, Department of Homeland Security, Department of Justice

The Cyber Incident Annex discusses policies, organization, actions, and responsibilities for a coordinated, multidisciplinary, broad-based approach to prepare for, respond to, and recover from cyber-related incidents of national significance impacting critical national processes and the national economy. This annex describes the framework for federal cyber incident response coordination among federal departments and agencies and, on request, state, local, tribal, and private-sector entities.

This framework may be utilized in any incident of national significance with cyber-related issues, including significant cyber threats and disruptions; crippling cyber attacks against the Internet or critical infrastructure information systems; technological emergencies; or presidentially declared disasters. Cyber-related incidents of national significance may result in activation of both ESF #2—Communications and the Cyber Incident Annex. When processes in both annexes are activated, the Department of Homeland Security National Cyber Security Division (NCSD) continues its responsibilities under this annex and also fulfills its responsibilities as described in ESF #2.

A cyber-related incident of national significance may take many forms: an organized cyber attack, an uncontrolled exploit such as a virus or worm, a natural disaster with significant cyber consequences, or other incidents capable of causing extensive damage to critical infrastructure or key assets. Large-scale cyber incidents may overwhelm government and private-sector resources by disrupting the Internet and/or taxing critical infrastructure information systems. Complications from disruptions of this magnitude may threaten lives, property, the economy, and national security. Rapid identification, information exchange, investigation, and coordinated response and remediation often can mitigate the damage caused by this type of malicious cyberspace activity.

The federal government plays a significant role in managing intergovernmental (federal, state, local, and tribal) and, where appropriate, public–private coordination in response to cyber incidents of national significance. Federal government responsibilities include:

- Providing indications and warning of potential threats, incidents, and attacks
- Information sharing both inside and outside the government, including best practices, investigative information, coordination of incident response, and incident mitigation
- Analyzing cyber vulnerabilities, exploits, and attack methodologies
- Providing technical assistance
- Conducting investigations, forensics analysis, and prosecution
- Attributing the source of cyber attacks
- Defending against the attack
- Leading national-level recovery efforts.

These activities are the product of, and require, a concerted effort by federal, state, local, and tribal governments, and nongovernmental entities such as private industry and academia.

### Nuclear/Radiological Incident Annex

**Coordinating Agencies**: Department of Defense, Department of Energy, Department of Homeland Security, Environmental Protection Agency, National Aeronautics and Space Administration, Nuclear Regulatory Commission

The Nuclear/Radiological Incident Annex provides an organized and integrated capability for a timely, coordinated response by federal agencies to terrorist incidents involving nuclear or radioactive materials (incidents of national significance), and accidents or incidents involving such material that may or may not rise to the level of an incident of national significance. This annex describes how the coordinating agencies and cooperating agencies support DHS's overall coor-

dination of the response to a nuclear/radiological incident of national significance. In addition, this annex describes how the coordinating agencies lead the response to incidents of lesser severity.

The actions described in this annex may be implemented (1) concurrently with, and as an integral part of, the NRP for all nuclear/radiological incidents or accidents considered to be Incidents of National Significance; or (2) independently for all other nuclear/radiological accidents or incidents considered to be below the threshold of an incident of national significance and, therefore, not requiring overall federal coordination by DHS.

This annex applies to nuclear/radiological incidents, including sabotage and terrorist incidents, involving the release or potential release of radioactive material that poses an actual or perceived hazard to public health, safety, national security, and/or the environment. This includes terrorist use of radiological dispersal devices (RDDs, or "dirty bombs") or improvised nuclear devices (INDs) as well as reactor plant accidents (commercial or weapons production facilities), lost radioactive material sources, transportation accidents involving nuclear/radioactive material, and foreign accidents involving nuclear or radioactive material.

The level of federal response to a specific incident is based on numerous factors, including the ability of state, local, and tribal officials to respond; the type and/or amount of radioactive material involved; the extent of the impact or potential impact on the public and environment; and the size of the affected area. In situations where threat analysis includes indications that a terrorist incident involving radiological materials could occur, actions are coordinated in accordance with the preincident prevention protocols set forth in the NRP base plan.

This annex:

- Provides planning guidance and outlines operational concepts for the federal response to any nuclear/radiological incident, including a terrorist incident, that has actual, potential, or perceived radiological consequences within the

United States or its territories, possessions, or territorial waters, and that requires a response by the federal government.

- Acknowledges the unique nature of a variety of nuclear/radiological incidents and the responsibilities of federal, state, local, and tribal governments to respond to them.

- Describes federal policies and planning considerations on which this annex and federal agency-specific nuclear/radiological response plans are based.

- Specifies the roles and responsibilities of federal agencies for preventing, preparing for, responding to, and recovering from nuclear/radiological incidents.

- Includes guidelines for notification, coordination, and leadership of federal activities, and coordination of public information, congressional relations, and international activities.

- Provides protocols for coordinating federal government capabilities to respond to radiological incidents. These capabilities include, but are not limited to:

  - The Interagency Modeling and Atmospheric Assessment Center (IMAAC), which is responsible for production, coordination, and dissemination of consequence predictions for an airborne hazardous material release

  - The Federal Radiological Monitoring and Assessment Center (FRMAC), established at or near the scene of an incident to coordinate radiological assessment and monitoring

  - The Advisory Team for Environment, Food, and Health (known as "the Advisory Team"), which provides expert recommendations on protective action guidance.

## Oil and Hazardous Materials Incident Annex

**Coordinating Agencies**: Environmental Protection Agency, U.S. Coast Guard (DHS)

This annex describes roles, responsibilities, and coordinating mechanisms for managing certain oil and hazardous materials pollution incidents that are

determined to be incidents of national significance. This annex addresses those oil and hazardous materials incidents of national significance that are managed through concurrent implementation of the NRP and the National Oil and Hazardous Substances Pollution Contingency Plan (NCP), but are not ESF #10—Oil and Hazardous Materials Response activations. Procedures for oil and hazardous material incidents of national significance for which ESF #10 is activated are addressed in the ESF #10 annex.

The NCP provides the organizational structure and procedures for federal response to releases of oil and hazardous materials in the United States and its territories, accidental or intentional. The NCP addresses incident prevention, planning, response, and recovery. The hazardous materials addressed under the NCP include certain substances considered weapons of mass destruction (i.e., chemical agents, biological agents, and radiological/nuclear material).

The NCP establishes structures at the national, regional, and local levels that are used to respond to thousands of incidents annually that never rise to the level of an incident of national significance. When an incident of national significance does occur, these NCP structures remain in place to provide hazard-specific expertise and support. This annex describes how the NCP structures work with NRP coordinating structures during incidents of national significance.

It is expected that most incidents of national significance involving oil and hazardous materials are managed through an ESF #10 activation, but it is possible that an incident of national significance involving oil and hazardous materials could occur for which ESF #10 would not be activated. Some oil and hazardous materials incident responses may be initiated under the NCP alone, or under this annex as an incident of national significance, then transition to ESF #10 after a Stafford Act declaration is made (or after ESF #10 is activated via the NRP federal-to-federal support mechanism). Federal on-scene coordinators (OSCs) have independent authority under the NCP to respond to an oil or hazardous materials incident and may initiate initial response activities before the DHS determines whether the incident is an incident of national significance and/or the president declares a Stafford Act major disaster or emergency.

NCP structures and response mechanisms remain in place during an incident of national significance involving an actual or potential release of oil or hazardous materials, and coordinate with NRP mechanisms as described in this annex.

### Terrorism Incident Law Enforcement and Investigation Annex

**Coordinating Agency**: Federal Bureau of Investigation (DOJ)

The purpose of this annex is to facilitate an effective federal law enforcement and investigative response to all threats or acts of terrorism within the United States, regardless of whether they are deemed credible and/or whether they escalate to an incident of national significance. To accomplish this, the annex establishes a structure for a systematic, coordinated, unified, timely, and effective national law enforcement and investigative response to threats or acts of terrorism. This annex provides planning guidance and outlines operational concepts for the federal law enforcement and investigative response to a threatened or actual terrorist incident within the United States, and acknowledges and outlines the unique nature of each threat or incident, the capabilities and responsibilities of the local jurisdictions, and the law enforcement and investigative activities necessary to prevent or mitigate a specific threat or incident.

When acts of terrorism, threats, or detection of terrorist plans are recognized, the U.S. government attempts to apprehend and prosecute directly, or assist other governments in prosecuting, the responsible individuals. To ensure the policies established in applicable presidential directives are implemented in a coordinated manner, this annex provides overall guidance to federal, state, local, and tribal agencies concerning the federal government's law enforcement and investigative response to potential or actual terrorist threats or incidents that occur in the United States, particularly those involving WMDs.

The law enforcement and investigative response to a terrorist threat or incident within the United States is a highly coordinated, multiagency state, local, tribal, and federal responsibility. In support of this mission, the following federal agencies have primary responsibility for certain aspects of the overall law enforcement and investigative response:

- Department of Defense (DOD)
- Department of Energy (DOE)
- Department of Health and Human Services (HHS)
- Department of Homeland Security (DHS)
- Department of Justice/Federal Bureau of Investigation (FBI)
- Environmental Protection Agency (EPA)

The attorney general was given the lead responsibility for criminal investigations of terrorist acts or terrorist threats by individuals or groups inside the United States, or directed at U.S. citizens or institutions abroad, under Homeland Security Presidential Directive No. 5. Acting through the FBI, the attorney general, in cooperation with other federal departments and agencies engaged in activities to protect our national security, also coordinates the activities of the other members of the law enforcement community to detect, prevent, preempt, and disrupt terrorist attacks.

Although not formally designated under this annex, other federal departments and agencies may have authorities, resources, capabilities, or expertise required to support terrorism-related law enforcement and investigation operations. Agencies may be requested to participate in federal planning and response operations, and may be requested to designate liaison officers and provide other support as required.

## RECOVERY

The recovery function is not easy to classify; it often begins in the initial hours and days following a disaster event and can continue for months and in some cases years, depending on the severity of the event (Figure 7-13). Unlike the response function, where all efforts

FIGURE 7-13   New York City, New York, September 27, 2001—The remaining section of the World Trade Center is surrounded by a mountain of rubble following the September 11 terrorist attacks. (Photo by Bri Rodriguez/FEMA News Photo)

have a singular focus, the recovery function or process is characterized by a complex set of issues and decisions that must be made by individuals and communities. These issues include the following:

- Rebuilding homes
- Replacing property
- Resuming employment
- Restoring businesses
- Permanently repairing and rebuilding infrastructure

Since the establishment of DHS, the recovery function has remained relatively unchanged, though minor changes affecting the nomenclature and classification of the available assistance, as well as some relief programs and grants, have occurred. Because the recovery function has such long-lasting impacts and usually high costs, the participants in the process are numerous. They include all levels of government, the business community, political leadership, community activists, and individuals. The major players and programs will be listed here and changes, if any, will be described.

Given that the federal government plays the largest role in providing the technical and financial support for recovery, this section will focus on the federal role. It will discuss the structure and the various programs available to assist individuals and communities in the postdisaster environment and will briefly reference the various national voluntary organizations that provide some assistance for recovery. Sidebar 7-13 provides some quick facts about recovery.

## SIDEBAR 7-13   **Quick Facts on Recovery**

- In the period from 1990 to 1999, FEMA spent more than $25.4 billion for declared disasters and emergencies compared to $3.9 billion in current dollars for 1980–1989.
- For the 1990–1999 period, more than $6.3 billion was provided in grants for temporary housing, home repairs, and other disaster-related needs for individuals and families. An additional $14.8 billion went to states and local governments for cleanup and restoration projects, including more than $1.37 billion for mission-assigned work undertaken by other federal agencies.
- In the 1990s, a total of 88 declarations were issued for hurricanes and typhoons, for which FEMA obligated more than $7.78 billion for disaster costs. The most costly to FEMA was Hurricane Georges in 1998, followed closely by Hurricane Andrew in 1992.
- The most frequently declared disaster type was flooding resulting from severe storms,

with more than $7.3 billion committed by FEMA for response and recovery costs. The most costly were the Midwest floods in 1993 and the Red River Valley floods in 1997.
- By November 2002, FEMA had given a total of $306,102,000 in disaster recovery funding for the victims of September 11 attacks. The distribution of different programs is as follows:
  - Temporary home housing: mortgage and rental assistance ($76,275,000), minimal home repair ($1,450,000), transient accommodations ($1,225,000), rental assistance ($26,150,000)
  - Individual family grants ($25,400,000)
  - Crisis counseling assistance and training program ($162,400,000)
  - Unemployment assistance ($13,200,000)
  - Legal services ($2,000)

*Source*: Federal Emergency Management Agency, www.fema.gov.

## DISASTER RECOVERY OPERATIONS IN THE NATIONAL RESPONSE PLAN

The National Response Plan addresses the recovery needs of communities affected by incidents of national significance through the application of ESF #14, Long-Term Community Recovery and Mitigation. This ESF provides the framework on which the various federal government agencies that support state, regional, local, and tribal governments, nongovernmental organizations (NGOs), and the private sector provide available programs and resources to enable community recovery, especially long-term community recovery, and to reduce or eliminate risk from future incidents. For this ESF, FEMA is the coordinating agency. There are six individual primary agencies.

Ultimately, it is the state, local, and tribal governments (as well as the private sector) who define for themselves what constitutes risk reduction and long-term community recovery priorities. Like all aspects of the NRP, federal resources are provided to supplement the ongoing activities at the local level—to provide support, not to take over.

Federal support is tailored to the type, extent, and duration of the event and the predicted long-term recovery period, and on the availability of federal resources. Long-term community recovery efforts are focused on permanent restoration of infrastructure, housing, and the local economy, with attention to mitigation of future impacts of a similar nature, when feasible. In recognition of the importance of using the disaster recovery period to increase the resilience (thereby reducing the vulnerability) of the affected area, ESF #14 directs federal agencies to apply loss reduction building expertise in the rebuilding of critical infrastructure.

According to ESF #14, the coordinating, primary, and support agencies are tasked to:

- Assess the social and economic consequences in the impacted area and coordinate federal efforts to address long-term community recovery issues resulting from an incident of national significance.
- Advise on the long-term recovery implications of response activities and coordinate the transition from response to recovery in field operations.
- Work with state, local, and tribal governments, NGOs, and private-sector organizations to conduct comprehensive analysis of local economy impacts, and determine how to bring economic recovery to the affected communities.
- Identify appropriate federal programs and agencies to support implementation of the long-term community recovery plan, and ensure coordination of these programs.
- Avoid duplication of assistance, and coordinate to the extent possible program application processes and planning requirements to streamline assistance.
- Determine responsibilities for recovery activities, and provide a vehicle to maintain continuity in program delivery among federal departments and agencies, and with state, local, and tribal governments and other involved parties, to ensure follow-through of recovery and hazard mitigation efforts.

Each of the primary and support agencies have distinct programs aimed at facilitating recovery, based on their individual agency-specific expertise. The following subsections describe each agency's recovery function.

### Department of Agriculture

Provides emergency loans for the agricultural sector, technical assistance for agricultural market recovery, rural housing assistance, technical assistance for resource conservation, and technical and financial assistance for emergency watershed protection.

### Department of Commerce Economic Development Administration

Provides general economic recovery and growth assistance, technical assistance in community planning, and economic assessment expertise.

### Federal Emergency Management Agency

Provides technical assistance in community and state planning; recovery and mitigation grant and insurance programs; outreach and public education; building science expertise; and natural hazard vulnerability/risk assessment expertise. FEMA's many recovery programs are detailed later in this chapter.

### Department of Housing and Urban Development

Provides building technology technical assistance, and assistance for housing; community redevelopment and economic recovery; public services; infrastructure; mortgage financing; and public housing repair and reconstruction.

### Department of the Treasury

Provides economic and financial resilience and vitality, including reliability of public and private payments systems and financial flows, and removal of impediments to economic activity.

### Small Business Association

Provides long-term loan assistance to homeowners, renters, businesses of all sizes, and nonprofit organizations for repair, replacement, mitigation, relocation, or code required upgrades of incident-damaged property. Loan assistance is provided to small businesses to address adverse economic impacts due to the incident.

### Department of Commerce

Provides assistance through three different sub-components:

- **Economic and Statistics Administration**: Performs economic impact assessments.
- **National Institute of Standards and Technology**: Provides building science expertise.
- **National Oceanic and Atmospheric Administration**: Provides natural hazard vulnerability analysis expertise and coastal zone management.

### U.S. Army Corps of Engineers

Provides technical assistance in community planning and civil engineering, and natural hazard risk assessment expertise, and supports the development of national strategies and plans related to housing and permanent housing, debris management, and the restoration of public facilities and infrastructure.

### Department of Energy

Assists in the economic assessment of an incident based on degradation to energy infrastructure. Provides the appropriate support and resources to assist in energy infrastructure restoration. Provides technical advice in radioactive debris management.

### Department of Health and Human Services

Provides expertise in long-term health and medical concerns and mental health services.

### Department of Homeland Security

Provides assistance through three separate components (other than FEMA):

- **Border and Transportation Security Directorate, Transportation Security Administra-** **tion**: Coordinates security of the nation's transportation system in times of national emergency.
- **Information Analysis and Infrastructure Protection Directorate**: Provides technical expertise in protective measures for critical infrastructure.
- **Private-Sector Liaison**: Provides expertise in private-sector capabilities and services; provides coordination with private-sector organizations.

### Department of the Interior

Provides technical assistance in community planning, and natural and cultural resources expertise; community liaison for federally owned lands and facilities; and natural hazard vulnerability analysis expertise.

### Department of Labor

Conducts incident unemployment programs; provides job training and retraining assistance and expertise in economic assessment.

### Department of Transportation

Provides technical assistance in transportation planning and engineering and transportation assistance programs.

### Environmental Protection Agency

Provides technical assistance for planning for contaminated debris management and environmental remediation.

### Tennessee Valley Authority

Provides technical expertise in federal lands stewardship and electrical grid operations.

### American Red Cross

Provides mass care services; individual immediate and long-term family services; postevent mitigation; referral support; and health and mental health services.

## COORDINATION OF DISASTER RECOVERY

The practical work of implementing the recovery process occurs at the Joint Field Office. Two organizational structures, or branches, divide the recovery assistance functions. These branches assess state and local recovery needs at the outset of the disaster and relevant time frames for program delivery. The Human Services branch coordinates assistance programs to help individuals, families, and businesses meet basic needs and return to self-sufficiency. It is responsible for the donations management function. The Infrastructure Support branch coordinates assistance programs to aid state and local governments and eligible private nonprofit organizations to repair or replace damaged public facilities. The two branches assist in identifying appropriate agency assistance programs to meet applicant needs, synchronizing assistance delivery and encouraging incorporation of mitigation measures where possible. In addition to the work of the disaster recovery centers (DRCs), applicant briefings are conducted for local government officials and certain private nonprofit organizations to inform them of available recovery assistance and how to apply.

Federal disaster assistance available under a major disaster falls into three general categories: individual assistance, public assistance, and hazard mitigation assistance. Individual assistance is aid to individuals, families, and business owners. Public assistance is aid to public and certain private nonprofit entities for emergency services and the repair or replacement of disaster-damaged public facilities. Hazard mitigation assistance is funding available for measures designed to reduce future losses to public and private property.

A detailed description of the first two types of assistance follows.

## FEMA'S INDIVIDUAL ASSISTANCE RECOVERY PROGRAMS

Individual assistance programs are oriented to individuals, families, and small businesses, and the programs include the Individuals and Households Program, SBA loans, disaster unemployment assistance, legal services, special tax considerations, and crisis counseling. The disaster victim must first register for assistance and establish eligibility before receiving this assistance. These programs are described next.

### INDIVIDUALS AND HOUSEHOLDS PROGRAM

The Individuals and Households Program (IHP) is a program coordinated jointly by FEMA and the affected states. When a major disaster is declared, the IHP provides both money and services to people in the declared areas whose property has been damaged or destroyed and whose losses are not covered by insurance. To receive assistance under this program, disaster victims must register for assistance and first have their eligibility established.

IHP has two separate programs that address the needs of individuals and households. The Housing Assistance program works to ensure that people whose homes are damaged by a disaster have a safe place to live while it is repaired or replaced. The Other Needs Assistance (ONA) program provides financial assistance to individuals and households who have disaster-related expenses or serious needs, but who do not qualify for Small Business Administration (SBA) loans (see next subsection). These two programs are designed to provide funds for expenses that are not covered by insurance. They are available only to U.S. citizen homeowners and renters, noncitizen nationals, or qualified aliens. The following is a list of the types of assistance available through this program and what each provides:

- **Temporary Housing**—Funding that covers the cost of renting an alternate house or apartment when a victim's residence is uninhabitable due to disaster damage.
- **Repair**—Funding that covers the cost of repair to damage that was caused by the disaster, but which was not covered by insurance. These repairs must be geared toward making the home "safe and sanitary" to qualify.
- **Replacement**—Funding to cover the cost of replacing a home destroyed by a disaster.
- **Permanent Housing Construction**—Funding for the construction of a new home. This type of assistance occurs only in very unusual situations, in remote locations where no other type of housing is possible.
- **Other Needs Assistance (ONA)**—Funding for necessary and serious needs caused by the disaster. This includes medical, dental, funeral, personal property, transportation, moving and storage, and other expenses that FEMA approves. To receive ONA, the victim may first need to apply for an SBA loan.

## SMALL BUSINESS ADMINISTRATION (SBA) DISASTER LOANS

Following federally declared disasters, the U.S. Small Business Administration (SBA) normally provides federally subsidized loans to repair or replace homes, personal property, or businesses that sustained damages not covered by insurance. For many individuals the SBA disaster loan program is the primary form of disaster assistance. The SBA can provide three types of disaster loans to qualified homeowners and businesses:

1. Home disaster loans to homeowners and renters to repair or replace disaster-related damage to home or personal property

2. Business physical disaster loans to business owners to repair or replace disaster-damaged property, including inventory, and supplies
3. Economic injury disaster loans, which provide capital to small businesses and to small agricultural cooperatives to assist them through the disaster recovery period

## DISASTER UNEMPLOYMENT ASSISTANCE

The Disaster Unemployment Assistance (DUA) program provides unemployment benefits and reemployment services to individuals who have lost their jobs as a result of the disaster. Benefits begin with the date the job was lost, and can be continued for up to 26 weeks after the presidential declaration date. The DUA program is available to people who are not covered by other unemployment insurance programs or who cannot qualify for other unemployment compensation.

## LEGAL SERVICES

Following a disaster, the Young Lawyers Division of the American Bar Association may be contracted by FEMA to provide free legal assistance to disaster victims. These services are provided to low-income individuals who, prior to or because of the disaster, are unable to afford adequate legal services to meet their postdisaster-related needs. Legal advice under this program is limited to cases that will not result in any attorney or other fees. The assistance that participating lawyers provide typically includes the following:

- Assistance with insurance claims (life, medical, property, etc.)
- Counseling on landlord/tenant problems
- Assisting in consumer protection matters, remedies, and procedures
- Replacement of wills and other important legal documents destroyed in a major disaster

## SPECIAL TAX CONSIDERATIONS

Taxpayers who have sustained a casualty loss from a declared disaster may deduct that loss on the federal income tax return for the year in which the casualty actually occurred, or elect to deduct the loss on the tax return for the preceding tax year. To qualify, victims' losses must be greater than 10% of the adjusted gross income for the tax year by at least $100. Additionally, the Internal Revenue Service (IRS) can expedite refunds due to taxpayers in a federally declared disaster area. This service is available to any taxpayer in a federally declared disaster area.

## CRISIS COUNSELING

The Crisis Counseling Assistance and Training Program (CCP) is designed to provide supplemental funding to states for short-term crisis counseling services. Two separate portions of the CCP can be funded: immediate services and regular services. A state may request either or both types of funding. The immediate services program is intended to enable the state or local agency to respond to the immediate mental health needs with screening, diagnostic, and counseling techniques, as well as outreach services such as public information and community networking. The regular services program is designed to provide up to 9 months of crisis counseling, community outreach, and consultation and education services to people affected by the disaster. To be eligible for crisis counseling services funded by this program, the person must be a resident of the designated area or must have been located in the area at the time the disaster occurred. The person must also have a mental health problem that was caused by or aggravated by the disaster or its aftermath, or he or she must benefit from services provided by the program.

## PUBLIC ASSISTANCE PROGRAMS

Public assistance, oriented to public entities, is designed to facilitate the repair, restoration, recon-

FIGURE 7-14  New York City, New York, October 30, 2001—FEMA/New York State Disaster Field Office personnel meet to coordinate federal, state, and local disaster assistance programs. (Photo by Andrea Booher/FEMA News Photo)

struction, or replacement of public facilities or infrastructure damaged or destroyed by a federally declared disaster. Eligible applicants include state governments, local governments and any other political subdivision of a state, Native American tribes, and Alaska Native villages. Certain private nonprofit (PNP) organizations may also receive assistance, including educational, utility, irrigation, emergency, medical, rehabilitation, and temporary or permanent custodial care facilities, and other PNP facilities that provide essential services of a governmental nature to the general public.

As soon as is possible and practical following a disaster declaration, the state, assisted by FEMA, briefs state, local, and PNP officials to inform them of the assistance available and how to apply for it (Figures 7-14 and 7-15). To receive this assistance, a Request for Public Assistance must be filed with the state within 30 days of the time the area is designated as eligible. Following the briefing, a "Kickoff Meeting" is conducted where damages are discussed, needs assessed, and a plan of action put in place. A team made up of federal, state, and local representatives initiates the project, including documenting the eligible facilities, the eligible work, and the eligible cost for

FIGURE 7-15   New York City, New York, October 20, 2001—Disaster Field Office staff continue to work with other agencies operating near Ground Zero to provide information about disaster assistance programs. (Photo by Andrea Booher/FEMA News Photo)

fixing the damages to every public or PNP facility identified by state or local representatives. The team prepares a project worksheet (PW) for each project. Projects are grouped into the following categories:

- Category A: Debris removal
- Category B: Emergency protective measures
- Category C: Road systems and bridges
- Category D: Water control facilities
- Category E: Public buildings and contents
- Category F: Public utilities
- Category G: Parks, recreational, and other

FEMA reviews and approves the PWs and obligates the federal share of the costs (75% or more) to the state. The state then disburses funds to local applicants.

## OTHER FEDERAL AGENCY DISASTER RECOVERY FUNDING

Other federal agencies have programs that contribute to social and economic recovery. Most of these additional programs are triggered by a presidential declaration of a major disaster or emergency under the Stafford Act. However, the secretary of the Department of Agriculture and the administrator of the Small Business Administration have specific authority relevant to their constituencies to declare a disaster and provide disaster recovery assistance. All of the agencies are part of the structure of the National Response Plan. Appendix 7-1 provides a complete list of all disaster recovery programs available after a disaster declaration.

## CONCLUSION

The motives behind the establishment of the Department of Homeland Security are almost as numerous as the number of agencies it involved: politics, power, public relations, or a real need to improve the federal response and recovery systems because of the new spectrum of threats made apparent by the September 11 attacks. For whatever reason or combination of reasons, a system that had demonstrated its operational capabilities in both natural disasters and terrorism events in Oklahoma City, New York, and the Pentagon is undergoing significant change. As a result of the integration of different agencies and the need for new procedural system to operate together, the National Response Plan (NRP) has been developed with the National Incident Management System (NIMS). These two documents are now the references and guidelines that determine how the nation's first responders and agencies involved in response operate. The extensive funding provided by the government through the DHS has allowed the initiation of training and equipping of the nation's first responders and this effort will continue for the foreseeable future in order to build a strong, uniform, and highly capable response force.

The effort to include citizens and the private sector as active partners is commendable. Programs developed under the Citizen Corps Councils provide the opportunity to build strong communities. However, they have been poorly supported by the political leadership and are underfunded. Further collaboration with the business sector will allow for enhanced preparedness and protection of the critical infrastructure and provide a better understanding of its vulnerabilities and how to respond if it is attacked.

As a final point, it is essential to bear in mind that the massive integration of many agencies into one has its drawbacks: The independency is compromised and the overall redundancy of the system decreases. The NRP and NIMS define how different agencies operate together but it should not jeopardize or change the agencies' own integrity and mission. Although redundancy is an attribute that all organizations try to get rid of, it is also what often saves the day during a crisis situation. "Too efficient" systems with minimal backup, no duplication of function, and low flexibility/adaptability have been shown to be more vulnerable to unexpected situations, to fail in a worse manner, and to be less agile when responding to and dealing with an emergency. Thus, an excessive integration to reduce redundancy can cause the involved agencies to depend on each other rather than empower each other—and this might make the way for a catastrophic chain reaction of failure to occur in certain conditions.

## CASE STUDY 1
## The Space Shuttle Columbia Disaster

### The Event

On February 1, 2003, the Space Shuttle *Columbia*, flying mission STS-107, reentered Earth's atmosphere following its 28th successful space flight that began on January 16 of that year. It was carrying seven astronauts, including Commander Rick D. Husband, Pilot William C. McCool, Payload Commander Michael P. Anderson, Mission Specialists David M. Brown, Kalpana Chawla, and Laurel Blair Salton Clark, and Payload Specialist Ilan Ramon. The flight had been delayed a total of 13 times since its originally scheduled lift-off date of January 11, 2001.

On January 16, 2003, when the shuttle finally lifted off, a piece of insulation on one of the shuttle's fuel tanks broke off about 82 seconds into the flight. The event was considered inconsequential by mission specialists. However, because of the speed the shuttle was traveling at the time (1,650 mph), and the delicate nature of the shuttle's protective thermal skin, the insulation caused a small breach that did not pose any problems until the "burn" period experienced upon reentry.

During the reentry burn period (which began at 8:44 a.m.), several stages of shuttle positioning and speed, according to normal procedural systems, caused the shuttle to slow down considerably from its 17,500-mph speed. The friction caused by the shuttle entering the Earth's atmosphere at over 20 times the speed of sound, which results in an incredible release of energy, caused the leading edge of the wings to rise to as much as 3,000 degrees Fahrenheit.

Ground control crews began to notice failures in many of the instruments in the left wing. Progressively, more problems arose, but the control teams were having trouble with determining the root of the problems and with communicating with the crew to gain more insight into what may have been happening. The last transmission from the crew came at 8:59 a.m., which was cut off after just one word. At 9:05 a.m., a loud explosion was heard over Texas, and evidence that the shuttle had begun to disintegrate was clear to the naked eye.

The destruction of the shuttle showered debris across an area of hundreds of square miles in East Texas and Western Louisiana (a very small amount of material was also found in Arkansas). In total, over 2,000 individual debris fields were noted by recovery crews. As had been true with the Space Shuttle *Challenger*, the event was witnessed by the entire nation via breaking news reports. NASA immediately issued a warning to the public that all debris should be considered hazardous material, with the potential to cause injuries or death, and that any information on the location of debris should be immediately reported to local authorities. (Wikipedia, 2005)

## The Response

The response to the shuttle disaster has been called the largest deployment of civilian government agencies in history.

Due to the large area within which the debris was falling, scores of police and fire departments were immediately called to action by reports from citizens. As true first responders, these officials began, albeit without any real organization, to collect and document the shuttle debris. It was almost guaranteed that, beyond the initial seven astronauts and the space shuttle, there would be no additional fatalities, injuries, or destruction caused by the disaster. However, the work hours and resources required for such a large operation were assuredly going to be excessive—and likewise a strain on the state and local agencies involved.

President Bush immediately assessed the situation with FEMA and DHS officials, and issued emergency declarations for the states of Texas and Louisiana. It is important to note that these declarations were made in the absence of any formal request for assistance from the governors of either of those states. It was later declared by the administration that this action was considered appropriate because the space shuttle *Columbia* itself was considered federal property, and therefore the authority to make such declarations existed.

The disaster declaration, as per the Stafford Act, authorized the Federal Emergency Management Agency (FEMA) under Emergency Support Function (ESF) #5 to coordinate federal aid and the management of resources used by all responders in the response and recovery to the disaster. FEMA announced that Michael Brown, FEMA Deputy Director and Acting Undersecretary of the newly created Department of Homeland Security, would lead FEMA's efforts in what was considered a "search, find, and secure" operation.

From the onset, the agencies' priorities were three-fold: ensure public safety, retrieve evidence-pieces of the shuttle that could ultimately determine the cause of the tragedy, and reimburse expenses of state and local governments and private citizens who may have sustained property damage as a result of the accident and search. NASA quickly identified potential hazardous materials, such as tanks containing toxic substances or unexploded pyrotechnic devices, and once found, the Environmental Protection Agency (EPA) secured the material. The EPA also worked with state and local authorities to clear school campuses and public access areas, and tested air and water samples taken along the flight path for shuttle contaminates. Using the resources of the Emergency Response and Removal Service (ERRS) contractors and the U.S. Coast Guard (USCG) Gulf Strike Team, EPA found no evidence of hazardous material in the atmosphere or drinking water supplies. Early in the recovery effort, teams from NASA, the Federal Bureau of Investigation (FBI), National Guard, Urban Search and Rescue (US&R) organizations, the Department of Public Safety and others conducted a successful search in East Texas to recover and bring home the bodies of *Columbia*'s crew.

On February 2, FEMA announced that its principal mission was to assist the state and local response agencies in mapping the debris fields and collecting any debris reported or found. The agency reported that they had coordinated the following activities:

- Established an Interagency Initial Operating Facility (IOF) at Barksdale Air Force Base in Louisiana. Representatives from NASA, FEMA, the FBI, the EPA, and the Department of Defense were to be assembled there to coordinate response activities.
- Assigned liaisons from FBI, EPA, the Department of Transportation, the General Services Administration, and the Department of Defense to FEMA's Regional Operations Center in Denton, Texas. FEMA assigned state liaisons to the Texas State Emergency Operations Center and the State Command Post in Lufkin, Texas.
- Began the process of establishing two disaster field offices (DFOs) in Lufkin, Texas, and at the Barksdale Air Force Base in Louisiana. The

Lufkin DFO would serve as the primary operational DFO for all operations, including staging assets and deploying field teams for search, find, and secure operations. Barksdale Air Force Base in Louisiana would serve as the investigative center and storage location. A third (satellite) DFO was set up the next day at the Fort Worth Naval Air Station.

- Deployed special Mobile Emergency Response Systems (MERS) communications equipment to Lufkin, Texas.
- Announced that EPA had deployed HAZMAT teams to collect debris, mobilized Airborne Spectral Photo-Imaging of Environmental Contaminants Technology (ASPECT) aircraft to help locate debris using infrared sensors to detect hazardous chemicals and deployed the Trace Atmospheric Gas Analyzer Unit to provide mobile analytical support.
- Announced that the U.S. Coast Guard (now part of DHS) had deployed members of its Gulf Strike Team, based in Mobile, Alabama, to Lufkin to assist with debris recovery operations there. One of three located throughout the country, Gulf Strike Team personnel are specially trained and equipped to respond to incidents involving oil or hazardous chemical spills. (FEMA 3, 2003)

These teams had been deployed within hours to the disaster area to assist local fire, law enforcement, and emergency management authorities already on site. More than 60 agencies, including public and private groups, responded with personnel, supplies, and equipment. The Lufkin DFO was the regional center of all search-related operations. This was the first major response performed by the newly created Department of Homeland Security.

By the next day, February 3, FEMA had established a Joint Information Center (JIC) at the Lufkin Civic Center in Lufkin, Texas, to serve as the distribution point for information disseminated to the public, and to which the public could go to retrieve information. The JIC was comprised of representatives from FEMA, the EPA, NASA, the American Red Cross (ARC), the U.S. Forest Service, The U.S. Coast Guard, the Department of Health and Human Services (HHS), and several other agencies involved in the response at the federal and state levels. FEMA also announced that additional U.S. Coast Guard strike teams and the Texas and Louisiana National Guard were participating in the search, that water quality was being tested in both states, and that hazardous spills were being addressed.

On February 5, four days after the shuttle disaster, FEMA released a fact sheet describing the procedures by which materials were to be collected by state and local response agencies. The following are the guidelines from that fact sheet:

"The following guidelines are designed to assist public service personnel to determine when and how to collect and document space shuttle material. If the material is less than 18 inches in length and does not appear to be hazardous, then it may be collected under the following guidelines:

"**PRIVATE CITIZENS ARE NOT AUTHORIZED TO COLLECT MATERIAL**

"The following trained personnel are authorized to collect non-hazardous materials:

- Local, state or Federal Law Enforcement Personnel
- Fire, Medical, or Emergency Services Personnel
- U.S. Forest Service or Texas Forest Service
- Federal Emergency Management Agency (FEMA)
- Environmental Protection Agency (EPA)
- National Aeronautics and Space Administration (NASA)

"Only non-hazardous material may be collected under these guidelines. If the material includes any of the following, officials should contact **936-699-1032** or **936-699-1034** to report what they have found so that specially trained personnel can be deployed:

- **Stored Energy**: High pressure tanks and cylinders. Landing gear and tires.
- **Monomethyl Hydrazine**: Clear liquid stored in tanks, strong fishy odor.
- **Nitrogen Tetroxide**: Greenish liquid or brownish vapor, stored in tanks, bleach-like odor.
- **Ammonia**: Clear liquid, stored in tanks, very strong ammonia smell.

- **Pyrotechnic Devices**: Landing gear, window frames, crew seats, hatches and antennae.
- **Biological Material**: Any biological material, including human or animal remains.

"The following procedure should be followed by authorized, trained personnel if the identified material is non-hazardous:

- Photograph items before they are moved.
- Carefully document the location of the items (to include GPS data if available).
- Attach a tag to the item with the location the item was found and the name and phone number of the individual collecting the item. Include any information you think may be relevant to the investigation. Documentation for large items may be recorded with permanent marker directly on the hardware.
- Wear gloves (preferably not cloth) when handling items and do not open, adjust or move any switches, components or boxes.
- If possible, seal the item in a plastic bag.
- Transport the item to your local command post.

"If an item is marked SECRET, CONFIDENTIAL, or SSOR do not leave this item unattended before handover to NASA personnel. With any questions or for more information, please contact DPS at the Lufkin Emergency Operation Center, **936-699-1077**." (FEMA 5, 2003)

On February 6, the president amended the original disaster declaration to include any state within which shuttle debris was found. Additionally, the declaration was amended such that FEMA was authorized to reimburse a full 100% of the costs incurred by local and state agencies in their efforts to retrieve shuttle materials. (FEMA 6, 2003) By this point 115 pieces of shuttle material had been found by 174 officials searching in Louisiana. Texas was using 800 National Guard troops, 353 Department of Public Safety personnel, and 140 Forest Service employees in the search. Additionally, the EPA had collected over 1,100 bags of hazardous materials through the efforts of 370 employees working in 60 teams. (FEMA 7, 2003)

March 1 marked one month of operations in the response and recovery of the shuttle disaster. By this point there were over 5,200 federal and state officials working on the response, and four collection centers had been established to accept the debris that had been located. (FEMA 8, 2003) On March 27, a Bell 407

helicopter, involved in the search for shuttle debris, crashed in poor weather. Two members of the crew, Texas Forest Service employee Charles Krenek and pilot Jules F. Mier, Jr., died, and three other crew members were injured. This event brought the death toll of the disaster to nine. Air operations in the search were suspended until April 10, until it was determined that flights could resume under the safest possible conditions. (FEMA 10, 2003)

On April 17, FEMA announced that it would be handing over operational control of the recovery mission to NASA on April 30, nearly three months following the disaster. Also announced were the following updates on the progress of the search:

- Ground crews have searched over 83% of the 704,000 assigned acres.
- Air operations have searched 577 (92%) of the 629 grids (2 by 2 mile) assigned areas.
- Water operations have concluded.
- More than 79,900 pounds of shuttle material has been shipped to Kennedy Space Center in Florida. That represents approximately 37% of the weight of the craft.
- All reported debris in Louisiana has been picked up.
- Under the FEMA Public Assistance Program, Texas has been obligated $2.6 million and Louisiana has been obligated $395,000 for approved county/parish shuttle debris recovery related activities. (FEMA 9, 2003)

FEMA turned over control of the recovery operation to NASA on April 30. The same day, NASA opened the Columbia Recovery Operation (CRO) office at the Johnson Space Center in Houston. FEMA closed the disaster field office in Lufkin, Texas, on May 10. On May 5, FEMA released a recap of the search for the Space Shuttle *Columbia* debris material. This announcement included the following final statistics about the disaster recovery:

- After three months, search personnel recovered more than 82,500 pieces of shuttle debris equaling a total weight of 84,800 pounds, or almost 40 percent of the total dry weight of the shuttle.
- Ground, water and air searches combined covered more than 2.28 million acres.
- Water operations successfully identified more than 3,100 targets and covered 23 square miles.

- More than 16,500 ground search personnel and their support personnel searched an unprecedented 680,748 acres.
- Total man-hours utilized in the recovery effort amounted to approximately 1.5 million.
- Under the FEMA Public Assistance program, $10 million is the amount projected for Texas to reimburse eligible costs associated with the recovery effort. As of May 1, $3.98 million has been obligated. For Louisiana, projected reimbursable payments are $500,000 while $396,000 has been obligated.
- Outside Texas and Louisiana, searches have been concluded in New Mexico and California. Searches continue in Nevada and Utah.
- No debris has been found west of Littlefield, Texas, or east of Fort Polk, Louisiana.
- More than 130 federal, state and local agencies have participated in the recovery effort.
- Approximately 25,000 personnel took part in the recovery operation.
- The operation was supported by more than 270 organizations including businesses and volunteer groups.

**EPA Involvement**

FEMA tasked the Environmental Protection Agency with the management of all hazardous materials found in the search area. This disaster marked new territory for many of the agencies involved, including EPA and NASA, which had never before worked together on a project. Additionally, as NASA had warned repetitively that all shuttle debris should be considered hazardous, this was to be one of EPA's greatest operational challenges to date. More than 1,900 employees from the agency were deployed.

EPA's response was based out of Region 6, headquartered in Dallas, Texas. EPA's primary mission in the response effort was to protect public health and the environment, and their first task was to remove shuttle material from school property—a task they completed by February 4, only 3 days following the disaster. The search teams were set up so that an EPA team accompanied each 20-person search crew in order to handle any debris found within the search grids. In addition, EPA personnel responded to any other reports of potential debris sites that were called in to FEMA DFOs. Finally, EPA was charged with staffing the four local debris collection centers that

were established to process the tens of thousands of pieces of shuttle material that were collected over the course of the recovery operation.

To handle such a large operation, EPA had national teams suspend regular operations and deploy to Region 6, where the disaster had occurred, to help staff the 24-hour-per-day demands of the shuttle response. On the day of the disaster, EPA initiated flights of their Airborne Spectral-Imagery of Environmental Contaminants Technology (ASPECT) aircraft, which was able to locate shuttle parts containing potentially hazardous materials. Based on these flights they were able to determine that there were no major concentrations of hazardous materials present in the debris fields that could pose a major health hazard to the human populations in the surrounding areas. EPA also mobilized their Trace Atmospheric Gas Analyzer vehicle, which has the ability to collect real-time outdoor air quality samples while in motion.

On average, each EPA team processed between 10 and 15 sites per day, with the goal of processing a county every 3 to 5 days (per team). EPA dive teams conducted searches of small ponds and lakes, while side-scan sonar was utilized in larger bodies of water to locate debris.

Finally, EPA was tasked with the data management of collected shuttle debris. The location, description, and other information about each piece was collected in the field in handheld computers, and uploaded each night onto a central computer database, in order to assist NASA in determining the cause of the crash and other investigative goals. (EPA, 2003)

**All Agency Involvement**

The following federal agencies participated:

- Defense Coordinating Element
- Defense Criminal Investigation Service
- Department of Defense
- Department of Health and Human Services
- Department of the Interior
- Department of Transportation
- Environmental Protection Agency
- Federal Bureau of Investigation

- Federal Emergency Management Agency
- General Services Administration
- National Aeronautics and Space Administration
- National Imagery and Mapping Agency
- National Transportation Safety Board
- National Weather Service
- Naval Research Laboratory
- Office of Personnel Management
- U.S. Air Force
- U.S. Army
- U.S. Army Corp of Engineers
- U.S. Attorney's Office
- U.S. Coast Guard
- U.S. Fire Service
- U.S. Fish and Wildlife
- U.S. Forest Service
- U.S. Marshal Service
- National Park Service
- U.S. Navy
- Urban Search and Rescue
- and others.

Participating state agencies and other entities included these:

- Arkansas National Guard
- Colorado Forest Service
- Florida Division of Forestry
- Louisiana Department of Wildlife and Fisheries
- Louisiana National Guard
- Louisiana Office of Emergency Preparedness
- Louisiana State Police
- Maryland Task Force 1
- New Mexico National Guard
- North Carolina Forest Service
- Oklahoma National Guard
- Stephen F. Austin University
- Texas Department of Mental Health Mental Retardation
- Texas Army National Guard
- Texas Commission on Environmental Quality
- Texas Division of Emergency Management
- Texas Department of Public Safety
- Texas Department of Criminal Justice
- Texas Department of Transportation

- Texas Engineering Extension Service
- Texas Fish & Wildlife Department
- Texas Forest Service
- Texas National Resources Information System Service
- Texas Task Force 1
- Texas Water Development Board
- University of Texas Center for Space Research
- Virginia Department of Forestry
- and others.

Participating local agencies and other entities included the following:

- Angelina County Economic Development Partnership
- Angelina County Sheriff's Office
- Arlington Police Department
- Broward County Sheriff
- City of Lufkin
- City of San Diego Fire Department
- City of Dallas Fire Department
- City of Ft. Worth Fire Department
- Ft. Worth Independent School District
- Galveston County Sheriff
- Houston Police Department
- Jasper County Sheriff
- Kern County Fire Department
- San Augustine County Sheriff,
- and others.

Participating volunteer agencies were as follows:

- Alpine Rescue Team
- American Red Cross
- Civil Air Patrol
- The Salvation Army
- The Texas Baptist Men
- and others.

In support of EPA, the U.S. Navy was assigned to coordinate water search operations. An operations base was set up at Toledo Bend Reservoir. There were eight dive teams working the reservoir: three U.S. Navy, two EPA, one each from the city of Galveston, city of Houston, and the Texas Department of Public

Safety. In addition, six boats equipped with side and multibeam scanning sonar looked for dive targets, four on the reservoir and two on Lake Nacogdoches. The Navy also deployed various handheld sonar units and an autonomous unit that were programmed to search underwater areas independently. About 130 personnel worked the water search operation.

Following a tremendous initial search effort by local governments and volunteers, four base camps were established to house interagency crews at the request of the Texas Forest Service. These crews relieved the search burden on state and local resources by bringing in firefighting crews from other parts of the nation. Crews from 39 states joined the effort. In total, about 4,500 personnel arrived and about 155 crews of 20 people each daily combed through NASA-assigned search areas in a corridor 240 by 10 miles wide from Ellis County in the west to Toledo Bend Reservoir in the east. Four crew base camps were set up: Nacogdoches (1,100 personnel), Palestine (about 1,000), Hemphill (about 1,000), and Corsicana (about 1,350). A mobilization unit was established at Longview Airport to assist crew arrival, travel to and from base camps and departure. Since February 14, these out-of-state crews had expended nearly 132,000 man-hours on the search.

Extensive air searches were used in the search. Operating out of two facilities, one in the Lufkin area and one in the Palestine area, 33 helicopters and nine fixed-wing aircraft flew search grids over the 240 by 10 mile corridor seeking possible debris sites. Possible sites were relayed to ground crews for inspection.

The state of Texas rushed to assist local communities in the initial search, and continued to support the federal agencies responding to the event. The Texas Department of Public Safety's Division of Emergency Management coordinated the state response. Among state agency personnel committed were the following: 353 state troopers, about 800 National Guard, four aircraft, 17 helicopters, 140 Texas Forest Service personnel, 35 horse-mounted search teams, 20 Texas Department of Transportation personnel, 27 Texas Commission of Environmental Quality personnel, and various other units such as dogs and handlers, mapping support personnel, and game wardens.

**Conclusion**

As a test of the response capabilities, many have argued that the Department of Homeland Security was given an easy assignment—there were only seven initial fatalities, no injuries, and very little destruction. However, from a coordination standpoint, the event was colossal. As previously mentioned, it was the single greatest mobilization of civil service employees in the history of the nation, and with very few exceptions, the operation was carried off without a hitch. All local and state costs were reimbursed by the federal government, and many working relationships were created in the response and recovery phases when counterparts were able to work face to face in a relatively low-stress environment. The event proved that FEMA had retained its agency status within DHS, and was able to continue functioning as it had before the Homeland Security Act was signed just 4 months earlier.

## REFERENCES

Bullock & Haddow, LLC. 2003. *Madison County Terrorism Annex to Basic Emergency Response Plan. North Carolina.*

EPA. 2003. *Response to the Columbia Space Shuttle Incident.* <www.epa.gov/columbia>

FEMA 1. 2003. *President Declares Emergency in Texas and Louisiana in Response to Space Shuttle Tragedy.* FEMA Press Release (February 1). <www.fema.gov/news/newsrelease.fema?id=2406>

FEMA 2. 2003. *FEMA to Lead Search, Find, and Secure Mission Following Space Shuttle Tragedy.* FEMA Press Release (February 1). <www.fema.gov/news/newsrelease.fema?id=2405>

FEMA 3. 2003. *FEMA Puts Federal Resources into Action to Assist State and Local Authorities in Search, Find and Secure Mission for Columbia Debris.* FEMA Press Release (February 2). <www.fema.gov/news/newsrelease.fema?id=2407>

FEMA 4. 2003. *FEMA Establishes Joint Information Center for Columbia Debris Search, Find, and Secure Mission at Lufkin Civic Center.* FEMA Press Release (February 3). <www.fema.gov/news/newsrelease.fema?id=2409>

FEMA 5. 2003. Columbia *Material Collection Guidelines: Fact Sheet.* FEMA Press Release (February 5). <www.fema.gov/news/newsrelease.fema?id=2414>

FEMA 6. 2003. *President Amends Columbia Emergency Declaration to Include All States.* FEMA Press Release (February 6). <www.fema.gov/news/newsrelease.fema?id=2416>

FEMA 7. 2003. *FEMA Updates Search, Find and Secure Activities for Columbia Emergency.* FEMA Press Release (February 6). <www.fema.gov/news/newsrelease.fema?id=2415>

FEMA 8. 2003. *Good Progress Made in One Month of Shuttle Recovery.* FEMA Press Release (March 1). <www.fema.gov/news/newsrelease.fema?id=2458>

FEMA 9. 2003. *FEMA Will Hand On-Going Recovery Operations to NASA April 30.* FEMA Press Release (April 17). <www.fema.gov/news/newsrelease.fema?id=2534>

FEMA 10. 2003. *Recap of the Search for Columbia Shuttle Material.* FEMA Press Release (May 5). <www.fema.gov/news/newsrelease.fema?id=2808>

Wikipedia. 2005. *Space Shuttle Columbia Disaster.* <http://en.wikipedia.org/wiki/Space_Shuttle_Columbia_disaster>

## CASE STUDY 2
## The London Terror Attacks, July 7, 2005

On Thursday, July 7, 2005, just before 9 a.m., four suicide bombers blew themselves up; three on London subway trains and one on a bus. The explosions resulted in the deaths of 56 people, including the bombers, and injured more than 700 others. The entire London subway system was closed for the remainder of the day, and cellular telephone systems were jammed, leading to commuter chaos. The following timeline illustrates the attacks and the step-by-step response by British authorities.

8:50 a.m.   Three explosions occur almost simultaneously on three London underground trains: between Aldgate and Liverpool Street stations on the Circle Line; between Russell Square and King's Cross stations on the Piccadilly Line; and at Edgware Road station on the Circle Line.

At first, police are only aware of the Aldgate/Liverpool Street train attack. The Russell Square/King's Cross blast was not reported until 8:56, and the Edgware blast at 9:17. A review of technical data and witness accounts showed the three bombs actually went off within about 50 seconds.

9:47   A No. 30 bus on Upper Woburn Place near Tavistock Square is destroyed by a fourth explosion. Pictures show the roof of the double-decker bus ripped off and witnesses report seeing body parts in the road, Reuters reports.

10:02   Scotland Yard says it is dealing with a "major incident."

10:20   Metropolitan Police post a message on their website reporting that a major transportation incident has happened in London and that it is responding to six metro stations and one confirmed explosion in a public bus. Cause, severity, and impact of the explosions is not known at this point.

10:47   Home Secretary Charles Clarke says multiple London blasts have caused "terrible injuries."

11:15   European Union commissioner for justice and security affairs Franco Frattini tells reporters in Rome that the blasts in London are terrorist attacks.

11:35   London police chief tells Reuters news agency there are "indications of explosives" at one of the blast sites.

12:00 p.m.   British Prime Minister Tony Blair says the "barbaric" London blasts are terrorist attacks and were designed to coincide with the G8 summit in Scotland. He will return to London.

12:15   A group calling itself the Group of al-Qaeda of Jihad Organization in Europe lays claim to the blasts, posting a statement on an Islamist website. The claim cannot be independently verified.

12:27   Police and hospital officials tell Reuters that a total of 185 people are wounded across London, 10 of them seriously and 7 critically.

12:30   Metropolitan Police confirmed explosions in three metro stations and one public bus and continues its presence on the incident sites. At the time the police does not provide a number about the injuries but underlines that there are multiple casualties.

12:51   Emergency services personnel tell CNN writer William Chamberlain that all survivors had been evacuated from King's Cross station, leaving the dead below ground "in the double digits."

12:53   Britain's Home Secretary Charles Clarke tells the House of Commons there were four explosions in central London and the underground system will be closed all day. They would decide later in day whether to resume bus services. Earlier six attacks were reported.

2:38    U.S. law enforcement sources say the British government has said that at least 40 people have been killed. London hospitals report at least 300 wounded, the Associated Press reports.

3:26    London deputy police chief Brian Paddick says police had no warning of the attacks and have not received any claims of responsibility. He says police are keeping an open mind over who carried out the attacks and that it is unclear whether a claim of responsibility by al-Qaeda is genuine or whether suicide bombers were involved. No arrests have been made in connection with the attacks.

3:41    Assistant chief ambulance officer Russell Smith says the service has treated 45 patients with serious or critical injuries. A further 300 patients have been treated for minor injuries.

4:30    London Police announce that the Metropolitan Police Service Casualty Bureau has been opened and ask the public to call the hotline if they are concerned about their loved ones who may have been affected by the incidents. The police announced the number of the confirmed fatalities as 33 for the first time and mentioned that the incidents are conducted by terrorists.

4:32    Transport authorities say Docklands Light Railway services in east London and mainline rail services have resumed, except out of King's Cross and Victoria stations. Buses in central London are also returning to service. All underground services remain suspended.

5:43    Prime Minister Tony Blair says that Britain will not be intimidated by terrorism and promises intense police and security services action to bring those behind the bombings to justice. "I would also pay tribute to the stoicism and resilience of the people of London who have responded in a way typical of them," says Blair.

5:49    The United Nations Security Council passes a resolution condemning the London attacks and expressing "outrage and indignation at today's appalling terrorist attacks against the people of the United Kingdom that cost human life and caused injuries and immense human suffering."

7:15    Metropolitan police updates the number of confirmed fatalities as 37 and confirms that the incidents involved four explosive devices.

This timeline is based on multiple sources including CNN, and the London Metropolitan Police media releases:

www.cnn.com/2005/WORLD/europe/07/07/london.
   timeline/index.html
www.met.police.uk/news/op_theseus/response1.htm
www.met.police.uk/news/op_theseus/response2.htm
www.met.police.uk/news/op_theseus/response3.htm
www.met.police.uk/news/op_theseus/response4.htm

**Observations and Comments on Incident**

**London Metropolitan Police**: London Metropolitan Police immediately responded to all potential incident scenes and fulfilled its first response responsibility. The unique aspect of the incident management by the Metropolitan Police was its consistent and persistent behavior in terms of releasing information to the media and the public. The department did not speculate on the incidents and their outcomes and public impacts at any time. Metropolitan Police chose to release factual information only when the validity of the information was confirmed by credible sources, in many cases its investigators or cooperating government officials. The first casualty numbers were announced about 4:30 p.m. by the department. Until then different sources in the media were reporting varying numbers of casualties (between 2 and 90). (*Source*: Multiple London Metropolitan Police Press Releases and media coverage on July 7, 2005)

**London Fire Brigade**: Around 200 firefighters were called to explosions at Aldgate, Edgware Road, and King's Cross London underground stations and an explosion on a bus at Tavistock Square on Thursday, July 7. Twelve fire appliances with 60 firefighters attended the incident at Edgware Road, 12 fire appliances with 60 firefighters attended the incident at King's Cross, 10 fire appliances with 50 firefighters attended the Aldgate incident, and 4 fire appliances with 20 firefighters were called to Tavistock Square. Throughout the morning several new specialist fire rescue units were deployed to work with the other emergency services to evacuate casu-

alties and make the incidents safe. (*Source*: London Fire Brigade, www.london-fire.gov.uk/news/statement.asp)

**London Emergency Medical Services**: The response of the emergency medical service units to the bomb attacks in London has generally been assessed as "adequate" by experts. The incident claimed more than 50 lives, left more than 700 hurt, and kept about 100 overnight in hospital, 22 of whom were in critical condition as of July 8. Hospitals responding to the crisis included St. Mary's hospital in Paddington, the Royal Free hospital in Hampstead, St. Thomas' hospital, and Great Ormond Street children's hospital, which does not have an emergency department but took in 22 patients. Hospitals in London were put on major incident alert within minutes of the first explosion, which occurred at 0851 BST in the third carriage of an underground train traveling in a tunnel 100 meters from Liverpool Street station. Less than a mile away, at the Royal London hospital in Whitechapel, medical staff put into place a well-rehearsed strategy to cope with the first of 208 patients. The shock waves from the blast were the cause of the most frequently seen injuries on that day, which are particularly traumatic for air-filled parts of the body. The waves can cause perforated eardrums, collapsed lungs, and perforated bowels. But the force can also devastate soft tissue—the blast was responsible for many of the limbs lost during the attacks. Smoke inhalation resulting in lung damage, burns, and ripped skin caused by debris such as glass shards were also common injuries. (*Source*: "Medical Teams Praised for Reaction to Bombings," www.newscientist.com/article.ns?id=dn7649)

**Leadership and Crisis Communications**

U.K. Prime Minister Tony Blair was in the G8 summit in Gleneagles, Scotland, when he learned about the terror attacks that hit the capital of his country and several citizens and noncitizens. At 12 p.m. that day Tony Blair appeared before the media in Gleneagles and gave a three-and-a-half-minute-long speech about the day's terrorist incidents. A full transcript of the speech can be found at www.number-10.gov.uk/output/Page7853.asp.

Mr. Blair's style of communication on that day has demonstrated his leadership skills and expertise in crisis communications. An analytical piece about the way he delivered his speech marks the following nuances in his speech as critical to conveying the right message the right way:

He demonstrated his passion for his people and did not choose to hide his emotions.

He shared his emotions (grief) but also gave a strong image that communicated that he is there and ready to deal with the problem.

He improvised his speech instead of reading it, which proved that it wasn't "business as usual" for him.

He used many long pauses to communicate the gravity of the situation.

He avoided speculations and focused on stating the limited number of facts he was informed about.

He sincerely communicated his condolences to the families who lost loved ones in the attacks.

He used strong and direct vocabulary to describe the events ("barbaric").

The analysis above is based on an analytical piece written by T. J. Walker. (*Source*: Walker, T. J., "Crisis Communications with Class," www.mediatrainingworldwide.com, 212-764-4955) The video of the full speech can be found at http://relay.westminsterdigital.co.uk/demand.php?c=number10/statements&m=statementFull2005-07-07.wmv&.wvx.

## REVIEW QUESTIONS

1. According to your perspective, list the most important differences between the NRP and the FRP.

2. Do you believe that the response capabilities of the new Department of Homeland Security have been adequately tested?

3. If you were an appointed local emergency manager, what do you think about the information provided in this chapter? What are the pros and cons for you in this emerging structure from a response perspective? Answer the same question from a regional emergency manager officer and a FEMA high-level officer point of view.

4. Find an updated version of the National Incident Management System (NIMS) and compare its organization scheme to the ICS organization. Who is involved (personal title and agencies) in the picture? Is anyone left out?

5. The establishment of the Department of Homeland Security is seen by some scholars and experts as a "militarization" of the emergency management field. Do you agree with this view in terms of response? Explain why or why not.

## REFERENCES

American Corporate Council Association <www.acca.com/infopaks/homeland/legislativechart.pdf>

American Patriot Friends Network <www.apfn.org ANSER>

Center for Arms Control and Non-Proliferation <www.armscontrolcenter.org/terrorism/homeland%20security/UpdatedDHSAgencies.pdf>

Centers for Disease Control and Prevention <www.cdc.gov>

Coppola, D. 2003. *Terrorism Annex for North Carolina Counties* (August). Washington, DC: TerrBullock & Haddow LLC.

Department of Agriculture <www.usda.gov>

Department of Defense <www.dod.gov>

Department of Energy <www.doe.gov>

Department of Health and Human Services <www.dhhs.gov>

Department of Homeland Security <www.dhs.gov>

Department of Justice <www.doj.gov>

Domestic Terrorism Concept of Operations Plan <www.fema.gov>/pdf/rrr/conplan/conplan.pdf>

The Environmental Protection Agency <www.epa.gov>

Federal Emergency Management Agency <www.fema.gov>

Federal Radiological Emergency Response Plan <www.nrt.org/production/nrt/home.nsf/0/5c23c5d58074d6e48525660c005b56b5?OpenDocument>

Federal Response Plan <www.fema.gov>/pdf/rrr/frp/frp2003.pdf>

Federation of American Scientists <www.fas.org>

International Association of Emergency Managers <www.iaem.org>

*Journal of Homeland Security* <www.homelandsecurity.org>

National Disaster Medical System <http://ndms.dhhs.gov>

National Oil and Hazardous Substances Pollution Contingency Plan <www.epa.gov>/oilspill/ncpover.htm>

National Response Plan <www.nemaweb.org/docs/national_response_plan.pdf>

North Carolina Department of Emergency Management <www.dem.dcc.state.nc.us>

NOVAD <www.novad.org>

Nuclear Regulatory Commission <www.nrc.gov>

Ready.gov <www.ready.gov>

U.S. Coast Guard <www.uscg.mil>

*Washington Post.* 2005. "War Plans Drafted to Counter Terror Attacks in U.S." (August 8), p. A1.

White House <www.whitehouse.gov>

# APPENDIX 7-1
## NRP Disaster Recovery Programs

| Program | Agency | Assistance provided | Activating mechanism | Eligibility |
|---------|--------|---------------------|----------------------|-------------|
| Emergency Haying and Grazing | Department of Agriculture (USDA), Farm Service Agency (FSA) | Emergency authority to harvest hay or to graze land devoted to conservation and environmental uses under the Conservation Reserve Program. | AWD | I/B |
| Emergency Loans | USDA, FSA | Low-interest loans to family farmers and ranchers for production losses and physical damage. | PD; designated by Secretary of Agriculture or Administrator, FSA (physical losses only) | I/B |
| Noninsured Crop Disaster Assistance Program | USDA, FSA | Direct payments to reduce financial losses resulting from a natural disaster that causes production loss or prevents planting of crops grown commercially for food or fiber, for which federal crop insurance is not available. | AWD | I |
| Emergency Conservation Program | USDA, FSA | Cost-share payments to rehabilitate farmlands damaged by natural disasters and to carry out emergency water conservation or water-enhancing measures during times of severe drought, in cases when the damage or drought is so severe that federal assistance is necessary. | AWD | I/B |
| Agricultural Marketing Transition Act (AMTA) Program | USDA, FSA | Direct payments to eligible producers of program crops that comply with AMTA requirements. | AWD | I/B |
| Conservation Reserve Program (CRP) | USDA, FSA | Voluntary program that offers annual rental payments, incentive payments for certain activities, and cost-share assistance to establish approved cover on eligible cropland. | AWD | I/B |

*(continues)*

APPENDIX 7-1 (*continued*)

| Program | Agency | Assistance provided | Activating mechanism | Eligibility |
|---|---|---|---|---|
| Farm Operation Loans | USDA, FSA | Loans and loan guarantees to be used for farm operating costs. | N/P | I |
| Farm Ownership Loans | USDA, FSA | Direct loans, guaranteed loans, and technical assistance for farmers in acquiring or enlarging farms or ranches; making capital improvements; promoting soil and water conservation; and paying closing costs. | AWD | I |
| Emergency Food Assistance (Emergency Food Stamp and Food Commodity Program) | USDA, Food and Nutrition Service (FNS) | Direct payments to states for specified uses. | PD; declaration by the Secretary of Agriculture | S/I |
| Food Distribution | USDA, FNS | Donations of USDA-purchased food. | PD; declaration by Secretary of Agriculture and compliance with eligibility criteria | F/S/L/N |
| Emergency Watershed Protection (EWP) | USDA, Natural Resources Conservation Service (NRCS) | Direct payments and technical assistance to install structural and nonstructural measures to relieve imminent threats to life and/or property, and to purchase floodplain easements. Technical assistance such as site evaluations, design work, and installation inspections also are provided through the program. | AWD; triggered by NRCS State Conservationist | S/L/N/B/I |
| Water Resources | USDA, NRCS | Project grants for the installation of preventive measures such as dams, channels, flood warning systems, purchasing easements, floodplain delineation, and land treatment. Advisory and counseling services also are available. | N/P | S/L/N |
| Resource Conservation and Development (RC&D) | USDA, NRCS | Technical assistance and local project costs. Projects may include land and water conservation, resource improvements, recreational development, and waste disposal projects. | AWD loans to finance | L/N |
| River Basin Project | USDA, NRCS | Technical assistance. Special priority is given to projects designed to solve problems of upstream rural community flooding, water quality improvement that comes from agricultural nonpoint sources, wetlands preservation, and drought management for agricultural and rural communities. Special emphasis is placed on helping state agencies develop strategic water resource plans. | AWD; triggered by NRCS State Conservationist | F/S/L |
| Soil Survey | USDA, NRCS | Technical assistance. Objective is to maintain up-to-date, published surveys (and soil survey data in other formats) of | N/P | S/L/N/B/I |

APPENDIX 7-1 (*continued*)

| Program | Agency | Assistance provided | Activating mechanism | Eligibility |
|---|---|---|---|---|
| | | counties or other areas of comparable size for use by interested agencies, organizations, and individuals; and to assist in the use of this information. | | |
| Federal Crop Insurance Program | USDA, Risk Management Agency (RMA) | Direct payments of insurance claims. Insurance against unavoidable cause of loss such as adverse weather conditions, fire, insects, or other natural disasters beyond the producer's control. | No activating cause of mechanism is needed, but availability is based on crop-specific sales, closing dates, and the availability of crops in particular counties | I |
| Business and Industrial Loan Program (B&I) | USDA, Rural Business Service | Guaranteed and direct loans up to $10 million. Possible disaster uses include drilling wells, purchasing water, or tying into other water programs. | AWD | B/N/T and public bodies |
| Rural Housing Site Loans | USDA, Rural Housing Service (RHS) | Loans for the purchase and development of housing and necessary equipment that becomes a permanent part of the development (e.g., water and server lines). | AWD | N |
| Rural Rental Housing Loans | USDA, RHS | Loans for the purchase, building, or repair of rental housing. Funds can also be used to provide water and water disposal systems. | AWD | I/S/L/B |
| Emergency Community Water Assistance Grants (ECWAG) | USDA, Rural Utilities Service (RUS) | Project grants to help rural residents obtain adequate water supplies. | PD | S/L/N |
| Water and Waste Disposal Loans and Grants | USDA, RUS | Project grants and direct and guaranteed loans to develop, replace, or repair water and waste disposal systems in rural areas and towns having populations of 10,000 or less. | AWD | L/N/T |
| Voluntary Organizations Recovery Assistance | American Red Cross, Mennonite Disaster Service, Salvation Army, and member organizations of the National Voluntary Organization Active in Disaster | Mass care (shelter and feeding), welfare inquiries, health and mental health service, child care, home repairs (labor and funding), emergency communications, debris removal, burn services, cleaning supplies, personal property, distribution of supplies, transportation, loan personnel, and other specialized programs and services. | Disaster event | I |
| Economic Adjustment Program—Disaster Economic Recovery Assistance | Department of Commerce (DOC), Economic Development Administration (EDA) | Planning and technical assistance grants to state and local governments for strategic recovery planning and implementation to focus on job retention/creation to help offset the economic impacts of a major disaster. | PD; requires supplemental appropriation (S) | S/L/N/T |
| Economic Adjustment Program—Disaster Economic Recovery Assistance | DOC, EDA | Revolving loan fund grants to state and local governments to provide a source of local financing to support business and economic recovery after a major disaster where other financing is insufficient or unavailable. | PD; SA | S/L/N/T |

(*continues*)

APPENDIX 7-1 (*continued*)

| Program | Agency | Assistance provided | Activating mechanism | Eligibility |
|---|---|---|---|---|
| Economic Adjustment Program—Disaster Economic Recovery Assistance | DOC, EDA | Infrastructure construction grants to address local recovery implementation needs for new or improved publicly owned infrastructure after a major disaster, support job creation and retention, leverage private investment, and help accelerate and safeguard the overall economic recovery of the disaster-impacted area. | PD; SA | S/L/N/T |
| Corporation for National Service (CNS) Programs | CNS | Volunteers of all ages/backgrounds provide short/long-term response and recovery assistance. They are available through the community or national deployment. | PD | F/S/N/T |
| Beach Erosion Control Projects | Department of Defense (DOD), U.S. Army Corps of Engineers (USACE) | Specialized services. USACE designs and constructs the project. | Decision of the Chief of Engineers | S/L |
| Emergency Rehabilitation of Flood Control Works or Federally Authorized Coastal Protection Works | DOD, USACE | Specialized services to assist in the repair and restoration of public works damaged by flood, extraordinary wind, wave, or water action. | Approval by HQUSACE | S/L/N/I |
| Emergency Water Supply and Drought Assistance Programs | DOD, USACE | Emergence supplies of clean drinking water for human consumption and construction of wells. | Assistant Secretary of the Army for Civil Works designates the area as "drought distressed" | L |
| Flood and Postflood Response, Emergency Operations | DOD, USACE | Specialized services, such as flood fighting and rescue, protection of federally constructed shore or hurricane projects, and postflood response assistance. | Designation by USACE district commander | S/L |
| Watercourse Navigation: Protecting, Clearing, and Straightening Channels | DOD, USACE | Specialized services, such as clearing or removing unreasonable obstructions to navigation in rivers, harbors, and other waterways or tributaries. | Decision of the Chief of Engineers | S/L |
| Community Disaster Loan Program | Department of Homeland Security (DHS) | Program provides loans not greater than 25% of the local government's annual operating budget. | PD | L |
| Cora C. Brown Fund | DHS | Grants to disaster victims for unmet disaster-related needs. | PD; designation for individual assistance | I |
| Crisis Counseling Assistance and Training Program (CCP) | DHS: Department of Health and Human Services (HHS) | Grants to states providing for short-term counseling services to disaster victims. | Governor's request | I, via S |
| Fire Suppression Assistance Program | DHS | Project grants. DHS approves a grant to a state on the condition that the state takes measures to mitigate natural hazards, including consideration of nonstructural alternatives. | Decision by DHS | S |

APPENDIX 7-1 (*continued*)

| Program | Agency | Assistance provided | Activating mechanism | Eligibility |
|---|---|---|---|---|
| Hazard Mitigation Grant Program (HMGP) | DHS | Project grants to implement hazard mitigation plans and prevent future loss of lives and property. | PD | L/N, via S |
| Individuals and Households Grant (IHG) Program | DHS | Grants to individuals administered by the state. Objective is to provide funds for the expenses of disaster victims that cannot be met through insurance or other assistance programs. | PD; designation for individual assistance: Requires specific request by State Governor | I, via S |
| Legal Services | DHS | Free legal advice and referrals. Assistance includes help with insurance claims, counseling on landlord–tenant and mortgage problems, assistance with home repair contracts and consumer protection matters, replacement of legal documents, estate administration, preparation of guardianships and conservatorships, and referrals. | PD; designation for individual assistance | I |
| National Flood Insurance Program (NFIP) | DHS | Insurance benefits against losses from floods, mudflow, or flood-related erosion. | AWD | I/B/S |
| NFIP, Community Assistance Program | DHS | Grants to states for technical assistance to resolve floodplain management issues. | AWD | S/L |
| Public Assistance Program | DHS | Project grants. Funds can be used for clearing debris, emergency measures, and repairing or replacing damaged structures, roads, utilities, public buildings, and infrastructure. | PD; designation for public assistance | L/N, via S |
| Disaster Housing Program | DHS | Direct-payment grants and services. Grants include transient accommodation reimbursement, and home repair, rental, and mortgage assistance. Services may include a mobile home. | PD; designation for individual assistance | I |
| Regulatory Relief for Federally Insured Financial Institutions | Federal Deposit Insurance Corporation (FDIC) and other federal regulatory agencies | Specialized services. Supervisory agencies can grant regulatory relief to insured institutions. Regulatory relief includes lending assistance, extensions of reporting and publishing requirements, waivers from appraisal regulations, and implementation of consumer protection laws. | PD; other disaster that affects the ability of a federally insured financial institution to provide normal services | N/B |
| Donation of Federal Surplus Personal Property | General Services Administration (GSA) | Donation of surplus personal property to eligible recipients. | N/P | S/L/N/ public airports |
| Disposal of Federal Surplus Real Property | GSA | Sale, exchange, or donations of property and goods. | N/P | S/L/N |
| Disaster Assistance for Older Americans | HHS, Administration on Aging | Direct payments to state agencies focused on aging-related services. | PD | I, via S |

*(continues)*

APPENDIX 7-1 (*continued*)

| Program | Agency | Assistance provided | Activating mechanism | Eligibility |
|---|---|---|---|---|
| Mental Health Disaster Assistance | HHS, Public Health Service | Project grants to provide emergency mental health and substance abuse counseling to individuals affected by a major disaster. | Supplemental appropriation by Congress relating to PD | I, via S |
| Community Development Block Grant (CDBG) Program—Entitlement Grants Planning and Development (CPD) | Department of Housing and Urban Development (HUD), Community | Formula grants to entitlement communities. Preferred use of funding is for long-term needs, but funding may also be used for emergency response activities. | Supplemental appropriation by Congress relating to PD | L |
| CDBG—State's Program | HUD, CPD | Formula grants to states for nonentitlement communities. Preferred use of funding is for long-term needs, but funding may also be used for emergency response activities. States establish methods of fund distribution. | Supplemental appropriation by Congress relating to PD | L, via S |
| Mortgage Insurance for Disaster Victims Program (Section 203(h)) | HUD | Provides mortgage insurance to protect lenders against the risk of default on loans to qualified disaster victims whose homes are located in a presidentially designated disaster area and were destroyed, requiring reconstruction/replacement. Insured loans may be used to finance the purchase or reconstruction of a one-family home that will be the principal residence of the homeowner. | PD | I |
| Reclamation States Emergency Drought Relief Act of 1991 | Department of the Interior (DOI), Bureau of Reclamation | Loans, grants, use of facilities, construction, management and conservation activities, and purchase of water for resale or for fish and wildlife services. Temporary drought assistance may include the drilling of wells, installation of equipment, improved reporting of conditions. | Request for drought assistance and approval by Commissioner of Reclamation | F/S/N/I |
| Disaster Unemployment Assistance (DUA) | Department of Labor (DOL), DHS | Direct payments of DUA benefits and reemployment assistance services. Objective is to provide assistance to individuals who are ineligible for regular unemployment compensation programs and who are left jobless after a major disaster. | PD; designation for individual assistance. PD may be limited to DUA only | I, via S |
| Employment: Job Training Partnership Act (JTPA), National Reserve Emergency Dislocation Grants | DOL, Employment and Training Administration | Program provides states with grant money to provide individuals with temporary jobs and/or employment assistance. | PD | I, via S |
| Price-Anderson Act | American Nuclear Insurers and Nuclear Regulatory Commission (NRC) | Payment of liability claims that arise from a nuclear power reactor accident. Insurance-provided assistance may compensate victims for increased living | AWD | I |

APPENDIX 7-1  (*continued*)

| Program | Agency | Assistance provided | Activating mechanism | Eligibility |
|---|---|---|---|---|
| | (for commercial nuclear power plants); Department of Energy (for DOE facilities) | expenses after an evacuation, unemployment, business losses, environmental cleanup, reduced property values, and costs associated with bodily injury. | | |
| Price-Anderson Act | NRC | Insurance reimburses states and municipalities for costs necessarily incurred in providing emergency food, shelter, transportation, or police services in evacuating the public after a nuclear power reactor accident. | AWD | S/L |
| Economic Injury Disaster Loans (EIDLs) | Small Business Administration (SBA) | Direct long-term, low-interest loans to small businesses and agricultural cooperatives. Loans are only available to applicants with no credit available elsewhere, and the maximum amount of an EIDL is $1.5 million. | PD; declaration of a disaster by the Secretary of Agriculture and/or SBA-declared disaster | B |
| Physical Disaster Loans (Business) | SBA | Direct long-term, low-interest loans to businesses and nonprofit organizations. Loans provided to repair or replace uninsured property damages caused by disasters. Loans limited to $1.5 million. | PD or SBA declaration | N/B |
| Physical Disaster Loans (Individual) | SBA | Direct long-term, low-interest loans to homeowners and renters to repair or replace uninsured damages caused by disasters to real and personal property. Loan amounts limited to $200,000 to repair or replace real estate, and to $40,000 to repair or replace personal property. | PD or SBA declaration | I |
| Social Security Assistance | Social Security Administration (SSA) | Advisory and counseling services to process SSA survivor claims, assist in obtaining necessary evidence for claim processing, resolve problems involving lost or destroyed SSA checks, and reprocess lost or destroyed pending claims. | PD; AWD | I |
| International Donations | Department of State (DOS) | Donations including goods and cash. | Request for international coordination assistance from DHS's Donations Coordinator | I |
| Transportation: Emergency Relief Program | Department of Transportation (DOT), Federal Highway Administration (FHWA) | Formula and project grants to repair roads. FHWA can provide (1) up to $100 million in funding to a state for each natural disaster or catastrophic failure; and (2) up to $20 million in funding per year for each U.S. territory. Special legislation may increase the $100 million per state limit. | PD; AWD | F/S |
| Alcohol and Tobacco Tax Refund | Department of the Treasury, Bureau of Alcohol, Tobacco and Firearms | Specialized services to provide federal alcohol and tobacco excise tax refund to business that lost assets in a disaster. | PD | B |

*(continues)*

APPENDIX 7-1 (*continued*)

| Program | Agency | Assistance provided | Activating mechanism | Eligibility |
|---|---|---|---|---|
| Savings Bonds Replacement or Redemption | Treasury, Bureau of Public Debt | Specialized services. Bureau of Public Debt expedites replacement of U.S. Savings Bonds lost or destroyed as a result of a disaster. | PD | I |
| Taxes: Disaster Assistance Program | Treasury, Internal Revenue Service (IRS) | Advisory and counseling services. IRS provides information about casualty loss deductions, claim procedures, and reconstruction of lost financial records. | PD | I/B |
| Forbearance on VA Home Loans | Department of Veterans Affairs (VA) | Encourage lenders to extend forbearance to any borrowers who have VA home loans and who are in distress as a result of disaster; provide incentives to such lenders. | PD | I |
| Coastal Zone Management: Hazards, Environmental Recovery, and Mitigation | DOC, National Oceanic and Atmosphieric Administration (NOAA) | Assistance to state and local governments in mitigation and recovery/restoration planning, postevent permitting assistance, water-level data for storm surge and flooding prediction and mitigation. | PD for postevent; AWD from coastal state(s) for preevent planning | S |
| Reestablishing Local Survey Networks | DOC, NOAA | Provision of survey mark data to local and state agencies for reestablishing their geodetic control networks: reestablishment of national network if warranted. | PD; AWD depending on funding availability | S/L |
| Coastal Zone Management Administration Awards | DOC, NOAA | Grants to states for the management of coastal development to protect life and property from coastal hazards. | AWD requires supplemental appropriation by Congress relating to PD for poststorm coastal hazard mitigation and recovery activities | S/L/T via S |
| Coastal Zone Management Fund | DOC, NOAA | Emergency grants to state coastal zone management agencies to address unforeseen or disaster-related circumstances. | AWD subject to amounts provided in appropriation acts: no funds currently appropriated | S/L/T via S |
| Technical Support | DOC, NOAA, National Weather Service | Technical assistance for weather, water, and climate warning systems and critical information dissemination systems. Poststorm data acquisition activities. | AWD | F/S/L/N/T |
| Technical Support | DOC, National Institute of Standards and Technology | Disaster damage surveys, assistance in procurement of consulting services, evaluation of structural and fire performance of buildings and lifelines. | Federally declared disasters to buildings and lifelines, on cost-reimbursable basis | F/S/L |

*Source*: DHS, the Federal Response Plan January 2003.

*Abbreviations*:

| | |
|---|---|
| presidential declaration (PD) | individual/family (I) |
| available without declaration (AWD) | nonprofit organization (N) |
| federal agency (F) | Indian tribe (T) |
| state agency (S) | business (B) |
| locality (L) | not provided (N/P) |

# 8

# Communications

## INTRODUCTION

Communicating messages to the general public is a critical and underdeveloped aspect of effective emergency management. These messages come in three basic forms: risk, warning, and crisis. Risk communications involves alerting and educating the public to the risks they face and how they can best prepare for and mitigate these risks in order to reduce the impacts of future disaster events. Warning communications involves delivering a warning message in time for individuals and communities to take shelter or evacuate in advance of a disaster event. Crisis communications involves providing timely and accurate information to the public during the response and recovery phases of a disaster event.

The emergency management community has vast experience in practicing risk and warning communications. Preparedness programs have been an active part of emergency management in this country for decades, and public education programs conducted by the Federal Emergency Management Agency (FEMA), the American Red Cross, the Salvation Army, local fire departments, and other public- and private-sector agencies have disseminated millions of

brochures and checklists describing the risks of future disaster events and the steps that individuals and communities can take to reduce and prepare for them. In recent years, these programs have embraced new technologies to disseminate this information, including video and, most significantly, the Internet. There is a wealth of knowledge supported by scientific research concerning effective means to communicate hazard risk messages for natural disaster and selected technological disaster risks.

The design and implementation of warning systems has similarly advanced in the past decades. From the Civil Defense sirens to the Emergency Broadcast Network to weather radios, warning systems alerting the public to sudden or impending disaster events have become more sophisticated and widely used. Broadcasting timely information that allows individuals to make appropriate shelter and evacuation decisions is at the core of the warning systems designed for natural hazards such as tornadoes and tsunamis. Watch and warning notices for floods and hurricanes provide individuals and community leaders with valuable information on the path and potential destructiveness of severe storms that could result in flooding events. The public media—television, radio, and most recently the Internet—are the mechanisms most often used by emergency officials to issue watch and warning notices.

The importance of communicating with the public during the response and recovery phases of a natural or technological disaster event has only recently been fully embraced by emergency officials. Too often in the past, little value was placed on communicating with the public during and after a disaster event, and emergency officials had little training and less interest in this area. This changed in the 1990s as FEMA, under the direction of James Lee Witt, made a commitment and marshaled the resources to develop and implement an aggressive public affairs program designed to deliver timely and accurate messages to the public in a time of crisis. The messages focused on what measures government and private sector officials were taking to help a community in responding to and recovering from a disaster event and the methods by which individuals and communities could apply for and receive federal, state, and local disaster relief. FEMA established a working partnership with the media to deliver these messages through press conferences, individual interviews, satellite feeds, radio actualities, and the Internet. Another means of communication is *Recovery Times*, a newspaper supplement published by FEMA and distributed by local newspaper outlets. In time, the FEMA public affairs model has been embraced by state and local emergency officials.

The new terrorist threat has introduced new hazards that are not fully understood, a new risk perception among members of the public concerned about becoming the victim of a terrorist attack (no matter how unlikely that risk may be), new response and recovery (mostly cleanup) procedures and practices, new information uncertainties, new restrictions of releasing information to the public, and new demands for public information. Do the communications models developed in the past for communicating risk, warning, and crisis messages concerning natural and technological hazards apply to terrorism-related communications? Will the traditional delivery systems— television, Internet, radio, and print—adequately

disseminate terrorism-related information? Will emergency and government officials find a balance between the need to provide timely and accurate information to the public and the need to conduct criminal investigations?

These are the types of questions that are addressed in this chapter, which includes sections on risk communications, warning communications, and crisis communications. A case study of the October 2002 sniper attacks in Washington, D.C., is also included in the chapter.

## RISK COMMUNICATIONS

The federal government, through the Department of Homeland Security (DHS), has initiated several programs to achieve a goal of community and individual resilience to the effects of terrorism and other disasters. One of the primary methods employed to achieve such preparedness is public education.

Public education has long been recognized as an effective method for decreasing the damaging potential of hazards and risks, and the media are often central in such projects (Mullis, 1998). Furthermore, the role of the media in previous risk-related public education endeavors dealing with natural and technological hazards and public health issues has been well documented. From teaching citizens to build tornado-resistant safe rooms to minimizing tsunami drowning and preventing teen pregnancy, public and private agencies have partnered with, cooperated with, or utilized the various players collectively referred to as the mass media to achieve the goal of reducing public risk.

While the news media's reporting on risks has often been blamed for inciting a "culture of fear" (Glassner, 1999) in which people are afraid of a multitude of risks that have only a minute chance of ever occurring, the news media have also been integral in helping to create what could be considered the most risk-free era in recorded history (Walsh, 1996). However, no studies have been conducted to measure the efficacy of the media in informing and educating the public about terrorism and other "intentional" hazards.

The new focus on terrorism within the borders of the United States has brought to question the degree of risk faced by individual Americans. Although the topic has become a daily concern of all media outlets, the effect that this new attention has had on decreasing the vulnerability of the average citizen to that particular hazard is questionable. Citizens have indicated through polls that the threat of terrorist attacks on American soil is one of their primary concerns, and they have looked to their leaders for guidance on personal preparedness for such a threat. The federal government has recognized this concern and has sought to confront the preparedness issue through actions taken by DHS to address national vulnerabilities. DHS has also embarked on a public education campaign the likes of which has not been seen since the Civil Defense drills of the 1950s taught citizens to "duck and cover" during air raids (Waugh, 2000). The media has been involved in this effort from the beginning, and regardless of their goals, intentions, or the level to which they have actually partnered with the federal government in their actions, it is likely that the news media have never before played such a central role in risk communication.

With such a great quantity of headlines, stories, editorials, investigative reports, and briefings related to terrorism, it would seem that all citizens should be able to decode from the barrage of messages relayed by DHS the information they need to protect themselves. However, considering that never before have the media and government risk communicators focused on any one subject so intensely, established risk perception and communication models are largely ineffective. DHS and the emergency management community in general must ask the following questions now and before planning future activities:

- How can risk communicators best make contact with the general public?
- Can the news media serve as an effective risk communicator for terrorism in the United States?
- Do the established risk communications models apply to terrorism and other intentional hazards?

## EMERGENCY MANAGEMENT AND RISK COMMUNICATION IN THE UNITED STATES

The most widely practiced form of emergency management in the United States, and the only form practiced by FEMA, is comprehensive emergency management (CEM). This four-phase cyclical system groups actions into the general categories of mitigation, preparedness, response, and recovery. For a given hazard there are generally pre-event actions (mitigation and preparedness) and post-event actions (response and recovery) performed. The response phase includes the immediate period of reaction after a disaster occurs (when critical emergency resources are required). Recovery includes the long-term rebuilding that begins after the emergency functions related to disaster response are no longer required. Mitigation is defined as any activity that prevents or reduces the impact of a disaster, and preparedness involves predisaster planning and training addressing the possibility of future disasters (Waugh, 2000). Like response, disaster preparedness is also always managed at the local level and is considered to be more of a local government responsibility than any of the other phases of CEM.

Preparedness generally consists of training the local first responders and educating the public about ways to prepare for specific hazards within specific communities. A hazard is an event or physical condition that has the potential to cause fatalities, injuries, property damage, infrastructure damage, agricultural loss, damage to the environment, interruption of business, or other types of harm or loss (FEMA, 1997). The risk associated with a hazard is identified as the probability (likelihood) of the hazard occurring, multiplied by the consequence of the hazard should it occur. For many hazard risks, public education is seen as the most effective means to reduce both the likelihood and consequence components significantly. Emergency management public education efforts utilize numerous resources, including in-school education, distribution of pamphlets and fact sheets, and inserts in phone books and utility mailings, among many others. However, it is the use of the various forms of the news media that has often been seen as the most effective means of public education.

The federal government took a more active role in community preparedness during the Clinton administration while FEMA was under the direction of James Lee Witt (a move taken by several governments throughout the world during the same period). Director Witt espoused the idea that the emergency response community must shed the view that the media were adversaries and work to form media partnerships in order to be more effective in public disaster preparedness education. Witt worked to institutionalize such tasks as creating media education materials and public service announcements, ensuring availability of "approved" hazard experts, providing training in emergency management terminology and actions for reporters and anchor people, and promot-

ing more responsible reporting by the media. The success of these changes was measured through the increased resilience of communities to hazards in which such changes in individual behavior were known to be the primary means of reducing vulnerability (such as during tsunamis and tornadoes).

In the wake of the September 11, 2001, terrorist attacks and the anthrax mail attacks shortly thereafter, the "all-hazards" approach of the federal government focused its efforts on preparedness and mitigation (prevention) of future terrorist attacks (Figure 8-1). Although terrorism had been considered a high-risk hazard by the federal government for some time, it was not necessarily on the minds of the American public. After these events, however, terrorism became an obvious primary concern of both the government and its citizens. Terrorism was no longer seen as something that affected isolated locations known to be

FIGURE 8-1   New York City, New York, September 27, 2001—FEMA workers needed to stay current with the news in regard to the terrorist attacks on the World Trade Center and the Pentagon. (Photo by Bri Rodriguez/FEMA News Photo)

at high risk and was instead regarded as a hazard that could affect anyone at any place and any time, a hazard that could result in a mass casualty event (one that overwhelms the capacity of local health officials to respond). Additionally, the possibility of terrorists employing weapons of mass destruction (WMD)—chemical, biological, radiological, explosive, or nuclear—became a reality.

On November 25, 2002, President Bush signed into law the Homeland Security Act of 2002, investing in the new DHS the mission of protecting the United States from further terrorist attacks, reducing the nation's vulnerability to terrorism, and minimizing the damage from potential terrorist attacks and natural disasters. DHS began working to organize the federal response to the consequences of disasters but concentrated its efforts on preparedness and response capabilities to combat terrorism (as is evident by changes in federal funding trends). DHS officials were still operating under the same constraints of the previous administration in terms of what they could do to increase preparedness at the community level. DHS repeatedly acknowledged that, even in the event that a terrorist attack be declared a national disaster, local communities would need to be prepared to be self-sufficient for a minimum of 48 hours. However, public demand for more federal action and information required DHS to address these public education needs.

The Ready.gov campaign is DHS's primary effort to increase individual citizen preparedness at the community level. It is essentially a website that offers citizens explicit directions detailing what they can do to prepare themselves and their families for all hazards, including terrorism. Other efforts at informing the public, which are equal components in the larger public education effort, include the five-color-coded Homeland Security Alert System and specific public announcements, such as the well-known "duct tape and plastic" incident (in which DHS Director Tom Ridge made a general appeal to people in the United States to buy those items to protect themselves from the effects of a possible WMD terrorist attack).

Personal preparedness from disasters, as described by the Ready.gov website, includes three major com-

ponents. Specifically, they are "get a kit" (one that contains materials to ensure potable water, food, clean air, first aid, and special needs items), "make a plan" (in which individuals or families determine actions to be taken in the event of specific disasters), and "be informed" (which involves general information about hazards and their specific personal mitigation and preparedness measures). To measure the effectiveness of a citizen's degree of terrorism-hazard preparedness, these three components must be used as performance measures. For the specific case of terrorism, "vigilance" (or actively looking for and reporting suspicious behavior that could be linked to terrorism) is included as a performance measure for personal terrorism preparedness (DHS, 2003).

Since late 2004, DHS has added two components to their Ready.gov site to expand on the specific groups that may benefit from the preparedness information they provide. The first group is the business community. The website instructs business owners and administrators on how to (1) plan to stay in business, (2) talk to your people, and (3) protect your investment. The second group is children.

## PAST RESEARCH FOCUSING ON RISK COMMUNICATION: THE POWER OF THE NEWS MEDIA

According to acclaimed risk communication experts Baruch Fischhoff, M. Granger Morgan, Ann Bostrom, and Cynthia Atman, risk communication is "communication intended to supply laypeople with the information they need to make informed, independent judgments about risks to health, safety, and the environment" (Morgan *et al.*, 2002). Creating messages that satisfy these high ideals requires extensive time, experience, and planning and is therefore more often successful in educating the public about old risks that are well understood than new risks such as terrorism. Although it would seem from a purist's point of view that anything short of the aforementioned definition would not suffice, some authors have defined risk communication to be the mere action of reporting on any existing or proposed hazard regardless of the story's ability to result in any increase in public awareness, knowledge, or preparedness (Willis, 1997).

The news media play a significant role in disaster and emergency management both before and after disasters occur. The media are well recognized for the invaluable service they have consistently performed during the initial critical moments of a disaster, when the emergency response efforts are mobilized. In these events, the media serve to transmit warning messages and alerts and give instructions on where to evacuate, where to seek medical care and shelter, and where to go for more specific information (Mileti, 1999). Jim Willis (1997) writes, "there may be no other area of journalism [than risk communication] where the Fourth Estate has such an awesome responsibility." Furman (2002) contends that the media's ability to educate people during these times is in many cases more likely to save lives than many other components of emergency response, adding that "people will die if they don't get good information." The emergency response community has embraced the media for their capability in response, recognizing that they will be the primary, if not the only, means of informing large masses of potential victims (McCormick Tribune Foundation, 2002).

With regard to the preparedness phase of emergency management, the primary risk communication tasks that have been assumed by the media include raising citizen awareness to the presence of an existing or future hazard and providing information to those citizens regarding prevention or protection (Burkhart, 1991). The effectiveness of the media as a conduit of educational information has been studied extensively, most notably in the area of public health. A great number of these studies have shown a positive correlation between the use of the media and an increase in the promoted knowledge or behavior. Phyllis Piotrow (1990) and a team of researchers working in Nigeria found that the promotion of family planning and clinic sites on local television played a significant role in the number of people

utilizing those services. Charles Westoff and German Rodriguez (1995) found that there was a strong correlation between patients who reported that they had been exposed to family planning messages in the media and the use of contraceptives by those same patients.

Witzer (1997) writes that "exposure to electronic and print media is associated with later marriage and with greater knowledge and use of family planning among men and women in Sub-Saharan Africa." Jones, Beniger, and Westoff (1980) found that there was a strong correlation between mass media coverage of the adverse affects of the birth-control pill and discontinuation rates among users. Similar results were found relating to sex education among young adults (Brown and Keller, 2000) and early initiation of breast feeding (McDivitt *et al.*, 1993). Nelken (1987) found in one study that more than 60% of Americans learn about cancer prevention from the media, whereas less than 20% do so from physicians.

With natural and technological hazards, the behavioral modifications and preparatory measures taken by recipients as a result of media risk communication also look promising. Mitigation specialists at FEMA claim that the media's role in community and citizen preparedness is critical if such efforts are to succeed (FEMA, 1998). Dennis Mileti (1999) found that personal preparedness was most likely to be undertaken by those people who are most attentive to the news media but that other attributes are often necessary in conjunction with that attention. Media risk communication has been widely credited as an important supplemental component to official communication in public preparedness to hazards (Burkhart, 1991). Singer and Endreny (1993) contend that there are many factors determining how people view hazards (including personal experience and contact with other people), but with hazards that are extreme in consequence and rare in occurrence (such as terrorism) the media are the most influential source of information. James Walsh (1996) found that several studies indicate that people use the media for obtaining information on hazards more than any other source.

The primary source of the news media's ability to effectively communicate and educate most likely lies in the institutionalized methods of attracting viewers and providing timely information that has been developed and refined over centuries. Burkhart (1991) writes, "in the preparedness phase, the mass media are positioned between the actors who evaluate a threat and decide upon a message, and the media audience." Burkhart adds that it is the media's ability to influence perceived risk and the credibility of the source of information that gives them such power over public behavior. McCombs and Shaw's (1972) research, which found that audiences not only are alerted to important issues by the media but that they learn "how much importance to attach to an issue or topic from the emphasis the media place on it" supports Burkhart's convictions.

This positive view of the media as a successful risk communicator comes not without contention. There are many social scientists who feel that the media, for various reasons, are ineffective at informing the public about the risks they face. Winston (1985) feels that it is the "built-in, organizational, competitive, and institutional biases" that prevent the media from informing citizens about hazards. These biases are coupled with procedural standards that can also make effective communication of risk difficult. For instance, Singer and Endreny (1993) report that the media inform about "events rather than issues, about immediate consequences rather than long-term considerations, about harms rather than risks," and Wenham (1994) describes how the media "tell how bad things are, while [emergency management agencies] make things better." Burkhart (1991) feels that it is a deficiency of knowledge about hazards and disaster management among journalists that makes them unable to effectively communicate due to both a lack of understanding of the most basic concepts and their inability to act as a "surrogate for the layman, to absorb and transform technical information to a public that is often even less well-prepared to grasp technical information and concepts." Such criticisms are repeated by Singer and Endreny (1993). There are other, similar reasons identified by research efforts

that sought to explain the media's risk communication deficiencies, including restrictions of time and space that prevent adequate knowledge transfer (Willis, 1997) and the media's insistence on taking control of the selection and presentation of message format that leads to a decrease in message effectiveness (Burkhart, 1991).

There is another subgroup of studies that find the news media to be largely ineffective as a risk communicator but assign less blame to them for such problems. Raphael (1986) turns the focus of the blame onto the public, stating that "citizens often display a magical belief in goodness and protection and a sense of generalized risk, which may explain why people pay less attention to preparedness information provided by the media outside of the context of an emergency." Jerry Hauer from the New York City Office of Emergency Management feels that it is the tendency of the emergency management community to exclude the media from training and drills due to the fear that the media will leak operational plans to terrorists and the fear that the media will cause mass public panic that has prevented them from being able to be effectively inform the public (McCormick Tribune Foundation, 2002). This position is supported by Burkhart (1991), who states, "Media are often limited by the nature of the information they receive," and Bremer and Bremer (2002), who state, "Terrorism presents a major dilemma to political leaders in terms of how to get enough attention without bringing too much attention to the problem." Furman (2002) adds, "It is difficult to educate the American people because there's very little we can tell them to do. . . . You're faced with the problem of just how much you want to tell the American people, because, in the end, there's very little we can give them."

There is a third type of research that claims that while the news media are, in fact, ineffective at educating the public, they still play a vital role in risk communication. McCallum, Hammond, and Morris (1990) state that, "regardless of reservations about their ability to play the role effectively, the media do carry considerable information about certain hazards and risks to most people." This view of the media as informer is fairly widespread. Willis (1997) states that while the media too often avoid contributing to the solution to the problems, they are effective at raising attention to issues and communicating degrees of urgency. Mullis (1998) further promotes this argument, stating that the media are effective at initiating preparedness activities. Burkhart (1991) found that while media warnings were too imprecise to be effective, they "were able to get people talking to other people about the danger mentioned in media warnings." Cohen (1963) succinctly characterized this phenomenon as follows: "The press may not be successful much of the time in telling its readers what to think, but it is stunningly successful in telling them what to think about."

## ACCURACY OF INFORMATION

A second area that must be examined when considering the ability of the media to communicate risk is the ability of the media to do so in a way that gives members of the public an accurate perception of their personal risk of victimization. In what is probably one of the earliest descriptions of the media's power to influence public risk perception and, likewise, preparedness and mitigative behavior, Walter Lippmann (1922) writes in his acclaimed *Public Opinion* that

> We shall assume that what each man does is based not on direct and certain knowledge, but on pictures made by himself or given to him. If his atlas tells him that the world is flat, he will not sail near what he believes to be the edge of our planet for fear of falling off.

Willis (1997) writes that because the media's depiction of public health and safety-related issues has either an indirect or a direct effect on public behavior, the media's responsibility to be as accurate as possible in their presentation of such hazards is vital. In the case of terrorism, DHS has established a five-color-coded Homeland Security Alert System that is intended to inform the public about the current risk of a terrorist attack within the United States. At certain times, the risk is raised in specific locations, such as a city, a landmark, or a building. While the media often

refer to this system when it goes up or down in severity, they also provide exhaustive unrelated information that heavily influences public perception. It is this perception that people must use in judging their own risk and, likewise, preparing themselves appropriately. It is important for the media not to understate risks because people will otherwise not expend the time and money needed to adequately prepare themselves, but exaggerating the risk of a hazard can have drastic consequences, including stress-related health problems and financial and economic effects including business and tourism losses.

Thus far, research has found that the media tend to overstate the risk of the hazards on which they focus (which also tend to be those that are the least likely to occur), while they understate commonly occurring hazards (Singer and Endreny, 1993). Altheide (2002) found that almost 80% of Americans feel that they are subject to more risk than their parents were 20 years ago, when in fact evidence has shown that we have a "competitive advantage in terms of disease, accidents, nutrition, medical care, and life expectancy" and that the media's portrayal of risk is mainly to blame. One reason this occurs is that the media do not have the time or resources to ensure the accuracy of their reports beyond reasonable doubt. Willis (1997) found that while scientists use elaborate methods of ensuring the validity of their findings, journalists depend on secondary or tertiary sources that confirm or refute their primary source, all of whom may be incorrect in their assumptions. Warner (1989) feels the problem lies in the media's tendency to use vivid imagery in reporting risk, such as comparing the number of people who die as a result of smoking as equivalent to three fully seated jumbo jets crashing every day. Singer and Endreny (1993) claim that daily reporting of rare hazards, which tend to be more "newsworthy," make these events subject to the availability heuristic. Walsh (1996) notes that over 2 million Americans canceled travel plans to Europe in 1986 because of fears of terrorism, when their actual risk would have been reduced significantly more if they had lost 10 pounds and traveled to Europe as planned.

Related to this concern that the media do not give the public accurate perceptions of risks is the fear that the public will become emotionally afraid of risks rather than becoming aware of their dangers. This distinction is important because it determines the types of preparedness measures citizens take in response to the messages they receive and the rationality with which those actions are made. When people are presented with a risk, they are more likely to take preventive and preparatory measures if they are led to believe that the risk is a danger that can be managed rather than one that they should fear. Past research has found that increasing the levels of public fear can actually cause a decrease in public preparedness behavior (Mullis, 1998). Unfortunately, it may be that the nature of media culture promotes and even amplifies fear by attempting to draw viewers through entertainment and "framing." Walsh (1996) contends that the media pay attention only to issues and situations that frighten viewers, "filling coverage with opinions rather than facts or logical perspective." Furedi (1997) takes a slightly different but related alternative stance on the subject in stating that "the media's preoccupation with risk is a symptom of the problem and not its cause," as the media can only amplify fear that already exists.

## ESSENTIAL COMPONENTS OF EFFECTIVE RISK COMMUNICATION

Numerous components of effective risk communication have been identified as vital to the success of an effective campaign. Morgan and his colleagues (2002) conclude that effective risk communication requires authoritative and trustworthy sources. They add that if the acting communicators are perceived by the public as having a vested personal interest in the result of such preparedness, they may be skeptical about the communicators' intentions. Dennis Mileti (1999) contends that several characteristics must be considered in creating the messages, including the following: amount of material, speed of presentation, number of arguments, repetition, style, clarity, ordering, forcefulness, specificity, consistency, accuracy, and extremity of the position advocated. These characteristics are adjusted depending on whether the communicators intend to attract attention or enhance the acceptance of

their message (Mileti, 1999). Singer and Endreny (1993) claim that in order for a message to be considered comprehensive, it should contain an annual mortality associated with the hazard (if known), the "spatial extent" of the hazard, the time frame associated with the hazard, and the alternatives for mitigating the hazard.

Communicators must also ensure that their messages are understood by those whom they are trying to reach, which undoubtedly changes from community to community depending on the demographic makeup of each. Mileti (1999) writes, "Most hazard-awareness and education programs have assumed a homogeneous 'public,' and have done little to tailor information materials to different groups." He adds that hazard-awareness programs are more effective if they rely on multiple sources transmitting multiple messages through multiple outlets and that radio and television are best at maintaining hazard awareness, whereas printed materials tend to provide more specific instructions on what should be done.

These are obviously high standards when considering the strict time, length, and content guidelines within which journalists must work. Highlighting the difficulty of both creating and analyzing such endeavors and the need for such a study as this, Morgan and his colleagues (2002) write, "As practiced today, risk communication is often very earnest but also surprisingly ad hoc. Typically, one can find neither a clear analysis of what needs to be communicated nor solid evidence that messages have achieved their impact. Nor can one find tested procedures for ensuring the credibility of information."

## FUTURE RESEARCH TO IMPROVE NEWS MEDIA RISK COMMUNICATION

The objectives of future research projects should be (1) to determine how effective the news media have been as a conduit of information to citizens as part of a larger terrorism-related public education campaign being conducted by DHS and (2) to develop a risk communications model by which media-provided public education pertaining to terrorism and other intentional hazards can be most effectively applied. Media reports in print, television, and radio formats should be examined for their content to (1) see if they meet the minimum information requirements established by risk communication experts, (2) determine if responsibility for preparedness is focused on the individual or the government, and (3) determine if an accurate portrayal of risk has been made. Surveys should be conducted with a random representative sample of American citizens to determine (1) the levels to which they have prepared for terrorism, (2) by what information they were motivated to do so, and (3) if their perception of risk reflects the level of risk portrayed by DHS and other federal sources. All collected and analyzed data should be used to determine which forms of risk communication are most effective at creating a more informed, prepared citizenry and to generate a list of risk communications' "fundamental requirements" relating to the task of terrorism that builds on established risk communications models. From these models, strategic

recommendations can be targeted to the various agencies and industries that regularly perform risk communication.

## EXISTING GOVERNMENT PUBLIC AWARENESS CAMPAIGNS

Ready.gov, with its partners in the public, private, and voluntary sectors, is promoting three basic steps individuals and families can take to be prepared for a terrorist incident—get a kit, make a plan, and be informed (see Figure 8-2). The "Overview" portion of the website (see Sidebar 8-1) provides information for families. This website also includes information for business preparedness, information for children, and basic information on explosives, chemical and biological agents, nuclear and radiological issues, and natural disasters. Sidebar 8-2 presents some of the Ready.gov fact sheets.

---

SIDEBAR 8-1    **Ready.gov "Overview"**

### Introduction: What Is Ready.gov All About?

Terrorists are working to obtain biological, chemical, nuclear and radiological weapons, and the threat of an attack is very real. Here at the Department of Homeland Security, throughout the federal government, and at organizations across America we are working hard to strengthen our Nation's security. Whenever possible, we want to stop terrorist attacks before they happen. All Americans should begin a process of learning about potential threats so we are better prepared to react during an attack. While there is no way to predict what will happen, or what your personal circumstances will be, there are simple things you can do now to prepare yourself and your loved ones.

Some of the things you can do to prepare for the unexpected, such as assembling a supply kit and

developing a family communications plan, are the same for both a natural or man-made emergency. However, as you will see throughout the pages of **Ready.gov**, there are important differences among potential terrorist threats that will impact the decisions you make and the actions you take. With a little planning and common sense, you can be better prepared for the unexpected.

### STEP 1: Get a Kit of Emergency Supplies

Be prepared to improvise and use what you have on hand to make it on your own for *at least* three days, maybe longer. While there are many things that might make you more comfortable, think first about fresh water, food and clean air. Consider putting together two kits. In one, put everything needed to stay where you are and make it on your

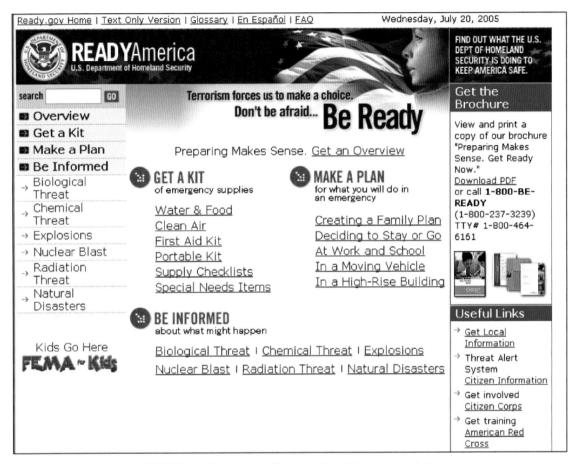

FIGURE 8-2   Department of Homeland Security Ready.gov website.

own. The other should be a lightweight, smaller version you can take with you if you have to get away.

You'll need a gallon of water per person per day. Include in the kits canned and dried foods that are easy to store and prepare. If you live in a cold weather climate, include warm clothes and a sleeping bag for each member of the family.

Start now by gathering basic emergency supplies—a flashlight, a battery-powered radio, extra batteries, a first aid kit, toilet articles, prescription medicines and other special things your family may need. Many potential terrorist attacks could send tiny microscopic "junk" into the air. Many of these materials can only hurt you if they get into your body, so think about creating a barrier between yourself and any contamination. It's smart to have something for each member of the family that covers their mouth and nose.

Plan to use two to three layers of a cotton t-shirt, handkerchief or towel. Or, consider filter masks, readily available in hardware stores, which are rated based on how small a particle they filter. It is very important that the mask or other material fit your face snugly so that most of the air you breathe comes through the mask, not around it. Do whatever you can to make the best fit possible for children.

Also, include duct tape and heavyweight garbage bags or plastic sheeting that can be used to seal windows and doors if you need to create a barrier between yourself and any potential contamination outside.

## STEP 2: Make a Plan for What You Will Do in an Emergency

Be prepared to assess the situation, use common sense and whatever you have on hand to take care of yourself and your loved ones. Depending on your circumstances and the nature of the attack, the first important decision is deciding whether to stay or go. You should understand and plan for both possibilities.

*Develop a Family Communications Plan*: Your family may not be together when disaster strikes, so plan how you will contact one another and review what you will do in different situations. Consider a plan where each family member calls, or e-mails, the same friend or relative in the event of an emergency. It may be easier to make a long-distance phone call than to call across town, so an out-of-state contact may be in a better position to communicate among separated family members. You may have trouble getting through, or the phone system may be down altogether, but be patient.

*Staying Put*: There are circumstances when staying put and creating a barrier between yourself and potentially contaminated air outside, a process known as "shelter-in-place," can be a matter of survival. Choose an interior room or one with as few windows and doors as possible. Consider pre-cutting plastic sheeting to seal windows, doors and

air vents. Each piece should be several inches larger than the space you want to cover so that you can duct tape it flat against the wall. Label each piece with the location of where it fits.

If you see large amounts of debris in the air, or if local authorities say the air is badly contaminated, you may want to "shelter-in-place." Quickly bring your family and pets inside, lock doors, and close windows, air vents and fireplace dampers. Immediately turn off air conditioning, forced air heating systems, exhaust fans and clothes dryers. Take your emergency supplies and go into the room you have designated. Seal all windows, doors and vents. Watch TV, listen to the radio or check the Internet for instructions.

*Getting Away*: Plan in advance how you will assemble your family and anticipate where you will go. Choose several destinations in different directions so you have options in an emergency. If you have a car, keep at least a half tank of gas in it at all times. Become familiar with alternate routes as well as other means of transportation out of your area. If you do not have a car, plan how you will leave if you have to. Take your emergency supply kit and lock the door behind you. If you believe the air may be contaminated, drive with your windows and vents closed and keep the air conditioning and heater turned off. Listen to the radio for instructions.

*At Work and School*: Think about the places where your family spends time: school, work and other places you frequent. Talk to your children's schools and your employer about emergency plans. Find out how they will communicate with families during an emergency. If you are an employer, be sure you have an emergency preparedness plan. Review and practice it with your employees. A community working together during an emergency also makes sense. Talk to your neighbors about how you can work together.

## STEP 3: Be Informed about What Might Happen

Some of the things you can do to prepare for the unexpected, such as assembling a supply kit and developing a family communications plan, are the same for both a natural or man-made emergency. However there are important differences among potential terrorist threats that will impact the decisions you make and the actions you take.

### Specific Terrorist Threats

- A biological attack is the deliberate release of germs or other substances that can make you sick. Many agents must be inhaled, enter through a cut in the skin or eaten to make you sick.
- A chemical attack is the deliberate release of a toxic gas, liquid or solid that can poison people and the environment.

- A nuclear blast is an explosion with intense light and heat, a damaging pressure wave and widespread radioactive material that can contaminate the air, water and ground surfaces for miles around.
- A radiation threat or "Dirty Bomb" is the use of common explosives to spread radioactive materials over a targeted area.

Be prepared to adapt this information to your personal circumstances and make every effort to follow instructions received from authorities on the scene. Above all, stay calm, be patient and think before you act. With these simple preparations, you can be ready for the unexpected.

*Source*: Department of Homeland Security, www.ready.gov.

---

SIDEBAR 8-2   **"Be Informed" Ready.gov Fact Sheets**

### Be Informed—Biological Threat

A biological attack is the deliberate release of germs or other biological substances that can make you sick. Many agents must be inhaled, enter through a cut in the skin, or be eaten to make you sick. Some biological agents, such as anthrax, do not cause contagious diseases. Others, like the smallpox virus, can result in diseases you can catch from other people.

### *If There Is a Biological Threat*

Unlike an explosion, a biological attack may or may not be immediately obvious. While it is possible that you will see signs of a biological attack, as was sometimes the case with the anthrax mailings, it is perhaps more likely that local health-care workers will report a pattern of unusual illness

or there will be a wave of sick people seeking emergency medical attention. You will probably learn of the danger through an emergency radio or TV broadcast or some other signal used in your community. You might get a telephone call or emergency response workers may come to your door.

In the event of a biological attack, public health officials may not immediately be able to provide information on what you should do. It will take time to determine exactly what the illness is, how it should be treated, and who is in danger. However, you should watch TV, listen to the radio, or check the Internet for official news, including the following:

- Are you in the group or area authorities consider in danger?

- What are the signs and symptoms of the disease?
- Are medications or vaccines being distributed?
- Where?
- Who should get them?
- Where should you seek emergency medical care if you become sick?

### Protect Yourself

If you become aware of an unusual and suspicious release of an unknown substance nearby, it doesn't hurt to protect yourself. Quickly get away. Cover your mouth and nose with layers of fabric that can filter the air but still allow breathing. Examples include two to three layers of cotton such as a t-shirt, handkerchief or towel. Otherwise, several layers of tissue or paper towels may help. Wash with soap and water, and contact authorities.

### Symptoms and Hygiene

At the time of a declared biological emergency, if a family member becomes sick, it is important to be suspicious. Do not automatically assume, however, that you should go to a hospital emergency room or that any illness is the result of the biological attack. Symptoms of many common illnesses may overlap. Use common sense, practice good hygiene and cleanliness to avoid spreading germs, and seek medical advice.

### Be Informed—Chemical Threat

A chemical attack is the deliberate release of a toxic gas, liquid, or solid that can poison people and the environment.

### Possible Signs of Chemical Threat

- Many people suffering from watery eyes, twitching, choking, having trouble breathing or losing coordination
- Many sick or dead birds, fish or small animals

### If You See Signs of Chemical Attack

- Quickly try to define the impacted area or where the chemical is coming from, if possible.
- Take immediate action to get away.
- If the chemical is inside a building where you are, get out of the building without passing through the contaminated area, if possible.
- Otherwise, it may be better to move as far away from where you suspect the chemical release is and "shelter in place." Read more at Staying Put, www.Ready.gov/text/stay
- If you are outside, quickly decide what is the fastest escape from the chemical threat. Consider if you can get out of the area, or if you should follow plans to "shelter in place."

### If You Think You Have Been Exposed to a Chemical

If your eyes are watering, your skin is stinging, and you are having trouble breathing, you may have been exposed to a chemical.

- If you think you may have been exposed to a chemical, strip immediately and wash.
- Look for a hose, fountain, or any source of water, and wash with soap if possible, being sure not to scrub the chemical into your skin.
- Seek emergency medical attention.

### Be Informed—If There Is an Explosion

- Take shelter against your desk or a sturdy table
- Exit the building ASAP
- Do not use elevators
- Check for fire and other hazards
- Take your emergency supply kit if time allows

### If There Is a Fire

- Exit the building ASAP.
- Crawl low if there is smoke.
- Use a wet cloth, if possible, to cover your nose and mouth.

- Use the back of your hand to feel the upper, lower, and middle parts of closed doors.
- If the door is not hot, brace yourself against it, and open slowly.
- If the door is hot, do not open it. Look for another way out.
- Do not use elevators.
- If you catch fire, do not run. Stop-drop-and-roll to put out the fire.
- If you are at home, go to a previously designated meeting place.
- Account for your family members, and carefully supervise small children.
- Never go back into a burning building.

### If You Are Trapped in Debris

- If possible, use a flashlight to signal your location to rescuers.
- Avoid unnecessary movement so that you don't kick up dust.
- Cover your nose and mouth with anything you have on hand. (Dense-weave cotton material can act as a good filter. Try to breathe through the material.)
- Tap on a pipe or wall so that rescuers can hear where you are.
- If possible, use a whistle to signal rescuers.
- Shout only as a last resort. Shouting can cause a person to inhale dangerous amounts of dust.

### Be Informed—Nuclear Blast

A nuclear blast is an explosion with intense light and heat, a damaging pressure wave, and widespread radioactive material that can contaminate the air, water, and ground surfaces for miles around. While experts may predict at this time that a nuclear attack is less likely than other types, terrorism by its nature is unpredictable.

### If There Is a Nuclear Blast

- Take cover immediately, below ground if possible, though any shield or shelter will help protect you from the immediate effects of the blast and the pressure wave.
- Quickly assess the situation.
- Consider if you can get out of the area or if it would be better to go inside a building and follow your plan to "shelter in place."
- In order to limit the amount of radiation you are exposed to, think about shielding, distance, and time.
  - Shielding: If you have a thick shield between yourself and the radioactive materials, more of the radiation will be absorbed and you will be exposed to less.
  - Distance: The farther away you are from the blast and the fallout, the lower your exposure.
  - Time: Minimizing time spent exposed will also reduce your risk.

Use available information to assess the situation. If there is a significant radiation threat, health-care authorities may or may not advise you to take potassium iodide. Potassium iodide is the same stuff added to your table salt to make it iodized. It may or may not protect your thyroid gland, which is particularly vulnerable, from radioactive iodine exposure. Consider keeping potassium iodide in your emergency kit, and learn what the appropriate doses are for each of your family members. Plan to speak with your health-care provider in advance about what makes sense for your family.

### Be Informed—Radiation

A radiation threat, commonly referred to as a "dirty bomb" or "radiological dispersion device" (RDD), is the use of common explosives to spread radioactive materials over a targeted area. It is not a nuclear blast. The force of the explosion and radioactive contamination will be more localized. While the blast will be immediately obvious, the presence of radiation will not be clearly defined until trained personnel with specialized equipment are on the scene. As with any radiation, you want to try to limit exposure.

### *If There Is a Radiation Threat or "Dirty Bomb"*

To limit the amount of radiation you are exposed to, think about shielding, distance, and time.

- Shielding: If you have a thick shield between yourself and the radioactive materials, more of the radiation will be absorbed and you will be exposed to less.
- Distance: The farther away you are away from the blast and the fallout, the lower your exposure.

- Time: Minimizing time spent exposed will also reduce your risk.

As with any emergency, local authorities may not be able to immediately provide information on what is happening and what you should do. However, you should watch TV, listen to the radio, or check the Internet often for official news and information as it becomes available.

*Source*: Department of Homeland Security, www.ready.gov.

## WARNING COMMUNICATIONS

In March 2002, the White House Office of Homeland Security unveiled a new terrorist warning system called the Homeland Security Advisory System (HSAS). The system was color coded with accompanying written descriptions that identified the threat level for a possible terrorist attack at any given time (see Figure 8-3). Currently DHS provides a detailed

FIGURE 8-3    Homeland Security Advisory System.

explanation of how the HSAS works (see Sidebar 8-3).

Since its inception, concerns have been raised about the level of information provided through the HSAS. These concerns are shared by both the general public and members of the first responder community (e.g., police, fire, and emergency medical technicians) as well as local officials responsible for ensuring public safety. Several organizations have expanded on the information provided by DHS by developing additional guidance on actions that individuals, families, neighborhoods, schools, and businesses should take. Recommendations developed by the American Red Cross and released in August 2003 are presented in Appendixes 8.1 through 8.5. A copy of "California State Agency Guidance: Homeland Security Advisory System," developed by the Governor's Office for Emergency Services in California, is presented in Appendix 10 at the end of the book.

The Partnership for Public Warning (PPW) was formed in January 2002 as a "partnership between the private sector, academia, and government entities at the local, state, and federal levels" (Partnership for Public Warning, 2003). PPW is a nonprofit entity with a stated mission "to develop consensus on processes, standards, and systems that will provide the right

### SIDEBAR 8-3   **Understanding the Homeland Security Advisory System**

The world has changed since September 11, 2001. We remain a nation at risk to terrorist attacks and will remain at risk for the foreseeable future. At all Threat Conditions, we must remain vigilant, prepared, and ready to deter terrorist attacks. The following Threat Conditions each represent an increasing risk of terrorist attacks. Beneath each Threat Condition are some suggested Protective Measures, recognizing that the heads of federal departments and agencies are responsible for developing and implementing appropriate agency-specific Protective Measures:

1. **Low Condition (Green)**: This condition is declared when there is a low risk of terrorist attacks. Federal departments and agencies should consider the following general measures in addition to the agency-specific Protective Measures they develop and implement:
   - Refining and exercising as appropriate preplanned Protective Measures
   - Ensuring personnel receive proper training on the Homeland Security Advisory System and specific preplanned department or agency Protective Measures
   - Institutionalizing a process to assure that all facilities and regulated sectors are regularly assessed for vulnerabilities to terrorist attacks and all reasonable measures are taken to mitigate these vulnerabilities
2. **Guarded Condition (Blue)**: This condition is declared when there is a general risk of terrorist attacks. In addition to the Protective Measures taken in the previous Threat Condition, federal departments and agencies should consider the following general measures in addition to the agency-specific Protective Measures that they will develop and implement:

   - Checking communications with designated emergency response or command locations
   - Reviewing and updating emergency response procedures
   - Providing the public with any information that would strengthen its ability to act appropriately
3. **Elevated Condition (Yellow)**: An Elevated Condition is declared when there is a significant risk of terrorist attacks. In addition to the Protective Measures taken in the previous Threat Conditions, federal departments and agencies should consider the following general measures in addition to the Protective Measures that they will develop and implement:
   - Increasing surveillance of critical locations
   - Coordinating emergency plans as appropriate with nearby jurisdictions
   - Assessing whether the precise characteristics of the threat require the further refinement of preplanned Protective Measures
   - Implementing, as appropriate, contingency and emergency response plans
4. **High Condition (Orange)**: A High Condition is declared when there is a high risk of terrorist attacks. In addition to the Protective Measures taken in the previous Threat Conditions, federal departments and agencies should consider the following general measures in addition to the agency-specific Protective Measures that they will develop and implement:
   - Coordinating necessary security efforts with federal, state, and local law enforcement agencies or any National Guard or other appropriate armed forces organizations
   - Taking additional precautions at public events and possibly considering alternative venues or even cancellation

- Preparing to execute contingency procedures, such as moving to an alternate site or dispersing their workforce
- Restricting threatened facility access to essential personnel only

5. **Severe Condition (Red)**: A Severe Condition reflects a severe risk of terrorist attacks. Under most circumstances, the Protective Measures for a Severe Condition are not intended to be sustained for substantial periods of time. In addition to the Protective Measures in the previous Threat Conditions, federal departments and agencies also should consider the following general measures

in addition to the agency-specific Protective Measures that they will develop and implement:

- Increasing or redirecting personnel to address critical emergency needs
- Assigning emergency response personnel and prepositioning and mobilizing specially trained teams or resources
- Monitoring, redirecting, or constraining transportation systems
- Closing public and government facilities

*Source*: Department of Homeland Security, www.dhs.gov.

information about dangers to life and property to the right people, in the right places and the right times, so that those in harm's way can take timely and appropriate action to save lives, reduce losses and speed recovery—whether from natural disasters, accidents, or acts of terrorism" (Partnership for Public Warning, 2003).

In May 2003, PPW published "A National Strategy for Integrated for Public Warning Policy and Capability," which examined the current status of public warning systems, practices, and issues across the United States. The report stated,

> Working together in partnership, the stakeholders should assess current warning capability, carry out appropriate research and develop the following:
>
> - A common terminology for natural and man-made disasters
> - A standard message protocol
> - National metrics and standards
> - National backbone systems for securely collecting and disseminating warnings from all officials sources
> - Pilot projects to test concepts and approaches
> - Training and event-simulation programs
> - A national multimedia education and outreach program

*Source*: Partnership for Public Warning, 2003.

## TERROR ALERTS BECOME MORE SPECIFIC

Critics of the Homeland Security Advisory System have complained since its inception that the warnings it provides are much too vague, or are geographically much too broad to be useful for local or even state emergency management agencies. The nation consists of about 700,000 law enforcement officers, and a population of 300 million, all of which were affected by these vague terror alerts by being asked to increase vigilance. So bad was this problem that, in 2003, the nation's governors called the lack of effective communications their number one concern in the war on terror.

Later that year, then–DHS Secretary Tom Ridge met with the governors at their annual conference, giving a public address aimed at soothing their concerns. He assured them that the flow of information would increase, but that it would probably never increase to the amount that the governors were asking. At this meeting, Ridge told the governors that they would be asked to select five staff members who would be given high-level security clearances. In conjunction with the governors, they would be given access to a secure website that would provide details about specific alerts, but they would not be allowed to pass the information on to lower ranks. Ridge also promised the governors flexibility to determine their state's security priorities in heightened alerts, after 150 key locations designated by the federal government had been locked down.

As Ridge promised, the terror alerts did become more location specific, as was seen in late 2004 and mid-2005. On August 1, 2004, the HSAS was raised to Orange for the financial sector in New York City, Washington, D.C., and northern New Jersey. This was the first time a specific geographic threat was issued. The warning was given after intelligence analysis and reports pointed to a possible attack on those sectors after al-Qaeda surveillance was detected. That advisory was retracted on November 10 of that same year, more than 3 months later, after permanent protective measures were put in place. Then, after the July 7, 2005, terror attacks on the subway and bus systems in London, the HSAS terror alert level was raised to Orange for the mass transit portion of the transportation sector (including regional and intercity passenger rail, subways, and bus systems). While this was not done because of any specific intelligence indicating that an attack was due to occur in the United States, it allowed for further protective measures to be put into place in case a previously undetected attack was to occur. These measures included the following:

- Additional law enforcement
- Bomb-detecting K-9 teams
- Increased video surveillance
- Spot testing in certain areas
- Additional perimeter barriers
- Extra intrusion detection equipment
- Increased inspections of trash receptacles and other storage areas

## CRISIS COMMUNICATIONS

Communications has become an increasingly critical function in emergency management. The dissemination of timely and accurate information to the general public, elected and community officials, and the media plays a major role in the effective management of disaster response and recovery activities. Communicating policies, goals, and priorities to staff, partners, and participants enhances support and promotes a more efficient disaster management operation.

During the 1990s, FEMA established a strong communications capability that worked very effectively in numerous natural disasters and during the response to the bombing at the Murrah Federal Office Building in Oklahoma City. There are many similarities between communicating public messages during a terrorist crisis and communicating public messages during a crisis caused by a natural hazard. Former New York Mayor Rudy Giuliani successfully implemented a communications strategy in the aftermath of the World Trade Center attacks that was very similar to the FEMA model.

However, there are significant differences between natural and terrorist events and communications, especially in the area of information collection and dissemination to the public. The anthrax incidents and the sniper attacks in the Washington, D.C., metropolitan area clearly highlighted one of the most significant differences: the need to share timely information with the public during an ongoing crisis versus the needs of the criminal investigators to protect and hold close information as they seek to identify and detain the parties responsible for the incident. This very delicate balancing act will likely be repeated time and again in the years to come; how officials, the public, and the media will come to terms with this issue is not especially clear at this time.

In this section we will examine the underlying concepts of the FEMA model and examine some of the research conducted to date on crisis communications during a terrorist crisis.

## THE FEMA MODEL

The mission of an effective disaster communications strategy is to provide timely and accurate information to the public. The foundation of an effective disaster communications strategy is built on the four critical assumptions:

- Customer focus
- Leadership commitment
- Inclusion of communications in planning and operations
- Media partnership

### Customer Focus

An essential element of any effective emergency management system is a focus on customers and customer service. This philosophy should guide any communications with the public and with all partners in emergency management. A customer service approach includes placing the needs and interests of individuals and communities first, being responsive and informative, and managing expectations. The FEMA emergency information field guide illustrates the agency's focus on customer service and its strategy of getting messages out to the public as directly as possible. The introduction to the guide states the following:

> As members of the Emergency Information and Media Affairs team, you are part of the frontline for the agency in times of disaster. We count on you to be ready and able to respond and perform effectively on short notice. Disaster victims need to know their government is working. They need to know where and how to get help. They need to know what to expect and what not to expect. Getting these messages out quickly is your responsibility as members of the Emergency Information and Media Affairs team. (FEMA, 1998)

The guide's mission statement reinforces this point further:

> To contribute to the well-being of the community following a disaster by ensuring the dissemination of information that:
>
> - Is timely, accurate, consistent, and easy to understand
> - Explains what people can expect from their government
> - Demonstrates clearly that FEMA and other federal, state, local, and voluntary agencies are working together to provide the services needed to rebuild communities and restore lives. (FEMA, 1998)

The customers for emergency management are diverse. They include internal customers, such as staff, other federal agencies, states, and other disasters partners. External customers include the general public, elected officials at all levels of government, community and business leaders, and the media. Each of these customers has special needs, and a good communications strategy considers and reflects their requirements.

### Leadership Commitment

Good communications start with a commitment by the leadership of the emergency management organization to sharing and disseminating information both internally and externally. The director of any emergency management organization must endorse and promote open lines of communications among the organization's staff, partners, and public in order to effectively communicate (Figure 8-4). This leader must model this behavior in order to clearly illustrate that communications is a valued function of the organization.

In the 1990s, FEMA Director James Lee Witt embodied FEMA's commitment to communicating with the FEMA staff and partners, the public, and the

**FIGURE 8-4** Arlington, Virginia, September 15, 2001—FEMA Director Joe McAllbaugh talks to the media about FEMA's role in the response and recovery operations under way at the Pentagon after the September 11 terrorist attacks. (Photo by Jocelyn Augustino/FEMA News Photo)

media. Witt was a very strong advocate for keeping FEMA staff informed of agency plans, priorities, and operations. He characterized a proactive approach in communicating with FEMA's constituents, and his accessibility to the media was a significant departure from that of previous FEMA leaders. Director Witt exhibited his commitment to effective communications in many ways:

- During a disaster response, he held media briefings daily, and sometimes two or three times a day. He would hold special meetings with victims and their families.
- He led the daily briefings among FEMA partners during a disaster response.
- He devoted considerable time to communicating with members of Congress, governors, mayors, and other elected officials, during times of disaster and nondisaster.
- He met four or five times a year with the state emergency management directors, FEMA's principal emergency management partners.
- He gave speeches all over this country and around the world to promote better understanding of emergency management and disaster mitigation.

Through Witt's leadership and commitment to communications, FEMA became an agency with a positive image and reputation. Communications led to increased success in molding public opinion and garnering support for the agency's initiatives in disaster mitigation.

### Inclusion of Communications in Planning and Operations

The most important part of leadership's commitment to communications is inclusion of communications in all planning and operations. This means that a communications specialist is included in the senior management team of the emergency management organization. It means that communications issues are considered in the decision-making processes and that

a communications element is included in all organizational activities, plans, and operations.

In the past, communicating with external audiences, or customers, and in many cases internal customers was neither valued nor considered critical to a successful emergency management operation. Technology has changed the equation. In today's world of 24-hour television and radio news and the Internet, the demand for information is never-ending, especially in an emergency response situation. Emergency managers must be able to communicate critical information in a timely manner to their staff, partners, the public, and the media.

To do so, the information needs of the various customers and the best methods by which to communicate with these customers must be considered at the same time that planning and operational decisions are being made. For example, a decision process on how to remove debris from a disaster area must include discussion of how to communicate information on the debris removal operation to community officials, the public, and the media.

During the many major disasters that occurred in the 1990s, Director Witt assembled a small group of his senior managers who traveled with him to the sites of disasters and worked closely with him in managing FEMA's efforts. This group always included FEMA's director of public affairs. Similarly, when planning FEMA's preparedness and mitigation initiatives, Witt always included staff from Public Affairs in the planning and implementation phases. Every FEMA policy, initiative, or operation undertaken during this time included consideration of the information needs of the identified customers, and a communications strategy to address these needs was developed.

### Media Partnership

The media plays a primary role in communicating with the public. No government emergency management organization could ever hope to develop a communications network comparable to those networks already established and maintained by television, radio, and newspaper outlets across the country. To effectively provide timely disaster information to the public, emergency managers must establish a partnership with their local media outlets.

The goal of a media partnership is to provide accurate and timely information to the public in both disaster and nondisaster situations. The partnership requires a commitment by both the emergency manager and the media to work together; it also requires a certain degree of trust between both parties.

Traditionally, the relationship between emergency managers and the media has been tenuous. Conflicts have arisen as a result of the emergency manager's need to respond quickly and the media's need to obtain information on the response so it can report it just as quickly. These conflicts sometimes resulted in inaccurate reporting and tension between the emergency manager and the media. The loser in such conflicts is always the public, which relies on the media for its information.

It is important for emergency managers to understand the needs of the media and the value they bring to facilitating response operations. An effective media partnership provides the emergency manager with a communications network to reach the public with vital information. Such a partnership provides the media with access to the disaster site, access to emergency managers and their staff, and access to critical information that informs and ensures the accuracy of the reports before they reach the public.

An effective media partnership helps define the roles of the emergency management organizations, manage public expectations, and boost the morale of the relief workers and the disaster victims. All of these factors can speed the recovery of a community from a disaster event and promote preparedness and mitigation efforts designed to reduce the loss of life and property from the next disaster event.

### Communications Infrastructure

FEMA built a substantial communications infrastructure to support these communications objectives. Resources were devoted to hiring and training staff with experience in working with the media and com-munity and providing these employees with the tools they needed to be successful. FEMA built and maintained a television studio with satellite capabilities and an audio studio with radio broadcast capabilities. The agency also established an interactive website where radio actualities and print information could be posted instantaneously. FEMA hired still and video photographers who were dispatched to the field, filing their photos electronically each night. These photos were then made available to media outlets around the country via the Internet.

Local emergency managers developed similar capabilities on a smaller scale in communities around the country. A research project conducted by graduate students at George Washington University found that many jurisdictions in the Washington, D.C., metro area have built varying degrees of communications infrastructure such as communications plans, web and fax communication capabilities, and trained staff that served them well during recent natural and man-made events. A copy of the research project is presented in Appendix 11.

### Terrorism Application

As noted earlier, Mayor Giuliani was an effective communicator in the aftermath of the World Trade Center attacks. He quickly assumed the role of principal government spokesperson, providing information, solace, and comfort to victims and their families, fellow New Yorkers, the nation, and the world through a series of planned and unplanned media events and interviews over the course of the days and months after September 11. Giuliani has been praised for his candor, his sensitivity, and his availability during these efforts. He has set a standard by which public officials will be judged in future tragedies.

In Washington, D.C., a different communications scenario surfaced in the days and weeks after the first anthrax-contaminated letter was discovered in the office of then U.S. Senate Majority Leader Tom Daschle in October 2001. A series of public officials and scientists issued often-conflicting information to the public as both the officials and the public struggled to understand the nature and the reach of the anthrax threat. The failure to communicate accurate and timely information reduced public confidence in the government response and increased the confusion and misinformation surrounding the events.

What factors made Mayor Giuliani's efforts successful and caused the situation in Washington to worsen? What type of information and infrastructure support did Giuliani have that may or may not have been available to the public officials in Washington? Was the commitment to inform the public different in New York City than it was in Washington, D.C.?

A study of the anthrax attacks funded by The Century Foundation concluded that "the timely flow of information from experts to the public via the mass media will be the nation's best protection against panic and potential disaster" (Thomas, 2003). To reach this goal, the media and public officials will need to change the way they work together and possibly establish new protocols for determining the methods by which sensitive information is collected and disseminated to the public. These issues must ultimately be balanced against the public's right to know. As the study found, the public is often smarter and better informed than both the media and public officials believe (Thomas, 2003).

A report entitled "What Should We Know? Whom Do We Tell?: Leveraging Communications and Information to Counter Terrorism and Its Consequences" found that the dissemination of information before a terrorist incident is as critical, if not more so, as delivering timely and accurate information during and after a crisis (Chemical and Biological Arms Control Institute, 2002). Preincident planning and coordination and public education and awareness campaigns are critical elements in establishing clear lines of communications among responding agencies, significantly improving the opportunities to collect accurate information and make it available to the public through the mass media. Again, changes in current practices and relationships among responders and with the media must occur to meet the information needs before, during, and after future terrorist attacks (Chemical and Biological Arms Control Institute, 2002).

The Washington, D.C., sniper attacks provide valuable insight into the difficulties in communicating with the public during an ongoing crisis. The tension between the need to provide timely and complete information when such information was lacking and the need to avoid compromising an ongoing criminal investigation was clearly evident during this nearly month-long crisis. A case study of this event and its media coverage is presented at the close of this chapter.

## 9/11 COMMISSION FINDINGS ON FIRST RESPONDER COMMUNICATIONS

The National Commission on Terrorist Attacks Against the United States, also known as the 9/11 Commission, found that inadequate communications contributed greatly to hindering the ability of responding agencies to respond to the events that unfolded, and directly led to the high number of police and fire department employees who were killed when the towers collapsed. It was discovered during the after-action review that many of these first responders were unable to communicate either with each other or with their commanders, and many of the open channels were quickly overcome by the heavy traffic. The following excerpt from the commission report describes these troubles:

> The attacks of September 11, 2001, overwhelmed the response capacity of most of the local jurisdictions where the hijacked airliners crashed. . . . The inability to communicate was a critical element at the World Trade Center, Pentagon, and Somerset County, Pennsylvania, crash sites, where multiple agencies and multiple jurisdictions responded. The occurrence of this problem at three very different sites is strong evidence that compatible and adequate communications among public safety organizations at the local, state, and federal levels remains an important problem.

The commission recommended that more funding and research be set aside to ensure that first responder interoperable communication is improved to prevent these issues in the future. On July 13, 2004, Senator

Stabenow of Michigan proposed an amendment to the Homeland Security Appropriations Bill that would provide funding for interoperable communications grants to states and local communities to allow first responders to buy and upgrade their communications equipment. As of late July 2005, Congress had yet to address these concerns with any budget allocations.

The First Response Coalition (FRC), an association of citizens, individual first responders, and advocacy groups concerned about first responder issues (formed in 2004), has developed a white paper, "It's Time To Talk: Achieving Interoperable Communications for America's First Responders." This report addresses the scope of the communications interoperability problem, examines the reasons public safety departments cannot communicate, and the importance of interoperability to first responders and the communities they protect. It also explores the barriers to interoperability, including cost, lack of coordinated planning, and scarcity of spectrum resources. The paper concludes with the First Response Coalition's plan to make public safety communications interoperability a national priority and create a funding mechanism that will allow first responders to obtain the communications equipment and infrastructure they desperately need. This report can be found on the FRC website, www.firstresponsecoalition.org.

## CONCLUSION

The experience of emergency managers with natural disasters provides at minimum a guide to the development of effective terrorism-related communications strategies. However, there is much work to be done to adapt existing risk, warning, and crisis communications models to the new hazards, the new partners, and the new dynamic between response and recovery and criminal activity associated with the new terrorist threat. One thing will remain constant: Communication with the public about the terrorist threat must receive the same attention and resources that are now going to new technologies, new training pro-

grams, and new organizations. It has never been more important that public officials talk to the public, and it has never been more difficult than it is now. If this problem is not addressed properly, it can only compound in the worst way the terrible consequences of any terrorist incident.

## CASE STUDY 1
### Washington, D.C., Sniper Attacks

**Introduction**

In America's post-911 era of terror awareness, the extreme actions of groups like al Qaeda are no longer necessary to spark detrimental anxiety-based social reactions. The two "snipers" who placed the nation's capital under a state of siege for 3 weeks with one rifle and a box of bullets confirmed this fact. Washington, D.C.'s latest duct-tape and plastic "panic buying" spree, set off by the Department of Homeland Security's momentary "Terrorism Threat Index" increase, illustrates that the mere hint of a future event can now induce "irrational" behavior. Clearly, the emergency management community can no longer simply blame the media for such strong public sentiments.

Controlling public fear is a public safety task that falls squarely on the shoulders of local government, but like other terrorism preparedness and response functions, fear management must be supported by the federal government to be effective. There exists a rapidly growing need for agencies to adopt formal fear management capabilities staffed by appropriately trained, dedicated officials. In many cases of terrorism, fear is the greatest emergency that must be managed, and irresponsible or inadequate attempts to do so can actually increase the public's risk. Using the recent sniper crisis as an example, this case study will examine the roots of public fear and the often-distorted reality of risk and will propose methods by which emergency management agencies can successfully manage fear should a terror-based event occur within their jurisdiction.

## Background

The residents of the Washington, D.C., metropolitan area[1] were confronted with a dramatically heightened sense of personal vulnerability in the $12^1/_2$ months leading up to the sniper crisis. On September 11, 2001, during the worst terrorist attack to take place on American soil, the city became the target of two hijacked airplanes.[2] Less than 1 month later, several letters containing anthrax were mailed to federal government offices, resulting in the closing of several buildings,[3] a mass prophylaxis with the antibiotic Cipro, and the death of several Washington, D.C., postal workers. Ever-increasing security measures became impossible to avoid, with numerous streets surrounding federal buildings closed to the public, military vehicles with mounted machine guns positioned around the Pentagon, and all the while the media reporting that the emergency response capabilities of the Washington, D.C., government would be severely deficient should a mass casualty event occur in the near future (Ward, 2001).

It was easy to surmise that, to international and "homegrown" terrorists alike, Washington, D.C., was a likely target. Reported levels of stress among area residents were much higher than those observed throughout the rest of the country, as indicated by several polls (Diaz and O'Rourke, 2002). By the time the sniper announced his presence on the morning of October 3, 2002, by killing four people, Washingtonians had already been pushed to the limits of their psychological stress tolerance.

## Reactions and Actions

To study this case, we must first examine the reactions and actions of the authorities (the police department and other government officials), the media, and the public. These three groups were intimately linked by the virtual dearth of information that was available. The links can be simplified through the understanding that the authorities gathered and analyzed the information, the media broadcast the information, and the public received the information and acted upon it. The information flow diagram shown in Figure 8-5 depicts these links.

The following pages provide a broader understanding of each of these groups' actions in order to offer insight into why each may have acted as they did.

## The Authorities

The individuals considered the "authorities" include the local, state, and federal government officials who were involved with the various aspects related to the response to the sniper crisis. Because this was primarily a law enforcement response to an event that involved only conventional weapons, the local police departments were the lead agencies involved.[4] These authorities were the sole source of credible information during the crisis.

The Montgomery County Police Department (MCPD) was the first to become involved in the crisis on the morning of October 3, primarily because the majority of killings had taken place in Montgomery County, Maryland. Having authority in the affected jurisdiction, the MCPD put forth Chief Charles Moose as the official spokesperson for the media.[5] Although

---

[1]Includes the District of Columbia, Northern Virginia, and several counties in Maryland. The population of this region, according to the 2000 census, is 4,922,640 (FAIR, 2002b).

[2]While only one plane crashed into a building in the Washington, D.C., metropolitan area (the Pentagon), it is believed that the plane that crashed into a Pennsylvania field was heading for either the White House or the United States Capitol (Lochhead, 2002).

[3]As of late November 2002, the Brentwood Postal Facility, where the three postal workers who contracted anthrax worked, remained closed, with no planned reopening in the near future (Fernandez, 2002).

[4]Presidential Decision Directive-39 (PDD39), signed by President Clinton in 1995, gives the Department of Justice, through the Federal Bureau of Investigation (FBI), lead agency authority in incidents where weapons of mass destruction are used or if the event is considered terrorism (Watson, 2000). The sniper crisis was never officially classified as such, so Chief Moose remained in command.

[5]Initially, MCPD spokeswoman Captain Nancy Demme was issuing statements to the media, but Chief Moose assumed the public relations role upon further consideration of the severity of the crisis.

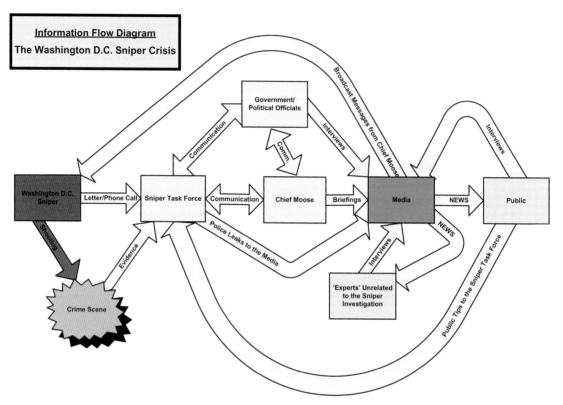

**FIGURE 8-5**   Information flow diagram during the Washington, D.C., sniper crisis.

Chief Moose could provide only basic information concerning the characteristics of the victims and the locations of the shootings, he was immediately recognized as the leader in the crisis.[6] For the remainder of the crisis, the media (and likewise, the public) continued to look to Chief Moose for information and guid-

---

[6]Chief Moose, who holds a Ph.D. in urban studies, was seen not only as a trustworthy leader but also as the lead decision maker. It was important that he addressed the media, considering all information passed through his hands—something a spokesperson of a lower rank could not claim. Moose was credited for his on-camera compassion, shedding tears on occasion and uttering comments throughout the crisis that showed his "human" side. At one point, for instance, he urged parents to spend more time with their children (Sun and Ly, 2002).

ance. In fact, even though FBI agents ultimately arrested the suspects outside of Chief Moose's jurisdiction, it was Chief Moose who officially announced the arrest.

Chief Moose proclaimed that this was one of the greatest challenges he has ever faced (Stockwell, Ruane, and White, 2002). He had never been required to fulfill such an important public relations role. The crisis quickly escalated to an international scale, and Chief Moose became the one man the world turned to for information so desperately sought. Chief Moose faced a major problem in that he often did not have very much information to give, and when he did, he felt that giving anything specific would jeopardize the investigation.

Chief Moose provided very little information detailing the actual risk people faced. He would regularly assure the public that police were doing their best to keep people safe and that the bulk of police resources were focused on solving the case, but he could not tell people how concerned they should be about personal safety. On at least one occasion he even stated that "we've not been able to assure anyone their safety in regards to this situation" (Ruane and Stockwell, 2002).

The Washington, D.C., Metropolitan Police Department (MPD) publicly issued a list of "Tips for Staying Safe." This list told residents to keep moving when outside, to walk in a rapid zigzag pattern, and to avoid brightly lit open spaces. It also stated, "Remember that a sniper with the right equipment can shoot accurately from about 500 yards, the equivalent of five football fields" (Hurdle, 2002). These tips did not give any indication to residents of what their actual risk from the sniper might be. Some residents followed the advice they were given in these messages, but it is arguable that the lack of Chief Moose's endorsement of the tips prevented them from being widely observed.

School administrators became major players in the response to the sniper threat. Several schools were closed in the Richmond, Virginia, area after a sniper letter proclaiming that children were not safe was found at a shooting scene. Schools in other areas of Virginia and Maryland were closed as well, though no specific threats were given to the administrators of those schools as in Richmond. These closings were said to have been the result of a fear of liability among school administrators (*Economist*, 2002) and were not based on solid evidence. While they claimed that "there was no other way to guarantee students' safety" (Gettleman, 2002), the fact remained that they did not want to be held responsible for making a decision to let school stay in session and then have a child shot in their "jurisdiction" during such a high-profile crisis. In fact, none of the schools shut down during the sniper crisis were shut down after the September 11 terrorists attacks or after any other unsolved murders in the area (Reel, 2002). A further explanation could be heard in

the words of Henrico County Public School Superintendent Mark Edwards, who stated, "The decision was not based on any specific threats, but on 'the volume of concern'" (Gettleman, 2002). Such statements strengthened arguments that these actions were based on a reaction to fear, not the risk itself. Of course, it is undeniable that there existed a genuine concern for the safety of the children in the motivation of these decisions, echoed by Montgomery County Superintendent Jerry West, who said, "We have always taken very seriously every day the level of threat to our children. We have always consistently done everything we can do to keep our children safe" (Schulte, 2002). The closing of schools became a focus of media attention and undoubtedly affected public opinion about personal safety.[7]

Politicians also become involved in the public reaction to the crisis, and in several cases used the events to further their own agendas. Kathleen Kennedy Townsend, in her gubernatorial campaign in Maryland, began attacking her opponent's opposition to a federal ban on assault weapons, stating that the gun control would be an answer to the voters' fears (Fineman, 2002). Connie Morella, campaigning for the House of Representatives, said, "I'm still knocking on doors, and when I do that, I think I'm a comfort to the people at home. I mean, if I'm out there doing that, people say, 'Hey, it must be all right'" (Barker, 2002).

There is finally the issue of unnamed authorities passing unreleased information to the media. It is important to stress both the detriment and opportunities presented by these insider "leaks." In numerous instances, the press learned of confidential information that was either never to be shared or not to be released immediately, and they broadcast that information, to the obvious dismay of Chief Moose. While on many occasions these leaks increased the tensions observed between the Sniper Task Force officials and

---

[7]In a *Washington Post* poll, 82% of respondents said that they approved of the way their local schools were handling the situation (*Washington Post*, 2002b).

the media, it cannot be overlooked that leaks were directly attributed to the capture of the two suspects.

## The Media

The media was virtually the only bridge of information between the authorities and the public (see Figure 8-5 earlier). Media agencies gleaned information from a myriad of sources, but the only information broadcast that could be deemed "factual" or "credible" almost always came directly from Chief Moose. In addition, that which was leaked was usually confirmed or denied by Chief Moose. Media coverage, in regards to air time, was almost total when the crisis began and immediately after each successive victim. Regular news shows became dominated by the case, and there were constant "special reports" with additional information that was considered "related" to the case.

Coverage of the sniper crisis spanned the globe, and early on there were as many international news agencies as national ones camped outside the Montgomery County Police Department. The number of articles seen in the national and international press surged with each successive shooting, peaking immediately after the capture of Muhammad and Malvo. The actual daily number of articles, taken from major national and international newspapers, is displayed in Figure 8-6.

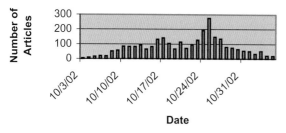

FIGURE 8-6  Number of articles related to the sniper crisis[8] appearing in 47 major international newspapers.

[8]Numbers attained by searching for the keyword "sniper," using the Lexis/Nexis "general news search" of 47 major newspapers from throughout the world.

The media had a particularly strong influence in this crisis. Because the events were statistically so rare, and there were so few victims overall, there were startlingly few people outside of the immediate families and close friends of those victims who had any personal experience with "sniping" events.[9] In light of this fact, it is safe to say that members of the public received more than 99% of their information concerning the crisis from the media.[10] To put this statistic in perspective, it can be compared to the findings of an *L.A. Times* poll in which respondents claimed their "feelings about crime" were based 65% on what they read and saw in the media, and 21% on experience[11] (Walsh, 1996, p. 9).

The media agencies often looked to alternate sources of information to achieve a competitive edge over one another. It was not uncommon to see "serial killings" experts speaking on news talk shows or to see "geographic profiling" experts doing the same (most notably after Chief Moose announced that geographic profilers were being used in the case). None of these alternate sources could provide any factual information outside of what was already known by the

[9]Many people were affected by the secondary effects of the sniper, such as long traffic jams caused by roadblocks or school closings. However, as the direct consequence of the sniper was death or injury caused by shooting, only a very small group was *directly* affected.

[10]Fear of crime, often cited as being overestimated by the public, is also mainly established through media coverage. In the 1990s, when the murder rate in the United States dropped by 20%, the murder coverage on network newscasts increased by 600%. As a result, 62% of Americans "believed crime was soaring, and described our society as 'truly desperate' about crime" (Jacobson, 2001).

[11]The findings of this poll have been reinforced by other studies on the subject. When Esther Madriz, a professor at Hunter College in New York City, interviewed women in New York City about their fears of crime they frequently responded with the phrase "I saw it in the news." The interviewees identified the news media as both the source of their fears and the reason they believed those fears were valid. Asked in a national poll why they believe the country has a serious crime problem, 76% of people cited stories they had seen in the media. Only 22% cited personal experience (Glassner, 1999, p. xxi).

public, as they were not directly connected to the investigation (see Figure 8-5).

As stated earlier, there existed an explicit tension between the media and Chief Moose. This rift was most visible on October 9, when Chief Moose lashed out at the press for publishing information pertaining to a message written on a tarot card found at the school where a 13-year-old boy was shot. In another instance that angered Chief Moose, CNN reported, hours before the information was officially released, that the thirteenth shooting victim had died (Shales, 2002). Chief Moose's public scolding of the media (the result of a combination of sustained high levels of stress and inexperience with such high-profile events), however, was limited after the initial statements made in relation to the tarot card.

A fact that must be noted for its uniqueness is that the media was obviously used by the police as a direct mode of communication with the sniper. Chief Moose would "speak" to the sniper using cryptic messages at regularly scheduled press conferences without giving the media any prior indication that he would be doing this. Chief Moose did acknowledge his recognition of this important role the media played, one they were more than willing to fulfill.

**The Public**

The general public includes, for the sake of this case study, the people of the Washington, D.C., and Richmond, Virginia, metropolitan areas. These people were the vulnerable group involved in the crisis—the sniper's targets. They were also the target of the media's and the authorities' information. The public was not only a target of these other players (including the sniper) but also a major source of information and action. The public demand for information fueled the media frenzy that occurred. Their fear of the sniper was the driving force in many of the decisions, rational or irrational, that were made by the authorities. Finally, the public was an integral component in the hunt for the sniper, and it was tips received from several members of the public that eventually led the police to Malvo and Muhammad.

Public action and reaction became the subject of many stories. This exhibited behavior became the focus of countless articles, detailing "newsworthy" actions that were performed in the name of safety.

Examples of such actions, followed by percentages of the affected population who admitted to performing them derived from a *Washington Post* poll (if available), include the following:

- Used different gas stations than one normally used (Morin and Deane, 2002)—36%.
- Avoided stores/shopping centers close to highways (Morin and Deane, 2002)—32%.
- Crouched down while pumping gas (Ropeik, 2002a).
- Ran or weaved through parking lots (Walker, 2002).
- Avoided outdoor activities (Irvin and Mattingly, 2002)—44%.
- Kept constant movement in public places (Eccleston, 2002).
- Stayed at home except when absolutely necessary (Johnson and Finer, 2002)—13%.
- Drove when one would normally have taken Metro (*Washington Post*, 2002b)—11%.
- Watched or listened to the news more than usual (*Washington Post*, 2002b)—71%.

Gas station attendants were witness to much of this fear because so many people believed that the stations were a preferred target location of the sniper. One attendant reported that "some people, when they get out of their cars, they are so scared that their hands shake, and they can't get their [credit] cards into the [gas pumps]" (Nakamura and Davis, 2002).

The public was a responsible recipient of this flood of information, and generally followed any behavioral advice they were given by the authorities. They learned the meaning of terms like "Code Blue" and "Code Red,"[12] how to identify .223-firing assault

[12]School security codes—Code Blue signifies that all outdoor activities are canceled and positive ID is required to enter the building, and Code Red signifies that students are locked in their classroom in case a threat actually exists within the building (Lambert, 2002).

rifles, the meaning of ballistics tests and what government agency conducts them, and how to identify box trucks, Chevy Astro Vans, and ladder racks. The public was told to call in their tips to the FBI tip line, and by the time the sniper was caught, over 90,000 calls had been placed (Whitlock, 2002).

What the public did not do, however, was panic. As much as the media wrote stories detailing the "paralyzing fear" experienced by the average person, life did go on with civility. There were no events where people were pushing each other over to get inside the "safety" of a store, for example. The public was fearful but intelligent, receptive to advice, and obviously able to process information well enough to locate the sniper within 24 hours once they learned the car and license plate information.

### So Why Was Everyone So Afraid?

In their article "Rating the Risks," Paul Slovic, Baruch Fischhoff, and Sarah Lichtenstein (1979) begin as follows: "People respond to the hazards they perceive." The exhibited responses to the sniper at personal, local, regional, and even federal levels would indicate that sources influencing risk perception during the crisis existed at extreme levels. In this section, the sniper crisis will be compared to models developed in recent and historical research in order to better explain the peculiar public risk behavior observed. This examination will be structured according to the four "Risk Perception Fallibility" conclusions of Slovic, Fischhoff, and Lichtenstein found in their 1979 article "Rating the Risks."

*Risk Perception Fallibility Conclusion 1*: "Cognitive limitations, coupled with the anxieties generated by facing life as a gamble, cause uncertainty to be denied, risks to be distorted, and statements of fact to be believed with unwarranted confidence."

People tend to fear a risk less as they become better informed, with more specific details of the risk. However, the amount a person can discover about a risk will almost never be complete, as the actual likelihood or consequence most risks pose cannot be quantified in a way that addresses the specific threat faced by individuals (even well-known risks such as

cancer or heart disease) (Ropeik, 2002c). The more uncertainty a risk poses, or, as Slovic, Fischhoff, and Lichtenstein state, "the more of a gamble something is," the more people will fear it. The sniper, who could strike anyone, anywhere, at any time, presented citizens in the Washington, D.C., metropolitan area with the ultimate in uncertainty.

In the face of uncertainty, people will consciously or subconsciously make personal judgments based on very imperfect information in order to establish some individual concept of the risk they face (Slovic, Fischhoff, and Lichtenstein, 1979). These judgments based on uncertainties and imperfect information often cause people to wrongly perceive their own risk, more often in a way that overstates reality. There could scarcely have been more uncertainty in regards to the public's knowledge of useful information in the sniper crisis. Members of the public were constantly told by the media that the police had very little to work with, because the sniper was leaving few clues at crime scenes (Patrick, 2002). People had no idea how great of a threat the sniper was in comparison to other public safety threats the police handled during routine action because these statistics were never released. Considering the amount of resources police dedicated, it would appear that the threat to public safety was greater than anything people in the area had ever faced, and considering the ineffectiveness of the actions of the police in catching the sniper (such as the systems of roadblocks),[13] the public could assume only that the police were powerless to combat this "enormous" threat. Many other factors external to the investigation gave an impression of dire seriousness and great uncertainty as well. Every time a media "expert" would attempt to define the sniper's actions,

---

[13]In one of the most comprehensive roadblock systems set up after the October 22 shooting (which occurred during the morning rush-hour traffic), one person was quoted in the *Washington Post* as saying that, after getting off the highway and onto the back roads, "I didn't see a single police car on the way in [to his job in College Park, Maryland]. If you're trying to stop someone, you'd have to have a tighter net, and that simply wasn't there. I was a novice trying to make my way through, and it was fairly easy" (Layton and Shaver, 2002).

stating that he would likely not strike in place X or at time Y, the sniper would strike in that place or at that time. The great number of white vans in circulation gave the impression that the sniper was everywhere.[14] The fact that schools were being closed, outdoor activities were regularly canceled, the government was talking of bringing in the national guard, and the New York–based Guardian Angels were in the area pumping gas only strengthened the public's view that the risk was greater than it actually was. Frequent talk that the crisis may be the result of terrorism propagated the idea that the sniper might be just the first in a series of snipers that could become a regular part of life in America.[15] In a survey that asked citizens of the Washington, D.C., metropolitan area how concerned they were that they might personally become a victim of the sniper, 19% said a great deal and 31% said somewhat scared—a total of 50% (*Washington Post*, 2002b).

*Risk Perception Fallibility Conclusion 2*: "Perceived risk is influenced (and sometimes biased) by the imaginability and memorability of the hazard. People may, therefore, not have valid perceptions even for familiar risks."

People are more afraid of those things that they can imagine or that they can remember. These easily available risks, as they are called, tend to be overestimated in regards to their likelihood of occurrence. Generally, people tend to fear what they hear about repetitively or

constantly. This phenomenon is referred to as the *availability heuristic*, which states that people perceive an event to be likely or frequent if instances of the event are easy to imagine or recall. This is a perception bias that can be correct when considering events that are, in fact, frequently observed, such as in the case of those who believe that automobile accidents are common because almost everyone they know has been involved in one. However, when a risk that is spectacular but not necessarily common receives constant media attention, such as high-school shootings did in the 1990s (particularly the Columbine attack),[16] people often wrongly assume that similar events are very likely to occur. In the case of the sniper, where coverage in newspapers and on television, radio, and the Internet was constant, receiving front-page placement every day from October 4 until the suspects were captured on October 24,[17] it would follow that people would likely assume their personal risk was greater than it actually was. Again, the omnipresence of white vans and white box trucks, both intimately associated with the sniper crisis through the police and the media, gave people a constant reminder of the sniper. Many of the decisions by government officials to close schools, restrict the movement of students, and cancel outdoor activities altered people's daily lives in such a way that they were made constantly aware of the crisis around them. In addition, seeing sniper victims on TV who were similar to themselves, doing things they regularly did, made it easy for people to imagine succumbing to the same fate.

In an October 13 *Washington Post* poll that asked participants if they felt most threatened by the sniper shootings, the anthrax letters, or the September 11 attacks, 44% responded the sniper shootings, 29% responded the September 11 attacks, and 13% responded the anthrax letters (*Washington Post*,

---

[14]Mark Warr, a sociology professor at the University of Texas, Austin, writes, "People may experience fear merely in anticipation of possible threats or in reaction to environmental clues (e.g., darkness, graffiti) that imply danger" (Warr, 2000). To many people, the sight of ever-present white vans was a constant reminder that the sniper was still at large. To some, the sight of a white van was influential enough to elicit a physical response; a Connecticut business traveler, working in the area in a white Chevy van, stated "I pull into a gas station, and people jump down. Little kids point and say, 'Look, the sniper'" (Snyder, 2002).

[15]During the sniper crisis, it was reported in several newspapers that an al Qaeda suspect in Belgium had admitted during interrogations that members of al Qaeda had been trained in the terrorist training camps to shoot targets from 50 to 250 meters. The suspect added that al Qaeda planned to use snipers to kill U.S. senators while they were golfing (Reid, 2002).

[16]In 1999, two students of Columbine High School in Littleton, Colorado, shot and killed 13 of their classmates. The extensive media coverage led to the public perception that school shootings were on the rise, when in fact, the incidence of school shootings was actually falling that year (Kisken, 2001).

[17]As of November 15, the sniper case was still receiving daily front-page coverage in the *Washington Post*.

2002b). Slovic and his colleagues (1979) described how events that are "out of sight [are] effectively out of mind." It would follow that the opposite was true of the sniper: that which is always in sight is always on people's minds.

*Risk Perception Fallibility Conclusion 3*: "[Risk management] experts' risk perceptions correspond closely to statistical frequencies of death. Laypeople's risk perceptions [are] based in part on frequencies of death, but there [are] some striking discrepancies. It appears that for laypeople, the concept of risk includes qualitative aspects such as dread and the likelihood of a mishap being fatal. Laypeople's risk perceptions were also affected by catastrophic potential."

It can be difficult for people to exactly understand the statistics they are given, and even more difficult for them to conceptualize how those statistics apply to them personally. Furthermore, these statistics tend to do little to affect the way people perceive the risks that are calculated. This is not to say that the average person lacks sufficient intelligence to process numbers; it is just that the numbers are not the sole source of influence on public risk perception. In ranking their risks, people tend to rely more on qualitative factors than on the quantitative likelihood of a hazard resulting in personal consequence (Slovic, Fischhoff, and Lichtenstein, 1979). People are generally more concerned with the consequences than the likelihoods of risks.

In consideration of the statistics provided to the public by the media, it is important to examine their quality and usefulness to the recipients. While it is clear that everyone knew the number of people killed by the sniper, few knew the actual number of people living in the affected area or the actual murder rate in "normal" years within that same area. Without complete information the given statistics were meaningless and likely misleading. In fact, in the absence of complete information, people assumed that their chances of becoming a sniper victim were much greater than they really were. Economists have classified this tendency of people to overestimate unknown or unclear risks as "risk-ambiguity aversion" (*Economist*, 2002). However, even if the statistics were straightforward, it is difficult for people to understand

how those numbers affect them as individuals, even if they are risk "experts" (Jardine and Hrudey, 1997).

Paul Slovic, Baruch Fischhoff, and Sarah Lichtenstein (1980), in their article "Facts and Fears: Understanding Perceived Risk," proposed that there are 18 risk characteristics that influence public risk perception. These qualitative measures have helped to explain what attributes of a risk cause public fear. According to their measures, the risk of being killed by the sniper ranks among the most feared risks, as it is dreaded, has consequences that are fatal, "affects me," is new, is not easily reduced, is uncontrollable, among other reasons. The sniper risk, not surprisingly, falls close to terrorism and crime on the authors' ranking of risks' ability to elicit fear.

*Risk Perception Fallibility Conclusion 4*: "Disagreements about risk should not be expected to evaporate in the presence of 'evidence.' Definitive evidence, particularly about rare hazards, is difficult to obtain. Weaker information is likely to be interpreted in a way that reinforces existing beliefs."

The sniper announced his presence with a true mass-murder event.[18] The initial news reports described an ensuing crisis that left open the possibility that the murders may continue at an equally high rate of incidence (five killings in 16 hours). By the end of October 3, police had little to work with, and there was little hope that the sniper would be quickly captured. The public had been told from the very beginning that they were dealing with a killer who was a grave threat to public safety. Due to psychological factors described in the previous three Risk Perception Fallibility Conclusions, people were made to believe they were at high risk. This became the frame of reference in which the public was to define the sniper risk, and one that would now be very difficult to alter.

The crisis continued for 3 weeks. Many (often heavily editorialized) articles did try to enlighten peo-

[18]The sniper was by definition, both a serial killer and a mass murderer. Serial killers are defined as people who kill several people over a period of days, weeks, or years, killing in cycles, shifting between active and "cooling off" periods, while mass murderers kill several people at one time, usually in one location, over a couple of hours without a "cooling off" period (Macalester College, 2002).

ple about their actual personal risk, some even giving detailed statistics that illustrated to the public that their vulnerability to the sniper was extremely low. Unfortunately, not only did these articles rarely (if ever) get front-page coverage but they were greatly outnumbered by articles telling people that their lives were in grave danger from the sniper. In the end, it was not the "long-shot" statistics nor the articles that told people to remain calm that were believed but the fear-mongering and sensational articles given priority coverage by newspapers and news networks. This is not surprising, considering the findings of Slovic, Fischhoff, and Lichtenstein's research. They state that "people's beliefs change slowly and are extraordinarily persistent in the face of contrary evidence. New evidence appears reliable and informative if it is consistent with one's initial belief; contrary evidence is dismissed as unreliable, erroneous, or unrepresentative." They add that "convincing people that the catastrophe they fear is extremely unlikely is difficult under the best conditions. Any mishap could be seen as proof of high risk, whereas demonstrating safety would require a massive amount of evidence" (Slovic, Fischhoff, and Lichtenstein, 1979), evidence that is sometimes impossible to obtain in an accurate or timely manner.

This stoicism is compounded by the fact that once people make their initial judgments, they believe with overwhelming confidence that their beliefs are correct. This phenomenon, called the *overconfidence heuristic*, suggests that people often are unaware of how little they know about a risk and how much more information they need to make an informed decision. More often than not, people believe that they know much more about risks than they actually do. With regard to the sniper, having overconfidence in incorrect information was inevitable considering the nature of the media coverage. For instance, with "expert" profilers giving descriptions of the killer's "most likely" demographics as a lone young, white male, it is no surprise that everyone was caught off guard when the pair turned out to be two black males (Fears and Thomas-Lester, 2002). However, with no confirmed information provided about the suspects prior

to their arrest, there logically should have been no surprise no matter what race or age he, she, or they were.

This phenomenon has been linked to media coverage of other spectacular events in the past, specifically in regard to the way in which people's rating of risks depends on the amount of media coverage a risk receives. For example, one study showed that the percentage of crimes covered by the media that involve perpetrators and victims of different races is of a greater proportion than occurs in reality. In other words, one is more likely to see a news story describing a white victim of a black attacker than a story depicting a black victim of a black attacker, even though the latter is more common. This inconsistency in coverage is seen as the main reason Caucasians overestimate their likelihood of being a victim of interracial crime by a factor of 3 (Twomey, 2001). Paul Slovic wrote in his 1986 article "Informing and Educating the Public about Risk" that "strong beliefs are hard to modify" and "naïve views are easily manipulated by presentation format."

Often, it is only time that can change people's opinions about the risks they personally face. One major reason people are more scared of a new risk than an old risk is that they have not been able to gather enough information to alter their initial impression. After time has passed, and they realize that their expectations for victimization have not been realized for themselves or anybody that they know, they begin to question the validity of their views. Had the sniper not been caught, the general public would have gained a more accurate appreciation of how small their chance of becoming a victim was, much in the manner that people are no longer as concerned about the child abductions that seemed to plague the United States during 2001.[19] Fortunately, the sniper was caught before this hypothesis could be tested.

---

[19]After a media frenzy followed a series of high-profile child abductions during the early summer of 2001, there was great apprehension reported among parents who began to fear for the safety of their children. Later reports showed that the majority of child abductions were due to child custody disputes and not performed by strangers. The frenzy quickly died down once public knowledge about these facts became more common (STATS, 2002).

**Reality—Statistics of the Crisis**

"Of all the grim facts surrounding [the] Oklahoma City [bombing], perhaps the grimmest is the one nobody talks about: against the backdrop of everyday American tragedy, 167 deaths is not many. . . . In a typical year, guns kill 38,000 Americans and about that many die on our roads. These numbers routinely go up or down 2% or 3%—half a dozen Oklahoma bombings—without making the front page" (political commentator Robert Wright, *Time*, May 1995; cited in Walsh, 1996, p. 18).

In the 3 weeks during which the sniper terrorized more than 5 million people in the Washington, D.C., metropolitan area, shooting 13 people and killing 10, "routine" crime took place virtually unnoticed. In the District of Columbia alone, there were 239 assaults with a deadly weapon, 32 people shot, and 22 people murdered (Barger, 2002). This accounts for just 10% of the total area where the sniper operated, so it can be assumed that there were far more of these "routine" murders than 22. However, not one of these crimes merited front-page coverage in the newspapers.

In the previous section it was necessary to put aside statistics in order to understand public risk perception, but now the statistics alone must be analyzed to determine how the real risk people faced during those 3 fearful weeks from the sniper compared to the other risks they face in their daily lives without second thought. Richard Wilson of Harvard University writes in his article "Analyzing the Daily Risks of Life" that "to compare risks we must calculate them" (1979, p. 57). To calculate the statistical risk that the citizens of the Washington, DC, metropolitan area faced, it is necessary to ascertain the population of the area where the sniper operated. These statistics will not be perfect by any means, as they cannot account for the ever-increasing zone in which the sniper operated (*Economist*, 2002). Additionally, although the sniper operated within a large geographic area, there was not an equal distribution of murders across the total area (Montgomery County was the location of seven of these murders, for example). However, these statistics will be more accurate in terms of personal risk (see description in footnotes 24 and 25), because the virtually random selection of victims who were performing a wide range of activities brings the population and personal risk almost to equality.

To achieve this rough estimate of personal risk, it would be possible to consider the number of victims, divided into the total population of the affected area, spread out over the period in which the sniper was operating. This would not be accurate in projecting future risk, however, because the operating environment changed for the sniper in the early morning of October 3. When the police were not aware of his presence, it was possible for the sniper to repeatedly attack within a short period of time. Shortly after initiation of the crisis, when the sniper's presence was officially recognized, his attacks required more time[20] (presumably for more detailed planning). It is therefore necessary to estimate how the murders would have progressed over the course of a year in the context of a post-awareness scenario. In operating under this assumption, it can be said that the four murders that took place on the morning of October 3 would have likely been only one murder had the police been on alert for the sniper. In that case, the statistics to work with are as follows:

- Number of people shot (adjusted for post-awareness): 10
- Number of people killed (adjusted for post-awareness): 7
- Population, Washington, DC, metropolitan area[21]: 4,922,152
  - (83.16% of total sniper-area population)
- Population, Richmond-Petersburg metropolitan area[22]: 996,512
  - (16.84% of total sniper-area population)
- Population, total affected area: 5,919,152

[20]In addition, the sniper attacks waned in frequency over time, but this factor will not be considered because the sampling period was too short to derive a long-term frequency (*Economist*, 2002).

[21]2000 census information (FAIR, 2002a).

[22]2000 census information (FAIR, 2002b).

- Number of days the sniper operated (10/2/02–10/24/02)[23]: 23
- Multiplier (for 365 day average): 15.870
- National murder rate: 5.5/100,000
- Washington, DC, metropolitan area murder rate: 7.4/100,000
- Richmond-Petersburg metropolitan area murder rate: 11.1/100,000

Using these numbers, we may derive the following population risk factors for the people living in the area where the sniper operated:

- Chance of being shot by the sniper in the next 12 months[24]: 2.7/100,000 or 1/37,297
- Chance of being killed by the sniper in the next 12 months[25]: 1.9/100,000 or 1/53,325

Comparing these figures against the risks that people face in their daily lives with little or no concern will put the real risk from the sniper into statistical perspective. Table 8-1 lists the likelihood of death from various causes, listed in order of decreasing risk. According to these figures, a person was more likely to be accidentally poisoned or to die in a car accident than to be shot and possibly killed by the sniper. As previously noted, the other risks have higher variance between individual and population risk, as more can be done on the personal level to mitigate them (such as wearing a seatbelt or a life preserver), but the fact remains that for the average of all people these statistics are accurate.

## Lessons Learned and Future Implications

Now that the sniper crisis has been compared to risk perception models and the population risk statistics have been calculated, we can ask the question,

---

[23]The murders that took place before this date were committed for the purposes of robbery or passion and are therefore not included in the analysis of population risk.

[24]The number of people in the affected area (5,919,152) divided by the number of people shot during the sniper crisis (10—adjusted), times the year-adjustment multiplier (15.870).

[25]The number of people in the affected area (5,919,152) divided by the number of people killed during the sniper crisis (7—adjusted), times the year-adjustment multiplier (15.870).

---

TABLE 8-1   **Likelihood of Death from Various Causes**

| Hazard | Annual risk | Lifetime risk |
|---|---|---|
| 2000 Murder Rate: Sniper area (weighted)[a] | 1/12,870 | 1/167 |
| 2000 Murder Rate: National | 1/18,182 | 1/236 |
| Car accident[b] | 1/18,752 | 1/244 |
| Accidental fall | 1/20,728 | 1/270 |
| Accidental poisoning | 1/22,388 | 1/292 |
| Murdered with a gun | 1/25,196 | 1/328 |
| **Shot by sniper** | 1/37,297 | 1/484 |
| Hit by car while walking | 1/45,117 | 1/588 |
| **Killed by sniper** | 1/53,325 | 1/693 |
| Drowning (accidental) | 1/77,308 | 1/1,008 |
| Fire/smoke inhalation | 1/81,487 | 1/1,062 |
| Lightning | 1/4,262,813 | 1/55,578 |

[a]The combined Washington, D.C., metropolitan area (WMA)/ Richmond-Petersburg metropolitan area (RPMA) combined crime rate was found by taking the crime rate of the WMA (7.1/100,000) and multiplying it by the WMA percentage of total population area (83.16%), then taking the RPMA crime rate (11.1/100,000) and multiplying it by the RPMA percentage of total population (16.84%), to give a combined crime rate of 7.77/100,000. WMA and RPMA 2000 murder rate data taken from *Crime in the United States*, 2000 (FBI, 2001).

[b](Memmott, 2002b)—All figures other than those associated with the sniper are attributed to this source.

"Should the public have been so deeply fearful during the sniper crisis?" The answer, according to these established models is yes, they definitely should have been, considering the information they received. However, according to the statistical data and risk comparison, they did not need to be so afraid, and there are ways in which the media, emergency responders, and other federal, state, and local government officials can limit this type of fear in the future.

### 1. Respond Separately to the Event and to the Fear

The authorities, namely the police and the government officials, dedicated a vast amount of resources to the sniper investigation because of the high level of public fear and concern, not because of some recognized disproportionate threat to public safety.[26] Conversely, they did little, if anything, to treat the fear itself. When emergency management agencies respond in this way, they can actually amplify the level of anxiety by signaling to the public that their crippling fears are justified[27] and move emergency management and police resources away from routine but necessary public safety work. These actions increase people's susceptibility to other health-related risks by preventing them from exercising and through the damaging physiological effects of fear-induced stress.[28] Variations of the statement "People will never feel safe again until the sniper is caught," repeated in every newspaper, echoed the primary motivation behind this large-scale response.

In the future, police and government officials should treat the event and the fear of the event as two separate problems that need to be addressed separately. This is a need that has already been recognized in past crime and terrorism crises (Warr, 2000). There should be a separate function of emergency management—a "Fear Management Team" consisting of members with backgrounds in sociology, psychology, emergency management, public education, and public relations, among others. This team would have several sub-functions, as follows:

---

[26]This is not an uncommon action for authorities to take. For instance, the EPA's Science Advisory Board discovered that "agency resources tend to be directed to problems 'perceived' to be the most serious rather than those that actually pose the greatest threat." (Walsh, 1996).

[27]Barry Glassner writes in *The Culture of Fear* that "the turnabout in [American] domestic public spending over the past quarter century, from child welfare and antipoverty programs to incarceration, did not [. . .] produce reductions in *fear* of crime. Increasing the number of cops and jails arguably has the opposite effect: It suggests that the crime problem is all the more out of control" (Glassner, 1999).

[28]James Walsh (1996), author of *True Odds: How Risk Affects Your Everyday Life*, writes, "When European terrorism reared up in 1986, 2 million Americans changed their travel plans The reality, of course, was that most of these people could have done a lot more to enhance their life expectancies by losing 10 pounds and going to Europe as planned."

- *Measure levels of public fear*: There are established ways in which fear can be measured in real-time status, including by conducting surveys, recognizing behavioral indicators (what people are doing to avoid what they fear—changes in routine, for example), and establishing recognition-triggers for "transient public episodes of fear" (how a population is acting as a whole in response to fear—drops in the number of public transportation users, for example) (Warr, 2000). Emergency management can only respond to a high level of fear if they know it exists. Not all events will be as obvious as the sniper crisis.

- *Develop an informed, educational public relations message*: As a part of regular emergency management operations, a trusted leader with decision-making power must be identified and put forth to communicate with the public through the media. The members of the Fear Management Team would process information culled from their monitoring of public fear to create communications through the trusted official in a manner that adequately and accurately addresses public fear. They would develop mental models that give emergency responders a clear understanding of what exactly the public does and does not understand about the risk and what they believe emergency responders are doing and/or are able to do to ensure their security. They would work directly with the emergency response team to inform them about the exact information the public needs to correct or adjust their belief in order to more closely match reality. They would work with government officials as well, helping them to inform the public through reinforcement of the messages given by the emergency response spokesperson.

- *Address public fear directly*: The Fear Management Team would coordinate the services of mental health specialists in an effort to further reduce public fear to more "healthy" levels. These public health officials would address the public directly, through media outlets, or through community groups.[29] Because they would have information directly related to the crisis, they would be able to make accurate and informed communications through the media (unlike the uninformed "experts" that were prevalent during the sniper crisis who did not have access to secure information). The information would not be compromised by this team, because it would not be necessary to share the specifics—however, the public would recognize that the team members, as trusted public health officials, were making informed decisions and would more likely invest more faith in these opinions in adjusting their perceptions.

• *Assist local government/community authorities in decision making*: Both local government and community groups must respond to crises, and their actions often directly affect the public. School superintendents need to know when it is appropriate to cancel school, and community groups need to know when public events must be postponed. Without direction from emergency response (the most "informed" source of information), they will not act with consistency and will likely send a mixed message to the public. In addition, the overreaction by one influential government or community leader can lead to secondary responses from other less organized or less informed groups.[30] This Fear Management Team would serve as an advisory board for government and community groups, ensuring that

their leaders are able to make decisions based on the most complete and current information, and allowing the groups to work in consensus rather than as separate entities.

### 2. Increase Responsible Reporting by the Media

The media have a responsibility to ensure that during crisis events, public safety information reaches a wide audience in a timely and accurate manner, a duty they are recognizing and embracing more each year (Moore, 2002). However, most newspaper and television news employees have never received crisis communications training and therefore have no idea how to fulfill this role. The media operate as a business and are motivated primarily by ratings and viewer and reader numbers, which ensure steady income generation; the media cannot be expected to cease provisions of blanket coverage during extreme events such as the sniper crisis. The industry functions within a time-compressed environment in which editors often must develop stories using incorrect or incomplete information. Journalists will continue to proactively seek information on crises using their own means, and there will always be leaks made to the media by emergency management and public officials.

The media is adroit at using scare tactics and fear-mongering to harness public attention and often does little to calm nerves once that attention is obtained. These agencies must learn as an industry that they can contribute to public safety by providing accurate, responsible, and useful information while still maintaining these traditional "shock" methods to attract viewers, and thereby preserve a competitive edge without sacrificing integrity. For the media to participate in a crisis response constructively, they need to add to the glut of sensationalism a balance of rationality—a reality check for the public to process information and judge individual risk. If they broadcast a message that says, "Four of the victims were shot while pumping gas at local gas stations," for example, they need to qualify this statement by adding, "however, there have been approximately 10.5 million gas transactions made at over 1000 gas stations in the affected area during the crisis so far" (Memmott,

---

[29]In Loudoun County, Maryland, a community group formed after 9/11 to help people cope with the stress gave free public seminars to help people cope with the sniper stress (Helderman and Goldenbach, 2002).

[30]Barry Glassner, author of *The Culture of Fear*, wrote, "Since the first sniper shooting October 2, a sort of domino effect has spurred decision-makers: School systems have decided, in conference calls with local law enforcement arranged through the Washington Council of Governments, to suspend all outdoor activities. Then day-care centers and youth soccer leagues have followed the lead of their public school systems, and the smaller community groups have fallen into line" (Reel, 2002).

2000b) in order to give adequate perspective to the original statement. Emergency management must recognize the media as willing participants in the process and provide them with this information that may not be readily available otherwise.

The media should recognize and act upon the public's tendency to anchor and adjust[31] in forming perceptions on risk. This cannot be denied. If a story informs citizens that "this is the greatest number of law enforcement officers ever dedicated to a criminal investigation in county history,"[32] readers may incorrectly infer that their lives are at greater risk than ever before,[33] and all future information will be processed within this context. If they are later told in an article that is given proportional emphasis,[34] for instance,

that, "although 10 people have been killed by the sniper in the past 3 weeks, there are an average of 38 people killed in traffic accidents alone during the same time period in the Washington, D.C., metropolitan area" (Memmott, 2002b), they will be able to rank their personal risk more appropriately.

Media agencies must also avoid irresponsible reporting aimed at "creating" stories. Martha Moore of *USA Today* cites as an example of this phenomenon the many cases in which local news stations will make announcements, before a coming storm for example, that "people should prepare by stocking up on batteries and water before the stores run out of these items." Following this statement, the news agency will post teams at local stores to report that people are crowding these local stores in order to get their hands on the few remaining batteries and bottles of water that remain, causing successive waves of panic buying[35] (Moore, 2002). Similar situations occurred during the sniper crisis. The media would report that "gas stations are the preferred location of the sniper," and then run stories showing how people were not going to gas stations, which had the snowball effect of making consumers progressively more afraid to visit gas stations.

The media agencies are not villains. Quite to the contrary, they are a vital component to emergency management without which risk communication would be nearly impossible. Also, not all of today's media reporting is misinformed or irresponsible. There are many news agencies that employ reporters who are trained or knowledgeable in crisis communications and risk perception and who regularly practice the suggestions made above. For example, in a *USA Today* article titled "How to Cope? Keep Guard and Spirits Up," the author suggested that residents of the D.C. area "take a lesson from people in other nations who confront such fears every day: Get on with life—but be more alert than ever to dangers and more kind than ever to others" (Memmott, 2002a). The knowl-

---

[31]The anchoring and adjustment heuristic states that people use a natural starting point as a first approximation in analyzing how a risk affects them. The initial anchoring point is then adjusted as more information is received (Slovic, Fischhoff, and Lichtenstein, 1979). Anchors are generally set according to the first information a person receives about a risk.

[32]In a CNN article titled "Sniper Probe 'Unprecedented' for Region," it was reported that "a conservative estimate would put at 1,000 the number of officers and experts from various federal, state, and local law enforcement officers assigned to the case, and the size of the investigation grows with each new development—and shooting—in the case" (Loughlin, 2002).

[33]Irresponsible reporting has not only caused undue stress on numerous occasions, but has hurt local economies as well. In the 1990s the media widely reported on a crime wave against tourists in Florida, which resulted in 10 murders. Barry Glassner (1999), author of *The Culture of Fear*, writes that the event was labeled a crime wave only because the media chose to label it as such. "Objectively speaking, ten murders out of 41 million visitors did not even constitute a ripple, much less a wave, especially considering that at least 97% of all victims of crime in Florida are Floridians. Although the Miami area had the highest crime rate in the nation during this period, it was not tourists who had most cause for worry. One study showed that British, German, and Canadian tourists who flock to Florida each year to avoid winter weather were more than 70 times more likely to be victimized at home." This type of reporting made many tourists think twice before traveling to Florida, and the tourism industry suffered as result.

[34]Often, articles that proclaim bad news are given front-page coverage and are in great quantity while those reporting good news are given secondary status and appear less frequently (Johnson, 2002).

[35]The phenomenon observed when people irrationally stock up on certain "survival" groceries they believe will be needed but unavailable after a disaster occurs.

edge and experience of reporters like this must be shared across the industry. The journalist's goal is to provide the public with timely information; the extent to which that information is both accurate and effective depends largely upon the level of cooperation provided by emergency management.

### 3. Establish Public Risk Perception and Risk Communication Training Standards for Emergency Management, Government Officials, and the Media

The federal government requires both emergency responders and public officials to complete training and prove competencies in performing many of the tasks associated with their job duties. While many first responders who communicate directly with the public are trained in public relations and communications, they are often not trained in crisis communications, risk perception, or risk communication. Their support teams, who provide the information on which their public response is based, are just as likely to lack adequate training in these areas. A statement from an ATF agent who described the extensive damage a .223 bullet fired from a rifle does to the human body or the MPD safety tip that reminded residents that a sniper could hit victims from 500 yards are examples of statements that neither provided useful information to the public nor controlled fear. If emergency responders and government officials are to effectively treat the fear associated with a crisis, they must be trained in methods that have proven successful in the past and develop a clear understanding of what drives human fear. Training in these studies will not become institutional unless the need is recognized throughout the emergency management sector. These training opportunities must also be made available to the media in order to ensure a comprehensive approach to fear management. If this training is conducted through a partnership between media and emergency management, interpersonal relationships will likely be created, thus further enhancing fear management.

If training in risk perception and risk communication became a requirement for emergency management public relations-related tasks, fear management would become a routine organizational function. The

existence of a Fear Management Team, as proposed above, would be better understood and utilized across all functions of emergency management agencies if management-level employees had a more comprehensive understanding of its purpose. Industry observance of this requirement would be more accepted if the federal or state government covered the costs for this training as they do for many other law enforcement and public safety programs.

Chief Moose did an outstanding job as a crisis manager and leader, but he did little to combat fear directly. Considering the lack of experience among emergency response officials with terrorism in the United States, it is unlikely that many of them would be prepared to take on such a difficult task as fear management. However, if the threat of terrorism is growing, as the FBI and the Department of Homeland Security claim it is, then the need for such training is obvious.

### 4. Seize the Opportunity during Periods of Increased Public Attention for Risk Education

Almost every person in the Washington, D.C., metropolitan area and likely the entire United States can say with confidence that they know what a .223 caliber bullet is and what it looks like, can identify Bushmaster as a brand of rifle, can tell approximately how far (in meters) a sniper can hit a target, can describe a box truck, and knows what a ladder rack on a Chevy Astro Van looks like. When people are afraid, they pay attention and they learn. It cannot be overlooked that despite the number of police looking for the sniper, it was a truck driver who located the sniper after learning the make, model, and license plate number of the sniper's vehicle on the news.

People will listen to emergency response and government suggestions if the source of information is trusted and holds decision-making authority.[36] These

---

[36]People tend to heed government suggestions, so they should be rational and helpful, and most importantly, carefully thought out. During the anthrax crisis, when public fear was at epidemic levels, 36% of Americans were washing their hands after opening mail as the U.S. Postal Service had instructed them to do. In areas where

rare mass-education opportunities must not be wasted. Emergency managers have a moral obligation under such circumstances to inform people of the real risks they face and tell them what it is they need to do to protect themselves from those risks. Telling people to weave while going through a parking lot during the sniper crisis is likely to make people think twice about going to the store, but it is unlikely that the information will save more than a few, if any, lives. Telling people that if they feel the need to drive long distances to purchase gas in order to feel safe, then they must also be sure to wear their seat belt because car accidents are a much more likely killer than the sniper, instantly contributes to a decrease in thousands of peoples' risk.

## Modified Information Flow Diagram— The Road Ahead

On March 1 the emergency management functions of the federal government were officially transferred into the Department of Homeland Security Secretary. Tom Ridge has been given exactly one year to reorganize and improve the functions of 22 absorbed agencies in a way that more effectively prevents, prepares for, responds to, and recovers from future terrorist attacks (and natural and technological disasters). Concurrently, the states have been spending billions of their own dollars to prevent and prepare for terrorist attacks, primarily following the direction of the federal government. This opportunity to improve current emergency management systems must not pass by without a full examination of the vital importance of managing public fear.

The information flow diagram shown in Figure 8-7 is provided as a possible solution to managing fear at the local level. The diagram depicts how a Fear Management Team would operate within the overall flow of crisis information and within the range of emergency management activities. Federally funded crisis communications training is displayed in order to indicate the likely recipients of this training. Although this design is simplified, it can be easily adapted to suit the needs of almost any local emergency response to a crisis that captures extensive public attention. Figure 8-7 does not directly address where the additional resources provided in federally declared disasters would apply or how the command structure would accommodate these resources, as it remains to be seen how the DHS reorganization will alter existing response systems.

## Conclusion

Fear is irrational only if people have enough information about a hazard to perform a personal risk analysis, find that the likelihood of the hazard affecting them is smaller than or equal to risks they face on a daily basis with little or no thought, and are still afraid. When there are little or no means for people to gather information to make informed personal risk analyses, they tend to overestimate personal vulnerability because of incomplete and often incorrect information. Only information can combat fear, and only the government (in partnership with the media) can provide for that need.

On November 7, 2002, two people in New York City were hospitalized and confirmed to be infected with bubonic plague—the first cases in that city in more than 100 years. Bubonic plague is a disease that is historically one of the greatest killers of man, decimating over a third of the population of Europe during the Middle Ages. To the people of New York City, this disease was dreaded, new, fatal, globally catastrophic, involuntary, and notoriously hard to control. Why did fear not reign in New York when this information hit the newsstands? The answer lies in the way the information was first reported by Dr. Thomas Frieden, the health commissioner of New York City (a city that has

---

people had actually contracted anthrax-related sicknesses, handwashing incidence was higher—45% in Washington, D.C., and 57% in Trenton, New Jersey—this from an attack that killed only 5 of over 400 million people. People were not acting irrationally, but listening to the advice they had been told by their government (Pelton, 2001). The government warned the public not to hoard the antibiotic Cipro, but the media reported they were stockpiling the drug to such an extreme as to cause pharmacy shortages. Surveys showed that only 4% of Americans had bought the antibiotic against the advice of the government.

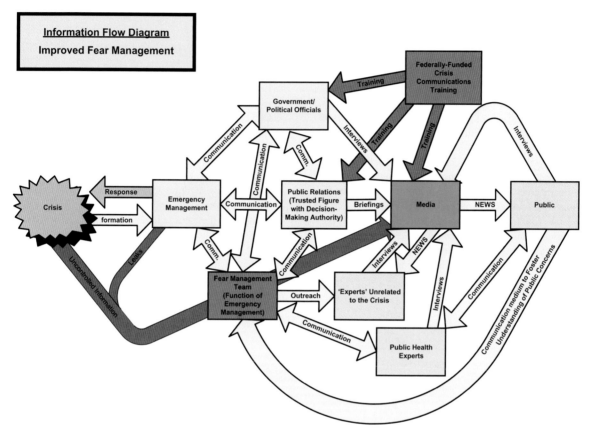

**FIGURE 8-7**    Information flow diagram: improved fear management.

in recent years experienced two major health crises—the first U.S. outbreak of West Nile virus and the anthrax letters in 2001). After announcing the two cases of the disease, Dr. Frieden made the following statement:

> Bubonic plague does not spread from person to person. There is no risk to New Yorkers from the two individuals who are being evaluated for plague. Those patients became ill within 48 hours of arriving in New York City. Therefore, we are confident that their exposure occurred in New Mexico. More than half of the plague cases in the United States are in New Mexico. A wood rat and fleas from the rodent that were found on the couple's property in Santa Fe, New Mexico, tested positive in July for plague. Bubonic plague is a bacterial disease in rodents transmitted to humans through the bites of infected fleas. (*CNN*, 2002)

The story barely lasted a week.

# REVIEW QUESTIONS

1. Identify and discuss the four critical assumptions underlying the crisis communications efforts of the Federal Emergency Management Agency (FEMA) in the 1990s.
2. Discuss the role of the mass media in risk and crisis communications.
3. Review the content and communication delivery mechanisms used in the Department of Homeland Security's Ready.gov campaign. Do you feel this is useful information that could effectively prepare the public for a disaster?
4. How would you reengineer the Homeland Security Advisory System (HSAS)? How many alert levels would you include, what colors and titles would you associate with each alert level, and what preparedness messages designed for individuals and communities would you associate which each alert level?

5. In reviewing the case study of the Washington, D.C., sniper attacks, it is clear that Montgomery County Police Chief Charles Moose was the principal government spokesperson and appeared in front of the media daily. In many of his media appearances, Chief Moose had little information to share with the media and the public principally because of the sensitive nature of the ongoing criminal investigation to identify and comprehend the snipers. These media appearances were a unique opportunity for Chief Moose to deliver preparedness messages to the community. Identify those preparedness messages that Chief Moose did deliver to the community over the course of the sniper crisis and provide suggestions of additional preparedness messages he could have delivered.

# REFERENCES

Airline Industry Information (AII). 2002. *BALPA Issues Advice to Concerned Crew Traveling to Washington, DC.* October 18.

Altheide, D. L. 2002. *Creating Fear: News and the Construction of Crisis.* New York: Aldine de Gruyter.

Anderson, P. 2002. *Sniper Suspect Linked to Tacoma Shootings.* Seattlepi.com. October 28. <http://seattlepi.nwsource.com/local/93210_tacoma28ww.shtml>

Ansell, J., and F. Wharton. 1992. *Risk: Analysis, Assessment, and Management.* Chichester, England: John Wiley & Sons.

Atwater, B. F., C. V. Marco, J. Bourgeois, W. C. Dudley, J. W. Hendley II, and P. H. Stauffer. 1999. *Surviving a Tsunami— Lessons Learned from Chile, Hawaii, and Japan.* Washington, DC: USGS Information Services.

*The Australian.* 2002. "Sniper Search Goes Airborne." *The Australian.* October 17, p. 8.

Barger, B. 2002. "At the Intersection of Bravado and Fear." *The Washington Post.* November 3, p. B2.

Barker, J. 2002. "Montgomery Seeks to Ensure Safety of Voters." *The Baltimore Sun.* October 22, p. 1B.

Bremer, A. L., and P. Bremer III. 2002. "The Terrorist Threat." In *Terrorism: Informing the Public.* N. Ethiel (ed.). Chicago: McCormick Tribune Foundation.

Brown, J. D., and S. N. Keller. 2000. "Can the Mass Media Be Healthy Sex Educators?" *Family Planning Perspectives*, vol. 32, no. 5, pp. 255–256.

Bullock, J. 2003. Several interviews over a two-month period with the former FEMA chief of staff. Washington, DC.

Burkhart, F. N. 1991. *Media, Emergency Warnings, and Citizen Response.* Boulder, CO: Westview Press.

CBS News. 2002. *A Deadly Journey? Crimes and Clues.* <www.cbsnews.com/htdocs/maryland_murders/frame-source.html',540,400>

Centers for Disease Control and Prevention. 2002. *Suicide in the United States.* National Center for Injury Prevention and Control. <www.cdc.gov/ncipc/factsheets/suifacts.htm>

Chemical and Biological Arms Control Institute. 2002. *What Should We Know? Whom Should We Tell? Leveraging Communication and Information to Counter Terrorism and Its Consequences.* Michael J. Powers, Project Director. Washington, DC. December 2002.

Clines, F. 2002a. "Widening Fears, Few Clues as 6th Death Is Tied to Sniper." *New York Times.* October 5, p. A1.

Clines, F. 2002b. "The Hunt for a Sniper." *New York Times.* October 15, p. A1.

CNN. 2002. *Bubonic Plague Suspected in NYC Visitors*. CNN.com. November 7. <www.cnn.com/2002/health/11/07/ny.plague/index.html>

Cohen, B. C. 1963. *The Press and Foreign Policy*. Princeton, NJ: Princeton University Press.

Connor, T., and H. Kennedy. 2002. "Cops Flood Site of VA Shooting." *Daily News* (New York). October 20, p. 3.

Coppola, C. P., MD. Series of interviews. Dr. Coppola operated on the 13-year-old boy who was shot at the middle school in Bowie, Maryland, on October 7, 2002.

Coppola, D. 2002. Research on public risk perception in Mexico City, Mexico.

De Morales, L. 2002. "Did on-the-Spot Coverage Put Lawmen on the Spot?" *The Washington Post*. October 24, p. C1.

Department of Homeland Security (DHS). 2003. Ready.gov website. Washington, DC: DHS. <www.ready.gov>

Diaz, K., and L. O'Rourke. 2002. "D.C. Area Breathes Easier, But Not Deeply." *Star Tribune* (Minneapolis). October 25, p. 20A.

Disaster Management Center. 1995. *Disaster Preparedness*. The University of Wisconsin. <http://dmc.engr.wisc.edu/courses/preparedness/BB04-intro.html>

Dishneau, D. 2002. "Virginia Shooting Linked to Sniper Spree." *The Toronto Star*. October 6, p. A9.

Ebner, J., and L. Herring. 2002. *In Disasters, Panic Is Rare; Altruism Dominates*. American Sociological Association. August 7. <www.asanet.org/media/panic.html>

Eccleston, R. 2002. "Killings Have Washington Terrorized." *The Australian*. October 14, p. 12.

*Economist*. 2002. "The Logic of Irrational Fear." October 19.

Enders, J. 2001. "Measuring Community Awareness and Preparedness for Emergencies." *Australian Journal of Emergency Management*, Spring 2001, pp. 52–59.

FAIR. 2002a. *Washington, D.C. PMSA*. Federation for American Immigration Reform. <www.fairus.org/html/msas/042dcwdc.htm>

FAIR. 2002b. *Richmond-Petersburg Metropolitan Area*. Federation for American Immigration Reform. <www.fairus.org/html/msas/042varip.htm>

Fears, D., and A. Thomas-Lester. 2002. "Blacks Express Shock at Suspects' Identity." *The Washington Post*. October 26, p. A17.

Federal Bureau of Investigation. 2001. *Crime in the United States, 2000*. The Federal Bureau of Investigation (FBI) Uniform Crime Reports. Washington, DC: FBI. October 22.

Federal Emergency Management Agency (FEMA). 1998. "Making Your Community Disaster Resistant: Project Impact Media Partnership Guide." Washington, DC: FEMA.

Federal Emergency Management Agency (FEMA). 1997. *Multi Hazard: Identification and Assessment*. Washington, DC: FEMA.

Fernandez, M. 2002. "Brentwood Postal Plant Fumigation Postponed." *The Washington Post*. November 13, p. B3.

Fineman, H. 2002. "The 'Anxiety Election.'" *National Affairs*. October 21, p. 32.

Furedi, F. 1997. *Culture of Fear: Risk-Taking and the Morality of Low Expectation*. London: Cassell.

Furman, M. 2002. "Good Information Saves Lives." In *Terrorism: Informing the Public*. N. Ethiel (ed.). Chicago: McCormick Tribune Foundation.

Gettleman, J. 2002. "The Hunt for a Sniper: The Scene." *New York Times*. October 21, p. A14.

Glassner, B. 1999. *The Culture of Fear*. New York: Basic Books.

Government Printing Office. 2002. *US Code Title 28, Part II, Chapter 33, Section 540B*. <www.access.gpo.gov/uscode/uscmain.html>

Haddow, G. 2003. Several interviews over a two-month period with the former FEMA deputy chief of staff. Washington, DC.

Helderman, R., and A. Goldenbach. 2002. "Autumn's Diversions Disrupted." *The Washington Post*. October 20, p. T3.

Higham, S., and S. Kovaleski. 2002. "Encounters with Sniper Suspects." *The Washington Post*. November 3, p. A1.

*Houston Chronicle*. 2002. "Sniper's Score: 5 Shots, 5 Dead." October 4, p. A1.

Hurdle, J. 2002. "Holidaying in the Line of Fire." *The Daily Telegraph* (London). October 19, p. 4.

Instituto Ciudadano de Estudios Sobre la Inseguridad A.C. 2002. *Primera Encuesta Nacional sobre Inseguridad Publica en las Entidades Federativas*. Mexico City. May.

Irvin, C. W., and D. Mattingly. 2002. "Anxiety Becomes Part of Daily Routine." *The Washington Post*. October 17, p. T3.

Jacobson, L. 2001. "Media—The Perception of Panic." *McGill Tribune* via U-Wire. November 14.

Jardine, C. G., and S. E. Hrudey. 1997. "Mixed Messages in Risk Communication," *Risk Analysis*, vol. 17, no. 4, pp. 489–498.

Johnson, D., and J. Finer. 2002. "Sniper Casts Shadow of Fear over Weekend." *The Washington Post*. October 13, p. C1.

Johnson, P. 2002. "Out in TV Land, 'Local News Is in Bad Shape.'" *USA Today* Online. November 11.

Johnson, P., and M. Moore. 2002. "Media Reports Touch Raw Nerves in Washington." *USA Today*. October 10, p. 2A.

Jones, E. F., J. R. Beniger, and C. F. Westoff. 1980. "Pill and IUD Discontinuation in the United States, 1970–1975: The Influence of the Media." *Family Planning Perspectives*, vol. 12, no. 6, pp. 293–300.

Kennedy, H., M. Mbugua, and R. Pienciak. 2002. "Cops Hunt Two Targets." *The Daily News* (New York). October 24, p. 2.

Kisken, T. 2001. "Climate of Fear Overblown, Sociologist Says." *Ventura County Star*. November 6, p. B1.

Kornblut, A. 2002. "Elusive Sniper Joins DC's Nightmares." *The Boston Globe*. October 20, p. A1.

Kovaleski, S., and M. Ruane. 2002a. "Hundreds of Leads to a Gunman." *The Washington Post*. October 7, p. A1.

Kovaleski, S., and M. Ruane. 2002b. "Boy, 13, Shot by Sniper at School." *The Washington Post*. October 8, p. A1.

Kovaleski, S., and M. Williams. 2002. "Experts Suggest Motive Is Tied to Crafts Store." *The Washington Post.* October 16, p. A13.

Kurtz, H. 2002. "The Leak that Sank the Suspects." *The Washington Post.* October 25, p. C1.

*LA Times.* 2002. "Americans Fear Sniper More Than Terrorists." *Los Angeles Times.*

Lambert, R. 2002. "The Washington Sniper Is Not the Only Fear Stalking the United States Right Now." *The Times* (London). October 18.

Layton, L., and K. Shaver. 2002. "Experts, Travelers Question Efficacy of Massive Dragnets." *The Washington Post.* October 23, p. A17.

Lichtblau, E., and D. van Natta. 2002. "The Hunt for a Sniper." *New York Times.* October 25, p. A1.

Lippmann, 1922. (Reissue Edition Jane 12, 1997) New York, NY: Free Press.

Lochhead, C. 2002. "One Year Later." *San Francisco Chronicle.* September 12, p. A17.

Loughlin, S. 2002. *Sniper Probe "Unprecedented" for Region.* CNN Washington Bureau. October 24.

Macalester College. 2002. *Serial Killers.* <www.macalester.edu/~psych/whathap/UBNRP/serialkillers/serialkillers.html>

McCallum, D. B., S. L. Hammond, and L. Morris. 1990. *Public Knowledge of Chemical Risks in Six Communities.* Washington, DC: Georgetown University Medical Center, Institute for Health Policy Analysis.

McCombs, M., and D. Shaw. 1972. "The Agenda-Setting Function of Mass Media." *Public Opinion Quarterly,* vol. 36, pp. 176–187.

McCormick Tribune Foundation. 2002. "Terrorism: Informing the Public." Cantigny Conference Series. N. Ethiel (ed.). Chicago: McCormick Tribune Foundation.

McDivitt, J. A., S. Zimicki, R. Hornik, and A. Abulaban. 1993. "The Impact of the Healthcom Mass Media Campaign on Timely Initiation of Breastfeeding in Jordan." *Studies in Family Planning,* vol. 24, no. 5, pp. 295–309.

Memmott, M. 2002a. "How to Cope? Keep Guard and Spirits Up." *USA Today.* October 18, p. 6A.

Memmott, M. 2002b. "Fear May Be Overwhelming, But So Are the Odds." *USA Today.* October 18, p. 6A.

METRO. 1998. *Washington Metropolitan Area Transit Authority.* National Transit Database. <www.ntdprogram.com/NTD/Profiles.nsf/1998+30+Largest+Agencies/3030/$File/P3030.PDF>

Miga, A. 2002a. "Sniper 'Witness' Arrested." *The Boston Herald.* October 19, p. 3.

Miga, A. 2002b. "Death Penalty Sought for Sniper." *The Boston Herald.* October 26, p. 1.

Miga, A., and K. Rothstein. 2002. "Zeroing In." *The Boston Herald.* October 24, p. 1.

Mileti, D. S. 1999. *Disasters by Design.* Washington, DC: Joseph Henry Press.

Miller, J. 2002. "Who? How? When? What? Where?" In *Terrorism: Informing the Public.* N. Ethiel (ed.). Chicago: McCormick Tribune Foundation.

Moore, M. T. 2002. *Presentation at the NAS Natural Disasters Roundtable.* Washington, DC: National Academy of Sciences. October 31.

Morello, C., C. Davenport, and H. Harris. 2002. "Pair Seized in Sniper Attacks." *The Washington Post.* October 25, p. A1.

Morello, C., and J. Stockwell. 2002. "No Attacks, No Arrests, No Shortage of Anxiety." *The Washington Post.* October 14, p. A1.

Morello, C., and J. White. 2002. "8th Killing Linked to Sniper." *The Washington Post.* October 12, p. A1.

Morgan, M. G., B. Fischoff, A. Bostrom, and C. J. Atman. 2002. *Risk Communication: A Mental Models Approach.* Cambridge: Cambridge University Press.

Morin, R., and C. Deane. 2002. "Half of Area Residents in Fear, Post Poll Finds." *The Washington Post.* October 24, p. A1.

Mullis, J.-P. 1998. "Persuasive Communication Issues in Disaster Management." *Australian Journal of Emergency Management,* Autumn 1998, pp. 51–58.

Nakamura, D., and P. Davis. 2002. "Suddenly, D.C. Gas Looks Cheap Enough." *The Washington Post.* October 15, p. A7.

Naudet, J., and G. Naudet. 2001. *September 11 Documentary.* CBS. Two-hour film shot during the September 11 World Trade Center attack response.

Nelken, D. 1987. *Selling Science: How the Press Covers Science and Technology.* New York: W. H. Freeman.

Nielsen, S., and J. Lidstone. 1998. "Public Education and Disaster Management: Is There Any Guiding Theory?" *Australian Journal of Emergency Management,* Spring 1998, pp. 14–19.

*Ottawa Citizen.* 2002. "Canadians Told to Avoid Washington." *The Ottawa Citizen.* October 13, p. A8.

Partnership for Public Warning. 2003. www.partnership for public warning.org/PPW.

Patrick, A. 2002. "Eight Dead, But Still No Real Clues." *Sunday Age* (Melbourne). October 13, p. 1.

Pelton, T. 2001. "36% of Americans Wash Up After Handling Mail." *The Baltimore Sun.* December 18, p. 8A.

Perspectives.org. 2002. *Friend's Apparent Accidental Shot Lodges Near Brain.* <www.perspectivescs.org/guns/example2.htm>

Phillips, C. 2002. "Malvo Spent Childhood Looking for Father Figure." *The Seattle Times.* November 21, p. A1.

Pienciak, R., and H. Kennedy. 2002. "Sniper's Ransom." *The Daily News* (New York). October 22, p. 3.

Piotrow, P. T., J. G. Rimon, K. Winnard, D. L. Kincaid, D. Huntington, and J. Convisser. 1990. "Mass Media Family Planning Promotion in Three Nigerian Cities." *Studies in Family Planning,* vol. 21, no. 5, pp. 265–274.

Raphael, B. 1986. *When Disaster Strikes: How Individuals and Communities Cope with Catastrophes.* New York: Basic Books.

Rashbaum, W., and K. Flynn. 2002. "Sniper Hits a Teacher at Stuyvesant Town." *New York Times.* October 3, p. B1.

Reel, M. 2002. "A Region Running Scared?" *The Washington Post.* October 19, p. A1.

Reid, T. 2002. "Al Qaeda Trained Snipers for US Attacks." *The Times* (London). October 19, p. 21.

Rennie, D. 2002. "Sniper Stretches City's Nerves to Breaking Point." *The Daily Telegraph* (London). October 22, p. 10.

Ropeik, D. 2002a. "Fear Factors in an Age of Terrorism." MSNBC Online. October 15.

Ropeik, D. 2002b. "We should fear too much fear." *Milwaukee Journal Sentinel.* October 23, p. 23A.

Ropeik, D. 2002c. *Presentation on Risk Perception.* The National Academy of Sciences Roundtable on Natural Disasters. October 31.

Ruane, M., and J. Stockwell. 2002. "Montgomery Bus Driver Fatally Shot." *The Washington Post.* October 23, p. A1.

Schulte, B. 2002. "Schools Shaken by Threat But Won't Shut Down." *The Washington Post.* October 23, p. A1.

Self Knowledge. 2002. *Definition of Fear.* <www.selfknowledge. com/35217.htm>

Shales, T. 2002. "TV News Feels Its Way in Dark Times." *The Washington Post.* October 23, p. C1.

Shrader-Frechette, K. S. 1991. *Risk and Rationality.* Berkeley: University of California Press.

Singer, E., and P. M. Endreny. 1993. *Reporting on Risk: How the Mass Media Portray Accidents, Diseases, Disasters, and Other Hazards.* New York: Russell Sage Foundation.

Slovic, P. 1986. "Informing and Educating the Public about Risk." *Risk Analysis,* vol. 6, no. 4, pp. 403–415.

Slovic, P., B. Fischhoff, and S. Lichtenstein. 1996. "Cognitive Processes and Societal Risk Taking." In *Cognition and Social Behavior.* Potomac, MD: Lawrence Erlbaum Associates, pp. 165–184.

Slovic, P., B. Fischhoff, and S. Lichtenstein. 1980. "Facts and Fears: Understanding Perceived Risk." In *Societal Risk Assessment: How Safe Is Safe Enough?* New York: Plenum.

Slovic, P., B. Fischhoff, and S. Lichtenstein. 1979. "Rating the Risks." *Environment,* vol. 21, no. 3, pp. 14–20, 36–39.

Snyder, D. 2002. "Fear Is Traveling the Lanes of I-95." *The Washington Post.* October 21, p. A14.

STATS. 2002. *Abducting the Headlines.* <www.stats.org/ newsletters/0208/abduction.htm>

Stephen, A. 2002. *America—Andrew Stephen Reports on Panic in Washington.* New Statesman, Ltd. October 22.

Stockwell, J., M. Ruane, and J. White. 2002. "Man Shot to Death at Pr. William Gas Station." *The Washington Post.* October 10, p. A1.

Sun, L. H., and P. Ly. 2002. "Story 'Not About Me,' Reserved Moose Says." *The Washington Post.* October 28, p. A10.

Thomas, P. 2003. *The Anthrax Attacks.* New York: The Century Foundation. June 1.

Timberg, C., and M. Shear. 2002. "Dragnet Comes Up Empty Again." *The Washington Post.* October 21, p. A1.

Tresniowski, A., J. S. Podesta, M. Morehouse, and A. Billups. 2002. "Stalked by Fear." *People* magazine. October 28, p. 58.

Twomey, J. 2001. "Media Fuels Fear About Youth Crime." *The Baltimore Sun.* May 13, p. 1C.

Vulliami, E. 2002. "America Stays Indoors as Sniper Roams Free." *The Observer.* October 13, p. 1.

Walker, W. 2002. "Terror Grips D.C. Region." *Toronto Star.* October 23, p. A20.

Wallace, C. 2002. *A New Kind of Killer?* ABC News. October 15.

Walsh, J. 1996. *True Odds: How Risk Affects Your Everyday Life.* Santa Monica, CA: Merritt Publishing.

Ward, B. 2001. "History's Lessons Lost in the Turmoil." *The Ottawa Citizen.* September 18, p. A10.

Warner, K. E. 1989. "The Epidemiology of Coffin Nails." In *Health Risks and the Press: Coverage on Media Coverage of Risk Assessment and Health.* Washington, DC: The Media Institute.

Warr, M. 2000. "Fear of Crime in the United States: Avenues for Research and Policy." In *Measurement and Analysis of Crime and Justice,* pp. 451–489.

*Washington Post.* 2002a. "Crime and Justice." *The Washington Post.* October 3, p. B2.

*Washington Post.* 2002b. "Washington Area Sniper Poll." *The Washington Post.* October 24.

Watson, D. 2000. *Statement of Mr. Dale Watson, Asst. Director, FBI Counterterrorism Division, before the Subcommittee on National Security.* U.S. House of Representatives. March 22.

Watson, R. 2002. "Suburbs in Terror of the Beltway Sniper after Boy Is Shot." *The Times* (London). October 8.

Waugh, W. L., Jr. 2000. *Living with Hazards, Dealing with Disasters: An Introduction to Emergency Management.* New York: M.E. Sharpe.

Wenham, B. 1994. "The Media and Disasters: Building a Better Understanding." In *International Disaster Communications: Harnessing the Power of Communications to Avert Disasters and Save Lives.* Washington, DC: The Annenberg Washington Program.

Westoff, C. F., and G. Rodriguez. 1995. "The Mass Media and Family Planning in Kenya." *International Family Planning Perspectives,* vol. 21, no. 1, pp. 26–31, 36.

Whitlock, C. 2002. "The Sniper Case: Out of 90,000 Calls, Just 3 Broke It Open." *Post Gazette* (Pittsburgh). October 25. <www.post-gazette.com/nation/20021025probenat2p2.asp>

Wiggins, C. 2002. "Warm Waters Attract People and Sharks." *The Standard* (Baker County). March 27.

Willis, J. 1997. *Reporting on Risks: The Practice and Ethics of Health and Safety Communication.* Westport, CT: Praeger.

Wilson, R. 1979. "Analyzing the Daily Risks of Life." *Technology Review,* vol. 81, no. 4, pp. 41–46.

Winston, J. A. 1985. "Science and the Media: The Boundaries of Truth." *Health Affairs,* vol. 6, pp. 5–23.

Witzer, M. 1997. "In Sub-Saharan Africa, Levels of Knowledge and Use of Contraceptives Are Linked to Media Exposure." *International Family Planning Perspectives,* vol. 23, no. 4, pp. 183–184.

## APPENDIX 8-1

### Citizen Guidance on the Homeland Security Advisory System, created by DHS and the American Red Cross

| Risk of Attack | Recommended Actions for Citizens |
|---|---|
| **GREEN**<br>Low Risk | → Develop a family emergency plan. Share it with family and friends, and practice the plan. Visit www.Ready.gov for help creating a plan.<br>→ Create an "Emergency Supply Kit" for your household.<br>→ Be informed. Visit www.Ready.gov or obtain a copy of "Preparing Makes Sense, Get Ready Now" by calling 1-800-BE-READY.<br>→ Know how to shelter-in-place and how to turn off utilities (power, gas, and water) to your home.<br>→ Examine volunteer opportunities in your community, such as Citizen Corps, Volunteers in Police Service, Neighborhood Watch or others, and donate your time.<br>→ Consider completing an American Red Cross first aid or CPR course , or Community Emergency Response Team (CERT) course . |
| **BLUE**<br>Guarded Risk | → *Complete recommended steps at level green.*<br>→ Review stored disaster supplies and replace items that are outdated.<br>→ Be alert to suspicious activity and report it to proper authorities. |
| **YELLOW**<br>Elevated Risk | → *Complete recommended steps at levels green and blue.*<br>→ Ensure disaster supply kit is stocked and ready.<br>→ Check telephone numbers in family emergency plan and update as necessary.<br>→ Develop alternate routes to/from work or school and practice them.<br>→ Continue to be alert for suspicious activity and report it to authorities. |
| **ORANGE**<br>High Risk | → *Complete recommended steps at lower levels.*<br>→ Exercise caution when traveling, pay attention to travel advisorie.<br>→ Review your family emergency plan and make sure all family members know what to do.<br>→ Be Patient. Expect some delays, baggage searches and restrictions at public buildings.<br>→ Check on neighbors or others that might need assistance in an emergency. |
| **RED**<br>Severe Risk | → *Complete all recommended actions at lower levels.*<br>→ Listen to local emergency management officials.<br>→ Stay tuned to TV or radio for current information/instructions.<br>→ Be prepared to shelter-in-place or evacuate, as instructed.<br>→ Expect traffic delays and restrictions.<br>→ Provide volunteer services only as requested.<br>→ Contact your school/business to determine status of work day. |

## APPENDIX 8-2
### American Red Cross Homeland Security Advisory System Recommendations for Families

| | |
|---|---|
| **SEVERE**<br>*(Red)* | • *Complete recommended actions at lower levels*<br>• Listen to radio/TV for current information/instructions<br>• Be alert to suspicious activity and report it to proper authorities immediately<br>• Contact business/school to determine status of work/school day<br>• Adhere to any travel restrictions announced by local governmental authorities<br>• Be prepared to shelter in place or evacuate if instructed to do so by local governmental authorities<br>• Discuss children's fears concerning possible/actual terrorist attacks |
| **HIGH**<br>*(Orange)* | • *Complete recommended actions at lower levels*<br>• Be alert to suspicious activity and report it to proper authorities<br>• Review disaster plan with all family members<br>• Ensure communication plan is understood/practiced by all family members<br>• Exercise caution when traveling<br>• Have shelter in place materials on hand and understand procedure<br>• Discuss children's fears concerning possible terrorist attacks<br>• If a need is announced, donate blood at designated blood collection center |
| **ELEVATED**<br>*(Yellow)* | • *Complete recommended actions at lower levels*<br>• Be alert to suspicious activity and report it to proper authorities<br>• Ensure disaster supplies kit is stocked and ready<br>• Check telephone numbers and e-mail addresses in your family emergency communication plan and update as necessary<br>• If not known to you, contact school to determine their emergency notification and evacuation plans for children<br>• Develop alternate routes to/from school/work and practice them |
| **GUARDED**<br>*(Blue)* | • *Complete recommended actions at lower level*<br>• Be alert to suspicious activity and report it to proper authorities<br>• Review stored disaster supplies and replace items that are outdated<br>• Develop an emergency communication plan that all family members understand<br>• Establish an alternate meeting place away from home with family/friends |
| **LOW**<br>*(Green)* | • Obtain copy of <u>Terrorism: Preparing for the Unexpected</u> brochure from your local Red Cross chapter<br>• Develop a personal disaster plan and disaster supplies kit using Red Cross brochures <u>Your Family Disaster Plan</u> and <u>Your Family Disaster Supplies Kit</u><br>• Take a Red Cross CPR/AED and first aid course |

## APPENDIX 8-3
### American Red Cross Homeland Security Advisory System Recommendations for Neighborhoods

| | |
|---|---|
| **SEVERE**<br>*(Red)* | • *Complete recommended actions at lower levels*<br>• Listen to radio/TV for current information/instructions<br>• Be alert to suspicious activity and report it to proper authorities immediately<br>• Adhere to any travel restrictions announced by local governmental authorities<br>• Be prepared to shelter in place/evacuate and assist neighbors who are elderly or have special needs to do the same |
| **HIGH**<br>*(Orange)* | • *Complete recommended actions at lower levels*<br>• Be alert to suspicious activity and report it to proper authorities<br>• Check on neighbors who are elderly or have special needs to ensure they are okay. Review disaster plan with them<br>• If a need is announced, contact nearest blood collection agency and offer to organize a neighborhood blood drive |
| **ELEVATED**<br>*(Yellow)* | • *Complete recommended actions at lower levels*<br>• Be alert to suspicious activity and report it to proper authorities<br>• Have neighborhood meeting in order to identify neighbors who are elderly or have special needs. Assist them in development of a personal disaster plan and disaster supplies kit if requested. |
| **GUARDED**<br>*(Blue)* | • *Complete recommended actions at lower level*<br>• Be alert to suspicious activity and report it to proper authorities<br>• Ask the local Red Cross chapter to offer a presentation called "Preparing for the Unexpected" at an upcoming neighborhood meeting |
| **LOW**<br>*(Green)* | • Have neighborhood meeting to discuss emergency plans and establish a 'Neighborhood Watch'<br>• Obtain copies of <u>Terrorism: Preparing for the Unexpected</u> brochure from your local Red Cross chapter and distribute at neighborhood meeting<br>• Promote or arrange for people in the neighborhood to take a Red Cross CPR/AED and first aid course |

## APPENDIX 8-4

## American Red Cross Homeland Security Advisory System Recommendations for Schools

| | |
|---|---|
| **SEVERE**<br>*(Red)* | • *Complete recommended actions at lower levels*<br>• Listen to radio/TV for current information/instructions<br>• Be alert to suspicious activity and report it to proper authorities immediately<br>• Close school if recommended to do so by appropriate authorities<br>• 100% identification check (i.e.-driver's license retained at front office) and escort of anyone entering school other than students, staff and faculty<br>• Continue offering lessons from Masters of Disaster "Facing Fear: Helping Young People Deal with Terrorism and Tragic Events" curriculum<br>• Ensure mental health counselors available for students, staff and faculty |
| **HIGH**<br>*(Orange)* | • *Complete recommended actions at lower levels*<br>• Be alert to suspicious activity and report it to proper authorities<br>• Review emergency plans<br>• Offer Masters of Disaster "Facing Fear: Helping Young People Deal with Terrorism and Tragic Events" lessons in grades K-12<br>• Prepare to handle inquiries from anxious parents and media<br>• Discuss children's fears concerning possible terrorist attacks |
| **ELEVATED**<br>*(Yellow)* | • *Complete recommended actions at lower levels*<br>• Be alert to suspicious activity and report it to the proper authorities<br>• Ensure all emergency supplies stocked and ready<br>• Obtain copies of <u>Terrorism: Preparing for the Unexpected</u> brochure from your local Red Cross chapter and send it home with students in grades K-12, staff and faculty |
| **GUARDED**<br>*(Blue)* | • *Complete recommended actions at lower level*<br>• Be alert to suspicious activity and report it to proper authorities<br>• Conduct safety training/emergency drills following the school's written emergency plan for all grades<br>• Ensure emergency communication plan updated and needed equipment is purchased<br>• Continue offering lessons from 'Masters of Disaster" curriculum for grades K-8 regarding emergency preparedness for natural disasters |
| **LOW**<br>*(Green)* | • Use Red Cross <u>Emergency Management Guide for Business and Industry</u> to develop written emergency plans to address all hazards including plans to maintain the safety of students, staff, and faculty, as well as an emergency communication plan to notify parents in times of emergency. Disseminate relevant information to families of children, staff and faculty.<br>• Initiate offering "Masters of Disaster" curriculum for grades K-8 regarding emergency preparedness for natural disasters<br>• Ensure selected staff members take a Red Cross CPR/AED and first aid course |

## APPENDIX 8-5

# American Red Cross Homeland Security Advisory System Recommendations for Businesses

| | |
|---|---|
| **SEVERE**<br>*(Red)* | • *Complete recommended actions at lower levels*<br>• Listen to radio/TV for current information/instructions<br>• Be alert to suspicious activity and report it to proper authorities immediately<br>• Work with local community leaders, emergency management, government agencies, community organizations, and utilities to meet immediate needs of the community<br>• Determine need to close business based on circumstances and in accordance with written emergency plan<br>• Be prepared to work with a dispersed or smaller work force<br>• Ensure mental health counselors available for employees |
| **HIGH**<br>*(Orange)* | • *Complete recommended actions at lower levels*<br>• Be alert to suspicious activity and report it to proper authorities<br>• Review emergency plans to include continuity of operations and media materials on hand<br>• Determine need to restrict access to business or provide private security firm support/reinforcement<br>• Contact vendors/suppliers to confirm their emergency response plan procedures<br>• If a need is announced, contact nearest blood collection agency and offer to organize a blood drive |
| **ELEVATED**<br>*(Yellow)* | • *Complete recommended actions at lower levels*<br>• Be alert to suspicious activity and report it to proper authorities<br>• Contact private security firm for security risk assessment and to determine availability of support/reinforcement<br>• Contact voluntary organizations you support to determine how you can provide assistance in case of emergency |
| **GUARDED**<br>*(Blue)* | • *Complete recommended actions at lower level*<br>• Be alert to suspicious activity and report it to proper authorities<br>• Dialogue with community leaders, emergency management, government agencies, community organizations and utilities about disaster preparedness<br>• Ensure emergency communication plan updated to include purchase of needed equipment.<br>• Ask the local Red Cross chapter to provide a "Terrorism: Preparing for the Unexpected" presentation at your workplace for employees |
| **LOW**<br>*(Green)* | • Use Red Cross Emergency Management Guide for Business and Industry to develop written emergency plans to address all hazards. Include an emergency communication plan to notify employees of activities; designate an off-site 'report to' location in case of evacuation.<br>• Develop continuity of operations plan to include designating alternate work facility/location for business<br>• Arrange for staff to take a Red Cross CPR/AED and first aid course<br>• Obtain copies of Terrorism: Preparing for the Unexpected and Preparing Your Business for the Unthinkable brochures from your local Red Cross chapter for distribution to all employees/management as appropriate. |

# 9

# Technology

## INTRODUCTION

While addressing the Piedmont Triad Partnership (a North Carolina business association) in 2003, Department of Homeland Security (DHS) Undersecretary Charles McQueary stated that, "If I were asked to describe the Department of Homeland Security, I would say it's a story about science and technology." This quotation clearly asserts the emphasis that DHS has and continues to place on homeland security technologies. The actual amounts dedicated to technology research and development only serve as further testimony in support of McQueary's statements. Technology is the fastest developing field related to the homeland security drive, and it is changing and improving as it proceeds. Technology has brought changes not only in the field of emergency management but throughout governments, national laboratories, research and development facilities, and universities, and it is likely to even affect the way scientific work in conducted in the future.

DHS announced from the beginning of its establishment that it "is committed to using cutting-edge technologies and scientific talent" for a safer country and formed the Directorate of Science and Technol-ogy (S&T) for this purpose. The S&T Directorate was tasked under the original development plans with assuming the research needs of the new department, and for organizing the scientific, engineering, and technological resources of the country in order to adapt their use to the newly recognized needs under the counterterrorism drive created by the September 11, 2001, terrorist attacks. Universities, the private sector, and the federal laboratories have all become important DHS partners in this endeavor.

Billions of dollars have already been spent by the Department of Homeland Security and other agencies with related missions on developing and exploiting technologies for use in the fight against terrorism and, on occasion, for emergency management in general. As is true in all areas of research, not all of the technology developed has been successful, though many innovative and useful systems have resulted. Also, because many feel the push toward technologies is not necessarily decreasing vulnerabilities, but is instead increasing reliance on technologies that could fail, there exists dissent over the actual overall value of technology as a homeland security tool. Regardless of these issues, it is undeniable that the way of life in the United States has changed as result of this great investment by the federal government. This chapter will examine that investment and offer different views on its value.

## OVERVIEW OF INVOLVED AGENCIES AND BUDGET

Although the Department of Homeland Security has the most obvious stake in homeland security–related research efforts, many other agencies are involved in these R&D efforts dispersed throughout the federal government. As DHS was gaining prominence and emerging as a leading agency for these issues, ongoing research and scientific programs conducted under the various different organizations were almost instantly given new direction and resources to respond to the new threats of terrorism. Table 9-1 lists the agencies involved in the homeland security R&D field and their recent budgets. Overall, the total federal investment in homeland security R&D is around

$4.43 billion in FY 2006, up almost 5% from the FY 2005 budget ($4.22 billion). Figures 9-1 and 9-2 show the distributions of funding by agencies and years.

## DEPARTMENT OF HOMELAND SECURITY

Before the establishment of DHS, most R&D efforts dealing with issues relevant to homeland security were dispersed among a wide variety of agencies, and this situation still remains. However, the clear trend since 2003 has been to make DHS a focus for such R&D, and as of 2006 almost 30% of all research and development funding is managed by DHS. Inside DHS, the S&T Directorate has been established in order to coordinate and manage research and development efforts. For the first 3 years of the directorate's existence, R&D efforts were dispersed throughout the various directorates and independent agencies (the Coast Guard, for example). However, as of FY 2006, all R&D efforts were consolidated under S&T. A more

TABLE 9-1  **Federal Homeland Security R&D Appropriations (in millions of dollars)**

| Agency | FY 2002 | FY 2003 | FY 2004 | FY 2005 | FY 2006 |
|---|---|---|---|---|---|
| Agriculture | 175 | 155 | 40 | 161 | 172 |
| Commerce | 20 | 16 | 23 | 73 | 82 |
| DOD | 259 | 212 | 267 | 362 | 394 |
| Energy | 50 | 48 | 47 | 92 | 81 |
| DOD | 266 | 737 | 1,028 | 1,243 | 1,287 |
| EPA | 95 | 70 | 52 | 33 | 94 |
| HHS | 177 | 1,653 | 1,724 | 1,796 | 1,802 |
| NASA | 73 | 73 | 88 | 88 | 92 |
| NSF | 229 | 271 | 321 | 326 | 329 |
| DOT | 106 | 7 | 3 | 0 | 0 |
| All others | 48 | 47 | 32 | 42 | 92 |
| **TOTAL** | **1,499** | **3,290** | **3,626** | **4,216** | **4,425** |

*Source*: Office Of Management Budget, *2003 Report to Congress on Combating Terrorism*, and *Budget of the U.S. Government FY 2006.*

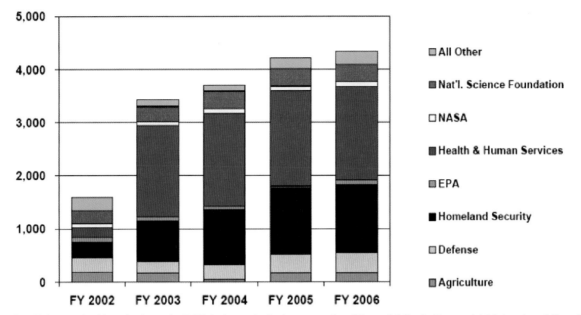

FIGURE 9-1   Federal homeland security R&D budget authority by agency (in millions of dollars). (*Source:* AAAS, based on Office of Management and Budget data, March 2005)

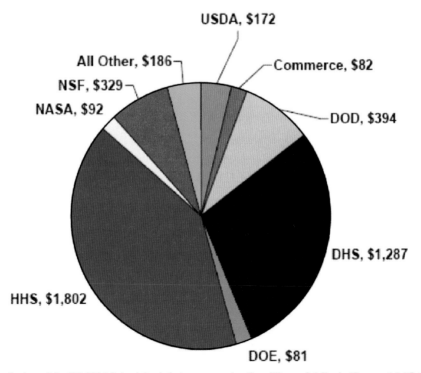

FIGURE 9-2   Distribution of the FY 2006 federal funds between agencies (in millions of dollars). (*Source:* AAAS, based on Office of Management and Budget data, February 2005)

detailed description of S&T and the research this directorate conducts follows.

## DHS DIRECTORATE OF SCIENCE AND TECHNOLOGY

The S&T Directorate is led by an undersecretary of homeland security. This official is responsible for managing technology research and development through the administration of four separate offices:

- **Office of Plans, Programs, and Budget (PPB)**—Provides the strategic and technical vision for S&T and its research, development, testing, and evaluation (RDT&E) process. The primary goals of the office are to align research and development efforts with the DHS mission and objectives, identify the needs of those who will be using the end products of the technology, and formulate technology investment plans to produce solutions to homeland security problems that have been identified.
- **The Homeland Security Advanced Research Projects Agency (HSARPA)**—Engages industry, academia, government, and other sectors in innovative research and development, rapid prototyping, and technology transfer to meet the operational needs of DHS.
- **The Office of Research and Development (ORD)**—Executes the directorate's RDT&E of programs within the national and federal laboratories (see later discussion), establishes the University Centers of Excellence (see later discussion), and maintains the nation's enduring research and development complex dedicated to homeland security.
- **The Office of Systems Engineering and Development (SED)**—Oversees the development of specialized pilot systems in the field through the use of local program offices, which apply technologies that have been developed for real-world situations.

Several strategic objectives have been identified for the S&T Directorate, which guide its overall mission. These objectives, as stated by DHS, are as follows:

- Develop and deploy state-of-the art, high-performance, low-operating-cost systems to prevent, detect, and mitigate the consequences of chemical, biological, radiological, nuclear, and explosive attacks.
- Develop equipment, protocols, and training procedures for response to and recovery from chemical, biological, radiological, nuclear, and explosive attacks.
- Enhance the technical capabilities of the directorate's operational elements and other federal, state, local, and tribal agencies to fulfill their homeland security–related missions.
- Develop methods and capabilities to test and assess threats and vulnerabilities, and prevent technology surprise and anticipate emerging threats.
- Develop technical standards and establish certified laboratories to evaluate homeland security and emergency responder technologies, and evaluate technologies for SAFETY Act certification.
- Support U.S. leadership in science and technology.

## S&T DIRECTORATE PORTFOLIOS

The DHS Science and Technology Directorate conducts and funds research in several designated program areas, also referred to as *portfolios,* which have been organized into three main categories: (1) countermeasures, (2) support to department components, and (3) cross-cutting. The programs and their portfolios, are discussed next.

### Countermeasures Portfolios

The Countermeasures Portfolios are those that are designed to protect the nation against the use of weapons of mass destruction (WMDs). These portfolios focus on program execution related to addressing vulnerabilities and assessing risks related to biological, chemical, radiological and nuclear, and high explosives weapons:

- Biological—Provides research to reduce the probability and potential consequences of a biological attack on the nation's civilian population, its infrastructure, and its agricultural system.
- Chemical—Provides research for reducing the nation's vulnerability to chemical attacks on its civilian population and infrastructure.
- Radiological and nuclear—Provides research to develop and deploy technologies for detection of radiological materials at international borders and in domestic transit (primarily at the nation's ports), and provides an effective intervention capability at the local, state, and federal levels.
- High explosives—Provides the concepts, technologies, systems analysis, and procedures to interdict terrorists' use of explosives against transportation targets, buildings, critical infrastructure, and population centers.

### DHS Component Support Portfolios

These portfolios support the various DHS components in order to increase the capabilities of operational end users, to assist them in securing the nation from terrorist attacks, and to enhance their ability to conduct their missions:

- Border and Transportation Security—Focuses on preventing the entry of terrorists and instruments of terrorism, while ensuring the efficient flow of lawful traffic and commerce.
- Critical Infrastructure Protection—Develops tools to anticipate, identify, and analyze risks in critical infrastructure, and deploys systems to reduce those risks.
- Cyber Security—Engages in research, development, testing, and evaluation activities related to improving cyber security.

- Emergency Preparedness and Response—Supports the planning, prevention, response, and recovery from natural and man-made disasters and terrorist events including technology development for the emergency responder community.
- Threat and Vulnerability, Testing and Assessment—Develops capabilities to evaluate extensive amounts of diverse threat information.
- U.S. Coast Guard—Provides new technologies to improve the performance of all Coast Guard missions and maritime transportation systems.
- U.S. Secret Service—Focuses on the development, acquisition, and deployment of prevention-oriented countermeasures to support the Secret Service protective mission.

### Cross-Cutting Portfolios

Cross-Cutting Portfolios address vulnerabilities and assess risks that support overarching issues spanning all countermeasures and component portfolios:

- Emerging Threats—Anticipates and defines potential threats arising from new scientific and technological advances and terrorist use of existing capabilities in new or unexpected manners.
- Rapid Prototyping—Accelerates the deployment of advanced technologies to address urgent user requirements.
- Standards—Develop standards and protocols for tools and personnel, ensuring a robust capability to defend against and respond to any crisis situation.
- Programs—Engages the academic community to create learning and research environments in areas critical to homeland security.

## S&T BUDGET

The amount of funding under the overall Department of Homeland Security budget dedicated to science and technology has steadily risen each year since the department's creation. This growth signifies the

Table 9-2   **Department of Homeland Security R&D Budget**

|                       | FY 2004        | FY 2005          | FY 2006          |
| --------------------- | -------------- | ---------------- | ---------------- |
| R&T Directorate budget | $912,751,000   | $1,115,450,000   | $1,368,446,000   |

steadily increasing role that technology is taking on in modern emergency management, especially in the area of terrorism prevention and response. It is important to remember that these funds are only in addition to similar project funds being supplied by many other federal agencies, which together comprise a much larger homeland security–related research and development budget. Table 9-2 and Figure 9-3 illustrate the DHS-specific S&T budget allocation.

The S&T Directorate is responsible for setting the national agenda and giving direction and setting priorities for R&D efforts in other department and agencies, regardless of the funding source. S&T is unique among federal R&D agencies in that it has responsi-

bility for the entire cycle of science and technology (i.e., from product research to bringing the product to the market and deploying it).

The S&T Directorate has established the Homeland Security Advanced Research Project Agency (HSARPA). This agency, based on the existing model of the Defense Advanced Research Project Agency (DARPA) in the Department of Defense, distributes the resources within the directorate; awards money for the extramural grants; develops and tests potential technologies; and accelerates or prototypes development of technologies for deployment. The directorate has also created a Homeland Security Advisory Committee consisting of 20 members appointed by the

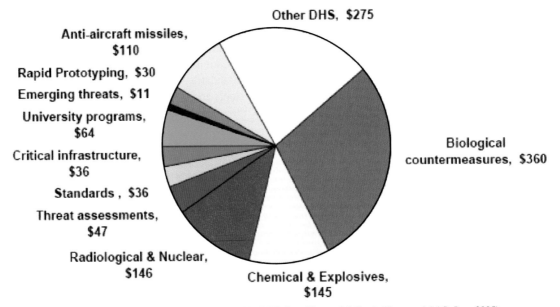

FIGURE 9-3   S&T budget allocations within DHS (in millions of dollars). (*Source:* AAAS, June 2005)

## SIDEBAR 9-1   Information Management

The National Strategy for Homeland Security, released by the White House in 2002, stated that "Information contributes to every aspect of homeland security and is a vital foundation for this effort." The critical issues related to homeland security that drove this initial effort during the creation of DHS were the many disparate databases dispersed among federal, state, and local entities and systems, between which information could not be easily or even possibly shared—either horizontally (across the same level of government) or vertically (between federal, state, and local governments).

Despite spending some $50 billion on information technology per year, two fundamental problems had prevented the federal government from building an efficient government-wide information system:

1. Government acquisition of information systems has not been routinely coordinated, and hundreds of systems have been acquired over time.
2. Legal and cultural barriers often prevent agencies from exchanging and integrating information.

As a result, the national vision announced in the national strategy for information management is to build a national "system of systems" to share the essential homeland security information horizontally and vertically, and to develop common awareness of threats and vulnerabilities. This task fell under the Critical Infrastructure Assurance Office of the Department of Commerce, which has since been transferred into the Department of Homeland Security. The major initiatives outlined in the National Strategy that address information management include:

- Integrate information sharing across the federal government.

- Integrate information sharing across state and local governments, private industry, and citizens to enhance the timely dissemination of information from the federal government to state and local homeland security officials. The different efforts under way are:
  - The FBI and other federal agencies are augmenting the information available in their crime and terrorism databases
  - State and local government use of secure intranet to increase the flow of classified federal information to state and local entities
  - A secure video conferencing capability connecting officials in Washington, D.C., with all government entities in every state
  - The expansion of the .gov domain on the Internet for use by state governments (already completed), to ensure the legitimacy of government websites and enhance searches of all federal and state websites, thereby allowing information to be accessed more quickly.
- Adopt common "meta-data" standards for electronic information relevant to homeland security to integrate terrorist-related information from databases of all government agencies responsible for homeland security.
- Improve public safety emergency communications to disseminate information about vulnerabilities and protective measures, as well as allow first responders to better manage incidents and minimize damage.
- Ensure reliable public health information to assure prompt detection, accurate diagnosis, and timely reporting and investigation of disease epidemics.

*Source*: Department of Homeland Security, 2003, www.dhs.gov

undersecretary representing first responders, citizen groups, researchers, engineers, and businesses to provide science and technology advice to the undersecretary. DHS has also created a new federally funded research and development center (FFRDC), the Homeland Security Institute, to act as a think tank for risk analyses, simulations of threat scenarios, analyses of possible countermeasures, and strategic plans for counterterrorism technology development.

The various federal agencies involved in homeland security R&D are listed in Sidebar 9-2.

The S&T Directorate focuses on four areas: weapons of mass destruction, information (see Sidebar 9-1) and infrastructure, laboratories and research facilities, and maritime research. Each is described in the following sections, and the directorate's FY 2006 programs are listed in Sidebar 9-3.

---

SIDEBAR 9-2   **Federal Agencies Involved in Homeland Security R&D**

**Department of Homeland Security**—DHS R&D increased $44 million, or 3.6%, to $1.3 billion in 2006, after increases of more than $200 million in each of the previous 3 years. Unlike in previous years, where the R&D budget was divided up among various DHS components, such as the Border and Transportation Security Directorate and the Coast Guard, in 2006 S&T will be receiving 100% of the R&D allocation for the department. Some facts about this allocation include:

- 56% (the majority) of DHS R&D funds will be used for development activities.
- The largest part of the portfolio would continue to be biological countermeasures.
- Large increases for new DHS R&D priorities are offset by cuts in other areas of the DHS R&D portfolio.

**Department of Health and Human Services**—In FY 2006, the entire $1.8 billion in Department of Health and Human Services (HHS) homeland security R&D funding is going to biodefense research. The vast majority of these research activities is performed through the National Institutes of Health (NIH) and the Centers for Disease Control and Prevention (CDC).

**Department of Defense**—The Department of Defense (DOD) increased its homeland security R&D by 8.7% in FY 2006, up to $394 million from the previous year. Nearly all of the investment

would come from the various defense agencies, particularly the Defense Advanced Research Projects Agency (DARPA), which focuses primarily on military applications in areas such as biological warfare defense, and the Chemical and Biological Defense Program (CBDP). While these agencies focus primarily on overseas military applications, their R&D results could provide benefits to civilian populations.

**Department of Agriculture**—Most of the U.S. Department of Agriculture's (USDA's) homeland security R&D funding in 2006 is dedicated to the renovation of animal research and diagnostic facilities at the National Centers for Animal Health in Ames, Iowa, that would be the heart of a USDA-wide food and biosafety initiative aimed at securing the U.S. food supply against both natural and terrorist threats.

**Environmental Protection Agency**—Funding for homeland security R&D within the EPA almost tripled between FY 2005 and FY 2006, rising to $94 million. Drinking water security research is one of two priorities addressed by EPA, involving efforts to develop better surveillance and laboratory networks for drinking water supplies to counter potential terrorist threats. The second priority involves decontamination, in an effort to develop better technologies and methods for decontaminating sites after terrorist sites occur. Most of the EPA's R&D

activities are conducted at the National Homeland Security Research Center (NHSRC) in Cincinnati.

**National Institutes of Standards and Technology**—The National Institute of Standards and Technology (NIST), under the Department of Commerce, funds R&D on cryptography and computer security, providing scientific and technical support to DHS in these areas.

**National Science Foundation**—The National Science Foundation (NSF) funds research to combat bioterrorism in the areas of infectious diseases and microbial genome sequencing; these programs increased to $329 million in FY 2006.

**Department of Energy**—The focus of the Department of Energy's (DOE's) R&D efforts involves countering terrorist threats to energy facilities, most notably those that house radiological or nuclear materials.

*Source*: American Association for the Advancement of Science (www.aaas.org)

---

### SIDEBAR 9-3   FY 2006 Science & Technology Directorate Programs

**$362 million for biological countermeasures**—Contains the single largest budget component within the DHS R&D budget. Much of this funding is dedicated to the continued construction of the National Biodefense Analysis and Countermeasures Center in Maryland. A $23 million allocation is dedicated to breaking ground on construction of a National Bio and Agrodefense Facility (NBAF), a $450 million total project with a scheduled completion of 2010 to enhance DHS capabilities to respond to food- or animal-borne terrorist threats. Finally, a biological pathogen detection system is being developed and deployed in top threat cities.

**$102 million for chemical countermeasures**—This budget rose 93% over FY 2005, primarily for the development of a warning system to detect the presence of low-volatility chemical agents (LVAs).

**$15 million for explosives countermeasures**—Funding in this area, which seeks to address terrorist attacks involving explosive agents, fell 25% over the previous year.

**$246 million for radiological and nuclear countermeasures**—A primary focus of this component is to test and improve detection technologies and system architectures deployed at U.S. ports of entry and at other critical transportation nodes. This includes a radiation detection pilot project at the Port Authority of New York and New Jersey. Additional resources will be directed toward advances in neutron sources suitable for use in port facilities for cargo containers, allowing for detection at greater distances. Some of these resources and activities from this portfolio will be redirected to the construction of a Domestic Nuclear Detection Office (DNDO).

**$47 million for threat and vulnerability assessments**—This component addresses technologies that analyze and evaluate threats, especially in information technologies. Funding for FY 2006 fell 29% from FY 2005 levels.

**$36 million for standards development**—New standard development will focus on validation of existing, high-priority, high-use technology for detection such as polymeric chain reaction (PCR) devices, Raman spectrophotometers, spectroscopy-based radiation portal monitors, neutron detectors, high-energy X-ray interrogation systems, neutron interrogation systems, trace explosive detection devices, and explosion mitigation devices. A database of standard protocols for use by incident command centers will be made available to state and local agencies. The Standards Program, as part of an interagency team and experts from the private sector and many DHS agencies, is developing a list of prioritized requirements for chemical, biological, radiological, nuclear, and explosive (CBRNE) countermeasures standards. In addition, a report and database on existing CBRNE countermeasures standards will be issued.

**$94 million for support of DHS components**—The Bureau of Transportation Security is developing the next generation of container security and communications systems to detect intrusion, location, contents, and tampering. The S&T Directorate is driving toward full border and transportation intelligence fusion and the ability to detect contraband at ports of entry. The Emergency Preparedness and Response (EP&R) portfolio is completing capability assessments in four pilot cities and developing technology systems solutions utilizing new developments in CBRNE countermeasures and emergency response equipment through its Regional Technology Integration (RTI) Initiative. Upon completion of the assessment phase, the S&T Directorate will help provide integrated urban area all-hazards detection and emergency response based on risk and technology readiness level. Also, the EP&R portfolio is implementing the Interagency Modeling and Atmospheric Analysis Center (IMAAC), which serves to fully support federal, state, and local responders during incidents of national significance. IMAAC conducts training in high-threat urban areas and utilizes results of field experiments and participation in the National Exercise Program (NEP) to improve models for hazards predictions.

**$64 million for university programs**—Research areas for future Centers of Excellence continue to be evaluated and established. Additional classes of scholars and fellows will be awarded in FY 2006, working toward the S&T Directorate goal of a steady state of highly talented and diverse students.

**$110 million for countermeasures for man-portable air defense systems (MANPADS)**—This budget rose 80% over FY 2005 levels, in support of defense against portable anti-aircraft missiles.

**$117 million for R&D consolidation**—In FY 2006, the process of consolidating all DHS R&D into the S&T Directorate will be completed.

**$11 million for emerging threats**

**$21 million for rapid prototyping**

**$6 million for the Safety Act**

**$21 million for interoperable communication**

**$21 million for critical infrastructure protection**

**$17 million for cyber security**

*Source*: Department of Homeland Security. 2005. *Budget in Brief.*

## WEAPONS OF MASS DESTRUCTION

The DHS website states, "The S&T Directorate will tap into scientific and technological capabilities to provide the means to detect and deter attacks using weapons of mass destruction. S&T will guide and organize research efforts to meet emerging and predicted needs and will work closely with universities, the private sector, and national and federal laboratories." This effort can be subdivided into two fields: chemical and biological, and radiological and nuclear. In both fields, the directorate's aim is to carry research to develop sensors to detect such weapons from production to employment. The different organizations within the federal sector that will support and serve the R&D efforts of S&T are detailed in the following section.

## CHEMICAL AND BIOLOGICAL DEFENSE INFORMATION AND ANALYSIS CENTER (WWW.CBIAC.APGEA.ARMY.MIL)

The Chemical and Biological Defense Information and Analysis Center (CBIAC) is a DOD Information Analysis Center (IAC), administratively managed by the Defense Technical Information Center (DTIC). The center serves as the DOD focal point for information related to chemical and biological defense technology. Its function is to generate, acquire, process, analyze, and disseminate chemical and biological science and technology information in support of military resources, the chemical and biological defense research, development, and acquisition community, and other federal, state, and local government agencies. The CBIAC accomplishes its mission by the following means:

- Identifying and acquiring relevant data and information from all available sources and in all media
- Processing data and acquisitions into suitable storage and retrieval systems
- Identifying, developing, and applying available analytical tools and techniques for the interpretation and application of stored data and acquisitions
- Disseminating focused information, data sets, and technical analyses to managers, planners, scientists, engineers and military field personnel for the performance of mission related tasks
- Anticipating requirements for chemical and biological science and technology information.
- Identifying and reaching out to emerging chemical and biological defense organizations

## DEFENSE THREAT REDUCTION AGENCY (WWW.DTRA.MIL/CB/CB_INDEX.HTML)

The Defense Threat Reduction Agency (DTRA) safeguards national interests from weapons of mass destruction (chemical, biological, radiological, nuclear, and high explosives) by controlling and reducing the threat and providing quality tools and services for the war fighter. DTRA performs four essential functions to reach its mission: combat support, technology development, threat control, and threat reduction. Moreover, the agency's work covers a broad spectrum of activities:

- Shaping the international environment to prevent the spread of weapons of mass destruction
- Responding to requirements to deter the use and reduce the impact of such weapons
- Preparing for the future as WMD threats emerge and evolve

The activities concerning homeland security are as follows:

- DTRA draws on the disparate chemical and biological weapons defense expertise within the DOD to increase response capabilities.
- The Advanced Systems and Concepts Office (ASCO) stimulates, identifies, and executes high-impact seed projects to encourage new thinking, address technology gaps, and improve the operational capabilities of DTRA.

## DEPARTMENT OF STATE (WWW.STATE.GOV)

The Department of State is a very useful source of information that provides assessment of potential chemical and biological weapons, and analyzes what different countries and groups have as resources.

## CENTERS FOR DISEASE CONTROL AND PREVENTION (WWW.CDC.GOV)

The Centers for Disease Control and Prevention (CDC) is recognized as the lead federal agency for protecting the health and safety of people by providing credible information to enhance health decisions and promoting health through strong partnerships. CDC serves as the national focus for developing and applying disease prevention and control, environmental health, and health promotion and education activities designed to improve the health of the people of the United States, with the mission to promote health and quality of life by preventing and controlling disease, injury, and disability. CDC provides information about the effects and treatment for exposure to chembio weapons and has valuable experts within its 12 centers, institutes, and offices. The most prominent and relevant ones are as follows:

- The National Center for Chronic Disease Prevention and Health Promotion prevents premature death and disability from chronic diseases and promotes healthy personal behaviors.
- The National Center for Health Statistics provides statistical information that will guide actions and policies to improve the health of the American people.
- The National Center for HIV, STD, and TB Prevention provides national leadership in preventing and controlling human immunodeficiency virus infection, sexually transmitted diseases, and tuberculosis.
- The National Center for Infectious Diseases prevents illness, disability, and death caused by infectious diseases in the United States and around the world.
- The National Immunization Program prevents disease, disability, and death from vaccine-preventable diseases in children and adults.
- The Epidemiology Program Office strengthens the public health system by coordinating public health surveillance; providing support in scientific communications, statistics, and epidemiology; and training in surveillance, epidemiology, and prevention effectiveness.
- The Public Health Practice Program Office strengthens community practice of public health by creating an effective workforce, building information networks, conducting practice research, and ensuring laboratory quality.

## LAWRENCE LIVERMORE NATIONAL LABORATORY (WWW.LLNL.GOV/HSO/)

The Lawrence Livermore National Laboratory provides information about nuclear and radiological weapons. Its activities are explained more broadly in the research and development section.

## U.S. NUCLEAR REGULATORY COMMISSION (WWW.NRC.GOV)

The U.S. Nuclear Regulatory Commission (NRC) is an independent agency established to regulate civilian use of nuclear materials. The NRC's mission is to regulate the nation's civilian use of by-product, source, and special nuclear materials to ensure adequate protection of public health and safety, to promote the common defense and security, and to protect the environment. The NRC's regulatory mission covers three main areas:

- *Reactors*: Commercial reactors for generating electric power and nonpower reactors used for research, testing, and training
- *Materials*: Uses of nuclear materials in medical, industrial, and academic settings and facilities that produce nuclear fuel
- *Waste*: Transportation, storage, and disposal of nuclear materials and waste, and decommissioning of nuclear facilities from service

The NRC carries out its mission by conducting several activities but most of them are not directly related to the homeland security purpose. The commission performs them as part of its mission to regulate the normal use of radiological material, but many of its capabilities and resources can be used during a radiological or nuclear incident. The major contribution fields are commission direction setting and policy making; radiation protection; establishment of a regulatory program; nuclear security and safeguards information on how to promote the common defense and security; public affairs; congressional affairs; state and tribal programs; and international programs.

## INFORMATION AND INFRASTRUCTURE

DHS has been given the primary responsibility for detecting and deterring attacks on the national information systems and critical infrastructures, and the S&T Directorate is developing a national research and development enterprise to support this mission. The three main issues concerning information and infrastructure are as follows: Internet security, telecommunication, and the security systems. The directorate coordinates and integrates several organizations to accomplish its mission, as discussed next.

### NATIONAL INFRASTRUCTURE PROTECTION CENTER (WWW.NIPC.GOV)

The National Infrastructure Protection Center (NIPC) operates directly under DHS and gives information about current efforts and possible threats coming from cyberspace. The center produces infrastructure warnings under the titles of assessments, advisories, alerts, and information bulletins (Info-Bulletins), which are developed and distributed in a manner that is consistent with DHS's advisory and information-sharing system.

These threat warning products are based on material that is significant, credible, timely and that address cyber and/or infrastructure dimensions with possibly significant impact. These products will often be based on classified material and include dissemination restrictions, but the center will then seek to develop a sensitive "tear-line" version for distribution to critical sector coordinators, general law enforcement authorities, state and local authorities, and others as appropriate. Some details about each product are as follows:

- Assessments address broad, general incident or issue awareness information and analysis that is both significant and current, but they do not necessarily suggest immediate action.

- Advisories address significant threat or incident information that suggests a change in readiness posture, protective options, and/or response.
- Alerts address major threat or incident information addressing imminent or in-progress attacks targeting specific national networks or critical infrastructures.

### FEDERAL COMPUTER INCIDENT RESPONSE CENTER (WWW.FEDCIRC.GOV)

The Federal Computer Incident Response Center (FedCIRC) is the federal civilian government focal point for computer security incident reporting and providing assistance with incident prevention and response. The center became part of DHS's Information Analysis and Infrastructure Protection (IAIP) Directorate beginning March 2003 and focuses on four major activities:

- *Incident Prevention*: The center provides a patch authentication and dissemination capability that can assist organizations in identifying and patching known vulnerabilities specific to their systems. The center provides informational notices and advisories about current threats and vulnerabilities.
- *Incident Reporting*: The center receives incident reports from federal agencies/departments that allow it to identify deliberate targeting efforts and other trends. By sharing sanitized incident information in return, all civilian agencies/departments can withstand or quickly recover from attacks against U.S. information resources.
- *Incident Analysis*: The center has a partnership with CERT/CC and offers Incident and Vulnerability Notes to illustrate the range of adverse events affecting federal agencies/departments as reported.
- *Incident Response*: The center provides personnel, appropriate remediation, and recovery activities for the aftermath.

## SANS Institute (www.sans.org)

The SANS (Systems Administration, Audit, Network, Security) Institute is active in the fields of information security research, certification, and education and provides a platform for professionals to share their lessons learned, to conduct research, and teach the information security community. Besides the various training programs and resources aimed at informing its members and the community, the following centers are part of SANS:

- *Internet Storm Center*: This center was created to detect rising Internet threats. It uses advanced data correlation and visualization techniques to analyze data from a large number of firewalls and intrusion detection systems in over 60 countries. Experienced analysts constantly monitor the Storm Center data feeds and search for trends and anomalies in order to identify potential threats. When a potential threat is detected, the team immediately begins an intensive investigation to gauge the threat's severity and impact. The Storm Center may request correlating data from an extensive network of security experts from across the globe, and possesses the in-house expertise to analyze captured attack tools quickly and thoroughly. Critical information is then disseminated to the public in the form of alerts and postings.
- *Center for Internet Security (CIS) and SCORE*: CIS formalizes the best practice recommendations once consensus between the SANS Institute and SCORE is reached and the practices are validated. Those latter become minimum standards benchmarks for general use by the industry. Both organizations rely on and have a very broad contact with the field experts.

## CERT Coordination Center (www.cert.org)

The CERT Coordination Center (CERT/CC) is located at the Software Engineering Institute (SEI), a federally funded research and development center at Carnegie Mellon University in Pittsburgh, Pennsylvania. SEI had been charged by DARPA in 1988 to set up a center to coordinate communication among experts during security emergencies and to help prevent future incidents.

The CERT/CC is part of the larger SEI Networked Systems Survivability Program, whose primary goals are to ensure that appropriate technology and systems management practices are used to resist attacks on networked systems and to limit damage and ensure continuity of critical services in spite of successful attacks, accidents, or failures. The areas of work of the center can be summarized as follows:

- *Vulnerability Analysis and Incident Handling*: Analyze the state of Internet security and convey that information to the system administrators, network managers, and others in the Internet community. In these vulnerability and incident-handling activities, a higher priority is assigned to attacks and vulnerabilities that directly affect the Internet infrastructure (for example, network service providers, Internet service providers, domain name servers, and routers).
- *Survivable Enterprise Management*: Help organizations protect and defend themselves. To this end, risks assessments that help enterprises identify and characterize critical information assets and then identify risks to those assets have been developed, and the enterprise can use the results of the assessment to develop or refine their overall strategy for securing their networked systems.
- *Education and Training*: The center offers training courses to educate technical staff and managers of computer security incident response teams as well as system administrators and other technical personnel within organizations to improve the security and survivability of each system. The center's staff also take part in developing curricula in information security and has compiled a guide, *The CERT® Guide to System and Network Security Practices*, published by Addison-Wesley.

- *Survivable Network Technology*: The center focuses on the technical basis for identifying and preventing security flaws and for preserving essential services if a system is penetrated and compromised. The center does research for new approaches to secure systems and analysis of how susceptible systems are to sophisticated attacks and finding ways to improve the design of systems. Another focus is on modeling and simulation. The center has developed "Easel," a tool that is being used to study network responses to attacks and attack mitigation strategies. And finally, the center is also developing techniques that will enable the assessment and prediction of current and potential threats to the Internet. These techniques involve examining large sets of network data to identify unauthorized and potentially malicious activity.

## NATIONAL COMMUNICATIONS SYSTEM (WWW.NCS.GOV)

Through the National Communications System (NCS), DHS supports the telecommunications critical infrastructure and research and development of tools and technology to prevent disruption or compromise of these services. The NCS was established in 1963 as a "single unified communications system to serve the president, Department of Defense, diplomatic and intelligence activities and civilian leaders." The NCS mandate included linking, improving, and extending the communications facilities and components of various federal agencies, focusing on interconnectivity and survivability. The NCS's national security and emergency preparedness (NS/EP) capabilities were broadened in 1984 when it began coordinating and planning NS/EP telecommunications to support crises and disasters.

With the U.S. Information Agency being absorbed into the U.S. State Department in October 2000, the NCS membership currently stands at 23 members. The NCS also participates in joint industry–government planning through its work with the president's National Security Telecommunications Advisory Committee (NSTAC), with the NSC's National Coordinating Center for Telecommunications (NCC), and with the NCC's subordinate Information Sharing and Analysis Center (ISAC).

The NCS comprises numerous programs and committees that represent the majority of the national efforts in the field of communication for national emergencies and crisis. The President's National Security Telecommunications Advisory Committee (NSTAC) and the Office of the Manager NCS (OMNCS) have been given the tasks of providing access control, priority treatment, user authentication, and other survivability features supporting NS/EP telecommunications to the Advanced Intelligent Network (AIN). The OMNCS has established an AIN Program to address the emerging technology and an associated AIN Program Office to plan, coordinate, and oversee the effort. Two very important examples of initiatives are the following:

- The Alerting and Coordination Network (ACN) provides a stable emergency voice communications network connecting telecommunications service providers' Emergency Operations Centers (EOCs) and Network Operations Centers (NOCs) to support NS/EP telecommunications network restoration coordination, transmission of telecommunications requirements and priorities, and incident reporting when the Public Switched Telephone Network (PSTN) is inoperable, stressed, or congested. The ACN is operational 24 hours a day, 7 days a week, to support the National Coordinating Center (NCC) during normal and emergency operations.
- The Emergency Notification Service (ENS) is a full-time service established to notify critical government personnel during emergencies using multiple communication channels, including telephone, Short Message Service (SMS), pager, and e-mail. Within minutes of receiving an activation order from an authorized representative of an organization, an automated process makes

multiple attempts to reach intended recipients until they confirm delivery or until a predetermined number of attempts have been made. After 30 minutes, a report detailing confirmation of delivery is returned to the originator of the notification. Messages can be recorded in advance or when the notification is initiated and can be sent as a general notification or a sensitive notification.

To initiate, coordinate, restore, and reconstitute NS/EP telecommunications services or facilities, the NCS continues to develop new capabilities and reevaluate or upgrade older ones. The NCS's current capabilities are given in Sidebar 9-4. The current initiatives going on under the NCS's National Coordination Center for Telecommunications can be summarized as follows:

- In January 2000, the national coordinator for Security, Infrastructure Protection, and Counterterrorism designated the NCC-ISAC as the Information Sharing and Analysis Center for telecommunications. The NCC-ISAC will facilitate voluntary collaboration and information sharing among its participants, gathering information on vulnerabilities, threats, intrusions, and anomalies from telecommunications industry, government, and other sources. The NCC-ISAC will analyze the data with the goal of averting or mitigating impact on the telecommunications infrastructure.
- The NCC-ISAC uses an Information Sharing and Analysis System (ISAS) to analyze the information provided by the NCC-ISAC participants. The ISAS incorporates capabilities for automated correlation of inputs with other inputs and

SIDEBAR 9-4  **NCS Current Capabilities**

The Communications Resource Information Sharing (CRIS) initiative provides a directory of readily available federal telecommunications assets, services, and capabilities that may be shared with other government agencies to support NS/EP needs. Participation is voluntary and limited to NCS members and their affiliates, and assets are only available if their use does not interfere with departmental or agency missions or operations.

The Government Emergency Telecommunications Service (GETS) is a nationwide NS/EP switched voice and voice band data communications service that provides authorized local, state, and federal government users with communications during disasters by using surviving PSTN resources. GETS provides access authorization, enhanced routing, and priority treatment in local and long-distance telephone networks and is accessible through a dialing plan and personal identification number (PIN). GETS uses three major types

of networks: the major long-distance networks provided by interexchange carriers (AT&T, MCI WorldCom, and Sprint); the local networks provided by local exchange carriers (Bell operating companies and independent companies, cellular carriers, and personal communication services); government-leased networks (including the Federal Telecommunications System and the Defense Information System Network).

The National Technology Coordination Network (NTCN) connects participating government and industry organizations via a multimodal conferencing bridge. The bridge links disparate communications systems and allows for voice communications including dedicated line, high-frequency radio, satellite telephone, and switched wireline telephone. Telecommunications industry participants are connected to the bridge through the National Telecommunications Alliance's Alerting and Coordination Network (ACN). The ACN is a nonpublic network system developed to provide communications and coordination capabilities to industry members during Public Network (PN) outages.

The Shared Resources (SHARES) High Frequency (HF) Radio Program provides a single interagency emergency message handling system to transmit NS/EP information during disasters by consolidating HF radio resources belonging to 91 federal and federally affiliated organizations. SHARES stations are in every state and at 20 overseas locations. The network consists of 1,101 HF radio stations located in the United States and abroad, 335 emergency planning and response personnel, and over 250 HF frequencies. It also provides the federal community a forum for addressing issues affecting HF radio operability. The manager of NCC is responsible for day-to-day operations of

SHARES, while the manager of NCS is responsible for the overall SHARES program.

The Federal Communications Commission (FCC) established the Telecommunications Service Priority (TSP) program in 1988 to provide priority provisioning and restoration of NS/EP telecommunication services. Under the TSP program, service vendors are authorized and required to provision and restore services with TSP assignments before services without such assignments. As a result, a telecommunications service with a TSP assignment will receive full attention by the service vendor before any non-TSP service. Non-federal government users who request TSP restoration or provisioning must be sponsored by a federal organization.

*Source*: Telecommunications Service Priority, 2003

all-source information. The ISAS provides advanced automation, analysis, modeling, data fusion, and correlation processes to support the near real-time exchange of critical information, assessments, and warning information involving vulnerabilities, threats, and affecting the telecommunications infrastructure.

The last issue for emergency communication is wireless communication. Wireless network congestion was widespread on September 11, 2001, and with wireless traffic demand estimated at up to 10 times the normal amount in the affected areas and double nationwide, the need for wireless priority service became critical and urgent. Since the early 1990s OMNCS has worked to develop and implement a nationwide cellular priority access capability in support of NS/EP telecommunications. As a result of a petition filed by the NCS in October 1995, the FCC set the wireless Priority Access Service (PAS) as voluntary. For example, the Wireless Priority Service

(WPS), the NCS program implementation of the FCC PAS, is the wireless complement to the wire line Government Emergency Telecommunications Service (GETS). GETS utilizes the PSTN to provide enhanced wire line priority service to qualified NS/EP personnel.

But as a result of the events of September 11, 2001, the National Security Council issued the following guidance to the Office of the Manager, National Communications System (OMNCS):

> NCS has to move forward on implementing an immediate solution using channel reservation capability from one vendor for the Washington, DC, area; based on lessons learned in DC, the NCS will make a recommendation on whether to expand the immediate solution to other metro areas.
>
> In parallel, the NCS will proceed with deploying a priority access queuing system for wireless nationwide.

The two proposed solutions are discussed in more detail in Sidebar 9-5.

SIDEBAR 9-5  **NCC Wireless Priorities**

In the early 1990s, the OMNCS initiated efforts to develop and implement a nationwide cellular priority access capability in support of national security and emergency preparedness (NS/EP) telecommunications and pursued a number of activities to improve cellular call completion during times of network congestion. Subsequently, as a result of a petition filed by the NCS in October 1995, the FCC released a Second Report and Order (R&O) on wireless Priority Access Service (PAS). The R&O offers federal liability relief for NS/EP wireless carriers if the service is implemented in accordance with uniform operating procedures. The FCC made PAS voluntary, found it to be in the public interest, and defined five priority levels for NS/EP wireless calls.

Wireless Priority Service (WPS), the National Communications System (NCS) program implementation of the FCC PAS, is the wireless complement to the wireline Government Emergency Telecommunications Service (GETS). GETS utilizes the Public Switched Telephone Network (PSTN) to provide enhanced wireline priority service to qualified NS/EP personnel. WPS users are authorized and encouraged to use GETS to better their probability of completing their NS/EP call during periods of wireless and wireline network congestion. Wireless network congestion was widespread on September 11, 2001. With wireless traffic demand estimated at up to 10 times normal in the affected areas and double nationwide, the need for wireless priority service became a critical and urgent national requirement.

Reacting to the events of September 11, 2001, the National Security Council issued the following guidance to the National Communications System (NCS):

**Immediate Solution**

With the White House guidance in October 2001, the NCS began immediate acquisition of service for the Washington, D.C., metropolitan area and recommended and proceeded with services for New York City as well. The February 2002 Olympics in Salt Lake City also warranted immediate service. The NCS entered into subcontracts with the Immediate WPS service providers, T-Mobile (previously VoiceStream) and Globalstar. T-Mobile's implementation of the Immediate Solution became operational during May 2002 in Washington and New York. By November 2002, T-Mobile supported 2,084 WPS users in Washington and 725 in New York, for a total of 2,809 WPS cellular users. Globalstar also supported 1,506 customers as well.

**Nationwide Solution**

Due to the requirement for nationwide WPS coverage, multiple carriers and multiple access technologies are needed. WPS is based on the two digital access technologies most widely available in the United States, GSM (i.e., Cingular, Nextel, and T-Mobile) and Code Division Multiple Access (CDMA) (i.e., Sprint PCS and Verizon Wireless). Nationwide WPS is provided in two major phases, Initial Operating Capability (IOC) and Full Operating Capability (FOC). IOC is a GSM-based solution only, consisting of priority radio channel access at call origination. IOC began December 31, 2002, and it satisfied the requirements of the FCC Second R&O for invocation of the service on a call-by-call basis by dialing the WPS prefix (*272) at the start of each NS/EP WPS call. FOC provides a full, end-to-end capability, beginning with the NS/EP wireless caller, through the wireless networks, through the interexchange Carrier (IXC) and/or local exchange carrier (LEC) wireline networks, and to the wireless or wireline called party. T-Mobile began deploying WPS FOC in December 2003. Cingular (and formerly AT&T Wireless) began deploying WPS FOC in July 2004. Nextel also deployed WPS in July 2004, and will upgrade

to FOC beginning in April 2005. As of May 2005, there were over 11,500 WPS users. It is the objective of NCS to provide the WPS capability to an estimated NS/EP wireless user population of 200,000 GSM users and 150,000 CDMA users.

*Source*: National Communications System, www.ncs.gov.

## LABORATORIES AND RESEARCH FACILITIES

The research and development function is the most important aspect of the S&T Directorate. It will rely on several existing agency programs to accomplish this task: Department of Defense (DOD), Department of Energy (DOE), and Department of Agriculture (USDA) programs, among others. A significant portion of the funding attached to these programs comes from DOD's newly created National Bioweapons Defense Analysis Center, responsible for nearly the entire biological countermeasures portfolio.

DHS intends to establish an Office for National Laboratories that will coordinate DHS interactions with DOE national laboratories with expertise in homeland security. The office has the authority to establish a semi-independent DHS headquarters laboratory within an existing federal laboratory, national laboratory, or FFRDC to supply scientific and technical knowledge to DHS; the most recent indications are that DHS plans to do so with at least five national labs. In addition to Livermore, DHS has initial plans to establish four other labs-within-labs at Los Alamos, Sandia, Pacific Northwest, and Oak Ridge National Laboratories. DHS will also establish one or more university-based centers for homeland security.

The national and federal laboratory system possesses significant expertise in the area of weapons of mass destruction in addition to massive computing power. These labs include the following:

- *DOE National Nuclear Security Administration Labs*: Lawrence Livermore Laboratory, Los

Alamos National Laboratory, Sandia National Laboratory.

- *DOE Office of Science Labs*: Argonne National Laboratory, Brookhaven National Laboratory, Oak Ridge National Laboratory, Pacific Northwest National Laboratory, other DOE Laboratories.
- *Department of Homeland Security Labs*: Environmental Measurements Laboratory, Plum Island Animal Disease Center.
- *Department of Health and Human Services Labs*: HHS operates several laboratories focused on wide-ranging health and disease prevention issues.
- *U.S. Customs Laboratory and Scientific Services*: The U.S. Customs Laboratory and Scientific Services do testing to determine the origin of agricultural and manufactured products.

This section starts with an overview of the facilities cited above and relevant programs and then discusses other R&D activities, such as university-based center approach, and partnerships between DHS and other agencies.

### LAWRENCE LIVERMORE NATIONAL LABORATORY (WWW.LLNL.GOV)

The Homeland Security Organization at Lawrence Livermore National Laboratory (LLNL) provides comprehensive solutions integrating threat, vulnerability, and trade-off analyses, advanced technologies, field-demonstrated prototypes, and operational capabilities to assist federal, state, local, and private entities in defending against catastrophic terrorism. The center is also dedicated to pursuing partnerships with universities and the private sector to fulfill its mission. A summary of the programs going on is given in Appendix 9-1 at the end of this chapter.

## Los Alamos National Laboratory (www.lanl.gov)

Los Alamos National Laboratory (LANL) is a Department of Energy (DOE) laboratory, managed by the University of California, and is one of the largest multidisciplinary institutions in the world. The Center for Homeland Security (CHS) was established in September 2002 to engage the laboratory's broad capabilities in the areas of counterterrorism and homeland security. It provides a single point of contact for all external organizations.

The organization's emphasis is in the key areas of nuclear and radiological science and technology, critical infrastructure protection, and chemical and biological science and technology. Current LANL projects with a key role in homeland security include the following:

- BASIS (the Biological Aerosol Sentry and Information System), a biological early warning system that was tested and installed at the 2002 Salt Lake City Winter Olympics
- A novel nuclear detector, the Palm CZT Spectrometer, is also in development and deployment, providing real-time gamma and neutron detection and isotope identification in a handheld device
- LANL has also been active in the anthrax bacterial DNA analysis and the computerized feature identification tool known as GENIE, for Genetic Image Exploitation.

## Sandia National Laboratory (www.sandia.gov)

The Sandia National Laboratories have been active since 1949 in the development of science-based tech-

nologies that support national security. Through science and technology, people, infrastructure, and partnerships, Sandia's mission is to meet national needs in four key areas, including nuclear weapons, nonproliferation and assessments, military technologies and applications, and energy and infrastructure assurance (see Appendix 9-2).

## Argonne National Laboratory (www.anl.gov)

Argonne is one of the DOE's largest research centers. It is also the nation's first national laboratory, chartered in 1946. Argonne's research falls into four broad categories: basic science, scientific facilities, energy resources programs, and environmental management.

Industrial technology development is an important activity in moving benefits of Argonne's publicly funded research to industry to help strengthen the nation's technology base. Appendix 9-3 summarizes the homeland security–related programs and projects developed by the lab.

## Brookhaven National Laboratory (www.bnl.gov)

Established in 1947 on Long Island, New York, Brookhaven National Laboratory (BNL) is a multiprogram national laboratory operated by Brookhaven Science Associates for the DOE. Six Nobel Prizes have been awarded for discoveries made at BNL. Brookhaven has a staff of approximately 3,000 scientists, engineers, technicians, and support people and hosts more than 4,000 guest researchers annually. Brookhaven National Laboratory's role for the DOE is to produce excellent science and advanced technology with the cooperation, support, and appropriate involvement of our scientific and local communities. The fundamental elements of BNL's role in support of the four DOE strategic missions are the following:

- To conceive, design, construct, and operate complex, leading edge, user-oriented facilities in response to the needs of the DOE and the international community of users.

- To carry out basic and applied research in long-term, high-risk programs at the frontier of science.
- To develop advanced technologies that address national needs and to transfer them to other organizations and to the commercial sector.
- To disseminate technical knowledge, to educate new generations of scientists and engineers, to maintain technical capabilities in the nation's workforce, and to encourage scientific awareness in the general public.

Major programs that are managed at the laboratory include the following:

- Nuclear and high-energy physics
- Physics and chemistry of materials
- Environmental and energy research
- Nonproliferation
- Neurosciences and medical imaging
- Structural biology

## OAK RIDGE NATIONAL LABORATORY (WWW.ORNL.GOV)

The Oak Ridge National Laboratory (ORNL) is a multiprogramming science and technology laboratory managed for DOE by UT-Battelle, LLC. Scientists and engineers at ORNL conduct basic and applied research and development to create scientific knowledge and technological solutions that strengthen the nation's leadership in key areas of science; increase the availability of clean, abundant energy; restore and protect the environment; and contribute to national security.

ORNL's National Security Directorate's missions are as follows: to provide federal, state, and local government agencies and departments the technology and expertise to support national and homeland security needs; and to develop for, or transfer technology to, industry so it can be used in support of national or homeland security objectives as well as to enhance America's economic competitiveness in world markets. The different centers and programs of the laboratory are given in Appendix 9-4.

## PACIFIC NORTHWEST NATIONAL LABORATORY (WWW.PNL.GOV)

The Pacific Northwest National Laboratory (PNNL) is a DOE laboratory that delivers breakthrough science and technology to meet selected environmental, energy, health, and national security objectives; strengthen the economy; and support the education of future scientists and engineers.

PNNL's mission in national security supports the U.S. government's objectives against the proliferation of nuclear, chemical, and biological weapons of mass destruction and associated delivery systems. About one-third of PNNL's $600 million annual research and development budget reflects work in national security programs for the Departments of Energy, Defense, and most other federal agencies. The focus is on issues that concern the Air Force, Army, Defense Advanced Research Projects Agency, Defense Threat Reduction Agency, Navy, and nuclear nonproliferation.

Scientists and engineers at PNNL are finding ways to diagnose the life of the Army's Abrams tank, developing technologies that verify compliance with the Comprehensive Nuclear Test Ban Treaty, helping North Korea secure spent nuclear fuel in proper storage canisters, and training border enforcement officials from the United States and foreign countries. Some of PNNL's national security projects are listed in Appendix 9-5.

## OTHER DOE LABORATORIES AND OBJECTIVES (WWW.ENERGY.GOV)

The Department of Energy also has other affiliated organizations in addition to the ones cited above that focus on the same issues. A quick summary is provided in Appendix 9-6.

## Environmental Measurements Laboratory (www.eml.doe.gov)

The Environmental Measurements Laboratory (EML), a government-owned, government-operated laboratory, is directly part of the Science and Technology (S&T) Directorate. The laboratory advances and applies the science and technology required for preventing, protecting against, and responding to radiological and nuclear events in the service of homeland and national security.

EML's current programs focus on issues associated with environmental radiation and radioactivity. Specifically, EML provides DHS with environmental radiation and radioactivity measurements in the laboratory or field, technology development and evaluation, personnel training, instrument calibration, performance testing, data management, and data quality assurance. Examples of these programs are given in Appendix 9-7.

The two unique facilities of the lab are as follows:

- *Environmental Chamber:* A 25-cubic-meter facility, the only one in the United States, that can generate atmospheres with controlled aerosols and gases for calibration and testing of new instruments
- *Gamma Spectrometry Laboratory:* A fully equipped laboratory with high-efficiency, high-resolution gamma sensors

## Plum Island Animal Disease Center (www.ars.usda.gov/plum/)

The Plum Island Animal Disease Center (PIADC) became part of DHS on June 1, 2003. While the center remains an important national asset in which scientists conduct basic and applied research and diagnostic activities to protect the health of livestock on farms across the nation from foreign disease agents, it also has the new mission to help DHS to protect the country from terrorist threats, including those directed against agriculture.

The U.S. Department of Agriculture (USDA) is responsible for research and diagnosis to protect the nation's animal industries and exports from catastrophic economic losses caused by foreign animal disease (FAD) agents accidentally or deliberately introduced into the United States. While continuing its mission, it will also work closely with DHS personnel to fight agroterrorism. The common goals for the organization are given in Appendix 9-8.

While the island setting and biocontainment facilities of PIADC permit safe and secure research by operating at a Biosafety Level 3, the DHS has no plans in the near or long term for a Biosafety Level 4 facility.

## Department of Health and Human Services Labs (www.hhs.gov)

The Department of Health and Human Services operates several laboratories focused on different health and disease prevention issues. The laboratories have extensive programs, and more details can be found in a later section.

## U.S. Customs Laboratory and Scientific Services (www.customs.gov/xp/cgov/import/operations_support/labs_scientific_svcs)

It is one of the principal responsibilities of the Science Officers to manage the Customs Gauger/Laboratory Accreditation program. The program calls for the accreditation of commercial gaugers and laboratories so that their measurements and analytical results can be used by customs for entry and admissibility purposes. The staff edits and publishes the *Customs Laboratory Bulletin* which, as a customs-scientific journal, is circulated internationally and provides a useful forum for technical exchange on subjects of general customs interest. Appendix 9-9 provides an overview of the existing laboratories and their specializations.

## ACADEMIC RESEARCH INSTITUTIONS

Universities, their research centers, institutes, and qualified staff represent a very important portion of the scientific research in the United States. These facilities represent an estimated one-third of the total federal budget available for R&D activities. The S&T Directorate has already started to show its recognition of the importance of these institutions in the overall homeland security R&D effort through both awarding them R&D grants and by funding Homeland Security Centers of Excellence on their campuses.

### Homeland Security Centers of Excellence

The Science and Technology Directorate, through its Office of University Programs, is furthering the homeland security mission by engaging the academic community to create learning and research environments in areas critical to homeland security. Through the Homeland Security Centers of Excellence program, DHS has invested in university-based partnerships to develop centers of multidisciplinary research where important fields of inquiry can be analyzed and best practices developed, debated, and shared. The department's Homeland Security Centers of Excellence (HS-Centers) bring together the nation's best experts and focus its most talented researchers on a variety of threats that include agricultural, chemical, biological, nuclear/radiological, explosive, and cyber terrorism as well as the behavioral aspects of terrorism.

These are the current HS-Centers:

- DHS selected the University of Southern California (partnering with the University of Wisconsin at Madison, New York University, North Carolina State University, Carnegie Mellon University, Cornell University, and others) to house the first HS-Center, known as the Homeland Security Center for Risk and Economic Analysis of Terrorism Events (CREATE). The department is providing the University of Southern California and its partners with $12 million over the course of 3 years for the study of risk analysis related to the economic consequences of terrorist threats and events. (Awarded November 2003.)

- Texas A&M University and its partners were awarded $18 million over the course of 3 years for the Homeland Security National Center for Foreign Animal and Zoonotic Disease Defense. Texas A&M University has assembled a team of experts from across the country, which includes partnerships with the University of Texas Medical Branch, University of California at Davis, University of Southern California and University of Maryland. Texas A&M University's HS-Center will work closely with partners in academia, industry, and government to address potential threats to animal agriculture including foot-and-mouth disease, Rift Valley fever, Avian influenza, and brucellosis. Their research on foot-and-mouth disease will be carried out in close collaboration with Homeland Security's Plum Island Animal Disease Center. (Awarded April 2004.)

- The University of Minnesota and its partners were awarded $15 million for the Homeland Security Center for Food Protection and Defense, which will address agro-security issues related to post-harvest food protection. The University of Minnesota's team includes partnerships with major food companies as well as other universities including Michigan State University, University of Wisconsin at Madison, North Dakota State University, Georgia Institute of Technology, Rutgers University, Harvard University, University of Tennessee, Cornell University, Purdue University and North Carolina State University. (Awarded April 2004.)

In FY 2006, $64 million in funding will be available for university programs. DHS released a broad agency announcement in 2005 for proposals for the next round of grants for the HS-Center program. The focus area for this next center is high-consequence event preparedness and response. The center will perform research into preparation for disasters—high-consequence events—with special emphasis on acts of terrorism. Its research will address the technical, systemic, behavioral, and organizational challenges such events pose. The center will engage in mission-oriented research to significantly enhance the capabilities of first responders and others.

## MARITIME RESEARCH

The scope of the S&T Directorate encompasses the pursuit of a full range of research into the use, preservation, and exploitation of the national waterways and oceans. The U.S. Coast Guard Research and Development Center is in charge of conducting research to support defense of this resource and of the homeland.

## U.S. COAST GUARD (WWW.USCG.MIL)

The Research and Development (R&D) Center is the Coast Guard's sole facility performing research, development, test, and evaluation (RDT&E) in support of the Coast Guard's major missions of maritime mobility, maritime safety, maritime security, national defense, and protection of natural resources. The center has as its mission "to be the Coast Guard's pathfinder, anticipating and meeting future technological challenges, while partnering with others to shepherd the best ideas into implementable solutions."

The Coast Guard RDT&E program produces two types of products: the development of hardware, procedures, and systems that directly contribute to increasing the quality and productivity of the operations and the expansion of knowledge related to technical support of operating and regulatory programs. Some of the programs are included in Appendix 9-10.

## R&D EFFORTS EXTERNAL TO DHS

## DEPARTMENT OF HEALTH AND HUMAN SERVICES

### National Institutes of Health

The National Institutes of Health's (NIH's) most relevant effort in homeland security R&D is in bioterrorism-related research. It has conducted work in the field for much longer than the existence of the Department of Homeland Security, but it emerged as a high-priority R&D agency after the 2001 anthrax mail situation. Budget allocations, which tend to be a reliable predictor of federal priorities, have clearly indicated that this dedication to bioterrorism detection and countermeasures remains. In the FY 2006 budget, NIH saw an increase in funding (even though it was only 0.4% over FY 2005), to $1.8 billion. Analysts have shown, however, that despite the small increase in overall funding, a smaller amount of construction costs in FY 2006 translate to an actual increase in biodefense R&D funding of 8%.

With $1.7 billion in funding going to grant-funded research, NIH is clearly the leader within the federal government for homeland security R&D efforts. Most of this amount is funded by the National Institute of Allergy and Infectious Disease (NIAID). The 2006 priorities for NIAID include the clinical development of vaccines for several diseases with bioterrorism applications including plague and tularemia, and also the funding of preclinical development of potential therapies for use in bioterrorism attacks.

In addition to the funds dedicated to NIAID, the secretary of HHS has been allocated $97 million for funding the development of medical countermeasures against nuclear, radiological, and chemical terrorism threats. Several of the NIAID initiatives are provided in Appendix 9-11.

### Centers for Disease Control and Prevention (CDC)

Another agency of HHS, the Centers for Disease Control and Prevention (CDC), which funds bioterrorism R&D at its own laboratories, receives the rest of the related R&D funding allocated in HHS. The amount received by CDC is less than $100 million and is focused on the surveillance of biological terrorism indicators. The majority of CDC terrorism activities are not research and development in nature, and include the management of the Strategic National Stockpile (SNS), and funding for state and local responders to upgrade their abilities to prepare for and manage WMD events.

## DEPARTMENT OF DEFENSE

The Department of Defense (DOD) has had a fluctuating budget for homeland security R&D since 2001. In FY 2006, DOD enjoyed an increase in R&D funding of 8.7%, to a total allocation of $394 million. The vast majority of DOD R&D funding is provided through the Defense Advanced Research Projects Agency (DARPA), which works mainly on applications that serve the needs of the military (e.g., biological warfare defense and the Chemical and Biological Defense Program). The outcome of this research, however, often has applications that can be applied by civilian first responders despite the military origin of the projects that generated them.

## DEPARTMENT OF AGRICULTURE

Like DOD, USDA has witnessed fluctuating R&D budgets since the September 11 terrorist attacks. FY 2004 was the year in which their funding was cut the most, while most other years it remained at well over $150 million per year. Since 9/11, USDA has invested a considerable amount of research effort toward developing security mechanisms to protect dangerous pathogens, which could be used as terror weapons, which are located in many laboratories dispersed throughout the United States. Much of the more recent increases in funding, mainly FY 2005 and FY 2006, were dedicated to renovating facilities that performed animal research and diagnosis at the National Centers for Animal Health in Ames, Iowa. These efforts are aimed at protecting the U.S. food supply from acts of sabotage and terrorism—both of which could have potentially devastating effects on the U.S. economy. The FY 2006 funding for USDA homeland security R&D efforts is $172 million.

## ENVIRONMENTAL PROTECTION AGENCY

The Environmental Protection Agency (EPA), which has seen steady but small federal allocation of homeland security R&D funding since September 11, experienced an enormous increase in funding in FY 2006. The EPA allocation jumped over 185%, from $33 million in FY 2005 to $94 million in FY 2006. EPA research related to homeland security is divided between two focus areas: drinking water security research (which would involve EPA efforts to develop better surveillance and laboratory networks for drinking water supplies to counter potential terrorist threats) and decontamination research (to develop better technologies and methods for decontaminating terrorist attack sites). EPA also conducts threat and consequence assessments and testing potential biodefense and other decontamination technologies. Much of this work is conducted at EPA's National Homeland Security Research Center (NHSRC) in Cincinnati. EPA R&D efforts are detailed in Appendix 9-12.

## NATIONAL INSTITUTE OF STANDARDS AND TECHNOLOGY

The Department of Commerce (DOC) is home to the National Institute of Standards and Technology (NIST), which funds R&D in cryptography and computer security, and which provides scientific and technical support to DHS in these areas. Examples of NIST projects are presented in Appendix 9-13.

## NATIONAL SCIENCE FOUNDATION

The National Science Foundation (NSF) funds research to combat bioterrorism in the areas of infectious diseases and microbial genome sequencing. These programs increased to $329 million in FY2006.

## CONCLUSION

Homeland security represents an entirely new spectrum of issues of R&D and technology and an opportunity to revitalize old issues under the homeland security umbrella. Establishing DHS and the S&T Directorate brought a new, major player into the federally supported R&D efforts. There was much discussion and disgruntlement within the research community concerning the lack of involvement of NSF in the development of the homeland security R&D agenda. In fact, several people questioned the need for the S&T as opposed to just increasing NSF or NIST's portfolios.

With a spectrum of activity varying from research to development to deployment, and a span of subjects from bioterrorism to personal protective equipment, from communication tools to nonproliferation, and from detection devices to mass production of vaccines, the S&T Directorate has been given a monumental task. The directorate not only coordinates the R&D facilities of many organizations but also has the authority to set priority in others. The proposed university-based HS-Centers provide a level of new funding that has not been available for some time and provide one of the best funded opportunities for specific R&D to benefit emergency management.

Although the context of change leaves little room for conclusions, the extraordinary budget given to the S&T Directorate either in existing programs or in new ones will provide the emergency management and first responder communities new capabilities never before imagined. It is to be hoped that these technological "toys" do not give a false sense of confidence and overshadow the real requirements of building an improved capacity to mitigate, prepare for, respond to, and recover from the risks of terrorism (Figure 9-4).

The changes that can be implied with the establishment of the university-based centers should be watched closely. These centers will probably provide the first and most concrete platform for the announced partnership, or "integration," of academia, the private sector, and the federal government in support of homeland security. The establishment and progress of these centers should be followed carefully and will answer two fundamental questions:

1. How ready are these sectors to work together? That is, can the most basic goal of survival and safety of the homeland be a motivation strong enough to overcome the sectors' administrative and functional differences?
2. Will real integration occur? The R&D field may be the place to show if integration at the large scale as proposed by the DHS is really possible or not. This field is probably the most appropriate one because research, development, and deployment are very close functions. But still this task may be more difficult than it seems because it involves many different organizations, whose cooperation, successes, or failures can put the success of the whole organization at risk.

FIGURE 9-4  New York City, New York, September 29, 2001—Lobby of hotel near the World Trade Center site. (Photo by Andrea Booher/FEMA News Photo)

## REVIEW QUESTIONS

1. Identify 10 specific areas of research (with their programs) that the DHS encompasses and were previously not included in FEMA or any other existing laboratories/research centers.

2. Explain in your own words the establishment of HSARPA and its scope and objectives.

3. Make a quick search about the missions and goals of the National Science Foundation (NSF) and the National Institute for Science and Technology (NIST). What is your position in the debate to put the R&D function of homeland security under the DHS or as an extension of NIST or NSF? Explain your reasoning.

4. Develop an agenda as if you were applying on behalf of your university to be a university-based HS-Center. Who are the partners (academic and private) in your region that you would like to join? What would be the strengths of this team? What specialties does your university already have that could be applied to homeland security R&D?

5. Develop a basic scheme showing all the research topics under the four major areas on which the DHS S&T Directorate focuses. Does it seem consistent to you? Would you add or subtract any topic to adjust it?

# REFERENCES

American Association for the Advancement of Science <www.aaas.org>

Argonne National Laboratory <www.anl.gov>

Brookhaven National Laboratory <www.bnl.gov/world>

Centers for Disease Control and Prevention <www.cdc.gov>

CERT Coordination Center <www.cert.org>

Chemical and Biological Defense Information and Analysis Center <www.cbiac.apgea.army.mil>

Defense Threat Reduction Agency <www.dtra.mil/cb/cb_index.html>

Department of Agriculture <www.usda.gov>

Department of Defense <www.dod.gov>

Department of Energy <www.doe.gov>

Department of Energy Laboratories <www.energy.gov>

Department of Health and Human Services <www.dhhs.gov>

Department of Homeland Security <www. dhs.gov>

Department of Justice <www.doj.gov>

Department of State <http://usembassy.state.gov>

Environmental Measurements Laboratory <www.eml.doe.gov>

Environmental Protection Agency <www.epa.gov>

Federal Computer Incident Response Center <www.fedcirc.gov>

Federal Emergency Management Agency <www.fema.gov>

Federal Response Plan <www.fema.gov/pdf/rrr/frp/frp2003.pdf>

Lawrence Livermore National Laboratory <www.llnl.gov/hso>

Los Alamos National Laboratory <www.lanl.ov/worldview>

Medical Treatment of Radiological Casualties <www.appc1.va.gov/emshg/docs/Radiologic_Medical_Countermeasures_051403.pdf>

National Communications System <www.ncs.gov>

National Infrastructure Protection Center <www.nipc.gov>

National Institute of Standards and Technology <www.nist.gov>

National Institutes of Health <www.nih.gov>

National Personal Protective Technology Laboratory <www.cdc.gov/niosh/npptl/default.html>

National Response Plan <www.nemaweb.org/docs/national_response_plan.pdf>

National Strategy for Homeland Security <www.whitehouse.gov/homeland/book>

Oak Ridge National Laboratory <www.ornl.gov>

Pacific Northwest National Laboratory <www.pnl.gov>

Plum Island Animal Disease Center <www.ars.usda.gov/plum>

RAND Science and Technology Institute <www.rand.org>

Sandia National Laboratory <www.sandia.gov>

SANS Institute <www.sans.org>

Telecommunications Service Priority. 2003. Welcome to the TSP Website. National Coordination Center for Telecommunications (NCC). TSP Website. December 4. http://tsp.ncs.gov/.

U.S. Coast Guard <www.uscg.mil>

U.S. Customs Laboratory and Scientific Services <www.customs.gov/xp/cgov/import/operations_support/labs_scientific_svcs>

U.S. Nuclear Regulatory Commission <www.nrc.gov>

# APPENDIX 9-1

## Lawrence Livermore National Laboratory Programs

### Chemical and Biological Countermeasures

Various efforts are addressing the national need for technologies to quickly detect, identify, and mitigate the use of chemical and biological threat agents against U.S. civilian populations. The principal program is the Chemical and Biological National Security Program (CBNP).

- **Biological Aerosol Sentry and Information System (BASIS)**. This joint Livermore–Los Alamos system uses a network of aerosol collectors and a central deployable field laboratory to provide early warning of biological attack. BASIS has been deployed at the 2002 Winter Olympics and elsewhere.

- **Advanced Biodetection Technology**. Miniaturized PCR technology developed at LLNL forms the basis for today's most advanced commercial biodetectors.
- **Biological Signatures**. Analyses of virulence genes and pathogen pathways to develop targeted DNA and/or protein assays that recognize even engineered organisms are performed.
- **Forensic Science Center**. This center has expertise and instrumentation for the complete chemical and isotopic analysis of nuclear materials, inorganic materials, organic materials (e.g., chemical warfare agents, explosives, illegal drugs), and biological materials (e.g., toxins, DNA).
- *In-Situ* **Chemical Sensors**. These are portable chemical sensors, for both attended and unattended operation, that can variously detect waterborne species, airborne volatiles, and particulates. Also on the way are specialized coatings, based on a range of polymers and novel materials, for improved field sampling and sample concentration.
- **Remote Chemical Sensing**. These are remote sensing systems capable of detecting and identifying a wide range of gases from high overhead and characterizing effluent materials by their spectral fingerprints. The program in chemical signatures analyzes weapons production processes to predict the emissions and other observables indicative of weapons activity.

## Nuclear and Radiological Countermeasures

This thrust area focuses on developing technical capabilities aimed at countering the threat of terrorist use of a nuclear or radiological device in or near a U.S. population center.

- **Nuclear Emergency Response**. LLNL scientists and engineers participate in the Nuclear Emergency Search Team (NEST), which responds in the event of a terrorist incident involving nuclear or radiological materials.

- **Cargo Container Security**. The Intermodal Container Evaluation and Experimental Facility provides unbiased testing of commercially available and prototype technologies for detecting nuclear materials inside cargo containers.
- **Radiation Detection**. The center is developing advanced radiation detection technologies, such as the handheld Cryo3, which uses electromechanical cooling instead of liquid nitrogen and thus is well suited for field deployment.
- **Detection and Tracking System**. This rapidly deployable network of correlated radiation detectors and cameras can detect, characterize, and track nuclear or radioactive material carried inside vehicles moving at up to freeway speeds.

### Systems Analysis and Studies

This program area focuses on identifying and understanding gaps in U.S. preparedness and response capabilities and the associated opportunities for technology.

- **Homeland Security Analysis**. Systems studies are conducted to evaluate the effectiveness of alternative approaches to early detection, interdiction, and mitigation of damage to the U.S. homeland from a range of possible threats, emphasizing weapons of mass destruction and the disruption of information systems.
- **Vulnerability Assessment**. Ongoing LLNL efforts are assessing vulnerabilities of the U.S. energy infrastructure to physical and cyber attack.
- **Outreach to Operational Entities**. LLNL interacts with representative state, regional, and local agencies to develop, test, and evaluate capabilities for preventing, detecting, and responding to WMD terrorism in real-world settings.

### Information Analysis and Infrastructure Protection

This thrust area is aimed at developing tools and capabilities for gathering, manipulating, and mining vast quantities of data and information for the dual purpose of detecting early indications and warnings of terrorist intentions, capabilities, and plans and of identifying and mitigating vulnerabilities to critical U.S. infrastructures.

- **Computer Incident Advisory Center (CIAC)**. CIAC is operated by LLNL as the Department of Energy's cyber alert and warning center. CIAC notifies the complex of vulnerabilities that are being exploited, specifies countermeasures to apply, and provides profiles of attacks. CIAC also develops cyber defense tools and technologies and provides cyber security training.
- **Information Operations and Assurance**. The Information Operations and Assurance Center provides technologies and expertise to exploit information technology as a defensive strategy and to defend critical infrastructures against attack.
- **International Assessments**. Livermore has one of the strongest capabilities in the United States for all-source analysis of foreign WMD activities by weapons states, proliferators, and terrorists, including early-stage foreign technology development and acquisition as well as patterns of cooperation.
- **Nuclear Threat Assessment**. LLNL's Nuclear Threat Assessment Center is the national center for evaluating nuclear threats and illicit nuclear trafficking cases.

### Border and Transportation Security

Activities in this area address opportunities for technology to enhance U.S. border and transportation security, from nuclear detection systems for maritime and air cargo to automated facial screening of airline passengers to integrated data management systems for immigration and border control.

- **Concrete-Penetrating Radar**. Micropower impulse radar (MIR) developed at LLNL can "see" many feet into concrete rubble; it was used at the World Trade Center rubble pile to search for survivors.

- **Baggage Screening Technologies**. Candidate technologies for improved screening of passengers and baggage are in various stages of development, including computed tomography (CT), X-ray scanning, gamma-ray imaging, neutron interrogation, and ultrasonic and thermal imaging.
- **Truck-Stopping Device**. This simple mechanical device attaches to the back of a tanker truck and can be triggered by highway patrol officers to keep a hijacked truck from becoming a motorized missile.

### Emergency Preparedness and Response

This program thrust develops technical capabilities for minimizing the damage and recovering from any terrorist attacks that do occur and works with local, regional, state, and federal first responders to ensure that the tools developed meet real-world needs.

- **National Atmospheric Release Advisory Center (NARAC)**. NARAC is the premiere capability in the United States for real-time assessments of the atmospheric dispersion of radionuclides, chemical and biological agents, and particulates. In addition to its essential role in emergency response, NARAC can also be used to evaluate specific scenarios for emergency response planning. The LINC (Local Integration of NARAC with Cities) program was recently established to facilitate access to NARAC by local and state agencies to better plan for and respond to toxic releases.
- **Joint Conflict and Tactical Simulation (JCATS)**. JCATS models urban and rural conflicts involving the movement of up to tens of thousands of people, vehicles, weapons, etc., occurring over large areas (up to half the surface of the globe) down to encounters within buildings. In addition to evaluating military tactics, JCATS can be used to assess strategies for protecting cities, industrial sites, and critical U.S. infrastructure against terrorist attack.

- **Homeland Operational Planning System (HOPS)**. HOPS is being developed, in partnership with the California National Guard, specifically for homeland security planning and analysis. HOPS analyses provide insight into the

vulnerabilities of elements of U.S. infrastructure and the likely consequences of strikes against potential terrorist targets.

*Source*: Lawrence Livermore National Laboratory.

# APPENDIX 9-2
## Sandia National Laboratory Programs

### Nuclear Weapons

The primary mission is to ensure the U.S. nuclear arsenal is safe, secure, reliable, and can fully support the nation's deterrence policy. The initiatives are as follows:

- Enhance the capabilities of radiation-hardened microelectronics to address national security issues.
- Develop simulation capabilities to model the entire nuclear weapon life cycle.
- Deliver advanced robotics systems to monitor proliferation activities, clean up hazardous sites, and disassemble old munitions.
- Improve the methods and practices used to support product delivery.
- Incorporate pulsed power technology into defense applications.
- Develop distributed information systems for the nuclear weapons complex.

### Nonproliferation and Assessments

Sandia's Nonproliferation and Assessments program reduces U.S. vulnerability to weapons of mass destruction (WMD). These include nuclear, biological, and chemical weapons, as well as nonconventional WMDs such as the highjacked civilian airlines used to commit acts of war against our nation.

- Develop technologies for early detection of proliferation activities.
- Provide leadership for policies and technologies that will bring deterrence, nonproliferation, and

nuclear energy into a constructive synergy for the 21st century.
- Develop new technologies to protect the United States from chemical and biological threats.

### Military Technologies and Applications

The Military Technologies and Applications program develops high-impact responses to national security challenges, and the existing integrated science expertise allows developing technologically superior weapons and security systems. The initiatives are as follows:

- Further develop applications of collectively intelligent systems.
- Enhance the capabilities of distributed information-rich systems to provide timely and effective solutions to critical national security issues and help divert emerging threats.
- Support Sandia's directed energy research efforts.
- Enhance technologies to defeat difficult targets.
- Continue demilitarization efforts to rid the globe of landmines.
- Improve waste legacy to dispose of the materials that cannot be reused, to store and recycle the materials that can be put to use, and to clean up contaminated areas.

### Energy and Infrastructure Assurance

The Energy and Infrastructure Assurance program supports Sandia's core purpose of helping secure the nation through technology. The goal is to enhance the surety (safety, security, and reliability) of energy and other critical infrastructures, and efforts are made in the areas of energy research, earth sciences, transportation systems, risk management technologies, environmental stewardship, and nuclear waste management. Sandia is also actively working to improve the nation's critical infrastructure surety. The focus is on infrastructure elements in the areas of transportation, electric power grid, oil and gas distribution, telecommunications, finance and banking, and vital human services. The initiatives in this matter are as follows:

- Energy Efficiency and Renewable/Fossil Energy, where much of the work centers on partnering with industrial suppliers and users of the technology.
- Critical infrastructure protection. The Sandia National Laboratories have a number of capabilities that can be applied to assist the nation in improving infrastructure surety as its primary goal is to guarantee the surety of the nuclear weapons stockpile.

- Nuclear energy. The Nuclear Energy Technology program provides relevant and defensible technical information and effective approaches for making or supporting critical decisions concerning the safety and reliability of nuclear systems. The major program areas are Nuclear Reactor Safety, Light Water Reactor Technology, International Nuclear Safety, DOE Nuclear Facilities Safety, and Risk Assessment.
- Office of Science
- Water initiative. Sandia is solving technological challenges innate to water safety, security, and sustainability and thus, enhance national security.

*Source*: Sandia National Laboratory.

# APPENDIX 9-3
## Argonne National Laboratory Programs

### Emergency Preparedness

The mission of the group is to help increase the knowledge, skills, and effectiveness of emergency managers, planners, and responders in the United States and overseas who are dealing with technological and natural disasters. It incorporates a variety of analytical tools and methods, such as exercise planning, evaluation, and review; planning standards and criteria; response planning models; classroom and field training; computer simulations; guidance and policy manuals. The programs are as follows:

- **Consequence Management**: The aim is to develop and improve planning, training, exercising, and communication systems that prepare emergency professionals to successfully manage the consequences of high-impact disasters. The program also provides detection and modeling technologies, information systems, and decision support tools that strengthen preparedness and response efforts.

- **Chemical Stockpile Emergency Preparedness Program (CSEP)**: This program is a national initiative intended to enhance resources, training, public education, and plans for an accidental release of chemical weapons agent from any of the continental U.S. stockpile storage installations. The program involves a unique integrated effort, including not only the eight U.S. Army Soldier and Biological Chemical Command (SBCCOM) storage installations, but also the 10 states and 39 counties that could be affected. The Decision and Information Sciences (DIS) provides a wide variety of scientific and technical support, including the following:
  - Policy and guidance development

- Training in emergency exercise evaluation, local response methods, emergency risk communications, and planning
- Emergency exercise scenario preparation, exercise control, and exercise evaluation
- Emergency planning methods development, modeling support, software development, and site-specific assistance

DIS collaborates with Oak Ridge National Laboratory and Pacific Northwest National Laboratory in this endeavor. DIS has contributed a number of key products and services to the national CSEP Program such as developing an installation-based team of emergency planners; initiating the national emergency exercise program; modeling potential agent deposition patterns to enable development of personal protective equipment specifications; developing and implementing a quality assurance program for each installation's meteorological towers; conducting emergency spokesperson training for installation and community leaders to interact with the media during an accident; drafting national guidance on how communities should use memorandums of understanding to enter into mutual aid agreements; developing the Alabama Special Population Planner to enable GIS-based emergency planning for special populations and special facilities; and inventing the Emergency Response Synchronization Matrix to facilitate multi-jurisdictional emergency planning.

- **The Alabama Special Population Planner (SPP)**: This is the first geographic information system (GIS)-based software tool designed to facilitate emergency planning for "special populations" and "special facilities." By using its tools and data, SPP allows users to develop specific plans to meet the unusual emergency planning problems posed by special populations and special facilities.
- **Chemical Incident Modeling**: Preparedness for the always possible chemical spills from the many industrial chemicals transported requires good science on the likely human impacts of the spread as well as a means of transferring that information in an easy-to-use form for the first

responder. The lab has developed a methodology for determining Initial Isolation and Protective Action Distances (PAD) appearing in the 2000 Emergency Response Guidebook. The objective for choosing the PADs specified in the guidebook was to balance the need to adequately protect the public from exposure to potentially harmful substances against the risks and expenses that could result from overreacting to a spill.

- **Policy and Guidance Development**: The lab has prepared guidance documents that provide information about hazardous materials, emergency plans, procedures, equipment, training, drills, and exercises needed to prepare for and respond to HAZMAT emergencies.
- **Preparedness Evaluation**: Careful review of plans and procedures along with on-site assessments of personnel, equipment, training, and facilities helps provide a complete picture of an organization's ability to react quickly and effectively during a crisis to protect lives, property, and the environment. The organization has assisted different federal, state, and local governments in developing and improving their emergency preparedness and response capabilities.
- **Synchronization Matrix**: As the complexity of emergency response planning increases because of expanding interjurisdictional and organizational interactions, it becomes exceedingly more difficult for a person to understand and visualize the interplay of a complete set of response plans, procedures, and checklists and to manage them within a synchronized community response. The lab has a systems-based process solution by which emergency planners and responders can coordinate, integrate, and synchronize their emergency plans. Argonne's emergency response synchronization matrix (ERSM) was developed to organize the increasingly complex interjurisdictional response necessary to meet the Chemical Stockpile Emergency Preparedness Program (CSEPP) response requirements.
- **Risk Communication**: Communicating effectively through the media requires an understanding of the media's role and constraints. As the

key decision makers and public affairs officials lack all the tools they need to anticipate media response and to convey information in a way that ensures it will be correctly interpreted and disseminated, Argonne has developed a full-service, full-cycle approach to planning, training, and exercising.

- Planning services focus on the creation and implementation of strong and effective risk communication plans for all-hazards, specific hazards, and specific emergencies, such as acts of terrorism.
- Training courses build skills and explore the conceptualization and operation of a successful emergency information effort from Joint Information Center/System to spokesperson training.
- Exercise support includes scenario development and preplanning as well as execution of realistic tests of the emergency information program.
- Product development includes multimedia materials to enhance public outreach and education efforts and to enhance public information/affairs programs and staff skills and knowledge.

### Environmental Assessment Division

The Environmental Assessment Division (EAD) develops and applies tools and approaches to help prevent natural and man-made disasters, improve response to ongoing incidents, and address the consequences of incidents. EAD's experience helps analysts, decision-makers, and first responders to:

- Reduce the nation's vulnerability to an attack.
- Manage the flow of information during an incident.
- Address issues related to recovery after an event.

Efforts to reduce vulnerability to terrorist actions parallel EAD's ongoing activities to safeguard the workplace and the environment from vandalism, human error, and adverse natural events. These efforts include the following: risk mitigation and assessment

for critical facilities and systems, hazardous waste management, advanced modeling and analysis, web-based risk management training, and web-based information management.

EAD also has experience modeling the potential effects of attacks on the general population and economy, as well as addressing environmental issues associated with chemical warfare agents, explosives, industrial chemicals, and nuclear materials.

Other activities include the following:

- Integrate information management tools across the entire spectrum of homeland security threats is critical to analysts, decision makers, and first responders.
- Conduct real-time threat analysis for determining appropriate emergency response actions (e.g., sheltering, decontamination, evacuation, and addressing the situation of individuals with special needs in times of emergency).
- Address recovery and cleanup efforts including chemical and nuclear damage assessment, gaseous dispersion modeling, surface and groundwater modeling, hazardous material transportation, and public awareness.

### Nonproliferation

The mission of the Nonproliferation and National Security Department (NNS) is to carry out research and development, provide technical support, and build prototype systems in order to further U.S. government initiatives and policies in nuclear materials safeguards and security, arms control treaty verification, nonproliferation of weapons of mass destruction, Material Protection Control and Accountability initiatives for nuclear materials in Russia and the NIS, and related national security areas. The lab works were also directed to international safeguards, leading to innovative concepts such as safeguard seals, short-notice random inspections; mail table declarations, and zone approaches. The NNS Department is currently working on establishing capabilities in counterterrorism and critical infrastructure protection.

*Source*: Argonne National Laboratory.

## APPENDIX 9-4
## Oak Ridge National Laboratory Centers and Programs

**Technology Advantage Center**

The center functions as a clearinghouse and broker for technologies that can be used in protecting the nation against threats to its safety and security. To identify candidate technologies, the center is developing an automated search engine that uses intelligent software agents to perform tailored, high-speed searches of relevant electronic information. Augmenting the search engine is a network of contacts that spans government, industry, academia, and other sources, ensuring that the latest information in emerging technologies is included.

The center can also assist customers with technology testing, technology road map preparation, rapid prototyping, and technology implementation.

The center has assessed the capabilities of a "See Inside Rooms" technology for a DOD agency and orchestrated the vision for Objective Force Warrior, a major U.S. Army science and technology initiative, including a comprehensive review of high-tech solutions that will be available by 2010 and 2018.

The programs that the center is working on are as follows: biological countermeasures, radiological and nuclear countermeasures, chemical and high explosives countermeasures, critical infrastructure protection, information synthesis and analysis, vulnerability/threat assessment, and wireless communication and network.

**Technological Capabilities**

The various technological capabilities of the Oak Ridge National Laboratory are as follows:

- **Chemical/Biological  Detection**:  Advanced biosensors, advanced multifunctional biochips, chemical mass spectrometer, calorimetric spectrometer for chem-bio detection, countermeasures to attacks on water supplies, infrared laser array for chem-bio agent detection (LADAR), infrared camera to detect and track chemical plume
- **Equipment**: Military equipment condition monitoring, technologies for the assessment of heat damage to composite materials and structure
- **Mass Spectroscopy**: Boarding pass analyzer, calorimetric spectroscopy
- **Models and Simulations** of GIS, Landscan, HPAC, SensorNet
- **Multipurpose Technologies**: Compact high-power light source for LADAR, graphite foam, innovative integration of electronics, microsensor array platform
- **Personal Protection**: Advanced ceramic and countermine, biochip, inorganic membranes, microclimate conditioning
- **Sensors:** DOE industrial wireless program, integrated multichannel sensors, fiber-optic sensor suite of skills, sensor-based tagging and tracking, ultra-weak-signal sensing, nanophotonic sensor materials/systems
- **Software**: IntelAgents, Total Online Access Data System (TOADS)

*Source*: Oak Ridge National Laboratory.

## APPENDIX 9-5
### Pacific Northwest National Laboratories Programs

**Homeland Security**

Pacific Northwest National Laboratories (PNNL) is assessing the vulnerability of critical infrastructures across the nation as well as teaming with organizations to ensure the air and sea ports are protected from the threat of terrorist attacks. Around the globe, PNNL is training border enforcement officials to thwart the smuggling of chemical, biological or nuclear materials across foreign borders. The lab works on the following:

- Sensors and electronics for threat detection
- Cyber security and information assurance
- Information visualization
- Dynamic Information Analysis Laboratory
- Atmospheric monitoring and research
- Center for Coastal Security and Protection
- Weapons of Mass Destruction Emergency Response

**High-Tech Crime Fighting**

The aim is to develop technological capabilities and tools to investigate crime precisely and rapidly, assess possible risks of consequences, and determine whether incidents of unknown reasons are accidental or voluntary. Some of the programs are as follows:

- Investigating airline crashes for reason of crash
- Getting to the root of the agro-terror problem
- Tools for law enforcement agents to access, enter, and transfer large amounts of information at the crime scenes
- Tracking down deadly pathogens with mass spectrometry
- Visualization software to analyze large amount of compiled data
- Developing methods for assessing accuracy and strength of forensic evidence

- Establishing the Critical Infrastructure Protection and Analysis Center to research and develop tools to safeguard key assets
- Handwriting analysis tool
- Nonintrusive weapon detection

**Information Security Resource Center**

The Information Security Resource Center (ISRC) provides support to the Department of Energy Security Policy Staff in the Office of Security by serving as a Center of Excellence for information security issues. The ISRC provides programmatic and technical support in the areas of information security, facility surveys and approvals, foreign ownership, and control or influence and maintains the DOE Incident Tracking and Analysis Center (ITAC). The ISRC also helps to identify and mitigate security threats and vulnerabilities and provides awareness to the DOE complex through the publication of advisory notices and crosstalks.

**Pacific Northwest Center for Global Security**

The Pacific Northwest Center for Global Security was established in October 1998 by the Department of Energy's Pacific Northwest National Laboratory, with four principal objectives:

- *Coordinate* the arms control, proliferation prevention, emergency response, and regional security activities of the PNNL, serving as the point of contact on nonproliferation and global security issues, and providing a window to the laboratory's scientific and technical resources
- *Partner* with organizations throughout the Pacific Northwest, particularly universities and nongovernmental organizations, on nonproliferation and global security activities
- *Position* the National Nuclear Security Administration (NNSA) and the Pacific Northwest National Laboratory to respond to changing

conditions of the post–Cold War environment by emphasizing the broader issues of global security and addressing both the traditional and non-traditional aspects of proliferation prevention and regional stability

- *Inform* the laboratory about the current state of global security and nonproliferation, and introduce scholars and policy makers to laboratory programs and staff through a seminar series, workshops, and conferences.

One central purpose of PNNL's global security activities is to help minimize the conditions under which nations or peoples proliferate weapons of mass destruction. A second purpose is to develop a better understanding of the threats posed by environmental, energy, and information security issues and to reduce those threats, especially in regions where the stakes of tension and instability are raised by the presence of weapons of mass destruction. The center combines traditional approaches to global security, such as reducing stockpiles of weapons of mass destruction

with nontraditional approaches (such as economic transition, energy, and environmental security) that increase regional stability.

### Real-Time Engine Diagnostics-Prognostics

Artificial intelligence aims to increase battlefield readiness by diagnosing engine problems in tanks before costly repairs are needed. PNNL is developing REDI-PRO, or Real-time Engine Diagnostics-Prognostics, a prototype system to diagnose and predict failures and abnormal operations in the M1 Abrams main battle tank's turbine engine.

### Information Technology

A new software tool known as Starlight being developed at PNNL enables the user to sift through the blizzard of information to discover trends or hidden information. Using Starlight's interactive, investigative tools, it is possible to characterize data, query and search for information, and visualize results using high-fidelity, 3-D graphics.

*Source*: Pacific Northwest National Laboratories.

## APPENDIX 9-6
### Other Department of Energy Objectives and Laboratories

### Nuclear Security

The Department of Energy, through the National Nuclear Security Administration (NNSA), works to enhance national security through the military application of nuclear energy. The NNSA also maintains and enhances the safety, reliability, and performance of the United States' nuclear weapons stockpile, including the ability to design, produce, and test, in order to meet national security requirements.

NNSA has four missions with regard to National Security:

- To provide the U.S. Navy with safe, militarily effective nuclear propulsion plants and to ensure the safe and reliable operation of those plants

- To promote international nuclear safety and nonproliferation
- To reduce global danger from weapons of mass destruction
- To support U.S. leadership in science and technology

### Intelligence

The DOE has stewardship of vital national security capabilities, from nuclear weapons to leading-edge research and development projects. These capabilities, and related DOE programs, are important not only to the national strength but, within the framework of international cooperation, to the lessening of global threats.

## Counterterrorism

Department activities are focused on protecting our nuclear weapons secrets but also place a high priority on protecting the other sensitive scientific endeavors and on combining with other departmental elements in the efforts to defeat terrorism.

## Weapons of Mass Destruction

DOE is an integral part of the United States' efforts to reduce global danger from weapons of mass destruction. The deputy administrator for defense nuclear nonproliferation within NNSA is responsible for the enhancement of national security through the following four-part strategy:

- Protecting or eliminating weapons and weapons-usable nuclear material or infrastructure and redirecting excess foreign weapons expertise to civilian enterprises
- Preventing and reversing the proliferation of weapons of mass destruction
- Reducing the risk of accidents in nuclear fuel cycle facilities worldwide
- Enhancing the capability to detect weapons of mass destruction, including nuclear, chemical, and biological systems.

## Emergency Response

As a high-visibility shipper of radioactive material, the U.S. Department of Energy and its transportation activities have come under intense scrutiny from Congress, states, tribes, local governments, and the public. An underlying concern is the adequacy of emergency-preparedness along DOE shipping corridors. The Environmental Management Program implements the complex-wide Transportation Emergency Preparedness Program (TEPP) to address preparedness issues for nonclassified/nonweapons radioactive material shipments. As an element of the DOE Comprehensive Emergency Management System, TEPP provides support to DOE and other federal, state, tribal, and local authorities to prepare for a response to a transportation incident involving DOE shipments of radioactive material. TEPP is implemented on a regional basis, with a TEPP coordinator designated for each of the eight DOE Regional Coordinating Offices.

## Oversight

The Office of Independent Oversight and Performance Assurance (OA) is the independent oversight organization for the secretary of energy and for the administrator of the National Nuclear Security Administration. As a corporate resource, it conducts evaluations to verify that the department's safeguards and security interests are protected, that the department can effectively respond to emergencies, and that site workers, the public, and the environment are protected from hazardous operations and materials.

*Source*: Department of Energy.

## APPENDIX 9-7
### Selected Environmental Measurements Laboratory Programs

**Modeling Atmospheric Transport**

In collaboration with the World Meteorological Organization (WMO), Global Atmosphere Watch (GAW), the Chinese Academy of Meteorological Sciences, and the Chinese Academy of Sciences, measurements are being made using EML's Surface Air Sampling System at Mt. Waliguan in Qinghai Province in central China. The measurements will be used to study the transport process in the atmosphere and will provide unique scientific data for global atmospheric modeling. This collaboration is part of EML's role as a World Calibration Center for Radioactivity in GAW.

**International Environmental Sample Archive**

EML's International Environmental Sample Archive (IESA) maintains a unique and extensive archive of environmental samples collected throughout the world. Many of these were collected during the period of atmospheric nuclear weapons testing and have unique isotopic compositions. These samples can be used for the following: quality control—test newly developed instruments and techniques;

nonproliferation—identify signatures of nuclear proliferation; background—determine global variations of signatures.

**Nonproliferation Treaties**

As a federal laboratory, EML supports DOE's national security mission through its detection and deterrence activities for the nonproliferation treaties. EML has been designated as the U.S. Radionuclide Laboratory in support of the International Monitoring System. Development and evaluation of detection systems to aid international weapons inspectors in verification compliance will cross over into counterterrorism applications.

**EML's Global Radioactivity Sampling Network**

EML has maintained a worldwide network of aerosol and deposition sampling stations for more than 40 years. Currently, there are 10 domestic sites. The network serves to identify any new sources of radioactivity released into the environment.

*Source*: Environmental Measurement Laboratory.

## APPENDIX 9-8
### USDA/DHS Common Activity Goals

- Develop new strategies to prevent and control foreign or emerging animal disease epidemics through a better understanding of the nature of infectious organisms; their pathogenesis in susceptible animals; the host immune responses; the development of novel vaccines; and the development and improvement of diagnostic tests.
- Conduct diagnostic investigations of suspected cases of foreign or emerging animal diseases in

the United States or in countries abroad through cooperation with animal health international organizations.
- Test imported animals and animal products to assure they are free of foreign animal disease agents.
- Assess risks involved in importation of animals and animal products from countries where epidemic foreign animal diseases occur.

- Produce and maintain materials used in diagnostic tests for foreign animal diseases.
- Test and evaluate vaccines for foreign animal diseases and maintain the North American foot-and-mouth disease vaccine bank.
- Train veterinarians and animal health professionals in the diagnosis and recognition of foreign animal diseases through courses at PIADC and at other domestic and international locations.
- Contribute to DHS's biological countermeasures program in the S&T Directorate, which seeks to

reduce the probability and potential consequences of a biological attack on the nation's civilian population and its agricultural system.

- Concentrate on high-consequence biological threats, including agricultural diseases such as foot-and-mouth disease and high-volume contamination of food supplies.

*Source*: Plume Island Animal Disease Center and DHS.

# APPENDIX 9-9
## U.S. Customs Laboratories

### Research Laboratory

The Research Laboratory is a centralized research facility that provides scientific support to Customs Headquarters and the field laboratories. The laboratory develops new analytical methods and evaluates new instrumentation for application by the field laboratories. Analytical services are also provided to Customs' legal and regulatory functions and to other headquarters offices that may need scientific support, including quality assurance for the Customs Drug Screening Program and technical assistance for the Canine Enforcement Program and for international drug training programs. The Research Laboratory is an important resource in addressing tariff classification issues for high-technology products, in developing statistical data to confirm the country of origin of imported commodities, and in providing a sound technical foundation for Intellectual Property Rights (IPR) enforcement involving copyrights, trademarks, and patents.

### New York Laboratory

In addition to the analysis of imported merchandise, the New York Laboratory does the following:

- Provides scientific advice for the ruling program and preentry assessment of the National Commodity Specialist Division.
- Provides technical information on drawback cases.
- Responds to requests for scientific advice to assistant chief counsel and the Department of Justice on issues before the Court of International Trade.
- Provides narcotic test kit training by our forensic chemists to Customs officers and agents.
- Manages a computerized database of chemicals entered under the HTS, which as of now consists of 5,000 entries.
- Has a strong textile program, and provides training in the use of the textile field kit.
- Has on staff the National Petroleum Chemist responsible for the East Coast.

It also specializes in metals, chemicals, textiles and footwear, building stone, consumer products, polymers and plastics, paper and food products.

### Chicago Laboratory Customs Service Area

This laboratory is located in Chicago's Customhouse and is a full-service laboratory, providing technical advice and analytical services to Customs officers and other entities on a wide range of issues and imported commodities. These services assist Customs officers in meeting the primary Customs mission of collecting revenue based on import duties and enforcing Customs and related laws. The Chicago Laboratory has a Customs-only tensile tester capable of determining certain physical characteristics of industrial fasteners and other steel articles. The laboratory has had a strong involvement in the geological identification of building stones under the harmonized tariff schedule. Because of its northern location, NAFTA issues and Canadian merchandise are prevalent. In the forensics area, the Chicago laboratory is, at present, the only Customs laboratory with the capability to enhance video and audio tapes for Customs enforcement officers. The laboratory also has a mini photo processor to develop standard color-print film, can provide enlargements, and can process black-and-white film.

## Savannah Laboratory (Including San Juan Branch) Customs Service Area

This laboratory is a full-service analytical laboratory with capabilities for chemical and physical testing of all types of commodities, narcotics and other controlled substances. The laboratory specializations are generally related to textile and apparel analyses. The laboratory is designated as Customs' testing facility for wool, which includes determining clean content and wool grade. Additionally, the laboratory is uniquely capable of determining if upholstery fabrics meet tariff requirements and for determining tensile strengths of textile products.

## New Orleans Laboratory Customs Service Area

The services provided by the New Orleans Laboratory include analyses of a broad range of imported and exported commodities and merchandise to determine whether said merchandise is properly described by the required documentation or identified as contraband according to its physical and chemical nature. This laboratory is also responsible for providing technical support in areas such as drawback, classification

issues, and regulatory audit functions as well as for criminal and civil investigations. In addition to the normal work of a U.S. Customs Field Laboratory, the New Orleans Laboratory has three areas of specialization:

- Raising fingerprints off of objects is an expertise developed by this laboratory so that the Customs Service would have this capability in-house. State-of-the-art instrumentation is available that can digitize fingerprints and match the prints electronically to known fingerprints in its database. Furthermore, the instrument will be able to match raised prints to the FBI's Automated Fingerprint Identification System (AFIS) database once that system is released.
- One of the three National Petroleum Chemists is assigned to the New Orleans laboratory. The major duties of this position include the following: refinery foreign trade zone operations, country-of-origin determination of petroleum, analysis of petroleum products for composition, review of applications for drawback of petroleum products, and review of Public Gauger/Laboratory facilities for compliance to Customs regulations.
- The only biologist in the Customs Service is on staff at this laboratory. One of the major duties of this position is to introduce new ways of analyzing samples of a biological nature to the laboratory system.

## Los Angeles Laboratory Customs Service Area

Within its service area, the Los Angeles Laboratory does the following:

- Provides preentry technical advice on classification of commodities.
- Analyzes entered merchandise for compliance with Customs laws and/or other agency requirements enforced by Customs.
- Examines merchandise for technical conformity with copyright, patent, trademark, and marking laws.

- Provides Customs officers with advice on sampling and handling of hazardous materials and chemicals.
- Supports Customs efforts on technical issues concerned with commercial fraud and drawback enforcement.
- Advises the Department of Justice on technical matters related to Customs laws.
- Provides forensic support such as analysis of controlled substances and technical advice in forensic areas to Customs officers.
- Provides general scientific support to Customs officers in the service area of textiles analysis (mostly finished wearing apparel) and specialized textile analyses such as printed/dyed fabrics and hand/power-loomed fabrics. Conducts intellectual property rights analysis, motor testing, hazardous materials handling and analysis.

### San Francisco Laboratory Customs Service Area

The San Francisco laboratory is a full-service laboratory that provides technical advice and analytical services to Customs officials and other agencies on a wide range of imported and exported commodities. Available to the technical staff are analytical instruments such as optical spectrophotometers, scanning electron microscopes, gas chromatograph-mass spectrometers, gas and liquid chromatographs, and X-ray diffraction meters and spectrographs.

Many samples of wearing apparel, footwear, building stone, metal products, foods, beverages, chemicals, and controlled substances are analyzed each year in the laboratory. Expedited services are provided on samples involving intellectual property rights (IPR), textiles that require quota, and visa and forensics. If samples cannot be brought to the laboratory, mobile laboratories are available to conduct on-site examinations.

Because of the laboratory's location on the Pacific Rim, there is an emphasis and greater expertise in that commerce which includes the following: textiles, including intermediates of the manufacturing process as well as finished wearing apparel; oriental food and beverages; and electronics. And because of the very significant value of petroleum importations, the laboratory specializes in petroleum chemistry. A special emphasis of this work targets the country of origin of crude oil and some of its finished products such as aviation fuel.

*Source*: U.S. Customs and Border Protection.

## APPENDIX 9-10
## U.S. Coast Guard Programs

### Intelligent Waterway System

- **Vessel Traffic Management Research**: The present methods, used to gather and distribute vessel traffic and marine safety information, need improvement. New approaches are needed to improve the timeliness of information, increase overall distribution capacity and quality, and conform to the operation of modern navigation systems. This project aims to investigate, develop, test, and demonstrate technologies, methods, and standards useful for providing future vessel traffic management safety and mobility information using fully automated means. Particular emphasis will be placed on information interfaces that automatically gather and deliver safety and mobility information to the marine operator.
- **Waterways Information Network**: Effective, efficient information exchange with the maritime public and cooperating agencies is the key element to close performance gaps in several areas of marine and navigation safety, but there is no standardized method to exchange and improve the timeliness of waterway relevant information within the larger USCG, federal, state, port, and responsible party "stakeholder" communities.

This project aims to develop a low-cost, seamless information infrastructure to exchange security, navigation, marine safety, and other data with other agencies, the maritime industry, and the public.

## Risk Competency

- **Port State Control Targeting Matrix (PSCTM)**: Based on a standard statistical analysis, none of the five risk factors associated with the PSCTM were statistically significant in predicting noncompliance. Hence, it does not adequately meet the needs of the Coast Guard to identify those foreign-flagged vessels that pose the greatest risk to our ports. This program aims to produce an improved PSCTM that will adjust the risk factors so that Coast Guard personnel can identify and board vessels that are more likely to pose safety or environmental threats to the nation's ports and waterways.

- **Planning and Management**: The Coast Guard pursues, under the constraint of limited resources, a multiplicity of risk-based performance goals, including public safety, environmental protection, and marine commerce. Due to the ever-changing demands on the resources and capabilities for effectively managing the safety of ports, waterways, and maritime industry, the Coast Guard needs to develop the guidelines and technical frameworks that will support a marine safety core competency in Coast Guard risk-based decision-making (RBDM). This research will develop risk-based approaches that can optimize existing decision-making processes in the field. Some programs concerning oil spill response are also available, and more detail can be found on the U.S. Coast Guard website.

*Source*: U.S. Coast Guard.

## APPENDIX 9-11
### National Institute of Allergies and Infectious Diseases

**Partnerships in Product Development**

In addition to awarding contracts for second-generation smallpox and anthrax vaccines, the National Institute of Allergies and Infectious Diseases (NIAID) has expanded other collaborative opportunities with industry. Though the Biodefense Partnerships program, which is a new mechanism that encourages private-sector research and development of countermeasures and a similar initiative that includes academia—cooperative research for the development of vaccines, adjuvant, therapeutics, immunotherapeutic and diagnostics for biodefense and SARS—NIAID is funding 31 grants to companies to develop high-priority biodefense products.

**Basic Research**

NIAID awarded eight Regional Centers of Excellence for Biodefense and Emerging Infectious Diseases Research. This nationwide network of multidisciplinary academic centers is conducting wide-ranging research on infectious diseases and the development of diagnostics, therapeutics, and vaccines. In addition, through partnerships with other agencies and companies around the world, NIAID has made a significant investment in sequencing pathogen genomes. Finally, dozens of grants made to individual investigators at academic institutions nationwide are opening new avenues for improving the existing ability to prevent, diagnose, and treat diseases caused by potential agents of terrorism.

**Biodefense Research Resources and Facilities**

NIAID is funding the construction of new biosafety laboratories around the country to address the serious shortage of such facilities to safely conduct research on biodefense and emerging infectious diseases. It also has developed and expanded contracts to screen new drugs; develop new animal models; establish a reagent and specimen repository; and provide researchers with genomic, proteomic, and bioinformatic resources.

**Immunology**

NIAID is funding research to better understand the body's own protective mechanisms. In particular, one recent large-scale grant is funding sophisticated studies of the human innate immune system. Another new set of grants has established a network of researchers focused on studies of the human immune system and biodefense.

*Source*: National Institutes of Health.

# APPENDIX 9-12
## Environmental Protection Agency Programs

On September 24, 2002, EPA announced the formation of the Homeland Security Research Center (NHSRC) headquartered in Cincinnati, Ohio. The NHSRC—part of the Office of Research and Development (ORD)—manages, coordinates and supports a variety of research and technical assistance efforts to provide state-of-the-art scientific knowledge and technology to emergency responders, building owners, drinking and wastewater utility operators, health departments, and others to enhance their ability to quickly detect contamination and respond effectively.

The center provides a management structure that ensures effective design and oversight of research, and facilitates interaction with EPA program offices and regions, other federal agencies, the private sector, and research partners. The NHSRC's team of world-renowned scientists and engineers is dedicated to understanding the terrorist threat, communicating the risks, and mitigating the results of attacks. EPA's National Homeland Security Research Center, guided by the road map set forth in the EPA's Strategic Plan for Homeland Security, ensures rapid production and distribution of security-related products.

EPA research and development efforts focus on five primary areas:

- **Threat and Consequence Assessment** addresses human exposure to chemical, biological, and radiological contaminants to define dangerous levels of these contaminants and establish protective cleanup goals.
- **Decontamination and Consequence Management** focuses on decontamination of buildings and outdoor environments, as well as the safe disposal of contaminated materials.
- **Water Infrastructure Protection** is charged with protecting the nation's drinking water supplies and infrastructure, as well as wastewater collection, treatment, and disposal.
- **Response Capability Enhancement** works directly with emergency responders and local governments to provide tools and information needed to make informed decisions in the event of an attack.
- **Technology Testing and Evaluation** evaluates technologies that show potential for use in homeland security applications. These evaluations are used by water utilities, building owners, emergency responders, and others to make informed decisions when purchasing security technology.

*Source*: Environmental Protection Agency.

## APPENDIX 9-13

### National Institute of Science and Technology Projects

#### Strengthening Structural and Fire Safety Standards

An essential tool in the fight against terrorism is a solidly built and protected infrastructure. NIST is contributing to this goal on a number of fronts aimed at strengthening structural and fire safety standards in buildings.

- **Investigation of the World Trade Center (WTC) buildings' collapse**: A 24-month federal building and fire safety investigation to study the structural failure and subsequent progressive collapse of several WTC buildings following the terrorist attacks of September 11, 2001, in New York City.
- **On-site survey of Pentagon structural and fire damage**: In October 2001, a NIST expert in building and fire research participated in an on-site survey of the Pentagon structural and fire damage as part of a team organized by the American Society of Civil Engineers and led by the U.S. Army Corps of Engineers. The Army Corps of Engineers subsequently funded a team of NIST experts to review and evaluate the performance of the Pentagon's structural system.
- **Anthrax air flow study**: NIST engineers provided help in understanding how spores may have spread through the buildings. NIST experts in ventilation systems and air quality used a sophisticated NIST-developed computer model to understand different ways in which air flow may have transported spores.
- **Coordinated national strategy for protecting critical infrastructures**: NIST is actively discussing the development of a coordinated national strategy in this area with the relevant agencies—FEMA, the Department of Defense, the Department of Transportation, and the General Services Administration; state and local

building and emergency management officials; and private organizations.

#### Improved Materials for Structures

NIST is helping the engineering and construction industries improve building materials, enabling stronger, longer lasting structures, be they bridges, buildings, or off-shore oil rigs.

#### Cyber Security Standards and Technologies

NIST helps secure electronic information through programs that develop national and international standards for IT security and improve awareness of and capabilities for security solutions. Sample projects are as follows:

- The development of cryptographic standards and methods to protect the integrity, confidentiality, and authenticity of information resources. In December 2001, NIST and the Department of Commerce announced the newest and strongest yet encryption standard for the protection of sensitive, nonclassified electronic information.
- Partnership with government and industry to establish more secure systems and networks by developing, managing, and promoting security assessment tools, techniques, services, and supporting programs for testing, evaluation, and validation.
- The development of guidelines to address topics such as risk management, security program management, certification and accreditation, and security training and awareness.

#### Cyber Security of Electric Power and Industrial Control Systems

NIST is working with companies and industry organizations to identify the types of vulnerabilities that exist and to develop security requirements for the real-time systems that control the power grid and critical industrial production processes. A Process Control Security Requirements Forum has been established to identify and assess threats and risks to process control information and functions, make and promote the adoption of security requirements recommendations, and promote security awareness and integration of security considerations in the life cycle of electric power and industrial process control systems.

**Enhanced Threat Detection and Protection**

- **Ensuring proper doses for irradiation of mail**: NIST is a member of a White House task force led by the Office of Science and Technology Policy to ensure that mail intended for Congress and other federal government offices is properly irradiated to kill anthrax bacteria. NIST also is advising federal officials on possible construction of a dedicated radiation source near Washington, D.C., for future mail sanitation.

- **Weapon detection technologies and standards**: With funding from the National Institute of Justice (NIJ), NIST researchers have completed work on new performance standards and operational requirements for both walk-through and handheld metal detectors. The researchers have also created a sophisticated measurement system that uses specialized computer software to evaluate detector effectiveness. Another NIST research group has received funding from the NIJ and the Federal Aviation Administration (FAA) to investigate a new technology for weapons detection based on low-energy, millimeter-size electromagnetic waves.

- **Detection of chemical, biological, radiological and other threats**: As the primary reference laboratory for the United States, NIST develops standards, protocols, and new test methods to ensure that chemical and biological compounds can be measured accurately. This includes extensive, ongoing programs for the detection of chemical, biological, radiological, nuclear, and explosive threats.

**Tools for Law Enforcement**

For most of its 100-year history, NIST has worked closely with law enforcement, corrections, and criminal justice agencies to help improve the technologies available for solving and detecting crimes and for protecting law enforcement officers. Some of the projects are as follows:

- **Standards for biometrics**: NIST efforts to improve the technologies and standards available for definitive identification of individuals—techniques such as fingerprinting, face recognition, and DNA analysis—have taken on added urgency.

- **Standards for forensic DNA typing**: Since the development of DNA typing methods more than 10 years ago, NIST has developed a series of Standard Reference Materials (SRMs) that can be used by forensic and commercial laboratories to check the accuracy of their analyses.

- **Enhanced surveillance cameras**: By mimicking the eye and surrounding the camera with liquid instead of air, NIST researchers (with interagency Technology Support Working Group funding) hope to improve the performance of surveillance cameras substantially. This, in turn, may improve the reliability of other technologies, such as face recognition within airports.

- **Protective vests and helmets**: At its ballistic research test facility, NIST develops the test methods and conducts the evaluations needed to continually improve standards for testing the performance of bullet- and knife-resistant vests, helmets, and face shields, as well as car windows and body armor, and to keep up with changing materials and technologies.

- **Standards for bullets and casings**: NIST is developing reference material bullets and casings that forensic labs will be able to use with their own instruments to determine whether their analyses produce ballistic signatures that match those supplied by NIST.

- **Forensic tools for investigating computer or magnetic data evidence**: NIST computer scientists are helping to speed up the detection process dramatically with a new tool, the National Software Reference Library. Working with software manufacturers and others who provided copies of their programs, NIST collected "signature" formats for more than 6 million different computer files. The library allows law enforcement agencies to eliminate 25% to 95% of the total files in a computer, concentrating only on those that really might contain evidence.
- **Crimes involving pipe bombs or handguns**: NIST chemists, in conjunction with the NIJ, have come up with a reliable way to associate the composition of unfired gunpowder or ammunition with residues collected at handgun or pipe bomb crime scenes. NIST now is preparing a smokeless powder reference material that forensic laboratories will be able to use in checking the accuracy of their bomb and gunpowder residue analyses.

**Emergency Response**

- **Protecting first responders**: Existing standards for emergency responders' protective gear were drafted with accidents—not terrorism—in mind. With funding from the NIJ, NIST is facilitating the development of a suite of national chemical and biological protective equipment standards. A standard for a self-contained breathing apparatus to withstand biological and chemical assault was deemed the highest priority and has been developed. Standards for other types of breathing apparatus are in the pipeline, as are standards for personal protective suits. Standards for chemical and biological detectors also have been given a high priority.
- **Standardization of communications for first responders**: NIST, again with funding from the NIJ, is working with the public safety community to standardize techniques for wireless telecommunications and IT applications. NIST is also working with standards development organizations to have first responder requirements included within the scope of standardization efforts.
- **Development and standardization of web-based technologies**: NIST is also working on the development, deployment, and standardization of web-based technologies for integrating sensors, real-time video, smart tags, and embedded microprocessor devices to provide next-generation personnel support for remote monitoring, control, and communications in the field. This technology can enable rapid access to real-time sensor and video information and allow sharing and collaborative use of IT applications.
- **Simulation tools**: To address the need to provide accurate and thorough simulations, NIST is helping to establish a framework to allow a broad range of simulation systems to share information, including models and results. NIST is working with the response community, industry, and academia to identify information sources, simulation systems, and data requirements; develop an emergency response simulation framework and standard interfaces; and develop and demonstrate distributed simulations using commercial software and the new framework.
- **Search and rescue robots**: A NIST project aimed initially at protecting emergency personnel by minimizing the amount of time rescuers spend searching earthquake-damaged buildings has helped provide a new tool for rescue workers at the World Trade Center. Since one of NIST's goals is to foster cooperation among robotics researchers around the world, NIST supplies its test arenas to two international robotics conferences, which include competitions to see how well search-and-rescue robots perform on the NIST arena.

*Source*: National Institute of Standards and Technology.

# 10

# The Future of Homeland Security

## INTRODUCTION

This chapter is provided to identify and briefly explain several of the most pressing issues confronting the role of emergency management and disaster assistance programs in homeland security, both in general and specific to the Department of Homeland Security (DHS). Just as the Federal Emergency Management Agency (FEMA) has been the federal government leader in the national emergency management system since its 1979 inception, DHS has assumed a similar leadership role in the creation and management of a national system to ensure the security of the nation.

A measure of how effectively DHS can perform in this leadership position, and exactly what role emergency management and disaster assistance functions will ultimately play within DHS and the national homeland security system, has not been adequately developed. Their long-term performance outlook, as a result, remains very uncertain at this time.

We believe that FEMA's history offers two important lessons for DHS as it progresses in its difficult mission. The first of these lessons is that it is critical for DHS to take all of the necessary steps to ensure that the nation's emergency management and disaster assistance capabilities, especially those at the federal government level, are not marginalized. Additionally, these emergency management agencies must given the tools that enable them to effectively manage the new terrorist threat with which they have been confronted. The second lesson is that terrorism, in all of its forms, must not become the singular risk driving DHS policy. In the absence of an all-hazards approach, the scene will surely be set for a catastrophic disaster from any one of the many more likely natural and technological hazards faced by the nation. At minimum, the experience of Hurricane Katrina should serve as a wake-up call for DHS in this regard.

## THE FEMA HISTORY LESSON

Prior to 1979, federal emergency management and disaster preparedness, response, and recovery programs and capabilities were scattered among numerous federal government agencies, including the White House. There was little if any coordination among these disparate parts. Communicating with the federal government during a disaster had become such a problem that the National Governor's Association petitioned then-President Jimmy Carter, to consolidate all federal programs into a single agency.

On April 1, 1979, President Carter signed the executive order that established the Federal Emergency Management Agency, moving federal disaster programs, agencies, and offices from across the federal government into a single executive branch agency. The director of FEMA was charged with integrating these diverse programs into one cohesive operation capable of delivering federal resources and assistance through a new concept called the Integrated Emergency Management System. This system was centered on an all-hazards approach.

With the election of President Ronald Reagan in 1980, the focus of FEMA's policies and programs shifted dramatically from an all-hazards approach to a single focus on nuclear attack planning through its Office of National Preparedness. At the same time, agency leadership and personnel struggled to integrate its many diverse programs. This focus on a single low-probability/high-impact event and the inability of the agency's many parts to function effectively as one led to the disastrous responses to Hurricane Hugo, the Loma Prieta earthquake, and Hurricane Andrew. There were numerous calls for the abolition of FEMA, including from several members of Congress.

President Bill Clinton was elected in 1992 and appointed the first experienced emergency manager as director of FEMA. Under James Lee Witt's leadership, FEMA once again adopted an all-hazards approach, became a customer-focused organization that worked closely with its state and local emergency management partners and effectively responded to an unprecedented series of major disasters across the country. These included major natural disasters but also terrorist events such as the first World Trade Center bombing and the Oklahoma City bombing.

The new FEMA successfully launched a national community-based disaster mitigation initiative, Project Impact, and for the first time reached out to the nation's business community to partner in emergency management at the national and community levels.

By the time of the election of President George W. Bush in 2000, FEMA had gained the trust of the public, the media, its partners, and elected officials in all levels of government. FEMA functioned as a single agency as envisioned when it was created in 1979 and possessed one of the most favorable brand names in government.

Upon taking office in 2001, the Bush administration began to deconstruct FEMA. It was assumed that a program like Project Impact, which focused on individual and private-sector responsibility, would thrive under a Republican administration. Instead it was eliminated as not being effective, and funding for other natural disaster mitigation programs was dramatically reduced. However, the effect of Project Impact was given national media attention after an earthquake struck Seattle and the Mayor of Seattle credited his city's participation in the Project Impact program for the minimal losses the city experienced as a result of that quake.

The emphasis on the national security functions of FEMA was highlighted when new FEMA Director Joe Allbaugh reinstated the Office of National Preparedness and all indications were that FEMA would once again focus on national security issues.

This process was accelerated after the September 11, 2001, terrorist attacks. FEMA became part of the new Department of Homeland Security (DHS) and the all-hazards approach, while acknowledged in speeches, was replaced by a single focus on terrorism. More importantly, the director of FEMA no longer reported directly to the president and was replaced in the president's cabinet by the DHS secretary. In the latest DHS reorganization announced in July 2005, the FEMA of the 1990s has been disassembled and its parts spread throughout the Department of Homeland Security.

## LESSONS FOR HOMELAND SECURITY FROM THE FEMA EXPERIENCE

The writer George Santayana once famously said "Those who ignore history are doomed to repeat it." There are two critical lessons to be learned from the

FEMA experience that provide some perspective on how the Department of Homeland Security may function in the future.

First and foremost, it will take time for DHS to become a functioning organization. DHS was cobbled together in much the same way that FEMA was, bringing together an estimated 178,000 federal workers from 22 agencies and programs in a very short space of time. It took FEMA nearly 15 years and several reorganizations to effectively coordinate and deliver the full resources of the federal government to support state and local governments in responding to major disasters. DHS is less than 3 years old and it is already undertaking its first reorganization. If FEMA's experience is any kind of indicator, it will be at least a decade before DHS will achieve full functionality.

Second, the single focus on a low-probability/high-impact event (i.e., a major terrorist attack similar to September 11) will undermine DHS's capabilities in responding to high-probability/low-impact events. A FEMA staffer once said that you don't plan for the maximum event possible; you plan for the maximum event probable. This is especially critical for the former FEMA response and recovery and preparedness and mitigation programs now located in various places in DHS. In terms of natural and traditional man-made disasters (hurricanes, earthquakes, hazardous materials incidents, etc.), these programs' capabilities have been marginalized. The 2004 hurricanes in Florida and the resulting congressional and media investigations of fraud and incompetence that characterized the federal response are clear evidence of the negative impact this single focus can have in an all-hazards world.

At this time, DHS seems intent on repeating the mistakes that FEMA made in its past. These mistakes will impact all of the department's functions but none more so than the traditional emergency management functions that were once managed by FEMA: mitigation, preparedness, response and recovery.

DHS's primary mission is to prevent a terrorist attack on American soil. The emergency management and disaster assistance functions once centered in FEMA contribute little to this mission. However, should another terrorist event occur in the future, as everyone including President Bush and Vice President Cheney concede it will, these emergency management and disaster assistance functions will be critical to preparing our people, reducing the impact, and mounting an effective response and recovery that gets Americans back on their feet quickly. Marginalizing these capabilities as it pursues its primary mission is a mistake FEMA made in the past and one that DHS cannot afford to repeat now and in the future.

## THE FUTURE OF EMERGENCY MANAGEMENT IN HOMELAND SECURITY

Maintaining and enhancing the nation's emergency management system, especially the role of the federal government in this system, does not conflict with the primary mission of DHS. In fact, it is a critical element in the overall homeland security strategy. However, we feel several steps should be taken to ensure the health and vitality of the nation's emergency management system and to return the federal government to a leadership role in this area.

### REESTABLISH FEMA AS AN EXECUTIVE BRANCH AGENCY

In March 2004, former FEMA Director James Lee Witt in testimony before a joint hearing of two House Government Reform subcommittees strongly recommended that FEMA be removed from the Department of Homeland Security and be reestablished as an executive branch agency that reports directly to the president. Mr. Witt stated, "FEMA, having lost its status as an independent agency, is being buried beneath a massive bureaucracy whose main and seemingly only focus is fighting terrorism while an all-hazards mission is getting lost in the shuffle." (Peckenpaugh, 2004)

Moving FEMA out of DHS and consolidating its traditional mitigation, preparedness, response, and recovery programs will ensure that the all-hazards approach will be reinstated and that FEMA and its state and local partners will once again focus on dealing with all manner of disaster events including terrorist attacks. Emergency management professionals will once again be in charge of preparing the public, reducing future impacts through hazard mitigation, and managing the resources of the federal government in support of state and local governments in responding to major disasters and fostering a speedy and effective recovery from these events.

This system worked very well in the 1990s when the United States had the most sophisticated and efficient emergency management system in the world. This system effectively responded to hundreds of major natural disasters across the country and successfully managed the federal response to the Oklahoma City bombing and the September 11 attacks in New York City and at the Pentagon. This system also produced comprehensive preparedness and training programs and the first national community-based hazard mitigation initiative.

Currently, the federal emergency management and disaster assistance capabilities that once resided in FEMA are scattered throughout DHS and cannot be effectively managed or coordinated. Consolidating these functions in a reestablished FEMA outside of DHS will not conflict with DHS's primary mission to prevent terrorist attacks on American soil and will enhance those critical elements in the homeland security system that will be called on when the next event occurs.

## ENCOURAGE COMMUNITY-BASED HOMELAND SECURITY

Since September 11, 2001, the federal government has taken the lead in homeland security and the vast majority of policy and program initiatives have focused on federal capabilities and responsibilities. With the exception of the Citizen Corps program and web-based awareness campaigns such as Ready.gov, very little has been done to effectively involve the American public in homeland security activities.

The "Redefining Readiness" study conducted by the New York Academy of Medicine identified numerous problems with the assumptions of homeland security planners in developing smallpox and dirty bomb plans without input from the public. Involving the public in developing community-based homeland security plans is critical to the successful implementation of these plans.

This study and others have discovered that a large segment of the public is ready and willing to participate in these planning efforts and to be part of a community-based effort to deal with the new homeland security threats. What are needed are the mechanisms for involving the public in this process.

A good model for such a mechanism is Project Impact, the former FEMA initiative to develop disaster-resistant communities. At its height, more than 225 Project Impact communities were functioning across the country with support from FEMA. Each community had created a community partnership that involved all stakeholders in the community including the business sector in identifying community risks, identifying what could be done to mitigate these risks, and developing and implementing a plan to take action to reduce the impacts of future disaster events in their community.

The Project Impact model is based on an all-hazards approach, and including the new risks from terrorism into this model would be very simple. The city of Tulsa, Oklahoma, has done just that, successfully incorporating homeland security efforts into its Project Impact programs that were originally developed to address flood and tornado risks.

The bottom line is that the general public must be involved in the development and implementation of community homeland security plans and DHS and its partners in state and local government should invest more resources in developing the planning processes needed to involve the public in the nation's homeland security system.

### IMPROVE COMMUNICATIONS

Communicating with the public is another area that needs to be improved if the nation is going to have a truly effective homeland security system. To date, DHS has shown little interest in communicating with the public and when it has the results have not always been positive—the "duct tape and plastic" fiasco serves as a classic example. DHS and its state and local partners need to address three factors to improve its communications with the American people.

First, there must be a commitment from the leadership not only at DHS and its state and local partners, but at all levels of government including the executive level to communicate timely and accurate information to the public. This is especially important in the response and recovery phases to a terrorist incident.

In a disaster scenario, the conventional wisdom that states information is power, and that hoarding that information helps to retain such power, is almost categorically reversed. Withholding information during disaster events generally has an overall negative on the well-being of the public, and on the impression the public forms about involved authorities. In practice, sharing of information is what generates authority and power, when that information is useful and relates to the hazard at hand. Two shining examples of this fact are the actions of former FEMA Director James Lee Witt and former New York City Mayor Rudy Giuliani. Both leaders went to great lengths to get accurate and timely information to the public in a time of crisis, and their efforts both inspired the public and greatly enhanced the effectiveness of the response and recovery efforts they guided.

To date, DHS leadership and the political leadership have been reluctant to make this commitment to share information with the public. This is something that must change if they expect the American people to fully comprehend the homeland security threat and to become actively engaged in homeland security efforts. Few citizens have any idea of what actual terrorism risks they face, and fewer can actually relate those risks in any comparable fashion to the risks they face everyday without notice.

Second, homeland security officials at all levels must resolve the conflict between sharing information with the public in advance and in the aftermath of a terrorist incident that has value for intelligence or criminal prosecution purposes. This is directly linked to the commitment issue discussed in the previous paragraphs and has been repeatedly cited by homeland security officials as reasons for not sharing more specific information with the public.

This is a very difficult issue that, in the past, DHS has tried to ignore. However, the continued frustration among the public and state and local officials with the Homeland Security Advisory System (HSAS) is just one sign that this issue will not solve itself nor just go away.

Also at issue is the question of when to release relevant information to the public without compromising intelligence sources and/or ongoing criminal investigations. This is an issue that rarely if ever confronts emergency management officials dealing with natural and unintentional man-made disasters. Therefore, there is little precedent or experience for current homeland security officials to work with in crafting a communications strategy that balances the competing need for the public to have timely and accurate information with the need to protect intelligence sources and ongoing criminal investigations. To date, the needs of the intelligence and justice communities have clearly been judged to outweigh those of the public.

Members of Congress and DHS Secretary Michael Chertoff have spoken recently about reworking the HSAS. This would be a critical first step in reestablishing trust with the public for the warning system. From this starting point, if the commitment is there among the homeland security leadership, additional communications mechanisms can be developed to ensure that the public gets timely and accurate information both in advance of any terrorist incident and during the response and recovery phases in the aftermath of the next terrorist attack.

Third, more effort must be invested by federal departments and agencies to better understand the principal terrorist threats that our nation faces (i.e., biological, chemical, radiological, nuclear, and explosives) and develop communications strategies that educate and inform the public about these threats with more useful information. The 2001 Washington, D.C., anthrax incident is a perfect example of uninformed or misinformed public officials sharing what is often conflicting and, in too many instances, wrong information with the public.

The nation's public officials must become better informed about these principal risks and be ready and capable of explaining complicated information to the public. As the anthrax incident made clear, this is not a luxury, but a necessity if the response to similar incidents in the future is to be successful.

Decades of research and a new generation of technologies now inform emergency managers as they provide information about hurricanes, tornadoes, earthquakes, and hazardous materials incidents to the public. A similar research effort must be undertaken for these five new terrorist risks and communications strategies developed that will ensure that homeland security officials at all levels are capable of clearly explaining to the public the hazards these threats pose.

These communications strategies must consider how to communicate to the public when incomplete information is all that is available to homeland security officials. In the vast majority of cases, this partiality of information is probable. A public health crisis will not wait for all the data to be collected and analyzed, nor will the public. Homeland security officials must develop strategies for informing the public effectively, as the crisis develops, by forming effective messages that are able to explain to the public how what is being said is the most accurate information available based on the information that, likewise, is available—despite its incomplete nature. Clearly, this is not an easy task, but it not an impossible task either. The public will expect to a growing degree that such communications efforts are made, so the sooner such a system is in place the better the next incident will be managed.

## PARTNER WITH THE BUSINESS SECTOR

DHS and numerous business groups, such as the Business Roundtable, acknowledge that an effective partnership between government and business must be established as part of the nation's homeland security efforts. This is only logical considering that almost 85% of the nation's infrastructure is privately held.

However, in the 4 years since the attacks of September 11, 2001, no such partnership has been established. There has been some progress and cooperation, but there is no overall strategy in place to incorporate the business sector into the government's emergency management planning for homeland security.

Numerous issues must be resolved before such a strategy can be designed and implemented. A significant issue that must be addressed is how the government will protect and use confidential information it is asking or requiring the business community to provide. The business community, which has vast institutional knowledge about this privacy issue as well as countless other issues that have been presented in the homeland security approach, must be included in the planning process not only for terrorism planning but also for natural disaster management.

One possible avenue for establishing and nurturing an effective partnership with the business sector is to start at the community level. Issues such as what the government will do with confidential information is likely to be less critical at the community level, allowing for lessons to be learned in progressive steps. Additionally, there is an established history of public–private partnerships in emergency management at the community level, many of which started with FEMA's Project Impact program. To illustrate this point, the following message received by our team of authors from Kathleen Criss, CBCP, emergency management coordinator for the University of Pittsburgh Medical Center, is provided:

> I want to share with you the PA Region 13 program, which has been acknowledged as one of the first and is considered a national best practice for regional mutual aid by

FEMA and several other organizations. Robert Full, Chief of Allegheny County Emergency Services and the nominated Chair of the PA Region 13 Counter Terrorism Task Force, has been actively working with the business community since 1999. A public/private partnership was established during the Year 2000 planning and continues today to address "all hazards" and homeland security concerns.

There is a formal plan in place to activate the Business Liaison role in the Allegheny County Emergency Operations Center during a crisis; this plan has been tested several times through actual disaster events and drills. We are currently working on IT solutions to improve emergency communications, alerting capabilities, and resource sharing at times of disaster. Members of the business community were also invited to attend hazard mitigation training courses with first responders, participate in workshops to improve security in chemical and other "critical infrastructure" organizations, and planning meetings to document the County's hazard mitigation plan for submission to the Commonwealth of Pennsylvania. We also participate regularly in annual disaster drills—from planning to the final after action report and follow-up to correct deficiencies. (Criss, 2005)

Ms. Criss indicated in her message that she has been working closely with officials at DHS to promote their efforts as a best practice to other areas of the country and "that DHS does understand this problem and is trying to the best of its ability to work with these existing groups to improve its own programs, where possible. It is not a quick or easy process to implement. It takes trust and dedication from the public and private sectors to begin this relationship to allow the two sides to work together for the betterment of the community its serves." (Criss, 2005)

There are other examples of public–private partnerships working in homeland security that are built on the attributes noted by Ms. Criss. We believe that this bottom-up approach to developing public–private partnerships may be the best avenue for homeland security officials at all levels to pursue.

## CONCLUSION

We believe that the FEMA experience from 1979 to the present is a harbinger of what fate the Department of Homeland Security may befall as it struggles in the coming decade to establish an integrated and effective national homeland security system. At a minimum, FEMA's experiences should serve as a cautionary tale for homeland security officials at the federal, state, and local levels of government.

Reestablishing FEMA as the leader of the nation's emergency management system, supporting community-based homeland security efforts involving the general public, communicating timely and accurate information to the public, and establishing a strong and vital partnership with the business sector could ease DHS's growing pains and pave the way for the establishment of a comprehensive homeland security system in this country.

One final note on the FEMA experience. At the core of FEMA's success in the 1990s was its focus on the needs of its customers, the American people. FEMA policies and programs from that period were driven by the needs of disaster victims and by the needs of community residents who wanted to reduce the terrible impacts of future events. Since its inception in 2002, the Department of Homeland Security and its partners in the federal government have been focused almost exclusively on their own needs. Policies and programs have been designed and implemented that meet the needs of these governmental departments and agencies and that were not informed by the needs of the public, their supposed customers.

If the officials at DHS and working in homeland security at the state and local levels change one thing in the future, it is critical that they shift their focus from themselves to the public, and that they plan and implement policies and programs with the full involvement of the public and their partners. It worked very well for FEMA, so there is no reason why it should not do the same for DHS.

# REFERENCES

Criss, Kathleen. 2005. E-mail message to George Haddow (July 14).

Peckenpaugh, Jason. 2004. "Regional Homeland Security Offices Will Be Small." GovExec.Com (March 24). <www.govexec.com/story_page.cfm?articleid=28072&printerfriendlyVers=1&>

# Appendix 1: List of Acronyms

| | | | |
|---|---|---|---|
| AAAS | American Association for the Advancement of Science | CIA | Central Intelligence Agency |
| AAR | Association of American Railroads | CIAC | Computer Incident Advisory Center |
| ACN | Alerting and Coordination Network | CIG | Central Intelligence Group |
| AFIS | FBI's Automated Fingerprint Identification System | CIO | Chief Information Officer |
| | | CIRG | Critical Incident Response Group |
| AFSA | Armed Forces Security Agency | CJCS | Chairman of the Joint Chiefs of Staff |
| AIN | Advanced Intelligent Network | CM | Consequence Management |
| AMS | Aerial Measuring System | CMU | Crisis Management Unit |
| AMSA | Association of Metropolitan Sewerage Agencies | CONPLAN | Domestic Terrorism Concept of Operations Plan |
| AMWA | Association of Metropolitan Water Agencies | CP | Command Post |
| | | CPC | Community Preparedness Corps |
| ARAC | Atmospheric Release Advisory Capability | CPR | Cardiopulmonary Resuscitation |
| | | CRIS | Communications Resource Information Sharing |
| ARG | Accident Response Group | CSEPP | Chemical Stockpile Emergency Preparedness Program |
| ARS | Agricultural Research Service | | |
| ASCO | Advanced Systems and Concepts Office | CSI | Container Security Initiative |
| ATA | American Trucking Associations | CSREES | Cooperative State Research, Education and Extension Service |
| BASIS | Biological Aerosol Sentry and Information System | | |
| | | CSS | Central Security Service |
| BIA | Business Impact Analysis | CTO | Chief Technology Officer |
| CBD | Chemical and Biological Defense | DARPA | Defense Advanced Research Project Agency |
| CBIAC | Chemical and Biological Defense Information and Analysis Center | | |
| | | DCI | Director of Central Intelligence |
| CBNP | Chemical and Biological National Security Program | DEST | Domestic Emergency Support Team |
| | | DFO | Disaster Field Office |
| CBR | Chemical, Biological, Radiological | DHS | Department of Homeland Security |
| CBRNE | Chemical, Biological, Radiological, Nuclear Material or High-Yield Explosive | DHS-BTS | Department of Homeland Security—Directorate of Border Transportation Security |
| CDBG | Community Development Block Grant | | |
| CDC | Centers for Disease Control and Prevention | DHS-IAIP | Department of Homeland Security—Directorate of Information Analysis and Infrastructure Protection |
| CDRG | Catastrophic Disaster Response Team | | |
| CEN | Community Emergency Networks | DHS-OPSL | Department of Homeland Security—Office for Private Sector Liaison |
| CERCLA | Comprehensive Environmental Response, Compensation, and Liability Act | | |
| | | DHS-OSLGC | Department of Homeland Security—Office for State/Local Government Coordination |
| CERT | Community Emergency Response Teams | | |
| CERT/CC | CERT Coordination Center | DHS-S&T | Department of Homeland Security—Directorate of Science and Technology |
| CFO | Chief Financial Officer | | |
| CFR | Code of Federal Regulations | DHS-USCG | Department of Homeland Security—The United States Coast Guard |
| CHS | Center for Homeland Security | | |

| DIA | Defense Intelligence Agency | FEMA | Federal Emergency Management Agency |
|---|---|---|---|
| DIS | Decision and Information Sciences | FERC | Federal Energy Regulatory Commission |
| DMA | Defense Mapping Agency | FFRDC | Federally Funded Research and |
| DMA 2000 | Disaster Mitigation Act 2000 | | Development Center |
| DMAT | Disaster Medical Assistance Teams | FNS | Food and Nutrition Service |
| DMORT | Disaster Mortuary Operational Response | FOC | Nationwide Full Operational Capability |
| | Teams | FOSC | Federal On-Scene Coordinator |
| DOC | Department of Commerce | FRERP | Federal Radiological Emergency |
| DoD | Department of Defense | | Response Plan |
| DOE | Department of Energy | FRMAC | Federal Radiological Monitoring and |
| DOI | Department of the Interior | | Assessment Center |
| DOJ | Department of Justice | FRP | Federal Response Plan |
| DOL | Department of Labor | FS | Forest Service |
| DOS | Department of State | FY | Fiscal Year |
| DOT | Department of Transportation | GAW | Global Atmosphere Watch |
| DRC | Disaster Recovery Centers | GETS | Government Emergency |
| DRF | Disaster Relief Fund | | Telecommunications Service |
| DTCTPS | FBI Domestic | GIS | Geographic Information System |
| | Terrorism/Counterterrorism Planning | GSA | General Services Administration |
| | Section | HF | High Frequency |
| DTIC | Defense Technical Information Center | HHS | Department of Health and Human |
| DTRA | Defense Threat Reduction Agency | | Services |
| DUA | Disaster Unemployment Assistance | HMRU | Hazardous Materials Response Unit |
| EAD | Environmental Assessment Division | HOPS | Homeland Operational Planning System |
| EDS | Electronic Detection Systems | HQ EOC | Headquarters Emergency Operation |
| ELES | Emergency Law Enforcement Services | | Center |
| EMI | FEMA's Emergency Management | HR | House of Representatives |
| | Institute | HS-Center | Homeland Security Centers of |
| EML | Environmental Measurements | | Excellence |
| | Laboratory | HSARPA | Homeland Security Advanced Research |
| EMT | Emergency Medical Technicians | | Project Agency |
| ENS | Emergency Notification Service | HSPD | Homeland Security Presidential |
| EOC | Emergency Operations Centers | | Directive |
| EP&R | Directorate of Emergency Preparedness | HUD | Department of Housing and Urban |
| | and Response | | Development |
| EPA | Environmental Protection Agency | IAC | Information Analysis Center |
| ERSM | Emergency Response Synchronization | IAEM | International Association of Emergency |
| | Matrix | | Managers |
| ESF | Emergency Support Function | ICE | Bureau of Immigration & Customs |
| EST | Emergency Support Team | | Enforcement |
| ETD | Electronic Trace Detectors | ICS | Incident Command System |
| FAA | Federal Aviation Administration | IESA | International Environmental Sample |
| FBI | Federal Bureau of Investigation | | Archive |
| FCC | Federal Communications Commission | IFG | Individual and Family Grant |
| FCC | Federal Coordinating Centers | IHP | Individuals and Households Program |
| FCO | Federal Coordinating Officer | IOC | Nationwide Initial Operational |
| FedCIRC | Federal Computer Incident Response | | Capability |
| | Center | IPR | Intellectual Property Rights |

| | | | |
|---|---|---|---|
| ISAC | Information Sharing and Analysis Center | NIAID | National Institute of Allergy and Infectious Diseases |
| ISAS | Information Sharing and Analysis System | NIH | National Institutes of Health |
| ISRC | Information Security Resource Center | NIIMS | National Interagency Incident Management System |
| ITAC | DOE Incident Tracking and Analysis Center | NIJ | National Institute of Justice |
| IXC | Interexchange Carrier | NIMA | National Imagery and Mapping Agency |
| JCATS | Joint Conflict and Tactical Simulation | NIMS | National Incident Management System |
| JIC | Joint Information Centers | NIPC | National Infrastructure Protection Center |
| JOC | Joint Operations Center | | |
| LADAR | Laser Array for Chem-Bio Agent Detection | NIST | National Institute of Standards and Technology |
| LEC | Local Exchange Carrier | NJIC | National Joint Information Center |
| LEPPC | Local Emergency Prevention and Preparedness Councils | NNS | Nonproliferation and National Security Department |
| LFA | Lead Federal Agency | NNSA | National Nuclear Security Administration |
| LINC | Local Integration of NARAC with Cities | NOAA | National Oceanographic and Atmospheric Administration |
| LLNL | Lawrence Livermore National Laboratory | NOC | Network Operations Centers |
| MIR | Micropower Impulse Radar | NPDES | National Pollutant Discharge Elimination System |
| MMST | Metropolitan Medical Strike Team | | |
| MRA | Mortgage and Rent Assistance | NPIC | National Photographic Interpretation Center |
| MRC | Medical Reserve Corps | | |
| MSCA | Military Support to Civil Authorities | NPS | National Pharmaceutical Stockpile |
| NAP | Nuclear Assessment Program | NPSC | National Processing Service Centers |
| NARAC | National Atmospheric Release Advisory Center | NRC | Nuclear Regulatory Commission |
| | | NRMRL | National Risk Management Research Laboratory |
| NASA | National Aeronautics and Space Administration | | |
| | | NRO | National Reconnaissance Office |
| NASCIO | National Association of State Chief Information Officers | NRP | National Response Plan |
| | | NRT | National Response Team |
| NCCC | National Civilian Community Corps | NS/EP | NCS's National Security and Emergency Preparedness |
| NCP | National Oil and Hazardous Substances Pollution Contingency Plan | | |
| | | NSA | National Security Agency |
| NCS | National Communications System | NSF | National Science Foundation |
| NDMS | National Disaster Medical System | NSF | National Strike Force |
| NDPO | National Domestic Preparedness Office | NSFCC | National Strike Force Coordination Center |
| NEMA | National Emergency Management Association | NSTAC | President's National Security Telecommunications Advisory Committee |
| NEPPC | National Emergency Prevention and Preparedness Council | | |
| | | NCC | National Coordinating Center for Telecommunications |
| NERC | North American Electric Reliability Council | | |
| | | NTCN | National Technology Coordination Network |
| NEST | Nuclear Emergency Search Team | | |
| NHBEM | National Health Bureau of Emergency Management | NVOAD | National Volunteer Organizations Against Disasters |
| NIA | National Intelligence Authority | NWP | Neighborhood Watch Program |

| | | | |
|---|---|---|---|
| OA | Office of Independent Oversight and Performance Assurance | SANS | System, Audit, Network, Security |
| | | SAR | Search and Rescue |
| OCPM | Office of Crisis Planning and Management | SBA | U.S. Small Business Administration |
| | | SBCCOM | U.S. Army Soldier and Biological Chemical Command |
| OEP | Office of Emergency Preparedness | | |
| OES | Office of Emergency Services | SCO | State Coordinating Officer |
| OIG | Office of Inspector General | SEB | State Emergency Boards |
| OMNCS | Office of the Manager, NCS | SEI | Software Engineering Institute |
| ONA | Other Needs Assistance | SERT | State Emergency Response Team |
| ORNL | Oak Ridge National Laboratory | SFA | Support Federal Agency |
| OSC | FBI Federal On-Scene Commander | SFHA | Special Flood Hazard Areas |
| OSHA | Occupational Safety and Health Administration | SHARES | Shared Resources |
| | | SIOC | Strategic Information and Operations Center |
| OSS | Office of Strategic Services | | |
| PAD | Protective Action Distances | SMS | Short Message Service |
| PAS | ISAS Priority Access Service | SNS | Strategic National Stockpile |
| PDA | Preliminary Damage Assessment | SPP | Special Population Planner |
| PFA | Primary Federal Agency | SRM | Standard Reference Materials |
| PHS | U.S. Public Health Service | STI | Science and Technology Information |
| PIADC | Plum Island Animal Disease Center | TARU | Technical Advisory Response Unit |
| PIN | Personal Identification Number | TEMA | Tennessee Emergency Management Agency |
| PN | Public Network | | |
| PNNL | Pacific Northwest National Laboratory | TEPP | DOE Transportation Emergency Preparedness Program |
| PNP | Private Non profit | | |
| POC | Point of Contact | TOADS | Total Online Access Data System |
| PSCTM | Port State Control Targeting Matrix | TOC | Transitional Operational Capability |
| PSN | Public Switched Network | TSA | Transportation Security Agency |
| R&D | Research and Development | TSP | Telecommunications Service Priority |
| RAP | Radiological Assistance Program | | |
| RBDM | (Coast Guard) Risk-Based Decision Making | TWIC | Transportation Worker Identification Card |
| RDD | Radiological Dispersal Device | US&R | Urban Search & Rescue |
| RDT&E | Research, Development, Test and Evaluation | USCG | U.S. Coast Guard |
| | | USDA | U.S. Department of Agriculture |
| REAC/TS | Radiation Emergency Assistance Center/Training Site | USFA | U.S. Fire Administration |
| | | VA | Department of Veterans Affairs |
| REPPC | Regional Emergency Prevention and Preparedness Council | VIPS | Volunteers in Police Service |
| | | VMI | Vendor Managed Inventory |
| RISC | Regional Interagency Steering Committee | VOAD | Voluntary Organization Active in Disaster |
| RJIC | Regional Joint Information Center | VSAT | Vulnerability Self Assessment Tools |
| ROC | Regional Operation Center | | |
| RRT | Regional Response Team | WMD | Weapons of Mass Destruction |
| S&T | Science and Technology Directorate | WMD-CST | Weapons of Mass Destruction Civil Support Teams |
| S/REOC | State and/or Regional Emergency Operations Centers | | |
| | | WMO | World Meteorological Organization |
| SA | Submitted Amendment | WPS | Wireless Priority Service |
| SAC | FBI Special Agent in Charge | WTC | World Trade Center |

# Appendix 2: U.S.A. Patriot Act Summary

H.R.3162

Title: To deter and punish terrorist acts in the United States and around the world, to enhance law enforcement investigatory tools, and for other purposes.

Sponsor: Rep Sensenbrenner, F. James, Jr. [WI-9] (introduced 10/23/2001) Cosponsors: 1

Related Bills: H.R.2975, H.R.3004, S.1510

Latest Major Action: 10/26/2001 Became Public Law No: 107-56.

Note: H.R. 3162, the USA PATRIOT Act, incorporated provisions of two earlier anti-terrorism bills: H.R. 2975, which passed the House on 10/12/2001; and S. 1510, which passed the Senate on 10/11/2001. Provisions of H.R. 3004, the Financial Anti-Terrorism Act, were incorporated as Title III in H.R. 3162.

SUMMARY AS OF:

10/24/2001—Passed House, without amendment. (There is 1 other summary)

Uniting and Strengthening America by Providing Appropriate Tools Required to Intercept and Obstruct Terrorism (USA PATRIOT ACT) Act of 2001—Title I: Enhancing Domestic Security Against Terrorism—Establishes in the Treasury the Counterterrorism Fund.

(Sec. 102) Expresses the sense of Congress that: (1) the civil rights and liberties of all Americans, including Arab Americans, must be protected, and that every effort must be taken to preserve their safety; (2) any acts of violence or discrimination against any Americans be condemned; and (3) the Nation is called upon to recognize the patriotism of fellow citizens from all ethnic, racial, and religious backgrounds.

(Sec. 103) Authorizes appropriations for the Federal Bureau of Investigation's (FBI) Technical Support Center.

(Sec. 104) Authorizes the Attorney General to request the Secretary of Defense to provide assistance in support of Department of Justice (DOJ) activities relating to the enforcement of federal criminal code (code) provisions regarding the use of weapons of mass destruction during an emergency situation involving a weapon (currently, chemical weapon) of mass destruction.

(Sec. 105) Requires the Director of the U.S. Secret Service to take actions to develop a national network of electronic crime task forces throughout the United States to prevent, detect, and investigate various forms of electronic crimes, including potential terrorist attacks against critical infrastructure and financial payment systems.

(Sec. 106) Modifies provisions relating to presidential authority under the International Emergency Powers Act to: (1) authorize the President, when the United States is engaged in armed hostilities or has been attacked by a foreign country or foreign nationals, to confiscate any property subject to U.S. jurisdiction of a foreign person, organization, or country that he determines has planned, authorized, aided, or engaged in such hostilities or attacks (the rights to which shall vest in such agency or person as the President may designate); and (2) provide that, in any judicial review of a determination made under such provisions, if the determination was based on classified information such information may be submitted to the reviewing court ex parte and in camera.

Title II: Enhanced Surveillance Procedures—Amends the Federal criminal code to authorize the interception of wire, oral, and electronic communications for the production of evidence of: (1) specified chemical weapons or terrorism offenses; and (2) computer fraud and abuse.

(Sec. 203) Amends rule 6 of the Federal Rules of Criminal Procedure (FRCrP) to permit the sharing of grand jury information that involves foreign intelligence or counterintelligence with Federal law enforcement, intelligence, protective, immigration, national defense, or national security officials (such officials), subject to specified requirements.

Authorizes an investigative or law enforcement officer, or an attorney for the Government, who, by authorized means, has obtained knowledge of the contents of any wire, oral, or electronic communication or evidence derived there from to disclose such contents to such officials to the extent that such contents include foreign intelligence or counterintelligence.

Directs the Attorney General to establish procedures for the disclosure of information (pursuant to the code and the

FRCrP) that identifies a United States person, as defined in the Foreign Intelligence Surveillance Act of 1978 (FISA).

Authorizes the disclosure of foreign intelligence or counterintelligence obtained as part of a criminal investigation to such officials.

(Sec. 204) Clarifies that nothing in code provisions regarding pen registers shall be deemed to affect the acquisition by the Government of specified foreign intelligence information, and that procedures under FISA shall be the exclusive means by which electronic surveillance and the interception of domestic wire and oral (current law) and electronic communications may be conducted.

(Sec. 205) Authorizes the Director of the FBI to expedite the employment of personnel as translators to support counterterrorism investigations and operations without regard to applicable Federal personnel requirements. Requires: (1) the Director to establish such security requirements as necessary for such personnel; and (2) the Attorney General to report to the House and Senate Judiciary Committees regarding translators.

(Sec. 206) Grants roving surveillance authority under FISA after requiring a court order approving an electronic surveillance to direct any person to furnish necessary information, facilities, or technical assistance in circumstances where the Court finds that the actions of the surveillance target may have the effect of thwarting the identification of a specified person.

(Sec. 207) Increases the duration of FISA surveillance permitted for non-U.S. persons who are agents of a foreign power.

(Sec. 208) Increases (from seven to 11) the number of district court judges designated to hear applications for and grant orders approving electronic surveillance. Requires that no fewer than three reside within 20 miles of the District of Columbia.

(Sec. 209) Permits the seizure of voice-mail messages under a warrant.

(Sec. 210) Expands the scope of subpoenas for records of electronic communications to include the length and types of service utilized, temporarily assigned network addresses, and the means and source of payment (including any credit card or bank account number).

(Sec. 211) Amends the Communications Act of 1934 to permit specified disclosures to Government entities, except for records revealing cable subscriber selection of video programming from a cable operator.

(Sec. 212) Permits electronic communication and remote computing service providers to make emergency disclosures to a governmental entity of customer electronic communications to protect life and limb.

(Sec. 213) Authorizes Federal district courts to allow a delay of required notices of the execution of a warrant if immediate notice may have an adverse result and under other specified circumstances.

(Sec. 214) Prohibits use of a pen register or trap and trace devices in any investigation to protect against international terrorism or clandestine intelligence activities that is conducted solely on the basis of activities protected by the first amendment to the U.S. Constitution.

(Sec. 215) Authorizes the Director of the FBI (or designee) to apply for a court order requiring production of certain business records for foreign intelligence and international terrorism investigations. Requires the Attorney General to report to the House and Senate Intelligence and Judiciary Committees semi-annually.

(Sec. 216) Amends the code to: (1) require a trap and trace device to restrict recoding or decoding so as not to include the contents of a wire or electronic communication; (2) apply a court order for a pen register or trap and trace devices to any person or entity providing wire or electronic communication service in the United States whose assistance may facilitate execution of the order; (3) require specified records kept on any pen register or trap and trace device on a packet-switched data network of a provider of electronic communication service to the public; and (4) allow a trap and trace device to identify the source (but not the contents) of a wire or electronic communication.

(Sec. 217) Makes it lawful to intercept the wire or electronic communication of a computer trespasser in certain circumstances.

(Sec. 218) Amends FISA to require an application for an electronic surveillance order or search warrant to certify that a significant purpose (currently, the sole or main purpose) of the surveillance is to obtain foreign intelligence information.

(Sec. 219) Amends rule 41 of the FRCrP to permit Federal magistrate judges in any district in which terrorism-related activities may have occurred to issue search warrants for searches within or outside the district.

(Sec. 220) Provides for nationwide service of search warrants for electronic evidence.

(Sec. 221) Amends the Trade Sanctions Reform and Export Enhancement Act of 2000 to extend trade sanctions to the territory of Afghanistan controlled by the Taliban.

(Sec. 222) Specifies that: (1) nothing in this Act shall impose any additional technical obligation or requirement on a provider of a wire or electronic communication service or other person to furnish facilities or technical assistance; and (2) a provider of such service, and a landlord, custodian, or other person who furnishes such facilities or technical assistance, shall be reasonably compensated for such reasonable expenditures incurred in providing such facilities or assistance.

(Sec. 223) Amends the Federal criminal code to provide for administrative discipline of Federal officers or employees who violate prohibitions against unauthorized disclosures of information gathered under this Act. Provides for civil actions against the United States for damages by any person aggrieved by such violations.

(Sec. 224) Terminates this title on December 31, 2005, except with respect to any particular foreign intelligence investigation beginning before that date, or any particular offense or potential offense that began or occurred before it.

(Sec. 225) Amends the Foreign Intelligence Surveillance Act of 1978 to prohibit a cause of action in any court against a provider of a wire or electronic communication service, landlord, custodian, or any other person that furnishes any information, facilities, or technical assistance in accordance with a court order or request for emergency assistance under such Act (for example, with respect to a wiretap).

Title III: International Money Laundering Abatement and Anti-Terrorist Financing Act of 2001—International Money Laundering Abatement and Financial Anti-Terrorism Act of 2001-Sunsets this Act after the first day of FY 2005 if Congress enacts a specified joint resolution to that effect.

Subtitle A: International Counter Money Laundering and Related Measures—Amends Federal law governing monetary transactions to prescribe procedural guidelines under which the Secretary of the Treasury (the Secretary) may require domestic financial institutions and agencies to take specified measures if the Secretary finds that reasonable grounds exist for concluding that jurisdictions, financial institutions, types of accounts, or transactions operating outside or within the United States, are of primary money laundering concern. Includes mandatory disclosure of specified information relating to certain correspondent accounts.

(Sec. 312) Mandates establishment of due diligence mechanisms to detect and report money laundering transactions through private banking accounts and correspondent accounts.

(Sec. 313) Prohibits U.S. correspondent accounts with foreign shell banks.

(Sec. 314) Instructs the Secretary to adopt regulations to encourage further cooperation among financial institutions, their regulatory authorities, and law enforcement authorities, with the specific purpose of encouraging regulatory authorities and law enforcement authorities to share with financial institutions information regarding individuals, entities, and organizations engaged in or reasonably suspected (based on credible evidence) of engaging in terrorist acts or money laundering activities. Authorizes such regulations to create procedures for cooperation and information sharing on matters specifically related to the finances of terrorist groups as well as their relationships with international narcotics traffickers.

Requires the Secretary to distribute annually to financial institutions a detailed analysis identifying patterns of suspicious activity and other investigative insights derived from suspicious activity reports and investigations by Federal, State, and local law enforcement agencies.

(Sec. 315) Amends Federal criminal law to include foreign corruption offenses as money laundering crimes.

(Sec. 316) Establishes the right of property owners to contest confiscation of property under law relating to confiscation of assets of suspected terrorists.

(Sec. 317) Establishes Federal jurisdiction over: (1) foreign money launderers (including their assets held in the United States); and (2) money that is laundered through a foreign bank.

(Sec. 319) Authorizes the forfeiture of money laundering funds from interbank accounts. Requires a covered financial institution, upon request of the appropriate Federal banking agency, to make available within 120 hours all pertinent information related to anti-money laundering compliance by the institution or its customer. Grants the Secretary summons and subpoena powers over foreign banks that maintain a correspondent bank in the United States. Requires a covered financial institution to terminate within ten business days any correspondent relationship with a foreign bank after receipt of written notice that the foreign bank has failed to comply with certain judicial proceedings. Sets forth civil penalties for failure to terminate such relationship.

(Sec. 321) Subjects to record and report requirements for monetary instrument transactions: (1) any credit union; and (2) any futures commission merchant, commodity trading advisor, and commodity pool operator registered, or required to register, under the Commodity Exchange Act.

(Sec. 323) Authorizes Federal application for restraining orders to preserve the availability of property subject to a foreign forfeiture or confiscation judgment.

(Sec. 325) Authorizes the Secretary to issue regulations to ensure that concentration accounts of financial institutions are not used to prevent association of the identity of an individual customer with the movement of funds of which the customer is the direct or beneficial owner.

(Sec. 326) Directs the Secretary to issue regulations prescribing minimum standards for financial institutions regarding customer identity in connection with the opening of accounts.

Requires the Secretary to report to Congress on: (1) the most timely and effective way to require foreign nationals to provide domestic financial institutions and agencies with appropriate and accurate information; (2) whether to require foreign nationals to obtain an identification number (similar to a Social Security or tax identification number) before opening an account with a domestic financial institution; and (3) a system for domestic financial institutions and agencies to review Government agency information to verify the identities of such foreign nationals.

(Sec. 327) Amends the Bank Holding Company Act of 1956 and the Federal Deposit Insurance Act to require consideration of the effectiveness of a company or companies in combating money laundering during reviews of proposed bank shares acquisitions or mergers.

(Sec. 328) Directs the Secretary take reasonable steps to encourage foreign governments to require the inclusion of the name of the originator in wire transfer instructions sent to the United States and other countries, with the information to remain with the transfer from its origination until the point of disbursement. Requires annual progress reports to specified congressional committees.

(Sec. 329) Prescribes criminal penalties for Federal officials or employees who seek or accept bribes in connection with administration of this title.

(Sec. 330) Urges U.S. negotiations for international cooperation in investigations of money laundering, financial crimes, and the finances of terrorist groups, including record sharing by foreign banks with U.S. law enforcement officials and domestic financial institution supervisors.

Subtitle B: Bank Secrecy Act Amendments and Related Improvements—Amends Federal law known as the Bank Secrecy Act to revise requirements for civil liability immunity for voluntary financial institution disclosure of suspicious activities. Authorizes the inclusion of suspicions of illegal activity in written employment references.

(Sec. 352) Authorizes the Secretary to exempt from minimum standards for anti-money laundering programs any financial institution not subject to certain regulations governing financial record keeping and reporting of currency and foreign transactions.

(Sec. 353) Establishes civil penalties for violations of geographic targeting orders and structuring transactions to evade certain record keeping requirements. Lengthens the effective period of geographic targeting orders from 60 to 180 days.

(Sec. 355) Amends the Federal Deposit Insurance Act to permit written employment references to contain suspicions of involvement in illegal activity.

(Sec. 356) Instructs the Secretary to: (1) promulgate regulations requiring registered securities brokers and dealers, futures commission merchants, commodity trading advisors, and commodity pool operators, to file reports of suspicious financial transactions; (2) report to Congress on the role of the Internal Revenue Service in the administration of the Bank Secrecy Act; and (3) share monetary instruments transactions records upon request of a U.S. intelligence agency for use in the conduct of intelligence or counterintelligence activities, including analysis, to protect against international terrorism.

(Sec. 358) Amends the Right to Financial Privacy Act to permit the transfer of financial records to other agencies or departments upon certification that the records are relevant to intelligence or counterintelligence activities related to international terrorism.

Amends the Fair Credit Reporting Act to require a consumer reporting agency to furnish all information in a consumer's file to a government agency upon certification that the records are relevant to intelligence or counterintelligence activities related to international terrorism.

(Sec. 359) Subjects to mandatory records and reports on monetary instruments transactions any licensed sender of money or any other person who engages as a business in the transmission of funds, including through an informal value transfer banking system or network (e.g., hawala) of people facilitating the transfer of money domestically or internationally outside of the conventional financial institutions system.

(Sec. 360) Authorizes the Secretary to instruct the United States Executive Director of each international financial institution to use his or her voice and vote to: (1) support the use of funds for a country (and its institutions) which contributes to U.S. efforts against international terrorism; and (2) require an auditing of disbursements to ensure that no funds are paid to persons who commit or support terrorism.

(Sec. 361) Makes the existing Financial Crimes Enforcement Network a bureau in the Department of the Treasury.

(Sec. 362) Directs the Secretary to establish a highly secure network in the Network that allows financial institutions to file certain reports and receive alerts and other information regarding suspicious activities warranting immediate and enhanced scrutiny.

(Sec. 363) Increases to $1 million the maximum civil penalties (currently $10,000) and criminal fines (currently $250,000) for money laundering. Sets a minimum civil penalty and criminal fine of double the amount of the illegal transaction.

(Sec. 364) Amends the Federal Reserve Act to provide for uniform protection authority for Federal Reserve facilities, including law enforcement officers authorized to carry firearms and make warrant less arrests.

(Sec. 365) Amends Federal law to require reports relating to coins and currency of more than $10,000 received in a non-financial trade or business.

(Sec. 366) Directs the Secretary to study and report to Congress on: (1) the possible expansion of the currency transaction reporting requirements exemption system; and (2) methods for improving financial institution utilization of the system as a way of reducing the submission of currency transaction reports that have little or no value for law enforcement purposes.

Subtitle C: Currency Crimes—Establishes as a bulk cash smuggling felony the knowing concealment and attempted transport (or transfer) across U.S. borders of currency and monetary instruments in excess of $10,000, with intent to evade specified currency reporting requirements.

(Sec. 372) Changes from discretionary to mandatory a court's authority to order, as part of a criminal sentence,

forfeiture of all property involved in certain currency reporting offenses. Leaves a court discretion to order civil forfeitures in money laundering cases.

(Sec. 373) Amends the Federal criminal code to revise the prohibition of unlicensed (currently, illegal) money transmitting businesses.

(Sec. 374) Increases the criminal penalties for counterfeiting domestic and foreign currency and obligations.

(Sec. 376) Amends the Federal criminal code to extend the prohibition against the laundering of money instruments to specified proceeds of terrorism.

(Sec. 377) Grants the United States extraterritorial jurisdiction where: (1) an offense committed outside the United States involves an access device issued, owned, managed, or controlled by a financial institution, account issuer, credit card system member, or other entity within U.S. jurisdiction; and (2) the person committing the offense transports, delivers, conveys, transfers to or through, or otherwise stores, secrets, or holds within U.S. jurisdiction any article used to assist in the commission of the offense or the proceeds of such offense or property derived from it.

Title IV: Protecting the Border—Subtitle A: Protecting the Northern Border—Authorizes the Attorney General to waive certain Immigration and Naturalization Service (INS) personnel caps with respect to ensuring security needs on the Northern border.

(Sec. 402) Authorizes appropriations to: (1) triple the number of Border Patrol, Customs Service, and INS personnel (and support facilities) at points of entry and along the Northern border; and (2) INS and Customs for related border monitoring technology and equipment.

(Sec. 403) Amends the Immigration and Nationality Act to require the Attorney General and the Federal Bureau of Investigation (FBI) to provide the Department of State and INS with access to specified criminal history extracts in order to determine whether or not a visa or admissions applicant has a criminal history. Directs the FBI to provide periodic extract updates. Provides for confidentiality.

Directs the Attorney General and the Secretary of State to develop a technology standard to identify visa and admissions applicants, which shall be the basis for an electronic system of law enforcement and intelligence sharing system available to consular, law enforcement, intelligence, and Federal border inspection personnel.

(Sec. 404) Amends the Department of Justice Appropriations Act, 2001 to eliminate certain INS overtime restrictions.

(Sec. 405) Directs the Attorney General to report on the feasibility of enhancing the Integrated Automated Fingerprint Identification System and other identification systems to better identify foreign individuals in connection with U.S. or foreign criminal investigations before issuance of a visa to, or permitting such person's entry or exit from, the United States. Authorizes appropriations.

Subtitle B: Enhanced Immigration Provisions—Amends the Immigration and Nationality Act to broaden the scope of aliens ineligible for admission or deportable due to terrorist activities to include an alien who: (1) is a representative of a political, social, or similar group whose political endorsement of terrorist acts undermines U.S. antiterrorist efforts; (2) has used a position of prominence to endorse terrorist activity, or to persuade others to support such activity in a way that undermines U.S. antiterrorist efforts (or the child or spouse of such an alien under specified circumstances); or (3) has been associated with a terrorist organization and intends to engage in threatening activities while in the United States.

(Sec. 411) Includes within the definition of "terrorist activity" the use of any weapon or dangerous device.

Redefines "engage in terrorist activity" to mean, in an individual capacity or as a member of an organization, to: (1) commit or to incite to commit, under circumstances indicating an intention to cause death or serious bodily injury, a terrorist activity; (2) prepare or plan a terrorist activity; (3) gather information on potential targets for terrorist activity; (4) solicit funds or other things of value for a terrorist activity or a terrorist organization (with an exception for lack of knowledge); (5) solicit any individual to engage in prohibited conduct or for terrorist organization membership (with an exception for lack of knowledge); or (6) commit an act that the actor knows, or reasonably should know, affords material support, including a safe house, transportation, communications, funds, transfer of funds or other material financial benefit, false documentation or identification, weapons (including chemical, biological, or radiological weapons), explosives, or training for the commission of a terrorist activity; to any individual who the actor knows or reasonably should know has committed or plans to commit a terrorist activity; or to a terrorist organization (with an exception for lack of knowledge).

Defines "terrorist organization" as a group: (1) designated under the Immigration and Nationality Act or by the Secretary of State; or (2) a group of two or more individuals, whether related or not, which engages in terrorist-related activities.

Provides for the retroactive application of amendments under this Act. Stipulates that an alien shall not be considered inadmissible or deportable because of a relationship to an organization that was not designated as a terrorist organization prior to enactment of this Act. States that the amendments under this section shall apply to all aliens in exclusion or deportation proceedings on or after the date of enactment of this Act.

Directs the Secretary of State to notify specified congressional leaders seven days prior to designating an organization as a terrorist organization. Provides for organization redesignation or revocation.

(Sec. 412) Provides for mandatory detention until removal from the United States (regardless of any relief from removal) of an alien certified by the Attorney General as a suspected terrorist or threat to national security. Requires release of such alien after seven days if removal proceedings have not commenced, or the alien has not been charged with a criminal offense. Authorizes detention for additional periods of up to six months of an alien not likely to be deported in the reasonably foreseeable future only if release will threaten U.S. national security or the safety of the community or any person. Limits judicial review to habeas corpus proceedings in the U.S. Supreme Court, the U.S. Court of Appeals for the District of Columbia, or any district court with jurisdiction to entertain a habeas corpus petition. Restricts to the U.S. Court of Appeals for the District of Columbia the right of appeal of any final order by a circuit or district judge.

(Sec. 413) Authorizes the Secretary of State, on a reciprocal basis, to share criminal- and terrorist-related visa lookout information with foreign governments.

(Sec. 414) Declares the sense of Congress that the Attorney General should: (1) fully implement the integrated entry and exit data system for airports, seaports, and land border ports of entry with all deliberate speed; and (2) begin immediately establishing the Integrated Entry and Exit Data System Task Force. Authorizes appropriations.

Requires the Attorney General and the Secretary of State, in developing the integrated entry and exit data system, to focus on the use of biometric technology and the development of tamper-resistant documents readable at ports of entry.

(Sec. 415) Amends the Immigration and Naturalization Service Data Management Improvement Act of 2000 to include the Office of Homeland Security in the Integrated Entry and Exit Data System Task Force.

(Sec. 416) Directs the Attorney General to implement fully and expand the foreign student monitoring program to include other approved educational institutions like air flight, language training, or vocational schools.

(Sec. 417) Requires audits and reports on implementation of the mandate for machine readable passports.

(Sec. 418) Directs the Secretary of State to: (1) review how consular officers issue visas to determine if consular shopping is a problem; and (2) if it is a problem, take steps to address it, and report on them to Congress.

Subtitle C: Preservation of Immigration Benefits for Victims of Terrorism—Authorizes the Attorney General to provide permanent resident status through the special immigrant program to an alien (and spouse, child, or grandparent under specified circumstances) who was the beneficiary of a petition filed on or before September 11, 2001, to grant the alien permanent residence as an employer-sponsored immigrant or of an application for labor certification if the petition or application was rendered null because of the disability of the beneficiary or loss of employment due to physical damage to, or destruction of, the business of the petitioner or applicant as a direct result of the terrorist attacks on September 11, 2001 (September attacks), or because of the death of the petitioner or applicant as a direct result of such attacks.

(Sec. 422) States that an alien who was legally in a nonimmigrant status and was disabled as a direct result of the September attacks may remain in the United States until his or her normal status termination date or September, 11, 2002. Includes in such extension the spouse or child of such an alien or of an alien who was killed in such attacks. Authorizes employment during such period.

Extends specified immigration-related deadlines and other filing requirements for an alien (and spouse and child) who was directly prevented from meeting such requirements as a result of the September attacks respecting: (1) nonimmigrant status and status revision; (2) diversity immigrants; (3) immigrant visas; (4) parolees; and (5) voluntary departure.

(Sec. 423) Waives, under specified circumstances, the requirement that an alien spouse (and child) of a U.S. citizen must have been married for at least two years prior to such citizen's death in order to maintain immediate relative status if such citizen died as a direct result of the September attacks. Provides for: (1) continued family-sponsored immigrant eligibility for the spouse, child, or unmarried son or daughter of a permanent resident who died as a direct result of such attacks; and (2) continued eligibility for adjustment

of status for the spouse and child of an employment-based immigrant who died similarly.

(Sec. 424) Amends the Immigration and Nationality Act to extend the visa categorization of "child" for aliens with petitions filed on or before September 11, 2001, for aliens whose 21st birthday is in September 2001 (90 days), or after September 2001 (45 days).

(Sec. 425) Authorizes the Attorney General to provide temporary administrative relief to an alien who, as of September, 10, 2001, was lawfully in the United States and was the spouse, parent, or child of an individual who died or was disabled as a direct result of the September attacks.

(Sec. 426) Directs the Attorney General to establish evidentiary guidelines for death, disability, and loss of employment or destruction of business in connection with the provisions of this subtitle.

(Sec. 427) Prohibits benefits to terrorists or their family members.

Title V: Removing Obstacles to Investigating Terrorism—Authorizes the Attorney General to pay rewards from available funds pursuant to public advertisements for assistance to DOJ to combat terrorism and defend the Nation against terrorist acts, in accordance with procedures and regulations established or issued by the Attorney General, subject to specified conditions, including a prohibition against any such reward of $250,000 or more from being made or offered without the personal approval of either the Attorney General or the President.

(Sec. 502) Amends the State Department Basic Authorities Act of 1956 to modify the Department of State rewards program to authorize rewards for information leading to: (1) the dismantling of a terrorist organization in whole or significant part; and (2) the identification or location of an individual who holds a key leadership position in a terrorist organization. Raises the limit on rewards if the Secretary State determines that a larger sum is necessary to combat terrorism or defend the Nation against terrorist acts.

(Sec. 503) Amends the DNA Analysis Backlog Elimination Act of 2000 to qualify a Federal terrorism offense for collection of DNA for identification.

(Sec. 504) Amends FISA to authorize consultation among Federal law enforcement officers regarding information acquired from an electronic surveillance or physical search in terrorism and related investigations or protective measures.

(Sec. 505) Allows the FBI to request telephone toll and transactional records, financial records, and consumer reports in any investigation to protect against international terrorism or clandestine intelligence activities only if the investigation is not conducted solely on the basis of activities protected by the first amendment to the U.S. Constitution.

(Sec. 506) Revises U.S. Secret Service jurisdiction with respect to fraud and related activity in connection with computers. Grants the FBI primary authority to investigate specified fraud and computer related activity for cases involving espionage, foreign counter-intelligence, information protected against unauthorized disclosure for reasons of national defense or foreign relations, or restricted data, except for offenses affecting Secret Service duties.

(Sec. 507) Amends the General Education Provisions Act and the National Education Statistics Act of 1994 to provide for disclosure of educational records to the Attorney General in a terrorism investigation or prosecution.

Title VI: Providing for Victims of Terrorism, Public Safety Officers, and Their Families—Subtitle A: Aid to Families of Public Safety Officers—Provides for expedited payments for: (1) public safety officers involved in the prevention, investigation, rescue, or recovery efforts related to a terrorist attack; and (2) heroic public safety officers. Increases Public Safety Officers Benefit Program payments.

Subtitle B: Amendments to the Victims of Crime Act of 1984—Amends the Victims of Crime Act of 1984 to: (1) revise provisions regarding the allocation of funds for compensation and assistance, location of compensable crime, and the relationship of crime victim compensation to means-tested Federal benefit programs and to the September 11th victim compensation fund; and (2) establish an antiterrorism emergency reserve in the Victims of Crime Fund.

Title VII: Increased Information Sharing for Critical Infrastructure Protection—Amends the Omnibus Crime Control and Safe Streets Act of 1968 to extend Bureau of Justice Assistance regional information sharing system grants to systems that enhance the investigation and prosecution abilities of participating Federal, State, and local law enforcement agencies in addressing multi-jurisdictional terrorist conspiracies and activities. Authorizes appropriations.

Title VIII: Strengthening the Criminal Laws Against Terrorism—Amends the Federal criminal code to prohibit specific terrorist acts or otherwise destructive, disruptive, or violent acts against mass transportation vehicles, ferries, providers, employees, passengers, or operating systems.

(Sec. 802) Amends the Federal criminal code to: (1) revise the definition of "international terrorism" to include activities that appear to be intended to affect the conduct of government by mass destruction; and (2) define "domestic terrorism" as activities that occur primarily within U.S. jurisdiction, that involve criminal acts dangerous to human life, and that appear to be intended to intimidate or coerce a civilian population, to influence government policy by intimidation or coercion, or to affect government conduct by mass destruction, assassination, or kidnapping.

(Sec. 803) Prohibits harboring any person knowing or having reasonable grounds to believe that such person has committed or to be about to commit a terrorism offense.

(Sec. 804) Establishes Federal jurisdiction over crimes committed at U.S. facilities abroad.

(Sec. 805) Applies the prohibitions against providing material support for terrorism to offenses outside of the United States.

(Sec. 806) Subjects to civil forfeiture all assets, foreign or domestic, of terrorist organizations.

(Sec. 808) Expands: (1) the offenses over which the Attorney General shall have primary investigative jurisdiction under provisions governing acts of terrorism transcending national boundaries; and (2) the offenses included within the definition of the Federal crime of terrorism.

(Sec. 809) Provides that there shall be no statute of limitations for certain terrorism offenses if the commission of such an offense resulted in, or created a foreseeable risk of, death or serious bodily injury to another person.

(Sec. 810) Provides for alternative maximum penalties for specified terrorism crimes.

(Sec. 811) Makes: (1) the penalties for attempts and conspiracies the same as those for terrorism offenses; (2) the supervised release terms for offenses with terrorism predicates any term of years or life; and (3) specified terrorism crimes Racketeer Influenced and Corrupt Organizations statute predicates.

(Sec. 814) Revises prohibitions and penalties regarding fraud and related activity in connection with computers to include specified cyber-terrorism offenses.

(Sec. 816) Directs the Attorney General to establish regional computer forensic laboratories, and to support existing laboratories, to develop specified cyber-security capabilities.

(Sec. 817) Prescribes penalties for knowing possession in certain circumstances of biological agents, toxins, or delivery systems, especially by certain restricted persons.

Title IX: Improved Intelligence—Amends the National Security Act of 1947 to require the Director of Central Intelligence (DCI) to establish requirements and priorities for foreign intelligence collected under the Foreign Intelligence Surveillance Act of 1978 and to provide assistance to the Attorney General (AG) to ensure that information derived from electronic surveillance or physical searches is disseminated for efficient and effective foreign intelligence purposes. Requires the inclusion of international terrorist activities within the scope of foreign intelligence under such Act.

(Sec. 903) Expresses the sense of Congress that officers and employees of the intelligence community should establish and maintain intelligence relationships to acquire information on terrorists and terrorist organizations.

(Sec. 904) Authorizes deferral of the submission to Congress of certain reports on intelligence and intelligence-related matters until: (1) February 1, 2002; or (2) a date after February 1, 2002, if the official involved certifies that preparation and submission on February 1, 2002, will impede the work of officers or employees engaged in counterterrorism activities. Requires congressional notification of any such deferral.

(Sec. 905) Requires the AG or the head of any other Federal department or agency with law enforcement responsibilities to expeditiously disclose to the DCI any foreign intelligence acquired in the course of a criminal investigation.

(Sec. 906) Requires the AG, DCI, and Secretary of the Treasury to jointly report to Congress on the feasibility and desirability of reconfiguring the Foreign Asset Tracking Center and the Office of Foreign Assets Control to provide for the analysis and dissemination of foreign intelligence relating to the financial capabilities and resources of international terrorist organizations.

(Sec. 907) Requires the DCI to report to the appropriate congressional committees on the establishment and maintenance of the National Virtual Translation Center for timely and accurate translation of foreign intelligence for elements of the intelligence community.

(Sec. 908) Requires the AG to provide a program of training to Government officials regarding the identification and use of foreign intelligence.

Title X: Miscellaneous—Directs the Inspector General of the Department of Justice to designate one official to review allegations of abuse of civil rights, civil liberties, and racial and ethnic profiling by government employees and officials.

(Sec. 1002) Expresses the sense of Congress condemning acts of violence or discrimination against any American, including Sikh-Americans. Calls upon local and Federal law enforcement authorities to prosecute to the fullest extent of the law all those who commit crimes.

(Sec. 1004) Amends the Federal criminal code with respect to venue in money laundering cases to allow a prosecution for such an offense to be brought in: (1) any district in which the financial or monetary transaction is conducted; or (2) any district where a prosecution for the underlying specified unlawful activity could be brought, if the defendant participated in the transfer of the proceeds of the specified unlawful activity from that district to the district where the financial or monetary transaction is conducted.

States that: (1) a transfer of funds from one place to another, by wire or any other means, shall constitute a single, continuing transaction; and (2) any person who conducts any portion of the transaction may be charged in any district in which the transaction takes place.

Allows a prosecution for an attempt or conspiracy offense to be brought in the district where venue would lie for the completed offense, or in any other district where an act in furtherance of the attempt or conspiracy took place.

(Sec. 1005) First Responders Assistance Act—Directs the Attorney General to make grants to State and local governments to improve the ability of State and local law enforcement, fire department, and first responders to respond to and prevent acts of terrorism. Authorizes appropriations.

(Sec. 1006) Amends the Immigration and Nationality Act to make inadmissible into the United States any alien engaged in money laundering. Directs the Secretary of State to develop a money laundering watch list which: (1) identifies individuals worldwide who are known or suspected of money laundering; and (2) is readily accessible to, and shall be checked by, a consular or other Federal official before the issuance of a visa or admission to the United States.

(Sec. 1007) Authorizes FY 2002 appropriations for regional antidrug training in Turkey by the Drug Enforcement Administration for police, as well as increased precursor chemical control efforts in South and Central Asia.

(Sec. 1008) Directs the Attorney General to conduct a feasibility study and report to Congress on the use of a biometric identifier scanning system with access to the FBI integrated automated fingerprint identification system at overseas consular posts and points of entry to the United States.

(Sec. 1009) Directs the FBI to study and report to Congress on the feasibility of providing to airlines access via computer to the names of passengers who are suspected of terrorist activity by Federal officials. Authorizes appropriations.

(Sec. 1010) Authorizes the use of Department of Defense funds to contract with local and State governments, during the period of Operation Enduring Freedom, for the performance of security functions at U.S. military installations.

(Sec. 1011) Crimes Against Charitable Americans Act of 2001—Amends the Telemarketing and Consumer Fraud and Abuse Prevention Act to cover fraudulent charitable solicitations. Requires any person engaged in telemarketing for the solicitation of charitable contributions, donations, or gifts to disclose promptly and clearly the purpose of the telephone call.

(Sec. 1012) Amends the Federal transportation code to prohibit States from licensing any individual to operate a motor vehicle transporting hazardous material unless the Secretary of Transportation determines that such individual does not pose a security risk warranting denial of the license. Requires background checks of such license applicants by the Attorney General upon State request.

(Sec. 1013) Expresses the sense of the Senate on substantial new U.S. investment in bioterrorism preparedness and response.

(Sec. 1014) Directs the Office for State and Local Domestic Preparedness Support of the Office of Justice Programs to make grants to enhance State and local capability to prepare for and respond to terrorist acts. Authorizes appropriations for FY 2002 through 2007.

(Sec. 1015) Amends the Crime Identification Technology Act of 1998 to extend it through FY 2007 and provide for antiterrorism grants to States and localities. Authorizes appropriations.

(Sec. 1016) Critical Infrastructures Protection Act of 2001— Declares it is U.S. policy: (1) that any physical or virtual disruption of the operation of the critical infrastructures of the United States be rare, brief, geographically limited in effect, manageable, and minimally detrimental to the economy, human and government services, and U.S. national security; (2) that actions necessary to achieve this policy be carried out in a public-private partnership involving corporate and nongovernmental organizations; and (3) to have in place a comprehensive and effective program to ensure the continuity of essential Federal Government functions under all circumstances.

Establishes the National Infrastructure Simulation and Analysis Center to serve as a source of national competence to address critical infrastructure protection and continuity through support for activities related to counterterrorism, threat assessment, and risk mitigation.

Defines critical infrastructure as systems and assets, whether physical or virtual, so vital to the United States that their incapacity or destruction would have a debilitating impact on security, national economic security, national public health or safety, or any combination of those matters.

Authorizes appropriations.

# Appendix 3: Homeland Security Act of 2002

SUMMARY AS OF:

11/19/2002—Passed Senate, amended. (There are 3 other summaries)

Homeland Security Act of 2002—Title I: Department of Homeland Security—(Sec. 101) Establishes a Department of Homeland Security (DHS) as an executive department of the United States, headed by a Secretary of Homeland Security (Secretary) appointed by the President, by and with the advice and consent of the Senate, to: (1) prevent terrorist attacks within the United States; (2) reduce the vulnerability of the United States to terrorism; (3) minimize the damage, and assist in the recovery, from terrorist attacks that occur within the United States; (4) carry out all functions of entities transferred to DHS; (5) ensure that the functions of the agencies and subdivisions within DHS that are not related directly to securing the homeland are not diminished or neglected except by a specific Act of Congress; (6) ensure that the overall economic security of the United States is not diminished by efforts, activities, and programs aimed at securing the homeland; and (7) monitor connections between illegal drug trafficking and terrorism, coordinate efforts to sever such connections, and otherwise contribute to efforts to interdict illegal drug trafficking. Vests primary responsibility for investigating and prosecuting acts of terrorism in Federal, State, and local law enforcement agencies with proper jurisdiction except as specifically provided by law with respect to entities transferred to DHS under this Act.

(Sec. 102) Directs the Secretary to appoint a Special Assistant to carry out specified homeland security liaison activities between DHS and the private sector.

(Sec. 103) Creates the following: (1) a Deputy Secretary of Homeland Security; (2) an Under Secretary for Information Analysis and Infrastructure Protection; (3) an Under Secretary for Science and Technology; (4) an Under Secretary for Border and Transportation Security; (5) an Under Secretary for Emergency Preparedness and Response; (6) a Director of the Bureau of Citizenship and Immigration Services; (7) an Under Secretary for Management; (8) not more than 12 Assistant Secretaries; and (9) a General Counsel. Establishes an Inspector General (to be appointed under the Inspector General Act of 1978). Requires the following individuals to assist the Secretary in the performance of the Secretary's functions: (1) the Commandant of the Coast Guard; (2) the Director of the Secret Service; (3) a Chief Information Officer; (4) a Chief Human Capital Officer; (5) a Chief Financial Officer; and (6) an Officer for Civil Rights and Civil Liberties.

Title II: Information Analysis and Infrastructure Protection—Subtitle A: Directorate for Information Analysis and Infrastructure Protection; Access to Information—(Sec. 201) Establishes in the Department: (1) a Directorate for Information Analysis and Infrastructure Protection, headed by an Under Secretary for Information Analysis and Infrastructure Protection; (2) an Assistant Secretary for Information Analysis; and (3) an Assistant Secretary for Infrastructure Protection.

Requires the Under Secretary to: (1) access, receive, and analyze law enforcement and intelligence information from Federal, State, and local agencies and the private sector to identify the nature, scope, and identity of terrorist threats to the United States, as well as potential U.S. vulnerabilities; (2) carry out comprehensive assessments of vulnerabilities of key U.S. resources and critical infrastructures; (3) integrate relevant information, analyses, and vulnerability assessments to identify protection priorities; (4) ensure timely and efficient Department access to necessary information for discharging responsibilities; (5) develop a comprehensive national plan for securing key U.S. resources and critical infrastructures; (6) recommend necessary measures to protect such resources and infrastructure in coordination with other entities; (7) administer the Homeland Security Advisory System; (8) review, analyze, and make recommendations for improvements in policies and procedures governing the sharing of law enforcement, intelligence, and intelligence-related information and other information related to homeland security within the Federal Government and between the Federal Government and State and local government agencies and authorities; (9) disseminate Department homeland security information to other appropriate Federal, State, and local agencies; (10) consult with the Director of Central Intelligence (DCI) and other appropriate Federal intelligence, law enforcement, or other elements to establish collection priorities and strategies for information relating the terrorism threats; (11) consult with State and local governments and private entities to ensure appropriate exchanges of information relating to such threats; (12) ensure the protection from unauthorized disclosure of homeland security and intelligence information; (13) request additional information from appropriate entities relating to threats of terrorism in the United States; (14) establish and utilize a secure communications and information technology infrastructure for receiving and analyzing data; (15) ensure the compatibility and privacy protection of shared information databases and analytical tools; (16) coordinate training and other support to facilitate the identification and sharing of information; (17) coordinate activities with elements of the intelligence community, Federal, State, and local law enforcement agencies, and the private sector; and (18) provide intelligence and information analysis and support to other elements of the Department. Provides for: (1) staffing, including the use of private sector analysts; and (2) cooperative agreements for the detail of appropriate personnel.

Transfers to the Secretary the functions, personnel, assets, and liabilities of the following entities: (1) the National Infrastructure Protection Center of the Federal Bureau of Investigation (other than the Computer Investigations and Operations Section); (2) the National Communications System of the Department of Defense; (3) the Critical Infrastructure Assurance Offices of the Department of Commerce; (4) the National Infrastructure Simulation and Analysis Center of the Department of Energy and its energy security and assurance program; and (5) the Federal Computer Incident Response Center of the General Services Administration.

Amends the National Security Act of 1947 to include as elements of the intelligence community the Department elements concerned with analyses of foreign intelligence information.

(Sec. 202) Gives the Secretary access to all reports, assessments, analyses, and unevaluated intelligence relating to threats of terrorism against the United States, and to all information concerning infrastructure or other vulnerabilities to terrorism, whether or not such information has been analyzed. Requires all Federal agencies to promptly provide to the Secretary: (1) all reports, assessments, and analytical information relating to such threats and to other areas of

responsibility assigned to the Secretary; (2) all information concerning the vulnerability of U.S. infrastructure or other U.S. vulnerabilities to terrorism, whether or not it has been analyzed; (3) all other information relating to significant and credible threats of terrorism, whether or not it has been analyzed; and (4) such other information or material as the President may direct. Requires the Secretary to be provided with certain terrorism-related information from law enforcement agencies that is currently required to be provided to the DCI.

Subtitle B: Critical Infrastructure Information—Critical Infrastructure Information Act of 2002—(Sec. 213) Allows a critical infrastructure protection program to be so designated by either the President or the Secretary.

(Sec. 214) Exempts from the Freedom of Information Act and other Federal and State disclosure requirements any critical infrastructure information that is voluntarily submitted to a covered Federal agency for use in the security of critical infrastructure and protected systems, analysis, warning, interdependency study, recovery, reconstitution, or other informational purpose when accompanied by an express statement that such information is being submitted voluntarily in expectation of such nondisclosure protection. Requires the Secretary to establish specified procedures for the receipt, care, and storage by Federal agencies of critical infrastructure information voluntarily submitted. Provides criminal penalties for the unauthorized disclosure of such information.

Authorizes the Federal Government to issue advisories, alerts, and warnings to relevant companies, targeted sectors, other governmental entities, or the general public regarding potential threats to critical infrastructure.

Subtitle C: Information Security—(Sec. 221) Requires the Secretary to establish procedures on the use of shared information that: (1) limit its re-dissemination to ensure it is not used for an unauthorized purpose; (2) ensure its security and confidentiality; (3) protect the constitutional and statutory rights of individuals who are subjects of such information; and (4) provide data integrity through the timely removal and destruction of obsolete or erroneous names and information.

(Sec. 222) Directs the Secretary to appoint a senior Department official to assume primary responsibility for information privacy policy.

(Sec. 223) Directs the Under Secretary to provide: (1) to State and local government entities and, upon request, to private entities that own or operate critical information systems, analysis and warnings related to threats to and vulnerabilities of such systems, as well as crisis management support in response to threats to or attacks upon such systems; and (2) technical assistance, upon request, to private sector and other government entities with respect to emergency recovery plans to respond to major failures of such systems.

(Sec. 224) Authorizes the Under Secretary to establish a national technology guard (known as NET Guard) to assist local communities to respond to and recover from attacks on information systems and communications networks.

(Sec. 225) Cyber Security Enhancement Act of 2002— Directs the U.S. Sentencing Commission to review and amend Federal sentencing guidelines and otherwise address crimes involving fraud in connection with computers and access to protected information, protected computers, or restricted data in interstate or foreign commerce or involving a computer used by or for the Federal Government. Requires a Commission report to Congress on actions taken and recommendations regarding statutory penalties for violations. Exempts from criminal penalties any disclosure made by an electronic communication service to a Federal, State, or local governmental entity if made in the good faith belief that an emergency involving danger of death or serious physical injury to any person requires disclosure without delay. Requires any government entity receiving such a disclosure to report it to the Attorney General.

Amends the Federal criminal code to: (1) prohibit the dissemination by electronic means of any such protected information; (2) increase criminal penalties for violations which cause death or serious bodily injury; (3) authorize the use by appropriate officials of emergency pen register and trap and trace devices in the case of either an immediate threat to a national security interest or an ongoing attack on a protected computer that constitutes a crime punishable by a prison term of greater than one year; (4) repeal provisions which provide a shorter term of imprisonment for certain offenses involving protection from the unauthorized interception and disclosure of wire, oral, or electronic communications; and (5) increase penalties for repeat offenses in connection with unlawful access to stored communications.

Subtitle D: Office of Science and Technology— (Sec. 231) Establishes within the Department of Justice (DOJ) an Office of Science and Technology whose mission is to: (1) serve as the national focal point for work on law enforcement technology (investigative and forensic technologies, corrections technologies, and technologies that support the judicial process); and (2) carry out programs that improve the safety and effectiveness of such technology and improve technology access by Federal, State, and local law enforcement agencies. Sets forth Office duties, including: (1) establishing and maintaining technology advisory groups and performance standards; (2) carrying out research, development, testing, evaluation, and cost-benefit analyses for improving the safety, effectiveness, and efficiency of technologies used by Federal, State, and local law enforcement agencies; and (3) operating the regional National Law Enforcement and Corrections Technology Centers (established under this Subtitle) and establishing additional centers. Requires the Office Director to report annually on Office activities.

(Sec. 234) Authorizes the Attorney General to transfer to the Office any other DOJ program or activity determined to be consistent with its mission. Requires a report from the Attorney General to the congressional judiciary committees on the implementation of this Subtitle.

(Sec. 235) Requires the Office Director to operate and support National Law Enforcement and Corrections Technology Centers and, to the extent necessary, establish new centers through a merit-based, competitive process. Requires such Centers to: (1) support research and development of law enforcement technology; (2) support the transfer and implementation of such technology; (3) assist in the development and dissemination of guidelines and technological standards; and (4) provide technology assistance, information, and support for law enforcement, corrections, and criminal justice purposes. Requires the Director to: (1) convene an annual meeting of such Centers; and (2) report to Congress assessing the effectiveness of the Centers and identifying the number of Centers necessary to meet the technology needs of Federal, State, and local law enforcement in the United States.

(Sec. 237) Amends the Omnibus Crime Control and Safe Streets Act of 1968 to require the National Institute of Justice to: (1) research and develop tools and technologies relating to prevention, detection, investigation, and prosecution of crime; and (2) support research, development, testing, training, and evaluation of tools and technology for Federal, State, and local law enforcement agencies.

Title III: Science and Technology in Support of Homeland Security—(Sec. 301) Establishes in DHS a Directorate of Science and Technology, headed by an Under Secretary for Science and Technology, to be responsible for: (1) advising the Secretary regarding research and development (R&D) efforts and priorities in support of DHS missions; (2) developing a national policy and strategic plan for, identifying priorities, goals, objectives and policies for, and coordinating the Federal Government's civilian efforts to identify and develop countermeasures to chemical, biological, radiological, nuclear, and other emerging terrorist threats; (3) supporting the Under Secretary for Information Analysis and Infrastructure Protection by assessing and testing homeland security vulnerabilities and possible threats; (4) conducting basic and applied R&D activities relevant to DHS elements, provided that such responsibility does not extend to human health-related R&D activities; (5) establishing priorities for directing, funding, and conducting national R&D and procurement of technology systems for preventing the importation of chemical, biological, radiological, nuclear, and related weapons and material and for detecting, preventing, protecting against, and responding to terrorist attacks; (6) establishing a system for transferring homeland security developments or technologies to Federal, State, and local government and private sector entities; (7) entering into agreements with the Department of Energy (DOE) regarding the use of the national laboratories or sites and support of the science and technology base at those facilities; (8) collaborating with the Secretary of Agriculture and the Attorney General in the regulation of certain biological agents and toxins as provided in the Agricultural Bioterrorism Protection Act of 2002; (9) collaborating with the Secretary of Health and Human Services and the Attorney General in determining new biological agents and toxins that shall be listed as select agents in the Code of Federal Regulations; (10) supporting U.S. leadership in science and technology; (11) establishing and administering the primary R&D activities of DHS; (12) coordinating and integrating all DHS R&D activities; (13) coordinating with other appropriate executive agencies in developing and carrying out the science and technology agenda of DHS to reduce duplication and identify unmet needs; and (14) developing and overseeing the administration of guidelines for merit review of R&D projects throughout DHS and for the dissemination of DHS research.

(Sec. 303) Transfers to the Secretary: (1) specified DOE functions, including functions related to chemical and biological national security programs, nuclear smuggling programs and activities within the proliferation detection program, the nuclear assessment program, designated life sciences activities of the biological and environmental research program related to microbial pathogens, the Environmental Measurements Laboratory, and the advanced

scientific computing research program at Lawrence Livermore National Laboratory; and (2) the National Bio-Weapons Defense Analysis Center of DOD.

(Sec. 304) Requires the HHS Secretary, with respect to civilian human health-related R&D activities relating to HHS countermeasures for chemical, biological, radiological, and nuclear and other emerging terrorist threats, to: (1) set priorities, goals, objectives, and policies and develop a coordinated strategy for such activities in collaboration with the Secretary to ensure consistency with the national policy and strategic plan; and (2) collaborate with the Secretary in developing specific benchmarks and outcome measurements for evaluating progress toward achieving such priorities and goals.

Amends the Public Health Service Act to: (1) authorize the HHS Secretary to declare that an actual or potential bioterrorist incident or other public health emergency makes advisable the administration of a covered countermeasure against smallpox to a category or categories of individuals; (2) require the HHS Secretary to specify the substances to be considered countermeasures and the beginning and ending dates of the period of the declaration; and (3) deem a covered person to be an employee of the Public Health Service with respect to liability arising out of administration of such a countermeasure.

Extends liability to the United States (with an exception) with respect to claims arising out of an administration of a covered countermeasure to an individual only if: (1) the countermeasure was administered by a qualified person for the purpose of preventing or treating smallpox during the effective period; (2) the individual was within a covered category; or (3) the qualified person administering the countermeasure had reasonable grounds to believe that such individual was within such category. Provides for a rebuttable presumption of an administration within the scope of a declaration in the case where an individual who is not vaccinated contracts vaccinia. Makes the remedy against the United States provided under such Act exclusive of any other civil action or proceeding against a covered person for any claim or suit arising out of the administration of a covered countermeasure.

(Sec. 305) Authorizes the Secretary, acting through the Under Secretary, to establish or contract with one or more federally funded R&D centers to provide independent analysis of homeland security issues or to carry out other responsibilities under this Act.

(Sec. 306) Directs the President to notify the appropriate congressional committees of any proposed transfer of DOE life sciences activities.

(Sec. 307) Establishes the Homeland Security Advanced Research Projects Agency to be headed by a Director who shall be appointed by the Secretary and who shall report to the Under Secretary. Requires the Director to administer the Acceleration Fund for Research and Development of Homeland Security Technologies (established by this Act) to award competitive, merit-reviewed grants, cooperative agreements, or contracts to public or private entities to: (1) support basic and applied homeland security research to promote revolutionary changes in technologies that would promote homeland security; (2) advance the development, testing and evaluation, and deployment of critical homeland security technologies; and (3) accelerate the prototyping and deployment of technologies that would address homeland security vulnerabilities. Allows the Director to solicit proposals to address specific vulnerabilities. Requires the Director to periodically hold homeland security technology demonstrations to improve contact among technology developers, vendors, and acquisition personnel.

Authorizes appropriations to the Fund. Earmarks ten percent of such funds for each fiscal year through FY 2005 for the Under Secretary, through joint agreement with the Commandant of the Coast Guard, to carry out R&D of improved ports, waterways, and coastal security surveillance and perimeter protection capabilities to minimize the possibility that Coast Guard cutters, aircraft, helicopters, and personnel will be diverted from non-homeland security missions to the ports, waterways, and coastal security mission.

(Sec. 308) Requires the Secretary, acting through the Under Secretary, to: (1) operate extramural R&D programs to ensure that colleges, universities, private research institutes, and companies (and consortia thereof) from as many areas of the United States as practicable participate; and (2) establish a university-based center or centers for homeland security which shall establish a coordinated, university-based system to enhance the Nation's homeland security. Authorizes the Secretary, through the Under Secretary, to: (1) draw upon the expertise of any Government laboratory; and (2) establish a headquarters laboratory for DHS and additional laboratory units.

(Sec. 309) Allows the Secretary, in carrying out DHS missions, to utilize DOE national laboratories and sites through: (1) a joint sponsorship arrangement; (2) a direct contact

between DHS and the applicable DOE laboratory or site; (3) any "work for others" basis made available by that laboratory or site; or (4) any other method provided by law. Allows DHS to be a joint sponsor: (1) with DOE of one or more DOE national laboratories; and (2) of a DOE site in the performance of work as if such site were a federally funded R&D center and the work were performed under a multiple agency sponsorship arrangement with DHS Directs the Secretary and the Secretary of DOE to ensure that direct contracts between DHS and the operator of a DOE national laboratory or site for programs or activities transferred from DOE to DHS are separate from the direct contracts of DOE with such operator.

Establishes within the Directorate of Science and Technology an Office for National Laboratories that shall be responsible for the coordination and utilization of DOE national laboratories and sites in a manner to create a networked laboratory system to support DHS missions.

(Sec. 310) Directs the Secretary of Agriculture to transfer to the Secretary the Plum Island Animal Disease Center of the Department of Agriculture and provides for continued Department of Agriculture access to such Center.

(Sec. 311) Establishes within DHS a Homeland Security Science and Technology Advisory Committee to make recommendations with respect to the activities of the Under Secretary.

(Sec. 312) Directs the Secretary to establish the Homeland Security Institute, a federally funded R&D center. Includes among authorized duties for the Institute: (1) determination of the vulnerabilities of the Nation's critical infrastructures; (2) assessment of the costs and benefits of alternative approaches to enhancing security; and (3) evaluation of the effectiveness of measures deployed to enhance the security of institutions, facilities, and infrastructure that may be terrorist targets.

(Sec. 313) Requires the Secretary to establish and promote a program to encourage technological innovation in facilitating the mission of DHS, to include establishment of: (1) a centralized Federal clearinghouse to further the dissemination of information on technologies; and (2) a technical assistance team to assist in screening submitted proposals.

Title IV: Directorate of Border and Transportation Security—Subtitle A: Under Secretary for Border and Transportation Security—(Sec. 401) Establishes in DHS a Directorate of Border and Transportation Security to be headed by an Under Secretary for Border and Transportation

Security. Makes the Secretary, acting through the Under Secretary for Border and Transportation Security, responsible for: (1) preventing the entry of terrorists and the instruments of terrorism into the United States; (2) securing the borders, territorial waters, ports, terminals, waterways, and air, land, and sea transportation systems of the United States; (3) carrying out the immigration enforcement functions vested by statute in, or performed by, the Commissioner of Immigration and Naturalization immediately before their transfer to the Under Secretary; (4) establishing and administering rules governing the granting of visas or other forms of permission to enter the United States to individuals who are not citizens or aliens lawfully admitted for permanent residence in the United States; (5) establishing national immigration enforcement policies and priorities; (6) administering the customs laws of the United States (with certain exceptions); (7) conducting the inspection and related administrative functions of the Department of Agriculture transferred to the Secretary; and (8) ensuring the speedy, orderly, and efficient flow of lawful traffic and commerce in carrying out the foregoing responsibilities.

(Sec. 403) Transfers to the Secretary the functions, personnel, assets, and liabilities of: (1) the U.S. Customs Service; (2) the Transportation Security Administration; (3) the Federal Protective Service of the General Services Administration (GSA); (4) the Federal Law Enforcement Training Center of the Department of the Treasury; and (5) the Office for Domestic Preparedness of the Office of Justice Programs of the Department of Justice (DOJ).

Subtitle B: United States Customs Service—(Sec. 411) Establishes in DHS the U.S. Customs Service (transferred from the Department of the Treasury, but with certain customs revenue functions remaining with the Secretary of the Treasury). Authorizes the Secretary of the Treasury to appoint up to 20 new personnel to work with DHS personnel in performing customs revenue functions.

(Sec. 414) Requires the President to include a separate budget request for the U.S. Customs Service in the annual budget transmitted to Congress.

(Sec. 416) Directs the Comptroller General to report to Congress on all trade functions performed by the executive branch, specifying each agency that performs each such function.

(Sec. 417) Directs the Secretary to ensure that adequate staffing is provided to assure that levels of current customs revenue services will continue to be provided. Requires the Secretary to notify specified congressional committees prior to taking any action which would: (1) result in any significant reduction in customs revenue services (including hours of operation provided at any office within DHS or any port of entry); (2) eliminate or relocate any office of DHS which provides customs revenue services; or (3) eliminate any port of entry.

(Sec. 419) Amends the Consolidated Omnibus Budget Reconciliation Act of 1985 to create in the Treasury a separate Customs Commercial and Homeland Security Automation Account to contain merchandise processing (customs user) fees. Authorizes appropriations for FY 2003 through 2005 for establishment of the Automated Commercial Environment computer system for the processing of merchandise that is entered or released and for other purposes related to the functions of DHS.

Subtitle C: Miscellaneous Provisions—(Sec. 421) Transfers to the Secretary the functions of the Secretary of Agriculture relating to agricultural import and entry inspection activities under specified animal and plant protection laws.

Requires the Secretary of Agriculture and the Secretary to enter into an agreement to effectuate such transfer and to transfer periodically funds collected pursuant to fee authorities under the Food, Agriculture, Conservation, and Trade Act of 1990 to the Secretary for activities carried out by the Secretary for which such fees were collected.

Directs the Secretary of Agriculture to transfer to the Secretary not more than 3,200 full-time equivalent positions of the Department of Agriculture.

(Sec. 423) Directs the Secretary to establish a liaison office within DHS for the purpose of consulting with the Administrator of the Federal Aviation Administration before taking any action that might affect aviation safety, air carrier operations, aircraft airworthiness, or the use of airspace.

(Sec. 424) Requires the Transportation Security Administration to be maintained as a distinct entity within DHS under the Under Secretary for Border Transportation and Security for two years after enactment of this Act.

(Sec. 425) Amends Federal aviation law to require the Under Secretary of Transportation for Security to take certain action, if, in his discretion or at the request of an airport, he determines that the Transportation Security Administration is not able to deploy explosive detection systems at all airports required to have them by December 31, 2002. Requires the Under Secretary, in such circumstances, to: (1) submit to specified congressional committees a detailed plan for the deployment of explosive detection systems at such airport by December 31, 2003; and (2) take all necessary action to ensure that alternative means of screening all checked baggage is implemented.

(Sec. 426) Replaces the Secretary of Transportation with the Secretary of Homeland Security as chair of the Transportation Security Oversight Board. Requires the Secretary of Transportation to consult with the Secretary before approving airport development project grants relating to security equipment or the installation of bulk explosive detection systems.

(Sec. 427) Directs the Secretary, in coordination with the Secretary of Agriculture, the Secretary of Health and Human Services, and the head of each other department or agency determined to be appropriate by the Secretary, to ensure that appropriate information concerning inspections of articles that are imported or entered into the United States, and are inspected or regulated by one or more affected agencies, is timely and efficiently exchanged between the affected agencies. Requires the Secretary to report to Congress on the progress made in implementing this section.

(Sec. 428) Grants the Secretary exclusive authority to issue regulations with respect to, administer, and enforce the Immigration and Nationality Act (INA) and all other immigration and nationality laws relating to the functions of U.S. diplomatic and consular officers in connection with the granting or refusal of visas, and authority to refuse visas in accordance with law and to develop programs of homeland security training for consular officers, which authorities shall be exercised through the Secretary of State. Denies the Secretary authority, however, to alter or reverse the decision of a consular officer to refuse a visa to an alien.

Grants the Secretary authority also to confer or impose upon any U.S. officer or employee, with the consent of the head of the executive agency under whose jurisdiction such officer or employee is serving, any of these specified functions.

Authorizes the Secretary of State to direct a consular officer to refuse a visa to an alien if the Secretary of State deems such refusal necessary or advisable in the foreign policy or security interests of the United States.

Authorizes the Secretary to assign employees of DHS to any diplomatic and consular posts abroad to review individual visa applications and provide expert advice and training to consular officers regarding specific security threats relating to such applications and to conduct investigations with respect to matters under the Secretary's jurisdiction.

Directs the Secretary to study and report to Congress on the role of foreign nationals in the granting or refusal of visas and other documents authorizing entry of aliens into the United States.

Requires the Director of the Office of Science and Technology Policy to report to Congress on how the provisions of this section will affect procedures for the issuance of student visas.

Terminates after enactment of this Act all third party screening visa issuance programs in Saudi Arabia. Requires on-site personnel of DHS to review all visa applications prior to adjudication.

(Sec. 429) Requires visa denial information to be entered into the electronic data system as provided for in the Enhanced Border Security and Visa Entry Reform Act of 2002. Prohibits an alien denied a visa from being issued a subsequent visa unless the reviewing consular officer makes specified findings concerning waiver of ineligibility.

(Sec. 430) Establishes within the Directorate of Border and Transportation Security the Office for Domestic Preparedness to: (1) coordinate Federal preparedness for acts of terrorism, working with all State, local, tribal, county, parish, and private sector emergency response providers; (2) coordinate or consolidate systems of communications relating to homeland security at all levels of government; (3) direct and supervise Federal terrorism preparedness grant programs for all emergency response providers; and (4) perform specified other related duties.

Subtitle D: Immigration Enforcement Functions—(Sec. 441) Transfers from the Commissioner of Immigration and Naturalization to the Under Secretary for Border and Transportation Security all functions performed under the following programs, and all personnel, assets, and liabilities pertaining to such programs, immediately before such transfer occurs: (1) the Border Patrol program; (2) the detention and removal program; (3) the intelligence program; (4) the investigations program; and (5) the inspections program.

(Sec. 442) Establishes in the Department of Homeland Security (DHS) the Bureau of Border Security, headed by the Assistant Secretary of the Bureau of Border Security who shall: (1) report directly to the Under Secretary; (2) establish and oversee the policies for performing functions transferred to the Under Secretary and delegated to the Assistant Secretary by the Under Secretary; and (3) advise the Under Secretary with respect to any policy or operation of the Bureau that may affect the Bureau of Citizenship and Immigration Services.

Directs the Assistant Secretary to: (1) administer the program to collect information relating to nonimmigrant foreign students and other exchange program participants; and (2) implement a managerial rotation program.

Establishes the position of Chief of Policy and Strategy for the Bureau of Border Security, who shall: (1) make immigration enforcement policy recommendations; and (2) coordinate immigration policy issues with the Chief of Policy and Strategy for the Bureau of Citizenship and Immigration Services.

(Sec. 443) Makes the Under Secretary responsible for: (1) investigating noncriminal allegations of Bureau employee misconduct, corruption, and fraud that are not subject to investigation by the Inspector General for DHS; (2) inspecting and assessing Bureau operations; and (3) analyzing Bureau management.

(Sec. 444) Authorizes the Under Secretary to impose disciplinary action pursuant to policies and procedures applicable to FBI employees.

(Sec. 445) Requires the Secretary of Homeland Security to report on how the Bureau will enforce relevant INA provisions.

(Sec. 446) Expresses the sense of Congress that completing the 14-mile border fence project near San Diego, California, mandated by the Illegal Immigration Reform and Immigrant Responsibility Act of 1996 should be a priority for the Secretary.

Subtitle E: Citizenship and Immigration Services—(Sec. 451) Establishes in DHS a Bureau of Citizenship and Immigration Services, headed by the Director of the Bureau of Citizenship and Immigration Services, who shall: (1) establish the policies for performing and administering transferred functions; (2) establish national immigration services policies and priorities; and (3) implement a managerial rotation program.

Authorizes the Director to implement pilot initiatives to eliminate the backlog of immigration benefit applications.

Transfers all Immigration and Naturalization Service (INS) adjudications and related personnel and funding to the Director.

Establishes for the Bureau positions of: (1) Chief of Policy and Strategy; (2) legal adviser; (3) budget officer; and (4) Chief of the Office of Citizenship to promote citizenship instruction and training for aliens interested in becoming naturalized U.S. citizens.

(Sec. 452) Establishes within the DHS a Citizenship and Immigration Services Ombudsman, with local offices, to:

(1) assist individuals and employers resolve problems with the Bureau; (2) identify problem areas; and (3) propose administrative and legislative changes.

(Sec. 453) Makes the Director responsible for (1) investigating noncriminal allegations of Bureau employee misconduct, corruption, and fraud that are not subject to investigation by the Inspector General of DHS; (2) inspecting and assessing Bureau operations; and (3) analyzing Bureau management.

(Sec. 454) Authorizes the Director to impose disciplinary action pursuant to policies and procedures applicable to FBI employees.

(Sec. 456) Sets forth transfer of authority and transfer and allocation of appropriations and personnel provisions.

(Sec. 457) Amends the INA to repeal the provision permitting fees for adjudication and naturalization services to be set at a level that will ensure recovery of the costs of similar services provided without charge to asylum applicants.

(Sec. 458) Amends the Immigration Services and Infrastructure Improvements Act of 2000 to change the deadline for the Attorney General to eliminate the backlog in the processing of immigration benefit applications to one year after enactment of this Act.

(Sec. 459) Directs the Secretary to report on how the Bureau of Citizenship and Immigration Services will efficiently complete transferred INS adjudications.

(Sec. 460) Directs the Attorney General to report on changes in law needed to ensure an appropriate response to emergent or unforeseen immigration needs.

(Sec. 461) Directs the Secretary to: (1) establish an Internet-based system that will permit online information access to a person, employer, immigrant, or nonimmigrant about the processing status of any filings for any benefit under the INA; (2) conduct a feasibility study for online filing and improved processing; and (3) establish a Technology Advisory Committee.

(Sec. 462) Transfers to the Director of the Office of Refugee Resettlement of the Department of Health and Human Services (HHS) INS functions with respect to the care of unaccompanied alien children (as defined by this Act).

Sets forth the responsibilities of the Office for such children, including: (1) coordinating and implementing the care and placement of unaccompanied alien children who are in Federal custody, including appointment of independent legal counsel to represent the interests of each child; (2) identifying and overseeing individuals, entities, and facilities to house such children; (3) family reunification; (4) compiling, updating, and publishing at least annually a State-by-State list of professionals or other entities qualified to provide guardian and attorney representation services; (5) maintaining related biographical and statistical information; and (6) conducting investigations and inspections of residential facilities.

Directs the Office to: (1) consult with juvenile justice professionals to ensure such children's safety; and (2) not release such children upon their own recognizance.

Subtitle F: General Immigration Provisions—(Sec. 471) Abolishes INS upon completion of all transfers from it as provided for by this Act.

(Sec. 472) Authorizes the Attorney General and the Secretary to make voluntary separation incentive payments, after completion of a strategic restructuring plan, to employees of: (1) INS; (2) the Bureau of Border Security of DHS; and (3) the Bureau of Citizenship and Immigration Services of DHS.

(Sec. 473) Directs the Attorney General and the Secretary to conduct a demonstration project to determine whether policy or procedure revisions for employee discipline would result in improved personnel management.

(Sec. 474) Expresses the sense of Congress that: (1) the missions of the Bureau of Border Security and the Bureau of Citizenship and Immigration Services are equally important and should be adequately funded; and (2) the functions transferred should not operate at levels below those in effect prior to the enactment of this Act.

(Sec. 475) Establishes within the Office of Deputy Secretary a Director of Shared Services who shall be responsible for: (1) information resources management; and (2) records, forms, and file management.

(Sec. 476) Provides for budgetary and funding separation with respect to the Bureau of Citizenship and Immigration Services and the Bureau of Border Security.

(Sec. 477) Sets forth reporting and implementation plan provisions.

(Sec. 478) Directs the Secretary to annually report regarding: (1) the aggregate number of all immigration applications and petitions received, and processed; (2) regional statistics on the aggregate number of denied applications and petitions; (3) application and petition backlogs and a backlog elimination plan; (4) application and petition processing periods; (5) number, types, and disposition of grievances and plans to improve immigration services; and (6) appropriate use of immigration-related fees.

Expresses the sense of Congress that: (1) the quality and efficiency of immigration services should be improved after the transfers made by Act; and (2) the Secretary should undertake efforts to guarantee that such concerns are addressed after such effective date.

Title V: Emergency Preparedness and Response—(Sec. 501) Establishes in DHS a Directorate of Emergency Preparedness and Response, headed by an Under Secretary.

(Sec. 502) Requires the responsibilities of the Secretary, acting through the Under Secretary, to include: (1) helping to ensure the effectiveness of emergency response providers to terrorist attacks, major disasters, and other emergencies; (2) with respect to the Nuclear Incident Response Team, establishing and certifying compliance with standards, conducting joint and other exercises and training, and providing funds to the Department of Energy and the Environmental Protection Agency for homeland security planning, training, and equipment; (3) providing the Federal Government's response to terrorist attacks and major disasters; (4) aiding recovery from terrorist attacks and major disasters; (5) building a comprehensive national incident management system with Federal, State, and local governments to respond to such attacks and disasters; (6) consolidating existing Federal Government emergency response plans into a single, coordinated national response plan; and (7) developing comprehensive programs for developing interoperative communications technology and helping to ensure that emergency response providers acquire such technology.

(Sec. 503) Transfers to the Secretary the functions, personnel, assets, and liabilities of: (1) the Federal Emergency Management Agency (FEMA); (2) the Integrated Hazard Information System of the National Oceanic and Atmospheric Administration, which shall be renamed FIRESAT; (3) the National Domestic Preparedness Office of the FBI; (4) the Domestic Emergency Support Teams of DOJ; (5) the Office of Emergency Preparedness, the National Disaster Medical System, and the Metropolitan Medical Response System of HHS; and (6) the Strategic National Stockpile of HHS.

(Sec. 504) Requires the Nuclear Incident Response Team, at the direction of the Secretary (in connection with an actual or threatened terrorist attack, major disaster, or other emergency in the United States), to operate as an organizational unit of DHS under the Secretary's authority and control.

(Sec. 505) Provides that, with respect to all public health-related activities to improve State, local, and hospital preparedness and response to chemical, biological, radiological, and nuclear and other emerging terrorist threats carried out by HHS (including the Public Health Service), the Secretary of HHS shall set priorities and preparedness goals and further develop a coordinated strategy for such activities in collaboration with the Secretary.

(Sec. 506) Defines the Nuclear Incident Response Team to include: (1) those entities of the Department of Energy that perform nuclear or radiological emergency support functions, radiation exposure functions at the medical assistance facility known as the Radiation Emergency Assistance Center/Training Site (REAC/TS), radiological assistance functions, and related functions; and (2) Environmental Protection Agency entities that perform such support functions and related functions.

(Sec. 507) Includes in the homeland security role of FEMA: (1) all functions and authorities prescribed by the Robert T. Stafford Disaster Relief and Emergency Assistance Act; and (2) a comprehensive, risk-based emergency management program of mitigation, of planning for building the emergency management profession, of response, of recovery, and of increased efficiencies. Maintains FEMA as the lead agency for the Federal Response Plan established under Executive Orders 12148 and 12656. Requires the FEMA Director to revise the Plan to reflect the establishment of and incorporate DHS.

(Sec. 508) Directs the Secretary, to the maximum extent practicable, to use national private sector networks and infrastructure for emergency response to major disasters.

(Sec. 509) Expresses the sense of Congress that the Secretary should: (1) use off-the-shelf commercially developed technologies to allow DHS to collect, manage, share, analyze, and disseminate information securely over multiple channels of communication; and (2) rely on commercial sources to supply goods and services needed by DHS.

Title VI: Treatment of Charitable Trusts for Members of the Armed Forces of the United States and Other Governmental Organizations—(Sec. 601) Sets forth requirements a charitable corporation, fund, foundation, or trust must meet to designate itself as a Johnny Micheal Spann Patriot Trust (a charitable trust for the spouses, dependents, and relatives of military and Federal personnel who lose their lives in the battle against terrorism that is named after the first American to die in such service following the September 11th terrorist attacks). Requires at least 85 percent of each Trust corpus to be distributed to such survivors and prohibits more than 15 percent from being used for administrative purposes. Prohibits: (1) any Trust activities from violating any prohibition against

attempting to influence legislation; and (2) any such Trust from participating in any political campaign on behalf of a candidate for public office. Requires: (1) audits of each Trust that annually receives contributions of more than $1 million; and (2) Trust distributions to be made at least once a year. Provides for the notification of Trust beneficiaries.

Title VII: Management—(Sec. 701) Makes the Secretary, acting through the Under Secretary for Management, responsible for the management and administration of DHS. Details certain responsibilities of the Under Secretary with respect to immigration statistics. Transfers to the Under Secretary functions previously performed by the Statistics Branch of the Office of Policy and Planning of the Immigration and Naturalization Service (INS) with respect to: (1) the Border Patrol program; (2) the detention and removal program; (3) the intelligence program; (4) the investigations program; (5) the inspections program; and (6) INS adjudications.

(Sec. 702) Requires a chief financial officer, a chief information officer, and a chief human capital officer to report to the Secretary. Requires the chief human capital officer to ensure that all DHS employees are informed of their rights and remedies under merit system protection and principle provisions.

(Sec. 705) Requires the Secretary to appoint an Officer for Civil Rights and Civil Liberties who shall: (1) review and assess information alleging abuses of civil rights, civil liberties, and racial and ethnic profiling by employees and officials of DHS; and (2) make public information on the responsibilities and functions of, and how to contact, the Office.

(Sec. 706) Requires the Secretary to develop and submit to Congress a plan for consolidating and co-locating: (1) any regional offices or field offices of agencies that are transferred to DHS under this Act, if their officers are located in the same municipality; and (2) portions of regional and field offices of other Federal agencies, to the extent such offices perform functions that are transferred to the Secretary under this Act.

Title VIII: Coordination With Non-Federal Entities; Inspector General; United States Secret Service; Coast Guard; General Provisions—Subtitle A: Coordination with Non-Federal Entities—(Sec. 801) Establishes within the Office of the Secretary the Office for State and Local Government Coordination to oversee and coordinate Department homeland security programs for and relationships with State and local governments.

Subtitle B: Inspector General—(Sec. 811) Places the DHS Inspector General under the authority, direction, and control of the Secretary with respect to audits or investigations, or the issuance of subpoenas, that require access to sensitive information concerning intelligence, counterintelligence, or counterterrorism matters; criminal investigations or proceedings; undercover operations; the identify of confidential sources; and certain matters of disclosure.

Amends the Inspector General Act of 1978 to: (1) give such Inspector General oversight responsibility for internal investigations performed by the Office of Internal Affairs of the United States Customs Service and the Office of Inspections of the United States Secret Service; and (2) authorize each Inspector General, any Assistant Inspector General for Investigations, and any special agent supervised by such an Assistant Inspector General to carry a firearm, make arrests without warrants, and seek and execute warrants. Allows the latter only upon certain determinations by the Attorney General (exempts the Inspector General offices of various executive agencies from such requirement). Provides for the rescinding of such law enforcement powers. Requires the Inspector General offices exempted from the determinations requirement to collectively enter into a memorandum of understanding to establish an external review process for ensuring that adequate internal safeguards and management procedures continue to exist to ensure the proper utilization of such law enforcement powers within their departments.

Subtitle C: United States Secret Service—(Sec. 821) Transfers to the Secretary the functions of the United States Secret Service, which shall be maintained as a distinct entity within DHS.

Subtitle D: Acquisitions—(Sec. 831) Authorizes the Secretary to carry out a five-year pilot program under which the Secretary may exercise specified authorities in carrying out: (1) basic, applied, and advanced research and development projects for response to existing or emerging terrorist threats; and (2) defense prototype projects. Requires a report from the Comptroller General to specified congressional committees on the use of such authorities.

(Sec. 832) Permits the Secretary to procure temporary or intermittent: (1) services of experts or consultants; and (2) personal services without regard to certain pay limitations when necessary due to an urgent homeland security need.

(Sec. 833) Authorizes the Secretary to use specified micro purchase, simplified acquisition, and commercial item acquisition procedures with respect to any procurement

made during the period beginning on the effective date of this Act and ending on September 30, 2007, if the Secretary determines that the mission of DHS would be seriously impaired without the use of such authorities. Requires a report from the Comptroller General.

(Sec. 834) Requires the Federal Acquisition Regulation to be revised to include regulations with regard to unsolicited proposals.

(Sec. 835) Prohibits the Secretary from entering into a contract with a foreign incorporated entity which is treated as an inverted domestic corporation. Sets forth requirements for such treatment. Authorizes the Secretary to waive such prohibition in the interest of homeland security, to prevent the loss of any jobs in the United States, or to prevent the Government from incurring any additional costs.

Subtitle E: Human Resources Management—(Sec. 841) Expresses the sense of Congress calling for the participation of DHS employees in the creation of the DHS human resources management system.

Amends Federal civil service law to authorize the Secretary, in regulations prescribed jointly with the Director of the Office of Personnel Management (OPM), to establish and adjust a human resources management system for organizational units of DHS. Requires the system to ensure that employees may organize, bargain collectively, and participate through labor organizations of their own choosing in decisions which affect them, subject to an exclusion from coverage or limitation on negotiability established by law. Imposes certain requirements upon the Secretary and the OPM Director to ensure the participation of employee representatives in the planning, development, and implementation of any human resources management system or system adjustments.

Declares the sense of Congress that DHS employees are entitled to fair treatment in any appeals that they bring in decisions relating to their employment.

Terminates all authority to issue regulations under this section five years after enactment of this Act.

(Sec. 842) Prohibits any agency or agency subdivision transferred to DHS from being excluded from coverage under labor-management relations requirements as a result of any order issued after June 18, 2002, unless: (1) the mission and responsibilities of the agency or subdivision materially change; and (2) a majority of the employees within the agency or subdivision have as their primary duty intelligence, counterintelligence, or investigative work directly related to terrorism investigation. Declares that collective bargaining units shall continue to be recognized unless such conditions develop. Prohibits exclusion of positions or employees for a bargaining unit unless the primary job duty materially changes or consists of intelligence, counterintelligence, or investigative work directly related to terrorism investigation. Waives these prohibitions and recognitions in circumstances where the President determines that their application would have a substantial adverse impact on the Department's ability to protect homeland security.

Subtitle F: Federal Emergency Procurement Flexibility— (Sec. 852) Provides that the simplified acquisition threshold to be applied for any executive agency procurement of property or services that is to be used to facilitate the defense against or recovery from terrorism or nuclear, biological, chemical, or radiological attack and that is carried out in support of a humanitarian or peacekeeping operation or a contingency operation shall be: (1) $200,000 for a contract to be awarded and performed, or a purchase to be made, inside the United States; or (2) $300,000 for a contract to be awarded and performed, or a purchase to be made, outside the United States.

(Sec. 854) Authorizes the head of each agency to designate certain employees to make such procurements below a micro-purchase threshold of $7,500 (currently $2,500) under the Office of Federal Procurement Policy Act.

(Sec. 855) Permits executive agencies to apply to any such procurement specified provisions of law relating to the procurement of commercial items, without regard to whether the property and services are commercial items. Makes the $5 million limitation on the use of simplified acquisition procedures inapplicable to purchases of property or services to which such provisions apply.

(Sec. 856) Requires executive agencies to use specified streamlined acquisition authorities and procedures for such procurements. Waives certain small business threshold requirements with respect to such procurements.

(Sec. 857) Requires the Comptroller General to review and report to specified congressional committees on the extent to which procurements of property and services have been made in accordance with requirements of this Subtitle.

(Sec. 858) Requires each executive agency to conduct market research to identify the capabilities of small businesses and new entrants into Federal contracting that are available to meet agency requirements in furtherance of defense against

or recovery from terrorism or nuclear, biological, chemical, or radiological attack.

Subtitle G: Support Anti-terrorism by Fostering Effective Technologies Act of 2002—Support Anti-terrorism by Fostering Effective Technologies Act of 2002 or SAFETY Act—(Sec. 862) Authorizes the Secretary to designate anti-terrorism technologies that qualify for protection under a risk management system in accordance with criteria that shall include: (1) prior Government use or demonstrated substantial utility and effectiveness; (2) availability for immediate deployment in public and private settings; (3) substantial likelihood that such technology will not be deployed unless protections under such system are extended; and (4) the magnitude of risk exposure to the public if such technology is not deployed. Makes the Secretary responsible for administration of such protections.

(Sec. 863) Provides a Federal cause of action for sellers suffering a loss from qualified anti-terrorism technologies so deployed. Prohibits punitive damages from being awarded against a seller.

(Sec. 864) Requires sellers of qualified anti-terrorism technologies to obtain liability insurance in amounts certified as satisfactory by the Secretary.

Subtitle H: Miscellaneous Provisions—(Sec. 871) Authorizes the Secretary to establish, appoint members of, and use the services of advisory committees as necessary.

(Sec. 872) Grants the Secretary limited authority to reorganize DHS by allocating or reallocating functions within it and by establishing, consolidating, altering, or discontinuing organizational units.

(Sec. 873) Requires the Secretary to comply with Federal requirements concerning the deposit of proceeds from property sold or transferred by the Secretary. Requires the President to submit to Congress a detailed Department budget request for FY 2004 and thereafter.

(Sec. 874) Requires each such budget request to be accompanied by a Future Years Homeland Security Program structured in the same manner as the annual Future Years Defense Program.

(Sec. 876) Provides that nothing in this Act shall confer upon the Secretary any authority to engage in war fighting, the military defense of the United States, or other military activities or limit the existing authority of the Department of Defense or the armed forces to do so.

(Sec. 878) Directs the Secretary to appoint a senior DHS official to assume primary responsibility for coordinating policy and operations within DHS and between DHS and other Federal departments and agencies with respect to interdicting the entry of illegal drugs into the United States and tracking and severing connections between illegal drug trafficking and terrorism.

(Sec. 879) Establishes within the Office of the Secretary an Office of International Affairs, headed by a Director, to: (1) promote information and education exchange on homeland security best practices and technologies with friendly nations; (2) identify areas for homeland security information and training exchange where the United States has a demonstrated weakness and another friendly nation has a demonstrated expertise; (3) plan and undertake international conferences, exchange programs, and training activities; and (4) manage international activities within DHS in coordination with other Federal officials with responsibility for counter-terrorism matters.

(Sec. 880) Prohibits any Government activity to implement the proposed component program of the Citizen Corps known as Operation TIPS (Terrorism Information and Prevention System).

(Sec. 881) Directs the Secretary to review the pay and benefit plans of each agency whose functions are transferred to DHS under this Act and to submit a plan for ensuring the elimination of disparities in pay and benefits throughout DHS, especially among law enforcement personnel, that are inconsistent with merit system principles.

(Sec. 882) Establishes within the Office of the Secretary the Office of National Capital Region Coordination, headed by a Director, to oversee and coordinate Federal homeland security programs for and relationships with State, local, and regional authorities within the National Capital Region. Requires an annual report from the Office to Congress on: (1) resources needed to fully implement homeland security efforts in the Region; (2) progress made by the Region in implementing such efforts; and (3) recommendations for additional needed resources to fully implement such efforts.

(Sec. 883) Requires DHS to comply with specified laws protecting equal employment opportunity and providing whistle blower protections.

(Sec. 885) Authorizes the Secretary to establish a permanent Joint Interagency Homeland Security Task Force, composed of representatives from military and civilian agencies, for the purpose of anticipating terrorist threats and taking actions to prevent harm to the United States.

(Sec. 886) Reaffirms the continued importance of Federal criminal code proscriptions on the use of the armed forces as posse comitatus and expresses the sense of Congress that nothing in this Act shall be construed to alter the applicability of such proscriptions to any use of the armed forces to execute the laws.

(Sec. 887) Requires the annual Federal response plan developed by DHS to be consistent with public health emergency provisions of the Public Health Service Act. Requires full disclosure of public health emergencies, or potential emergencies, among HHS, DHS, the Department of Justice, and the Federal Bureau of Investigation.

(Sec. 888) Transfers to DHS the authorities, functions, personnel, and assets of the Coast Guard, which shall be maintained as a distinct entity within DHS. Prohibits the Secretary from substantially or significantly reducing current Coast Guard missions or capabilities, with a waiver of such prohibition upon a declaration and certification to Congress that a clear, compelling and immediate need exists. Requires the DHS Inspector General to annually review and report to Congress on performance by the Coast Guard of its mission requirements. Requires the Commandant of the Coast Guard, upon its transfer, to report directly to the Secretary. Prohibits any of the above conditions and restrictions from applying to the Coast Guard when it is operating as a service in the Navy. Directs the Secretary to report to specified congressional committees on the feasibility of accelerating the rate of procurement in the Coast Guard's Integrated Deepwater System from 20 to ten years.

(Sec. 889) Requires the inclusion in the President's annual budget documents of a detailed homeland security funding analysis for the previous, current, and next fiscal years.

(Sec. 890) Amends the Air Transportation Safety and System Stabilization Act, with respect to the September 11th Victim Compensation Fund of 2001, to limit "agents" of an air carrier engaged in the business of providing air transportation security to persons that have contracted directly with the Federal Aviation Administration on or after February 17, 2002, to provide such security and that had not been or are not debarred within six months of that date.

Subtitle I: Information Sharing—Homeland Security Information Sharing Act—(Sec. 891) Expresses the sense of Congress that Federal, State, and local entities should share homeland security information to the maximum extent practicable, with special emphasis on hard-to-reach urban and rural communities.

(Sec. 892) Directs the President to prescribe and implement procedures for Federal agency: (1) sharing of appropriate homeland security information, including with DHS and appropriate State and local personnel; and (2) handling of classified information and sensitive but unclassified information. Authorizes appropriations.

(Sec. 893) Requires an implementation report from the President to the congressional intelligence and judiciary committees.

(Sec. 895) Amends the Federal Rules of Criminal Procedure to treat as contempt of court any knowing violation of guidelines jointly issued by the Attorney General and DCI with respect to disclosure of grand jury matters otherwise prohibited. Allows disclosure to appropriate Federal, State, local, or foreign government officials of grand jury matters involving a threat of grave hostile acts of a foreign power, domestic or international sabotage or terrorism, or clandestine intelligence gathering activities by an intelligence service or network of a foreign power (threat), within the United States or elsewhere. Permits disclosure to appropriate foreign government officials of grand jury matters that may disclose a violation of the law of such government. Requires State, local, and foreign officials to use disclosed information only in conformity with guidelines jointly issued by the Attorney General and the DCI.

(Sec. 896) Amends the Federal criminal code to authorize Federal investigative and law enforcement officers conducting communications interception activities, who have obtained knowledge of the contents of any intercepted communication or derivative evidence, to disclose such contents or evidence to: (1) a foreign investigative or law enforcement officer if the disclosure is appropriate to the performance of the official duties of the officer making or receiving the disclosure; and (2) any appropriate Federal, State, local, or foreign government official if the contents or evidence reveals such a threat, for the purpose of preventing or responding to such threat. Provides guidelines for the use and disclosure of the information.

(Sec. 897) Amends the Uniting and Strengthening America by Providing Appropriate Tools Required to Intercept and Obstruct Terrorism Act (USA PATRIOT ACT) of 2001 to make lawful the disclosure to appropriate Federal, State, local, or foreign government officials of information obtained as part of a criminal investigation that reveals such a threat.

(Sec. 898) Amends the Foreign Intelligence Surveillance Act of 1978 to allow Federal officers who conduct electronic surveillance and physical searches in order to acquire foreign intelligence information to consult with State and local law enforcement personnel to coordinate efforts to investigate or protect against such a threat.

Title IX: National Homeland Security Council— (Sec. 901) Establishes within the Executive Office of the President the Homeland Security Council to advise the President on homeland security matters.

(Sec. 903) Includes as members of the Council: (1) the President; (2) the Vice President; (3) the Secretary; (4) the Attorney General; and (5) the Secretary of Defense.

(Sec. 904) Requires the Council to: (1) assess the objectives, commitments, and risks of the United States in the interest of homeland security and make recommendations to the President; and (2) oversee and review Federal homeland security policies and make policy recommendations to the President.

(Sec. 906) Authorizes the President to convene joint meetings of the Homeland Security Council and the National Security Council.

Title X: Information Security—Federal Information Security Management Act of 2002—(Sec. 1001) Revises Government information security requirements. Requires the head of each agency operating or exercising control of a national security system to ensure that the agency: (1) provides information security protections commensurate with the risk and magnitude of the harm resulting from the unauthorized access, use, disclosure, disruption, modification, or destruction of the information; and (2) implements information security policies and practices as required by standards and guidelines for national security systems. Authorizes appropriations for FY 2003 through 2007.

(Sec. 1002) Transfers from the Secretary of Commerce to the Director of the Office of Management and Budget (OMB) the authority to promulgate information security standards pertaining to Federal information systems.

(Sec. 1003) Amends the National Institute of Standards and Technology Act to revise and expand the mandate of the National Institute of Standards and Technology to develop standards, guidelines, and associated methods and techniques for information systems. Renames the Computer System Security and Privacy Advisory Board as the Information Security and Privacy Board and requires it to advise the Director of OMB (instead of the Secretary of Commerce) on information security and privacy issues pertaining to Federal Government information systems.

Title XI: Department of Justice Divisions—Subtitle A: Executive Office for Immigration Review—(Sec. 1101) Declares that there is in the Department of Justice (DOJ) the Executive Office for Immigration Review (EOIR), which shall be subject to the direction and regulation of the Attorney General under the INA.

(Sec. 1102) Amends the INA to grant the Attorney General such authorities and functions relating to the immigration and naturalization of aliens as were exercised by EOIR, or by the Attorney General with respect to EOIR, on the day before the effective date of the Immigration Reform, Accountability and Security Enhancement Act of 2002.

Subtitle B: Transfer of the Bureau of Alcohol, Tobacco and Firearms to the Department of Justice—(Sec. 1111) Establishes within DOJ, under the Attorney General's authority, the Bureau of Alcohol, Tobacco, Firearms, and Explosives (the Bureau). Transfers to DOJ the authorities, functions, personnel, and assets of the Bureau of Alcohol, Tobacco and Firearms (BATF), which shall be maintained as a distinct entity within DOJ, including the related functions of the Secretary of the Treasury.

Provides that the Bureau shall be headed by a Director and shall be responsible for: (1) investigating criminal and regulatory violations of the Federal firearms, explosives, arson, alcohol, and tobacco smuggling laws; (2) such transferred functions; and (3) any other function related to the investigation of violent crime or domestic terrorism that is delegated to the Bureau by the Attorney General.

Retains within the Department of the Treasury certain authorities, functions, personnel, and assets of BATF relating to the administration and enforcement of the Internal Revenue Code.

Establishes within the Department of the Treasury the Tax and Trade Bureau, which shall retain and administer the authorities, functions, personnel, and assets of BATF that are not transferred to DOJ.

(Sec. 1113) Amends the Federal criminal code to authorize special agents of the Bureau, as well as any other investigator or officer charged by the Attorney General with enforcing criminal, seizure, or forfeiture laws, to carry firearms, serve warrants and subpoenas, and make arrests without warrant for offenses committed in their presence or for felonies on reasonable grounds. Authorizes any special agent to make seizures of property subject to forfeiture to the United States. Sets forth provisions regarding seizure, disposition, and claims pertaining to property.

(Sec. 1114) Establishes within the Bureau an Explosives Training and Research Facility at Fort AP Hill in Fredericksburg, Virginia, to train Federal, State, and local law enforcement officers to: (1) investigate bombings and explosions; (2) properly handle, utilize, and dispose of explosive materials and devices; (3) train canines on explosive detection; and (4) conduct research on explosives. Authorizes appropriations.

(Sec. 1115) Transfers the Personnel Management Demonstration Project to the Attorney General for continued use by the Bureau and to the Secretary of the Treasury for continued use by the Tax and Trade Bureau.

Subtitle C: Explosives—Safe Explosives Act—(Sec. 1122) Rewrites Federal criminal code provisions regarding the purchase of explosives to create a new "limited permit" category. Prohibits a holder of a limited permit: (1) from transporting, shipping, causing to be transported, or receiving in interstate or foreign commerce explosive materials; (2) from receiving explosive materials from a licensee or permittee whose premises are located outside the holder's State of residence; or (3) on more than six separate occasions during the period of the permit, from receiving explosive materials from one or more licensees or permittees whose premises are located within the holder's State of residence.

Requires license, user permit, and limited permit applicants to include the names of and identifying information (including fingerprints and a photograph of each responsible person) regarding all employees who will be authorized by the applicant to possess explosive materials. Caps the fee for limited permits at $50 for each permit. Makes each limited permit valid for not longer than one year.

Modifies criteria for approving licenses and permits. Requires the Secretary of the Treasury to issue to the applicant the appropriate license or permit if, among other conditions: (1) the applicant is not a person who is otherwise prohibited from possessing explosive materials (excluded person); (2) the Secretary verifies by inspection or other appropriate means that the applicant has a place of storage for explosive materials that meets the Secretary's standards of public safety and security against theft (inapplicable to an applicant for renewal of a limited permit if the Secretary has verified such matters by inspection within the preceding three years); (3) none of the applicant's employees who will be authorized to possess explosive materials is an excluded person; and (4) in the case of a limited permit, the applicant has certified that the applicant will not receive explosive materials on more than six separate occasions during the

12-month period for which the limited permit is valid. Authorizes the Secretary to inspect the storage places of an applicant for or holder of a limited permit only as provided under the code. Requires the Secretary of the Treasury to approve or deny an application for licenses and permits within 90 days.

Requires the Secretary: (1) upon receiving from an employer the name and other identifying information with respect to a person or an employee who will be authorized to possess explosive materials, to determine whether such person or employee is an excluded person; (2) upon determining that such person or employee is not an excluded person, to notify the employer and to issue to the person or employee a letter of clearance confirming the determination; and (3) upon determining that such person or employee is an excluded person, to notify the employer and issue to such person or employee a document that confirms the determination, explains the grounds, provides information on how the disability may be relieved, and explains how the determination may be appealed.

(Sec. 1123) Includes among aliens who may lawfully receive or possess explosive materials any alien who is in lawful non-immigrant status, is a refugee admitted under the INA, or i3s in asylum status under the INA and who is: (1) a foreign law enforcement officer of a friendly government; (2) a person having the power to direct the management and policies of a corporation; (3) a member of a North Atlantic Treaty Organization or other friendly foreign military force; or (4) lawfully present in the United States in cooperation with the DCI and the shipment, transportation, receipt, or possession of the explosive materials is in furtherance of such cooperation.

(Sec. 1124) Requires: (1) licensed manufacturers, licensed importers, and those who manufacture or import explosive materials or ammonium nitrate to furnish samples and relevant information when required by the Secretary; and (2) the Secretary to authorize reimbursement of the fair market value of samples furnished, as well as reasonable shipment costs.

(Sec. 1125) Sets penalties for the destruction of property of institutions receiving Federal financial assistance.

(Sec. 1127) Requires a holder of a license or permit to report any theft of explosive materials to the Secretary not later than 24 hours after discovery. Sets penalties for failure to report.

(Sec. 1128) Authorizes appropriations.

Title XII: Airline War Risk Insurance Legislation—(Sec. 1201) Amends Federal aviation law to extend the period during which the Secretary of Transportation may certify an air carrier as a victim of terrorism (and thus subject to the $100 million limit on aggregate third-party claims) for acts of terrorism from September 22, 2001, through December 31, 2003.

(Sec. 1202) Directs the Secretary of Transportation to extend through August 31, 2003, and authorizes the Secretary to extend through December 31, 2003, the termination date of any insurance policy that the Department of Transportation (DOT) issues to an American aircraft or foreign-flag aircraft against loss or damage arising out of any risk from operation, and that is in effect on enactment of this Act, on no less favorable terms to such air carrier than existed on June 19, 2002. Directs the Secretary, however, to amend such policy to add coverage for losses or injuries to aircraft hulls, passengers, and crew at the limits carried by air carriers for such losses and injuries as of such enactment, and at an additional premium comparable to the premium charged for third-party casualty under the policy.

Limits the total premium paid by an air carrier for such a policy to twice the premium it was paying for its third party policy as of June 19, 2002. Declares that coverage in such a policy shall begin with the first dollar of any covered loss incurred.

(Sec. 1204) Directs the Secretary of Transportation to report to specified congressional committees concerning: (1) the availability and cost of commercial war risk insurance for air carriers and other aviation entities for passengers and third parties; (2) the economic effect upon such carriers and entities of available commercial war risk insurance; and (3) the manner in which DOT could provide an alternative means of providing aviation war risk reinsurance covering passengers, crew, and third parties through use of a risk-retention group or by other means.

Title XIII: Federal Workforce Improvement—Subtitle A: Chief Human Capital Officers—Chief Human Capital Officers Act of 2002—(Sec. 1302) Requires the heads of Federal departments and agencies currently required to a have Chief Financial Officer to appoint or designate a Chief Human Capital Officer to: (1) advise and assist agency officials in selecting, developing, training, and managing a high-quality, productive workforce in accordance with merit system principles; and (2) implement the rules and regulations of the President and the Office of OPM and civil service laws.

Requires such Officer's functions to include: (1) setting the agency's workforce development strategy; (2) assessing workforce characteristics and future needs; (3) aligning the agency's human resources policies and programs with organization mission, strategic goals, and performance outcomes; (4) developing and advocating a culture of continuous learning to attract and retain employees with superior abilities; (5) identifying best practices and benchmarking studies; and (6) applying methods for measuring intellectual capital and identifying links of that capital to organizational performance and growth.

(Sec. 1303) Establishes a Chief Human Capital Officers Council (consisting of the Director of OPM, the Deputy Director for Management of the Office of Management and Budget, and the Chief Human Capital Officers of executive departments and other members designated by the Director of OPM) to advise and coordinate the activities of the agencies of its members on such matters as modernization of human resources systems, improved quality of human resources information, and legislation affecting human resources operations and organizations.

(Sec. 1304) Directs OPM to design a set of systems, including metrics, for assessing the management of human capital by Federal agencies.

Subtitle B: Reforms Relating to Federal Human Capital Management—(Sec. 1311) Requires each agency's: (1) performance plan to describe how its performance goals and objectives are to be achieved; and (2) program performance report to include a review of the goals and evaluation of the plan relative to the agency's strategic human capital management.

(Sec. 1312) Authorizes the President to prescribe rules which grant authority for agencies to appoint candidates directly to certain positions for which there exists a severe candidate shortage or a critical hiring need.

Allows OPM to establish quality category rating systems for evaluating applicants for competitive service positions under two or more quality categories based on merit rather than numerical ratings. Requires agencies that establish a quality category rating system to report to Congress on that system, including information on the number of employees hired, the impact that system has had on the hiring of veterans and minorities, and the way in which managers were trained in the administration of it.

(Sec. 1313) Sets forth provisions governing Federal employee voluntary separation incentive payments. Requires each agency, before obligating any resources for such payments, to submit to OPM for modification and approval a plan outlining the intended use of such payments and a proposed organizational chart for the agency once such payments have been completed. Requires such plan to include the positions and functions affected, the categories of employees to be offered such payments, the timing and amounts of payments, and how the agency will subsequently operate. Limits voluntary separation incentive payments to the lesser of: (1) the amount of severance pay to which an employee would be entitled; or (2) an amount determined by the agency head, not to exceed $25,000. Sets forth provisions regarding the repayment and waiver of repayment of such incentive payments upon subsequent employment with the Government. Authorizes the Director of the Administrative Office of the United States Courts to establish a substantially similar program for the judicial branch. Continues existing voluntary separation incentives authority until expiration.

Amends Federal employee early retirement provisions to apply to employees who are: (1) voluntarily separated by an agency undergoing substantial delayering, reorganization, reductions in force, functions transfer, or workforce restructuring; or (2) identified as being in positions that are becoming surplus or excess to the agency's future ability to carry out its mission effectively; and (3) within the scope of the offer of voluntary early retirement on the basis of specific periods or such employee's organizational unit, occupational series, geographical location, and/or skills, knowledge, and other factors related to a position. Expresses the sense of Congress that the implementation of this section is intended to reshape, and not downsize, the Federal workforce.

(Sec. 1314) Includes students who provide voluntary services for the Government as "employees" for purposes of provisions authorizing agency programs to encourage employees to commute by means other than single-occupancy motor vehicles.

Subtitle C: Reforms Relating to the Senior Executive Service—(Sec. 1321) Repeals recertification requirements for senior executives.

(Sec. 1322) Changes the limitation on total annual compensation (basic pay and cash payments) from the annual rate of basic pay payable for level I of the Executive Schedule to the total annual compensation payable to the Vice President for certain senior level executive and judicial employees who hold a position in or under an agency that has been certified as having a performance appraisal system which makes meaningful distinctions based on relative performance.

Subtitle D: Academic Training—(Sec. 1331) Revises agency academic degree training criteria to allow agencies to select and assign employees to academic degree training and to pay and reimburse such training costs if such training: (1) contributes significantly to meeting an agency training need, resolving an agency staffing problem, or accomplishing goals in the agency's strategic plan; (2) is part of a planned, systemic, and coordinated agency employee development program linked to accomplishing such goals; and (3) is accredited and is provided by a college or university that is accredited by a nationally recognized body.

(Sec. 1332) Amends the David L. Boren National Security Education Act of 1991 to modify service agreement requirements for recipients of scholarships and fellowships under the National Security Education Program to provide for recipients to work in other Federal offices or agencies when no national security position is available.

Title XIV: Arming Pilots Against Terrorism—Arming Pilots Against Terrorism Act—(Sec. 1402) Amends Federal law to direct the Under Secretary of Transportation for Security (in the Transportation Security Administration) to establish a two-year pilot program to: (1) deputize volunteer pilots of air carriers as Federal law enforcement officers to defend the flight decks of aircraft against acts of criminal violence or air piracy (Federal flight deck officers); and (2) provide training, supervision, and equipment for such officers.

Requires the Under Secretary to begin the process of training and deputizing qualified pilots to be Federal flight deck officers under the program. Allows the Under Secretary to request another Federal agency to deputize such officers.

Directs the Under Secretary to authorize flight deck officers to carry firearms and to use force, including lethal force, according to standards and circumstances the Under Secretary prescribes. Shields air carriers from liability for damages in Federal or State court arising out of a Federal flight deck officer's use of or failure to use a firearm. Shields flight deck officers from liability for acts or omissions in defending the flight deck of an aircraft against acts of criminal violence or air piracy, except in cases of gross negligence or willful misconduct.

Declares that if an accidental discharge of a firearm results in the injury or death of a passenger or crew member on the aircraft, the Under Secretary: (1) shall revoke the deputization of the responsible Federal flight deck officer if such discharge was attributable to the officer's negligence; and (2) may temporarily suspend the pilot program if the Under Secretary

determines that a shortcoming in standards, training, or procedures was responsible for the accidental discharge.

Prohibits an air carrier from prohibiting a pilot from becoming a Federal flight deck officer, or threatening any retaliatory action against the pilot for doing so.

Declares the sense of Congress that the Federal air marshal program is critical to aviation security, and that nothing in this Act shall be construed as preventing the Under Secretary from implementing and training Federal air marshals.

(Sec. 1403) Directs the Under Secretary, in updating the guidance for training flight and cabin crews, to issue a rule to: (1) require both classroom and effective hands-on situational training in specified elements of self-defense; (2) require training in the proper conduct of a cabin search, including the duty time required to conduct it; (3) establish the required number of hours of training and the qualifications for training instructors; (4) establish the intervals, number of hours, and elements of recurrent training; (5) ensure that air carriers provide the initial training within 24 months of the enactment of this Act. Directs the Under Secretary to designate an official in the Transportation Security Administration to be responsible for overseeing the implementation of the training program; and (6) ensure that no person is required to participate in any hands-on training activity that such person believes will have an adverse impact on his or her health or safety.

Amends the Aviation and Transportation Security Act to authorize the Under Secretary to take certain enhanced security measures, including to require that air carriers provide flight attendants with a discreet, hands-free, wireless method of communicating with the pilot of an aircraft.

Directs the Under Secretary to study and report to Congress on the benefits and risks of providing flight attendants with nonlethal weapons to aide in combating air piracy and criminal violence on commercial airlines.

(Sec. 1404) Directs the Secretary of Transportation to study and report within six months to Congress on: (1) the number of armed Federal law enforcement officers (other than Federal air marshals) who travel on commercial airliners annually, and the frequency of their travel; (2) the cost and resources necessary to provide such officers with supplemental aircraft anti-terrorism training comparable to the training that Federal air marshals receive; (3) the cost of establishing a program at a Federal law enforcement training center for the purpose of providing new Federal law enforcement recruits with standardized training comparable to Federal air marshal training; (4) the feasibility of implementing a certification program designed to ensure that Federal law enforcement officers have completed aircraft anti-terrorism training, and track their travel over a six-month period; and (5) the feasibility of staggering the flights of such officers to ensure the maximum amount of flights have a certified trained Federal officer on board.

(Sec. 1405) Amends Federal aviation law to require the Under Secretary to respond within 90 days of receiving a request from an air carrier for authorization to allow pilots of the air carrier to carry less-than-lethal weapons.

Title XV: Transition—Subtitle A: Reorganization Plan—(Sec. 1502) Requires the President, within 60 days after enactment of this Act, to transmit to the appropriate congressional committees a reorganization plan regarding: (1) the transfer of agencies, personnel, assets, and obligations to DHS pursuant to this Act; and (2) any consolidation, reorganization, or streamlining of agencies transferred to DHS pursuant to this Act.

(Sec. 1503) Expresses the sense of Congress that each House of Congress should review its committee structure in light of the reorganization of responsibilities within the executive branch by the establishment of DHS.

Subtitle B: Transitional Provisions—(Sec. 1511) Outlines transitional provisions with regard to assistance from officials having authority before the effective date of this Act; details of personnel and services to assist in the transition; acting officials during the transition period; the transfer of personnel, assets, obligations and functions; and the status of completed administrative actions, pending proceedings and civil actions, and Inspector General oversight. Prohibits DHS use of any funds derived from the Highway Trust Fund, the Airport and Airway Trust Fund, the Inland Waterway Trust Fund, or the Harbor Maintenance Trust Fund, with a specified exception for certain security-related funds provided to the Federal Aviation Administration.

(Sec. 1514) Provides that nothing in this Act shall be construed to authorize the development of a national identification system or card.

(Sec. 1516) Authorizes and directs the Director of OMB to make additional necessary incidental dispositions of personnel, assets, and liabilities in connection with the functions transferred by this Act.

Title XVI: Corrections to Existing Law Relating to Airline Transportation Security—(Sec. 1601) Amends Federal aviation law to require the Administrator of the Federal Aviation Administration (FAA), along with the Under Secretary of Transportation for Security, to each conduct research (including behavioral research) and development activities to develop, modify, test, and evaluate a system, procedure, facility, or device to protect passengers and property against acts of criminal violence, aircraft piracy, and terrorism and to ensure security.

Directs the Secretary of Transportation (currently, the Under Secretary) to prescribe regulations prohibiting disclosure of information obtained or developed in ensuring security under this section if the Secretary of Transportation decides disclosing such information would: (1) be an unwarranted invasion of personal privacy; (2) reveal a trade secret or privileged or confidential commercial or financial information; or (3) be detrimental to the safety of passengers in transportation. Sets forth similar provisions requiring the Under Secretary to prescribe regulations prohibiting the disclosure of information obtained or developed in carrying out security under authority of the Aviation and Transportation Security Act (PL107-71).

(Sec. 1602) Increases the maximum civil penalty to $25,000 for a person who violates certain aviation security requirements while operating an aircraft for the transportation of passengers or property for compensation (except an individual serving as an airman).

(Sec. 1603) Revises certain hiring security screener standards to allow a national (currently, only a citizen) of the United States to become a security screener.

Title XVII: Conforming and Technical Amendments—(Sec. 1701) Sets forth technical and conforming amendments.

(Sec. 1706) Transfers from the Administrator of General Services to the Secretary of Homeland Security law enforcement authority for the protection of Federal property.

(Sec. 1708) Establishes in DOD a National Bio-Weapons Defense Analysis Center to develop countermeasures to potential attacks by terrorists using weapons of mass destruction.

(Sec. 1714) Amends the Public Health Service Act to define "vaccine" to mean any preparation or suspension, including one containing an attenuated or inactive microorganism or toxin, developed or administered to produce or enhance the body's immune response to a disease and to include all components and ingredients listed in the vaccine's product license application and product label.

# Appendix 4: List of State Emergency Management Offices

Alabama Emergency Management Agency
5898 County Road 41
P.O. Drawer 2160
Clanton, Alabama 35046-2160
1-205-280-2200
1-205-280-2495 FAX
http://www.aema.state.al.us/

Alaska Division of Emergency Services
P.O. Box 5750
Fort Richardson, Alaska 99505-5750
1-907-428-7000
1-907-428-7009 FAX
http://www.ak-prepared.com

American Samoa Territorial Emergency
    Management Coordination (TEMCO)
American Samoa Government
P.O. Box 1086
Pago Pago, American Samoa 96799
1-011-684-699-6415
1-011-684-699-6414 FAX

Arizona Division of Emergency Management
5636 E. McDowell Road
Phoenix, Arizona 85008
(602) 244-0504 or 1-800-411-2336
http://www.dem.state.az.us

Arkansas Department of Emergency Management
P.O. Box 758
Conway, Arkansas 72033
1-501-730-9750
1-501-730-9754 FAX
http://www.adem.state.ar.us

California Governor's Office of Emergency Services
P.O. Box 419047
Rancho Cordova, California 95741-9047
1-916-845-8510
1-916-845-8511 FAX
http://www.oes.ca.gov/

Colorado Office of Emergency Management
Division of Local Government
Department of Local Affairs
15075 South Golden Road
Golden, Colorado 80401-3979
1-303-273-1622
1-303-273-1795 FAX
www.dola.state.co.us/oem/oemindex.htm

Connecticut Office of Emergency Management
Military Department
360 Broad Street
Hartford, Connecticut 06105
1-860-566-3180
1-860-247-0664 FAX
http://www.mil.state.ct.us/OEM.htm

Delaware Emergency Management Agency
165 Brick Store Landing Road
Smyrna, Delaware 19977
1-302-659-3362
1-302-659-6855 FAX
http://www.state.de.us/dema/index.htm

District of Columbia Emergency Management Agency
2000 14th Street, NW, 8th Floor
Washington, DC 20009
1-202-727-6161
1-202-673-2290 FAX
http://www.dcema.dc.gov

Florida Division of Emergency Management
2555 Shumard Oak Boulevard
Tallahassee, Florida 32399-2100
1-850-413-9969
1-850-488-1016 FAX
www.floridadisaster.org

Georgia Emergency Management Agency
P.O. Box 18055
Atlanta, Georgia 30316-0055
1-404-635-7000

1-404-635-7205 FAX
http://www.State.Ga.US/GEMA/

Office of Civil Defense
Government of Guam
P.O. Box 2877
Hagatna, Guam 96932
1-011-671-475-9600
1-011-671-477-3727 FAX
http://ns.gov.gu

Guam Homeland Security/Office of Civil Defense
221B Chalan Palasyo
Agana Heights, Guam 96910
1-671-475-9600
1-671-477-3727 FAX

Hawaii State Civil Defense
3949 Diamond Head Road
Honolulu, Hawaii 96816-4495
1-808-733-4300
1-808-733-4287 FAX
http://www.scd.state.hi.us

Idaho Bureau of Disaster Services
4040 Guard Street, Building 600
Boise, Idaho 83705-5004
1-208-334-3460
1-208-334-2322 FAX
http://www.state.id.us/bds/bds.html

Illinois Emergency Management Agency
110 East Adams Street
Springfield, Illinois 62701
1-217-782-2700
1-217-524-7967 FAX
http://www.state.il.us/iema

Indiana State Emergency Management Agency
302 West Washington Street
Room E-208 A
Indianapolis, Indiana 46204-2767
1-317-232-3986
1-317-232-3895 FAX
http://www.ai.org/sema/index.html

Iowa Division of Emergency Management
Department of Public Defense
Hoover Office Building
Des Moines, Iowa 50319
1-641-281-3231
1-641-281-7539 FAX
http://www.state.ia.us/government/dpd/emd/index.htm

Kansas Division of Emergency Management
2800 S.W. Topeka Boulevard
Topeka, Kansas 66611-1287
1-785-274-1401
1-785-274-1426 FAX
http://www.ink.org/public/kdem

Kentucky Emergency Management
EOC Building
100 Minuteman Parkway Building. 100
Frankfort, Kentucky 40601-6168
1-502-607-1682
1-502-607-1614 FAX
http://kyem.dma.state.ky.us

Louisiana Office of Emergency Preparedness
7667 Independence Boulevard
Baton Rouge, Louisiana 70806
1-225-925-7500
1-225-925-7501 FAX
http://www.loep.state.la.us

Maine Emergency Management Agency
State Office Building, Station 72
Augusta, Maine 04333
1-207-626-4503
1-207-626-4499 FAX
http://www.state.me.us/mema/memahome.htm

CNMI Emergency Management Office
Office of the Governor
Commonwealth of the Northern Mariana Islands
P.O. Box 10007
Saipan, Mariana Islands 96950
1-670-322-9529
1-670-322-7743 FAX
http://www.cnmiemo.org/

National Disaster Management Office
Office of the Chief Secretary
P.O. Box 15
Majuro, Republic of the Marshall Islands
    96960-0015
1-011-692-625-5181
1-011-692-625-6896 FAX

Maryland Emergency Management Agency
Camp Fretterd Military Reservation
5401 Rue Saint Lo Drive
Reistertown, Maryland 21136
1-410-517-3600
1-877-636-2872 Toll-Free

1-410-517-3610 FAX
http://www.mema.state.md.us

Massachusetts Emergency Management Agency
400 Worcester Road
Framingham, Massachusetts 01702-5399
1-508-820-2000
1-508-820-2030 FAX
http://www.state.ma.us/mema

Michigan Division of Emergency Management
4000 Collins Road
P.O. Box 30636
Lansing, Michigan 48909-8136
1-517-333-5042
1-517-333-4987 FAX
http://www.michigan.gov/msp/1,1607,7-123-1593_
3507—,00.html

National Disaster Control Officer
Federated States of Micronesia
P.O. Box PS-53
Kolonia, Pohnpei—Micronesia 96941
1-011-691-320-8815
1-001-691-320-2785 FAX

Minnesota Division of Emergency Management
Department of Public Safety
Suite 223
444 Cedar Street
St. Paul, Minnesota 55101-6223
1-651-296-2233
1-651-296-0459 FAX
http://www.dps.state.mn.us/emermgt/

Mississippi Emergency Management Agency
P.O. Box 4501—Fondren Station
Jackson, Mississippi 39296-4501
1-601-352-9100
1-800-442-6362 Toll Free
1-601-352-8314 FAX
http://www.mema.state.ms.us
http://www.memaorg.com

Missouri Emergency Management Agency
P.O. Box 16
2302 Militia Drive
Jefferson City, Missouri 65102
1-573-526-9100
1-573-634-7966 FAX
http://www.sema.state.mo.us/semapage.htm

Montana Division of Disaster & Emergency Services
1100 North Main
P.O. Box 4789
Helena, Montana 59604-4789
1-406-841-3911
1-406-444-3965 FAX
http://www.state.mt.us/dma/des/index.shtml

Nebraska Emergency Management Agency
1300 Military Road
Lincoln, Nebraska 68508-1090
1-402-471-7410
1-402-471-7433 FAX
http://www.nebema.org

Nevada Division of Emergency Management
2525 South Carson Street
Carson City, Nevada 89711
1-775-687-4240
1-775-687-6788 FAX
http://dem.state.nv.us/

Governor's Office of Emergency Management
State Office Park South
107 Pleasant Street
Concord, New Hampshire 03301
1-603-271-2231
1-603-225-7341 FAX

New Jersey Office of Emergency Management
Emergency Management Bureau
P.O. Box 7068
West Trenton, New Jersey 08628-0068
1-609-538-6050 Monday–Friday
1-609-882-2000 ext 6311 (24/7)
1-609-538-0345 FAX
http://www.state.nj.us/oem/county

New Mexico Department of Public Safety
Office of Emergency Services & Security
P.O. Box 1628
13 Bataan Boulevard
Santa Fe, New Mexico 87505
1-505-476-9600
1-505-476-9695 FAX
http://www.dps.nm.org/emergency/index.htm

Emergency Management Bureau
Department of Public Safety
P.O. Box 1628
13 Bataan Boulevard
Santa Fe, New Mexico 87505

1-505-476-9606
1-505-476-9650
http://www.dps.nm.org/emc.htm

New York State Emergency Management Office
1220 Washington Avenue
Building 22, Suite 101
Albany, New York 12226-2251
1-518-457-2222
1-518-457-9995 FAX
http://www.nysemo.state.ny.us/

North Carolina Division of Emergency Management
116 West Jones Street
Raleigh, North Carolina 27603
1-919-733-3867
1-919-733-5406 FAX
http://www.dem.dcc.state.nc.us/

North Dakota Division of Emergency Management
P.O. Box 5511
Bismarck, North Dakota 58506-5511
1-701-328-8100
1-701-328-8181 FAX
http://www.state.nd.us/dem

Ohio Emergency Management Agency
2855 W. Dublin Granville Road
Columbus, Ohio 43235-2206
1-614-889-7150
1-614-889-7183 FAX
http://www.state.oh.us/odps/division/ema

Office of Civil Emergency Management
Will Rogers Sequoia Tunnel 2401 N. Lincoln
Oklahoma City, Oklahoma 73152
1-405-521-2481
1-405-521-4053 FAX
http://www.odcem.state.ok.us/

Oregon Emergency Management
Department of State Police
595 Cottage Street, NE
Salem, Oregon 97310
1-503-378-2911 ext. 225
1-503-588-1378
http://www.osp.state.or.us/oem/oem.htm

Palau NEMO Coordinator
Office of the President
P.O. Box 100

Koror, Republic of Palau 96940
1-011-680-488-2422
1-011-680-488-3312

Pennsylvania Emergency Management Agency
P.O. Box 3321
Harrisburg, Pennsylvania 17105-3321
1-717-651-2001
1-717-651-2040 FAX
http://www.pema.state.pa.us

Puerto Rico Emergency Management Agency
P.O. Box 966597
San Juan, Puerto Rico 00906-6597
1-787-724-0124
1-787-725-4244 FAX

Rhode Island Emergency Management Agency
645 New London Avenue
Cranston, Rhode Island 02920-3003
1-401-946-9996
1-401-944-1891 FAX
http://www.state.ri.us/riema/riemaaa.html

South Carolina Emergency Management Division
1100 Fish Hatchery Road
West Columbia South Carolina 29172
1-803-737-8500
1-803-737-8570 FAX
http://www.state.sc.us/epd

South Dakota Division of Emergency Management
500 East Capitol
Pierre, South Dakota 57501-5070
1-605-773-6426
1-605-773-3580 FAX
http://www.state.sd.us/state/executive/military/sddem.htm

Tennessee Emergency Management Agency
3041 Sidco Drive
Nashville, Tennessee 37204-1502
1-615-741-4332
1-615-242-9635 FAX
http://www.tnema.org

Texas Division of Emergency Management
5805 N. Lamar
Austin, Texas 78752
1-512-424-2138
1-512-424-2444 or 7160 FAX
http://www.txdps.state.tx.us/dem/

Utah Division of Emergency Services and
    Homeland Security
1110 State Office Building
P.O. Box 141710
Salt Lake City, Utah 84114-1710
1-801-538-3400
1-801-538-3770 FAX

Vermont Emergency Management Agency
Department of Public Safety
Waterbury State Complex
103 South Main Street
Waterbury, Vermont 05671-2101
1-802-244-8721
1-802-244-8655 FAX
http://www.dps.state.vt.us

Virgin Islands Territorial Emergency Management—
    VITEMA
2-C Contant, A-Q Building
Virgin Islands 00820
1-340-774-2244
1-340-774-1491

Virginia Department of Emergency Management
10501 Trade Court
Richmond, VA 23236-3713
1-804-897-6502
1-804-897-6506
http://www.vdem.state.va.us

State of Washington Emergency Management
    Division
Building 20, M/S: TA-20
Camp Murray, Washington 98430-5122
1-253-512-7000
1-253-512-7200 FAX
http://www.emd.wa.gov

West Virginia Office of Emergency Services
Building 1, Room EB-80, 1900 Kanawha
    Boulevard, East
Charleston, West Virginia 25305-0360
1-304-558-5380
1-304-344-4538 FAX
http://www.state.wv.us/wvoes

Wisconsin Emergency Management
2400 Wright Street
P.O. Box 7865
Madison, Wisconsin 53707-7865
1-608-242-3232
1-608-242-3247 FAX
http://emergencymanagement.wi.gov/

Wyoming Emergency Management Agency
5500 Bishop Boulevard
Cheyenne, Wyoming 82009-3320
1-307-777-4920
1-307-635-6017 FAX
http://wema.state.wy.us

# Appendix 5: List of State Homeland Security Contacts

**Alabama**
James Walker, Jr.
Homeland Security Director
Alabama Department of Homeland Security
P.O. Box 304115
Montgomery, AL 36103-4115
1-334-956-7250
1-334-223-1120 FAX

**Alaska**
BG Craig Campbell
Box 5800
Ft. Richardson, AK 99505-0800
1-907-428-6003
www.ak-prepared.com/homelandsecurity

**Arizona**
Frank Navarette
Homeland Security Director
1700 West Washington Street, 3rd Floor
Phoenix, AZ 85007
1-602-542-7030
www.homelandsecurity.az.gov/

**Arkansas**
Col. Wayne Ruthven
Director
Box 758
Conway, AR 72033
1-501-730-9781
www.adem.state.ar.us

**California**
Matt Bettenhausen
Director of the Office of Homeland Security
State Capitol, First Floor
Sacramento, CA 95814
1-916-324-8908
www.oas.ca.gov/operational/oeshome.nsf/1?openform

**Colorado**
Joe Morales

Executive Director, CO Office of Public Safety
700 Kipling Street
Denver, CO 80215
1-303-239-4398
www.ops.state.co.us

**Connecticut**
James Thomas
Commissioner of Homeland Security
450 Capitol Ave
Hartford, CT 06106
1-860-418-6394
www.ct.gov/oem/site/default.asp

**Delaware**
David Mitchell
Acting Homeland Security Director
Director, Emergency Management
Tatnall Building, 2nd Floor
William Penn Street
Dover, DE 19901
1-302-659-2240
www.delawarepublicsafety.com

**District of Columbia**
Ed Reiskin
Deputy Mayor for Public Safety
1350 Pennsylvania Avenue, NW #327
Washington, DC 20004
1-202-727-4036
www.dcema.dc.gov/dcema/site/default.asp

**Florida**
Kenneth Tucker
Deputy Commissioner, Florida Dept. of L.E.
Box 1489
Tallahassee, FL 32302-1489
1-850-410-8300
www.fdle.state.fl.us/osi/domesticsecurity/

**Georgia**
Matt Sherberger

Acting Director of Homeland Security
P.O. Box 1456
Atlanta, GA 30371
1-404-624-7030
www.gahomelandsecurity.com/

**Hawaii**
BG Robert Lee
Adjutant General
3949 Diamond Head Road
Honolulu, HI 96816-4495
1-808-733-4246
www.scd.state.hi.us

**Idaho**
MG Jack Kane
Adjutant General
4040 West Guard Street
Boise, ID 83705-5004
1-208-422-5242
www.bhs.idaho.gov

**Illinois**
Carl Hawkinson
Deputy Chief of Staff of Public Safety
Homeland Security Advisor
207 State House
Springfield, IL 62706
1-217-524-1486
www.state.il.us/iema/index.htm

**Indiana**
Eric Dietz
Executive Director, State Emergency Management Agency
Indianapolis, IN 46204
1-317-232-3986
www.in.gov/sema

**Iowa**
MG Ron Dardis
Homeland Security Advisor
Adjutant General of Iowa
Hoover State Office Bldg.
1305 E. Walnut
Des Moines, IA 50319
1-515-252-4211
www.iowahomelandsecurity.org

**Kansas**
BG Todd Bunting
Homeland Security Advisor

Adjutant General of Iowa
2800 SW Topeka
Topeka, KS 66611-1287
1-785-274-1011
www.accesskansas.org/kdem/

**Kentucky**
Keith Hall
Director of Homeland Security
200 Metro Street
Frankfort, KY 40622
1-502-564-2081
homelandsecurity.ky.gov

**Louisiana**
MG Bennett C. Landreneau
Adjutant General and Director
Louisiana Office of Emergency Preparedness
7667 Independence Blvd.
Baton Rouge, LA 70806
1-504-278-2812
www.ohsep.louisiana.gov/default.htm

**Maine**
BG John Libby
Adjutant General
Homeland Security
1 State House Station
Augusta, ME 04333-0001
1-207-626-4205
www.state.me.us/portal/homelandsec.html

**Maryland**
Dennis Schrader
Homeland Security Director
State House, 100 State Circle
Annapolis, MD 21401
1-410-974-2389
www.mema.state.md.us

**Massachusetts**
John Cohen
Homeland Security Policy Advisor
Executive Office of Public Safety
1 Ashburton Place, Rm. 2133
Boston, MA 02108
1-616-727-3200
www.mass.gov/mema

**Michigan**
COL Tadarial Sturdivant

Director of State Police
Contact: Capt. John Ort
713 South Harrison Road
East Lansing, MI 48823
517-336-6157
www.michigan.gov/homeland

**Minnesota**
Michael Campion
Acting Commissioner of Public Safety
Director, Homeland Security
DPS, North Central Life Tower
445 Minnesota Street, Suite 1000
St. Paul, MN 55101
1-651-215-1527
www.dps.state.mn.us/homesec/mohshome.asp

**Mississippi**
Dewitt Fortenberry, Jr.
Commissioner of Public Safety
Director, Homeland Security
P.O. Box 4501
Jackson, MS 39296-4501
1-601-987-1499
www.homelandsecurity.ms.gov

**Missouri**
Michael Chapman
Director, Missouri Homeland Security
P.O. Box 749
Jefferson City, MO 65102
1-573-522-3007
www.homelandsecurity.mo.us

**Montana**
Dan McGowan
Acting Homeland Security Advisor
Department of Military Affairs–HAFRC
Montana Disaster and Emergency Services
1900 Williams Street
P.O. Box 4789
Helena, MT 59604-4789
1-406-841-3911
www.state.mt.us/dma/des/default.asp

**Nebraska**
Rick Sheehy
P.O. Box 94848
Lincoln, NE 68509-4848
1-402-471-2256
www.nebema.org

**Nevada**
Giles Vanderhoof
Homeland Security Advisor
2525 S. Carson Street
Carson City, NV 89710
1-775-684-4556
homelandsecurity.nv.gov

**New Hampshire**
Bruce Cheney
State Homeland Security Advisor
Director, Office of Emergency Management
10 Hazen Drive
Concord, NH 03305
1-603-271-6911
www.nh.gov/homelandsecurity/

**New Jersey**
Sidney Caspersen, Director
N.J. Office of Counterterrorism
P.O. Box 091
Trenton, NJ 08625
1-609-341-5050
www.state.nj.us/njhomelandsecurity/

**New Mexico**
Tim Manning
NM Homeland Security Director
P.O. Box 1628
Santa Fe, NM 87507-1628
1-505-476-0267
www.dps.nm.org/emergency/index.htm

**New York**
James McMahon
Director, Office of Public Security
Executive Chamber
633 3rd Avenue, 38th Floor
New York, NY 10017
1-212-867-7060
info@security.state.ny.us
www.state.ny.us/security/

**North Carolina**
Bryan Beatty
Secretary, Dept. of Crime Control and Public Safety
4701 Mail Service Center
Raleigh, NC 27699
1-919-733-2126
www.ncgov.com/asp.subpages/safety_security.asp

**North Dakota**
Doug Friez
Homeland Security Coordinator/Emergency Management
 Director
Fraine Barracks Lane, Bldg. 35
Fraine Barracks
Bismark, ND 58504
1-701-328-8100
www.state.nd.us/dem/homesec.html

**Ohio**
Kenneth L. Morckel
Director of Public Safety
1970 W. Broad St.
Columbus, OH 43223-1102
1-614-466-3383
www.homelandsecurity.ohio.gov

**Oklahoma**
Major Kerry Pettingill
Director
Oklahoma Office of Homeland Security
Department of Public Safety
Box 11415
Oklahoma City, OK 73136-0415
1-405-425-7296
1-405-425-7295 FAX
kpetting@dps.state.ok.us
www.homelandsecurity.ok.gov

**Oregon**
Beverlee Venell
Director, Office of Homeland Security
400 Public Service Bldg.
Salem, OR 97310
1-503-378-3725
www.oregon.gov/osp/opss/

**Pennsylvania**
Jonathan Duecker
Director, Pennsylvania Office of Homeland Security
2605 Interstate Drive
Harrisburg, PA 17110
1-717-651-2715
www.homelandsecurity.state.pa.us

**Puerto Rico**
Rosaida Melendez
Homeland Security Advisor
La Fortaleza

P.O. Box 9020082
San Juan, PR 00902-0082
1-787-724-0388

**Rhode Island**
MG Reginald Centracchio
Adjutant General
222 State House
Providence, RI 02903
1-401-275-4333
www.riema.ri.gov/

**South Carolina**
Robert M. Stewart
Chief, S.C. Law Enforcement Division (SLED)
P.O. Box 21398
Columbia, SC 29221-1398
1-803-737-9000

**South Dakota**
John A. Berheim, Director
Division of Emergency Management
500 East Capitol Avenue
Pierre, SD 57501
1-605-773-3450
www.state.sd.us/homeland/

**Tennessee**
MG (Ret.) Jerry Humble
215 Eighth Avenue, North
Nashville, TN 37203
1-615-532-7825
www.state.tn.us/homelandsecurity/

**Texas**
Steve McCraw
Director, Office of Homeland Security
P.O. Box 12428
Austin, TX 78711
1-512-936-1882
www.texashomelandsecurity.com

**Utah**
Nannette Rolfe
Director, Division of Emergency Services
210 State Capitol
Salt Lake City, UT 84114
1-801-538-3400
www.cem.utah.gov

**Vermont**
Chris Reinfurt
Commissioner, VT State Police
103 South Main Street
Waterbury, VT 05671-2101
1-802-241-5357
www.dps.state.vt.us/homeland/home_main.html

**Virginia**
George Foresman
Assistant to the Governor for Commonwealth Preparedness
202 N. 9th Street, 5th Floor
Richmond, VA 23219
1-804-225-3826
www.commonwealthpreparedness.virginia.gov

**Washington**
MG Timothy J. Lowenberg
Adjutant General and Director
State Military Department
Washington Military Dept., Bldg. 1
Camp Murray, WA 98430-5000
1-253-512-8201
emd.wa.gov

**West Virginia**
James Spears
Secretary, Dept. of Military Affairs and Public Safety
State Capitol Complex, Bldg. 6, Room B-122
Charleston, WV 25305
1-304-558-3795
www.state.wv.us/wvoes

**Wisconsin**
General Al Wikening
Administrator, Emergency Management
P.O. Box 7865
Madison, WI 53707-7865
1-608-242-3210
www.wisconsin.gov/state/core/domestic_prep.html

**Wyoming**
Joe Moore, Director
Wyoming Office of Homeland Security
Herschler Building, First Floor East
122 W. 25th Street
Cheyenne, WY 82002-0001
1-307-777-4663
wyohomelandsecurity.state.wy.us

**American Samoa**
Leiataua Birdsall V. Ala'ilima
Special Assistant to the Governor
Office of Territory Emergency Mgmt.
American Samoa Government
Pago, Pago, AS 96799
1-011-684-633-4116

**Guam**
Frank Blas
Homeland Security Advisor
P.O. Box 2950
Hagatna, GU 96932
1-671-475-9600/9602

**Northern Mariana Islands**
Jerry Crisostomo
Special Advisor for Homeland Security
Caller Box 10007
Saipan, MP 96950
1-670-664-2280

**Virgin Islands**
MG Cleave A. McBean
Adjutant General
21-22 Kongens Gade
St. Thomas, VI 00802
1-340-712-7710

# Appendix 6: List of Corporation for National and Community Service (CNCS) Homeland Security Grantees

GRANT ANNOUNCEMENT—$10.3 MILLION TOTAL

## ALABAMA

Colbert County Commission, $75,744

This new RSVP project will serve Colbert County, engaging 200 RSVP volunteers in assisting law enforcement, fire departments, and emergency management services. Volunteers will assist fire and law enforcement with clerical work, neighborhood and business watches, presentations on public safety, meetings on homeland security strategies, and volunteer recruitment. Partners include the County Health Department, the Tennessee Valley Authority, and the Northwest Alabama Regional Airport.

## ALASKA

Municipality of Anchorage, $300,000

The Municipality of Anchorage Department of Health and Human Services will assist homebound seniors and an estimated 4,500 physically or developmentally disabled residents of Anchorage prepare to respond to a disaster. Various municipal agencies, the Office of Emergency Management, police and fire departments, American Red Cross, and the Police Chaplains Association will provide training and technical assistance in emergency preparedness and disaster response. Volunteers will act as instructors and will provide education, screening, and supplies to identified residents in need. Department staff will facilitate and coordinate the project by establishing and maintaining a database of the residents in need of these services.

## CALIFORNIA

American Red Cross of Greater Los Angeles, $349,125

The American Red Cross, in partnership with the Governor's Office on Service and Volunteerism (GO SERV), will implement homeland security–related projects in Los Angeles, San Francisco, and Sacramento. Twenty-four AmeriCorps members will provide community disaster/emergency-preparedness education and training to individuals, families, and community- and faith-based organizations, including Neighborhood Watch and Citizen Corps groups, with an emphasis on seniors living in the Los Angeles, San Francisco, and Sacramento metropolitan areas. In addition to reaching 24,000 local residents, the AmeriCorps members will provide continuity and contingency planning assistance to 300 community- and faith-based organizations, schools, and businesses to increase their organizational capacity in the event of an emergency or disaster.

## COLORADO

Valley Community Fund, $217,400

Valley Community Fund, in conjunction with the San Luis Valley American Red Cross, will develop the capacity of San Luis Valley citizens to become the first line of defense in case of emergencies and disasters. The project will mobilize 5,885 volunteer citizens throughout the San Luis Valley and will recruit and train 200 volunteers to support and sustain activities. The San Luis Valley American Red Cross is the only local volunteer group that, in response to disasters, supports firefighters, search-and-rescue crews, and law enforcement as well as the affected population. The project intends to educate one in four members of the community in order to develop citizens as the first line of defense. The intended outcome will be a community educated in disaster preparedness, schoolchildren educated in disaster preparedness and response, the establishment of trained disaster response teams of at least six people in all six counties, and nurses trained in first aid, CPR, and disaster health service.

CONNECTICUT

The American Radio Relay League, Inc., $181,900

The American Radio Relay League (ARRL) plans to expand its program to 5,200 certified emergency volunteers. ARRL is the national association for Amateur Radio and is the national leader in emergency communications by volunteers who operate their own equipment on their time at no cost to any government, organization, or corporation. The Certified Emergency Radio volunteers serve their local communities and work side by side with emergency medical teams, police and fire departments, and Offices of Emergency Management to stabilize communities with reliable emergency communications service. The Homeland Security Grant will allow the ARRL to train more volunteers by funding the Amateur Radio Emergency Communication Course, which will revise its training curriculum to ensure that new elements of emergency preparedness and homeland security are included.

DISTRICT OF COLUMBIA

Executive Office of the Mayor, $400,000

The Executive Office of the Mayor will recruit, train, and place 2,000 new volunteers in a capacity to support the city in homeland security activities. Placements will be in pre-existing organizations such as Emergency Medical Technician Corps and Volunteers in Police Service and will allow for their expansion. Volunteers will assist or develop local Neighborhood Watch Programs. Neighborhood Citizen Corps teams will be established, with Community Emergency Response Team (CERT) and volunteer management training. The project will strengthen homeland security through community building efforts, volunteer preparation for disaster response, and building and developing volunteer opportunities within the city.

Disaster Resistance Neighborhood Program—Red Cross, $99,174

Eight AmeriCorps members will serve with the Red Cross to develop Disaster Resistant Neighborhood Programs across eight wards encompassing 39 Advisory Neighborhood Commissions in the District. They will promote disaster safety through an organized effort at the neighborhood level, led by neighborhood volunteers. In addition to working with the wards' City Council members, ANC commissioners, and other community-based organizations, the AmeriCorps members will also participate on Disaster Action Teams and present community disaster education to volunteers. The eight members will form four teams of two; each team will be assigned to cover two wards.

FLORIDA

City of Orlando, $400,000

The City of Orlando will engage, train, and empower citizens in volunteer service to protect people and neighborhoods in the event of a disaster. The project will mobilize approximately 3,500 volunteers and will engage 1,400 new volunteers in three years. The city will establish a centralized Homeland Security Volunteer Office to coordinate homeland security training programs and recruit, screen, and track volunteers. Volunteers will partake in a homeland security certification program that will provide them with proficiency in assisting special populations, recruiting volunteers, and collaborating with community leaders on neighborhood disaster preparedness.

Florida Commission on Community Service, $328,000

The Florida Commission on Community Service will subgrant funds to Volunteer Florida. Volunteer Florida empowers volunteer centers throughout Florida to mobilize seniors and veterans to serve in local homeland security initiatives. The volunteer centers have seven program options to implement homeland security programs at the centers. Some programs include: Community Emergency Response Teams, which will be established or expanded according to center needs; Florida Division of Emergency Management's program to help small businesses become more disaster resistant; Event Watch, which will provide additional security for community events that are potential terrorist targets; and Front Porch Florida, which will engage underrepresented populations in implementing improvement programs in their communities.

Florida AmeriCorps Community Emergency Support Initiative, $434,000

Under this grant to the Florida Department of Community Affairs, the AmeriCorps Community Emergency Support Initiative will organize and assign five-member teams to each of the seven emergency management regions in the state. Along with the regional managers for emergency, they will create Citizen Emergency Response Teams. Members will be part of a "train the trainer" model that will multiply the capacity of the emergency management division in each region by training 150 trainers. In addition, members will recruit 1,000 volunteers and implement 70 projects, including weatherizing the homes of senior citizens and economically disadvantaged community residents in areas prone to natural disasters. Senior citizens and people with disabilities are a special target of this program, both as beneficiaries and as prospective volunteers.

Florida Department of Elder Affairs, $235,977
The Department of Elder Affairs will train 20 AmeriCorps members to educate elderly populations in disaster preparedness through community presentations in eight counties in north Florida. In addition, members will train schoolteachers in the use of American Red Cross curricula such as "Facing Fear" and "Masters of Disasters." Members will help to establish three joint volunteer centers working in education for managing disasters. The department will subgrant the program to the local American Red Cross to recruit and train members. The Red Cross plans to involve its community- and school-based partners. The chapter has memorandums of understanding with 25 community- and faith-based agencies, and the proposal states that the chapter plans to utilize its AmeriCorps members and volunteers to work with these agencies.

United Way of Central Florida, $81,772
This new RSVP project will serve Polk County, utilizing 150 RSVP volunteers to focus on disaster preparedness/response and Neighborhood Watch/public safety activities. Volunteers will receive Community Emergency Response Teams (CERT) training to improve community readiness, lead Crime Patrol and Neighborhood Watch patrols, provide administrative support to local deputy and fire offices, and inform neighborhoods on Red Cross Family Disaster Planning. Partners include fire departments, emergency management services, Freedom Corps, the American Red Cross, law enforcement, and public schools.

IOWA
Iowa Commission on Volunteer Service, $136,985
In a project established by the Iowa Commission on Volunteer Service, 16 AmeriCorps members will teach the Red Cross's "Masters of Disaster" and "Facing Fear" programs and other community disaster education materials to students in 28 school districts statewide to help them understand and cope with acts of terrorism and other disasters. The members will also use these materials to educate 320 community groups and will recruit a cadre of 40 volunteers to ensure the program's sustainability. Members will also recruit 200 additional volunteers to assist with service activities.

KENTUCKY
Kentucky Association of Senior Service Corps, $114,330
The Kentucky Association's RSVP project will mobilize 200 RSVP volunteers in five counties (Logan, Simpson, Warren, Calloway, and Graves) that are currently not served by RSVP. The project will focus on crime reduction, Neighborhood

Watch, and school safety, in addition to serving other community needs. Placement of volunteers will be in a variety of community organizations, including police departments, Red Cross chapters, health departments, school systems, and the Salvation Army.

Green River Development District, $123,800
The Green River Development District will operate its program in seven rural counties. AmeriCorps members will be placed in a number of rapid response agencies to educate 1,000 individuals about public safety, public health, and disaster preparedness issues; train 600 volunteers in disaster preparedness and relief; and assist in developing closer collaboration among local agencies in areas of disaster response, health service, and other related areas. Currently, Green River Development District has 18 AmeriCorps members serving who are trained in disaster preparedness and have previously provided disaster relief to the state.

MARYLAND
National Association of Community Health Centers, $434,000
The National Association of Community Health Centers will use its grant to establish the Community Emergency and Disaster Response Initiative at five sites across the country, with a total of 35 AmeriCorps members. The initiative's primary goal is to establish training and resources, disaster and emergency preparedness, and response and recovery strategies for community health center users and other residents in five communities. AmeriCorps members will be trained as trainers and equipped to use the Federal Emergency Management Agency's disaster preparedness curriculum in health centers. The grant will address the concerns revealed by a post-September 11 survey conducted by the association, which reported that 91 percent of the health centers are not adequately prepared for a public health emergency involving bioterrorism. The five sites are: San Francisco Community Clinic Consortium; Grace Hill Neighborhood Health Center, St. Louis, MO; Syracuse Community Health Center, Syracuse, NY; Unity Health Services, Washington, DC; and Michigan Primary Care Association, Okemos, MI.

Volunteer Frederick, Inc., $115,725
This new RSVP project will mobilize 550 volunteers to serve Frederick County, home to Camp David and Fort Detrick. The project's volunteers will work with 52 volunteer stations serving community needs through Neighborhood Watch/ Public Safety, Disaster Preparedness/Response, Youth

Education, and Senior Assistance activities. Partners include law enforcement, fire departments, food banks, the YMCA, Big Brothers/Big Sisters, Safe Kids Coalition, the Red Cross, emergency management services, and hospitals. Some volunteers will train to become members of Disaster Action Teams, freeing up trained emergency workers, building disaster response infrastructure, and serving as administrative officers at fire departments. Other programs will include serving in the Sheriff's Office Community Assistance Patrol program and assisting the Frederick Memorial Hospital as liaisons in the Emergency Department.

Civic Works, Inc., $123,948
Civic Works, Inc., will use its grant to train AmeriCorps members in three areas: community outreach and education; volunteer recruitment and management; and disaster response activities. Members will disseminate public health, bioterrorism, and disaster preparedness information to 5,000 residents in Baltimore at community fairs, community association meetings, church groups, schools, and door-to-door. AmeriCorps members will also recruit and train 50 additional volunteers to help meet the program's goal of reaching 20,000 residents in 20 different communities. In the event of an emergency, members can also provide relief to rescue workers, search-and-rescue services, first aid, coordination of supplies, and other support to relief efforts.

MICHIGAN
Detroit Medical Center, $200,000
The Southeast Michigan Weapons of Mass Destruction, Bioterrorism and Disaster Preparedness Consortium will mobilize an estimated 6,000 volunteers. These volunteers will provide local preparedness planning, make Detroit a trauma-ready city by developing a readiness response team for bioterrorism, and focus on all aspects of health care and trauma services that may be needed in the event of a disaster. The strategies of the project include expansion of the community-wide immunization program, development and dissemination of public-health and disaster-preparedness information, and the continued staging of citywide disaster-preparedness trials. The Consortium comprises the fire, police, and EMS teams of Detroit, the Detroit Medical Center, Wayne State University School of Medicine, and the John D. Dingell/Veterans Administration Medical Center.

MINNESOTA
Community Net, $100,000

This new RSVP project, with 400 RSVP volunteers, will serve Olmsted, Goodhue, Rice, and Wabasha counties. Teams of volunteers will be trained to assist with the Public Health Emergency Response Plan and will participate in disaster response exercises to strengthen preparedness and conduct training in other counties. A group of volunteers will assist police, fire, and sheriff's offices with clerical work and ticketing, allowing trained professional personnel to respond to emergencies. Other volunteers will be trained as probation monitors, supervising clients and assisting probation staff with paperwork. Partners include the Olmsted County Public Health Department, the Red Cross, and social services.

MONTANA
Western Montana Area VI Agency on Aging, $104,266
This RSVP project will serve Lake, Mineral, and Ravalli counties, including the Flathead Indian Reservation that lies within Lake County. Some 254 RSVP volunteers will serve with volunteer stations working in Public Safety, Youth Crime, Disaster Response/Preparedness, Public Health, and Health Education activities. Volunteers will assist law enforcement in patrols, expand neighborhood watch groups, provide administrative assistance, develop strategy development plans, and man emergency management office dispatch services, freeing up staff time. The volunteers also will educate the public about the Rocky Mountain Laboratories, a biomedical research lab, to alleviate fear of the facility. Partners include the American Red Cross, Head Start, Kids First, YMCA, and Lake County Youth Court.

Richland County Health Department, $88,718
This new RSVP project will serve the sparsely populated northeastern area of Richland and McCone counties. RSVP will utilize 250 volunteers in homeland security activities through the Richmond Health Network. Volunteer teams will assist the Local Emergency Preparedness Committee in implementation of its emergency plan; work with law enforcement to develop Neighborhood Watch and community policing programs; and staff a Seniors Outreaching to Seniors program that will locate, assess the needs of, educate, and empower seniors and others with special needs related to emergency response. The Richland Health Network is a collaborative effort of the Richland County Health Department, the Sidney Health Center, and the County Commission on Aging.

NEW JERSEY
New Jersey Department of Education, $248,000

New Jersey's location close to New York City, along with the density and diversity of its population, make it a possible target for terrorist attacks. The grant will be used by the New Jersey Department of Education to establish the New Jersey Secure Corps, a statewide initiative with the main objective of creating and activating a Volunteer Organization Active in Disasters (VOAD) in each of the state's 21 counties. Each VOAD will function as the central coordination unit for disasters and emergencies. Members will make at least 20 community presentations to teach residents about bioterrorism and the ways in which they can prepare as a community for a bioterrorist attack. In addition, members will create a statewide database that will link all volunteers who have expressed an interest in becoming involved in disaster preparedness with organizations in the area, according to the volunteer's skills, availability, and geographic location.

## NEW YORK

American Red Cross in Greater New York, $500,000
American Red Cross in Greater New York will recruit and train 310 leaders who will mobilize 5,000 coordinated volunteers with the ability to respond quickly, appropriately, and in effective ways should a disaster or another act of terrorism occur. For the training of leaders and mobilization of volunteers, the collaborative project will utilize the New York State Emergency Management Office, New York State Offices for Aging, the New York State Commission on National and Community Service, Retired and Senior Volunteer Programs of New York, Volunteer Organizations Active in Disaster, and the New York State Department of Education. The goal is to strengthen homeland security, log 3,600,000 hours of volunteer service in one year, and create Citizen Corps Councils.

Center for Court Innovation, $484,000
The New York City Public Safety Corps will enhance homeland security by assisting criminal justice officials (police, probation officers, judges) as they perform their duties by working directly with victims and by engaging local residents in solving neighborhood public safety problems. The project expands the New York Red Hook Public Safety Corps into other areas of New York City.

Forty full-time AmeriCorps members will address five principal objectives: to free up police, prosecutors and court staff to focus on pressing duties; to provide critical manpower support in case of an emergency; to address conditions of disorder that, if left unchecked, create a climate where crime would flourish; to build partnerships between criminal justice agencies and neighborhood residents, generating substantial neighborhood volunteers; and to be a visible presence in neighborhoods to communicate that someone who cares and helps is always nearby. Members will help identify community security concerns, develop new solutions to these concerns, and recruit volunteers to participate in projects addressing these concerns.

New York State Corps Collaboration, $293,760
With the New York State Corps Collaboration, 36 AmeriCorps members will serve to develop an infrastructure to address disaster preparation, mitigation, and response in the smaller towns in New York State. Some 36 members will serve in teams of 12 members each in three areas. In Component 1, 12 members assigned to host sites at Red Cross chapters across the state will assist Red Cross personnel and volunteers in emergency preparedness and receive training in Shelter Operations and Mass Care. In Component 2, 12 members will work to develop and strengthen Volunteer Organizations Active in Disaster in 12 areas to be determined by the Red Cross; members will survey existing resources and help build a database for local emergency management. In Component 3, 12 members will serve in one of the group's existing youth corps to identify, recruit, screen, and facilitate the training of 500 local volunteers.

Pace University, $247,973
The Pace University Community and Volunteer Mobilization AmeriCorps program will recruit and train members and volunteers dedicated to the recovery and rehabilitation of the downtown and Chinatown areas of New York City that were devastated on September 11. Members will help build sustainable infrastructure in three areas: Public Health and Public Safety Training Program Infrastructure, in which members will help fire and police departments and local hospitals create a disaster/emergency plan for the downtown area, conduct community asset mapping to determine existing services, and create a public health and public safety manual; Web Volunteer Bulletin Board/Technical and Community Training Network/ Infrastructure, in which members will create a web network that will serve as a clearinghouse to help the downtown community identify volunteers to help with post–September 11 activities and serve as a quick response communication network for future needs; and English as a Second Language activities, in which members will help improve the English language skills of area immigrants so that they can understand when there is an emergency, how to respond, and how to help

others who do not speak English. Additionally, this activity will help community residents with job application skills, a particular need as 25 percent of community residents lost jobs due to September 11.

The Valley, $248,087

With the AmeriCorps Public Safety Program, members will be placed within the central administrative office and at firehouses of the New York Fire Department, allowing firefighters to attend to other urgent needs. The members will also promote public and fire safety awareness through community and school presentations, and forge relationships between the fire department and local communities by assisting with the department's minority recruitment efforts and outreach to people of color.

NORTH CAROLINA

North Carolina Commission on Volunteerism and Community Service, $119,900

The Commission on Volunteerism and Community Service will engage 2,000 volunteers to support homeland security and disaster relief activities statewide. The commission will have 100 local volunteer coordinators prepared to serve at disaster sites and will establish a statewide volunteer management database to support the mobilization of volunteers. A public awareness campaign about the volunteer efforts will be utilized to generate public interest in volunteer opportunities throughout North Carolina.

OHIO

Ohio Community Service Council, $450,000

The Ohio Community Service Council will forge statewide and local partnerships with the Ohio Emergency Management Agency, the Ohio Volunteer Center Association, and the Ohio RSVP Directors Association to better facilitate the volunteer needs of emergency systems in Ohio. Pilot Citizen Corps Councils will be developed as part of the State of Ohio Security Task Force for the purpose of supporting and promoting the engagement of citizen volunteers in homeland security roles. Volunteer centers in nine Ohio regions will assess the volunteer needs of the community, train agencies in volunteer management, promote citizen involvement, and mobilize and support volunteers assigned to emergency response roles.

OKLAHOMA

City of Tulsa, $275,000

The City of Tulsa will develop and implement a citywide volunteer mobilization strategy to meet the city's needs in

the event of a disaster. Community units will be created in order to connect people within a community and assist neighborhoods in becoming safe and secure in public safety, public health, and disaster preparedness and relief. The community units will, among other activities, assess vulnerabilities, educate the public about the multiethnic fabric of the community, and fill the volunteer needs of emergency and police response agencies. A Language and Culture Bank will be established, providing language translation required by official first responders. The city will also create a process to mobilize volunteers for disaster response.

OREGON

Oregon Trail Chapter, American Red Cross, $136,392

Serving with the Oregon Trail Chapter of the American Red Cross, 11 AmeriCorps members will respond to disasters, recruit and train disaster responders, teach community disaster preparation and health and safety classes, and mobilize 400 new volunteers who will provide 1,500 hours of service. During the first year of implementation, sites for the AmeriCorps members will be at Oregon Red Cross Chapters, and the plan is to expand outside of the Red Cross in the future. AmeriCorps members will be serving directly with local community- and faith-based organizations.

PENNSYLVANIA

American Red Cross—Southeast Pennsylvania Chapter, $323,000

The American Red Cross—Southeast Pennsylvania Chapter will create an alliance of over 100 nonprofits in the Greater Philadelphia area to form the Southeastern Pennsylvania Voluntary Organizations Active in Disaster. The alliance, joined by United Way, will empower and mobilize citizens of southeastern Pennsylvania to help neighbors prevent, prepare for, and respond to disasters. Initially the alliance will mobilize 400 new volunteers. The goal is to eventually mobilize 7,000 volunteers to attend to victims for the initial 72 hours following a disaster and an additional 1,000 trained volunteers to build a coordinated disaster response system.

SOUTH CAROLINA

South Carolina AmeriCorps Defense Brigade, $297,476

The South Carolina Military Department will support the 25-member South Carolina AmeriCorps Defense Brigade. The AmeriCorps members will identify and prepare 600 volunteers to deliver homeland defense services to individuals and communities in an effort to increase public awareness about potential threats to homeland security, as well as develop and manage a database of volunteers.

## TENNESSEE

Tennessee Commission on National and Community Service, $150,000

The Tennessee Commission will fortify the statewide homeland security infrastructure by developing and strengthening relationships with local councils and statewide disaster agencies. The Tennessee Office of Homeland Security will focus primarily on the mobilization of 1,000 volunteers a year. Partners in the project include the Tennessee Emergency Management Agency. Local homeland security councils and disaster response organizations will assist in identifying opportunities for various kinds of volunteers to support homeland security.

## TEXAS

City of Austin, $400,000

The Office of Emergency Management will coordinate 300 volunteers to form the volunteer teams of Disaster Ready Austin, and the Austin Police Department's Civil Defense volunteer program will be expanded by 200 volunteers. The emergency management office will develop a long-term corps of volunteers who will provide direct emergency management services to the community. The Austin Police Department currently has a force of 100 Civil Defense volunteers. The Civil Defense expansion will support airport police by providing supplemental security, assisting in duties that do not require a peace officer's license, and preparing for mobilization in the event of a natural or man-made disaster. Some partners in the project are the American Red Cross, Salvation Army, Senior and Law Enforcement Together, Neighborhood Advocates for Emergency Preparedness, and Austin Area Interreligious Ministries.

## VIRGINIA

Mercy Medical Airlift, $253,400

Mercy Medical Airlift's Volunteer Pilot Homeland Security Transportation Network will build on the established volunteer "Angel Flight" pilots program, which serves ten states (Delaware, Kentucky, Maryland, Michigan, North Carolina, Ohio, Pennsylvania, Tennessee, Virginia, West Virginia) and the District of Columbia. The program plans to increase volunteer pilot participation to 400 pilots regionally, with a minimum of 5,000 pilots nationwide. The Angel Flight program currently provides only preplanned charitable long-distance medical transportation for needy patients and their

families. The increase in the number of volunteer pilots will decrease the current response time by establishing two pilot groups who can respond on either 1- or 6- hours' notice. In the third year of the grant, the program will be replicated in five other regional volunteer pilot organizations. Examples of the volunteer pilot air transportation system include flying emergency blood shipments to hospitals, key relief agency officials to disaster sites, and "booties" to rescue dogs working at "Ground Zero."

American National Red Cross Rapid Response Corps, $371,978

Thirty AmeriCorps members serving with the American National Red Cross Rapid Response Corps will be placed at American Red Cross chapters across the country. Member activities as will be designed to increase the chapter's capacity to provide integrated community education and outreach efforts focused on homeland security. Specific activities will be determined by each operating site's needs.

## WASHINGTON

Pierce County Neighborhood Emergency Teams, $250,000

The Pierce County Department of Emergency Management and Pierce County Sheriff's Department plan to expand the Pierce County Neighborhood Emergency Teams (PC-NET) to over 100 neighborhoods from the existing eight. PC-NET, a local adaptation of the national CERT teams, will expand in scope to include crime prevention and homeland security. The volunteers will be recruited and trained to serve as trainers of neighborhood residents in crime prevention, assessment and reporting of terrorist threats, and emergency response to disaster. The resident training will prepare neighborhoods to be self-sufficient for up to 72 hours without professional emergency response.

## WEST VIRGINIA

Council on the Southern Mountains RSVP, $100,000

This new RSVP project will serve the West Virginia counties of McDowell, Wyoming, and Raleigh. The project's 200 RSVP volunteers will be assigned roles in Neighborhood Watch/Public Safety activities, Health Education, Child Literacy, and Disaster Preparedness. Teams of volunteers will work with the Red Cross, National Guard, and FEMA to assist families in a faster recovery from disaster in a flood plain area of McDowell. The volunteers will establish Neighborhood Watches and seek to reduce crime by 40 percent through education and training. Partners include law enforcement agencies, hospitals, rural health-care clinics, physicians, pharmaceutical companies, education systems, AmeriCorps, West Virginia Extension Services, and emergency management services.

WISCONSIN

Housing Authority of the City of Milwaukee, $225,000

The Housing Authority of the City of Milwaukee will recruit and utilize 2,000 multigenerational volunteers for disaster preparedness and response. The Authority's Public Safety Staff, Milwaukee Area Technical College, the Sheriff's Department, American Red Cross, and FEMA will provide training in emergency preparedness, crime prevention, basic responder skills, team organization, risk reduction, and two-way radio communication. Volunteers will establish a Block Watch program, be trained in the rescue and relocation of children, create a school Emergency Response Handbook, organize an intergenerational volunteer network with seniors and youth, and provide CERT training to be utilized in disaster response. The goal of the project is to engage a variety of ages to work together to build a secure community.

Volunteer Center of Racine, $100,000

Racine County will engage 237 community members as RSVP volunteers in order to provide support in areas of public safety, public health, and disaster preparedness and relief. A partial list of partners for the community wide effort include Volunteer Center of Racine, Racine County Emergency Management, Wisconsin Emergency Management Agency, FEMA, Neighborhood Watch, American Red Cross, schools, law enforcement, and the fire department. The volunteers will provide homeland security awareness, assist with food distribution, and focus on transportation in the event of a disaster.

ADVOCAP, Inc., $125,000

The establishment of RSVP in Winnebago and Green Lake Counties will utilize 250 volunteers in homeland security roles. Various teams of trained volunteers will provide recommendations to improve home security through home safety checks for elderly and disabled citizens, serve with TRIAD to provide outreach and safety information to citizens, and become trainers in disaster preparedness. Programs which will utilize the volunteers include TRIAD, Green Lake Sheriff's Office, the American Red Cross chapter, schools, Habitat for Humanity, meal sites, senior centers, and social service departments.

# Appendix 7: Centers for Disease Control (CDC) Preparedness and Planning Information Sites

## PREPARATION & PLANNING

On this page:
- *General*
- *Businesses*
- *Health-care Facilities*
- *State & Local*
- *National*
- *Legal & Planning Issues*
- *Contacts*
- *Other Resources*

## GENERAL INFORMATION

- *Safety in a Power Outage* NEW!
  What to do when the power goes out unexpectedly.

- *Bioterrorism Preparedness FAQ*

- *Chemical Agents: Facts About Sheltering in Place* (*también en español*)
  How to find temporary shelter in an emergency (http://www.bt.cdc.gov/planning/Shelteringfacts.pdf)

- *Chemical Agents: Facts About Evacuation* (*también en español*)
  Knowing when and how to evacuate an area in an emergency (http://www.bt.cdc.gov/planning/evacuationfacts.pdf)

- *Chemical Agents: Facts About Personal Cleaning & Disposal of Contaminated Clothing* (*también en español*)
  What to do if you come in physical contact with dangerous chemicals (http://www.bt.cdc.gov/planning/personalcleaningfacts.pdf)

## PREPAREDNESS FOR BUSINESSES

- *Emergency Preparedness for Business*
  Instructions to building occupants, actions to be taken by facility management, and first responder notification procedures. From the National Institute for Occupational Safety and Health (NIOSH)

- *Notice to Readers: Protecting Building Environments from Airborne Chemical, Biologic, or Radiologic Attacks*
  MMWR 2002 Sep 6;51(35):789. (http://www.cdc.gov/mmwr/PDF/wk/mm5135.pdf)

- *Guidance for Protecting Building Environments from Airborne Chemical, Biological, or Radiological Attacks*
  May 2002. From the National Institute for Occupational Safety and Health, CDC (http://www.cdc.gov/niosh/bldvent/pdfs/2002-139.pdf)

## PREPAREDNESS FOR HEALTH-CARE FACILITIES

- *Bioterrorism Readiness Plan: A Template for Health-care Facilities* (http://www.cdc.gov/ncidod/hip/Bio/13apr99APICCDCBioterrorism.PDF)

- *Hospital Preparedness for Mass Causalities*
  Provided by the Advancing Health in America Policy Forum.

## STATE & LOCAL PREPAREDNESS

- *Continuation Guidance for Cooperative Agreement on Public Health Preparedness and Response for Bioterrorism—Budget Year Four*
  The Centers for Disease Control and Prevention (CDC) announces the availability of FY2003 funding for continuation of the cooperative agreements to upgrade state and local public health jurisdictions' preparedness for and response to bioterrorism, other outbreaks of infectious disease, and other public health threats and emergencies.

- *Public Health Preparedness and Response Capacity Inventories*
  Voluntary assessments of state and local capacity to respond to bioterrorism, infectious disease outbreaks, and other public health threats and emergencies. Includes measures to assess progress toward meeting the benchmarks and critical and enhanced capacities in the Grant Guidance for FY2002 Supplemental Funds for Public Health Preparedness and Response to Bioterrorism (Announcement 99051).

- *Notice to Readers: Protecting Building Environments from Airborne Chemical, Biologic, or Radiologic Attacks*
  MMWR 2002 Sep 6;51(35):789. (http://www.cdc.gov/mmwr/PDF/wk/mm5135.pdf)

- *Guidance for Protecting Building Environments from Airborne Chemical, Biological, or Radiological Attacks*
  May 2002. From the National Institute for Occupational Safety and Health, CDC (http://www.cdc.gov/niosh/bldvent/pdfs/2002-139.pdf)

- *Notification Procedures for State and Local Public Health Officials*

- *Preparing at the Local Level for Events Involving Weapons of Mass Destruction*
  Emerging Infectious Diseases 2002 Sep;8(9):1006-1007. (http://www.cdc.gov/ncidod/EID/vol8no9/pdf/01-0520.pdf)

- *Public Health Response to Biological & Chemical Terrorism: Interim Planning Guidance for State Public Health Officials* (http://www.bt.cdc.gov/file-formats.asp"\l"pdf

## NATIONAL PREPAREDNESS

- *Community Reaction to Bioterrorism: Prospective Study of Simulated Outbreak*
  Emerging Infectious Diseases 2003 June;9(6):708-712.

- *Planning against Biological Terrorism: Lessons from Outbreak Investigations*
  Emerging Infectious Diseases 2003 May;9(5):515-519. (http://www.cdc.gov/ncidod/EID/vol9no6/pdfs/02-0769.pdf)

- *Fear of Bioterrorism and Implications for Public Health Preparedness*
  Emerging Infectious Diseases 2003 April;9(4):503-505. (http://www.cdc.gov/ncidod/eid/vol9no4/pdfs/02-0593.pdf)

- *Continuation Guidance for Cooperative Agreement on Public Health Preparedness and Response for Bioterrorism—Budget Year Four*
  The Centers for Disease Control and Prevention (CDC) announces the availability of FY2003 funding for continuation of the cooperative agreements to upgrade state and local public health jurisdictions' preparedness for and response to bioterrorism, other outbreaks of infectious disease, and other public health threats and emergencies.

- *Cooperative Agreement Award Notice and Grant Guidance*
  Guidance for CDC bioterrorism funding for states.

- *Bioterrorism and Public Health Preparedness: The CDC's Program in Brief*
  Brief description of bioterrorism and CDC role.

- *Bioterrorism Preparedness FAQ*

- *Strategic National Stockpile*
  National repository of pharmaceuticals & medical supplies.

- *Epi-X: The Epidemic Information Exchange*
  Secure, web-based communications network connecting CDC with state and local health departments, poison control centers, and other public health professionals.
- *Biological and Chemical Terrorism: Strategic Plan for Preparedness and Response*
  Recommendations of the CDC Strategic Planning Workgroup.
  MMWR Recommendations and Reports 2000 Apr 21;49(RR-4);1-14. (http://www.cdc.gov/ mmwr/PDF/RR/RR4904.pdf)
- *Public Health Assessment of Potential Biological Terrorism Agents*
  Emerging Infectious Diseases 2002 Feb;8(2):225-230. (http://www.cdc.gov/ncidod/ EID/vol8no2/pdf/01-0164.pdf)
- *Strengthening National Preparedness for Smallpox: An Update*
  Emerging Infectious Diseases 2001 Jan-Feb;7(1):155–157. (http://www.cdc.gov/ ncidod/eid/vol7no1/pdfs/luduc.pdf)
- *National Bioterrorism Preparedness and Response Initiative* (http://www.bt.cdc.gov/ file-formats.asp"\l"pdf)
  Slide set. Provides an overview and general information about the bioterrorism preparedness and response activities.
- *Emergency and Environmental Health Services*
  From the National Center for Environmental Health. Description of NCEH involvement in providing national and international leadership for the coordination, delivery, and evaluation of emergency and environmental health services.
- *Centers for Public Health Preparedness*
  Program focusing on information technology and training in support of bioterrorism preparedness and emergency response.

## LEGAL AND PLANNING ISSUES

- *Regulations to Control Communicable Diseases*
  42 U.S.C. 264 (From United States Code Annotated; Title 42; The Public Health And Welfare; Chapter 6a—Public Health Service; Subchapter Ii—General Powers And Duties; Part G—Quarantine And Inspection).
- *Interstate Quarantine*
  From United States Code Annotated; Title 42; The Public Health And Welfare; Part 70. On U.S. Government Printing Office site.
- *Foreign Quarantine*
  From United States Code Annotated; Title 42; The Public Health And Welfare; Part 71. On U.S. Government Printing Office site.

## CONTACTS FOR PREPARATION AND PLANNING

- *Bioterrorism Preparedness and Response Program*
  Program questions: 404-639-0385
- *Emergency Preparedness and Response Branch*
  Provided by the National Center for Environmental Health.
- *Health Agency Locator (HAL)*

## OTHER RESOURCES

- *Smallpox Preparation & Planning*
- *Anthrax Preparation & Planning*

# Appendix 8: Selected Websites for Additional Information

Americorps—www.americorps.org

Animal and Plant Health Inspection Service—
www.aphis.usda.gov

Citizen Corps—www.citizencorps.gov

Corporation for National and Community Service—
www.nationalservice.org

Department of Homeland Security—www.dhs.gov

Federal Emergency Management Agency—
www.fema.gov

Immigration and Nationalization Service—www.ins.gov

Medical Reserve Corps—www.medicalreservecorps.gov

National Association of Counties—www.naco.org

National Governors' Association—www.nga.org

National League of Cities—www.nlc.org

Neighborhood Watch—www.usaonwatch.org

Office for Domestic Preparedness—
www.ojp.usdoj.gov/odp

Office for National Preparedness—www.fema.gov/onp

Senior Corps—www.seniorcorps.org

Transportation Security Administration—
www.tsa.dot.gov

United States Coast Guard—www.uscg.mil

United States Conference of Mayors—
www.usmayors.org

United States Customs Service—
www.customs.ustreas.gov

United States Secret Service—www.ustreas.gov/usss/

USA Freedom Corps—www.usafreedomcorps.gov

Volunteers in Police Service—www.policevolunteers.org

*Source*: Institute for Crisis, Disaster and Risk Management, George Washington University—www.gwu.edu/gelman/guides/sciences/crisis.html

## FEDERAL GOVERNMENT

### U.S. Department of Homeland Security

This official site features press releases and other documents that define the role and work of DHS. Emphasis is on these areas: emergencies and disasters, travel and transportation, immigration and borders, research and technology, and threats and protection. Much of the focus is on terrorism, but natural disasters and other emergencies are also addressed. This is a good source for remarks by government officials on issues related to terrorism and national security.

Location: www.dhs.gov

www.tsa.gov Transportation Security Administration

www.cbp.gov Customs and Border Protection

www.ice.gov Immigration and Customs Enforcement

www.fletc.gov Federal Law Enforcement Training Center

www.fema.gov Federal Emergency Management Agency

www.fema.gov/nims National Incident Management System

www.training.fema.gov/EMIWEB/ FEMA's Emergency Management Institute (EMI) serves as the national focal point for the development and delivery of emergency management training to enhance the capabilities of federal, state, local, and tribal government officials, volunteer organizations, and the public and private sectors to minimize the impact of disasters on the American public.

www.uscg.mil United States Coast Guard

www.ustreas.gov/usss/ United States Secret Service

www.customs.ustreas.gov United States Customs Service

www.hsarpa.gov Homeland Security Advanced Research Project Agency

www.ojp.usdoj.gov/odp Office of Domestic Preparedness. The principal DHS component responsible for preparing the country for acts of terrorism.

*Other DHS sites:*

www.ready.gov DHS website designed to educate Americans about preparedness and response to a national emergency.

www.ndms.gov

**Federal Emergency Management Agency (FEMA)**

Part of the Department of Homeland Security, the FEMA site includes information about ongoing disaster responses, various response plans, key emergency management officials at the state and local levels, documents, and other resources.

Location: www.fema.gov

**U.S. Environmental Protection Agency/Chemical Emergency Preparedness and Prevention Office (CEPPO)**

EPA's CEPPO site covers prevention, risk management, preparedness, emergency response, and counterterrorism. Also includes information on regulations, software, publications, and links to related websites. This is a key site for information dealing with hazardous materials, chemical accidents, and oil spills.

Location: www.epa.gov/ceppo

**U.S. Geological Survey**

This site has sections covering land-based natural hazards (earthquakes, floods, volcanoes).

Location: www.usgs.gov

**National Oceanographic and Atmospheric Administration/Office of Response and Restoration**

This site provides access to tools, information, and software for responders to oil spills, chemical accidents, hazardous materials releases, and ship groundings.

Location: http://response.restoration.noaa.gov/index.html

**NASA Disaster Finder**

Disaster Finder is a web-based search tool designed and maintained by NASA Goddard Space Flight Center. Links are categorized within the Disaster Finder database according the Disaster services section of the *Taxonomy of Human Services: A Conceptual Framework with Standardized Terminology and Definitions for the Field*. This taxonomy provides a classification system that allows organizations maintaining human services databases to index and access community resources based on the specific types of disaster services they provide.

Location: http://disasterfinder.gsfc.nasa.gov/

## STATE AND LOCAL EMERGENCY ORGANIZATIONS

**National Emergency Management Association (NEMA)**

NEMA is an organization of state-level emergency management officials. The NEMA online library provides full-text access to documents and presentations from NEMA committees. This site also includes information on NEMA membership, conferences, job listings, and a directory of emergency management contacts by state.

Location: www.nemaweb.org

**International Association of Emergency Managers (IAEM)**

IAEM is an association of local (city and county) emergency management officials. This site provides information on IAEM activities and membership. Selected issues of the newsletter are available online, as well as a bulletin board and discussion list.

Location: www.iaem.com

**National Governors' Association (NGA)**

The National Governors' Association Center for Best Practices (NGAC) provides support to governors in responding to the challenges of homeland security and other emergency management issues. From the NGA home page, visit the site index and scroll to the homeland security and technology division. This will lead to sections on bioterrorism, emergency management, and homeland security. Within these sections are links to several substantial, full-text publications, including a two-volume governors' guide to emergency management, domestic preparedness checklist, and presentations from the NGA Bioterrorism Summit.

Location: www.nga.org/

**Center for State Homeland Security**

Created to help states fulfill their critical homeland security role, this site provides access to full-text articles, legislation, and reports from government agencies and research institutes in a variety of areas, including counterterrorism, public health, and infrastructure protection. It also provides links to state agencies responsible for homeland security and/or emergency management.

Location: www.cshs-us.org

## NONGOVERNMENT ORGANIZATIONS

**American Red Cross (Disaster Services)**

This site gives an overview of the work of the American Red Cross, including reports on Red Cross projects worldwide. It also includes news coverage of disasters and relief efforts.

Location: www.redcross.org

**Disaster Relief**

Sponsored by the American Red Cross, this site features an extensive collection of news stories on disasters back to 1996. The "Library" provides the full text of Red Cross disaster preparedness pamphlets and an extensive collection of disaster statistics. It also includes links to disaster-related sites, including state emergency management offices.

Location: www.disasterrelief.org

**National Memorial Institute for the Prevention of Terrorism**

A nonprofit organization created after the 1995 bombing of the Alfred P. Murrah Federal Building in Oklahoma City dedicated to the prevention and mitigation of terrorist events. While their initial focus was directed toward preparation and response for the traditional "first responder" community, they have extended their research by congressional mandate to include research into social and political issues related to all forms of terrorism. The website includes links to multiple online databases, as well as an extensive library of documents and reports including an interlibrary loan and reference service, and a terrorism-related conference calendar.

Location: www.mipt.org

## UNIVERSITY RESEARCH CENTERS

**University of Colorado/Natural Hazards Center (NHRAIC)**

This site includes links to a number of valuable research sources. These include the full text of articles from newsletters and journals published by the center, working papers, conference papers, and more. The site also provides access to the HazLit Database, an online catalog of over 22,000 items in the center's library.

Location: www.colorado.edu/hazards

**University of Delaware/Disaster Research Center (DRC)**

DRC has studied a broad range of disaster types, including hurricanes, floods, earthquakes, tornadoes, hazardous chemical incidents, plane crashes, civil disturbances, and riots. This site includes descriptions of current projects, as well as extensive bibliographies of DRC publications, including books, articles, preliminary papers, and more. Only some of the publications

are available as full-text versions online; others can be purchased through the center.

Location: www.udel.edu/DRC/

**Canadian Centre for Emergency Preparedness**

This center is a not-for-profit organization based in Ontario devoted to the promotion of emergency risk management to individuals, communities and organizations, in both government and the private sector, with the aim of reducing the risk, impact and cost of natural, human-induced and technological disasters.

Location: www.ccewp.ca

**George Washington Institute for Crisis, Disaster and Risk Management**

Location: www.gwu.edu/~icdrm/

Texas A&M University Hazard Reductions and Recovery Center has an extensive search site for links to disaster, hazard, risk and emergency management research centers (by type) as well as links to university disaster research centers university home pages and details of disaster research projects. Currently, the site only contains details from NSF-funded projects. These disaster research project descriptions are organized by the university that received the funding.

Location: www.hrrc.tamu.edu/

## COMMERCIAL SITES

**Disaster Central**

Maintained by emergency management researcher, consultant, and educator Claire Rubin, this site provides an extensive set of links to recent research reports and other documents on emergency management, terrorism, homeland security, state and local government, critical infrastructure, health and medicine, policy analysis, and risk management. This site is an excellent source for full-text documents online.

Location: www.disaster-central.com/

**National Homeland Security Knowledge Base**

This site provides an extensive set of links to U.S. and other government agencies as well as international and research organizations. Focus is on various threats to homeland security, including nuclear/radiological, biological, chemical, and explosive incidents, as well as natural disasters.

Location: www.twotigersonline.com/resources.html

## SPECIALIZED ORGANIZATIONS

### Earthquake Engineering Research Institute (EERI)

This site provides information on meetings sponsored by EERI as well as updates on seismic legislation. A catalog of EERI publications is available, but only a few select articles and reports are available in their full-text versions online.

Location: www.eeri.org

### Association of State Floodplain Managers

ASFPM is involved in floodplain management; flood hazard mitigation; the National Flood Insurance Program; and flood preparedness, warning, and recovery. This site includes information on conferences, publications, grants and fellowships, job listings, and links to related websites.

Location: www.floods.org

### National Hurricane Center/Tropical Prediction Center (NOAA)

NOAA issues watches, warnings, forecasts, and analyses of hazardous tropical weather. The site includes satellite and radar images, information on hurricane awareness, and historical storm-related data.

Location: www.nhc.noaa.gov/

## RISK ASSESSMENT AND RISK MANAGEMENT

### Risk and Insurance Management Society (RIMS)

This site provides a range of services for society members, including conference announcements, job listings, and a catalog of publications. Several articles from the last few issues of the society's magazine, *Risk Management*, are available online.

Location: www.rims.org/

### Risk World

Risk World provides extensive coverage of news on risk assessment and management with archives of news stories back to 1995. It also provides abstracts of papers from recent conferences and a collection of research reports, many of which are available online.

Location: www.riskworld.com/

### Society for Risk Analysis

Highlights of this site include the table of contents of the society's journal, links to sources of specific risk-related resources (data, models, technical reports, etc.), and a glossary of risk analysis terms.

Location: www.sra.org/

## BUSINESS AND INDUSTRY CRISIS MANAGEMENT/ORGANIZATIONAL CONTINUITY

### Disaster Resource Guide

This site consolidates educational, organizational, and vendor resources in the areas of safety/security, emergency/crisis management, and business continuity. It provides an extensive collection of full-text articles, as well as book reviews, descriptions of company programs, and links to related sites.

Location: www.disaster-resource.com/

### Emergency Management Guide for Business and Industry

This guide provides a step-by-step approach to emergency planning, response, and recovery for companies of all sizes. It requires Adobe Acrobat.

Location: www.fema.gov/library/bizindex.htm

### Disaster Recovery Institute International (DRII)

The highlight of this site is the complete text of "Professional Practices for Business Continuity Planners," a guide to and standards for developing and implementing business continuity plans. The site also includes information on DRII training and certification programs and links to related sites.

Location: www.dr.org

### DRI International Glossary of Terms

This site gives definitions of terms commonly used in the industry. It requires Adobe Acrobat.

Location: www.dr.org/gloss.htm

### Rothstein Associates (Recovery Resources)

This site includes a collection of full-text articles, the Disaster Recovery Forum, the Business Survival Newsletter, and related links. The Rothstein Catalog on Disaster Recovery lists hundreds of books, software, videos, and other materials.

Location: www.rothstein.com/

### www.ContingencyPlanning.com

This site includes the complete text of articles from *Contingency Planning & Management* magazine. It also includes an extensive collection of "Disruption Defenses," which are prevention, mitigation, response, and recovery recommendations for some of the more common business disruption threats.

Location: www.contingencyplanning.com/

### Survive: The Business Continuity Group

This site for business continuity professionals features training events and conferences, publications for purchase, news stories, and a directory of disaster recovery and contingency services and products. The complete texts of some feature stories and news items are available online.

Location: www.survive.com/

### The Lukaszewski Group

The Lukaszewski Group is a management consultant firm that offers services in many areas, including crisis and disaster management. The site features an extensive collection of articles, speeches, and presentations by Mr. Lukaszewski.

Location: www.e911.com/

### Business Continuity Institute

The Business Continuity Institute offers a range of services for members, including job postings, conference announcements, links to related sites, and an online bookstore. A highlight of the site is the collection of Business Continuity Planning Guides, the full texts of which are available online.

Location: www.thebci.org/

### Continuity Systems Limited

This U.K. firm provides a "Recovery Healthcheck" questionnaire online, the full text of a few articles by Ian Charters, disaster statistics, and "myths" about disasters.

Location: www.continuity.co.uk/

### Business Resumption Planning, Step by Step

From the company Datasure, this is a 13-step plan for business continuity. Other features of this site are a Business Resumption Checklist and guides to computer storage and power protection.

Location: http://datasure.com/stepby.html

### MLC and Associates, Inc.

This business continuity consulting firm provides in-depth descriptions of their services, including business continuity programs, simulations and exercises, continuity training, and data security.

Location: www.mlc2resq.com/

### SunGard Recovery Services—"Getting Started"

This site includes a 1-minute risk assessment, 10 tips for recovery, frequently asked questions, and case studies of several companies.

Location: http://recovery.sungard.com/home.html

## ARTICLE DATABASES

The databases listed here are good sources to search for journal articles and conference papers on crisis, disaster, and risk management.

### ABI/Inform

ABI/Inform is the primary database for business and management topics. This database indexes about 800 publications, including research journals, trade journals, and popular business magazines. It provides citations and abstracts for all articles; about half of the articles indexed include the full text.

### American Society of Civil Engineers

This database provides full-text access to 29 journals published by ASCE 1999 to present. Of particular interest is the journal *Natural Hazards Review*.

### Compendex

This database is a comprehensive index to more than 3,000 journals and conference proceedings from all areas of engineering. However, it includes only citations and abstracts.

### Emerald Library

This database provides full-text articles from over 130 management journals published by Emerald. The topics covered go from 1989 to the present.

### GEOBASE

GEOBASE is part of the OCLC FirstSearch family of databases; it indexes over 2,000 journals, books, conference proceedings, and reports on geography, geology, and ecology. The coverage is from 1980 to the present. Only citations and abstracts are provided.

GEOBASE is a good resource for topics dealing with natural and environmental disasters and hazards.

### PsycInfo
This database covers over 1,300 journals and books in psychology and related disciplines from 1987 to present. It is a good resource for topics on psychological, organizational, and social aspects of crisis, emergency, disaster, and risk management. It includes only citations and abstracts.

### Sociological Abstracts
This database indexes articles from about 800 journals relevant to sociology and related disciplines. It is useful for finding articles on social aspects of crisis, disaster, and risk management. The coverage is from 1963 to present and includes only citations and abstracts.

## PERIODICALS, TRADE JOURNALS, AND NEWSLETTERS

### *Disaster Recovery Journal*
Both the hardcopy journal and access to the online site are free.
Location: www.drj.com

### *Contingency Planning & Management*
Both the hardcopy journal and access to the online site are free. The site includes a searchable archive of past issues.
Location: www.contingencyplanning.com

### *Homeland Protection Professional*
Editorial calendar shows articles planned for upcoming issues. No articles are available online, but you can register for a free trial print subscription.
Location: www.hppmag.com/

### **Homeland Security Newsletter**
Published monthly by the Anser Institute, this newsletter contains original articles as well as links to articles from government sources, newspapers, and other popular press. Online subscriptions are available with archives back to 2002 available online.
Location: www.homelandsecurity.org/newsletter

## RESEARCH JOURNALS

These are professional research journals published in the area of crisis and emergency management. All sites provide instructions for submitting articles, a list of editorial board members, subscription information, and tables of contents and/or abstracts. Except as noted, these journals do not provide full-text articles online.

### *International Journal of Emergency Management*
This journal began publishing in 2001. Click on "Journals" in the left menu bar, then scroll to the journal title.
Location: www.inderscience.com/

### *Journal of Emergency Management*
This journal began publishing in 2003. Table of contents and abstracts are provided, but no full-text articles.
Location: www.pnpco.com/pn06001.html

### *Journal of Homeland Security and Emergency Management*
The first issue was published in 2004. Abstracts and full-text articles are available online.
Location: www.bepress.com/jhsem/

### *International Journal of Mass Emergencies and Disasters*
This journal began publishing in 1982. The site provides a table of contents and abstracts or 1995 to the present.
Location: www.usc.edu/schools/sppd/ijmed/

### *Disaster Prevention and Management*
This international journal is published by Emerald Press, covering a full range of disaster management topics.
Location: www.emeraldinsight.com/Insight/viewContainer.do?containerType=Journal&containerId=10806

### *Crisis Response Journal*
A new international publication aimed at the world's emergency responders, planners and disaster academics. Published quarterly from the United Kingdom.
Location: www.crisisresponsejournal.com

## ONLINE BOOKS

Although most books are still available only in print, some publishers are beginning to make entire books available online at no cost. Listed here are some titles that are available online.

### *Disasters by Design: A Reassessment of Natural Hazards in the United States*

Dennis Mileti. National Academy Press, 1999.
Location: www.nap.edu/books/0309063604/html/

### *Chemical and Biological Terrorism: Research and Development to Improve Civilian Medical Response*

Committee on R&D Needs for Improving Civilian Medical Response to Chemical and Biological Terrorism Incidents, Institute of Medicine, 1999.
Location: http://books.nap.edu/books/0309061954/html/

### *Disaster Response: Preparation and Coordination*

Eric Auf der Heide. Center for Excellence in Disaster Management and Humanitarian Assistance, 1989.
Location: www.coe-dmha.org/dr/flash.htm

### *The Long Road to Recovery: Community Responses to Industrial Disaster*

Edited by James K. Mitchell. United Nations University Press, 1996.
Location:      www.unu.edu/unupress/unupbooks/uu21le/uu21le00.htm

### *Reducing Disaster Losses Through Better Information*

Board on Natural Disasters, Commission on Geosciences, Environment, and Resources, National Research Council. National Academy Press, 1999.
Location: http://books.nap.edu/catalog/6363.html

Visit these publishers' home pages for announcements of new books, some of which may be available online.

- National Academy Press (http://books.nap.edu/)
- United Nations University Press (www.unu.edu/unupress/)

## HEALTH AND MEDICAL ORGANIZATIONS

### U.S. Department of Health & Human Services

The Department of Health and Human Services (DHHS) is the U.S. government's principal agency for protecting the health of all Americans and providing essential human services. U.S. Public Health Service agencies are listed below. All have varying programs with direct and indirect effects on Homeland Security.

Location: www.dhhs.gov
 www.nih.gov National Institutes of Health
 www.fda.gov Food and Drug Administration
 www.cdc.gov Centers for Disease Control and Prevention
 www.ihs.gov Indian Health Service
 www.hrsa.gov Health Resources and Services Administration
 www.samhsa.gov Substance Abuse and Mental Health Services Administration
 www.ahrq.gov Agency for Healthcare Research and Quality

### U.S. Centers for Disease Control and Prevention

This extensive site includes health standards and statistics, fact sheets on health information and disease prevention, and health-related news stories. Brochures, software, and other publications are available for download and by order from CDC.
Location: www.cdc.gov/

### Agency for Toxic Substances and Disease Registry (ATSDR)

This site features many news and information sources on toxic substances. Highlights include ToxFAQs, a series of summaries about hazardous substances; HazDat, a database that provides information on the release of hazardous substances from Superfund sites and from emergency events; and Minimal Risk Levels (MRLs) for hazardous substances. "Science Corner" is a gateway to environmental health information and resources on the web.
Location: http://atsdr1.atsdr.cdc.gov/cx.html

### Federal Emergency Management Agency/Rapid

This response information system site that focuses on terrorist incidents provides access to several databases, including characteristics of chemical, biological and radiological materials, first-aid measures, federal response capabilities, and information sources on potential weapons of mass destruction.
Location: www.rris.fema.gov/

### Disaster Mental Health Services

From the Department of Social Work at Walter Reed Army Medical Center, this guidebook is an introduction to the field of disaster mental health for clinicians and administrators. Adobe Acrobat is required to view many sections of the book.

Location: www.wramc.amedd.army.mil/departments/
socialwork/provider/DMHS.htm

**National Disaster Medical System (NDMS)**

The National Disaster Medical System is a section within
the U.S. Department of Homeland Security, Federal
Emergency Management Agency, Response Division,
Operations Branch, and is responsible for supporting
federal agencies in the management and coordination
of the federal medical response to major emergencies
and federally declared disasters.

Location: www.ndms.dhhs.gov

**Metropolitan Medical Response System**

Located within the Office of Domestic Preparedness at
DHS.

Location: www.mmrs.fema.gov

**National Association of County and City Health
Officials (NACCHO)**

This organization that represents the interests of and is
involved with issues concerning local public health
agencies. Website contains a separate Emergency Preparedness and Response section.

Location: www.nacho.org

**The Association of State and Territorial Health
Officials (ASTHO)**

The national nonprofit organization representing the state
and territorial public health agencies of the United
States, the U.S. Territories, and the District of Columbia. ASTHO's members, the chief health officials of
these jurisdictions, are dedicated to formulating and
influencing sound public health policy, and to assuring
excellence in state-based public health practice.

Location: www.astho.org

**Terrorism Resources for the Health Care Community**

A list of selected websites selected by the University of
Maryland Health Sciences and Human Services
Library to be useful to health care providers and con-
sumers containing terrorism-related material.

Location: www.hshsl.umaryland.edu/resources/terrorism.
html

## INTERNATIONAL DISASTER INFORMATION

**United Nations Relief Web**

This site covers news and information on humanitarian
emergencies and natural disasters, with a focus on

improving relief efforts. It includes a searchable database of over 50,000 documents dating to 1981 and an
extensive collection of maps.

Location: www.reliefweb.int

**Volunteers in Technical Assistance (VITA)**

VITA is a not-for-profit private volunteer organization
that provides technical information as requested by
developing countries. The site includes a section on
disasters.

Location: www.vita.org

**United Nations International Strategy for Disaster
Reduction (formerly IDNDR)**

ISDR focuses on creating disaster prevention strategies
and reducing social and economic disruption caused by
disasters. This site includes information about ISDR as
well as UN documents on disaster reduction.

Location: www.unisdr.org

**World Health Organization**

Part of WHO's mission is to provide aid during emergencies. This site provides extensive information on diseases and health topics and includes links to
health-related databases available free on the web.

Location: www.who.org

**Pan American Health Organization**

Regional office for the Americas of the World Health
Organization. Includes health statistics, reports on
health topics, links to related sources, and news on
health issues.

Location: www.paho.org

**United Nations Development Program**

UNDP partners with United Nations relief agencies
and helps countries to prepare for, avoid, and manage
complex emergencies and disasters. This site
provides extensive information and reports on UNDP
projects.

Location: www.undp.org

**European Community Humanitarian Office (ECHO)**

ECHO's role is to provide humanitarian aid in response to
natural disasters and armed conflict in countries outside
the European Union. This site includes statistics,
reports, and descriptions of ECHO's operations.

Location: http://europa.eu.int/comm/echo/en/index_en.
html

### International Federation of Red Cross/Red Crescent Societies

Reportedly the largest humanitarian organization in the world, the International Federation of Red Cross and Red Crescent Societies (IFRC) comprises 181-member Red Cross and Red Crescent societies, a secretariat in Geneva, and more than 60 delegations strategically located to support activities around the world.

Location: www.ifrc.org

## VOLUNTEER PROGRAM WEBSITES

### National Voluntary Organizations Active in Disaster

NVOAD assists with the coordination efforts of volunteer organizations in preparation and response to disasters. Many individual states have state-level VOADs that may or may not choose to become affiliated with the NVOAD.

Location: www.nvoad.org

### USA Freedom Corps

A coordinating council housed at the White House to encourage all citizens to volunteer opportunities within their communities. Included in the Freedom Corps umbrella are the national service organizations of Citizens Corps, AmeriCorps, Peace Corps, and Senior Corps, as well as multiple other organizations, many of which directly involve the response to disasters or emergencies.

Location: www.usafreedomcorps.gov

### Corporation for National and Community Service

A major organization developed to administer national service programs. The Corporation for National and Community Service includes the Senior Corps, Ameri-Corps, and Learn and Serve America.

Location: www.cns.gov

### Citizen Corps

Citizen Corps, a component of the USA Freedom Corps, created by President Bush to assist with the coordination of volunteer activities of citizens within the community in response to community emergencies. Citizen Corps is coordinated nationally by DHS. Included in the Citizen Corps programs are Volunteers in Police Service (VIPS), Community Emergency Response Teams (CERT), Medical Reserve Corps (MRC), Fire Corps, and Neighborhood Watch Program (NWP).

Location: www.citizencorps.gov

### Volunteers in Police Service (VIPS)

Volunteers in Police Service (VIPS) work to enhance the capacity of law enforcement at the state and local level through the use of volunteers. VIPS is a program within the Citizen Corps.

Location: www.policevolunteers.org

### Medical Reserve Corps

The Medical Reserve Corps develops community health and medical volunteers to respond to emergencies and disasters.

Location: www.medicalreservecorps.gov

### Neighborhood Watch Program

The Neighborhood Watch Program trains and utilizes citizens to provide for improved security within their own neighborhoods.

Location: www.usaonwatch.org

### Fire Corps

The Fire Corps program involves the development of citizen advocates supporting fire and EMS response within communities to increase capacity through utilizing citizens in support roles for fire and EMS.

Location: www.firecorps.org

# Appendix 9: SAFE Conference Report

**Homeland Security at the Community Level**

**Issues and Opportunities:**

**A Report on the First Annual Conference on The Community and Homeland Security**

San Francisco, CA

March 27–28, 2003

Damon Coppola

George Haddow

Jane Bullock

The SAFE Project

## ACKNOWLEDGMENTS

The SAFE Project and NCCD wish to gratefully acknowledge the support of the FAITHS Initiative of the San Francisco Foundation in hosting this conference. We also wish to thank Damon Coppola for his excellent job recording the proceedings and writing this final report.

## EXECUTIVE SUMMARY

The National Council on Crime and Delinquency (NCCD) and the SAFE Project (Securing America's Future for Everyone) hosted the First Annual Conference on the Community and Homeland Security on March 27 and 28, 2003, at the San Francisco Foundation in San Francisco, California. The conference brought local leaders, from several states, responsible for shaping homeland security programs and activities in their communities together with representatives from federal, state, local, nonprofit, private, and international organizations working on homeland security–related issues. The conference allowed all of these practitioners, participants, and representatives to voice their concerns and share their experiences, and gave them their first opportunity not only to work together to identify existing problems with homeland security at the local level, but to propose possible solutions to these problems. The conference began with a delivered message from United States Senator Barbara Boxer, who expressed her gratitude for the efforts of participants who had come together to make communities safer. Senator Boxer reaffirmed the need for a conference that addressed homeland security efforts at the community level and stated she was "pleased by [the participants'] commitment to build[ing] a coalition of experts at the local, state, and federal levels."

The primary concern of those in attendance was well stated by Carol Lopes (Berkeley, California), who said, "Though there has been a lot of progress, we are willfully unprepared. Community and neighborhood preparedness is the centerpiece of today's work. Our responsibility is to prepare a community before a disaster and assist after a disaster strikes. We must train a cadre of emergency prepared individuals who will interface well with first responders."

Four principal areas of concern emerged from these discussions, detailed in this report. They include: (1) greater access to resources to fund homeland security programs and projects at the community level; (2) greater access to practical information about application, eligibility, recruitment, retention, and other concerns; (3) the need for innovative and effective programming ideas; and (4) the need to focus on diverse and "special needs" populations. This report will explore these four issues as they were defined by the speakers and the participants, drawing directly from the presentations, panel discussions, and facilitated participant discussions.

## INTRODUCTION

The National Council on Crime and Delinquency (NCCD) and the SAFE Project (Securing America's Future for Everyone) hosted the First Annual Conference on the Community and Homeland Security on March 27 and 28, 2003, at the San Francisco Foundation in San Francisco, California.

The conference brought local leaders, from several states, responsible for shaping homeland security programs and activities in their communities together with representatives from federal, state, local, nonprofit, private, and international organizations working on homeland security–related issues. The conference allowed all of these practitioners, participants, and representatives to voice their concerns and share their experiences and gave them their first opportunity not only to work together to identify existing problems with homeland security at the local level, but to propose possible solutions to these problems.

The conference began with a delivered message from United States Senator Barbara Boxer, who expressed her gratitude for the efforts of participants who had come together to make communities safer. Senator Boxer reaffirmed the need for the conference that addressed homeland security efforts at the community level and stated she was "pleased by [the participants'] commitment to build[ing] a coalition of experts at the local, state, and federal levels."

The conference speakers focused their presentations on a multitude of homeland security programs and actions occurring within communities, while exploring a spectrum of topics spanning federal, state, local, private, and nonprofit organizational levels. Over the course of the two-day conference, several common threads emerged, the most significant being how to increase the effectiveness of homeland security efforts at the community level.

This idea was echoed by representatives from all levels of government and private and nonprofit groups and is illustrated through the following sample of statements made throughout the course of the conference:

- Jane Bullock (SAFE project): "The only way to accomplish anything in homeland security preparedness is for it to be grassroots-based. Top-down does not work. It must start neighborhood by neighborhood."
- Chuck Supple (GO SERV): "We must engage citizens to address problems in their own communities to have the greatest possible impact in community homeland security."
- Valli Wasp (Austin, Texas): "Preparedness must be addressed locally. We need to take this to 'homes'—get rid of the 'land,' get rid of the 'security'—this is about people protecting their homes. If you want people to listen to you, you have to go to where they live."
- Eileen Garry (U.S. Department of Justice): "Every good idea I have ever heard came from the local level."

In the process of examining Homeland Security at the community level, the group established that it was necessary to clarify the term "community." Both the speakers and the audience agreed that the "community" concept must be used with the greatest possible flexibility. Limiting the definition of community will effectively reduce the range of homeland security project options, possible sources of funding, and the pool of available participants in developed programs.

Jane Bullock (SAFE) stated, "The word 'community' can be geographic or organizational, and this conference has shown that the word can mean anything—a church, a mosque. . . . We must consider the word in the broadest way possible. Everyone needs to be a part of the partnership—neighborhoods, churches, unions, senior citizen centers, and many others." A related concern was that the term "homeland security" needed to be defined as it applies to the community level. Monique Morris (NCCD) rhetorically asked participants, "What is homeland security? What is terrorism? Is it a drug dealer? A traditional terrorist? Crime?"

The primary concern of those in attendance was well stated by Carol Lopes (Berkeley, California), who said, "Though there has been a lot of progress, we are willfully unprepared. Community and neighborhood preparedness is the centerpiece of today's work. Our responsibility is to prepare a community before a disaster and assist after a disaster strikes. We must train a cadre of emergency-prepared individuals who will interface well with first responders."

As the attendees primarily consisted of or represented local decision-makers who are seeking preparedness and protection from natural and technological disasters and terrorist attacks in their communities, the sentiments were well received. These attendees exhibited a collective frustration, voiced through their commentary and questions following each of the presentations and during a group discussion that ended the conference.

Four principal areas of concern emerged from these discussions, detailed in this report. They include the following:

- Resources: Greater access to resources to fund homeland security programs and projects at the community level
- Information: Greater access to practical information about application, eligibility, recruitment, retention, and other concerns
- Programming: The need for innovative and effective programming ideas
- Customizing: The need to focus on diverse and "special needs" populations

This report will explore these four issues as they were defined by the speakers and the participants, drawing directly from the presentations, panel discussions, and facilitated participant discussions. Each issue will be defined and placed in context to its source of concern and effect on local communities. The possible remedies identified by participants will be outlined. Finally, a section titled "Conclusions: Where Do We Go from Here?" will offer one viable and potentially effective solution to these issues derived directly from the group discussions.

## BACKGROUND

On November 25, 2002, President George W. Bush signed into law the Homeland Security Act of 2002, creating the new Department of Homeland Security (DHS) with a mission of protecting the United States from further terrorist attacks, reducing the nation's vulnerability to terrorism, and minimizing the damage from potential terrorist attacks and natural disasters.

The February 13, 2003, passage of the FY2003 omnibus appropriations bill included significant spending to state and local governments to support first-responder activities. For this purpose, the new DHS received approximately $2 billion in funding, less than the $3.5 billion that had been proposed. Most of this funding will go directly to the states. DHS officials have said that the states must pass along as much as 75 percent of the funding to local governments.

As of the date of the conference, the states had received only a limited amount of this funding, and in reality the states will likely manage to keep a considerable amount of this funding at the state level. If the states do pass the terrorism funding to local governments, they will likely offset these losses by canceling or reducing the amounts of other pass-through funding.

The most direct line funding for communities is through Citizens Corps activities, the Corporation for National and Community Service (CNCS) programs, and other volunteer-driven programs in the Departments of Health and Human Services (HHS) and Justice (DOJ). In FY2004, the new Department of Homeland Security is expected to make funds available to state and local governments through Citizens Corps, the Office of State and Local Government Coordination, the Directorate of Border and Transportation Security, and the Emergency Preparedness and Response Directorate (which is currently overseeing the Federal Emergency Management Agency [FEMA]). The FY2004 budget requests funding levels similar to FY2003 for state and local activities, with a strong emphasis on local support.

In addition, the Bush Administration's $79 billion dollar Supplemental to support the war in Iraq includes additional spending on homeland security. However, the state and local part of this bill is primarily reimbursement for increased security measures, not preparedness or mitigation.

The most promising initiative to support communities is new legislation being proposed in the Senate entitled the "Homeland Security Block Grant Act." This legislation, as written, would provide $3.5 billion directly to communities, each year until 2006, for community homeland security planning and coordination, special projects, development and maintenance of training facilities, best practices clearinghouses, and communication systems.

President Bush created the U.S.A. Freedom Corps in an effort to provide centralized coordination of the various volunteer-based organizations dispersed throughout the federal government, including Peace Corps, Citizen Corps, and the Corporation for National and Community Service. (Peace Corps volunteers work exclusively on international assignments and therefore will not be detailed in this report.) The mission of Freedom Corps is to promote volunteerism as an integral part of citizenship.

## CITIZEN CORPS

Citizen Corps was the "new piece," with FEMA tasked as the lead agency, owing to its relevant mission and its existing relationships with local communities. The program was developed to "harness the power of every individual through education, training, and volunteer service to make communities safer, stronger, and better prepared to respond to the threats of terrorism, crime, public health issues, and disasters of all kinds."

To accomplish this mission, Citizen Corps is working to develop a national network of state, local, and tribal Citizen Corps Councils, which will "tailor the activities to the community and build on community strengths to develop and implement a local strategy to have every American participate through personal responsibility, training, and volunteer service."

There are four Citizen Corps programs administered by three federal agencies—the Department of Justice, the Federal Emergency Management Agency, and the Department of Health and Human Services, individually described below.

### Department of Justice

- Neighborhood Watch: This crime prevention program, which has a 30-year history, engages volunteer citizen action to enhance security within local communities by encouraging citizens to report suspicious activity in their immediate neighborhoods. Citizen Corps hopes to double the number of neighborhood watch programs to 15,000 by 2005, while incorporating terrorism prevention into the program's mission. The program is partnered by the National Sheriffs' Association.

- Volunteers in Police Service (VIPS): This program provides training for civilian volunteers who assist local police departments by performing "nonsworn" duties, effectively freeing up officers to provide them with more time to spend on critical functions. This program is partnered by the International Association of Chiefs of Police.

### Federal Emergency Management Agency

- Community Emergency Response Teams (CERT): This program provides civilians with training in emergency management planning and response functions to bolster the capacity of local communities to respond to disasters. President Bush has proposed a threefold increase in the number people enrolled in CERT to 600,000 by 2005. Since its move into Citizen Corps, the program has added a new module that addresses terrorism preparedness.

### Department of Health and Human Services

- Medical Reserve Corps (MRC): This program utilizes the experience and knowledge of active and retired health-care professionals and citizens with an interest in public health issues to augment local health-care capacity in the event of large-scale local emergencies. The volunteers also work throughout the year to promote community public health issues. To date there have been 42 $50,000 grants administered throughout the country. There is expected to be an additional $8 million made available to Medical Reserve Corps in the near future.

## CORPORATION FOR NATIONAL AND COMMUNITY SERVICE

CNCS, created by President Bill Clinton, consists of three programs: Senior Corps, AmeriCorps, and Learn and Serve America. CNCS "provides opportunities for Americans of all ages and backgrounds to serve their communities and country." CNCS recruits volunteers to serve with national and community nonprofit organizations, faith-based groups, schools, and local agencies to help meet community needs in education, the environment, public safety, homeland security, and other areas. The three principal CNCS programs are described below.

### Senior Corps

This program is described as a network of programs that "tap the experience, skills, and talents of older citizens to meet community challenges." It includes three programs; Foster Grandparents (who serve as tutors and mentors to youths with special needs), Senior Companions (who help homebound seniors and other adults maintain independence in their own homes), and the Retired and Senior Volunteer Program (RSVP—volunteers conduct safety patrols for local police departments, participate in environmental projects, provide intensive educational services, and respond to natural disasters, among other activities). More than half a million Americans, age 55 and over, assist local nonprofits, public agencies, and faith-based organizations in carrying out their missions. The 2004 budget requests funding for 600,000 Senior Corps volunteers ($212 million).

### AmeriCorps

This program is described as a network of national service programs that "engage more than 50,000 Americans each year in intensive service to meet critical needs in education, public safety, health, and the environment." AmeriCorps members serve through more than 2,100 nonprofits, public agencies, and faith-based organizations, tutoring and mentoring youth, building affordable housing, teaching computer skills, cleaning parks and streams, running after-school programs, and helping communities respond to disasters. The AmeriCorps program includes AmeriCorps (volunteers serve 20 to 40 hours per week at local and national nonprofit organizations and community-based organizations, both secular and faith-based), AmeriCorps VISTA (focuses on eradicating poverty and helping to meet the needs of people in low-income communities), and AmeriCorps NCCC (National Civilian Community Corps—a residential program that supplies volunteers to nonprofit groups to provide for disaster relief, preserve the environment, build homes for low-income families, tutor children, and meet other challenges). The programs engage more than 55,000 Americans of all ages and backgrounds in service each year. The 2004 budget requests funding for 75,000 AmeriCorps volunteers ($554 million).

### Learn and Serve America

This program "supports service-learning programs in schools and community organizations that help nearly 1 million students from kindergarten through college meet community needs, while improving their academic skills and learning the habits of good citizenship." The 2004 budget requests $43 million for programs that could accommodate 1.65 million students.

As of the date of the conference, over 400 Citizen Corps Councils had been established in communities across the country, with more being formed almost every day. Citizen Corps hopes to have fifty-six state and territory Citizen Corps Councils formed by mid-2003.

## THE ISSUES

The following four principal areas of concern emerged from the discussions that transpired during the two-day conference.

### RESOURCES

Greater access to resources to fund Homeland Security programs and projects at the community level.

Most communities throughout the United States were operating within the constraints of lean fiscal budgets prior to the September 11 attacks. In the aftermath of those events, countless administrative, police, fire, and emergency management staff were called upon to fulfill new or expanded public safety roles. As a result, municipalities were forced to spend funds they could ill afford on these new costs, including overtime pay and expensive prevention and detection equipment. Steve Weston of the California Highway Patrol described how the new requirements created "a tremendous burden" on that law enforcement organization.

Although billions of dollars in federal funding to cover these costs have been promised, few have been granted. Additionally, both state and local governments are finding that many existing programs they have depended on are being cut, such as the Community Oriented Policing Services (COPS) program and the Local Law Enforcement Block Grant, to pay for increasing costs associated with the wars on terrorism and Iraq. Many communities are beginning to feel that "you can't seem to get funding unless you wrap the word 'counterterrorism' around [the project]" (Eileen Garry—DOJ).

Staff involved in initiating and promoting homeland security programs in communities are finding themselves particularly frustrated in their efforts as a result of this severe resource drought. One participant expressed the concern that "making us fundraisers, in addition to our programmatic [tasks], really stretches municipalities' resources thin. The raw numbers of people required for fundraising exhausts programs."

However, such fundraising actions are recognized as vital to any program's success, echoed by Doris Milldyke (Kansas), who said, "Money is the first goal, volunteers are the second." There undeniably exists a fervent desire to promote homeland security programs throughout America's communities, but so many of these project entrepreneurs are finding themselves impotent due to the shortage of available federal resources.

Another related concern of the participants was that funding made available for the local jurisdictions often became "bottlenecked" in the state offices, rarely trickling down to communities. Adam Sutkus, speaking on behalf of then California governor Gray Davis' GO SERV office, stated, "Because of the September 11 environment, there are many new funding streams." However, this came as little consolation to the local representatives.

Valli Wasp of Austin explained during her presentation that "it is very difficult to get local funds from the state, because it is all about control. It is a paternalistic, military-like relationship between the state and local communities." Jane Bullock of the SAFE Project explained, "Money must go to the locals [as required by program rules], but it may not reach them because of 'creative budgeting' at the state level."

Jane Bullock described how "funding can be a huge problem," but added that "additional money in the Homeland Security area is appearing" and that there "should be a 5-year window of increased spending." However, she described these prospects as "shaky."

All participants agreed that funding needs to be an active role of local Citizen Corps and other Homeland Security programs, but most expressed they needed advice and ideas. Speakers and participants alike voiced their frustration and called upon each other for both traditional and alternative means for securing much-needed resources.

The discussions revealed some surprising results, detailed below. These findings are grouped according to whether they apply to the federal government, the business sector, foundations (and other philanthropies), or creative fundraising.

### The Federal Government

Karen Marsh, representing the FEMA Citizen Corps program, described how Citizen Corps started after September 11, 2001, without any funding but was later appropriated $20 million that it eventually distributed to the states in August of 2002. Of this amount, 75 percent must be passed directly to the communities. Although these sources of funding "did not fare as well in 2003," $181 million has been requested for 2004. If this money materializes, it would be the primary source of funding for a majority of the programs discussed over the course of the conference.

A community block grant program, such as the one proposed in the "Homeland Security Block Grant Act," that provides funding directly to communities to augment the capabilities of first responders, is desperately needed. Ann Patton of Tulsa, Oklahoma, indicated that "block grants would be invaluable" in accomplishing these community homeland security goals.

In addition, Chuck Supple of GO SERV described how it is possible for Citizen Corps Councils to apply for AmeriCorps grants to bolster their programs, and Kristin Haggins of CNCS stated that with VISTA, you can get "human" grants instead of money.

### The Business Community

Business emerged as a vastly underused source for human, material, and financial resources. Participants agreed that local communities need to increase partnerships with the business community but acknowledged that "there [currently] exists no concrete strategy to reach them." Many in attendance stated that one way to increase chances of successfully garnering support from businesses is to ask for merchandise instead of cash donations.

Several participants and speakers relayed successes they had experienced in their own communities, including Ann Patton of Tulsa, Oklahoma, who partnered with several Tulsa McDonalds Restaurants to perform disaster communication through the McDonalds paper [meal] tray liners;

Joseph Bobot from Ohio, who successfully solicited donated Stokes Litters (stretchers) from a local business; and Valli Wasp of Austin, who secured a whole spectrum of donated products and services while working to help her local community prepare for the possible ramifications of the Y2K bug.

One participant suggested that staff involved in community-based homeland security "jump on the homeland security tradeshow bandwagon," referring to the widespread business showcases where homeland security–based products are marketed. Another questioned whether the Fortune 500 companies would, out of recognition of their corporate responsibility in the communities where they operate, endorse community-based homeland security programs. Jane Bullock (SAFE) added that participants should look to local hospitals and the banking and financial community to act as partners.

### Foundations

Though discussed in less detail than the preceding two groups, foundations and other philanthropic organizations were also identified as a potential source of funding. One participant stated that "we must create an awareness of both the business and philanthropic communities," referring to a recognition by those groups of both their responsibility to participate in such programs and the potential security and safety benefits of that participation. Chuck Supple stated that the state of California has only recently begun looking into support from foundations and philanthropies and that they have not yet identified a place for philanthropic involvement. He suggested that community foundation networks help in identifying areas for philanthropy involvement.

### Creative Fundraising Ideas

The most widely recognized need for communities regarding fundraising resources was that they find creative ways to solve their financial problems. Karen Marsh (Citizen Corps) expressed during her presentation that emergency managers need to focus on volunteer recruitment and donations. Her comments indicated an awareness that these municipal programs require support from nontraditional means for their success.

One participant noted that it has become necessary for the Citizen Corps Councils to reach out to every community "stratum," adding that "waiting for the federal government to offer communities money leads to nothing." Richard

Paige from Mendocino County, California, asserted that local Citizen Corps Councils need to attain 501(c)(3) non-profit status, adding, "This is not just a recommendation!"

The breadth of suggestions for creative fundraising methods was rather impressive and highlighted the need for a platform for sharing ideas among local community programs. In addition to those described above, the following ideas were proposed:

- Give tax breaks to businesses that make donations to Citizen Corps (participant).
- Secure program endorsement from local elected officials to increase the likelihood of consideration for funding (Norma Schroeder, California, EMSA).
- There are many "unofficial" Medical Reserve Corps throughout the community. The classification of "registered unit" can be given to existing MRC-type units if they meet preestablished requirements, therefore "put[ting] them in the loop without the otherwise-required $50,000 grant" (Norma Schroeder).
- Councils must establish close working relationships with police and fire departments, because they are critical partners in getting federal government funding (Jane Bullock, SAFE).
- Resources include more than money. They can be people, space, in-kind, and others (Ken Terao, Aguirre International).
- Communities should try to first establish a local program with which to seek funding, instead of first seeking money to start a nonexistent program (participant).

## Summary

The presentations and discussions by conference participants concerning resources identified several critical areas:

- Block grants to communities are an efficient means for providing federal funding for community homeland security efforts. Consideration should be given to expanding the use of Community Development Block Grants for homeland security efforts and passage of the "Homeland Security Block Grant Act."
- Communities should partner with the National Governor's Association, the United States Conference of Mayors, the League of Cities, and other professional associations seeking federal funding for community homeland security efforts.

- Creative funding ideas practiced in communities around the countries need to be identified and widely disseminated among community homeland security officials.
- New partnerships need to be established with the country's business and philanthropic communities to leverage their resources for community homeland security efforts.

## INFORMATION

Greater access to practical information about application, eligibility, recruitment, retention, and other concerns.

It was obvious to all of the participants that virtually everyone involved in coordinating homeland security programs at the community level was passionate about initiating or expanding programs in their own communities. However, there exists an overwhelming sense of frustration concerning the lack of access to information to help them pursue these goals.

Although the information they seek often does exist, participants voiced dismay that they had to search for it in what seems to them like countless locations due to a lack of any centralization. Ann Patton (Tulsa, Oklahoma) stated, "An information clearinghouse would be invaluable." Doris Milldyke (Kansas) noted that information on VIPS, MRS, and other programs is "notoriously difficult to find," adding, "We need a golden key for information on getting grants." During the discussion period, participants added that they are frustrated with the application process for Citizen Corps and that, because programs keep changing, they have difficulty "keeping up." One woman exclaimed, while explaining frustration over her inability to retrieve information from the Washington, DC, office of Citizen Corps, said, "Don't tell me to talk to my state!"

Karen Marsh of Citizen Corps explained during her presentation that every community throughout the United States and its territories is different, and therefore the Citizen Corps program was designed to be flexible. She added that Citizen Corps offers guidance to communities for setting up a local Citizen Corps Council. However, a point made by Ana-Marie Jones (Oakland, California) during her presentation on emergency planning described the danger of too much flexibility without sufficient guidance, "When you give 500 agencies money for plans, you get 499 different plans. You must coordinate and standardize."

Ann Patton later added that it would be helpful to have a model Citizen Corps program made available for design and planning purposes. Joanne Burke stated that GO SERV captures and documents best practices for people to draw upon, information of interest to most in attendance. Eileen Garry (DOJ) added that, based upon the participants' discussions, she would add a section to her web site showcasing available counterterrorism training available to state and local first-responders (www.counterterrorismtraining.org) in a section titled "Community Support."

### Summary

Access to accurate and timely information was identified by conference participants as critical to their efforts to design and implement community-based homeland security programs. Suggestions for improving access to this information included the following:

- Establishing an information clearinghouse to catalog homeland security information sources
- Establishing a web-based "Chat Room" for community officials to exchange ideas and best practices and to discuss current issues
- Establishing a "Funding Exchange" to share ideas on funding sources and creative funding ideas
- Partnering with the Department of Homeland Security and state homeland security operations to facilitate the flow of information on federal and state programs and funding opportunities to community officials.

### PROGRAMMING

The need for new and innovative programming ideas.

Another principal area of concern for the participants involved a wide range of programming issues. Homeland Security program staff in attendance expressed a strong desire to go beyond the traditional "cookie-cutter" approach in designing programs and utilizing volunteers. They agreed that all communities were different and thus had different needs.

Some in attendance felt that more direction from the state and federal levels was necessary ("We cannot just throw people and money at problems and expect to . . . see results," said Chuck Supple), while others felt that the ideas must originate within the community ("New ideas need to surface"). Ana-Marie Jones described how she discovered in

Oakland, California, that many teachers were overwhelmed by the thought of their responsibilities in times of disaster. Through her program, children were trained to keep quiet during emergencies, providing the teachers with more "peace of mind." All felt that there needed to be greater exploration to discover additional and improved program areas. Chuck Supple stated this position well in saying, "We've probably only thought of a 'minutia' of the areas where volunteers would be useful."

The speakers and participants were all more than happy to share several original and innovative ideas they had developed in their own communities, and to relay areas of concern they had encountered. Steve Weston of the CHP explained how many new skill sets were needed to handle the increased counterterrorism requirements of homeland security. His organization discovered that they had extensive language capabilities previously unknown to them that were valuable in their investigations.

Ann Patton described how she helped to develop a "Language and Culture Bank" in Tulsa, Oklahoma, that was effective in increasing preparedness and fear management throughout the many diverse communities in that city.

Doris Milldyke said, "We must market to local law enforcement the benefits of Citizen Corps, because many [departments] feel they already have more volunteers than [they] know what to do with." She added that states need to try to encourage the formation of regional Citizen Corps Councils in rural areas where local Citizen Corps Councils are unlikely to form. Jane Bullock (SAFE) expressed concern that public health issues were not adequately addressed by community homeland security programs.

The topic of volunteer training seemed to surface repeatedly throughout these discussions on programming. Adam Sutkus of GO SERV suggested that more courses that "train-the-trainer" were needed. Joanne Burke, also of GO SERV, advised that the twenty-hour CERT training program be built into other larger programs in a way that CERT becomes a required component.

Chuck Supple explained how trained citizens can have a great impact on the community, but insisted that the training must be significant. He added that the training brings people "in the door," thus allowing them to participate in additional programs. Mr. Supple advised participants to "create an opportunity, recruit, and use all volunteers," stating that, "not only those with significant skills are wanted. Training and preparation is part of Citizen Corps."

Even though the specific goals of homeland security programs may differ significantly from community to community, several speakers and participants agreed that the most fundamental driving force behind community Homeland Security programs should be "to knit the community together" (Ann Patton), and "to make neighborhoods where people know each other in the best of times and in the worst of times" (Carol Lopes).

There are literally infinite ways in which communities can tailor these programs to suit the needs of their citizens. The conference participants again expressed the need for a clearinghouse of such experience, advice, and information.

## Summary

In addition to the homeland security programming currently in place (i.e., CERT training, Medical RSVP, etc.), conference participants identified a need to design and implement programs that fully leveraged the capabilities of volunteers in the community. Several ideas were considered, including the following:

- The SAFE Project designed to develop volunteer programs in support of community emergency management and homeland security operations
- The development of Community Emergency Networks (CEN) designed to facilitate communications between community residents and local emergency and homeland security officials before, during, and after a disaster or terrorist incident

## CUSTOMIZING

The need to focus on diverse populations, including those with "special needs."

A major concern articulated by several of the speakers throughout the two-day conference was the need to address communities' "special needs populations." Presenters stressed the importance of considering these groups in project planning and shared examples of situations in which projects required adaptation to accommodate such groups.

Chuck Supple, who described California as a state where "the majority is a mixed minority," stressed, "National security depends on bringing people in communities of different backgrounds together." Amy Gaver (American Red Cross) said that there are over 100 languages spoken in the San Francisco Bay Area, but stressed that residents "love their diversity."

Valli Wasp (Austin, Texas) explained how the term "special needs" must be considered in multiple ways, describing

one example where the web site "Ready.gov" (DHS) has caused concern for citizens in Texas who don't have underground shelters in their houses to take cover in during certain emergencies as instructed to on the site.

Several speakers offered general advice to participants for working with special-needs populations. Carol Lopes stressed that participants must "ensure that the vulnerable populations are considered" in the planning and execution of programs. Maya Harris-West (Oakland, California) stated that accountability must be a vital component of any homeland security program, "especially in communities with a great distrust of police."

Ana-Marie Jones warned that "special needs communities are often isolated from services," adding that "[programs] must have a trusted leader who either speaks or has access to the languages of all representative groups—you need more than a 'Spanish press release.'" She suggested that participants "involve special needs communities before the disaster" to be effective. George Haddow (SAFE) echoed an earlier presenter's view that in certain special needs communities "people are more likely to respond to those that they know than a person with a gun and a badge."

Specific needs and characteristics of communities can be regarded as a benefit instead of a hindrance. Monique Morris (NCCD) explained how paramedics may be afraid or unwilling to go into more dangerous neighborhoods in times of disaster, but if people from those communities are trained through community homeland security projects, then those communities become safer even outside of disaster events. Ms. Morris also explained how tapping into religious groups that are central to many of these communities could greatly assist both fundraising and recruitment of volunteers. She added, "Design your mission to fit their mission, not the other way around."

## Summary

Servicing diverse and "special needs" populations must be a critical component of any community-based homeland security effort. A number of ideas for addressing these needs were discussed by participants, including the following:

- Reprogramming Community Development Block Grant (CDBG) funding targeted for "special needs" populations to include homeland security efforts
- Establishing "Language and Culture Banks" in communities to facilitate communications and information flow between public safety and emergency officials and special-needs populations

- Partnering with national associations and groups that represent the interests of special-needs populations such as the elderly, veterans, minority populations, children and the disabled
- Partnering with foundations and other philanthropic organizations such as the Annie E. Casey Foundation, which focuses its efforts and funding in disadvantaged communities
- Partnering with local emergency management/ homeland security and public health operations to help these groups identify and serve "special needs" populations in the community.

## CONCLUSIONS

Where do we go from here?

The conference concluded with a general participatory group discussion based on the topics that had been discussed over the 2-day period. This conversation quickly led to suggestions for change and future implications. The range of responses reflected the vast experience, insight, and motivation of the group.

One issue that repeatedly emerged was that there existed no centralized advocacy for funding, information, or programming that communities could turn to for assistance. George Haddow (SAFE) noted, "There has never been a grassroots network for emergency management, but the need is growing." One participant flatly stated that "we must organize at the grassroots level, or we will be having the same conversations next year." Another added, "Unity is the solution. Otherwise, we are just individual sitting ducks."

Ann Patton told the members of the group that they must "recognize it is our problem, and we need to fix it." To illustrate her point, she displayed a map depicting disaster-resistant communities across the nation and said, "We need to connect the dots" (and create a network of communities concerned with Homeland Security issues).

This network of concerned communities could be the "Golden Key" that Doris Milldyke spoke of during her presentation. Karen Marsh (Citizen Corps) described how Citizen Corps captures and documents best practices for communities to draw upon—these experiences need not only to be documented by all communities, but to be shared across all state and territorial borders.

A network would give all communities access to the experiences of the presenters and participants at the conference, and allow them to share their individual expertise as well. Norma Schroeder stated, "Community groups should be able to share lessons and experiences." Given ample access, planners would learn invaluable lessons on volunteer recruitment from people such as Monique Morris (NCCD). They would surely benefit from the programming success stories of groups like, and from other communities such as, Tulsa, Austin, and Oakland.

The tremendous benefits possible from such a "network of practitioners" make the necessity for its existence not only obvious but also immediate. Eileen Garry (DOJ) stated during her presentation that "the solutions to our problems are in this room." Only such a network would allow for the effective sharing of those solutions such that small local achievements can become widespread success stories. Conference participants agreed that such a network could address many of the needs identified over the course of the conference, including the following:

- Improving the flow of information on homeland security funding opportunities at all levels of government and in the business and philanthropic sectors to community officials
- Facilitating the sharing of best practices and ideas on community-based homeland security programs and activities
- Designing and implementing new community-based homeland security programming such as the SAFE Project and the Community Emergency Networks (CEN)
- Ensuring that special-needs populations in communities are identified and helped through programs such as the Language and Culture Bank and partnerships with advocacy groups.

## THE NEXT CONFERENCE

The First Annual Conference on Communities and Homeland Security closed with a clear message: Solving the identified problems is a priority for communities. One participant expressed concern that communities "cannot wait a year for the next conference." Others felt that the next conference should focus on additional issues that were only touched upon, such as volunteer liability, the assessment of risk, and mitigation.

One attendee suggested that subgroups be formed to tackle these individual areas of concern. Another stressed that there needs to be greater representation of stakeholders, including a wider representation of communities from across the country and more participation by both foundations and the media.

There was an overwhelming sense among the conference organizers, the speakers, and the attendees that the meeting brought several important issues to the table. Many of these practitioners agreed to work together in the interim via conference calls and online collaboration to develop real solutions. However, the need to address the creation of a formal platform to support a network of communities working together to solve these problems must be foremost in the consideration of any future meeting that is organized.

## THE COMMUNITY AND HOMELAND SECURITY CONFERENCE AGENDA

| Topic | Speaker |
|---|---|
| Welcome and Opening Remarks | Barry Krisberg, Ph.D., NCCD |
| "Homeland Security: A California Perspective" | Chief Dave Wilson, California Highway Patrol |
| "Citizen Corps and Homeland Security" Corps | Karen Marsh, Citizen |
| Panel Discussion— "Community-Based Programs and Homeland Security" | Panelists: Ann Patton, Tulsa, OK Carol Lopes, Berkeley, CA |
| Moderator: Barry Krisberg, Ph.D., NCCD | Ana-Marie Jones, Oakland, CA Maya Harris-West, Oakland, CA |
| "Integrating Citizen Corps into Statewide Community Response" | Chuck Supple, Executive Director, CA Governor's Office on Service and Volunteerism (GO SERV) |
| Panel Discussion— "New Approaches to Community-Based Homeland Security Programs" | Panelists: Valli Wasp, Austin, TX Doris Milldyke, Manhattan, KS Adam Sutkus, Sacramento, CA |
| Moderator: Jane Bullock, SAFE Project | |
| "National Efforts of the Corporation for National and Community Service (CNCS) and Citizen Corps" | Kristen Haggins, State Director of CNCS |
| "Volunteer Recruitment and Training" | Monique Morris, NCCD |
| "Statewide Medical Response Corps Formation, Programs, and Funding" | Norma Schroeder, Emergency Medical Services Authority (EMSA) |
| "Role of the Red Cross in Homeland Security" | Amy Gaver, American Red Cross |
| "How to Prepare a Community Homeland Security Plan" | Jane Bullock, SAFE Project |
| "How to Evaluate Community Homeland Security Programs" | Ken Terao, Aguirre International |
| "Counter-Terrorism Training and Resources" | Eileen Garry, U.S. Department of Justice |
| "Building Community Emergency Networks" | George Haddow, SAFE Project |
| "Next Steps: Forming a National Community NCCD Network" Group discussion and brainstorm | Facilitated by Barry Krisberg |

# Appendix 10: California State Agency Guidance: Homeland Security Advisory System

## California State Agency Guidance:
### Homeland Security Advisory System

O E S
CALIFORNIA ★
Governor's Office of
Emergency Services

March 20, 2003

**Purpose**

As memorialized in Homeland Security Presidential Directive 3, the Federal Government has implemented the Homeland Security Advisory System to provide a comprehensive and effective means to disseminate information regarding the risk of terrorist acts. The system provides warnings in the form of a set of graduated "Threat Conditions" that would increase as the risk of the threat increases. At each Threat Condition, State departments and agencies would implement a corresponding set of "Protective Measures" to further reduce vulnerability or increase response capability during a period of heightened alert. This document describes the Threat Conditions and provides guidance in creating and implementing the protective measures for State departments and agencies. The content and format were developed from existing, available information and input from the Intelligence and Early Warning Subcommittee of the State Strategic Committee on Terrorism. <u>Each State department and agency is responsible for determining what actions and plans are appropriate to that department or organization.</u>

**Federal Homeland Security Advisory System**

There are five Threat Conditions, each identified by a description and corresponding color. From lowest to highest, the colors and levels are:

| RED | SEVERE – A Severe risk of terrorist attacks |
|---|---|
| ORANGE | HIGH – A high risk of terrorist attacks |
| YELLOW | ELEVATED – A significant risk of terrorist attacks |
| BLUE | GUARDED – A general risk of terrorist attacks |
| GREEN | LOW – A low risk of terrorist attacks |

The higher the Threat Condition, the greater the risk of a terrorist attack. Risk includes both the probability of an attack occurring and its potential gravity. Threat Conditions may be for the entire State, or may be set for a particular geographic area or industrial sector.

California State Agency Guidance Document:
Homeland Security Advisory System
1

The assignment of a Threat Condition will prompt the implementation of an appropriate set of protective measures. The protective measures are the specific steps an organization should take to reduce its vulnerability or increase its ability to respond during a period of heightened alert. It is recognized that departments and agencies may have several preplanned sets of responses to a particular Threat Condition to facilitate a rapid, appropriate, and tailored response. Department and agency heads are responsible for developing their own protective measures and other antiterrorism or self-protection and continuity plans, as well as resourcing, rehearsing, documenting, and maintaining these plans. Likewise, they retain the authority to respond, as necessary, to risks, threats, incidents, or events at facilities within the specific jurisdiction of their department or agency, and, as authorized by law, to direct agencies and industries to implement their own protective measures. They will continue to be responsible for taking all appropriate proactive steps to reduce the vulnerability of their personnel and facilities to terrorist attack.

**Protective Measures**

Protective measures and activities for state agencies are recommended actions, not required actions. While each state agency should implement measures/activities appropriate to its own operating environment, the following general guidelines apply:

- The threat/risk goes up with each successive level.

- Responses are additive; each level incorporates all activities from the previous levels.

- Threat information may be general or indicated for different geographical regions of the state.

- Specific implementation must be determined by each agency in light of actual events; protective measures for a higher level than officially designated may be implemented by each agency. For example, if the threat advisory level is elevated from "Yellow" to "Orange" an agency may elect to implement not only "Orange" level suggested protective measures, but also some "Red" level protective measures.

- Measures are numbered for ease of use. For example, an organization may wish to state that it has implemented all measures for YELLOW, but added measures 70 and 73, etc.

The following pages present specific protective measures in response to the Homeland Security Advisory System [HSAS] threat level conditions.

## Recommended Protective Measures: GREEN – Low Condition
This condition is declared when there is a *low* risk of terrorist attacks.

**Measure 1.** Reviewing and revising current Emergency and Business Continuity/ Resumption Plans to include mitigation and contingency planning for conditions that current plans do not address such as biological, nuclear, incindiary, chemical, explosive threats and exposure

**Measure 2.** Ensure the agency is familiar with all of the requirements of the Standardized Emergency Management System (SEMS). All State agencies must comply with these requirements. Contact the Governor's Office of Emergency Services for further information.

**Measure 3.** Refining and exercising, as appropriate, preplanned Protective Measures.

**Measure 4.** Ensuring personnel receive proper training on the Homeland Security Advisory System and specific preplanned department or agency Protective Measures.

**Measure 5.** Institutionalizing a process to assure that all facilities are regularly assessed for vulnerabilities to terrorist attacks, and all reasonable measures are taken to mitigate these vulnerabilities.

**Measure 6.** All contractors and visitors must check or sign in and out of designated facilities or areas within the facility that are considered key command, control or communications centers or areas.

**Measure 7.** Ensure existing security measures are in place and functioning such as fencing, locks, camera surveillance, intruder alarms, and lighting. Identify those additional security measures and resources that can enhance the security at the higher Threat Condition levels (e.g. increased surveillance).

**Measure 8.** Review procedures for receiving and disseminating information transmitted via the state agency emergency notification system (as required by Management Memo 02-09).

**Measure 9.** Establish local, regional and system-wide threat and warning dissemination process, emergency communications capability, and contact information with law enforcement and security officials, including CHP and local FBI Field Offices. Emergency communications should have redundancy in both hardware and means to contact security officials, law enforcement agencies, and mobile field command centers.

**Measure 10.** Develop terrorist and security awareness and provide information and educate employees on security standards and procedures. Caution employees not to talk with outsiders concerning their facility or related issues.

California State Agency Guidance Document:
Homeland Security Advisory System
3

**Measure 11.** Advise all personnel at each facility to report the presence of unknown personnel, unidentified vehicles, vehicles operated out of the ordinary, abandoned parcels or packages, and any suspicious activities. Report suspicious information immediately to the California Highway Patrol

**Measure 12.** Develop procedures for shutting down and evacuation, or shelter in place, of facilities. Facilities located near critical community assets should be especially vigilant of security measures.

**Measure 13.** Incorporate security awareness and information into public education programs and notifications to emergency response organizations.

**Measure 14.** Survey *surrounding* areas to determine those activities that might increase the security risks that could affect the state facility (e.g. airports, government buildings, industrial facilities, pipelines.)

**Measure 15.** Ensure contingency and business continuity plans are current and include a response to terrorist threats.

**Measure 16.** Develop and implement hardware, software, and communications security for computer based operational systems.

*Intentionally Blank*

## Recommended Protective Measures: BLUE – Guarded Condition
This condition is declared when there is a *general* risk of terrorist attacks.

**Measure 17.** Ensure that a response can be mobilized and review facility security plans and procedures including bomb threat, chemical, biological or radiological threat and evacuation procedures. Ensure plans incorporate EOD and tactical teams as necessary, including accessibility to explosive detection capabilities such as K-9 teams or electronic air sampling devices.

**Measure 18.** Inspect perimeter fencing and repair all fence breakdowns. In addition, review all outstanding maintenance and capital project work that could affect the security of facilities.

**Measure 19.** Review all operations plans, personnel details, and logistics requirements that pertain to implementing higher Threat Condition levels.

**Measure 20.** Inspect all CCTV/Video Camera/VCR equipment and intercom systems where applicable to ensure equipment is operational.

**Measure 21.** Review and ensure adequacy of personnel and ID issuance and control procedures.

**Measure 22.** Require each visitor to check in at designated facilities or areas within the facility that are consider key command, control or communications centers or areas and verify their identification. Be especially alert to repeat visitors or outsiders who have no apparent business at the facility and are asking questions about the facility or related issues including the facility's personnel. Be familiar with vendors who service the facility and investigate changes in vendor personnel.

**Measure 23.** Inspect emergency supplies to ensure equipment is in good working order.

**Measure 24.** Provide the public with any information that would strengthen its ability to act appropriately.

**Measure 25.** At regular intervals, remind all personnel to be suspicious and inquisitive about strangers, particularly those carrying suitcases or other containers. Watch for unidentified vehicles on or in the vicinity of facilities. Watch for abandoned parcels or suitcases and any unusual activity.

**Measure 26.** Consider on-scene emergency medical care in case of delayed outside assistance. (I.e., Basic First Aid and CPR employee training).

**Measure 27.** Review and familiarize staff with their respective agency Department Operation Centers (DOC's) or Emergency Operation Centers (EOC's) activation criteria and procedures.

## Recommended Protective Measures: YELLOW – Elevated Condition
An Elevated Condition is declared when there is a *significant* risk of terrorist attacks.

**Measure 28.** Inform all security officials, with an operational need to know, of the increased threat. Communicate this information to agency employees who have an operational need to know. Reinforce awareness of responsibilities with employees.

**Measure 29.** Test security and emergency communications procedures and protocols. Post a Security Alert if appropriate. Check communications with designated emergency response or command locations.

**Measure 30.** Secure all buildings and storage areas not in regular use. Increase frequency of inspection and patrols within the facility including the interior of buildings and along the facility perimeter. Increase surveillance in areas considered key command, control or communications centers and areas such as truck docks, taxi lanes, and parking lots.

**Measure 31.** Check designated unmanned and remote sites at more frequent intervals for signs of unauthorized entry, suspicious packages, or unusual activities.

**Measure 32.** Reduce the number of access points for vehicles and personnel to minimum levels and periodically spot check the contents of vehicles at the access points. Be alert to vehicles parked for an unusual length of time in or near a facility.

**Measure 33.** Inspect all mail and packages coming into a facility. Do not open suspicious packages. Review the USPS "Suspicious Mail Alert" and the "Bombs by Mail" publications with all personnel involved in receiving mail and packages.

**Measure 34.** Network with CHP and local law enforcement intelligence units, i.e. FBI field offices, and liaison, as appropriate, with other departments.

**Measure 35.** Ensure that personnel with access to building plans and area evacuation plans be available at all times. Personnel should be able to seal off an area immediately. The staff required to implement security plans should be on call and readily available.

**Measure 36.** Increase security spot checks of vehicles and persons entering facilities.

**Measure 37.** Review and implement security measures for high-risk personnel, as appropriate.

**Measure 38.** Inform personnel of additional threat information as available. Implement procedures to provide periodic updates on security measures being implemented.

**Measure 39.** Ensure that an agency or facility response can be mobilized appropriately for the increased security level. Review communications procedures and back-up plans with all concerned.

**Measure 40.** Review with all facility employees the operations plans; personnel safety, security details, and logistics requirements that pertain to implementing increased security levels. Review notification/recall lists.

**Measure 41.** Confirm availability of security resources that can assist with 24/7 coverage as applicable.

**Measure 42.** Step up routine checks of unattended vehicles, scrutiny of packages and vehicles, and monitor critical facilities and key infrastructure to ensure they are properly secured.

**Measure 43.** Limit visitor access to key security areas and confirm that the visitor has a need to be there and is expected. All unknown visitors should be escorted while in these areas.

**Measure 44.** Advise CHP and local police agencies that the facility is at Elevated Condition (Yellow) and advise the measures being employed. Coordinate emergency plans as appropriate with nearby jurisdictions.

**Measure 45.** Resurvey the surrounding area to determine if activities near the facility could create emergencies and other incidents that could affect the facility (e.g. airports, government buildings, industrial facilities, railroads, other pipelines).

**Measure 46.** Instruct employees working alone at remote locations to check-in on a periodic basis.

**Measure 47.** Check to ensure all emergency telephone, radio, intercom, and satellite communication devices are in place and operational.

**Measure 48.** Direct all personnel at the facility to secure vehicles by locking them.

**Measure 49.** Interface with vendors and contractors to heighten awareness and report suspicious activity. Post signs or make routine public announcements that emphasize the need for all passengers to closely control baggage and packages to avoid transporting items without their knowledge.

**Measure 50.** Develop and implement a schedule for increasing the frequency of inspection including specific areas and item such as: telephone booths, garbage containers, and all public areas.

**Measure 51.** Assessing whether the precise characteristics of the threat require further refinement of the preplanned Protective Measures.

**Measure 52.** Implement, as appropriate, contingency and emergency response plans.

**Measure 53.** Keep all personnel involved in implementing antiterrorist contingency plans on call.

**Measure 54.** Secure and regularly inspect all buildings, rooms, and storage areas not in regular use.

**Measure 55.** At the beginning and end of each workday and at other regular and frequent intervals, inspect the interior and exterior of buildings in regular use for suspicious packages.

**Measure 56.** Examine mail (above the regular examination process) for letter or parcel bombs.

**Measure 57.** Check all deliveries to facility and loading docks.

**Measure 58.** Make staff and dependents aware of the general situation in order to stop rumors and prevent unnecessary alarm.

**Measure 59.** Operate random patrols to check vehicles, people, and buildings.

**Measure 60.** Implement additional security measures for high-risk personnel as appropriate.

*Intentionally Blank*

## Recommended Protective Measures: ORANGE – High Condition
A High condition is declared when there is a *high* risk of terrorist attacks.

**Measure 61.** Move cars and objects (e.g. crates, trash containers) at least 25 meters from buildings (where possible) particularly highly populated, mission related, or high profile buildings. Consider centralized parking. Move automobiles and other non-stationary items from station and terminal perimeters and other sensitive buildings or areas. Identify areas where explosive devices could be hidden.

**Measure 62.** Close and lock gates and barriers except those needed for immediate entry and egress. Inspect perimeter fences on a regular basis. Ensure that other security systems are functioning and are available.

**Measure 63.** Increase security manpower for additional surveillance, to act as a deterrent and prevent unauthorized access to secure areas, deploy specialty/technical resources, and enact local tactical plans, if applicable. The areas recommended for additional patrols should include parking areas and loading docks. Increase surveillance of critical locations.

**Measure 64.** Continue Low, Guarded and Elevated measures or introduce those that have not already been implemented.

**Measure 65.** Reduce facility access points to the absolute minimum necessary for continued operation. Restrict threatened facility access to essential personnel only.

**Measure 66.** Advise CHP and local police agencies that the facility is at a High Condition (Orange) and advise the measures being employed.

**Measure 67.** Consult with CHP and local authorities about control of public roads and accesses that might make the facility more vulnerable to terrorist attack if they were to remain open. Take additional precautions at public events and possibly consider alternative venues or even cancellation.

**Measure 68.** Implement centralized parking and shuttle bus service where feasible.

**Measure 69.** Schedule more frequent visits to remote sites and other locations that are potentially impacted.

**Measure 70.** Increase the frequency of call-ins from remote locations. Employees should not work alone in remote areas.

**Measure 71.** Check all security systems such as lighting and intruder alarms to ensure they are functioning. Install additional, temporary lighting if necessary to adequately light all suspect areas or decrease lighting to detract from the area.

**Measure 72.** Identify the owner of all vehicles parked at key command, control, or communications areas or other critical areas/facilities/ and have all vehicles removed which are not identified.

**Measure 73.** Strictly enforce control of entry. Inspect all vehicles entering key areas/facilities including the vehicle's cargo areas, undercarriage, glove boxes, and other areas where dangerous items could be concealed.

**Measure 74.** Limit access to designated facilities to those personnel who have a legitimate and verifiable need to enter the facility. Implement a procedure for positive identification of all personnel, allowing no exceptions. Evacuate all non-essential personnel.

**Measure 75.** Implement frequent inspection of key areas or facilities including the exterior and roof of all buildings and parking areas. Increase patrolling at night and ensure all vulnerable critical points are fully illuminated and secure.

**Measure 76.** Review procedures and make necessary preparations to activate Command Center(s) where applicable. Prepare to execute contingency procedures, such as moving to an alternate site or dispersing the workforce.

**Measure 77.** Coordinate security efforts with the California Highway Patrol. This should include enhancements to security efforts with Federal, State, and local law enforcement agencies or any National Guard or other appropriate armed forces organizations. **NOTE:** Any resource taskings will be in accordance with current policies and procedures.

**Measure 78.** Keep all personnel responsible for implementing antiterrorist plans on call.

**Measure 79.** Enforce centralized parking of vehicles away from buildings.

**Measure 80.** Increase patrolling of the facilities.

**Measure 81.** Protect all designated vulnerable points.

## Recommended Protective Measures: RED – Severe Condition
A Severe Condition reflects a *severe* risk of terrorist attacks.

**Measure 82.** Increase security patrol activity to the maximum level sustainable. Increase perimeter patrols and inspections of facility.

**Measure 83.** Postpone or cancel all non-vital facility work conducted by contractors, or continuously monitor their work as applicable.

**Measure 84.** Continue all Low, Guarded, Elevated and High Condition measures or introduce those that have not already been implemented.

**Measure 85.** Implement emergency and continuity plans as appropriate. Reduce restricted area access points to an operational minimum.

**Measure 86.** Augment security forces to ensure absolute control of key command, control or communications centers or areas and other potential target areas. Establish surveillance points and reporting criteria and procedures.

**Measure 87.** Remove unattended, unauthorized vehicles parked within 300 feet of a terminal building or station where passengers load or unload.

**Measure 88.** Increase or redirect personnel to address critical emergency needs.

**Measure 89.** Identify all vehicles within operational or mission support areas.

**Measure 90.** Search all vehicles and their contents before allowing entrance to facilities.

**Measure 91.** Control access and implement positive identification of all personnel.

**Measure 92.** Search all suitcases, briefcases, packages, etc., brought into the facility.

**Measure 93.** Conduct frequent checks of building exteriors and parking areas.

**Measure 94.** Minimize all administrative journeys and visits.

**Measure 95.** Coordinate the possible closing of public access roads and/or facilities with CHP and local authorities.

**Conclusion**

**Each State department and agency is responsible for determining what actions and plans are appropriate to that department or organization.** Along with emergency response preparation, each state department and agency should ensure Continuity of Government and Continuity of Operations. The above guidelines should be used as a catalyst for the review, refinement, and modification of existing emergency and business resumption plans, as needed. Contact the Governor's Office of Emergency Services for further assistance on emergency planning issues, or the California Highway Patrol for physical security issues.

# Appendix 11: Communicating During Emergencies

**By Jane A. Bullock, George D. Haddow, and Richard Bell**

(NOTE: Research support for this paper was provided by Lauren Block, Tracy R. Bolo, Amina Chaudary, Brain D. Cogert, David DeCicco, Aspasia Papadopoulos, Robert Paxton, and Michael Stinziano.)

## INTRODUCTION

Communicating with the public is one of the critical tasks facing emergency management agencies (EMAs). Reaching the widest possible audience with the most up-to-date, credible information can save lives and property, reduce public fears and anxiety, and maintain the public's trust in the integrity of government officials.

We recently conducted a survey of how EMA communicators had fared during a number of national disasters and terrorist attacks. Our concern about the adequacy of EMA communications planning has been heightened by a striking change in the intensity of media coverage. In describing their work with the press, our respondents used imagery very much like that which they applied to the emergency event itself. They found themselves swamped by a veritable "tidal wave" of reporters almost literally beating down their doors.

In this article we review the findings of our survey and interviews and lay out the principal suggestions we received from a cross-section of EMAs on putting the personnel and infrastructure in place to execute robust, flexible communications plans.

## METHODOLOGY

This article is based on responses to a questionnaire that we received from communicators involved in the following recent natural disasters or terrorist attack, including interviews in most cases with the principal spokesperson involved:

- Tropical Storm Allison, Harris County Texas, Office of Emergency Management, Mayor's Office, June 5–10, 2001
- The Hayman forest fire, Colorado, Public Affairs, U.S. Forest Service, Rocky Mountain Region, Summer 2000
- Attack on the Pentagon, northern Virginia, Office of the Assistant Secretary of Public Affairs and Media Relations, U.S. Department of Defense, September 11, 2001
- Attack on the Pentagon, northern Virginia, Capitol Police, September 11, 2001
- Sniper attacks, Washington, DC, metro area, Media Services, Montgomery County Police Department, Fall 2002
- Anthrax attack on Hart Senate Office Building, Washington, DC, October, 2001
- Anthrax attacks, Office of Communications, Division of Media Relations, Centers for Disease Control and Prevention, Fall 2001
- F4 level tornado, La Plata, Maryland, Maryland Emergency Management Agency, April 28, 2002

## PLANNING

Creating a communications plan on the fly during a crisis is an extremely daunting task. The absence of a plan virtually guarantees that communicators will not be able to reach the public as effectively as they would if they had a plan in place.

Producing a workable written plan is inherently an agency-by-agency process, contingent on available personnel, budget limitations, etc. By soliciting critical review of the plan from all the affected participants—the public, the press, other government agencies—EMAs have the opportunity to produce the best possible plan under the circumstances.

Some of the EMAs with whom we talked had highly elaborate communications plans. But regardless of length, they all agreed that their plans made them more effective during emergencies. And the EMAs who had been through a trial by fire without a written communications plan were equally adamant about putting such a plan in place as soon as possible.

## PEOPLE

The most well-written communications plan is not worth much without a strong commitment from elected officials and department managers to put the infrastructure in place to carry out the plan.

The spokesperson's credibility is a key to his/her effectiveness at representing the government, reassuring the public, and keeping the media happy. In some jurisdictions, the highest ranking elected official or the head of the department managing the crisis will be the lead communicator, giving them a kind of automatic credibility at the onset of an event (like New York Mayor Rudy Guiliani after 9/11).

Given the increasing intensity of media coverage, the media spokesperson plays an increasingly important role in ensuring the overall effectiveness of an EMA. In order to maintain the spokesperson's credibility as a source with the media, the spokesperson needs to be "at the table" for all senior management decisions. If reporters believe that a spokesperson is not fully integrated into the decision-making process, they will inevitably be more suspicious of the information they do receive.

By participating in decision making, the spokesperson can also play a vital internal role by making sure that decision-makers have fully considered how their decisions may play out in the media, giving them a better chance of avoiding public relations blunders.

After the terrorist attack on the Pentagon on September 11, 2001, Arlington County officials significantly upgraded its top public communications official. The change was more than just a title change (from Assistant County Manager for Public Information to Director of Communications and Public Affairs). The county also raised the position's salary and provided that the new director would report directly to the county manager. The job description for this new position includes the development of "a comprehensive communications program that will provide a cohesive image, identity, and brand message both externally and internally by optimizing the use of existing electronic resources (Internet, intranet, and cable television) and nonelectronic sources (print media) as well as developing new communications venues."

If possible, one person should be the principal spokesperson (the single voice/single face model). Nothing is likely to be more confusing to the media or the public than dealing with a constantly changing array of talking heads. (There's a reason almost all the daily White House press briefings are handled by one person!)

## MEDIA TRAINING

Learning to be a media spokesperson in the middle of a crisis is risky. There is no substitute for practical media training before a crisis arrives. In Harris County, Texas, the three authorized spokespeople had all been through a FEMA-approved 32-hour public information officer (PIO) course offered through the Texas Department of Public Safety's Office of Emergency Management. The Forest Service spokesperson during the 2002 Hayman forest fire had roughly 50 hours of formal media training.

In addition, the agency's public affairs staff worked with him on "war game" crises, creating what he called "murder boards" to put him through the kind of tough questioning he would encounter in a real crisis. And the Capitol Police officer who handled the anthrax attack on the Senate Hart Building was a media trainer himself with over 160 hours of training.

## INFRASTRUCTURE

### BUILDING AN EMERGENCY OPERATIONS CENTER

Just as some jurisdictions had no written EM plan, some did not have an Emergency Operations Center (EOC), although there was broad agreement that having a well-equipped EOC was the physical foundation for an effective communications effort.

For planning purposes, the EOC should have redundant communications capabilities, both internally and with the outside. No communications technology works every time. Land lines can fail; during the attack on the Pentagon, there were frequent problems with cell phones.

Without a well-equipped EOC, crisis managers face difficult hurdles staying on top of what is happening. After the September 11 attack on the Pentagon, local officials found that their EOC was ill equipped for the emergency management team to communicate with first responders or to receive accurate information from the scene. Phone lines were down, and the room was not equipped with radios or televisions. They were forced to delay press briefings until they could verify facts with first responders and people on-site.

EOCs should be designed with the media in mind. The Harris County, Texas, EOC has an on-site press room with telephone and computer access. EOCs can make life easier for television reporters by preparing video footage (called "B-roll") of scenes that reporters could use, like the interior of the Emergency Operations Center. EOCs can also prepare fact sheets and other printed background materials on the major threats that the agency has identified.

Communicators can also provide the press with special support if necessary. During the Hayman forest fire, the Forest Service gave out personal protective equipment to reporters (hard hats, fire clothes, etc.).

### CARVING THROUGH THE JURISDICTIONAL JUNGLE

The communications plan provides a framework for mapping and, where possible, negotiating communications procedures about how to handle one of the most common problems of the EMA universe, overlapping jurisdictions. Such overlaps are inherent in the nature of almost every large-scale emergency event. A comprehensive plan must include not only local, state, and federal law enforcement and emergency management agencies but also the spectrum of veterinary and public health agencies (in light of the threat of the use of biological, chemical, or radiological weapons by terrorists).

In the aftermath of the anthrax attacks, the Centers for Disease Control and Prevention has published a useful analysis of the similarities and differences in public health and law enforcement investigations and the steep learning curves for both sets of agencies in their collaborations. ("Collaboration Between Public Health and Law Enforcement: New Paradigms and Partnerships for Bioterrorism Planning and Response," Jay C. Butler et al., http://www.cdc.gov/ncidod/EID/vol8no10/02 0400.htm). The authors emphasis the importance of pre-existing relationships between law enforcement and public health agencies and the need for practice exercises, and call for adding liaisons who are cross-trained in the public health aspects of communicable diseases and in law enforcement and criminal investigations.

Even without a written communications plan, an informal prior agreement can be helpful in reducing confusion. In the case of the anthrax attack on the Hart Senate Office Building, there was no written plan. But the Capitol Police Board and the House and Senate leadership had previously determined that the Capitol Police would be the designated agency to handle media inquiries after any terrorist or criminal incidents within the Capitol complex. Members of

Congress—a group not known for being media-shy—conferred with the police spokesperson before holding their own press conferences, and the spokesperson attended these events, off camera, to provide guidance as needed.

In our study, several communicators highlighted the importance of maintaining clear channels of communications with all of the government agencies involved, regardless of which agency had been designated the lead communications agency. This cross-agency communications is essential for keeping everyone "on the same page" so that reporters do not get confusing or conflicting information from their contacts at other agencies. Up-to-date e-mail and fax lists are a relatively cheap way to distribute breaking information to other agencies in a timely way.

The Office of Emergency Management in Harris County used an Internet e-mail and pager software they developed to reach more than 140 media outlets in the region, 125 law-enforcement agencies, 54 fire departments, 29 cities, and selected individuals throughout the surrounding 41 counties. After Tropical Storm Allison, the office expanded the list of individuals requesting real-time information, adding more elected federal, state, and local officials and media outlets. (Copies of the Harris County plans can be downloaded from http://www.hcoem.org.)

## WORKING WITH THE MEDIA

### BUILDING PRIOR RELATIONSHIPS

The media play an integral part in EMA outreach efforts to keep the public informed and up-to-date. But without preexisting relationships with reporters, it's not uncommon or unexpected that in the heat of the moment, EMAs might come to look upon the press in a crisis as adversaries engaged in a "feeding frenzy" for new facts.

Planning is essential to building relationships with the media, so that EMAs and the media understand each other's needs and operating styles and how to work together as much as possible as allies. Both EMAs and

the press share a deep concern about protecting the health and welfare of the public. Far from being adversaries, reporters can be valuable allies, particularly in devising an effective communications plan in the first place.

Harris County's Office of Emergency Management had a policy of inviting reporters in twice a year to talk about how the agency could better meet the needs of the press. Such conversations are no guarantee, of course, against future disagreements. But such meetings do allow for EMAs and reporters to share each others' perspectives in a nonstressful environment, reducing the possibility of misunderstandings later on during crises. And such exchanges also allow EMAs to plan to meet the media's needs where possible. Another useful technique for improving media relations is to schedule meetings with the editorial boards of local media outlets.

## CONSERVING CREDIBILITY WITH THE MEDIA

Credibility is a dynamic asset in a crisis; a spokesperson can lose credibility quickly if the media and the public come to believe they're being misinformed or under-informed. Every effort should be made to ensure that whatever information is released to the public is accurate and up-to-date. As one PIO told us, his goal was to be "the first and best source of information, especially if it's bad news."

Misinformation only compounds one of the other common communications problems during crisis, the rapid spread of unfounded rumors, the rebutting of which can take up valuable time. During the Capitol Hill anthrax attack, many Capitol Hill reporters—who were used to covering policy debates, not terrorist attacks—were anxious about their own medical conditions, having been in the "hot zone" at some point. Congressional staffers, their usual sources of information, were also anxious about their own health and provided information often based on rumor, outside their areas of legislative expertise. Reporters, frustrated with what seemed to them to be the slow release of information, would go with these rumor sources and end up being forced to back-track later. Many of the communications managers in our survey said that combating such rumors was one of the most difficult tasks they faced during a crisis.

Limiting the amount of information that reaches the public poses a different kind of challenge. It is not uncommon for government or corporate managers to use the control of the release of information as a way of gaining or preserving bureaucratic power. But in a crisis, this withholding tendency can aggravate the public's anxieties. In Arlington County, Virginia, after the September 11 attack on the Pentagon, officials found that although they might not have any new, more specific information about what might happen next, citizens still wanted frequent updates and reassurances from their county government.

In a crisis management setting, withholding information may very well result in a loss of power and control. Our respondents agreed that one should lean in the direction of making more, rather than less, information available, consistent with law enforcement and public safety considerations.

In a full-blown media circus, even a vigorous attempt at openness may not be enough to halt a media feeding frenzy. One of the more striking examples of this press intensity came from the Montgomery County, Maryland, police during the Fall 2002 Washington, DC area sniper attacks. The department was already providing frequent media releases, one-on-one interviews, web updates, and as many as four press briefings a day.

But reporters wanted more. Some went so far as to peer through a half-inch opening in the window shades at the operations center, stealing a look at text on a dry erase board. Within seconds, they were questioning Montgomery County police chief Charles Moss about the information they had gleaned, showing little concern about whether their questions might endanger public safety.

## KEEPING ALTERNATIVE MEDIA CHANNELS OPEN

In addition to the traditional media (TV, radio, newspapers), EMAs have access to newer media like e-mail, web sites, and local cable TV, which can be used to reach the public directly. Because these tools also do not reach as wide an audience as traditional mass media, they should be seen as adjuncts, not substitutes.

These unmediated channels can be very effective tools for providing the public with a great deal of information without tying up large numbers of EMA staff. However, if an EMA is using a web site, it is essential that staff updates the site on a frequent basis; stale information drives users away.

The agencies we surveyed reported a wide range of satisfaction in using new media tools. In some cases, results were disappointing because too few people were aware of the local cable TV channel or did not know the agency had a web site. On the other hand, one agency reported over 1.6 million contacts on its web site from press, first responders, and the public and regarded the web site as a valuable component of its overall communications strategy.

## CONCLUSION

Communicating during emergencies is necessarily fraught with uncertainty: The unexpected is most likely to happen. No emergency communications plan can fully encompass all of the scenarios that may arise. But the findings from our survey show that EMAs can take steps to create a robust communications plans, train spokespeople, and build the infrastructure that will allow EMAs to roll with the punches and maximize their effectiveness at getting their messages to the press, the public, and other government agencies.

# Glossary of Hazard Terms

1. General Terms
2. Biological
3. Chemical
4. Radiological/Nuclear

## GENERAL TERMS

**Aerosol**   Fine liquid or solid particles suspended in a gas (for example, fog or smoke).

**Biological agents**   Living organisms or the materials derived from them that cause disease in or harm to humans, animals, or plants or cause deterioration of material. Biological agents may be used as liquid droplets, aerosols, or dry powders.

**Chemical agent**   A chemical substance that is intended to kill, seriously injure, or incapacitate people through physiological effects. Generally separated by severity of effect: lethal, blister, and incapacitating.

**Consequence management**   Measures to protect public health and safety, restore essential government services, and provide emergency relief to governments, businesses, and individuals affected by the consequences of terrorism. State and local governments exercise primary authority to respond to the consequences of terrorism (Source: Federal Response Plan [FRP] Terrorism Incident Annex, page TI-2, April 1999). The Federal Emergency Management Agency (FEMA) has been designated the lead agency for consequence management to ensure that the FRP is adequate to respond to terrorism. Additionally, FEMA supports the Federal Bureau of Investigation (FBI) in crisis management.

**Crisis management**   This is the law enforcement aspect of an incident that involves measures to identify, acquire, and plan the resources needed to anticipate, prevent, and/or resolve a threat of terrorism. The FBI is the lead agency for crisis management for such an incident (Source: FBI). During crisis management, the FBI coordinates closely with local law enforcement authorities to provide successful law enforcement resolution to the incident. The FBI also coordinates with other federal authorities, including FEMA (Source: Federal Response Plan Terrorism Incident Annex, April 1999).

**Cyber-terrorism**   Malicious conduct in cyber-space to commit or threaten to commit acts dangerous to human life or against a nation's critical infrastructures, such as energy, transportation, or government operations in order to intimidate or coerce a government or civilian population, or any sequence thereof, in furtherance of political or social objectives.

**Decontamination**   The process of making people, objects, or areas safe by absorbing, destroying, neutralizing, making harmless, or removing the hazardous material.

**Federal Response Plan (FRP)**   The FRP establishes a process and structure for the systematic, coordinated, and effective delivery of federal assistance to address the consequences of any major disaster or emergency declared under the Robert T. Stafford Disaster Relief and Emergency Assistance Act, as amended (42 U.S. Code [USC] et seq.). The FRP Terrorism Incident Annex defines the organizational structures used to coordinate crisis management with consequence management (Source: FRP Terrorism Incident Annex, April 1999).

**Infrastructure Protection**   Proactive risk management actions intended to prevent a threat from attempting to or succeeding at destroying or incapacitating critical infrastructures (for instance, threat deterrence and vulnerability defense).

**Lead agency**   The federal department or agency assigned lead responsibility under U.S. law to manage and coordinate the federal response in a specific functional area. The FBI is the lead agency for crisis management, and FEMA is the lead agency for consequence management. Lead agencies support the overall lead Federal agency (LFA) during all phases of the response.

**Lead federal agency (LFA)**   The agency designated by the president to lead and coordinate the overall federal response is referred to as the LFA and is determined by the type of emergency. In general, an LFA establishes operational structures and procedures to assemble and work with agencies providing direct support to the LFA in order to provide an initial assessment of the situation, develop an action plan, monitor and update operational priorities, and ensure each agency exercises its concurrent and distinct authorities under U.S. law and supports the LFA in carrying out the president's relevant policy. Specific responsibilities of an LFA vary according to the agency's unique statutory authorities.

**Mitigation**   Those actions (including threat and vulnerability assessments) taken to reduce the exposure to and detrimental effects of a WMD incident.

**Nonpersistent agent**   An agent that, upon release, loses its ability to cause casualties after 10 to 15 minutes. It has a high evaporation rate, is lighter than air, and will disperse rapidly. It is considered to be a short-term hazard; however, in small, unventilated areas, the agent will be more persistent.

**Persistent agent**   An agent that, upon release, retains its casualty-producing effects for an extended period of time, usually anywhere from 30 minutes to several days. A persistent agent usually has a low evaporation rate and its vapor is heavier than air; therefore, its vapor cloud tends to hug the ground. It is considered to be a long-term hazard. Although inhalation hazards are still a concern, extreme caution should be taken to avoid skin contact as well.

**Plume**   Airborne material spreading from a particular source; the dispersal of particles, gases, vapors, and aerosols into the atmosphere.

**Preparedness**   Establishing the plans, training, exercises, and resources necessary to achieve readiness for all hazards, including WMD incidents.

**Radiation**   High-energy particles or gamma rays that are emitted by an atom as the substance undergoes radioactive decay. Particles can be either charged alpha or beta particles or neutral neutron or gamma rays.

**Recovery**   Recovery, in this document, includes all types of emergency actions dedicated to the continued protection of the public or promoting the resumption of normal activities in the affected area.

**Response**   Executing the plan and resources identified to perform those duties and services to preserve and protect life and property as well as provide services to the surviving population.

**Terrorism**   The unlawful use of force or violence against persons or property to intimidate or coerce a government, the civilian population, or any segment thereof, in furtherance of political or social objectives. Domestic terrorism involves groups or individuals who are based and operate entirely within the United States and U.S. territories without foreign direction and whose acts are directed at elements of the U.S. government or population.

**Toxicity**   A measure of the harmful effects produced by a given amount of a toxin on a living organism.

**Weapons-grade material**   Nuclear material considered most suitable for a nuclear weapon. It usually connotes uranium enriched to above 90 percent uranium-235 or plutonium with greater than approximately 90 percent plutonium-239.

**Weapon of mass destruction**   Any destructive device as defined in 18 USC 921; any weapon that is designed or intended to cause death or serious bodily injury through the release, dissemination, or impact of toxic or poisonous chemicals or their precursors; any weapon involving a disease organism; or any weapon that is designed to release radiation or radioactivity at a level dangerous to human life (Source: 18 USC 2332a). In 18 USC 921, a destructive device is defined, with certain exceptions, to mean any explosive, incendiary, or poison gas, bomb, grenade, or rocket having a propellant charge of more than 4 ounces, or a missile having an explosive incendiary charge of more than 0.25 ounce, or a mine, or a device similar to the above; any type of weapon by whatever name known that will, or that may be readily converted to, expel a projectile by the action of an explosive or other propellant and that has any barrel with a bore of more 0.5 inch in diameter; any combination of parts either designed or intended for use in converting any device into any destructive device described above and from which a destructive device may be readily assembled.

*Source*: CDC, www.cdc.gov

## BIOLOGICAL

**Adventive**   Arrived in the geographical area specified from somewhere else by any means; not native (nonindigenous) to the area in which it has arrived.

**Alien**   Native somewhere else. Same as exotic and foreign.

**Anorexia**   Loss of appetite.

**Ataxia**   Lack of muscular coordination.

**Augmentative biological control**   Release of large numbers of a biological control agent to supplement the small numbers already present, in expectation of a greatly increased effect.

**Autochthonous**   Native; indigenous; this arcane word means the same as native and indigenous, and those are older and well-accepted expressions.

**Biological control**   The use of living natural enemies to control pests *or:* the active manipulation of antagonistic organisms to reduce pest population densities, either animal or plant, to noneconomically important levels.

**Biopesticide**   A living organism applied as an inundative biological control agent or augmentative biological control agent.

**Biorational pesticide**   A chemical such as a toxin or growth regulator derived from a living organism and applied either as the entire dead organism or as an extract from the organism; alternatively, the chemical or an analog of it synthesized in vitro. Use of biorational pesticides is usually considered to be chemical control not biological control.

**Carnivore**   An organism that feeds on animals.

**Classical biological control**   A form of inoculative biological control in which specialist natural enemies are imported from the supposed homeland of an adventive pest and released in small numbers in attempt to establish a permanent population. A variant form of classical biological control uses biological control agents imported from a third area, inhabited by a close relative of the target pest.

**Cleptoparasitism**   A form of multiple parasitism in which a parasite preferentially attacks a host that is already parasitized by another species.

**Coagulopathy**   Disorder of blood clot formation.

**Commensalism**   A situation in which two or more organisms of distant phylogeny use the same food resource without competition.

**Cyanosis**   Bluish discoloration of skin suggesting lack of oxygen to tissues.

**Dementia**   Mental deterioration.

**Detritivore**   An organism that feeds on detritus (decaying material).

**Diaphoresis**   Perspiration.

**Direct pest**   Said of a pest that damages the marketable part of a plant (e.g., the fruit).

**Dysarthria**   Difficulty of speech suggesting a neurological cause.

**Dyspepsia**   Epigastric discomfort secondary to indigestion.

**Dysphagia**   Difficulty in swallowing.

**Dysphasia**   Difficulty in arranging words in proper order due to a neurological lesion.

**Dysphonia**   Vocal impairment.

**Dyspnea**   Difficulty breathing.

**Ecchymosis**   Hemorrhagic discoloration of the skin.

**Ectoparasite**   A parasite that lives on the external surface of its host; examples include lice and fleas.

**Ectoparasitoid**   A parasitoid that lives on the external surface of its host, feeding on it and killing it in the process.

**Enanthem**   An eruption on the mucosal surface.

**Encapsulation**   A cellular defense strategy used by hosts of an endoparasitoid (or any other invading organism) to isolate it and deprive it of resources (oxygen and/or nutrients), so as to kill it.

**Encephalitis**   Inflammation of the brain.

**Endemic**   Occurring constantly in an area in small numbers, but allowing a switch to large numbers, at which time the population or species is said to be epidemic; the antonym of *endemic*.

**Endemism**   The condition of being native to and restricted to a specified area.

**Endocarditis**   An inflammation within the heart.

**Endoparasite**   A parasite that lives in another organism, feeding on it but not usually killing it (noun).

**Endoparasitoid**   A parasitoid that lives in another organism, feeding on it and killing it in the process.

**Endophage**   An organism that feeds inside another animal; the corresponding adjective is *endophagous*.

**Entomogenous**   Reproducing within insects; used mainly to describe habits of some nematodes.

**Epidemic**   Occurring in unusually large numbers; said of a population or species.

**Epistaxis**   Nosebleed.

**Erythema**   Redness of the skin from various causes.

**Exotic**   Native somewhere else. Kangaroos are exotic species as far as inhabitants of North America are concerned, but they are not exotic in Australia.

**Facultative parasitism**   A condition in which a free-living organism may exist by parasitism (parasitoidism) but does not rely upon this way of life.

**Facultative parasitoidism**   The condition of existing by parasitoidism but not relying upon this way of life.

**Gregarious parasitoid**   A parasitoid whose nutritional requirements are such that several can exist in the body of the host.

**Hematemesis**   Bloody vomitus.

**Hemifacial**   Involving one side of the face.

**Hemoptysis**   Bloody sputum.

**Hepatomegaly**   Enlargement of the liver.

**Host**   The living organism that serves as food for a parasite, parasitoid, or pathogen.

**Host-discrimination**   The selection of an appropriate host by a parasite or parasitoid, according to the species, developmental stage, and physiological condition (including absence of existing parasites/parasitoids) of that host.

**Host-specific**   A parasite, parasitoid, or pathogen that, at least in the area specified, is monophagous.

**Hyperparasite**   A parasite that lives on another parasite.

**Idiobiont**   A parasitoid whose host is rendered immobile by the parent of the idiobiont, and the said host is consumed in the location and stage it is in when attacked, or at least in a nearby location to which the parent of the idiobiont has moved it.

**Indirect pest**   Said of a pest that damages the unmarketed part of a plant (e.g., the leaves, when it is the fruit that is marketed).

**Inoculative biological control**   Importation and release of biological control agents in an area in which they are not already present, with intent to establish a permanent population.

**Inundative biological control**   Release of large numbers of a biological control agent relative to the numbers of a target species, in expectation of a rapid effect. There is no implication that the released biological control agent will establish a permanent population.

**Invasive**   A population or species that is expanding its range.

**Koinobiont** A parasitoid developing in a host that continues to be mobile and able to defend itself; hosts that are larvae often are not killed until they have prepared cryptic pupation retreats.

**Lethality** The ratio of the number of deaths to the number of afflicted patients.

**Leukopenia** A decrease in the number of white blood cells.

**Macule** A flat discoloration on the skin.

**Malaise** A perception of physical distress.

**Melena** Stools blackened by blood pigment.

**Meningitis** Inflammation of the membranes that envelop the brain.

**Myalgia** Muscular pain.

**Mydriasis** Markedly dilated pupil.

**Nuchal** Pertaining to the back of the neck.

**Osteomyelitis** Inflammation of the bone, usually due to a bacterial infection.

**Pancytopenia** A marked decrease of all blood cells.

**Papule** A small, raised lesion on the skin.

**Parasite** An organism that lives in or on the body of its host without killing the host, but usually debilitating it.

**Peritonitis** Inflammation of the membrane lining the abdominopelvic compartment.

**Persistence** The ability of a biological agent to remain in the environment while still retaining its capacity to cause casualties.

**Pest** An animal or plant that is deemed by mankind to be too numerous [this includes weeds].

**Petecchia** A tiny, hemorrhagic spot on the skin.

**Phoresy** The habit of gaining transport from one place to another on an animal (i.e., "hitching a ride").

**Photophobia** Abnormal intolerance to light.

**Predator** An organism that, during its development, consumes more than one prey individual.

**Prey** The living organism that serves as food for a predator.

**Prostration** Extreme exhaustion.

**Ptosis** Drooping of the upper eyelid.

**Pustule** Small collection of pus on the skin.

**Pyelonephritis** Inflammation of the kidneys, usually due to an infection.

**Rhinorrhea** Mucousy nasal discharge.

**Rigor** Exaggerated stiffening of the body.

**Sacroiliitis** Inflammation of the sacroiliac joint.

**Splenomegaly** Enlargement of the spleen.

**Spore** An inactive, resistant form of a bacterium.

**Synchronous** Occurring at the same time.

**Thrombocytopenia** A decrease in the absolute number of platelets.

**Vector** An animal that transmits a pathogen to plants or animals.

**Vesicle** A small, raised collection of clear, serous fluid on the skin.

*Sources*:

1. The Florida Integrated Pest Management and Biocontrol
2. http://biocontrol.ifas.ufl.edu/glossary.htm
3. http://www.bioterry.com/Manual/Appendix/ Glossary.asp

## CHEMICAL

**Abiotic** An abiotic system is one that is free of biological organisms. Abiotic transformations are those brought about by a nonbiological mechanism. Thus the modification of a chemical through heating or by the absorption of radiation is, strictly, an abiotic transformation or process.

**Absolute risk** Absolute Risk is the excess risk due to an exposure to a hazard.

**Acceptable Daily Intake** The Acceptable Daily Intake (ADI) is a measure of the quantity of a particular chemical in food that, it is believed, can be consumed on a daily basis over a lifetime without harm. Data for the calculation of an ADI may be derived from a variety of sources; often direct observation of human eating habits is used, but laboratory tests may also be appropriate. The concept of an ADI is most valuable when applied to chemicals which are not usually found in foods, such as additives or the residues of pesticides or veterinary drugs. ADIs may be defined both for humans and for animals and are widely used by organizations such as the World Health Organization.

**Acceptable risk**  The concept of acceptable risk is not particular easy to define. It is essentially a measure of the risk of harm, injury, or disease arising from a chemical or process that will be tolerated by a person or group. Whether a risk is "acceptable" will depend upon the advantages that the person or group perceives to be obtainable in return for taking the risk, whether they accept whatever scientific and other advice is offered about the magnitude of the risk, and numerous other factors, both political and social.

**ACGIH**  The American Conference of Governmental Industrial Hygienists.

**Acid**  Chemists use a variety of ways to define what they mean by an acid. The definition which is most readily understood, due to Arrhenius, is that an acid is a chemical which produces hydrogen ions when dissolved in water. The strength of an acidic solution is usually measured in terms of its pH (a logarithmic function of the $H^+$ ion concentration). Strongly acidic solutions have low pHs (typically around 0–3), while weakly acidic solutions have pHs in the range 3–6.

**Acidic solution**  See **Acid.**

**Action level**  The action level is the exposure level at which (USA) OSHA regulations take effect. This is generally one-half of the PEL.

**Acute effect**  An acute effect is one that involves severe symptoms that develop rapidly and may quickly reach a crisis.

**Acute hazard**  An acute hazard is one to which a single exposure may cause harm, but which is unlikely to lead to permanent damage.

**Acute toxicity**  See **Toxicity.**

**ADI**  See **Acceptable Daily Intake.**

**AIHA**  American Industrial Hygiene Association.

**Allergen**  An allergen is any material which produces an allergic reaction in an individual.

**Allergic contact dermatitis**  Allergic contact dermatitis is a type of skin hypersensitivity. Its onset may be delayed by several days to as much as several years for weaker sensitizers. Once sensitized, fresh exposure to the sensitizing material can trigger itching and dermatitis within a few hours.

**Allergy**  An allergy is the appearance of symptoms of disease, irritation, or discomfort upon exposure to a material, often one that has little effect on other people. Development of allergies is essentially an unwanted (or faulty) reaction of the immune system.

**All-or-none effect**  See **Quantal effect.**

**AMA**  The American Medical Association.

**Ambient standard**  See **Environmental quality standard.**

**Ames test**  The Ames test is used to assess whether a chemical might be a carcinogen. It assumes that carcinogens possess mutagenic activity and uses bacteria and mammalian microsomes to determine whether a chemical is a mutagen. Approximately 85 percent of known carcinogens are mutagens. The Ames test, therefore, is a helpful but not perfect predictor of carcinogenic potential.

**Analgesic**  An analgesic, such as aspirin, is a chemical that reduces the body's sensitivity to pain.

**Anoxia**  Anoxia is the absence of oxygen in blood, gases or human (or animal) tissues. It can be thought of as an extreme case of hypoxia, the lowering of oxygen levels.

**Argyria**  See **Argyrism.**

**Argyrism**  Argyria or argyrism is an irreversible bluish-black discoloration of the skin, mucous membranes, or internal organs caused by ingestion of, or contact with, various silver compounds.

**Asphyxiant**  An asphyxiant is a material capable of reducing the level of oxygen in the body to dangerous levels. Most commonly, asphyxiants work by merely displaying air in an enclosed environment. This reduces the concentration of oxygen below the normal level of around 19 percent, which can lead to breathing difficulties, unconsciousness, or even death.

**Asphyxiation**   See **Asphyxiant.**

**Atmosphere**   See **Units of pressure.**

**Auto-ignition temperature**   The auto-ignition temperature of a chemical is the lowest temperature at which a material will ignite without an external source of ignition.

**Base**   Chemists define the word *base* in a variety of ways. The simplest (though perhaps most limited) is that a base generates hydroxide ions (OH⁻) when dissolved in water. Typical bases according to this definition are the alkali hydroxides, such as sodium hydroxide or potassium hydroxide. The pH of a strongly basic solution will be in the range 11 to 14. Basic solutions are caustic and corrosive, but the most serious hazard they present is damage to the eyes. A strongly basic solution will attack the cornea very rapidly and may create sufficient damage to cause blindness. Safety glasses must therefore always be worn when handling bases.

**Basic solution**   See **Base.**

**Binary effect**   See **Quantal effect.**

**Biohazard**   A biohazard (biological hazard) is one which is posed to humans by a biological organism or by a material produced by such an organism.

**Breakthrough**   Breakthrough is the movement of a chemical through a protective material, such as a rubber glove. This may be due to gradual permeation of the chemical into and through the material or as a result of chemical or physical degradation of the material.

**Breakthrough time**   The breakthrough time is the time taken in standard tests for permeation of a chemical through a protective barrier (such as a rubber glove) to be detected.

**Carcinogen**   A carcinogen is a chemical known or believed to cause cancer in humans. The number of proven carcinogens is comparatively small, but many more chemicals are suspected to be carcinogenic.

**Carcinogenic**   A carcinogenic chemical is one which is believed to be capable of causing cancer; that is, acting as a carcinogen.

**CAS number**   The CAS registry number is a unique number assigned to a chemical by the Chemical Abstracts Service.

**Ceiling level**   The ceiling level, or ceiling value, is the maximum permissible concentration of a hazardous material in the working environment. This level should not be exceeded at any time. It is usually (but not invariably) set somewhat above the relevant time-weighted average for the chemical.

**Ceiling value (CV)**   See **Ceiling level.**

**Chronic hazard**   A chronic hazard is presented by a chemical that has the potential to cause long-term damage to health, often as a consequence of repeated or prolonged exposure to it.

**Chronic toxicity**   See **Toxicity.**

**Chrysiasis**   Chrysiasis is the development of a blue-grey pigmentation in skin and mucous membranes. May be caused by exposure to gold compounds.

**Clastogen**   A clastogen is a material which is capable of causing chromosomal breaks.

**CNS**   CNS is an acronym for *central nervous system*. A wide variety of chemicals may damage or depress the CNS, from relatively innocuous materials such as ethyl alcohol, which is a depressant when consumed in large amounts, to nerve gases and organomercury compounds, such as methylmercury hydroxide, which may be fatal if inhaled or absorbed through the skin in even tiny amounts.

**Combustible substances**   A combustible substance is any material that will burn.

**Copolymer**   A copolymer is a material created by polymerizing a mixture of two (or more) starting compounds. The resultant polymer molecules contain the monomers in a proportion that is related both to the mole fraction of the monomers in the starting mixture and to the reaction mechanism.

**Corrosive**   A corrosive material is one that causes damage to skin, eyes, or other parts of the body on contact. The technical definition is written in terms of "destruction, or irreversible damage to living tissue at the site of contact." Often this damage is caused directly by the chemical, but the action of some corrosive materials is a consequence of inflammation that they may cause. Concentrated acids are obvious examples of corrosive materials, but even dilute solutions of bases such as sodium or ammonium hydroxide may also be very corrosive, particularly in contact with the eyes.

**CTDs**   See **Repetitive strain injury.**

**Cumulative trauma disorders**   See **Repetitive strain injury.**

**Cutaneous hazard**   A cutaneous hazard is a chemical that may cause harm to the skin, such as defatting, irritation, skin rashes, or dermatitis.

**Cytotoxic**   A cytotoxic material is one that is harmful to cell structure and function and that may ultimately cause cell death.

**Degradation**   Degradation is the term generally used to describe the loss of resilience of material used for protective gloves. Degradation may cause the material to soften, swell, become hard and brittle, or in severe cases, disintegrate.

**Dermatitis**   Dermatitis is an inflammation of the skin that may be brought about by repeated contact with chemicals. A wide variety of chemicals may be responsible, especially those which can cause defatting of the skin, such as chlorinated solvents. Irritation, cracked skin, and blisters are common symptoms. Dermatitis may also arise if a person is susceptible to sensitization and is allergic to butyl rubber, latex, or other types of gloves designed to protect the skin from contact with chemicals. Dermatitis may seem a comparatively minor problem compared to the other hazards posed by chemicals but should be regarded as a potentially serious condition and not ignored.

**Desquamation**   Desquamation is the detachment of cells from the surface of an epithelium.

**Detoxify**   The word *detoxify* is used in at least two senses in safety. Detoxify is often used to indicate the treatment of a patient who has ingested or been exposed to a harmful chemical, in such a way as to lessen the effects of exposure. It is also used to

indicate the process by which a harmful material may be treated to render it harmless or less toxic.

**ECn**   ECn is a commonly used abbreviation that refers to the (exposure) concentration of a toxic material that has a defined effect upon n% of a test population.

**ED50**   The ED50 (Effective Dose 50) is the amount of material required to produce a specified effect in 50 percent of an animal population. (See qualification in the definition of **LD50**).

**EDn**   EDn is the usual abbreviation for the dose of a chemical which will have the expected effect upon n% of a test population.

**Embryotoxic**   An embryotoxic material is anything that can adversely affect the growth or development of the embryo.

**Embryotoxins**   Embryotoxins, such as aflatoxin, are naturally produced chemicals that retard the growth or affect the development of the unborn child. In serious cases they can cause deformities or death.

**Emetic**   An emetic is a substance that induces vomiting (emesis).

**Emission standard**   An emission standard is a regulatory limit on the amount of a toxic (or potentially toxic) chemical that may be emitted from a source (often but not necessarily some sort of industrial plant). Various forms of emission standard exist; the simplest is the so-called Uniform Emissions Standard (UES) which places the same limit on all emissions of a particular product.

**Environmental quality objective**   An environmental quality objective (or EQO) is typically a nonenforceable goal, which specifies a target for environmental quality that, it is hoped, will be met in some particular environment, such as a river, beach, or industrial site. EQOs are generally not set by regulation (unlike "Environmental Quality Standards") and often are cast in the rather vague form of generally desirable objectives, rather than as more concrete quantitative measures.

**Environmental quality standard**   An environmental quality standard is a value, generally defined by regulation, that specifies the maximum permissible concentration of a potentially hazardous chemical in an environmental sample, generally of air or water. (Sometimes also known as an ambient standard.)

**Epidemiology** Epidemiology is a scientific process that attempts to link the effects of factors such as lifestyle (for example, level of smoking or drinking) or exposure to toxic chemicals to disease and, if relevant, mortality. Statistical correlations are developed whose purpose is ultimately to indicate the degree of risk that someone with a particular exposure pattern, lifestyle, or genetic profile has of contracting a specific disease.

**ET50** ET50 is an abbreviation for the exposure time required for a defined effect to be observed among 50 percent of a population when that population is treated with a known amount or concentration of a toxicant.

**Etiologic agents** Microscopic organisms, such as bacteria or viruses, that can cause disease.

**Explosion limits** See **Flammability limits.**

**f/cc** f/cc or fcc is an abbreviation for fibers per cubic centimeter of air. (In crystallography, it is an abbreviation for face-centered cubic.)

**Flammable limits** The flammable limits refer to the conditions under which a mixture of a flammable material and air may catch fire or explode. If the percentage of flammable material in the air is between the minimum and maximum limits, the presence of a flame or a source of ignition is likely to lead to rapid combustion or explosion. Flammable limits for many materials are in the range 2 percent to 10 percent, but for some materials the limits are much wider. Ether, for example, has flammable limits of 1.7 percent to 48 percent, which is an unusually wide range. This, coupled with the low boiling point of ether (34.6°C) and high vapor pressure at room temperature (400 mm Hg at 18°) means that it is easy to create a potentially explosive mixture of ether in air and renders this compound an extreme fire hazard.

**Flashback** Flashback occurs when the flame in a gas torch burns back into the torch or hose; this is often accompanied by a hissing or squealing sound and a pointed or smoky flame.

**Flash point** The flash point of a chemical is the lowest temperature at which a flame will propagate through the vapor of a combustible material to the liquid surface. It is determined by the vapor pressure of the liquid, since only when a sufficiently high vapor concentration is reached can it support combustion. It should be noted that the source of ignition need not be an open flame but could equally be, for example, the surface of a hot plate or a steam pipe.

**Foreign matter** Foreign matter most commonly refers to the presence of unwanted or undesirable material present in foods or chemicals. When used in connection with foods, foreign matter may include packing materials inadvertently (or deliberately) included in the product, plant, or meat products that should have been removed in manufacture or processing; and vermin remains, stones, grit, sand, and so forth. Chemicals may be contaminated by a range of foreign matter, most commonly packing materials, such as glass or polystyrene chips.

**Genotoxic** Genotoxic chemicals are those that are capable of causing damage to DNA. Such damage can potentially lead to the formation of a malignant tumor, but DNA damage does not lead inevitably to the creation of cancerous cells.

**Graded effect** A graded effect is one whose severity is related continuously to dose. Increases in dose rate or exposure level thus have a steadily increasing (sometimes linear) effect upon the severity of symptoms.

**Guinea pig maximization test** The guinea pig maximization test is a widely-used test in the screening of contact allergens for the possibility that they may act as sensitizers in humans.

**Hematopoietic agent** A hematopoietic agent is a chemical that interferes with the blood system by decreasing the oxygen-carrying ability of hemoglobin. This can lead to cyanosis and unconsiousness. Carbon monoxide is one such agent, familiar to smokers.

**Hepatotoxin**   A hepatotoxin is a naturally-produced chemical capable of causing liver damage.

**Highly toxic**   The term *highly toxic* is to some extent imprecise, and exactly how it is defined varies from one regulatory or standards body to another. A typical (and widely-used) definition follows:

Highly toxic—A chemical falling within any of the following categories:

(a) A chemical with a median lethal dose (LD50) of 50 milligrams or less per kilogram of bodyweight when administered orally to albino rats weighing between 200 and 300 grams each.

(b) A chemical with a median lethal dose (LD50) of 200 milligrams or less per kilogram of body weight when administered by continuous contact for 24 hours (or less if death occurs within 24 hours) with the bare skin of albino rabbits weighing between 2 and 3 kilograms each.

(c) A chemical that has a median lethal concentration (LD50) in air of 200 parts per million by volume or less of gas or vapor, or 2 milligrams per liter or less of mist, fume or dust, when administered by continuous inhalation for 1 hour (or less if death occurs within 1 hour) to albino rats weighing between 200 and 300 grams each.

**Hypersensitivity**   See **Allergy.**

**Hypertonic**   A hypertonic solution contains a higher concentration of electrolytes than that found in body cells. If such a solution is allowed to enter the blood stream, the osmotic pressure difference between the blood and the cells will cause water to flow out of the cells, which will then shrink. This may cause serious harm or even be fatal. Consequently, it is essential when blood transfusions are given or blood replacement products are used that the electrolyte concentration in the material to be given to a patient matches that of the body.

**Hypotonic**   A hypotonic solution is one in which the concentration of electrolytes is below that in cells. In this situation, osmotic pressure leads to the migration of water into the cells in an attempt to equalize the electrolyte concentration inside and outside the cell walls. If the difference in concentration is significant, the cell walls may rupture, leading to the death of the cell. Consequently, it is vital that the electrolyte concentration of liquids used during blood transfusions be equal to that in cells.

**Hypoxia**   Hypoxia is a condition defined by a low supply of oxygen.

**Immunotoxic**   An immunotoxic chemical is one that is potentially harmful to the immune system.

**Inhibitor**   An inhibitor is a material that is added to a chemical to prevent an unwanted reaction. For example, 2,6-di-t-butyl-p-cresol may be added to tetrahydrofuran (THF) to prevent potentially dangerous polymerization. Inhibitors are often added to chemicals that tend to undergo self-induced free-radical polymerization.

**Insoluble**   An insoluble material is one that is incapable of dissolving to any significant extent in a specified solvent.

**Intraperitoneal**   Intraperitoneal is the term used when a chemical is contained within or administered through the peritoneum (the thin, transparent membrane that lines the walls of the abdomen). It may be abbreviated IP, IPN, or IPR on safety data sheets.

**Intravenous**   Intravenous indicates the introduction of a material into or through a vein. This is frequently abbreviated IV or IVN in LD50 values quoted on Material Safety Data Sheets.

**In vitro**   An in vitro biological study is one that is carried out in isolation from a living organism.

**In vivo**   An in vivo biological study is one that takes places within a living biological organism.

**Irritant**   An irritant is a chemical that may cause reversible inflammation on contact.

**Ketosis**   Ketosis is an excess of ketones in the body. This can be brought about by exposure to certain types of chemicals.

**LC50** (Lethal Concentration 50) is the concentration of a chemical that kills 50 percent of a sample population. This measure is generally used when exposure to a chemical is through the animal breathing it in, while the LD50 is the measure generally used when exposure is by swallowing, through skin contact, or by injection.

**LD50** (Lethal Dose 50) is the dose of a chemical that kills 50 percent of a sample population. In full reporting, the dose, treatment, and observation period should be given. Further, LD50, LC50, ED50 and similar figures are strictly only comparable when the age, sex, and nutritional state of the animals is specified. Nevertheless, such values are widely reported and used as an effective measure of the potential toxicity of chemicals.

**Level A** Level A is an EPA designation for the highest level of PPE required during an emergency response. This generally includes a totally encapsulated layer of clothing, together with self-contained respiratory equipment.

**Logistic effect** See **Quantal effect.**

**Median lethal concentration** The median lethal concentration is the concentration of a harmful chemical, generally in aqueous solution, that can be expected to cause the death of 50 percent of a specified population of organisms under a defined set of experimental conditions.

**MSDS** MSDS is a very widely used abbreviation for Material Safety Data Sheet. A MSDS contains details of the hazards associated with a chemical and gives information on its safe use.

**Multigeneration study** In a multigeneration study, several generations of animals (usually at least three generations) are exposed to a toxic chemical to test its effect. Exposure is typically continuous, rather than repeated dose.

**Mutagen** A mutagen is an agent that changes the hereditary genetic material that is a part of every living cell. Such a mutation is probably an early step in the sequence of events that ultimately leads to the development of cancer.

**Mutagenic** A mutagenic agent is one that is capable of causing mutations. It may also (but does not necessarily) act as a carcinogen.

**Mutation** A mutation is a heritable change in genetic material—in other words, a change that can potentially be passed from parent to child. This change may occur in a gene or in a chromosome and may take the form of a chemical rearrangement or a partial loss or gain of genetic material.

**Nephrotoxic** See **Nephrotoxin.**

**Nephrotoxin** A nephrotoxin is a naturally produced chemical that may cause kidney damage.

**Neurotoxin** A neurotoxin is a chemical whose primary action is on the CNS (central nervous system). Many neurotoxins are extremely toxic and must only be used under carefully controlled conditions.

**Nuisance material** A nuisance material is one that can cause transient irritation or discomfort but that has no long-term or systemic effects.

**Nystagmus** Nystagmus is an involuntary rapid motion of the eyes. It can be caused by exposure to a variety of chemicals, such as barbiturates, or may be a congenital condition. Any risk that chemical exposure may lead to this condition must be noted clearly on the MSDS.

**Occlusion** Occlusion is the trapping of hazardous material next to the skin. This keeps the material in contact with the skin for long periods of time, increasing the chance that dermal damage will occur.

**Occupational hygiene** Occupational hygiene is an applied science that is concerned with ensuring that standards of health in the workplace are maintained. It deals with the chemical, environmental, and physical factors that may affect the health of workers. The practice of occupational hygiene is increasingly dominated by regulatory standards designed to protect the workplace environment.

**Occupational overuse injuries** See **Repetitive strain injuries.**

**Odor threshold** The odor threshold is the lowest concentration of a vapor in air that can be detected by smell.

**Oxidizing agent** An oxidizing agent may be defined in various ways, depending on the context in which the phrase is used. In broad terms it is often taken to mean a chemical that can act as an electron acceptor.

**Oxygen deficient atmosphere** An oxygen deficient atmosphere is one in which the level of oxygen is below that of normal air, around 19.5 percent.

**Packing group** The packing group for a chemical indicates the degree of hazard associated with its transportation. The highest group is Group I (great danger); Group II is next (medium danger), while Group III chemicals present the lowest hazard (minor danger). Packing groups are often shown on MSDS data sheets for chemicals under the heading "Transport Information."

**Pascal** see **Units of pressure.**

**PEC** See **Predicted Environmental Concentration.**

**Permeability** Permeability is the ability of a chemical to pass through a material, such as a protective glove.

**Permeation rate** The Permeation rate is a measure of the rate at which a chemical will pass through protective material, such as that used for gloves. It is generally specified as the mass of material passing through unit area in unit time. For this value to be meaningful, the thickness of the protective material must also be specified.

**Peroxidizable materials** Peroxidizable materials can form peroxides in storage, generally when in contact with the air. These peroxides present their most serious risk when the peroxide-contaminated material is heated or distilled, but they may also be sensitive to mechanical shock. The quantity of peroxides in a sample may be determined using a simple peroxide test strip.

**Photoallergic contact dermatitis** Photoallergic contact dermatitis is a skin condition brought on by exposure to light following skin contact with certain types of chemicals, such as sulphonamides.

**Physical hazard** A physical hazard arises when use of a chemical is potentially dangerous due, for example, to the possibility of explosion, fire, or violent reaction with water. Peroxides, sulfuric acid, diethyl ether, and phosphorus

pentachloride are examples of materials that present physical hazards. Often, of course, such materials will also present health hazards due to their toxicity.

**Pictographs** Pictographs are widely-used pictorial representations of the hazards presented by chemicals.

**P.O.** Abbreviation for *per os*, meaning oral administration.

**Poison Class A or B** Poison Class A or B poisons are classified by the DOT into two classes. Those in Class A are highly toxic materials that, even in very small quantities, present a hazard to life. Examples are cyanogen, phosgene, and hydrocyanic acid. Class B poisons, though less toxic, are presumed to present a serious threat to health during transportation.

**Potentiation** Potentiation is the enhancement of the action of one chemical by the presence of a second.

**ppb** Parts per billion. Used to specify the concentration (by volume) of a gas or vapor at very low concentration or a dissolved material at high dilution.

**PPE** An abbreviation for personal protective equipment, PPE refers to whatever protective equipment may be used to insulate an individual from the chemical, thermal, explosive, or other hazards presented by the environment in which he or she is working. In most instances, the PPE will comprise such items as safety glasses, laboratory coat, protective shoes, and chemical-resistant gloves.

**ppm** Parts per million. Used to specify the concentration (by volume) of a gas or vapor at low concentration or a dissolved material at high dilution.

**Predicted Environmental Concentration** The Predicted Environmental Concentration is an indication of the expected concentration of a material in the environment, taking into account the amount initially present (or added to) the environment, its distribution, and the probable methods and rates of environmental degradation and removal, either forced or natural.

**Pulmonary** Relating to the lungs.

**PVA** Abbreviation for polyvinyl alcohol. This material has excellent resistance to organic solvents (though is somewhat water-soluble) so is widely used in protective clothing. PVA is a trademark of Ansell Edmont Co.

**Pyrophoric materials** Pyrophoric materials ignite spontaneously in air. Since a wide variety of chemicals will burn if heated sufficiently, it is usual to define a pyrophoric material as one that will ignite spontaneously at temperatures below about 45°C.

**QSAR** See **Structure-activity relationship.**

**Quantal effect** A quantal effect is one for which there are only two possible outcomes; the effect thus occurs or does not. In the field of safety, the context in which the term quantal effect is most widely used (and the most dramatic) is death.

**Quantitative structure-activity relationship** See **Structure-activity relationship.**

**REACH** Acronym for Registration, Evaluation, and Authorization of Chemicals. This is a new system to regulate chemical use in the EU, which will replace a large quantity of existing legislation and place controls on some chemicals that are not currently covered by regulation. As of summer 2003 this is a proposal, but it seems clear that new regulations will be promulgated in due course. The effect of the legislation will be to force companies to show that the chemicals they produce are safe for humans and for the environment.

**Recommended limit** For chemicals which are believed to be toxic, a recommended limit is often specified. This is the maximum quantity or concentration that is believed to be safe. It may be backed up by regulation or simply be an advisory limit.

**Reducing agent** A reducing agent may be defined in various ways, depending on the context in which the phrase is used. In broad terms it is often taken to mean a chemical which can act as an electron donor.

**Renal** The term *renal* describes an effect or process that relates to the kidneys.

**Repetitive strain injury** The term *repetitive strain injury (RSI)* refers to a wide range of musculoskeletal injuries, such as carpal tunnel syndrome, bursitis, or tendonitis. Such injuries are often also referred to as *work-related upper limb disorders, occupational overuse injuries*, or *cumulative trauma disorders*, but there is no suggestion that such problems can arise only in the workplace—they can equally well arise through activities performed in the home. RSI has become much more prominent with the rapid rise in computer use, which has resulted in many people complaining of hand, neck, and arm problems. However, other activities, such as repetitive use of a pipette or the playing of a musical instrument may also give rise to symptoms. RSI is potentially a very serious problem, and employers are under a legal obligation to minimize the risk of employees developing RSI.

**Reproductive toxin** A reproductive toxin is a naturally produced chemical that may cause birth defects or sterility.

**Respirable dust** Respirable dust is airborne material that is capable of penetrating to the gas-exchange region of the lungs.

**Rodenticide** A rodenticide is a term applied to any chemical used to kill rodents.

**Routes of entry** The routes of entry are the ways in which a toxic chemical can enter the body. Chemicals are easily swallowed or inhaled, and many chemicals are readily absorbed through the skin upon contact. The fourth route of entry is deliberate or accidental injection of the chemical under the skin through use of a hypodermic or as a result of an accident.

**RSI** See **Repetitive strain injury.**

**SAR** See **Structure-activity relationship.**

**SCBA** Abbreviation for self-contained breathing apparatus. Such an apparatus consists of a suitable face mask, combined with a hose and source of fresh air, generally in the form of a tank of compressed air. The SCBA may be incorporated into a full-body protection suit. It is important to recognize that use of a SCBA is not trivial, and they are not designed to be worn by those without training.

**Sensitizer**   A sensitizer is a chemical that may lead to the development of allergic reactions after repeated exposure.

**Short-term exposure limit** (STEL) This is the maximum permissible concentration of a material, generally expressed in ppm in air, for a defined short period of time (typically 5 or 15 minutes, depending upon the country). This "concentration" is generally a time-weighted average over the period of exposure. These values, which may differ from country to country, are often backed up by regulation and therefore may be legally enforceable.

**Stochastic**   A phenomenon is stochastic (random) in nature if it obeys the laws of probability.

**Structure-activity relationship**   The structure-activity relationship (SAR) is a means by which the effect of a drug or toxic chemical on an animal, plant, or the environment can be related to its molecular structure. This type of relationship may be assessed by considering a series of molecules and making gradual changes to them, noting the effect upon their biological activity of each change. Alternatively, it may be possible to assess a large body of toxicity data using intelligent tools such as neural networks to try to establish a relationship.

**Subacute toxicity**   See **Toxicity.**

**Subcutaneous**   *Subcutaneous* means below the skin. The subcutaneous toxicity of a chemical is important if the chemical is injected (deliberately or accidentally) or is forced through the skin by injury.

**Surfactant**   A surfactant lowers the surface tension of a liquid. Soaps and some components of detergents are typical surfactants.

**Synergistic effect**   It is not uncommon for the effect of two chemicals on an organism to be greater than the effect of each chemical individually or the sum of the individual effects. The presence of one chemical enhances the effects of the second. This is called a synergistic effect or synergy, and the chemicals are sometimes described as showing synergism.

**Synergy**   See **Synergistic effect.**

**Systemic poison**   Systemic poisons have an effect that is remote from the site of entry into the body.

**TDI**   See **Tolerable Daily Intake.**

**Teflon**   Teflon is a polymer that is widely used in safety clothing because of its excellent resistance to chemicals and heat. However, it has poor mechanical properties, so is generally combined with other materials to provide the required mechanical durability.

**Temperature rating**   The temperature rating is a measure of the highest (or occasionally lowest) temperature at which it is safe to use a product for a particular purpose. For example, temperature ratings are often quoted for electrical insulators, specifying the maximum temperature at which they provide adequate protection against electrical breakdown.

**Temporary safe reference action level**   The temporary safe reference action level of a potentially hazardous chemical is the maximum inhalation level at which, over a short period of time, the chemical is supposed not to present a significant hazard. The level of the chemical in the environment should nevertheless be reduced as rapidly as possible by improvements in ventilation, for example, or ameliorated through the use of suitable protection, such as breathing apparatus.

**Teratogen**   A teratogen is a chemical that may cause nonheritable genetic mutations or malformations in the developing foetus.

**Teratogenesis**   Teratogenesis is the production of nonheritable reproductive defects.

**TLV**   TLV (Threshold Limit Value) is the maximum permissible concentration of a material, generally expressed in parts per million in air for some defined period of time (often 8 hours, but sometimes for 40 hours per week over an assumed working lifetime). These values, which may differ from country to country, are often backed up by regulation and therefore may be legally enforceable.

**TLV-C**  TLV-C ceiling exposure limit; an exposure limit that should not be exceeded under any circumstances.

**Tolerable Daily Intake**  The Tolerable Daily Intake (TDI) is an estimate of the quantity of a chemical contaminant in food or water that can be ingested daily over a lifetime without posing a significant risk to health. "Contaminants" are different from "residues" in this context a contaminant is a chemical whose presence in food or water does not serve, and never has served, any useful purpose. TDIs are thus distinct from ADIs (the Acceptable Daily Intake), which relate to residues of chemicals that have been deliberately added to a product (for example, residues of pesticide sprays or antifungal agents).

**Tolerance**  Tolerance is the ability of an animal or plant to withstand single or repeated doses of a potentially harmful chemical without adverse effect.

**Torr**  See **Units of pressure.**

**Toxicant**  *Toxicant* is a comparatively rarely used term that describes any material that is potentially toxic.

**Toxicity**  The term *toxicity* is very widely used in a safety context, for obvious reasons. It is used in two contrasting senses: to denote the capacity to cause harm to a living organism and to indicate the adverse effects caused by a chemical. The degree of harm caused to an organism by exposure to a toxic chemical generally increases with exposure level but is also dependent upon the type of organism, the length of exposure, the physiological status of the organism (essentially its fitness) and its developmental stage. For example, some toxic chemicals have a more serious effect upon a developing fetus than upon an adult organism. Toxicity is often subdivided into:

- **Acute toxicity**  Adverse effects are observed within a short time of exposure to the chemical.

This exposure may be a single dose, or a short continuous exposure, or multiple doses administered over 24 hours or less.

- **Subacute (subchronic) toxicity**  Adverse effects are observed following repeated daily exposure to a chemical, or exposure for a significant part of an organism's lifespan (usually not exceeding 10 percent). With experimental animals, the period of exposure may range from a few days to 6 months.

- **Chronic toxicity**  Adverse effects are observed following repeated exposure to a chemical during a substantial fraction of an organism's lifespan (usually more than 50 percent). For humans, chronic exposure typically means several decades; for experimental animals, it is typically more than 3 months. Chronic exposure to chemicals over periods of 2 years using rats or mice may be used to assess the carcinogenic potential of chemicals.

**Trohoc**  Trohoc is a type of epidemiological study in which one identifies certain outcomes and then looks for possible causes. This backwards design has lead to the coining of the term trohoc (cohort spelled backwards).

**TSCA**  Toxic Substances Control Act. This regulates the manufacture, transport, and use of toxic substances.

**TSRAL**  See **Temporary safe reference action level.**

**Tumorigenic**  Tumorigenic is a description that can be applied to any material or phenomenon (a chemical, a radiochemical, radiation, etc.) capable of generating tumors.

**TWA**  (Time Weighted Average) This term is used in the specification of Occupational Exposure Limits (OELs) to define the average concentration of a chemical to which it is permissible to expose a worker over a period of time, typically 8 hours.

**Uniform emission standard**  See **Emission standard.**

**Units of pressure**  Units of pressure are often somewhat confusing, because of the different systems in use. A Torr (named after Torricelli) is the pressure produced by a column of mercury 1 mm high, so it equals 1/760th of an atmosphere. The Pascal is now widely used. This is the S.I. unit, and equals a force of one Newton per square meter (in turn, a Newton is the force required to give a 1 kilogram mass an acceleration of 1 meter per second). The Pascal is quite a small pressure, so we often use KiloPascals (kPa), equal to one thousand Pascals. 101.325 kPa equals one atmosphere. Pounds per square inch (psi) used to be common in the UK but has now been supplanted in virtually every country other than the United States by the S.I. unit. One atmosphere is approximately 15 psi.

**VDU**   See **Display screen equipment.**

**Vesicant**   A vesicant is a chemical that, if it can escape from the vein, causes extensive tissue damage, with vesicle formation or blistering.

**Very toxic**   The designation of a chemical as being very toxic is to some extent arbitrary. It is most commonly applied to chemicals whose ORL-RAT LD50 value is <25 mg kg$^{-1}$, but this should be taken as providing guidance only.

**Viton**   Viton is a hexafluoropropylene-vinylidene fluoride co-polymer that is widely used in protective clothing. Viton is a trademark of the DuPont Company.

**VOCs**   Volatile organic compounds.

**Work-related upper limb disorder**   See **Repetitive strain injury.**

**WULD**   See **Repetitive strain injury.**

**Xenobiotic**   A xenobiotic is a chemical (or, more generally, a chemical mix) that is not a normal component of the organism that is exposed to it. Xenbiotics, therefore, include most drugs (other than those compounds that naturally occur in the organism), as well as other foreign substances.

*Sources*:

1. The Physical and Theoretical Chemistry Laboratory, Oxford University, England
2. Chemical Safety Information—Glossary
3. http://physchem.ox.ac.uk/MSDS/glossary.html

## RADIOLOGICAL/NUCLEAR

**Absolute risk**   The proportion of a population expected to get a disease over a specified time period.

**Absorbed dose**   The amount of energy deposited by ionizing radiation in a unit mass of tissue. It is expressed in units of joule per kilogram (J/kg), and called "gray" (Gy).

**Activity (radioactivity)**   The rate of decay of radioactive material expressed as the number of atoms breaking down per second measured in units called becquerels or curies.

**Acute exposure**   An exposure to radiation that occurred in a matter of minutes rather than in longer, continuing exposure over a period of time.

**Acute radiation syndrome (ARS)**   A serious illness caused by receiving a dose greater than 50 rads of penetrating radiation to the body in a short time (usually minutes). The earliest symptoms are nausea, fatigue, vomiting, and diarrhea. Hair loss, bleeding, swelling of the mouth and throat, and general loss of energy may follow. If the exposure has been approximately 1,000 rads or more, death may occur within 2 to 4 weeks.

**Air burst**   A nuclear weapon explosion that is high enough in the air to keep the fireball from touching the ground. Because the fireball does not reach the ground and does not pick up any surface material, the radioactivity in the fallout from an airburst is relatively insignificant compared with a surface burst.

**Alpha particle**   The nucleus of a helium atom, made up of two neutrons and two protons with a charge of +2. Certain radioactive nuclei emit alpha particles. Alpha particles generally carry more energy than gamma or beta particles and deposit that energy very quickly while passing through tissue. Alpha particles can be stopped by a thin layer of light material, such as a sheet of paper, and cannot penetrate the outer, dead layer of skin. Therefore they do not damage living tissue when outside the body. When alpha-emitting atoms are inhaled or swallowed, however, they are especially damaging because they transfer relatively large amounts of ionizing energy to living cells.

**Americium (Am)**   A silvery metal, it is a man-made element whose isotopes Am-237 through Am-246 are all radioactive. Am-241 is formed spontaneously by the beta decay of plutonium-241. Trace quantities of americium are widely used in smoke detectors and as neutron sources in neutron moisture gauges.

**Background radiation**   Ionizing radiation from natural sources, such as terrestrial radiation due to radionuclides in the soil or cosmic radiation originating in outer space.

**Becquerel (Bq)**   The amount of a radioactive material that will undergo one decay (disintegration) per second.

**Carcinogen**   A cancer-causing substance.

**Chain reaction**   A process that initiates its own repetition. In a fission chain reaction, a fissile nucleus absorbs a neutron and fissions (splits) spontaneously, releasing additional neutrons. These, in turn, can be absorbed by other fissile nuclei, releasing still more neutrons. A fission chain reaction is self-sustaining when the number of neutrons released in a given time equals or exceeds the number of neutrons lost by absorption in nonfissile material or by escape from the system.

**Chronic exposure**   Exposure to a substance over a long period of time, possibly resulting in adverse health effects.

**Cobalt (Co)**   A gray, hard, magnetic, and somewhat malleable metal, cobalt is relatively rare and generally obtained as a by-product of other metals, such as copper. Its most common radioisotope, cobalt-60 (Co-60), is used in radiography and medical applications. Cobalt-60 emits beta particles and gamma rays during radioactive decay.

**Collective dose**   The estimated dose for an area or region multiplied by the estimated population in that area or region.

**Committed dose**   A dose that accounts for continuing exposures expected to be received over a long period of time (such as 30, 50, or 70 years) from radioactive materials that were deposited inside the body.

**Conference of Radiation Control Program Directors (CRCPD)**   An organization whose members represent state radiation protection programs.

**Contamination (radioactive)**   The deposition of unwanted radioactive material on the surfaces of structures, areas, objects, or people where it may be external or internal.

**Criticality**   A fission process in which the neutron production rate equals the neutron loss rate to absorption or leakage. A nuclear reactor is "critical" when it is operating.

**Cumulative dose**   The total dose resulting from repeated or continuous exposures of the same portion of the body, or of the whole body, to ionizing radiation.

**Curie (Ci)**   The traditional measure of radioactivity based on the observed decay rate of 1 gram of radium. One curie of radioactive material will have 37 billion disintegrations in 1 second.

**Cutaneous radiation syndrome (CRS)**   The complex syndrome resulting from radiation exposure of more than 200 rads to the skin. The immediate effects can be reddening and swelling of the exposed area (like a severe burn), blisters, ulcers on the skin, hair loss, and severe pain. Very large doses can result in permanent hair loss, scarring, altered skin color, deterioration of the affected body part, and death of the affected tissue (requiring surgery).

**Decontamination**   The reduction or removal of radioactive contamination from a structure, object, or person.

**Depleted uranium**   Uranium containing less than 0.7% uranium-235, the amount found in natural uranium.

**Deposition density**   The activity of a radionuclide per unit area of ground. Reported as becquerels per square meter or curies per square meter.

**Deterministic effects**   Effects that can be related directly to the radiation dose received. The severity increases as the dose increases. A deterministic effect typically has a threshold below which the effect will not occur.

**Deuterium** A nonradioactive isotope of the hydrogen atom that contains a neutron in its nucleus in addition to the one proton normally seen in hydrogen. A deuterium atom is twice as heavy as normal hydrogen.

**Dirty bomb** A device designed to spread radioactive material by conventional explosives when the bomb explodes. A dirty bomb kills or injures people through the initial blast of the conventional explosive and spreads radioactive contamination over possibly a large area—hence the term "dirty." Such bombs could be miniature devices or large truck bombs. A dirty bomb is much simpler to make than a true nuclear weapon.

**Dose (radiation)** Radiation absorbed by person's body. Several different terms describe radiation dose.

**Dosimeter** A small portable instrument (such as a film badge, thermoluminescent dosimeter [TLD], or pocket dosimeter) for measuring and recording the total accumulated dose of ionizing radiation a person receives.

**Enriched uranium** Uranium in which the proportion of the isotope uranium-235 has been increased by removing uranium-238 mechanically.

**Epidemiology** The study of the distribution and determinants of health-related states or events in specified populations and the application of this study to the control of health problems.

**Exposure (radiation)** A measure of ionization in air caused by X-rays or gamma rays only. The unit of exposure most often used is the roentgen.

**Fallout, nuclear** Minute particles of radioactive debris that descend slowly from the atmosphere after a nuclear explosion.

**Fissile material** Any material in which neutrons can cause a fission reaction. The three primary fissile materials are uranium-233, uranium-235, and plutonium-239.

**Fission (fissioning)** The splitting of a nucleus into at least two other nuclei that releases a large amount of energy. Two or three neutrons are usually released during this transformation.

**Fusion** A reaction in which at least one heavier, more stable nucleus is produced from two lighter, less stable nuclei. Reactions of this type are responsible for the release of energy in stars or in thermonuclear weapons.

**Gamma rays** High-energy electromagnetic radiation emitted by certain radionuclides when their nuclei transition from a higher to a lower energy state. These rays have high energy and a short wave length. All gamma rays emitted from a given isotope have the same energy, a characteristic that enables scientists to identify which gamma emitters are present in a sample. Gamma rays penetrate tissue farther than do beta or alpha particles but leave a lower concentration of ions in their path to potentially cause cell damage. Gamma rays are very similar to X-rays.

**Gray (Gy)** A unit of measurement for absorbed dose. It measures the amount of energy absorbed in a material. The unit Gy can be used for any type of radiation, but it does not describe the biological effects of the different radiations.

**High-level radioactive waste** The radioactive material resulting from spent nuclear fuel reprocessing. This can include liquid waste directly produced in reprocessing or any solid material derived from the liquid wastes having a sufficient concentration of fission products. Other radioactive materials can be designated as high-level waste, if they require permanent isolation. This determination is made by the U.S. Nuclear Regulatory Commission on the basis of criteria established in U.S. law.

**Hot spot** Any place where the level of radioactive contamination is considerably greater than the area around it.

**Ingestion** (1) The act of swallowing; (2) in the case of radionuclides or chemicals, swallowing radionuclides or chemicals by eating or drinking.

**Inhalation** (1) The act of breathing in; (2) in the case of radionuclides or chemicals, breathing in radionuclides or chemicals.

**Internal exposure**  Exposure to radioactive material taken into the body.

**Iodine**  A nonmetallic solid element. There are both radioactive and nonradioactive isotopes of iodine. Radioactive isotopes of iodine are widely used in medical applications. Radioactive iodine is a fission product and is the largest contributor to people's radiation dose after an accident at a nuclear reactor.

**Isotope**  A nuclide of an element having the same number of protons but a different number of neutrons.

**Kiloton (Kt)**  The energy of an explosion that is equivalent to an explosion of 1,000 tons of TNT. One kiloton equals 1 trillion (1,012) calories.

**Lead (Pb)**  A heavy metal. Several isotopes of lead, such as Pb-210, which emits beta radiation, are in the uranium decay chain.

**Low-level waste (LLW)**  Radioactively contaminated industrial or research waste such as paper, rags, plastic bags, medical waste, and water-treatment residues. It is waste that does not meet the criteria for any of three other categories of radioactive waste spent nuclear fuel and high-level radioactive waste; transuranic radioactive waste; or uranium mill tailings. Its categorization does not depend on the level of radioactivity it contains.

**Megaton (Mt)**  The energy of an explosion that is equivalent to an explosion of 1 million tons of TNT. One megaton is equal to a quintillion (1,018) calories.

**Nuclear energy**  The heat energy produced by the process of nuclear fission within a nuclear reactor or by radioactive decay.

**Penetrating radiation**  Radiation that can penetrate the skin and reach internal organs and tissues. Photons (gamma rays and X-rays), neutrons, and protons are penetrating radiations. However, alpha particles and all but extremely high-energy beta particles are not considered penetrating radiation.

**Pitchblende**  A brown to black mineral that has a distinctive luster. It consists mainly of urananite (UO2) but also contains radium (Ra). It is the main source of uranium (U) ore.

**Plume**  The material spreading from a particular source and traveling through environmental media, such as air or groundwater. For example, a plume could describe the dispersal of particles, gases, vapors, and aerosols in the atmosphere or the movement of contamination through an aquifer (for example, dilution, mixing, or adsorption onto soil).

**Plutonium (Pu)**  A heavy, man-made, radioactive metallic element. The most important isotope is Pu-239, which has a half-life of 24,000 years. Pu-239 can be used in reactor fuel and is the primary isotope in weapons. One kilogram is equivalent to about 22 million kilowatt-hours of heat energy. The complete detonation of a kilogram of plutonium produces an explosion equal to about 20,000 tons of chemical explosive. All isotopes of plutonium are readily absorbed by the bones and can be lethal depending on the dose and exposure time.

**Polonium (Po)**  A radioactive chemical element and a product of radium (Ra) decay. Polonium is found in uranium (U) ores.

**Radiation**  Energy moving in the form of particles or waves. Familiar radiations are heat, light, radio waves, and microwaves. Ionizing radiation is a very high-energy form of electromagnetic radiation.

**Radioactive contamination**  The deposition of unwanted radioactive material on the surfaces of structures, areas, objects, or people. It can be airborne, external, or internal.

**Radioactive decay**  The spontaneous disintegration of the nucleus of an atom.

**Radioactive material**  Material that contains unstable (radioactive) atoms that give off radiation as they decay.

**Radiological dispersal device (RDD)**  A device that disperses radioactive material by conventional explosive or other mechanical means, such as a spray.

**Radium (Ra)**  A naturally occurring radioactive metal. Radium is a radionuclide formed by the decay of uranium (U) and thorium (Th) in the environment. It occurs at low levels in virtually all rock, soil, water, plants, and animals. Radon (Rn) is a decay product of radium.

**Radon (Rn)**   A naturally occurring radioactive gas found in soils, rock, and water throughout the United States. Radon causes lung cancer and is a threat to health because it tends to collect in homes, sometimes to very high concentrations. As a result, radon is the largest source of exposure to people from naturally occurring radiation.

**Rem (roentgen equivalent, man)**   A unit of equivalent dose. Not all radiation has the same biological effect, even for the same amount of absorbed dose. Rem relates the absorbed dose in human tissue to the effective biological damage of the radiation. It is determined by multiplying the number of rads by the quality factor, a number reflecting the potential damage caused by the particular type of radiation. The rem is the traditional unit of equivalent dose, but it is being replaced by the sievert (Sv), which is equal to 100 rem.

**Roentgen (R)**   A unit of exposure to X-rays or gamma rays. One roentgen is the amount of gamma or X-rays needed to produce ions carrying 1 electrostatic unit of electrical charge in 1 cubic centimeter of dry air under standard conditions.

**Shielding**   The material between a radiation source and a potentially exposed person that reduces exposure.

**Sievert (Sv)**   A unit used to derive a quantity called *dose equivalent*. This relates the absorbed dose in human tissue to the effective biological damage of the radiation. Not all radiation has the same biological effect, even for the same amount of absorbed dose. Dose equivalent is often expressed as millionths of a sievert, or micro-sieverts ($\mu$Sv). One sievert is equivalent to 100 rem.

**Somatic effects**   Effects of radiation that are limited to the exposed person, as distinguished from genetic effects, which may also affect subsequent generations.

**Strontium (Sr)**   A silvery, soft metal that rapidly turns yellow in air. Sr-90 is one of the radioactive fission materials created within a nuclear reactor during its operation. Stronium-90 emits beta particles during radioactive decay.

**Surface burst**   A nuclear weapon explosion that is close enough to the ground for the radius of the fireball to vaporize surface material. Fallout from a surface burst contains very high levels of radioactivity.

**Tailings**   Waste rock from mining operations that contains concentrations of mineral ore that are too low to make typical extraction methods economical.

**Thermonuclear device**   A "hydrogen bomb." A device with explosive energy that comes from fusion of small nuclei, as well as fission.

**Thorium (Th)**   A naturally occurring radioactive metal found in small amounts in soil, rocks, water, plants, and animals. The most common isotopes of thorium are thorium-232 (Th-232), thorium-230 (Th-230), and thorium-238 (Th-238).

**Tritium (chemical symbol H-3)**   A radioactive isotope of the element hydrogen (chemical symbol H).

**Uranium (U)**   A naturally occurring radioactive element whose principal isotopes are uranium-238 (U-238) and uranium-235 (U-235). Natural uranium is a hard, silvery-white, shiny metallic ore that contains a minute amount of uranium-234 (U-234).

*Source*:

1.  Centers for Disease Control and Prevention
    http://cdc.gov

# References

Altheide, David L. 2002. *Creating Fear: News and the Construction of Crisis*. New York: Aldine de Gruyter.

Ansell, Jake, and Frank Wharton. 1992. *Risk: Analysis, Assessment, and Management*. Chichester: John Wiley & Sons.

Atwater, Brian F., Marco Cisternas V., Joanne Bourgeois, Walter C. Dudley, James W. Hendley II, and Peter H. Stauffer. 1999. *Surviving a Tsunami: Lessons learned from Chile, Hawaii, and Japan*. Washington, DC: USGS Information Services.

Baldwin, Thomas E. 2003. *Historical Chronology of FEMA Consequence Management Preparedness and Response to Terrorism*. Argonne, Illinois: Argonne National Laboratory.

Blanchard, Wayne. 2001. "The Emergency Manager." *IAEM Bulletin* (May).

Bohn, Kevin. 2003. "ACLU Files Lawsuit Against Patriot Act." *CNN* (July 30).

Bremer, Ambassador L., and Paul Bremer III. 2002. "The Terrorist Threat." In *Terrorism: Informing the Public*, edited by Nancy Ethiel. Chicago: McCormick Tribune Foundation.

Brookings Institution. 2003. "Protecting the American Homeland: One Year On." Washington, DC. January.

Brookings Institution. 2002. "Homeland Security: The White House Plan Explained and Examined." *A Brookings Forum* (September 4).

Brown, Jane D., and Sarah N. Keller. 2000. "Can the Mass Media Be Healthy Sex Educators?" *Family Planning Perspectives*. vol. 32. no. 5. pp. 255–256.

Brunker, Mike. 2002. "Sea Change for the Coast Guard." MSNBC (December 19).

Bullock, Jane. 2003. Several interviews over a two-month period with the FEMA Chief of Staff (Fmr.) Washington, DC. Unpublished Damon Coppola Intexvelnee.

Burkeman, Oliver. 2003. "U.S. to Fit Airliners with Anti-Missile Defenses." *The Guardian* (September 19).

Burkhart, Ford N. 1991. *Media, Emergency Warnings, and Citizen Response*. Boulder, Colorado: Westview Press.

Center for Defense Information. 2002. "Terror Alerts: The Homeland Security Advisory." September 1. <http://www.govexec.com/features/0902/0902s4.htm>

Central Intelligence Agency. 2002. "Terrorism: Guide to Chemical, Biological, Radiological and Nuclear Weapons Indicators." November.

Chabrow, Eric. 2003. "Share and Share Alike: Government Agencies Struggle to Overcome the Many Barriers to Collaboration." *Information Week* (September 1).

Cheng, Mae M. 2003. "Homeland Department May Contract Out Jobs." *Newsday* (September 14).

Citizen Corps web site <www.citizencorps.gov>

The City of Oklahoma. 1996. *Alfred P. Murrah Federal Building Bombing April 19, 1995*. Stillwater, Oklahoma: Fire Protection Publications. Oklahoma State University.

CNCS. 2003. "President Calls for More Americorps and Senior Corps Volunteers in 2004 Budget" (February 3). <http://www.nationalservice.org/news/pr/020303.html>

CNCS. 2002. "White House and CNCS Announce New Grants to Involve Volunteers in Homeland Security" (July 18). <http://www.nationalservice.org/news/pr/071802.html>

Cohen, Bernard C. 1963. *The Press and Foreign Policy*. Princeton, New Jersey: Princeton University Press.

*Columbus Dispatch*. 2003. "Security Risks in the Air." Editorial. (September 19).

Cook, David T. 2003. "Tom Ridge." *Christian Science Monitor* (September 15).

Coppola, Damon P. 2003. *Annotated Organizational Chart for the Department of Homeland Security*. Washington, DC: Bullock & Haddow, LLC.

Davis, Lance. 2003. "City Officials Respond to Orange Alert." *The National League of Cities* (February 17).

Department of Homeland Security (DHS). 2003. Ready.Gov web site. Washington, DC: DHS. <http://www.ready.gov>

Department of Homeland Security web site <http://www.dhs.gov>

Department of Homeland Security. 2003. "2004 Budget in Brief." <http://www.dhs.gov/interweb/assetlibrary/FY_2004_BUDGET_IN_BRIEF.pdf>

Department of Homeland Security. 2003. The National Strategy for the Protection of Physical Infrastructure and Key Assets, pp. 39–40. <www.dhs.gov>.

Department of Homeland Security. 2002. "The Department of Homeland Security" (June). <http://www.dhs.gov/interweb/assetlibrary/book.pdf>

Diamond, John, et al. 2003. "6 Fronts of the War on Terrorism." *USA Today* (September 11).

Disaster Management Center. 1995. *Disaster Preparedness.* Madison, Wisconsin: The University of Wisconsin. <http://dmc.engr.wisc.edu/courses/preparedness/BB04-intro.html>

Edmonson, R.G. 2003. "Blurring of the Lines." *Journal of Commerce* (August 11), p. 12.

Enders, Jessica. 2001. "Measuring Community Awareness and Preparedness for Emergencies." *Australian Journal of Emergency Management* (Spring), pp. 52–59.

Etzioni, Amitai. 2003. "Our Unfinished Post-9/11 Duty." *Christian Science Monitor* (September 11), p. 9.

Federal Emergency Management Agency. 2003. *A Nation Remembers, A Nation Mourns* (September). Washington, DC. FEMA.

Federal Emergency Management Agency. 2002. *Managing the Emergency Consequences of Terrorist Incidents—Interim Planning Guide for State and Local Government.* Washington, DC: FEMA.

Federal Emergency Management Agency. 2002. "Allbaugh Announces Citizen Corps' First Official Affiliate Program During National Fire Prevention Week" (October 10). FEMA Press Release.

Federal Emergency Management Agency. 2001. *Delivery of Individual Assistance Programs.* New York: FEMA, Office of Inspector General (September).

Federal Emergency Management Agency (FEMA). 1998. "Making Your Community Disaster Resistant: Project Impact Media Partnership Guide." Washington, DC: FEMA.

Federal Emergency Management Agency (FEMA). 1997. *Multi Hazard: Identification and Assessment.* Washington, DC: FEMA.

FFIS. 2003. "Federal Actions Affecting States." Federal Funds Information for States web site (February 14). <www.ffis.org/misc/sum.htm>

FindLaw. 2002. "Homeland Security Act of 2002" (November 19). <http://news.findlaw.com/wp/docs/terrorism/hsa2002.pdf>

Fitzpatrick, Dan. 2003. "Sounding the Alarm—Again." *Pittsburgh Post Gazette* (September 9). p. C12.

Foster. 2003. "Leave This Patriot Alone." *Milwaukee Journal Sentinel* (September 17) p.14A.

Furedi, Frank. 1997. *Culture of Fear: Risk-Taking and the Morality of Low Expectation.* London: Cassell.

Furman, Matt. 2002. "Good Information Saves Lives." In *Terrorism: Informing the Public,* edited by Nancy Ethiel. Chicago: McCormick Tribune Foundation.

Fusco, Anthony L. 1993. "The World Trade Center Bombing: Report and Analysis." U.S. Fire Administration. Washington, DC.

Gay, Lance. 2001. "How the New Antiterrorism Bill Could Affect You." *Scripps Howard News Service* (October 26).

Gedan, Benjamin. 2003. "Local Safety Officials Feel Unprepared Post September 11th Survey Suggests Funds Are Issue." *Boston Globe* (August 29) p. B2.

Ghent, Bill. 2003. "Senate Dems fault Bush over Homeland Security Funds." *Government Executive Magazine* (February 13).

Ghent, Bill. 2003. "White House Threatens Veto as Omnibus Deal Nears Hill." *Government Executive Magazine* (February 5).

Glassner, Barry. 1999. *The Culture of Fear.* New York: Basic Books.

Haddow, George. 2003. Several interviews over a two-month period with the FEMA Deputy Chief of Staff (Fmr.) Washington, DC. Damon Coppola.

Hall, Mimi. 2003. "Tracking of Foreign Visitors Hits Snags." *USA Today* (September 22) p. 1A.

Hall, Mimi. 2003. "Terrorist Risk Lists Leave Gap, Even Now." *USA Today* (August 11) p. 1A.

Hendrix, Anastasia. 2003. "Rights Group Slams Homeland Security Tactics." *San Francisco Chronicle* (May 29) p. A16.

Hughes, Amy C. 2003. "Summit tackles tough issues." *State Government News.* The Council of State Governments (August).

Hulse, Carl. 2003. "Congress Advances $29.4 Billion Plan for Security Agency." *New York Times* (September 18) p. A25.

Jones, Elise F., James R. Beniger, and Charles F. Westoff. 1980. "Pill and IUD Discontinuation in the United States, 1970–1975: The Influence of the Media." *Family Planning Perspectives.* vol. 12. no. 6. pp. 293–300.

Kaplan, Stan. 1997. "The Words of Risk Analysis." *Risk Analysis.* vol. 17 no. 4, p. 408.

Kayyem, N. Juliette, Chang E. Patricia. 2002. *Beyond Business Continuity: The Role of the Private Sector in Preparedness Planning.* pp. 3–4, August 2002 Business Continuity Institute.

Lebihan, Rachel. 2003. "Balancing Security and Privacy." *Australian Financial Review* (September 12) p. 64.

Lichtblau, Eric. 2003. "Administration Creates Center for Master Terror 'Watch List'." *New York Times* (September 17) p. A20.

Lumpkin, John J. 2003. "Bush Seeks $41.3B for Homeland Security." Newsday.com (January 31).

Marks, Alexandra. 2003. "With 9/11 More Distant, Alertness Wavers." *Christian Science Monitor* (August 5) p. 3.

Martin, Gary. 2003. "Homeland Defense Mission May Take Decades." *San Antonio Express News* (September 7) p. A12.

McCallum, D. B., S. L. Hammond, and L. Morris. 1990. *Public Knowledge of Chemical Risks in Six Communities.* Washington, DC: Georgetown University Medical Center, Institute for Health Policy Analysis.

McCombs, M., and D. Shaw. 1972. "The Agenda-Setting Function of Mass Media." *Public Opinion Quarterly.* vol. 36. pp. 176–187.

McCormick Tribune Foundation. 2002. "Terrorism: Informing the Public." In *Cantigny Conference Series*, edited by Nancy Ethiel. Chicago: McCormick Tribune Foundation.

McDivitt, Judith A., Susan Zimicki, Robert Hornik, and Ayman Abulaban. 1993. "The Impact of the Healthcom Mass Media Campaign on Timely Initiation of Breastfeeding in Jordan." *Studies in Family Planning.* vol. 24. no 5. pp. 295–309.

McGreevy, Patrick. 2003. "Security Aid Falls Short, Mayors Say." *Los Angeles Times* (September 18) Part 2, p. 3.

Means, Marianne. 2003. "Homeland Security; Desk Shuffling Is Not Enough." *San Diego Union Tribune* (September 7) p. G1.

Mehren, Elizabeth. 2003. "Latest Trend in Academia: Security." *Los Angeles Times* (September 14) p. 34.

Mileti, Dennis S. 1999. *Disasters by Design.* Washington, DC: Joseph Henry Press.

Miller, Judith. 2002. "Who? How? When? What? Where?" In *Terrorism: Informing the Public*, edited by Nancy Ethiel. Chicago: McCormick Tribune Foundation.

Mintz, John. 2003. "Government's Hobbled Giant; Homeland Security Is Struggling." *Washington Post* (September 7) p. A1.

Moretti, M. Mindy. 2003. "Homeland Security Task Force Presses Congress to Act." *NACo County News* (January 27).

Morgan, M. Granger, Baruch Fischoff, Ann Bostrom, and Cynthia J Atman. 2002. *Risk Communication: A Mental Models Approach.* Cambridge: Cambridge University Press.

Moritz, Owen. 2003. "Ferry Frisk in Riders' Future?" *Daily News* (July 2) p. 25.

Moscoso, Eunice. 2003. "Cities Await Security Funds." *Atlanta Journal and Constitution* (September 18) p. 8A.

Moscoso, Eunice. 2003. "September 11, Two Years Later." *Atlanta Journal and Constitution* (September 10) p. 6A.

Mullis, John-Paul. 1998. "Persuasive Communication Issues in Disaster Management." *Australian Journal of Emergency Management* (Autumn) pp. 51–58.

National Association of Counties. 2003. "Policy Agency to Secure the People of America's Counties." NACo home-page. <http://www.naco.org/programs/homesecurity/homelandpolicy.pdf>

National Governors Association. 2002. "States' Homeland Security Priorities." *NGA Center for Best Practices* (August 19).

National League of Cities. 2002. "Homeland Security: Practical Tools for Local Governments" (November). <http://www.nlc.org/nlc_org/site/files/reports/terrorism.pdf>

Nelken, D. 1987. *Selling Science: How the Press Covers Science and Technology.* New York: W. H. Freeman.

Nielsen, Samuel, and John Lidstone. 1998. "Public Education and Disaster Management: Is There Any Guiding Theory?" *Australian Journal of Emergency Management* (Spring) pp. 14–19.

Occhipinti, John D. 2002. "Allies at Odds." *Buffalo News* (December 22) p. H1.

Office of Management and Budget. 2003. "Department of Homeland Security." <http://www.whitehouse.gov/omb/budget/fy2004/homeland.html>

Patten, Wendy. 2002. "U.S. Homeland Security Bill: Civil Rights Vulnerable and Immigrant Children Not Protected." *Human Rights Watch* (November 21).

Peckenpaugh, Jason. 2002. "Building a Behemoth." *Government Executive Magazine.*

Physical Infrastructure and Key Assets, pp. 39–40, <http://www.dhs.gov>

Piotrow, Phyllis T., Jose G. Rimon, Kim Winnard, D. Lawrence Kincaid, Dale Huntington, and Julie Convisser. 1990. "Mass Media Family Planning Promotion in Three Nigerian Cities." *Studies in Family Planning.* vol. 21. no. 5. pp. 265–274.

*Pittsburgh Post Gazette.* 2003. "The Age of Insecurity." Editorial. (September 21) p. B7.

*Pittsburgh Post Gazette.* 2003. "Will They Listen to Rudman This Time?" Editorial. (July 7) p. A13.

Raphael, B. 1986. *When Disaster Strikes: How Individuals and Communities Cope with Catastrophes.* New York: Basic Books.

Richelson J. T., J. Gefter, M. Waters, M. Evans, M. Byrne, R. Rone, J. Martinez, J. Grant, M. Burroughs, 2003. "U.S. Espionage and Intelligence, 1947–1996," *Digital National Security Archive.* <http://nsarchive.chadwyck.com/esp_essay.htm>

Sataline, Suzanne. 2003. "Democratic Senators Call for Intelligence Reform." *St. Petersburg Times* p.6A

Shapiro, Jeffrey Scott. 2003. "America Risks Repeating a 'Fundamental Injustice.' " *Insight on the News* (September 15) p. 51.

Shenon, Philip. 2003. "High Alerts for Terror Get Harder to Impose." *New York Times* (September 13) p. A9.

Simon, Harvey. 2003. "Emphasis on Illegal Immigrants Could Have Security Tradeoffs." *Aviation Week's Homeland Security and Defense* (September 4) vol. 2. no. 36. p. 5.

Singer, Eleanor, and Phyllis M. Endreny. 1993. *Reporting on Risk: How the Mass Media Portray Accidents, Diseases, Disasters, and Other Hazards.* New York: Russell Sage Foundation.

Smith J. David. 2002. "Business Continuity Management: Good Practice Guidelines, System." CDI web site. <http://www.cdi.org/terrorism/alerts.cfm>.

Taylor, Gus. 2003. "Communities Shun Patriot Act." *The Washington Times.* July 21, 2003.

The United States Conference of Mayors. 2003. "Statement of Boston Mayor Thomas M. Menino, President, U.S. Conference of Mayors, on FY 2003 Omnibus Appropriations Bill." Report by *USCM* (February 13).

The United States Conference of Mayors. 2002. "One Year Later: A Status Report on the Federal-Local Partnership on Homeland Security." Report by *USCM* (September 9).

The United States Conference of Mayors. 2001. "A National Action Plan for Safety and Security in America's Cities." Report by *USCM* (December).

Thornton, Kelly. 2003. "Civilians Join Talks on Terror Preparedness." *San Diego Union Tribune* (April 30) p. B1.

*USA Today.* 2003. "MIA: Terror Database." (August 12) p. 12A.

Walker, Laura. 2003. "We Have Our Radios. Now What?" *Broadcasting and Cable* (August 18) p. 28.

Walsh, James. 1996. *True Odds: How Risk Affects Your Everyday Life.* Santa Monica: Merritt Publishing.

Warner, Kenneth E. 1989. "The Epidemiology of Coffin Nails." In *Health Risks and the Press: Coverage on Media Coverage of Risk Assessment and Health.* Washington, DC: The Media Institute.

Waugh, William L., Jr. 2000. *Living with Hazards, Dealing with Disasters: An Introduction to Emergency Management.* New York: M.E. Sharpe.

Wenham, Brian. 1994. "The Media and Disasters: Building a Better Understanding." In *International Disaster Communications: Harnessing the Power of Communications to Avert Disasters and Save Lives.* Washington, DC: The Annenberg Washington Program.

Westoff, Charles F., and German Rodriguez. 1995. "The Mass Media and Family Planning in Kenya." *International Family Planning Perspectives.* vol. 21. no. 1. pp. 26–31, 36.

The White House. 2002. "Department of Homeland Security Reorganization Plan" (November 25). <http://www.whitehouse.gov/news/releases/2002/11/reorganization_plan.pdf>

The White House. 2002. "Fact Sheet: Homeland Security Council." (October 29). <http://www.whitehouse.gov/news/releases/2001/10/20011029-16.html>

The White House. 1997. "50th Anniversary of the National Security Act of 1947." Office of the Press Secretary. <http://clinton4.nara.gov/WH/EOP/NSC/html/50thanniv.html>

http://www.whitehouse.gov/homeland/stateandlocal/index.html

Willis, Jim. 1997. *Reporting on Risks: The Practice and Ethics of Health and Safety Communication.* Westport, Connecticut: Praeger.

Winston, J. A. 1985. "Science and the Media: The Boundaries of Truth." *Health Affairs.* vol. 6. pp. 5–23.

Witwer, M. 1997. "In Sub-Saharan Africa, Levels of Knowledge and Use of Contraceptives Are Linked to Media Exposure." *International Family Planning Perspectives.* vol. 23. no. 4. pp. 183–184.

# Index